£17.95

British Politics
in Focus

Causeway Press

The Authors

Roy Bentley is a Senior Lecturer in Social Sciences and Access Coordinator at Oxford College of Further Education.

Alan Dobson is Head of Combined Humanities at Oldham Sixth Form College.

Maggie Grant is a Lecturer in Politics and Sociology at Mid-Warwickshire College.

David Roberts is Higher Education Coordinator at Great Yarmouth College.

Roy Bentley would like to thank Ruth for her help on Chapters 5, 7, 11 and 19.

The authors are grateful for the many helpful comments on the first edition. Please send comments on this edition to Causeway Press, PO Box 13, Ormskirk, Lancs, L39 5HP.

Editor at Causeway Press - Steve Lancaster
Cover design by David Weston (Waring Collins Partnership)
Graphic origination by Caroline Waring-Collins (Waring Collins Partnership)
Reader - Annemarie Work
Original artwork by Elaine Sumner and Caroline Waring-Collins (Waring Collins Partnership)

Acknowledgements

The publishers wish to thank the following for permission to reproduce photographs, cartoons and other illustrations: Austin, David 243, 253; Bell, Steve 37, 66, 150, 240, 487, 489, 521, 627 (t), 674 (t); Bennett, Felix 599; Brick 84, 90, 93, 130, 157, 336, 450, 498, 501, 507, 624, 665, 674 (b); Britton-Finnie, Sandy 61 (l); British Nationalist Party 42; Brown, Dave 440, 65; Central Office of Information 419; CIWF 355; Class War 42; Conservative Party 217 (tl); Countryside Alliance 332, 333; CRE 141; Crossley, Neil 111, 407, 435, 586; FOE/Greenpeace 343; Gibbard 26, 50 (t & m), 411 (t), 422; Guardian Newspapers 634; Hampshire Chronicle 16, 17; IFAW 328; Kent, John 297; Labour Party 217 (tm & b), 302 (br); Labour Research 389, 516; Lee, Stephen 390; Liberal Democrats 25, 217 (tr); LICC 478; New Statesman 525, 642; Newman, Nick 411 (b); Organ, Diana 382; Oxford City Council 560; Oxfordshire County Council 562; PA News 5, 112, 118, 351, 471 (r), 529; PCA 603; Pickthall, Colin 378; Pinn/Financial Times 461; Press Association 61 (r); Punch 399 (b), 591; Referendum Party 276; Rex Features 211(b), 537; Riddell/Observer 77, 386, 412, 617; Saatchi & Saatchi 50 (b), 302 (bl); Simmonds, Posy 136; Simonds, David 101, 146, 171, 175, 180, 416, 436, 579; Socialist Workers Party 42; Tarver, Richard 361; Times 683; Topham Picturepoint 211 (t & m), 249, 259, 372, 381, 399 (t), 423, 627 (b); Traynor, Ian 9, 280, 471 (l); West Lancs District Council 566; Winterbottom, Tony 287, 466, 547, 621.

Every effort has been made to locate the copyright owners of material used in this book. Any omissions brought to the attention of the publisher are regretted and will be credited in subsequent printings.

British Library Cataloguing in Publication Data
A catalogue record for this book is available from the British Library.

ISBN 1 873929 93 5

Causeway Press Limited
PO Box 13, Ormskirk, Lancs, L39 5HP

© Roy Bentley, Alan Dobson, Maggie Grant, David Roberts
1st impression, 1999

Printed and bound by Caledonian International Book Manufacturing Ltd, Glasgow

Contents

Part 1
Political argument

1 What is politics?

Introduction

What is the link between the Prime Minister discussing government policy with journalists outside Number 10 Downing Street, a lively debate in Parliament, a local Labour councillor addressing a public meeting about the planned closure of a hospital, and an informal conversation between Conservative backbenchers in the House of Commons tearoom? The answer is that these are all examples of political activity. Political activity, however, is not just activity involving politicians or people who belong to a political party. When, in early 1998, groups of disabled people gathered outside the gates of Downing Street to protest against threats to cut their benefits, many of the demonstrators did not belong to any political party, but their action was still political.

In its broadest sense, politics concerns the way in which people interact - how they make decisions and settle disputes. It is, therefore, concerned with power and the way in which power is distributed in society. Whilst power is most obviously held by the government and its agents, it is not exclusively held by them. Decisions are made at many different levels. Politics, therefore, operates at many different levels.

This chapter examines what exactly is meant by the terms 'politics' and 'political activity'. More specifically, it considers where political activity takes place in the UK and how power is distributed.

Chapter summary

Part 1 deals with the question 'what is politics?' It considers two approaches - politics as the study of conflict resolution and politics as the study of power.

Part 2 considers different types of political activity.

What is political activity? Who is involved in it? Where does it take place?

Part 3 discusses where political power is located in the UK. It provides an introduction to the British system of government.

Part 1 Definitions

Key issues

1. How can politics be defined?
2. What leads to conflict in society and how can it be resolved?
3. What is power and how does it differ from authority?
4. Why is politics necessary?

1.1 What is politics?

Decision making

People are social animals. They choose to live together in groups. Because people live together in groups, there is a need to make decisions - about how the resources available to the group are to be shared out, for example, or how conflicts which arise within the group are to be resolved. The study of politics is the study of how such decisions are made. It may also be the study of how such decisions should be made.

Since the resources available to any group are limited, questions inevitably arise about how the resources which are available should be distributed. Should everybody have an equal share, for example, or do some people deserve a bigger share than others? Since it is possible to increase the resources available to a group (by conquest, technological advance or better management of existing resources), further questions arise. For example, what (if any) strategy should be employed to increase resources and what is the best way to protect the resources which already exist? Since there is no single correct answer to such questions, different people have different ideas about what is the best action to take. According to some commentators, the conflict which arises from the expression of different views is at the heart of politics. The study of politics is the study of conflict resolution.

A. Politics as the study of conflict resolution

Modern society is highly complex. Individuals argue

over many different interests, values and beliefs. Conflict does not just take place between individuals, however. It also exists between larger groups - between countries as well as within them. According to one viewpoint, the aim of politics is to remove conflict so that people can live in reasonable harmony with each other. In other words, the aim of politics is to produce consensus - a general agreement over what people want and what they believe is right.

In general terms, it can be argued that conflict arises for two main reasons. First, it arises because of conflicting interests. And second, it arises because of conflicting values or beliefs.

Conflicting interests

In a country such as Britain, there is a complex web of interests which people want to expand and protect. Many of these interests are economic and financial. People want a job with good pay, a comfortable house, holidays and so on. They want a good education for their children, healthcare and security against poverty. Farmers and agricultural workers want a prosperous farming industry. Publishers want people to buy lots of books.

Although many of the interests, such as the desire for a good health system, are common to all people, difficulties and disagreement emerge because resources are limited and different people have different priorities. Some people might want more money to be spent on high-tech machinery in hospitals, for example, whilst others want more nurses to be employed at a better rate of pay. Since there may not be the resources to take both approaches, choices have to be made. It is the necessity of making such choices which leads to conflict.

Conflicting values

When people defend their interests, it does not necessarily mean that they are being selfish. Opponents of a new open cast mine, for example, might be furious that it is close to their homes, but they might also claim, with some justification, that to open the mine would be an ecological disaster because of the damage it would cause to the wildlife living on the site. Such arguments might produce support from people living miles away who are not personally affected by the project. Political activity, in other words, can spring from a set of values and beliefs as well as from self-interest. Equally, the way in which a conflict is resolved might owe more to the values and beliefs of the decision makers than to their personal interest in the matter.

B. Politics as the study of power

The sociologists Dowse & Hughes (1972) argue that politics is about power, claiming that 'politics occurs when there are differentials in power'. This suggests that:

> 'Any social relationship which involves power differentials is political. Political relationships would extend from parents assigning domestic chores to their children to teachers enforcing discipline in the classroom; from a manager organising a workforce to a general ordering troops into battle.' (Haralambos & Holborn 1995, p.501)

If people have power, it means that they are able to make other people do what they want them to do, even if the other people do not want to do it. Power is, therefore, the ability to influence the behaviour of another either by threat, sanctions or through manipulation. In all political situations, those who have power are able to reward those who conform and punish those who do not.

Power cannot be exercised unless there is some way of backing it up. This may be the direct threat of or the use of force, but it does not have to be. Power that is based on the direct threat of or the use of force is usually described as 'coercion'. But, individuals (or governments) often do not have to resort to coercion to get their own way. Rather, some forms of power are accepted as 'legitimate' (as fair and right) and people are obedient because of that. In Britain, for example, most people obey the laws made by the government even if they themselves do not agree with them. They do this because they accept that the government is legitimate. Power which is regarded as legitimate is usually described as 'authority'.

Civil disobedience

There is a fine line between authority and coercion. The British government may gain legitimate power by winning an election, but does it have the right to use coercion if people do not obey laws passed by the government? Should citizens have the right to protest against what they believe are unfair or unjust laws?

When people protest against what they believe are unfair laws, their action is usually described as 'civil disobedience'. According to Heywood (1994), there is an important difference between a criminal act and an act of civil disobedience. Whilst a criminal act is committed for selfish ends, an act of civil disobedience can be justified by reference to 'religious, moral and political principles' (Heywood 1994, p.216). Civil disobedience is, in other words, political whilst a criminal act is not. This is because civil disobedience uses ethical grounds to question the way in which power is used whilst a criminal act does not.

- Politics is the study of how decisions are made and should be made.
- Some writers claim that politics is the study of conflict resolution. They suggest that the aim of politics is to produce a consensus by resolving conflicts over interests and values in an acceptable way.
- Other writers claim that politics is about the exercise of power. There are two main ways of exercising power - by threatening or using force (coercion) or by making decisions which people regard as legitimate (authority).
- Unlike criminal acts, civil disobedience is a political act because it uses ethical grounds to question the way in which power is used.

Activity 1.1 *What is politics?*

Item A *What is politics?*

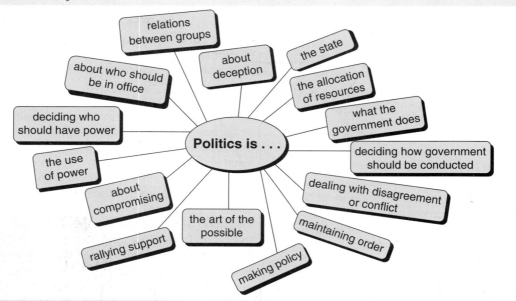

Item B *Weber's three types of authority*

Max Weber, a German sociologist who lived in the 19th century, distinguished between three different types of authority:

ii) Charismatic authority
Charismatic authority depends upon the special qualities of a leader. People are drawn to follow the leader because of the qualities which they believe that leader to have. Charismatic authority may die with the leader or continue to work through a group of chosen disciples.

i) Traditional authority
Traditional authority depends upon the belief in established customs and traditions. Those in authority expect obedience and loyalty on the grounds that established customs and traditions demand it. For example, the tradition of a hereditary monarchy demands that a new monarch commands as much obedience and loyalty as the previous monarch commanded.

iii) Rational-legal authority
Rational-legal authority depends upon a formal set of rules which gives those who hold authority the right to direct and command others and to take decisions on their behalf. It has a moral dimension in that citizens have freely handed power over to another person (or other people). So, a democratic government can be said to exercise rational-legal authority since the electorate hands over power to it through the ballot box.

It should be noted that Weber regarded these three categories as 'ideal types'. In the real world, authority might come from two or more of the three sources. Second, Weber believed that there was a fixed amount of power in any society. Since the amount of power is constant, power held by any individual or group is power not available to any other individual or group. And third, Weber suggested that power is always used to further the interests of those who hold it.

Item C *Lukes' three faces of power*

In a book published in 1974, Steven Lukes argued that power has three faces or dimensions.

i) Decision making

The first face of power is its open face - the power that can be seen to be exercised when a decision is taken. Suppose the government proposed a law in Britain. This proposal would be debated in Cabinet and in Parliament. Interest groups would lobby MPs. There might be demonstrations for or against the proposal. Eventually, the proposal might pass through Parliament, gain royal assent and become law. In this decision-making process, it would be relatively straightforward to identify where power lay.

iii) Manipulating desires

The third face of power goes one step further. Lukes suggests that power can be exercised through manipulation. People with power can persuade others that what is being offered is what is desired. For example, some feminists would argue that men exercise power over women in contemporary Britain by persuading them that being a mother and a housewife are the most desirable roles for women. In reality, feminists claim, women who occupy these roles are exploited by, and for the benefit of, men.

ii) Non-decision making

The second face of power is its secretive face. Power is exercised behind closed doors. Those who have the power to set the political agenda have the power to determine not only what can be discussed, but, more important, what cannot be discussed. Power is, therefore, not just about making decisions. It is also about preventing decisions being taken or about narrowing the choices which are considered. For example, a teacher might offer students the opportunity to decide whether to do a piece of homework that week or the following week. The class appears to have been given the opportunity to reach a decision. In reality, however, power still rests with the teacher who has limited the options open to the students. The students are not free to decide whether or not they do this particular piece of work, nor can they choose to reject doing homework altogether.

Item D *Disabled protesters outside the gates of Downing Street*

This photo shows disabled protesters outside the gates of Downing Street in January 1998.

Questions

1. Using Item A, write a paragraph explaining what is meant by 'politics'.

2. a) Which of Weber's three types of authority in Item B best describes the British political system today? Give reasons for your answer.

   b) Can you think of examples to illustrate the other two types of authority?

3. What does Item C tell us about the way in which politics works in Britain today?

4. a) Explain why what is happening in Item D is political.

   b) What does this picture tell us about the British political system?

Part 2 Political activity

Key issues

1. What is a political activity?
2. Who gets involved in politics?
3. Where does politics take place?

2.1 Types of political activity

Voting

When people either belong to or take a side over a particular issue, they are engaged in political activity. The most common political activity in Britain, as in most countries, is voting. In the general election held in May 1997, for example, 71.3% of the electorate turned out to vote (down from 77.7% in April 1992). Although a smaller percentage of the electorate tends to vote in local or European elections (just under 30% voted in the local elections of May 1998, for example, and only 36.5% voted in the European election of June 1994), these elections involve the political participation of far more people than any other activity.

Other types of political activity

Apart from voting, people have the opportunity of participating in the political process in a number of other ways. Writing to a local councillor, Member of Parliament (MP) or Member of the European Parliament (MEP), or to a local or national newspaper is one way of participating in the political process. Joining a pressure group or political party is another. But, whilst some people feel that paying their membership fee to a pressure group or political party is enough, others are prepared to spend a great deal of their spare time campaigning. There is, in other words, a scale of political participation. This scale ranges from complete inactivity at one end to full-time activity at the other end.

2.2 People involved in politics

Activism and apathy

During election campaigns, activists from the political parties go round from house to house, knocking on doors and canvassing support. On the doorstep, people are often prepared to air their views. When asked what sort of people, in their opinion, are involved in politics, most mention councillors, MPs and MEPs, but few mention themselves. Many say that they are disillusioned with politics and that it is not even worth voting since 'they're all the same'. The fact that they refer to politicians as 'they' rather than 'we' shows that they feel removed from the political process.

In reality, however, political activity covers a much wider area than many people realise. People are involved in political activity whenever they interact with others in any form of social activity. This is because any group, however large or small, involves an element of decision making - and, therefore, involves political activity.

If politics is about decision making, then everybody can be said to be involved in politics through their everyday participation with others. All members of society, after all, are members of groups - either because they are born into them (such as their family or ethnic group) or because they choose to join them (such as a sports club or religious group).

Although everybody participates in political activity in this broad sense, however, far fewer people choose to participate in political activity in the narrower sense of working for a political party or group, or of standing for office.

Why participate?

Those who do choose to get involved in politics in this narrower sense may do so for a number of reasons. First, they may hold a set of beliefs strongly and hope to persuade others to accept them. Second, they may want to bring about change and feel that participation in the political process is the best way to achieve this. Third, they may want to help others. Fourth, they may want to promote their own interests or the interests of their group. And fifth, they may enjoy exercising power over others and want to hold power for its own sake.

2.3 Where political activity takes place

A broad definition

If politics is taken in its broadest sense, then it is possible to argue that:

> 'Politics is at the heart of all collective human activity, formal and informal, public and private, in all human groups, institutions and societies, not just some of them, and it always has been and always will be.' (Leftwich 1984, p.63)

In this sense, political activity can be said to take place wherever one person tries to influence or change the behaviour of another. It takes place in any situation in which decisions have to be made or disagreements sorted out. It takes place wherever there is a power relationship between the participants. It takes place, therefore, at both the micro (small) level and at the macro (large) level.

The small picture

At the micro level, political activity can be identified, for example, within the family. Take the traditional 'nuclear' family, made up of two parents and two children. In such a family, the roles are clearly defined. The father goes out to work to support the family, whilst the mother stays at home to look after the children and the house. The children are expected to obey the wishes of the parents without question. What the father says, goes. There is, in other words, a power relationship in which the children are at the bottom and the father is at the top. When important decisions have to be made, it is the father who has the final say. But, families do not have to work like this, and, indeed, many do not. Many families, for example, have a single parent or, if there are two parents, make decisions jointly rather than allowing the father to have all the power. The point is that, in every family (whether it works as a traditional nuclear family or not), there is a power relationship which determines how decisions are made and disputes are settled. Activity within the family, therefore, can be described as 'political' at the micro level. The same is true of activity which takes place in the workplace or in school or college.

The big picture
At the macro level, political activity is, perhaps, easier to identify. The work of government ministers, the civil service, opposition MPs or MEPs and local councillors, for example, all comes under the heading of political activity at the macro level. Political activity takes place, therefore, where these people work - at Number 10 Downing Street, in Whitehall, in the British and European Parliaments or in the local council chamber.

It is not only in these places, however, that political activity takes place at the macro level. Since the position of most politicians is dependent on their election to office, it is necessary for them to gain and maintain their electors' support. To do this, they need to communicate with the electorate. As a result, the media is also the centre of a great deal of political activity at the macro level. It is on television or radio, or in the newspapers that politicians try to persuade their electors of the validity of their views. Politicians and political activists, therefore, attempt to gain positive exposure of their views in the media and they often stage events for the benefit of the media.

The fact that the media is the focus of a great deal of political activity does not mean, however, that political activity at the macro level is something which only takes place in public. On the contrary, most important decisions are made behind closed doors. Take, for example, the decisions made by the Cabinet. During a parliamentary session, the Cabinet meets each week to discuss what the Prime Minister decides are the key political issues of the day. What is discussed in Cabinet and many of the decisions which are reached, however, remain secret. Since part, or even the whole, of the decision-making process goes on in secret, it is sometimes difficult to find out exactly how a decision came to be made. It is, therefore, sometimes difficult

to be sure exactly where political activity takes place.

2.4 How political participation has changed

The general trends
Over the past 30 or so years, the nature of political participation has changed. In the first three decades after the Second World War, a large number of people joined conventional political organisations like trade unions and political parties. Between 1945 and 1978, the number of people who were members of trade unions grew from 7.87 million to 13.11 million and there were only eight years during this period when the number of members did not grow (Pelling 1987, pp.299-300). Between 1978 and 1996, however, membership of trade unions went down from 53% of the working population to 31% (Social Trends 1998). Similarly, membership of the two main political parties has declined in recent years:

'In the post-war era, there has been a substantial erosion in the overall pool of volunteers: since the early 1950s, Conservative Party membership plunged from 2.8 million to 780,000 in 1992, while individual membership of the Labour Party declined from just over a million to its nadir [lowest point] in the 1980s, before recovering to 400,000 in 1997.' (Norris 1997, p.78)

Unconventional participation
Young people, in particular, seem alienated from traditional forms of participation. Mark Evans (1997) argues that, in part, this is due to the British first-past-the-post electoral system which makes it difficult for new parties to grow. But, he also points out:

'Age differences in participation are complex. The young are less likely to vote than the old and are more likely to be alienated from conventional forms of participation. However, they are more likely to engage in unconventional forms of participation, such as protest politics. In short, it is not that young people do not participate in politics, rather that they participate differently. Under 35s are particularly interested in help for the homeless (73%), disabled rights (71%), animal rights (66%) and increased funding for the NHS (64%). Young people have been prominent in championing environmental causes and civil rights (in, for example, campaigns against the Criminal Justice Bill in 1994).' (Evans 1997, p.112 - slightly adapted)

Unconventional participation is not confined to the young, however. People of all ages and classes can be found protesting. The campaign against road building, for example, has support from many sections in the population.

For further information on political particpation see Chapter 7, Part 2.

Main points - Part 2

- The most common political activity in Britain is voting. Writing to elected representatives or the media, and joining a pressure group or political party are other political activities.
- Although the number of political activists is small, everybody participates in politics to some extent.
- Political activity takes place wherever one person tries to influence or to change the behaviour of another. At the micro level, it takes place within the family. At the macro level, it takes place at Westminster, Whitehall or Brussels. The mass media is also a focus of political activity, though not all political activity is openly reported.
- Over the past 30 years, political activity has changed. Fewer people join conventional political organisations. More people are engaged in unconventional political activity.

Activity 1.2 Political activity

Item A *The state of the nation*

This graph shows the results of a survey carried out by MORI between 21 April and 8 May 1995. Respondents were asked to say whether they were satisfied with the way each of the political institutions was doing its job. It should be noted, however, that the figures only include those who expressed a preference. For example, 50% of respondents said that they had no opinion about

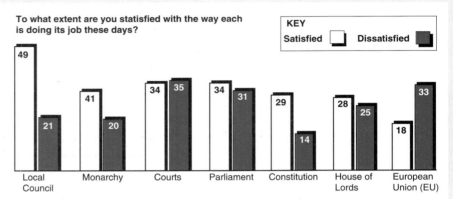

To what extent are you statisfied with the way each is doing its job these days?

KEY   Satisfied ☐   Dissatisfied ■

Local Council	Monarchy	Courts	Parliament	Constitution	House of Lords	European Union (EU)
49 / 21	41 / 20	34 / 35	34 / 31	29 / 14	28 / 25	18 / 33

whether the EU was doing a good job. The survey did not just ask about how satisfied people were with various institutions, it also asked how much people thought they knew about various subjects. Respondents were most confident that they knew about their rights as a citizen - 43% said they knew at least a fair amount about this, although 20% said they knew hardly anything. A third of respondents said that they knew at least a fair amount about the courts and the constitutional role of the monarchy and 32% said the same about their local council. Only 22%, however, said they knew a fair amount about the House of Lords and only 21% said they knew a fair amount about the British constitution. The institution people knew least about was the European Union (EU) - just 19% said they knew a fair amount about the EU, whilst as many as 39% said they knew hardly anything about it.

Adapted from *New Statesman and Society*, 2 June 1995.

Item B *Political apathy*

Yesterday John Prescott and his colleagues appealed to the press, radio and television to do their civic duty and help make 21 million English voters aware that 4,174 seats in 166 councils are at stake in the local elections (most Labour-held). They also revealed that, in Croydon (which the Tories want to recapture after Labour ended a century of single-party rule in 1994), two branches of Tesco will house polling stations - part of drive to raise voter awareness. In many European countries, they do not have this problem (see right) probably because constituencies are small enough for local residents to identify with elected representatives. Also, these representatives have greater freedom to act than their British counterparts (whose hands are tied by decisions made by central government).

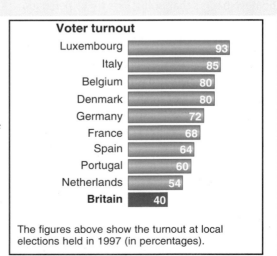

Voter turnout

Luxembourg	93
Italy	85
Belgium	80
Denmark	80
Germany	72
France	68
Spain	64
Portugal	60
Netherlands	54
Britain	40

The figures above show the turnout at local elections held in 1997 (in percentages).

Adapted from the *Guardian*, 22 April 1998.

Item C *Political activities performed by members of the Labour Party*

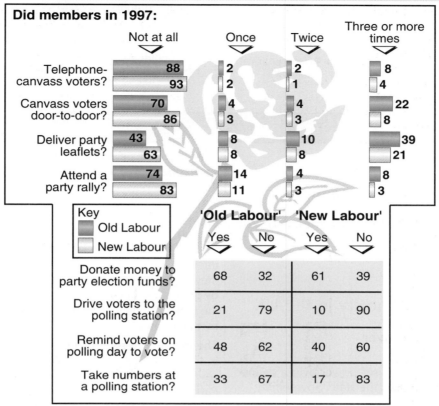

Did members in 1997:

	Not at all	Once	Twice	Three or more times
Telephone-canvass voters? (Old Labour)	88	2	2	8
Telephone-canvass voters? (New Labour)	93	2	1	4
Canvass voters door-to-door? (Old Labour)	70	4	4	22
Canvass voters door-to-door? (New Labour)	86	3	3	8
Deliver party leaflets? (Old Labour)	43	8	10	39
Deliver party leaflets? (New Labour)	63	8	8	21
Attend a party rally? (Old Labour)	74	14	4	8
Attend a party rally? (New Labour)	83	11	3	3

Key
Old Labour
New Labour

	'Old Labour'		'New Labour'	
	Yes	No	Yes	No
Donate money to party election funds?	68	32	61	39
Drive voters to the polling station?	21	79	10	90
Remind voters on polling day to vote?	48	62	40	60
Take numbers at a polling station?	33	67	17	83

This diagram examines the extent to which members of the Labour Party took part in political activity in 1997 (the year of Labour's general election victory). Those who joined the Labour Party before 1994 are described as 'Old Labour'. Those who joined the Labour Party after 1994 are described as 'New Labour'. All figures are percentages.

Adapted from Whiteley & Seyd 1998.

Item D *Political activities performed by Conservatives*

How often have you done the following activities during the last FIVE years?

	Never	Rarely	Occasionally	Frequently
Displayed an election poster in a window	51	8	23	18
Signed a petition supported by the party	53	14	26	8
Donated money to Conservative party funds	16	12	45	28
Delivered party leaflets	63	4	13	20
Attended a party meeting	53	13	19	15
Helped at a Conservative party function	58	9	17	16
Canvassed voters	77	6	9	9
Stood for office within the party organisation	89	2	4	5
Stood for office in local government or Parliament	94	1	2	3

This table shows the political activities performed by members of the Conservative Party. The survey was carried out in 1992.

Adapted from Whiteley et al. 1994.

Item E *Apathy in the UK.*

'I like it! It's a blatant appeal to public apathy.'

Questions

1. Devise a questionnaire to find out the extent to which people participate in political activity. Test your questionnaire on colleagues and friends, and write a short report discussing the findings.
2. What do Items A and B tell us about (a) the political institutions and (b) political activity in the UK?
3. Judging from Items C and D, how politically active is the average member of the Conservative and Labour parties? What conclusions can be drawn from this information?
4. What point is being made by Item E? Is there any evidence in Items A-D to support it?

Part 3 Politics in the UK

Key issues

1. How is power and authority exercised in the UK?
2. What is the UK's institutional framework?
3. Who exercises power?
4. Where did power lie in the Battle for Twyford Down?

3.1 Power and authority in the UK

A. The location of power

The state

The institution which exercises power over a defined area is usually described as the state. Sovereignty (that is, supreme power) normally lies with the state. All states have certain characteristics in common.

First, they have a territory with clearly defined geographical boundaries.

Second, membership is compulsory - all members of the population become citizens at birth.

Third, since the state is a sovereign body, it holds the ultimate legal power over its members. The state controls coercive bodies such as the military and the police and it can decide who may use force and to what extent it should be used. Laws made by the state can result in a citizen's imprisonment or even a citizen's death.

Fourth, the state delegates its power to certain institutions.

And fifth, all states have some kind of constitution (a set of rules) and a pattern of offices which have to be filled. In some countries, such as the USA, this constitution is written down in a document ('codified'). In the UK, it is not (see Chapter 4, Section 1.1).

Liberal democracies

The UK, like the USA and the other members of the EU, is a 'liberal democracy' (see Chapter 4, Section 1.3). Three basic types of power are involved in the running of liberal democracies:

The first type is **legislative power** - the power to make laws. In the UK, this power has been granted to Parliament. It is the role of Parliament to make new laws and to reform those already in existence.

The second type is **executive power** - the power to suggest new laws and to implement existing laws. In the UK, this power has been granted to the government and its departments. The government is helped to fulfill its role by the civil service, a permanent body of supposedly impartial state employees.

The third type is **judicial power** - the power to interpret laws and to make judgements about whether they have been broken or not. This power is exercised by the courts. These range from the House of Lords, the highest appeal court, to local courts presided over by magistrates.

The location of sovereignty

In the UK, it is possible to talk of 'parliamentary sovereignty' - the idea that power rests with Parliament. This is because Parliament has the power to make laws which cannot be challenged. Since, however, at regular intervals Parliament (or, at least the House of Commons) must submit itself to the people in elections, it could be argued that the people are sovereign because they have the power to decide who will rule them.

B. The institutional framework

The monarchy

The UK is a constitutional monarchy. In former times, the monarch possessed a great deal of political power, but this has now been eroded. Whilst the monarch remains the nominal head of state, the political role played by monarchs in the past is now undertaken by the Prime Minister and other members of government:

'The Queen personifies the state. In law, she is head of the executive, an integral part of the legislature, head of the judiciary, the commander-in-chief of the armed forces of the Crown and the "supreme governor" of the established Church of England. As a result, of a long process of evolution during which the monarchy's power has been progressively reduced, the Queen acts on the advice of her ministers. Britain is governed by Her Majesty's government in the name of the Queen.' (HMSO 1994, p.8)

The executive

The political power once exercised by the monarch,

is now, therefore, exercised by the executive - by the Cabinet which is chaired by the Prime Minister and by the government departments. Most government departments are headed by a Cabinet minister chosen by the Prime Minister. The Cabinet meets once a week at the Cabinet Room in Number 10 Downing Street, the Prime Minister's official residence.

Most Cabinet ministers are in charge of a government department - such as the Department of Health, the Department of Transport and so on. These ministers are responsible for a particular area of the government's work. Occasionally, however, a Cabinet minister is appointed 'without portfolio'. As well as choosing Cabinet ministers, the Prime Minister also chooses the junior ministers who work in government departments. At any one time, there are around 100 ministers in total. Periodically, the Prime Minister has a 'reshuffle' and sacks, promotes or moves ministers. Whilst ministers are, therefore, political appointees, they work in tandem with permanent civil servants who are state employees.

The legislature
Legislative power is exercised by Parliament which consists of two Houses, the House of Commons and the House of Lords. Each member of the House of Commons is elected by people living in a constituency (a geographical area). General elections must take place every five years, but they can be called before the five year term has been completed. The vast majority of candidates in general elections belong to a political party and they stand on behalf of that party. The political party which gains the largest number of seats in the House of Commons is usually invited to form a government (it is possible that the combined number of seats held by two or more parties might outnumber the largest party and, by making a coalition, these smaller parties might then be in a position to form a government). The Leader of the party invited to form the government becomes Prime Minister. The largest party outside government forms the official opposition. The Leader of the opposition normally chooses a 'shadow Cabinet'.

All proposed legislation must pass through a number of stages before it becomes law. Most proposals ('Bills') are first put forward in the House of Commons. They must pass through both the Houses of Parliament, however, before they can be sent to the monarch for royal assent. Once a Bill has received royal assent, it becomes law.

An adversarial system
When a party wins an election and forms a government, it is generally regarded as having a mandate (the authorisation) to put into practice the promises it made in its election manifesto. The British system of government, however, is **adversarial** - it relies on two sides being taken on any issue. It is,

there.
proposal
them. Since
majority in the
rely on its supporter
of the criticism made b,

The House of Lords
Members of the House of Lords
Labour government elected in 199,
legislation taking away the right of here
(Lords who gained their position by birthri,
vote on legislation (see Chapter 14, Section 3.5). Life peers sit in the Lords during their lifetime, but they do not pass on the right to sit in the Lords to their children. Two other groups sit in the House of Lords - the Lords Spiritual (the two Archbishops and other bishops from the Church of England) and the Lords Pastoral (Law Lords who sit in judgement when the House of Lords is used as a court of appeal).

3.2 Who exercises power in the UK?

Three models
Three main models have been developed to explain who exercises power in the UK - the pluralist model, the élite model and the Marxist model.

A. The pluralist model
According to the pluralist model, power is exercised by the mass of the population, rather than by a small, élite group. This conclusion is derived from two main arguments.

First, pluralists note that if a majority of people do not like what their representatives are doing, they can vote them out of office at the next election. Representatives, therefore, have to act in a way that is pleasing to the majority.

And second, pluralists claim that people are able to exercise power between elections by joining interest groups (such as political parties, trade unions and other pressure groups). Group activity, they argue, is vital to the successful functioning of the political system. Groups constantly compete to gain the attention of decision makers and it is the job of the decision maker to decide between the competing claims made by different groups.

The location of power
It follows from this, therefore, that what matters to pluralists about the distribution of power in society is not that it is uneven, but that it is widely dispersed rather than concentrated into the hands of the few. It also follows that, according to the pluralist model, the state acts impartially, responding to the demands of different popular pressures. No single group can possibly dominate in society since, for every force exerted by one group, there is an equal and opposite force exerted by other groups.

Pluralists argue that such a system is healthy because it encourages political participation, it

...nfluence over decision... ...power is dispersed rather than ...to the hands of a few and, at the ...me, it allows the view of minority groups to be voiced.

B. The élite model

Élite theorists suggest that power in the UK is held by a small minority of people who use it for their own ends. The unequal distribution of power in society, the model suggests, is not necessarily in the best interests of the majority of people. Rather, it benefits a ruling élite.

Classical élite theorists argue that all states are governed by an élite or conflicting élites and that the majority of the population is basically passive and uninterested in politics. Schumpeter, for example, defined the role of elections in liberal democracies as:

'That institutional arrangement for arriving at political decisions in which individuals acquire the power to decide by means of a competitive struggle for the people's vote.' (Schumpeter 1974, p.269)

Contrasts with the pluralist model

The élite model differs from the pluralist model in a number of ways.

First, whereas pluralists argue that political parties act as a route through which different interests can be expressed, élite theorists argue that this is not so. Élite theorists point out that political parties often prevent views and opinions being aired if they do not coincide with the particular party's stance.

Second, whilst pluralists concentrate on those groups which make an input into decision making, élite theorists point out that a process of non-decision making can operate to prevent certain interests reaching the political agenda. To put this in terms used by Lukes (1974), pluralists concentrate on the first face of power only, whilst élite theorists also consider the second face of power (see above Activity 1.1, Item C).

And third, élite theorists point out that interest groups are not equal in status. Some are more powerful than others and any dispute or disagreement is likely to favour the more powerful group. Those with more economic clout or a well-educated and articulate membership, for example, are more likely to shape the political agenda than those representing groups like the homeless, the poor or the elderly. Pluralists, on the other hand, imply that interest groups compete on a level playing field.

The Establishment

Studies of the British political system have led some élite theorists to suggest that there is a cohesive political class which monopolises power. This is sometimes described as the 'Establishment'. Members of the Establishment share the same sort of social and educational background and have a distinct set of values:

'A number of researchers have found that the majority of those who occupy élite positions in Britain are recruited from a minority of the population with highly privileged backgrounds. This appears to apply to a wide range of British élites including politicians, judges, higher civil servants, senior military officers and the directors of large companies and major banks...There is also evidence that there may be some degree of cohesion within and between the various élites.' (Haralambos & Holborn 1995, pp.518-19)

C. The Marxist model

Like most other liberal democracies, the UK is a capitalist country. The vast bulk of its wealth is owned by individuals rather than by the state. In simple terms, those who own and control the wealth are capitalists whilst the people they employ are workers. Although the capitalists are fewer in number than the workers, they tend to acquire political as well as economic power.

Marxists are fundamentally opposed to the capitalist system. They argue that it is responsible for the inequalities in British society and the unevenness of the distribution of power. Marxist studies of the British political system are, therefore, (unlike some pluralist or élitist studies) necessarily critical of the system.

Contrasts with the other models

The Marxist model is closer to the élite model than to the pluralist model. Like élite theorists, Marxists argue that a cohesive political élite exists in the UK. Also like some élite theorists, Marxists agree that the democratic institutions in the UK are a sham. It is not, therefore, in their conclusions that élite theorists and Marxists disagree. Rather, it is in the arguments they use to reach these conclusions. Marxists argue that the élite - the ruling class - has power because it controls and owns capital. The source of power lies, therefore, in the economic infrastructure (in the way in which the economic system works). Élite theorists, on the other hand, argue that the explanation for the domination of élites is psychological.

Marxists are particularly critical of the pluralist idea that the state is, in some way, neutral. On the contrary, Marxists argue, the capitalist system developed to protect the interests of those with economic power. Power is distributed in the state to ensure that this happens. One way in which the state does this is to manipulate people's views. The Marxist model, therefore, incorporates Lukes' third face of power (see above, Activity 1.1, Item C).

· Main points - Sections 3.1-3.2

- The institution which exercises power over a defined area is usually described as the state. Sovereignty (that is, supreme power) normally lies with the state. Britain is a liberal democracy. Legislative power is exercised by Parliament, executive power by the government and judicial power by the courts.
- It is debatable whether Parliament or the people are sovereign.
- The monarch is the nominal head of state. The political power once exercised by the monarch is now exercised by the government (executive).
- The British system is adversarial.
- Three main models have been developed to explain who exercises power in the UK: (1) the pluralist model - the mass of the population exercises power; (2) the élite model - a small minority of people exercise power; and (3) the Marxist model - the system is flawed because capitalists exercise power.

Activity 1.3 The British political system

Item A *The British political system*

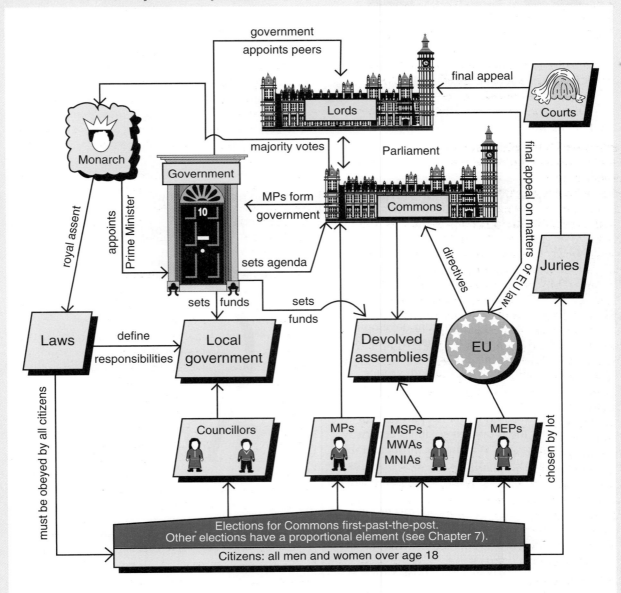

Item B *Political decision making in the UK*

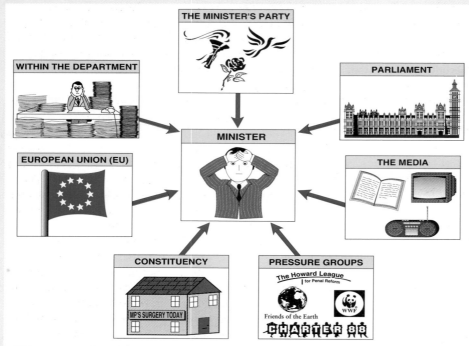

THE MINISTER'S PARTY

WITHIN THE DEPARTMENT

EUROPEAN UNION (EU)

MINISTER

PARLIAMENT

THE MEDIA

CONSTITUENCY

MP'S SURGERY TODAY

PRESSURE GROUPS

The Howard League for Penal Reform

Friends of the Earth

WWF

CHAPTER 88

This diagram shows the various pressures on a government minister. Similar diagrams could be drawn for any decision maker.

Questions

1. Use Item A to write a short passage explaining where power is exercised in the UK.

2. a) Which of the three models described in Section 3.2 above is illustrated by Item B? Explain how you know.

   b) Design a similar diagram to illustrate one of the other two models.

3. Where does political activity take place in the UK? Use Items A and B and your own diagram from 2b in your answer.

3.3 The Battle of Twyford Down - an exercise in power

A. Background

In the 1970s, the government published its plans to extend the M3 from Basingstoke to the proposed new M27 near Southampton. Twyford Down is located on this route, just east of Winchester. The campaign to save Twyford Down from development accelerated during the 1980s. It began as a local issue involving local groups and escalated into a major political battle involving pressure groups, central government in Westminster and the European Commission in Brussels.

The first option favoured by the Department of Transport was that the proposed six lane motorway would run to the west of Winchester through arable land, meeting the M27 on the north-west outskirts of Southampton. However, an alliance of local residents and landowners formed the Winchester M3 Joint Action Group. In 1976, pressure from this group resulted in a public inquiry which debated the route of the motorway again. As a result, a second route was proposed - that of improving the existing A33. In 1980, however, the newly elected Conservative government accepted recommendations for a fresh study. On 15 February 1983, a report was published recommending a third, completely new, route. This route entailed making a cutting east of St Catherine's Hill, through the heart of Twyford Down.

The three routes are shown in Box 1.1 below:

Box 1.1 The location of Twyford Down

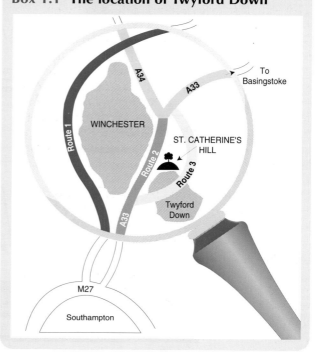

What was the significance of Twyford Down?

Twyford Down was an important historical site, an important environmental area and an area of outstanding natural beauty. The proposed route threatened two Scheduled Ancient Monuments (Celtic fields, bronze age settlements and an iron age village were located there), two Sites of Special Scientific Interest (SSSI) and one Area of Outstanding Natural Beauty.

In 1921, two masters from Winchester College bought Twyford Down to protect it from development. Later, in 1936, they gave it to the college in order to ensure its protection in the future.

In 1990, Winchester College sold the Down to the Department of Transport (DoT), claiming that it was a compulsory purchase. In 1993, however, a television documentary (*Dispatches*) claimed to have discovered that the college had previously (in 1982) dropped a High Court case which was delaying further road development in the area. In other words, the college had come to the conclusion that further road development would be beneficial and it was happy to sell Twyford Down to the DoT. The cutting route, it was argued, would be to the college's advantage since it would move the M3 further away from the college.

B. The battle

A petition was sent to the DoT in August 1993. When making decisions, the DoT does not act alone, but takes advice from a number of agencies - for example, the Countryside Commission (which aims to preserve the landscape), English Nature (which aims to conserve wildlife) and English Heritage (which aims to protect historical and archaeological sites). All three groups opposed the third route through Twyford Down.

The Twyford Down Association, set up in 1985, originally drew its members from the local area and included supporters of all the main political parties. As the fight continued, it broadened its membership, encouraging people throughout the country to join or to show solidarity. At the same time, environmental pressure groups, such as Friends of the Earth (FoE) and the Worldwide Fund for Nature (WWF) became involved, ensuring that the battle was increasingly fought on a national level.

Whilst protesters tried to pressurise the government into changing the route, supporters of the scheme, such as the Roads Lobby, pressed the government to go ahead as soon as possible.

Lobbying the government

In March 1991, the Twyford Down Association put forward an alternative to the cutting route. They suggested to Malcolm Rifkind, Secretary of State for Transport, that, rather than cutting through the Down, a tunnel (similar to the Channel Tunnel) could be dug under the Down. The DoT, however, decided that this option was too expensive (£80 million, compared to £60 million to cut through the Down) and would cause further delay. When John Browne, Conservative MP for Winchester, wrote to

the DoT suggesting that a toll tunnel could be dug using funds from the private sector, the reply was that the matter was closed - 20 years of debate and four public inquiries had given the protesters ample time to raise any objections they had. Besides, a toll tunnel might cause extra congestion on existing routes if traffic chose not to use it.

Lobbying the EU

In 1990, a complaint was lodged with the European Commission on the grounds that the British government had breached European law by failing to implement the EC's 1985 Environmental Assessment Directive which required that major projects should be submitted for approval before proceeding. The Environmental Commissioner, Carlo Ripa di Meana, made a public announcement that the Commission had decided to look further into the UK's implementation of this directive - not just in connection with Twyford Down, but also in connection with seven other road-building projects. He wrote personally to Malcolm Rifkind, asking him:

> 'not to proceed with work on these projects so that the environment will neither be lost nor damaged beyond repair.' (EC press release, 17 October 1991)

Prime Minister, John Major, was furious at what he saw as European interference in British affairs. He claimed that this matter had nothing to do with the European Union.

It is difficult to describe exactly what happened at the Commission since much of their activity takes place behind closed doors. Nevertheless, on 31 July 1992, the Commission announced that it would drop legal action against the British government in five out of the seven cases - including that relating to Twyford Down.

Non-violent direct action

In an attempt to put pressure on the government, the Twyford Down Association (in conjunction with other pressure groups, notably FoE) organised a number of high profile demonstrations. These culminated in a mass demonstration in June 1992. Demonstrators were of all ages and from many different backgrounds - from professional people like doctors and lawyers to those who had opted out of mainstream society like travellers and members of the so-called 'Donga tribe' ('Dongas' are medieval trackways or drovers' roads, some of which had survived on Twyford Down before the road construction).

Using the electoral system

When the general election date was announced in 1992, Barbara Bryant (a lifelong Conservative and member of the Twyford Down Association) organised a campaign to encourage voters in Winchester to vote tactically (ie to put aside personal party preferences and to vote for the candidate which had the best chance of defeating the Conservative candidate since it was the Conservative government which had allowed the cutting route to go ahead). The campaign was unsuccessful. The Conservative candidate was elected with 33,113 votes, a majority of 8,121. The combined votes of the Labour and Liberal Democrat candidates came to 29,909.

In September 1992, construction on the cutting through Twyford Down began.

Direct action

Some protesters felt that the only alternative left was direct action. Members of the Donga tribe, for example, pitched teepees at the Dongas' area of the Down, right in the path of the motorway route, and refused to move. Group 4, a security firm employed by the DoT, used physical force to remove the protesters.

Main points - Section 3.3

- **Plans to extend the M3 motorway were first considered in the 1970s. Three routes were considered. The third and final route involved cutting though Twyford Down.**
- **Twyford Down contained two Scheduled Ancient Monuments, two Sites of Special Scientific Interest (SSSI) and one Area of Outstanding Natural Beauty.**
- **Opponents of the route used the following tactics to pressurise the government into changing its mind:**

organising petitions; building a national campaign; suggesting an alternative (a tunnel); appealing to the EU; organising peaceful demonstrations; encouraging tactical voting; direct action.
- **The government faced pressure from opponents of the scheme, supporters of the scheme and the European Commission. The fact that a Conservative MP was elected in Winchester in 1992 may also have been taken into account.**

Activity 1.4 *The Battle of Twyford Down*

Item A   *A mass demonstration*

At the end of June, Friends of the Earth organised a march along the length of the M3 route. Designed as a focus for all Twyford Down supporters, it was an opportunity to pay our last respects to the Down. Although the European Commission had still not announced its decision, there was an understanding by the summer of 1992 that nothing now could save Twyford Down. There was, however, an increasing awareness of the potential that Twyford Down offered as an example of the damage the road-building programme was inflicting on the landscape of southern England. In Surrey, for example, the Devil's Punchbowl at Hindhead was threatened by plans to improve the A3 and campaigners there had recently 'borrowed' our idea and achieved excellent coverage in the press with a 'NO' shape produced by volunteers holding white boards skywards while standing in

The final mass march organised by the Twyford Down Association in June 1992.

the formation of NO. We strongly believed that whatever the outcome at Twyford Down, the greater the profile it achieved and the more the Department of Transport was forced to justify its decision to press ahead with the cutting, the better the chance of saving other special places. So, the rally in June was not seen as an empty gesture, but as part of a much wider campaign to put an end to the mindless destruction of an unchecked road building programme.

Adapted from Bryant 1996.

Item B *The government viewpoint*

We fully considered the scheme, its effects on such things as visual impact, heritage and conservation areas, ecology, water and drainage, noise and agriculture, and we have taken many steps to reduce the impact of the road, including turning the existing A33 back into downland habitat. Of course, everyone has a right to protest, providing they do so within the law. But, what we have seen here is people trespassing on the Department's land, stopping the rescue of ecological rich turf, and putting themselves at risk from construction equipment. We have had to employ a detective agency to obtain photographic evidence of trespass and serve notice on the trespassers. Because this was a civil offence, trespassers were removed from the property by security personnel using minimum force. No action was taken against protesters acting lawfully.

Comments made by Kenneth Carlisle, Parliamentary Under Secretary of State for Transport, in a television documentary broadcast in 1993.

Item C *The result*

This photograph shows the M3 extension at Twyford Down in November 1997.

Questions

1. 'The Battle of Twyford Down shows that power rests entirely with the British government'. Is this a fair statement? Use Items A and B in your answer.

2. Do pressure groups exercise any power? Use Item A in your answer.

3. What arguments might a protester use to counter those put forward in Item B?

4. a) Make a list of the different sorts of political activity which took place during the decision-making process which led to the scene shown in Item C.
   b) Describe which groups exercised power and how they exercised it.
   c) Does the Battle for Twyford Down provide evidence in support of the pluralist, élitist or Marxist model of power? Explain your answer.

References

Bryant (1996) Bryant, B., *Twyford Down*, Chapman and Hall, 1996.

Dowse & Hughes (1972) Dowse, R.E. & Hughes, J.A., *Political Sociology*, John Wiley & Sons, 1972.

Dunleavy et al. (1997) Dunleavy, P., Gamble, A., Holliday, I. & Peele, G., *Developments in British Politics 5*, Macmillan, 1997.

Evans (1997) Evans, M., 'Political participation' in *Dunleavy et al. (1997)*.

Haralambos & Holborn (1995) Haralambos, M. & Holborn, M., *Sociology: Themes and Perspectives*, HarperCollins, 1995.

Heywood (1994) Heywood, A., *Political Ideas and Concepts*, Macmillan, 1994.

HMSO (1994) Central Office of Information, *The British System of Government*, HMSO, 1994.

Leftwich (1984) Leftwich, A., *What is Politics?*, Basil Blackwell, 1984.

Lukes (1974) Lukes, S., *Power*, Macmillan, 1974.

Norris (1997) Norris, P., 'Political communications' in *Dunleavy et al. (1997)*.

Pelling (1987) Pelling, H., *A History of British Trade Unionism*, Pelican, 1987.

Schumpeter (1974) Schumpeter, J.A., *Capitalism, Socialism and Democracy*, Urwin, 1974.

Social Trends (1998) Office for National Statistics, *Social Trends 28*, HMSO, 1998.

Whiteley & Seyd (1998) Whiteley, P. & Seyd, P., *New Labour, New Grass Roots Party?* Paper presented at Keele University, April 1998.

Whiteley et al. (1994) Whiteley, P, Seyd, P. & Richardson, J., *True Blues*, Oxford University Press, 1994.

2 Political ideology

Introduction

Consider the following three statements: 'people are basically selfish and cannot be trusted'; 'the way to reduce crime is to make punishments more severe'; and, 'government should get off our backs'. Do you agree or disagree with each statement? Your answer to this question is important not just because it indicates how you feel about three separate and specific issues but also because it says something about the way in which you view the world. Although everyone views the world in their own, unique way, groups of people hold ideas, beliefs, prejudices, hopes and fears in common. In a group of ten people, for example, three might agree with all three of the above statements, five might agree with the first two statements but not the third whilst the remaining two might disagree with all three statements. Because groups of people view the world in a similar way, it is possible to identify reasonably coherent structures of thought which are shared by each group. These reasonably coherent structures of thought are known as 'ideologies'.

The identification and analysis of different ideologies is important because it provides explanations of how and why people act as they do and what direction society could or should follow. But such issues are analysed and explained in quite different ways depending on which ideology is used as a guide. It is rather as if each ideology provides us with a pair of glasses which produces its own version of the truth. Change the glasses and the political world is viewed quite differently.

In British politics, three key pairs of ideological glasses have been used to view the political landscape: liberalism, conservatism and socialism. This chapter examines the nature of these ideologies, their evolution and the differences between them.

Chapter summary

Part 1 describes the origin and meaning of the term 'ideology'. It examines ways in which ideologies can be used as analytical tools.

Part 2 looks at the core ideas of liberalism. It focuses on the way in which contemporary forms of liberalism evolved from classical liberalism.

Part 3 considers the meaning and development of conservatism - from Burke in the 18th century to

the emergence of the New Right and conservatism in the 1990s.

Part 4 explores the values and beliefs of socialism, including the impact of Marxism. The differences between democratic socialism and social democracy are analysed.

Part 5 provides an overview of other ideologies and discusses the role they play in British politics.

Part 1 What is an ideology?

Key issues

1. How did the term 'ideology' originate and develop?
2. What are political ideologies' concerns?
3. How can ideologies be used as analytical tools?

1.1 The origins and definition of the term 'ideology'

Origins of the term

The term 'ideology' was first used by the French writer Antoine Destutt de Tracy in his *Elements d'Ideologie*, written between 1801 and 1805. the new term referred to a 'science of ideas' which was to be the basis of a new and better way of conducting politics. This science of ideas was to be free from the kind of prejudice and bias often associated with the intolerance of religious beliefs. In this sense, ideology was not just concerned with ideas but was also a hunt for an objective, scientific and truthful approach to politics.

The problems with defining the term

Since then the term 'ideology' has been used in a number of ways. Eagleton (1991), for example, provides 16 separate definitions of the term and suggests that:

> 'Nobody has yet come up with a single adequate definition of ideology...This is not because workers in this field are remarkable for their low intelligence but because the term "ideology" has a whole range of useful meanings, not all of which are compatible with each other. To try to compress this wealth of meaning into a single comprehensive definition would thus be unhelpful even if it were possible.' (Eagleton 1991, p.1)

Four uses of the term

Whilst it may not be possible to come up with a single, suitable definition, it is possible to identify four distinct ways in which the term 'ideology' has been used.

First, Marx and Engels (1846) suggested that ideology was a set of false and misleading beliefs which provided legitimacy to the existing power structures and prevented the oppressed and exploited masses from seeing and seeking solutions to their oppression.

Second, the philosopher Karl Popper used the term 'ideology' in a negative sense and argued that ideologies were 'closed' systems of political thought:

> 'Ideologies claim a monopoly of truth, they seek to explain everything and in so doing refuse to tolerate rival views or opposing theories. An ideology is thus a "secular religion", which leads to intolerance, censorship and political repression.' (Heywood 1992, p.7)

Third, when people use the term 'ideology' in ordinary conversation they often use it as a term of abuse. A person who acts 'ideologically' is characterised as a person who is extreme, inflexible and intransigent. The implication is that people whose actions are motivated by ideology are completely committed to a set of beliefs which they follow blindly with their minds closed to alternative views. Those who are guided by ideology have a hidden agenda and are, therefore, not to be trusted.

And fourth, an ideology is:

> 'A set of ideas by which men posit, explain and justify the ends and means of organised social action, irrespective of whether such action aims to preserve, amend, uproot or rebuild a given social order.' (Seliger 1976, p.11)

The descriptive meaning of ideology

The term 'ideology' is most often used by political scientists in this way:

> **An ideology is a reasonably coherent structure of thought shared by a group of people. It is a means of explaining how society works and of explaining how it ought to work.**

Dobson (1992) describes this as the 'descriptive' meaning of ideology and argues that an ideology in this sense has four elements:

- a concept of human essence
- an idea about how history has developed and why
- the role of the state as it is and ought to be
- broad policy prescriptions based on its analysis.
(Dobson 1992, p.17)

1.2 Key questions

Ideology and human nature

What is the real nature of human beings? Should people be optimists and regard others as essentially trustworthy and able to make their own decisions with a minimum of interference or should they be pessimists who believe that people are flawed and in need of control? How important are people's backgrounds? Does experience shape people's behaviour or is character pre-determined?

Such questions may seem to be a long way from what is usually thought of as politics. But that is not so. Take the issue of censorship for example. Those 'optimists' who regard people as essentially trustworthy are likely to oppose censorship because, in their view, people are capable of making up their own minds about what they see, listen to or read. 'Pessimists', on the other hand, believe that people are essentially flawed and so, to them, censorship is necessary to ensure control.

Similarly, different views about human nature are often the basis of disputes about policy towards crime and punishment. Those who believe that experience shapes people's behaviour are likely to argue that crime is caused by poor social conditions and that improving these conditions would reduce crime. But those who believe that people's characters are pre-determined are likely to argue that some people are born criminals and it is in society's interest to keep these criminals locked up.

Ideology and the past

How strong a role should tradition play in our lives? Should changes in society be cautious and build on what we know about the past? Or, should changes mean a radical break with the past? The answer to these questions depends on how what happened in the past is interpreted. History is not simply a collection of facts or objective truths, it is a matter of judgement. For example, although all historians would agree that it was the Labour government elected in 1945 which set up the welfare state, not all historians would agree that this was a good thing. Indeed, some historians have argued that the setting up of the welfare state exacerbated Britain's economic and political decline whilst others have argued that it was a positive development which led to several decades of social stability. There is no correct answer here. Historians on both sides use the same evidence. The difference lies in their approach and their attitude towards that evidence. In other words, the way in which they interpret the past is determined by their ideological stance. And, this is not just the case with professional historians. It is also the case with anyone who formulates an argument which expresses a view of the past or cites a historical precedent.

The individual and the group

What kind of identity do we have or should we have? Should we see ourselves as individuals, members of a class, a community, a nation, a race? People need a sense of place in the world. But, what should be the basis for this? Given that people are all members of different groups, which one (if any) should be paramount? The position of an individual in society can cause particular disagreement. Some believe, for example, that the crucial unit is the individual and that individuals should be encouraged to pursue their own self-interest because, in this way, everybody would benefit. Others argue that this simply encourages selfishness and works against the wider interests of the community or against society as a whole. Still others argue that the nation or the race is the supreme unit and individuals only have any importance as part of such a group.

Ideology and the state

Given that the state consists of the government, civil service, police, judiciary, armed forces and so on, it is bound to be of primary significance to all ideologies even though there is considerable disagreement about what its role ought to be. Do we need a strong state or are our interests best served by a much more limited structure with fewer powers? Does the power of the state pose a threat to our freedom or enhance it? What should be the main priority of the state - order, greater equality, freedom? Is 'big government' a positive benefit because it can improve our lives through planning and the provision of social services or does this produce a 'nanny state' where people are reluctant to look after themselves and expect everything to be done for them from the cradle to the grave?

Conclusions

It is useful to unpick an ideology so that the component parts can be identified. But these parts are also interrelated. Views about human nature, for example, influence attitudes towards the role of the state. Those who believe that individuals are capable of managing their own affairs are likely to regard a powerful state as unnecessary and perhaps even a danger to individual freedom. Those who are more dubious about human nature probably prefer a strong state, if only to maintain order. It is this kind of interrelationship which helps to provide coherence and consistency to an ideology and, therefore, gives it a clearer identity.

It should be noted, however, that just because an ideology is called 'liberalism' or 'conservatism' that does not mean that it can only apply to the Liberal Party or the Conservative Party. It is true that ideologies are often heavily associated with a particular party, but the relationship is not entirely straightforward. Key liberal ideas, for example, have influenced both the Conservative Party and the Labour Party. Similarly, it could be argued that Margaret Thatcher was a liberal rather than a conservative when she was Leader of the Conservative Party. The activity which follows looks at a number of models which have been used to classify ideologies.

Main points - Part 1

- The term 'ideology' was first used at the beginning of the 19th century. Today, it is a difficult term to define because it is used in different ways.
- A definition accepted by most political commentators is: 'an ideology is a reasonably coherent structure of thought shared by a group of people. It is a means of explaining how society works and of explaining how it ought to work.'
- An ideology defined in this way has four main elements: (1) a view of human nature; (2) a view of history; (3) a view of the relative importance of the individual and the group; and (4) a view of the role of the state.
- Political parties are often influenced by more than one ideology. Key liberal ideas, for example, have not just influenced the Liberal Democrats. They have influenced the Conservative Party and Labour Party too.

Activity 2.1 Classifying ideologies

Item A *The linear model*

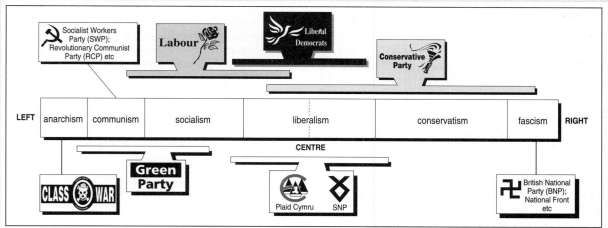

Political scientists who use the left/right linear model of the political spectrum argue that it reflects different political values about economic policy and different attitudes towards equality. Left wingers aim for greater equality and this is reflected in their economic policies. Those on the far left argue for a state-planned economy whilst socialists and liberals support a mixed economy. Right wingers claim that equality is either undesirable or impossible and support free market capitalism and privately owned property. The model is inconsistent, however. Some fascist regimes practised state ownership, for example, and anarchists are usually located on the left but they do not support state control.

Adapted from Heywood 1992.

Item B *Eysenck's model*

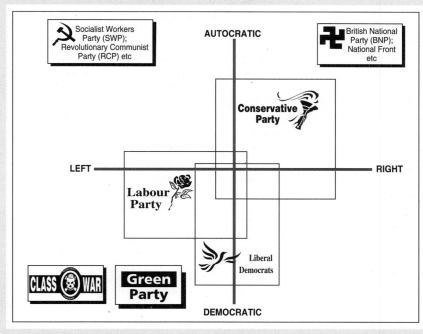

This diagram (left) is based on the model first suggested by Eysenck (1964). He accepted the left/right spectrum as the horizontal axis of his spectrum, but added a vertical axis. This vertical axis measured political attitudes which were, at one end, democratic (open and accountable) and, at the other end, autocratic (closed and not accountable). This model makes clear the similarities between extreme groups (for example, the fascists and communists) but also indicates the difference between them (for example, by placing the fascists on the extreme right and the communists on the extreme left).

Adapted from Heywood 1992.

Item C *The 'horseshoe' model*

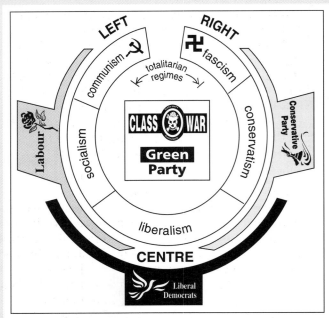

The 'horseshoe' model attempts to overcome the problems of the linear model by emphasising the similarities between the extremes. Both communist and fascist regimes have been described as repressive and authoritarian and so, in this model, they appear side by side. Critics argue that this overplays the similarities. In some respects, for example, Nazi Germany (a fascist state) was very different from the Soviet Union under Stalin (a communist state). For example, capitalism thrived under Nazism whilst it was eradicated by Stalin.

Adapted from Heywood 1992.

Item D *The political spectrum*

The origin of the terms 'left' and 'right' dates back to the French Revolution. Different groups sat in different positions at the first meeting of the Estates-General in 1789. Aristocrats who supported the king sat on his right while radicals sat on his left. As a result 'right' was used of reactionaries (people who opposed change or wanted the old system to remain) whilst 'left' was used of revolutionaries (people who wanted radical change). Today the left/right divide still exists but it no longer simply distinguishes between reactionaries and revolutionaries. Although some right wingers are reactionaries, others are not. Similarly, although some left wingers are revolutionaries, others resist change.

Adapted from Heywood 1992.

Questions

1. Using Items A-D, give the arguments for and against pinpointing a person's ideological stance using the terms 'left' and 'right'.

2. Devise a questionnaire that could be used to find out where people fit on the political spectrum.

3. a) What do Items A, B and C tell us about the ideological stance of the three major political parties in Britain?

   b) In your view, which of the three models gives the most realistic account of political debate in Britain today? Give reasons for your answer.

Part 2 Liberalism

Key issues

1. What is liberalism?
2. How did it develop?
3. What is the difference between 'classical' liberalism and 'progressive' liberalism?

2.1 The development of liberal ideas

A. The political roots of liberalism

The political roots of modern liberalism lie in the 17th and 18th centuries when new forces challenged the concentration of political power. The English Civil War of the 1640s led to the execution of Charles I and the creation of a short-lived republic. Although the monarchy was restored in 1660, James II was forced to flee the country in the 'Glorious Revolution' of 1688. It was in this context that the arguments of John Locke (1632-1704) had a considerable impact on the development of liberal ideas.

The writing of John Locke

Locke argued that all people have certain 'natural rights' (the right to life, liberty and property) which cannot be removed except by the agreement of the people themselves. It follows from this that government should be based on the consent of the people as a whole and government should only be tolerated as long as it is prepared to defend the rights of the people. If a government becomes tyrannical and denies its citizens their rights, then it is justifiable for these citizens to withdraw their consent and to rebel against it. To avoid tyranny, Locke argued, there should be limits to the powers of government. For example, the executive (the government) should be separate from the legislature (Parliament) so that power is not over-concentrated.

Locke's arguments made a major impact. For example, the *American Declaration of Independence* of 1776 justified the break with Britain in terms which Locke would have found familiar:

'Men are endowed by their creator with certain unalienable rights; that among them are life, liberty and the pursuit of happiness. That to secure these rights, governments are instituted among men, deriving their just powers from the consent of the governed; that whenever any form of government becomes destructive of these ends, it is the right of the people to alter or abolish it and to institute a new government.'

By emphasising the need for consent and for limits on the powers of government, Locke laid the philosophical basis for future liberal reforms.

B. The economic roots of liberalism

Adam Smith
In the 18th and 19th centuries the old economic order was challenged by the development of new industries and new ways of work in the Industrial Revolution. The old view was that the state should protect the economy against competition by maintaining high tariffs (a tariff is a tax or a duty placed on goods coming into the country) and by discouraging trade between nations. This view came under attack from liberal economists such as Adam Smith (1723-90). Smith criticised constraints on trade, arguing that the increasing importance of manufacturing and its voracious appetite for raw materials meant that the interests of factory and mine owners lay in widening trade as much as possible. The general prosperity of the country, he claimed, depended on a willingness to accept the forces of the market based on freedom and competition.

According to Smith there was a 'hidden hand of the market' which consisted of thousands of individual decisions made by buyers and sellers. Produce the right goods and profit would follow. Produce the wrong goods and the result was loss and failure. Prosperity depended on allowing people the freedom to make such decisions.

2.2 Classical liberalism

What is classical liberalism?
Locke, Smith and other writers who challenged the old order and emphasised the importance of freedom, choice and the needs of emerging capitalism helped to create and develop classical liberalism. Classical liberalism became enormously influential in British politics in the 19th century. Its core ideas can be identified as follows.

Classical liberalism and human nature
The liberal tradition is to be guardedly optimistic about human nature and about the capacity of people to run their own affairs. This approach stems from the belief that people are rational. Since people know what is in their own interests, they are, therefore, able and willing to make their own

choices (whether economic or political) with the minimum of interference.

The individual is at the heart of classical liberalism. Indeed, the purpose of politics is to enable individuals to develop their talents and abilities so that they can maximise their own happiness. The centrality of the individual is reinforced by the belief that all individuals possess 'inalienable rights' which it is the duty of the state to protect. The liberal philosopher John Stuart Mill (1806-73) argued that individuals should have complete freedom to do whatever they wanted so long as it did not harm others.

Classical liberalism and the past
Classical liberalism views society as an aggregate of individuals rather than a body having some kind of collective identity of its own. Reform (which is often equated with 'progress') is seen as both possible and desirable, especially when directed towards maximising the freedom of individuals to make their own choices. According to this view, therefore, social change is the result of individual self-improvement. The liberal view of history is that there is a steady progression towards the formation of a more just and fairer society based on rational principles.

Classical liberalism and the state
Liberal attitudes towards the state can be illustrated by the comment of the American President Thomas Jefferson who claimed 'that which governs best governs least'. There were two main reasons for such an approach. First, given the stress on the importance of individuals and their capacity for self-government, the role of the state was naturally seen to be minimal. And second, liberals realised that if individuals pursued their self-interest this could mean the emergence of leaders anxious to use their power for their own advantage. The state could become a source of tyranny. Common sense therefore dictated that such a possibility could be avoided by both limiting the overall power of the state and by separating the power it was given between different institutions so that it could not be concentrated into the hands of one person or group.

At the same time, liberals accepted that some exercise of state power was necessary to protect individual interests themselves - for example by preserving law and order and providing protection from external threats. But, they argued, the state should never be above the law.

The core of classical liberalism
Liberalism is concerned with three key concepts - freedom, equality and toleration.

1. Freedom
Freedom is important because liberalism is

concerned to allow the greatest possible freedom to the individual. The problem is where to draw the line. When are limits on freedom justified? What (if any) constraints should there be on what people can do in pursuit of their own interests?

2. Equality

Equality is closely linked with freedom. For example, by agreeing that all people should have equality before the law and equal political rights, liberals suggest that each individual should have an equal (though restricted) amount of freedom. Similarly, liberals support equality of opportunity but accept that this will not necessarily produce an equal outcome. Even if everybody has an equal opportunity to do something, some people will do it better than others. In this sense, equality, therefore, becomes the right to be unequal.

3. Toleration

Linked to the desire for freedom and equality is the liberal's ability to tolerate opposing viewpoints. The essence of toleration is to accept people and ideas which we dislike. By believing in the existence of natural rights, such as the freedom to worship, liberals are bound to apply such rights to everyone.

The essence of classical liberalism

According to Hall (1988), it is because concern about freedom, equality and tolerance is at the heart of classical liberalism that liberals are open-minded, rational, freedom-loving people. Their commitment to individual liberty makes them sceptical of the claims of tradition and prepared to question established authority. But, the commitment to individual liberty also means that liberals are often unwilling to interfere in people's private affairs. As a result, in the 19th century, liberal politicians supported minimal interference by the state.

2.3 Progressive liberalism

What is progressive liberalism?

Classical liberalism developed and gained popularity in the late 18th and early 19th centuries, at the time when Britain's industrial base was becoming established. But, industrialisation brought unforeseen social and political changes in its wake. Over time, these social and political changes modified the interpretation and application of classical liberalism.

The changing role of the state

Perhaps the most important way in which liberalism developed in the 19th century was in relation to the role of the state. Classical liberalism supported minimal interference by the state. The experience of industrialisation, however, raised questions about the legitimacy of this. Despite the Victorian emphasis on the virtue of 'self-help', the existence of widespread poverty led to calls for government intervention. Local authorities found that by building schools,

hospitals, libraries and houses they could make significant improvements. Besides, surveys carried out at the end of the 19th century found that many people living in poverty simply did not have sufficient means with which to help themselves even if they wanted to. As a result, some liberals began to argue for greater state intervention. T.H. Green, for example, argued that the pursuit of freedom must take into account the practical ability of people to develop their abilities whilst L. Hobhouse supported the need to intervene in the market place to secure basic rights such as a living wage. These new ideas, sometimes described as 'progressive liberalism', found their way into the political mainstream in the early part of the 20th century. The Liberal government of 1906 to 1914, for example, intervened in areas of life previously untouched by government by introducing old age pensions, national health insurance and unemployment insurance.

Progressive liberalism's 'golden age'

Progressive liberalism's period of greatest influence, however, came in the first three decades after the Second World War. This was mainly due to the work of two progressive liberals - John Maynard Keynes and William Beveridge. Keynes, an economist, argued that the government should be active in managing or manipulating the nation's economy by using a variety of fiscal and monetary policies such as the raising or lowering of taxes and the spending of public money on government-sponsored projects. Keynesian economic policies were pursued by both Labour and Conservative governments between 1945 and the mid-1970s (see Chapter 15, Section 1.3). Beveridge produced for the wartime government a report entitled *Social Insurance and Allied Services*. This report, published in 1942, became the blueprint for the welfare state which was set up by the post-war Labour government. The Beveridge Report was concerned with how best to deal with the problems caused by unemployment, sickness and low income. It recommended a system of insurance which would be organised by the state. All those in work would pay insurance to fund benefits for those who were ill or out of work. Healthcare and education were to be regarded as basic rights and to be provided free by the state (see also Chapter 3, Section 1.1).

2.4 Neo-liberalism

What is neo-liberalism?

Although progressive liberalism was the dominant ideology during the period of post-war consensus (1945-c.1975), Keynesian economics and the welfare state have increasingly come under attack. Since Margaret Thatcher's election as Conservative Party Leader (in 1975) and certainly since her election as

Prime Minister (in 1979), a new and distinctive type of liberalism has emerged - neo-liberalism. Neo-liberalism is usually associated with the New Right (see Section 3.3 below) and can be characterised as follows:

> 'Economic liberalism or neo-liberalism, often seen as the dominant theme within the New Right, draws heavily upon classical liberalism; it advocates that the frontiers of the state be rolled back and proclaims the virtues of private enterprise, the free market and individual responsibility. As such, neo-liberalism can be seen as a backlash against the steady growth of state power perpetrated [put into place] through much of the 20th century by liberal, socialist and conservative governments. Neo-liberals support an extreme form of individualism which leaves little room for public services or the provision of social welfare.' (Heywood 1994, p.11)

Main points - Part 2

- The political roots of liberalism lie in the 17th century with the writing of John Locke who argued that people have 'natural rights'.
- The economic roots of liberalism lie in the 18th century with the writing of Adam Smith who argued that prosperity depended on allowing people to trade in a free market.
- There are three core concepts at the heart of liberalism - freedom, equality and toleration. Liberalism has taken three forms: (1) classical liberalism (which focused on the needs of the individual); (2) progressive liberalism (which focused on what the state could do to help the individual); and (3) neo-liberalism (which rejected the approach of progressive liberalism and refocused on the needs of the individual).

Activity 2.2 Different types of liberalism

Item A *Classical and progressive liberalism*

(i) The spirit of self-help is the root of all genuine growth in the individual. Help from others is often weakening whilst self-help is strengthening. Whatever is done for men or groups takes away the incentive (encouragement) and necessity of doing it themselves. And where people are over-guided and over-governed, the inevitable tendency is for them to become comparatively helpless.

From Smiles 1859.

(ii) The working classes have done their best during the past 50 years to make provision without the aid of the state. But, it is insufficient. The old man has to bear his own burden while in the case of a young man who is broken down and who has a wife and family to maintain, the suffering is increased and multiplied to that extent. These problems of the sick, of the ill, of the men who cannot find means of earning a living are problems with which it is the business of the state to deal. They are problems which the state has neglected for too long.

Part of a speech made to Parliament by David Lloyd George on 15 June 1908.

Item B *Liberalism and the Liberal Democrats*

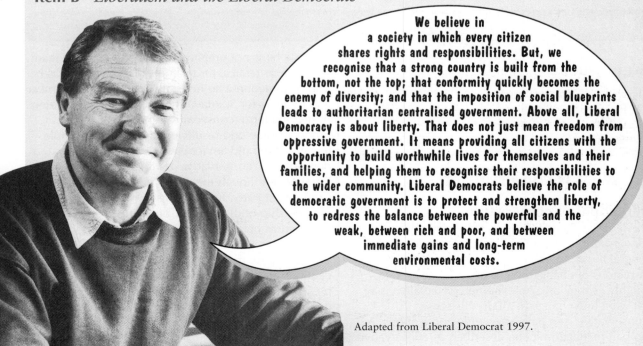

We believe in a society in which every citizen shares rights and responsibilities. But, we recognise that a strong country is built from the bottom, not the top; that conformity quickly becomes the enemy of diversity; and that the imposition of social blueprints leads to authoritarian centralised government. Above all, Liberal Democracy is about liberty. That does not just mean freedom from oppressive government. It means providing all citizens with the opportunity to build worthwhile lives for themselves and their families, and helping them to recognise their responsibilities to the wider community. Liberal Democrats believe the role of democratic government is to protect and strengthen liberty, to redress the balance between the powerful and the weak, between rich and poor, and between immediate gains and long-term environmental costs.

Adapted from Liberal Democrat 1997.

Item C *Neo-liberalism*

In 1979, the Conservatives came to power under the leadership of Margaret Thatcher with a clear and consistent neo-liberal programme. This was quite different from the consensus policies all the main parties had offered for the previous 30 years. The overall aim of the Thatcher governments from 1979 was to restore the UK's prosperity. This was to be achieved by relying on the free market, minimal government interference, and individual liberty and responsibility. The strategy was to create the conditions in which free enterprise could flourish. Policies can be grouped into four closely related areas:

This cartoon pokes fun at the faith which Prime Minister Margaret Thatcher (right) and her Chancellor Nigel Lawson (centre) placed in a free market. It was published in March 1985.

- the conquest of inflation
- reducing the size and cost of the state
- providing incentives for hard work and enterprise
- removing restrictions on the operation of the free market.

Yet, while the Thatcher governments wished to roll back state influence on economic life, at the same time, they supported a strong state in relation to public order, social morality and defence. Thatcherites were highly critical of what they saw as a breakdown of order and social stability and they tended to blame this on the spread of 'liberal' and permissive values.

Adapted from Adams 1993 and Heywood 1994.

Questions

1. Using the passages in Item A write an article explaining what classical liberalism and progressive liberalism have in common and how they differ.
2. To what extent do liberal principles guide the ideas outlined in Item B? Give reasons for your answer.

3. a) Judging from Item C, what is neo-liberalism and how does it differ from other forms of liberalism?
   b) 'Thatcherites not Liberal Democrats are the real heirs of classical liberalism.' Using Items A-C, give arguments for and against this view.

Part 3 Conservatism

Key issues

1. What is conservatism?
2. How did it develop?
3. What are the different strands of conservatism?

3.1 What is conservatism?

Definitions of conservatism

The term 'conservative' is used in ordinary conversation to describe a certain state of mind. In general terms, to be conservative is to be cautious, suspicious of change and to prefer to keep things roughly as they are. An extreme conservative may not want any change at all. In this sense, 'conservative' can have very wide applications. A football manager may be described as conservative because he is not prepared to experiment with team selection or tactics, for example. The same could be said of someone who finds anything other than meat and two veg for Sunday dinner unacceptably daring.

Using the term 'conservative' in this way can produce some odd results politically. For example, leaders of the old Soviet Union were frequently described as 'conservative' by the mass media in Britain even though they were all members of the Communist Party. In Britain itself, however, membership of the British Communist Party was regarded as being incompatible with conservatism.

As this example suggests, conservatism in a strict political sense means more than simply having a cautious attitude towards change and a tendency to prefer the status quo (though this is part of its definition). Conservatism as an ideology has distinct views on human nature, for example, and on the role of the state.

Conservatism and human nature

As with all ideologies, views about the nature of human beings underpin a great deal of conservative thinking. Conservatives tend to have few illusions or idealistic hopes about people. It is not just that they see people as being flawed. Rather, conservatives argue that experience shows that people are capable of a whole range of emotions and these different emotions motivate their behaviour in different ways. People are sometimes selfish, sometimes generous, sometimes inconsistent and sometimes quite logical. As a result, conservatives believe that it would be extremely dangerous to base politics on the belief that people are or could be completely rational or predictable in their dealings with one another.

Such views have considerable implications. They mean, for example, that the maintenance of peace and order in society requires a proper framework organised by the state and cannot be left to self-regulation by individuals. Equally, conservatives have little hesitation in blaming human nature for many of the imperfections and problems seen in society.

In addition, conservatives argue that it is a characteristic of human beings that talent and ability are not equally distributed. Therefore, any attempt to impose equality on society is doomed to failure either because natural inequalities are bound to reappear or because the enforcement of equality would require such drastic policies that the result would be a police state. Some conservatives argue that this natural inequality does not lead inevitably to the exploitation of the less privileged since those in a privileged position have a responsibility to use their advantages for the benefit of others.

Conservatism and the past

Edmund Burke

The conservative view of the past was first set out by Edmund Burke (1729-97) in his *Reflections on the Revolution in France* which was published in 1790, two years after the French Revolution began. Burke saw the French Revolution as a completely undesirable challenge to order, continuity and stability. He believed that society evolves over time and is the product of the gradually accumulated wisdom of the past. It certainly cannot be improved through rapid, especially violent, change. Nor can it be improved by following any kind of abstract idea or blueprint. Reform in society may be desirable sometimes, but it should always be gradual and built on experience. If it is not, the great danger is that a harmonious social fabric, sanctified by tradition, could be recklessly swept away and replaced by chaos.

Love of tradition

Burke's arguments are still highly relevant. Modern conservatism emphasises that society should be allowed to develop naturally so that it can reflect the deep needs, values and beliefs which have stood the test of time. Institutions which have evolved (such as Parliament) deserve respect precisely because they have this historic seal of approval. They have proved their worth. Similar arguments can be used to justify the importance of the ownership of property. Ownership is a reflection of the established rights of individuals and it is a source of stability.

Cautious support for change

So, if change is necessary, the conservative approach would be to base it on experience and to proceed cautiously. Take the British monarchy for example, This still remains intact, though the monarchy today is very different from that at the beginning of the century (for example, it is less remote than it used to be). Conservatives would argue that it is by responding to changing values and attitudes that the British monarchy has managed to survive in a period when many other monarchies have been discarded.

Opposition to idealistic blueprints

It is the conservatives' respect for tradition which makes idealistic blueprints for social reform a particular target for criticism. According to conservatives these are flawed in two ways. They are likely to be based on a lack of understanding of what people really want and, more dangerously, they can destroy something which works. Such a view can be illustrated by the rush to build tower blocks in the 1950s and 1960s. More accommodation was needed at the time, but it can be argued that many of the schemes subsequently failed because they did not take into account the long, established tradition of British people living in houses rather than flats. The result is that, 40 years later, many of these tower blocks are being pulled down.

Conservatism, the individual and the group

Whereas liberalism emphasises the importance of the individual as a basic unit, conservatism stresses the role played by the family and the nation. It is through the family that values can be passed from one generation to the next and, again, this contributes to social harmony. The nation, on the other hand, is typically seen by conservatives as a place where people live in harmony and share deep-seated values and interests. If conflict does occur, it is likely to be blamed on 'troublemakers'. Patriotism, therefore, becomes a source of identity and a stabilising influence because it provides people with a sense of place and a pride in national achievement. To conservatives, the nation is an expression of collective purpose and the symbols of nationhood (such as the flag, the national anthem and celebrations of past achievements or even past defeats) help to weld people together.

Conservatism and the state

Inevitably, to conservatives, the flaws in human nature alone require a controlling structure. Burke said that good order is the foundation of all good things and conservatism stresses the importance of the rule of law, duty and hierarchy. Here, the state is expected to play an important role. The task of the state, however, is not and cannot be to make people good. Rather, it is to provide a strong framework within which people can be protected while they pursue their own lives.

Conservative attitudes towards the state are also influenced by traditional respect for the values and virtues of leadership. If human nature is unreliable, then it is hardly surprising that mass participation in decision making is treated very cautiously and the importance of leadership is emphasised. Since talents, including leadership talent, are not equally distributed, society needs the guidance of the more able.

3.2 Different strands of conservatism

Conservatism and the Conservative Party

Just as liberalism contains two distinct strands (classical liberalism and progressive liberalism), it is possible to distinguish between a number of different strands of conservatism. In their analysis of the Conservative Party, Whiteley and his colleagues (1994) suggest that there are three distinct ideological tendencies within the Conservative Party. All three tendencies can be described as variations of conservatism.

1. Traditional conservatism

Whiteley and his colleagues (1994) suggest that traditional conservatism is derived from the values and attitudes traditionally held by the land-owning aristocracy. They categorise it as follows:

> 'It stresses patriotism and authority but often opposes social and political changes such as the emancipation of women, racial integration, the legalisation of abortion and easier divorce...It tends to oppose Britain's closer integration with Europe and is covertly, if not occasionally overtly, racist. Traditionalists are also strong supporters of the idea of social discipline and law and order; they strongly favour capital punishment and emphasise the importance of punishment as a means of dealing with crime...Traditionalists tend to oppose constitutional changes in society, preferring to retain old forms of government. They are strongly attached to the monarchy and to institutions like the House of Lords and would oppose constitutional changes like the introduction of a Bill of Rights.' (Whiteley et al. 1994, pp.130-1)

2. 'One nation' conservatism (see also Chapter 8, Section 2.1)

One nation conservatism was developed in the mid-19th century. This brand of conservatism was first outlined by Benjamin Disraeli (1804-81). Keen to broaden support for the Conservative Party, Disraeli argued that, despite class differences, the interests uniting the British people were of far greater significance than those dividing them. It was true that some were more privileged than others, but it was the duty of the more privileged to look after those in need. Heywood (1992) notes that Disraeli's argument had both a pragmatic and a moral strand. On the one hand, Disraeli realised that growing social inequality in Britain had the potential to lead to violent uprisings like those that had taken place in Europe in 1789, 1830 and 1848. Reform was, therefore, necessary on practical grounds because it would protect the long-term interests of the wealthy by ensuring that revolution was avoided. On the other hand, Disraeli argued that reform was necessary on moral grounds. This argument was based on the traditional conservative belief that society was naturally arranged in a hierarchy. Since those at the top of the hierarchy had more wealth and privileges than those at the bottom, those at the top had a greater responsibility to consider the needs of those less fortunate than themselves. In other words, in return for their privileged position, those at the top of the hierarchy had a moral obligation to alleviate the suffering of those at the bottom of the hierarchy.

The slogan 'one nation'

The slogan 'one nation' was given to this type of conservatism because of Disraeli's emphasis on the unity between classes. The British people, the term suggested, all belonged to one happy family, each with a particular role to play and each with a particular place within the family hierarchy.

Whiteley and his colleagues (1994) describe one nation conservatives as 'progressive' and argue that:

> '[One nation conservatism] was revived and revitalised by the post-war election defeat of the Conservatives and the perception arising from that defeat that the party needed to modernise itself...Progressives accept and support the Beveridge welfare state and Keynesian methods of macro-economic management...Progressivism stresses the importance of a social safety net to deal with poverty in addition to a limited redistribution of income and wealth. It espouses a paternalistic [father-like] commitment to caring for all members of the community and favours government intervention in the economy to regulate markets.' (Whiteley et al. 1994, p.131)

3. 'Liberal' conservatism

Whilst one nation conservatives accept that the government should play a positive role in economic management and the provision of welfare, 'liberal' conservatives disagree. Liberal conservatism (also called 'libertarian' conservatism) draws on classical liberalism and places it within a conservative framework.

Liberal conservatism is nothing new. Heywood (1992) notes that liberal ideas, especially liberal economic ideas about the free market, have been put forward by conservatives since the 18th century. These ideas are liberal because they support the greatest possible economic liberty and the least possible government regulation of the economy. Liberal conservatism, however, differs from liberalism because liberal conservatives argue that economic liberty is compatible with traditional conservative values such as the belief in authority and duty. Liberal conservatives, therefore, support free-market economics and regard state intervention in economic matters as unnecessary and a hindrance. On the other hand, unlike liberals, liberal conservatives do not believe that moral decisions can be left to the individual. They argue that a strong state is required to maintain public order and to ensure that traditional values are upheld.

Whiteley and his colleagues (1994) describe liberal conservatives as 'individualists' and categorise them as follows:

> 'Individualism is preoccupied with concerns over private property and the interests of the small businessman. It supports the idea of reduced government intervention in the economy. The most enthusiastic supporters of the Conservative government's privatisation programme can be found among this group. Individualists believe that the welfare state undermines self-reliance and enterprise and that the government should cut taxes and deregulate business. They also tend to oppose extensions to the welfare state, fearing that this will promote idleness and they are inclined to blame the victim when it comes to explaining the origins of poverty or unemployment.' (Whiteley et al. 1994, p.131)

3.3 The New Right

What is the 'New Right'?

Liberal conservatism has made an important impact on British politics since the mid-1970s. The key event was the election of Margaret Thatcher as Leader of the Conservative Party in 1975. Much of Thatcher's thinking was informed by liberal conservatism and, in government, she appointed colleagues with views similar to her own. As a result, liberal conservatism replaced one nation conservatism as the mainstream ideology in the Conservative Party. Since much of liberal conservative thinking fits with attitudes that are generally regarded as being 'right wing' and since

the revival of liberal conservatism is a relatively new phenomenon, those who subscribe to liberal conservative ideas are often said to belong to the 'New Right'. Like many political movements, the New Right is a loose coalition of writers, politicians and political activists whose views coincide on many, but by no means all, issues. Since the mid-1970s, the New Right has made its mark throughout the world. It was, for example, a major influence on American Presidents Ronald Reagan and George Bush during the 1980s.

The New Right in the late 1990s

In Britain, the influence of New Right ideology was at its greatest between 1984 and 1990, during which time Margaret Thatcher and like-minded ministers attempted to encourage individual responsibility, the acquisition of personal wealth (especially in shares and property), and a reduced role for the state. After Thatcher's resignation as Prime Minister in 1990, however, a conflict developed in the Conservative Party between those who wished to retain the momentum of the Thatcher years (and, therefore, to implement an even more radical New Right agenda) and those who wished to consolidate what had been achieved since 1979 (by reinstating one nation conservative values). This ideological conflict between 'revolutionaries' and 'consolidators' was a key theme of John Major's premiership and was reflected in the 1997 Conservative election manifesto (Conservative Party 1997, pp.1-3). It has also been cited by the political commentator John Gray as a crucial cause of the Conservatives 'cataclysmic defeat' on 1 May 1997. Gray argues that the Conservative Party's ideological divisions mean that the party no longer has a programme with the coherence of that elaborated by Thatcher:

> 'The Conservative Party is the site of a contest between two obsolete world views. Its damaging conflicts over Europe were symptoms of a deeper division between one nation Tories and Thatcherite free-marketeers. Neither faction has begun to understand the changes that have transformed British society and the global economy over the past decade.' (Gray 1997, p.22)

This ideological divide re-emerged during the leadership election which followed the Conservative defeat at the general election in 1997. The main contenders were a member of the New Right (John Redwood), a consolidator (Kenneth Clarke) and a candidate who promised to tread a path somewhere between these two extremes (William Hague). It was Hague who won the contest and a key test of his leadership will be whether he can heal divisions by forging a new Conservative ideological project.

Main points - Part 3

- In general terms, to be conservative is to be cautious, suspicious of change and to prefer to keep things roughly as they are. Conservatives tend to have few idealistic hopes about people.
- Many conservative ideas come from Edmund Burke. He opposed rapid change, arguing in support of tradition and gradual reform. For conservatives the family and the nation are the key units. They stress the importance of rule of law, duty and hierarchy.
- There are three main strands of conservatism: (1) traditional conservatism (which stresses patriotism and authority but opposes social reform and other threats to the status quo); (2) one nation conservatism (which argues that, despite class differences, the interests uniting British people are far greater than those dividing them); and (3) liberal conservatism (which supports the greatest possible economic liberty and the least possible government regulation and intervention).
- In the 1980s, the Conservative Party was dominated by liberal conservatives. After the resignation of Margaret Thatcher, ideological divisions emerged.

Activity 2.3 Conservative values

Item A Law and order

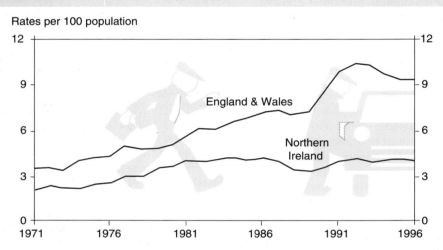

This graph shows the number of criminal offences recorded by the police between 1971 and 1996.

Adapted from Social Trends 1998.

Item B Conservative values (1)

Let us begin by recognising the scale of our defeat and of our problem. The Conservative Party was thought to be uncaring about unemployment, poverty, poor housing, disability and single parenthood. We were thought to favour greed and the unqualified pursuit of the free market. But, compassion is an essential ingredient of Conservatism. We have never lost it, but the world does not believe it. Conservatives have a scepticism about panaceas (blanket solutions) and about the possibility of governments solving problems with the flourish of a pen. But, that common sense approach must not mask the fact that concern for others and magnanimity are important qualities of Conservatism. The Conservative Party has always voiced unreserved support for the family. We believe that children are best brought up in stable family arrangements with two parents. But, we admire those many people who are doing an excellent job raising children on their own. The important thing is that people recognise the responsibility they have when they conceive children and do all they can to provide a warm, caring and balanced home for them. Our society has changed. For good or ill, many people nowadays do not marry and yet head stable families with children. For a younger generation, in particular, old taboos have given way to less judgemental attitudes. There remain many other people to whom the new norms seem all wrong. The Tory Party is conservative and not given to political correctness. Still, it never rejects the world that is. Tolerance is part of the Tory tradition.

Adapted from a speech made by Michael Portillo (Defence Secretary in John Major's government before losing his seat at the 1997 general election) on 9 October 1997.

Item C *Conservative values (2)*

	Strongly agree	Agree	Neither	Disagree	Strongly disagree			Strongly agree	Agree	Neither	Disagree	Strongly disagree
PLEASE TICK ONE BOX FOR EACH STATEMENT												
The Conservative Party should adjust its policies to capture the middle ground of politics	16	54	13	15	2		Unemployment benefit should ensure people a reasonable standard of living	14	60	13	11	2
The next Conservative government should establish a prices and incomes policy as a means of controlling inflation	12	31	12	32	14		The death penalty should be reintroduced for murder	36	33	7	17	7
A future Conservative government should privatise British Coal	12	44	17	22	5		Britain's present electoral system should be replaced by a system of proportional representation	5	17	12	43	24
Income and wealth should be redistributed towards ordinary working people	5	21	20	42	12		When it comes to raising a family, a woman's place is in the home	15	41	14	20	11
A future Conservative government should make abortions more difficult to obtain	12	22	19	35	13		Restrictions on immigration into Britain are too loose and should be tightened	54	37	5	3	1
The welfare state undermines individual self-reliance and enterprise	16	46	14	21	3		Conservatives should resist further moves to integrate the European Community	20	34	16	27	3

This survey of members of the Conservative Party was conducted between January and April 1992. In total, there were 2,467 respondents. The figures show the percentage of respondents giving each answer.

Adapted from Whiteley et al. 1994.

Questions

1. a) Using Item A write an article which gives a conservative account of the growth of crime in England and Wales and which provides recommendations for solving this problem.
   b) Would you say that your account conformed more with traditional conservatism, one nation conservatism or liberal conservatism? Give reasons for your answer.
2. What evidence is there in Item B to show that Michael Portillo is a conservative?
3. Using Items B and C, explain how conservatism differs from liberalism.
4. 'The principles which lie behind the Conservative Party are conservative principles.' Explain this statement using Items B and C
5. a) What do the answers in Item C tell us about the nature of conservatism in the Conservative Party in the early 1990s?
   b) Would you say that the majority of members of the Conservative Party were traditional conservatives, one nation conservatives or liberal conservatives? Give reasons for your answer.

Part 4 Socialism

Key issues

1. What is socialism?
2. How did it develop?
3. How does if differ from liberalism and conservatism?

4.1 The roots of socialism

A new ideology

The changes to British society brought about by the Industrial Revolution did not just result in the adaptation of existing ideologies such as liberalism and conservatism, they also led to the development of a new ideology - socialism. But, whilst liberalism and conservatism accepted and embraced the new capitalist economic order, socialism opposed it, aimed to change it and provided an alternative to it.

Capitalism

An industrial country whose wealth (ie land, raw materials and businesses) is owned mainly by individuals rather then by the state is a capitalist country. In simple terms, those who own and control the wealth are 'capitalists' (they have capital which they invest in businesses). Those who have no capital of their own but rely on being paid for their labour are 'workers'. Although the capitalists are fewer in number than the workers, they tend to acquire political power and social privileges as well as economic power.

Industrialisation in Britain was piecemeal. It relied upon individual initiative. New industrial enterprises were set up and owned by private individuals. On the whole, central government did not encourage or attempt to organise economic development. It certainly did not attempt to gain ownership of the new industrial enterprises. As a result, it was left to the owners of businesses to decide what conditions their workers should work in and how much they should be paid. Since the aim of these businesses was to make a profit, working conditions were often poor and wages low. In fact, during the early years of the Industrial Revolution, many working people had to endure appalling working and living conditions.

Conditions in the early 19th century

The following two passages indicate the sort of conditions poorly paid working families had to endure. The first passage is an extract from an account written by Lord Shaftesbury who toured poor areas:

> 'In the first house I turned into there was a single room. The window was very small and the light came in through the door. The young woman said, "Look there at that great hole; the landlord will not mend it. Every night I have to sit and watch, or my husband does, because that hole is over a common sewer and the rats come up 20 at a time. If we did not watch for them they would eat the baby up."'
> (Shaftesbury 1847)

The second passage comes from a report written by a parliamentary commission in 1843:

> 'If the statement of the mother be correct, one of her children, four years of age, works twelve hours a day with only an interval of a quarter an hour for each meal at breakfast, dinner and tea, and never going out to play: and two more of her children, one six and the other eight years of age, work in the summer from six am til dusk and in winter from seven in the morning til ten at night, fifteen hours.'
> (Second Report of the Children's Employment Commissioners, 1843)

It is in this context that socialism first developed.

Marx and Engels

Writers such as Karl Marx and Friedrich Engels criticised capitalism. They argued that the workers were being exploited by the capitalists. Once the workers realised the extent to which they were being exploited, they would rise up and overthrow the capitalists in a revolution. This revolution would lead to a new way of organising society - socialism. In a socialist society, people would share property and work cooperatively.

Capitalism in the late 19th century

By the late 19th century, the character of capitalism in Britain had changed. Although there was still a huge divide between rich and poor, living and working conditions had begun to improve. In part, this was due to the more active role taken by government - laws banning child labour and restricting the length of the working week were passed by Parliament, for example, and local councils were given powers to raise local taxes which could be spent on improving local living conditions. But, other factors also played a part. The growth and recognition of trade unions provided the workers with the machinery to take collective action, for example. The campaign for greater democracy led to the gradual extension of the franchise and, therefore, wider participation in politics. As a result, there was less alienation amongst the workers. Whilst groups of revolutionary socialists survived, the number of their supporters remained small. More and more socialists supported the idea that socialism could be achieved by peaceful means and by working within the existing system. This split between revolutionary socialists (usually referred to as 'communists') and reformist socialists intensified after the Bolsheviks (Russian communists) seized power in Russia in the revolution of October 1917. In Britain, the influence of revolutionary socialism has remained slight whilst reformist socialism has managed to enter the political mainstream.

4.2 What is socialism?

The nature of socialism

Socialism has two elements. It is both a criticism of capitalism and a blueprint for an alternative way of organising society. But these two elements are intertwined. It is through the criticism of capitalism that the alternative way of organising society becomes apparent. This criticism of capitalism can be divided into four areas.

First, the toll on workers in a capitalist system is immense since capitalists compete with each other in the fight for the highest possible profits. Workers are exploited and dehumanised, becoming no more than numbers on a balance sheet. In such circumstances, work has no meaning other than as drudgery which keeps together body and soul.

Second, capitalism produces vast inequalities in society. There is a huge gap between the 'super rich' at the top and the poor at the bottom. The mass of people reap little reward for their labour. Yet, it is their labour which actually creates the wealth in the first place. Capitalism by its very nature perpetuates inequalities.

Third, the so-called 'freedoms' which both conservatism and liberalism claim to support are merely a sham and an illusion. 'Freedom' in the conservative or liberal sense is only meaningful for the rich.

And fourth, capitalism is not even an efficient system since it wastes all kinds of limited resources. The emphasis on the market place and the scramble for profits means that little attention is paid to the interests of society as a whole. The rich, for example, are more likely to spend their money on building a large house for themselves than on building a hospital for the good of the community.

Socialism and human nature

The term 'socialism' itself provides an important clue about attitudes towards human nature. To socialists, people are social beings who thrive best in a close relationship with one another. People are not just motivated by selfish interests, but are capable of living harmoniously and cooperatively together as part of a community with a compassionate attitude towards all. Socialists do not agree that people are inherently flawed. Rather, they emphasise that people are largely the product of their upbringing and their environment. If people are selfish, greedy or uncaring, it is likely to be the result of acquiring such characteristics, probably because they are the dominant values in society. It follows from this that, if human capacities are to be developed, then the right environment must be created. This implies that socialists must seek a decisive change in the nature of society.

Socialists explain many types of anti-social behaviour, including crime, by arguing that such behaviour is determined, to a large extent, by material factors such as unemployment and poverty rather than by weaknesses in human nature. Eliminating these material problems would, therefore, be a major step towards solving many social problems.

Social utopianism

If such ideas are taken further, they can lead to socialist utopianism - a belief that a society could be created where better housing, schools, hospitals would produce a more cooperative, compassionate and peaceful society. But, not all socialists are utopians. Many socialists accept that Britain is a capitalist society where capitalist values predominate. Since they, as socialists, believe that the environment largely determines political behaviour, they expect people to be seduced by the values portrayed, for example, through advertising and through the media. The onus is on them, as socialists, to combat such values.

Socialist aims

The socialist view of human nature indicates that human happiness depends on reshaping society according to socialist values. There are two main aims:

- the promotion of greater equality by means of a redistribution of resources

from the wealthy to the rest
- the organisation of society through rational planning rather than by relying on market forces.

Socialism, the individual and the group

If the key unit in liberalism is the individual and in conservatism it is the family and the nation, the key unit in socialism is the group (or class). At the heart of socialism is the belief that people should join together and work collectively. Heywood explains this as follows:

> 'At its heart, socialism possesses a unifying vision of human beings as social creatures, capable of overcoming social and economic problems by drawing upon the power of the community rather than simply individual effort. This is a collectivist vision because it stresses the capacity of human beings for collective action, their willingness and ability to pursue goals by working together, as opposed to striving for personal self-interest.' (Heywood 1992, p.96)

Competition

Heywood then goes on to point out that socialists differ from both liberals and conservatives in their attitude towards competition. Liberals and conservatives not only regard competition between people as natural, they also regard it as desirable. Socialists, on the other hand, believe that, by its very nature, competition turns people against each other and, therefore, forces them to suppress or ignore their desire to cooperate. In simple terms, competition encourages selfishness and aggression whilst cooperation makes moral and economic sense. By working together rather than competing, the argument goes, people develop bonds between each other and are able to achieve more than could be achieved by working alone.

Responding to criticism

This belief in collective action has led to a great deal of criticism from non-socialists. Socialists have been accused, for example, of ignoring or suppressing individual freedom (by emphasising the needs of the group rather than the individual) and of lacking economic realism (since, it is claimed, economic success relies on competition). It should be noted, however, that socialism, like other ideologies, is ultimately no more than a framework upon which practical policies are based. Since Britain is a capitalist rather than a socialist state, it is perhaps understandable that the policies supported by most British socialists fall short of the ideal. Certainly, the new constitution agreed by Britain's mainstream socialist party, the Labour Party, in April 1995 attempts to combine a desire for collective action with an admission that competition is the basis for economic success.

Socialism and the past

Some socialist historians still subscribe to the view that:

> 'The history of all hitherto existing societies is the history of class struggles.' (Marx & Engels 1848, p.79)

But most accept that:

> 'Capitalism has not appeared to develop as Marx had predicted. Far from becoming more intense, class conflict has gradually been diluted by growing affluence.' (Heywood 1992, p.101)

Despite this, socialist historians are less likely to analyse developments in terms of individuals than are historians who subscribe to other ideologies. Socialists tend to argue that a 'great man' approach to history (an emphasis on the role of prominent individuals) is not very helpful. What matters is the changing relationship between different groups (classes) in society. By examining the past, socialists are able to understand how capitalism has been able to survive and to suggest ways in which a more just and fairer society, based on rational principles, can be established.

Socialism and the state

Socialists aim to transform society. Gaining control of the state is, therefore, crucial. Once office has been won, the state becomes the main vehicle of change. A central aim of socialists, for example, is the redistribution of wealth in society. In part, this can be achieved by the exercise of state power. A socialist government, for example, might introduce a system of progressive taxation so that the rich pay a larger proportion of their income in taxation than the poor. The money collected by the state in taxation could then be used to combat poverty and disadvantages. State power might also be used to defend the civil liberties of individuals and groups.

The role of the state, however, has become a source of considerable debate in British politics and faith in the beneficial effect of state activity has weakened even among socialists. The perceived failure of British nationalised industries in the 1970s, the experience of the Thatcher revolution in the 1980s, the collapse of 'state socialism' in the Soviet Union in 1991 and four successive general election defeats for the Labour Party (in 1979, 1983, 1987 and 1992) convinced many socialists in Britain that the state should not be seen as a neutral entity, simply obeying the wishes of the government of the day. Rather, it should be seen as a complex entity with many members and many interests of its own. Some of these interests might be quite unacceptable to socialists. As a result, previous certainties about the beneficial impact of the state as a weapon to achieve socialist objectives have been challenged.

4.3 Different strands of socialism

Classifying socialism

Like liberalism and conservatism, it is possible to identify different ways in which socialism has been adapted. In general terms, it is necessary to distinguish between revolutionary socialism and reformist socialism.

1. Revolutionary socialism

As suggested above (Section 4.1), one strand of British socialism is derived from the writing of Marx and Engels. This strand is known as 'revolutionary socialism' because its supporters believe that class conflict will inevitably result in the revolutionary overthrow of the capitalist system. Revolutionary socialists are also described as 'Marxists'. In the UK, revolutionary socialism or Marxism is regarded as an ideology on the extreme of the political spectrum (see Part 5 below).

2. Reformist socialism

Whilst Marxists argue that the irresistible forces of class conflict mean that the revolutionary overthrow of the capitalist system is inevitable, other socialists argue for a more gradual approach. Reformist socialists suggest that, even without a revolution, socialist parties can gain election to government and then introduce reforms which will gradually transform society. It is this path which has been followed by the British Labour Party.

Some political commentators distinguish between 'democratic socialism' and 'social democracy'. Whilst both take the reformist rather than the revolutionary path towards socialism, each has rather different aims.

Democratic socialism

Democratic socialists hope to use the existing democratic mechanisms in society to gain power and then to introduce a hardline socialist programme which transforms the state. Their aim, in effect, is to alter the balance of power in society to such an extent that the capitalist system ceases to exist. They differ from revolutionary socialists, therefore, in terms of tactics, but not in terms of aims.

Social democracy

Social democrats, on the other hand, accept that they are living in a capitalist society and do not expect to change the fundamental nature of this society. Rather, they hope to introduce reforms which redistribute resources in such a way that the majority benefit rather than just the few. Whilst social democrats might have similar ideals to democratic socialists, their views about what policies should be pursued are often quite different.

4.4 Socialism and New Labour

Socialism and the Labour Party

As noted above, in Britain the main socialist party is the Labour Party. Early in its history, the Labour Party abandoned any traces of revolutionary socialism. Throughout the party's history, however, there have been ideological battles between those who support democratic socialism and those who support social democracy, with each group trying to gain ascendancy in the party. A particularly acute battle was fought after Labour's 1979 election defeat, resulting in a temporary victory for the democratic socialists. By the time of the 1983 general election, the dominance of the democratic socialists ensured that Labour's election manifesto presented a clear socialist programme. That programme, however, was rejected by the electorate and Labour's heavy defeat was used by social democrats as justification for a change in direction and the adoption of social democratic values. By the time that Tony Blair was elected Leader in 1994, democratic socialism had been marginalised.

An ideological shift

Before Tony Blair was elected Leader of the Labour Party in 1994, the context within which changes to party procedure and party policy took place remained broadly within the social democratic tradition. During and after Tony Blair's successful leadership election campaign, however, it became clear that he stood outside the social democratic and democratic socialist traditions which had, up to this time, dominated the party. To signify this ideological shift, Tony Blair and his supporters made increasing use of the term 'New Labour' and one of Blair's first acts as Leader was to campaign (successfully) to replace the old Clause IV of the Labour Party constitution (which committed the party to clear socialist goals - see Box 2.1) with a new clause (which did not - see Box 2.2).

Blair and his supporters' precise ideological position

Box 2.1 The old Clause IV

The Labour Party's object is...to secure for the workers by hand or by brain the full fruits of their industry and the most equitable distribution thereof that may be possible upon the basis of common ownership of the means of production, distribution and exchange, and the best obtainable system of popular administration and control of each industry or service.

From Labour 1993.

Box 2.2 The new Clause IV

The Labour Party...believes that by the strength of our common endeavour we achieve more than we achieve alone, so as to create for each of us the means to realise our true potential and for all of us a community in which power, wealth and opportunity are in the hands of the many not the few, where the rights we enjoy reflect the duties we owe, and where we live together, freely, in a spirit of solidarity, tolerance and respect.

From Labour 1998.

is difficult to determine, but it owes something to two relatively new ideas (stakeholding and communitarianism) and one older idea (Christian socialism). Combined, these ideas have led to talk of a new approach to politics - a 'Third Way' (see Activity 2.4 below).

Stakeholding

Stakeholding has been popularised by, among others, Will Hutton. In his books (Hutton 1995 and 1997), Hutton argues that the consequence of vigorously pursuing free-market policies during the Thatcher and Major years was the serious growth of social divisions and alienation. To counter these problems, he proposes policies which are radical but non-socialist - policies designed to give people who are currently dispossessed a stake in society:

'Stakeholding is not a call for the socialisation of capitalism, big government or a new corporatism; rather it requires institutions, systems and a wider architecture which creates a better economic and social balance, and with it a culture in which common humanity and the instinct to collaborate are allowed to flower. The task is to get the institutions that lie between the state and the individual - pension funds, business firms, banks, universities, TECs, housing associations, trade unions, even satellite television stations - to operate in ways that reflect the costs that individualist action motivated by self-interest necessarily imposes on the rest of us.' (Hutton 1997, p.33)

Communitarianism

As the name suggests, communitarianism places great value on the idea of 'community'. Put simply, it has two main planks. First, it provides a strong critique of individualism, arguing that an individual's freedom of action should be restrained by consideration of the needs of the community. And second, it provides an alternative to reliance on the state, suggesting that, rather than coming from the centre, decisions should be made on a local, community level. As Robert Leach points out, it is understandable that emphasis on community should have an appeal to members of the Labour Party:

'Community could be linked with the values of fraternity, fellowship and cooperation, all key terms in the 19th century socialist lexicon but relatively neglected more recently in favour of various interpretations of equality.' (Leach 1998, p.39)

Like stakeholding, however, communitarianism accepts the existence of capitalism and claims that any divisions or alienation are the result, not of the structural characteristics of capitalism, but of trends which can be solved within the existing economic system if the right policies are adopted. Rather than seeking fundamental economic reforms, communitarians emphasise that individuals have certain responsibilities and duties as well as certain rights.

Christian socialism

Although Tony Blair has been careful not to make too much of his personal religious beliefs, he has made it clear that, like his predecessor John Smith, he is a committed Christian and that this informs his thinking. Indeed, Robert Leach points out that, not only does Christian socialism have deep roots, it also points in a distinct ideological direction:

> 'Christian socialism has been an influential element in Labour Party thinking since its earliest days. It imparted a strong ethical character to its socialism, which emphasised universal fellowship rather than class conflict.' (Leach 1998, p.40)

Links between the three ideas

Although it would be wrong to suggest that any one of these three ideas (stakeholding, communitarianism and Christian socialism) has dominated the thinking of Tony Blair and his supporters, there are elements in all three ideas which, once isolated, suggest a coherent approach:

> 'All of them involve a critique of individualism, the unrestrained pursuit of profit and unfettered market forces. All of them emphasise the importance of obligations as well as rights, inclusion rather than exclusion, and cooperation in place of unlimited competition. These are certainly not the ideas of the New Right. New Labour is, therefore, not to be identified with Thatcherism. Nor do these ideas have much in common with the Marxist left. They are all, however, largely consistent with the strong

strand of ethical socialism within the British Labour Party from its origins.' (Leach 1998, p.41)

Main points - Part 4

- Industrialisation led to the development of a new ideology - socialism - which provided a critique of capitalism and offered an alternative to liberalism and conservatism.
- At the heart of socialism is the belief that people should join together and work collectively. Socialists have two main aims: (1) the promotion of greater equality by means of a redistribution of resources from the wealthy to the rest; and (2) the organisation of society through rational planning rather than by relying on market forces.
- Revolutionary socialists argue that class conflict will bring the revolution which overthrows the capitalist system and transforms society. Reformist socialists argue that, without a revolution, socialist parties can form governments which gradually transform society.
- Reformist socialists can be divided into: (1) democratic socialists who hope to gain power and then to introduce a hardline socialist programme which transforms the state; and (2) social democrats who do not expect to change the nature of society - rather, they hope to give the majority a fairer deal.
- Throughout the Labour Party's history, there have been ideological battles between those who support democratic socialism and those who support social democracy.
- Some people argue that there has been an ideological shift in the Labour Party since Tony Blair became Leader in 1994.

Activity 2.4 Socialism and the Third Way

Item A *Socialism (1)*

Item B *Socialism (2)*

Socialism is the collective ownership by all the people of the factories, mills, mines, railways, land and all other instruments of production. Socialism means production to satisfy human needs and it means direct control and management of the industries and social services by the workers through a democratic government. Under socialism, all authority will originate from the workers who will be integrally united in socialist trade unions. All persons elected to any post in the socialist government, from the lowest to the highest level, will be directly accountable to the rank and file. Such a system would make possible the fullest democracy and freedom. It would be a system based on the most primary freedom - economic freedom. For individuals, socialism means an end to economic insecurity and exploitation. It means workers cease to be commodities bought and sold on the labour market. It means a chance to develop all individual capacities and potentials within a free community of free individuals. It means a classless society.

Adapted from Levin 1976.

Item C *The Third Way (1)*

The Labour government has been in power for nearly a year now and it is possible to identify a consistent pattern in its actions. The pattern that emerges is not neo-liberal or social democratic, but something different - a Third Way. This Third Way has four main elements. First, in many of the government's actions there is clearly a belief in the value of community, especially local communities. This is apparent, for example, in the move towards elected mayors and in the drive for devolution. Second, there is an emphasis on accountability. Schools and hospitals are being set performance targets, for example, and if they fail to meet their targets they will be closed or hit squads sent in. Third, and related to the notion of community accountability, there is a strong belief in individual responsibility. This is implicit in the Home Office's attitude towards criminal and anti-social behaviour. It also underlies the drive towards welfare reform - dependency is to be reduced by individuals taking more responsibility for their actions. Related to responsibility is the fourth main element - opportunity. Again this is crucial in welfare reform - unemployed young people, single parents and the disabled are to be given opportunities to work, for example. So, there it is - not 'liberty, fraternity and equality' but 'community, accountability, responsibility and opportunity'. Rearrange the order a bit and the initials produce 'CORA' - a worthy rival to Margaret Thatcher's TINA (there is no alternative) since this is a real alternative. Unlike neo-liberalism, CORA is not libertarian or individualistic. Individual rights do not have primacy - community responsibilities have at least equal status. Unlike social democracy, it is not egalitarian. The commitment to social justice relies on ensuring minimum standards and equality of opportunity, rather than on redistribution and equality of outcome. Unlike neo-liberalism, there is no automatic belief in the virtues of the free market. Unlike social democracy, there is no special commitment to the public sector or even to the mixed economy. Rather, there is a robust pragmatism. What's best is what works.

Adapted from the *New Statesman*, 6 March 1998.

Item D *The Third Way (2)*

According to the political commentator Charlie Leadbetter, the central belief of the Third Way is simple - cooperative self-help. The government's job is to help people to get together to help themselves. This requires a belief in self-help, self-reliance and self-improvement. The aim is to create a society which promotes individual initiative and endeavour. Unlike people on the right, however, Leadbetter believes that the government has an important role in this. He wants to help people recognise that they are interdependent and often need to cooperate to achieve their ends. Unlike the Old Left (Old Labour), he believes that the state suffers from many failings. The government's role is to help people find solutions that are mutually advantageous. It is not the state's role to impose those solutions or to provide them, but to underpin, facilitate and regulate them. The Third Way, Leadbetter argues, goes beyond the traditional positions of the New Right (anti-state, pro-market) and the Old Left (pro-public ownership, anti-market) to establish a new approach to public-private partnership and cooperative self-help. The best example of Third Way politics in action is the Northern Ireland peace settlement. It only works by being inclusive. Parties to the agreement have rights, but only if they fulfil responsibilities. The settlement promotes self-governance and devolution of power. The government has helped to set the framework, but the settlement will only work if those involved make it work. State and society must work together. The settlement is not just a political process but a cultural one as well - it will only work if people renegotiate their identity.

Adapted from the *Observer*, 10 May 1998.

Item E *The Third Way (3)*

This cartoon appeared in the *Guardian* on 23 September 1998. It shows the Liberal Democrat symbol hovering above William Hague (Conservative Party Leader) and Tony Blair (Labour Prime Minister) whilst Paddy Ashdown (Leader of the Liberal Democrats) has caught and cooked it.

Questions

1. How does socialism differ from (i) liberalism and (ii) conservatism? Use Items A and B in your answer.

2. a) 'A new type of socialism'. Judging from Items C and D, is this a fair description of the Third Way?
   b) On what grounds might some socialists be uneasy with the Third Way?

3. Write a caption to accompany the cartoon in Item E. The caption should explain what the cartoonist thinks about the Third Way and why this conclusion has been reached.

4. Herbert Morrison, Labour's Deputy Leader after World War II, said that socialism is whatever the Labour Party happens to be doing at any one time.
   a) What do you think he meant by this?
   b) Do you think this is a sufficient definition of socialism? Give reasons for your answer.

Part 5 Other ideologies

Key issues

1. What is the nature of ideologies on the extreme of the political spectrum?
2. Have any new ideologies developed since 1945?
3. What impact have extreme and new ideologies made on British politics?

5.1 Ideologies on the extreme of the political spectrum

What is an 'extreme' ideology?

Liberalism, conservatism and socialism are all mainstream ideologies. It is these ideologies which determine the parameters of political argument in Britain. Any ideas that fall outside the ideological framework constructed by them are regarded as 'extreme' and unacceptable. In other words, despite their differences, liberals, conservatives and socialists have much in common. Take the system of parliamentary democracy which exists in Britain for example. Most liberals, conservatives and socialists agree that Britain should have a system of parliamentary democracy - even if they disagree over exactly how this parliamentary democracy should be organised.

Those who support ideologies on the extreme of the political spectrum, however, reject mainstream politics and support political systems which are fundamentally different. There are three main ideologies on the extreme of the political spectrum - anarchism, Marxism and fascism.

Anarchism

The word anarchy comes from the ancient Greek for 'no rule'. Anarchists are people who oppose all forms of authority. An anarchist state would be a state without any form of government or any laws. People would make decisions amongst themselves within their community without compulsion.

Since anarchists oppose all forms of government, governments and people in authority are bound to feel threatened by the idea of anarchy, especially if (as has sometimes happened) anarchists are prepared to take violent action against them. The result is that in everyday language the term 'anarchy' is often used to mean chaos, disorder and mindless violence. This, most anarchists would argue, is an ugly distortion of the true meaning of the term.

Whilst all anarchists believe that all forms of government and authority should be abolished, there are two distinct types of anarchism.

Anarcho-capitalism

One type can be characterised as an ultra-extreme form of liberalism. It is sometimes called 'anarcho-capitalism'. Anarcho-capitalists take free-market economics to their logical conclusion. If a market is to be truly free, they argue, then there is no need for government. People should be free to do anything they like. The success or failure of their actions will be determined by the market. The market will be self-regulatory and so there is no need for regulations to be imposed from outside (by government). Turner suggests that:

> 'In concrete terms this would translate into the modern era as meaning, for example, no taxation, no compulsory education, no protection of minimum rights for workers in areas such as health and safety or redundancy, no regulation of what could or could not be used in the preparation of food or medicines. It is 19th century liberalism pushed to its logical extreme.' (Turner 1993, p.29)

Left-wing anarchism

The second type of anarchism is known as 'left-wing anarchism'. This can be characterised as an ultra-extreme form of socialism in that it is based on the premise that people are naturally able and willing to cooperate and work together collectively. If this is the case, then there is no need for government. Left to their own devices, people are perfectly capable of working together and resolving any differences between them. Turner suggests that there is a series of core principles which are shared by left-wing anarchists:

> 'The right to complete individual freedom, a complete rejection of authority of all forms, the establishment of a non-hierarchical society and an abiding belief that human nature is always essentially good. Where it is evidently bad, this is always a consequence of the deleterious [damaging] impact on humans of state exploitation and capitalist influences.' (Turner 1993, p.29)

Drawbacks

Unlike the other major ideologies, anarchism has not been put into practice on a large scale. Heywood suggests that this is because anarchism suffers from three drawbacks:

> 'First, its goal, the overthrow of the state and all forms of political authority, is often considered to be simply unrealistic. Certainly, the evidence of modern history from most parts of the world suggests that economic and social development is usually accompanied by a growth in the role of government, rather than its diminution [reduction] or complete abolition. Secondly, in opposing the state and all forms of

political authority, anarchists have rejected the conventional means of exercising political influence, forming political parties, standing for elections, seeking public office and so on. Anarchists have, therefore, been forced to rely upon less orthodox methods, often based upon a faith in mass spontaneity rather than political organisation. Thirdly, anarchism does not constitute a single, coherent set of political ideas. Although anarchists are united in their opposition to the institutions of the state and indeed other forms of coercive authority, they arrive at this conclusion from very different philosophical perspectives.' (Heywood 1992, p.195)

Marxism

It has already been noted (Section 4.3 above) that socialism can be divided into two strands. Whilst reformist socialists are able and willing to work within the existing capitalist system, revolutionary socialists (Marxists) hope to overthrow this system. Marxists may want the same end goal as reformist socialists, but their analysis of the current political situation and their tactics differ from them. For example, many Marxists are internationalists - they believe that a truly socialist society cannot be achieved until the working classes in countries all over the world rise up and overthrow capitalism. Because they are internationalists, they are not interested in existing state boundaries. As a result, they discourage patriotism. Because they believe that a revolution is a necessary precondition of socialism, they try to undermine the existing government by encouraging class conflict. Tactics include educating the workers (revealing to them the true nature of their exploitation) and participating in political action designed to alienate workers from the existing political system (in the hope that this will lead the workers to rise up and overthrow the government). Such an analysis and such tactics are not shared by reformist socialists. As a result, Marxists are often branded as the 'enemy within' and tend to be marginalised by mainstream politicians.

Fascism

Whilst Marxism is associated with the extreme left of the political spectrum, fascism is associated with the extreme right. Fascism is notoriously difficult to define. Hunt (1992), however, suggests that fascism is made up of eight separate elements.

First, fascists are aggressive nationalists. They believe that their nation is the best, that all citizens should be enthusiastically patriotic and, if necessary, military conquest should be embarked upon to solve struggles between nations.

Second, fascists are militarists. They admire organised violence and the military way of life.

Third, fascists are racists. This is a particularly important part of modern fascism. Contemporary British fascists, for example, argue that only white people should be allowed to live in Britain.

Fourth, fascists believe in charismatic leadership. Fascists place their leader on a pedestal and allow their leader to have absolute authority. They prefer dictatorial rule to democratic rule.

Fifth, the key unit to fascists is not the individual or the family but the state. The state is more important than the individual and, therefore, individuals should be prepared to sacrifice themselves for the good of the state.

Sixth, fascists despise Marxism. They despise it because it is internationalist (the opposite of nationalist) and because Marxists encourage class conflict. Class conflict damages the unity of the state.

Seventh, fascists are opposed to parliamentary government on the grounds that this type of government's fundamental concern is with the freedom of the individual rather than with the unity of the nation.

And finally, fascism revels in the irrational and mystical. Fascists assume that people are irrational and appeal to their irrationality. Fascists also construct myths which are used to bind their supporters together through rituals. For example, fascism often emphasises the idea of rebirth - the idea that fascism will bring economic, political and spiritual renewal. In this sense, fascism has much in common with religion.

5.2 'New' ideologies

Feminism and environmentalism

Just as liberalism, conservatism and socialism were all shaped by the Industrial Revolution, two new ideologies have emerged out of the profound socio-economic changes which have taken place since 1945 - feminism and environmentalism. Although the roots of both lie in the pre-war world, it is only in recent years that political scientists have begun to accept that they are distinct ideologies rather than tendencies within other ideologies. Significantly, neither ideology fits neatly on the left-right model of the political spectrum. Both aim to influence people on both the left and the right.

Feminism

As with most ideologies, it is difficult to provide a simple, succinct definition of feminism. Bryson, however, argues that:

'A starting point for all feminism is the belief that women and men are not equal in society and that women are systematically disadvantaged, subordinated or oppressed. Unlike traditional political thinking which has either defended or ignored gender inequality, feminism sees this as a central issue. As a political theory, feminism tries to understand the nature and causes of women's disadvantage and as a political movement it tries to change it.' (Bryson 1994, p.31)

Although the term 'feminism' was first used over 100 years ago and the origins of modern feminism can be traced back to the 18th century, it is only since the 1960s that political scientists have begun to take feminism seriously. Heywood points out that:

'Until the 1960s, sexual divisions were rarely considered to be politically interesting or important. If the very different social, economic and political roles of men and women were considered at all, they were usually regarded as "natural" and, therefore, as inevitable. For example, men, and probably most women, accepted that some kind of sexual division of labour was dictated by the simple facts of biology: women were suited to a domestic and household existence by the fact that they could bear and suckle children, while the greater physical strength of men suited them to the outdoor and public world of work...The growth of the women's movement and feminist thought since the 1960s, however, has severely tested such complacency.' (Heywood 1992, p.216)

Since the 1960s, three distinct strands of feminism have been identified - liberal feminism, socialist (or Marxist) feminism and radical feminism.

Liberal feminism

Liberal feminists argue that women and men have equal moral worth and deserve equal treatment. Women, therefore, should have the same rights as men and the same opportunities. Forbes summarises the key elements of liberal feminism as follows:

'Liberal feminists dismiss any talk of essential differences between women and men and are happy to propose changes that introduce formal and legal equality into the relations between the sexes. There is a stress on equal civil and economic rights, the need for education for women (and to change men), full partnership in work and an equal share in the information of laws.' (Forbes 1991, p.63)

Socialist feminism

According to socialist feminists, however, it is the capitalist system which is responsible for women's oppression. Capitalism ensures that women are exploited either as unpaid workers in the home or as part-time workers on low wages. To combat this, structural change is required:

'Socialist feminists believe that the relationship between the sexes is rooted in

the social and economic structure itself and that nothing short of profound social change, some would say social revolution, can offer women the prospect of genuine emancipation.' (Heywood 1992, p.232)

Radical feminism

Whilst liberal and socialist feminism owe something to existing ideologies, radical feminism goes beyond them. According to Bryson:

'Radical feminism claims that the oppression of women by men is the oldest and most universal form of inequality that there is. It also argues that male domination or "patriarchy" is not confined to the public worlds of politics and economic life but that it is based upon the most intimate areas of our lives...Many radical feminists reject the idea that women should try to compete with men by becoming like them. They argue instead that women are in many ways better than men...For some this means that "womanly values" should be more powerfully expressed in society as a whole. For others, it leads to the claim that all men are to be seen as "the enemy" and that lesbian separatism is the only solution. Many, however, reject this conclusion and are careful to distinguish between male power (which they oppose) and individual men (who may be good friends or husbands).' (Bryson 1994, pp.31-32)

Environmentalism

Worldwide population growth, industrial growth and scientific advance are three factors which, combined, have led to a growing concern about the relationship between human beings and the environment. Until the 1960s, politicians did not really concern themselves with the environment except to consider it as a resource bank to be exploited. Since then, however, there has been a realisation that many of the world's resources are finite and that current practices may be causing long-term, perhaps even irreversible, damage.

Impact of environmentalism

The growing concern about the damage that people are or may be doing to the environment is at the heart of the new ideology that has been called 'environmentalism'. The impact of this new ideology is great. Since the late 1980s, for example, all three major political parties in Britain have claimed that they have taken 'Green' issues on board. In other words, all three parties admit to having been influenced by environmentalism.

The main principle

Environmentalism is based upon the principle that there should be a balanced relationship between people and their environment. Whereas other ideologies are only or mainly concerned with the relationship between people, environmentalists are concerned about the relationship between people and the natural world. Environmentalists emphasise that people are just one species within a complex ecosystem and that (because of people's ability to manipulate the environment) their behaviour will determine whether or not that ecosystem survives. The implication of this is that people should consider long-term environmental consequences when making political decisions.

Sustainability

Central to environmentalism is the notion of sustainability. Sustainability is:

> 'The capacity of a system, in this case the biosphere [world] itself, to maintain its health and continue in existence. Sustainability sets clear limits upon human ambitions and material dreams because it requires that production does as little damage as possible to the fragile global ecosystem.' (Heywood 1992, p.267)

Take timber for example. In the world as a whole, an enormous amount of timber is being collected and used. At present, more trees are being cut down than are being planted. As a result, the total number of trees in the world is diminishing. Environmentalists argue that this is shortsighted. To carry on cutting down trees at the present rate is unsustainable since there will come a time when there are no trees left. In the long term, current practice will lead to an ecological disaster. To prevent this happening there should be a policy of sustainability - for every tree that is chopped down, for example, a new tree should be planted.

This idea has important implications. Whilst other ideologies assume that economic growth is a fundamental aim, environmentalists question whether economic growth is in people's long-term interest. As a result, some environmentalists argue that people should be taught to reject materialism and to look for personal fulfilment in a lifestyle based only on sustainable resources.

Main points - Part 5

- There are three ideologies on the extreme of the political spectrum - anarchism, Marxism and fascism - and two new ideologies - feminism and environmentalism.
- Anarchists are opposed to all forms of authority. An anarchist state would have no government or laws.
- Marxists share the same goals as many reformist socialists, but they differ in their tactics.
- Fascism has eight main elements - nationalism, militarism, racism, love of leadership, love of the state, hatred of Marxism, hatred of democracy, and a belief in the irrational.
- The starting point for feminism is that women are disadvantaged. There are three main strands - liberal feminism, socialist feminism and radical feminism.
- The starting point for environmentalism is that there should be a balanced relationship between people and their environment. A key term is 'sustainability' - the capacity of a system to maintain its health.

Activity 2.5 New and non-mainstream ideologies

Item A *Making assumptions*

(i) Every language reflects the prejudices of the society in which it evolved and English evolved through most of its history in a male-centred, patriarchal (male-dominated) society. We shouldn't be surprised, therefore, that its vocabulary and grammar reflect attitudes that exclude or demean women. Once we began looking at what the English language had to say at a subliminal level some things have become obvious. What standard usage says about males, for example, is that they are a species whilst females are a sub-species. From this, flows a thousand other enhancing and degrading messages all encoded in the language which we, in English speaking countries, learn when we are born.

(ii) A British Rail advertisement aimed at company executives included the following passage: 'Consider the effects long distance driving can have on an executive. Chances are when he arrives at his meeting he'll be feeling every inch of that journey. Worse, his tiredness may make him unresponsive and irritable. Would you feel happy about doing business with a man like that.'

(iii) Bill's attempts to interest XYZ company in his products had finally paid off. He was invited to make a presentation and was offered the use of a conference room in a letter signed John Liveridge, assistant to the president. When Bill signalled that he was set up, a woman and a man entered the room. The woman said to Bill, 'I'm Virginia Hancock and this is John Liveridge, my...'. Bill enthusiastically broke in, drowning her last word. 'I'm delighted to meet you, Mr Liveridge, and you too, Ginny.' Ms Hancock owned the company, Mr Liveridge was her assistant and Bill lost a customer.

All passages adapted from Miller & Swift 1989.

Item B   *Class War*

Item C   *Socialist Worker*

Item D   *British Nationalist*

Item E   *The three main political parties and the environment*

(i) The Labour Party

The foundation of Labour's environmental approach is that protection of the environment cannot be the sole responsibility of any one department of state. All departments must promote policies to sustain the environment. And Parliament should have an environmental audit committee to ensure high standards across government. Throughout this manifesto, there are policies designed to combine environmental sustainability with economic and social progress.

Adapted from Labour 1997.

(ii) The Conservative Party

Britain has an enviable track record in protecting the environment. Our rivers, beaches and water are cleaner and we are using our energy more efficiently. We are leading the world in reducing the level of greenhouse gases that cause global warming and pressing for policies which will enable the world to sustain development without long-term damage to our environment. We have clear objectives to build on this record.

Adapted from Conservative 1997.

(iii) The Liberal Democrats

Our aim - to make clean air, pure water and a decent environment a central priority of government. The problem - for too long, the environment has been damaged by greed and indifference. This cannot go on. From global warming to polluted rivers and asthma in children, everybody is already paying the cost of environmental damage. The longer action is delayed, the higher the cost will be. Our commitment - to save energy, cut traffic congestion, stop the unnecessary destruction of the countryside and stem the tide of pollution.

Adapted from Liberal Democrat 1997.

Questions

1. Look at Item A.
   a) What evidence is there in passage (ii) to support the view expressed in passage (i)?
   b) Why do you think some feminists argue that the way in which people use language is important?
   c) What does passage (iii) tell us about the impact of feminism?
2. a) Judging from Items B-D, what are the main priorities of anarchist, Marxist and fascist groups?
   b) What are the main differences between anarchism, Marxism and fascism?
3. The major chains of newsagents refuse to stock *Class War*, *Socialist Worker* and *British Nationalist*. Judging from Items B-D, why do you think this is so?
4. a) Judging from Item E, what is the evidence that the main political parties have been influenced by environmentalism?
   b) How would you rate each party's commitment to environmentalism? Give reasons for your answer.

References

Adams (1993) Adams, I., *Political Ideology Today*, Manchester University Press, 1993.

Bryson (1994) Bryson, V., 'Feminism', *Politics Review*, Vol.4.1, September 1994.

Conservative (1997) *You Can Only Be Sure With The Conservatives*, Conservative Party manifesto, Conservative Party, 1997.

Dobson (1992) Dobson, A., 'Ideology', *Politics Review*, Vol.1.4, April 1992.

Eagleton (1991) Eagleton, T., *Ideology*, Verso, 1991.

Eysenck (1964) Eysenck, H., *Sense and Nonsense in Psychology*, Penguin, 1957.

Forbes (1991) Forbes, I., 'The politics of gender' in *Wale* (1991).

Gray (1997) Gray, J., 'Conservatism RIP', *New Statesman*, 12 September 1997.

Hall (1988) Hall, J., *Liberalism, Politics, Ideology and the Market*, Paladin, 1988.

Heywood (1992) Heywood, A., *Political Ideologies: an Introduction*, Macmillan, 1992.

Heywood (1994) Heywood, A., *Political Ideas and Concepts: an Introduction*, Macmillan, 1994.

Hunt (1992) Hunt, S., 'Fascism and the race issue in Britain', *Talking Politics*, Vol.5.1, Autumn 1992.

Hutton (1995) Hutton, W., *The State We're In*, Jonathan Cape, 1995.

Hutton (1997) Hutton, W., *The State To Come*, Vintage, 1997.

Labour (1993) *Labour Party Rule Book 1993-4*, Labour Party, 1993.

Labour (1997) *New Labour - Because Britain Deserves Better*, Labour Party manifesto, Labour Party, 1997.

Labour (1998) *Labour Party Rule Book 1998*, Labour Party, 1998.

Lancaster (1998) Lancaster, S. (ed.), *Developments in Politics*, Vol.9, Causeway Press, 1998.

Leach (1998) Leach, R., *Political Ideas* in *Lancaster (1998)*.

Levin (1976) Levin, J., 'Levin speaks for socialism', *Weekly People*, 9 October 1976.

Liberal Democrat (1997) *Make the Difference*, Liberal Democrat manifesto, Liberal Democrats, 1997.

Marx & Engels (1846) Marx, K. & Engels, F., *The German Ideology* in McLellan (1977).

Marx & Engels (1848) Marx, K. & Engels, F., *The Communist Manifesto*, Pelican, 1967.

McLellan (1977) McLellan, D., *Karl Marx: Selected Writings*, Oxford University Press, 1977.

Miller & Swift (1989) Miller, C. & Swift, K., *The Handbook of Non-sexist Writing*, The Women's Press, 1989.

Seliger (1976) Seliger, M., *Politics and Ideology*, Allen & Unwin, 1976.

Shaftesbury (1847) Lord Shaftesbury, *Description of Frying Pan Alley*, 1847.

Smiles (1859) Smiles, S., *Self Help*, Penguin, 1986.

Social Trends (1998) Office for National Statistics, *Social Trends 28*, HMSO, 1998.

Turner (1993) Turner, R., 'Anarchism: what is it?', *Politics Review*, Vol.3.1, September 1993.

Wale (1991) Wale, W. (ed.), *Developments in Politics*, Vol.2, Causeway Press, 1991.

Whiteley et al. (1994) Whiteley, P., Seyd, P. & Richardson, J., *True Blues: the Politics of Conservative Party Membership*, Oxford University Press, 1994.

Part 2
British politics in context

Political developments since 1945

Introduction

When Tony Blair became Prime Minister after the 1997 general election, many political commentators argued that this was a momentous event. This was not just because the Labour Party secured its largest parliamentary majority ever. It was also because the Labour victory ended 18 years of Conservative rule. Under the leadership of Margaret Thatcher and John Major, the Tories won four successive general elections and, during their time in government, made a number of fundamental changes to British politics. This chapter examines the institutions and practices against which the Conservatives struggled during their years in power. It also assesses the Conservatives' successes and failures and considers the continuities and changes which have occurred since Labour won power.

Central to any discussion of politics since 1975 is the figure of Margaret Thatcher. She became the first female Leader of the Conservative Party in 1975 and the first woman Prime Minister in 1979. Under her leadership, the Conservatives won two further general elections in 1983 and 1987. By the time of her resignation, Thatcher had been Prime Minister for nearly 12 years, the longest continuous period in office of any Prime Minister this century. But, her importance is not only due to the fact that she managed to stay in office for so long. She was also responsible for a style of leadership and, most importantly, for a set of ideas and policies which came to be known as 'Thatcherism'. The extent to which Thatcherism meant a break with the consensus which had dominated post-war politics, the extent to which John Major extended or broke with Thatcherism and the impact of Thatcherism on New Labour are all central themes in this chapter.

Chapter summary

Part 1 provides the political context in which Thatcherism developed. In particular, it examines the post-war consensus and the attack mounted upon it by the New Right.

Part 2 focuses on the key ideas of Thatcherism and assesses successes and failures under Thatcher. It also explores the opposition to Thatcherism.

Part 3 looks at politics under John Major and examines reasons for the Conservative Party's defeat in the 1997 general election.

Part 4 examines the steps that Labour took to avoid defeat in the 1997 general election and analyses the election results.

Part 5 examines the performance of the New Labour government during its first 18 months in power. It looks at the government's policies, the principles that underlie them and the extent to which (if at all) the Labour government has established a 'Third Way'.

Part 1 The post-war consensus and its breakdown

Key issues

1. What is the 'welfare state' and why was it set up?
2. What was the post-war consensus?
3. Why did the post-war consensus break down?

1.1 What is the 'welfare state'?

The Beveridge Report

Although the post-war Labour government was responsible for setting up the welfare state, the principles which underlay it were laid down by a liberal, William Beveridge. Beveridge was a senior civil servant who had worked on welfare policy for many years. In 1941, he was commissioned by the Prime Minister, Winston Churchill, to write a report examining existing welfare schemes and suggesting ways of improving them. The Beveridge Report (Beveridge 1942) was published in 1942 and rapidly became a bestseller (it sold more than 100,000 copies in December 1942 alone).

Beveridge's ideas

In his report, Beveridge argued that social problems could not be treated in isolation. Rather, they were all linked. He identified five key social problems (the 'five giants') which any social welfare system must aim to overcome. These were:

- want
- disease
- ignorance
- squalor
- idleness.

By arguing that these 'five giants' were all linked, Beveridge suggested a new role for government. Whereas government had previously been reluctant to intervene in the affairs of individuals, the Beveridge Report gave government the philosophical justification for intervention. For the first time, it was conceded that poverty and underachievement might be the result of material, social conditions rather than individual failings. As a result, the ground was cleared for the state to set up institutions designed to help all, regardless of their ability to pay.

Beveridge's recommendations

Beveridge argued that there should be a single national insurance scheme to finance welfare provisions. Every worker would make a weekly contribution to this government-run scheme and this would protect them and their family 'from the cradle to the grave'. The scheme would provide:

- benefits for the unemployed, sick and disabled
- pensions for the old and widowed
- funeral grants
- maternity benefits.

Beveridge also expected the government to:

- provide family allowances
- create a national health service
- maintain full employment.

The 1945 general election

Churchill (a Conservative) did not immediately implement the Beveridge Report, arguing that winning the war was a priority. Whether the Conservatives would have implemented Beveridge's recommendations is a matter of speculation. When a general election was held in 1945, to the surprise of many commentators, Labour won with a large majority (393 seats to the Conservatives' 213). Significantly, the manifesto upon which Labour had fought the election had included a commitment to implement Beveridge's proposals. As the new ministers entered office, they did so with a secure mandate to fulfill their commitment.

The welfare state

The programme carried out by the post-war Labour government was an ambitious attempt to conquer Beveridge's 'five giants'.

Ignorance

Steps to defeat ignorance had already been taken by the previous government when it passed the Butler Education Act in 1944. This Act made secondary schooling compulsory and free for all children up to the age of 15 and it set up the tripartite system of grammar, secondary modern and technical schools.

This system was designed to ensure that all secondary school pupils received an education suited to their needs. The 1945-50 Labour government accepted this and decided that further educational reforms were not necessary. Education, however, was an exception. In other areas, the incoming government was prepared to introduce reforms which transformed the relationship between the individual and the state.

Disease

Perhaps the most radical measure introduced by Labour was that aimed at combating disease. To slay this 'giant' Labour set up a National Health Service (NHS). Before the NHS was created, most people had to pay for their own private health insurance or relied on charity. Only workers who paid into the state health scheme set up by the Liberal government of 1906-14 could receive free treatment. The 1946 National Health Act established the principle that healthcare should be provided for everybody by the state free at the point of delivery and that it should be funded out of National Insurance contributions. Hospitals and doctors, for the first time, were taken under state control.

Want, squalor and idleness

A number of further measures were taken to combat the interrelated problems of want, squalor and idleness. The most significant of these was the 1946 National Insurance Act which set up a full system of benefits covering:

- unemployment
- sickness
- maternity
- death.

Unlike previous schemes of social insurance, the 1946 Act provided a safety net for all who fell on hard times, whatever their status or previous level of contributions. It was this commitment to universal provision that was the Act's chief contribution to people's security.

Other measures taken by the Labour government included:

- a house building programme (over one million houses were built using government funds between 1945 and 1951)
- a series of measures 'nationalising' key industries (transferring them from private to state ownership with the aim of reducing exploitation and increasing long-term planning and investment)
- economic policies which were designed to reduce unemployment and raise living standards (unemployment never exceeded 320,000 during the period 1945 to 1955).

Keynesian economics

Central to the development of the welfare state was the economic approach devised by the economist J.M. Keynes (1883-1946). Keynes rejected laissez faire (free-market) policies. He argued that, if it was left to itself, the market would stabilise at a point below its full capacity (ie in recession). Since companies tended to lay people off and to reduce wages during a recession, unemployment was then bound to rise and people were bound to have less money to spend. As a result, there would be an inevitable fall in demand for new goods. This fall in demand would intensify the recession. Even more people would be laid off and demand would fall still further. In other words, a vicious circle would take hold of the economy.

Keynes also rejected the socialist view that the economy could be stimulated by simple redistribution of wealth to the poor. He argued that redistribution of wealth would destroy any incentive to achieve.

Keynes' solution was to argue that recessions could be overcome by government intervention. Instead of saving during a recession, governments should take the lead and borrow money to invest in new projects. These new projects would provide jobs and create wealth. The people who did these new jobs would have money to spend and, by spending this money, they would stimulate the economy. As a result of this stimulation, demand would increase and the economy would come out of recession. In other words, what Keynes proposed was 'demand management' in a mixed economy. In this mixed economy, if there was a rise in unemployment, the government would, if necessary, increase the Budget deficit by investing in new projects and lowering taxes. But, equally, when there was full employment and demand was threatening to rise too much (ie the economy was beginning to overheat), the government would reduce the Budget deficit, for example by raising taxes. This would dampen down demand.

1.2 The post-war consensus and its breakdown

What was the post-war consensus?

The post-war Labour government retained power until 1951. By then, the foundations of the welfare state had been laid. But, these foundations would not have come to anything if the Conservative government which took office in 1951 had immediately begun to dismantle them. That it chose not to do so indicates the extent to which the principles behind the welfare state had been accepted by both the public at large and by the political élite. Indeed, not only did the Conservative government elected in 1951 not attempt to dismantle the new welfare state, but every government elected between 1945 and 1979, whether Labour or Conservative, pledged to maintain and improve its main institutions and practices (the only exception being the first two years of the Heath government elected in 1970). Governments during this period also accepted that the best way to run the economy

was according to Keynesian principles. Indeed, Keynesian economics were regarded as the key to making the welfare state work successfully.

The term 'post-war consensus'

It is because there was substantial agreement between the two main political parties over the direction which foreign and domestic policy should follow that the term 'post-war consensus' was coined. During the period of post-war consensus the main parties agreed about aims and principles, but differed in emphasis and style. That does not mean that there was no conflict. Debates in the House of Commons were as heated as at any time in the past, for example. Rather, it means that the parameters within which conflict took place were clear and both main parties pursued similar policies. As Kavanagh remarks:

> 'The package of policies on the domestic front is familiar: full employment Budgets; the greater acceptance, even conciliation, of the trade unions; public ownership of the basic monopoly services and industries; state provision of social welfare requiring in turn high public expenditure and taxation; and economic management of a sort via a large public sector and a reduced role for the market.' (Kavanagh 1990, p.34)

Why did the consensus come about?

If substantial agreement exists as to what the post-war consensus was, far less agreement is to be found as to why this consensus came about. Middlemass (1979) and others have argued that the period of consensus had its origins in the 1920s and 1930s when Labour politicians first reached the highest levels of the British political system. This experience ensured that Labour politicians became committed to the existing system. Writers on the left, such as Miliband (1961), on the other hand, have maintained that members of the Labour Party and trade unions were already committed to the existing system and sought to contain working-class ambitions within it. The post-war consensus, Miliband argues, was achieved by the deradicalisation of working-class demands. Others argue that it was cooperation between the two main parties in the wartime coalition government, together with the collective effort of the nation in defeating the Nazis, which laid the basis for consensus. Still others have argued that the growth of public expenditure and controls during the war prepared both the public and politicians for the growth of the public sector when the welfare state was established after the war.

The breakdown of the consensus

All these interpretations emphasise the different elements of a complex process in which, for a relatively short period, a common view was held about how best to ensure political stability, prosperity and security for Britain's citizens. The consensus did not last, however. It began to break down in the face of economic and political developments which appeared to show that stability and prosperity could not be guaranteed by the policies adopted during the years of consensus.

Why did the consensus break down?

Cracks in the post-war consensus began to appear from 1968 onwards. In that year, students across Europe, the USA and Asia demonstrated against many of the ideas embodied in the post-war consensus. As important, in Britain economic performance was falling far behind that of its major competitors and the government found itself increasingly unable to manage the problems of unemployment, inflation and the balance of payments.

Edward Heath's experiment with free-market economics

Many political commentators and politicians felt new ideas were required. Amongst these was the Conservative Leader, Edward Heath. He argued that a radical policy of encouraging enterprise and free markets was necessary if Britain's economic prospects were to be improved. The debate was thrashed out at the Selsdon Park Hotel in 1969, with the results appearing in the Conservatives' manifesto for the 1970 general election. Although the Conservatives won the election, the Heath government was plagued by problems which forced it to abandon its free-market experiment in 1972 and to return to more orthodox post-war policies. Despite this, the consensus had been questioned. When a series of strikes paralysed the country in 1974, leading to a three-day week, Heath called an election.

1974 - a turning point?

The Conservatives lost the election in February 1974, but Labour did not secure an overall majority. A second election was held in October 1974 and Labour secured a small overall majority.

With hindsight, 1974 can be seen as a turning point. First, the Conservative defeat resulted in a serious reconsideration of policy which eventually resulted in Margaret Thatcher's election as Leader and the adoption of a New Right social market strategy (see Section 2.1 below for a definition of the term 'New Right'). And second, Labour came to power just as a series of domestic and world economic crises were about to break out. The Labour government proved incapable of managing these crises and this provided the context in which a (New Right) alternative to the post-war consensus could begin to appear attractive to the electorate.

The Labour government 1974-79

According to the mythology which developed after Margaret Thatcher's general election victory in 1979, the Labour government of 1974-79 lurched from crisis to crisis until it was eventually undone by the so-called 'winter of discontent'. Whatever the truth behind this interpretation of events, it is important to

be aware of it since it was used by the Thatcher governments to justify their attacks on the post-war consensus. By pointing to the mistakes made in the past, the Thatcher governments were able to present their policies as fresh and necessary. The Thatcherite view of the 1970s, therefore, highlights themes that set the agenda in the 1980s.

1. Inflation

The first of these themes was that the management of the economy under the terms of the post-war consensus led directly to high inflation. According to this view, the Labour government of 1974-79 had been unable to control inflation and this was a major cause of Britain's economic decline. In fact, the Labour government had been relatively successful in dealing with inflation. Following the doubling of oil prices in 1973, inflation grew rapidly throughout the industrialised West and, in Britain, it reached 23% by the end of 1974 (it rose to 26% in 1975). By the time of the general election of 1979, however, a range of deflationary measures had brought inflation down to 9.5%. Of course, inflation at 9.5% was still relatively high. But, the idea that inflation spiralled out of control in the late 1970s is an exaggeration. Those on the New Right, however, had good cause to make this claim since they argued that defeating inflation should be the government's priority rather than maintaining full employment.

2. Public spending

The second theme was that public spending in the 1970s led to a balance of payments crisis which also hastened Britain's economic decline. Again, whilst it is true that the Labour government inherited a large deficit in 1974 and, in 1976, was forced to ask for a loan from the International Monetary Fund (IMF), from 1976 the Labour government imposed strict limits on public expenditure with the result that the balance of payments problem had begun to ease by 1979. The Thatcherites made much of the deficit and the IMF loan. They blamed the inefficiency of nationalised industries (industries under public ownership) for the balance of payments problems and this paved the way for their programme of privatisation and tighter controls on public spending.

3. Trade unions

The third theme was that the country had been held to ransom by the trade unions. According to this view, by including the unions in the decision-making process and by attempting to work out an incomes policy with them, the Labour government had, in effect, handed power over to unelected union leaders. The result was that, when the union leaders did not get their own way, they seriously damaged Britain's industry by calling workers out on strike. This view was bolstered by evidence from the so-called 'winter of discontent'. When, in 1978, the unions refused Prime Minister Callaghan's call for a 5% wage ceiling, a rash of strikes in the public sector broke out. These strikes dominated the winter of 1978-79 and damaged Labour's chances at the 1979 election. Whilst the New Right could claim that the 'winter of discontent' showed that the power of the unions must be curbed, supporters of the unions could claim, with some justification, that the close relationship between the government and the unions between 1974 and 1978 had laid the foundations for economic recovery.

Main points - Part 1

- The ideas behind the welfare state were contained in the 1942 Beveridge Report and put into practice by the post-war Labour government.
- Beveridge's aim was to set up a social welfare system which combated the 'five giants' - want, disease, ignorance, squalor and idleness.
- The welfare state was designed to provide a safety net for people 'from the cradle to the grave'. For the first time, benefits were universal, an NHS was set up, free at the point of delivery, and efforts were made to ensure full employment.
- Every government elected between 1945 and 1979 (except Heath's in 1970), whether Labour or Conservative, pledged to maintain and improve the main institutions and practices of the welfare state. In other words, there was a 'post-war consensus'.
- 1974 was a turning point. First, Margaret Thatcher became Conservative Leader following the party's defeat in the October 1974 election. And second, the Labour government failed to solve the economic problems which arose in 1974-79. This provided a suitable environment for attacking the post-war consensus.

Activity 3.1 *The post-war consensus*

Item A *The welfare state*

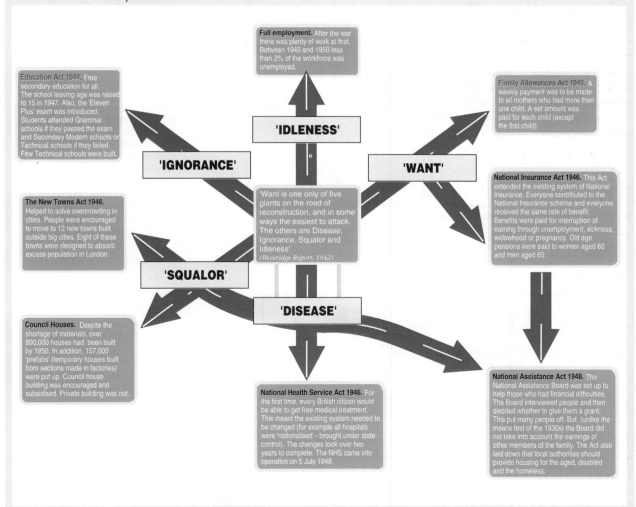

Full employment. After the war there was plenty of work at first. Between 1945 and 1950 less than 2% of the workforce was unemployed.

Education Act 1944. Free secondary education for all. The school leaving age was raised to 15 in 1947. Also, the 'Eleven Plus' exam was introduced. Students attended Grammar schools if they passed the exam and Secondary Modern schools or Technical schools if they failed. Few Technical schools were built.

Family Allowances Act 1945. A weekly payment was to be made to all mothers who had more than one child. A set amount was paid for each child (except the first child).

'IDLENESS'

'IGNORANCE'

'WANT'

'Want is one only of five giants on the road of reconstruction, and in some ways the easiest to attack. The others are Disease, Ignorance, Squalor and Idleness'
(Beveridge Report, 1942)

The New Towns Act 1946. Helped to solve overcrowding in cities. People were encouraged to move to 12 new towns built outside big cities. Eight of these towns were designed to absorb excess population in London.

National Insurance Act 1946. This Act extended the existing system of National Insurance. Everyone contributed to the National Insurance scheme and everyone received the same rate of benefit. Benefits were paid for interruption of earning through unemployment, sickness, widowhood or pregnancy. Old age pensions were paid to women aged 60 and men aged 65.

'SQUALOR'

'DISEASE'

Council Houses. Despite the shortage of materials, over 800,000 houses had been built by 1950. In addition, 157,000 'prefabs' (temporary houses built from sections made in factories) were put up. Council house building was encouraged and subsidised. Private building was not.

National Health Service Act 1946. For the first time, every British citizen would be able to get free medical treatment. This meant the existing system needed to be changed (for example all hospitals were 'nationalised' - brought under state control). The changes took over two years to complete. The NHS came into operation on 5 July 1948.

National Assistance Act 1948. The National Assistance Board was set up to help those who had financial difficulties. The Board interviewed people and then decided whether to give them a grant. This put many people off. But, (unlike the means test of the 1930s) the Board did not take into account the earnings of other members of the family. The Act also laid down that local authorities should provide housing for the aged, disabled and the homeless.

Item B   *Nationalised industries*

Discovering the Loss World

By the mid-1970s, the nationalised industries were making a loss. Critics began to argue that public ownership was inefficient and outdated.

Item D   *The IMF loan, 1976*

In November 1976, Britain was forced to apply for a £3 billion loan from the IMF. In return for the loan, the IMF demanded £5 billion in public spending cuts. The man in the water is the Prime Minister, Jim Callaghan.

Item E   *Labour isn't working*

This poster was produced during the 1979 general election campaign. Between 1974 and 1979, unemployment rose from 542,000 to 1,500,000. Throughout the period 1945-74, unemployment had remained below 1,000,000.

Item C   *The 'winter of discontent'*

In the late 1970s, Britain's economic decline was much aggravated by the oil crisis of 1973-4 (as a result of which the price of oil quadrupled). The huge rise in the price of oil resulted in inflation on a scale unknown since 1919. Inflation was then pushed up further by trade union pressure for enormous pay rises. With surging price rises and pressure from wage and other costs, unemployment re-emerged with levels unknown since the 1930s. There seemed to be a deep rot at the heart of the economy. The government at first tried to stem inflation with the so-called 'social contract' - an agreement negotiated with the unions. Unions agreed to moderate their wage demands in return for unspecified government policies geared to their needs, and especially geared towards job protection. There were no serious strikes until September 1978 when Ford car workers refused to accept the government's 5% guideline. After two months, they accepted a pay rise of 17%. This was the green light for others. Fire fighters won a 22% rise, bakers 14% and heating and ventilation engineers won no less than a 30% rise. Lorry drivers then planned a strike for January, raising the prospect of a winter without food and energy. When the lorry drivers won a rise of 17-20%, discontent spread to public service workers. A rash of local selective strikes by health service workers, refuse collectors and even grave diggers in Liverpool followed. By February 1979 (when the public-service workers won a 9% rise), the main crisis was over. But, correctly or not, the public feeling was of an industrial system out of control and a government in a state of near-paralysis.

Adapted from Morgan 1984 and 1992.

Questions

1.a) Judging from Item A, how did the welfare state attempt to combat Beveridge's 'five giants'?

b) Describe the links between the welfare state and the post-war consensus.

2. a) Take each of Items B, D and E explain the point being made by the picture.

b) What do the pictures tell us about how and why attitudes towards the post-war consensus were changing.

3. Judging from Items B-E, what led to the breakdown of the post-war consensus?

Part 2 Thatcherism, its record and its opponents

Key issues

1. What was the New Right?
2. What was Thatcherism?
3. What was the record of the Thatcher governments?
4. What opposition was there to Thatcherism?

2.1 The New Right

What was the 'New Right'?

During the 1970s, the political movement which became known as the 'New Right' emerged in Britain and the USA. It was from this movement that Margaret Thatcher drew her inspiration. The origins of the New Right can be traced to three main sources.

1. Friedman and Hayek

The first of these sources was the work of the academics Milton Friedman and F.A. Hayek. Although the two men disagreed over some fundamental issues, they made common cause in their support of the importance of free markets. A free market is a market in which the laws of supply and demand can operate without interference from any external source. Friedman and Hayek maintained that:

- markets play a crucial role in ensuring the maximum level of human freedom
- markets are better at distributing resources than planned economies
- inflation is the primary economic and political evil (an evil which can only be defeated by control of the money supply - see Chapter 15, Section 1.4).

2. Enoch Powell

The second major source of New Right ideas was the former Conservative MP and minister Enoch Powell. During the 1960s, Powell articulated a coherent critique of the consensus politics which had dominated post-war Britain. He argued against incomes policies, economic planning and high levels of public expenditure. Like Friedman and Hayek, Powell argued in favour of a free-market economy, claiming that a free market was the basis upon which individual freedom was built and was the best way of distributing resources. Indeed, as early as 1958, Powell had argued that inflation was a consequence of the growth of the money supply and public expenditure. He was also a nationalist. He resisted Britain's entry into the European Economic Community in 1973 and he made a number of interventions on the issue of immigration (he was forced to resign as a minister after making a speech which was condemned as promoting racism). Ironically, by the time his views entered the Conservative mainstream he had broken with the party.

3. Think tanks

The third major source of New Right ideas was a number of think tanks which gained importance in the 1970s and early 1980s. In particular, the Institute of Economic Affairs (set up in 1955), the Centre for Policy Studies (set up in 1974) and the Adam Smith Institute (set up in 1978) all set out to promote the ideas of New Right thinkers such as Hayek and Friedman.

New Right doctrine

According to the New Right, during the period of post-war consensus the government intervened in economic affairs when it should not. This resulted in economic decline and a loss of individual freedom and choice. At the same time, the government acted too timidly in areas where it alone should act - in law and order, in defence and in encouraging respect for authority. The solution to these problems was twofold. First, the government should intervene less. It should reduce its involvement in social affairs and nurture individual freedom, choice and responsibility. And second, the government should be more rigorous in enforcing law and protecting Britain's interests.

The debate over the term 'New Right'

The term 'New Right' has aroused controversy. Doubts about it centre upon two objections. First, some commentators argue that to describe the movement as 'right wing' ignores the fact that much of its impetus came from liberal ideas about reducing the role of government and the state. Barry (1987), for example, argues that 'New Liberals' would be a more accurate description (though it should be noted that this would not be entirely accurate since it would ignore the stress that the movement places on the restoration of the authority of the state and the family). The second objection is that the groups on the right which emerged in the 1970s were so diverse that they do not fit any one label.

A common goal

Whilst it may be true that the New Right is not a formally constituted entity and there is indeed a degree of diversity between the aims and emphases of different groups, it is possible to identify a common goal shared by them all:

> 'What all strands within the New Right share... is the rejection of many of the ideas, practices and institutions which have been characteristic of social democratic regimes in Europe and of the New Deal and Great Society programmes in the United States. The New Right is radical because it seeks to undo much that has been constructed in the last 60 years.' (Gamble 1988, p.27)

In other words, the New Right is unified in its attack on the post-war consensus - on Keynesian economics, on the welfare state and on state provision more generally. It is this which defines it as a distinct movement.

2.2 Thatcherism

What is Thatcherism?

The term 'Thatcherism' has also been criticised. In the 1980s, for example, Tony Benn argued that the term personalised the politics of the post-1979 period and, therefore, concealed its true nature. The term, he argued, acted as a smokescreen, encouraging opponents to concentrate on Thatcher's personality rather than on the policies she promoted. In addition, it has been argued (for example, by Riddell 1985) that use of the term grants to the Thatcher project a much higher level of ideological and political coherence than it actually ever had. It should be noted, however, that even Riddell, despite his reservations, decided to use the term since:

> 'However difficult it is to define, Thatcherism does have a meaning for those in the political world.' (Riddell 1985, p.6)

A definition

In a general sense, 'Thatcherism' can be defined as an attempt to establish a new political and ideological framework based on a mixture of liberal and authoritarian New Right ideas. More specifically, a number of different strands can be identified.

Most writers agree that Thatcher's personality and leadership style is a part of what is meant by 'Thatcherism'. How important this personal role was, however, is the subject of debate. Riddell, for example, says:

> 'Mrs Thatcher's views, prejudice and style have determined government actions more than any other single factor.' (Riddell 1985, p.6)

Gamble, on the other hand, argues that:

> 'Thatcherism cannot be reduced to the personal project of a single individual.' (Gamble 1988, p.22)

If controversy rages over Thatcher's personal role, greater agreement exists over the other strands which comprise Thatcherism. Most writers agree that ideology is an important component of Thatcherism. Equally, most writers agree that specific political circumstances (the apparent failure of the post-war consensus) provided the context in which Thatcherism could flourish. And finally, most writers agree that Thatcherism is associated with a specific set of policies and positions - in particular, a degree of authoritarianism new in post-war British politics, a particular style of government and a number of key policy elements.

The Key Elements of Thatcherism

With hindsight, it is possible to identify a number of themes which were woven together to create 'Thatcherism'. There was, however, no blueprint prepared in advance. Whatever their other differences, most commentators on Thatcherism agree that what we now know as 'Thatcherism' developed over time and, despite being based on New Right principles, was often a response to the unfolding of events. Looking back at the period as a whole, however, it is possible to identify seven key themes of the Thatcherite project.

1. A new way of managing the economy

In the early years of Thatcher's first administration, a new way of managing the economy - 'monetarism' - was tried (see also Chapter 15, Section 1.4). Monetarism is an economic theory which completely rejects the aims and techniques of economic management proposed by Keynes. Whilst the primary goal of Keynesianism is to maintain full employment, the primary goal of monetarism is to keep inflation under control - even if that means maintaining a high level of unemployment. Whereas Keynesian economists argue that the government should play an active role by managing demand, monetarists argue that the government's only role should be to control the money supply (the money supply is the total amount of money circulating in the economy). By adopting monetarism, the first Thatcher government took an important step in breaking with the post-war consensus.

2. Privatisation

If, as monetarist economists argued, the main cause of inflation was government borrowing, there was a need to reduce this borrowing. One way of doing this was to raise income by selling off (privatising) government-owned assets - in particular, the nationalised industries and services. According to the Thatcherites, privatisation would bring three benefits. First, it would raise government funds and, therefore, help to stem inflation. Second, it would improve the efficiency of the formerly nationalised industries since they would no longer enjoy monopoly status but would be subject to the rigours of the market. And third, since the money from privatisation would be raised by selling shares to the public, privatisation would encourage wider share ownership. This was considered desirable on the grounds that it encouraged people to participate in the economic and political life of the country. By the late 1980s, the government was using the term 'popular capitalism' to describe the society it was trying to create.

3. Curbing the unions

During the years of post-war consensus the relationship between government and unions was close even when the Conservatives were in power. The New Right, however, was hostile towards trade unions.

This hostility was due to three main factors. First, there was an element of fear of the unions. The miners' strike of 1974 led to the downfall of the Heath government. Similarly, the rash of strikes in the winter of 1978-79 discredited the Callaghan government. By the late 1970s, it seemed to those on the right that the unions had become a threat to the authority of government. Second, the New Right argued that the activities of trade unions distorted the working of the market by allowing the growth in wages to outstrip growth in productivity. Unions, in other words, were responsible for reducing the competitiveness of British industry and should be blamed for Britain's economic decline. And third, the New Right believed that incomes policies were a cause of inflation rather than a cure for it. Inflation could be reduced by controlling the money supply not by making agreements with trade unions. There was, therefore, no need for government to have any contacts with union leaders. For these reasons, the Thatcher governments decided that it was necessary to draw up legislation which would curb the power of the unions (see Chapter 5, Section 3.2).

4. Centralisation

That policies involving the centralisation of power should be at the heart of Thatcherism might seem strange since the New Right places great emphasis on individual freedom and the severing of the relationship between the state and the economy. But, the need to centralise power arises from a paradox which lies at the heart of New Right thought. As Gamble put it:

> 'The New Right would like to be conservatives but they are forced to be radicals. They have to struggle against the forces which have gravely undermined the market order and which, if left unchecked, will destroy it.' (Gamble 1988, p.32)

So, to achieve the desired break with the post-war consensus, the Thatcherites needed to concentrate as much power into their hands as possible whilst ensuring that alternative, opposition sources of power were controlled or removed.

5. Authoritarianism

An authoritarian stance is central to Thatcherite ideology. One of the criticisms levelled at government policies during the post-war consensus was that, by involving the state in activities it should play no part in, the credibility of the state had been undermined. A key plank of the Thatcher strategy, therefore, was to restore the authority of the state and to increase it. Authority was to be restored by removing the state from activity in areas where it ought not to have a role (for example by privatising nationalised industries). But, where the state should be strong, for example in the areas of law and order and defence, it was to be strengthened. As a result, the phrase 'free economy, strong state' has been applied to the Thatcherite project.

6. A new style of government

Even those commentators concerned to minimise the personal role of Margaret Thatcher do not seek to deny that her personal style of leadership made an impact. One commentator, Kavanagh (1990), argued that Thatcher's individual contribution to British politics can be described under four headings. First, she had an unusually decisive and confrontational style and forceful personality. Second, she was an activist in the Cabinet. She saw herself as the leading participant in Cabinet discussion and pushed ministers into what she believed was right rather than what was expedient. Third, she was a combative parliamentarian who was determined never to be bettered either at Question Time or in debate. And finally, there was her public image. Polls show that she rated low on compassion, but very high on decisiveness, resolution and principle. She was not a Leader about whom people were ambivalent. People tended to like her or loath her with great passion.

7. Victorian values

Margaret Thatcher and her supporters often looked back to the Victorian period for inspiration and to justify their attitudes. In her autobiography, Thatcher recalls:

> 'I never felt uneasy about praising "Victorian values"...The Victorians had a way of talking which summed up what we were now rediscovering - they distinguished between the "deserving" and the "undeserving poor". Both groups should be given help, but it must be help of a very different kind if public spending is not just going to reinforce the dependency culture.' (Thatcher 1993, p.627)

Thatcher also championed self-help and individualism and she admitted that one of her aims was to destroy socialism (which promoted collective rather than individual action). Famously, she claimed that there was 'no such thing as society':

> 'There are are individual men and women, and there are families. And no government can do anything except through people, and people must look to themselves first. It's our duty to look after ourselves and then to look after our neighbour.' (quoted in Thatcher 1993, p.626)

As these passages suggest, there was a moral dimension to Thatcherism and this informed many of the government's policies.

The Thatcher record

Since it was the intention of Thatcher and her supporters to bring fundamental and lasting change to Britain, some attempt must be made to assess both the record and the legacy of the Thatcher governments. Any judgement on this record should take into account both the aims of the government and the impact that policies had on people. In other words,

there are two key questions:
- did the government achieve what it set out to achieve?
- who benefited and who did not benefit from the policies?

A brief examination of the performance of the Thatcher governments in the areas of the economy, the NHS, defence, law and order, foreign policy and in the world beyond Whitehall should make it possible to answer these questions.

1. The economy
Economic policy under Thatcher focused on five main areas.

(i) Inflation
The fight against inflation was successful. From 1961, the rate of inflation in Britain had been higher than average compared to other industrialised countries. But, after three years in power, the Conservatives had reduced inflation to a rate comparable to that in other industrialised countries. By 1986, inflation was down to 2.5%. Although it then began to rise again, government policy was altered to ensure that it remained at a low level.

(ii) Control of public expenditure
Control of public expenditure was seen as a key means of controlling the money supply. Despite their pledges, however, the Thatcher governments were unable to reduce public expenditure. Indeed, overall it rose. Only by 1988-89 had the proportion of public expenditure in relation to GDP fallen back to its 1979 level. Overall public spending grew because some areas were expanded deliberately (eg defence and law and order) whilst other areas expanded as a result of economic strategy (for example, social security expenditure grew massively as a result of a large increase in unemployment). Also, attempts to control public spending were concentrated in a few areas such as housing, support for trade and industry and contributions to Europe. The novel aspect of the Thatcher years was not the attempt to control public spending, but the way in which it was targeted.

(iii) Taxation
Beginning in 1979, income tax rates were cut whilst indirect taxes, such as VAT, were raised. This was a big break with the past. It widened the gap between high and low earners because indirect taxes hit those on small incomes harder than those on high income (the lower the income of a family, the greater the proportion of that income which is spent on goods and services which charge indirect taxes).

(iv) Employment
Whilst the maintenance of full employment had been a priority for other governments, this was not the case with the Thatcher governments. High levels of unemployment were tolerated in the hope that this would bring greater economic efficiency. The number of unemployed people rose from 1.5 million in 1979 to 3.2 million in mid-1985. It then fell, gradually dipping below 2 million at the start of 1989, but, from late 1989, it began to rise again.

(v) Privatisation
A further break with the past was the privatisation programme which began slowly with the government reducing its holding in BP in 1979 and selling off its holding in Cable and Wireless in 1981. The first major sale was that of British Telecom in 1984. This was followed by a rash of sales. Between 1979 and 1990, the government raised £32.9 billion from privatisation.

2. The NHS
Spending on the NHS increased by nearly one third between 1979 and 1990, an increase from 14% to 16% of overall public spending. But, an ageing population and the huge cost of modern medicine meant that a greater increase in spending on the NHS was necessary just to maintain the existing quality of service. The Thatcher governments were less willing than previous governments to accept that ever greater amounts of public money should be spent on health care. In addition, it was whilst Thatcher was still Prime Minister that the review of the NHS began which was to lead to the most fundamental reform of the NHS for a generation. The 1991 health reforms, notably the creation of an internal market within the NHS, marked an important break with the past.

3. Defence
Unlike most governments since 1960, the Thatcher governments increased defence expenditure even when they cut other public spending programmes. Between 1978 and 1986, defence spending increased by 27%. Like previous governments, however, the Thatcher governments developed and maintained Britain's independent nuclear deterrent. In 1983, American Cruise and Pershing missiles were stationed in Britain. Also, Britain's ageing Polaris nuclear weapons system was replaced by the American Trident system.

4. Law and order (see also Chapter 18)
Until 1994, when poll evidence suggested that opinion was shifting, the Conservatives were always regarded as the party of law and order - a connection which Margaret Thatcher was keen to develop. For example, the first Thatcher government made the police a priority. Police officers were given a pay rise shortly after the 1979 election. Also, 9,500 officers were recruited in England and Wales between 1979 and 1983 and a process of re-equipment took place. The result was a 20% increase in expenditure on the police between 1979 and 1983. In addition to financial support, the police were given overwhelming political support - they were given uncritical support by the government during the miners' strike of 1984-85, for example, and criminal justice legislation strengthened the

police's position.

5. Foreign policy

The cornerstone of the Thatcher governments' foreign policy was the development of Britain's 'special relationship' with the USA. This was facilitated by the election of Ronald Reagan and then George Bush. Reagan's ideological stance was close to Thatcher's. Also, both agreed that the Soviet Union posed an increasing threat to the West and that a resolute response was needed if this was to be counteracted. Although a special relationship with the USA was not new, the intensity of Thatcher's pro-American stance was unusual.

(i) The European Community (EC)

In 1979, the Conservatives were thought to be far more pro-European than Labour, but, by 1990, the position had been reversed. In the early 1980s, the main government aim was to reduce the size of Britain's contribution to the EC budget. Thatcher made much of the fact that she was able to secure £3 billion in rebates from the EC between 1980 and 1984. In 1986, Thatcher signed the Single European Act. In 1988, however, Jacques Delors' proposals for European monetary and political union were vehemently opposed by Thatcher in her 'Bruges Speech'. This outlined her vision of Europe as a union of sovereign states cooperating together, but preserving their own economic interests and cultural and historical diversity. This was a stance which Thatcher retained until her resignation. It helps to explain her refusal to join the European Exchange Rate Mechanism until October 1990.

(ii) The Falklands War

According to Thatcher herself, the high point of her career came in the field of foreign policy:

'Nothing remains more vividly in my mind, looking back on my years in Number 10 than the 11 weeks in the spring of 1982 when Britain fought and won the Falklands War.' (Thatcher 1993, p.173)

Thatcher devotes two whole chapters of her memoirs to the Falklands War, a measure of its importance in her eyes. The significance of the war was as follows. First, it was a military success and, therefore, helped to erase the memories of the failure of Suez (in 1956, American pressure had forced the British government to withdraw its troops after they had invaded Egypt in an attempt to seize the Suez canal and overthrow the Egyptian President Colonel Nasser). Second, it marked a departure from other post-war governments which had been shy of military intervention. Third, there is little doubt that the war won prestige for Britain amongst its allies. And fourth (and perhaps most important), it helped to restore Margaret Thatcher's popularity at a time when it had reached an all-time low.

6. Beyond Whitehall (see also Chapter 16)

Conflict between local and central government reached a new level during the Thatcher years. On the financial front, the government passed legislation restricting local authorities' freedom to raise money and capping their expenditure. It also introduced the 'poll tax', an unpopular new system of local taxation. The key organisational change was the abolition of the Greater London Council (GLC) and the metropolitan counties (all controlled by Labour). Central government argued that the services provided by these bodies could be devolved to lower tier authorities, saving considerable sums of money. One consequence of organisational change was the growth of quangos - unelected bodies with the power to distribute public funds.

Main points - Sections 2.1-2.2

- The origins of the New Right can be traced to three main sources - the work of Milton Friedman and Frederick Hayek, the ideas of Enoch Powell, and the ideas generated by various think tanks.
- Although the term has been questioned, the New Right is unified in its attack on the post-war consensus - on Keynesian economics, on the welfare state and on state provision more generally.
- 'Thatcherism' can be defined as an attempt to establish a new political and ideological framework based on a mixture of liberal and authoritarian New Right ideas.

- The key elements in Thatcherism were: (1) a new way of managing the economy; (2) privatisation; (3) curbing the unions; (4) centralisation; (5) authoritarianism; (6) a new style of government and (7) Victorian values.
- In terms of meeting its objectives, the Thatcher governments had some success. For example, they succeeded in lowering inflation and income tax and restructuring local government. It is also clear, however, that some people gained (those with above average incomes), whilst others did not (those unemployed or on low incomes).

Activity 3.2 The impact of Thatcherism

Item A *Did the Conservative Party become Thatcherite?*

(i)

In Conservative Party politics people often talk about the 'left' and the 'right'. *Compared to other Conservative Party members,* where would you place your views on the scale below?

LEFT | | | | | | | | RIGHT
| 2 | 2 | 4 | 7 | 26 | 17 | 22 | 9 | 13 |

And where would you place your views in relation to British politics as a whole (not just the Conservative Party)?

LEFT | | | | | | | | RIGHT
| 0.3 | 0.2 | 1 | 2 | 18 | 18 | 28 | 16 | 17 |

(ii)

Please indicate whether you think the government should or should not do the following things, or doesn't it matter either way?

	Definitely should	Probably should	Doesn't matter	Probably should not	Definitely should not
Encourage private education	29	36	20	12	3
Spend more money to get rid of poverty	29	52	8	9	2
Encourage the growth of private medicine	17	35	16	25	7
Put more money into the NHS	31	49	8	11	2
Reduce government spending generally	14	46	9	27	4
Introduce stricter laws to regulate the trade unions	28	38	12	19	3

(iii)

	Srongly agree	Agree	Neither	Diasgree	Strongly disagree
The Conservative Party should adjust its policies to capture the middle ground of politics	16	54	13	15	2
The public enterprises privatised by the Conservative government should be subject to stricter regulation	24	48	12	14	1
A future Conservative government should privatise British Coal	12	44	17	22	5
The welfare state undermines individual self-reliance and enterprise	16	46	14	21	3
When somebody is unemployed, it is usually their fault	2	5	15	56	22
The next Conservative government should establish a prices and incomes policy as a means of controlling inflation	12	31	12	32	14

The information above comes from a survey of Conservative Party members carried out in early 1992. Overall, 3,066 Conservatives responded to the survey - 78% of those approached. All figures are percentages.

Adapted from Whiteley et al. 1994.

Item B *Did the electorate become Thatcherite (1)?*

Was there an ideological shift in Britain during the Thatcher period? Were the attitudes of the population transformed? Certainly, there is empirical evidence which shows that the electorate became less respectful of authority and more liberal on issues like pornography, abortion, capital punishment and equality for women between 1979 and 1987. In addition, the electorate came to reject both Thatcherite economic priorities and the idea that there was no alternative to government policies. There was little support for Victorian values and significant opposition to a wide variety of specific government decisions. Overall, Thatcher's missionary preaching has fallen on deaf ears. It is clear that anti-Thatcherite trends in social attitudes have continued. The British Social Attitudes Report published at the end of 1992 showed, for example, a clear trend in public opinion against free enterprise and towards intervention in the economy. Only a third of the population believed that private enterprise was the best way to solve economic problems. Only 29% agreed that 'the less government intervenes the better it is for the economy'. There was growing support for price control and for state subsidy to industry and 87% of respondents supported government funding of job-creating projects. At the same time, 65% favoured high taxes rather than lower spending - just 3% favoured cuts in taxes and in public spending.

Adapted from Marsh & Tant 1994.

Item C *Did the electorate become Thatcherite (2)?*

(i) Should the government aim to curb inflation (Column A) or to reduce unemployment (Column B)?

Date	A	B	Don't know
Oct 1976	54	36	10
Jun 1980	52	42	7
Nov 1980	30	62	8
Jan 1982	23	70	8
Nov 1982	21	73	6
May 1983	22	69	9
Jul 1984	18	75	7
Aug 1985	16	77	7
Feb 1986	15	78	7

(ii) Which is more to blame if people are poor? Lack of effort on their part (Column A), circumstances out of their control (Column B), or both (Column C)?

Date	A	B	C
Jan 1977	35	32	33
Mar 1985	22	50	28

(iii) Do you approve or disapprove of the following government policies?

Policy	Approve	Disapprove
Abolition of GLC	21	79
Banning of trade unions at GCHQ	31	69
Privatisation of British Gas	43	57
Privatisation of British Telecom	44	56
Poll tax	29	71
Privatisation of electricity and water	28	72

(iv) Do you agree that when somebody is unemployed it is usually his or her fault?

Date	Agree	Disagree
May 1986	10	90
Nov 1987	13	87

The tables above show the results of a survey of the public conducted in 1986. All figures are percentages.

Adapted from Crewe 1986.

Questions

1. Judging from Item A, would you say that Margaret Thatcher transformed the Conservative Party? Give reasons for your answer.
2. a) What is Thatcherism?
   b) Judging from Items B and C, would you say that Thatcherism won the hearts of the British people?
3. What is the evidence in Item C to support the arguments made in Item B?
4. Using the information in this section explain why Margaret Thatcher's period in office has been described as a 'turning point in post-war history'.

2.3 The opponents of Thatcherism

The extent of opposition

When considering the Thatcher years it is often easy to think of them as a period in which the political scene was so dominated by Margaret Thatcher and her ideas that there was no worthwhile opposition. This would, however, be far too simplistic a view. Throughout the Thatcher years there was a significant opposition to the policies that the government pursued. Nor, as is sometimes thought, did Thatcher and her allies sweep all before them at elections. Although the Conservatives under Margaret Thatcher won three general elections in a row, they never gained more than the 43.9% of the vote which they won in 1979. In other words, at each of the three general elections there were more opponents of Thatcher and her policies than there were supporters. Paradoxically, the extent of the opposition which was ranged against Thatcher may constitute the greatest tribute to her. It may also help to explain why her achievements did not match her rhetoric.

The Labour Party

Perhaps the least important practical source of opposition to the Conservatives during the Thatcher years was the Labour Party. Although it remained the official opposition to the government in Parliament, the party spent much of the 1980s engaged in internal struggles over constitutional and policy issues. These internal struggles were motivated by the realisation that the party was in crisis. Partly, this realisation was the consequence of electoral defeat. And partly, it arose out of:

- concern that the party had not performed well in government in the 1970s
- fear that the party was losing its core support the manual working class - or, at least, fear that the manual working class was shrinking
- an awareness that in Thatcherism it was facing an alternative ideological perspective to which it had to respond.

Internal struggles

It was the response of the left within the party to these

problems which precipitated the internal struggles. Led by Tony Benn, many on the left argued that the reason for the difficulties experienced in government after 1974 and the electoral defeat in 1979 was that the party leadership had betrayed its socialist principles. Based upon this analysis, the left argued that more radical socialist policies were required in order to counteract Thatcherism. In addition, changes to the party constitution were demanded, to make the leadership more accountable to the members. By 1981, a leftward shift in policy had been achieved. The party was committed to unilateral nuclear disarmament, the closure of American nuclear bases in Britain, withdrawal from the EEC, the repurchase of council houses sold to their tenants, the abolition of public schools and subsidised low fares for public transport. An Alternative Economic Strategy had been adopted which called for reflation, import controls, the 35-hour week, more public ownership, planning agreements and industrial democracy.

From SDP to Kinnock

The leftward shift resulted in a split in the Labour Party. Several prominent MPs on Labour's right wing broke away to form their own party - the Social Democratic Party (SDP). The Labour Party was attacked in the media for being out of touch and disunited. This image of impotence grew stronger after the Conservatives won the 1983 general election. It was only after the election of Neil Kinnock as Leader in 1983 that Labour began to rebuild itself as a credible opposition party with an internal cohesion and policies which appealed to the electorate.

The 'wets'

If the Labour Party's opposition was ineffective, so too was that from within the Conservative Party, even though there were those in the Cabinet in the early 1980s and on the backbenches who believed that government policy was mistaken. It should be noted, however, that whilst those who opposed Thatcher within the Conservative Party were known collectively as 'wets', the wets were by no means a unified group. The term was applied to all those who were suspicious and fearful of the consequences of pursuing a monetarist economic policy. Also, since the government had a large overall majority it was able to whip up sufficient support to avoid defeat.

Thatcher and the wets

Thatcher herself was aware of the problems which such opponents could create, but did not make a concerted effort to root out the wets in the Cabinet until September 1981. By then, she had concluded that:

> 'The differences between Cabinet ministers over the economic strategy - and myself and Jim Prior over trade union reform - were not just ones of emphasis but of fundamentals.' (Thatcher 1993, p.150)

Prior was shifted to Northern Ireland and replaced with the 'dry' Norman Tebbit whilst two other wets, Ian Gilmour and Christopher Soames, were both sacked.

Why the wets were ineffective

Although Gilmour in particular mounted a campaign against the government from the backbenches, three factors tended to undermine the wets' opposition to the Thatcherites. First, they had no coherent strategy. The only policies they suggested as alternatives were those which were perceived to have failed in the past. Second, from autumn 1981, the first signs of economic recovery appeared and undermined the pessimistic predictions of those who opposed the monetarist economic strategy. And third, in 1982 the Falklands War broke out. British success in the war was equated with growing economic success. Both were seen as evidence of the value of the resolute approach.

So, by the end of 1982, the wets' opposition had substantially been marginalised. There is no doubt that this diverse group of Conservatives did raise some difficult questions, but their rebellion was not sufficient to undermine the assurance of the Prime Minister that the course the government was following was the right one.

The trade unions

It was a key principle of the New Right that unions were undemocratic, disruptive of free markets and acted against the national, and often their own members', interests. Previous governments had attempted to control the power of trade unions, with a notable lack of success. The Thatcher governments adopted a gradualist approach and, most important, made changes to the civil law, not to the criminal law. This encouraged individual trade unionists and employers (rather than the government) to take action against strikes. The legislation passed between 1979 and 1990 is outlined in Chapter 5, Section 3.2.

Union opposition

Between 1979 and 1985, the unions challenged the government through a number of industrial disputes. The first important strike took place in the steel industry over issues surrounding pay and redundancy. It lasted from December 1980 to April 1981, with the government refusing to intervene to force the board of the (nationalised) steel industry to review its pay offer. When the strike was settled, the union had not secured the pay offer it wanted. This was regarded as a victory for the government. Later in 1981, workers at British Leyland went on strike over pay. Then, in 1982 a succession of strikes by rail workers, NHS workers and water workers caused considerable disruption. It was clear, however, that the show-down between the government and the unions would involve the miners (NUM).

The miners' strike

From the time when he had been appointed Energy Secretary in 1981, Nigel Lawson had built up supplies of coal at power stations and encouraged the electricity generating board to ensure that as much capacity as possible could be run using oil or nuclear fuel. Ian McGregor was appointed chair of the National Coal Board in September 1983. He formulated a plan to bring the coal industry into profit which required pits to be closed and jobs lost. The implementation of this plan was the immediate cause of the miners' strike which began in March 1984. In the year-long dispute which followed, all the means at the state's disposal were used to ensure the miners were defeated. At the same time, the NUM laid itself open to public hostility and court action by failing to call a ballot before the strike began. As a result, the NUM's funds were sequestrated by the courts.

The strike ended in March 1985 with defeat for the miners. For Thatcher and her supporters, this was a major victory:

'The coal strike was always about more than uneconomic pits. It was a political strike. And so, its outcome had a significance far beyond the economic sphere. From 1972 to 1985, the conventional wisdom was that Britain could only be governed with the consent of the trade unions. No government could really resist, still less defeat, a major strike; in particular a strike by the miners' union. Even as we were reforming trade union law and overcoming lesser disputes, such as the steel strike, many on the left and outside it used to believe that the miners had the ultimate veto and would one day use it. That day had come and gone.'
(Thatcher 1993, pp.377-78)

After the miners' strike, trade union opposition to Thatcherism was no longer a major issue.

Pressure groups

Three pressure groups were of particular significance - the Campaign for Nuclear Disarmament (CND), the Greenham Common women's protest against nuclear missiles and the anti-poll tax campaign.

CND

The first Thatcher government aimed to update Britain's independent nuclear deterrent and agreed to allow new American nuclear missiles to be stationed on British soil. This, combined with renewed fears of a nuclear war, led to a substantial revival of CND (which had lain dormant since the early 1960s). Estimates vary, but Young (1991) suggests that membership of CND rose from 2,000 in 1979 to 100,000 in 1981. Optimism that popular pressure would result in unilateral disarmament grew when the Labour Party adopted a unilateralist position at its 1982 conference.

Despite the evidence of popular support for CND (rallies were regularly attended by 250,000 people in the early 1980s), the government remained firm. Michael Heseltine, Secretary of State for Defence, waged a vigorous campaign against CND. But, it was probably the Falklands War and the general election which followed it that really undermined CND. With a unilateralist platform, the Labour Party suffered a humiliating electoral defeat in 1983. This suggested

that, despite CND's popularity, wide support remained for the government's nuclear policy. The rise to power of Mikhail Gorbachev in the Soviet Union in February 1984, moreover, signalled the start of a process which defused international tension and thereby removed the basis for much of CND's campaigning.

Greenham Common

It was at the time of CND's revival that the Greenham and other peace camps were established by women who were opposed to the siting of American nuclear missiles at air bases in Britain. The women developed a new type of protest with a specifically female focus. The Greenham women in particular attracted a great deal of attention in the mid-1980s. Although they became less significant as the decade wore on, the peace camps remained until the weapons were removed as a consequence of arms control agreements.

The anti-poll tax campaign

If nuclear disarmament was the focus of protest in the early Thatcher years, the poll tax (see Chapter 16, Section 2.5) was the focus later. Unlike CND, however, the anti-poll tax campaign was a success. Indeed, it played an important part in Thatcher's downfall. Although the campaign did use traditional means of protest such as rallies, public meetings and letter writing campaigns, its main strength was that huge numbers of people simply refused to pay. The bureaucratic chaos that non-payment brought not only revealed the depth of opposition to the tax, it demonstrated that the tax was unworkable.

Local government

Opposition to the Thatcher regime from local government was based on the principle that local authorities not controlled by Conservatives had a mandate to pursue policies different from those initiated by central government. In practical terms, this opposition took several forms. First, in the early Thatcher years, non-Conservative local authorities defied central government by ignoring demands for reduced expenditure. For example, South Yorkshire Council continued to operate a cheap fares policy. Second, after 1984 local authorities attempted to get round the budget cuts forced on them initially by raising the rates and then by 'creative accountancy'. Third, local authorities initiated campaigns against central government's plans to abolish the GLC and metropolitan counties. Later, they campaigned against the introduction of the poll tax. In addition, some councils (for example, Liverpool) mounted ideologically-inspired fights with central government.

In general, these tactics were unsuccessful. Local authority spending was capped. The GLC and metropolitan counties were abolished. The poll tax was introduced. Council houses were sold and building programmes cut.

Urban unrest

The final major source of opposition to Thatcherism was less focused, but nonetheless important. On a number of occasions in the 1980s, violence flared up in the inner cities. The first major outbreak of urban unrest was the Brixton riot of April 1981. This was followed by a week of rioting in July 1981 in Liverpool, London, Birmingham and eight other inner city areas. Although peace was restored and the government promised to examine and provide solutions to the people living in inner city areas, riots again broke out in October 1985.

Explaining the 1985 riots

Benyon (1986) notes:

> 'It does seem that in 1985, as in 1981, the areas in which disorder occurred share certain common characteristics. In addition, it seems that the riots themselves began in 1985, again as four years earlier, after similar events. The immediate precipitants or trigger events in each case involved police officers and black people, as they did in 1981. The trigger events are the sparks which ignite the tinder, the tinder being the underlying causes which give rise to the potential for disorder. There seem to be five characteristics which are common to the areas where rioting occurred in 1985.' (Benyon 1986, p.7)

These five characteristics were as follows. First, unemployment was high. Second deprivation was widespread. Third, racial disadvantage and discrimination were common. Fourth, there was a feeling of political exclusion and powerlessness. And fifth, there was mistrust and hostility towards the police.

Although the opposition to the government expressed by these outbreaks of urban unrest was sporadic and short-lived, it focused attention on those who, because of their colour or economic position, had been left behind by the Thatcherite enterprise economy.

Main points - Section 2.3

- **Throughout the Thatcher years there was a significant opposition to the policies that the government pursued.**
- **Although it remained the official opposition to the government in Parliament, the Labour Party spent much of the 1980s engaged in internal struggles. As a result, its opposition was largely ineffective - at least until Neil Kinnock became Leader in 1983.**
- **Opposition within the Conservative Party was also ineffective because the wets formed no coherent programme and they were overtaken by events (an improving economy and the Falklands War).**
- **Trade union opposition was broken by the miners' strike. Pressure group opposition was easily ignored (with the exception of the anti-poll tax campaign). Central government's powers ensured that resistance at local government level was broken.**
- **Urban unrest in 1981 and 1985 was sporadic and short-lived. It did, however, focus attention on those who did not benefit from the Thatcherite approach.**

Activity 3.3 Opposition to Thatcher

Item A   *Election results 1983 and 1987*

1983 general election

Party	Votes	%	No. seats
Con	13,012,316	42.4	397
Lab	8,456,934	27.6	209
Lib/SDP	7,780,949	25.4	23
Others	1,418,938	4.6	21

Con overall majority of 144

1987 general election

Party	Votes	%	No. seats
Con	13,760,583	42.3	376
Lab	10,029,807	30.8	229
Lib/SDP	7,341,633	22.5	22
Others	1,397,555	4.4	23

Con overall majority of 102

Adapted from Craig 1989.

Item B   *The opposition*

Again and again, attempts to reform or redefine the old consensus on 'one nation' lines failed. Those who hoped that the new Social Democratic Party (SDP) would break the mould were disappointed. Internal divisions followed electoral disaster in 1987. By 1989, the centre in British politics was split between the Liberal Democrats (a merger of the Liberal Party and the SDP), the Democrats (ex-SDP members whose Leader David Owen opposed the merger), the Liberal Party (Liberals who opposed the merger) and the Green Party. The Labour Party, too, was damaged by internal division and self-doubt. It seemed in long-term decline for sociological as well as ideological reasons. Large sections of the community, especially blacks in the urban ghettos, young unemployed in urban areas in the north and large numbers of people in Scotland seemed almost to contract-out from traditional forms of participation and civic involvement.

Adapted from Morgan 1992.

Item C *The Conservative and Labour parties in the 1980s*

Item D *CND demonstration*

More than 250,000 people attended this CND march through London in October 1981.

Questions

1. a) What do Items A-D tell us about the nature of the opposition faced by the Thatcher governments?
   b) Why do you think this opposition failed to make an impact on government policy?
2. Judging from Items A-C why do you think the opposition parties were ineffective during the Thatcher years?
3. 'There is no point in going on demonstrations when conviction politicians are in power.' Give arguments for and against this view, using Item D in your answer.

Part 3 John Major's premiership

Key issues

1. What led to Margaret Thatcher's downfall?
2. To what extent did Thatcherism survive under John Major?
3. What were John Major's objectives in 1990-92?
4. What problems did John Major face in 1992-97?

3.1 John Major's premiership 1990-92

The fall of Margaret Thatcher

Five factors combined to bring about Margaret Thatcher's downfall. The first was Britain's economic position in 1990. Inflation and unemployment were rising whilst consumer spending and manufacturing output were falling. Coxall (1991) notes that such developments, in the face of 13 years of Thatcherite economic policy, were not treated sympathetically by the electorate. The second factor was the poll tax. Popular hatred of this tax was particularly pronounced, with widespread protests and anti-payment campaigns attracting the headlines and considerable support. The third factor was Europe. By 1990, the Conservative Party was in disarray over its policy towards the European Community. From 1988, Margaret Thatcher began to take a strong line against moves towards European federalism. This led to a fierce debate within the party. The fourth factor was linked to the third. Between 1989 and 1990, a number of senior Cabinet ministers resigned, giving the impression that all was not well within the Conservative leadership (the Chancellor, Nigel Lawson, the Trade and Industry Secretary, Nicholas Ridley, and the Deputy Prime Minister, Geoffrey Howe, all resigned over Europe). The fifth factor was a series of election results which indicated that the unpopularity of the third Thatcher government was not just reflected in opinion polls (the Conservatives lost 13 seats in the 1989 Euro-election and big swings against them ensured that they lost the mid-Staffordshire and Eastbourne by-elections).

The leadership contest

The catalyst for a leadership contest was Geoffrey Howe's resignation speech on 13 November 1990. Its impact was sufficient to convince Michael Heseltine that he should mount a leadership challenge and the next day he announced his candidature. In the first ballot on 20 November, Conservative MPs had a straight choice between Margaret Thatcher and Michael Heseltine. Although

Thatcher won more votes than Heseltine, she was four votes short of the number needed to prevent a second ballot. At first, she said she would stand in that ballot. But, when she had interviewed members of the Cabinet and found that about 12 of them did not believe she would win, she decided to resign.

Thatcher's resignation allowed Douglas Hurd and John Major to enter the contest. Without intervening directly in the campaign, Thatcher made it clear that Major was her favoured candidate and this undoubtedly affected his chances of success. Heseltine's decision to challenge Thatcher was resented by a large number of Conservative MPs and Heseltine's supporters may have damaged his chances by 'talking up' his support. Hurd's chances were damaged by media reports which made much of his education at Eton and his privileged background. The second ballot was held on 27 November. Major won 185 votes, Heseltine 131 and Hurd 56. Although Major failed by two votes to gain a technical victory (50% of the vote plus one), the other candidates withdrew, leaving Major as Leader and Prime Minister.

John Major's government
Although few questioned the constitutional legitimacy of the way John Major became Prime Minister, many did question whether it was right that a Prime Minister should come to power not as a result of a general election, but as the result of a ballot within a party. Despite these criticisms, John Major waited until April 1992 before calling a general election.

Major's background
Like Margaret Thatcher whose background was modest (she was the daughter of a greengrocer), John Major did not come from a rich family. Unlike Thatcher, however, John Major did not owe his rise to his education. Whereas Thatcher went to Oxford University to study Chemistry, Major left school at 16 with just three 'O' levels. It was not until 1976 that Major was selected to stand for Parliament. He beat more than 300 prospective candidates to the safe seat of Huntingdon. Once elected as an MP in 1979, his rise to power was swift. In 1983, he became a minister for Social Security. Immediately following the 1987 general election, he entered Cabinet as Chief Secretary of the Treasury. In June 1989, after Geoffrey Howe was shuffled, Major became Foreign Secretary. But, he only remained at the Foreign Office for three months. In October 1989, Nigel Lawson resigned as Chancellor and Major replaced him. Just over a year later, he replaced Margaret Thatcher as Prime Minister:

> 'Extraordinarily, in the space of 16 months Mr Major had been Foreign Secretary, Chancellor and, now, Prime Minister. This was indeed a meteoric rise.' (Benyon 1991, p. 148)

John Major's first Cabinet
In choosing his Cabinet, Major demonstrated a desire to heal the wounds which had split the Conservative Party over the previous months. He did fail, however, to appoint a woman to the Cabinet, an omission for which he was criticised. A high proportion of the Cabinet had served in Thatcher's last Cabinet, although Major rewarded colleagues who had helped in his leadership campaign - Norman Lamont (Chancellor), David Mellor (Chief Secretary to the Treasury) and Chris Patten (Conservative Party chair). Most important, perhaps, was the inclusion of Michael Heseltine as Environment Secretary. Not only was this a senior post in its own right. It had added importance since the Environment Secretary was charged with dealing with the poll tax.

John Major's programme 1990-92
The policies which emerged in Major's first two years as Prime Minister demonstrated both a degree of change and considerable continuity. Major, it appeared, remained committed to the fundamentals of Thatcherism, but was keen to mitigate some of its more unpleasant side effects.

Change
The new regime was determined to present the image of 'capitalism with a caring face'. Kelly (1993) notes that, within weeks of taking power, the Major government announced £200 million of extra spending on hospitals, AIDS, London's homeless and social housing. The freeze on child benefit was removed and public sector pay increases above the rate of inflation were announced. Significantly, the government moved quickly to announce the end of the poll tax (in March 1991). It was to be replaced by the council tax.

The main theme until the 1992 general election was the establishment of a nation 'at ease with itself'. The implication was that the radical changes of the Thatcher years had been necessary, but the time for consolidation had arrived. This explains the launch of the Citizen's Charter in early 1991. The charter programme was meant to combine the Thatcherite insistence on high standards in public service with a new emphasis on partnership and cooperation, and a recognition of achievement.

Continuity
Not every initiative was characterised by a softening of the Thatcherite approach. Major's commitment to low inflation was as strong as Thatcher's, for example, and this remained the cornerstone of economic policy. In addition, Major was committed to further privatisation (notably of the coal industry and railways) and to a basic rate of income tax of 20p in the pound (a long-cherished Thatcherite dream). Moreover, the contracting-out of public services to the private sector, begun under Thatcher, was to be continued and extended. Here again, the Citizen's Charter had a role to play. By laying out in

charters the standards which had to be maintained, the government put pressure on public bodies to meet those standards or to suffer the consequences.

Major's objectives

On becoming Prime Minister, Major had four interrelated objectives. The first was to establish himself as a Prime Minister in his own right with a distinctive perspective and direction of his own. His early policy pronouncements and his more conciliatory and cooperative style were attempts to do this. The second was to heal the wounds in the Conservative Party which had developed over the last years of Thatcher's premiership. The third was to preserve the essence of Thatcherism, while softening its rough edges so as to make it appealing to the public once more. And, the fourth was to produce a climate in which sufficient numbers of voters would vote Conservative in the forthcoming general election.

The 1992 general election

When John Major announced the date of the 1992 general election, most commentators predicted a Labour victory or a hung Parliament. These predictions were based upon two main factors. First, most opinion polls showed the Conservatives lagging. And second, the economy remained in recession. In practice, however, such predictions proved to be wrong. The Conservative Party did lose 39 seats and its share of the vote fell to its fourth lowest since 1945. Despite this, however, the result was a Conservative victory and an overall majority of 21.

Why did the Conservatives win?

According to Crewe (1992), there were five main reasons for a Conservative victory in 1992. First, the size and distribution of the swing to Labour favoured the Conservatives. Second, many people did not believe that Neil Kinnock had the leadership qualities to be Prime Minister. Third, the Conservatives' negative campaigning made an impact - especially their assertion that a Labour government would raise taxation and allow inflation to rise. Fourth, there was a general fear that Labour was not competent to govern. And fifth, there was a last minute swing to the Conservatives amongst the middle classes and skilled working-class voters, especially in marginal seats in England.

3.2 John Major's premiership 1992-97

John Major's position after the election

The victory in April 1992 enormously strengthened Major's position both as Conservative Leader and as Prime Minister. He now had a popular mandate and, against the odds, he had won it largely on the basis of his personal popularity and campaigning skills. The honeymoon, however, did not last for long. By late 1994, just two years after the election, David McKie could write:

'No government since polling began had fallen as fast and as far from public favour as John Major's did between its election and its second anniversary in April 1994. Major himself was the least popular Prime Minister ever, yet his government's ratings were even worse than his own. On the issues where the Conservatives, even in bad times, had dominated Labour - their superior capacity for managing the British economy, their greater command in the fight against crime - Labour had taken the lead and showed no sign of relinquishing it.' (McKie 1994, p.3)

The problems faced by Major's government

The problems which the Major government had to face came thick and fast. They can be categorised under five headings.

1. Black Wednesday

In September 1990, Britain finally agreed to join the Exchange Rate Mechanism (ERM) of the European Monetary System (EMS). It did so when the pound's exchange rate was high. As Chancellor and then as Prime Minister, John Major made his support for Britain's participation in the EMS clear. In the 1992 Conservative election manifesto, for example, participation in the EMS in the long term was to be a central plank in government economic policy:

'Membership of the ERM is now central to our counter-inflation discipline...In due course we will move to the narrow bands of the ERM.' (Conservative 1992, p.6)

In the summer of 1992, however, the money markets began to exert pressure on the pound. Despite promising that the government would not pull out of the ERM and despite spending as much as £10 billion trying to protect the pound, on 16 September 1992 ('Black Wednesday') the Chancellor, Norman Lamont, was forced to take the pound out of the ERM and to devalue it. This was not just a reversal of government policy, it was also a humiliation. This was the first time since 1945 that a Conservative government had been forced to devalue the pound and it shattered the Conservatives' reputation for economic competence. Even when the economy recovered in 1995-97, no credit was given to the Conservatives.

2. Taxation

It is generally agreed that the crucial issue in the 1992 general election campaign was taxation. The Conservatives made a great deal of political capital by portraying Labour as a high tax party. Conservatives, they argued, cut taxes. They did not put them up. As late as 1 January 1994 John Major said:

'The Conservative Party remains the party of the lowest possible tax, the party of low income tax and the only party whose instinct is to cut tax and leave money with individuals and families and not take it for the state.' (John

Major's New Year Message, 1994)
Despite these words, in 1993 Britain's budget deficit was around £50 billion. To reduce this debt, more money had to be raised. As a result, Norman Lamont announced in his March 1993 budget that indirect taxes would be raised over the following three years. When Lamont was replaced by Kenneth Clarke in May 1993, Clarke continued the policy set in place by Lamont. In January 1994, the Labour Party was able to claim for the first time in 15 years that tax levels under a Conservative government exceeded the tax levels of the last Labour government. This embarrassment for the Conservatives was heightened when VAT was imposed on fuel in 1995. By the time of the 1997 general election, Labour could claim that the Conservatives had made 22 tax rises since 1992. This blunted what had been a potent Conservative weapon during the 1992 election campaign.

3. Euroscepticism

The third blow to the Major government was the way in which the split within the Conservative Party over Europe widened considerably in the period 1992-97. Although the government was able to secure a parliamentary majority in support of the Maastricht Treaty, arguments within the Conservative Party over the role which Britain should play in the EU continued. A stubborn group of anti-Europeans (the 'Eurosceptics') mounted an orchestrated campaign in Parliament and in the media and finally voted against the government, despite a three-line whip, in late November 1994. As a punishment, the Conservative whip was withdrawn from eight Conservative MPs (another, Richard Body, joined them voluntarily). Although the whip was restored to the eight in April 1995 and although John Major successfully fought a leadership contest in July 1995, the Eurosceptics' actions exposed the fundamental split within the party. This split emerged again during the 1997 election campaign - this time over the future of the pound, should the proposed single European currency be introduced. The government had carefully drawn up a 'wait and see' policy to keep both wings on board, but the Eurosceptics pressed hard for an outright rejection. The result was that Conservative divisions were exposed - without any effort to bring this about on Labour's part. It should be noted that parliamentary arithmetic played an important part in exposing the Conservative splits. When the whip was withdrawn from the Eurosceptics, the government technically became a minority government (due to by-election defeats and defections). Since the government's parliamentary majority depended on the support of Eurosceptics, they could exert a great deal of pressure on the government.

4. The 'sleaze' factor

In addition to the other problems facing the Major government, an unprecedented number of sexual and financial scandals involving Conservatives provided critics with the ammunition to accuse the government of sleaze. A number of the early scandals were exposed whilst the Conservatives were promoting their 'Back to Basics' campaign (a campaign launched in 1993 which aimed to encourage people to take responsibility for their actions, but was widely interpreted as meaning that the government supported old-fashioned family values). By exposing a number of sexual and financial indiscretions, the media gave the impression that the government was being hypocritical. More important, serious accusations were levelled against ministers - notably Neil Hamilton and Jonathan Aitken - that they had abused their positions by accepting payments in money and in kind in return for pursuing the interests of their paymasters. Although there was no question of senior ministers being involved in such activities, the fact that they refused to condemn their colleagues added to the impression that the government cared not about the public, but about a small élite. This impression was reinforced by complaints that Conservative supporters were being appointed to highly paid jobs in the unelected quangos which were rapidly growing in number as a result of Conservative policies.

5. The Labour Party

Following Labour's defeat in the 1992 general election, the Labour Leader Neil Kinnock resigned and John Smith was elected in his place. John Smith, it was generally agreed, had suitable credentials to pose a formidable threat to John Major at the next election, but he suffered a heart attack and died in May 1994. After Tony Blair was elected in John Smith's place in July 1994, Labour's opinion poll ratings reached record highs and they remained high until May 1997. This was due to four main factors:

- the image projected by Blair and his colleagues (they presented the Labour Party as united, modern and pro-gressive and attacked the Conservatives for being disunited, complacent and stale)
- the internal party reforms pushed through by the leadership (most notably, the campaign to change Clause IV in the Labour Party constitution)
- the policies adopted by the leadership (the main policies had been agreed two years before the 1997 general election took place and so the public knew much of what to expect in the Labour manifesto)
- the modernisation of the Labour Party's media and election machinery.

In addition, unlike in 1992 when the polls suggested that Neil Kinnock was an electoral liability, there was a consensus that Tony Blair was a competent and dynamic leader.

The way in which Labour repositioned itself in the period 1994-97 is explored in more detail in Section 4.1 below.

Policy initiatives 1992-97

The Major administration should not be judged just by the problems it faced. During the period 1992-97, there were significant developments in the following areas:

- steps towards peace in Northern Ireland (see Chapter 4, Section 3.4)
- reform of the civil service (see Chapter 13, Section 2.2)
- reform of local government (see Chapter 16, Section 2.6)
- restructuring of the police service and legislation on criminal justice (see Chapter 18, Sections 2.2 and 2.6).

The Major government's policy towards Europe is discussed in Chapter 6, Section 3.3. The Major government's management of the economy is discussed in Chapter 15, Section 3.2.

Main points - Part 3

- Margaret Thatcher's position was weakened by: (1) Britain's economic position in 1990; (2) the poll tax; (3) Conservative splits over Europe; (4) the resignation of Cabinet ministers; and (5) a series of poor election results for the Conservatives.
- Michael Heseltine's leadership bid resulted in the resignation of Thatcher and the elevation of John Major.
- The policies which emerged in Major's first two years as Prime Minister demonstrated both a degree of change (especially in terms of image) and considerable continuity (especially in terms of economic goals).
- Between 1992 and 1997, the Major government was besieged by the following problems - (1) loss of a reputation for economic competence; (2) the necessity to go back on a pledge not to raise taxes; (3) damaging splits over Europe; (4) sleaze; and (5) a revitalised Labour Party.

Activity 3.4 *John Major in power 1990-97*

Item A *Major's changing public image*

The newspaper on the left was published just after the Conservative victory in April 1992. The majority of newspapers supported Major in the 1992 general election. In March 1997, the *Sun* switched its allegiance from the Conservatives to Labour. Only a minority of newspapers supported Major in the 1997 general election.

Item B *Thatcherism and Major (1)*

This cartoon was first published in 1991. It shows the following members of John Major's Cabinet: (from the left) John Gummer (Agriculture Secretary), John MacGregor (Leader of the Commons), John Major (Prime Minister), Michael Heseltine (Environment Secretary), Chris Patten (Chancellor of the Duchy of Lancaster) and Norman Lamont (Chancellor of the Exchequer).

Item C *Thatcherism and Major (2)*

(i) The sharp contrast in style between Thatcher and Major does not necessarily indicate a similar marked change in policy and underlying philosophy. Indeed, the central thrust of the Thatcher free-market strategy has been maintained and extended. The introduction of executive agencies and market testing in the civil service has enthusiastically been carried forward. Compulsory competitive tendering in local government has been extended. The development of internal markets in health and education has been energetically pursued. Major's government has not hesitated to promote further privatisation (British Rail). The most obvious change was the replacement of the poll tax by the council tax, but this was a pragmatic political decision, not a change in philosophy. For a time, it appeared that Major would be less hostile to Europe than his predecessor, but this too has proved more a difference of style than substance. Indeed, to satisfy the Eurosceptics in his own party, Major has been increasingly obliged to demonstrate his toughness (by negotiating British opt-outs in the Maastricht Treaty, for example). If Major attached considerable weight to the competition policies which reflect one aspect of Thatcherism, he also emphasised the traditional conservative values which reflect another. This was most clearly shown in the ill-fated Back to Basics campaign. This revealed that Major was less cautious than his predecessor. She championed the same values without making specific commitments. There is one area where there has been a significant new departure - Northern Ireland. The Downing Street Declaration marked the beginning of a new phase in the search for peace.

Adapted from Leach 1995.

(ii) Nobody doubted that Margaret Thatcher had a particular agenda and a 'big idea'. She was the first Prime Minister to have an 'ism' named after her and she was a conviction politician. As such, she probably set impossible standards for any successor. From the start, John Major rejected any comparisons with Thatcher and he went out of his way to to reject the idea of 'Majorism'. Indeed, apart from the emphasis on active citizenship, it is difficult to find any distinctive Major effect on the political agenda. He was happy to preside over the Thatcher legacy. Indeed, for much of the time, Majorism equalled simply the absence of Thatcher.

Adapted from Kavanagh 1994.

(iii) From 1979, a key aim of the Conservatives was to reduce the role of the state in social and economic affairs. By 1990, this aim had only partially been met - largely because Conservative reforms have been driven as much by short-term necessity as longer-term ideological goals. Nevertheless, Thatcherite reforms did display increasing radicalism as their strategy unfolded - as shown by reforms in education, the civil service and employment policy in the third term, for example. Thatcherism is, therefore, a process which has unfolded over a number of years in an evolutionary manner. Under John Major, this evolutionary process has continued into a new, more radical period which can be termed 'late-Thatcherism'. Seen in this way, the Major period can be said to represent both continuity with and a development of Thatcherism under Margaret Thatcher. For example, the Major government did not merely administer Thatcherite schooling policies. In early 1991, it introduced a system of league tables for schools and in 1992 it introduced privatised school inspectors to replace Her Majesty's Inspectorate. Similarly, Major surprised political commentators by dramatically increasing the pace of change in the civil service.

Adapted from Kerr et al. 1997.

Item D *Major's style of leadership*

Between 1992 and 1997, John Major was transformed into an electoral liability. This happened for a host of reasons, but most importantly because of his perceived weakness, especially in relation to Tony Blair whose assault on the structure and policies of 'Old' Labour had made him appear confident and tough. Major's apparent weakness resulted from his inability to manage key aspects of policy and party management. The trend was set early in the 1992 Parliament with the events of 'Black Wednesday'. Not only did this undermine the reputation for economic competence established by the Conservatives over many years, it also exposed the deficiencies of Major as a leader. His handling of his Chancellor Norman Lamont (who stayed in office until May 1993) showed him as indecisive and dithering (he neither sacked nor effectively supported Lamont in September 1992). This pattern of policy miscalculation followed by party mismanagement then became a trend. Examples include:

- the management of the rebellion over the Maastricht Treaty
- the Back to Basics campaign
- the increase of VAT on fuel
- the 1995 leadership election
- the BSE crisis.

In addition, Major failed, at least at first, to condemn the actions of disgraced MPs. Not only did this give the impression he was soft on sleaze, it also reinforced the idea that he was weak and indecisive.

Adapted from Dobson 1998.

Questions

1. Explain the transformation in John Major's public image which is shown in Item A.
2. 'A continuation of Thatcherism'. Is this an accurate description of politics under John Major? Use Items B and C in your answer.
3. How far were the problems faced by John Major down to him and how far were they due to factors beyond his control? Use Items A-D in your answer.

Part 4 The 1997 general election

Key issues

1. What steps did Labour take to avoid defeat in the 1997 general election?
2. What were the main features of the 1997 general election result?
3. How can the 1997 general election result be explained?

4.1 The Labour Party under Tony Blair

Repositioning the Labour Party 1994-97

In order to understand the 1997 general election result, it is necessary to take into account not just the problems faced by the Major government (described in the previous section), but also the way in which the Labour Party repositioned itself following Tony Blair's election as Party Leader in 1994.

The economy

During the 1992 general election campaign, Labour had proved exceptionally vulnerable to Conservative attacks on its economic policies. This experience resulted in two main changes by the time of the 1997 general election.

First, many of the spending commitments made in 1992 were jettisoned. Unlike in 1992, this made it difficult for the Conservatives to claim in 1997 that Labour's pledges could only be fulfilled if income tax was raised, if government borrowing was raised (which would be inflationary), or both. In addition, of course, by 1997 Labour was able to argue that the Conservatives could no longer be trusted on taxation

since they had broken their 1992 pledge not to raise the tax burden. In particular, Labour was able to play on public outrage at the imposition of VAT on fuel.

And second, the Labour Party included in its manifesto pledges which would appeal to a wide cross-section of the electorate and not just to its traditional working-class base. Such commitments included:

- the introduction of a national minimum wage
- the imposition of a 'windfall tax' on the profits of the privatised utilities
- the establishment of a welfare-to-work programme designed to bring benefit claimants back into employment.

Tony Blair's leadership

The impact of Tony Blair's leadership on the revitalisation of the Labour Party was twofold. First, Blair's election as Leader provided the impetus for a number of important changes both in the structure and organisation of the Labour Party and in the policies officially supported by the Labour Party. And second, by projecting the image of a strong and decisive leader, Blair was able to stand in contrast to Major who was widely regarded as weak and indecisive (reversing the position in 1992 when Major was seen in a positive light and Kinnock was widely regarded as an electoral liability). The internal reforms and Blair's positive image are, of course, intimately related. Without the internal reforms and substantive changes in policy, Blair might not have appeared so strong and decisive. And, if he had not appeared so strong and decisive, there would not have been such a contrast with John Major. At the same time, by taking advantage of the positive image that was projected by the media, Blair was able to push through internal reforms and policy changes without the sort of division which had damaged the Labour Party in the past and was damaging the Conservative Party at the time.

It should be noted that the circumstances were ripe for change in the Labour Party. After losing four general elections in a row, there was consensus amongst the rank and file that a new approach should be tried. Also, the first steps on the road to reform had already been taken by Neil Kinnock and John Smith and so there was already some momentum towards change. Nevertheless, Blair's achievement was considerable. Further moves towards one member one vote (OMOV) for internal Labour Party ballots, the replacement of Clause IV of the Labour constitution and substantial changes with regard to policy all served to build the idea that Blair was a man in charge of his party who had the right credentials to lead the country. This was an electoral advantage both because it appealed to voters and because it attracted new Labour Party members who were willing to work for Labour during the election campaign.

Wooing Middle England

Labour Party leaders and strategists were aware that what the party had failed to do in 1992 was to win over sufficient voters in so-called 'Middle England' (which is largely made up of people in social group 'C1' - people with junior managerial or routine clerical administrative posts). Many of the policies adopted by the Labour Party after 1994 were meant to appeal directly to the aspirations and beliefs of this group. Labour's emphasis on reducing crime and direct taxation, for example, reflected concerns which were especially strong amongst Middle Englanders.

The policies and presentation intended to attract this group of voters were spectacularly successful. In the 1997 general election, some of Labour's most impressive gains were in areas of the country where large parts of Middle England were concentrated. In Greater London, gains of +12.4% were recorded, for example, and +11.4% in South East England (Dobson 1998).

Other key developments

It was not just the repositioning of the Labour Party and the positive image projected by its Leader which explains Labour's appeal in 1997. Three other developments were particularly significant. First, the Labour Party made a concerted effort to win support in the press. The result was that, for the first time in a general election, a majority of newspapers (with a significant majority of the total readership) supported Labour. Second, by skilfully coordinating their submissions to the Boundary Commission,

Labour Party officials and MPs were able to ensure that changes which were expected to disadvantage Labour in 20 seats were negligible. And third, the Labour Party made a concerted effort to capture the votes of women. They did this by sending out signals that a Labour government would take women's issues seriously (a Minister for Women was promised, for example), by encouraging more women candidates (all-women shortlists were promoted until they were outlawed in 1996) and by tailoring their policies to appeal to women.

4.2 The 1997 campaign and result

The campaign

On 17 March 1997, John Major stood on the steps of 10 Downing Street and announced that there would be a general election on 1 May. This was very nearly the last lawful date possible. There can be little doubt that the decision to leave the election as late as possible and to have a long campaign (the 1997 general election was one of the longest campaigns in recent British political history) reflected the weak position of the Conservatives in the polls. The government clearly hoped that, by leaving the election late, some of the credit for the growing economic prosperity of the past two years would be translated into votes for the Conservatives. The government also believed that a long campaign would maximise the opportunity for electors to see major Labour mistakes and inconsistencies.

In the event, the campaign was both long and dull, with little happening to lead any commentators to change their opinion that a Labour government was the likely outcome. The campaign is discussed in detail in Chapter 7, Section 3.6

The result

If the 1997 campaign was one of the dullest on record, the results were just the opposite. It was an election of records and superlatives (see Box 3.1).

Explaining Labour's victory

Whilst nobody could deny that the result of the 1997 general election was a decisive victory for Labour, the political commentator John Curtice has argued that it would be an exaggeration to describe the result as a 'landslide'. It is true that Labour won a huge overall majority in the House of Commons (an overall majority of 178), but an examination of the voting figures shows that the result was actually closer than the distribution of seats in the Commons suggests. In other words, the number of seats won by Labour was inflated by the way in which the electoral system works. Labour, so the argument goes, was always going to win a majority in the Commons, but a number of factors conspired to ensure that this majority, in terms of seats, was rather larger than might be expected by the numbers who actually voted Labour.

Box 3.1 The 1997 general election

- Tony Blair, at 43, became the youngest Prime Minister since Lord Liverpool in 1812.
- Labour's total of 418 seats (419, if the Speaker is included) was the party's highest ever.
- Labour's total of 13.5 million votes was its highest since 1951.
- Labour's share of the vote, at 43%, was its highest since 1966.
- The Liberal Democrats' total of seats (46) was the highest for any third party since the Liberals won 56 in 1929.
- With 165 seats, the Conservatives had their lowest number since 1906.
- The Conservatives' total of 9.6 million votes was the party's fewest since 1929.
- The Conservatives' share of the vote (30.7%) was their lowest since 1832.
- The Conservatives had not failed to win a seat in Wales since 1906.
- The Conservatives had never before failed to win a seat in Scotland.
- The number of Cabinet ministers to lose their seats (seven) was the highest since 1906 (when eight, including the Conservative Prime Minister, Arthur Balfour, were defeated).
- The number of women returned (120) was the highest ever.
- There were 259 new MPs, the highest number since 1945.
- Martin Bell was the first independent to sit for a British constituency since 1910.
- The nine black and Asian MPs elected was the highest number ever.
- Turnout in the election (71.4%) was the lowest since 1935.

Adapted from Cathcart 1997.

Long-term factors

The long-term factors which explain the size of Labour's victory are those described in the earlier part of this section and in the previous section. Put simply, by the time the general election was called, the Conservative Party appeared tired, divided and sleazy whilst the Labour Party appeared fresh, united and dynamic. In 1997, Labour no longer suffered from the problems that had resulted in defeat in 1992. Conversely, the problems that the Conservatives had faced since 1992 meant that they went into the 1997 election in a weak position. After 18 years of Conservative rule, there was a mood that it was 'time for a change'. In addition, the political commentator John Curtice has pointed out that:

'As in Scotland and Wales so across Great Britain as a whole, the Conservatives' principal problem is that their vote has become too geographically evenly spread.' (Curtice 1997, p.7)

The 'first-past-the-post' electoral system favours parties whose votes are concentrated in certain constituencies rather than being evenly spread.

Short-term factors

Whilst long-term factors produced the climate in which the election was fought, a number of short-term factors had an important bearing on the result. First, Labour's campaign tactics were important. Labour targeted key marginal constituencies and concentrated resources on them. This ensured that the party did rather better in most of these key marginals than it did nationally. In other words, it managed to win more seats than the national swing would suggest it should win. Second, there is clear evidence of anti-Conservative tactical voting:

'Encouraged by a number of campaigns, voters were provided with far more information in 1997 than ever before as to how to vote if they wished to remove the sitting Conservative MP. The evidence suggests that a substantial number of people did decide to take this option, with Conservative switchers, Labour supporters and Liberal Democrats all being willing to vote for the most promising anti-Conservative candidate.' (Dobson 1998, p.17)

Third, the work of party members contributed to the result. Whilst Labour was a growing and increasingly youthful party by 1997, Conservative membership was shrinking and ageing. As a result, the Conservatives were stretched during the campaign in a way that Labour was not. The Defence Secretary, Michael Portillo, for example, lost his seat partly because his constituency party workers had concentrated on a neighbouring constituency because they were short-staffed. And fourth, much of the coverage of the election campaign focused on issues that damaged rather than helped the Conservatives. For example, the first two weeks were dominated by sleaze. The publicity surrounding the disgraced former minister Neil Hamilton was particularly harmful not just because it focused attention on sleaze but also because it gave the impression that John Major was weak and ineffectual (Major was unable to prevent Hamilton's local association from adopting him as their candidate). Similarly, when attention turned to the European single currency, this issue highlighted divisions in the Conservative Party.

Putting the result into perspective

Labour won 44.4% of the vote in Great Britain (ie excluding Northern Ireland). This was considerably more than the Conservatives (31.5%), but, as John Curtice (1997) points out, it was a smaller share of the vote than the Labour Party won in all the elections held between 1945 and 1966. One reason for this lower share of the vote is the growth of the third party vote since the 1960s. In 1997, the Liberal Democrats won 17.2% of the vote in Great Britain, whereas the Liberals won less than 10% of the vote in all elections held between 1945 and 1966 (except in 1964 when they won 11.4%).

A second factor that should be taken into account is the low turnout. Whilst the turnout in general elections has dropped since the 1950s (turnout was higher than 75% in all elections between 1950 and 1966 and was over 80% in 1950 and 1951), turnout in 1997 was the lowest since 1935 (71.3% in the UK as a whole). Research by Curtice and Steed (1997) shows that turnout was much lower in traditionally strong Labour areas than in strong Conservative areas.

A third factor is the size of the Conservative vote. Although the Conservatives lost a quarter of their 1992 vote, they still managed to win 9.6 million votes and their share of the vote was 3% more than that won by Labour when it was badly defeated in 1983.

Main points - Part 4

- The repositioning of the Labour Party meant: (1) adopting economic policies with a broader appeal and fewer spending commitments; (2) making internal Labour Party reforms; (3) building a positive image for the Party Leader (unlike in 1992); (4) targeting new policies at 'Middle England'; (5) wooing the press; (6) minimising the impact of the Boundary Commission; and (7) attempting to win the votes of women.
- Whilst nobody could deny that the result of the 1997 general election was a decisive victory for Labour, the number of seats won by Labour was inflated by the way in which the electoral system works. Also, turnout was the lowest in a general election since 1935.
- A number of factors explain Labour's huge Commons majority: (1) the problems faced by the Conservative government; (2) the repositioning of Labour; (3) electoral geography (even spread of Conservative votes); (4) Labour's campaign tactics; (5) tactical voting; (6) party membership; and (7) the campaign.

Activity 3.5 The 1997 general election

Item A   The general election result (1)

Party	Total numbers of votes	MPs elected	Share of UK vote (%)	Share of GB[d] vote (%)
Labour	13,516,632	418	43.3	44.4
Change from 1992	+1,959,498	+147	+8.9	+9.2
Conservative[a]	9,592,999	165	30.7	31.5
Change from 1992	-4,456,509	-171	-11.1	-11.3
Liberal Democrat	5,242,894	46	16.8	17.2
Change from 1992	-755,552	+26	-1.0	-1.1
Welsh/Scottish Nationalists	782,570	10	2.5	2.6
Change from 1992	-3,778	+4	+0.2	+0.2
Referendum Party (not in existence in 1992)	811,827	0	2.6	2.7
Speaker	23,969	1	0.1	0.1
Change from 1992	+23,969	+1	+0.1	+0.1
Others[b]	524,928	1	1.7	1.7
Change from 1992	+91,058	+1	+0.4	+0.4
Northern Ireland parties[c]	790,778	18	2.5	–
Change from 1992	-5,685	+1	+0.2	–
Total votes	31,286,597	659		
Change from 1992	-2,335,172	+8		
United Kingdom turnout	71.4%			
Change from 1992	-6.3%			

Notes: (a) The figures for the Conservative Party exclude eight candidates in Northern Ireland who polled a total of 9,858 votes. (b) The figures for 'others' exclude all candidates and votes in Northern Ireland; they include Martin Bell, elected as Independent MP for Tatton (29,354 votes), 57 British National Party candidates (35,833 votes), 94 Green Party candidates (63,452 votes), 54 Liberal Party candidates (44,989 votes), 178 Natural Law Party candidates (28,073 votes), 53 Pro-Life Alliance candidates (18,545 votes), 64 Socialist Labour Party Candidates (52,110 votes), 16 Scottish Socialist Alliance candidates (9,740 votes), 194 UK Independence Party candidates (106,028 votes) and 309 'other' candidates who polled a total of 136,804 votes. (c) The figures for Northern Ireland parties include all candidates and parties. (d) GB stands for Great Britain.

Adapted from Curtice 1997.

Item B *The general election result (2)*

Voter category	Conservatives		Labour		Lib Dem	
All GB voters	31	(-12)	44	(+9)	17	(-1)
Men	31	(-8)	44	(+6)	17	(-1)
Women	32	(-11)	44	(+10)	17	(-1)
AB voters	42	(-11)	31	(+9)	21	(0)
C1	26	(-22)	47	(+19)	19	(-1)
C2	25	(-15)	54	(+15)	14	(-4)
DE	21	(-8)	61	(+9)	13	(0)
First-time voters	19	(-16)	57	(+17)	18	(-3)
Age 18-29	22	(-18)	57	(+19)	17	(0)
30-44	26	(-11)	49	(+12)	17	(-3)
45-64	33	(-9)	43	(+9)	18	(-2)
65+	44	(-3)	34	(-2)	16	(+2)
Home owners	35	(-12)	41	(+11)	17	(-3)
Council tenants	13	(-6)	65	(+1)	15	(+5)
Trade union members	18	(-9)	57	(+7)	20	(+2)

All figures are percentages. Change from 1992 in brackets. GB = Great Britain.

Adapted from Dobson 1998.

Questions

1. Item A shows that Labour won the 1997 general election by a large margin of seats.
   a) Why did Labour win by such a large margin?
   b) Was the result as clear-cut as the division of seats suggests? Explain your answer.
2. To what extent do you think Labour's electoral tactics were responsible for the result outlined in Items A and B? Explain your answer.
3. 'A great victory in seats, a modest success in other respects'. To what extent do Items A-C provide evidence for this assessment of Labour's performance in the 1997 general election?
4. a) What does Item C tell us about the 1997 general election result?
   b) What were the political consequences of this result?

Item C *The general election result (3)*

In the 1997 general election, the winner's bonus and the penalties against the party in second place operated with a particular vengeance. With 43.3% of the (UK) vote, Labour won 63.4% of the seats, producing a votes:seats ratio of 1:1.46. In contrast, with 30.7% of the vote, the Conservatives only gained 25.0% of all seats, producing a votes:seats ratio of 1:0.81. The size of the winner's bonus for Labour and the penalty for the main party in second place were larger than any since the war. In 1987, with a similar share of the vote to the Conservatives in 1997, Labour won 60 more seats. What this means is that, in 1997, it took, on average, 113,987 votes to elect every Liberal Democrat MP, 58,127 to elect every Conservative MP, but 32,318 votes to elect every Labour MP. This disproportionality was produced by certain factors - the size of the winner's bonus under the British 'first-past-the-post' system; the geographic distribution of party support; the effects of anti-Conservative tactical voting; and the difference in size of constituency electorates (in 1997, despite the work of the Boundary Commission, Conservative seats included on average about 5,000 more voters than Labour seats). The result is that if, in the next election, Labour and the Conservatives win exactly the same share of the vote (37%), a uniform swing would produce 341 Labour MPs and 254 Conservative MPs - an 87 seat winner's bonus for Labour. It would take a minimal swing of 8% to produce a hung Parliament and a vast swing of 11.6% for the Conservatives to gain an overall majority. This size of swing has only been achieved this century by Labour in 1945 (11.8%) and by the National Government in 1931 (14.4%).

Adapted from Norris 1997.

Part 5 New Labour in power

Key issues

1. What were the characteristics of the new Labour government?
2. What policies were pursued in Labour's first 18 months of power?
3. To what extent has the Labour government found a 'Third Way'?

5.1 The new Blair government

Personnel

The make-up of Tony Blair's first government was determined both by the Labour Party constitution (which stipulates that members of the shadow Cabinet must be appointed to posts in a new Labour government) and by Blair's own political preferences and considerations. There were a number of surprises. First, Chris Smith, shadow Health Secretary, became Secretary of State for Culture, Media and Sport (as the Department of National Heritage was renamed), whilst Frank Dobson was appointed as Secretary of State for Health. Second, Tony Blair's close colleague Peter Mandelson was appointed to the Cabinet Office as Minister without Portfolio and, despite not being a member of the Cabinet, became entitled to sit on a number of Cabinet committees. And third, Frank Field was appointed as Minister for Welfare Reform in the Department of Social Security (Field was not a shadow minister, but was an expert in the field of welfare reform). Significantly, few MPs who could be described as being 'Old' Labour (old-style left wingers) were appointed. The *Observer*'s headline 'Left feels the squeeze' is an accurate reflection of most commentators' analysis of Tony Blair's appointments (*Observer*, 4 May 1997).

The reshuffle of July 1998
Tony Blair's reshuffle in July 1998 affected 52 ministers. Three were promoted to the Cabinet, two promoted and three moved sideways within the Cabinet, and four sacked from the Cabinet (the Cabinet was reduced in size by one). One junior minister (Frank Field) resigned and nine were sacked. Ten new junior ministers were appointed from the backbenches, 16 junior ministers were promoted and four moved sideways (*Times*, 29 July 1998). A number of political commentators argued that the reshuffle was designed to strengthen Tony Blair's own position at the expense of the Chancellor, Gordon Brown. Supporters of Gordon Brown, it was argued, were sacked or moved sideways whilst those loyal to Blair were promoted (*Guardian*, 28 July 1998).

The new government's programme
The legislative programme announced by the new government had two main aims. First, a number of key manifesto commitments were to be implemented (to show the electorate that Labour would fulfil its promises). And second, the programme was designed to put New Labour ideas into practice. Key Bills in the first Queen's Speech are listed in Box 3.2.

Box 3.2 Key Bills in Labour's first Queen's Speech, 1997

1. Two Education Bills to reduce class sizes and raise school standards.
2. A Firearms Bill to introduce a ban on all handguns.
3. A Finance Bill to implement Gordon Brown's first Budget and to set up the welfare-to-work programme.
4. A Bill to give the Bank of England control over interest rates.
5. Referendum Bills for Scotland and Wales.
6. Devolution Bills for Scotland and Wales (subject to a positive result in the referendums).
7. A Crime and Disorder Bill (to deliver Labour's promise that it would be 'tough on crime and tough on the causes of crime').
8. A Low Pay Bill to set up a commission to recommend a minimum wage.
9. A Lottery Bill to channel lottery cash into education and health.
10. A Bill incorporating the European Convention on Human Rights.

In total, 52 separate pieces of legislation were passed during Labour's first parliamentary session. The session lasted for 19 months, the longest session for over 30 years (*Guardian*, 20 November 1998).

The second parliamentary session began on 24 November 1998. The Queen's Speech proposed 22 Bills, including a Bill designed to remove voting rights from hereditary peers. The smaller number of Bills reflected both a shorter parliamentary session and an anticipated lengthy struggle with the Lords. The key Bills are outlined in Box 3.3.

Box 3.3 Key Bills in Labour's second Queen's Speech, 1998

1. A Bill to reform the House of Lords.
2. Bills to reform disability benefits and widowers' pensions and introducing new tax credits for people on benefits and low pay.
3. A Bill introducing new trade union rights.
4. A Bill reducing the age of consent for homosexuals from 18 to 16.
5. A Bill to change the rules on legal aid.
6. A Bill providing for a London mayor and assembly.
7. A Bill scrapping the NHS internal market.

5.2 Labour in power

The economy
Driver and Martell (1998) point out that the Labour Party was elected to government in 1997 on a programme which rejected two of the defining characteristics of Labour economic policy-making since 1947:
- nationalisation (or, more precisely, the renationalisation of industries privatised by the previous Conservative governments)
- Keynesianism.

In other words, by the time of the 1997 general election, the Labour Party had finally accepted that the post-war consensus had been broken and that a new approach was necessary. The new government's economic policies were, in some ways, very close to those pursued by the previous Conservative administration (for example, as promised, the Labour government stuck to Conservative spending commitments during its first two years in office). On the other hand, there were significant innovations (for example, the Bank of England was given responsibility for setting interest rates and a Comprehensive Spending Review resulted in public spending being set for three years beginning in 1999). The management of the economy under Tony Blair is described in more detail in Chapter 15, Section 3.3.

The NHS
The 1997 Labour manifesto made a strong claim in relation to the NHS:

'Labour created the NHS 50 years ago. It is under threat from the Conservatives. We want to save and to modernise the NHS.' (Labour 1997, p.20)

In order to 'save the NHS', Labour made the pledges outlined in Box 3.4.

Box 3.4 Labour's manifesto pledges on the NHS

In its 1997 election manifesto, Labour made the following pledges on matters concerning the NHS:

- cut waiting lists
- end the Conservatives' internal market in healthcare
- cut down on bureaucracy and use the money on direct care for patients
- alter the primary healthcare system so that fundholding GPs do not have an advantage over other GPs in their area
- alter contracts between primary care teams and hospitals so that they last for three to five years rather than one year
- make hospital boards accountable to their local communities
- introduce a new Patient's Charter
- promote new developments in telemedicine
- appoint a new Minister for Public Health
- ban tobacco advertising
- establish a new independent Food Standards Agency
- raise spending on the NHS in real terms.

Labour's record after 18 months

In the first 18 months of office, the Labour government fulfilled or took steps towards fulfilling a number of these pledges. Four developments were particularly significant. First, a Minister of Public Health was appointed (Tessa Jowell) in May 1997. Second, although (in November 1997) it was announced that tobacco advertising would be banned, Formula One motor racing was controversially exempted from this ban. Third, when the results of the Comprehensive Spending Review were made public in July 1998, it was revealed that, between 1999 and 2002, health spending would rise by 4.7% a year (compared to an average of 2.5% between 1992 and 1997). And fourth, it was announced in the second Queen's Speech that there would be an NHS Bill which would:

- end the NHS internal market by replacing optional GP fundholders with a universal system of primary care groups led by GPs
- set up a Health Improvement Commission to carry out spot checks on NHS services
- enable ministers to recoup £2 million a week from insurance companies for treating the victims of road accidents
- compel drugs companies to comply with a new voluntary agreement on drugs prices.

Although the government pledged to save a great deal of money by cutting down on bureaucracy, that proved difficult to do in practice. Also, waiting lists rose in 1998.

There was disappointment in some quarters that the second Queen's Speech did not include a Bill setting up a Food Standards Agency. This was one of the Bills dropped to make sure that Lords reform had sufficient parliamentary time.

Welfare

Reform of the provision of welfare was a top priority and major headache for the Labour government in its first 18 months. The problem facing the government (like that facing previous governments) was that the cost of benefits was rising rapidly every year (more people were living longer and, therefore, drawing a pension for longer, for example), yet the money generated by government was not growing at a sufficient pace to fund these extra costs. Government, therefore, needed either to raise more money (through taxes) or to cut costs. Since the Labour government had made a pledge not to raise taxes, it had to find a way to cut costs. The dilemma facing the government was that simply cutting benefits or pensions would be politically risky whilst radical reform would be extremely complex.

The government's record in its first 18 months

The appointment of Frank Field as Minister of Welfare Reform was widely interpreted as a sign that the government was prepared to consider radical reform. But, there were soon rumours that he had poor relations with Harriet Harman, the Secretary of State for Social Security, and that the Treasury did not agree with his proposals. When Field resigned in July 1998 and Harman was sacked, commentators argued that the government had lost its way on welfare reform. By then, two particularly significant measures had been taken. First, the welfare-to-work programme was set up using money gained from a windfall tax on the privatised utilities. The scheme was designed to help the unemployed (especially young and long-term unemployed people) by providing subsidised work as a 'carrot' and withdrawal of benefit as a 'stick'. And second (amid much controversy) additional benefit payments given to lone parents were cut. Following the accusations that the government had lost its way on welfare reform, a programme of changes was outlined in the second Queen's Speech. The changes included:

- a shake-up of disability benefits (saving £750 million in the long term)
- the creation of a Disability Rights Commission
- the overhaul of benefits for widows and widowers (saving £500 million in the long term)
- the development of stakeholder pension schemes
- the provision for pension sharing on divorce
- a single gateway for all benefits, including a compulsory interview

- the introduction of the working families' tax credit and the disabled person's tax credit to help the low paid.

Education

One of Labour's main slogans in the run-up to the 1997 general election was 'education, education, education'. Behind this, was the belief that high educational standards were the key to ensuring the education system delivered what was required of it. In its first 18 months in power, there were four key developments. First, the Assisted Places scheme, introduced by the Conservatives, was abolished. This scheme had provided bright children from low income families with the funds to attend fee-paying schools. Second, when the results of the Comprehensive Spending Review were made public in July 1998, it was revealed that, between 1999 and 2002, education spending would rise by 5.1% a year (compared to an average of 1.4% between 1979 and 1997). Third, it was controversially announced that, beginning in 1998, students starting university courses would have to pay £1,000 a year in fees - a decision which caused great disquiet amongst many Labour MPs and supporters. And fourth, a white paper entitled *Excellence in Schools* was produced in 1997. This made the following provisions:

- national testing of nine year olds
- the closure of failing schools and their reopening with a new senior management team
- the continued promotion of diversity within the education system (ie private schools, religious schools and Grant Maintained schools would all remain)
- Grant Maintained schools were to be renamed 'foundation schools'
- the creation of Education Action Zones.

Two of these provisions were particularly controversial. First, the continued promotion of diversity within the education system could be interpreted as a sign that the government was not strongly committed to comprehensive education. And second, the Education Action Zones were to be set up where several schools in an area were all failing. Control of such schools would be taken from the LEA and placed in the hands of parents, local businesses and voluntary agencies who would be free to develop educational provision free from constraints such as the national curriculum. This was controversial because it took power away from the (elected) local authority and gave it to an unelected body.

Law and order

The 1997 Labour manifesto included a pledge to be 'tough on crime and tough on the causes of crime'. After coming to power, Labour focused on the first part of this pledge. The Crime and Disorder Act 1998, for example, contained a raft of measures intended to crack down on crime (see Chapter 18, Activity 18.9). Measures to deal with the causes of crime have included:

- the appointment of former chief constable Keith Hellawell as 'drugs tsar' - leader of a team set up to combat the relationship between drugs and crime
- providing jobs through the welfare-to-work programme (it was argued that crime can best be reduced by providing people with gainful employment)
- providing funds to install CCTV in town centres
- providing funds for local authorities to deal with crime-ridden estates.

The Labour government's record on law and order is considered in more deal in Chapter 18, Part 4.

The constitution

It has been noted by a number of commentators that constitutional questions provided one of the key points of difference between Labour and the Conservatives at the 1997 general election. They also mark a key difference between 'Old' and 'New' Labour (for example, Driver & Martell 1998, p.123). The new government has been vigorous in pursuing this constitutional agenda. The measures taken in the first 18 months are outlined in Box 3.5.

Box 3.5 Constitutional reform 1997-98

The following measures were taken between May 1997 and November 1998:

- referendums were held over the devolution of power to Scotland, Wales and London
- Bills were passed setting up new assemblies in Scotland and Wales
- a referendum on the setting up of a new assembly in Northern Ireland was held
- elections to the new Northern Ireland Assembly were held
- the European Convention on Human Rights was incorporated into British law
- the Jenkins Commission reported, recommending the Alternative Plus voting system for elections to Parliament.

In addition, three important constitutional measures were put forward in the second Queen's Speech:

- a Bill introducing a new proportional voting system for European elections (a Bill to this end was controversially blocked by the Lords at the end of the first parliamentary session in November 1998)
- a Bill setting up a London mayor and assembly
- a Bill abolishing the right of hereditary peers to vote.

Some politicians and commentators complained about the lack of progress on a Freedom of Information Bill (see Chapter 19, Section 5.4).

Northern Ireland

Following the 1997 general election, the Labour government quickly made it clear that securing an agreement over new constitutional arrangements in Northern Ireland was to be a priority. On 10 April 1998, a deal was struck - the Good Friday Peace Agreement. Referendums followed in Northern Ireland and in the Republic of Ireland in May 1998, producing a large majority in favour of the new constitutional settlement. Given that the peace process had ground to a halt in 1996-97, the Good Friday Peace Agreement was a major breakthrough and a triumph for the government in general and for Tony Blair and Mo Mowlam in particular. The peace process in Northern Ireland is examined in more detail in Chapter 4, Section 3.4 and Chapter 18, Section 1.3.

Beyond Whitehall

Beyond Whitehall, two areas have been of particular significance with regard to the Labour government's approach.

Local government

The Labour government introduced four main changes to local government in the first 18 months in power. First, as noted above, a Bill setting up a new London-wide authority and an elected mayor was included in the second Queen's speech. Second, the government made a commitment to establish regional assemblies where demand for them had popular support. Third, although most of the powers to control local government finance pioneered by the Conservatives were retained, capital receipts from the sale of council houses were released on a gradual basis and the Local Government Bill announced in the second Queen's Speech included the following provision.

> 'The "crude and universal" capping of council finances by Whitehall will end although John Prescott will still retain strong reserve powers.' (*Guardian*, 25 November 1998)

And fourth, plans to replace the committee system through which councillors control local authorities have been piloted and the Local Government Bill announced in the second Queen's Speech was designed to introduce the so-called 'Best Value' regime:

> 'This will replace compulsory competitive tendering under which councils have to invite private bids for selected services, such as refuse collection.' (*Guardian*, 25 November 1998)

There were also proposals to make all local authorities elect a third of their councillors every year and to allow voting beyond the traditional polling station, in supermarkets for example. The Labour government's plans for local government are considered in more detail in Chapter 16.

Europe and foreign affairs

The second area beyond Whitehall which is worthy of mention is that of European and foreign affairs. The Labour government adopted a distinctly less hostile tone towards the EU than its predecessors. However, it decided not to hold a referendum on the single European currency until after the next election. The Labour government's approach towards the EU is considered in more detail in Chapter 6, Section 3.3.

In terms of foreign affairs, much was made of the Foreign Secretary Robin Cook's reported claim that he would pursue an 'ethical' foreign policy. Critics have argued that Britain's close alliance with the USA and the continued exporting of arms to countries like Indonesia and Turkey (which have a poor record on human rights) have raised doubts about the government's commitment to this ethical dimension in practice. Also, according to the *Times* (23 September 1998), the Foreign Office's efforts to implement an ethical foreign policy were foiled by the Ministry of Defence and the Department of Trade and Industry.

5.3 The Third Way

The Third Way - a new consensus

Once the Labour Party had won power, talk of 'New Labour' gave way to discussion of a 'Third Way'. The emphasis on New Labour, it appears, was primarily for opposition, a campaigning device designed to demonstrate to a sceptical electorate that the party bearing the name 'Labour' in 1997 was different in every respect from the one which bore this name and failed in 1974-79. The Third Way, on the other hand, was a label designed to describe all that was distinctive about the Labour government's approach (see also Chapter 2, Activity 2.4). Central to the notion of a Third Way is the idea that it is possible to carve a middle path which is both radical and centrist at the same time. This middle path lies between Thatcherism on the right and democratic socialism on the left. It is inclusive - it is designed to appeal to former Conservative voters and to Liberal Democrats as much as to Labour voters. It is radical - it has a dynamic agenda for change. And it is consensual - the aim is to move ahead with the support of the mass of the people.

Criticisms of the Third Way

The idea that the government has found a distinctive Third Way has produced a great deal of debate. Central to criticism of the idea is the accusation that there is nothing really distinctive about the approach taken by the Labour government. Rather, it is, in effect, pursuing a Thatcherite agenda. This is the line taken by former Labour Deputy Leader Roy Hattersley. His criticisms apply not only to New Labour's economic policy, but also to key aspects of social policy. In education, for example, Hattersley argues that the government's failure to back the comprehensive ideal and its decision to charge students fees for tuition are two pieces of evidence that the Labour leadership has abandoned all that Labour historically stood for and has accepted a Thatcherite agenda. Talk of a 'Third Way', therefore, amounts to nothing more than a rhetorical device designed to camouflage the right-wing reality of the Blair project. This criticism was echoed by the group of critics who produced a special edition of the journal *Marxism Today* in October 1998. They argued that, while it is senseless to claim that Blairism is nothing but Thatcherism by another name, the Labour government has abandoned social democracy and submitted to the forces of capitalism. This is not a third way. Rather it is a variant on the Thatcherite way, more acceptable in some of its detail, but not substantially different in its ideological impetus nor in its economic and social policies.

Support for the Third Way

The political commentator, David Marquand argues that the government can be seen to be radical in its policy on the constitution, less so in relation to the welfare state and not at all in relation to the economy where its policies remain dictated by a free-market, business-oriented agenda. What the Blair government most certainly is not, he argues, is some new type of Thatcherism (Marquand 1998). Other commentators deny the very terms of the debate as defined by the critics above. From within the Labour Party and from academics such as Anthony Giddens (one of the intellectual architects of Blair's Third Way) and John Gray the view has emerged that any attempt to place the Labour Party on the ideological spectrum of right and left is to ignore the fact that history has invalidated this spectrum and that party programmes must now be characterised in different ways. The Labour government is carving out a third way because it is both radical and beyond traditional left-right distinctions (Giddens 1994 and 1998, and Gray 1995).

Main points - Part 5

- **There were few places for 'Old' Labour MPs in Tony Blair's first government. The reshuffle in July 1998 affected 52 ministers.**
- **In total, 52 separate pieces of legislation were passed during the first parliamentary session and 22 Bills were proposed for the second.**
- **Labour's approach in government shows signs of continuity with the previous administration (for example, in the approach to economic management) and innovation (for example, in constitutional reform).**
- **There is a debate about whether the Labour government's approach is distinctive. Some people argue that it is merely the Thatcherite agenda dressed up differently. Others argue that it is a new approach - the 'Third Way'.**

Activity 3.6 New Labour in power

Item A *The Third Way (1)*

Since taking office, New Labour has certainly been hyperactive, setting policy reviews in place here, legislating and innovating there. But, where is New Labour really going? Does Blair have a political project? Thatcherism from which Blair has learned so much certainly did have a project. Its aim was to transform the political landscape - to make us think in its terms and speak its language as if there were no other. It also had a strategy - an idea of where it wanted to go and how to get there. Above all, Thatcher knew that, to achieve radical change, politics must be conducted like a war and she clearly identified her enemies, dividing them into Wets v Drys and Us v Them. Blair clearly sees himself in the Thatcher mould and has worked hard to model himself on her style of leadership - with a great deal of success. Blair has also modelled his ambitions to make everything 'new' on Thatcherism's project of self renewal. The government talks about 'the Blair project' and the Third Way - a mysterious middle course on every question between all the existing extremes. But, the more this idea is examined, the less convincing it becomes. The problem is that the Third Way does not offer a strategic framework. It claims to be 'beyond left and right', but, in reality, it is smokescreen thrown up to evade the really hard questions of political principle. One of the problems is the claim that the Third Way is all-inclusive. It has no enemies. Everybody can belong. This suggests that, by some miracle, those who supported the ban on tobacco advertising could somehow come together with those who opposed the ban or that an ethical foreign policy could somehow co-exist with the sale of arms to Indonesia. Talk of a Third Way suggests that conflicts can be solved by effortlessly shifting the debate to a higher plane which is somehow above politics. But, a project to transform and modernise society in a radical direction which does not disturb any existing interests and has no enemies is not a serious enterprise.

Adapted from Hall 1998.

Item B   *Observer poll, April 1998*

1. HOW SUPPORT HAS SHIFTED *(figures in millions)*

	General election	Support lost	Support gained	Support April 1998
Labour	13.5	2.6	5.5	**16.4**
Conservative	9.6	2.8	2.3	**9.1**
Liberal Democrat	5.2	2.8	2.5	**4.9**
Other	2.1	1.3	0.2	**1.0**

2. LABOUR'S GROWING SUPPORT

Party	May 97(%)	April 1998	Change
Labour	44	**52**	+8
Conservative	31	**29**	-2
Liberal Democrat	17	**16**	-1
Other	7	**3**	-4

3. DO YOU AGREE OR DISAGREE WITH THE FOLLOWING?

(a) 'The Labour government has no principles; it is only interested in staying in power'

Figures in percentages	All	Lab	Con	LibDem
Agree	**28**	16	44	20
Disagree	**72**	84	54	79
Neither/don't know	**1**	0	2	1

(b) 'Paddy Ashdown is wrong to take the Liberal Democrats so close to Labour'

	All	Lab	Con	LibDem
Agree	**42**	32	58	37
Disagree	**50**	58	35	56
Neither/don't know	**8**	10	6	6

(c) 'On balance have the policies of the Labour government been good or bad (i) for you and your family (ii) for Britain as a whole?'

	(i)		(ii)	
Good	(i)	62	(ii)	75
Bad	(i)	32	(ii)	21
Don't know	(i)	6	(ii)	4

This poll was published after Labour had been in power for almost a year.

Item C   *The Third Way (2)*

Three quite different interpretations have so far been advanced to explain the Blair phenomenon. The first and dominant theory until May 1997 was that New Labour was simply a marketing concept and that Blairism was nothing more than an electoral strategy designed to win power by repackaging the Labour Party. The second interpretation to emerge was that Blairism is essentially Thatcherism with a human face. A third interpretation, however, is becoming increasingly convincing. This is that the Blair government is guided by an ideologically coherent political project which is significantly different from the discarded social democracy of Old Labour and the failed Thatcherism of the Conservatives. In other words, Blair means what he says. To talk of a Third Way is effectively to define Labour as a post-socialist party. The Blair project is, in essence, a programme of cultural engineering or renewal rather than a more familiar programme of economic or social engineering. Culture in this context does not mean 'high' culture (the supposedly enlightened and cultivated artistic pursuits of a society), but the ideas, beliefs, values and knowledge of the population in general. Since Blairism treats culture as of primary importance and regards economic and social issues and structures as secondary, it operates within a mental landscape quite different from that structured by the traditional left-right divide and the ideological battle between capitalism and socialism. The Third Way is a recognition that culture is malleable - what people think and, therefore, how they behave can be reshaped by manipulating the images, symbols and ideas that are presented to them. The decision to scrap Clause IV, for example, was in part meant to symbolise a cultural shift in the Labour Party. The cultural renewal which so dramatically transformed the Labour Party and its electoral fortunes, now that it is in power, can be applied equally successfully to Britain itself.

Adapted from Heywood 1998.

Item D   *Labour and the Liberal Democrats*

In November 1998, the Labour Party and Liberal Democrats issued a joint statement announcing that the Lab-Lib Cabinet committee would be expanded to get rid of the 'destructive tribalism' of the past. As a result, cooperation on constitutional reform would be followed by similar cooperation on health, education, welfare reform and moves towards European integration. This cartoon shows (from the left) Tony Blair, Paddy Ashdown (Leader of the Liberal Democrats) and William Hague (Leader of the Conservatives).

Item E *Change and continuity*

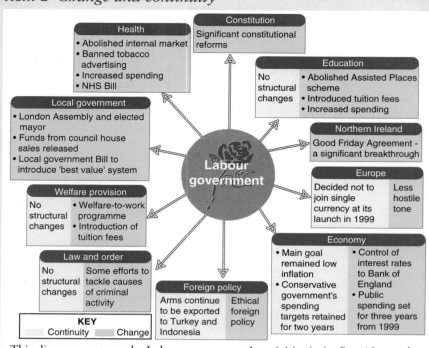

KEY
Continuity   Change

This diagram assesses the Labour government's activities in its first 18 months of power.

Questions

1. a) 'The Blair government is building a new consensus'. Using Items A-E, give arguments for and against this statement.

   b) Write an assessment of the Blair government's first 18 months in power.

2. What does Item B tell us about the Labour government at the end of its first year in office?

3. Using Items A and C give arguments for and against the view that the 'Third Way' is a meaningful term.

4. Judging from Items A-E, what (if anything) is distinctive about the Labour government?

References

Barry (1987) Barry, N., *The New Right*, Croom Helm, 1987.

Benyon (1986) Benyon, J., 'Turmoil in the cities', *Social Studies Review*, Vol.1.3, January 1983.

Benyon (1991) Benyon, J., 'The fall of Margaret Thatcher: the end of an era' in *Wale (1991)*.

Beveridge (1942) Beveridge, W., *Social Insurance and Allied Services*, Cmd 6404, HMSO, 1942.

Butler & Kavanagh (1997) Butler, D. & Kavanagh, D., *The British General Election of 1997*, MacMillan, 1997.

Cathcart (1997) Cathcart, B., *Were You Still Up for Portillo?*, Penguin, 1997.

Conservative (1992) Conservative Central Office, *The Conservative Manifesto 1992*, Conservative Party, 1992.

Coxall (1991) Coxall, B., 'The struggle for the Conservative leadership in 1990', *Talking Politics*, Vol.4.1, Autumn 1991.

Craig (1989) Craig, F.W.S., *British Electoral Facts 1832–1987*, Dartmouth, 1989.

Crewe (1986) Crewe, I., 'Has the electorate become Thatcherite?' in *Skidelsky (1986)*.

Crewe (1992) Crewe, I., 'Why did Labour lose (yet again)', *Politics Review*, Vol.2.1, September 1992.

Curtice (1997) Curtice, J., 'Anatomy of a non-landslide', *Politics Review*, Vol.7.1, September 1997.

Curtice & Steed (1997) Curtice, J. & Steed, M., 'The results analysed' in *Butler & Kavanagh (1997)*.

Dobson (1998) Dobson, A., 'The 1997 general election' in *Lancaster (1998)*.

Driver & Martell (1998) Driver, S. & Martell, L., *New Labour: Politics after Thatcherism*, Polity Press, 1998.

Gamble (1988) Gamble, A., *Free Economy, Strong State*, Macmillan, 1988.

Giddens (1994) Giddens, A., *Beyond Left and Right*, Polity Press, 1994.

Giddens (1998) Giddens, A., *The Third Way*, Polity Press, 1998

Gray (1995) Gray, J., *Enlightenment's Wake: Politics and Culture at the Close of the Modern Age*, Routledge, 1995.

Hall (1998) Hall, S., 'The great moving nowhere show', *Marxism Today*, November/December 1998.

Heywood (1998) Heywood, A., 'It's the culture, stupid: deconstructing the Blair project', *Talking Politics*, Vol.11.1, Autumn 1998.

Kavanagh (1990) Kavanagh, D., *Thatcherism and British Politics: an End to Consensus?*, Oxford University Press, 1990.

Kavanagh (1994) Kavanagh, D., 'A Major agenda?' in *Kavanagh & Seldon (1994)*.

Kavanagh & Seldon (1994) Kavanagh, D. & Seldon, A. (eds), *The Major Effect*, Macmillan, 1994.

Kelly (1993) Kelly, R., 'After Margaret: the Conservative Party after 1990', *Talking Politics*, Vol.5.3, Summer 1993.

Kerr et al. (1997) Kerr, P., McAnulla, S & Marsh, D., 'British politics under John Major' in *Lancaster (1997)*.

Labour (1997) *New Labour - Because Britain Deserves Better*, Labour Party manifesto, Labour Party, 1997.

Lancaster (1995) Lancaster, S. (ed.), *Developments in Politics*, Vol.6, Causeway Press, 1995.

Lancaster (1997) Lancaster, S. (ed.), *Developments in Politics*, Vol.8, Causeway Press, 1997.

Lancaster (1998) Lancaster, S. (ed.), *Developments in Politics*, Vol.9, Causeway Press, 1998.

Leach (1995) Leach, R., 'Political ideas' in *Lancaster (1995)*.

Marquand (1998) Marquand, D., 'The Blair Paradox', *Prospect*, May 1998.

Marsh & Tant (1994) Marsh, D. & Tant, T., 'British politics post Thatcher: a minor Major effect' in *Wale (1994)*.

McKie (1994) McKie, D., *The Guardian Political Almanac 1994/5*, Fourth Estate, 1994.

Middlemass (1979) Middlemass, K., *Politics in an Industrial Society*, André Deutsch, 1979.

Miliband (1961) Miliband, R., *Parliamentary Socialism*, Merlin, 1961.

Morgan (1984) Morgan, K.O., *The Oxford Illustrated History of Britain*, Oxford University Press, 1984.

Morgan (1992) Morgan, K.O., *The People's Peace: British History 1945-90*, Oxford University Press, 1992.

Norris (1997) Norris, P., 'Anatomy of a Labour landslide' in *Norris & Gavin (1997)*.

Norris & Gavin (1997) Norris, P. & Gavin, N.T. (eds), *Britain Votes 1997*, Oxford University Press, 1997.

Riddell (1985) Riddell, P., *The Thatcher Government*, Basil Blackwell, 1985.

Skidelsky (1986) Skidelsky, R. (ed), *Thatcherism*, Chatto & Windus, 1986.

Thatcher (1993) Thatcher, M., *The Downing Street Years*, HarperCollins, 1993.

Wale (1991) Wale, W. (ed), *Developments in Politics*, Vol.2, Causeway Press 1991.

Wale (1994) Wale, W. (ed), *Developments in Politics*, Vol.5, Causeway Press 1994.

Whiteley et al. (1994) Whiteley, P., Seyd, P. & Richardson, J., *True Blues: the Politics of Conservative Party Membership*, Oxford University Press, 1994.

Young (1991) Young, H., *One of Us*, Macmillan, 1991.

4 The British constitution

Introduction

A constitution is a system of rules which describes the structure and powers of government, the relationship between different parts of government and the relationship between government and citizen. The constitution is, therefore, an essential starting point for uncovering the structure and processes of government and the location of power in the political system. In many countries, the constitution has been codified (written down in a single document) and copies are widely available. The constitution of the USA, for example, is inexpensive and relatively short. It can be purchased in any decent bookshop in the USA. But, a comparable rule book cannot be purchased in the UK. This is not because the UK does not have a constitution. It is because the rules which describe the structure and power of government, and the relationship between government and citizen, are not found in any single document. The British constitution remains uncodified. Instead, the fundamental rules and principles underlying the operation of government in the UK are scattered among a variety of different sources.

   Supporters of the British constitution argue that its great strength is its capacity for evolution. The British constitution should not be written down in a single document, they argue, because it is constantly changing. Written, codified constitutions lack flexibility. Against this, a growing number of people argue for constitutional reform. They claim that the British constitution is out of date and undemocratic, drawbacks which could be remedied by producing a new written constitution. In its manifesto for the 1997 general election, the Labour Party promised a programme of constitutional reform. The Labour government formed after the election then began to take measures designed to put this programme into practice. This chapter begins by examining the British constitution as it is and then goes on to consider the arguments for and against, and the plans for, constitutional reform.

Chapter summary

Part 1 attempts to define the British constitution by examining the six main sources from which the constitution is derived. It also looks at the evolution of the constitution.

Part 2 analyses parliamentary sovereignty and the rule of law.

Part 3 asks what is meant by the term 'unitary state' and considers arguments for and against devolution. It also discusses the place of Northern Ireland in the UK.

Part 4 considers the role of the monarchy and attitudes towards it.

Part 5 examines pressure for constitutional reform and steps towards constitutional reform since 1997

Part 1 Defining the British constitution

Key issues

1. What do we mean by separation of the powers?
2. From what sources is the British constitution derived?
3. Which is better - a codified or an uncodified constitution?
4. How did the British constitution evolve into its present form?

1.1 The different parts of government

The tasks of government
Government involves three main tasks. First, there is the **legislative function**, the process of making laws. Second, there is the **executive role** of implementing the law and ensuring that legislative requirements are carried out. Third, there is the **judicial task** of law enforcement, of deciding whether laws have been broken and, if they have, of dispensing

punishment.

Constitutions usually define which people or institutions have the power to carry out these tasks. Some constitutions stipulate that legislative, executive and judicial powers should each be exercised by a different person or group. This is known as the **principle of the separation of the powers**. The object of such a principle is to avoid the concentration of power into the hands of a single person or group. Defining the different parts or branches of government (and the relationships between them) is, therefore, of central constitutional significance. It is a crucial element in establishing how a particular political system should work.

Sources of the British constitution

1. Statute law

A statute is an Act of Parliament. It is a written law which has been passed (approved) by Parliament and is enforceable by the law courts. Over time, some statutes have come to be regarded as having special significance because they contain rules relating to certain rights or duties of the citizen or to how the government of the country should be organised.

The Habeas Corpus Act of 1679 is an example of a statute of constitutional significance because it affords some protection for the citizen against wrongful imprisonment. The Act enables anyone who has been confined to demand to be brought before court for a just trial. In the past, this Act was used to free slaves, to free apprentices from cruel owners and to prevent husbands confining their wives without their consent.

Other examples of statute law are the Representation of the People Acts which stipulate the rules under which elections may take place and the Parliament Acts of 1911 and 1949 which place limits on the House of Lords.

Because (at least in theory) Parliament can pass any law it wishes, statute law takes precedence over the other sources of the constitution. But, that does not mean that it is all-powerful. In 1972, for example, Parliament passed the European Communities Act and Britain joined the European Economic Community (EEC). One of the conditions of membership of the EEC (which is now known as the EU - European Union) is that European law is binding on all member states and, therefore, takes precedence over domestic law. Despite this, it is possible to argue that statute law still takes precedence over European law since Parliament has the power to repeal the 1972 European Communities Act.

2. Common Law

Common law is law made by judges. It arises out of the custom that a decision made by one court of law must be followed by other courts facing similar facts. Judges are in this way bound by legal precedents. Much of the original law of civil liberties, for example, as well as the procedures to be followed by the courts in reviewing the actions of public bodies, is based on common law.

3. Royal prerogative

The royal prerogative is a set of privileges or powers held by the monarch. The royal prerogative includes the powers to:

- declare war
- make treaties
- take possession of or give up territory
- issue orders to armed forces
- do anything necessary to defend the realm
- in an emergency to confiscate or destroy property and intern aliens
- make appointments
- control and manage the civil service.

Although these powers are still exercised in the name of the monarch, in practice, they have passed to the Prime Minister and Cabinet:

'With rare exceptions (such as appointing the Prime Minister), acts involving the use of "royal prerogative" powers are nowadays performed by government ministers who are responsible to Parliament and can be questioned about particular policies. Parliamentary authority is not required for the exercise of these prerogative powers, although Parliament may restrict or abolish such rights.' (HMSO 1994, p.9)

Criticisms of prerogative powers

Since parliamentary authority is not required for the exercise of prerogative powers, these powers provide the executive (the government) with a means of by-passing the legislature (Parliament). Critics argue that this permits profoundly undemocratic government:

'The prerogative derives from the time when Britain was ruled according to the divine right of kings. Government ministers have inherited its powers which allow them to rule virtually by decree in many areas not covered by statute. These powers...lie behind the near absence in our constitutional arrangements of the kind of citizens' rights that exist in the United States. The prerogative is all about the power of government over the people and virtually nothing to do with the power of the people over government.' (*Independent on Sunday*, 17 July 1994)

4. Conventions

A convention is a practice which, through custom, is considered to be the appropriate or proper behaviour or procedure to follow in given circumstances. Constitutional conventions are, therefore, rules related to the exercise of governmental powers which, through precedent, are considered binding by and on those concerned, even though they are not enforced by the law courts. Examples include the doctrines of individual and collective ministerial responsibility (see Chapter 12, Section 2.3 and

Chapter 13, Section 1.3) and the rule that the assent of the monarch is required before Bills passed by the two Houses of Parliament can become law.

5. Works of authority
Certain books written by constitutional theorists are sometimes cited by politicians and others to establish appropriate procedures. Two major sources are Erskine May's *Parliamentary Practice*, first published in 1844, and *An Introduction to the Study of the Law of the Constitution* by A.V. Dicey, first published in 1885. Although these works have no definitive legal standing, appeals to them can be persuasive in settling disputes or uncertainties arising from interpretations of aspects of the constitution.

6. Treaties and laws of the European Union
As was suggested above, in practice, the treaties and law of the European Union now form a significant additional source of the British constitution. The implications of this are explored in Section 2.1 below.

Flexibility or rigidity?
Since the British constitution is uncodified and is derived from sources of varying status (statute law has greater weight than conventions or works of authority, for example), it does not provide an accessible and easily understood reference point for students of government or for the ordinary citizen. At least in theory, elements of the constitution can easily be changed. For example, even those constitutional rules laid down in statute law can be altered by the same processes which apply to any other piece of legislation. To some people, this is a major disadvantage since it means that, for example, hard-won civil rights could be abolished overnight by a political party which temporarily wins power.

Written, or codified, constitutions often contain sections which outline the basic rights of citizens and these usually have a special status preventing easy or quick alterations to them.

On the other hand, the British constitution's capacity to change can be seen as an advantage. The constitution can adapt to political changes and developments and is, therefore, less likely to contain rules and obligations which are out of date. Written constitutions tend to be much less flexible. They contain special rigid, often lengthy, procedures which must be followed before any constitutional changes can be introduced. As a result, such changes are usually rare. The USA's constitution, for example, has been altered only 26 times and the first ten amendments were made together in 1791, just four years after the constitution had been drawn up.

Main points - Section 1.1

- **Government involves three main tasks: (1) the legislative function; (2) the executive role; and (3) the judicial task of law enforcement.**
- **Constitutions define which people or institutions have the power to carry out the three tasks. Some stipulate that each task is carried out by a different person or group - the principle of the separation of the powers.**
- **The six main sources from which the British constitution is derived are statute law, common law, royal prerogative, constitutional conventions, various 'works of authority' and the treaties and law of the European Union.**
- **Uncodified constitutions are more flexible than codified constitutions. It is debatable whether flexibility is an advantage.**

Activity 4.1 The Constitution in Britain and the USA

Item A *The American constitution*

Articles 1-5 (adapted)
All legislative powers herein granted shall be vested in a Congress of the United States which shall consist of a Senate and a House of Representatives. The House of Representatives shall be composed of members chosen every second year by the people. The Senate shall be composed of two senators from each state chosen for six years. All Bills for raising revenue shall originate in the House of Representatives. Every Bill which shall have passed the House of Representatives and the Senate shall, before it becomes law, be presented to the President of the United States. If he approve, he shall sign it, but if not, he shall return it with his objections. If, after reconsideration, two-thirds of the House of Representatives shall agree to pass the Bill, it shall be sent, together with the objections, to the Senate, by which it shall likewise be reconsidered; and, if approved by two-thirds of that house, it shall become a law. The executive power shall be vested in a President of the United States of America. He shall hold his office during the term of four years. The President shall be Commander-in-Chief of the armed forces. He shall, from time to time, give to the Congress information of the state of the Union, and recommend to their

consideration such measures as he shall judge necessary and expedient. The judicial power of the United States shall be vested in the Supreme Court. The Congress, whenever two-thirds of both houses shall deem it necessary, shall propose amendments to this constitution, or, on the application of the legislatures of two-thirds of the several states, shall call a convention for proposing amendments, which in either case shall be valid as part of this constitution when ratified by the legislature of three-fourths of the several states or by conventions in three-fourths thereof.

Amendment 1 (adapted)
Congress shall make no law respecting of religion or prohibiting the free exercise thereof; or abridging the freedom of speech or of the press; or the right of the people peaceably to assemble and to petition the government for a redress of grievances.

Amendment 6 (adapted)
In all criminal proceedings, the accused shall enjoy the right to a speedy trial by an impartial jury of the state and district wherein the crime shall have been committed.

Item B *The sources of the British constitution*

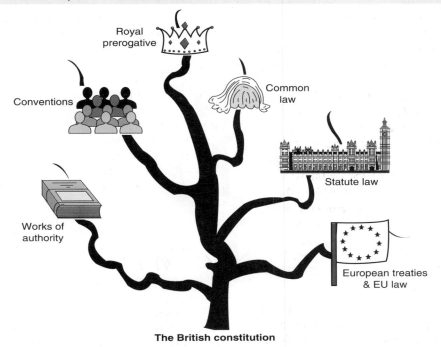

The British constitution

Adapted from Kingdom 1991.

Item C *The British constitution*

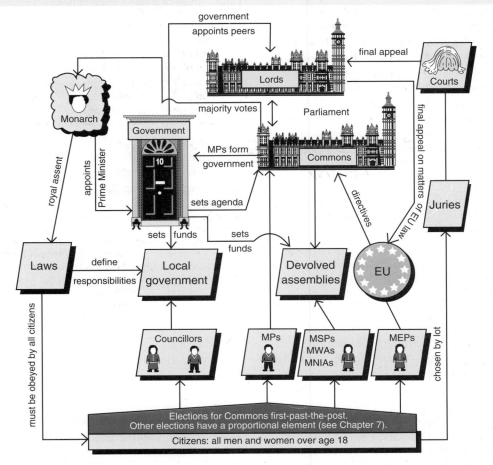

Item D   *The British and American constitutions compared*

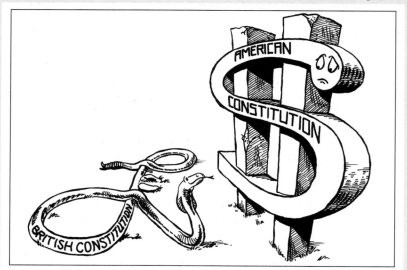

This cartoon compares the rigidity of the American constitution with the flexibility of the British constitution.

Questions

1. Judging from Items A and C, do you agree with the point being made in Item D? Give reasons for your answer

2. Using Item A, draw a diagram of the American constitution in a style similar to that used in Item C.

3. What are the advantages and disadvantages of a constitution derived from the sources shown in Item B?

4. Judging from Item C, would you say that the principle of separation of the powers is put into practice in the UK? Give reasons for your answer.

1.2 The early development of the British constitution

Evolution rather than revolution

One of the reasons why Britain does not have a codified constitution is that British political history over the past three centuries has followed an evolutionary rather than a revolutionary path. In other countries, written constitutions have been introduced following sudden and total changes to their political system. The French Revolution of 1789 led to the introduction of a written constitution, as did the Russian Revolution of 1917. Similarly, new written constitutions were introduced in Germany after defeat in 1918 and 1945, and India drew up a written constitution when British rule ended in 1947.

Absolute monarchy to constitutional monarchy

Until the 17th century there was no real separation of powers in the British system of government. Rather, there was a system of absolute monarchy. The monarch could overrule decisions made by Parliament. Ministers were merely personal advisers. Judges were appointed and removed by the monarch. It was only after the English Civil War of 1642-52 and the short period of republican government (Charles I was executed in 1649 and the monarchy was restored in 1660) that the power of the monarch was curtailed. When the monarchy was restored, the new king, Charles II, attempted to reassert royal power. But, this resulted in his exile (the so-called 'Glorious Revolution' of 1688) and the introduction of a Bill of Rights which granted Parliament protection against royal absolutism.

From the beginning of the 18th century, therefore, Britain was no longer governed by an absolute monarch. Constitutionally, although monarchs still exercised considerable power, they required the support of Parliament. The monarch's business was carried out by the Cabinet (the monarch's ministers). The Cabinet brought matters before Parliament for its approval. This system became known as a constitutional monarchy. Britain remains a constitutional monarchy today.

1.3 Development of the British constitution since 1700

The balanced constitution

The authoritative work detailing the theory of the 18th century constitution was Sir William Blackstone's *Commentaries upon the Laws of England*. Blackstone saw the principal institutions of government as providing a set of mutual checks and balances. The House of Commons could reject what the nobility (the Lords) had decided and vice versa. The monarch could act as a check on both Houses whilst they, in turn, had sanctions which could be used to check the executive power of the monarch's ministers.

According to Dearlove & Saunders (1991), this theory was, to some extent, borne out in practice. But, the practice of checks and balances was based largely on the patronage and corruption that a very small electorate permitted (even by the end of the 18th century, less than 5% of adult men and no women were permitted to vote - see Chapter 7, Section 1.4). The constitution, therefore, operated essentially in the interests of the aristocracy:

'[The constitution provided] state power to a narrow group of substantial landowners in loose alliance with merchants and the small towns which were able to return members to the Commons.' (Dearlove & Saunders 1991, p.24) This constitutional set-up was workable so long as the feudal system which supported it remained in place. But, by the later 18th century, the erosion of the old feudal system had been accelerated by the Industrial Revolution. Industrialisation produced a new class of wealthy factory owners who had considerable economic power, but no direct political power since their interests were not represented in Parliament or by members of the government. Economic and social developments, therefore, gave rise to political pressure which challenged the existing constitution.

The liberal constitution

Whilst the main constitutional concern in the 18th century was the balance of governmental powers within Parliament, the changes which occurred in the 19th century shifted the constitutional focus to divisions outside Parliament. For a while, this produced a 'golden period' of dominance for the House of Commons.

The principal division in the 19th century was between the aristocratic class (made up predominantly of landowners who wanted to preserve the status quo) and the new middle classes (made up predominantly of industrial capitalists who were resentful of the power of landed interests and were eager for political representation and power for themselves). Both groups wished to avoid granting any representation or power to the working class (the majority of the population). But, the middle classes needed the support of working-class reformers to push through any extension of the franchise and reform of the House of Commons.

This political conflict culminated in the Great Reform Act of 1832 which extended the vote to the new middle classes (see Chapter 7, Section 1.4). This meant that it was no longer possible for the Lords, through patronage, to control the composition of the House of Commons. The Act also redistributed the seats in the House of Commons to allow the newly developed industrial areas to be represented in Parliament. In addition, the powers of the monarch were further limited as the choice of Prime Minister and senior Cabinet members now passed to the Commons.

Bagehot and the liberal constitution

These developments increased the independence of the House of Commons and effectively ended the relevance of the theory of the 'balanced constitution'. This was noted by Walter Bagehot whose *The English Constitution*, published in 1867, provided an account of the relationships between the institutions of the state in the post-1832 period, a period in which the power of the new propertied middle classes grew substantially. According to Bagehot, the middle classes defined their interests in terms of 'liberty' and they wanted a 'liberal' constitution in which the role of the state would be restricted in order to protect individual freedom.

According to Bagehot, this liberal constitution contained two separate parts:
- the dignified
- the efficient.

The dignified part of the constitution was the House of Lords and the monarchy. Although these institutions were still publicly regarded as powerful (and, therefore, provided legitimacy to the constitution as a whole) their real powers had diminished. In reality, they had been taken over by the efficient parts - the House of Commons, the Prime Minister and Cabinet. It was with these efficient parts that power now lay. Bagehot claimed that the secret of the constitution was the very close relationship between the legislature and the executive. It was particularly significant that the Cabinet (the centre of executive power) was (after 1832) chosen by the House of Commons (the focal point of legislative power).

The liberal-democratic constitution

The liberal constitution described by Bagehot was not a democratic constitution. The vast majority of the adult population was still denied the vote, though this began to change in 1867, the year in which Bagehot's work was first published. Those in power grudgingly came to realise that some form of working-class political representation had to be introduced to avoid threats to the existing political and social order posed by the growth in ideas about equality and socialism. The 1867 Electoral Reform Act gave the vote to some workers and, therefore, began the process of creating a mass electorate.

The importance of a mass electorate

The growth of a mass electorate was of great importance constitutionally. It encouraged the development of mass parties. These parties came to dominate Parliament and government. The result was a constitutional shift with the brief period of the House of Common's predominance beginning to draw to a close. Power shifted to the Prime Minister and Cabinet who were chosen from the party with the majority in the House of Commons. At the same time, the growth of a mass electorate meant that parties could only govern if they gained the support of the electorate at election times. The need to consider public opinion added a new dimension to the constitution.

A.V. Dicey

Eighteen years after the 1867 Act the first edition of A.V. Dicey's *An Introduction to the Study of the Law of the Constitution* was published. This book remains one of the most influential works of authority on the British constitution. Although Dicey himself was no democrat, his account was able to accommodate some of the changes which had been taking place. According to Dicey, the 'twin pillars' of the British constitution are:

- **parliamentary sovereignty** (the supremacy of Parliament in making the law)
- **the rule of law** (the law as the ultimate source of authority to which all, including the organs of state, are subject).

To this legalistic interpretation, Dicey added a further dimension to the notion of sovereignty. He argued that, if **legal** sovereignty resided in Parliament, **political** sovereignty rested with the electorate because the electorate chooses parliamentary representatives. Dicey added that, because of the constitutional convention of ministerial responsibility (the principle that ministers are accountable to Parliament for the actions of government), the executive is also brought under the influence of the political sovereignty of the electorate.

Criticisms of Dicey's model

According to Birch (1964), Dicey's interpretation of the constitution represents an idealised view. It is based on the assumption of a one-directional flow of power from the electorate to Parliament to government. It, therefore, ignores the possibility that power also flows in the reverse direction. Birch also argues that Dicey's model fails to recognise the significant influences that parties and the Cabinet have exercised on Parliament since the Electoral Reform Act of 1867. In general, 20th century interpretations of the British constitution have acknowledged the pro-active role of the executive in the policy-making process (especially the role of the Prime Minister and Cabinet). Parliament is, therefore, presented in a more diminished reactive role and the electorate largely viewed as passive.

The balance of power

According to the liberal view, there is a need for restricted government and the safeguarding of individual freedoms. Despite criticism of the Dicey model, this view remained (and remains) strong. In 1929, for example, the Lord Chief Justice, Lord Hewart, in *The New Despotism*, bitterly criticised the inflated powers of the executive and argued that parliamentary sovereignty and the rule of law (Dicey's twin pillars) had been eroded. Against this, however, it can be argued that the developments in the late 19th century (the extension of the franchise and the change in the balance of power between the legislature and the executive) were achieved without fundamentally altering the structures of power or class in British society. A democratic element (a mass electorate) was added to the existing liberal constitution without altering the dominance of the ruling classes and without threatening the continuation of the existing capitalist economic system. The result was a liberal-democratic constitution and it is this which has formed the basis of the British political system in the 20th century.

Main points - Sections 1.2-1.3

- Britain does not have a codified constitution because British political history over the past three centuries has followed an evolutionary rather than a revolutionary path.
- Until the Glorious Revolution, there was no separation of powers in the British system of government, but absolute monarchy. Since then, Britain has been a constitutional monarchy.
- The 20th century liberal-democratic constitution emerged from the 19th century liberal constitution which itself evolved from the 18th century balanced constitution.
- Industrialisation was the key to the evolution of the liberal constitution from the balanced constitution. The growth of a mass electorate was the key to the evolution of the liberal-democratic constitution from the liberal constitution.
- Dicey's twin pillars of the British constitution are parliamentary sovereignty and the rule of law.

Activity 4.2 The evolution of the British constitution

Item A   *The liberal constitution*

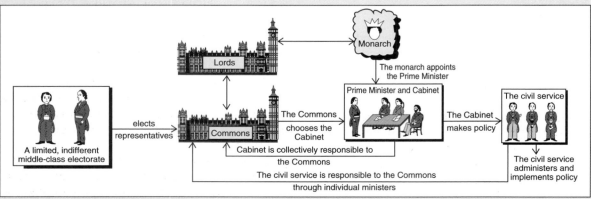

Adapted from Dearlove & Saunders 1991.

Item B *The liberal-democratic constitution*

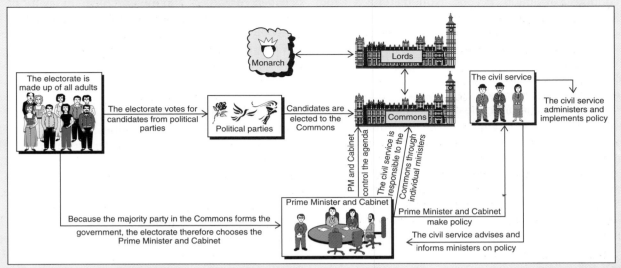

Adapted from Dearlove & Saunders 1991.

Item C *Dicey's two pillars of the constitution*

Two features have at all times since the Norman Conquest characterised the political institutions of England. The first of these features - royal supremacy - has now passed into the sovereignty of Parliament. The principle of parliamentary sovereignty means neither more nor less than this, namely that Parliament has the right to make or unmake any law whatever; and, further, that no person or body is recognised by the law of England as having the right to override or set aside the legislation of Parliament. The second of these features, which is closely connected with the first, is the rule or supremacy of law. When we say that the rule of law is a characteristic of the English constitution, we generally include under one expression at least three distinct though kindred conceptions. We mean in the first place that no man is punishable or can be lawfully made to suffer in body or goods except for a distinct breach of law established in the ordinary legal manner before the ordinary courts of the land. We mean in the second place not only that no man is above the law but that every man, whatever be his rank or condition, is subject to the ordinary law of the realm and amenable to the jurisdiction of the ordinary tribunals. Third, the general principles of the constitution (as, for example, the right to personal liberty or the right of public meeting) are the result of judicial decisions determining the rights of private persons in particular cases brought before the courts.

Adapted from Dicey 1885.

Questions

1. a) Identify the major constitutional differences between the liberal constitution and the liberal-democratic constitution as depicted in Items A and B.
   b) Explain when and how the liberal constitution changed into the liberal-democratic constitution.
2. Using Item C, re-write Dicey's interpretations of (i) parliamentary sovereignty and (ii) the rule of law using language more appropriate to today.
3. 'The British constitution's capacity to evolve is its major strength.' Using Items A-C explain this statement.

Part 2 Parliamentary sovereignty and the rule of law

Key issues

1. What does parliamentary sovereignty mean in theory and in practice?
2. To what extent does parliamentary sovereignty remain one of the two main pillars of the constitution?
3. What does rule of law mean in theory and in practice?
4. To what extent does rule of law remain one of the two main pillars of the constitution?

2.1 Parliamentary sovereignty

The principle of parliamentary sovereignty

According to the principle of parliamentary sovereignty, Parliament is the only body that can make law for the UK. No other authority can overrule or change the laws which Parliament has made. This principle, therefore, gives statute law precedence over the other sources of the constitution.

The principle of parliamentary sovereignty, however, cannot be found in any Act of Parliament. It is a part of common law which established itself as judicial rule in the late 17th century, following the 'Glorious Revolution' of 1688. Norton (1982 & 1988) points out that, if the principle of parliamentary sovereignty were to be part of statute law, it could not have the pre-eminence claimed for it. This is because parliamentary sovereignty implies that Parliament can pass, change or repeal any law it likes and is not bound by the laws made by previous Parliaments. If the principle of parliamentary sovereignty was found in an Act of Parliament, it would be possible for Parliament to repeal this Act and do away with the principle.

As it stands, the principle of parliamentary sovereignty means that British courts are obliged to enforce any law passed by Parliament. This is very different from the USA, for example, where the Supreme Court can declare a law passed by Congress to be unconstitutional.

Modifications

The principle of parliamentary sovereignty has been modified as the result of a number of political developments which have taken place in the 19th and 20th centuries.

Mass electorate

First, when the principle of parliamentary sovereignty was established, less than 5% of the adult male population and no women had the right to vote. Today, virtually all adults over the age of 18 have the right to vote. This development means that the most significant part of Parliament, the House of Commons, is now elected by popular vote. So, where does sovereignty now lie - with Parliament or with the electorate? Dicey's answer was to distinguish between **political** sovereignty resting with the electorate and **legal** sovereignty resting with Parliament. But this, as Norton has recognised, raises a problem:

> 'If one accepts that sovereignty is indivisible, how can one have two distinct bodies (the electorate and Parliament) each exercising sovereignty?' (Norton 1982, p.13)

This duality is further reflected in the assumption that government ministers are **legally** responsible to the monarch (strictly they are 'Ministers of the Crown') but, **by convention**, they are responsible to Parliament.

Referendums

Second, the use of referendums on three occasions in the 1970s and again in 1997 and 1998 also seems to have affected the notion of a sovereign Parliament. Referendums, it can be argued, remove decision making (or at least the confirmation of decisions) from Parliament. It could be argued, therefore, that referendums and parliamentary sovereignty are incompatible.

The party system

Third, the growth of a mass electorate in the late 19th century led to the development of the party system. This, in turn, altered the balance of power between Parliament and the executive (in favour of the executive). Since the government is now generally formed from the largest party in the House of Commons, it can usually rely on its majority to secure parliamentary approval for its proposals. Most laws are, therefore, now initiated not by Parliament, but by government. This may have affected parliamentary sovereignty.

Taking account of political realities

Fourth, the principle of parliamentary sovereignty implies no theory about the location of political power. If, in the final resort, political power rests on the use or threat of force then the principle has little relevance. If, however, power depends on popular consent, then what if this consent is withdrawn? What would that withdrawal of consent tell us about where sovereignty lies? Erskine May, writing in 1844, noted:

> 'The legislative authority of Parliament extends over the United Kingdom and all its colonies and foreign possessions; and there are no other limits to its power of making laws for the whole empire than those which are incident to all sovereign authority - the willingness of the people to obey or their power to resist.' (quoted in Silk 1989, p.37)

This serves as a reminder that the sovereignty of Parliament has always been limited by the need to take account of political realities.

Extra-parliamentary pressure

There have been occasions when powerful pressure groups have been able to frustrate attempts to implement legal measures. In other words, extra-parliamentary action has sometimes forced Parliament to revise or repeal laws it has made. In the 1970s, for example, trade unions forced Parliament to amend the 1971 Industrial Relations Act and in the late 1980s extra-parliamentary action forced the government to replace the poll tax with the council tax. These examples suggest that in practice the principle of parliamentary sovereignty is limited.

International agreements and treaties

The UK has, at various times, committed itself to international agreements and treaties which place upon it certain obligations. For example, in 1949 the UK joined NATO and, as a result, let go of some control over defence policy and foreign policy. Theoretically, of course, commitments like this do not infringe parliamentary sovereignty since Parliament could decide to ignore or cancel its commitments. But, in practice, the political (and often economic) consequences of so doing make such actions unlikely - the more so with the increasingly global nature of political and economic events and relationships.

Britain and the EU

Britain's membership of the EU has raised important

questions about the limitations on the sovereignty of the British Parliament. Under the terms of membership, Britain is a member of the EU 'in perpetuity'. EU law is binding on all member states and, therefore, takes precedence over British domestic law. The British Parliament can express its disapproval in the case of amendments to the Treaty of Rome (the founding treaty signed by all members of the EU), but otherwise EU legislation automatically becomes law within the UK, irrespective of what the British Parliament thinks about it.

On the face of it this seems to breach the principle of the sovereignty of Parliament. But (despite the enormous economic and political consequences of so doing), Parliament could agree to repeal previous legislation, withdraw from the EU and, by doing so, demonstrate that parliamentary sovereignty still exists.

Complete withdrawal from the EU, however, seems increasingly unlikely. Despite resistance from Eurosceptics, the continuing movement in Europe as a whole towards greater European integration is pulling Britain along this route too. The 1986 Single European Act and the Maastricht Treaty (see Chapter 6, Sections 1.1 and 1.2) can be seen as reducing Britain's sovereignty since they have extended the range of policy areas on which the EU can legislate.

The European Convention on Human Rights
There were concerns that the incorporation of the European Convention on Human Rights into British Law would further erode parliamentary sovereignty because judges would be given the power to strike down laws that breached the convention. The 1998 Human Rights Act (which comes into effect in 2000), however, limited the power of judges to declaring laws to be incompatible with the convention. Parliament will then be able to use a fast-track procedure to amend laws declared incompatible.

Main points - Section 2.1

- According to the principle of parliamentary sovereignty, Parliament is the only body that can make law for the UK. This gives statute law precedence over the other sources of the constitution.
- The principle of parliamentary sovereignty has been modified as the result of: the growth of a mass electorate; the use of referendums; the growth of a party system; political realities; extra-parliamentary pressure; signing international agreements.
- EU law is binding on all member states and, therefore, takes precedence over British domestic law. Parliament could repeal previous legislation and withdraw from the EU, but, in practice, this is unlikely.
- The incorporation of the European convention on Human Rights has not further eroded parliamentary sovereignty.

Activity 4.3 Limits on parliamentary sovereignty

Item A *The Factortame case*

Following the signing of the 1986 Single European Act, Spanish fishing vessels registered in Britain in order to qualify for a share of the fishing quota awarded to the UK. Two years later, however, the British government passed the Merchant Fishing Act 1988 ordering vessels to re-register and to satisfy additional nationality requirements. The vessels owned by Factortame Ltd and other Spanish companies failed to qualify and were prevented from fishing after 1 April 1989. These companies applied to the High Court for a ruling that the 1988 Act was incompatible with European law and, therefore, inoperable. The High Court referred the case to the European Court of Justice (ECJ) and ordered the Transport Secretary not to apply certain parts of the 1988 Act. The Transport Secretary, however, successfully appealed against this, on the grounds that no UK court had the power to suspend an Act of Parliament. On further appeal to the House of Lords, it was agreed that, under existing English law, no court could suspend an Act of Parliament. But, the case was referred to the ECJ on the question of whether or not EC laws confer on national courts the power and/or the obligation to restrain the government during the period taken for a final judgement to be made by the ECJ. In 1990, the ECJ ruled that British courts do indeed have power to suspend Acts which appear to breach a European law. Meanwhile, the European Commission had initiated an action against the British government. The ECJ ruling on this was that the requirements made in the 1988 Act contravened the 1986 Single European Act - they were discriminatory and contrary to article 52 of the EEC Treaty. The Spanish-owned fishing companies have lodged a claim for up to £20 million compensation for loss of profits during the 18 months they were unable to fish. In August 1997, the High Court ruled that the government would have to pay compensation. This ruling was upheld in the Court of Appeal in April 1998.

Adapted from Dowdle 1994 and the *Times*, 28 April 1998.

Item B   *The EU and sovereignty*

Membership of the EU has brought a new role for the British courts. Under the terms of EU membership, if there is a clash between the provisions of European law and domestic UK law, then the European law must win out. Under the provisions of the Treaty of Rome, cases which reach the highest domestic court of appeal (in Britain, the House of Lords) must be referred to the European Court of Justice. In 1990, the European Court of Justice (ECJ) in the Factortame case ruled that courts in the UK had the power to suspend an Act of Parliament which appeared to breach an EU law. The House of Lords then restrained the minister from enforcing the Act. The effect of this was to challenge the principle of parliamentary sovereignty because it challenged the idea that the decisions of Parliament are binding and can be set aside by no body other than Parliament. The ECJ's ruling meant that British courts could now set aside Acts passed by Parliament. This does not mean, however, that the principle of parliamentary sovereignty is dead. Parliament retains the power to repeal the 1972 European Communities Act. Furthermore, if Parliament passed an Act explicitly overriding European law, it is likely that the British courts would enforce the Act. Whilst the principle of parliamentary sovereignty may not be dead, it is clearly under challenge. The power of government is no longer concentrated in the Cabinet, but is shared with the European institutions. As a result, the constitution is not what it used to be.

Adapted from Norton 1994a.

Item C   *Two horses*

'The UK government has seated Parliament on two horses, one straining towards the preservation of parliamentary sovereignty, the other galloping in the general direction of Community [EU] law supremacy.' (De Smith in Street & Brazier 1981, p.91)

Item D   *Incorporation of the European Convention on Human Rights*

On 9 November 1998, the Human Rights Act received royal assent, giving British citizens a Bill of Rights of the kind taken for granted in virtually every other Western democracy. The new Act incorporates the European Convention on Human Rights into British Law and comes into effect in 2000 (giving judges time to be trained). Clare Dyer argues that this is a major development because, unlike most other democracies, Britain has never had a rights-based culture. Under British law, anything is permitted unless specifically prohibited. Parliament has traditionally been all-powerful, able to pass any law it wants with no concern for the rights of minorities. Under the new Act, parliamentary sovereignty will be preserved. Judges will not be drawn into political controversy by being asked (as judges are in Canada) to strike down laws voted on by the people's elected representatives. If a statute is unclear, judges will have to interpret it so as to conform to the convention. But, if the meaning is clear, judges will have to follow the law even if it breaches the convention. They will be limited to declaring the law 'incompatible'. Parliament will then be able to amend it using a fast-track procedure. Judges will, however, be able to override most secondary legislation (statutory instruments and regulations put out by government departments). Critics argue that parliamentary sovereignty is a myth used to prevent meaningful constitutional change. Hugo Young, for example, claims that the Human Rights Act is feeble and little more than tokenism because British judges do not have the same powers as European judges sitting in Strasbourg. If a new order of freedoms and rights is to be installed, Young argues, then Parliament's sovereign power to override it must be reduced as close as possible to zero.

Adapted from the *Guardian*, 8 July 1997 and 12 November 1998.

2.2 The rule of law

What is the rule of law?

According to Dicey, writing in 1885, the rule of law has three main elements.

- Nobody can be punished unless convicted of an offence by a court of law.
- The law applies equally to everyone.
- The general principles of the constitution (such as the right to personal liberty) do not stem from declarations made by rulers, they arise out of decisions made in individual cases by an independent judiciary.

Writing more than 100 years later, Grant describes the rule of law as follows:

'Essentially the concept of the rule of law seeks to equate law and justice, ie it seeks to ensure that the law and the legal system are fair and equitable. This is an idea which is hard - perhaps impossible to achieve in practice.' (Grant 1994, p.51)

Whilst Dicey argued that the rule of law had three main elements, Grant has identified five. By examining these five elements, she suggests, it is possible to see both the strengths and weaknesses of a constitution which relies on the rule of law.

1. Legal equality

The first element identified by Grant is legal equality, the idea that:

'Everyone, including governments should be equally subject to the same laws, and should have equal access to the law.' (Grant 1994, p.51)

Grant argues that, in reality, this ideal is not attained. Only the very rich or the very poor (who are eligible for legal aid) can afford to go to court. The majority of people cannot afford to take legal action. Also, some people are, in some sense, above the law. For example, MPs have parliamentary privilege which makes them immune from prosecution for libel or slander for what they say in Parliament. The monarch is above the law.

2. The just law

The second element is the 'just law', the idea that, under the rule of law, justice and the law are the same thing. There is, in other words, no such thing as an unjust law. The trouble with this idea is that there are occasions when the majority of people simply do not agree that a law is just. This happened with the poll tax. Although people were legally obliged to pay the tax, many simply refused to do so on the grounds that it was unjust. Grant also points out that the idea of the just law requires consistent legal practice. When judges give completely different sentences for the same crime or when miscarriages of justice are discovered, this undermines the rule of law.

3. Legal certainty

The third element is 'legal certainty', the idea that the law:

'Should amount to a clear statement of rights, obligations and limits to power, especially the power of state and government. It should not be uncertain, arbitrary, ambiguous or contradictory.' (Grant 1994, p.52)

The problem with this idea is that the law often relies to some extent on interpretation and is, therefore, uncertain. Grant cites the example of public order laws. On some occasions, the term 'offensive weapons' has been interpreted to mean articles such as keys and combs whilst on other occasions these articles would not fall under this heading. In addition, if the government is taken to court and found to have broken the law, it may choose to change the law rather than to follow the court ruling.

4. Innocent until proven guilty

The fourth element is the idea that everybody is innocent until proven guilty. Grant notes two problems with this. First, the 1994 Criminal Justice Act eroded the accused person's right to silence (see Chapter 18, Section 2.6). And second, media coverage may sometimes prejudice the attitudes of jurors before a trial has taken place.

5. Independence of the judiciary

The final element is the independence and impartiality of the judiciary (see also Chapter 17, Section 2.5). Grant notes that:

'Judges are largely separate from the executive and the legislature; they should be appointed on a non-political basis; senior judges can only be removed from office by a majority vote in both Houses of Parliament; their salaries are not subject to party debate; their decisions should not be questioned in Parliament; and their remarks in court are not subject to the laws of libel and slander.' (Grant 1994, p.53)

She adds, however, that, despite this, senior judges are

also members of the House of Lords and, therefore, part of the legislature as well as the judiciary. Also, the Lord Chancellor is a member of the judiciary, a member of the Cabinet (ie the executive) and a member of the House of Lords. In other words, the Lord Chancellor is a member of all three branches of government and this can lead to a conflict of interest.

The rule of law as a constitutional check

As a general principle, the rule of law reflects the liberal fear of arbitrary and excessive government. In those societies which have a written, codified constitution, protection against arbitrary government may be built in and overseen by the courts. In the USA, for example, the constitution provides the Supreme Court with the power to declare that laws passed by Congress are unconstitutional. No such check applies in the UK. This explains why Dicey regarded the rule of law as one of the twin pillars of the constitution. He claimed that the rule of law was an important balancing mechanism which kept in check parliamentary sovereignty. So, although the courts in the UK have no power to decide upon the content of laws passed by Parliament (because of parliamentary sovereignty), they may be called upon to review allegations that government ministers or officials have acted illegally.

Lack of effectiveness as a check

McAulsan & McEldowney (1985) doubt the effectiveness of the rule of law as a check. They argue that parliamentary sovereignty, which, in practice, means the wishes of the government of the day, has now taken precedence over the political and legal constraints embodied in constitutional conventions and in the rule of law. In the period after 1979, they claim, governments took a cavalier attitude to what Dicey understood as the rule of law. To back up this claim, they provide a list of examples of ministerial actions which, they allege, amount to 'abuse and excess of power'. In short, they argue that there has been:

> 'A general pattern of contempt for...the constraints on power imposed by the checks and balances...involved in a constitution based upon the concept of limited government.'
> (McAulsan & McEldowney 1985, p.32)

By the end of 1997, similar criticisms were being made of the Labour government.

Elective dictatorship

In a lecture delivered in 1976, Lord Hailsham claimed that the British system of government had become an 'elective dictatorship'. Because, he argued, governments in Britain are usually formed from the largest party represented in the House of Commons, the power arising from parliamentary sovereignty now effectively rests with the government. Yet, the checks on this power, such as the rule of law, are weak.

Effectiveness as a check

Jowell (1989) argues against the view that the rule of law is not effective as a check on the executive. He bases this argument on the fact that the courts have become more prepared to uphold the rule of law against actions of the executive which appear either to go beyond the powers granted by legislation or which may involve the bypassing of appropriate legal procedures. This development is reflected in the growing number of cases of judicial review and the growing number of judgements being made against government (see Chapter 17, Section 2.5).

To Dicey and other 19th century liberals who supported limited government, the rule of law was a way of excluding discretionary action by ministers and officials. But, the greater scope of government activity in the 20th century (for example the administration of the welfare state) has necessitated wide discretionary powers. The rule of law is, therefore, not now seen so much as a way of precluding official discretion, but as a protection against the abuse of discretion. It is in this sense that Jowell refers to the rule of law as a 'principle of institutional morality'. The rule of law in this sense provides limits and restricts the abuses of power which can occur under any government in modern times.

Main points - Section 2.2

- **Dicey argued that the rule of law has three main elements - nobody can be punished unless convicted by a court; the law applies equally to everyone; and, the general principles of the constitution arise out of decisions made by an independent judiciary.**
- **Grant (1994) argued that the rule of law has five main elements - legal equality; just law; legal certainty; innocent until proven guilty; and, the independence of the judiciary.**
- **Dicey claimed that the rule of law was one of the twin pillars of the constitution since it provided a check on parliamentary sovereignty.**
- **Some commentators argue that it is not an effective check because the government effectively has the power to do what it wishes (it is an 'elective dictatorship').**
- **Jowell (1989) argues that it is an effective check because the courts have become more willing to uphold the rule of law against executive actions.**

Activity 4.4 *The rule of law as a check*

Item A *The Tameside dispute (1)*

Section 68 of the 1944 Education Act states that, if the Secretary of State for Education is satisfied that any Local Education Authority has acted or is proposing to act unreasonably, then the Secretary of State may give whatever directions seem expedient. In March 1975, Tameside council (a Labour council) drew up plans to convert secondary schools into comprehensives. The proposals were approved by the Secretary of State in November 1975 and the plans were due to come into operation in September 1976. But, at the local elections in May 1976, the Conservatives won control of the council and, in June, they informed the Secretary of State that the plans would not be carried out. On 11 June, the Secretary of State gave a direction under Section 68 requiring the council to implement its predecessor's plans. On 18 June, the High Court ordered the council to do this. On 26 July, however, the Court of Appeal overruled the High Court and, on 2 August, the House of Lords agreed with the Court of Appeal. The basis of this final decision was that the minister could give a valid direction only if he was satisfied that no reasonable local authority could have decided as the Conservative majority did. Since the minister could not be satisfied, he could not issue a valid direction.

Adapted from Griffith 1985.

Item B *The Tameside dispute (2)*

Of course, judges may pass judgements on the acts of ministers, as they have recently done in the Tameside dispute. To this extent, the rule of law applies and prevails here as in other free countries. But, once the courts are confronted with an Act of Parliament, all they can do is to find out its meaning, if they can, and then apply it justly and mercifully as the language of the law permits. So, of the two pillars of our constitution, it is the sovereignty of Parliament which is paramount in every case.

Adapted from Hailsham 1976.

Item C *The judiciary and the executive*

When a governing party has an overall majority of 178 and the opposition is weak, who will curb any possible abuse of power? Senior judges will. Between 1992 and 1997, they provided stout opposition both in Parliament and in the courts. In Parliament, for example, important modifications were made to Michael Howard's Crime (Sentences) Act and his Police Act (both passed in 1997) as a direct result of opposition by senior judges in the House of Lords. The role of the courts is more subtle. When hearing applications for judicial review of ministerial decisions, judges interpret Acts of Parliament as authorising only those actions that Parliament 'must have intended'. Usually, it is impossible to show that judges' interpretation was wrong. Occasionally, though, Parliament can tell the courts what it really did intend. This happened in 1996 after an asylum seeker from Zaire successfully challenged new regulations which deprived her of benefits. The Social Security Secretary, Peter Lilley, then asked Parliament to reverse the Court of Appeal's decision by passing new legislation. Despite opposition in the Lords, this was passed. Within a few months, however, lawyers had found a provision in the National Assistance Act of 1948 obliging local councils to provide temporary accommodation for people in need and a High Court Judge ruled that this provision could be used by asylum seekers to obtain benefits and accommodation. The judge argued that, because the new Act did not spell out the desire to deprive asylum seekers of benefits and accommodation, Parliament cannot possibly have intended to do this. But, quite clearly, that was the real intention of the new legislation. Significantly, the judgement was upheld on appeal.

Adapted from the *Guardian*, 6 May 1997.

Item D *The British constitution*

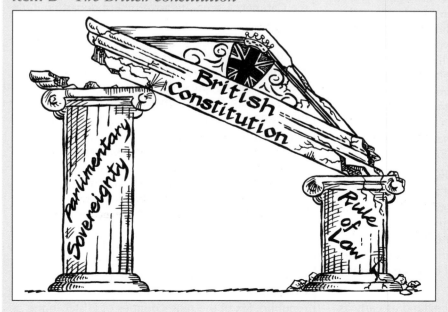

Questions

1. In what way do Items A, B and C support Jowell's argument about the willingness of courts to uphold the rule of law?

2. How accurate is the view of the constitution presented in Item D?

3. 'The rule of law is an important check on the executive'. Using Item C, give arguments for and against this statement.

4. Judging from Items A-D, to what extent do you think the rule of law is (i) applicable and (ii) desirable?

Part 3 A unitary state

Key issues

1. What is a unitary state?
2. What are the arguments for and against devolution in Scotland and Wales?
3. What steps have been taken towards devolution in Scotland and Wales?
4. Why did violence erupt in Northern Ireland and what steps have been taken to bring permanent peace?

3.1 A unitary state

What is a unitary state?

A state is described as unitary when the powers of government are held by a central authority, or set of authorities. Local or regional authorities may exist, but any powers they possess will have been granted to them by the central authority and could be withdrawn by that authority. This differs from a federal state, such as the USA, where the constitution guarantees certain powers to regional governments and to the central government.

Through various statutes, the UK is a union of England, Wales, Scotland and Northern Ireland. It is said to be a unitary state because any form of regional or local government which has existed or does exist cannot legally do anything unless it has been empowered to do so by Acts of Parliament. Parliamentary sovereignty also means that any such powers could be limited or removed by future statutes.

But, to say that the UK, constitutionally, is a unitary state does not go very far in explaining how this operates politically. The term 'central authority of the state' suggests that power is exercised legitimately, whilst the term 'authority' is a dimension of power that implies consent by those over whom it is exercised. Maintaining consent in Scotland, Wales and in particular in Northern Ireland has at times been problematic for British governments:

> 'The notion of a unitary state which lies at the heart of Britain's unwritten constitution no longer fits the territorial map it seeks to govern.' (Evans 1997, p.22)

The development of the UK

The United Kingdom developed as the result of a series of Acts of Union made between England and its neighbours. England has been and remains the dominant nation. Historically, it owed this dominance to its military supremacy (though union with Scotland was not achieved by force of arms).

Wales

Wales had been conquered by England as early as 1282. But, it was not until the 16th century that it was brought into union with England - by Acts passed in 1536 and 1542. An indication of English supremacy was the decision enshrined in the Acts to forbid the use of the Welsh language in the administration of the country. In addition, in 1746, Parliament decided that the term 'England' in any Act of Parliament automatically included Wales, a provision which did not change until 1967.

In 1907, Wales began to be viewed as a distinctive entity by the government - a separate Welsh Secretary of Education was created. In 1957, the new post of Minister of State for Wales was established. This was upgraded to Cabinet rank in 1964. A Welsh Office was set up in Cardiff, though much administration remained based in Whitehall. In a referendum held in September 1997, the Welsh electorate voted narrowly in favour of a Welsh Assembly with devolved powers.

Scotland

Scotland was brought into union with England in two stages. In 1603, James VI of Scotland became James I of England. Complete political union did not occur, however, until the Act of Union in 1707 which disbanded the Scottish Parliament and led to government from London. Unlike Wales, Scotland was not incorporated into the UK by conquest. It negotiated the terms of its entry into the Union. As a result, it retained its own legal and educational system as well as a distinctive form of local government and its own established church.

Scotland began to be viewed as a distinctive entity earlier than Wales. The position of Secretary of State for Scotland was established in 1885. Since 1892 the Secretary of State for Scotland has been a member of the Cabinet. A separate government department, the Scottish Office, was set up to deal with Scottish affairs in 1928. In September 1997, Scottish electors voted clearly in favour of a devolved Parliament for Scotland with tax-varying powers. As a result, elections for a Scottish Parliament are due to be held in 1999, with the Parliament operational from the following year.

Northern Ireland

The completion of the conquest of Ireland was achieved in Tudor times. But, opposition to British rule continued. An Act of Union passed in 1800 brought the whole of Ireland into the UK and it remained part of the UK until the end of 1921. Nationalist opposition to control from Westminster led to the Irish Treaty of 1921 which divided Ireland into two. The south of Ireland became a dominion (a self-governing territory belonging to the British Commonwealth) and then, in 1949, an independent republic. Six of the nine counties of Ulster in the north of Ireland have remained as part of the UK. Between 1922 and 1972, Northern Ireland was self-governing. In 1972, however, direct rule from Westminster was imposed and a Secretary of State of Cabinet rank was created. In 1998, after lengthy peace talks and a referendum in the North and South, elections were held for a new Northern Ireland Assembly.

3.2 Devolution

What is devolution?

Devolution means the transfer of power from a superior to an inferior political body. According to Bogdanor (1979), devolution has three elements:

- it involves the transfer of power to a subordinate elected body
- it involves the transfer of power on a geographical basis
- it involves the transfer of functions at present exercised by Parliament.

Since Parliament retains the power to suspend the devolved Parliament or assembly, parliamentary supremacy remains intact:

'Devolution is the delegation of central government powers without the giving up of sovereignty.' (Simpson 1998, p.7)

In practical terms, therefore, devolution involves the setting up of an elected regional assembly whose powers and responsibilities are carefully defined. Normally, these powers would not include the control of defence or foreign policy (areas which would still be dealt with by the central government). The new elected regional assembly may or may not have tax-varying powers. Whether it does or not, a devolved assembly is by no means independent. It is still bound by decisions made by central government.

Devolution is, therefore, different from federalism and separatism. Federalism involves the division of sovereignty between two levels of government which then become (in theory at least) autonomous. Separatism, on the other hand, refers to the creation of a self-governing independent state with complete control over its internal and external affairs.

Scottish and Welsh nationalism

Although Scotland and Wales are both part of the UK, they have retained their own distinctive cultures:

'The formation of the United Kingdom occurred over a long period of time during which special measures were taken to permit a degree of distinctiveness to its component parts. Little effort was made, unlike in France for example, to impose uniformity throughout the state. The United Kingdom was a unified state rather than a unitary or uniform state. It responded to pressures.' (Mitchell 1994, p.128)

It is the 'degree of distinctiveness' in the component parts of the UK which led to the growth of nationalism in Scotland and Wales and the demand for devolution or 'home rule'.

Scottish nationalism

Scottish nationalism arises from the fact that Scotland negotiated the terms of union in 1707:

'As a result, it was able to retain its own distinctive institutions...which have helped to nurture the strong sense of national identity in Scotland. Scots are well aware that they were once an independent nation and could be so again. The Union with England which was considered so advantageous at one time could be broken if it ceased to work to Scotland's benefit.' (Gamble 1993, p.75)

Gamble goes on to point out that Britain's economic decline, the development of the EU and the discovery of North Sea oil have all contributed to Scottish discontent with rule from Westminster. This discontent was exacerbated by the fact that four successive general elections between 1979 and 1992 resulted in a Conservative government even though the vast majority of Scottish people did not vote Conservative. According to Mitchell (1994), since 1945, about 75% of people living in Scotland have supported some measure of home rule.

Welsh nationalism

Welsh nationalism is centred on the Welsh language and traditional Welsh culture. As a result, it has a less widespread appeal than Scottish nationalism since it tends to alienate non-Welsh speakers who make up a large part of the Welsh population:

'Many of the modern battles of Welsh nationalism have been around the status of the Welsh language. Wales has an estimated 500,000 Welsh speakers out of a total population of 2.7 million. Much of the effort of Welsh nationalists has been to ensure that the Welsh language is protected and that its official status is recognised...Apart from these expressions of cultural nationalism, Wales has been affected only to a small extent by nationalist movements.' (Gamble 1993, p.82)

Arguments for devolution

Supporters of devolution argue that it would disperse power more fairly, make government more efficient and better serve people's loyalties:

'Giving power to new assemblies, it is claimed, would relieve a major burden on central government. By allowing decisions to be taken close to the local area affected by them, they would also be more efficient - targeted on the area's needs and probably taken more quickly than at national level. By being closer to the people and being seen to be closer...the assemblies would engage the attention and loyalties of citizens; they would be "their" assemblies. That support would also be an important dynamic in encouraging cooperation and support in the implementation of policies.' (Norton 1994, pp.9-10)

It is also argued that, since pressures for some degree of decentralisation have reached a stage where they can no longer be ignored, then:

'Britain can only be held together if some power concentrations at the centre are dispersed.' (Holliday 1997, p.237)

Arguments against devolution

Arguments against devolution tend to emphasise the cost of establishing a new tier of government and the difficulties of administering this extra tier:

'By interposing a new layer between central and local government, the potential for delay would be increased, as would the potential for clashes between central and regional government. Another layer of government may also produce greater confusion as to the responsibilities of the different layers. Who should the citizen complain to? Who should be held responsible if the dustbins aren't emptied?' (Norton 1994, p.10)

Opponents of devolution also argue that devolution is the first step on the road to complete independence and to the break-up of the United Kingdom. The 1992 Conservative election manifesto, for example, claimed that devolution proposals:

'Do not intend to bring about separation, but run that risk. They could feed, not resolve, grievances that arise in different parts of Britain. They would deprive Scotland and Wales of their rightful seats in the United Kingdom Cabinet, seats the Conservatives are determined to preserve...The plans for devolution put forward by the other parties would have a grave impact not just on Scotland and Wales but also on England. They propose new and costly regional assemblies in England for which there is no demand.' (Conservative 1992, p.47)

Devolution in Scotland

The electoral success of the nationalist parties in the general election of 1974 brought devolution onto the political agenda. The Labour government's weak position in Parliament led to a deal in which referendums were conceded. These referendums were held on 1 March 1979 (see Chapter 7, Section 3.7). Whilst the result of the Welsh referendum was conclusive (there was clearly little popular support for devolution), the Scottish result was inconclusive. A majority voted in favour of devolution. The majority, however, was not large enough for devolution to be implemented.

In the short term, the result of these referendums was a major blow for the nationalists. But, the issue of home rule, especially in Scotland, gradually re-emerged.

Growing support for devolution 1987-97

Between the general election of 1987 (when the Conservatives received their lowest share of the vote in Scotland since mass enfranchisement was introduced) and 1997, there was growing support for some degree of home rule. During this period, two main camps emerged. On the one hand, the Scottish National Party (SNP) rejected devolution because it did not go far enough. Instead, it aimed for independence within the EU. On the other hand, the Labour Party and Liberal Democrats were committed to devolution and joined together in the Scottish Constitutional Convention (SCC). The SCC was a forum for all Scottish groups committed to devolution. It was set up in 1989:

'To reach agreement on how Scotland ought to be governed.' (SCC 1989, p.1)

During the 1992 general election campaign, hopes were high amongst those in favour of devolution that the Conservatives would suffer further losses and the case for devolution would then become irresistible. In fact, the Conservatives gained one seat and an extra 1.7% in their vote. Although this was a minor gain, it was interpreted by the media as a victory for the unionist cause. Following the election, the Conservative government published a re-evaluation of its position on devolution. This document made it clear that the government favoured the status quo:

'Since the Act of Union and in particular over the last 100 years or so there has evolved the framework for the governance of Scotland which is basically sound and which has shown itself adaptable to changing circumstances.' (HMSO 1993, p.11)

The Conservatives continued with this policy until May 1997.

The 1997 general election

The 1997 general election results in Scotland suggested that the Conservatives had underestimated support for devolution. For the first time, they failed to return a single MP to Westminster. Over three-quarters of the Scottish seats went to the Labour Party, even though Tony Blair caused controversy by comparing the tax-raising powers of a Scottish Parliament with those of a parish council and by saying that even after a Scottish Parliament had been set up:

'Sovereignty rests with me as an English MP, and that's the way it will stay.' (quoted in Sell 1998, p.204)

The SNP share of the vote in Scotland in the 1997 general election was 22%, a marginal percentage increase compared to 1992, though on a lower turnout. Although the SNP received a smaller number of actual votes than in 1992, it increased its number of seats from three to six. Following the election, the SNP's official attitude towards devolution changed. The party decided that, tactically, it would support the campaign for a Scottish Parliament in the forthcoming referendum and it would then participate in the Parliament - as a 'stepping stone to independence' (Holliday 1997, p.235). This remains the ultimate goal of the SNP. So, both the SNP and the Conservatives supported the argument that devolution would lead eventually to full independence. The Conservatives feared this, however, whilst the SNP hoped for it.

The 1997 referendum

In September 1997, the Scottish electorate voted convincingly for a devolved Parliament on a turnout of 60.1%. By a smaller, but still clear, majority, members also opted for that Parliament to have tax-varying powers. The outcome was, therefore, the Yes-Yes result for which Labour, the Liberal Democrats and the SNP (but not the Conservatives) had been campaigning.

The new Parliament

As a result of the Yes-Yes result in the referendum, elections for the Scottish Parliament are due to be held in 1999 and the 129-member Parliament will start to operate in 2000. The voting system for the Scottish Parliament is a version of the Additional Member system (see Chapter 7, Section 4.1) - 73 MSPs (Members of the Scottish Parliament) are to be elected using the 'first-past-the-post' or 'plurality' system currently used for general elections whilst the other 56 MSPs are to be elected by proportional representation - seven from each of Scotland's existing Euro-constiutuencies. Following the election, the largest party will choose the Scottish First Minister (a sort of Prime Minister for Scotland) and the First Minister will choose a Cabinet. With the introduction of a proportional element in the electoral system and with four main political parties contesting the seats, some form of coalition government is likely. The Scottish Parliament will take over all powers except those expressly retained by Westminster. It will have limited tax-varying powers (up to 3p in the pound).

Devolution in Wales

The 1979 referendum in Wales showed that there was little support for devolution there at the time. Yet, as in Scotland (if to a lesser extent), interest in home rule grew between 1979 and 1997. There were two main reasons for this. The first was the 'democratic deficit' which had grown during the Conservative years in power after 1979:

'The Conservative Party was a minority party in Wales, but it had nevertheless filled the ministerial positions at the Welsh Office, even appointing a succession of Englishmen to the post of Secretary of State. Local government,

the bastion of the Labour Party, had been downgraded and many powers had been passed to quangos, to which Welsh Conservatives, who could not otherwise get elected to office, could be appointed.' (Bradbury 1998, p.7)

The second reason was economic. Between 1979 and 1997, Wales' economic links with the British economy had weakened and its links with the EU had strengthened:

'In this context there was concern that the interests of Wales were not well represented by the Welsh Office in comparison to other European regions which had their own Assembly to protect regional interests.' (Bradbury 1998, p.7)

The Welsh nationalist party, Plaid Cymru (which is committed to independence for Wales) won 10% of the vote in Wales and four of the 40 Welsh seats in the 1997 general election. Labour's 55% of the vote produced 36 seats. As in Scotland, the Conservatives failed to win a single seat in Wales.

The 1997 referendum

The result of the referendum held in September 1997 confirmed that support for devolution was far less widespread than in Scotland. On a low turnout of little over 50%, there was a majority of just 0.6% in favour of a Welsh Assembly. In other words, only a quarter of the Welsh electorate positively supported devolution. In part, this result has been explained by suspicion in North Wales (where more people speak Welsh and support for Plaid Cymru is much stronger) that a Cardiff-based Assembly would increase the power of an English-speaking South Wales political élite. As well as a north-south divide, there is also an east-west divide with most western counties of Wales voting for an Assembly and most of the eastern counties which border England voting against.

The Welsh Assembly

As in Scotland, elections to the Welsh Assembly will take place in 1999 and the Assembly will come into operation in 2000. Also as in Scotland, a version of the Additional Member voting system will be used with 40 members being elected by first-past-the-post and an additional 20 members being elected by proportional representation (four each from the five Welsh Euro-constituencies). Unlike Scotland, however, the Assembly will not have tax-varying powers. It will operate within a budget set by Whitehall. Also, it will not have the power to pass primary legislation (laws), but only the power to deal with secondary legislation (statutory instruments and regulations put out by government departments). The Assembly will take over control of some of the activities currently carried out by the Welsh Office and by Welsh quangos.

Main points - Sections 3.1-3.2

- The UK is a union of England, Wales, Scotland and Northern Ireland. It is a unitary state because regional or local government cannot legally do anything unless it has been empowered to do so by Acts of Parliament.
- Devolution involves the setting up of an elected regional assembly whose powers and responsibilities are carefully defined. Whether a devolved assembly has tax-varying powers or not, it is still bound by decisions made by central government.
- Supporters argue that devolution disperses power more fairly, makes government more efficient and better serves people's loyalties. Opponents emphasise the cost of establishing a new tier of government and the difficulties of administering it. They also argue that devolution is likely to lead to complete independence.
- A majority of those who voted in referendums held in 1997 supported devolution in both Scotland and Wales (in Wales, the majority was very small). As a result, plans are being implemented to set up a Scottish Parliament and a Welsh Assembly.

Activity 4.5 Devolution in Scotland and Wales

Item A The new assemblies' electoral system

Each voter will have two votes - one for a local constituency candidate and one for a political party. The local constituency candidates are elected on a 'first-past-the-post' system. The additional members are elected on a proportional basis from party lists (if two additional members are elected from a party then the top two candidates on the party's list are elected.

73   56

Welsh Assembly

40   20

Item B Devolution in Wales

The Labour government worked on the assumption that the 1997 referendum result gave a sufficient mandate to press ahead with the creation of a Welsh Assembly. The narrowness of the referendum result, however, produced a feeling that the Assembly would be on probation. Large sections of the population and large geographical areas were still to be won over. One of the first issues was whether Labour and the Liberal Democrats would genuinely encourage new people into politics and whether the Assembly would take account of different opinions in Wales through the consultative regional committee system that was proposed in the government's small print. In the longer term, the pressure is on parties to seek to develop the Assembly as a useful institution, furthering the interests of Wales in a way that would neither disrupt the British system of government nor promote separatist nationalism. Only in these circumstances would the hesitancy and division be dissolved.

Adapted from Bradbury 1998.

Item C The new assemblies' structure and power

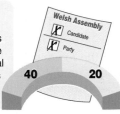

The Scottish Parliament

First Minster

chooses / Cabinet

Cabinet

Dept.   Dept.   Dept.

Cabinet ministers head departments

MSPs elect First Minister

First Minister and Cabinet set agenda and propose laws

129 MSPs

Parliament approves or rejects ministers' proposals

Powers - Scotland

The Scottish Parliament will have wide legislative powers, though Westminster will retain control over areas such as foreign affairs and defence. Ministers from the Scottish Parliament will be able to deal directly with the EU and the Scottish Parliament will scrutinise EU legislation. The Scottish Parliament will have tax-varying powers, but even without using them it could switch resources within a £14 billion block grant to match a legislative programme. There is no reason why it could not lower or even abolish tuition fees for students, for example. It could set new speed limits on roads, devolve primary health care to local authorities (a favoured option) or intervene to save industries regarded as strategic. The role of the Scottish Secretary sitting in the Westminister Cabinet is to be retained. In cases of serious dispute between Westminster and the Scottish Parliament, the Law Lords will arbitrate.

Estimated running costs per year of Scottish Parliament £20-30 million

The Welsh Assembly

Leader

Sets agenda with help of executive

Executive
10 members

Committee   Committee   Committee

MWAs elect leader

60 MWAs

Assembly approves or rejects proposals

Powers - Wales

The Welsh Assembly will have committees dealing with some matters now handled by the Welsh Office. It will have no tax-varying powers, nor will it be able to make or amend laws. Rather, it will have to work within an annual budget, currently £7 billion, set by Whitehall. Unlike Scotland which will develop a Parliament on Westminster lines, there will be no ministers and the Welsh Assembly will be headed by a Leader rather than a First Minister. According to the Labour government, however, the ten-member executive in the Welsh Assembly will have substantial policy-making powers.

Estimated running costs per year of Assembly £20 million

3.3 The consequences of devolution

Devolution and the Westminster Parliament

The devolution of power to Scotland and Wales is likely to affect both the composition of Parliament in Westminster and its procedure. In particular, because the devolved Scottish Parliament will have the power to make laws, there is a need to provide an answer to the so-called 'West Lothian question'.

The West Lothian question

When the debate over devolution began in the 1970s, the Labour MP for West Lothian, Tam Dalyell, pointed out that, if devolution went ahead, there would be an imbalance in terms of power. Whilst a devolved Scottish Parliament would allow the Scots alone to legislate on matters such as health and education, Scottish MPs would still sit at Westminster. Since health and education legislation for England would be decided at Westminster, Scottish MPs would have a say over English health and education legislation whilst English MPs would not have a say over Scottish health and education legislation. The question (the West Lothian question) was - how could this imbalance be overcome?

Peter Lynch suggests that there are five main responses which could be made to the West Lothian question:

- devolve power to the English regions
- reduce the number of Scottish and Welsh MPs
- restrict the voting rights of Scottish MPs so they cannot vote on matters affecting the rest of the UK (the so-called 'in-out' arrangements)
- set up a federal structure
- ignore the West Lothian question on the grounds that the British constitution has many inconsistencies.
  (Lynch 1996, pp.49-50)

Scottish over-representation

Closely related to the West Lothian question is the fact that Scotland is over-represented in the House of Commons:

> 'Scotland has been over-represented in the House of Commons since 1918, gaining 11% of the UK's seats despite having only 8.8% of the UK's population and also being over-represented in terms of the size of Scotland's electorate compared to the UK's electorate.'
> (Lynch 1996, p.47)

Between 1944 and 1997, the over-representation of Scottish MPs was guaranteed by law. The creation of a Scottish Parliament, however, made it difficult to justify this over-representation and, in July 1997, the government announced that this law would be repealed:

> 'Scotland has had a privileged position because it joined England as an equal in the Treaty of Union in 1707. The figure of 72 MPs was enshrined in legislation and it is that section of the Act that is to be repealed.'
> (*Guardian*, 24 July 1997)

If the Boundary Commission uses the same guidelines as it uses for drawing up English constituencies (areas with an average of 70,000 voters), the number of MPs from Scotland will drop from 72 to 58-60. This plan is due to come into effect in time for the election of 2007.

The reduction in the number of Scottish MPs at Westminster will affect the composition of the Commons. In party terms, it is likely that the Labour Party will lose out (in 1997, Labour won 56 of the 72 seats). In regional terms, fewer Scottish MPs will mean a smaller Scottish bloc and what Lynch (1998) calls the 'Englishing' of the House.

A new role for MPs

Devolution has important constitutional implications when it comes to the role of MPs at Westminster. Once the Scottish Parliament and Welsh Assembly are running, the role of Scottish and Welsh MPs in the Commons will change significantly:

> '[Scottish MPs] will not be able to pursue issues such as education, health, local government or the environment...because these will no longer be the functions of Westminster and Whitehall...The policy concerns of Scottish MPs are limited to defence, foreign policy and other policy areas which are reserved to UK government. Welsh MPs will be in a somewhat ambiguous position as they will be able to deal with all policy areas at Westminster, but require a separate mechanism to address issues which are the preserve of the Welsh Assembly.'
> (Lynch 1998, p.99)

Since the role of Scottish MPs, and Welsh MPs to some extent, will be restricted, it may be that their prospects of serving in government are limited. The appointment of a Scottish MP as Health Secretary might appear to be rather odd, for example, given that health policies in the minister's constituency would be outside the minister's control. If the prospects for Scottish MPs are limited, this is likely to affect recruitment.

Procedures in Parliament

Devolution will not only affect the composition of the Commons, it will also affect its procedures. For example, the Select Committee on Scottish Affairs and the Scottish and Welsh grand committees (Commons committees set up in 1979 to oversee Scottish and Welsh affairs) will all be redundant. In addition, Westminster's legislative functions will be reduced as there will be no specifically Scottish legislation passing through Parliament. There will, therefore, be no future role for the Scottish Standing Committee which currently deals with the passage of Bills concerning Scotland.

Although the government made it clear that a Secretary of State for Scotland and a Secretary of State for Wales would continue to be members of the Cabinet after devolution was implemented, Lynch (1998) argues that it is unlikely that these posts will survive in the long term. Once the transitional phase is completed, there would be little for them to do and they would have little legitimacy as representatives of Scottish or Welsh interests.

The SNP and independence

It was noted above that the Conservatives and SNP were united in their view that devolution would result, in the long term, in independence for Scotland. In May 1998, the SNP made it clear that, if the party gained an overall majority in the Scottish Parliament, then it would hold a referendum to find out if Scottish people supported independence. If that referendum found that the Scottish people did want independence, then the SNP would take the necessary steps to secure it. An independent Scotland would necessitate the repeal of the Act of Union. If a referendum did find that a majority of Scots favoured independence, therefore, there would be a major constitutional crisis since the principle that the people's will is sovereign would come into conflict with the principle of parliamentary sovereignty. It should be noted, however, that there is a precedent - in 1921, Britain repealed the Act of Union with Ireland (see Section 3.4 below).

Devolution and England

It was noted above that one response to the West Lothian question is to devolve power to English regions. If English regional assemblies were set up, the argument goes, then they could be responsible for the same policy areas as the Scottish Parliament, leaving MPs responsibility for matters which concern the UK as a whole - such as defence and foreign policy. The argument also usually assumes that the Welsh Assembly is upgraded so that it is responsible for policy making rather than just administering policy. If these measures were taken, it is concluded, the West Lothian question would become an irrelevance because all MPs would have the same areas of responsibility.

The Labour Party's pledge

Although, before the 1997 general election, the Labour Party retreated from plans to set up elected English regional assemblies, that remains a long-term goal. In 1997, the Labour Party made the following pledge in its manifesto:

> 'The Conservatives have created a tier of regional government in England through quangos and regional offices. Meanwhile, local authorities have come together to create a more coordinated regional voice. Labour will build on these developments through the establishment of regional chambers to coordinate transport, planning, economic development, bids for European funding and land use planning...In time we will introduce legislation to allow the people, region by region, to decide in a referendum whether they want directly elected regional government.' (Labour 1997, pp.34-5)

Steps taken since May 1997

As the first step towards fulfilling this pledge, the Regional Development Agencies Bill was included in the Labour government's first Queen's Speech. The result was the setting up of (unelected) Regional Development Agencies (RDAs). The purpose of RDAs is as follows:

> 'They are meant to spearhead regional economic strategies, bring a measure of coherence to an institutional environment which resembles a jungle, and orchestrate partnerships between public, private and third-sector bodies in each region. In these ways, the government hopes that the RDAs will rejuvenate the regional economies of England because only two regions - London and the South East - meet or exceed the average GDP per head in the European Union.' (Morgan 1998, p.vi)

The RDAs have a further purpose, too - to promote the benefits of organising on a regional basis. This is also the side effect of another government reform - the reform of the voting system for the European elections (see Chapter 7, Section 3.5). As a result of this reform, the UK is divided into 12 constituencies. The borders of these constituencies are also the borders used by most government departments and civil servants. By recognising these borders, the government promotes organisation on a regional basis. Nevertheless, as the manifesto pledge made clear, the Labour government will not push regionalism. Rather, it intends to respond to popular demand:

> 'Both Labour and the Liberal Democrats talk of a rolling programme of devolution in England, with each region travelling towards its own chamber, assembly or Parliament at a speed regulated by public demand...The pattern of devolution in England, therefore, will be

uneven and some regions may never decide to create their own tier of regional institutions. Further, nobody is talking about giving regional Parliaments law-making powers or, indeed, tax-raising powers of real significance.' (Leaman 1998, p.17)

The exception is London. In a separate pledge, the Labour Party promised to hold a referendum on the setting up of an elected mayor and London-wide authority. Following a referendum in May 1998, work on this assembly began (see Chapter 16, Section 1.3).

A trend towards regionalism?

Although, in most regions, there is little evidence of a burning desire for regional government, the Campaign for a Northern Assembly has been in operation since the mid-1990s and the Labour government is reported to be looking seriously at how quickly an assembly for the North East of England can be set up (*Guardian*, 8 May 1998). Certainly, the trend is towards greater regionalism:

'There is a growing regional dimension to public policy, recognised by the Conservatives when they created Government Offices for the regions, by Labour's regional development agencies and by the European Union. Like it or not, public business has to be done at regional level.' (Leaman 1998, p.17)

Main points - Section 3.3

- The West Lothian question: is it fair that Scottish MPs at Westminster have a say in legislation affecting, for example, education in England, when English MPs will have no say in legislation affecting education in Scotland?
- The five main responses to the West Lothian question are: devolve power to the English regions; reduce the number of Scottish and Welsh MPs; 'in-out' arrangements; set up a federal structure; ignore the West Lothian question.
- Devolution will result in fewer Scottish MPs at Westminster. It will also change parliamentary procedure at Westminster.
- The Labour government has taken some steps towards regional government.

Activity 4.6 *The consequences of devolution*

Item A *Growing regionalism*

There are signs that the apparently permanent British separation between a strong regional cultural life and an integrated, centralised political life is about to break down. First, regions will become political units in their own right when the Bill changing electoral procedure in Euro-elections is passed. Second, four regions - Scotland, Wales, Northern Ireland and London - will have directly elected assemblies by 2000. London will also have an elected mayor. Although central government intends to police the Mayor via its Government Office for London (with 350 civil servants and a cost of £314 million per year), mayoral candidates are likely to demand that London is made into a region. Third, there are some signs of regionalism in England. For example, the 22 local authorities in Yorkshire and Humberside have formed a 'Regional Assembly' to provide a strategic talking shop and a means of monitoring the new Regional Development Agency (RDA) for the region. Also the nine RDAs set up by the Labour government will operate as yet more super-quangos, remote from any organised political control. Whether this level of indifference will endure is hard to predict. But, the level of regional competition and consciousness is likely to rise sharply as elected politicians in Scotland and Wales begin to claim credit for policies that boost economic growth. Fourth, even at Westminster there are signs of regional consciousness. From October 1998, Labour whips will begin to use the new regional boundaries (they used different regional boundaries before). Regional meetings of Labour MPs will occur more often. And fifth, the civil service is organised in Government Offices for the Regions. If regional assemblies develop, civil servants might answer both to their parent department in Whitehall and their regional assembly.

Adapted from Dunleavy & Weir 1998.

This cartoon was drawn in response to signs in 1998 that the Labour government was taking steps to promote regional government.

Item B *An English Parliament*

If devolution is good for Scotland, then why not throughout the UK? We should be thinking about the position of England in a renegotiated and looser union. One idea is a federal system for the whole of the UK with regional assemblies in England taking the same role as those in Northern Ireland, Scotland and Wales. Supporters point to the popular demand for regionalism in the North and in London. They also point out that there is a growing regional dimension to public policy and argue that policy makers should be made accountable through elected assemblies. The federal system is neat but flawed. There would be little support for different health service laws or systems of student finance in different regions of England. Even if there was, the victims would be local authorities which would have to play second fiddle to regional bosses. A more effective alternative would be to create an English Parliament made up of the MPs elected from English constituencies. This would have full powers over legislation affecting only England. One of its jobs would be to decentralise central government functions within England and to make regional bureaucracies accountable. If this Parliament was drawn from a House of Commons elected by proportional representation, it would be sensitive to opinion in all parts of England. Regional interests could be articulated in a new democratic second chamber elected on a system of regional PR. For this to work, local government would need to be strengthened. That would be the best way to ensure proper decentralisation.

Adapted from Leaman 1998.

Item C *The regional division of votes and seats in 1997*

	% vote			MPs elected		
	Lab	Con	Lib Dem	Lab	Con	Lib Dem
Wales	55	20	12	34	0	2
Scotland	46	18	13	56	0	10
England	44	34	18	329	165	34
North	61	22	13	32	3	1
North West	54	27	14	60	7	2
Yorks/Humberside	52	28	16	46	7	2
London	49	31	15	57	11	6
East Midlands	48	34	13	31	14	0
West Midlands	48	34	14	44	14	1
East Anglia	38	39	18	8	14	0
South East	32	41	21	36	73	8
South West	26	37	31	15	22	14

This table shows the regional distribution of UK votes and seats for the three main parties at the 1997 general election.

Adapted from Holliday 1997.

Questions

1. a) Judging from this section, what are the likely consequences of devolution?
   b) 'Devolution will mean the end of the unitary state'. Give arguments for and against this view.
2. Using Items A and B give arguments for and against (a) a federal UK and (b) an English Parliament.
3. Judging from Item C, how do the regions differ in terms of their political complexion?

3.4 Northern Ireland

The problem of legitimacy

From the standpoint of the Westminster government, the problem of legitimacy, of maintaining consent to the central authority of the British state, has been at its most critical in the case of Northern Ireland.

Britain's relations with Ireland have been troubled ever since the first English landing in 1169. The roots of the recent 'Troubles' lie in the 17th century when, after a period of conquest, some 170,000 settlers (Protestants, mainly from Scotland) made the journey to Ireland and were given parcels of land which had been snatched from the Catholics who lived there. From this time onwards, the population of Ireland has been politically divided along religious lines. It is this division which has given rise to the constitutional problem of securing consent from all sections of the population. Put simply, following the partition of Ireland, a majority in Northern Ireland (mainly Protestants) remained loyal to Britain whilst a substantial minority (mainly Catholic) did not willingly give its consent to rule by Westminster. For British governments, the long-term problem has been how to achieve a constitutional settlement which is acceptable to both communities.

Ireland before partition

Following the British occupation of Ireland in the early 17th century, the indigenous Catholic population suffered great oppression. In 1649, Oliver Cromwell brought an army to Ireland to take revenge for the 'great rebellion' of 1641 in which Catholic rebels killed c.12,000 Protestant settlers. Not only did this lead to great loss of life, also:

> 'The percentage of the land of Ireland owned by Catholics which had shrunk by the time of the great rebellion to 59% was reduced by Cromwellian land settlement to a mere 22%. After further Catholic humiliation in great events to come it was to shrink by 1695 to 14% and by 1714 still further to 7%.' (Kee 1980, p.48)

The Battle of the Boyne and its consequences

Perhaps the most important of the 'great events' Kee refers to was the Battle of the Boyne in 1690. This battle was fought between the forces of the Protestant William of Orange and the Catholic James II. The victory of William is still celebrated by the Protestant 'Orange lodges' in Northern Ireland on 12 July each year.

William of Orange's victory established a Protestant ascendancy which:

> 'Proceeded to consolidate its position by enacting a penal code against the Catholics designed essentially not to punish the Catholics for their beliefs nor to convert them to any form of Protestantism, but to prevent them from obtaining as a group property, position, influence or power. The penal laws ratified, as it were, the identification of opposed classes in terms of religion. They secured the privileges of planters, settlers, speculators and adventurers in land and ensured that the great mass of the native stock of the country should be deprived of land, property, education and the prospects of advancement.' (De Paor 1970, p.17)

The penal code ensured that divisions between the Catholic and Protestant communities widened. It helps to explain why, in the long term, demands for Irish self-rule have tended to come from Catholics whilst the Protestants have tended to favour close ties with Britain.

The rebellion of 1798 and Act of Union

Despite divisions between the Protestant and Catholic communities, on occasions Protestants and Catholics have joined forces. For example, in 1791, Wolfe Tone (a Protestant) set up the Society of United Irishmen, an organisation whose aim was to unite Protestants and Catholics and to remove British rule from Ireland. Tone's attempt to bring over French troops failed in 1796, however, and the 'rebellion' of May 1798 only led to brutal reprisals.

The rebellion of 1798 was the catalyst for the abolition of the Irish Parliament and the passing of the Act of Union 1800. The whole of Ireland remained part of the UK from 1801 (when the Act came into force) until the end of 1921. A significant number of Irish people, however, never accepted the legitimacy of the Union.

Ireland in the 19th century

Throughout the 19th century, politicians in Parliament struggled to solve the 'Irish Question'. The problem was that there were deep divisions within Irish society. The majority of Catholics were nationalists who wanted some degree of home rule (devolution) whilst the majority of Protestants (most of whom lived in Ulster in the north) were unionists who supported the status quo. In part, this was a religious and a geographical divide. In part, it was a divide which reflected the relative status of Catholics and Protestants (in general, Catholics remained second class citizens). And in part, this was a divide which deepened because of changes which took place in the 19th century:

> 'Protestant unionism (support for unity with mainland Britain under the English crown) was the product of 19th century economic change. Unionism in its modern form was a response to the integration of industrial Ulster into the economy of mainland Britain and to the threat to that integration which was posed by the prospect of political separation.' (Moran 1985, p.50)

The struggle for home rule 1886-1914

By the end of the 19th century, politicians in Westminster had failed to find a compromise. Two Home Rule Bills had been defeated (in 1886 and 1893), but the very fact that they had been proposed meant that nationalists had high expectations and unionists felt under threat. In 1912, matters came to the boil. The general election of 1910 resulted in Irish Nationalist MPs holding the balance of power in the British Parliament. The Irish Nationalists made a deal with the Liberals. In return for a Home Rule Bill, they would support the Liberals in Parliament. In 1912, this Bill was passed in the Commons, but rejected by the Lords. Due to the Parliament Act of 1911, however, rejection by the Lords was only temporary. By the summer of 1914, the Bill would be law.

Outside Parliament, opposition to the Home Rule Bill was formidable. The Ulster Unionists set up an armed force to resist home rule (the Ulster Volunteer Force) and the Conservative Party, including the Leader Andrew Bonar Law, argued that the use of force would be justified to resist home rule. In response, nationalists set up their own armed groups (the Irish Citizen Army and the Irish Volunteers). Civil war seemed inevitable. The government agreed that Ulster could opt out of home rule for six years.

The Easter Uprising

The outbreak of the First World War had a profound effect upon the development of Irish politics. First, it ensured that the threatened civil war did not break out. Second, in 1916, a group of republicans (nationalists who wanted Ireland to become an independent republic) staged a rebellion against British rule on Easter Sunday 1916. The rebellion was easily crushed by British troops and the leading rebels were executed. Although this rebellion failed, it was a turning point. The rebels showed that they were prepared to die for their beliefs and this made a deep impression. Before 1916, the majority of people in Ireland wanted home rule rather than independence. After 1916, however, the mood changed. People began to support and vote for republicans. The main beneficiary was the republican party Sinn Fein which had been set up in 1905. In the general election of 1918, Sinn Fein won three-quarters of the Irish seats. Instead of going to Westminster, these MPs set up their own Irish Parliament, Dail Eireann. The Dail issued a declaration of independence and began recruiting an army - the Irish Republican Army (IRA). The aim was to provoke the British government into fighting a war:

> 'The sooner fighting is forced and a general

state of disorder is created throughout the country, the better it will be for the country.' (part of a speech made to the Sinn Fein Executive by Michael Collins, Head of the IRA and Minister of Finance in the Dail, in February 1919)

Civil war 1919-21

Michael Collins' wish was granted. Between 1919 and 1921, a war was fought between Irish and British troops. In 1921, the British government finally agreed to negotiate with Sinn Fein. A ceasefire was agreed in July and, in December, a treaty was signed. This treaty was a compromise. Southern Ireland would be a self-governing dominion (the Irish Free State), whilst six of the nine countries of Ulster (Northern Ireland) would remain part of the UK. Ireland, therefore, was to be partitioned.

Northern Ireland

Following the signing of the treaty in December 1921, British troops were withdrawn from the new Irish Free State and it was left to its own devices. It was no longer part of the UK. Over the years, the Irish Free State gradually loosened its ties with the UK. In 1937, it renounced the oath of loyalty to the British monarch. In 1949, it became a republic and left the British Commonwealth.

The six counties of Ulster which made up Northern Ireland remained part of the UK. The British Parliament remained in overall charge. But, the Northern Irish Parliament, set up in 1921, looked after day-to-day affairs. Between 1921 and 1972, the British government did not interfere in the running of Northern Ireland. Downing notes that:

'The characteristics of successive Northern Ireland Cabinets show remarkable consistency. Up to 1969, every member of the Cabinet was a Protestant and a member of the Unionist Party and all but three were members of the Orange Order [a society set up in 1795 to defend Protestant privilege]. Of the six members of the first Cabinet in 1921, four of them were still in office 14 years later. Twenty years tenure of office was not unusual...All the ministers shared a common vision and political stance; they tended to view all questions about the constitution, the administration of justice and the role of government in the economy from a narrow Ulster Unionist perspective. They all shared the same fears of Catholicism and socialism. After all, they had gone into Ulster politics to protect and maintain the Union with Britain...Anything that threatened this Union was a threat to the state itself.' (Downing 1989, p.103)

Gerrymandering

Although there was a large Catholic minority in Northern Ireland (c.33% of the population in 1921), the Protestant majority ensured that Protestants maintained their privileged position. One way of doing this was by ensuring that electoral boundaries were set in such a way that the Catholic electorate would have minimal representation:

'The population of the city of Londonderry is roughly three-fifths Catholic and nationalist...and two-fifths Protestant and unionist. This population distribution has remained more or less constant ever since the foundation of the state. For the state's first 50 years, the Corporation of Londonderry was composed the other way round: three-fifths Protestant and unionist and two-fifths Catholic and nationalist. This effect was achieved by "gerrymandering" or concentrating large numbers of people with majority political views in overlarge political districts and their opponents in smaller ones so that, in representation district by district, the latter are bound to win. Thus in Londonderry 87% of the large Catholic population were placed in one ward which returned eight seats while 87% of the much smaller Protestant population were placed in two wards which returned 12 seats. Year after year there was a Protestant and unionist majority of 12 to eight.' (Kee 1980, p.229)

Catholic disadvantage

Lack of political representation ensured that the Catholic population remained socially disadvantaged. Catholics formed a disproportionately large percentage of those in low-paid, unskilled jobs. They were under-represented in the police force, higher grades of the civil service and universities, but over-represented in terms of unemployment. Although this was not entirely due to discrimination (for example, most Catholics would not have wanted to take a job in the police force even if it was offered to them), there was a direct link between the Protestants' political control and the Catholics' lack of opportunity:

'Key localities with Catholic majorities were gerrymandered to produce Protestant councils: these councils in turn gave jobs and houses to Protestants in preference to Catholics.' (O'Brien & O'Brien 1985, pp.168-9)

The beginning of the 'Troubles'

The turning point was the setting up of the Civil Rights Association (CRA) in 1967. The aim of the CRA was to win civil rights for Catholics by peaceful mass demonstration. Protestant politicians, however, saw the marches organised by the CRA as a direct challenge to Protestant dominance. Heavy-handed tactics were used by the police to break up the marches. The atmosphere became tense and, following the annual Orange parades in July 1969, violent clashes between Catholics and Protestants broke out. These clashes culminated in the 'Battle of the Bogside' which began on 12 August. The Bogside is a Catholic area in Londonderry ('Derry' to nationalists). When police tried to take control of the Bogside, Catholics set up barricades and fought them off, declaring the area 'free Derry'. Since the police appeared to have lost control, the British government agreed to intervene and sent in British troops to restore order. These troops arrived on 14 August 1969.

The British troops soon lost the support of the Catholic community - especially when 'internment' (imprisonment without trial) was introduced in August 1971 (see Chapter 18, Section 1.3). By then, paramilitary groups on both sides had begun a campaign of bombing and shooting.

On 20 January 1972, 'Bloody Sunday', British troops killed 13 men taking part in a civil rights march. Although troops claimed that they had been fired upon first, the march was shown on television and it shocked many people in Britain. It seemed that civil war was about to break out. On 24 March 1972, the British government suspended the Northern Ireland Parliament and direct rule from Britain began. Between 1969 and 1998 over 3,500 people were killed in violent incidents in Northern Ireland.

Peace initiatives since 1969

Since 1969, the response of the British government to events in Northern Ireland has moved through a number of phases. Generally, there has been bipartisan agreement between Labour and the Conservatives and so policies have reflected different approaches rather than party political divisions.

Phase 1 - Crisis management 1969-75
Between 1969 and 1975, British policy was incoherent and at the level of crisis management (see McCullagh & O'Dowd 1986).

Phase 2 - Criminalisation 1975-85
Between 1975 and 1985, containment and stabilisation became paramount and the British government pursued a policy of 'criminalisation' (see Chapter 18, Section 1.3).

Phase 3 - Searching for a constitutional settlement
Although the policy of criminalisation remained in place, a new phase began in 1985 with the signing of the Anglo-Irish Agreement.

The Anglo-Irish Agreement
Crucially, the Anglo-Irish Agreement established that the Republic of Ireland had the right to be consulted over policy formulation in Northern Ireland, though executive responsibility remained with Westminster. In other words, by establishing, for the first time, structures by which the Republic of Ireland might participate in the government of Northern Ireland, the agreement meant the first change in the constitutional

status of Northern Ireland since 1921. In Northern Ireland, the unionists opposed the agreement on the grounds that it was the first step towards a united Ireland, and Sinn Fein (the political wing of the IRA) opposed the agreement on the grounds that it strengthened partition. In 1991, the Northern Ireland Secretary, Peter Brooke, suspended the Anglo-Irish Agreement to allow for constitutional talks. These talks finally broke down in November 1992.

The Downing Street Declaration
Just over a year later, in December 1993, the British and Irish governments issued what became known as the 'Downing Street Declaration', an attempt to pull together the different positions. In this declaration the following statement was made:

'The British government agrees that it is for the people of Ireland alone, by agreement between the two parts respectively to exercise their rights of self-determination on the basis of consent freely and concurrently given, North and South, to bring about a united Ireland if that is their wish...The British and Irish governments reiterate that the achievement of peace must involve a permanent end to the use of or support for paramilitary violence. They confirm that, in these circumstances, democratically mandated parties which establish a commitment to exclusively peaceful methods and which have shown that they abide by the democratic process are free...to join in dialogue in due course.'
(quoted in the *Guardian*, 16 December 1993)

Although, in the short term, the terms of this declaration were rejected by both the unionists and by Sinn Fein, it was this declaration which paved the way for the IRA ceasefire which was declared on 31 August 1994. Once this ceasefire had been declared, it made a lasting peaceful settlement more likely than at any time since the violence began in 1969 since it provided the opportunity for political discussions between the different parties and interest groups.

The Framework Document
As part of the peace process, the British and Irish governments issued the Framework Document in February 1995 (see Box 18.1 in Chapter 18, Section 1.3 for its provisions). This document outlined what a settlement might look like and was intended as a starting point for negotiations. It was rejected out of hand by unionist politicians, however. Then, further attempts to secure an agreement in 1995-97 stumbled over the question of when paramilitary groups (on both the nationalist and unionist sides) would begin to decommission their weapons.

The Mitchell Report
In an attempt to deal with the problem of decommissioning weapons, an international commission, chaired by Senator George Mitchell, was set up in December 1995 by the British and Irish

governments as part of their Twin Track Initiative (a parallel phase of preparatory talks was also set in motion to prepare the ground for all-party talks). In January 1996, the Mitchell Report was published. It argued that:

> 'It was unrealistic to expect decommissioning before all-party talks, but some decommissioning should take place during the talks. The report also outlined six principles of non-violence and democratic procedure to which all parties should subscribe.' (Aughey 1997, p.246)

John Major, who was heavily dependent on Unionist votes to maintain his majority in the Commons, accepted the Mitchell principles but demanded that the IRA begin disarming before joining all-party talks. For the IRA, this was a last straw. The following month, it detonated a large bomb in Canary Wharf, signalling an end to the ceasefire and an end to this round of the peace process.

The response of the British government to the Mitchell Report was to announce elections to the Northern Ireland Assembly (proposed in the Framework Document) as a 'gateway' to all-party talks. These elections were held in May 1996, but Sinn Fein never took up its seats and the SDLP resigned from it in July 1996.

The Good Friday Peace Agreement

Following the 1997 general election, the Labour government quickly made it clear that securing an agreement over new constitutional arrangements in Northern Ireland was to be a priority. On the one hand, the government reassured unionists by making it clear that a united Ireland was not a realistic option. On the other hand, the government made it clear that Sinn Fein would be welcome at the peace talks if it restored its ceasefire. The IRA ceasefire was duly restored on 19 July 1997 and the all-party talks began on 10 September. By 10 April 1998, a deal had been struck - the Good Friday Peace Agreement (see also Activity 4.7 below and Chapter 18, Section 1.3). Referendums followed in Northern Ireland and in the Republic in May 1998. Both referendums produced a large majority in favour of the new constitutional settlement.

One effect of the settlement and the outcome of the referendums is that both the British and Irish governments have conceded modifications to their constitutional claims to Northern Ireland:

> 'The Irish government has finally agreed to rescind [cancel] its territorial claim on Northern Ireland enshrined in Articles 1 and 2 of the Irish constitution...The new constitutional commitment instead expresses a hope for the unification of the people rather than the soil of Ireland. Britain has agreed to repeal the Government of Ireland Act 1920. And, it has agreed to pass legislation allowing the Secretary of State to be empowered to hold referendums on Northern Ireland every seven years "if it appears likely to him or her that a majority of those voting would express a wish that Northern Ireland should cease to be part of the UK and form part of a united Ireland".' (*Observer*, 12 April 1998)

In June 1998, elections for the new Irish Assembly were held. The SDLP emerged with the largest number of first preference votes and the Ulster Unionists with the largest share of seats. David Trimble became First Minister.

Main points - Section 3.4

- Since Protestant settlers took land from native Catholics in the 17th century, the population of Ireland was politically divided along religious lines, making it difficult to secure consent from all sections of the population.
- Following a civil war in 1919-21, Ireland was partitioned. The South became independent and the North continued to be part of the UK.
- Between 1921 and 1972, the British government did not interfere in the running of Northern Ireland. Direct rule began in 1972 after the 'Troubles' broke out.
- Between 1969 and 1998, British attempts to find a peaceful solution in Northern Ireland went through three phases - (1) crisis management 1969-75; (2) criminalisation 1975-85; and (3) searching for a new constitutional settlement 1985-98.
- The 1985 Anglo-Irish Agreement meant a change in constitutional status since the Irish Republic had a say in the government of Northern Ireland for the first time.
- Although several initiatives were made under John Major, it was only after the 1997 general election that all-party talks were held. The result was the Good Friday Agreement, referendums and elections to the new assembly.

Activity 4.7 The Good Friday Peace Agreement

Item A *Terms of the deal (1)*

The Good Friday Agreement creates three interconnecting bodies of government:

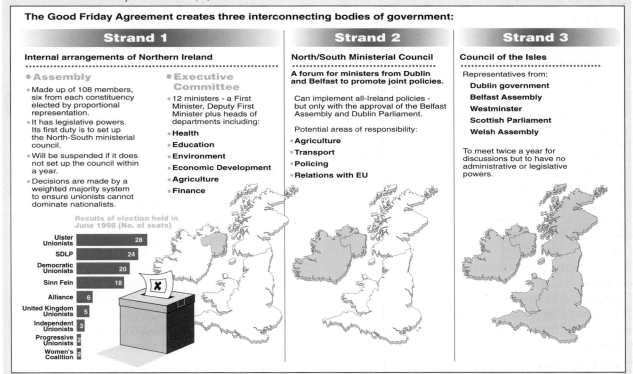

Strand 1

Internal arrangements of Northern Ireland

● **Assembly**

- Made up of 108 members, six from each constituency elected by proportional representation.
- It has legislative powers. Its first duty is to set up the North-South ministerial council.
- Will be suspended if it does not set up the council within a year.
- Decisions are made by a weighted majority system to ensure unionists cannot dominate nationalists.

● **Executive Committee**

- 12 ministers - a First Minister, Deputy First Minister plus heads of departments including:
  - ● Health
  - ● Education
  - ● Environment
  - ● Economic Development
  - ● Agriculture
  - ● Finance

Results of election held in June 1998 (No. of seats)

Party	Seats
Ulster Unionists	28
SDLP	24
Democratic Unionists	20
Sinn Fein	18
Alliance	6
United Kingdom Unionists	5
Independent Unionists	3
Progressive Unionists	2
Women's Coalition	2

Strand 2

North/South Ministerial Council

A forum for ministers from Dublin and Belfast to promote joint policies.

Can implement all-Ireland policies - but only with the approval of the Belfast Assembly and Dublin Parliament.

Potential areas of responsibility:
- ● Agriculture
- ● Transport
- ● Policing
- ● Relations with EU

Strand 3

Council of the Isles

Representatives from:
- **Dublin government**
- **Belfast Assembly**
- **Westminster**
- **Scottish Parliament**
- **Welsh Assembly**

To meet twice a year for discussions but to have no administrative or legislative powers.

Adapted from the *Guardian*, 11 April and 29 June 1998.

Item B *Terms of the deal (2)*

The Good Friday Agreement

- ● Elected Northern Ireland Assembly of 108 members
- ● Controlling executive committee made up of 12 ministers
- ● North-South body set up by and responsible to Assembly
- ● Release of paramilitary prisoners to be accelerated
- ● A British-Irish Council bringing together representatives from the Scottish Parliament and Welsh Assembly with counterparts from Belfast, Dublin and Westminster
- ● Reform of the Royal Ulster Constabulary
- ● Promise of decommissioning

Adapted from the *Guardian*, 11 April 1998.

Item C *Constitutional implications of the settlement*

As part of the Good Friday Agreement, a British-Irish Council (BIC) is to be set up. Lawmakers from the Republic will meet regularly with members of the British Parliament, the Northern Ireland Assembly and with representatives of the new assemblies for Scotland and Wales. The idea is that the BIC will promote the harmonious and mutually beneficial development of relationships between all these people. The BIC will meet in different formats - at summit level twice per year and at ministerial level on a regular basis (with relevant ministers from each institution meeting on a revolving basis - as happens in the EU's Council of Ministers). The aim is that the BIC will exchange information, discuss, consult and try to reach agreement on matters of mutual interest - for example, transport links or environmental issues. This body could, therefore, develop into a body which results in significant constitutional change for the UK. It is possible to see, for example, how a full federal system might evolve in the UK as relations of the various devolved bodies with Westminster is redefined.

Adapted from the *Guardian*, 11 April 1998.

Questions

1. Why do you think (a) nationalists and (b) unionists were able to support the Good Friday Agreement? Use Items A and B in your answer.

2. 'An important change to the UK's constitution'. Do Items A and B suggest that this is a fair assessment of the Good Friday Agreement? Explain your answer.

3. Judging from Items A-C, to what extent do you think recent developments in Northern Ireland affect the UK's position as a unitary state?

Part 4 The monarchy

Key issues

1. What is the monarch's constitutional position?
2. What are the actual powers of the monarch?
3. Is the monarchy under threat?

4.1 A constitutional monarchy

Government and monarch

The formal way of describing the British government is to say that the UK has a parliamentary government under a constitutional monarchy. Norton (1992) points out that this has resulted in the development of a whole series of institutions whose relationships are governed by convention rather than embodied in statute. The term 'parliamentary government under a constitutional monarchy', says Norton:

> 'Refers to government through rather than by Parliament, with the system being presided over by a largely ceremonial monarch. Government is elected through Parliament and is expected to formulate - to 'make' - public policy. The role of Parliament is to scrutinise and, if necessary, modify that policy before giving its assent. The monarch - as a neutral figure representing the unity of the nation - then formally gives the final seal of approval.' (Norton 1992, pp.30-31)

The constitutional position

Apart from the period 1649-60, England has had a monarchy based on the hereditary principle since the 10th century. Today, it is commonly thought that the monarch is a symbolic head of state only, performing primarily ceremonial functions such as visiting or entertaining leaders of foreign countries or opening new buildings. In Bagehot's terms (see Section 1.3 above), it is thought that the monarch carries out some of the 'dignified', as opposed to the 'efficient', parts of the constitution.

The official view of the monarch's constitutional position, however, is as follows:

> 'The Queen personifies the state. In law, she is head of the executive, an integral part of the legislature, head of the judiciary, the commander-in-chief of the armed forces of the Crown and the "supreme governor" of the established Church of England. As a result of a long process of evolution during which the monarchy's absolute power has been progressively reduced, the Queen acts on the advice of her ministers. Britain is governed by Her Majesty's government in the name of the Queen. Within this framework, and in spite of a trend during the past 100 years towards giving powers directly to ministers, the Queen still takes part in some important acts of government. These include summoning, proroguing (discontinuing until the next session without dissolution) and dissolving Parliament; and giving royal assent to Bills passed by Parliament. The Queen also formally appoints many important office holders.' (HMSO 1994, p.8)

The monarchy and political power

Although, as the above passage indicates, the monarch does have an important political role to play, in practice, power has substantially been removed from the personal control of the monarch. A formal link remains and is reflected in official titles such as 'Her Majesty's government', but executive power has come to be employed by ministers or their agents even though still nominally vested in the Crown. As Norton puts it:

> 'Ministers remain legally responsible to the Queen for their actions, but, by convention, are responsible to Parliament.' (Norton 1982, p.14)

In addition, membership of the EU has made an impact. Since EU law takes precedence over UK law, it is, therefore, no longer the case that all laws effective in the UK receive royal assent.

There are, however, two areas where there is at least the potential for the personal exercise of power by the monarch.

1. The power to appoint the Prime Minister

By convention, the monarch invites the Leader of the largest party in the House of Commons to form a new government after a general election has been held. There is, however, always the possibility of a 'hung' Parliament - a Parliament in which no single party has an overall majority of seats in the Commons. If this was to happen, the choice of Prime Minister and, therefore, the choice of the party or parties from which the government could be drawn might not be obvious. In such a case, the monarch would play a decisive political role in determining the nature of the government.

2. The power to dissolve Parliament
The power of the monarch to dissolve Parliament could also lead to the monarch's personal involvement in politics. Suppose, for example, that a newly formed minority government wished to call a general election in an attempt to strengthen its position. The monarch could decide not to dissolve Parliament and invite the Leader of another party to form a coalition government. Constitutional precedents offer no clear guidance in such a case.

4.2 Is the monarchy under threat?

Changing views on the monarchy
There is some evidence to suggest that attitudes towards the monarchy began to change in the 1990s. Certainly, it seems that, by the late 1990s, members of the royal family were not as popular as they had been in the past. In the 1950s, for example, the monarchy was seemingly above criticism. When the broadcaster and journalist Malcolm Muggeridge wrote an article which asked whether Britain really needed a Queen, he was sacked by a Sunday newspaper and by the BBC. Not only does this indicate the strength of support for the monarchy in the 1950s. It also suggests how deferential people were towards the royal family. Even in the 1980s, 85% plus of people told opinion pollsters that they supported the monarchy. By 1994, however, opinion had shifted significantly. A survey carried out by NOP in August 1994 found that:

- 66% thought that the monarchy should continue indefinitely
- 26% wanted the monarchy to abolished at some point
- 9% said that the monarchy should end now
- 12% said that the monarchy should end when the Queen died
- 5% said that the monarchy should end some time after the Queen died.

The same poll showed that support for the monarchy varied according to age:
'People who are aged 55 plus respect the institution in copious numbers: 74% in favour, 25% against. But, among the under 35s, 48% respect the monarchy but 51% don't.' (*Guardian*, 19 September 1994)
There are two main reasons for this decline in popularity. First, the behaviour of individual members of the royal family has failed to meet the

standards expected of prominent public figures. The well-publicised break-up of a number of marriages, including that of the heir to the throne, and other personal scandals gave the impression that the royal family was in crisis. And second, the cost of supporting the monarchy has been criticised. It is true that the Queen agreed to pay income tax for the first time and to cut the civil list (the list of members who receive public funds to pay for their expenses in performing public duties) in November 1992. Nevertheless, criticisms of the cost of maintaining a royal family have continued to surface. In July 1998, for example, there were criticisms of the amount of taxpayers' money spent on trivial excursions:

'For example, the taxpayer picked up a £2,565 bill to allow the Duke of York to attend a golf tournament last July. That Prince Andrew is a keen golfer is well known...But, does he really need to fly from London to Prestwick at our expense?...The Prince of Wales, it emerges, is flown to the most mundane events from his Highgrove house - £2,938, for example, to attend a royal film performance. Travelling by car appears out of the question.' (*Guardian*, 1 July 1998)
The same article revealed that, overall, the royal family cost £45 million a year to maintain plus £30 million on top for security. This made the British royal family the most expensive in Europe.

The impact of Diana's death
In a poll taken on 8-9 August 1997 (three weeks before Diana's death), only 48% of respondents agreed that Britain would be worse off without a royal family - compared to 70% in a parallel poll held in 1994 (*Guardian*, 12 August 1997). This was the first time that support for the royal family had fallen below 50%. Following the death of Princess Diana on 31 August 1997, however, the picture became less clear. Initially, there was a great deal of public and media criticism of the royal family's response to Diana's death. At the same time, however, the outpouring of grief from such a large section of the population suggested that many people retained some kind of allegiance to the monarchy as an institution. A poll taken for the *Observer* shortly after Diana's death suggested that support for the monarchy had leapt up, though a large majority of people wanted the institution to be modernised (see Item B in Activity 4.8 below). This suggests that, although outright abolition of the monarchy still had only minority support at the end of the 1990s, attitudes towards the royal family were continuing to change.

4.3 Arguments for and against the monarchy

The monarchy - arguments for
Those in favour of retaining the monarchy more or

less in its present form put forward the following arguments. First, despite some bad publicity, it is still a popular public institution. Second, the monarchy symbolises national unity and purpose both to the outside world and to people living in Britain. It helps to integrate British society. Third, through its maintenance of British traditions the monarchy provides continuity in an otherwise rapidly changing society. Fourth, the cost of sustaining the monarchy (according to the *Guardian*, 1 July 1997, £75 million per year) is less than the income generated through tourism and trade generated by the monarchy. It is also a great deal less than the cost of supporting a presidency in some countries (for example the USA). Fifth, the hereditary principle keeps the royal family above party politics. A disassociation from party politics would be essential in the event of a hung Parliament since the monarch would need to make decisions about the formation of a new government. Any alternative (such as a presidency) would involve elections which would automatically introduce a party political element.

The monarchy - arguments against

Arguments against a monarchy include the following. First, the hereditary principle is not acceptable in a democratic society. People should gain positions on merit, not because they happen to be born into a particular family. Second, far from uniting the nation, the privileges enjoyed by the extended royal family emphasise to ordinary people just how great a divide there is from top to bottom in British society. Third, the popularity of the monarchy has declined and no longer commands universal support. Fourth, because of the behaviour of individual members of the royal family, the monarchy no longer provides a model of idealised family life. Fifth, the cost of maintaining a monarchy is too great. It is an unnecessary burden on the taxpayer. Income generated by tourism does not directly feed back into the public purse and, in any case, abolishing the monarchy would not necessarily reduce tourism. And finally, there is no reason why the functions of Head of State could not be performed by an elected President or even by the holder of an existing post - the Labour MP Tony Benn, for example, has suggested that the Speaker of the House of Commons could be given the power to dissolve Parliament and to choose the Prime Minister (see Chapter 14, Section 2.1 for a description of the Speaker's role).

Republicanism in Britain

During the 1990s, there was increasing speculation about what would happen if Britain was to become a republic (a republic is a state whose head is not a monarch). Most British republicans argue that the monarchy should be replaced by an elected President with limited powers rather than a strong executive President like that in the USA or France:

> 'A British President would be a figurehead and honest broker, chosen by a college of politicians, as in Germany, or elected directly by the people, as in Ireland. Members of the royal family would be free to stay in Britain, just as members of the Hapsburg royal family are free to live in the Republic of Austria. But, the wealth and buildings they held in the public name would be taken away.'
> (*Independent on Sunday*, 28 October 1994)

It should be noted that, traditionally, republicanism has been associated with those on the political left. During the 1990s, however, calls for a major re-think on the future of the monarchy came from the radical right, too.

Main points - Part 4

- The UK has a parliamentary government under a constitutional monarchy. Although the monarch's duties are mainly ceremonial, some important powers remain - especially (1) appointing the Prime Minister; and (2) dissolving Parliament.
- By the late 1990s, attitudes towards the monarchy were changing. The main reason for this was the behaviour of members of the royal family which failed to meet the standards expected of prominent public figures.
- Following Diana's death, support for the monarchy as an institution appeared to rise, but a large majority of people wanted the monarchy to change.

- Supporters of the monarchy argue that: (1) it is still popular; (2) it symbolises national unity; (3) it provides continuity in a rapidly changing society; (4) it is cost effective; and (5) the hereditary principle keeps the royal family above part politics.
- Opponents of the monarchy argue that: (1) its privileges emphasise the divide in British society (2) its popularity has declined; (3) it no longer provides a model of idealised family life; (4) its cost is too great; (5) an elected representative could perform its functions; and (6) the hereditary principle is not acceptable in a democracy.

Activity 4.8 Attitudes towards the monarchy

Item A *Respect for the monarchy*

Item B *Modernising the monarchy*

Demos' report on the monarchy - main points

- Automatic right of succession of the heir to the throne should be abolished and the public should have the right of veto over a new monarch.

- Royals should receive state education and be treated on the NHS.

- The monarch should not automatically be head of the Church of England.

- The monarch should become a roving ambassador to "heal bitterness about Britain's past around the world".

- The Speaker of the Commons should take responsibility for appointing the Prime Minister and dissolving Parliament.

- The need for royal assent allowing Bills to become law should be abolished.

- A Minister of Justice should take responsibility for appointing judges.

- The Royal Household should be replaced by a civil service-run Office of the Monarchy.

In September 1998, the think tank Demos published a report which argued that the monarchy required dramatic reform if it was to match public expectations. The report ruled out a republic. Instead, it aimed to modernise the monarchy by allowing it to keep its ceremonial role, but removing its political and religious functions. The Queen would lose her power to dissolve Parliament, appoint Prime Ministers or give the Royal Assent to Bills. Church and Crown would be separated. The report also called for a democratic monarch whose legitimacy is drawn from the will of the people. There would be no automatic right of succession. Rather, the people would be asked whether they support the heir to the throne in a referendum. If the heir was rejected, a second referendum would be held. If the next in line was also rejected, there would be a third referendum. The report also suggested regular referendums throughout a reign to ensure the monarch retains the support of the people. Other ideas in the report include: abolishing the civil list, replacing royal courtiers with civil servants and setting up an independent honours commission. In a poll published on 6 September 1998, 60% of people thought the monarchy should be modernised and 49% thought the Queen should give up her political role.

Adapted from the *Guardian*, 7 September 1998.

Item C *Changing attitudes towards the monarchy*

1. How many marks out of 10 would you give the Queen as Britain's head of state and Prince Charles as Prince of Wales for the way they carry out their roles?

% giving 10 out of 10	1981	1997
Queen	71%	10%
Charles	58%	5%

3. Which of these options would you prefer:

a The monarchy should continue in its present form	12%
b The monarchy should continue but be modernised	74%
c The monarchy should be replaced with a republic when the queen dies	5%
d The monarchy should be replaced with a republic as soon as possible	7%

4. If the monarchy does continue when the Queen dies, do you think the crown should pass to Prince Charles or straight to Prince William?

Charles	38%
William	53%

2. Assuming that the monarchy continues, do you agree or disagree with each of these statements?

	Agree	Disagree
a The Royal Family should become much more informal, and less concerned with preserving their traditional ways	81%	15%
b The Royal Family is out of touch with ordinary people in Britain	79%	17%
c The Royal Family should not take part in field sports such as fox-hunting and grouse-shooting	62%	23%
d The Queen should start to give interviews like other public figures	49%	39%
e The Queen should give up functions such as signing new laws, opening Parliament and formally appointing a Prime Minister and stick to purely ceremonial duties	37%	57%

The table above shows the findings of a survey carried out by ICM shortly after Diana's death. A random sample of 511 adults was interviewed by telephone.

Adapted from the *Observer*, 14 September 1997.

Item D *Reaction to news of Diana's death*

This photograph shows a mourner in Hyde Park praying against a tree during the funeral service for Diana, Princess of Wales. The service was relayed to Hyde Park on giant screens from Westminster Abbey. It was held on 6 September 1997.

Questions

1. How accurate is the view of the monarchy portrayed in Item A? Use Items B-D in your answer.
2. a) How would the role of the monarch change if the proposals outlined in Item B were put into practice?
   b) What are the benefits and drawbacks of these proposals?
3. What do Items C and D reveal about attitudes towards the monarchy?

Part 5 Constitutional reform

Key issues

1. Why has pressure for constitutional reform developed?
2. What are the arguments for and against a written constitution?
3. What would a reformed constitution look like?

5.1 Pressure for reform

The origins of the debate

According to Norton, the British constitution:

> 'Used to be a subject of praise, but little discussion. Today, it is a subject of discussion, but little praise.' (Norton 1989, p.10)

It is Norton's thesis that debate about constitutional reform has only developed since the 1960s. It was during the 1960s and 1970s, that governments first appeared ineffectual in the face of rising unemployment and inflation. This apparent weakness, he argues, led not just to criticism of individual politicians, but to criticism of the system of government itself.

At first, the call for constitutional reform came from a small number of outspoken critics. Lord Hailsham's warning in 1976 that Britain was becoming an elective dictatorship, for example, received attention because it was a view not often heard in public.

Calls for reform since the late 1980s

It is only since the late 1980s that support for constitutional reform has begun to reach the political mainstream. This was due to three main factors:

- the formation of the constitutional reform group Charter 88 in 1988
- the Conservative Party's electoral success between 1979 and 1997
- a growth in interest in constitutional reform in the Labour Party.

These three factors are interlinked. Charter 88 was

set up in 1988 partly because this was the tricentenary of the 'Glorious Revolution' (supporters of Charter 88 argued that it was time that a new constitutional settlement replaced that made in 1688). But, 1988 was also the year after the Conservative Party had won its third general election victory in a row. In that election, just 32% of the electorate voted Conservative - 68% either voted for another party or did not vote at all. Frustration with the Conservatives' monoploy on power raised a number of questions about Britain's constitutional arrangements:

- Should there be electoral reform to prevent a single minority party dominating?
- Should there be devolution of power so that regions could be governed by local people?
- What about the unelected institutions like the House of Lords and the monarchy - shouldn't they be democratised?

Frustration with the Conservatives' monopoly on power also sparked an interest in constitutional reform in the Labour Party:

'Labour's conversion to the cause of constitutional reform is a relatively recent one. Up until the late 1980s, the dominant view within the party was that constitutional reform was a waste of time. There were more important matters for a Labour government to address, such as poverty and unemployment. But, Neil Kinnock's Policy Review from 1987 began to change Labour's approach to the constitution.' (Driver & Martell 1998, p.121)

Members of Charter 88 were able to play on this new interest in constitutional reform in the Labour Party and lobbied hard in an attempt to shape the party's policies.

A changing landscape

Frustration is not in itself enough to explain why constitutional reform rose up the political agenda. In 1992, Philip Norton pointed out that:

'The constitution of the UK is ever changing. Some changes are essentially at the margins (the creation of a new parliamentary committee, for example), others are more fundamental (the passage of the 1972 European Communities Act, for example). The constitution of 1991 is markedly different to that of 1961.' (Norton 1992, p.38)

By the time that the Conservatives were voted out of office in 1997, there had been a number of significant developments with constitutional implications. These are outlined in Box 4.1.

As a result of these developments, by the time of the 1997 general election, support for constitutional reform had gathered pace.

Box 4.1 Constitutional developments 1992-97

1. The ratifying of the Maastricht Treaty raised questions about Britain's sovereignty.
2. What many saw as an erosion of civil liberties suggested the advantages of a Bill of Rights.
3. The centralisation of power (the reduction of the powers of local government, for example) and the increasing use of unelected quangos led to calls for greater democracy and accountability.
4. The uncovering of miscarriages of justice led to calls for judicial reform
5. Corruption in the House of Commons and criticisms of its unrepresentative make-up led to calls for the modernisation of parliamentary procedures.

5.2 Constitutional reform since 1997

Labour's pledges

In its 1997 general election manifesto, the Labour Party pledged to make the constitutional reforms outlined in Box 4.2.

Box 4.2 Labour's pledges on constitutional reform

In its 1997 general election manifesto, the Labour Party pledged:

- to abolish the right of hereditary Lords to sit and vote in the House of Lords
- to set up a special select committee in the Commons to review its procedures
- to hold a referendum on the voting system for elections to the House of Commons
- to draw up a Freedom of Information Act
- to hold referendums and, if they supported the idea, to set up assemblies in Scotland and Wales
- to hold a referendum and, if it supported the idea, to set up a directly elected strategic authority and mayor for London
- to incorporate the European Convention on Human Rights into British law
- to hold a referendum on whether to join a single European currency.

Adapted from Labour 1997.

Compared to the constitutional reform programmes of other post-war governments, this was a formidable and radical package of reform. Indeed, one commentator suggested the package added up to:

'The most important constitutional changes proposed by a major political party this century.' (Rush 1997, p.39)

Criticisms of Labour's programme

Naturally, a package of reform like this was controversial. Predictably, it came under criticism from the right. Less predictably, perhaps, it also came under criticism from the left. These criticisms, from left and right, are summarised below.

1. The reforms do not go far enough

Some critics argued that the reforms did not go far enough. With a majority of 178, it was argued, the government could do what it liked. Rather than proceeding in small steps, it should take advantage of its strong position and bring its long-term aims forward. For example, rather than tinkering with the House of Lords by ending hereditary peers' right to vote, the government should take immediate steps to replace the Lords with an elected second chamber.

2. The pledges are being watered down

Some critics argued that some of the reforms that had been pledged were being watered down because some leading ministers lacked enthusiasm for them. In 1998, for example, it became clear that this was the case with the promised Freedom of Information Bill (see also Chapter 19, Section 5.4). Although a Bill was drawn up by David Clark, the Cabinet minister responsible, opposition from the Home Secretary, Jack Straw, ensured that it was delayed. In July 1998, Clark was sacked in Tony Blair's first reshuffle and in September it was reported that:

> 'Home Secretary Jack Straw is to weaken the government's Freedom of Information Bill...In a policy U-turn, Mr Straw is to scrap a commitment given by David Clark, responsible for freedom of information before being sacked, to announce a draft Bill this month. Straw will also abandon the fight for the measure to be included in the Queen's Speech.' (*Guardian*, 30 September 1998)

3. The reforms lack coherence

Some critics argued that the Labour Party had not really looked at the constitutional reform package as a whole. As a result, it lacked coherence. For example, devolution in Scotland and Wales would have a knock-on effect in England, but it was unclear how the government intended to deal with this. Similarly, removing hereditary peers from the Lords on the grounds that they had no place in a democratic system begged the question of what to do about the monarchy since monarchs are chosen by blood-line rather than by election.

4. Piecemeal legislation doesn't work

As early as 1994, it was pointed out that introducing piecemeal legislation had ended up achieving little in the past and what was needed was a new approach:

> 'Past efforts show that officials will be obstructive and little will be achieved if the new government attempts constitutional reform by introducing piecemeal legislation. This is what happened in Harold Wilson's first government. A Bill was introduced to reform the House of Lords. But, the Commons was divided between those who wanted abolition, those who wanted other changes, or no change, and those who supported the Bill. Eventually the Bill had to be abandoned...To bring about a new constitutional settlement, it is necessary to introduce a new way of law making. Rather than introducing separate laws for each area of change, a new government should set up a non-partisan Constitutional Convention. This would draw up a package of measures which would then be submitted to the people in a referendum.' (*Observer*, 20 November 1994)

5. The proposed reforms are dangerous

Some critics (mainly in the Conservative Party) argue that the proposed reforms are dangerous. A number of reasons are given for this accusation. First, it is alleged that devolution will soon lead to the break-up of the Union and a revival of English nationalism. This, it is suggested, could lead to great hostility and bitterness between the various nations which made up the UK. Second, it is argued that electoral reform will lead to weak, coalition government which will cause instability and uncertainty. Third, some critics argue that reform of the Lords will lead to a dangerous rivalry between the two legislative chambers. And fourth, Eurosceptics are worried that the government will manipulate the referendum on the single currency to ensure that a Yes vote is secured. If that happens, they claim, Britain's sovereignty will be fatally undermined.

6. Some of the reforms are unnecessary

Some critics argue that the plethora of referendums promised by the government is a sign of weakness. It is, they argue, the job of government to govern and it should rely on its electoral mandate, not keep going back to the people for confirmation. In particular, supporters of the single currency argue that the government had no need to promise a (potentially embarrassing) referendum. Rather, the government (as happened when there were calls to hold a referendum on the Maastricht Treaty) should have kept its options open. Other critics (mainly Conservatives) argue that Britain's constitution was working satisfactorily before 1997 and should have been left alone.

Prospects for change

Writing in 1997, Patrick Dunleavy expressed further doubts about whether the Labour government had either the time or the genuine inclination to make fundamental change to the constitution. He pointed out that, in practice, there is a strong incentive for a government to preserve both the two-party system and a flexible, unfixed constitution. The existing system, he argued, gave the following advantages to the two main parties:

- an electoral system which protected Labour and the Conservatives from third-party competition and bolstered the two parties' internal unity
- permanent control of Parliament through the whip systems and the 'usual channels' which guaranteed the government passage of its Bills and allowed the main opposition the scope to debate, criticise and question
- great freedom for the executive (which the opposition could later enjoy in its turn)
- extensive protection from judicial interference or controls
- scope to rearrange the constitution, administrative arrangements, the rights of citizens or the provisions of laws. (Dunleavy 1997, p.130)

Not only did these vested interests provide a great incentive not to push reforms too far, there was also the question of parliamentary time and the rest of the government's programme. Yet, despite all this, by the end of its first 18 months of office, the Labour government had made progress on devolution and the elected mayor and assembly in London. A Commons Select Committee had been set up to examine parliamentary procedures. The Jenkins Commission had produced its recommendations on voting reform for elections to the Commons. The Human Rights Act had received royal assent, ensuring that the European Convention on Human Rights would be incorporated into British Law from 2000. A Bill proposing that hereditary peers lose their voting rights had been announced in the second Queen's Speech. And, the Labour government had invited senior Liberal Democrats to sit on a Cabinet Committee considering constitutional reform (chaired by the Prime Minister). Not only did this suggest that constitutional reform was being taken seriously, it also signalled an inclusive approach and one less likely to make decisions on the basis of the Labour Party's future electoral success. At the end of the 20th century, it seems safe to say, the prospects for substantial constitutional change remained higher than at any point since 1945.

5.3 Should Britain have a written constitution?

A written constitution - arguments against
When people talk of a 'written constitution' what they mean more precisely is a constitution that has been codified (drawn up in a single document). Although part of the British constitution is written (statute law, for example), part is not. Supporters of the current system argue that this is its strength. Since the constitution is not cast in stone, it is able to evolve and develop according to circumstances. It has a flexibility which codified constitutions do not have.

Norton (1988) points out that three main arguments are used against the introduction of a written constitution.

1. A written constitution is unnecessary
The first argument is that a written constitution is unnecessary. Not only is the current system flexible, it has a number of checks and balances built into it. For example, there is a degree of balance between the executive, legislature and judiciary. The executive does not always manage to win the day. Opposition within Parliament or outside pressures sometimes force the government's hand (as, for example, over the poll tax). Also, judgements in the courts may curb government excesses.

2. A written constitution is undesirable
The second main argument is that a written constitution is undesirable. A written constitution would mean that any dispute over the structure and powers of government, the relationship between different parts of government and the relationship between government and citizen would be settled by a court. Power would, therefore, be transferred from the executive (which is an elected body) to the judiciary (which is an unelected body). Also, in its role of interpreting the constitution, the judiciary would have the power to declare laws and actions unconstitutional. In other words, judges would have to make political decisions. Political decisions, supporters of this point of view argue, should be left to politicians.

3. A written constitution is unachievable
The third argument is that a written constitution is unachievable. There are two main reasons for this. First, it would be difficult to gain a consensus about what exactly should be written down in the constitution. And second, under the existing constitution there is no way of introducing a new constitution. Norton explains that:

> 'There is no body that can authorise or legitimise it. An Act of Parliament creating a new constitution or stipulating the procedures for creating one would derive its legitimacy from the doctrine which it sought to destroy. The one thing that Parliament cannot do is use its power under the doctrine of parliamentary sovereignty to destroy that doctrine, because its legitimacy to do so derives from the very power which it seeks to destroy. Hence, to create a new, written constitution we would have to start from scratch, disavow, by some means, our existing constitution. And that would cause constitutional and political turmoil that would not be worth enduring.'

(Norton 1988, pp.12-13)

A written constitution - arguments for

There are four main arguments in support of the idea that Britain should have a written constitution.

1. To protect against arbitrary government

According to Norton, the main argument in favour of a written constitution is that it would keep in check the power of the executive:

> 'The principal argument for change derives from the perception that power in Britain has become too centralised. The old checks and balances identified by Dicey have been eroded, leaving the executive pre-eminent in the political system and able to get enacted, as Acts of Parliament, whatever measures it wants.' (Norton, 1988, p.10)

Those who support a written constitution, therefore, tend to argue that there is a need to limit government in Britain and that codifying the constitution is the best means to achieve this end. A written constitution would describe and entrench:

- the structure and powers of government
- the relationship between different parts of government
- the relationship between government and citizen.

It would, therefore, prevent arbitrary government since any disputes would be solved by (new) constitutional judicial procedures. The argument is similar to that made by Lord Hailsham in 1976 - namely that Britain has, in effect, become an elective dictatorship and the only way to curb the power of the executive is to write down precisely where its powers lie.

2. To protect citizens' rights

Linked to the above argument is the idea that citizens' rights can only be properly protected if they are entrenched in a written constitution. At present, a government with an overall majority can add or remove citizens' rights simply by introducing a Bill and relying on its parliamentary majority to pass it. Take for example the Criminal Justice Act which became law in November 1994 (see also Chapter 18, Section 2.6). This law restricts the right of people to protest and specifically targets minorities such as squatters and hunt saboteurs. Under a written constitution, the government would not be able to introduce legislation targeting minorities in this way or restricting citizens' rights. The only way to do this would be to amend the constitution - which would be a deliberately difficult and lengthy process.

3. To bring the constitution up to date

It was noted above (Section 2.1) that parliamentary sovereignty has been profoundly affected by Britain's membership of the EU. Since parliamentary sovereignty is no longer fully intact, there is, therefore, a need for a new constitutional settlement. In addition, some powers are being devolved to the new assemblies in Northern Ireland, Scotland and Wales and devolution for the English regions is on the agenda. As a result, the constitutional relationship between the centre and the regions will need to be redefined. Again, this would require a new constitutional settlement.

4. To move into line with the rest of the EU

The UK is the only country in the EU without a written constitution. If a written constitution was adopted in the UK, therefore, it would bring the UK into line with its European partners.

Main points - Part 5

- The debate about constitutional reform has only developed since the 1960s and it only reached the mainstream in the late 1980s. This was due to frustration with the political system and a changing political landscape.
- In its 1997 election manifesto, the Labour Party made eight pledges with regards to constitutional reform.
- Critics of Labour's package of reforms have argued that the reforms (1) do not go far enough; (2) are being watered down; (3) lack coherence; (4) will be lost if introduced piecemeal; (5) are dangerous; and (6) are unnecessary.
- Despite doubts about whether the government had either the time or the commitment to make fundamental reforms, the prospects for substantial change remained higher at the end of the 20th century than at any point since 1945.

Activity 4.9 Constitutional reform

Item A Prospects for substantial reform (1)

It is usual for politicians to talk about constitutional reform in an ethical, neutral way and to act in their party's interests. The links established between Labour and the Liberal Democrats in 1997 might decisively alter this pattern and open up the first real possibility of substantial change since 1945. But, the ambitions of a would-be great reform government can all too easily come to grief. There are many pitfalls. Ministers might give in to conservative Whitehall briefings. Constitutional legislation might be squeezed out by more immediate and urgent political concerns. The balance of a party's popularity might change. Good intentions might fade in the face of the natural desire for a government to keep a grip on power for its own protection. Nevertheless, in what looks likely to be a low-key government, constitutional reforms could still provide a grand theme for change.

Adapted from Dunleavy 1997.

Item B *A reformed British constitution*

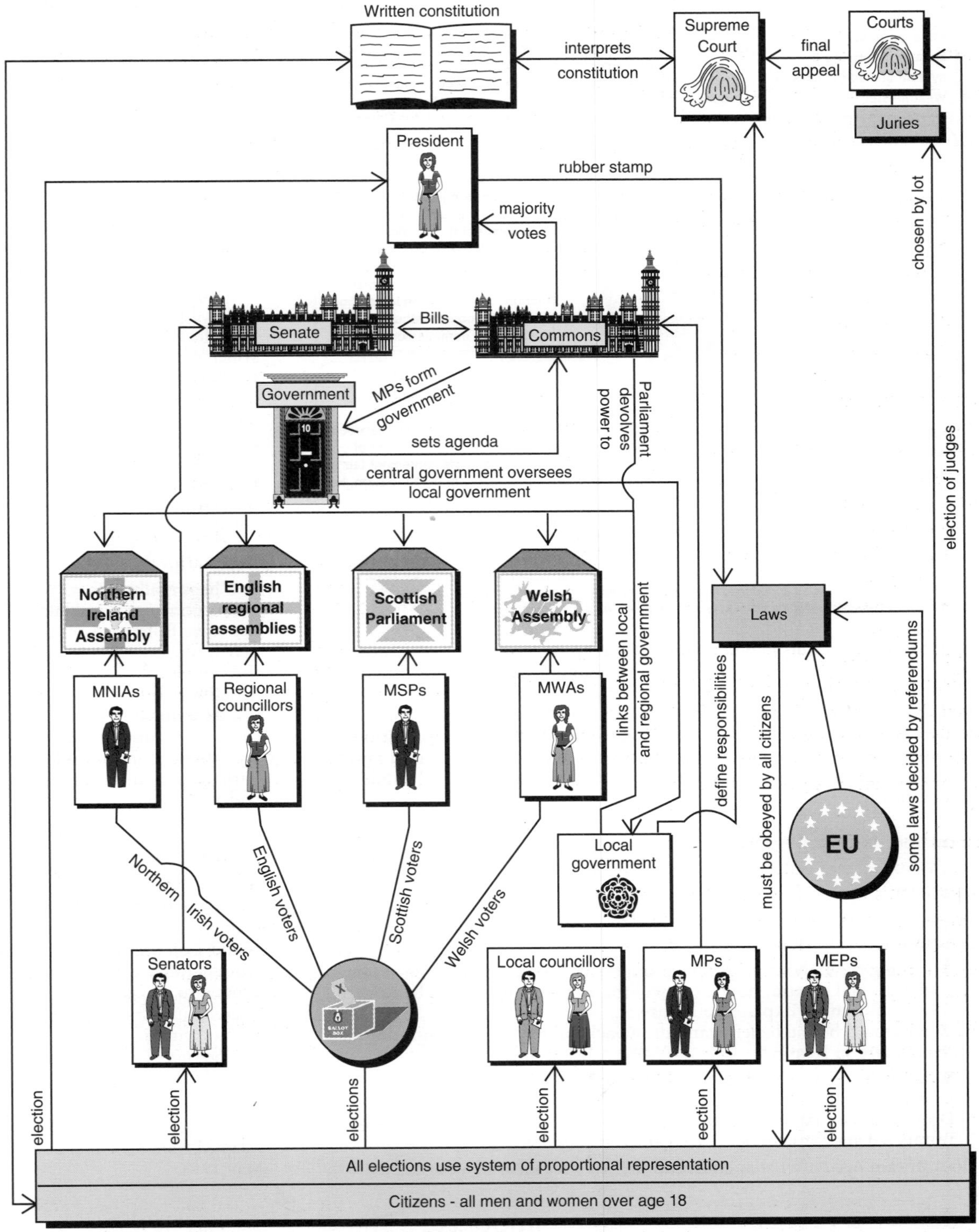

Written constitution

interprets constitution

Supreme Court

final appeal

Courts

Juries

President

rubber stamp

majority votes

Senate

Bills

Commons

Government

MPs form government

sets agenda

devolves power to

Parliament

central government oversees local government

Northern Ireland Assembly

English regional assemblies

Scottish Parliament

Welsh Assembly

Laws

MNIAs

Regional councillors

MSPs

MWAs

links between local and regional government

define responsibilities

must be obeyed by all citizens

chosen by lot

election of judges

some laws decided by referendums

EU

Local government

Northern Irish voters

English voters

Scottish voters

Welsh voters

Senators

Local councillors

MPs

MEPs

election

election

elections

election

eection

election

All elections use system of proportional representation

Citizens - all men and women over age 18

This diagram shows what the British constitution would look like if Charter 88's demands were put into effect.

Item C The Lord Chancellor and constitutional reform

Electoral reform
He is 'unpersuaded' by the case for reforming the system of electing MPs to Westminster.

The House of Lords
He believes in the need for gradual, step-by-step change. The government intends to legislate to remove hereditary peers during this Parliament, but concedes that there could be some delay within that time scale. An elected second chamber is a question for the future and he sees no need to increase the powers of a second chamber in order to check the Commons once hereditary peers have gone.

* Human rights
The government's intention is to incorporate the European Convention on Human Rights into British Law. It intends to adopt the New Zealand model, rather than the Canadian solution. Unlike the Canadian version, the New Zealand model does not allow the courts to strike down Acts of Parliament. Lord Irvine is also cautious about the need for a formal commission to promote human rights cases. He is keen that, even with their enhanced role, judges should be kept out of politics and should continue to be appointed in the same way as they are now.

** Freedom of Information
He envisages legislation during the second parliamentary session. He is aware of the problems, especially those to do with exemptions and how they are to be policed. He prefers enforcement of freedom of information legislation through the courts rather than an independent commission.

Devolution
He is proud of the plans for Scottish devolution, believing that the extensive devolution of powers, the legal framework for resolving disputes between Edinburgh and London and a reduction in the number of Scottish MPs at Westminster, will make the settlement fair to people in England and, therefore, stable in the long term. He does not believe in imposing devolution onto English regions except where there is very clear evidence that it is wanted - and he does not yet see any such evidence.

Lord Irvine

* The European Convention on Human Rights was incorporated into British law in November 1998.
** In September 1998, it was announced that legislation was to be delayed until after the second parliamentary session, whilst the Bill was redrafted. (see Chapter 19, Section 5.4).

The information in this diagram comes from an interview with the Lord Chancellor, Derry Irvine, a key figure in the Labour government's programme of constitutional reform. After the 1997 general election, Irvine was appointed to chair Cabinet committees concerned with devolution, the incorporation of the European Convention on Human Rights and freedom of information. Irvine said that he had no single blueprint for a brand new constitution. He favours change only when the status quo is not working efficiently and democratically.

Adapted from the *Observer*, 27 July 1997

Questions

1. Judging from Items A and D, what likelihood is there of substantial constitutional reform under Labour?

2. a) Assuming the Labour government implements its election promises on constitutional reform, how close will the British constitution be to that shown in Item B? Explain your answer.
   b) What would be the benefits and drawbacks of having a constitution like that shown in Item B?

3. a) What do Items C and D tell us about the thinking behind Labour's proposed constitutional reform?
   b) Do you agree that the proposed constitutional reforms 'will not solve Britain's democratic deficit'? Explain your answer.

4. Does Britain need a written constitution? Give reasons for your answer.

Item D Prospects for substantial reform (2)

Labour's constitutional programme contains a paradox. All the reforms involve dispersing power from the centre. Yet, at the same time, the government is exercising unprecedented central control. The apparent contradiction is easily explained, however. Tony Blair's project is not really the dispersal of power. He believes he can transform society and nothing must stand in his way. New Labour feels justified in stifling dissent because it wants to be the single party which expresses the interests of the nation as a whole. So, party is swallowed up by Leader and country is swallowed up by party, in the national interest. The emphasis on constitutional reform is a way of filling the ideological vacuum left by the collapse of socialism at the end of the Cold War. It suits Blair to sound radical to deflect criticism that he is really a Tory. Yet, the constitutional programme will not solve Britain's democratic deficit. Fragmenting power, through devolution for example, actually increases central control (on the principle of divide and rule). It will do nothing to correct the imbalance of power between Parliament and executive that widened under Thatcher. A Bill of Rights will politicise the judiciary and only judges who are 'on message' will be appointed. Removing the hereditary peers will make the Lords a giant quango. In 1997, Peter Mandelson argued that the age of representative democracy may be coming to an end, giving way to referendums, focus groups, lobbies, citizens' movements and the internet. This is an abdication of leadership. Representative government must not only represent, it must also govern.

Adapted from the *Observer*, 17 May 1998.

References

Aughey (1997) Aughey, A., 'Northern Ireland' in *Dunleavy et al.* (1997).

Birch (1964) Birch, A.H., *Representative and Responsible Government*, Allen & Unwin, 1964.

Bogdanor (1979) Bogdanor, V., *Devolution*, Oxford University Press, 1979.

Bradbury (1998) Bradbury, J., 'Yr ie bychan - the little yes: the 1997 Welsh Assembly referendum', *Politics Review*, Vol.7.4, April 1998.

Conservative (1992) Conservative Party election manifesto, *The Best Future for Britain*, Conservative Central Office, 1992.

Dearlove & Saunders (1991) Dearlove, J. & Saunders, P., *Introduction to British Politics: Analysing a Capitalist Democracy*, Polity Press, 1991.

De Paor (1970) De Paor, L., *Divided Ulster*, Penguin, 1970.

Dicey (1885) Dicey, A.V., *An Introduction to the Study of the Law of the Constitution*, Macmillan, 1959.

Dowdle (1994) Dowdle, J.L., 'The Glomar explorer, the common fisheries policy and the Factortame case', *Talking Politics*, Vol.6.3, Summer 1994.

Downing (1989) Downing, T. (ed), *The Troubles*, Thames Macdonald, 1989.

Driver & Martell (1998) Driver, S. & Martell, L., *New Labour: Politics after Thatcherism*, Polity Press, 1998.

Dunleavy (1997) Dunleavy, P., 'The constitution' in *Dunleavy et al. (1997)*.

Dunleavy & Weir (1998) Dunleavy, P. & Weir, S., 'Home rule for Yorkshire?', *New Statesman Special Supplement*, 26 June 1998.

Dunleavy et al. (1993) Dunleavy, P., Gamble, A., Holliday, I. & Peele, G., *Developments in British Politics 4*, Macmillan, 1993.

Dunleavy et al. (1997) Dunleavy, P., Gamble, A., Holliday, I. & Peele, G., *Developments in British Politics 5*, Macmillan, 1997.

Evans (1997) Evans, M., 'Democracy and constitutionalism in Britain', *Politics Review*, Vol.7.2, November 1997.

Gamble (1993) Gamble, A., 'Territorial Politics' in *Dunleavy et al. (1993)*.

Grant (1994) Grant, M., 'The rule of law - theory and practice', *Talking Politics*, Vol.7.1, Autumn 1994.

Griffith (1985) Griffith, J.A.G., *The Politics of the Judiciary*, Fontana, 1985.

Hailsham (1976) Lord Hailsham, 'Elective dictatorship', the 1976 Dimbleby Lecture reprinted in *The Listener*, 21 October 1976.

HMSO (1993) *Scotland in the Union: a Partnership for Good*, HMSO, Cmnd 2225, 1993.

HMSO (1994) Central Office of Information, *The British System of Government*, HMSO, 1994.

Holliday (1997) Holliday, I., 'Territorial politics' in *Dunleavy et al. (1997)*.

Jowell (1989) Jowell, J., 'The rule of law today' in *Jowell & Oliver (1989)*.

Jowell & Oliver (1989) Jowell, J. & Oliver, D. (eds), *The Changing Constitution*, Clarendon Press, 1989.

Kee (1980) Kee, R., *Ireland: a History*, Abacus, 1980.

Kingdom (1991) Kingdom, J., *Government and Politics in Britain: an Introduction*, Polity Press, 1991.

Labour (1997) Labour Party election manifesto, *New Labour - Because Britain Deserves Better*, Labour Party, 1997.

Lancaster (1997) Lancaster, S., *Developments in Politics*, Vol.8, Causeway Press, 1997.

Leaman (1998) Leaman, A., 'Devolution's coming home', *New Statesman*, 30 January 1998.

Lynch (1996) Lynch, P., 'Labour, devolution and the West Lothian question', *Talking Politics*, Vol.9.1, Autumn 1996.

Lynch (1998) Lynch, P., 'Devolution and a new British political system', *Talking Politics*, Vol.10.2, Winter 1997-8.

McAulsan & McEldowney (1985) McAulsan, P. & McEldowney, J.F. (eds), *Law Legitimacy and the Constitution*, Sweet & Maxwell, 1985.

McCullagh & O'Dowd (1986) 'Northern Ireland: the search for a solution', *Social Studies Review*, March 1986.

Mitchell (1994) Mitchell, J., 'Devolution' in *Wale (1994)*.

Moran (1985) Moran, M., *Politics and Society in Britain. an Introduction*, Macmillan, 1985.

Morgan (1998) Morgan, K., 'Let's get regionalism right this time', *New Statesman Special Supplement*, 26 June 1998.

Norton (1982) Norton, P., *The Constitution in Flux*, Martin Robertson, 1982.

Norton (1988) Norton, P, 'Should Britain have a written constitution?', *Talking Politics*, Vol.1.1, Autumn 1988.

Norton (1989) Norton, P., 'The changing constitution - part 2', *Contemporary Record*, Vol.3.2, November 1989.

Norton (1992) Norton, P, 'The Constitution' in *Wale (1992)*.

Norton (1994) Norton, P., 'The constitution in question', *Politics Review*, Vol.3.4, April 1994.

Norton (1994a) Norton, P., 'Europe and the constitution', *Talking Politics*, Vol.6.3, Summer 1994.

O'Brien & O'Brien (1985) O'Brien, M. & O'Brien, C.C., *Ireland: a Concise History*, Thames and Hudson, 1985.

Rush (1997) Rush, M., 'Thinking about the constitution' in *Lancaster (1997)*.

SCC (1989) Scottish Constitutional Convention, *Towards a Scottish Parliament*, Scottish Constitutional Convention, 1989.

Sell (1998) Sell, G., 'Scottish nationalism in the 1990s', *Talking Politics*, Vol.10.3, Spring 1998.

Silk (1989) Silk, P., *How Parliament Works*, Longman, 1989.

Simpson (1998) Simpson, D., *UK Government and Politics in Context*, Hodder & Stoughton, 1998.

Street & Brazier (1981) Street, H. & Brazier R.(eds), *Constitutional and Administrative Law*, Penguin, 1981.

Wale (1992) Wale, W. (ed), *Developments in Politics*, Vol.3, Causeway Press, 1992.

Wale (1994) Wale, W. (ed), *Developments in Politics*, Vol.5, Causeway Press, 1994.

5 The social context

Introduction

Politics in the United Kingdom does not function in a vacuum. It operates in a context which is the product of historical, geographical, social and economic factors. There is, in other words, a distinct political culture. This political culture is passed on from generation to generation, but it is not static. The political culture changes as society changes.

Since 1945, British society has changed in many important ways. Take class, gender and ethnicity for example. Not only have there been objective changes since the 1940s (for example, it is now illegal to pay a woman less than a man for the same work), attitudes have changed, too. People in public positions now talk the language of equal opportunities, even if their actions do not always live up to their rhetoric. As a result, the contemporary way of life is very different from that which existed after the Second World War. This chapter examines these social changes.

Social changes are closely intertwined with economic changes. Since 1945, Britain's industrial base has changed dramatically. Whilst the old manufacturing industries have declined, service industries and new industries have grown up. The growth of service industries and new industries has meant that old ways of work are no longer appropriate. In particular, the role of trade unions has been challenged and reappraised. This chapter considers how economic change has affected the way in which people live their lives and it assesses the developing role of the trade unions.

Chapter summary

Part 1 defines and examines the key political terms 'political socialisation' and 'political culture'.

Part 2 considers the importance of class, gender and ethnicity. To what extent do these social factors determine the nature of British political culture?

Part 3 describes the social impact of economic change since 1945. The impact of de-industrialisation and the changing role of trade unions are analysed.

Part 1 What is the 'social context'?

Key issues

1. What is 'political socialisation' and how does it take place?
2. What do we mean by 'political culture'?
3. Is there cultural diversity or uniformity?

1.1 Political socialisation

What is 'socialisation'?

The term 'socialisation' refers to the way in which people, through interaction with members of their family and other social groups, learn how to become members of society. Political socialisation is the process by which people acquire their attitude towards politics. People are not born with political dispositions. They have to acquire them as children and then as adults. Two models have been developed to explain the process of political socialisation - the primacy and recency models.

The primacy model

Some studies of political socialisation focus on childhood on the grounds that this is a time when people are particularly susceptible to the influence of others. This emphasis on childhood has been described as the 'primacy model'. Research has found that children acquire political attitudes quite early on in their lives, mainly from their parents. There is, for example, some continuity of voting patterns between parents and children (see, for example, Butler & Stokes 1971). Research suggests that by the age of 10 or 11 children have acquired party loyalties, a sense of national identity and a rudimentary knowledge of their country's main political institutions.

The recency model

Other studies have suggested that political socialisation is a lifelong process. This idea has been described as the 'recency model'. According to this model:

'Socialisation experiences have a greater impact the closer in time they are to the political context.' (Kavanagh 1983, p.45) So, experiences in adulthood are likely to be more important than childhood experiences because they are closer in time to the occasion when an adult performs a political action. The recency model also draws attention to 'zeitgeist effects' - the impact of personalities, issues and events associated with certain periods in adults' lives. For example, the 1960s is often seen as a period which affected a whole generation.

Agencies of socialisation

According to Rush (1992) the main agencies of political socialisation are the family, peer groups, the Church, the education system, the mass media and political parties. Only political parties within this list are overtly and consciously intent on political socialisation as a main aim. The other items on the list can be defined as agencies of political socialisation for the following reasons.

The family

The family is a small, intimate group that, in the early years, has a near monopoly of a child's cognitive, emotional and physical development. Through socialisation, the child learns attitudes, values and ways of looking at the world. Also, the family is located within the class and social structure of this country and this influences the life of the child in profound ways. The family can be seen as a power structure in miniature. Families can operate in authoritarian or democratic styles and, in so doing, can influence the way in which children think.

Peer groups

Peer groups are people who associate with each other on the basis of equal status. Children's peers are usually thought to have a particular significance. Friendship groups and work groups, however, are important throughout people's lives. Peer groups act as reference points for individuals and in so doing influence the attitudes and behaviour of individuals.

The Church

As Britain has become increasingly secular, the influence of the Church has declined. Nevertheless, the Church (or synagogue, or mosque) is still afforded a special place in social and political life and it does seek to influence the attitudes and behaviour of people. In the past, the Church of England was described as 'the Tory Party at prayer'. But, in the 1980s and 1990s, leading figures in the Church were highly critical of the Conservative government and provided an alternative vision of society. Under Labour, the Church has continued to lobby and push for its views and values to be adopted.

The education system

The education system provides a place in school for all children aged five to 16. So, for around 15,000 hours in a child's life, the education system is responsible for that child's development. Ironically, little (and in some schools none) of that time is spent learning about contemporary politics. Yet, schools play an important part in political socialisation since children learn how to survive in a hierarchical, bureaucratic organisation which provides a framework for the bulk of their waking lives.

The mass media

Finally, the mass media provides a view of the world beyond an individual's immediate experience. Newspapers, radio, film and television reach millions of people and they undoubtedly make some impact on people's attitudes and behaviour. Precisely what impact they make is the subject of debate. This is discussed more fully in Chapter 19.

Imitation, instruction and motivation

Political scientists argue that socialisation takes place through imitation, instruction and motivation. According to Rush these terms can be defined as follows:

> '[Imitation is] the copying of the behaviour of other individuals or groups of individuals and is generally most important in childhood... [Instruction is] the more or less intended learning of appropriate behaviour through formal education and less formally through discussion groups and other activities such as vocational training...[Motivation is] the learning of appropriate behaviour by experience, by a process of trial and error.' (Rush 1992, p.104)

Political socialisation - problems

The very concept of political socialisation is problematic. One difficulty is that no satisfactory way has been devised to find out how far early experiences in a child's life compare with later experiences as an adult when it comes to determining political behaviour. Behaviour is not just determined by socialisation alone. Personal and situational factors operating at the time affect how an individual responds to events. A second difficulty is that no satisfactory way has been devised to judge the effects of socialisation, particularly when much socialisation is not overt but is simply part of a pattern of everyday assumptions. Even when socialisation is overt, individuals can appear not to respond to the process. In other words, it is necessary to devise a sophisticated model of political socialisation or there is a danger of ending up with an 'over-socialised' view which simply regards people as puppets waiting to be manipulated.

1.2 Political culture

Definition

'Political culture' is a difficult term to define. According to Kavanagh it is:

'A shorthand expression to denote the set of values within which the political system operates.' (Kavanagh 1983, p.49)

This set of values is the product of historical, geographical, social and economic factors. Since these factors change over time, political culture is not static. It changes as society changes.

Since the values within which the political system operates vary from country to country, each country has its own political culture. For example, not only does the USA's political system differ from the British system institutionally, it also differs culturally. American citizens have different expectations of their government from British citizens. They expect their politicians to behave in ways which would seem alien to British citizens. In other words, a different set of values pervades political life in the USA and it is this different set of values which distinguishes it culturally from political life in Britain.

Subcultures

Of course, not all citizens can be expected to accept the same set of values and so, within a single country, it is possible for different political cultures to co-exist. Take, for example, attitudes towards the settlement of political disputes by the use of violence. The vast majority of British people oppose the use of violence to settle disputes, but a small minority disagree with (dissent from) this view. In some cases, a dissenting minority whose members share similar values may be said to belong to a subculture. When people talk of 'the political culture', what they usually mean, more precisely, is the **dominant** political culture.

The Marxist view

Marxists such as Miliband (1972) have argued that the ruling class, which has economic and political power, has developed a strong degree of control over British society. The ruling class has successfully promoted a dominant value system which endorses the status quo and, therefore, consolidates the position of the rich and powerful. This promotion of dominant values takes place through institutions such as the education system, the mass media and the main political parties. So, while consensus might be a feature of political life, it is a consensus imposed by the ruling class to facilitate its interests. But, while the ruling class might appear to be successful in imposing its view of the world, there is always the potential for the working class to resist and for class conflict to break out.

The civic culture

In their seminal study of political culture in five different countries, Almond & Verba (1963) classified differences in political involvement and awareness and found three broad types of political culture:

- **parochial** cultures where people only had a limited awareness of government and did not feel affected by its policies
- **subject** cultures where individuals knewabout their government and might even express strong support for it, but did not expect to have any influence over it
- **participant** cultures where people knew about their government and expected to act in ways which influenced it.

Definition of a civic culture

Almond & Verba argued that Britain was a prime example of a fourth type of political culture - a **civic culture**. A civic culture is a hybrid which mixes elements of a subject culture with elements of a participant culture. It is, they argued, because it is a hybrid that it is the most appropriate culture for a stable democracy. According to Kavanagh, a civic culture can be defined as follows:

'It is a mixed culture in which the subject orientations allow the élites the initiative to and freedom to take decisions, while the participant orientations make the élites sensitive to popular preferences.' (Kavanagh 1983, p.60)

So, in a country with a civic culture, ordinary citizens (the 'subjects') allow decision makers (the 'élites') the freedom to make any decisions they feel appropriate so long as these decisions take into account public opinion.

Deference

Central to this view of British political culture is the notion of 'deference' (accepting that others are superior and that their lead should be followed). As early as 1867, the writer Walter Bagehot argued that a key characteristic of British people was their tendency to defer to those in authority. It was this, he argued, which explained why, on the whole, the British people were law-abiding and there was little support for radical change. Almond & Verba agreed with Bagehot's view and incorporated it into their civic culture ('civility') model, arguing that the British people have a tendency to accept decisions made by those in authority (ie they are deferential) and this tendency has resulted in peace and stability. As Moran points out, this deference component in the civility model can take three forms:

'It may assert that the British defer to the high born, defer to all figures in public authority or defer to social and economic hierarchies.' (Moran 1989, p.36)

Criticism of Almond and Verba's model

Almond & Verba's view of political culture in the UK

has been criticised for its emphasis on consensus and homogeneity (uniformity) where none exists. Critics have argued that the idea that the UK is or ever has been homogenous is simplistic. Pimlott (1989) points out, for example, that even during the period of so-called 'post-war consensus' between 1945 and 1979 (see Chapter 3, Section 1.2), there was considerable political conflict. The revival of nationalism in Scotland and Wales in the 1970s and the 'Troubles' in Northern Ireland, for example, indicated that there were important regional variations in political culture. Writing just after this period in 1981, Kavanagh argued that Almond & Verba's civic culture was in decline:

'There is no great confidence in the political institutions, though there is also no desire for radical changes...[There is] more dissatisfaction with the specific performance of government than the system as a whole. The recent years of slow economic growth have led to greater social tensions, group rivalries and growing dissatisfaction with the incumbent authorities...What does seem clear is that the traditional bonds of social class, party and common nationality are waning and with them the restraints of hierarchy and deference.'
(Kavanagh 1981, p.73)

Since 1981, there is evidence that dissatisfaction with government and politicians has grown (see Item C in Activity 5.1, for example) and that the traditional bonds of class, party and nationality have broken down further (see Chapter 9, Parts 1 and 2). Also, lower turnouts at general elections in the 1990s and support for fundamental constitutional reform (as indicated by the 1997 referendum supporting Scottish devolution, for example) suggest that dissatisfaction with the system and not just with the specific performance of government has developed since 1981.

A cultural revolution?

During the 1980s, the Thatcher governments set out to alter fundamentally the political culture. The dominant political culture of the 1970s was regarded as a reason for Britain's poor economic performance and the Thatcher governments aimed to create a new culture of self-reliance, enterprise and market values. There is little evidence, however, to suggest that the Thatcher governments achieved this aim. In reviewing the eighth *British Social Attitudes Survey*, published in 1991 and covering the Thatcher years, the *Guardian* commented:

'Its consistent conclusion is not how much of a mark but how little Mrs Thatcher's radicalism has left on British society. The people's devotion to state provision of welfare, especially the NHS, survives undiminished. The preference for maintaining public spending rather than cutting taxes has grown. And, as Mrs Thatcher's government in its search for growth and for tax incentives

widened the gap between rich and poor, support has swelled for redistribution of wealth to help the have-nots.' (*Guardian*, 20 November 1991)

This view was confirmed by the fourteenth *British Social Attitudes Survey*, subtitled *The end of Conservative Values*, published in 1997. Reviewing the whole 18 years of Conservative rule from 1979 to 1997, it claimed that the period had failed to produce the revolution in the nation's political attitudes that the Thatcherites had hoped for. The *Guardian* summarised the report as follows:

'People remained attached to state provision in health. Those who bought their own homes did not, as the Conservatives hoped, take on Tory allegiances too. They continued to doubt the much advertised benefits of a flexible jobs market. Attitudes hardened on welfare and people liked the tougher line on law and order, but they also increasingly backed the cases for sweeping constitutional change which both Mrs Thatcher and John Major fiercely opposed.' (*Guardian*, 19 November 1997)

By continuing with certain Conservative policies (dictated in part by the acceptance of Conservative spending plans for the first two years of office), the Labour government elected in 1997 runs the risk of finding itself out of step with key aspects of the nation's political values.

Cultural diversity

Research also suggests that there is now a fragmentation in society and a cultural diversity which pervades all aspects of social and political life (see, for example, Taylor 1997). This diversity has developed as traditional class divisions have changed and new important divisions in society based on gender, race and region have emerged. John Gray argues that a new political culture is emerging:

'The Britain that has been disclosed by Diana's death is not new. It produced the electoral landslide of 1 May. But, it has not yet been fully mapped. It is hugely at variance with the picture of a culture that is rooted in the past. It is not a country that reveres traditional values. Still less does it defer to any authority which seeks to impose them.' (*Guardian*, 3 November 1997)

Others have argued that people's behaviour after Princess Diana's death meant that the authority of tradition has been 'blown away' and the social hierarchies and class structures of the past have gone (for example, Barnett 1997, p.88). According to this view, the UK has become more inclusive, more expressive and more emotional.

Cool Britannia

Another example of a conscious attempt to create a new culture for Britain came with the notion of 'Cool

Britannia'. The phrase was coined in 1967 by the Bonzo Dog Doo Dah Band (they recorded a satirical version of 'Rule Britannia') and was revived in the spring of 1996 when Ben & Jerry chose it to name a new flavour of ice cream:

> 'Then the madness started...Cool Britannia as a headline, as a fashion-page phrase, as a usefully flexible pun for articles about anything modern and British...Then the sub-editors' little secret became an editors' craze, a magazine cover concept, a commonplace on News at Ten... By 1997, Cool Britannia meant rock bands and restaurants, football managers and fashion designers, Union Jacks on everything; by the beginning of this year, it was the short-hand for the government's entire arts policy; this spring it has virtually become short-hand for the government itself.' (*Guardian*, 5 May 1998)

Rebranding Britain

The phrase was popular because it fitted with the idea that Britain needed to be 'rebranded' - an idea fuelled by a pamphlet produced by the think tank Demos in 1997 in which the author, Mark Leonard, claimed that:

> 'A gulf has opened up between the reality of Britain as a highly creative and diverse society and the perception around the world that Britain remains a backward looking island immersed in its own heritage.' (Demos 1997)

This idea was taken up by the Labour leadership (not least because they could claim with some justification to have rebranded the Labour Party) and, for some months after the 1997 general election, there was a conscious attempt to promote Cool Britannia:

> 'Within weeks of taking office, the government renamed the deliberately fusty-sounding Department of National Heritage as the dynamic sounding Department of Culture, Media and Sport. "Cool Britannia is here to stay", wrote Chris Smith, the ministry's new controller.' (*Guardian*, 5 May 1998)

There was also a concerted effort to promote links between the popular culture and government - with rock stars being invited for drinks with the Prime Minister, for example, and Arts Minister Mark Fisher making an appearance at the Glastonbury Festival.

Criticisms

By spring 1998, however, the relationship between the government and the creative world had deteriorated as the government introduced policies which disappointed its supporters (notably lack of financial support for the arts and more restrictive rules for benefit claimants). The most damning attack came from comedian Ben Elton:

> 'To me, the most gruesome aspect of the current Cool Britannia thing is the way that politicians are trying to latch onto it. I don't mind Radio 1 trying to be trendy, but I can do without the Labour Party wanting to strut its funky stuff. I did not vote Labour because they've heard of Oasis and nobody is going to vote Tory because William Hague has a baseball cap. It's sad, it really is. Leaders should never, ever try to look cool - that's for dictators.' (*Radio Times*, 18-24 April 1998)

Tony Blair hit back at his critics, however, by claiming that Cool Britannia was not about trendiness and style, but about jobs, investment and industry. As the *Guardian* (20 April 1998) pointed out, the debate exposed the dangers of seeking to define Britishness.

Main points - Part 1

- Two models are used to explain 'socialisation' (the way in which people learn how to become members of society). The primacy model focuses on childhood experiences. The recency model focuses on adult experiences.
- The main agencies of socialisation are the family, peer groups, the Church, the education system, the mass media and political parties. It is difficult to measure the impact of each, however, and difficult to judge the effects of socialisation.
- The term 'political culture' is a shorthand way of describing the dominant set of values within which a society operates. Political culture can change according to place and time.
- The idea that Britain has a 'civic culture' (where ordinary citizens allow decision makers to make any decisions they think appropriate so long as public opinion is taken into account) has been criticised for exaggerating consensus and uniformity.
- The Thatcherites' attempt to fundamentally alter British culture failed. There is evidence, however, of greater cultural diversity and fragmentation.

Activity 5.1 Political socialisation and political culture

Item A *Political socialisation*

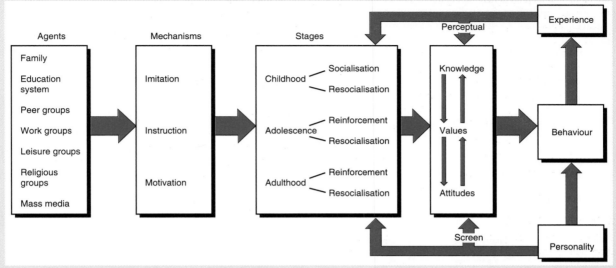

Adapted from Rush 1992.

Item B *The Floral Revolution*

One of the great puzzles of public life until 1997 was the extraordinary gulf between the institutions of government - Westminster, Whitehall, Buckingham Palace, the judiciary - and the culture of most people. Government institutions were dominated by the Great and the Good, by tradition, suits, solemnity, emotionless behaviour, protocol, formality, deference and hypocrisy. In contrast, from the 1960s onwards, the culture of the people came to embrace a different set of values - feelings, honesty, informality, humour, meritocracy, the personal, the admission of weakness and vulnerability, the casual and the female. There were many representatives of the people's culture in entertainment and television, in business and in sport. But, until Tony Blair, it is impossible to think of a major public figure in politics or royalty who embraced the new culture - with one remarkable exception, Diana. Diana redefined the nation, enfranchising groups that had previously felt disenfranchised. The Floral Revolution is a new kind of revolution. There are more traditional components - the defeat of the old Establishment, the demise of the old-style Royal family, possibly even the end of the monarchy. But, above all, the Floral Revolution heralds the victory of the new culture over the old, the legitimacy and authority of the self, the embrace of new social groups, the support for diversity. Diana, in redefining a nation, redefined each and every one of us.

Adapted from the *Observer*, 7 September 1997

Item C *Who do the British people trust?*

Table (i)

Do you trust...	1987	1991	1994	1996
British police not to bend the rules in trying to get a conviction?	52	49	47	51
judges to stand up to a government which wishes them to reach a particular verdict?	n/a	n/a	n/a	48
local councillors of any party to place the needs of their area above the interests of their party?	31	25	31	28
top civil servants to stand firm against a minister who wants to provide false information to Parliament?	46	n/a	27	28
politicians of any party in Britain to tell the truth when they are in a tight corner?	n/a	n/a	9	9

Table (ii) Do you trust the following?

Group	1983	1993	Change
Teachers	79	84	+5
Doctors	82	84	+2
Clergy	85	80	-5
Newsreaders	63	72	+9
Judges	77	68	-9
Ordinary people	57	64	+7
The police	61	63	+2
Civil servants	25	37	+12
Trade union officials	18	32	+14
Business leaders	25	32	+7
Politicians generally	18	14	-4
Government ministers	16	11	-5
Journalists	19	10	-9

All figures are percentages.

Table (i) is based on information which appeared in the 14th *British Social Attitudes Survey*, published in 1997. It shows the percentage of respondents who agreed that each category could be trusted 'just about always' or 'most of the time'. Table (ii) shows the results of a survey carried out by MORI in 1993. Respondents were asked whether or not they trusted each of the different types of people in the list to tell the truth.

Item D   A shifting revolution

The old Establishment was caught on the hop. There was no trickle-down effect in the grief for Diana. Rather this was a movement from the bottom up that did not so much proclaim the birth of a new order as illustrate how unconcerned we were with the old one. What I am suggesting is that a culture can shift. A mood can change. New forms can emerge and yet many old structures can stay in place. The mistake is to presume that cultural shifts are somehow less 'real' or less 'meaningful' than the traditional manifestations of political power. The strength of the dominant culture is precarious because it rests on assumptions about the way we live which are no longer tenable. The people on the streets felt at home, at ease and that they belonged together. They did not need an official sanctioning and those whose job it is to give it may well feel redundant. Something that was perceived as only going on at the edge has moved inwards and the centre cannot hold because it suddenly appears as one little sub-culture jostling alongside the others for our attentions.

Adapted from the *Independent*, 19 September 1997.

Item E   Branding Britain

SMELL	
Under 25s	*Over 55s*
Pollution/fumes	Fresh and green
Carbon monoxide	Flowers/roses/garden
Rubbish	Bakery bread
Dirty smell	The seasons
Stuffy/stale room	Hot days
Takeaways	Fish and chips
Ethnic food	Pollution

TOUCH	
Under 25s	*Over 55s*
Concrete	Wool/tweed
Grit	Velvet
Cement	Cotton
Hard	Warm/soft
Steel	Wet grass
Paving stones	Picking apples
Rough	Tender

HEARING	
Under 25s	*Over 55s*
Noisy busy	Big Ben
Music and dancing	Classical music
Non-stop 24 hours	Brass bands
Trends	Silence
Shouting	Peaceful
Traffic	Birdsong
Cars/planes/trains	Chit chat

TASTE	
Under 25s	*Over 55s*
Fish and chips/fries	Fish and chips
Roasts/beef/lamb	Roast beef
Egg and bacon	Sausage and mash
Sausage and mash	Home cooking
Cabbage/bland	Mint sauce
Takeaways	Yeast

The tables (above and left) show the results of research commissioned by Renegade, a new advertising agency, in 1997. Adopting American neuro-linguistic programming techniques, the agency hoped to offer an insight into the 'collective subconscious of Britain'. In a series of nationwide interviews, members of the public were asked to describe Britain in terms of smell, touch and hearing. The left-hand column shows the response of people aged under 25. The right-hand column shows the response of people aged over 55. The lists show the seven most popular responses.

Questions

1. a) Using Item A, make a list of people, groups and institutions that have helped to shape your attitudes towards politics.
   b) Put the items on the list in order of priority.
   c) Why is it difficult to produce an adequate model of political socialisation?

2. a) What do Items B and D tell us about British political culture in the late 1990s?
   b) Explain why political culture is a difficult term to define.

3. Using Items B-D, give arguments for and against the view that Almond and Verba's civic culture model is an adequate explanation of political culture in Britain at the end of the 20th century.

4. Look at Item E.
   a) What does it tell us about Britain's political culture?
   b) In what ways does it support the notion of cultural diversity by age?

Part 2 Social factors

Key issues

1. How important is class as a means of analysing British society?
2. To what extent do gender and ethnicity determine the position and role of people living in Britain?
3. How has British society changed since 1945?

2.1 Social class

The importance of class

According to Pulzer who wrote an analysis of British politics in the 1960s:

'Class is the basis of British party politics; all else is embellishment and detail.' (Pulzer 1967, p.98)

Today, most British people are aware of social class. If they were asked, most people would be willing to locate themselves within the class structure. Yet, in the early 1990s, John Major frequently asserted that Britain was becoming:

'A genuinely classless society in which people can rise to whatever level that their own abilities and their own good fortune may take them from wherever they started.' (comment made by John Major at a press conference held on 20 November 1990)

John Major's assertion raises important questions such as:

- to what extent does Britain remain a class-based society?
- does class still determine behaviour and attitudes?
- is class still the driving force behind British politics?

Before it is possible to answer these questions, however, it is necessary to understand what exactly is meant by the term 'social class'.

Definitions of class

One of the difficulties with determining the importance of social class is that class is defined in many different ways. Income, wealth, education, accent, dress, work, lifestyle, and housing may all be taken into account when discussing class. Most definitions of social class, though, are economic in origin and are derived from the work of the political philosopher Karl Marx.

Marx and class

Writing in the 19th century, Marx defined social class in terms of economic relationships. He argued that in a capitalist society there are two main social classes:

- the **capitalist class** (or bourgeoisie)
- the **working class** (or proletariat).

The capitalist class is a relatively small group made up of those who own and control land and businesses. They are the 'capitalists' because they have capital (money) to invest. The working class, on the other hand, is a large group - the majority of the population - made up of people who only have their labour to sell. Members of the working class hire out their labour in return for wages.

Class conflict

Marx claimed that, in a capitalist society, the capitalist class derives its wealth and income from the exploitation of the working class. In a factory, for example, it is the workers who produce wealth by actually making the manufactured goods. But, much of the wealth created by the workers is taken away by the owners in the form of profits (the capitalist class is a non-producing class - it does not actually produce anything). Marx argued that, since the workers receive scant reward for their labour, they are being exploited. Over time, he said, this exploitation was bound to alienate the working class and bring the workers into conflict with the capitalists. In short, it was inevitable that a struggle between the classes would arise with the workers struggling to improve their pay and conditions whilst the capitalists struggled to maintain and improve the size of their profits.

Class and power

Marx also pointed out that, in a capitalist society, the capitalist class is able to control the state in accordance with its broad overall interests. The capitalist class is, therefore, also the ruling class. Those in power in a capitalist society inevitably protect the interests of the capitalists rather than the workers. Although Marx recognised that there was an intermediate stratum (the 'middle class' as it could be called today), he regarded this group as a temporary phenomenon.

Weber's definition

Most subsequent definitions of social class have taken issue with the model proposed by Marx. The German sociologist Max Weber, for example, argued that Marx's division of society into two classes was too simple. Although Weber agreed with Marx that class should be seen in economic terms and that the major class division is between those who own land and businesses and those who do not, he argued that other factors such as differing skills should be taken into account.

As a result, Weber's model of social class includes four categories:

- the propertied upper class
- propertyless white collar workers (managers, administrators and professionals)
- the petit bourgeoisie (small property owners)
- the manual working class (which is divided into two groups - skilled workers and unskilled workers - the division reflecting the fact that skilled workers tend to be paid more than unskilled workers).

Weber also introduced the notion of an expanding

middle class. He argued that, by developing skills, it is possible for unskilled manual workers or (more often) their children to change class.

The Registrar General's classification

Weber's distinction between skilled and unskilled workers has been taken further in the Registrar General's occupational definition of social class, the definition normally used in government reports and surveys. The Registrar General divides the British population into five classes according to occupation. These five classes are described in Box 5.1.

Box 5.1 The Registrar General's definition of class

Class 1
Professional — Accountant, doctor, dentist, solicitor, university lecturer.

Class 2
Managerial and technical — Manager, teacher, librarian, farmer.

Class 3 (Non-manual)
Clerical and minor supervisory — Clerk, shop assistant, police officer, sales representative.

Class 3 (Manual)
Skilled manual — Electrician, tailor, bus driver, printer, cook.

Class 4
Semi-skilled manual — Agricultural worker, postal worker telephone operator, builder.

Class 5
Unskilled manual — Labourer, window cleaner, office cleaner.

It is important to note that the Registrar General does not just take economic rewards into account when deciding which occupation fits into which class. The prestige of an occupation is also taken into account. This explains why, for example, a relatively low paying occupation such as university lecturer is included in Class 1.

Changes for the 2001 Census

Criticism of the Registrar General's classification has led to a modified scale for the Census in 2001. The scale has been expanded to eight classes and will be based on employment status (whether employers, self-employed or employees) and the nature of employment conditions (ranging from secure, salaried employment with promotion prospects and autonomy - complete freedom of action - to people who have never worked and the long-term unemployed).

The eight classes are described in Box 5.2

The IPA's definition

One further definition of class should be described since it is commonly used by the media. This is the division of society into six classes by the Institute of Practitioners in Advertising (IPA). Advertisers use the sixfold division to work out where to place an advert and which groups to

Box 5.2 Changes to the Registrar General's classification

Class 1 Higher managerial and professional occupations
    1.1 Employers in large organisations (eg corporate managers)
    1.2 Higher professionals (eg doctors or barristers).

Class 2 Lower managerial and professional occupations (eg journalists, actors, nurses).

Class 3 Intermediate occupations (eg secretary, driving instructor).

Class 4 Small employers and own account workers (eg publican, taxi driver).

Class 5 Lower supervisory, craft and related occupations (eg pumber, butcher, train driver).

Class 6 Semi-routine occupations (eg shop assistant, traffic warden).

Class 7 Routine occupations (eg waiter, road sweeper).

Class 8 Never worked/long-term unemployed

target when selling a particular product. The IPA's definition has been adopted by political commentators not least because political parties have to 'sell' their image and polices in much the same way that a company has to sell its brand name and products. The six classes are defined in Box 5.3.

Box 5.3 The IPA's definition of class

Class A Higher managerial, administrative or professional
Class B Intermediate managerial, administrative, or professional
Class C1 Supervisory or clerical, and junior managerial, administrative or professional
Class C2 Skilled manual workers
Class D Semi-skilled and unskilled manual workers
Class E State pensioners or widows (no other earnings), casual or lowest grade workers, or long-term unemployed.

Concluding remarks

It should be clear from the different ways of defining class described above that different researchers use different criteria when undertaking their research. This means that it is important to be clear exactly what criteria have been used because the results of two studies using two different sets of criteria are not strictly comparable.

Class and politics in Britain

The class structure 1945 to c.1970

For the first 25 years after the Second World War, most political commentators agreed that social class was the driving force behind British politics. Studies were conducted to show that people voted on a class basis (see Chapter 9, section 1.1). The two-party system was seen as a reflection of the British class system - the Conservative Party represented the capitalist class whilst the Labour Party represented the working class. This attitude was summed up by Butler & Stokes in 1971:

'Our findings on the strength of links between class and partisanship in Britain echo broadly those of every other opinion poll or voting study...the pre-eminent role [of class] can hardly be questioned.' (Butler & Stokes 1971, p.102)

This conclusion was also supported by those who wrote from a Marxist perspective. For example, Westergaard & Resler argued that voting Labour was:

'The outcome of a general sense of class identity: of common interests to be protected or advanced. Asked why they vote as they do, manual working-class Labour supporters usually refer to the fact that the party is - or is supposed to be - the party of the working class.' (Westergaard & Resler 1976, p.364)

Similarly, Miliband claimed that the Conservative Party's function was:

'To aggregate the different interests of the dominant class.' (Miliband 1972, p.187)

The class structure has changed since c.1970

More recently, however, the claim has been made that the class structure has changed fundamentally. Saunders (1990), for example, notes that social mobility between the classes has increased and divisions between the classes are more fluid. Inequalities in income and wealth, he claims, are less marked than used to be the case and there has been a major expansion of middle-class occupations. He describes the spread of share ownership and house ownership and the growing consumption of consumer durables. Ownership and control of industry, he argues, are no longer in the hands of a capitalist class, but in the hands of millions of shareholders and professional managers. The upper class no longer has the power and privileges that it once had. Traditional working-class communities have disappeared as heavy industries such as shipbuilding and mining have declined. New industries have developed without the traditional lines of demarcation between the classes. Bonnett (1994) pursues this theme and claims that Britain's industrial structure has changed dramatically. There has been a shift away from the mass production of standardised products to flexible specialisation in production and products. There has also been a shift away from the old centres of capitalism (in Europe) to a new, global system of capitalism. One result of these changes is a decline of class-based politics and institutions.

The impact of class dealignment

The decline in class-based politics and institutions, it is claimed, is reflected in changing voting patterns (see Chapter 9, Section 1.1). Proportionally fewer working-class people voted Labour in the early 1990s than used to be the case in the 1950s and a growing number of the middle classes began to vote for third parties rather than for the Conservative Party. This, it is argued, forced the political parties to change their image. Labour has worked hard to rid itself of its 'cloth cap' image whilst the 'hunting, shooting and fishing' image of the Conservative leadership has been replaced by claims of classlessness. All the parties now claim to represent the national interest rather than a particular section of society. Some commentators even argue that political behaviour can be better explained by reference to new social movements - such as feminism or environmentalism - rather than to class.

Classlessness

It is in the context described above that John Major began to argue that Britain was becoming a classless society in which everybody would have opportunities to fulfil their ambitions, regardless of their class background. Adonis & Pollard point out that this view of classlessness did not mean that class differences would entirely disappear:

'The classless society is not a society without classes, but the age-old goal of a meritocratic society providing means for people to advance by ability regardless of class origins.' (Adonis & Pollard 1997, p.15)

They go on to assert that:

'The use of the term "classless society" has insidious effects. Not only does it beg the existence of the classes it has linguistically abolished: it helps foster the fallacy, now deeply rooted in Britain, that the single test of a healthy society lies in the existence of ladders for those with ambition and ability but low class background.' (Adonis & Pollard 1997, p.15)

New Labour and classlessness

In fact, Major's view is not far from that expressed by Tony Blair when he was Leader of the Labour opposition:

'Our task is to allow more people to become middle class. The Labour Party did not come into being to celebrate working-class people having a lack of opportunity and poverty, but to take them out of it.' (*Sunday Times*, 1 September 1996)

In the mid-1990s, commentators began to comment on New Labour politicians' marked reluctance to use the word 'class' in their speeches. In part, this was a matter of image. One way of presenting a new and modern image was to drop the sort of dialogue used in the past (especially the 'class warrior' rhetoric employed by the hard left). In part, it was a tactical device. By appealing to society as a whole rather than to a single class, New Labour could hope for votes from society as a whole. And in part, it was evidence of an ideological shift - a tacit admission of a decline in class-based politics.

The class structure has not changed since c.1970

Against the views expressed above, however, some commentators have argued that class is still an important political phenomenon. German (1996), for example, notes the major inequalities of income and wealth in Britain. These inequalities, together with disparities in educational opportunities and housing patterns and the other measures of class differences, she claims, provide sufficient evidence to show that class is still an important means of analysing British

society. Miliband sums up this viewpoint as follows:
  'Notwithstanding a torrent of propaganda to the contrary, advanced capitalist countries are now and will remain highly structured and hierarchical societies...The substance of life experience for everyone in these societies remains utterly shaped by the fact of class and class inequalities.' (Miliband 1989, pp.203-4)

Main points - Section 2.1

- 'Class' is a difficult term to define. Depending on the definition used, society is divided into two classes (Marx), four classes (Weber), five classes (Registrar General), six classes (IPA) or seven classes (Oxford Mobility Study).
- Most commentators agree that class was the driving force behind British politics during the period 1945-c.1970.
- Some commentators argue that the class structure has changed since c.1970 and that class is a less significant factor than it used to be. Some people have even argued that Britain is becoming a 'classless' society.
- Other commentators argue that inequalities, together with disparities in educational opportunities and housing patterns, mean that society is still shaped by class.

Activity 5.2 A classless society?

Item A *The class structure*

Item C *Changing views on the class struggle 1975-96*

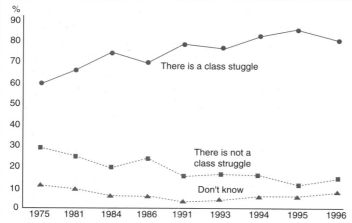

This graph shows the result of surveys conducted between 1975 and 1996. Respondents were asked whether or not they thought there was a class struggle.

Figures from Allan 1994 and the *New Statesman*, 23 August 1996.

Item B *Case studies*

1. Ned is aged 44. He works on the production line in the car assembly plant at Ford Dagenham. He has worked there for 16 years. He earns £6.50 an hour and works a 39 hour week. If he is five minutes late he loses five minute's pay. He lives in Bexleyheath, South London in a house which he owns. He is married with two children. He left school at 16.
2. Anna is aged 31. She works as a gardener and for her husband's computer consultancy. She was brought up on a council estate and went to a Roman Catholic girls' comprehensive school. She says that the school was responsible for ensuring that she is well spoken. If she had enough money, she would send her children to a private school. Both her parents were Irish and working class. She lives in the village of Botesdale near Diss in Norfolk with her husband and two children. She is a member of the Conservative Party.
3. Charles is aged 37. He is a banking director at a merchant bank. He lives with his wife in a large old house in Cornwall and commutes weekly to a London flat. He was educated at a private school and at Exeter University. His father was in the army and his mother trained as a painter. Charles earns between £60,000 and £150,000 a year. He says he is unusual in the City because he has only voted once. He describes himself as 'essentially conservative'. He says that he would send his children to state schools.
4. Andrew is aged 73. He is the 11th Duke of Devonshire and lives at the family home, Chatsworth in Derbyshire. Chatsworth is owned by a family charitable trust and is open to the public for seven months of the year. It has 175 rooms and a garden of 100 acres. It is surrounded by an estate of 11,000 acres. A total of 175 people work at Chatsworth and on its estate.

Adapted from the *Observer*, 12 December 1993.

Item D *The classless society (1)*

According to Adonis and Pollard, their book is about the segregation of modern Britain. Britain, they argue, cannot be understood apart from its class system which separates its people as clinically today as it did half a century ago when George Orwell described it as 'the most class-ridden country under the sun'. The classes have changed, but the barriers between them remain the same - money, education, family and occupation (or the lack of them). Class divisions are intensifying as the distance between the top and bottom widens and the classes at both extremes grow in size and identity. This growing division, they claim, is obvious to everyone - except crucially to most of the nation's élite which for reasons of fear and self-interest is struggling to eliminate class from the realm of respectable debate. To achieve this, the élite has developed two tactics. The first is the use of the term 'underclass' to denote a minority isolated from the mainstream majority. The second is the transformation of this mainstream into a 'classless society'. This is a myth and distortion in equal measure. Almost every visible and saleable aspect of modern life betrays the class hierarchy from Harrow to Hackney, sushi to sausages, sharp suit to shell suit, *FT* to *Sun*, Porsche to Escort, Channel Four to Radio One.

Adapted from Adonis & Pollard 1997.

Item E *The classless society (2)*

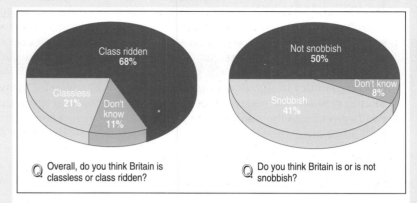

These charts are based on the results of a survey carried out by ICM on 3 and 4 July 1998.

Questions

1. Suppose you had been asked to conduct a survey to find out the class background of the students in your school or college. Write down the criteria you would use. Devise a questionnaire. Conduct the survey and write a report.
2. Describe your own class using (i) the Registrar General's classification (ii) the changes to the Registrar General's classification to be introduced for the 2001 Census and (iii) the IPA's definition. Give reasons for your choices.
3. How accurate are the class differences portrayed in Item A?
4. Identify the class of each person profiled in Item B. Explain how you reached your conclusion.
5. Give the arguments for and against the view that Britain is becoming a classless society. Use Items C-E in your answer.

2.2 Gender

The importance of gender

It is not just class that determines the position and role of people in British society. Other social factors are important. Take gender, for example. Although there is some evidence to suggest that in Britain there is less discrimination against women today than was once the case, there is overwhelming evidence that women have less chance of achieving high status and high earnings than men. Women may have won equality in the eyes of the law, but they have yet to win equality of opportunity. This section considers the importance of gender in British society.

Feminism

Feminists are supporters of and campaigners for equality between women and men (see also Chapter 2, Section 5.2). Although the origins of British feminism are usually traced to the late 18th century when Mary Wollstonecraft wrote *A Vindication of the Rights of Women* (published in 1792), the feminist movement since then has ebbed and flowed. As there have been two periods of intense feminist action, commentators often talk about two 'waves' of feminism.

First wave feminism

'First wave' feminism refers to the period beginning in the late 19th century when women in Britain (and other countries) mobilised and campaigned to win the right to vote (see Chapter 7, Section 1.4). But, although the right to vote was the focus of the campaign, the goal of many 'first wave' feminists was much wider. They hoped to eradicate inequalities between men and women. For example, when women finally won equal voting rights with men in 1928, Ray Strachey (who wrote a history of first wave feminism and took part in the campaign herself) pointed out:

'There are aspects of equality which cannot be won by law. These are changes of thought and outlook which even yet have not arrived. Above all, economic equality with men is still a distant dream. The struggle for these things goes on and must go on. But, the main fight is over and the main victory is won.' (Strachey 1928, pp.384-5)

The problem (from the feminists' point of view) was that winning the right to vote did not automatically mean that the problems outlined by Strachey were tackled. In fact, rather than encouraging women to campaign for further changes, electoral reform led to a period of 40 years in which feminism was marginalised. Bouchier suggests reasons for this:

'After several years of being nervously sensitive to women's issues, politicians realised that women were simply not voting on such issues as a group; nor did they have an effective political party of their own; nor were women entering politics in significant numbers. All three conditions are necessary before a group can begin to turn the democratic system to its own advantage.' (Bouchier 1983, p.16)

Second wave feminism

It was not until the late 1960s that a 'second wave' of feminism began. Its origins lie in the USA but it soon spread to Britain. Mitchell (1971) suggests three reasons for the resurgence of feminism in the 1960s. First, the late 1960s was a time of political turbulence. Many young people joined groups which aimed to change or upset the Establishment. Women who participated in these groups gained political experience and, at the same time, encountered a great deal of sexism (prejudice against them because of their sex). Women were expected to make the tea, for example, and to follow the lead of male leaders. As a result, some women began to argue that there was a need to struggle against male domination. Second, the contradictions in many women's lives led to the need for them to get together to reconsider their role. For example, the 1960s were the age of sexual liberation, yet women were often treated as little more than sex objects. A growing number of married women went out to work, yet it was commonly argued that a woman's place was in the home. These contradictions encouraged women to challenge the status quo. And third, the 1960s presented women with new opportunities which raised their awareness of their position in society. The number of women who entered higher education and embarked on careers grew rapidly. The development of the contraceptive pill gave women greater freedom to choose when and whether to have children. This greater awareness encouraged women to take political action.

The problem that has no name

The development of the new wave of feminism was sparked by a number of influential books, including Germaine Greer's *The Female Eunuch* and Betty Freidan's *The Feminine Mystique*. The latter was published in 1963 and summed up what Freidan described as the 'problem that has no name':

'The problems lay buried, unspoken for many years in the minds of American women. It was a strange stirring, a sense of dissatisfaction, a yearning that women suffered in the middle of the 20th century in the United States. Each suburban housewife struggled with it alone. As she made beds, shopped for groceries, matched slip cover material, ate peanut butter sandwiches, chauffeured Cub Scouts and Brownies, lay beside her husband at night, she was afraid to ask even of herself, the silent question: is this all?' (Freidan 1963, p.1)

In order to challenge the view that women should be satisfied with domestic life especially when it served to restrict their opportunities in employment, politics and public life, Freidan helped to set up NOW (the National Organisation of Women), a group which served as a blueprint for many British feminists. Women's groups began to spring up throughout Britain:

'Here women began to explore the ways that their lives were constrained in the private realm of home and the social forces forced upon girls and then women. In these man-free meetings, women discovered a new confidence. They began to name the male practices which contributed to their lack of freedom and attempted to devise alternative ways of behaving to escape the traps of male logic, language and power games.' (Forbes 1991, p.62)

The Women's Liberation Movement

Collectively the women's groups which sprung up in Britain were known, at first, as the Women's Liberation Movement. In the 1970s, the Women's Liberation Movement agreed on seven demands which must be met before equality with men could be achieved. These were as follows:

1. Equal pay now.
2. Equal education and job opportunities.
3. Free contraception and abortion on demand.
4. Free 24 hour childcare.
5. Legal and financial independence for all women.
6. An end to all discrimination against lesbians.
7. Freedom for all women from intimidation by the threat or the use of violence or sexual coercion, regardless of marital status, and an end to all laws, assumptions and institutions that perpetuate male dominance and men's aggression towards women.

Women in Britain in the 1990s

Examination of five areas should clarify the position of women in Britain in the 1990s.

1. Women's legal status

The Prime Minister, Stanley Baldwin, argued in 1928, after the Electoral Reform Bill was passed, that:

'The inequality of women, if there be such a thing, will not now depend on any creation of the law. It will never again be possible to blame the state for any position of inequality. Women will have, with us, the fullest rights.' (Speech in the House of Commons, 29 March 1928)

It was not until 1975, however, that the Equal Pay Act 1970 came into force. Before then, the law allowed employers to pay women at a lower rate of pay for doing the same job as a man. Similarly, it was not until 1975 that the Sex Discrimination Act was passed. Before then, the law did not allow the idea that a woman might be discriminated against because of her sex.

Although the Equal Pay Act and Sex Discrimination Acts mean that, in theory, men and women are now equal before the law, in reality this legislation has lacked teeth. Bassnett, for example, argues that:

> 'The vagueness of the Sex Discrimination Act which came into force with the Equal Pay Act left so many legal loopholes that anyone set against implementing the Act could manage to do so with regular impunity, a fact borne out by the difficulty women have had in winning cases of sexual discrimination in employment.' (Bassnett 1986, p.141)

2. Women at work
The number of women in work is growing whilst the number of working men is declining. According to Edward Balls, between 1970 and 1994 female employment rose by a fifth whilst male employment fell be the same amount (*Guardian*, 5 September 1994). By September 1996, there were more women in employment than men - 11,248,000 against 11,236,000 (*Guardian*, 20 December 1998). West argues:

> 'However, shifts in the division of labour do not amount to fundamental transformations. Women's integration into employment has largely been through part-time work. Job segregation actually remains very marked, despite women's inroads into some male-dominated occupations. Masculine, sexist cultures persist in many workplace environments, despite formal commitments to equal opportunities. And, there is little evidence of change in the domestic division of labour. Motherhood still depresses women's lifetime earnings and, other things being equal, tends to be associated with downward occupational mobility (as many women re-enter the workforce at a lower level than when they left it).' (West 1997, p.127)

Consequences of these changes
Women often find that employers assume that, because they are women, they are suited to particular kinds of work (usually caring, non-competitive roles) and not suited to other kinds of work (such as management, engineering or scientific research). Because an invisible barrier (sexual discrimination) prevents women breaking into these areas of work, commentators have talked of a 'glass wall' blocking women's way forward. Similarly, even when women are allowed into what were previously regarded as male occupations, they often find that they are not promoted as often as men or that they are not promoted at all. Again, an invisible barrier - a 'glass

ceiling' blocks their way upwards. For example, while women's access to the highest grades of management improved threefold between 1975 and 1995, this is only a rise from 1% to 3% of all highest grade managers (Pascall 1995). Women only hold 1.7% of executive directorships of the *Financial Times* Stock Exchange (FTSE-100) companies and only accounted for:

- 9% of the top civil service grades
- 6% of university chancellors and vice chancellors
- 8% of local government chief executives and chief officers.
(*Labour Research*, January 1997)

3. Women at home
Although the traditional attitude that women (especially married women) should stay at home and tend to the needs of their children and husband is changing, women still do most of the domestic work in Britain. This was graphically illustrated by market research carried out by Mintel in July 1993:

> 'Mintel tried to interview couples who equally shared grocery shopping, cooking and doing the laundry, but had to abandon the search after finding only one man in 100 did his fair share of housework. Fewer than one woman in ten thinks her partner shares cooking equally, while nearly two men in ten think they do...Only 20% of working women report that their male partner equally shares any single domestic task, whereas 85% say they almost always do all the laundry, ironing and a similar number say they are entirely responsible for cooking the main meal.' (*Guardian*, 21 December 1993)

The findings of the Mintel survey were confirmed by a study carried out in 1995 (HMSO 1995).

Work and domestic responsibilities
A major reason why 80% of part-time jobs are taken by women is that women are expected to combine work with their domestic responsibilities. Since few employers make any provision for childcare, it is women who generally break their careers to look after their family. Until recently, this expectation was reflected in law. Companies had a statutory obligation to provide maternity leave but not paternity leave. As a result of the Labour government's decision to sign the Social Chapter, however, this changed in June 1998. From that month, all companies were obliged to provide all employees (men and women) with a minimum of three months unpaid leave. As Peter Baker pointed out:

> 'This is a significant step towards recognising the importance of family-friendly employment practice and the role of fathers.' (*Observer*, 7 December 1997)

Indeed there is some evidence that attitudes towards paternity leave were changing before the EU Directive was implemented:

'In 1992, the CBI found that 76% of the firms they surveyed granted paternity leave. In 1987, only 32% of companies allowed fathers time off for the birth of a child.' (*Guardian*, 16 September 1997)

Nevertheless, the fact that statutory paternity leave is unpaid means that many men will be unable to take it and, besides, provision of paternity leave is only a small step on the way to changing attitudes about who is responsible for childcare.

4. Women and education

Some feminists argue that girls are disadvantaged at school because of the sexist attitudes of some teachers and because of the different socialisation of boys and girls - boys are encouraged to be assertive and competitive whilst girls are encouraged to be quiet and non-competitive. It is argued that this has affected educational performance and the choice of subjects (girls are less inclined to take science and technology-based subjects). But, even if girls do have to overcome such obstacles, figures compiled by the government show that girls are increasingly outclassing boys at every level up to and including A level. At the age of 14, for example, two thirds of girls but only half of boys reached the expected standard in non-core national curriculum subjects. In the core national curriculum subjects, girls outperformed boys in English, achieved the same results in Maths and performed only slightly worse than boys in science. (*Guardian*, 26 November 1997). The 1996 examination results showed that:

'Girls were outperforming boys in all 15 of the most popular GCSE subjects...[and at A level] girls were ahead in 13 of the most popular subjects, including subjects where traditionally boys have done better than girls.' (Denscombe 1997, pp.20-1)

Women in higher education

In higher education, the number of female students has increased dramatically in the last 30 years (Social Trends 1998). In 1970-71 there were twice as many male students as female students. By 1995-96, the number of female undergraduates (529,000) was greater than the number of male undergraduates

(519,000). Differences in subject choice remain, however and women are still more likely to be found in the less prestigious institutions (Pilkington 1997). A government survey notes:

'The concern is not simply that females do not undertake science, engineering and technology (SET) degree courses but also that those that do are much less likely than their male counterparts to pursue careers, or to find employment, in related occupations or professions. Whereas in 1995-6, 59% of males who obtained employment shortly after graduating from SET courses took up a science, engineering and technology occupation, only 39% of females did so, thus further eroding female involvement in these subjects.' (Social Trends 1998, p.62)

5. Women and politics

Although women have been able to stand as candidates in parliamentary elections since 1918, women are still under-represented in Parliament and on local councils. The evidence to support these assertions and possible reasons are considered in Chapter 11.

Main points - Section 2.2

- **Like class, gender is an important social factor.**
- **First wave feminism resulted in women winning the right to vote. Second wave feminism (which began in the 1960s) focused on the role women were expected to play. The aim was to achieve equality of opportunity.**
- **Although the Equal Pay Act (1970) and Sexual Discrimination Act (1975) mean that men and women are equal before the law, in reality this legislation lacks teeth. At work, women are still, on average, paid less than men. They are less likely to be promoted and more likely to have part-time and/or low paid work. Women are also still expected to carry out most domestic tasks.**
- **Girls are outperforming boys in education at every level up to A level. Although the number of female undergraduates has risen dramatically over the last 30 years, women are reluctant to pursue degrees and careers in science and engineering.**

Activity 5.3 *Women in the late 1990s*

Item A   *The glass ceiling*

Research published today by the Equal Opportunities Commission reveals that men are being left out in the cold when it comes to part-time and flexible working, while women are still failing to move into the boardroom. The male unemployment rate is 1.5 times that of women, yet only 16% of part-time jobs are filled by men. A million more part-time jobs have been created in the past 10 years, making a total of 5.6 million, of which 84% are filled by women. But, in the highest echelons of industry, women are still failing to crack the glass ceiling. The Commission's report shows that only 3.3% of boardroom directors are women. Even when they make it to the boardroom, they tend to have non-executive appointments. Male directors earn more - their average is £88.390, but for women directors it is £71,638. There is also a disparity in managerial salaries with men paid £34,855 on average whilst women earn £30,569 on average. Also, the culture of long hours excludes many working mothers.

Adapted from the *Times*, 28 July 1997.

Item B   Women at work (1)

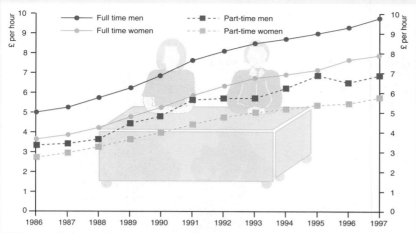

This graph shows the average gross hourly earnings of adult employees in Britain between April 1986 and April 1997.

Adapted from the New Earnings Survey 1997.

Item D   Division of household tasks

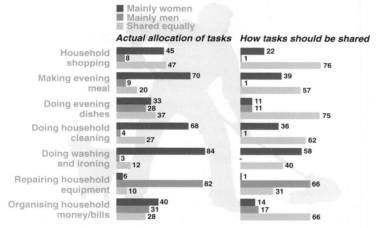

This chart shows the results of a survey carried out in 1995. Respondents were asked how domestic tasks were actually allocated and how they should be shared.

Adapted from HMSO 1995.

Item C   Why are men being held back?

Pity the young male graduate looking for work. Whereas 11% of men are still unemployed six months after leaving university, for female graduates the figure is 7.1%. While male unemployment stands at 9.1%, the figure for women is 3.6%. When it comes to getting a job, women have won the war of words. If a woman experiences problems developing her career, the 'glass ceiling' is to blame. For men, it can only be incompetence. Last year, 108,000 women and 106,000 men graduated from UK universities reflecting the slightly larger number of women in the population as a whole. Yet, while 29 universities offer degrees in women's studies, there are no degrees in men's studies. University courses in women's health, women in business and women and technology are also available. Most universities have 'advisers to women students' specifically designated to assist them. No such posts exist to help men. The media are far from blameless. Discrimination against women is newsworthy whilst that which disadvantages men is mostly ignored. The WISE campaign (Women Into Science and Engineering), now in its twelfth year, has increased the number of women taking up careers in engineering. There is no counterpart aiming to encourage men into female-dominated careers - in nursing, personnel management, teaching or social work for example. Very little has been done to attract unemployed men into these jobs. As the feminists continually say when the boot is on the other foot - how can employers of these workers ignore half the population?

Adapted from the Times, 27 March 1997.

Item E   Women at work (2)

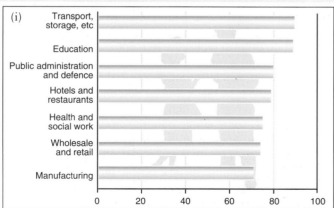

This chart shows women's earnings as a percentage of men's in selected areas of employment in April 1997.

Adapted from Social Trends 1998.

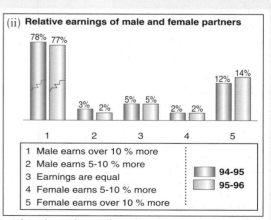

This chart shows the relative earnings of male and female partners in 1994-96.

Item F *Superwoman*

Questions

1. Explain why gender is a useful tool to use when analysing what kind of society exists in Britain.
2. a) Judging from Items A, B and E, what evidence is there to suggest that women lack equal opportunities in the workplace?
   b) Is there any evidence to suggest that old prejudices are being broken down?
3. a) Describe the main points being made in Item C.
   b) What arguments might be used to counter the points made in Item C?
4. What conclusions can be drawn from the data in Item D?
5. What does Item F tell us about the pressures that women face in contemporary Britain?

2.3 Ethnicity

What is 'ethnicity'?

What is the colour of your skin? Think of ways in which your life might have been different if your skin had been a different colour. Where were your parents and grandparents born? Think of ways in which your life has been shaped by your family and how your family environment would have been different if your parents or grandparents had come from a different culture.

Along with class and gender, sociologists argue that ethnicity is a key social factor. 'Ethnicity', however, is a difficult term to define. According to a House of Lords ruling in 1983, an ethnic group is a group in society which has:

- a distinct cultural identity
- a long, shared history
- a common geographical origin or common descent
- a common language
- a common literature peculiar to the group
- a common religion.

Using these criteria, it is possible to divide the British population into a number of ethnic groups. The majority of the population belongs to a single, dominant ethnic group (white Britons descended from white Britons) whilst the remainder of the population belongs to a number of ethnic minority groups - for example, white Britons descended from Irish immigrants or black Britons descended from West Indian immigrants. Although, as these examples indicate, some ethnic minority groups are white, all black and Asian Britons belong to ethnic minority groups. As a result, the issues of skin colour (race) and racism (prejudice against people because of their skin colour) are closely linked to any discussion of ethnicity.

The term 'black'

In the past, many studies failed to distinguish between different ethnic groups, lumping people together as 'blacks' and 'whites'. There were a number of problems with this. First, 'black' took on a dual meaning, sometimes referring to all black people and sometimes referring only to African-Caribbean groups. Second, this classification did not take account of the way in which some black and Asian people see themselves. Modood (1988), for example, argues that many people from the Indian subcontinent do not define themselves as 'black'. Third, some critics argue that the black-white distinction is unlikely to improve race relations since it encourages polarisation. As a result, it is difficult to find a suitable shorthand to describe non-white members of ethnic minority groups. In this book, either specific ethnic groups are named or the term 'black and Asian' is generally used. Quotations using other terms have not been altered however.

Using ethnicity

By dividing up society along ethnic lines, sociologists are able to target groups in society and find out how different ethnic backgrounds affect the life chances of different groups of people. This means of classification includes consideration of cultural factors as well as skin colour and, therefore, provides a more complex model than that based simply on skin colour alone. For example, a study showing that Indian Britons do better at school than both Bangladeshi Britons and African-Caribbean Britons, but not as well as white Britons, may be of greater use than a study which simply shows that, overall, white Britons do better at school than 'black' Britons since it allows politicians to target resources to areas which need it (areas where Bangladeshi Britons live, for example). Having said this, however, it should not be assumed that each ethnic culture is uniform. Gilroy (1987) warns against 'ethnic absolutism' - the idea that once a researcher has identified which ethnic group a person belongs to, then that person's behaviour can be predicted. Ethnicity is dynamic and flexible. It is not fixed.

PSI survey

This view was supported by the Policy Studies Institute in a national survey of ethnic minorities which discovered that mixed marriages and partnerships were increasing (PSI 1997). Half of the African-Caribbean men born in Britain and a third of African-Caribbean women have a white partner. Mixed marriages have become so common that nearly half of 'African-Caribbean' children have one white parent. Also, about one in five British-born Indians has a white partner.

Grounds for optimism

Some commentators see grounds for optimism. Stuart Hall, for example, argues that the homogeneity (uniformity) of the British is giving way to plurality and diversity:

> 'For the first time, the ethnic minorities are now being allowed into the mainstream on the basis of negotiation. The alternatives offered in the 1960s and 1970s were assimilation [behaving like white Britons] or difference and permanent exclusion. They refused assimilation; they were never prepared to be white British. But, globalisation is now allowing a new negotiation. They can be British and different - be both themselves and British.' (Stuart Hall quoted in the *Observer*, 28 December 1997)

Historical background

British history has been shaped by waves of immigration. Romans, Saxons, Angles, Vikings and Normans all settled in Britain and helped to shape British culture. In the 19th century, thousands of Irish people fled the famine and settled in Britain. During the 1930s and 1940s, Jews and others fled to Britain to escape Nazi persecution.

Records of black people in Britain stretch back to the period of Roman occupation (there is evidence that soldiers recruited in Africa served in Britain and some are known to have settled here). Walvin (1984) notes that there has been a small but continuous black and Asian presence in Britain for the last 500 years. The growth of the British Empire played a part in this. As British contact with black and Asian people grew, small black communities established themselves in Britain. It was, however, only after 1945 that substantial numbers of black and Asian people settled in Britain.

Post-war immigration

During the 1950s and early 1960s, Britain experienced an economic boom which led to an acute labour shortage. This shortage was met, in part, by encouraging the immigration of workers, mainly from the New Commonwealth countries (countries which had formed part of the British Empire). In the 1950s, most of these workers came from the West Indies and, in the 1960s, most came from the Asian subcontinent. Many of these immigrants were employed in unskilled and low paid jobs which the indigenous white population was unwilling to take. This had immediate and serious consequences:

> 'Partly because of low pay, partly because of their relative newness and partly because of implicit discriminatory practices on the part of both public and private authorities, black people found themselves forced into cheap rented housing, much of it located in the already decaying inner areas of Britain's cities. So, from their arrival, black people suffered from economic and housing disadvantage, to which was added other forms of disadvantage resulting from lack of attention to their needs, particularly with regard to education. Finally, in terms of social interaction, black people suffered from the hostility of their erstwhile hosts. Centuries of colonialism had left their mark in terms of popular stereotypes of black people as being pagan, uncivilised, inherently inferior to Europeans and ignorant. These images were reflected in white attitudes and behaviour.' (Taylor

1993, p.146, slightly adapted)

Immigration control
Throughout the 1950s, immigration remained unchecked. Between 1955 and 1957, for example, more than 40,000 people each year emigrated from New Commonwealth countries into Britain. In the early 1960s, however, increasingly strident calls began to be made in favour of immigration control. The Notting Hill riots in 1958 drew attention to growing racial tension (white youths shouting racist slogans clashed with black and Asian youths in the Notting Hill area of London over several days). And, in 1962, the government passed the first of what was to become a string of Immigration Acts designed to restrict the influx of immigrants. Further Acts were passed in 1968, 1971 and 1981. According to Wilson (1984), each Act was designed to shut the door on black and Asian immigration whilst leaving it open for white immigrants, with the result that:

'The most brutal and wide-ranging racism which occurs day after day is not the work of fascist minority parties but of Her Majesty's government. It is the racism written into and demanded by Britain's immigration laws.' (Wilson 1984, p.72)

Combating racism
Although tighter immigration controls have restricted the number of new immigrants (especially black and Asian immigrants) settling in Britain, a number of measures have been taken to combat racism within Britain. Race Relations Acts were passed in 1965, 1968 and 1976. Since 1976, racial discrimination has been outlawed (both 'direct' or intentional discrimination and 'indirect' or unintentional discrimination) and the Commission for Racial Equality (CRE) has been given investigative and legal powers to counter racism. But, whilst restrictions on immigration have been effective, measures to combat racism have not:

'Despite three Race Relations Acts (in 1965, 1968 and 1976) and over 20 years of inner city policy initiatives, black people in Britain still suffer widely from racial discrimination and racial disadvantage. While a few have broken through to public prominence...black people are generally under-represented in high status occupations. They find it much more difficult to secure jobs and...live disproportionately in the poorest, most neglected and most deprived parts of the country.' (Taylor 1993, pp.162-3)

A measure of this deprivation and discontent was the outbreak of a number of serious riots in inner cities during the early 1980s. Although the government denied that racial tension explained the outbreak of these riots, Lord Scarman, who was appointed to investigate the causes of the rioting in Brixton, felt able to conclude:

'The evidence which I have received...leaves no doubt in my mind that racial disadvantage is a fact of current British life. It was, I am sure, a significant factor in the causation of the Brixton disorders. Urgent action is needed if it is not to become an endemic [widespread], ineradicable [indestructible] disease threatening the very survival of our society.' (Scarman 1981, p.209)

Britain's black and Asian population
The 1991 population census revealed that out of a total population of 54.81 million, 51.80 million people were white whilst 3.01 million were black. The three largest groups of black and Asian Britons were Indian Britons (840,000), Caribbean Britons (500,000) and Pakistani Britons (467,000). In 1991, therefore, just 5.5% of the total population was black and Asian. This was a rise from 2.3% in 1971 and 3.9% in 1981.

Playing the race card
The Runnymede Trust (Runnymede 1991) notes that white people often overestimate how many black and Asian people live in Britain. In 1978, for example, Margaret Thatcher warned that Britain might be 'swamped' with immigrants, a warning repeated by the Conservative MP Nicholas Fairbairn in the 1992 general election campaign. In May 1993, the Conservative MP Winston Churchill went even further:

'Tory backbencher Winston Churchill ignited a blazing row last night by demanding an end to the "relentless flow" of immigrants. In some of the most inflammatory remarks made in years on the race issue, Mr Churchill, grandson of the wartime leader, said that unless urgent action was taken, the British way of life was under threat.' (*Daily Mail*, 29 May 1993)

It is clear from the 1991 census figures that comments such as these are deliberately provocative.

Racism in the late 1990s
In the late 1990s, right-wing politicians and the tabloid newspapers turned their attention to asylum seekers. In 1997, the result was headlines like 'Dover deluge' (*Daily Mail*) and 'Giro Czechs' (the *Sun* referring to the asylum claims of a group of travellers from the Czech Republic). Although the numbers involved were small (2,240 applications for asylum were granted in 1996 according to the *Guardian*, 22 November 1997), the issue was exploited and linked to general fears about national identity. Norman Tebbit, a former leading Conservative politician, expressed these fears at a fringe meeting at the 1997 Conservative Party conference:

'Multiculturalism is a divisive force. One cannot uphold two sets of ethics or be loyal to two nations, any more than a man can have two masters. It perpetuates ethnic divisions because nationality is in the long term more about culture than ethnics. Youngsters of all races born here should be taught that British history is their history, or they will forever be foreigners holding British passports and this kingdom will become a Yugoslavia.' (*Guardian*, 8 October 1997)

The fact that politicians still choose to 'play the race card' in the late 1990s is significant. It suggests that they feel there is popular support for such attitudes. Indeed, there is evidence to confirm that is the case. Surveys of public attitudes suggest that racist attitudes are widespread - for example, around a third of white people in Britain admit to having racist attitudes (IPPR 1997).

The consequences of racism

Racial harassment
These racist attitudes lead to serious consequences. A report published in 1997 suggested that 250,000 people a year are victims of racial harassment (PSI 1997). And, in 1995-96, there were 12,222 recorded racial attacks in England and Wales, a 3% increase on the previous year with nearly 500 attacks involving serious physical violence (*Observer*, 21 September 1997).

Poverty
Black and Asian groups suffer in other ways too. For example, black and Asian groups are far more likely than whites to be found in the poorest fifth of the population and far less likely to be in the richest fifth (Rowntree 1995). Youth (ages 16 to 24) unemployment rates in 1996-97 for certain black and Asian groups were more than double those for white people of the same age:

> 'In Spring 1995, black youths were almost three times as likely to be unemployed as white youths. By 1996-97 the rate for this group had improved but was still just over double the rate for white youths.' (Social Trends 1998, p.87)

Low status
While there has been a certain movement of black and Asian groups into non-manual employment, especially self-employment (Richardson 1996), people from black and Asian groups are generally unlikely to find high status jobs. For example, in 1996 people from black and Asian groups accounted for:
- 0% of High Court judges
- 0% of Chief Police Officers
- 0.97% of officers in the armed forces
- 0.34% of senior civil servants (grades 1-5)
- 0% of chairs of quangos.
  (*Guardian*, 2 October 1997)

Educational disadvantage
One reason why people from black and Asian groups are under-represented in the professions is because they have been educationally disadvantaged, though there is no uniform pattern in educational achievement (at compulsory school level) for all ethnic minorities. After reviewing the evidence, the 1995 Ofsted Report stated:

> 'On average, African-Caribbean pupils (of both sexes) achieved below the level attained by other groups. Asian pupils, on the other hand, achieved almost as well as, or better than, whites of the same class and gender.' (Gilborn & Gipps 1996, p.180)

Within the Asian student population, pupils of Indian origin tend to achieve the highest results and Bangladeshis the lowest.

A significant problem for some groups is the rate of exclusion from school. This is six times higher for African and African-Caribbean groups than for whites (*Guardian*, 6 September 1996).

There are some signs, however, that the educational position is changing. People from black and Asian groups are now much more likely than white people to continue their education after the age of 16. Also, apart from African-Caribbean men and Bangladeshi women, people from black and Asian groups are now more likely to go to university (PSI 1997). The TUC Report *Pride and Prejudice*, however, revealed that, despite going through further and higher education:

> 'A greater proportion of black people than whites were not able to translate their skills into high paid employment.' (*Voice*, 22 and 29 December 1997)

The Labour government and racism
In its 1997 general election manifesto, the Labour Party made a pledge to protect people from racist harassment and attacks:

> 'Britain is a multiracial and multicultural society. All its members must have the protection of the law. We will create a new offence of racial harassment and a new crime of racially motivated violence to protect ethnic minorities from intimidation.' (Labour 1997, p.23)

Speaking in October 1997, Home Secretary Jack Straw made it clear that the Labour government would fulfil this pledge. Straw announced that his Crime and Disorder Bill would contain provisions to allow judges to pass heavier sentences for any crime which has a racial element:

> 'Those who commit racist crimes should expect severe punishment. Where there is a racialist element then conviction should always attract a higher and more severe penalty.' (Jack Straw quoted in the *Guardian*, 3 October 1997)

Despite this, the Labour government was criticised by Herman Ouseley, Chief Executive of the Commission for Racial Equality, on the grounds that, although Labour had taken many initiatives in their first months in office:

> 'There were few signals that ministers intended to do much different on race equality.' (*Guardian*, 21 October 1997)

Main points - Section 2.3

- Like class and gender, ethnicity is an important social factor.
- An ethnic group is a group in society which has a distinct cultural identity, a long, shared history, a common geographical origin or common descent, a common language, a common literature, peculiar to the group or a common religion. Since all black and Asian Britons belong to ethnic minority groups, the issues of race and racism are closely linked to any discussion of ethnicity.
- The census of 1991 revealed that 5.5% of the British population was black and Asian. Despite this and despite tight immigration controls, some politicians

on the right still argue that Britain is in danger of being 'swamped' by immigrants or that Britain's identity is being undermined by black and Asian people.
- Studies show not only that many white Britons are racists, but also that many violent attacks are racially motivated. People from black and Asian groups are disadvantaged in other ways too. They are, on average, poorer than whites and are under-represented in high status jobs. Some people from black and Asian groups are educationally disadvantaged, though there are signs that this may be changing.

Activity 5.4 Racism in Britain

Item A *Crime, pay and unemployment by ethnic group*

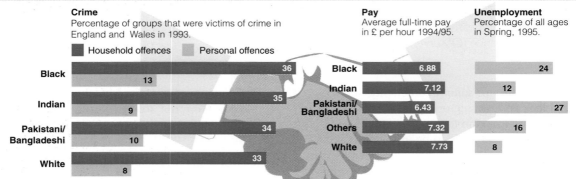

Crime
Percentage of groups that were victims of crime in England and Wales in 1993.

■ Household offences   ■ Personal offences

	Household	Personal
Black	36	13
Indian	35	9
Pakistani/Bangladeshi	34	10
White	33	8

Pay
Average full-time pay in £ per hour 1994/95.

Black	6.88
Indian	7.12
Pakistani/Bangladeshi	6.43
Others	7.32
White	7.73

Unemployment
Percentage of all ages in Spring, 1995.

Black	24
Indian	12
Pakistani/Bangladeshi	27
Others	16
White	8

These charts are based on the findings of a report entitled *Social Focus on Ethnic Minorities* which was published by the Office for National Statistics in August 1996.

Item B *Ethnic minority groups*

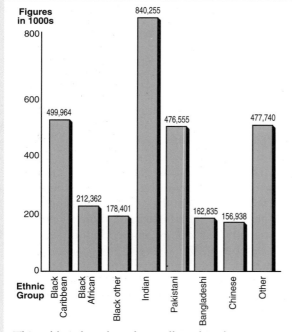

Figures in 1000s

Ethnic Group	Figures
Black Caribbean	499,964
Black African	212,362
Black other	178,401
Indian	840,255
Pakistani	476,555
Bangladeshi	162,835
Chinese	156,938
Other	477,740

This table is based on data collected in the 1991 census.

Item C *Racism in Britain (1)*

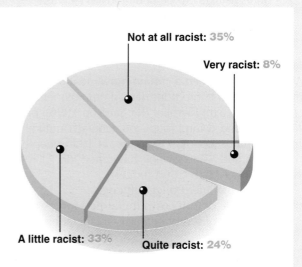

Not at all racist: 35%
Very racist: 8%
A little racist: 33%
Quite racist: 24%

This chart shows part of the results of a survey published by the European Union Eurostat Statistical Office in 1997. Pollsters questioned more than 16,000 people from EU member states about their attitudes to race. The replies from British respondents are given in the chart above.

Adapted from the *Guardian*, 20 December 1997.

Item D *Racism in Britain (2)*

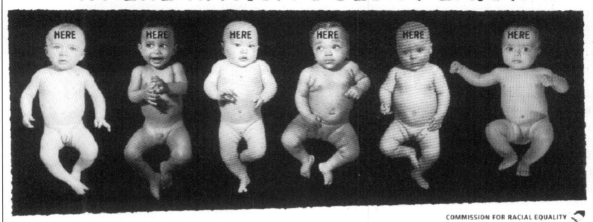

THERE ARE LOTS OF PLACES IN BRITAIN WHERE RACISM DOESN'T EXIST.

HERE HERE HERE HERE HERE HERE

COMMISSION FOR RACIAL EQUALITY

This poster was produced by the Commission for Racial Equality (CRE) as part of a three year campaign to combat racism.

Item E *Racism in Britain (3)*

Mal and Linda moved to the Ryelands estate in Lancaster in 1991, sinking their life savings into a corner store with an upstairs flat. Since then, the mixed-race couple have been the victims of more than 1,500 documented racial incidents. Attempted murder, stonings, obscene graffiti, vandalism, arson attacks and death threats have changed their lives and relationships forever. Now, after six years of living hell, this couple has something to celebrate. On 2 October 1997, in a landmark ruling by the High Court, the couple won an appeal to sue Labour-run Lancaster city council for its alleged failure to protect them from violent racist tenants. Recently the couple's plight received national attention - at the Labour Party conference. This time on Mischief Night (as 4 November is known in Lancaster), chants of 'if you want the Paki out clap your hands; if you want the Paki dead stamp your feet' will be confronted by supporters from across the country, including the National Assembly Against Racism. In his lonely pursuit of justice, Mal now channels his anger into exposing the inaction of the council and the police. 'Throughout this violent campaign, the authorities have been very slow to react and for a long time the racists seemed able to carry on these attacks unchallenged. I look at myself and wonder what I have done to deserve this', he said.

Adapted from the *Guardian*, 29 October 1997.

Questions

1. Using Items A-F, give arguments for and against the view that Britain is moving towards racial harmony.

2. a) 'Ethnicity is an important social factor'. Explain this statement using Items A and B.
   b) What use should politicians make of the information in Item A?

3. What conclusions about British people's attitudes can you draw from Item C?

Item F *Racism in Britain (4)*

Powerful forces are transforming the position of black and Asian people in Britain - globalisation, the legacy of empire, the relatively tolerant disposition of the host population, the determination of black and Asian people. Britain has the potential to become a new kind of multi-ethnic, multicultural society, a true creature of the global era. But, the changes are still patchy. Mixed couples and mixed peer groups are now common on many of London's streets. Black culture has transformed white youth culture. Young Asians are emerging as powerful role models. Yet, none of this is reflected at the political level. It is unofficial rather than official, bubbling under rather than defining what we are. Blair's notion of inclusivity remains little more than rhetoric. There have been welcome measures such as the tightening up of the law on racial violence, but nothing to lend decisive weight to cultural change. Until the visibility of blacks and Asians in government, the civil service, the armed forces, corporate life and the law are transformed, all the changes will remain incomplete. There are two sides to ethnic relations. The new and encouraging exists alongside continuing discrimination and old patterns of racial violence. If Labour fails to make a decisive move forward, the resulting disappointment may stall or even reverse the process of change. Instead of new role models and achievement, the talk will be of continuing violence, a pervasive drugs culture and inter-ethnic gang warfare.

Adapted from the *Observer*, 28 December 1997.

4. a) What is the point being made by the poster in Item D?
   b) Explain why a three year campaign was necessary.

5. a) Using Items C-F, list measures that might be taken to combat racism.
   b) What role should the government play in combating racism?

Part 3 The social impact of economic change

Key issues

1. How has de-industrialisation affected Britain's workforce?
2. How has the role of trade unions developed?

3.1   The impact of de-industrialisation

What is de-industrialisation?

In the 19th century, Britain's wealth was primarily derived from its manufacturing base. The majority of the working population was employed in the extraction of raw materials and in manufacturing industries rather than in service industries. But today, the position is the reverse. Manufacturing industries have declined whilst service industries have grown.

The decline of Britain's manufacturing base has been described as 'de-industrialisation' (see also Chapter 15, Section 2.2). Although de-industrialisation began before 1979, since then the process has accelerated. Between 1979 and 1995, for example, the number of jobs in manufacturing industry fell from 6.75 million to 4 million. During the same period manufacturing output only grew by 12% which was lower than the EU average and much lower than Japan or the USA (Anderton 1996, p.59).

The origins of de-industrialisation

The traditional view of British working practices can be summarised as follows. In the years following the Second World War, the labour force was predominantly male. Men expected to work full-time in a single job for many years, even for the whole of their working lives. Unmarried women might work, but they would be expected to stop work once they were married. There was a general expectation that there would be 'full' employment.

This traditional view has been challenged by the process of de-industrialisation which has led to a changed labour force, new working practices and new employment levels.

The changing nature of the labour force

In the 1990s, the labour force is no longer predominantly male. According to Victor Keegan:

> 'Since the start of the 1970s, the size of the male labour force has risen by barely more than 300,000 to 15.4 million while the female labour force has increased by 3.1 million to 11.7 million. But, these figures conceal what is happening underneath because the "labour force"...includes the self-employed, the unemployed, the armed forces and people on training and related schemes. All of these are disproportionately

> male preserves. Strip them out and you find that, in December 1993, the actual number of women with jobs was 10.53 million compared to 10.85 million men with jobs.' (*Guardian*, 9 April 1994)

This growing number of women in work is both a reflection of and a consequence of the process of de-industrialisation. Traditionally, many men had jobs in manufacturing industries. But, these jobs have disappeared as Britain's manufacturing base has declined. Whilst jobs in the manufacturing industries have disappeared, jobs in service industries have been created. Many of these new jobs have been taken by women rather than by men.

The growth of part-time work

One reason why many jobs in service industries have been taken by women rather than by men is that many of these jobs are part-time (and low paid). Research has shown that the number of part-time jobs has risen dramatically since 1979. Whilst the number of part-timers in 1981 was 3.9 million (about the same as that in 1971) between 1981 and 1996 the number rose to 6.1 million (Anderton 1997, p.38). *Labour Research* noted in 1994:

> 'The number of part-timers in Britain has risen by a third since the Conservatives came to office [in 1979]. There are now just under 21 million employees of which 5.88 million (28%) work part-time. Fifteen years ago when unemployment was lower and manufacturing played a more decisive role in the economy there were more than 22 million employees of which 4.4 million (19.7%) worked part-time. The extent of part-time working, however, varies greatly between the sexes. While employees are now divided almost equally between men and women, only 10.5% of men work part-time compared with 46.4% women. Put another way, four in five part-timers are women. There is also a major variation between industries with 7.3% of production industry employees working part-time and 35.6% of service industry workers.' (*Labour Research*, July 1994, p.6)

The benefits of part-time work

Many employers prefer to take on part-timers because part-timers do not make the same demands on employers as full-time workers. Part-timers can be sacked more easily than full-timers, they can be paid lower rates of pay, and employers often do not have to pay part-timers' national insurance or pension contributions. At the same time, surveys show that a large majority of women are prepared to take part-time work because it is possible to combine part-time work with domestic responsibilities. One of the findings of a survey carried out by Labour Market Trends in 1996, for example, was that:

> 'The majority of part-time workers, particularly women aged 25-39 do not want a full-time job. For many women, part-time work enables them to spend time at home bringing up children. Only a very small proportion of part-time workers state that they would prefer to have a full-time job.' (Anderton 1997, p.42)

Men, on the other hand, are often reluctant to take part-time work:

> 'There are now 2.1 million unemployed males (against 630,000 women) many of whom are still locked into a culture shock. They still think of jobs in terms of a Golden Age (not that it seemed golden at the time) which may have vanished for good. They can't take the full-time "men's" jobs in industry because there simply aren't enough of them and they are culturally - and financially - unprepared to apply for part-time "women's" jobs.' (*Guardian*, 9 April 1994)

New ways of work

De-industrialisation has changed not just the composition of the labour force, but the way in which people work. Increasingly, there is a move away from the old-style, 'nine to five', full-time jobs to new ways of work. More and more people are job sharing, on 'flexitime' (flexible working hours) or on short-term contracts.

Teleworking

In the 1980s, it was predicted that, owing to technological developments, there would be a massive growth in 'teleworking' - working from home using computer and telephone links (and, therefore, saving employers costs such as light, heat and office rent). Although there has been some growth in teleworking (British gas has introduced compulsory teleworking to save money by closing offices, for example), there has not been the massive growth that was predicted:

> 'In 1986 the former National Economic and Development office (NEDO) predicted that by 1995 over 3 million people would be working from home on computer networks, and by 2010 that figure would have risen to 5 million. But, a study for the Employment Department in 1993 estimated that only one in 200 workers (125,000 in all) were genuine home-based teleworkers. Although this figure excludes the self-employed, nearly all of the country's 3.3 million self-employed would have to be teleworking to bear out NEDO's prediction.' (*Labour Research*, October 1995, p.13)

Frank Duffy, an expert in the planning, design and history of offices, explains the slow growth of teleworking as follows:

> 'The new technology doesn't mean that we'll work at home more, as was predicted in the 1980s, simply because people like to meet face to face. And that's how business is best done.' (*Guardian*, 28 January 1998)

Hot desking

Whether people work at home or in offices, however, there is a shift away from old ways of work. To stay in business in city centres, for example, organisations need to cut costs. Some are doing this by ridding themselves of costly office blocks and introducing new practices such as 'hot desking':

> '[Hot desking] works like this: you check into the office and request a workstation, like checking into a hotel and requesting a room. You are allocated a free desk for a set time and you take your possessions out of a locker and wheel them in a golf caddie to the allocated space. When you have finished you store them away and relinquish the space to the next user.' (*Guardian*, 3 December 1993)

This practice allows smaller amounts of office space to be organised more efficiently:

> 'Staff have no desks. Instead the office is divided (if that's not too mechanical a word) into a number of areas that allow people to work in many different ways. There are meeting areas if you must have a meeting; hideaway cubicles if you need peace and quiet for an hour or two; a "club" room where people can meet casually. Post is delivered, college or inns-of-court style, to pigeon holes. In effect, you can always find the kind of work space you need without having a designated office or desk of your own.' (*Guardian*, 28 January 1998)

The impact of de-industrialisation

That the choice of many is between unsatisfactory employment or unemployment is a consequence of de-industrialisation. The decline of Britain's manufacturing base has led to a net loss in the number of jobs available. Whilst the unemployment rate between 1945 and 1975 never rose above 1 million, since 1979 it has soared. For much of the 1980s, more than 3 million people were unemployed. High rates of unemployment have resulted in a realignment of the labour force.

The 30-30-40 society

Will Hutton describes the current employment market as the 30-30-40 society in the sense that:

- 30% of adults are either unemployed or economically inactive
- 30% of adults have jobs which are,

in one way or another, insecure

- 40% of adults have reasonably secure jobs which range from self employ-ment to full-time employment. (Hutton 1997)

It was the decline of secure, full-time jobs that was so dramatic in the 1980s. The result was the creation of a new group of insecure workers with limited employment rights and few holiday, pension and sickness benefits.

The target model

Another way of looking at British society in the late 1990s is to imagine an archery target with four rings (see Box 5.4). At the centre, there is the core group of workers with secure, full-time jobs. This group is continually shrinking. In the first ring out from the centre, there is the peripheral labour force which consists of part-time employees and employees on temporary contracts. These workers are generally less skilled and receive lower pay than the core group and they can be taken on or laid off according to demand. In the next ring out, there are the short-term unemployed (people unemployed for less than a year). When demand is high, people in this group move into the periphery. When demand is reduced, people from the periphery join the ranks of the short-term unemployed. And finally, in the outer ring there is a large and growing group of long-term unemployed. Members of this group find it incredibly hard to find a job. Many have never had a job. They exist on state benefits and the 'black economy'.

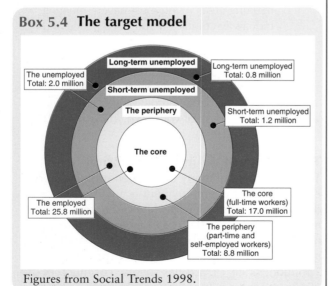

Box 5.4 The target model

Long-term unemployed

The unemployed
Total: 2.0 million

Long-term unemployed
Total: 0.8 million

Short-term unemployed

The periphery

Short-term unemployed
Total: 1.2 million

The core

The employed
Total: 25.8 million

The core
(full-time workers)
Total: 17.0 million

The periphery
(part-time and
self-employed workers)
Total: 8.8 million

Figures from Social Trends 1998.

The debate about an 'underclass'

Some authors (for example, Dahrendorf 1992) have described the large and growing group of long-term unemployed as a separate 'underclass' with a distinct culture - a 'dependency culture' - of its own. Members of this underclass, it is argued, are responsible for their own plight:

'The underclass does not refer to a degree of poverty, but to a type of poverty. It is not a new concept. I grew up knowing what the underclass was; we just didn't call it that in those days. In the small Iowa town were I lived, I was taught by my middle-class parents that there were two kinds of poor people. One class of poor people was never even called "poor". I came to understand that they simply lived with low incomes... Then there was another set of poor people, just a handful of them. These poor people didn't lack just money. They were defined by their behaviour. Their homes were littered and unkempt. The men in the family were unable to hold a job for more than a few weeks at a time. Drunkenness was common. The children grew up ill-schooled and ill-behaved and contributed a disproportionate share of the local juvenile delinquents.' (Murray 1996, p.23)

According to this view from the New Right, members of the underclass choose to live in a cycle of deprivation. Other authors (for example, Walker & Walker 1994 and 1997), however, argue that this cycle of deprivation could be broken by providing more jobs and a higher level of income.

Labour's Social Exclusion unit

In August 1997, the Labour government announced its intention of addressing the problem of 'social exclusion' with the creation of a 'Social Exclusion Unit'. The name of the unit is significant because it reveals something of the unit's aims and approach. These were devised largely by Geoff Mulgan, director of the think tank Demos and a government adviser. He insists on using the term 'social exclusion' rather than the 'poor' or 'the underclass' because:

'Poverty is only one attribute of those at the bottom of the heap. They are more properly defined as excluded because they live outside the worlds of work, of education, of sociability itself.' (*New Statesman*, 29 August 1997)

Mulgan dismisses Will Hutton's notion of a 30-30-40 society. He also dismisses criteria of poverty such as the Council of Europe's 'decency threshold' (which classes as poor all workers earning below two-thirds of the average wage - 48% of the British workforce) or the definition used by the Low Pay Unit (which classes as poor those living in families earning half the average wage or less - 17% of the population). He argues that many people move in and out of poverty and so are not a fit subject for government assistance. Instead:

'He focuses on the 8-10% who stay poor - who leave school with no qualifications, who live in areas where nearly 50% of crimes are committed, and who provide most of the single-parent families and drug addicts.' (*New Statesman*, 29 August 1997) Mulgan's idea is that a deal should be made between these people and the state. To do this, it will be necessary to decentralise the provision of welfare and to bring together the various agencies that deliver welfare - a task which would require fundamental changes to the way in which welfare provision is delivered. This explains why the announcement of the setting up of the Social

Exclusion Unit was described by Peter Mandelson as: 'The most important innovation we have made.' Similarly, Tony Blair claimed that this new unit, which would report directly to him, would prove a vital force in tackling poverty and fulfilling his vision of a 'one nation Britain' (*Guardian*, 9 December 1997).

Critics, however, noted the lack of extra financial resources to fund any new policies recommended by the Social Exclusion Unit.

Main points - Section 3.1

- The decline of Britain's manufacturing base has been described as 'de-industrialisation'. Although de-industrialisation began before 1979, since then the process has accelerated.
- In the 1990s, the labour force is no longer predominantly male. One reason why many jobs have been taken by women rather than by men is that they are part-time and low paid. Many employers prefer to take on part-timers because part-timers do not make the same demands on employers as full-time workers.
- De-industrialisation has changed not just the

composition of the labour force but the way in which people work. Increasingly, there is a move away from the old-style, 'nine to five', full-time jobs to new ways of work.
- De-industrialisation has resulted in a net loss of jobs and the development of a group of long-term unemployed people. There is a debate about whether this group should be described as an 'underclass'. The Labour government's Social Exclusion Unit aims to address the problems faced by this group.

Activity 5.5 The impact of de-industrialisation

Item A *De-industrialisation*

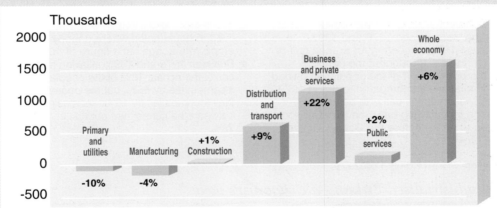

This chart shows the anticipated overall employment change in Britain 1994-2001 by broad industrial sector.

Adapted from Institute for Employment Research 1995.

Item B *The underclass*

It is a word you won't find in the party manifestos, but it's at the back of politicians' minds whenever they speak about schools, jobs and especially law and order. And, although it is rarely said out loud, it fuels the frenetic debate about the family and morality. The word is 'underclass' - the growing army of have-nots most politicians would like to pretend does not exist. Just under 19 million people live on the margins of poverty (on an income of less than £105 per week). They are much more likely to be ill than the better-off, to smoke, eat badly, indulge in petty crime, beat their children. They are caught in a vicious circle of poverty - bad housing, unemployment, low pay, poor diet and dismal schools. And, they find themselves increasingly excluded from mainstream society. The government's own figures show nearly 14% are now totally dependent on welfare. That's about 8 million people and even this is an underestimate because of the thousands of people, most of them young, who don't register in any statistics. Throughout this century people have defined themselves by their work. They were miners, engineers and so on and they were predominantly male. But, as the manufacturing industries collapsed, more jobs were taken by women and millions of badly educated men could no longer define themselves. 'I'm a printer' could be said with pride. 'I'm on benefit' is a mark of exclusion.

Adapted from the *Observer*, 13 April 1997.

Item C   *Unemployment*

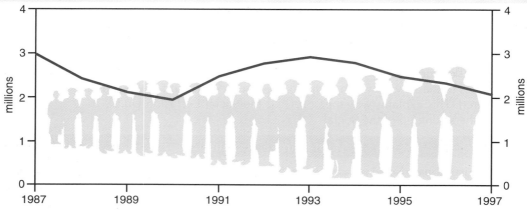

This chart shows the number of people claiming unemployment benefit 1971-97. It should be noted that, between 1979 and 1997, the Conservative government changed the way in which unemployment figures were calculated on 32 occasions (*Labour Research*, January 1997). On all but one of these occasions, the number of people unemployed fell after the adjustment.

Item D   *The rich and the poor, 1979-97*

- The richest 1%, about 448,000 people, own 17% of the UK's privately owned wealth.
- The richest 5% own 36% of the total of privately owned wealth.
- The wealthiest 10% own just under half the total of privately owned wealth - 48%.
- The richest 25% own nearly three-quarters of private wealth - 72%.
- There was little change in the distribution of wealth at the top between 1979 and 1997, with the wealthiest 10% accounting for around half of all wealth in the UK throughout the period.
- In 1997, the poorest half of the population owned only 7% of total wealth compared to 8% in 1979 when the Conservatives came to power.
- Although the income gap between rich and poor had started to widen before the Conservatives

came to power in 1979, it accelerated sharply during the 1980s.
- The widening gap meant that the number of people living below the official poverty line of half average earnings grew from 5 million in 1979 to 13.7 million in 1995 - an increase of 174%.
- Of the 13.7 million people living in poverty in 1997, the largest single group was single parents. The figures show that 31% of British children lived in households where nobody was in full-time employment, against a figure of 18% in 1979.
- Between 1979 and 1995, allowing for housing costs, the richest 10% of the population saw their incomes rise by 65%, but the poorest 10% saw their incomes fall by 13% - increasing the gap between the richest and poorest in the country by 78%.

Adapted from *Labour Research*, May 1997.

Item E   *De-industrialised Britain - a cartoonist's view*

This cartoon appeared in the *Guardian* on 13 June 1994.

Questions

1. Judging from Items A-E, what have been the social consequences of economic change?
2. What impact has de-industrialisation made on the labour market? Use Items A, C and E in your answer.
3. a) Judging from Items B and D, what is the evidence that an 'underclass' has developed?
   b) How useful is the term 'underclass'?
4. a) What does Item D tell us about the way in which the distribution of wealth changed under the Conservatives, 1979-97?
   b) What were the social consequences of this?
5. What point is being made by Item E?

3.2 The developing role of trade unions

The origins of trade unions

Trade unions developed in Britain in the late 18th and early 19th century in response to the new ways of work which resulted from the industrial revolution. Whereas, individually, workers found that they had little chance of persuading employers to improve pay or conditions at work, they found that, collectively, they had a great deal of bargaining power. As a result, workers in the same industry set up organisations whose function was to represent them in disputes with their employers. These organisations became known as trade unions. By the end of the 19th century, workers in most industries had the opportunity of joining a union. In 1868, a number of unions set up a national body, the Trades Union Congress (TUC). Since 1868, the TUC has met annually to consider matters of common interest to its members.

The Labour Representation Committee

In 1900, the TUC made the decision to support a new Labour Representation Committee (LRC) which would put up candidates in parliamentary elections. Unions agreed to charge a levy on each of their members to help fund the election of these candidates. In 1906, the LRC changed its name to the Labour Party. The Labour Party and the trade unions have maintained close ties ever since (see Chapter 8, Sections 2.1-2.3).

The growth of unions

Although the first unions encountered a great deal of opposition from employers and governments, by the end of the 19th century they had managed to gain legal recognition and over 2 million members. Trade union membership had grown to 7.8 million by 1945 and reached its peak of 13.4 million in 1979.

The unions and politics

Although the main role of trade unions is to protect and improve the pay and conditions of the workers whom they represent (an industrial and economic function), there is an underlying political element in their work. By organising and representing the workers, the unions ensure that employers cannot hire and fire at will and that the interests of the workers must be taken into account. A union's ultimate weapon is to call a strike. By withdrawing their labour, the workforce ensures that the employer loses profits. A strike or a threat of strike, therefore, puts pressure on the employer to meet the union's demands. On a large scale, this can have important political implications. Since unions represent many different groups of workers, it is possible that if one group is in dispute then unions representing other groups will take action in support of this group. There is, in short, the possibility that the workers, rather than the employers or the politicians, will use their collective power to dictate what industrial policy should be. It is because this is a possibility that many employers and politicians have been or remain hostile to trade unions.

On occasion, the reaction to union action has been dramatic. In 1926, for example, when the unions called for a general strike (a strike by all union members), the Conservative government was convinced that the unions intended to overthrow the government. A national emergency was declared and troops and volunteers used to break the strike. In fact, the General Strike lasted for just 13 days. Its defeat was followed by the passing of anti-union legislation (just as anti-union legislation was passed by the government after the miners' strike of 1984-85).

Despite enduring hostility from the government on occasions, however, trade union links with the Labour Party have ensured that the point of view of the unions is represented in Parliament.

The decline of unions since 1979

The age of corporatism

Governments and employers have not always been hostile to unions. During the Second World War and for the following 30 years, unions were tolerated and even involved in policy making at government level. This was the period of 'corporatism' (see Chapter 10, Section 3.1). The setting up of the welfare state after 1945 meant a huge growth in the public sector. Since the government was responsible for setting the wages and working conditions of public sector employees, it was imperative for it to maintain good relations with the unions (since strikes in the public sector could be politically damaging). Besides, the successful management of the public sector would ensure national economic success. Between 1945 and 1979, Labour and Conservative governments alike included trade unionists in policy making as a matter of course.

Industrial strife in the 1970s

The involvement of unions in government policy making did not, however, prevent significant industrial disputes from taking place. In the 1970s a number of major strikes were called. A miner's strike in 1974 significantly contributed to the downfall of Edward Heath's government and the so-called 'winter of discontent' of 1978-79 saw widespread strike action amongst public sector employees. As a result, by 1979 unions were being blamed by opponents for Britain's economic decline and polls showed that a majority of the population agreed that unions had too much power (see Chapter 3, Section 1.2).

Unions since 1979

Since 1979, not only have unions been excluded from government policy making, they have also been the subject of a number of hostile laws. Throughout the 1980s, union membership declined rapidly. This was due to public disaffection with the unions, government hostility towards the unions, and the rapid decline of manufacturing and other strongly unionised industries (such as the coal industry). This combination of government hostility to unions and de-industrialisation has forced unions to reconsider their role, as John Monks, General Secretary of the TUC, made clear in the following passage:

> 'The re-awakening of trade unions as a central force in public life will depend on our efforts to convince workers, especially those in newly developing industries and services that it is in their interests to join and play an active part in the movement. Equally, it is up to unions to show to employers, politicians and the community that we have a positive contribution to make to the development of public policy. The new trade unionism will not be the same as that of the 1960s or 1970s...We are determined to focus our resources on the key issues, such as jobs, the rights of people at work and developing a union response to new management styles.' (*Guardian*, 31 August 1994)

Trade unions and the Labour government

In 1997, many in the trade union movement believed that the best chance for improvement in their fortunes lay with the election of a Labour government. Union density (the percentage of the workforce holding trade union membership) had fallen from 39% in 1989 to 31.1% by 1996 (*Labour Research*, July 1997) and membership had fallen to below 7 million by the time of the 1997 general election. In addition, the cumulative effect of trade union legislation had dramatically reduced the ability of the unions to take actions on behalf of their members.

At the first meeting of the TUC after the 1997 general election, delegates welcomed Labour's commitments on employee rights and minimum standards but John Edmonds, the General Secretary of the GMB, criticised the Labour government's endorsement of 'labour flexibility' (*Guardian*, 9 September 1997). Also, Tony Blair upset some unionists at the TUC conference:

> 'Prime Minister Tony Blair's address caused raised eyebrows when he told unions to "modernise your political structures as we have done in the Labour Party". Warning that there could be no return to "industrial warfare", he went on: "I will watch very carefully to see how the culture of trade unionism develops."' (*Labour Research*, October 1997, p.3)

By the end of the Labour government's first year in office, relations between the government and the unions had deteriorated. A row had broken out over Labour's manifesto commitment that:

> 'Where a majority of the relevant workforce vote in a ballot for the union to represent them, then the union should be recognised.' (Labour Party 1997, p.17)

The TUC argued that this meant that a majority of those who vote in a ballot whilst the Confederation of British Industry (CBI) argued that it meant a majority of the workforce as a whole. According to Roy Hattersley:

> 'Officially and probably genuinely, Tony Blair wants the CBI and TUC to agree the procedure between themselves. Nobody believes that this is possible. For the TUC's public policy is no compromise and no surrender. Some union leaders actually believed Blair would accept their demands. Then they discovered the formula which, in the absence of agreement, Blair intends to impose...Trade union rights will only be established if 40% of the total workforce vote in favour or two-thirds of all employees take part in the ballot...Trade union leaders are offended by the idea that a Labour government - for which they have waited so long and paid so much - should be constantly and visibly on the employers' side.' (*Observer*, 12 April 1998)

- Trade unions are organisations whose function is to represent employees in disputes with their employers. Their main role is to protect and improve pay and working conditions, but there is also an underlying political element in their work.
- Between 1945 and 1979, union membership grew and governments included unions in decision making.
- Between 1979 and 1997, union membership

declined, unions were excluded from government decision making and nine major Acts were passed restricting union activity.
- Most unionists welcomed the election of a Labour government in 1997. There was some disappointment, however, with the government's failure to support the unions in the dispute with the CBI over union recognition.

Activity 5.6 *Unions in the 1990s*

Item A *Trade union legislation 1979-97*

A. Employment Act 1980
1. No new closed shop agreements to be made unless at least 80% of workers vote for them in a ballot.
2. Employees who lose their jobs through refusal to join a union on principle to be eligible for compensation.
3. Government to fund union ballots.
4. Picketing and secondary action severely limited.

B. Employment Act 1982
1. Existing closed shop agreements to be put to the vote and only to remain if at least 80% of workers vote in favour.
2. Compensation (See A.2 left) to be increased.
3. Sympathy action, 'political' strikes and action against non-unionised companies made illegal.

C. Trade Union Act 1984
1. Strikes only lawful if majority vote for them in a ballot.
2. Union leaders to be elected if members request it.
3. Unions obliged to hold ballot every 10 years on whether members want to continue to pay into the political fund (which goes to the Labour party).

D. Public Order Act 1986
Created new offences of riot, violent disorder and affray which could be used against marchers and pickets.

E. Employment Act 1988
1. Illegal to dismiss worker for not joining union, even if 80%+ have voted for closed shop.
2. Illegal to strike in support of closed shop agreement.
3. Illegal for union to discipline a member who refuses to join in strike action.

F. Employment Act 1989
Reduced rights to time off for trade union duties.

G. Employment Act 1990
1. Illegal for employer to refuse job on grounds that applicant does not belong to a union.
2. All secondary or sympathy action illegal.

H. Trade Union Reform and Employment Rights Act 1993
1. Strike ballots fully postal and employers to be notified before and after ballot.
2. Individuals have right to go to court to challenge strikes.
3. Unions prevented from poaching other unions' members.
4. Union members to write every three years if they want employer to deduct union dues from pay.
5. Information on union funds and salaries to be accessible to members.

Adapted from Dorey 1991, Allan et al. 1994 and *Labour Research*, May 1997.

Item B *New Labour and the unions (1)*

The election of a Labour government could have a major impact on industrial relations and, in particular, on collective bargaining. Even though collective bargaining is generally seen as a matter of 'voluntary' agreements between employers and unions, it will be set in a very different atmosphere from the last 18 years. Gone will be the Tories' promotion of individualism and self-interest and, hopefully, also finished is their programme of constantly shifting the power balance in favour of employers. Governments can affect collective bargaining both by creating a particular legal and economic framework and through their own actions as

a major employer in areas like the NHS and civil service. The most obvious impact which the new Labour government will have is through its commitment to introducing a statutory minimum wage. The impact of this on collective bargaining will, of course, depend on the level at which the minimum wage is set. The second commitment which will directly affect collective bargaining is the decision to join the Social Chapter. This will bring in a number of new rights and encourage greater consultation and employee representatives.

Adapted from *Labour Research*, June 1997.

Item C   *New Labour and the unions (2)*

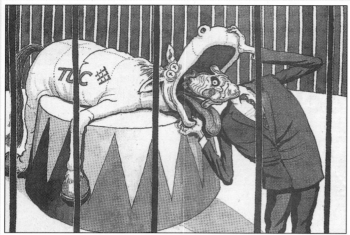

This cartoon was published on 10 September 1997, at the time of the first TUC Congress to be held after the general election. The cartoonist William Low (who drew before and during the Second World War) portrayed the TUC as a carthorse - slow and unwieldy but very strong. Steve Bell (who drew the cartoon above) often parodies this image by portraying the TUC as a pantomime horse. Not only does this suggest that the TUC lacks any real power, it also suggests that the head sometimes moves in a different direction from the rest of the body.

Item D   *Trade union membership (1)*

Date	Union membership
1979	12,128,000
1980	12,172,000
1981	11,601,000
1982	11,005,000
1983	10,510,000
1984	10,082,000
1985	9,855,000
1986	9,585,000
1987	9,243,000
1988	9,127,000
1989	8,964,000
1990	8,854,000
1991	8,633,000
1992	7,999,000
1993	7,808,000
1994	7,553,000
1995	7,275,000
1996	7,215,000

This chart provides information about membership of trade unions between 1979 and 1996.

Adapted from *Labour Market Trends*, June 1997.

Item E   *Trade union membership (2)*

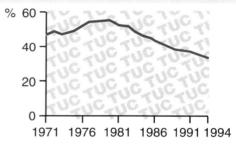

This graph shows trade union membership as a percentage of people in employment (excluding those in the armed forces).

Adapted from Social Trends 1997.

Item F   *Trade unions and new working practices*

The new leadership is reorganising the TUC so that it becomes more pragmatic and open. This is, in part, a response to falling numbers - the continuing decline particularly affects the once dominant manual and skilled workers unions. Today, the largest union is Unison which is largely concentrated in public (or former public) services. Union membership is highest amongst teachers whilst actors and university lecturers have bucked the declining trend. TUC General Secretary John Monks says he wants to create a non-party trade unionism which will sustain itself by its effectiveness and innovation. In this, he finds support from Labour. The TUC has not demanded, and will not demand, a special place in government once more. Instead, it has adopted a programme known as 'new unionism' which emphasises self-help. Union membership now stands at around 31% of all employees. The fall last year was less than 1%, the smallest for a decade. Optimists see the decline as reaching a plateau. But, nobody expects a fundamental change. The trends towards part-time work, greater professionalism of the workforce, flexible and individual contracts, more rapid hire and fire, the pressures of domestic and global competition, the ability of new technologies to give workers individual workspace in which union organisation is irrelevant - all of these can be at best neutral to trade unionism, but are more often damaging to it. The Labour government will not, politically or industrially, cut against the prevailing trend. The unions have to prove they can survive in stormy waters. The waters have become a little warmer, that is all.

Adapted from an article in the *New Statesman's* 1998 Trade Union Guide.

Questions

1. a) Judging from Items D and E, what were the consequences of the legislation outlined in Item A?
   b) Can you think of any other reasons to explain the trends shown in Items D and E?

2. a) Judging from Items B, C and F how did the election of a Labour government in May 1997 affect the prospects of trade unions?
   b) Do trade unions have a role to play in the future? Use Items B, C and F in your answer.

3. Look at Item C. What point is the cartoonist making about the relationship between the TUC and the new Labour government?

References

Adonis & Pollard (1997) Adonis, A. & Pollard, D., *A Class Act*, Hamish Hamilton, 1997.

Allan et al. (1994) Allan, P., Benyon, J. & McCormick, B., *Focus on Britain 1994*, Perennial Publications, 1994.

Almond & Verba (1963) Almond, G. & Verba, S., *The Civic Culture: Political Attitudes and Democracy In Five Nations*, Princeton University Press, 1963.

Almond & Verba (1981) Almond, G. & Verba, S., *The Civic Culture Revisited*, Little Brown (Boston, USA), 1981.

Anderton (1996) Anderton, A., *The Student's Economy in Focus 1996-7*, 1996.

Anderton (1997) Anderton, A., *The Student's Economy in Focus 1997-8*, 1996.

Barnett (1997) Barnett, A., *This Time. Our Constitutional Revolution*, Vintage, 1997.

Bassnett (1986) Bassnett, S., *Feminist Experiences*, Allen & Unwin, 1986.

Bonnett (1994) Bonnett, K., 'Power and politics' in *Haralambos (1994)*.

Bouchier (1983) Bouchier, D., *The Feminist Challenge*, Macmillan, 1983.

Butler & Stokes (1971) Butler, D. & Stokes, D., *Political Change in Britain*, Penguin 1971.

Dahrendorf (1992) Dahrendorf, R., 'Footnotes to the discussion' in *Smith (1992)*.

Demos (1997) Leonard, M., *Britain TM*, Demos, 1997.

Denscombe (1997) Denscombe, M., *Sociology Update*, Olympus Books UK, 1997.

Dorey (1991) Dorey, P., 'Politics and the trade unions', *Politics Review*, Vol.1.1, September 1991.

Forbes (1991) Forbes, I., 'The politics of gender' in *Wale (1991)*.

Freidan (1963) Freidan, B., *The Feminine Mystique*, Norton (New York), 1963.

German (1996) German, L., *A Question of Class*, Bookmarks, 1996.

Gilborn & Gipps (1996) Gilborn, D. & Gipps, C., *Recent Research on the Achievement of Ethnic Minority Pupils*, OFSTED, 1997.

Gilroy (1987) Gilroy, P., *There Ain't No Black in the Union Jack*, Hutchinson, 1987.

Haralambos (1994) Haralambos, M. (ed.) *Developments in Sociology*, Vol.10, Causeway Press, 1994.

Haralambos (1996) Haralambos, M. (ed.) *Developments in Sociology*, Vol.12, Causeway Press, 1996.

Haralambos (1997) Haralambos, M. (ed.) *Developments in Sociology*, Vol.13, Causeway Press, 1997.

HMSO (1995) Social and Community Planning Research, *Social Focus on Women*, HMSO, 1995.

Hutton (1997) Hutton, W., *The State to Come*, Vintage, 1997.

IPPR (1997) Institute for Public Policy Research (IPPR), *A Report on a Survey Conducted by NOP (Social and Political) on behalf of IPPR*, IPPR, 1997.

Kavanagh (1981) Kavanagh, D., 'Political culture in Great Britain: the decline of the civic culture' in *Almond & Verba (1981)*.

Kavanagh (1983) Kavanagh, D., *British Politics, Continuities and Change*, Oxford University Press, 1983.

Labour (1997) Labour Party manifesto, *New Labour Because Britain Deserves Better*, Labour Party, 1997.

Lister (1996) Lister, R. (ed.), *Charles Murray and the Underclass: the Developing Debate*, Institute of Economic Affairs, 1996.

Miliband (1972) Miliband, R., *The State in Capitalist Society*, Weidenfeld and Nicholson, 1972.

Miliband (1989) Miliband, R., *Divided Societies*, Oxford University Press, 1989.

Mitchell (1971) Mitchell, J., *Women's Estate*, Penguin, 1971.

Modood (1988) Modood, T., 'Black, racial equality and Asian identity', *New Community*, Vol.14.3, 1988.

Moran (1989) Moran, M., *Politics and Society in Britain. An Introduction*, Macmillan, 1989.

Murray (1996) Murray, C., 'The Emerging British Underclass' in *Lister (1996)*.

Pascall (1995) Pascall, G., 'Women on top? Women's careers in the 1990s', *Sociology Review*, Vol.4.3, 1995.

Pilkington (1997) Pilkington, A., 'Ethnicity and education' in *Haralambos (1997)*.

Pimlott (1989) Pimlott, B., 'Is the post-war consensus a myth?', *Contemporary Record*, Summer 1989.

PSI (1997) Policy Studies Institute, *Ethnic Minorities in Britain*, Policy Studies Institute, 1997.

Pulzer (1967) Pulzer, P.G., *Political Representation and Elections*, Allen & Unwin, 1967.

Richardson (1996) Richardson, J., 'Race and Ethnicity' in *Haralambos (1996)*.

Rowntree (1995) Joseph Rowntree Foundation, *Inquiry into Income and Wealth*, Joseph Rowntree Foundation, 1995.

Runnymede (1991) *Runnymede Trust Bulletin*, No.247, July/August 1991.

Rush (1992) Rush, M., *Politics And Society. An Introduction to Political Sociology*, Harvester Wheatsheaf, 1992.

Saunders (1990) Saunders, P., *Social Class and Stratification*, Routledge, 1990.

Scarman (1981) Lord Scarman, *The Scarman Report*, Penguin, 1981.

Smith (1992) Smith.D. (ed.), *Understanding the Underclass*, Policy Studies Institute, 1992.

Social Trends (1997) Government Statistical Service, *Social Trends*, Vol.27, HMSO, 1997.

Social Trends (1998) Government Statistical Service, *Social Trends*, Vol.28, HMSO, 1998.

Strachey (1928) Strachey, R., *The Cause*, Virago, 1979.

Taylor (1997) Taylor, P., *Investigating Culture and Identity*, Collins Educational, 1997.

Taylor (1993) Taylor, S., 'The politics of immigration and race in Britain' in *Wale* (1993).

Wale (1991) Wale, W. (ed.), *Developments in Politics*, Vol.2, Causeway Press, 1991.

Wale (1993) Wale, W. (ed.), *Developments in Politics*, Vol.4, Causeway Press, 1993.

Walker & Walker (1994) Walker, C. & Walker, A., 'Poverty and the poor' in *Haralambos* (1994).

Walker & Walker (1997) Walker, C. & Walker, A., 'Poverty and social exclusion' in *Haralambos* (1997).

Walvin (1984) Walvin, J., *Passage to Britain*, Penguin, 1984.

West (1997) West, J., 'Gender and work: continuity and change in the sexual division of labour' in *Haralambos* (1997).

Westergaard & Resler (1976) Westergaard, J. & Resler, H., *Class in a Capitalist Society*, Penguin, 1976.

Wilson (1984) Wilson, A., *Finding a Voice*, Virago, 1984.

6 Europe and the international context

Introduction

All too often Europe has been portrayed as something out there - just another factor in Britain's external relations, albeit a factor which can influence domestic decisions. Such a picture is misleading. The European Union (EU) is far more significant than any other international organisation to which Britain belongs. When Britain decided to join the EEC - European Economic Community (as it then was) - in 1972, the government signed a number of treaties. These treaties have all the characteristics of a written constitution and are binding within the UK. The treaties set out the powers and responsibilities of the European Union's institutions and their decision-making procedures. They also provide the means of settling disputes through the European Court. Since 1973, membership of the EU has made an impact on a wide range of domestic policies - including trade policy, agricultural policy, environmental policy and social policy, to give just a few examples.

With the passing of the Single European Act in 1986 and the ratification of the Maastricht Treaty in 1993, the ties between member states have become closer and there is pressure to make them closer still. Some member states want to move towards political and economic union. Others (including Britain) are concerned that this would mean an unacceptable loss of sovereignty. In Britain, there is intense debate over the exact role that Britain should be playing within the EU. Some politicians have even argued that Britain should withdraw from the EU altogether.

This chapter concentrates on the European Union, but it also looks at how Britain's role and status in the world has changed since 1945. In particular, it examines the international organisations to which Britain belongs (such as NATO, the United Nations and the Commonwealth) and considers the role which Britain plays within these organisations.

Chapter summary

Part 1 looks at the development of the European Union. Why was it first set up and how has it developed since then?

Part 2 focuses on the organisation of the EU. It looks at how decisions are made and the balance of power between the various institutions.

Part 3 analyses the present debate over the direction which the EU should take. Should it cement ties and become a federation or loosen ties and become a confederation of nation states?

Part 4 looks at globalisation. What is it? What are the consequences for the nation state? How does globalisation affect Britain and Europe?

Part 5 examines Britain's changing role and status in the world since 1945. How has Britain's role changed? What is Britain's relationship with the international organisations to which it belongs?

Part 1 The development of the European Union

Key issues

1. What led to the foundation of the European Economic Community in 1958?
2. Why was Britain not one of the founder members of the EEC?
3. What are the main developments since Britain joined in 1973?

1.1 Historical background

Origins of the EEC

The term 'European Union' has evolved as the organisation has evolved. At first, the organisation was known as the 'European Economic Community' (EEC) or 'Common Market' but, after the Single European Act was passed in 1986, the name changed to 'European Community' (EC). In 1993, after the ratification of the Maastricht Treaty, the name changed again from European Community to 'European Union' (EU). The evolution of the name reflects changes in the structure and nature of the organisation.

What led to the EEC?
Three factors are central to the origins of the EEC. First, at the end of the Second World War, European politicians were very aware that both world wars had followed a similar pattern. Twice, Germany had invaded France through Belgium, Luxembourg and the Netherlands (the 'Benelux' countries). It seemed to some politicians, therefore, that the best way of avoiding a third war was for European countries to work together politically, economically and perhaps even militarily. Second, the vast majority of countries in Europe had been involved in the Second World War. Not only had a great deal of fighting taken place in these countries, the economies in many of them had been stretched to breaking point. As a result, European countries did not have the resources to rebuild their economies on their own. Economic necessity led them towards cooperation. And third, the end of the Second World War was soon followed by the outbreak of the Cold War. Europe quickly became divided between the East (dominated by the Soviet Union) and the West (dominated by the USA). The Cold War encouraged Western European countries to cooperate with each other.

First moves towards union
The idea of a united Europe was first put forward in public by the British Prime Minister, Winston Churchill, in a speech made on 19 September 1946. Churchill advocated the building of a 'United States of Europe'. It is ironic that a British politician should have been the first to suggest European union since Britain refused to become a founding member of the EEC.

The first step towards a united Europe was made by the Benelux countries when they joined together to establish the Benelux customs union which came into effect in January 1948.

This was soon followed by the setting up of the Organisation for European Economic Cooperation (OEEC). The OEEC was set up to administer 'Marshall Aid' - a massive programme of financial aid set up by the USA to encourage economic recovery in Europe ($13 billion was distributed in four years). Although Marshall Aid (named after American Secretary of State, George Marshall) was offered to East European countries, they refused it on the grounds that it would lead to American interference in their domestic affairs (see Section 5.2 below). Consequently, members of the OEEC all came from Western Europe.

The Schuman plan
The next important step on the road to European union came in 1950 when Jean Monnet, a French

civil servant, and Robert Schuman, French Foreign Secretary, formulated what became known as the Schuman plan. Their aim was twofold. First, they wanted to promote economic recovery in both France and West Germany by pooling both countries' coal and steel industries. And second, they hoped to make war between the two countries impossible by placing their key industries under joint authority.

The ECSC
The Schuman plan was announced in 1950 and led to the creation of the European Coal and Steel Community (ECSC). The ECSC came into operation in 1952 after six countries (France, West Germany, Italy and the Benelux countries) signed the Treaty of Paris in 1951. The aim of the ECSC was to:

> 'Establish a common market for coal and steel, to ensure supplies, to promote expansion and modernisation of production and to provide better employment conditions.' (HMSO 1992, p.3)

In addition, the ECSC was the first European organisation to have a supranational structure. A supranational organisation is one in which institutions are created which have powers above that of any individual nation's government. The supranational structure of the ECSC became the blueprint for the structure of the EEC.

Supranationalism v intergovernmentalism
By the time the ECSC was set up, disagreements over the future shape of Europe had begun to emerge. The British government was particularly suspicious of supranational organisations, favouring instead intergovernmental organisations (in which each member state has the right to veto any measure to protect its national interests). Geddes notes that:

> 'Tension between supranationalists and intergovernmentalists became apparent at the May 1948 Congress of Europe in the Hague where over 700 prominent Europeans met to discuss the future of the continent. The outcome of the meeting was the creation of the Council of Europe in May 1949...Britain's preference for intergovernmentalism prevailed in the Council of Europe: decisions in its Council of Ministers are taken on the basis of unanimity.' (Geddes 1993, p.21)

Whilst the Council of Europe represented a triumph for intergovernmentalists, the creation of the ECSC represented a triumph for supranationalists.

The Messina conference and the creation of the EEC
In 1955, the foreign ministers of the ECSC member states met at Messina in Italy and agreed to set up a committee to consider further progress towards European integration. This committee's report led to the drawing up of the two Treaties of Rome which were signed by the six ECSC members in March

1957. One Treaty established the European Atomic Energy Community (Euratom) to coordinate members' development of nuclear energy. The second set up the European Economic Community:

> 'Its founding Treaty was premised on an "ever closer union of the peoples of Europe". It abolished trade barriers and customs duties and established a common external tariff, thereby making the EEC a customs union. The EEC was also designed to promote the free movement of people, goods, services and capital within a common market. The member states transferred to the EEC powers to conclude trading agreements with international organisations on their behalf.' (Geddes 1993, p.24)

The EEC formally came into existence on 1 January 1958.

Britain's early relations with Europe

Although the British government was invited to join the negotiations which led to the foundation of the EEC, it refused to become involved on the grounds that joining a supranational organisation would endanger national sovereignty. It was argued that, if Britain joined the EEC, it would lose the right to follow independent economic and defence policies. There were a number of reasons for Britain's aloofness. Britain was geographically separate from mainland Europe and, unlike its neighbours, had not been subject to conquest in recent times. In addition, Britain still had strong ties with countries outside Europe. Although the British Empire broke up after 1945, Britain still retained trading links with former colonies, especially those in the British Commonwealth. And third, the British government believed that it had a 'special relationship' with the USA.

EFTA

In response to the creation of the EEC, Britain attempted to establish a free trade area which covered all members of the OEEC (including the six members of the EEC). France, however, rejected this idea and negotiations failed. Instead, Britain and six countries which belonged to the OEEC but not to the EEC (Austria, Norway, Sweden, Denmark, Portugal and Switzerland) formed the European Free Trade Association (EFTA) in 1960. The aim of EFTA was to dismantle barriers to trade between members (so that trade would increase amongst members) and to provide a base from which to negotiate with the EEC over the creation of a single European market. During the 1960s, however, it became apparent that Britain's trade was growing faster with the EEC than it was with EFTA.

Britain's attempts to join the EEC

When the British government realised that the EEC was becoming a powerful trading bloc, it applied to join the EEC. Britain's first application was made in

1961. Negotiations continued until 1963 when the French President, Charles de Gaulle, vetoed Britain's application. Britain reapplied in 1967, but again this application was vetoed by de Gaulle. It was only after de Gaulle retired in 1969 that the British government was able to negotiate its entry into the EEC. In 1971, the Prime Minister, Edward Heath, held talks with de Gaulle's successor Pompidou. The following year, Heath signed the Treaty of Accession and on 1 January 1973, Britain became a member of the EEC (together with two other new members - Ireland and Denmark).

The EEC referendum, 1975

When Britain joined the EEC in 1973, it was confronted by a number of problems. First, most British politicians did not share the vision of those Euro-enthusiasts who looked forward to the creation of a European superstate. Although the British government, by joining the EEC, had accepted the EEC's supranational structure, many politicians accepted this only reluctantly. Second, friction arose because Britain had not been a member from the start. As a result, Britain had to accept existing policies and regulations which it had played no part in developing. Third, there was a price to pay for membership, in the short term at least. Since Britain had substantial trading links with non-EEC countries (especially Commonwealth countries) its contribution to EEC funds was particularly high (trading with non-EEC countries was penalised). On the other hand, because Britain's agricultural sector was highly efficient, it did not benefit from the EEC's Common Agricultural Policy (CAP) as much as other member states.

Rather than addressing each of these problems and tackling them head-on:

> 'British membership of the EC was advocated on pragmatic economic grounds. Britain thought it was joining a common market - an economic organisation - and played down the political consequences of membership.' (Geddes 1993, p.33)

Concern about membership of the EEC came to a head after the general election of October 1974. The new Labour government came to office with the pledge to renegotiate Britain's terms of membership and to hold a referendum. This referendum was held in June 1975. There was a 64% turnout and 67% voted in favour of remaining in the EEC.

Margaret Thatcher and the EEC

On becoming Prime Minister in 1979, Margaret Thatcher launched an attack on the EEC because Britain's contribution to the EEC Budget was too high (Britain was the second largest contributor to the EEC Budget even though it had the third lowest GDP per capita of all members). The result was a long and fierce battle over Britain's contribution.

The issue was not settled until 1984 when a rebate was agreed.

The Single European Act 1986

The second major development in the Thatcher years was the passing of the Single European Act in 1986. This Act was supported by Thatcher and her allies on the grounds that a free, single market would mean greater deregulation and less governmental intervention (and therefore greater economic growth), but it was also supported by the President of the European Commission, Jacques Delors, on the grounds that it would restart the move towards greater European integration. The result has been an ongoing debate about the future direction of Europe. This debate has yet to be resolved.

Main points - Section 1.1

- Political, military and economic factors led to the development of the EEC after the end of the Second World War.
- The EEC came into existence in 1958, a year after six countries signed the Treaty of Rome.
- Britain was not a founder member of the EEC, but it applied to join in 1961. This application was rejected, as was an application in 1967. Britain finally joined in 1973. Britain's membership was given popular support in a referendum held in 1975.
- During Margaret Thatcher's premiership, Britain's contribution to the EEC budget was reduced and the Single European Act was signed.

Activity 6.1 *The development of the EEC*

Item A *The evolution of the EEC*

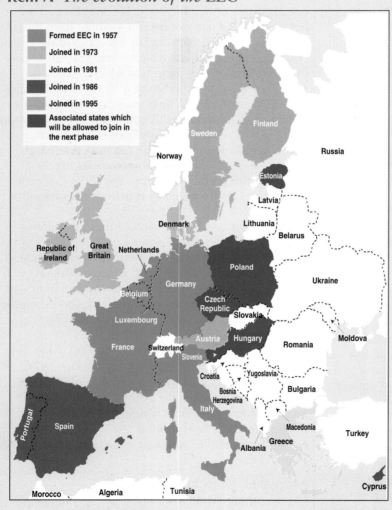

Legend:
- Formed EEC in 1957
- Joined in 1973
- Joined in 1981
- Joined in 1986
- Joined in 1995
- Associated states which will be allowed to join in the next phase

Item B *De Gaulle's veto*

(i) After refusing to join the community we are building, after creating a free trade area with six other states (EFTA), and after trying to prevent a real beginning for the Common Market, Britain has now applied for membership - on its own terms. But, Britain is insular, maritime, linked by trade, markets and food supply to very different and often very distant lands. How can Britain be brought into this system? How far is it possible for Britain to accept a truly common tariff? For this would involve giving up all Commonwealth preferences and treating as null and void obligations entered into with the Free Trade Area. It is possible that one day Britain might manage to transform itself sufficiently to become part of the EEC. In that case, the Six would open their door and France would raise no obstacle.

Adapted from a speech made by President de Gaulle in January 1963.

(ii) To tell the truth Britain's attitude is easy to explain. Having seen more clearly the great changes sweeping the world - the enormous power of the USA, the growing power of the Soviet Union, the revitalised power of the EEC, the new power of China and the growing independence of Commonwealth countries, its future is at stake. Moreover, financial difficulties and social problems force Britain to seek a framework both to safeguard itself and to play a leading role in the world.

Adapted from a speech made by President de Gaulle in September 1967.

Item C *A common tariff*

Trade between the EEC and the rest of the world was regulated so that every EEC member charged the same tariff (tax on imported goods) when trading with non-members. This had two advantages. It encouraged trade within the EEC and it prevented non-members from selling goods to the member with the lowest tariff on the understanding that this member would then sell on the goods to the other members. This common external tariff had been achieved by 1968.

Item D *Britain and the EEC*

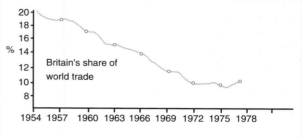

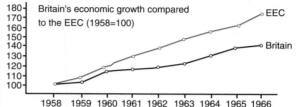

Industrial production 1959-67			
	1959	**1963**	**1967**
Britain	105	119	133
W. Germany	107	137	158
France	101	129	155
Italy	112	166	212
USA	113	133	168
Japan	120	212	347

This table gives comparisons with industrial production in 1958 (=100)

Adapted from Coates 1994.

Questions

1. Suppose Items A and C were used to illustrate an article entitled: 'The evolution of the EEC, 1958-98'. Write the article to accompany the pictures.
2. Judging from Item B, why did President de Gaulle veto Britain's two applications to join the EEC in the 1960s?
3. Using Items B and D, explain why Britain was not one of the founding members of the EEC and why it applied to join the EEC in the 1960s.

1.2 The Maastricht Treaty

Creating a European Union

At the Maastricht summit in December 1991, the 12 heads of state of the European Community agreed on a Treaty on European Union which changed the provisions laid down by the Treaty of Rome and made new commitments. The Maastricht Treaty, as it is usually known, set out to strengthen political and economic ties between member states:

> 'The effect of the Treaty was to form a European Union, to enlarge the area of policy competence of this Union beyond that enjoyed by the European Community and to strengthen further the European Parliament. It laid down a timetable for economic and monetary union. The final stage of the process

will involve the introduction of a single currency and the establishment of a Committee of the Regions. The Treaty also contained a protocol (the Social Chapter) giving force to the Social Charter, previously agreed by heads of government in 1989.' (Norton 1995, p.29)

By the end of 1993, all member states had ratified the Treaty, though a number of opt-out clauses were agreed with Britain and Denmark. As a result of these opt-outs, the Treaty does not have the same effect throughout the Union.

What does the Maastricht Treaty aim to achieve?

The Maastricht Treaty is a long and complicated document. Its passage through the British Parliament was painfully slow even though it had the backing of the government and the main opposition parties. This

Box 6.1 Main provisions of the Maastricht Treaty

1. The Treaty embodies the principle of subsidiarity. In other words, action should be taken at Community level only if its objectives cannot be sufficiently achieved by the member states acting alone.
2. The Treaty introduces the concept of Union citizenship, complementing existing national citizenship and conferring new rights for citizens of the Union to vote in elections to the European Parliament and local elections in whichever member state they live.
3. The Treaty introduces measures of institutional reform, including new powers for the European Parliament, some extension of qualified majority voting in the Council of Ministers and the establishment of a new advisory Committee of the Regions.
4. The Treaty strengthens control of the Community's finances.
5. The Treaty provides for the establishment of a common foreign and security policy conducted on an intergovernmental basis rather than within the existing framework of Community law.
6. The Treaty endorses a commitment to stepping up intergovernmental cooperation on interior and judicial issues, such as asylum and immigration policy and fighting international crime, terrorism and drug trafficking.
7. The Treaty provides for moves towards economic and monetary union.

Adapted from HMSO 1992.

was due to the opposition of backbench Conservatives who were concerned about the implications of some provisions in the Treaty.

By ratifying the Maastricht Treaty, member states created a European Union (hence the name-change from EC to EU) with three main pillars. The European Community forms one pillar, foreign and security policy forms a second pillar and justice and home affairs forms the third pillar. Whilst the European Community functions by means of a mix of supranational and intergovernmental institutions (described in Part 2 below), members agreed that in the spheres of foreign affairs, defence, home affairs and justice they should proceed through intergovernmental cooperation.

Although some member states wanted a commitment to greater federalism to be explicitly stated in the text of the Treaty, the British government fiercely opposed the use of the word 'federal'. Instead, the text of the Treaty uses the term 'ever closer union':

> 'This Treaty marks a new stage in the process of creating an ever closer union among the peoples of Europe, in which decisions are taken as closely as possible to the citizen.' (quoted in Nugent 1994, p.65)

Provisions of the Treaty

The main provisions of the Maastricht Treaty are summarised in Box 6.1 above.

Controversies

1. Federalism

The Maastricht Treaty raised questions about the direction in which the EU should head. Central to this was the question of federalism.

What is a federal system?

A federal system of government is a system where different levels of government coexist and remain autonomous. If, for example, a federal state has a national government and regional governments, the regional governments are not subordinate to the national government. Rather, the two layers of

government have their own areas of responsibility and they have control over these areas. The aim of a federal system is to ensure that decisions are made at an appropriate level. Matters concerning everyone are dealt with by national government, whilst matters concerning a particular region only are dealt with by regional government. Geddes claims that federal systems of government share five main features (see Box 6.2).

Box 6.2 Federal systems

Federal systems share the following five features:
1. Two levels of government, a general and regional.
2. Formal distribution of legislative and executive authority and sources of revenue between the two levels.
3. A written constitution.
4. An umpire - a supreme or constitutional court - to adjudicate in disputes between the two levels.
5. Central institutions, including a bicameral [two chamber] legislature within which the upper chamber will usually embody territorial representation, as in the case with the US Senate and the German Bundesrat.

Adapted from Geddes 1993.

The opposite to a federal system of government is a unitary system of government. The British system of government is unitary (see Chapter 4, Section 3.1). The powers of government in the UK are held by a central authority. Local authorities exist, but any powers they possess have been granted to them by central government and could be withdrawn by central government.

Geddes notes that Eurosceptics in Britain use the term 'federalism' in a distinct way:

> 'For its opponents, a "federal Europe" means a European superstate with a huge, centralised Brussels bureaucracy limiting the sovereign authority of member states. Advocates, on the other hand, see federation as...a means of decentralising power, not centralising it.' (Geddes 1993, p.13)

See Section 3.1 below for a summary of the arguments for and against federalism.

2. EMU

The commitment to economic and monetary union (EMU) has proved to be one of the most controversial parts of the Treaty. The Treaty laid down provisions which were intended to ensure:

- the disappearance of national currencies - they would be replaced by a single European currency (at first called the 'ECU', now called the 'Euro')
- the setting up of a European central bank (with powers to set interest rates for the whole EU).

Britain withdrew from the Exchange Rate Mechanism in 1992 (see Chapter 15, Section 3.4) and other members of the EU faced difficulties in meeting the convergence criteria laid down by the Treaty. In May 1998, however, 11 member states agreed to go ahead with EMU, beginning in January 1999.

3. The Social Chapter

A second controversial provision in the Treaty was the protocol (the Social Chapter) giving force to the Social Charter previously agreed by heads of government in 1989. The aim of this protocol was to harmonise laws on the social rights of workers to prevent unfair competition between member states through the exploitation of the workforce. Health and safety regulations, a common minimum wage and an agreed maximum number of working hours are all examples of measures covered by the Social Chapter. John Major's government negotiated an opt-out from the Social Chapter, claiming that it is an unnecessary intervention which would significantly increase the costs faced by employers. On its election in May 1997, however, the Labour government announced both that it would sign up to the Social Charter (it did so in June 1997) and that a minimum wage would be introduced.

4. Subsidiarity

A third area of controversy was the commitment to apply the principle of subsidiarity - the principle that decisions should be taken at the lowest appropriate level. The problem was that different people used the term in different ways and it was, therefore, unclear exactly what sort of future was implied by making a commitment to apply the principle. As in so many other areas, the debate over the term 'subsidiarity' boiled down to a debate about whether or not the EU should move towards federalism.

1.3 The 1997 Amsterdam Treaty

Impact of the Maastricht Treaty

Although the Maastricht Treaty was finally ratified by all member states, the ratification process revealed widespread popular discontent with the European project. In Denmark, for example, the Treaty was actually rejected in a referendum (held in June 1992) before being ratified after a second referendum (in May 1993). In France, there were mass demonstrations against the Treaty. In Britain, the Treaty bitterly divided the ruling Conservative Party and their supporters. Polls held throughout the 1990s suggested that developments in Europe were failing to capture the popular imagination in many EU member states (see Box 6.3).

Box 6.3 **Support for EU membership**

	Good thing %	Bad thing %
Ireland	83	3
Netherlands	78	9
Luxembourg	71	10
Italy	69	6
Greece	60	8
Portugal	56	6
Spain	53	9
Denmark	53	22
EU average	49	14
France	48	14
Belgium	42	18
Finland	39	25
Germany	38	15
UK	36	23
Austria	31	24
Sweden	31	48

This graph shows the results of a survey conducted by the European Commission in March 1998. Respondents were asked whether they thought membership of the EU was a 'good thing' or a 'bad thing'.

The 1997 Amsterdam Treaty

By the time that the 1997 Amsterdam Treaty was agreed, the optimistic mood which had been widespread amongst federalists in the early 1990s had changed. The grand vision of a federalist future had receded. The new key word was 'flexibility' - member states were to be allowed to integrate at their own pace, opting out when they disagreed with measures acceptable to the majority of states. It should be noted that, by 1997, the main priority of many officials was to ensure that economic and monetary union went ahead as planned. To safeguard this project, they were prepared to make compromises or postpone controversial decisions. As a result, decisions about reforming the EU's decision making rules (a crucial area given the commitment to enlargement) were shelved:

> 'More than five years since the leap towards political union and two years since talks began on the revamped version, the "Son of Maastricht" has lurched towards life as an exercise in cautious compromise, a 150-page reflection of the defensive inward-looking mood of the Union.' (*Times*, 18 June 1997)

The provisions of the Amsterdam Treaty are outlined in Item D of Activity 6.2 below.

- The Maastricht Treaty, signed in December 1991 and ratified by the end of 1993, changed the provisions laid down by the Treaty of Rome and made new commitments.
- The Treaty created a European Union with three pillars. Those who signed made a commitment to work towards 'ever closer union'.
- In Britain, the Treaty created three areas of

controversy - over economic and monetary union, over the Social Chapter, and over subsidiarity (the principle that decisions should be taken at the lowest appropriate level).
- By the time that the 1997 Amsterdam Treaty was agreed, the mood amongst European politicians and bureaucrats had changed. The Amsterdam Treaty was 'an exercise in cautious compromise'.

Activity 6.2 *Maastricht and its consequences*

Item A   *The Maastricht Treaty and federalism (1)*

(i)

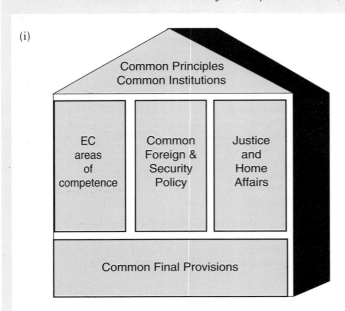

Common Principles
Common Institutions

EC areas of competence

Common Foreign & Security Policy

Justice and Home Affairs

Common Final Provisions

(ii) The negotiation of the Maastricht Treaty was marked by a clash between two rival views of the future of the EU. One shared by Germany and the federalist smaller states saw the EU as a tree with all its activities brought together in one set of institutions, eventually creating a single federal state. According to this view, the EU is a single, growing, living organism with one trunk, its roots sunk in the rich European soil. The rival metaphor, backed by France and Britain, was that of the temple. Supporters of this view wanted different policy areas split off from each other in separate pillars. Unity was provided by the 'pediment' - the part of the Treaty which covered policy areas common to all members. It was this architectural version which won out.

Adapted from Lodge 1993 and the *Independent on Sunday*, 11 September 1994.

Item B   *The Maastricht Treaty and federalism (2)*

The Maastricht Treaty was criticised by its opponents for bringing a federal superstate. Like the Single European Act, however, it simply amends, refines and extends key provisions of the existing treaties. It is paradoxical that the most centralised of the EU member states, the UK, should have drawn this conclusion from a treaty geared towards decentralised, devolved and regionalised decision making. Indeed, it is the provisions for decisions to be taken at levels lower than that of national governments which annoyed the British government. The Maastricht Treaty set up a new Committee of the Regions to achieve this. Only the British government wanted to appoint national government nominees to this new body. The federal and non-federal characteristics of the EU post-Maastricht can be listed as follows:

Federal characteristics
1. Important policy responsibilities are exercised at both the central (EU) and the regional (member state) levels.
2. Well developed institutions exist at both levels.
3. The Court of Justice is a central judicial body with the authority to rule on disputes between the two levels.
4. There is common citizenship.

Non-federal characteristics
1. Although the power of the centre (EU) has grown, the balance between the two levels is tipped very much in favour of the regional (member state) level.
2. Control of financial resources remains with the regional level. The EU budget is just 3% of total national budgets.
3. The EU's political structure is not well ordered or based on established and shared principles.
4. The rights of EU citizenship are extremely limited.

Adapted from Lodge 1993 and Nugent 1994.

Item C *Subsidiarity*

The subsidiarity principle means that decisions made by Parliaments, governments and other authorities are to be taken as close as possible to the citizen. In other words, decisions are taken at the lowest possible level (preferably by the local or regional authority). Decisions are taken at a higher level only if there is a good reason. Article 3b of the Maastricht Treaty defines subsidiarity as follows: 'The Community shall act within the limits of the powers conferred upon it by this Treaty and of the objectives assigned to it therein. In areas which do not fall within its exclusive competence, the Community shall take action, in accordance with the principle of subsidiarity, only if and in so far as the objectives of the proposed action cannot be sufficiently achieved by the member states and can, therefore, by reason of the scale or effects of the proposed action, be better achieved by the Community. Any action of the Community shall not go beyond what is necessary to achieve the objectives of this Treaty.' But subsidiarity does not just apply to legislative powers. The Treaty claims to mark: 'A new stage in the process of creating an ever closer union among the peoples of Europe, in which decisions are taken as closely as possible to the citizen.' Subsidiarity is, therefore, one of the fundamental characteristics of the EU and expresses the principle that member states preserve their individual identities.

Adapted from OOPEC 1992.

Questions

1. Why was the ratification of the Maastricht Treaty such an important event in the history of the European Community? Use Items A and B in your answer.

2. 'The aim of the Maastricht Treaty was to produce a federal Europe.' Using Items A-C, give arguments for and against this view.

3. Using Item C, explain why the principle of subsidiarity is supported by (a) politicians who support a federal Europe and (b) politicians who oppose a federal Europe. Given that the principle is supported by these different groups, how useful is it?

4. Judging from Item D, why has the 1997 Amsterdam Treaty been described as 'an exercise in cautious compromise'?

Item D *The Amsterdam Treaty*

Amsterdam Treaty, June 1997

Agreed

- Human rights - discrimination on basis of gender, race, religion, sexuality and age outlawed.

- Free movement of people guaranteed (but UK and Ireland keep border controls).

- Laws on immigration, visas, asylum and divorce to be common throughout EU.

- Europol - intelligence gathering agency - to begin operations.

- Budgetary deficits to be regulated once single currency introduced.

- Employment strategy to be coordinated between member states.

- Social Chapter to be incorporated into Treaty now that UK has signed.

- High ranking civil servant to coordinate common foreign and security policy.

- More powers and codecision procedure for EP.

No agreement

- Virtually no progress on institutional reform.

- Merger of WEU (a defence union to which several member states belong) with EU blocked by UK, Finland, Sweden and Ireland.

Adapted from the *Guardian*, 19 June 1997.

Part 2 The organisation of the European Union

Key issues

1. How are decisions made in the EU?
2. What is the role of the different institutions?
3. Where is power located?

2.1 How the EU works

EU institutions

An important characteristic of the EU is its mixture of supranational and intergovernmental institutions. This mixture ensures that, in some areas, member states are able to veto proposals which they feel are disadvantageous whilst, in other areas, decisions are made at the European level and must be implemented by members regardless of their reservations. Decisions in the EU are made by four main institutions - the Council of Ministers, the European Commission, the European Parliament and the European Court of Justice. Two consultative bodies also make an impact on some decisions - the Economic and Social Committee and the Committee of the Regions.

A. The Council of Ministers

The Council of Ministers is the EU's ultimate decision-making body. Its job is to discuss and approve (or reject) proposals drawn up by the Commission. Unlike other EU institutions, members of the Council of Ministers directly represent the interests of their member state. The Council has the power to issue regulations, directives, decisions, recommendations or resolutions:

> 'The Council has the power to make regulations (or Community laws) which are binding on member states and directly applicable. Directives are equally binding as to the aims to be achieved, but leave national authorities to decide on the methods of carrying them out. In addition, the Council can issue decisions binding those to whom they are addressed, whether member states, firms or private individuals. Recommendations and opinions are not binding. The Council can also indicate a general policy direction through resolutions.' (HMSO 1992, pp.17-18)

A revolving council

The Council of Ministers is, in reality, not a single council. It is a series of councils. The ministers responsible for the matter under discussion attend. So, if, for example, an environmental matter is under discussion, then the environment minister from each member state attends. The member state holding the presidency of the Council of Ministers chairs its meetings. The presidency is held by each member state for six months on a rota basis. The three areas most commonly discussed by the Council are foreign affairs, economics and finance, and agriculture. The Council of Foreign Ministers has a coordinating role, though there is a tendency to refer matters to the twice-yearly summits of heads of government (see below).

COREPER

Before proposals are put before the Council, they are considered by the Committee of Permanent Representatives (COREPER) which is made up of senior civil servants from the member states. This committee is able to resolve many of the issues under discussion and often the meeting of the Council of Ministers which follows acts merely as a rubber stamp. The Council of Ministers has its own staff of 2,000.

Voting procedure

The voting procedure used by the Council of Ministers depends on the matter under discussion. Some matters require **unanimity**. Some matters are decided by a **simple majority**. And some matters are decided by **qualified majority** voting. Under the qualified majority voting system, each member state is allocated a certain number of votes (Britain has ten, for example, whilst Luxembourg has two). Each member state is given roughly one vote for every four million people in its population, but the system is designed to favour the smaller states (to prevent their views always being swamped). Larger states, therefore, do not always have one vote for every four million people (Britain has ten votes, for example,

even though its population is over 50 million). The system ensures that no single member state can block a proposal. At least three member states (including two of the big states) must vote against a proposal for it to fail. The number of matters decided by the qualified voting system increased after the passing of the Single European Act in 1986 and was further extended after the Amsterdam Treaty was signed in 1997.

The European Council

Established in 1974, the European Council was set up to try to break the log-jam in Community policy making. The European Council brings together all the heads of member governments, their foreign ministers and the President of the Commission. Meetings are held twice a year (though extra meetings may be called in exceptional circumstances). They are always held in the country of the member state holding the presidency of the Council of Ministers. The aim of these meetings is to discuss major policy issues:

> 'The growing dominance of the European Council...is one of the biggest EU changes since its inception. When it began in the early 1970s, the idea was that heads of government should meet informally for a fireside chat. Now each presidency works towards a climax of decisions at summits normally held in June and December. And the conclusions from each summit tend to map out the agenda for the whole EU.' (*Economist*, 8 March 1997)

B. The European Commission

The Commission is the permanent bureaucracy of the EU. The President of the Commission is chosen by the European Council but is also subject to the European Parliament's formal approval. The Commission is headed by a college of commissioners, or 'executive', whose members are nominated by the member states in consultation with the President. The number of commissioners appointed from January 1995 was 20 (two each from the five largest members, namely Britain, Germany, France, Italy and Spain, and one each from the ten other member states). Further enlargement will probably mean that members currently nominating two commissioners will only be allowed to nominate one (so that new members can nominate a commissioner).

The Commission's role

The Commission's primary responsibility is to initiate European legislation. Each commissioner has responsibility for a particular sector which is allocated by the President of the Commission - for example, the two British commissioners appointed in 1995, Leon Brittan and Neil Kinnock, were given responsibility for trade relations with developed countries and transport respectively. Commissioners have to abandon any national allegiance. Since 1995, the length of tenure of office has been set at five years.

The bureaucracy

The Commission has a large administrative staff of around 15,000 people, based in both Brussels and Luxembourg. The Commission works, in theory, in all the members' languages, though, in practice, English and French predominate. Around 15% of the Commission's staff are employed in linguistic work (translating and interpreting). It should be noted that, although the Commission is often criticised for being over-bureaucratic, in fact:

> 'The Commission employs fewer people than the French Ministry of Culture and the British Lord Chancellor's office, neither of which is a major department of state. It is smaller than the governments of cities like Amsterdam and Madrid.' (Geddes 1993, pp.43-4)

Civil servants working for the Commission must be completely neutral and objective. They must act in the interests of the EU as a whole, rather than for their individual member states.

The role of the Commission has been described by a British government pamphlet as follows:

> 'The European Commission is the executive organ of the Community, ensuring that Community rules and provisions of the Treaties are implemented and observed correctly. It puts forward policy proposals and executes the decisions taken by the Council [of Ministers]. It attends all Council meetings, where it participates in discussions as an equal partner. The Commission administers the structural funds established by the Community, prepares a draft Budget which must be approved by the Council and the European Parliament and negotiates international agreements on behalf of the Community.' (HMSO 1992, p.18)

Powers

The Commission can investigate any complaint that the principles laid down in the treaties signed by member states have been breached and impose fines if it finds that rules have been broken or disregarded. When requested by an individual state, it can consider whether there is a case for a temporary waiving of rules. If a member state does not fulfil its obligations, the Commission can take it to the European Court of Justice (see below).

C. The European Parliament

The European Parliament (EP) is located in Strasbourg. Since 1979, its members (Members of the European Parliament - MEPS) have been directly elected every five years. The number of MEPs has risen from 518 in 1989 to 626 in 1995. This reflects the growth of the EU (in 1990, for example, East and West Germany were unified and in 1995 three new member states joined the EU). Under the terms of the 1997 Amsterdam Treaty, the number of MEPs has been set at a maximum of 700. This figure was set in anticipation of new members after further enlargement.

The number of MEPs elected by each member state is determined roughly by population. In 1995, for example, Germany returned 99 MEPs whilst the UK and France returned 87 and Luxembourg returned six. Members sit in the EP according to party group rather than nationality. The 1997 Amsterdam Treaty laid down regulations to govern the conduct and duties of MEPs.

The powers of the EP have been restricted by the fact that the final decision on legislation remains with the Council of Ministers. For this reason, the EP has often been accused of being little more than a talking shop. Since the late 1980s, however, the EP's formal and informal influence has been growing.

Cooperation procedure

When the Single European Act came into operation in 1987, the so-called 'cooperation procedure' gave the EP new powers. The cooperation procedure allows the EP to become involved in the decision-making process at a number of different stages:

> 'Under the cooperation procedure, there is a second reading process. On first reading, the Council is confined to adopting "common positions" which must be referred back to the EP. In making the reference back, the Council is obliged to provide the EP with explanations for common positions - including giving reasons for any EP amendments which have been rejected - and, if the EP is dissatisfied, it can exert further pressure at its second reading by amending or rejecting common positions by votes that include an absolute majority of its members.' (Nugent 1994, p.176-77)

Although, under the cooperation procedure, the EP cannot veto measures outright, it can put considerable pressure on the Commission and the Council:

> 'If the Parliament rejects the Council's position, then unanimity by the Council is required for the proposal to come into force as Community law. If the Parliament proposes amendments, the Council votes by qualified majority where the Commission endorses them and unanimously where the Commission has been unable to do so.' (HMSO 1992, p.21)

Codecision procedure

The Maastricht Treaty gave the European Parliament further powers by introducing the codecision procedure. This works as follows:

'[The codecision procedure] is similar to the cooperation procedure up to the point when the EP issues its second reading position. The procedure then changes, for if the Council cannot accept the EP's position as indicated by a vote of the majority of its component members, and if the differences between the two institutions cannot be resolved in a Conciliation Committee composed of an equal number of representatives from both the Council and the Parliament, the EP can prevent the text from being adopted (again by a vote of an absolute majority of its members) if the Council seeks to press ahead. In other words, the EP has a potential veto on legislative proposals which are subject to this procedure.' (Nugent 1994, p.177)

The 1997 Amsterdam Treaty extended the use of the codecision procedure. It removed the old cooperation procedure and replaced it with the codecision procedure in all cases except those dealing with economic and monetary union. The aim was to provide the European Parliament with a greater role in decision making and to make decision making more transparent.

D. The European Court of Justice

The Court of Justice has 15 judges - one from each member state. Judges are appointed by member states for a period of six years. There are six advocates general who assist the judges by analysing the arguments of those in dispute. The Court sits in Luxembourg.

The role of the Court of Justice is to interpret European law and to make decisions which are binding on member states. It rules on the interpretation and application of EU laws and sorts out disputes between member states. Given the scope of the treaties, a very wide range of matters can be brought before the Court. It is, in effect, the Supreme Court of the European Union.

Due to the increasing workload of the Court of Justice, the Single European Act provided for a Court of First Instance to be set up. This Court listens to and makes judgements on points of law only. There is the right of appeal from this Court to the Court of Justice.

Norton points out that the Court of Justice is the Court of last resort in the EU:

'Under the terms of EU membership, if there is a conflict between the provisions of European law and domestic UK law, then the European law is to prevail. The 1972 European Communities Act provided that any dispute over the interpretation of Community Treaties (and the laws made under them) was to be treated as a matter of

law. Under the provisions of the Treaty of Rome, cases which reach the highest domestic court of appeal (in the case of the UK, that means the House of Lords) must be referred to the Court of Justice...for a definitive ruling. Lower courts may also request a ruling from the Court of Justice on the meaning and interpretation of the treaties. There is no appeal from a decision of the Court of Justice.' (Norton 1995, p.30)

The European Court of Justice should not be confused with the European Court of Human Rights. The European Court of Human Rights was established by the Council of Europe which has twice as many members as the EU. The European Court of Human Rights examines violations of the 1950 European Convention on Human Rights.

E. The Economic and Social Committee

The Economic and Social Committee (ESC) is based in Brussels. Lists of nominees are put forward by each member country and the 222 members of the committee are appointed from these lists by the Council of Ministers. To ensure that a broad spectrum of interests is represented, membership is divided into three equally sized groups - employers, workers and interest groups. Each member state's list of nominees is supposed to reflect this division.

The ESC is a consultative body, but, since 1972, it has been able to deliver opinions without being consulted. Numerous articles in treaties require the Council of Ministers to consult the ESC, but its opinions are not binding. Despite this, Nugent argues, the committee plays an important role:

'First, it provides a useful forum in which representatives of sectional interests can come together on a largely cooperative basis to exchange views and ideas. Second, it is a consultative organ that gives some limited - but in most cases only very limited - opportunities for interests to influence Community policy and decision making. (Nugent 1994, p.217)

F. The Committee of the Regions

Established by the Maastricht Treaty, the Committee of the Regions is a consultative body which is meant to be the guardian of the principle of subsidiarity - the principle that decisions should be taken at the lowest appropriate level (see Section 1.2 above).

The membership and structure of the Committee of the Regions is similar to that of the ESC. Under the terms of the Maastricht Treaty, the committee must be consulted by the Council of Ministers and Commission whenever the ESC is consulted. Also, when the committee considers that specific regional interests are involved, it can issue an opinion on the matter.

Main points - Part 2

- The EU has a mixture of supranational and intergovernmental institutions. Decisions are made by four main bodies.
- The Council of Ministers is, in reality, a revolving series of councils. The Council has the power to make decisions binding on all members.
- The Commission is the permanent bureaucracy of the EU whose primary responsibility is to initiate European legislation.

- The power of the European Parliament is restricted by the fact that the final decision on legislation remains with the Council of Ministers.
- The role of the European Court of Justice is to interpret European law.
- Two consultative bodies make an impact on European decisions - the Economic and Social Committee and the Committee of the Regions.

Activity 6.3 *Decision making in the EU*

Item A *The EU decision-making process*

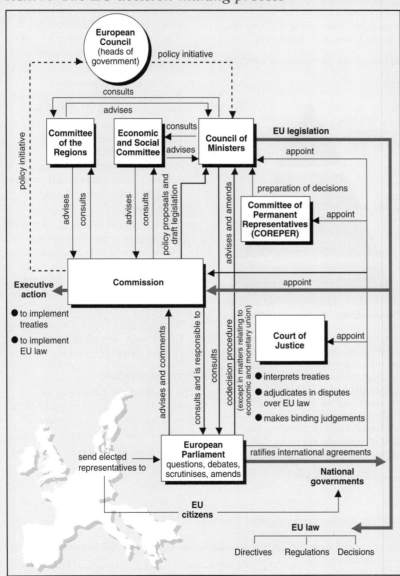

Adapted from Mazey & Richardson 1993.

Item B *The qualified majority voting system (1)*

Before 1995, the 12 members of the EU had a total of 76 votes in the Council and a measure could be blocked by 23 (or more) votes - a minimum of two large states and one small state voting against the measure. In March 1994, the British government proposed that the blocking threshold remain at 23 votes even after the new members joined the EU in January 1995. The main argument was that this was a question of protecting national sovereignty, especially as the number of decisions which required qualified majority voting had grown and was likely to grow. Most other members argued against this on the grounds that retaining the 23 vote blocking mechanism would make it too easy to reject proposals and EU business would grind to a halt. The 1997 Amsterdam Treaty extended qualified majority voting to 11 new areas of policy. In 1998, a qualified majority required 62 votes. A measure could be blocked, therefore, by 26 (or more) votes - a minimum of two large states and either Spain or two small states.

Adapted from the *Guardian*, 20 March 1994 and 30 January 1995, and the *Independent* 16 June 1997.

Item C   *The qualified majority voting system (2)*

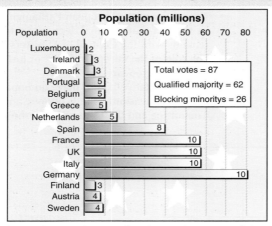

This chart shows the population of each member state of the EU and the number of votes each member state has in the Council of Ministers.

Adapted from the *Guardian*, 16 March 1994 and *Observer*, 14 September 1997.

Item E   *The Council of Ministers*

The output of the Council of Ministers is comparable to that of a government. Every working day, hundreds of officials from the member states meet in Brussels to discuss texts drawn up by the Commission. National interests are then promoted and defended as negotiation and bargaining takes place. The outcome is an agreed text which is adopted by the Council at one of its 100 or so sessions each year. In about 70% of cases, the agreement is reached at the level of experts meeting in working groups; 15-20% is decided upon by senior national officials meeting in COREPER; 10-15% is discussed and decided by the ministers in Council. The final adoption of measures is always and only done by the ministers meeting in

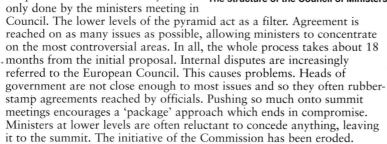

The structure of the Council of Ministers

Council. The lower levels of the pyramid act as a filter. Agreement is reached on as many issues as possible, allowing ministers to concentrate on the most controversial areas. In all, the whole process takes about 18 months from the initial proposal. Internal disputes are increasingly referred to the European Council. This causes problems. Heads of government are not close enough to most issues and so they often rubber-stamp agreements reached by officials. Pushing so much onto summit meetings encourages a 'package' approach which ends in compromise. Ministers at lower levels are often reluctant to concede anything, leaving it to the summit. The initiative of the Commission has been eroded.

Adapted from Hayes-Renshaw 1998 and the *Economist*, 8 March 1997.

Item D   *The European Parliament*

Criticisms of the European Parliament (EP)

- The EP is not a truly representative body. In the 1994 European elections, for example, only 36% of people bothered to vote. This suggests that most people do not believe that participation in such elections is worthwhile. It also means that MEPs cannot claim with any justification to have a mandate for their vision of Europe.

- The EP is expensive. In 1994, it cost over £500 million to run it. The cost of maintaining an MEP is much greater than maintaining an MP.

- The EP is not a proper Parliament. MEPs from different countries belong to different political parties which are only linked by a system of weak alliances. Parliamentary democracy cannot function properly without political parties being organised on a Europe-wide basis.

- The continued existence of the EP only makes sense if there are plans for its power to continue to evolve. This assumes that an EP with greater powers is desirable. If it is not, then the EP should be abolished immediately.

- British MEPs are in a minority in the EP and, therefore, cannot protect Britain's interests.

Recommendation

The work of the EP should be confined to consultation and MEPs should be nominated or elected from national Parliaments.

Adapted from the *Times*, 13 April 1995.

Questions

1. a) Using Items A and E, describe the different stages that a proposal has to go through before becoming law.
   b) Where is power located in the EU?
   c) Isolate the intergovernmental and supranational elements in the decision-making process. Would you say that the balance is right? Give reasons for your answer.
   d) What evidence is there of a 'democratic deficit'?

2. Using Items B and C, give arguments for and against the view that qualified voting should be extended.

3. 'The European Parliament plays an important role now and it should play an even more important role in the future.' Do you agree with this statement? Use Item D in your answer.

4. 'It is the EU's chief decision maker but it lacks accountability.' Is that an accurate description of the Council of Ministers? Use Item E in your answer.

Part 3 The future direction of the European Union

Key issues

1. What are the arguments for and against greater federalism?
2. What are the likely consequences of enlargement?
3. Where do the main British political parties stand on the European question?

3.1 The debate over federalism

The EU's political agenda

When the EEC was set up, it had a political as well as an economic agenda. That was the reason why, to begin with, the British government chose not join. This political agenda was ambitious. For many of those involved in the setting up of the EEC, the hope was that one day the organisation would evolve into a kind of United States of Europe. Although, after it joined, the British government played down the political consequences of membership, they have already been extensive:

> 'The British constitution has changed significantly over the past 25 years. It has undergone its most dramatic change as a result of British membership of the European Community. That has limited the role of government and Parliament in policy making, injecting new supranational bodies into the process (supranational bodies which enjoy supremacy over the national institutions). The effect has been to undermine and potentially destroy the basic tenets, and consequences, of the traditional constitution.' (Norton 1995, p.40)

The Single European Act and Maastricht Treaty have raised questions about the direction in which the EU should head. Central to this debate is the question of federalism (see Section 1.2 above for an explanation of the term 'federalism'). Should the EU continue in the direction of a federal system or should it become a loose confederation of nation states?

Arguments for a federal Europe

According to Pinder:

> 'The essence of the federal case is this: it is time to replace relations among states based on their relative power by relations among people based on law...The European nation state is too small a polity [political structure] to cope with the needs of society in the age of modern technology. We must complement it with a wider polity to do the things that our states can no longer do separately.' (Pinder 1991, p.5)

Pinder goes on to argue that a number of steps have been taken towards a federal Europe and a number of other steps could easily be taken. For example, two layers of government already exist (government at national and at European level). A written constitution could easily be drawn up from the Treaty of Rome and other treaties signed by the member states. The European Court of Justice can be seen as a kind of supreme court. The European Parliament and Council of Ministers can be seen as a nascent two-chamber legislature with the Commission as an executive. Certainly, if member states have the political will, the framework for a federal Europe is in place.

Countering arguments against federalism

The main argument used against a federal Europe is that it inevitably leads to a loss of national sovereignty. There are a number of ways of countering this argument.

First, there is the argument that national sovereignty is compromised as soon as a country joins the EU:

> 'The United Kingdom became a member of the EC on 1 January 1973. Under the terms of membership, policy-making competence in certain sectors of public policy moved upwards from the institution of the British state to the institutions of the EC, principally the Commission and the Council of Ministers... Once a measure of EC law has been approved by the Council of Ministers, it has legal force. This is a condition of membership...The assent of the British Parliament is not required.' (Norton 1995, pp.26-27)

Second, there is the argument that, in practice, a nation's sovereignty was by no means absolute before it entered the EU. Britain's 'special relationship' with the USA, for example, meant that informal pressures determined Britain's foreign policy. Similarly, on a number of occasions, pressure from the money markets (rather than Parliament) has determined economic policy. And third, there is the argument that, in fact, federalism does not lead to a loss of national sovereignty at all. In a federal Europe, decisions that affected the whole of the EU would be made at European level whilst decisions affecting an individual nation would be made by that nation's government. The advantage of making decisions at the European level would be that there would be a degree of harmony amongst member states, whilst regional differences could be preserved.

Inevitable evolution?

Some federalists argue that the logic of the development of the EU up to now suggests that, in time, the remaining barriers between members will be broken down. The Single European Act, for example, has already created a single market within the EU in which the free movement of goods, people, services and capital is ensured. Since goods, people, services and capital can now move freely around the EU, it is argued, there is no good reason to have 15 different national currencies. It would be far better to have a single European currency (see Chapter 15, Section 3.4). Similarly, it makes sense for the EU to negotiate on behalf of its members (as happened during the Uruguay round of the GATT negotiations, for example - see Chapter 15, Section 4.2 for information on GATT and the World Trade Organisation) rather than each member to negotiate on its own behalf. There is a tendency for the world to form bigger interest blocs and the EU is a formidable interest group in international negotiations.

Greater security

It is perhaps no surprise to find that the most committed federalists are found in the Benelux countries. Before the EU was formed, small countries like these had very little international clout, but membership of the EU has provided them with a significant voice in deciding matters which affect them. It has also provided them with a degree of security - both politically and economically. Such benefits, federalists argue, would be greater in a truly federal Europe.

Other arguments

A number of other arguments are used in favour of European federalism. First, it is argued that federalism would bring great social benefits to citizens of the EU. Workers, for example, could expect to find the same basic minimum standards of health and safety in the workplace throughout the EU. Second, it is argued that federalism would help to combat the ultra-nationalism that has led to the growth of neo-Nazi movements and it would ensure that political instability (like that which led to civil war in Yugoslavia) would be unthinkable. Third, there is the argument that greater harmonisation would mean less regulation and less bureaucracy. The result would be greater economic prosperity as well as political stability.

Arguments against federalism

The threat to national security

The main argument used by those opposed to a federal Europe is that federalism is a threat to national sovereignty. Sovereignty requires autonomy, but the existence of supranational institutions, by definition, restricts a nation's freedom of manoeuvre:

> 'Opponents of the EC argue that a loss of sovereignty in a democratic political system reduces the rights of citizens to exercise control over the decision-making authority. The ultimate recourse of the British electorate is to "kick the rascals out" by voting for a

change of government at a general election. However, if national government is no longer the sovereign authority, then national elections and policy preferences expressed in them may make little difference if they run counter to preferences agreed at Community level.' (Geddes 1993, p.11)

Whilst most Eurosceptics in the UK accept that membership of the EU brings benefits to trade and the economy, they are reluctant to agree to moves which might further restrict national sovereignty. For many, the EU should be a free trade area and no more.

Diversity is too great

The second main argument against a federal Europe is that there is too great a diversity between the member states for a United States of Europe to be a practical possibility. There are different cultures, different languages, different standards of living and different types of economy. Imposing uniformity is not the solution. The differences between member states should be recognised and accommodated.

The question of enlargement (or 'widening') is important in this context. If, in the near future, the EU was to expand to an organisation of 20 to 30 states, there would be even greater diversity. Harmonisation would be proportionately more difficult and less practical. A larger EU is, therefore, likely to be a less federal-minded EU.

Democratic deficit

A third argument against a federal Europe is that the Commission is over-bureaucratic and the Parliament is an expensive burden. Opponents of federalism note that there is, at present, only one chamber in the Parliament and that the Commission takes on both a legislative and an executive role. Commissioners are not elected and MEPs are not really accountable to the electorate. EU institutions are remote from ordinary people and to transfer more power to them would be to transfer power to unknown bureaucrats. In short, there is a democratic deficit that would be exacerbated in a federal Europe.

Linked to the above argument is the Eurosceptics' claim that the march towards a federal Europe is taking place without the consent of the majority of people living in the EU:

> 'It is now abundantly clear that a strong federalist current is carrying the European Community towards a destination which has never been approved or even discerned by a majority of our fellow citizens. Almost daily, speeches are made, conferences held or proposals put forward which reflect this trend.' (Vander Elst 1991, p.11)

Other arguments

Other arguments against a federal Europe include the

following. First, Eurosceptics argue that nationalism (or 'patriotism') is a virtue:

> 'Nationalism has many advantages: it reconciles classes; smooths over regional differences; and gives ordinary people a sense of community, pride and history.' (Sked 1989)

Replacing the nation state with a supranational superstate would destroy this valuable motivating force. Second, Eurosceptics argue that a federal Europe is an idealistic dream rather than a practical reality. It would cause more problems than it solved. And third, they argue that, in a federal Europe, the will of the small nations would swamp that of the larger nations. Inevitably, therefore, Britain would end up losing out.

3.2 Enlargement

A growing community

In its first 30 years, the EU doubled in size from six members in 1958 to 12 by 1988. In 1995, three new members joined. So far, enlargement has been a slow and relatively painless process. EU institutions have managed to evolve in line with increased membership, without changing the decision making process in a fundamental way. In particular, member states have retained their vetoes over certain issues. Commentators and politicians agree, however, that an EU with, for example, 30 members would have to be a very different organisation from that which now exists. With the end of the Cold War and the break-up of the Soviet Union, many states in eastern Europe are aiming to gain membership of the EU and an EU of 30 members is not beyond the bounds of possibility. The question is whether existing members will allow the EU to be widened in this way.

A two-tier or multi-speed Europe?

The question of enlargement has raised the possibility of a two-tier or multi-speed Europe. Within the EU, there is a division between those members who are keen to speed up the process towards political and economic union (most of the original six members have been especially keen to speed up the process) and those who are reluctant to move in this direction (the British government has been especially reluctant). A possible consequence of this division within the EU is the development of two tiers, with one tier accepting a single currency and moving towards greater political cooperation at the European level and the second tier opting out of

such arrangements. Enlargement is likely to encourage this process since new members will come into the EU with different expectations. Some will be better equipped to move towards political and economic union than others. As a result, a multi-speed Europe is a possibility with different members working towards 'ever closer union' at different rates.

Opposition to enlargement

Many federalists are opposed to further enlargement of the EU in the near future for two main reasons. First, they argue that enlargement would drain off resources from the stronger states since they would have to subsidise the new, weaker members. And second, new coalitions would be formed, changing the balance of power in the EU and possibly preventing greater political union.

Moves towards enlargement since 1994

The first applications for membership of the EU from the former Soviet bloc came in 1994 when Poland and Hungary put their names forward. A flood of applications then followed. In 1995, Bulgaria, Romania, Slovakia, Estonia, Latvia and Lithuania applied. They were joined in 1996 by the Czech Republic and Slovenia. At the Cardiff summit in 1998, the applications of all ten were approved by the European Council, as was the application of Cyprus which had been made in 1990. These 11 countries are due to join the EU in two waves with the Czech Republic, Estonia, Hungary, Poland, Slovenia and Cyprus joining first and the others later. It should be noted, however, that none of the applicants was expected to meet the entry criteria before 2002 at the earliest.

The entry criteria set by the EU's Copenhagen summit in 1993 are concerned both with applicants' political systems and their economic position:

> 'Politically, these include guarantees of democracy, human rights and protection of minorities. Economically, they require a functioning market economy, the capacity to cope with the single market and acceptance of the goal of EMU [economic and monetary union].' (*Economist*, 19 July 1997)

When the application of Turkey (first made in 1987) was considered at the Cardiff summit in 1998, it was refused partly because of Turkey's record on human rights and partly because of continuing and bitter opposition from Greece.

Main points - Sections 3.1-3.2

- A federal system of government is a system where different levels of government coexist and remain autonomous. The aim is to ensure that decisions are made at an appropriate level.
- The main argument in favour of federalism is that it is time to replace relations among states based on

power by relations based on law.
- The main argument used by those opposed to a federal Europe is that federalism is a threat to national sovereignty.
- The debate over enlargement is linked to that over federalism.

Activity 6.4 Further enlargement of the EU

Item A *Expansion to the east*

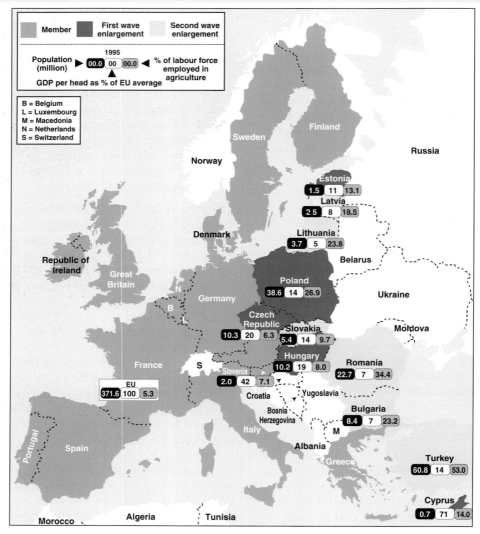

This map shows existing members of the EU and those countries which have applied to join.

Adapted from the *Economist*, 19 July 1997.

Item B *Arguments against enlargement*

Take the simple matter of everyday business. First, with an EU of even 21, far less legislation will be passed. In the Council of Ministers, it already takes three hours to go round the table letting each minister have a say. Second, the Commission acts by consensus but, with more commissioners, consensus will be harder to reach. Third, the need to translate into additional languages can only slow procedures down. And fourth, the new Parliament building in Strasbourg is not big enough to house greater numbers. The first wave of enlargement is to be carried out without increasing members' financial contributions. That means cutting the same cake 21 different ways and so less will be done. Expansion would bring 100 million new consumers, but with only a third of the purchasing powers of existing EU consumers. Price differences are staggering. Poland alone could destroy the carefully designed 'fortress Europe' policy aimed at keeping out unwanted immigrants and criminals. And, with over 25% of Poles working on the land, fundamental reform of the Common Agricultural Policy is necessary or massive subsidies will have to be paid to Polish smallholders.

Adapted from the *Independent on Sunday*, 20 July 1997.

Item C   *Arguments in favour of enlargement*

For those who support a European single market but fear monetary and political union, enlargement is the answer. Enlargement will vastly increase the size of the single market whilst, at the same time, making political or economic integration difficult, if not impossible because of institutional difficulties. Like John Major's government, the Blair government supports enlargement on the grounds that it will weaken the commitment of the Franco-German centre to integration and federalism. One of the aims of the British presidency in 1998 was to make serious progress on the enlargement issue. To the extent that the Cardiff summit recognised the firm commitment to membership of 11 applicant countries, this was done (though a great deal of fine detail was left to the Austrian presidency). As a result, it is clear that Europe is moving at five speeds at least. The fastest lane is that of the 11 who are entering the single currency. Then come Britain, Sweden, Denmark and Greece which will stay out of the Euro at first. Trailing them are the five-plus-one fast-track applicants; then the other five; then Turkey. The challenge will be to keep the convoy moving forward without breaking up.

Adapted from the *Economist*, 20 December 1997 and Pilkington 1999.

Item D   *An enlarged EU*

This cartoon shows a body builder (an enlarged EU) kicking sand in the face of Uncle Sam (the USA) as he runs past him.

Questions

1. a) Judging from Items A-D, what will be the benefits and drawbacks of a larger EU?
   b) What reforms will the EU need to make if enlargement is to be a success?

2. a) Judging from Items A-C, what are the likely consequences of enlargement?

   b) Using Item B, explain why many federalists are opposed to enlargement.

3. What point is being made by Item D? How accurate a prediction is it? Explain your answer.

3.3 Where British political parties stand on Europe

A contentious issue

Divisions over Europe are nothing new. Ever since the formation of the EEC, British politicians have been divided about the extent to which Britain should become involved in the European project. Indeed, the positions adopted by the two main parties have fluctuated so much that, at different times, both have been predominantly pro-European and predominantly anti-European. With the exception, perhaps, of the Heath government which negotiated Britain's entry into the EEC, no British government has adopted an unreservedly pro-European stance. As a result, the UK has earned the reputation of being a semi-detached member of the EU.

What affects attitudes towards the EU?

Ashford (1992) claims that three factors affect the attitudes towards the EU adopted by the main parties.

First, he contrasts the adversarial nature of the British system with that of other European countries, such as Germany, which have a more consensual style of politics. Regardless of which party has been in power in Britain, criticism has been made of the government's stance on Europe by the opposition parties. This has led to governments being reluctant to accept moves towards greater integration and, in turn, it has led to a lack of enthusiasm towards the EU amongst the British electorate.

Second, due to divisions within parties, there have never been clear-cut proposals over Britain's future role in Europe.

And third, both main parties are concerned that their ideological self-image is under threat from further European integration. Many Conservative supporters can see the advantage of a single market, for example, but oppose giving up economic sovereignty to achieve this. Similarly, although most Labour supporters agree with the provisions of the

Social Chapter, some regard the EU as a capitalist club which is incompatible with socialism.

The Conservative Party and Europe

With hindsight, it is possible to see mainstream Conservative thinking over Europe going through four distinct phases in the period since 1945.

Phase 1 - Detached from Europe (1945-61)

The first phase was dominated by Churchill's view of what Britain's relationship with Europe should be. In one sense, Churchill was a supporter of European integration. He said in 1946:

> 'If Europe is to be saved from infinite misery and indeed from final doom, there must be an act of faith in the European family. We must build a kind of United States of Europe.' (quoted in Lipgens 1981, p.319)

But, Churchill's 'United States of Europe' did not include Britain. Britain was to encourage its European neighbours to unite, but it was to remain aloof. This reflected Churchill's view that Britain was still a great power with worldwide obligations (to the Empire, for example). Britain, in other words, was not just geographically detached from Europe, it should remain politically detached as well. When Churchill became Prime Minister in 1955, the decision was taken not to participate in the Messina conference (see above, Section 1.1). Although Britain was invited to become a founder member of the EEC, the invitation was turned down.

Phase 2 - Pro-Europeanism (1961-75)

The second phase began when Harold Macmillan, Conservative Prime Minister, applied to the EEC for entry in 1961. This phase lasted from 1961 to 1975. It is characterised by the pro-European stance adopted by the Conservative leadership. Justifying his party's apparent U-turn, Macmillan said in 1961:

> 'Most of us recognise that, in a changing world, if we are not to be left behind and to drop out of the mainstream of the world's life, we must be prepared to change and adapt our methods. All through history, this has been one of the main sources of our strength.' (Hansard, 2 August 1961)

Macmillan, therefore, supported membership of the EEC on the grounds of pragmatism. Although Britain's application to join the EEC was vetoed in 1963 and again in 1967, the Conservative leadership continued to press for membership. Edward Heath, a pro-European, became Leader of the Conservative Party in 1965 and it was he who finally signed the Treaty of Accession in 1972. Having negotiated Britain's entry into the EEC, the Conservative leadership then supported continued membership when the referendum on this issue was held in 1975.

Phase 3 - Transition (1975-87)

The third phase began in 1975 when Margaret Thatcher was elected Leader of the Conservative

Party and lasted until 1987. Whilst in opposition between 1975 and 1979, Thatcher began to criticise the over-bureaucratisation of the EEC and she complained about the amount Britain contributed to the EEC budget. When she became Prime Minister in 1979, her attitude was markedly different from that of Edward Heath. Although she remained committed to membership of the EEC, she made it clear that her aim was to get the best deal for Britain (regardless of what that meant for the other members). Between 1979 and 1984 the EEC agenda was dominated by the question of how much members (especially Britain) should contribute to the EEC Budget. This was finally resolved when it was agreed that Britain should receive a rebate. Then, between 1984 and 1987 the British government was at the heart of plans to create a single market in Europe. This idea clearly reflected the deregulatory policies which the Thatcher government pursued in Britain. Ironically, however, it was the Single European Act which became the root of conflict in the Conservative Party.

Phase 4 - Division (from 1987)

The fourth phase began after the Single European Act came into operation in 1987 and still continues. Whilst the majority of Conservatives approved the idea of a single European market, the full implications of the Single European Act took many of them by surprise and alienated them. By 1988, Margaret Thatcher had joined the ranks of the disaffected. In her Bruges Speech of September 1988, she criticised what she saw as growing federalism, arguing instead that:

> 'My first guiding principle is this: willing and active cooperation between independent and sovereign states is the best way to build a European Community.' (Thatcher 1988)

The Bruges Speech was a turning point since Thatcher's Euroscepticism was not shared by some of her Cabinet colleagues. Divisions over Europe were then instrumental in Thatcher's downfall. And, they soon reappeared when John Major became Prime Minister.

Although, in the run-up to the Maastricht Treaty, Major's negotiation of opt-outs appeased the majority of Conservatives, hard-line Eurosceptics began to emerge. After the 1992 general election, the Major government's forced departure from the Exchange Rate Mechanism (ERM) increased antagonism to the whole European project and the goverment's small majority ensured that backbench rebellion could have serious consequences. The Eurosceptics took advantage of this and put pressure on the government. This culminated in the withdrawal of the whip from eight backbench MPs in November 1994. Although the whip was restored in April 1995, the Conservative Party remained deeply divided on Europe.

This division within the party deeply affected government policy. John Peterson notes that once

Britain had left the ERM:

> 'Over the next four years, Major and members of his Cabinet often seemed forced to scorn the EU just to occupy a middle ground within the Conservative Party.' (Peterson 1997, p.24)

Perhaps the best example of this is the policy of non-cooperation which was adopted by the British government after the EU imposed a ban on the export of British beef. In response to this ban:

> 'The UK vetoed all proposed EU measures which required a unanimous vote whether they related to beef or not, while demanding that a timetable be agreed for lifting the ban.' (Peterson 1997, p.25)

This policy of non-cooperation (which ended in June 1996) not only ensured that relations between Britain and other EU members deteriorated, it also gave a great deal of credibility to the Labour Party's claims that the Conservatives were failing to provide the lead which Britain needed in Europe.

The Conservative Party and Europe since 1997

Europe remained a divisive issue in the Conservative Party during the run-up to the 1997 general election and has remained one since the party's defeat. Following that defeat, William Hague was elected Party Leader. As Robert Leach points out, there were four reasons why Hague could take his time before making a firm commitment about the party's position on Europe:

- because the election defeat brought a strong will to unite
- because some leading pro- and anti-Europeans had failed to be re-elected and the others were marginalised by the parliamentary arithmetic
- because the fear that the Conservative Party would be outflanked by rival anti-European parties had vanished with the failure of the Referendum Party and others
- because parties in opposition can wait on events before making major policy statements.
  (Leach 1998, p.34)

Despite this, within weeks of the 1997 Conservative Party conference, Hague made a firm pledge against joining the single currency for the following ten years. He then consolidated this strong anti-European stance with a number of speeches which made his opposition to further integration very plain. In a speech made in France in May 1998, for example, he argued that the original idea of economic, strategic and political integration was outdated in a globalised high-tech world and he defended 'diversity, pluralism and the nation state' (*Independent*, 20 May 1998).

In the autumn of 1998, Hague held a ballot of all Conservative Party members asking them whether they supported his policy on Europe. A majority (84% of votes cast) backed the policy on a turnout of 60%.

The Labour Party and Europe

Labour and Europe 1945-75

As with the Conservative Party, mainstream Labour thinking was hostile towards the EEC at first. It was not until Labour won power in 1964 that the pro-European wing of the party managed to gain an ascendancy. The party voted in support of an application to join the EEC in 1967, but 36 Labour backbenchers voted against their party. The split in the party between pro- and anti-Europeans remained, festering, until Labour formed the government again in 1974. Most commentators agree that the split was the main reason why Harold Wilson agreed to a referendum in 1975.

Labour and Europe 1975-83

Although the electorate voted in the 1975 referendum by a substantial majority to remain in the EEC, a significant minority of Labour MPs and supporters remained opposed to membership on the grounds that the EEC was a capitalist club which would hinder rather than foster socialism. After Labour's general election defeat in 1979, this faction gained the upper hand in the Labour Party. The anti-European direction in which the Labour Party seemed to be heading was one reason why several senior Labour MPs left the party to form the SDP (see Chapter 8, Section 4.1) in 1981.

Labour fought and lost the 1983 general election on an anti-European platform - its 1983 manifesto committed a Labour government to withdraw from the EEC. The scale of the defeat, however, was so great that the party was forced to re-evaluate its policies.

Transformation after 1983

Under the leadership of Neil Kinnock (1983-92), the Labour Party was transformed into an overwhelmingly pro-European party. This transformation came about for a number of reasons.

First, the Labour Party remained in opposition throughout the 1980s. This frustrated the party's supporters who felt helpless in the face of the Thatcher 'revolution'. Many began to look to Europe to offset the worst excesses of Thatcherism. Second, the pro-European Liberal/SDP Alliance had taken away votes from Labour in the 1983 general election. Third, the Social Charter and the social dimension of changes agreed by the EC appealed ideologically to Labour supporters. And fourth, a pro-European stance made sense tactically in the late 1980s since it became clear that the Conservative Party was moving gradually towards an anti-European position.

Labour and Europe 1992-97

Although divisions over Europe in the Labour Party remained at the time of the party's defeat in the 1992 general election, they were much less obvious than those in the Conservative Party and they remained so throughout John Major's second term in office. Labour's strategy remained consistent:

- to present a united front (in contrast to the open divisions within the Conservative Party)
- to criticise the Conservative government's obstructionist tactics and its Eurosceptic rhetoric
- to argue that a Labour government would take a positive lead in Europe whilst still managing to protect Britain's national interests.

When Tony Blair and John Prescott were elected as Leader and Deputy Leader in 1994, this was widely regarded as a victory for the pro-Europeans. But, any hopes of movement towards the federalist camp were quickly dashed. Faced by a Europhobic press and opinion polls which showed that most British people were lukewarm about moves towards further integration, the Labour leadership (like the Conservative leadership) argued that its main priority was to protect British interests within the EU. In a speech delivered in Bonn in June 1996, for example, Tony Blair said he was aiming for:

'Relations based on national interest, which demands that we are a leading player in Europe; succeeding in Europe, not failing; winning, not losing; walking tall in Europe, not skulking on the sidelines; constructive and engaged, not simply because the interests of Europe demand it, but above all because the interests of Britain demand it.' (quoted in the *Independent*, 19 June 1996)

Significantly, the Labour Party followed the Conservative lead and made a commitment to hold a referendum before joining the single currency.

In the run-up to the 1997 general election, the Labour Party was able to make a great deal of political capital out of its stance on Europe. During the election campaign, Conservative divisions on Europe re-emerged and the issue was:

'The single most prominent in the press coverage of the campaign.' (Butler & Kavanagh 1997, p.140)

As Dobson notes:

'Europe worked wholeheartedly against the Conservatives and, without doubt, its continued prominence as an issue contributed mightily to the Labour landslide.' (Dobson 1998, p.21)

Labour and Europe since May 1997

The new Labour government acted quickly to signal a change in approach and attitude. Within days of the election, the Foreign Secretary, Robin Cook, announced that Britain would sign the Social Chapter and, within a month, Cook had appointed an MEP to be his European parliamentary private

secretary - to handle liaison with the European Parliament (no MEP had been appointed to such a post before). At the same time, Doug Henderson began work as the first Minister for Europe (previously a civil servant not a minister had been sent to represent Britain in inter-governmental talks), bringing Britain into line with other EU members.

These moves suggested a change of style and attitude and that has persisted. There is, however, rather less evidence of a change in substance. Although Britain has been far more willing to negotiate and accept compromises rather than to seek confrontation, there is still a big divide between those member states who, ultimately, have a federalist agenda and the British position - where the fundamental aim remains the building of a loose alliance of nation states. This divide was apparent during the negotiations over the 1997 Amsterdam Treaty when Britain blocked the merging of the WEU (a defence union) with the EU and when Tony Blair argued that no further institutional reform would be needed for successful enlargement (a claim that many other members would hotly dispute). And, it was apparent in 1998 when it was agreed that 11 member states would be going ahead with the single currency in January 1999, leaving Britain (and three other member states) on the sidelines. The Labour government had already announced (in October 1997) that it would not join the single currency until 2002 at the earliest.

The other parties and Europe

The Liberal Democrats

The Liberal Democrats are organised on federal lines (see Chapter 8, Section 4.2) and so it is no surprise to learn that they are enthusiastic supporters of greater European integration. As early as 1951, Liberals were arguing that Britain should join the European Coal and Steel Community and the Liberal Party was the only mainstream party to support Britain's entry into the EEC in 1957. The Liberal Democrats can, therefore, claim to have a long tradition of pro-Europeanism. Their long-term aim is for a federal Britain within a federal Europe.

Although the Liberal Democrats remain the most pro-European of the main parties, in recent years they have adopted a 'Euro-realist' approach and accept the need for some reforms. In a policy paper published in 1996, for example, they attacked EU decision making as 'unnecessarily secretive and largely unaccountable'. They back an extension of qualified majority voting in an enlarged EU and call for more open government.

The Nationalist parties and the Green Party

Both the Scottish Nationalist party (SNP) and Plaid Cymru (the Welsh nationalists) were originally opposed to Britain's entry into the EEC. But, since 1988, the SNP has adopted a pro-European stance. The SNP now calls for an independent Scotland within a federal EU. Plaid Cymru remains suspicious of the EU, not least because it has been heavily influenced by Green politics. Like the Green Party, Plaid Cymru is critical of an organisation whose priority is economic growth rather than environmental protection.

Parties in Northern Ireland

In Northern Ireland, the Social and Democratic Labour Party (SDLP) is a keen supporter of greater European integration, on the grounds that it will help to heal divisions in Northern Ireland. The official Unionists are opposed to Britain's membership of the EU, but accept that withdrawal is unlikely. The Democratic Unionist Party fears domination by Catholics in the EU and its Leader, Ian Paisley, has denounced what he sees as 'Popish influences' in the European Parliament.

Main points - Section 3.3

- Although the Conservative Party was pro-European between 1961 and 1975, important divisions within the party have developed since 1987.
- After the Major government was forced to leave the ERM in 1992, these divisions grew worse (partly due to the parliamentary arithmetic) and they affected government policy.
- The Labour Party remained divided over and often hostile towards Europe until after its election defeat

in 1983. Since then it has developed into a pro-European party.
- Moves initiated by the Labour government elected in 1997 suggest a change in style rather than substance. As previous governments, the Labour government supports a loose confederation of nation states.
- The Liberal Democrats are organised along federal lines and support greater European integration. They remain the most pro-European of the main parties.

Activity 6.5 *British political parties and the EU*

Item A *Labour Party manifesto 1997*

With a new Labour government, Britain will be a leader in Europe. Our vision of Europe is of an alliance of independent nations choosing to cooperate to achieve goals they cannot achieve alone. We oppose a European federal superstate. We need a fresh start in Europe with the credibility to achieve reform. We have set out a detailed agenda for reform:

- rapid completion of the single market
- high priority for enlargement of the EU
- urgent reform of the Common Agriculture Policy
- greater openness and democracy in EU institutions with open voting in the Council of Ministers and more effective scrutiny of the Commission by the European Parliament
- Retention of the national veto over key matters of national interest (taxation, defence, immigration, decisions over the Budget, treaty changes) while considering the extension of qualified majority voting in limited areas
- Britain to sign the Social Chapter.

Adapted from Labour 1997.

Item B *The Conservatives and Europe*

From the late 1980s, the Thatcherite right became increasingly concerned about the political agenda of the EU (supposed Eurofederalism) and the threat this was perceived to pose to national sovereignty. The government's belated entry into and forced departure from the Exchange Rate Mechanism in 1992 increased antagonism to the whole European project and turned the prospect of the single currency into the issue on which the right was determined to make a stand. For many Conservatives, a single European currency undermines their core beliefs in national independence and sovereignty. Yet, for other leading figures in the Conservative Party, the UK's future is inseparably bound up with Europe. For them, it is unthinkable that a Conservative government should ever contemplate leaving the EU. All the most significant developments concerning Europe had taken place under Conservative governments (joining the EEC and signing the Single European Act, for example). Failure to work with Britain's European partners would not only endanger the country's new and precariously won prosperity, but also disown the party's legacy of achievement on Europe.

Adapted from Leach 1998.

Item C *Taking a lead in Europe (1)*

This cartoon appeared in the *New Statesman* on 2 January 1998, as Britain began its six month term of presidency of the EU.

Item D   *Taking a lead in Europe (2)*

(i) If the Labour government wants to achieve anything in Europe, it would help if it spared us the usual leadership pretensions. Robin Cook did not get off to a good start when he immediately claimed an equal role for Britain among the 'big three' in Europe (Britain, France and Germany). Foolishly, he discarded Italy which has a larger GDP and is likely to join EMU earlier than Britain. Crucially, however, he still does not seem to understand that it has taken the French and Germans more than one parliamentary term to forge a relationship, built on mutual trust and close cooperation, which is strong enough to bridge continuing differences over individual policies. Britain should learn from its past failures and should not expect equal influence when it is not even prepared to commit itself to monetary union.

Adapted from Kaiser 1998.

(ii) Britain is not a leader in Europe. It cannot be. It lacks the resources, the policies and the history. The new Labour government has used the rhetoric of leadership in order, it seems, to make our accommodation with the EU more palatable - a tactic that may have had some success. Britain's challenge is not to lead, but to catch up with its partners. The other members of the EU, for all their welcome of a less divided and unpredictable British government, are not disposed to follow a British lead. They are sceptical of its economic performance, wary of its employment and welfare policies and, in any case, they have a leader - Germany.

Adapted from Lloyd 1998.

(iii) The UK presidency was supposed to mark a new era of British engagement (which it achieved) and 'leadership' (which it did not achieve). Britain mostly performed a difficult task honourably, steering the single currency to its birth while remaining outside the Euro zone. The main problem was the inflation of expectations that came with the rhetoric about 'Britain's leading role in Europe' when the presidency was launched last December. The emptiness of that claim was summed up last week when Gordon Brown left the room as the Euroland club of the 11 single currency members carried on the real business of the evening without him. The broad consensus is that the British presidency was not a great success.

Adapted from the *Guardian*, 9 June 1998.

Item E   *The record of the British presidency, January to June 1998*

PRAISE	GRUMBLE
● Steered the single currency to its birth, despite remaining outside the euro zone.	● Buddied-up with Washington rather than Brussels.
● Resolved mad cow crisis. EC will allow the export of British beef to resume shortly.	● Failed to pursue a distinctive European foreign policy.
● Helped resolve EU/US row over the Cuba and Iran embargoes.	● Failed to consult EU partners during the near-war crisis with Iraq.
● Gordon Brown's economic reforms endorsed by EU finance ministers.	● Foreign Secretary Cook's bodged Israel visit.
● Kept the Millenium Bug high on the EU agenda.	● Cook's failure to speak for EU members in Kosovo crisis and Cyprus row between Turkey and Greece.
● Allowed business to participate in devising EU regulations through Business Test Panels.	
● Action to achieve the climate change targets agreed at Kyoto.	● Allowed row over appointing head of Euro Bank to become a crisis.
● Brought in ban on drift-net fishing.	● Perceived as arrogant by other EU members.
● Set out plans to reform the Common Agriculture Policy.	

Adapted from the *Guardian*, 9 June 1998.

Questions

1. a) What does Item A tell us about the Labour Party's position on Europe?
   b) In what ways is the Labour Party's position on Europe different from that of the Conservative Party?
2. Using Item B, explain why the Conservative Party has split over Europe.
3. How accurate is the cartoon in Item C in explaining (a) the Labour Party's position on Europe and (b) the Conservative Party's position on Europe? Explain your answers.
4. a) Judging from Items D and E, what difficulties did the Labour government face during its first 18 months in office in trying to fulfil its manifesto pledge to take a lead in Europe?
   b) Assess the government's chances of fulfilling this pledge.

Part 4 Globalisation

Key issues

1. What is globalisation?
2. What are the consequences for the nation state?
3. How does globalisation affect Britain and Europe?

4.1 What is globalisation?

A definition

The term 'globalisation' has been defined as follows:
'Globalisation is about the dissolution of the old structures and boundaries of national states and communities. It is about the increasing transnationalisation of economic and cultural life, frequently imagined in terms of the creation of a global space and community in which we shall all be global citizens and neighbours.' (Robins 1997, p.2)

Globalisation, therefore, refers to a process of increasing international dependence in which countries become more integrated with one another economically and culturally.

Multinational companies

In terms of economics, the economies of nation states are now part of a global economic system. Multinational companies (also known as 'transnationals') have interests in many countries and sell their products to world markets. If conditions become more favourable in one country than another, then the multinational company can shift investment and production to take advantage of these conditions. As a result, those who control multinational companies have a great deal of power (both economic and political power) and national borders diminish in significance because they are no longer a barrier to the movement of capital, goods and (to a lesser extent) labour.

In terms of culture, the development of multinational companies has ensured that Western culture - such as Coca Cola, McDonald's hamburgers or pop music - can be found in the remotest corners of the world. Susan Strange, who is pessimistic about the impact of globalisation, argues that:
'[Globalisation] can refer to anything from the internet to a hamburger. All too often, it is a polite euphemism for the continuing Americanisation of consumer tastes and cultural practices.' (Strange 1996, p.xii)

Globalisation has also taken place in political terms. Most nations are involved in international organisations such as the United Nations (UN), North Atlantic Treaty Organisation (NATO) or International Monetary Fund (IMF).

The main components of globalisation

Globalisation, therefore, can be said to have three main components:

1. Growth of international trade

One component of globalisation is a growing dependency on international trade. Integral to globalisation is the making of new international trade agreements which tear down protectionist barriers. These trade agreements are policed by the World Trade Organisation (see Box 6.4).

> ### Box 6.4 The World Trade Organisation (WTO)
>
> The WTO was set up in 1995 as the successor to the General Agreement on Tariffs and Trade (GATT). Its main tasks are:
> - administering and implementing international trading agreements
> - acting as a forum for international trade negotiations
> - helping to resolve trade disputes (ultimately through decisions which governments are obliged to follow)
> - reviewing national trade policies
> - cooperating with other international institutions involved in global economic policy making.

2. Growth of foreign investment

A second component of globalisation is the growth of foreign investment - especially the investment of multinational companies. Multinational companies might set up plants in a particular country to escape protectionist barriers, to take advantage of cheaper labour or to gain access to local markets. Sometimes, multinational companies have a base in a particular country. Recently, however, there has been a trend towards 'stateless firms' - companies which have a base in no single country, but are run by international boards and are quoted on different stock exchanges.

3. Growth of international financial markets

A third component of globalisation is the growth of international financial markets. This growth has been made possible by developments in information technology and telecommunications. These developments, however, have only facilitated what was already a fast-growing trend. Over recent years, a global economy has developed with 24-hour trading taking place around the world. When the London stock market opens, traders have already analysed what has happened in Hong Kong and Tokyo. When Wall Street opens in New York in the afternoon (London time), traders are influenced by signals from London. In turn, the day's trading in Tokyo and Hong Kong is affected by what happened on Wall Street. As a result, a small financial shock in one country can be transmitted around the world, multiplying in intensity. This is what happened in 1997. When the heavily indebted Thai economy plunged into crisis, this had a knock-on effect in South Korea, Indonesia and other Asian countries. This, in turn, sent financial markets spiralling down in Japan, prompting concern that the downturn would be transmitted to Europe and the USA.

Two views of globalisation

Free-market liberal viewpoint

Many free-market liberals argue that globalisation is a positive development because it promotes world economic growth by allowing economic activities to take place where they can be carried out most cheaply. It also benefits consumers by allowing the free movement of goods, improving competition and choice.

Socialist viewpoint

Many socialists see globalisation as the latest stage in the development of international capitalism. They argue that the real beneficiaries are multinational companies not consumers. Increasing economic growth threatens the environment, making problems like global warming worse. Also, it is the rich countries which benefit most from globalisation - poor countries are exploited as a reservoir of cheap labour. This has a knock-on effect in other countries around the world. Low wages in poor countries tend to lead to lower wages elsewhere.

4.2 The political consequences of globalisation

Is the nation state under threat?

Globalisation is not just an economic phenomenon, it has important political consequences. Indeed, some people argue that globalisation has changed the relationship between economic activity and political activity:

'Globalisers argue that both quantitative and qualitative changes are taking place in the relationship between economic activity in the realm of global markets and political activity in the realm of inter-state relations. These activities represent more than just the internationalisation of economic activity. They represent a fundamental evolution in the relation between market power and state authority. In the major governance structures of the global order, we are witnessing a shift from public to private regulation and from territorial to trans-territorial forms of authority.' (Higgott & Reich 1997)

The implications of this for nation states are far reaching. Susan Strange argues that governments in nation states have lost the authority over society and the economy that they used to have:

'Where states were once the masters of markets, now it is the markets which, on many crucial issues, are the masters over the

government of states.' (Strange 1996, p.4)

Andrew Gamble points out that this claim is not new - it was being made in the 1970s - but, recent developments have strengthened it:

'A kind of popular wisdom has begun to emerge, particularly since the collapse of communism in Europe and the reunification of the world economy, that the nation state has become an anachronism [out of date] and is facing forces which it can no longer control. Power is being drained from it and acquired by other actors, particularly transnational companies and banks.' (Gamble 1997, p.359)

The implications of this are as follows:

- important economic decisions are not determined by national governments but by global financial markets and changing patterns of international trade
- national governments which attempt to resist global markets (for example, by protecting uncompetitive industries) suffer low economic performance, currency depreciation and low investment.

Having put the case, Gamble then argues that it is 'overblown'. He points out that global markets have existed as long as capitalism has existed and global trade has always been affected by decisions made by governments. There is little evidence, he claims, that national governments are impotent when it comes to dealing with global trade. Other writers, however, are not so sure. Crouch and Streeck, for example argue that:

'Hesitant to reveal to their voters the dirty secret that it is no longer they who determine their country's economic policies, national governments must somehow manage to extract from the democratic process policies that conform to the "general will" of global capitalism - the will of the markets.' (Crouch & Streeck 1997, p.11)

Fragmentation of nation states

Although it might be expected that globalisation would result in a tendency to think in terms beyond the nation state, that does not necessarily happen. Indeed, one unexpected response to globalisation has been the growth of nationalism within nation states:

'An increasing number of ethnic and linguistic groups within nation states are now identifying themselves as nations. Ethnic conflicts have broken out in the former republics of the Soviet Union, in Yugoslavia and in many of the former colonial territories in Africa. In the Islamic world, religious fundamentalism has been identified with new forms of nationalism, for example in the Iranian revolution and the civil war in Afghanistan. Even in the UK, there has been a resurgence of Irish, Scots and

Welsh nationalism in the last 30 years.' (Taylor et al. 1995, p.218)

So, globalisation does not just exert external pressure on nation states (pressure from the global financial markets, for example), it also produces internal pressure and a tendency to fragment. One explanation for this is that the process of globalisation has led people to question the power and legitimacy of the nation state and to look instead at new political structures. It is significant, for example, that the Scottish National Party's stance has changed from a simple demand for Scottish independence to a demand for independence within the EU. This change reflects a recognition that, in a global economy, complete independence is unrealistic. As an independent member of a transnational organisation (the EU), however, Scottish interests would be protected. As a result, the party suggests, there is a good case for severing ties with the rest of the UK.

The global democratic deficit

If it is accepted that globalisation has shifted power away from national governments, that raises questions about where that power has gone, who exercises it and how they exercise it. These are important questions, especially for anyone who is concerned with democratic accountability. For example, if decisions that were once made by national governments are now being taken by multinational companies, that means that decisions which were once taken by elected representatives are now being taken by unelected appointees. The problem is that political mechanisms above the level of the nation state either do not exist or they are extremely unwieldy. In short, there is a democratic deficit at the global level. Quite how this democratic deficit might be filled is unclear:

> 'We live in a complex interconnected world where there are certain issues and policies which are appropriate for local government or nation states, others for individual regions of the world and still others - for instance, the regulation of the world economy, elements of the environment, aspects of world health (the spread of malaria, the spread of Aids, or the risks from a post-antibiotic culture) - which need new institutions and mechanisms of accountability.' (Held 1997, p.28)

4.3 The impact of globalisation

Globalisation and the Labour government

The transformation of the Labour Party into a party which is pro-market, pro-business, anti-inflationary, and anti-tax-and-spend owes much to the leadership's views on globalisation. Tony Blair, for example, has made it quite clear that he believes that globalisation constrains governments and restricts their freedom of movement:

> 'The determining context of economic policy is the new global market. That imposes huge

limitations of a practical nature...on macroeconomic policies.' (quoted in the *Financial Times*, 22 May 1995)

That does not mean, however that the Labour leadership believes that governments cannot affect economic development. On the contrary, it believes that government has a key role:

> 'In a market economy, companies are the engines of wealth creation, but government has a supportive and collaborative role to play.' (CPP 1997, p.2)

The Labour government, therefore, is aware of the limits that globalisation places on what it can do, but is also aware of the possibilities for autonomous action.

Globalisation and the EU

Commentators are divided about the relationship between the EU and globalisation. Some argue that the EU acts as a constraint on globalisation because, although the EU is a powerful trading bloc, it is protectionist and has a social agenda. Companies, including multinationals, must accept and maintain certain standards in the treatment of their employees, for example, if they wish to trade in the EU. Others argue that globalisation is accelerated by the EU. They point out that multinational companies are strong supporters of a single market in the EU because the removal of barriers between countries benefits them (by allowing them to organise on a Europe-wide basis). Supporters of this viewpoint also point to evidence of the influence exerted on the development of the EU by organisations such as the European Round Table (set up by chief executives of top European companies) and the American Chamber of Commerce (which represents American multinationals in Brussels).

It should be noted that some Eurosceptics use the argument that Britain will never be able to enjoy the full fruits of globalisation while it remains in the EU because moves towards a federal structure hinder globalisation:

> '[A European superstate] would run counter to globalisation because it would be centralised, protectionist and bureaucratic, rather than dynamic, enterprising and responsive to rapidly changing costs and markets in the fastest-growing economies in the world in East Asia and North America. Maintaining British sovereignty is presented as a means by which Britain can maximise the opportunities which globalisation provides.' (Gamble 1997, p.361)

In contrast, supporters of the EU argue that, by pooling sovereignty, the EU provides the mechanisms for ensuring that high levels of income and welfare are enjoyed by its members:

> 'The pooling of sovereignty is inescapable in a global economy because interdependence creates problems which can no longer be solved at the national level.' (Gamble 1997, p.361)

Main points - Part 4

- Globalisation refers to a process of increasing international dependence in which countries become more integrated with one another economically and culturally.
- Some people argue that, as a result of globalisation, nation states have lost the authority over society and the economy that they used to have.

- An unexpected response to globalisation has been the growth of nationalism within nation states and the fragmentation of nation states.
- Some commentators argue that the EU acts as a constraint on globalisation. Others argue that globalisation is accelerated by the EU.

Activity 6.6 *The impact of globalisation*

Item A   *Globalisation and the nation state*

The process of globalisation has fundamentally changed the world in which we live. This is not entirely new, but today we are experiencing a more intensive interconnectedness than ever before. More than a trillion dollars change hands daily in the foreign exchange markets. Multinational companies dominate national and international economic transactions. Such developments fall far short of creating an integral world order, but they have significant consequences. We need to develop institutions that reflect the multiplicity of issues, questions and problems which affect and bind people together irrespective of whether they are in one nation state or another. Environmental problems provide an obvious illustration. For example, factories emitting toxic waste can be locally monitored and challenged, nationally regulated and supervised, regionally checked for cross-national standards and risks, and globally evaluated in the light of their impact on health, welfare and the economic opportunities of others. Given this model, nation states can no longer be the sole centres of legitimate power within their own borders. They need to be relocated within an overarching democratic framework.

Adapted from Held 1997.

Item C   *Globalisation and the EU*

This cartoon shows the USA and Asia about to do battle with the EU.

Item B   *The impact of globalisation (1)*

According to its critics, globalisation means world domination by powerful multinational corporations. It means that jobs and livelihoods are at the whim of the international financial markets. It also means that the great god of global free trade, bringing prosperity to all, is a false one. The essential point about globalisation, however, is that even its supporters accept that it is not perfect. There are winners and there are losers, and there can be unwelcome side effects. One of these, indeed, may be the concentration of power in the hands of too small a number of big corporations. But, even corporate giants have no guarantee of being king of the hill forever - Japanese and Korean industrial giants, for example, came from nowhere to challenge American and European domination. Multinationals, it is true, do not pay higher wages than they have to. Workers in a Nike shoe factory in the Philippines get paid a fraction of what is paid to their counterparts in the USA. But, they get paid more than they would be by a local entrepreneur. The best way to ensure workers are exploited is to ban foreign trade and investment. Take Eastern Europe during the Cold War, for example. Cut off from competition with the rest of the world, its industries became grossly inefficient. Clamping down on world trade now would condemn the poorest countries to permanent wretchedness.

Adapted from the *Sunday Times*, 17 May 1998.

Item D   *The impact of globalisation (2)*

No country can protect itself from the worldwide spread of new technologies. The result is not a universal free market, but an anarchy of sovereign states, rival capitalisms and stateless zones. Globalisation could be a great advance. Potentially, it could create a many-centred world in which different cultures and regimes cooperate without domination or war. But, that is not happening. In a world in which there are no constraints or regulations on market forces, peace is continually at risk. Slash and burn capitalism destroys the environment and kindles conflict over scarce resources. Minimal government intervention in the economy ensures that states are competing not only for markets, but for survival. The global market as it is presently organised does not allow the world's peoples to coexist harmoniously. It forces them to become rivals for resources whilst making no provision for conservation of these resources. Only a framework of global regulation can ensure that the world economy works in the service of human needs. Yet, the replacement of a global free market by a managed regime is, at present, nearly as Utopian a project as a universal free market.

Adapted from Gray 1998.

Part 5 Britain and the world

Key issues

1. How has Britain's role in the world changed since 1945?
2. What is Britain's relationship with the Commonwealth, NATO and the United Nations?
3. How does membership of these organisations affect decision making in the UK?

5.1 Britain and the Commonwealth

Britain and its empire

In 1945, Britain was an imperial power. The British Empire covered 11.5 million square miles and included over 400 million inhabitants. This vast empire was controlled by imperial staff in the colonies and by staff in London where three departments of state had imperial responsibility (the Dominions Office, Colonial Office and India Office).

By 1945, the British Parliament had granted independence to a number of former colonies, such as Canada, Australia and South Africa. These former colonies (or 'dominions' as they were known) were self-governing, but the British government retained ties with them and some influence over them. In 1914, for example, the British government declared war on behalf of the whole Empire (including the dominions) without consultation. During the war, however, the dominions were consulted on an equal basis and, in 1919, they signed the peace treaties individually and joined the League of Nations individually.

The Statute of Westminster

In the inter-war period, these dominions gained further autonomy:

> 'At the 1926 Imperial Conference the dominions were described as: "autonomous communities within the British Empire, equal in status, in no way subordinate one to another in any respect of their domestic or external affairs, though unified by a common allegiance to the Crown and freely associated as members of the British Commonwealth of Nations." This principle was legally formulated in the Statute of Westminster, an Act passed by the British Parliament in 1931.' (HMSO 1992a, p.5)

It was the Statute of Westminster which laid the legal foundations of the Commonwealth.

The dominions affected by the Statute were Australia, Canada, Newfoundland (which became a province of Canada in 1949), the Irish Free State, New Zealand and South Africa. All had a number of characteristics in common. First, they all had a developed economy. Second, all (except South Africa) had majority populations descended from white settlers. Third, all (except South Africa) had universal suffrage and a parliamentary system based on that of Britain. And fourth, all agreed to continued allegiance to the British monarch (who was represented in each dominion by a Governor General).

Decolonisation

Although some colonies had pressed for the end of British rule before 1945, it was only after the Second World War was over that the process of decolonisation began in earnest (see Item A in Activity 6.7). This was due to a number of factors.

Raised expectations

First, during the war the British government raised expectations in the colonies and, after the war was over, people in the colonies pressed for these expectations to be realised. Many colonies had sent troops to fight for the Allied cause, for example. After the war was over, there were hopes that their contribution would be rewarded by freedom from imperial control. Similarly, in 1941, Britain had signed the Atlantic Charter which committed it to 'uphold the rights of all people to choose the form of government under which they will live.' But, people in the colonies had no choice over the form of government under which they lived. They hoped that British government propaganda which had claimed that the Allies were fighting to preserve freedom of choice and the right to self-determination would mean an end to imperial rule once the war was over.

Britain's economic position

Second, the war drained Britain economically. The Empire had become simply too expensive to maintain. It was only after the war that the British government realised that this was the case.

Domino effect

Third, decolonisation gained a momentum of its

own. Once independence had been granted to one colony, it was harder to argue against independence for other colonies. The result was a 'domino effect' - the colonies fell like a stack of dominoes, one after another.

An irresistible pressure

Fourth, it should be noted that no imperial power was able to resist the pressure to decolonise after the war. This suggests that support for independence in the colonies did not depend upon the type of imperial rule (different imperial powers ruled in different ways). Rather, it suggests that the pressure to decolonise became irresistible.

Changing attitudes in Britain

And fifth, pressure to decolonise did not just come from the colonies. There was a change of attitude in Britain. Although some people supported fighting to preserve the Empire, most British politicians took the pragmatic view that decolonisation was inevitable and should, therefore, be put into practice in as painless a manner as possible. According to Simpson (1986) official policy towards the Empire in the 1940s and 1950s had two elements:

- the desire to protect strategic interests in order to maintain its position as a world power
- a desire to promote the welfare of people living in the colonies and to prepare them for self-government when Britain withdrew.

The process of decolonisation

The process of decolonisation was spectacular. By 1980, only 15 dependent territories remained under British control and most of these were small islands with small populations (such as the Falkland Islands, the Cayman Islands and the British Virgin Islands). The loss of its Empire undoubtedly affected Britain's status. Before the Second World War, Britain was regarded as a major power. The post-war world, however, was dominated by two superpowers the Soviet Union and the USA. Britain's loss in status led the American Secretary of State, Dean Acheson, to comment in a speech made in December 1962, 'Great Britain has lost an Empire and has not yet found a role.'

The Commonwealth

The Commonwealth is a free association of 54 sovereign independent states which evolved from the former British Empire. It is an international organisation which contains both developing and developed countries working in cooperation together. Membership of the Commonwealth is voluntary. Although the British monarch is the head of the Commonwealth, the position is only ceremonial. In 1949, it was decided that allegiance to the Crown was not a necessary criterion for Commonwealth membership. This allowed former

colonies to become republics (states without a monarch at their head), but to retain membership of the Commonwealth. Many current members of the Commonwealth are republics.

Those countries which were members of the Commonwealth before 1949 still (in theory at least) accept the British monarch as their head of state and are often referred to as the 'Old Commonwealth', whilst those members who gained independence from British rule after 1945 are often referred to as the 'New Commonwealth'.

The importance of the Commonwealth

From the British point of view, membership of the Commonwealth is important because:

> 'The Commonwealth enables Britain to play a responsible part alongside other nations in aiding the development and stability of the Third World. Britain participates fully in all Commonwealth activities (most of Britain's aid to developing countries goes to Commonwealth member states) and welcomes it as a means of consulting and cooperating with people of widely differing cultures.' (HMSO 1992a, p.1)

Close cultural, educational, sporting and some economic links exist between Commonwealth countries. But, members find it difficult to make political decisions together. The members have very different types of government and often very different policy aims.

Changing nature of the Commonwealth

The character of the Commonwealth has altered as new members have joined. Before 1960, it was dominated by white nations. Since then, black nations have been in the majority. By 1968, 12 of the 28 members were from Africa.

The changing nature of the Commonwealth has led to a number of political conflicts - notably over white rule in Rhodesia (now Zimbabwe) in the late 1960s and over the system of apartheid in South Africa that remained in place between 1948 and 1994. Following South Africa's withdrawal from the Commonwealth in 1961, there was growing division and tension within the Commonwealth along racial lines. In 1971, Commonwealth heads of government met in Singapore and drew up a code of ethics, known as the 'Singapore Declaration'. It was signed by all members and covered human rights, racial equality, economic freedom and support for the United Nations. Tension within the Commonwealth over South Africa continued, however. In the 1980s, the main issue was whether or not Commonwealth countries should impose economic sanctions on South Africa as a means of protesting about the continuation of repression of the black majority population under the Apartheid regime. The British government argued against sanctions, whilst most other Commonwealth countries supported them.

Following the release from prison of Nelson Mandela in 1990, sanctions were lifted. In April 1994, the first ever democratic elections were held in South Africa and Nelson Mandela was elected President. Shortly after the elections, South Africa rejoined the Commonwealth.

Organisation of the Commonwealth

The Commonwealth Secretariat was established in London in 1965. Its duties are to promote Commonwealth cooperation and to provide the central organisation for joint consultation between member states. In 1976, it was granted observer status at the United Nations. Meetings take place regularly between member states at various levels - from heads of government down to officials concerned with individual projects. The Secretariat provides information and policy advice to member governments on a wide range of issues. Since it is neutral, the Secretariat can also provide arbitration in the event of dispute.

The Secretary-General

The Commonwealth Secretary-General is head of the Secretariat and has access to all heads of governments. The Secretary-General is elected by Commonwealth heads of government. The Secretariat is based in London and staffed by over 400 officials from 30 countries. It is financed through contributions from member governments. Contributions are related to capacity to pay and are based on population and national income. In 1996-97, Britain paid 30%, Canada 19%, Australia 9.7%, India 3.3% and New Zealand 2.2%. Other members paid between 1.4% and 0.3%. The Secretariat provides technical assistance through the separately funded Commonwealth Fund for Technical Cooperation (CFTC).

Main points - Section 5.1

- In 1945, Britain ruled a huge empire. Between 1945 and 1980, however, a process of decolonisation occurred.
- The Commonwealth is a free association of 54 sovereign independent states which evolved from the former British Empire. The Statute of Westminster of 1931 laid the legal foundations of the Commonwealth.
- The character of the Commonwealth changed as new members joined. Before 1960, it was dominated by white nations. Since then, black nations have been in the majority.
- The Commonwealth is run by a Secretariat headed by a Secretary-General elected by Commonwealth heads of government.

Activity 6.7 *The Commonwealth*

Item A *Decolonisation 1945-98*

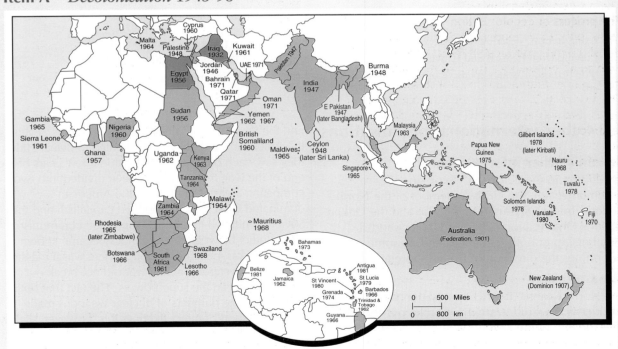

This map shows the countries which belonged to the British Empire and the dates at which independence was achieved.

Item B *The Singapore Declaration, 1971*

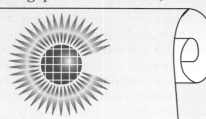

The Singapore Declaration, 1971

1 We believe that international peace and order are essential to the security and prosperity of mankind.

2 We believe in the liberty of the individual - in equal rights for all regardless of race, colour, creed, political belief.

3 We recognise racial prejudice as a dangerous sickness - we will each combat this evil within our own nations.

4 We oppose all forms of colonial domination. We are committed to furthering the principle of self-determination.

5 We believe that the wide disparities of wealth now existing between different sections of mankind are too great to be tolerated. We seek to overcome poverty, ignorance and disease and to achieve a more equitable society.

6 We believe that international cooperation is essential to remove the causes of war.

Adapted from an information sheet produced by the Commonwealth Secretariat in 1993.

Item C *Benefits of the Commonwealth*

The Commonwealth has countries queuing up to join. Mozambique and Cameroon were admitted in 1995. Yemen and Rwanda are anxious to follow. Fiji has just been re-admitted and the Palestine National Authority has expressed interest in applying after 1999 when it is due to achieve sovereignty. So, why the interest? The Commonwealth is a unique meeting place. Its 54 members range from the world's most populous nation (India) to one of its smallest (Tuvalu). Members embrace virtually every major global grouping (such as the G7 and the EU). A quarter of the world's population is represented, a fifth of global trade accounted for. As a result, it presents unrivalled opportunities for states, particularly smaller ones, to forge strategic alliances and to make their voices heard. For developing countries, aid is a factor. The Commonwealth's own fund for technical cooperation is peanuts (amounting to c.£28 million), but membership of the club does make access to the bilateral programmes of the big countries much easier. More important, however, is the networking. Whereas the UN places emphasis on the big players, the Commonwealth tries to treat members as equals. The network promotes unlikely alliances. Zimbabwe, for example, has growing commercial ties with Cyprus. The Commonwealth has other advantages too. Meetings share a common language, for example, meaning that discussions are interpreter-free and consequently much more lively. Also, big nations are waking up to the trading opportunities given that the Asian tiger economies are represented.

Adapted from the *Independent on Sunday*, 19 October 1997.

Questions

1. Using Item A, describe the process of decolonisation. What evidence is there of a domino effect?
2. Judging from Items B and C, what is the role and the purpose of the Commonwealth?
3. 'For Britain, it is an expensive burden.' Is this a fair assessment of the Commonwealth? Give reasons for your answer.

5.2 Other international organisations

Britain's other international ties

In addition to the European Union and the Commonwealth, the UK is a member of the North Atlantic Treaty Organisation (NATO) and the United Nations Organisation (UNO or UN for short). Membership of both influences and, to some extent, determines the direction of Britain's foreign policy.

The Cold War

The North Atlantic Treaty Organisation (NATO) is a product of the Cold War which broke out shortly after the end of the Second World War and lasted until the collapse of Soviet Communism in 1991.

What was the 'Cold War'?

The Second World War broke Europe's domination of world affairs and resulted in the emergence of the USA and the Soviet Union (USSR) as 'superpowers'. Even as the Americans and Soviets cooperated to defeat Hitler, they saw each other as rivals. Within a few years of the end of the war, the world had been divided into two competing areas of influence - the American-dominated West which supported capitalism and the Soviet-dominated East which supported communism. The conflict between the two blocs became known as the 'Cold War' because, although there was a massive build-up of weapons, actual war did not break out directly between the superpowers. The fact that both sides had large numbers of nuclear weapons made them stop short of direct fighting. It is, however, slightly misleading to talk of a 'cold' war since this implies that there was no real combat. In fact, both superpowers backed or fought wars in countries outside Europe (such as Korea, Vietnam and Afghanistan) and millions died as a result.

Why did the Cold War break out?

The Cold War developed out of what happened in the final stages of the Second World War. Soviet troops pushed the Nazis back through Eastern Europe into Germany whilst the troops of the Western Allies (the USA, Britain and France) crossed the Channel and pushed the Nazis back though France and the Benelux countries. Soviet troops occupied Eastern Europe, therefore, and the troops of the Western Allies occupied Western Europe.

Suspicions between the two superpowers stretched right back to the Russian revolution of 1917 and beyond. The USA was as fierce a champion of capitalism as the Soviet Union was a champion of communism. Suspicions remained throughout the Second World War and were exacerbated by the American announcement of the Marshall Plan in June 1947. Under this plan the USA promised a massive programme of financial aid to rebuild the stricken European economy. Although this aid was offered to Eastern European countries, they rejected it. Stalin claimed that the Marshall Plan was a plot to spread American control by economic rather than military means. In reply, the USSR set up the 'Molotov Plan' in July 1947. This tied Eastern Europe to the USSR in a series of trade agreements.

Germany after 1945

When Germany finally surrendered in 1945, the country was divided into four zones, each zone occupied by one of the victorious Allies - the USA, Britain, France and the Soviet Union. Berlin, the capital, was also divided into four zones. Suspicion between the Soviet Union and the other three Allies led to these temporary zones becoming pawns in the early phase of the Cold War. Whilst cooperation between the Western Allies led to the removal of barriers between their zones, the Soviet Union kept its zone separate. When, in 1948, the Soviet Union tried to prevent the other allies crossing Soviet-controlled territory to bring goods into their zones in Berlin, the Western Allies sent in supplies by air for more than a year until the Soviets finally relented. This, the 'Berlin Airlift', was typical of a Cold War confrontation.

The confrontation over Berlin had two main consequences. First, the division of Germany into East Germany (the Soviet zone) and West Germany (the other three zones) became fixed. In 1949, the American, British and French zones were amalgamated and the area became the Federal Republic of Germany (West Germany) with its own Western-style government and constitution. In response to this, the Soviet Union set up the German Democratic Republic (East Germany) with a Soviet-style government and constitution. And second, the Berlin Airlift revealed that the Western Allies could force the Soviets to back down if they combined their forces. The result was the formation of a military alliance - the North Atlantic Treaty Organisation (NATO).

NATO

The origins of NATO are closely linked to the signing of the Brussels Treaty in March 1948. This Treaty bound Britain, France and the three Benelux countries to assist each other in the event of armed aggression against any one of them from the Communist East. It was drawn up in response to a British initiative.

The Canadian Secretary of State for Foreign Affairs picked up on this initiative and suggested that the idea of a mutual defence system be extended to include Canada and the USA. The result was the development of a single defence system for the North Atlantic and Western Europe. On 4 April 1949, the North Atlantic Treaty was signed by the foreign ministers of 12 states - the original five members plus Canada, Denmark, Iceland, Norway, Italy, Portugal and the USA.

The need for a mutual defence organisation was (it was argued) immediately underlined when, in July 1949, news reached the West that the Soviet Union had successfully test-exploded an atom bomb for the first time. Until then, the USA had been the only country with nuclear capability in the world (the first atom bomb was test-exploded in the USA in July 1945). Once both superpowers had nuclear capability, an arms race began with huge amounts of money being poured into projects designed to build more and bigger nuclear weapons with more and more sophisticated delivery systems. NATO (like its counterpart, the Warsaw Pact) soon became a nuclear umbrella behind which its members sought protection. Greece and Turkey joined NATO in 1952, West Germany joined in 1955 and Spain joined in 1982.

NATO's role

NATO's main aim was to safeguard its members against aggression from the Soviet bloc. To achieve this, a great deal of political cooperation and joint defence planning was necessary. In theory, all members were to be equal, but, in practice, NATO was dominated by the USA from the start. There were two main reasons for this:

1. First, the USA was the only state capable of matching the might of a potential Soviet attack.
2. And second, the European members were more concerned with economic recovery than possible rearmament.

Although the British government prided itself on its 'special relationship' with the USA and its independent nuclear deterrent, in reality, Britain's nuclear stockpile was soon minuscule compared with that of the USA. Consequently, the USA's military dominance ensured that it dominated NATO policy.

NATO after 1991

After the collapse of Soviet Communism in 1991, NATO began searching for a new role. When a NATO summit was held in November 1991:

'A new strategy called "Strategic Concept" was

adopted, by which Britain and its allies acknowledged that the threat of a full-scale attack on all NATO's European fronts has been removed. At the same time, there are other possible risks - notably ethnic rivalries and territorial disputes - which could involve outside powers or spill over into NATO countries. In addition, account has to be taken of a substantial nuclear arsenal held in the republics of the former Soviet Union; Russia in particular remains the largest military power in Europe. There are other dangers outside Europe where developing states have modern weapons of mass destruction that could reach NATO territory.' (HMSO 1993, p.51)

NATO members, therefore, agreed that NATO should remain as the bastion of defence and security in Europe, but that smaller, more flexible reaction forces should be deployed. These reaction forces should have a more multinational nature than was the case in the past (when the USA provided the majority of personnel).

Enlargement

At the Madrid summit in July 1997, NATO's Secretary-General, Javier Solana, announced that three new members would be admitted to NATO in 1999 - namely, Poland, Hungary and the Czech Republic. He also announced that Slovenia and Romania were prime candidates for future membership (but named no date) and that the three Baltic republics (Latvia, Lithuania and Estonia) were 'aspiring members'. Although the decision to enlarge NATO was expected, it was controversial:

> 'Concerns remain over the military effectiveness of the newcomers, the cost to them and existing members, ratification problems in the US Senate and Russian sensitivities.' (*Guardian*, 9 July 1997)

Despite signing a 'cooperation accord' in May 1997 (which gives Russia a voice but not a veto over NATO decisions which affect its security), Russia condemned NATO's decision to accept the three new members.

The United Nations

The League of Nations

The first truly international organisation was the League of Nations, established after the First World War. The idea was that all countries in the world would join the League and, if there was a dispute between two countries, the League would decide which country was in the right. If one country broke international law (for example, by invading another country), the other members of the League would join together and take action against that country. The League of Nations suffered from the start because the USA refused to join it. It was then discredited when Japan invaded Manchuria in 1931,

Italy invaded Ethiopia in 1935, and it proved unable to prevent the outbreak of the Second World War.

Origins of the UN

The idea for a United Nations Organisation was developed during the Second World War. Churchill, Roosevelt and Stalin agreed at the Tehran conference in 1943 that a new international organisation should be set up to replace the League of Nations. Between August and October 1944, a conference was held in Washington DC to work out the final plans. The result was the United Nations Charter. This Charter was signed by 51 states in San Francisco in June 1945. The main aim of the UN is to secure peace throughout the world. It also works to eradicate suffering and poverty.

Membership of the UN is open to all states which accept the aims of the Charter. The main institutions of the UN are the Security Council, the General Assembly, the Secretariat and the International Court of Justice (see Activity 6.8, Item D).

The Security Council

The Security Council consists of five permanent members (Britain, France, China, Russia and the USA - the victors in the Second World War) and ten other members elected every two years by the General Assembly. The permanent members have the power to veto draft resolutions. During the Cold War, this power was often used to block resolutions because it was felt that one side or the other was trying to manipulate the UN to its own advantage. As a result, it was difficult for the UN to function properly. Since the end of the Cold War, however, there has been a degree of optimism that the UN will be able to play a more positive role in international affairs.

Peacekeeping

UN peacekeeping since the collapse of Soviet Communism in 1991 has had mixed fortunes. Military action against Iraq in 1990-91 had full UN backing and achieved its aim of forcing the Iraqis out of Kuwait, but this was achieved only at the cost of a great deal of loss of life. UN intervention in the former Yugoslavia contributed to the establishment of peace in the region. But, UN intervention in Somalia was widely regarded as a failure (not least because air strikes resulted in the deaths of many civilians). Interviewed eight weeks after being appointed to office, the Secretary General of the UN, Kofi Annan, argued that the UN's role is changing in respect to peacekeeping:

> 'Mr Annan's message is that the UN is shifting away from its traditional preoccupations with peacekeeping and international security to the economic and social problems many feel need urgent attention. "I will encourage governments to embrace a broader definition of security - security that includes economic wellbeing and the ability of people to fulfil themselves", he said.' (*Guardian*, 28 February 1997)

UN aid agencies

Although UN peacekeeping operations capture most public attention, the UN's aid agencies carry out work that helps to prevent war breaking out in the first place. The best known of these agencies are the World Health Organisation (WHO) and UNICEF (the UN's children fund). As a result of UNICEF's immunisation programme, the number of children in the developing world who have been immunised has risen from less than 5% in 1974 to 80% in 1991. A third agency, the UN Educational, Scientific and Cultural Organisation (UNESCO) aims to change people and politics through education. Its activities range from literacy programmes to campaigns to preserve ancient monuments. However, because it deals in ideas and culture, it is the most controversial UN agency. In 1985, Britain withdrew from UNESCO, officially because it had doubts about the effectiveness with which the organisation pursued its objectives. On 1 July 1997, however, Britain rejoined UNESCO, fulfilling a pledge made by the Labour Party in opposition.

Most of the UN aid agencies' work takes place in under-developed countries. Long-term projects are designed to improve the local economy whilst short-term projects help to provide food and medical relief. Despite the work of the UN agencies, however, the gap between the rich and poor nations has widened.

Main points - Section 5.2

- NATO is a product of the Cold War which developed after 1945. It was set up in 1949 to serve as a single defence system for the North Atlantic and Western Europe.
- NATO's main aim was to safeguard its members against aggression from the Soviet bloc. Since the Soviet Union's collapse in 1991, NATO's main aim has been to maintain defence and security in Europe.
- The United Nations was set up after the Second World War. It is an international organisation which has a peacekeeping role and runs a number of aid agencies.
- The main institutions of the UN are the Security Council, the General Assembly, the Secretariat and the International Court of Justice

Activity 6.8 *The UN and NATO*

Item A *The UN Charter*

The preamble to the United Nations Charter states that: 'We are determined to save succeeding generations from the scourge of war which twice in our lifetime has brought untold misery to mankind.' The aims of the UN can be summarised as follows:
1. To maintain international peace and security.
2. To settle international disputes in conformity with justice and international law.
3. To achieve international cooperation in solving international problems and to promote respect for human rights and fundamental freedoms for all without distinction as to race, sex, language or religion.

UN members are committed:
1. To refrain from the threat or use of force against the territory or political independence of any state.
2. To seek solutions to disputes by peaceful means.

The Charter recognises and permits the right of the individual or collective defence against armed attack and the existence of regional arrangements designed to maintain peace and security.

Adapted from an information sheet produced by the UN's London office.

Item B *The role of the UN*

The problem of what to do with a delinquent state has been complicated by a change in the nature of conflict since the end of the Cold War. Before, most wars had been between states and the few civil wars were mostly wars fuelled by East-West competition for influence in the developing world. Since then, inter-state wars have become rare and most conflicts are now within states. This has spawned a new kind of delinquency - the delinquency of the dictator or oligarchy or ethnic group that governs its country so cruelly, corruptly, selfishly, or just plain badly that civil strife becomes inevitable. Preventive action is all the rage these days. But, how can the international community take measures to prevent internal conflict without falling foul of the very norms it wants to uphold? International law is very clear. There is nothing in the UN Charter that authorises the UN to intervene in matters which are within the domestic jurisdiction of states. It is this insistence on the sovereign right of states to run their own affairs without foreign interference which has prevented the UN General Assembly from approving ideas for the prevention, management and resolution of conflict and for post-conflict peace building that Secretary General Boutros Ghali put forward in a number of papers. They are well-founded and coherent ideas, but in an age of internal conflicts they seem altogether too intrusive to developing countries.

Adapted from Goulding 1998.

Item C *The post-Cold War world*

The West has not yet developed a clear foreign policy direction for the 21st century, but it needs one rather urgently. The world is in the early stages of what promises to be one of its most tumultuous periods. Gone are the certainties of the Cold War world. By going back to a multi-power system, there is greater risk. Now, policy makers have to calculate the reactions of a number of other powers before formulating any major policies. There is, therefore, a risk that the reactions of the various powers will collide over any

policy. The probable main contenders for power in the 21st century are the USA, Russia, China, the EU and some new Muslim entity. These powers have little in common and are likely to misunderstand each other and miscalculate each other's reactions. They will inhabit a world which is ever more dangerous since technologically it will be a world capable of doing more damage by nuclear and other means.

Adapted from the *Economist*, 24 December 1994 and 6 January 1995.

Item D *How the UN works*

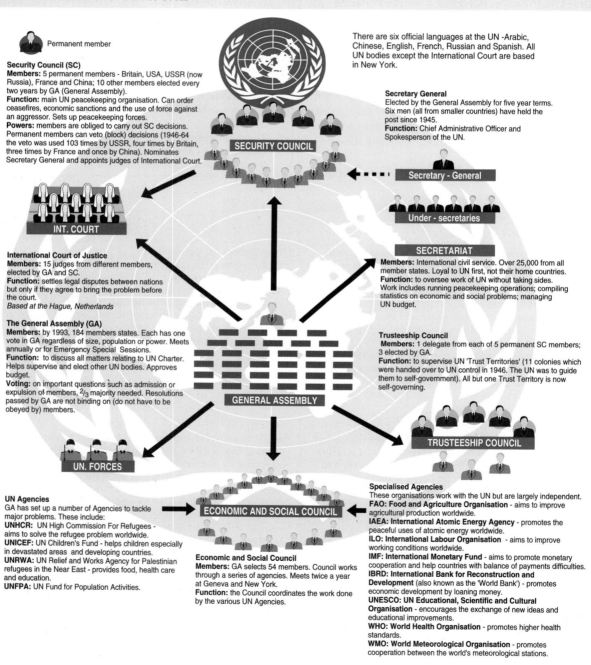

Questions

1. Judging from Items B and D, how does the UN attempt to achieve the aims set out in Item A? Why do you think the UN had difficulties fulfilling its role during the Cold War?
2. a) 'The world has become a safer place since the end of the Cold War.' Using Items B and C, give arguments for and against this view.
   b) Does the UN have a role to play in the new millennium? Explain your answer.
3. Why do you suppose Britain joined both the UN and NATO? Is there still any reason to belong to both organisations?

References

Ashford (1992) Ashford, N., 'The political parties' in *George (1992)*.

Butler & Kavanagh (1997) Butler, D. & Kavanagh, D., *The British General Election of 1997*, Macmillan, 1997.

Coates (1994) Coates, D., *The Question of UK Decline*, Harvester Wheatsheaf, 1994.

CPP (1997) Commission on Public Policy, *Promoting Prosperity: Report of the Commission on Public Policy and British Business*, Vintage Books, 1997.

Crouch & Streeck (1997) Crouch, C. & Streeck, W., 'Introduction: the future of capitalist diversity' in *Crouch & Streeck (1997a)*.

Crouch & Streeck (1997a) Crouch, C. & Streeck, W. (eds), *Political Economy of Modern Capitalism: Mapping Convergence and Diversity*, Sage, 1997.

Dobson (1998) Dobson, A., 'The 1997 general election: explaining a landslide' in *Lancaster (1998)*.

Dunleavy et al. (1997) Dunleavy, P., Gamble, A., Holliday, I. & Peele, G., *Developments in British Politics 5*, Macmillan, 1997.

Gamble (1997) Gamble, A., 'Conclusion: politics 2000' in *Dunleavy et al. (1997)*

Geddes (1993) Geddes, A., *Britain in the European Community*, Baseline Books, 1993.

George (1992) George, S. (ed.), *Britain and the European Community*, Clarendon, 1992.

Goulding (1998) Goulding M., 'A wider role for the UN', *New Statesman*, 13 March 1998.

Gray (1998) Gray, J., 'Globalisation - the dark side', *New Statesman*, 13 March 1998.

Hayes-Renshaw (1998) Hayes-Renshaw, F., 'Council of Ministers', *Politics Review*, Vol.7.3, February 1998.

Held (1997) Held, D., 'How to rule the world', *New Statesman*, 29 August 1997.

Higgott & Reich (1997) Higgott, R., & Reich S., 'Globalisation and sites of conflict: towards definition and taxonomy', paper presented at the International Studies Association annual convention, Minneapolis, March 1997.

HMSO (1992) Central Office of Information, *Britain in the European Community*, HMSO, 1992.

HMSO (1992a) Central Office of Information, Britain and the Commonwealth, HMSO, 1992.

HMSO (1993) Central Office of Information, *Overseas Relations and Defence*, HMSO, 1993.

Kaiser (1998) Kaiser, W., 'Europe - the British getting it right at last', *Parliamentary Brief*, Vol.5.3, January 1998.

Labour (1997) *New Labour - Because Britain Deserves Better*, Labour Party manifesto, Labour Party, 1997.

Lancaster (1995) Lancaster, S. (ed.), *Developments in Politics*, Vol.6, Causeway Press, 1995.

Lancaster (1998) Lancaster, S. (ed.), *Developments in Politics*, Vol.9, Causeway Press, 1998.

Lancaster (1999) Lancaster, S. (ed.), *Developments in Politics*, Vol.10, Causeway Press, 1999.

Leach (1998) Leach, R., 'Political ideas' in *Lancaster (1998)*.

Lipgens (1981) Lipgens, W., *European Integration*, Vol.1, Oxford University Press, 1981.

Lloyd (1998) Lloyd, J., 'A very British lead', *New Statesman*, 2 January 1998.

Lodge (1993) Lodge, J., 'Europe' in *Wale (1993)*.

Mazey & Richardson (1993) Mazey, S. & Richardson, J., 'Pressure groups and the EC', *Politics Review*, Vol.3.1, September 1993.

Norton (1995) Norton, P., 'The constitution' in *Lancaster (1995)*.

Nugent (1994) Nugent, N., *The Government and Politics of the European Union*, Macmillan, 1994.

OOPEC (1992) Office for Official Publication of the European Communities (OOPEC), *From Single Market to European Union* (in the series *Europe on the Move*), OOPEC, 1992.

Peterson (1997) Peterson, J., 'Britain, Europe and the world' in *Dunleavy et al. (1997)*.

Pilkington (1999) Pilkington, C., 'Europe' in *Lancaster (1999)*.

Pinder (1991) Pinder, J., *The Federal Case*, European Movement, 1991

Robins (1997) Robins, K., 'What is globalisation?', *Sociology Review*, Vol. 6.3, February 1997.

Simpson (1986) Simpson, W., *Changing Horizons*, Stanley Thornes, 1986.

Sked (1989) Sked, A., *Good Europeans?*, an occasional paper, The Bruges Group, 4 November 1989.

Strange (1996) Strange, S., *The Retreat of the State*, Cambridge University Press, 1996.

Taylor et al. (1995) Taylor, P., Richardson, J., Yeo, A., Marsh, Z, Trobe, K & Pilkington, A., *Sociology in Focus*, Causeway Press, 1995.

Thatcher (1988) Thatcher, M., *Britain in the European Community*, Conservative Political Centre, 1988.

Vander Elst (1991) Vander Elst, P., *Resisting Leviathan*, The Claridge Press, 1991.

Wale (1993) Wale, W. (ed.), *Developments in Politics*, Vol.4, Causeway Press, 1993.

Part 3
Representation

7 Democracy & elections

Introduction

If there is one thing that all politicians from the main political parties in Britain can agree on, it is that democracy is the best form of government. It is only when they are asked what exactly they mean by 'democracy' and how it should be delivered that the differences between them become apparent. In Britain it is assumed that everyone supports democracy and that the British system of government is democratic. The trouble is that the term 'democracy' (which comes from two ancient Greek words - **demos** meaning 'the people' and **cratos** meaning 'power') covers a wide range of meanings. For example, Communist China describes itself as 'democratic'. Yet, the system of government there is very different from the system of government in Britain.

This chapter describes the main characteristics of democratic political systems and examines the development of democracy in Britain. Since one of the features of a smoothly functioning democracy is that the majority of people participate, in some way, in decision making, the chapter considers to what extent people in Britain participate in politics. Perhaps the most obvious way in which people participate in politics is by voting in elections. This chapter examines the electoral system in Britain in some detail and considers alternative electoral systems. This raises the question of electoral reform. What are the arguments for and against electoral reform in Britain and why has the debate over electoral reform risen up the political agenda in recent years?

Chapter summary

Part 1 defines the term 'democracy' and examines the development of democracy in Britain.

Part 2 looks at political participation in Britain. Who participates and why? In what different ways do people participate in politics?

Part 3 describes the current electoral system in Britain. It considers the range of different types of

election and includes a case study of an election campaign.

Part 4 evaluates alternative electoral systems. What alternative systems are available? How do they work? What are the arguments for and against electoral reform in Britain?

Part 1 Democracy

Key issues

1. What are the main characteristics of a democratic political system?
2. What different forms can a democratic political system take?
3. How did democracy develop in Britain?

1.1 The main characteristics of democratic political systems

Aristotle's *Politics*

The distinction between democracy and other political systems had already been established by the 4th century BC when the Greek philosopher Aristotle wrote his *Politics*, the earliest surviving attempt to catalogue different political systems. Aristotle

distinguishes between **democracy** (rule by the many), **oligarchy** (rule by the few) and **monarchy** (rule by one).

Aristotle was aware that there is an important difference between how political systems work ideally and how they work in practice. In the *Politics*, he claimed that all existing political systems were imperfect because their rulers aimed at their own interests rather than at the interests of all. Oligarchs, for example, promoted their own interests (the interests of the rich) at the expense of poor. Democrats promoted their own interests (the interests of the poor) at the expense of the rich. By associating oligarchy with the rich and democracy with the poor, Aristotle adds an economic dimension to his definition of these political systems. Indeed, he argues that, in a state where there are only a few poor people but these few poor people were the rulers, that state should be defined as a democracy.

Defining 'democracy'

Aristotle's line of argument indicates that a simple definition of democracy as 'rule by the many' is not sufficient. Most modern political scientists would agree with this conclusion:

> 'Democracy is the most valued and also the vaguest of political terms in the modern world...The ancient Greek word "democracy" means rule by the demos which can be translated as either rule by "the people" or by "the mob", depending upon one's ideological preference. By itself, democracy means little more than that, in some undefined sense, political power is ultimately in the hands of the whole adult population and that no smaller group has the right to rule. Democracy only takes on a more useful meaning when qualified by one of the other words with which it is associated, for example liberal democracy, representative democracy...or direct democracy.' (Robertson 1986, p.8)

1.2 Direct democracy

Ancient Athens

According to the traditional view, the birthplace of democracy was ancient Athens. By the 5th century BC, a form of 'direct democracy' had developed in Athens. Athens at that time was an independent self-governing city state. Due to the survival of the writing of the ancient Greeks and the rediscovery of this writing during the Renaissance, Athens' experiment with democracy became an important influence on the development of political culture in Western Europe. The popularity of democracy in Britain today is due, in part, to the fact that Athenian democracy was admired so much in the past.

The city state of Athens in the 5th century BC had a total population in the region of 250,000 people. But, this figure includes women, children and slaves, none of whom were full citizens and none of whom, therefore, had a right to vote or to participate in the democratic process. Historians estimate that Athens had around 40,000 (male) citizens when its democracy was at its height in the years following the Battle of Marathon in 490 BC.

The Athenian system

Every Athenian citizen had the right to attend meetings of the Assembly, a meeting of the citizen body which was called more than 40 times per year (see Box 7.1). Decisions at the Assembly were taken on the basis of a majority vote and any proposals which were passed by a majority became law. Because every citizen had the right to speak and to vote at the Assembly, every citizen had the chance of directly determining what the laws should be. It is because of this that the system is known as direct democracy.

Box 7.1 The Athenian system

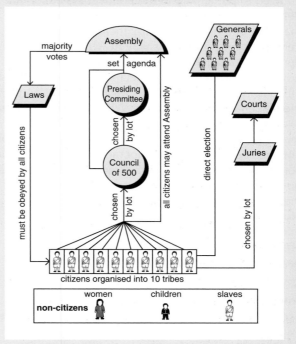

Each citizen belonged to one of ten 'tribes' and each year 50 members of each tribe were chosen by lot to serve on the Council. It was the Council which prepared the agenda for each meeting of the Assembly. Also, the Council chose a rotating presiding committee which in turn chose a presiding officer by lot. The presiding officer held office for a single day and no citizen was allowed to hold this office more than once. All roles concerned with government were, therefore, shared out between citizens who were chosen by lot. Citizens held office for one year and were then replaced by others. The only exception was the election of ten generals. These generals were chosen by direct election and they could stand for election more than once.

Applying the Athenian model

The Athenian system established a number of democratic principles or ideals, some of which have survived in modern democracies:

- every citizen should have the right to vote and to hold office
- the duty of all citizens is to participate actively in the system
- decisions should be made by a majority vote.

Some elements of the Athenian system have not proved as long lasting. The idea that the presiding officer should be chosen randomly by lot and should only serve for a day, for example, has found few supporters since the 5th century BC. Most modern democrats would disapprove of the idea that people in executive positions should be untrained and unelected. And, whilst most modern democrats would embrace the idea that every citizen should be allowed to participate in the political system, their definition of citizenship would normally be wider than that of the Athenians (by including women). Perhaps the most obvious way in which modern democracies differ from the Athenian model, however, is in the lack of direct involvement of most citizens in decision making. Obviously, the size of the citizen body is important. Whereas it is possible to accommodate 40,000 citizens in one place for a meeting, it is not so easy to accommodate 40 million citizens. Besides, direct democracy requires time and commitment. In a direct democracy, citizens need to be informed of what issues need to be resolved and the arguments for and against a particular decision. Not only does this beg the question of who should inform them, it also means that people have to be prepared to spend a large amount of their time preparing for and taking decisions.

Recent experiments in direct democracy

Since the 5th century BC, there have been a few experiments with direct democracy. For example, the Swiss constitution incorporates elements of direct democracy by allowing frequent referendums. Many states in the USA also frequently hold referendums and, in recent years, increasing use has been made of 'initiatives' - devices through which an individual or group can propose legislation by securing the signatures of a required number of voters and then having the issue put to the electorate to accept or reject (Watts 1997, p.45). Unlike initiatives, it should be noted, referendums are organised by the government. It is the government (not the public) which decides whether to hold the referendum, the wording of the question and the timing of the event.

The future

There is an argument that, given the rapid development of communications technology, direct democracy is possible in a large society today (every citizen could vote for or against a new law by pressing a button on a home computer, for example). The Labour government elected in May 1997 has moved a little way in this direction by setting up an on-line consultation on its Freedom of Information white paper and by allowing members of the public to e-mail questions to the Chancellor of the Duchy of Lancaster. In addition, the government has set up a 'People's Panel' in conjunction with MORI, the polling organisation, to test reaction to its policies. According to David Clark (the minister responsible for setting this up), this panel of 5,000 randomly selected members of the public would 'help us find out what people think about how the services they use are delivered' (MORI http://www.mori.com/polls/panel.htm). Critics, however, have seen this as a gimmick, arguing that the consultation of focus groups gives an illusion of public participation rather than a genuine public involvement

in decision making.

In general, it should be noted, apart from decisions made on a very small scale where direct democracy is sometimes employed, representative democracy is the norm and is likely to remain so at least in the near future.

1.3 Representative democracy

What is a representative democracy?

Whereas in a direct democracy every citizen is able to participate directly in decision making, in a representative democracy citizens elect representatives to make decisions for them. In Britain, for example, voters elect Members of Parliament (MPs) to represent them. These MPs meet in an assembly (the House of Commons) which is responsible for making laws. Every MP has the right to speak and vote for or against proposed laws. Proposals become law if a majority of MPs vote in favour of them.

By voting for a representative, citizens hand over the responsibility for making decisions to someone else. This has important implications.

Representatives and accountability

Although the voters have handed over responsibility for making decisions to their representative, that does not necessarily mean that they have no further part to play in the political process. A key to representative government is that the representatives are, in some way, accountable to the electorate. Or, to put it the other way round, the electorate, in some way, exercises control over the representatives. Unless representatives act in a way that meets with the approval of the majority of the electorate, for example, they (or their party) will not be re-elected. The fear of this affects the representatives' behaviour. On the other hand, by handing over responsibility for making decisions to someone else, citizens hand over the opportunity of making a personal contribution to the formation of legislation.

Representatives and constituents

The exact role played by the representative, therefore, becomes crucially important (see also Chapter 11, Section 3.2). Whereas some representatives argue that it is their duty only to do what their electors or their party have instructed them to do, others argue that, once elected, it is their duty to act according to their conscience. It is the latter view which was famously put forward by Edward Burke in a speech to his constituents in Bristol in 1774:

> 'Your representative owes you not his industry only but his judgements; and he betrays, instead of serving you, if he sacrifices to your opinion.'

Burke's view has made a lasting impression on British politicians and it is often used by MPs to justify their behaviour. The problem is that it is a licence for MPs to ignore the wishes of their constituents and their party leadership. On the other hand, the view that representatives should only do what they are instructed to do by their constituents (or party) is equally difficult to sustain. How can representatives know what the majority of their constituents think about a particular issue? And even if they do know, adhering only to the wishes of the majority can, on occasion, lead to tyranny for the minority (something which democracy is supposed to prevent). In other words, representative democracy raises a whole range of problems which do not arise in a direct democracy.

Participatory democracy
In order to overcome the problems described above, another model of democracy - 'participatory democracy' - has been suggested as a compromise between direct democracy and representative democracy. Hancock (1996) suggests that:

'[Participatory democracy] combines the pragmatic advantages of representative democracy with the theoretical attractions of direct democracy. It allows all citizens a greater say in policy issues through such mechanisms as public inquiries, advisory referendums and consultative bodies.' (Hancock 1996, p.7)

Liberal democracy (see also Chapter 4, Section 1.2)
Britain and other industrialised countries in the West are often described as 'liberal democracies'. According to Heywood:

'The liberal element in liberal democracy is a belief in limited government, the idea that the individual should enjoy some protection from arbitrary government. The second element, democratic government, reflects the idea that government should, in some way, be tied to the will of the people.' (Heywood 1991, p.57)

Ideas about liberal democracy evolved in the 19th century in Britain and they can be summarised as follows:

- government should be limited and its purpose should be the removal of obstacles to individual wellbeing
- the market should have a paramount role and state interference should be minimal
- the state should play a 'night-watchman role'
- the franchise should be gradually extended from men with property to members of the working class.

Civil liberties
Central to a liberal democracy is the existence of civil liberties - for example, freedom of speech, freedom of assembly and freedom to dissent. In Britain, these civil liberties are safeguarded by the 'rule of law' (a 19th century concept) and the separation of the powers (the maintenance of a separate executive and judiciary). The rule of law guarantees equality before the law and ensures that the powers of rulers can be curtailed by laws enforceable in courts (see Chapter 4, Section 2.2). The separation of the powers ensures that independence is maintained and that power is fragmented.

Evolution
As ideas about liberal democracy evolved, Dearlove & Saunders argue that:

'Its radical and egalitarian ideals were softened so that, in practice, democratic politics worked within the prevailing system of power in economy and society. Democracy ceased to embody the cry from below for the overthrow of the limited liberal state and the competitive market society to which it was connected. Instead, democracy came to embody the more limited claim that the working class had the right to compete within the established state institutions and within the established society, with the clear expectation that they would not use the state to intervene to effect fundamental change.' (Dearlove & Saunders 1984, p.26)

In the 20th century liberal democracies have come to have a number of defining characteristics (see Box 7.2).

Box 7.2 Liberal democracies
1. Liberal democracies are representative democracies. Political authority is based on popular consent.
2. Popular consent must be given by the whole adult population, with no groups excluded.
3. Elections must be free and fair.
4. There must be open competition for power and a real choice between the individuals, groups and parties which put up candidates for election.

Parliamentary democracy
There are different ways in which liberal democracies work. The two main ways are through a parliamentary system or through a presidential system. According to Norton:

'[The term "parliamentary democracy"] distinguishes the system from those in which the executive and legislature are elected independently of one another and in which one does not depend for its continuance in office on the confidence of the other.' (Norton 1991, p.22)

So, in the USA which has a presidential form of democracy, the elections for President and for Congress are held separately and the President forms a separate administration. By contrast, the UK is a parliamentary democracy and the government is formed from whichever party can command a majority in the House of Commons.

Criticisms of parliamentary democracy

Marxists are critical of parliamentary democracy on the grounds that it is a sham in which the democratic parliamentary institutions provide a smokescreen for the exploitation of the majority of the population. Raymond Williams, for example, argued that parliamentary democracy can be defined as:

> 'The coexistence of political representation and participation within an economic system which admits no such rights, procedures or claims.' (Williams 1981, p.3)

So, for Marxists, parliamentary elections merely serve to permit competing political élites, all of which fundamentally represent ruling class interests, to alternate in positions of power. Parliamentary democracy conceals the location of real power which is based on wealth and capital. This is even true when the Labour Party forms the government since the power of capital still predominates. In support of this argument, Marxists point to the growth in power of capitalist organisations outside and beyond the state - such as multinational companies, the International Monetary Fund (IMF) and the EU. The growing power of these institutions exposes the limitations of parliamentary democracy.

Criticism of parliamentary democracy also comes from the right. For example, Lord Hailsham, a former Conservative minister, suggested in 1976 that parliamentary democracy brought the danger of an 'elective dictatorship'. Writing in 1978 when Labour was in power, he said:

> 'It is only now that men and women are beginning to realise that representative institutions are not necessarily guardians of freedom but can themselves become engines of tyranny. They can be manipulated by minorities, taken over by extremists, motivated by the self-interest of organised millions. We

need to be protected from our representatives no less than our former masters.' (Hailsham 1978, p.13)

Hailsham feared that an elected government had few checks on its power. As a result, parliamentary democracy should be constrained. This would be achieved by returning to limited government, a period of stability, legislative restraint and constitutional reform.

It should be noted that Parliament itself has only one democratic element, the House of Commons. The House of Lords is an unelected second chamber and the monarch retains certain prerogative powers.

Main points - Sections 1.1-1.3

- Democracy means that power is ultimately in the hands of the whole population and no smaller group has the right to rule.
- When citizens make political decisions themselves and do not rely on representatives, this is known as 'direct democracy' (examples include 5th century BC Athens and the frequent use of referendums and initiatives in the USA).
- In a representative democracy, citizens elect representatives to make decisions for them. By doing this, citizens hand over the responsibility for making decisions to someone else.
- Representatives are, in some way, accountable to the electorate, but it is unclear whether they can or should take into account their voters' wishes when making decisions.
- Today, liberal democracies are representative democracies whose authority stems from the whole adult population voting in fair and free elections where there is open competition.
- In a parliamentary democracy, the legislature and executive are elected at the same time. This form of democracy has come under attack from both left and right.

Activity 7.1 *Different forms of democracy*

Item A *What is democracy? (1)*

Democracy is a simple idea based on two principles - popular control and political equality. Democracy requires that the rules and policies of any group should be subject to control by all its members. Also, the members of the group should have equal influence over the framing of its rules and policies. In a small group, these two principles can be realised directly. In a larger group, they can only be realised indirectly through the agency of chosen representatives. In a representative democracy, popular control means exercising control over the decision makers. It should be noted that democracy is not an all or nothing affair. It is a matter of degree - of the extent to which the two principles of popular control and political equality are realised in practice. The answer to the following four questions can be used to measure the level of democracy in a country. First, what kind of electoral system is used - is it free and fair? Second, how open and accountable is the government? Third, what civil and political rights exist (for example, is there freedom of speech)? And fourth, does the political and social culture encourage democracy to flourish at all levels in society?

Adapted from Beetham 1993.

Item B *What is democracy? (2)*

Quality	%
Living in a free country	64
An equal society	38
Voting for a government in elections	31
Strong and effective government	27
Popular control over government	17
A free-market economy	13

A survey carried out in 1994 asked people to choose two qualities out of a list of six that they felt were 'most important about democracy'. The results of this survey are shown above.

Adapted from Weir 1994.

Item C *Teledemocracy*

On 26 February 1998, the *Guardian* reported that a ground-breaking exercise in teledemocracy had been launched in Minnesota, USA, when an on-line debate began between the people and the candidates for the state's governorship. The idea was that, for two weeks, 14 candidates would participate in an on-line debate on six key topics selected by the non-profit making organisation Minnesota E-Democracy. Candidates (who were campaigning for selection within their own parties before the final run-off for Governor in November) were allowed 300-word responses to each issue and subsequent rebuttals of any accusations made by their opponents. Media commentators then posted instant analyses of the debate on-line, and a public e-mail forum, open to anyone, scrutinised the issues and politicians' responses in parallel. On hearing about this project, one *Guardian* reader argued that this was yet another scientific advance that did not result in progress. First, it reduced politics to the level of a game show. Second, it removed the need for a Parliament and handed control of decision making to the media and to those who control the media. And third, it set up every choice as a calculation of material benefit, removing consistency of values from the reckoning and making policy options merely a product to be marketed. 'We do actually still need representational politics', the reader concluded.

Adapted from the *Guardian*, 26 February and 5 March 1998.

Item D *Innovations proposed for the new Scottish Parliament*

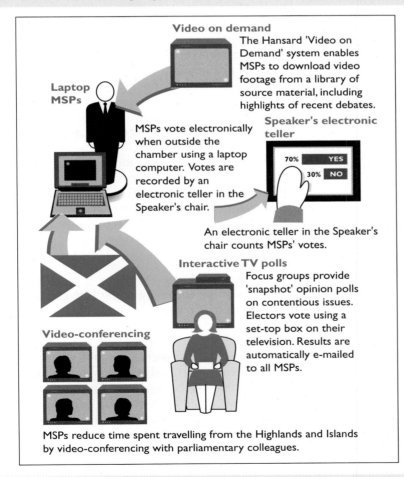

Video on demand
The Hansard 'Video on Demand' system enables MSPs to download video footage from a library of source material, including highlights of recent debates.

Laptop MSPs
MSPs vote electronically when outside the chamber using a laptop computer. Votes are recorded by an electronic teller in the Speaker's chair.

Speaker's electronic teller
70% YES
30% NO
An electronic teller in the Speaker's chair counts MSPs' votes.

Interactive TV polls
Focus groups provide 'snapshot' opinion polls on contentious issues. Electors vote using a set-top box on their television. Results are automatically e-mailed to all MSPs.

Video-conferencing
MSPs reduce time spent travelling from the Highlands and Islands by video-conferencing with parliamentary colleagues.

As architects compete to build a 'millennium chamber' in Edinburgh to house the new Scottish Parliament, Labour strategists are already planning to make it the most technologically advanced in the world (see diagram left). E-mail and on-line information systems are now common in legislatures around the world, but ministers and British Telecom want to go further. They believe electronic voting systems and video-conferencing will improve efficiency. Interactive television can be used to order 'snapshot' opinion polls on contentious issues. Boxes will be connected to televisions to enable a representative sample of Scots to vote on government proposals. The system will create an informal national focus group which ministers hope will re-engage voters with the political process. MSP stands for 'Member of the Scottish Parliament'.

Adapted from the *Guardian*, 18 August 1997.

Questions

NB *It might be useful to refer back to the diagram outlining the British political system in Chapter 1 (Item A in Activity 1.3) when answering these questions.*

1. a) Judging from Items A and B, what is democracy?
   b) Are there elements in Britain that could be described as undemocratic? Explain your answer.

2. In Item B, only 17% of respondents thought that 'popular control over government' was crucial in a democracy.
   a) Make a list of ways in which control is exercised over decision makers in Britain.
   b) What does the list tell us about democracy in Britain?
   c) Why do you think only 17% of respondents in 1994 chose this quality?

3. What are the advantages and disadvantages of the so-called 'teledemocracy' outlined in Items C and D?

1.4 The development of democracy in Britain

Britain and democracy before the 19th century

In Britain, the evolution from absolute monarchy to representative democracy was a slow and complex process. Gradually, the power of the monarchy was handed over to elected representatives and democratic mechanisms and controls developed. Unlike in France where the revolution of 1789 swept away the monarchy for good, in Britain, civil war in the 17th century was followed by the restoration of the monarchy. It is the lack of a decisive break in the past which explains the survival of undemocratic elements (such as the unelected monarchy and House of Lords) in the British political system today.

Although Parliament's control of public finance and law making has been guaranteed since 1688, other democratic elements are much more recent. In 1688, for example, less than 5% of the adult population had the right to vote. This was still the case in 1830. Given that the provision of fair and free elections is a basic component of representative democracy, it seems reasonable to argue that Britain should not be regarded as a legitimate democracy until fair and free elections were established. The struggle for the universal right to vote (also known as the 'franchise' or 'suffrage') and the development of fair electoral practice occurred during the 19th and early 20th centuries.

The electoral system in the early 19th century

At the beginning of the 19th century, the British electoral system was far from democratic. It was not just that less than 5% of adults had the right to vote or that bribery and corruption were prevalent. The electoral system did not provide the means for fair and equal representation. The right to vote (and to stand for election) was restricted to men and was dependent on a property qualification - only those who owned property worth a certain value were eligible to vote. These voters were able to vote in two types of constituencies - counties and boroughs (boroughs were towns which had, at some time, been granted a royal charter). Voters elected two MPs in each county and two MPs in each borough. But, the number of voters in each county and borough varied widely. Some boroughs had several thousand voters whilst some had less than 50.

Impact of the Industrial Revolution

As the Industrial Revolution gained momentum and new towns began to develop, the populations of these new towns found themselves without any representation at all. Thomas Paine, writing in 1791, noted:

> 'The county of Yorkshire which contains nearly a million of souls sends two county Members [MPs]; and so does the county of Rutland which contains not a hundredth part of that number. The town of Old Sarum which contains not three houses sends two Members [MPs]; and the town of Manchester which contains upwards of sixty thousand of souls is not admitted to send any.' (Paine 1791, p.51)

Constituencies with populations small enough for each voter to be bribed were known as 'pocket boroughs' because the MP who bribed the voters had them 'in his pocket'. Constituencies with only a handful of voters were known as 'rotten boroughs' - their population had once been large but, due to demographic changes, had dwindled.

Electoral procedures

Elections at the beginning of the 19th century were not conducted by secret ballot. They were 'open'. When an election was announced a large wooden platform (the 'hustings') was built in a public place. Candidates made speeches from the platform and then the voters were asked to vote by a show of hands. If the vote between two candidates was close then a 'poll' could be demanded. Each voter would have to go up onto the platform and prove that he had a vote. He would then have to state publicly which candidate he supported. This system was a recipe for corruption and intimidation. Bribery was rife and it was common, for example, for landlords to threaten to evict their tenants unless they voted for the candidate supported by the landlord.

Demands for reform

A variety of social and political factors combined to

produce reform. The development of new ways of work and living conditions, the growth of population and towns and the formation of the working and capitalist classes, for example, combined to produce a new set of relations in Britain. In addition, the lessons of the French Revolution, the spreading of new, radical ideas and growing popular discontent piled pressure on the legislators. The result was gradual reform which gained a momentum of its own. The First Reform Act was passed in 1832, but it was not until 1928 that universal suffrage was achieved.

The extension of the franchise in the 19th century

During the 19th century three Electoral Reform Acts and a number of other Acts affecting electoral procedure were passed.

Great Reform Act 1832

The First Reform Act (also known as the 'Great' Reform Act) was passed in 1832. This Act abolished 56 rotten boroughs (which had elected a total of 112 MPs) and changed the law so that 30 boroughs with a population of under 4,000 elected one rather than two MPs. This meant that there were 142 'spare' MPs. These 142 MPs were now to be elected by voters who lived in the new industrial towns. The Act also reduced the property qualification with the result that the total number of voters rose by 200,000. In addition, an electoral register was established for the first time. Although the net result was that still just 7% of the adult population had the right to vote, this Act was of immense importance because it established the principle that there should be fair and equal representation. It also conceded that the franchise could be broadened.

Second Reform Act 1867

Despite the efforts of the Chartists (a mass movement of mainly working people who demanded universal suffrage in the late 1830s and 1840s) it was not until 1867 that the Second Reform Act was passed. Like the First Reform Act, the distribution of MPs was changed - 45 boroughs with a population under 10,000 were to elect one MP rather than two and the 45 'spare' MPs were to be elected by voters in the new industrial towns and in London. Again, the property qualification was lowered in the boroughs with the result that all male householders living in boroughs could vote. The property qualification in the counties was not lowered. The result of these changes was that a million new voters were added to the register. For the first time, therefore, it was possible to talk of a 'mass' electorate. This had important consequences. For example, it forced the political parties to set up national organisations and it encouraged MPs to consider working-class interests for the first time (since many of their constituents belonged to the working class). Nevertheless, still just 16% of the adult population was enfranchised after the Second Reform Act was passed.

Anti-corruption Acts 1872 & 1883

The Second Reform Act was followed shortly by the Secret Ballot Act of 1872. This Act put an end to open elections by introducing the secret ballot. Its aim was to stamp out electoral corruption and it was strengthened in 1883 by the Corrupt and Illegal Practices Act. This Act standardised the amount candidates were allowed to spend on election expenses and made it an offence to attempt to bribe voters. These two Acts went a long way to ensuring that elections became free and fair.

Third Reform Act 1884-85

The Third Reform Act of 1884-85 was in fact made up of two separate Acts - the Franchise Act of 1884 and the Redistribution of Seats Act of 1885. The Franchise Act lowered the property qualification in the counties so that all male householders were allowed to vote. This added another 2.5 million voters to the register. The Redistribution of Seats Act abolished boroughs with a population of under 15,000 and changed the law so that boroughs with fewer than 50,000 inhabitants were to return one MP, not two as before. This meant that, for the first time, single-member constituencies became the rule. Although more than 5 million men had the right to vote after the Third Reform Act was passed, this was only around 28% of the total adult population.

By the end of the 19th century, therefore, it is possible to argue that, in relative terms, some progress had been made towards free and fair elections. But, the majority of the adult population remained disenfranchised.

Electoral reform in the early 20th century

By the beginning of the 20th century, most disenfranchised men could expect to gain the vote in the near future. Looking back over the previous 30 years, they could see that there was a tendency to reduce the property qualification slowly. It seemed only a matter of time, therefore, before all men had the right to vote.

The same, however, could not be said of women. Although a small number of women had argued for the vote before 1867, it was only after the Second Reform Act had been passed that large numbers of women began to mobilise and to campaign for the vote. By then, it seemed that the principle that there should be universal suffrage had been conceded by Parliament. Women began to argue that, if the vote was to be extended to more and more men, there was no reason why they should be excluded. It is, perhaps, no accident that, at first, this campaign was mainly waged by middle-class women. They saw that less-educated men of lower social status were being given the vote whilst they remained disenfranchised. Whilst their campaign in the late 19th century was conventional and muted, at the beginning of the 20th century it boiled up into a major confrontation with the patriarchal (male-dominated) state.

The suffragists and suffragettes

Women who campaigned to win the vote became known as suffragists or suffragettes:

- the term 'suffragist' is usually used of those women who were members of the National Union of Women's Suffrage Societies (NUWSS)
- the term 'suffragette' is usually used of those women who were members of the Women's Social and Political Union (WSPU).

The NUWSS was founded in 1897 when suffragist groups from all over Britain joined together to form a single campaigning organisation. The NUWSS used peaceful, moderate, law-abiding tactics. By 1914, over 600 local groups had joined the NUWSS and it had over 100,000 members. Throughout the period 1897 to 1914, the NUWSS continued to lobby MPs, gather petitions and organise peaceful rallies.

The WSPU was set up by Emmeline Pankhurst and her daughters in 1903. Unlike the NUWSS, the WSPU believed that because peaceful, law-abiding tactics had not won women the vote, more forceful action was necessary. Members of the WSPU began a campaign of direct action to draw attention to their cause. Suffragettes made public protests and, if arrested, always chose prison rather than paying a fine. From 1909, imprisoned suffragettes began to go on hunger strike and were subsequently force-fed by the authorities. These tactics certainly brought great publicity, but opponents argued that the publicity was damaging to the cause.

World War I

When war broke out in 1914, despite the efforts of the suffragists and suffragettes, women still did not have the right to vote. As soon as war was declared, however, the WSPU called a truce and redirected its efforts into helping the war effort. During the First World War, women made an important contribution by taking over the work that had previously been done by men. This allowed men to go and fight. When the war was over, the government promised to support the extension of the franchise to women. Historians are divided as to whether the earlier campaign for women's suffrage speeded up or slowed down the granting of the right to vote to women. Without doubt, it ensured that the issue remained close to the top of the political agenda.

Representation of the People Act 1918

More new voters were added to the register in 1918 than had been added in all previous Electoral Reform Acts combined. The Representation of the People Act which was passed in 1918 raised the number of voters from 7.7 million in the 1910 general election (the last general election to be held before the outbreak of the First World War) to 21.4 million in the general election held in 1918.

During the debate over this Act in Parliament, MPs argued that it was wrong that men who had served in the British army during the First World War should not have the vote. They also agreed that women should be rewarded for their contribution to the war effort. As a result, all men over the age of 21 and all women over the age of 30 were given the right to vote. Women under the age of 30 remained disenfranchised on the grounds that they lacked maturity. In reality, MPs feared that women under the age of 30 were more radical than older women and were worried that they would lose their seats if younger women were given the right to vote. A separate Act in 1918 gave women over the age of 30 the right to stand for election as MPs.

Equal Franchise Act 1928

By the mid-1920s, most people agreed that it was ridiculous to allow men aged 21 the vote but not women. Since fashionable young women in the 1920s were known as 'flappers', people talked of the 'flapper vote'. The Equal Franchise Bill of 1928 at last gave women the vote on the same terms as men. The historian A.J.P. Taylor notes:

> 'The British electoral system reached theoretical democracy only in April 1928. An Act promoted by the government for no particular reason then lowered the voting age for women from 30 to 21. Joynson-Hicks, a Conservative MP, promised the 'flapper' vote in the excitement of a public meeting and the government felt that they must honour this promise. The Act of 1928 added about five million new voters to the register.' (Taylor 1965, p.332)

Acts since 1928

Since 1928 several further Acts have been passed. These are listed in Box 7.3.

Box 7.3 Electoral Reform Acts 1928-98

1. The Representation of the People Act 1949 abolished additional votes for university graduates and for those owning business premises and land in constituencies other than those in which they lived. It also removed the six month residence qualification.
2. In 1969, the minimum voting age was lowered from 21 to 18.
3. The Representation of the People Act 1985 gave British citizens living abroad the right to vote for a period of five years after they had left Britain.
4. In 1989, this period was extended to 20 years and those who were too young to register as voters before they left Britain became eligible to vote.

Main points - Section 1.4

- Before the 19th century, less than 5% of British adults had the right to vote and bribery and corruption were rife. The electoral system did not provide the means for fair and equal representation.
- During the 19th century, three Electoral Reform Acts were passed gradually broadening the electorate so that, by 1900, 28% of adults could vote.
- After the Second Reform Act was passed in 1867, women began to agitate for the vote. At first they used peaceful means, but, in the early 20th century, suffragettes used direct action.
- When the First World War broke out, the suffragettes joined in the war effort. After the war, the Representation of the People Act was passed, giving all men over 21 and women over 30 the vote.
- Since 1928 the voting age of men and women has been the same (age 18 since 1969).

Activity 7.2 *The evolution of democracy in Britain*

Item A *The six points of the people's charter*

The Chartist movement in the 1830s and 1840s was the first nationwide protest movement. It attracted the support of many thousands of people, but the government refused to listen to Chartist demands. Although the Chartists failed to achieve their demands in the short term, five out of the six points were achieved in the long term. The second point refers to the introduction of a secret ballot. The fourth point - the payment of MPs - was introduced in 1911. Before 1911, MPs were unpaid and this made it very difficult for the working class to gain representation in Parliament. The sixth point (electing a new Parliament each year) is the only one not to have been put into practice.

The Six Points OF THE PEOPLE'S CHARTER.

1. A VOTE for every man twenty-one years of age, of sound mind, and not undergoing punishment for crime.
2. THE BALLOT.—To protect the elector in the exercise of his vote.
3. NO PROPERTY QUALIFICATION for Members of Parliament —thus enabling the constituencies to return the man of their choice, be he rich or poor.
4. PAYMENT OF MEMBERS, thus enabling an honest trades-man, working man, or other person, to serve a constituency, when taken from his business to attend to the interests of the country.
5. EQUAL CONSTITUENCIES, securing the same amount of representation for the same number of electors, instead of allowing small constituencies to swamp the votes of large ones.
6. ANNUAL PARLIAMENTS, thus presenting the most effectual check to bribery and intimidation, since though a constituency might be bought once in seven years (even with the ballot), no purse could buy a constituency (under a system of universal suffrage) in each ensuing twelvemonth; and since members, when elected for a year only, would not be able to defy and betray their constituents as now.

Item B *Extension of the franchise*

(i) Electorate and population.

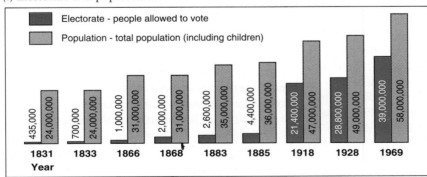

Legend:
- Electorate - people allowed to vote
- Population - total population (including children)

Year	Electorate	Population
1831	435,000	24,000,000
1833	700,000	24,000,000
1866	1,000,000	31,000,000
1868	2,000,000	31,000,000
1883	2,600,000	35,000,000
1885	4,400,000	36,000,000
1918	21,400,000	47,000,000
1928	28,800,000	49,000,000
1969	39,000,000	58,000,000

(ii) Percentage of adults (18 years and over) allowed to vote.

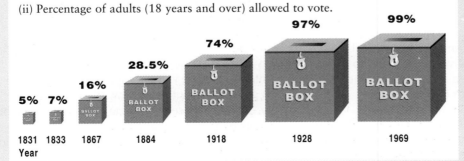

Year	Percentage
1831	5%
1833	7%
1867	16%
1884	28.5%
1918	74%
1928	97%
1969	99%

Item C *Patriarchy*

The channels of democracy in our society - trade unions, political parties, local councils, Parliament - were set up by men, for men. They are not designed to allow women's participation. They ignore important areas of women's lives. They must be forced to change. We have grown used to the idea that we are living in a democracy. But, we women are still, in effect, fighting for the franchise. We will not be the silent majority.

Adapted from Coote & Campbell 1982.

Item D *Suffragette banner*

This banner was produced in the early 20th century.

Questions

1. 'Britain has a long tradition of democratic government.' Give arguments for and against this statement.

2. a) What does Item A tell us about democracy in Britain in the 1830s?

   b) Give arguments for and against the view that annual elections (point 6) would strengthen democracy in Britain.

3. What do Items B and D tell us about the development of democracy in Britain?

4. a) Explain why the extension of the franchise, on its own, is not sufficient to guarantee democracy. Use Item C in your answer.

   b) How might the extension of the franchise lead to greater democracy?

Part 2 Political participation

Key issues

1. Why is the level of political participation important?
2. How do people participate?
3. What factors determine the level of participation?

2.1 Political participation and democracy

Participation in a direct democracy

In a direct democracy, every citizen has the chance to make an impact on every decision put before the citizen body. There is, therefore, a great deal of incentive to participate in political decision making. By participating, citizens make sure that their views are heard and taken into account. If they do not participate, those citizens with opposing views might be able to gain a majority. Citizens, therefore, have a direct and vested interest in participating.

Participation in a representative democracy

In a representative democracy, however, the mass of citizens do not have a direct input into political decision making. Representatives are elected to make decisions on their behalf. As a result, the question of political participation is rather different.

Some people argue that there is no need for citizens to become involved in politics, other than to vote at elections. After all, those who are elected as representatives have the time, the skills and the access to information that ordinary citizens do not

have and are, therefore, in a far better position to make decisions (see, for example, Held 1987 for a discussion of this viewpoint). Others, however, argue that a high level of political participation is important because it ensures that popular control is exerted on decision makers. Decision makers, supporters of this viewpoint claim, take into account the views of those who are politically active. Activists constantly monitor the work of decision makers and hold them accountable for their actions (see, for example, Beetham 1993).

Participation and representation

The debate over participation is, therefore, similar to that over representation (see above Section 1.3). Those who subscribe to Burke's view that representatives should act according to the dictates of their conscience, rather than the wishes of their constituents or party imply that, once representatives are elected, they have no obligation to listen to anyone else. Therefore, ordinary citizens should leave their representatives alone so that they can get on with decision making without interference. On the other hand, those who argue that representatives should act in accordance with the wishes of the majority of their constituents imply that political participation should be encouraged. Ordinary citizens should be constantly informing their representatives of their views so that the representative has firm guidance about what view is held by the majority. Similarly, those who argue that it is the duty of representatives to ensure that a party's manifesto commitments are carried out suggest that people should join political parties to ensure that their manifestos prioritise the issues they feel strongly about.

Participation and democracy

It is clear, therefore, that the level of political participation can determine, to some extent, the behaviour of decision makers. In states with low levels of political participation, decision makers have greater leeway to impose their will than they do in states with high levels of political participation. But, this does not necessarily mean that a state with a high level of political participation is more democratic than a state with a low level. Beetham points out that:

> 'We should be careful not to confuse democracy with participation, or to define it in terms of the level of citizen participation. To do this would produce the bizarre conclusion that the societies under Communist rule were the most democratic because they had the highest levels of voter turnout and the most active and widespread involvement of citizens in party life and public affairs. The problem with such "participation" from a democratic point of view was that it delivered very little control over the agenda or personnel of government for the citizen body because it was largely subject to control by the government itself.' (Beetham 1993, pp.8-9)

2.2 How do people participate?

Different types of participation

Apart from voting in local, general, European and by-elections, ordinary people in Britain have the opportunity of participating in the political process in a number of other ways. Writing a letter to a local councillor, MP or MEP, for example, is one type of political participation. Joining a pressure group or a political party is another. But, whilst some people feel that paying their membership fee to a pressure group or political party is enough, others are prepared to spend a great deal of their spare time campaigning. There is, in other words, a scale of political participation. This scale ranges from complete inactivity at one end to full-time activity at the other end.

Since political participation in a representative democracy is a means by which popular control can be exerted on decision makers, it is understandable that people should act collectively. By demonstrating that a large number of people have the same viewpoint, individual supporters of that viewpoint increase the pressure on decision makers to act in their favour. That is why activities such as collecting and signing petitions, marches and rallies and mass lobbies of MPs at Westminster are organised. Linked to this type of activity are the publicity stunts and other forms of direct action that are reported in the media. People and groups are well aware that the mass media plays a part in setting the political agenda and they design their political activity accordingly.

In their study of political participation in Britain, Parry and his colleagues (Parry et al. 1991) identified 23 political actions (see below, Activity 7.3, Items D and E).

2.3 How active are people in Britain?

Measuring participation

It is easy to measure the level of participation in elections since the turnout is measured as a matter of course. It is less easy to measure the other ways in which people participate in the political process. Nevertheless, the survey carried out by Parry and his colleagues in 1984-85 attempted to measure the extent to which people in Britain participate in the political process (Parry et al. 1991). This survey found that, whilst the vast majority of people participate in general elections, only a minority of people participate beyond general elections. In terms of elections, 82.5% of respondents said that they had voted in the previous general election, but only 27.7% said that they had voted in most local elections. In addition:

> 'Outside of elections when the individual has to put in more effort, the rate of political participation declines even further. In contacting politicians or decision makers where one might simply write a letter or leave a telephone message, those who had managed to do so "at least once in the last five years" were few - 20.7% in the case of a local councillor and only 9.7% for a Member of Parliament. A similar pattern applies to involvement in groups. Not more than about one in ten had been active in an informal or formal group to raise an issue. For party campaigning numbers shrank to single digits.' (Parry & Moyser 1993, p.20)

In the survey, respondents were asked which of the 23 different political actions identified by Parry and his colleagues they had done in the last five years. Those who answered that they had done more than four of these actions made up just 23% of the respondents. In other words, only a quarter of people in Britain can, in any sense, be described as 'political activists'. Britain, it seems, is a country with a low level of political participation. But, according to Parry and his colleagues, this is not unusual:

> '[People] may be aware of politics and even have an interest in it, but they tend not to speak out all that much beyond the confines of the voting booth. In this, however, they are not perhaps atypical of [unlike] ordinary people in other West European democracies.' (Parry et al. 1991, p.47)

Changing levels of participation

It was noted in Chapter 1 (Section 2.4) that, over the

past 30 or so years, the nature of political participation has changed. Whilst, in the first three decades after the Second World War, more and more people joined conventional political organisations like trade unions and political parties, from the mid-1970s membership of these organisations began to fall. Since then, people have increasingly been drawn to unconventional forms of political participation (joining single-issue groups, for example), a trend which has accelerated in recent years:

> 'The late 1990s are witnessing a dramatic upsurge in single-issue protest activity and unconventional forms of political participation...In the late 1980s, the bulk of survey data pointed to the "steady state" of political participation in the UK...In the late 1990s, this is no longer the case.' (Evans 1997, p.110)

Evans lists five explanations for changing levels of political participation. These can be summarised as follows:

1. **The impact of globalisation**
   Globalisation has shifted the focus of power, moving it away from Westminster. The new political structures which are emerging as a result of globalisation encourage people to participate in new ways.

2. **The impact of de-industrialisation**
   De-industrialisation has loosened the old social controls which had developed during industrialisation. As a result, there has been a shift in culture which is manifested, in part, in new forms of political participation.

3. **The statist thesis**
   Britain is a strong, centralised state and the growth in unconventional political participation is a response to the fact that opportunities for success using conventional channels are limited.

4. **The new class thesis**
   Whilst political protest used to be the preserve of the working class, changes in the class structure mean that it is now a middle-class phenomenon. This explains why political activity has changed its nature.

5. **The party dealignment thesis**
   Since people are less loyal to a single party than they used to be, they are more open to the appeal of single-issue groups. Conversely, the growth of single-issue groups has encouraged party dealignment.

Political apathy amongst the young

The low level of interest in politics expressed by young people has been a particular cause of concern for some commentators. Electoral turnout fell among 18 to 24 year olds to 68% in the 1997 general election. Membership of the youth wings of the main political parties is low and relatively few are involved in pressure group activity (Cole 1997). The think tank Demos has claimed that only 6% of 15-34 year olds describe themselves as 'very interested in politics', and concluded that 'an entire generation has opted out of party politics' (Wilkinson & Mulgan 1995, p.99). As noted in Chapter 1, Section 2.4, however, there is the counter-argument - namely that:

> 'It is not that young people do not participate in politics, rather that they participate differently. Under 35s are particularly interested in help for the homeless (73%), disabled rights (71%), animal rights (66%) and increased funding for the NHS (64%). Young people have been prominent in championing environmental causes and civil rights (in, for example, campaigns against the Criminal Justice Bill in 1994).' (Evans 1997, p.112)

Who are the activists?

Parry and his colleagues (1991) discovered that the minority of the population which is politically active is not typical of the nation as whole. This conclusion was reached by examining four characteristics - class, gender, party identification (which political party a person supports) and political outlook (whether a person holds 'moderate' or 'extreme' views).

In terms of class it was found that the majority of activists came from the 'salariat' - people who are relatively wealthy and who have professional and managerial occupations. Parry & Moyser argue that:

> 'This arises because class is associated with the possession of social and economic resources like education and wealth. These are the resources that ease the entry of the individual into the political arena.' (Parry & Moyser 1993, p.21)

Gender and party identification, however, seem to play little part in determining how active people are. Activists are no more likely to be men than women and, whilst people who support different political parties may differ in the type of activities they choose, there is little difference in the level of participation between supporters of the main parties. Although party identification does not seem to determine how active people are, political outlook does. Those with more 'extreme' views on both the right and the left tend to be more active than those with more moderate views.

These findings suggest that the average activist is well educated, earns more than the average wage and holds views which are more 'extreme' than the views of most people.

Main points - Part 2

- Some people argue that, in a representative democracy, there is no need for people to particpate in politics (except voting). Others argue that a high level of participation is important.
- Research shows that only a small minority of people in Britain are poitically active (though most vote in general elections).
- The nature of participation has changed over the last 30 years. People are more reluctant to join trade unions and political parties, but there has been a dramatic upsurge in single-issue protest activity.
- Levels of political participation are particularly low amongst young people.
- Political activists tend to be well educated, earn more than the average wage and to be more extreme in their views than others.

Activity 7.3 *Political participation in Britain*

Item A *Turnout at general elections 1945-97*

Year	% turnout
1945	72.8
1950	83.9
1951	82.6
1955	76.8
1959	78.7
1964	77.1
1966	75.8
1970	72.0
1974 (Feb)	78.8
1974 (Oct)	72.8
1979	76.0
1983	72.7
1987	75.3
1992	77.7
1997	71.4

This table shows the percentage of voters who voted in general elections between 1945 and 1997.

Adapted from Craig 1989 and Butler & Kavanagh 1997.

Item C *Non-registration*

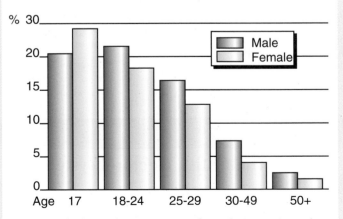

This graph shows the percentage of people not registered to vote in 1991, by age.

Adapted from the *Guardian*, 24 October 1995.

Item B *Political involvement*

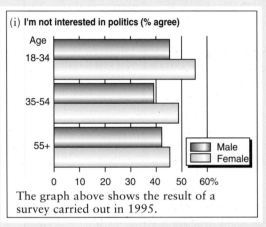

(i) I'm not interested in politics (% agree)

The graph above shows the result of a survey carried out in 1995.

Adapted from the *Guardian*, 24 October 1995.

(ii) A survey of nearly 9,000 people born in the same week in 1970 reveals that 'Thatcher's children' (people who have grown up and had most of their education under the Tories) are significantly more detached from politics than people in their 30s. Asked whether they were interested in politics, nearly 60% of men and nearly 75% of women said they had 'no interest' or were 'not very interested' in politics. In a similar survey six years ago, the same question was put to 12,000 people born in 1958. Researchers found lower apathy ratings then - 45% among men and 66% among women. The phenomenon of apathetic first-time voters is a familiar one. What is different is that the disenchantment with politics has remained as these voters have grown older. A significant proportion of the 27 year olds interviewed in the survey said they would not vote in the 1997 general election - the second general election in which they could vote. The survey also showed that educational qualifications influenced whether people were engaged in politics. Of the men born in 1970 who had gained no educational qualifications, 41% said it made no difference which party was in power, compared with 21% of graduates. Among women the proportions were 33% and 19% respectively.

Adapted from the *Times*, 23 March 1997.

Item D   *The level of political activity in Britain (1)*

Action	%
Voting in elections	
1 Local	**68.8**
2 General	**82.5**
3 European	**47.3**
Party campaigning	
4 Fund raising	**5.2**
5 Canvassed	**3.5**
6 Clerical work	**3.5**
7 Attended rally	**8.6**

Action	%
Group activity	
8 Informal group	**13.8**
9 Organised group	**11.2**
10 Issue in group	**4.7**
Contacting	
11 MP	**9.7**
12 Civil servant	**7.3**
13 Councillor	**20.7**
14 Town Hall	**17.4**
15 Media	**3.8**

Action	%
Protesting	
16 Attended protest meeting	**14.6**
17 Organised petition	**8.0**
18 Signed petition	**63.3**
19 Blocked traffic	**1.1**
20 Protest march	**5.2**
21 Political strike	**6.5**
22 Political boycott	**4.3**
23 Physical force	**0.2**

This table shows the 23 political actions identified in the survey carried out by Parry and his colleagues in 1984-85. The figures show the percentage of respondents who had performed these activities in the last five years.

Adapted from Parry et al. 1991 and Parry & Moyser 1993.

Item E   *The level of political activity in Britain (2)*

The level of participation was measured by finding out how many of the 23 activities listed in Item D had been performed by individuals over the past five years. Seven categories of participants were produced.

Category	Proportion of the population (%)	Average number of actions
1 Almost inactives	**25.8**	**2.05**
2 Just voters	**51.0**	**3.53**
3 Contacting activists	**7.7**	**6.54**
4 Direct activists	**3.1**	**6.96**
5 Collective activists	**8.7**	**7.13**
6 Party campaign activists	**2.2**	**10.03**
7 Complete activists	**1.5**	**15.75**
Whole population	**100.0**	**4.21**

(1) **Almost inactives** - people who barely 'spoke out' on anything even at election time. (2) **Just voters** - people who vote but do not participate in other ways. (3) **Contacting activists** - people who take part in contacting activities. (4) **Collective activists** - people who participate by working through pressure groups. (5) **Direct activists** - people who participate in protests. (6) **Party campaign activists** - people who actively work for a political party. (7) **Complete activists** - people who were involved in most of the 23 activities.

Adapted from Parry et al. 1991 and Parry & Moyser 1993.

Questions

1. Why is the level of political participation in Britain important?

2. a) Using Items A-C, give arguments for and against the view that most British people do not care about politics.
   b) What factors would you say determine the level of political participation in the UK?

3. Would you expect the level of participation to have grown since the survey mentioned in Items D and E was carried out? Give reasons for your answer.

4. Draw up a questionnaire and find out the level of political activity of your colleagues. Are the results above or below the average? Suggest reasons for the results.

Part 3 The British electoral system

Key issues

1. What kind of electoral system operates in the UK?
2. How do local, general, European and by-elections differ?
3. What happened in the 1997 election campaign?
4. When and why are referendums called?

3.1 The British electoral system

Britain's plurality system

The system of voting for local and general elections in Britain and for general elections in Northern Ireland is often described as a 'first-past-the-post' (FPP) or 'simple majority' system. Both terms are slightly inaccurate. Cowley & Dowding point out:

'Britain has a plurality system, sometimes misleadingly called "first-past-the-post". In order to win a constituency, a candidate requires a plurality of the votes; that is, he or she needs more votes than any other single candidate. A majority system (which Britain is also sometimes incorrectly called) is where a candidate requires more votes than all the other candidates put together.' (Cowley & Dowding 1994, p.19)

The system of voting for local and general elections in Britain works as follows. Each elector has one vote which is used to elect a candidate. The candidate with the most votes in a constituency wins the seat. Candidates can win seats with less than 50% of the vote. For example, suppose there was a constituency with three candidates standing. It is possible for one candidate to win 34% of the vote and the other two to win 33% of the vote. In this case the candidate with 34% of the vote would win the seat.

Electoral rules

All British citizens are entitled to vote at parliamentary elections provided that they are aged 18 or over and are not disqualified. Citizens of other Commonwealth countries and citizens of the Republic of Ireland who are resident in Britain are also eligible to vote so long as they are aged 18 or over and not disqualified. Further, British citizens living abroad are eligible to vote for up to 20 years after they have left Britain and those who were too young to vote when they left Britain are able to register when they reach the age of 18.

The following people are disqualified from voting in parliamentary elections:
- members of the House of Lords
- patients detained under mental health legislation
- sentenced prisoners
- people convicted within the last five years of corrupt or illegal electoral practices.

Those eligible to vote are only able to vote if they are registered in a constituency (British citizens living abroad register in the constituency in which they were living before they went abroad). Electoral registers are updated annually. Voters in England, Scotland and Wales must have registered by 10 October and voters in Northern Ireland must have registered by 15 September or their names will not appear on the register. The new register comes into operation on 16 February each year. Voting in elections in Britain is voluntary (in some countries it is compulsory and voters who fail to vote can be fined).

The Boundary Commission

Since the movement of people within Britain results in some areas gaining and some areas losing population, the boundaries of constituencies are periodically altered so that the size of population within each constituency is roughly equal. The exact location of each constituency's borders is determined by the Boundary Commission - an independent body chaired by the Speaker of the House of Commons. The Boundary Commission makes its decisions after receiving representations from political parties. It recommends new constituency boundaries every ten to 15 years. These changes can have important political consequences and MPs monitor the work of the Boundary Commission closely. By the time of the 1997 general election, for example, decisions made by the Boundary Commission had resulted in:
- the creation of eight additional parliamentary seats (making a total of 659 constituencies)
- significant changes in 418 existing seats
- minor changes in a further 76 seats.

As a result, only 157 seats remained completely unchanged. Before the new boundaries were settled, many commentators argued that the changes would prove beneficial to the Conservatives, giving them the advantage in around 20 seats. But, this did not happen:

'In the end, partly because Labour were more skilful in coordinating their submissions to the Boundary Commission, the final advantage to the Conservatives was negligible.' (Butler & Kavanagh 1997, p.22)

In the 1997 general election, Labour-held constituencies still, on average, contained 6,500 fewer voters than Conservative-held constituencies.

Over-representation in Scotland and Wales

In addition to inequality of population between individual seats, there has historically been an over-representation of MPs from Scotland and Wales in the House of Commons. This is because the Redistribution of Seats Act (1944) guaranteed both countries a minimum number of seats. In 1997, the two countries combined had 19 more seats than their population strictly allowed. In recent general elections, this has been to Labour's advantage since Labour is stronger than the Conservatives in these areas. In 1997, the government announced that, because Scotland was set to have its own Parliament, the relevant part of the Redistribution of Seats Act would be repealed and Scottish constituencies be drawn up by the Boundary Commission. The result is likely to be a fall in the number of Scottish MPs (from 72 to 58-60). This change is to be made in time for the general election of 2007.

3.2 General elections

Electoral procedures

A government's term of office is subject to a five year maximum. But, the government can decide to call a general election at any time within that five year period. That means that, unless the government loses a vote of confidence in the House of Commons or the full term has run, the Prime Minister can call a general election at the time when there is maximum party advantage to be gained.

Dissolving Parliament

Formally speaking, a general election is called when Parliament is dissolved by the monarch on the advice of the Prime Minister. When a decision has been made to dissolve Parliament, the monarch directs the Lord Chancellor to fix the Great Seal to the Royal Proclamation which dissolves the old Parliament and calls the new one. The Lord Chancellor and Secretary of State for Northern Ireland are then directed to issue the Writs of Election. Polling takes place within 17 days of the dissolution of Parliament, not including week-ends, bank holidays and days of public thanksgiving or mourning. If the monarch were to die after Parliament was dissolved, then polling would be delayed for two weeks. Whilst the general election is in progress, senior civil servants take over the day to day running of the country - though the Cabinet can be reassembled if there is a crisis.

The five formal stages of general elections are outlined in Box 7.4.

Box 7.4 The formal stages of general elections

1. Royal Proclamation.
2. Issue of Writs, as soon as possible after the royal proclamation - usually the same day.
3. Publication of the notice of election, not later than the second day after the writ is received.
4. Delivery of nomination papers, not later than the sixth day after the royal proclamation.
5. Polling day, on the eleventh day after the last day for delivery of nomination papers (that is, about three to four weeks after the election is announced).
Adapted from HMSO 1991.

By convention, polling day is a Thursday. There is, however, nothing to prevent the Prime Minister choosing another day.

Candidates

Candidates for parliamentary elections must be aged 21 or over. They must be British citizens, citizens of another Commonwealth country or citizens of the Republic of Ireland. Those disqualified from standing for election include the following:

'undischarged bankrupts; people sentenced to more than one year in prison; clergy of the Church of England, Church of Scotland, Church of Ireland and Roman Catholic Church; members of the House of Lords; and people holding offices listed in the House of Commons Disqualification Act 1975. This includes judges, civil servants, some local

government officers, members of the regular armed forces or the police service, some members of public corporations and government commissions and members of Parliaments or assemblies of countries outside the Commonwealth.' (HMSO 1991, pp.12-13)

Candidates must return nomination papers to their local Returning Officer during the period between the publication of the notice of election and six days after the proclamation summoning the new Parliament. Nomination papers must be signed by ten electors from the constituency and must state the candidate's full name, address and description (six words maximum). Candidates must also put down a deposit of £500. This is returned to candidates who receive 5% or more of the votes cast.

Spending limits

There are strict limits on how much each candidate can spend in their constituency. In the 1997 general election, candidates could spend £4,965 plus 4.2p per elector in borough constituencies (the more densely populated urban areas). In county constituencies (less densely populated rural areas), they could spend £4,965 plus 5.6p per elector. During the campaign, candidates may post one communication to each household free of charge. All other expenses are subject to the limit. After the election, the candidate's agent must declare all election expenses within 35 days. Until 1998, the amount spent by national party organisations was not limited. They could spend what they liked on party election broadcasts, other publicity and national campaigning. The Neill Report (published in October 1998), however, recommended caps on what parties could spend (see Chapter 8, Section 1.3). The Labour government agreed to introduce legislation following the Neill Report's recommendations. It also announced a cap on the forthcoming elections for the Scottish Parliament (£1.5 million) and Welsh Assembly (£600,000).

3.3 By-elections

Electoral procedures

By-elections are called when a sitting MP dies or retires from the Commons before Parliament is dissolved. They may also take place if the High Court rules that election law has been broken, though this is a very unusual event. The formal procedure for calling a by-election is as follows:

'When a by-election is to be held, the Speaker of the House of Commons issues a warrant to the Clerk of the Crown directing the Clerk to issue a Writ of Election. The writ is usually issued on the same day as the Speaker's warrant. If a vacancy occurs while Parliament is meeting, the motion for a new writ is usually moved by the party to which the former MP belonged. If the House is not meeting, the Speaker can issue a warrant if two MPs certify that a seat is vacant and notice is given in the London Gazette.' (HMSO 1991, pp.14-15)

Procedural rules
Once a by-election has been called, the same procedural rules apply as in a general election with the exception that candidates are allowed a higher rate of expenses. National interest in by-elections tends to be high as they are regarded as barometers of public opinion between general elections. Because of this, the Representation of the People Act 1989 set a different maximum level of expenses in by-elections. This figure was £19,863 in 1997 plus 14.1p per elector in borough constituencies and £19,863 plus 18.6p per elector in county constituencies.

Recent trends
Until the 1970s, by-elections tended to have a low turnout and it was assumed that there was less interest in them than in general elections because the formation of a government was not at stake. Since 1970, however, media attention and active campaigning by the major political parties have boosted turnout to levels nearer to those found in general elections. Governments find it very hard to maintain support in by-elections as many voters use the opportunity to register a protest vote. They can do this knowing that, generally, this will not mean defeat for the government since only one seat is at stake (see Chapter 9, Section 5.3).

Case study of the Winchester by-election
In the 1997 general election, the Winchester constituency elected a Liberal Democrat candidate, Mark Oaten, with a majority of only two votes (the Conservatives came second). As the result was so close, there were numerous recounts and the election result was announced late - at 6.30pm on 2 May. During the counting process, 233 ballot papers were disqualified by the Returning Officer, including two cases of 'personation' (voting in someone else's name). In addition, 55 ballot papers were not counted because the officials in charge of the polling stations had failed to ensure that they were stamped properly. The stamping process perforates the ballot paper and is designed to stop fraud. A further factor that may have affected the outcome is the candidature of a political maverick who described himself on the ballot paper as the 'Liberal Democrat Top Choice for Parliament' candidate. This may have confused the electorate. When the result was announced, the beaten Conservative candidate, Gerry Malone, announced that he would challenge the result in the High Court. When the case came to court, it was ruled that, since the Representation of the People's Act provides that unstamped ballot papers should be counted, the 55 unstamped papers should be counted before the judge. The result was

that Malone received 22 votes, Oaten 18 and the rest were scattered among the other candidates. This meant that Malone would have won the seat by two votes. The High Court ruled that the election result should be null and void and that a by-election should be held. This was the first time since 1911 that such an event had happened. Matthew Oaten was 'ceremoniously thrown out of Parliament by the Speaker' (*Guardian*, 19 November 1997) who also decided the date of the by-election. On this occasion, the cost was to be born by the Home Office. The by-election was held on 20 November 1997, some six months after the general election. Unsurprisingly, the campaign provoked considerable interest among the mass media. The result was a victory for the Liberal Democrats who won the seat by a majority of 21,000 votes.

A number of reasons were advanced to account for the dramatic change in the votes compared to the general election. First, the local electorate may have resented the fact that Gerry Malone had taken the case to the High Court. Second, Malone himself blamed anti-Scottish racism (he had been a Scottish MP before becoming the MP for Winchester in 1992). And third, the political climate in November 1997 was very different from that in April and May.

As a result of these events, Winchester was transformed from a very safe Conservative seat (with a majority of more than 23,000 in 1992) to the most marginal seat in the country, to a Liberal Democrat seat with a 21,000 majority.

3.4 Local elections

Electoral procedure
Councillors are elected to serve four year terms. They are elected using the same plurality system that is used in parliamentary elections. But, different councils (see Chapter 16, Part 1 for a description of the different types of council) elect councillors at different times. County councils, for example, hold a 'clean sweep' election every four years. At the end of a four year term, all county councillors resign at the same time and an election is fought to fill the seats. Once elected, the councillors keep their seats for the following four years. Metropolitan district councils, on the other hand, use a system of partial renewal. Metropolitan district councils are divided into multi-seat wards (a ward is an administrative area) and elections take place every year. So, suppose a ward has three seats held by councillors A, B and C. In the first year councillor A's seat comes up for election. In the second year, councillor B's seat comes up. And in the third year councillor C's seat comes up. In the fourth year there is no district election. If a ward has two rather than three seats then there is no election in two of the four years. If a ward has four seats then one seat comes up for election each year. When local government was reorganised in the 1970s, the

third type of council - rural (or 'shire') districts - was able to select either system. As a result, one third of rural districts use the partial renewal system whilst the other two thirds hold a clean sweep election in the year mid-way between county council elections.

One advantage of the partial renewal system is that it means there is an election every year. This encourages participation and keeps local parties active. In a consultation paper issued in 1998, the government made it clear that it would prefer to move to annual elections for all seats in local government (DoE 1998). A disadvantage is that a party might become very unpopular and lose seats all over the country, but that party could still retain control of councils for the forthcoming two or three years because not all representatives in a ward come up for election at once.

Local elections are usually held on the first Thursday in May. Turnout in local elections is generally much lower than in general elections.

3.5 European elections

Electoral procedure
Since 1979, voters have had the opportunity to vote in the elections for the European Parliament once every five years. In the European election of 1994, voters in the UK elected 87 Members of the European Parliament (MEPs). Of the 87 MEPs, 71 were elected in England, eight in Scotland, five in Wales and three in Northern Ireland. In England, Scotland and Wales, the same plurality system was used as in parliamentary elections between 1979 and 1994. In Northern Ireland, however, a system of proportional representation was used - the Single Transferable Vote system (see Section 4.1 below for a description of this voting system).

New electoral procedure
In order to bring mainland Britain into line with other members of the EU, in March 1998 the House of Commons passed a measure proposing a system of proportional representation in mainland Britain for the 1999 Euro-elections. The system chosen by the government was a 'Closed List' system (see also Section 4.1 below). This would mean that voters would have a choice of parties, not candidates, on their ballot papers. Also, instead of being divided into 87 separate constituencies, mainland Britain would be divided into 12 regions, varying in size from North East England with 2 million voters and four MEPs to South East England (excluding London) with 5 million voters and 11 MEPs. In every case, seats would be divided between the parties according to the proportion of the vote achieved in that region (a quota would be calculated to determine how many votes are needed to win a

seat). The seats would then be allocated to candidates on the regional lists devised by the political parties. So, if a party won four seats in a region, the top four candidates on its regional list would be elected. In Northern Ireland, the STV system would remain.

At the end of the 1997-98 parliamentary session, the government's proposals for a Closed List system were defeated in the House of Lords. In response, the government included a new Bill proposing the Closed List system in its second Queen's Speech (delivered in November 1998). By the end of 1998, a deal had been struck between the government and the Lords ensuring that the new system would be in operation in time for the 1999 Euro-elections.

Electoral rules
Those qualified to vote in parliamentary elections are qualified to vote in European elections. In addition, members of the House of Lords are allowed to vote in European elections. Similarly, those qualified to stand as candidates in parliamentary elections are qualified to stand in European elections. In addition, peers and members of the clergy of the Church of England, the Church of Scotland, the Church of Ireland and the Roman Catholic Church may stand. Candidates must be nominated by 30 electors and must put down a deposit of £5,000. This is returned if the candidate receives 5% of the vote in England, Scotland and Wales or one quarter of the electoral quota at any stage in the electoral process carried out in Northern Ireland. Candidates can stand in countries other than their home state (for example, the Eurosceptic businessman James Goldsmith stood as a candidate in France in June 1994), but candidates can only stand in one seat. The election expenses for Euro-candidates in 1994 were a maximum of £10,000 plus 4.3p per elector.

Main points - Sections 3.1-3.5

- **The system of voting for local and general elections in Britain and for general elections in Northern Ireland is a plurality system, often inaccurately described as 'first-past-the-post'.**
- **In the 1999 European elections, voters in England Scotland and Wales will use a system of proportional representation for the first time.**
- **With a few exceptions all British citizens over the age of 18 can vote in elections and stand as candidates.**
- **The Boundary Commission ensures that roughly the same number of people is contained within the borders of every constituency.**
- **There are clear rules governing when elections can be held, the timetable to be followed, who can stand and how much they can spend. These rules depend upon the type of election that is being held.**

Activity 7.4 Elections in the UK

Item A *Electoral procedure*

(i) A polling station

Most polling stations are in schools but other buildings are used. A presiding officer is responsible for ensuring that secrecy is maintained and there is no electoral malpractice.

(ii) The count

Sealed ballot boxes are taken to the count together with unused and spoilt ballot papers. The count is presided over by the returning officer.

(iii) Voting in the 1997 general election

Voters casting their votes on 1 May 1997.

Item B *Tidying up the electoral mess*

The Labour MP Jeff Rooker thinks that the way in which we run elections is old-fashioned and should be modernised. Take, for example, the count. Current electoral practice is to count every one of the thousands of ballot papers by hand. This means that election results are almost always modestly wrong. Rooker argues that voting machines should be introduced. More important, perhaps, he also supports fixed-term elections. Since the present system allows the Prime Minister to choose the election date, he argues, this gives too great an advantage to the party in power. Other proposed reforms include an end to the practice of holding elections on Thursday (allowing polling on Saturday and Sunday morning, as happens in other European countries), the introduction of controls over national as well as constituency spending in British elections and the setting up of an independent Electoral Commission. An Electoral Commission would ensure fair play and listen to complaints. Since 1867, this has been the job of the courts. But using the courts is slow and costly.

Adapted from the *Guardian*, 25 April 1994.

Item C *Elections in Winchester 1997*

General election result (May 1997)			
Electorate 78,884			Turnout 78.7%
Oaten, M	**Lib Dem**	**26,100**	**42.1%**
Malone, G	Con	26,098	42.1%
Davis, P	Lab	6,528	10.5%
Strand, P	Ref[1]	1.598	2.6%
Huggett, R	Top[2]	640	1.0%
Rumsey, D	UK Ind[3]	476	0.8%
Browne, J	Ind AFE[4]	307	0.5%
Stockton, P	Loony	307	0.5%
Con to Lib Dem swing 7.4%		**Lib Dem majority 2**	

By-election result (Nov 1997)			Key
Oaten, M	**Lib Dem**	**37,000**	1. Referendum Party;
Malone, G	Con	15,450	2. Top Choice Liberal
Davis, P	Lab	944	Democrat; 3. UK
Page, R	Ref	521	Independence Party;
Sutch, D	Loony	316	4. Independent Against A
Huggett, R	Top	59	Federal Europe; 5.
Barry, R	Nat Law[5]	48	Natural Law Party; 6.
Everest, R	Euro Con[6]	40	European Conservative
Majority 21,556 Turnout 68.7%			Party
Swing 19.8% Con to Lib Dem			

The Liberal Democrats have captured Winchester constituency using textbook tactics. During the last 15 years, they have built a strong local government base, a strong local party and a detailed knowledge of the constituency. 'This time', says their by-election agent, Candy Piercy, 'we ran our most sophisticated campaign ever.' They can now target individual houses and voters with specific election material, 'getting more bang for our bucks'.

Adapted from the *Guardian*, 22 November 1997 and Austin 1997.

Item D   *Altering constituency borders*

In an ideal world, all parliamentary constituencies would have an equal number of votes, making the power of each vote exactly the same. In the real world, this doesn't happen. Some of the discrepancies result from the over-representation of Scotland and Wales - hard to avoid when you're dealing with remote areas like the Western Isles, less defensible perhaps in Glasgow inner city seats. But, some of the discrepancies arise because of the drift of population. Normally, the discrepancy between Conservative-held and Labour-held seats expands between boundary reviews. Electorates fall in the inner city where Labour is strong and they grow in Tory-voting suburbia. A boundary review tries to adapt the constituency maps to these changes, which means that the Tories are always the likely (if temporary) gainers. The review completed in 1995 narrowed the gap but far from eradicated it. That is why the Labour Party was pleased with the outcome while the Conservatives tried to pretend they were not too upset.

Average number of voters in Labour and Conservative seats before and after the boundary review completed in 1995.

	Old boundaries	New boundaries
Conservative	71,509	68,457
Labour	62,176	64,292

Adapted from the *Guardian*, 9 October 1995.

Questions

1. a) You have been given Item A as illustrations to accompany an article entitled, 'Electoral procedure at British general elections'. Write the article.
   b) Which aspects of electoral procedure could be improved? Use Items A and B in your answer.
2. 'Britain has a fair electoral system'. Give arguments for and against this statement. Use Items A,B and D in your answer.
3. Look at Item C. List ways in which electoral procedures for the general election and by-election would (a) have differed and (b) remained the same.
4. Do you think Britain should have fixed-term elections? Explain your answer.
5. Using Item D, explain why the work of the Boundary Commission is important.

3.6 General election campaigns

Introduction

Although some people claim that a fresh general election campaign begins the day after an election result is declared, it is only once the Prime Minister has asked the monarch to dissolve Parliament that the political parties begin to campaign in earnest. General election campaigns proper usually last from three to four weeks and are, perhaps, the most intense three to four weeks that politicians have to face in the political cycle. Before the development of the mass media, Party Leaders travelled round the country addressing election rallies and meeting ordinary voters. Today, they use the television and radio to communicate their ideas. They still make speeches and meet ordinary voters, but this is done in front of the cameras. As a result, their words and actions are not just designed to appeal to the audience at the meeting they are attending. They are intended to appeal to the wider audience at home.

Every general election campaign has its own characteristics, but there are some factors which all general election campaigns have in common. This section looks at campaigning in general and then at a particular campaign - the 1997 general election campaign. The influence that general election campaigns have on the result of elections is considered in Chapter 9, Section 5.4.

A. Campaigning in general

All general election campaigns are run on two levels - the national level and the local level.

At the national level, the party leadership decides upon the themes and tactics which it feels will project the best image for the party throughout the nation and it outlines the party's policies in a manifesto. Leading members of the main parties become the focus of intense media coverage and they attempt to use this to persuade wavering voters to vote for their party. In addition, the national parties organise nationwide advertising campaigns and party election broadcasts and they may organise rallies or other political meetings or events.

At the local level, parliamentary candidates and their agents run campaigns in their constituency. Again, a high public profile is important and much time and effort is spent on generating publicity. All parties rely on volunteers to deliver leaflets and to knock on doors and canvass support.

Party election broadcasts

Although parties are permitted to pay for political adverts in the press or on billboards, they are not allowed to pay for political adverts on television or radio. Instead, free airtime is allocated to parties by broadcasters who 'follow the criteria laid down in the Broadcasting Act' (Butler & Kavanagh 1997, p.155). The criteria for allocating party election broadcasts have been consistent since 1947. The amount of time each party is allowed is determined, in part, by the number of candidates it puts up for election and, in part, by its strength in the previous Parliament. Parties which lack parliamentary representation (such as the Green Party) are allocated a five minute broadcast if they contest at least 50 seats. In the run-up to the 1997 general election, this position was challenged by Sir James Goldsmith, on behalf of the Referendum Party. He argued in the High Court that, because his party was standing in 500 seats, he should be allocated three broadcasts. His petition for a judicial review, however, was unsuccessful.

Between 1964 and 1979, party election broadcasts were allocated to the Conservatives, Labour and Liberal parties on a ratio of 5:5:3. The creation of the Alliance brought a revision to 5:5:4 in 1983 and 5:5:5 in 1987. In 1992 and 1997 the ratio reverted to 5:5:4. In 1997, it was estimated that the Conservative and Labour election broadcasts were watched by some 11.2 million people across all four channels, while the Liberal Democrat broadcasts attracted some 10.1 million viewers (Norris 1998). These figures were well down on the 1992 election. The future of election broadcasts looks uncertain as television executives fear that the public finds them boring. A consultation paper issued by the BBC and the Independent Television Commission suggests that there should be a reduction both in the time allowed for election broadcasts and in the number of party political broadcasts. It also argues that, for the smaller parties, the threshold of 50 contested seats should be raised (*Guardian*, 21 January 1998).

B. The 1997 general election campaign

The timing of a general election can be crucial. It is generally agreed, for example, that if James Callaghan had called an election in the summer or autumn of 1978, Labour would have won. But, Callaghan waited until May 1979. By then, the mood of the electorate had changed and Labour was defeated by the Conservatives.

In 1997, John Major waited until almost the last date possible before calling the general election. This was largely due to the opinion polls which resolutely showed a large Labour lead:

> 'Choosing an election date proved as difficult for John Major as it had five years earlier... This time there was a difference: the economy was set fair...but the opinion polls were disastrous. In 1992, it had been the opposite.' (Butler & Kavanagh 1997, p.75)

Major waited for the opinion polls to improve, but he waited in vain. When he did finally announce the date of the election on Monday 17 March, the announcement was immediately controversial. Since Parliament was due to go into Easter recess at the end of the week, there would be just three more days to do parliamentary business. This meant that Gordon Downey's report on sleaze, which was due to be published the following week, could not be considered by the Commons Standards and Privileges Committee (since the committee would be suspended). According to opponents, the timing of the election announcement was a deliberate ploy by

the government to avoid embarrassing revelations.

Certainly, the length of the campaign announced on 17 March was unusually long - 44 days from the announcement of the poll to polling day (Denver 1997). This was a deliberate tactic by the Conservatives, designed to 'put Tony Blair under pressure and to expose Labour's policies to intensive scrutiny' (Butler & Kavanagh 1997, p.82). But, the strategy backfired and, instead, it was the Conservatives who came under intense scrutiny, especially in the early stages of the campaign when the issue of sleaze dominated the media coverage.

Some commentators feel that the 1997 campaign made little impact, arguing that the election was lost for the Conservatives as early as 1992. Peter Riddell, for example argues:

> 'The decisive events of [the 1997] election occurred in autumn 1992 when sterling was forced out of the exchange rate mechanism and Tory divisions over Europe became chronic, and in the summer of 1994 when Tony Blair was elected Labour Leader. As a result, the public concluded the Tories had run out of steam and that it was time for a change, and that the Blairite Labour Party was no longer a threat.' (*Times*, 1 May 1997)

The Americanisation of the campaign

For some commentators, the 1997 election marked a further 'Americanisation' of the election campaign with an emphasis on leaders, personalities, image politics, simplistic soundbites, reliance on the mass media, negative campaigning, paid advertising, and saturation opinion polling. However, Scammell argues that:

> '[The new techniques introduced since the 1980s] have come from within; a response to changing political and electoral circumstances in Britain and the growth of new communications technology. American techniques have been grafted on (for example, recognition of the importance of television, photo-opportunities, direct mail, telephone canvassing) and rejected (presidential style debates, paid political advertising, campaign spending limits).' (Scammell 1995, p.291)

Similarly, Kavanagh (1995) has argued that the continuing importance of political parties in the UK will mitigate against the wholesale adoption of American techniques.

A post-modern campaign?

The changes in election campaigning, during this century, have also been characterised as a move from the pre-modern, to the modern, to the post-modern campaign (see Box 7.5 below).

The pre-modern campaign involved direct communication between voters and candidates,

Box 7.5 Pre-modern, modern and post-modern election campaigns

	Pre-modern	Modern	Post-modern
Campaign organisation	Local and decentralised	Nationally coordinated	Nationally coordinated but decentralised operations
Preparations	Short-term and ad-hoc campaign	Long campaign	Permanent campaign
Central coordination	Party leaders	Central headquarters, more specialist consultants and party officials	More outside consultants, pollsters and specialist campaign departments
Feedback	Local canvassing	Opinion polls	Opinion polls, focus groups, internet web sites
Media	National and local press, local handbills, posters and pamphlets. Radio leadership speeches	Television broadcasting through major territorial channels	Television narrow casting through fragmented channels, selective mailshots, selective advertisements
Campaign events	Local public meetings. Limited whistle-stop leadership tours	Media mangement. Daily press conferences. Themed photo opportunities. TV party political broadcasts. Billboard wars	Extension of media management to 'routine' politics, leadership speeches, policy launches etc.
Costs	Low budget and local costs	Higher costs for producing television party political broadcasts	Higher costs for consultants, research and television advertisements

Adapted from Norris 1997.

local campaigns and voluntary party workers canvassing the streets. The modern campaign was characterised by greater professionalism, coordination and centralisation. The post-modern campaign, on the other hand, involves:

> 'The emergence of a more autonomous and less partisan press, following its own "media logic", the growing fragmentation and diversification of electronic media outlets, programmes and audiences, and, in reaction to all these developments, the attempts by the parties to reassert control through strategic communications and media management during the permanent campaign.' (Norris 1998, p.117)

An example of post-modern campaign practice is Labour's decision to set up its Millbank campaign headquarters independently of their party headquarters at Walworth Road. During the 1997 election campaign, 80 staff were employed there, aided by the latest computer technology to rebut Conservative claims and to direct Labour's campaign in a tightly organised operation.

Norris admits that there are still elements of all three types of campaign in existence, but suggests that the direction is towards the post-modern campaign. In support of this analysis, Butler and Kavanagh claim:

> 'The 1997 election campaign will be looked back upon as one that neither changed the outcome of the election nor contained any memorable events, but it will be remembered as one where the techniques of controlled electioneering took a quantum leap forward.' (Butler & Kavanagh 1997, p.243)

What Butler and Kavanagh mean by 'techniques of controlled electioneering' is that the main political parties desperately tried to manage the media (see also Chapter 19 Section 4.3). Labour was particularly

successful at doing this and much attention was focused on the main architect of the party's media campaign - Peter Mandelson. Butler and Kavanagh go so far as to describe the 1997 election as a landmark for 'Mandelsonisation'.

Policy issues

Apart from attacking the Conservatives, Labour also claimed to be pushing a positive message on key social issues. Throughout the campaign, the polls suggested that Labour led on the policy issues which most concerned the electorate:

> 'On health, the most important issue for 68% of the electorate, Labour was preferred by 51%, Conservatives by 13%. On education, thought an important issue by 61%, Labour was preferred by 41%, Conservatives by 18%. Only on law and order, then third most important issue for 51% of the electorate, did the Conservatives have a narrow lead over Labour of 32% to 30%.' (Robins 1998, p.4)

Yet, it was the economy that was seen as crucial. Indeed, it was the 'loss of the Conservatives' reputation for economic competence [which] probably contributed more than any other factor to their defeat in 1997' (King 1998, p.187). Kellner supports this argument and suggests that the economy played a triple role in Labour's victory:

> 'First, Labour neutralised tax as an issue. Second, the memories of the economic failure in the early 1990s prevented the Tories from gaining credit from the more recent economic recovery. Third, many voters accepted Tory claims that Britain is booming - but they, personally, were not gaining from it.' (*Observer*, 4 May 1997)

Conservative divisions over Europe were important issues in the second third of the campaign because they distracted attention from the Conservatives' attacks on Labour for the proposed 'windfall tax' on the privatised public utilities and from the supposed threat posed by a revival of trade union power. Labour continued to emphasise social issues, especially education, throughout the campaign. The Liberal Democrats attempted to position themselves to attract support from those unhappy with the two main parties. They decided to play down proposals for constitutional reform and focus instead on key social themes of education, health and crime. In addition, they decided to concentrate on 50 key target seats with Paddy Ashdown very much to the fore (Fisher 1997).

Conservative demoralisation

In the last third of the campaign the Conservatives appeared to be demoralised, in part because the opinion polls gave little cause for comfort as the campaign neared its end. Peter Mandelson claimed that their campaign lacked 'a strategy and message and discipline' (Butler & Kavanagh 1997, p.239). John Major abandoned his soapbox (seen as an important feature of the 1992 election) early on in the campaign, but continued to tour the country seeking support. From within his own party, however, he was criticised for weak leadership and lack of clarity over key policy areas, especially Europe (many Conservative candidates failed to reflect the national party line in their local election manifestos, adding fuel to these criticisms). By 1997, Conservative Party membership had fallen. Many of the remaining members were elderly and, therefore, less likely to be out on the streets actively campaigning. A shortage of active party workers meant that in seats that were thought to be impregnable, for example that of Michael Portillo (then Secretary of State for Defence), activists were dispatched to help in neighbouring constituencies (Dobson 1998). This allowed Labour to make unexpected gains - including the seat of Michael Portillo.

The final days of the campaign

In the last few days of the campaign, John Major travelled to Northern Ireland, Scotland and Wales to oppose Labour's plans for constitutional change, especially devolution. He argued that:

> '[Supporters] had 72 hours to make sure that the system of government that had prevailed in this country for a very long time is protected and enshrined.' (Butler & Kavanagh 1997, p.111)

The Labour leadership held its nerve, wary of making any last minute mistakes that might cost votes, and scarcely able to believe that it might be on the threshold of a sweeping victory.

Cost of the campaign

Large sums of money were spent on national campaigning by all the parties in attempts to win votes. The Neill Report shows that the Labour Party spent £25.7 million, the Conservative Party spent £28.3 million and the Liberal Democrats spent £2.3 million (see Box 7.6).

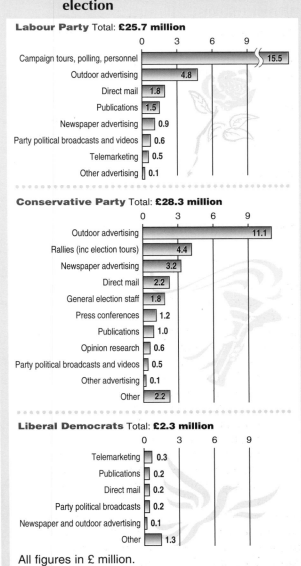

Box 7.6 Spending in the 1997 general election

Labour Party Total: **£25.7 million**

	£ million
Campaign tours, polling, personnel	15.5
Outdoor advertising	4.8
Direct mail	1.8
Publications	1.5
Newspaper advertising	0.9
Party political broadcasts and videos	0.6
Telemarketing	0.5
Other advertising	0.1

Conservative Party Total: **£28.3 million**

	£ million
Outdoor advertising	11.1
Rallies (inc election tours)	4.4
Newspaper advertising	3.2
Direct mail	2.2
General election staff	1.8
Press conferences	1.2
Publications	1.0
Opinion research	0.6
Party political broadcasts and videos	0.5
Other advertising	0.1
Other	2.2

Liberal Democrats Total: **£2.3 million**

	£ million
Telemarketing	0.3
Publications	0.2
Direct mail	0.2
Party political broadcasts	0.2
Newspaper and outdoor advertising	0.1
Other	1.3

All figures in £ million.

Adapted from information in the Neill Report recorded in the *Guardian*, 14 October 1998.

Following the 1997 general election, there were calls for reform of the system of funding. Critics argued that the existing system was flawed because parties were able to spend unlimited amounts nationally whilst expenditure at the local level was carefully limited. The Neill Report suggested that there should be a cap of £20 million on all parties at the next general election and that this should then be index-linked for future elections. The Labour government welcomed the findings of the Neill Report and the Home Secretary promised legislation before the next general election.

What went wrong with the Conservatives' campaign?

After reviewing the 1997 election campaign, John Curtice (1997) claimed that voters look for a party which 'gives the impression of being responsible and effective stewards of the nation as a whole'. In 1997, this was Labour rather than the Conservatives. Peter Riddell suggests that this may have been for the following reasons:

'First, the Tories' divisions over Europe resurfaced with a vengeance as a result of the defiance of the leadership line on a single European currency by so many candidates...[The] Tories would have been better advised to emphasise the economy and their education and housing proposals. Second, Labour and Mr Blair fought a near faultless campaign. Technically, the party has been a generation ahead of the Tories in its concentration of resources on target seats and voters. Labour has been more imaginative...[The] usual dissenters have toed the party line. This has prevented the mistakes that have dogged past Labour campaigns. But, all this much hyped, and often rather self-important activity, has been secondary to Mr Blair's changes in the strategy and direction of the party. Third, the Tories were always battling uphill against a time-for-a-change mood. That has neutralised attempts by the Tory Party to deploy its strong points...And, of course, the whole campaign has been fought against the background of polls pointing, with just one

exception, to a Labour landslide.' (*Times*, 1 May 1997)

Main points - Section 3.6

- **General election campaigns are the most intense period in the political cycle. All are run on both the national level and the local level. The timing of a general election can be crucial.**
- **Party election broadcasts are allocated according to the number of candidates put up by a party and the party's strength in the previous Parliament.**
- **The 1997 general election campaign was unusually long (44 days), but made little impact on the election result.**
- **Some commentators have argued that American techniques are increasingly being used in election campaigns. Others claim that there has been an evolution from pre-modern to post-modern campaigns.**
- **During the 1997 election campaign, Labour won on the policy issues whilst the Conservatives appeared divided and became demoralised. Both parties spent over £20 million on the campaign. Concerns about the amount spent led to the Neill Report which recommended caps on future election campaign expenditure.**

Activity 7.5 *The 1997 election campaign*

Item A   *The 1997 election campaign*

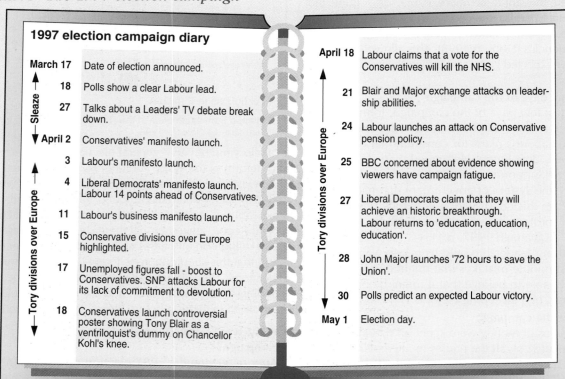

1997 election campaign diary

Sleaze / Tory divisions over Europe

March 17	Date of election announced.
18	Polls show a clear Labour lead.
27	Talks about a Leaders' TV debate break down.
April 2	Conservatives' manifesto launch.
3	Labour's manifesto launch.
4	Liberal Democrats' manifesto launch. Labour 14 points ahead of Conservatives.
11	Labour's business manifesto launch.
15	Conservative divisions over Europe highlighted.
17	Unemployed figures fall - boost to Conservatives. SNP attacks Labour for its lack of commitment to devolution.
18	Conservatives launch controversial poster showing Tony Blair as a ventriloquist's dummy on Chancellor Kohl's knee.

Tory divisions over Europe

April 18	Labour claims that a vote for the Conservatives will kill the NHS.
21	Blair and Major exchange attacks on leadership abilities.
24	Labour launches an attack on Conservative pension policy.
25	BBC concerned about evidence showing viewers have campaign fatigue.
27	Liberal Democrats claim that they will achieve an historic breakthrough. Labour returns to 'education, education, education'.
28	John Major launches '72 hours to save the Union'.
30	Polls predict an expected Labour victory.
May 1	Election day.

Item B *An insider's account*

The vital decisions were made a long time ago - in some cases, three years ago. We knew that the Tories were planning to attack us on tax and spend, as in 1992. It was, therefore, essential to prevent their attacks from having credibility. In 1959, Labour was criticised for making spending commitments without showing how they would be paid for. Then, in 1992, we lost because we made commitments with huge sums of money attached to them which needed increases in tax. I wanted to find a way between these two positions. The windfall tax showed that we could create jobs, but avoided the charge that we wanted something for nothing. At the same time, we outlined the principles of a fair tax system without making huge spending commitments. The other key strategic decision, made more than a year ago, was to air controversial policies months in advance of the campaign. By the time the campaign started, some areas that might have been controversial had been exhausted - such as the minimum wage and devolution. The aim was always to set the agenda. The one thing we hadn't anticipated was sleaze becoming an issue. Yet, it dominated the first two weeks. And then, it was divisions over Europe. At which point, Mawhinney (Conservative Party Chairman) announced that everything was going according to plan!

Adapted from an article by Gordon Brown in the *New Statesman*, Special Election Edition, May 1997.

Item C *The Leaders during the campaign*

The Stamina Factor: Final Figures

John Major:
Age: 54
Freshness rating: ★★
Miles travelled: 10,040
Constituencies visited: 56
Hours spent campaigning on the streets: 91
Interviews: More than 200
Press conferences and rallies: 28
Average working day: 19 hours
Opinion poll high: 37%. Low: 28%.

High points: Being mobbed in East London by Bangladeshis chanting: 'Long Live John Major'.
His off-the-cuff speech to morning press conference on single currency.
Low points: Discovery that ministers had broken ranks to oppose single currency, followed by open rebellion within his party.

Tony Blair:
Age: 43
Freshness rating: ★★★★★
Miles travelled: 10,000
Constituencies visited: 60
Hours spent campaigning on the streets: 40
Interviews: 420
Press conferences and rallies: 59
Average working day: 18 hours
Opinion poll high: 55%. Low: 42%.

High points: Unscripted speech to party faithful in Edinburgh when he spelt out his core beliefs and policies without being fazed by the failure of his lapel microphone.
Low points: Confusion over Labour's devolution policy when comparing a Scottish Parliament to an English parish council.

Paddy Ashdown:
Age: 56
Freshness rating: ★★★
Miles travelled: 17,300
Constituencies visited: 64
Hours spent campaigning on the streets: 45
Interviews: 200
Press conferences and rallies: 29
Average working day: 18.5 hours
Opinion poll high: 19%. Low: 9%.

High points: (personal) Birth of his grandson, Mathius. **(political):** Impromptu speech to hundreds of supporters outside packed rally in Oxford.
Low points: Having to sit between Lords Jenkins and Steel while they conceded the Liberal Democrats would never achieve power.

Adapted from the *Times*, 1 May 1997.

Item D *Campaign statistics*

Labour activists called on more people (12% of the electorate, versus 11% for the Tories). They out-leafleted the Tories 75% to 66%. They reached more potential voters by billboards (55% to 53%) and they reached as many through their party election broadcasts. People working for the Labour Party rang up in excess of two million people, double the number of calls made by the Tories, and Labour had more active helpers on the ground (in all, four million people did some work for Labour during the campaign - more than three times as many as the number working for the Tories). Only on sending letters signed by the Party Leaders were they equalled by the Tories. It is true that Labour was hugely outgunned on delivering videos through electors' letterboxes - but by the Referendum Party, not the Tories (22% of households recalled receiving the Referendum Party's video). Crucially, Labour's machine was even stronger in the marginal constituencies. In Gloucester, for example, five times as many people were canvassed by Labour as by the Conservatives, eight times as many were phoned and four times as many were conscious of Labour's billboards. In a poll, 41% of people in Gloucester said that Labour was making the most effort to win them over, compared with 16% for the Tories.

Adapted from an article by Bob Worcester in the *New Statesman*, Special Election Edition, May 1997.

Item E *Labour Party poster*

This poster appeared on billboards during the 1997 general election campaign.

Questions

1. Collect newspaper cuttings and keep a diary during a local election campaign. At the end of the campaign:
    a) explain in what ways the campaign was different from a general election campaign and in what ways it was the same.
    b) describe the techniques used by party members to win votes during the campaign.
2. a) Write an analysis of the 1997 general election campaign using Items A-E.
    b) How do you think your analysis would have differed if the Conservatives had won the election?
3. Describe the different techniques used by the political parties to win support during the 1997 general election campaign. Which techniques were most and which were least successful? Why?

3.7 Referendums

What are referendums?

One of the problems with representative democracy is that when a party is elected to govern the country, there is no way of knowing whether the electorate supported all, or only some parts, of the party's programme. It is possible, for example, that voters for a particular party liked that party's economic policies, but did not like its policies on education. Elections are not fought on a single question and so it is never clear which parts of a government's programme have popular support.

One way of finding out whether voters support a particular policy is to ask them to vote Yes or No to a single question on that policy. A vote on a single issue is known as a referendum (the plural is either 'referendums' or 'referenda'). Since the electorate is asked to vote directly on a particular issue, holding a referendum is a way of exercising direct democracy within a system of representative democracy.

Another form of direct democracy, which is similar to a referendum, is the 'initiative'. This is:

> '[A device] through which an individual or group may propose legislation by securing the signatures of a required number of qualified voters, and then having the issue put to the people to accept or reject.' (Watts 1997, p.45).

The use of referendums

Although referendums have not been held often in Britain, they are common in some European countries as well as in Australia and the USA. Batchelor notes that:

> 'In Switzerland, referendums and initiatives are regularly used as instruments of direct democracy and if 100,000 voters sign a petition demanding constitutional change, the initiative goes to a binding national vote. Also, all federal laws, decrees and long-term treaties must be voted on if at least 50,000 (less than 1% of the population) demand a referendum. From 1950 to 1986, Switzerland held no fewer than 190 referenda [267 by 1993], deciding to permit females voting in elections, to pursue free trade with the EC and to reject limits on the number of resident foreign workers. So keen are the Swiss on

referenda, David Butler has described them as "the one truly addicted nation". The Republic of Ireland, Norway, France, the Netherlands and Belgium have all resolved constitutional or other issues by this means. By 1992, five countries had voted on membership of the European Community and/or the Treaty of Maastricht. A further referendum was held in 1993 when Denmark reversed its 1992 rejection of Maastricht.
> (Batchelor 1994, p.172)

As the above examples suggest, referendums are commonly held to answer questions of a constitutional or moral nature. Indeed, Bogdanor argues that:

> 'The main function of the referendum is to offer constitutional protection, to prevent laws being changed without the consent of the people.' (*Guardian*, 22 November 1991)

Arguments in favour of holding referendums

Supporters of the use of referendums have made the following points in their favour. First, they encourage political participation, act as an educational device and mobilise consent. Second, they provide a single clear answer to a specific question. Third, they increase the legitimacy of major measures of government. Fourth, they are needed where a party system is either too rigid or no longer delivers the policy choices voters are seeking (this was the argument put forward by the Referendum Party in the 1997 general election in Britain - namely, that a referendum was needed on Britain's future relationship with Europe because all the main parties were in favour of further European integration). Fifth, referendums can strengthen the constitution when they are used as a means of confirming changes in the way we are governed. Sixth, referendums can help legislators keep in touch with the public mood and they can provide legislators with the justification for introducing key reforms.

Arguments against holding referendums

Against this, however, opponents of referendums have used the following arguments. First, their use undermines the sovereignty of Parliament. After all (so the argument goes), the people vote for their representatives at elections and, by so doing, they pass responsibility for decision making on to these representatives. Since the people's consent is given to the party of government at election time, there is no need to hold referendums between elections. Second, if the government alone decides whether or not to hold a referendum, it is likely that referendums will essentially be a conservative weapon. Governments will only hold them for pragmatic reasons (this is where the initiative provides a contrast to the referendum since, with an initiative, it is the voters themselves who decide to seek change). Third, the phrasing of the question is very important. If the government chooses the wording, it might well be able to determine the outcome it desires. Fourth, voters may lack sufficient information to give a considered judgement. As a result, there is a need for them to be provided with information before the referendum takes place. The question of who provides this information and how it is provided is a thorny one. This became apparent in the build-up to the referendum in Northern Ireland in 1998. A leaked government document stated that:

'Government officials will be used to manipulate the media/public.' (*Guardian*, 28 March 1998)

This problem was recognised in the Neill Report of October 1998 which suggested that governments should remain neutral when referendums were held. The Home Secretary, Jack Straw, disagreed with this view, however. In evidence to the House of Commons Home Affairs Committee, he said:

'It seems unrealistic to expect the government to be neutral on an issue to which ministers have devoted substantial energy and resources in getting through Parliament.' (*Guardian*, 21 October 1998)

Fifth, it is possible that an issue may be too complex to allow a Yes or No answer to a simple question. And finally there is the problem of public apathy. Low turnout might mean that the result of a referendum lacks credibility. The more referendums that are held, the lower the turnout is likely to be since people tend to suffer from voting fatigue.

Referendums in the UK

Northern Ireland 1973

It was not until 1973 that a referendum was held in the UK. The electorate for this referendum was confined to people living in Northern Ireland. Voters were asked in this referendum (held on 8 March 1973) whether they wished to remain in the UK or to join the Republic of Ireland. The result was a large majority in favour of remaining in the UK. But, the referendum was boycotted by all shades of nationalist opinion, including supporters of Sinn Fein and the SDLP.

The government decided to hold this referendum in the hope that, by clearly demonstrating the views of the population of Northern Ireland, it would be easier to encourage politicians on all sides to discuss, in a constructive manner, how to resolve the

conflict in the province. But, the size of the electorate became a contentious issue. Republicans and nationalists argued that the population of the whole of Ireland should be allowed to vote in the referendum, rather than only the people of Northern Ireland. Because of the boycott, the voting figures became rather meaningless and government intentions were undermined.

EEC 1975

In 1975, the whole of the UK participated in a referendum held on the issue of whether Britain should remain a member of the European Economic Community (see also Chapter 6, Section 1.1). The UK had entered the EEC in 1973 when the Conservative Party under Edward Heath was in power. But, in the vote in Parliament on this issue in 1973, 69 Labour MPs had defied the Labour whip and voted with the Conservatives. When Labour won the general election in 1974, the party was still divided over the issue and the Labour Leader, Harold Wilson, promised a referendum to test public opinion. Batchelor argues that this referendum was called for reasons of political expediency:

'When Harold Wilson found that he could not unite the 1974 Labour government on the issue of the UK's membership of the EEC, he found it expedient to call a referendum so that the electorate could decide - and thus let the Labour Party off the hook. Labour's zeal for such participatory exercises might have been regarded with less cynicism if the 1983 manifesto, which advocated the UK's withdrawal from the EC, had suggested a similar consultation exercise.' (Batchelor 1992, p.22)

In the House of Commons, a free vote was held and 396 MPs voted to stay in the EEC whilst 170 voted to leave. As a result, the government issued a simplified white paper arguing in favour of continued membership. All those entitled to vote in the referendum were then provided with a statement for and a statement against membership drawn up by the two main campaigning organisations.

It should be noted that in the run-up to the referendum, the pro-EEC campaigning group collected ten times as much money in donations as the anti-EEC group. Also, most of the press supported the pro-EEC campaign. The referendum was held on 5 June 1975 and the following question appeared on ballot papers:

'The government have announced the results of re-negotiation of the UK's terms of membership of the European Community. Do you think that the UK should remain in the EEC?' (Keesings, 16-22 June 1975)

A large majority of voters voted in favour of remaining in the EEC.

Devolution 1979

The third occasion on which referendums were held in the UK came on 1 March 1979 when the people of

Scotland and Wales voted on whether or not they wished to accept the devolution proposals passed by Parliament in the Scotland Act 1978 and the Wales Act 1978. The vote was complicated by the fact that Labour backbenchers managed to secure in the Acts the need for 40% of the electorate as a whole to vote in favour of devolution. If 40% of the electorate as a whole did not vote in favour of devolution, then the Act would be repealed.

In Scotland, a majority of those voting voted in favour of the devolution proposals. But, because there was a relatively low turnout, the total voting in favour of devolution was less than 40% of the electorate as a whole. As a result, the Scotland Act 1978 was repealed. In Wales, there was little support for devolution and the Wales Act 1978 was also repealed. It should be noted that, even if large enough majorities had been obtained in favour of devolution, there was no guarantee that the provisions of the two Acts would be implemented. Bruce Millan, Secretary of State for Scotland at the time when the referendums were held, said:

> 'Obviously the House, as well as the Secretary of State, will take full account of the referendum. Nevertheless, it is ultimately an advisory referendum in the sense that the House will make the final decision.' (Keesings, 20 April 1979)

The question of a referendum over Maastricht and EMU

Vociferous demands for a referendum were made at the time when the Maastricht Treaty was being debated by Parliament in 1993 (see Chapter 6, Section 1.2). Speaking in the House of Lords, Margaret Thatcher claimed:

> 'People have been the great bulwark against over-mighty rulers and the surest defence of the rights of individuals. Their powers are at the heart of our nationhood. The majority of our people want Britain to be in Europe, and so do I. They want to keep intact our Parliament too and they do not want to diminish its powers or its authority or its prestige. In my view, we have surrendered too many powers already. We should surrender no more unless the people wish it. It is the people's turn to speak. It is their powers of which we are the custodians.' (Hansard, 14 July 1993)

The Leaders of both the Conservative Party and the Labour Party, however, opposed a referendum in Britain in 1993.

Although the Maastricht Treaty was ratified without a referendum, both Labour and the Conservatives gave guarantees in their 1997 general election manifestos that there would be a referendum on membership of the single European currency.

Devolution 1997

The fourth occasion on which referendums were held in the United Kingdom was in 1997 when the Labour government carried out its manifesto commitment to hold referendums in Scotland and Wales on its devolution proposals (see also Chapter 4, Section 3.2). In some ways, this was a re-run of the 1979 referendums. But, by 1997, support for devolution was greater. Also, the referendums were held early in the lifetime of the Labour government when its popularity was high.

In the 1992 general election, Labour had promised to introduce assemblies for Scotland and Wales without a referendum, claiming that the general election itself would provide a mandate for change. The decision to change this policy and to hold referendums was taken by the party leadership, without consultation either within the Welsh or Scottish Labour Party or with other bodies like the Scottish Constitutional Convention. Deacon and Lynch (1996) argued that the decision to hold referendums reflected a fear of pushing through important proposals for constitutional change without a mandate from the Scottish and Welsh electorates. A further change in policy came when the Labour leadership decided to include two questions in the referendum for Scotland. The first question asked whether the voter supported the setting up of a new assembly. The second question asked whether the new assembly should have tax-varying powers. This question was designed to weaken the Conservative Party's campaign which claimed that Scottish voters would be forced to pay an extra 'tartan' tax to a Parliament that they never really wanted. Unlike in 1979, a simple majority of those voting in both referendums determined the outcome.

Labour moved rapidly to bring forward its plans for devolution. The Referendums Bill was published in May 1997, setting out the questions that would be asked. This was followed by white papers detailing the structure, membership, elections and powers of the two assemblies.

The campaign in Scotland

An energetic Yes-Yes campaign (so-called because there were two questions) was launched in Scotland with the support of the Labour Party, Liberal Democrats and Scottish Nationalist Party (SNP). The SNP's support was conditional since the party's position was that devolution should be considered only as a first step towards independence. The only major party not to support devolution was the Conservative Party. However, the fact that the Conservatives had lost all their parliamentary seats in Scotland in the 1997 general election weakened their position. By way of contrast, the fact that all parliamentary seats had been won by supporters of devolution was taken by supporters of the Yes-Yes campaign as a mandate for change (Denver 1997). From the start, opinion polls indicated a broad level of support for the proposals in Scotland. As a result, there was little doubt about the outcome of the devolution question, though less certainty about the outcome for the tax-varying question.

The campaign in Wales
In Wales, a low-key Yes campaign was fought, again with the Liberal Democrats and Plaid Cymru supporting Labour's proposals and the Conservatives opposing them. Labour arranged matters so that the two referendums were held a week apart in September 1997 with the Scottish event held first in the hope that this would build up support in Wales where the outcome was uncertain.

The results
In the event, the result in Scotland was decisively Yes-Yes, with 74.3% for a Scottish Assembly and 63.5% in favour of tax-varying powers, on a turnout of 60.1%. In Wales, the result was much closer to call with the majority for devolution a mere 6,721 (0.6%) on a turnout of 50.1%.

Unlike the devolution referendums in 1979, the 1997 referendums can be considered as a more fundamental exercise in direct democracy because they were pre-legislative. Lynch (1998) argues that:

'Rather than relying solely on a general election mandate to institute major reforms, Labour has utilised the referendum as a device to deliver change through "popular consent", not change through "elective dictatorship".' (Lynch 1998, p.96)

Mayor of London 1998
The Labour government followed the referendum success over devolution with a referendum in May 1998 on proposals that Londoners should be able to elect a mayor and a Greater London Assembly (see also Chapter 16, Section 1.3). The government was so concerned about voter apathy that:

'It instructed returning officers to count as valid as many ballot papers as possible, including ones marked with smiley faces...Papers bearing no crosses but marked with the words "I agree" or "OK" will also be considered valid.' (*Times*, 6 May 1998)

The vote took place on the same day as the local council elections, but this did little to enhance interest in the referendum. Only one-third of Londoners bothered to vote in the referendum with voting as low as 25% in some boroughs. Voter apathy was partly attributed to the fact that all the main parties were urging a Yes vote and partly to the perception that the Mayor and new assembly would have little real power.

Northern Ireland 1998
Following the 1998 Northern Ireland peace settlement (see also Chapter 4, Section 3.4), a referendum took place there in May 1998. Whilst, formally speaking, the point of the referendum was to permit the people of Northern Ireland to vote on the peace settlement, the political intention of the referendum was to marginalise the paramilitaries and others who opposed the deal. Both Tony Blair and his predecessor John Major (whose Downing Street Declaration in 1993 had paved the way for peace) worked for the Yes campaign, sharing a platform in Belfast and actively campaigning throughout the province. The Conservatives and Liberal Democrats also supported the Yes campaign, as did the SDLP, Sinn Fein and the Ulster Unionists (who were led by David Trimble). Opposition to the settlement was led by Ian Paisley's Democratic Unionists. They received support from some dissident Ulster Unionists.

When the referendum was held on 22 May 1998, a large majority voted Yes (71%).The legitimacy of the referendum, however, did not only depend on a simple majority. A high turnout and a significant Yes vote from the Unionist population were also required. After the referendum, most commentators agreed that a majority of Unionists had indeed voted Yes, though this was disputed by Ian Paisley (*Observer*, 24 May 1998).

Main points - Section 3.7
- One way of finding out whether voters support a particular policy is to ask them to vote Yes or No to a single question on that policy. This is known as a referendum.
- Referendums are usually held to answer questions of constitutional or moral nature.
- Supporters argue that referendums encourage participation, increase legitimacy, make the system more flexible, strengthen the constitution and keep legislators in touch.
- Opponents argue that referendums undermine the sovereignty of Parliament, are conservative and weighted in favour of the government, oversimplify complex issues and threaten legitimacy if turnout is low.
- In Britain, referendums have been held on Northern Ireland (1973 and 1998), the EEC (1975), devolution (1979 and 1997) and the mayor of London/Greater London Assembly (1998).

Activity 7.6 Referendums in the UK

Item A   *Referendums in the UK*

Date	Electorate	Issue	Yes vote	%	No vote	%	Turnout (%)
8 March 1973	Northern Ireland	Should Northern Ireland remain part of the UK?	591,820	98.9	6,463	1.1	58.1
5 June 1975	United Kingdom	Do you think that the UK should remain in the EEC?	17,378,581	67.2	8,470,073	32.8	63.2
1 March 1979	Scotland	Devolution for Scotland	1,230,937	51.5	1,153,500	48.3	62.9
1 March 1979	Wales	Devolution for Wales	243,048	20.3	956,330	79.7	58.3
11 September 1997	Scotland	Devolution for Scotland	1,775,045	74.3	614,400	25.7	60.1
		Tax-varying powers	1,512,889	63.5	870,263	36.5	60.1
18 September 1997	Wales	Devolution for Wales	559,419	50.3	552,698	49.7	50.1
7 May 1998	London	Mayor and Greater London Assembly	1,230,715	72.0	47,8413	28.0	33.0
22 May 1998	Northern Ireland	Support for the peace settlement	676,966	71.1	274,879	28.9	81.0

This table shows the results of the eight referendums held in the UK between 1973 and 1998. Although 51.5% of voters in the referendum in Scotland in 1979 voted for devolution, this came to just 32.8% of the total electorate. The Scotland Act 1978 was, therefore, repealed. In Wales in 1979, the 20.3% who voted in favour of devolution came to just 11.9% of the total electorate and so the Wales Act 1978 was repealed. In 1997, the decisions on devolution in Scotland and Wales were based on a simple majority of those voting.

Item B   *The referendum in Northern Ireland, 1998*

What the vote will mean

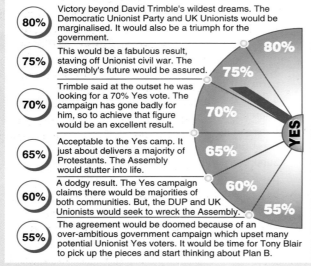

80% Victory beyond David Trimble's wildest dreams. The Democratic Unionist Party and UK Unionists would be marginalised. It would also be a triumph for the government.

75% This would be a fabulous result, staving off Unionist civil war. The Assembly's future would be assured.

70% Trimble said at the outset he was looking for a 70% Yes vote. The campaign has gone badly for him, so to achieve that figure would be an excellent result.

65% Acceptable to the Yes camp. It just about delivers a majority of Protestants. The Assembly would stutter into life.

60% A dodgy result. The Yes campaign claims there would be majorities of both communities. But, the DUP and UK Unionists would seek to wreck the Assembly.

55% The agreement would be doomed because of an over-ambitious government campaign which upset many potential Unionist Yes voters. It would be time for Tony Blair to pick up the pieces and start thinking about Plan B.

Adapted from the *Guardian*, 23 May 1998.

Item C   *Referendums - arguments for*

Referendums are good not bad, and though there is a serious constitutional argument based on parliamentary sovereignty to be made against them, we do not agree with it. Our parliamentary system is not enough. It is essential that voters should be entitled to choose the path for the future. It is desirable to involve the nation in big debates about its destiny. We need more opportunities of this kind to revive citizenship. Parliament is not enough, but referendums are not enough either. We should see the use of referendums on key issues as part of the essential regeneration of public life. That is why it is essential that referendums are part of the parliamentary process and not struggling against it. A referendum on an open-ended question is no use to anyone. For example, it makes no sense to ask 'do you support or oppose the UK's participation in a single European currency?' because, for most people, the answer will always depend on the circumstances. The only question that is both meaningful and responsible is one to approve or disapprove a specific course of action at the time it is proposed to take it.

Adapted from the *Guardian*, 4 April 1996.

Item D   *Referendums - arguments against*

Free politics is a process of compromise between group interests and ideals. In any problem, there is no one unique compromise and no reason why options should be reduced to a binary Yes/No, Either/Or form. Doing so can exclude large groups in the middle. Suppose, for example, that, in the mid-1990s, the people of Northern Ireland had been asked: 'Are you in favour of a united Ireland or should Northern Ireland remain part of the United Kingdom?' Quite apart from people wanting to know what exactly was on offer if they voted for unity, public opinion surveys at the time showed that a majority of people did not want either option. Rather, they supported the idea that Northern Ireland should be administered by both governments jointly with internal, devolved democracy. Referendums, in other words, can polarise opinion that might otherwise accept varying political compromises reached by elected politicians, even if nobody, not even a majority, would agree to any of them fully. Referendums can also exclude real alternatives. Take the question: 'Are you in favour of either first-past-the post or the alternative vote?' This excludes all the other voting systems that people might prefer to the two mentioned. It is a misunderstanding of the nature of government to work on the assumption that bits and pieces of it can be separated out and put to referendums without unexpected consequences on the rest. Joining or not joining the single European currency is a complex economic decision. Any government that gets itself off the hooks of short-term political dilemmas by tossing their reddest meat to the electorate has surrendered responsibility for what it is elected to do - to govern well or to suffer defeat.

Adapted from the *Guardian*, 6 February 1997.

Questions

1. Look at Item A.
   a) Why do you think these referendums were held?
   b) Would you agree that these referendums were a useful exercise in democracy? Give reasons for your answer.
2. Using Items A and B, analyse the results of the 1998 referendum in Northern Ireland.
3. In what circumstances, if at all, do you think referendums should be held? Use Items C and D in your answer.

Part 4 Electoral reform

Key issues

1. What types of electoral systems are available and how do they work?
2. What is the difference between majority and proportional systems?
3. What are the arguments for and against electoral reform in Britain?

4.1 Different voting systems

The range of voting systems
A Royal Commission appointed in 1911 to examine voting systems claimed that there were over 300 voting systems either actually in existence or potentially available. In other words, every country in the world could have a different voting system and there would still be systems that remained unused.

Despite this great diversity, many of these 300 or more voting systems have much in common - they differ only in terms of practical details.

Variations on the British system
Whilst most plurality systems (like the British system) operate with single-seat constituencies, it is possible to have multi-seat constituencies. These fall into two main categories. The first is the system which operated in Britain after the Great Reform Act of 1832 and lasted until 1945 in some seats. It is exactly the same as the single-seat constituency system except that there are two or more seats. Voters have as many votes as there are seats, but can only vote once for a single candidate. If there are two seats in the constituency, then the two candidates to have accumulated the highest number of votes win. The second kind of multi-seat constituency permits voters to have just one vote. Again, the seats are allocated to the candidates who receive the highest number of votes. This system is used in Japan and is known as the 'Single Non-transferable Vote' system. The aim is to reduce the bias towards major parties which tends to be a feature of plurality systems.

Majority systems
Majority systems include mechanisms to ensure that the winning candidate achieves more than 50% of the vote in a constituency. The three best known of these systems are the Alternative Vote system, the Supplementary Vote system and the Second Ballot system. All three systems assume that the country is divided into single-member constituencies. None of the systems is proportional because none ensures that, overall, the results of general elections reflect the number of votes cast for each party.

1. The Alternative Vote system
Under the Alternative Vote system, voters have the opportunity of ranking all the candidates whose names appear on the ballot paper in order of preference. As in the British plurality system, candidates stand for election in a constituency and one member is elected in each constituency.

If any candidate receives more than 50% of first preferences in the initial ballot then that candidate is elected. If, however, no candidate receives more than 50% of first preferences, then the candidate with the lowest number of first preferences is eliminated and that candidate's second preferences are redistributed to the other candidates. If no candidate has reached 50% of the vote after this redistribution, then the candidate with the lowest number of votes after the redistribution is eliminated and that candidate's second preferences are redistributed. This process is continued until a candidate gains more than 50% of the vote.

Voters are not obliged to indicate preferences on their ballot paper. They may vote for a single candidate because they do not want to support another candidate should their candidate be eliminated. In safe seats, there may be little point in indicating preferences since it is likely that a candidate will gain more than 50% of the vote without the need for any redistribution of votes. In marginal seats, however, second preferences might be crucial. Indeed, the system might encourage electoral pacts between two parties at the expense of a third since the two parties which made the pact could then recommend to their supporters which party to nominate as their second preference.

Advantages and disadvantages
Supporters of this system emphasise that it retains constituency representation and it ensures that the winning candidate has more than 50% of the vote. Critics argue that the system leads to disproportional support for the centre parties because, while they are not voters' first choice, they are nearly always voters'

second choice. The Alternative Vote system is used in elections to the Australian House of Representatives.

2. The Supplementary Vote system

A variation of the Alternative Vote system has been proposed by the Labour MP Dale Campbell Savours. This is called the Supplementary Vote system. Under this system, voters have just two preference votes. They can mark a cross in the first preference column for one candidate and in the second preference column for a second candidate. Candidates who win more than 50% of first preferences in the initial ballot are automatically elected. But, if no candidate gains more than 50% of the vote, only two candidates remain in the race - the two candidates with the highest number of first preferences. The second preferences from the losing candidates are then redistributed. Second preferences for eliminated candidates are discarded and those for the two remaining candidates added to their total. After this, whichever of the two remaining candidates has the greatest number of votes wins the seat. The winning candidate, therefore, does not necessarily need to win more than 50% of the votes cast.

Advantages

According to the Plant Report - the Labour Party's inquiry into alternative voting systems, commissioned in 1990 (Labour 1993) - the Supplementary Vote system has several advantages. First, like the Alternative Voting system, it is constituency based and is likely to produce strong governments. Second, it is easy to understand. And third, since only the top two candidates remain after first preferences are counted, it does not allow a third-placed candidate to come through the middle.

3. The Second Ballot system

As the name implies, the Second Ballot system includes the provision for voting to take place on two separate occasions. In the first ballot, voters vote for their favourite candidate. If any candidate wins more than 50% of the vote in a constituency, then that candidate is elected. But, if no candidate wins more than 50%, a second ballot is held, usually a week or two later. In some variations of this system, only the two candidates with the highest number of votes in the first ballot are allowed to stand in the second ballot. This ensures that the successful candidate in the second ballot achieves an absolute majority. In other variations, either all the earlier candidates are allowed to stand or there is a threshold in the first ballot (10% of the vote, for example) and only those who crossed the threshold (by winning more than 10% of the vote, for example) are allowed to stand in the second ballot. Some variations even allow newcomers to stand in the second ballot.

Advantages and disadvantages

This system is in no sense proportional and does

nothing to ensure a fair representation for small parties. It does, however, allow genuine choice since voters can vote for their favourite party in the first ballot, knowing that their vote will not be wasted since they will probably be able to cast a second vote in the second ballot. The system also encourages pacts between parties - parties which put up candidates in the first ballot agree not to stand in the second ballot to ensure that their allies have a better chance of being elected.

A version of the Second Ballot system is used in France. Only those candidates who win more than 12.5% of the vote in the first ballot are allowed to stand in the second ballot.

Proportional systems

Majority voting systems do not ensure that, overall, the results of general elections reflect the number of votes cast for each party. After all, a successful candidate in a majority system might have won just 51% of the vote. That means that, in a sense, 49% of votes in that constituency have been wasted. In the country as a whole, a party might have won many thousands of votes but not have won even one seat. This is what happened in the European elections in Britain in 1989. The Green Party won 15% of the vote nationally. But, it did not win a single seat. In a system which was truly proportional, the Green Party would have won 15% of the seats.

Proportional systems - systems of proportional representation (PR) - do not work on a single-member constituency basis. In fact, the bigger the number of representatives elected in a single constituency the more proportional the result because the election of a large number of representatives means that smaller parties have a greater chance of winning seats. Ideally (for those who support PR), a whole country should be a single multi-member constituency. The voters can then vote for their favourite party and seats can be allocated to the parties on the basis of the number of votes each has secured.

Urwin (1987) argues that PR has two conflicting aims:

- it attempts to ensure that party representation mirrors as closely as possible the level of support for various parties over the country as a whole
- it aims to provide voters with some degree of choice not only between the parties but also between individual candidates.

There are two main systems of PR - the List system and the Single Transferable Vote system. The List system comes closer to achieving the first aim whilst the Single Transferable Vote system some closer to achieving the second aim.

1. The List system

The List system involves multi-member constituencies. In a Closed List system, each party submits a list of candidates for each constituency, but the ballot paper contains a list of political parties rather than a list of individual candidates. Seats are allocated to each party according to the proportion of votes won (a quota is calculated to determine how many votes are needed to win a seat). The number of seats allocated to a party is then filled by the requisite number of candidates from that party's list, starting with the candidate at the top of the list. The system is 'closed' because voters are not able to express a preference for a particular candidate. In an Open List system voters are able to vote for individual candidates and the party vote is determined by adding together all the votes cast for the different candidates in that party. Seats are then allocated to a party according to the proportion of votes won by that party. If a party wins one or more seats, candidates are elected according to the number of votes they won (with the candidate who won most votes for that party being elected first and so on).

A version of the Closed List system has been proposed for the 1999 European elections in Britain (see Section 3.5 above).

How the system works

In its most basic form, a whole country is a single constituency (this is the case in Israel and the Netherlands). So, suppose that a country had 100 seats in its Parliament and it used a Closed List system with three parties 'A, B and C' putting up lists for an election. If Party A won 45% of the vote, Party B won 40% of the vote and Party C won 15% of the vote, then the top 45 candidates on Party A's list would be elected. Similarly, the top 40 candidates on Party B's list and the top 15 on Party C's list would be elected.

The List system is used in many countries including Sweden, Norway, Belgium, Spain and Finland. The exact details of how it works vary from country to country. Catt & Shaw (1990) explain how the List system works in Sweden:

> 'Sweden is divided into constituencies which each return a number of representatives (averaging 11). Parties put forward a slate of candidates in each area. Voters vote for one list and may alter the order in which the party has placed the candidates. Seats are allocated by the use of quota to the parties according to the strength of their support. Parties then allocate these seats to their candidates according to the preferences marked by the voters (no alteration means voters accept the order given by the party). A few extra seats (11% of the total) are used to give national proportionality if this has not been achieved by the constituency results. Before it wins any seats, a party must pass a "threshold"; it must gain 12% of the vote in a constituency or 4% of the national vote. Any mid-term vacancy is filled by the next most popular candidate on that party's list.' (Catt & Shaw 1990, pp.15-16)

Criticisms of the Closed List system

Critics of the Closed List system argue that, since the lists of candidates are drawn up by party headquarters, voters have no real choice over individual candidates. In addition, the size of constituencies means that the links between a representative and the local community are broken. MPs do not individually have a constituency and so there is no sense of local MPs being accountable to their electors.

2. The Single Transferable Vote system

The Single Transferable Vote system (STV) was created in the 19th century and is based upon the idea that votes should be given to candidates rather than parties. The country is divided into multi-member constituencies and parties may put up as many candidates in each constituency as there are seats. Voters have the opportunity of ranking all the candidates whose names appear on the ballot paper in order of preference. Alternatively, they can vote for just one or two candidates if they choose to do so.

Box 7.7 The formula used to calculate the quota

The formula most often used for calculating the quota is as follows:

$$Q = \frac{(\text{number of votes cast})}{(\text{number of seats in the constituency} + 1)} + 1$$

Seats are allocated according to a quota system (see Box 7.7 above). If any candidate reaches the quota on first preferences, then that candidate is elected. If the candidate receives more first preferences than are required by the quota, then the surplus votes are redistributed to that candidate's second preferences on a proportional basis (in other words, all the candidate's second preferences are counted and the surplus votes redistributed proportionally amongst the other candidates). This redistribution may allow other candidates to reach the quota. If that happens and a candidate (or more than one candidate) gains more votes than are needed for the quota, the second preferences of that candidate (or candidates) are redistributed in the same way. If, however, seats still remain unfilled, the candidate with the least number of votes is eliminated and that candidate's second preferences are redistributed. This process is continued until all the seats are filled. As a result, third, fourth and even fifth placed preferences may be brought into the calculation.

It is difficult in a multi-member constituency to hold by-elections and different versions of STV use different methods. Some versions hold a ballot of the whole constituency using the Alternative Vote system since only one seat is to be filled. Some versions ballot only part of the constituency. And still others do not hold a ballot at all. They elect the candidate who, according to the original ballot, would have been next to win a seat.

The STV system is currently used in the Republic of Ireland, in Australia (for the Senate) and in Northern Ireland (for European elections). It is also the system chosen for the elections to the new Northern Ireland Assembly.

Hybrid systems

1. The Additional Member System

After the Second World War, the Allies created the Additional Member system in West Germany. Of the four wartime Allies, Britain and the USA used a plurality system whilst France and the Soviet Union used proportional systems. As a result, the Additional Member system is a mixture (a hybrid) which combines a Regional List system with a single-member constituency plurality system.

The Additional Member system remains the system used in Germany and has been adopted in Hungary. Also, a version of the Additional Member system will be used to elect members of the Welsh and Scottish Assemblies.

The country is divided into single-member constituencies and into regions. The same number of representatives is elected by each. Voters have two votes - one for a constituency candidate and one for a party. In each constituency, a candidate is elected by a simple majority. The remaining seats are then allocated from regional party lists of candidates on a proportional basis. The share of seats won by a party in the constituency election is compared to the proportion of the vote won by the party overall. If there is a discrepancy, this is corrected by the allocation of seats from the regional party lists. Parties which won fewer constituency seats than was merited by their proportion of the party vote gain extra regional seats and vice versa. By this means, the overall result is proportional. To qualify for this redistribution of seats in Germany, parties need to cross a 'threshold'. They must win either at least three constituency

seats or 5% of the party vote.

2. The Alternative Vote Plus system

The Alternative Vote Plus system is very similar to the Additional Member system. The only real difference is that the single-member seats are elected by the Alternative Vote system (see above) rather than by a simple majority. There is then a top-up of additional seats on a regional or area basis to provide a total number of MPs which is proportional to the total votes cast for the different parties in the region or area as a whole. In both the Additional Member system and the Alternative Vote Plus system, a key decision is the proportion of seats which are top-up seats. If the proportion is as high as 50% (as in Germany, for example), then the overall result of the election is such that proportionality is achieved. If a lower percentage is chosen, then the degree of proportionality declines. This is illustrated in Box 7.8.

Box 7.8 The 1997 general election result (excluding Northern Ireland) under an AV Plus system

Actual result in 1997	Con	Lab	Lib Dem	Nats	Others
	165	418	46	10	1
How AV Plus changes the outcome					
75% local:25% top-up seats	179	338	106	17	1
83% local:17% top-up seats	163	371	93	13	1
90% local:10% top-up seats	143	396	90	11	1

Adapted from the *Observer*, 20 September 1998.

Advantages and disadvantages

Supporters of hybrid systems claim that they retain the best feature of plurality and majority systems, namely the fact that everyone has a local MP, and remove the worst feature, namely the fact that some parties are grossly over-represented in Parliament. Critics argue that two classes of representative are created - those who have to fight for re-election in their constituency and those whose re-election is ensured if they remain at the top of the party list. Also, since constituencies elect only a proportion of the representatives, they are very large and representatives correspondingly more remote.

Main points - Section 4.1

- There are three main types of voting system - majority systems, proportional systems and hybrid systems. Unlike proportional and hybrid systems, majority systems do not ensure that, overall, the results of elections reflect the number of votes cast for each party.
- There are three main types of majority system - the Alternative Vote system, Supplementary Vote system and Second Ballot system.
- There are two main types of proportional representation (PR) - the List system and the Single

Transferable Vote system (STV).
- The Additional Member system and Alternative Vote Plus system are hybrid systems - a mixture of a majority system (representatives are elected in single-member constituencies by a simple majority vote or by the Alternative Vote System) and a proportional system (additional members are elected from regional party lists with the number of additional members elected reflecting the overall proportion of the vote won by the party).

Activity 7.7 Different voting systems

Item A   *The Alternative Vote system*

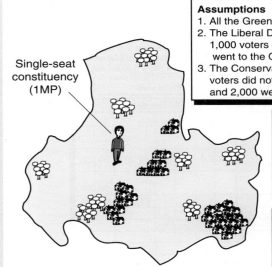

Single-seat constituency (1MP)

Assumptions
1. All the Green voters voted Liberal Democrat for their second preference.
2. The Liberal Democrat candidate's second preferences were split as follows: 1,000 voters did not have a second preference; 1,000 went to Labour; and 5,000 went to the Conservatives.
3. The Conservative candidate's second preferences were split as follows: 500 voters did not have a second preference; 5,000 went to the Liberal Democrats; and 2,000 went to Labour.

BALLOT PAPER
Election of One Member of the House of Commons

Directions. - Mark your vote on this ballot paper by placing the numbers 1,2 and 3 in the squares respectively opposite the names of the candidates so as to indicate the order of your preference for them

CANDIDATES
☐ Smith (Labour Party)
☐ Jones (Conservative Party)
☐ Adams (Liberal Democrat)
☐ Roberts (Green Party)

Candidates & parties	Votes	%
Smith (Lab)	10,000	40
Jones (Con)	7,500	30
Adams (Lib Dem)	7,000	28
Roberts (Green)	1,000	4

Note: Total votes = 25,000 To be elected using the Alternative Vote system, a candidate needs to gain 12,751 votes.

Item B   *The Single Transferable Vote system*

Notes

Stage 1. This shows first preferences. Since Evans has 36 more than quota, she is elected and 36 of her votes need to be redistributed.

Stage 2. All of Evans' second preferences are counted (see Box 7.9). Since Evans received a surplus of 36 votes out of a total of 144, each second preference vote = 144/36 = 0.25 of a vote. So, Vine receives 0.25 x 80 = 20 votes and so on.

Stage 3. No other candidate has yet reached the quota and so Pearson is excluded. He received 30 first preferences and 16 second preferences. The first preferences are redistributed at face value (if anybody chose Evans as a second preference, their third preference is counted since Evans has already reached the quota). The second preferences are redistributed at 0.25 of a vote. If voters did not choose a second preference (or only chose Pearson and Evans), the vote is non-transferable (see relevant line).

Stage 4. No other candidate has yet reached the quota and so Lennon is excluded. The same procedure is followed as Stage 3.

Stage 5. Stewart has been elected and has seven votes more than the quota. Since this surplus is less than the difference between the two candidates with fewest

Number of valid votes: 647   Number of seats: 5   Quota: $\frac{647}{5+1}$ = 108

Candidates		Stage 1	Stage 2		Stage 3		Stage 4		Stage 5	
Name	Party	First preferences	Transfer of Evan's surplus		Exclusion of Pearson		Exclusion of Lennon		Exclusion of Wilcocks	
Evans	B	**144**	- 36	**108**		**108**		**108**		**108**	Elected
Augustine	W	95		95	+ 1	96		96	+ 32	**128**	Elected
Harley	W	91	+ 1	92	+ 1	93		93	+ 15	**108**	Elected
Stewart	G	66	+ 2	68	+ 1	69	+ 46	**115**		**115**	Elected
Wilcocks	W	60		60		60		60	- 60	-	
Lennon	G	58		58		58	- 58	-			
Cohen	B	55	+ 9	64	+ 5	69	+ 2	71	+ 1	72	
Vine	B	48	+20	68	+23	91	+ 6	97	+ 7	**104**	Elected
Pearson	B	30	+ 4	34	- 34	-		-			
Non-transferable					+ 3	3	+ 4	7	+ 5	12	
Total		647		647		647		647		647	

votes, the surplus is not redistributed as it cannot affect the order. Rather, Wilcocks is excluded and the same procedure followed as Stage 3 (except that, if anybody chose Evans and Stewart as a second and third preference, their fourth preference is counted). Two further candidates are elected and two candidates now have surplus votes. Since the combined surplus (27 votes) is not enough to make any difference to the order of the bottom two candidates, Vine is elected even though she did not quite reach the quota.

Box 7.9

Evans' 2nd prefs
Vine	80
Cohen	36
Pearson	16
Stewart	8
Harley	4
Total	**144**

Adapted from ERS 1997.

Item C *The Additional Member system*

Table 1 Result of constituency election		
Party	Votes	Seats
A	184,000	5
B	116,000	3
C	55,000	1
D	50,000	0

Table 2 Final overall result			
Party	Constituency results	Additional seats	Total seats
A	5	1	6
B	3	1	4
C	1	0	1
D	0	1	1

ASSUMPTIONS

1. The region is made up of 9 single-seat constituencies and 3 additional seats. The electorate in the region, therefore, elects a total of 12 members.
2. Additional seats are allocated as follows:
a) The total number of votes for each party is divided by the number of single-seat constituencies already won, plus one. The first additional seat is allocated to the party which now has the highest number of votes (ie Party D) in Table 3).
b) The party's original total number of votes is re-divided by its new total number of seats plus one. The next additional seat is then allocated to the party with the highest total of votes (ie Party A) in Table 3).
c) The process is repeated until all additional seats are allocated (ie Party B in Table 3 also receives an additional seat).

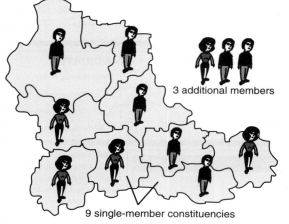

3 additional members

9 single-member constituencies

Table 3 Allocation of Additional Seats				
Party:	A	B	C	D
Directly elected seats	5	3	1	0
Number of votes	184,000	116,000	55,000	50,000
Divide by: 1				50,000
2			27,500	25,000
3				
4		29,000		
5				
6	30,667			
7	26,286			

The diagram above shows how the Additional Member system would work in an area divided into nine constituencies with three additional members. In Germany, a region with nine constituencies would elect nine additional members. It is assumed that four parties (A-D) won enough votes to cross the threshold and that each party in the region won the national average. Under the Jenkins Commission proposals, most areas would elect one additional member, but in some areas there would be two additional members.

Adapted from Watts 1994.

Questions

1. a) Using Item A explain which of the three candidates would have won under the Alternative Vote system.
   b) Explain how the election would have worked if the Supplementary Vote System had been used.
   c) What are the benefits and drawbacks of (i) the Alternative Vote system and (ii) the Supplementary Vote system?

2. Look at Item B.
   a) Explain why the five candidates with the highest number of first preferences are not the same five to be elected.
   b) What problems do you think the STV system is designed to solve?
   c) What are the benefits and drawbacks of the STV system?

3. a) Why do you think the Additional Member system (Item C) has been described as a 'hybrid' system?
   b) What are the benefits and drawbacks of the Additional Member system?

4.2 The debate over electoral reform in Britain

Recent developments

In recent years, the debate over electoral reform in Britain has risen up the political agenda, not least because, between 1979 and 1992, the Conservatives won an overall majority in four general elections in a row. Critics pointed to the fact that in none of these elections did the Conservatives receive more than 50% of the vote. In fact, the highest share of the vote they achieved was 43.9% in 1979. In other words, for four terms a majority of voters was governed by a party which they did not vote for. This trend continued in 1997 when Labour won a huge Commons majority (of 178 seats) and yet only received 43.3% of the popular vote (in the UK as a whole). Critics argue that this is the fault of the British electoral system and so the system should be changed. This section considers arguments for and against electoral reform. It begins with a critique of the current system.

Arguments in favour of the current plurality system

Strong government

Supporters of the plurality system currently used to elect MPs and local councillors argue that its great strength is the fact that it produces strong single-party governments. Since most general elections result in a single party having an overall majority, that means that the winning party is able to implement its proposed programme without interference from other parties. It is able, therefore, to fulfil the promises that it made to the electorate. As George Foulkes, a

Labour MP and opponent of electoral reform, points out:

> 'Our present voting system at least ensures that government decisions are made by the party which has the most votes - admittedly usually the largest minority. However, experience elsewhere has shown that PR often puts crucial government decisions in the hands of very small minorities, possible extremists, who hold the balance of power.' (Foulkes 1992, p.9)

It is also the case that coalition governments (which other electoral systems are likely to produce) are the result of compromise deals between parties after a general election. So, the programme of such governments has not been directly voted on by the electorate.

Links between MP and constituents

A second argument in favour of the present electoral system is that it ensures that there are strong links between an MP and the local community. Small single-member constituencies mean that local people can air their grievances directly with their MP. Foulkes argues that:

> 'It is an historic and essential part of our democracy that all constituents know that they have an MP who has a duty to pursue individual problems and constituency issues on their behalf, either individually or collectively.' (Foulkes 1992, p.8)

Watts (1994) points out that MPs have sole responsibility for the area which they represent and, once elected, they represent all those who live in the area, not just those who voted for them.

Easy to understand

A third argument in favour of the current electoral system is that it is based on a readily understood principle - everyone has a vote and the candidate with the most votes is the winner. Watts notes that:

> 'The system is easy to understand especially for the voter who marks an X on the ballot paper. It has the alleged merits of simplicity and familiarity and, as such, is widely accepted. The demand for change comes especially from those who have something to gain from it and the alternatives they propose can, in most cases, be said to be more complex and not without other problems. Primarily, they would jeopardise our system based on a parliamentary majority for one party and transfer power to the minority parties who would benefit from them. A bias in favour of the strong would be replaced by an undue influence given to the weak.' (Watts 1994, p.7)

Provides a mandate

A further argument in favour of the current system is that, by providing an outright winner (most of the

time), the current system ensures that a single party is provided with a mandate to carry out its programme. There is (usually) no need for post-election trade-offs and coalitions. The party with the most seats normally has an overall majority and is, therefore, able to carry out its programme without having to be compromised by the smaller parties. This allows strong government and maintains the principle that a party in government should be elected on the strength of its proposed programme and then judged on its actions. Coalitions with other parties would give undue influence to small parties which do not represent the opinion of a large section of the population.

It works

Finally, it can be argued that the current electoral system should be preserved simply because it works and has been proved to work over many years. All other electoral systems are flawed and so there is little point in replacing one flawed system with another.

Arguments against the current electoral system

Wasted votes

Perhaps the greatest drawback of the current electoral system is that in each constituency perhaps as many as 70% of the votes are wasted. Votes cast for the losing candidates are wasted in the sense that they are ignored in seat allocation. Votes that add to the winning candidate's majority are wasted in the sense that they give no extra benefit to the party whose candidate has won. As a result, the number of seats won by each party nationally is in no way proportional to the number of votes cast for each party. For example, in the 1997 general election, the Liberal Democrats won 16.7% of the vote nationally but they won just 7% of the seats. Indeed, under the current system it is possible for a party to win fewer votes than another party but more seats. This happened in February 1974 when Labour won 301 seats with 37.2% of the vote whilst the Conservatives won just 297 seats with 37.9% of the vote.

A minority's choice

A second drawback with the current electoral system is that the winning party rarely wins an outright majority of the total votes cast. In fact, this century there have only been two occasions when, nationally, a single party has won more than 50% of the vote in a general election - in 1900, when the Conservative and Liberal Unionists won 50.3% of the vote, and in 1931, when the Conservatives won 55% of the vote. In 1935, candidates standing for the National Government won a total of 53.3% of the vote, but the National Government was a coalition and the biggest party within the coalition (the Conservatives) won just 47.8% of the vote. The fact that the government is normally formed by a party which has only won a minority of the total vote means that more people voted against it than for it.

Regional imbalance

A third drawback is that the current electoral system has resulted in regional imbalance. For example, in the 1997 general election not a single Conservative MP was elected in Scotland or Wales despite the fact that the party attracted 17.5% and 19.6% of the vote in these regions. Britain's 'electoral geography' means that some parties gain an electoral advantage whilst others do not. This was a particular problem for the Conservatives in the 1997 election. Curtice and Steed (1997), for example, argue that the Conservatives 'have become a relatively small party whose vote is geographically relatively evenly spread from one part of the country to another'. Compared to Labour and even the Liberal Democrats whose votes are more unevenly distributed, this places the Conservatives at a disadvantage when it comes to translating votes into seats.

Over-importance of marginals

Critics of the current system also point out that general elections are decided by what happens in a small number of marginal constituencies. In other words, some votes matter more than others. Usually, around 500 seats are 'safe' seats. In these seats, the result is almost a foregone conclusion. The winning party gains many more votes than it needs to win. Votes for the other parties count for little. In marginal seats, however, every vote is important. The result in marginals determines the complexion of the government. In other words, the vote of a few hundred thousand voters in marginal seats can determine the fate of the country as a whole.

Link between MPs and constituents

Whilst supporters of the current system argue that the link between an MP and the local community is important, some critics argue that this is a weak argument. In reality, MPs cannot possibly represent all those who live in the area. According to Plant:

'The critic will point out that, within many existing constituencies, there are very significant social, political, economic, ethnic and religious cleavages which undermine the idea that constituencies are, in some sense, natural communities.' (Plant 1992, p.47)

And, besides, it is possible to look at the concept of representation rather differently. Plant suggests that supporters of PR believe that Parliament should not be made up of individuals who each claim to speak on behalf of a particular area. Rather:

'It should be seen as a microcosm of society. That is to say, the Parliament should represent all shades of opinion if they are numerically significant. The Parliament should reflect in proportion these shades of opinion. The root idea of the microcosmic view is that of the representative sample. On this understanding

of representation, a representative is a person whose characteristics and opinions reflect those of a wider group of people. When we say that a committee is representative, we mean it reflects the composition of some wider groupings which are believed to have an interest in the work or the outcomes of the committee. In this sense, we can say that a Parliament is representative when it reflects in a proportionate way, wider society.' (Plant 1992, p.47)

In other words, according to this view, a system which divides the country into small single-seat constituencies is likely to produce a Parliament which is less representative than a system which divides the country into large multi-seat constituencies.

Elective dictatorship

In addition, whilst supporters of the current system argue that it encourages strong government which does not rely on coalitions, critics point to the danger of a single party becoming entrenched in power. They also point out that the political parties themselves are, in effect, coalitions. A single party in government has to make deals with members of its own party in the same way that coalition governments have to make deals. The difference is that in a coalition these deals are made openly. Besides, PR does not necessarily lead to coalition government:

'There are plenty of other countries that have PR which have majority or one party governments. Spain elected its third majority Socialist government on PR in 1989. Sweden has had a left majority in Parliament and a one-party Labour government for 28 out of the last 34 years - with PR.' (Rooker 1992, p.8)

Accountability

Critics of PR argue that accountability is diminished if the clear line between a government and the electorate is lost through coalition politics. However, Temple (1995) argues that:

'In systems where long-term coalitions are the norm, there is evidence to suggest that voters vote in anticipation of certain partnerships. In many systems, the parties announce their preferred coalition partner in advance so that voters can vote in anticipation of proposed governments.' (Temple 1995, p.54)

In other words, a coalition government can be just as accountable to the electorate as a single-party government.

Complexity

Finally, it should be pointed out that although systems such as the Single Transferable Vote are mathematically complex, all voters have to do on the ballot paper is to indicate their order of preference. It is the Returning Officer who is responsible for working out the result. There is, therefore, no reason why voters should not be able to cope with other voting systems.

4.3 Electoral reform since 1997

The Plant Commission

Until 1997, the Conservative grip on power ensured that electoral reform remained low on the political agenda. During their years in opposition, however, the Labour Party began to consider alternatives to the plurality system currently used to elect MPs and local councillors in Britain. In 1990, the Labour Party set up the Plant Commission to investigate electoral reform and, in April 1993, the final Plant Report was published. The Plant Commission recommended:

- a version of the Additional Member system for a Scottish Parliament
- a regional List system for European elections and for elections to Labour's proposed second chamber
- the Supplementary Vote system for elections to the House of Commons.

Although none of the Plant Commission's recommendations was binding on the Labour Party, these recommendations helped to set the party's agenda in the run-up to the 1997 general election. In Labour's 1997 election manifesto, a pledge was made to create a Scottish Parliament and a Welsh Assembly both of which would be 'elected by an Additional Member system' (Labour 1997, p.33). Second, the manifesto confirmed that:

> 'We have long supported a proportional voting system for election to the European Parliament.' (Labour 1997, p.37)

And third, it was confirmed that John Smith's promise of a referendum on electoral reform for the Commons (made in 1993) would be fulfilled:

> 'We are committed to a referendum on the voting system for the House of Commons. An independent commission on voting systems will be appointed early to recommend a proportional alternative to the first-past-the-post system.' (Labour 1997, pp.32-3)

The Labour government's reforms

After a year in office, the Labour government had made some headway in fulfilling these manifesto pledges. By June 1998, five firm announcements had been made concerning new electoral arrangements and, on each occasion, the decision was made to introduce a system which had at least an element of proportionality. The government announced:

- a regional Closed List system for the 1999 European elections (see above, Section 3.5)
- a version of the Additional Member system for elections to the new Scottish and Welsh assemblies (see Box 7.10)

- STV for elections to the new Northern Ireland Assembly
- a version of the Additional Member system for elections to the London Assembly
- the Supplementary Vote system for the election of the Mayor of London.

Box 7.10 The Scottish Parliament and Welsh Assembly

The Scottish Parliament
In Scotland, there will be a unicameral (single chamber) body of 129 members. Voters will have two votes - one for their local constituency (73 members will be elected by the plurality system used in general elections) and one for the 56 additional members who will be elected using a Closed List system. In order to elect these additional members, the electorate will be divided into eight regions (with the same borders as the eight Euro-constituencies in Scotland in operation in 1994) and seven candidates will be elected from each of the eight regions on a proportional basis.

The Welsh Assembly
In Wales, there will be 40 single-member constituencies matching the 40 Westminster constituencies. The 20 additional members will be elected from closed party lists - four additional members from each of five regions. As in Scotland, the borders of each region will coincide with the borders of Euro-constituencies.

In addition, a five-strong commission, headed by Roy Jenkins, the retiring Leader of the Liberal Democrats in the Lords, was set up in December 1997 with the following brief:

> '[The commission is to] consider and recommend any appropriate system or combination of systems in recommending an alternative to the present system [and it is to] observe the requirement for broad proportionality, the need for stable government, an extension of voter choice and the maintenance of a link between honourable members and geographical constituencies.' (*Guardian*, 2 December 1997)

The Jenkins Report

The Jenkins Commission published its report in October 1998. This report recommended the Alternative Vote Plus system for general elections. Approximately 80-85% of MPs (530-60 in total) would be elected by the Alternative Vote system in single-member constituencies and around 15-20% of MPs (98-132 in total) would be elected in a top-up system from larger constituencies. There would be 80 of these top-up constituencies. Only parties which contested half of the single-member constituencies in the top-up area would be eligible to have candidates standing for top-up seats. Voters would be able to cast their votes in the top-up part of the ballot paper for either the party or for an individual candidate. In other words, the system would allow both an open list and a closed list. The idea behind this was that, normally, the candidates at the top of the party list would be expected to win, but, on occasion, a candidate who was particularly popular but low on the list might win. The recommendations of the Jenkins Commission are summarised in Box 7.11.

Box 7.11 The Jenkins Commission's recommendations

1. Constituency borders for elections to the House of Commons would be completely redrawn, reducing 659 constituencies to 530-60.

2. Every voter would have two votes. One vote would go to a constituency candidate. The other would go to a top-up MP. Electors would number constituency candidates in order of preference. The ballot paper would look something like this:

Constituency vote
This vote will help decide who is the constituency MP. Rank the candidates in order of preference (1 for your preferred candidate, then 2, 3 etc). Rank as many candidates as you wish.

Second vote
This vote will help decide the total number of seats for each party in the county. You may vote either for one party or, if you wish, for one of the listed candidates. A vote for a listed candidate will also be counted as a vote for that candidate's party.

Constituency vote		Second vote	
Collins *Conservative*		Conservative	Anderson / Coleman / Smith
Crosby *Liberal Democrat*		Labour	Baxter / Franklyn / Jones
Morgan *Labour*		Liberal Democrat	Newton / Hussain / Morison
Newman *Green Party*		Natural Law	Delaney / Shab
Quine *Natural Law Party*			

3. Any constituency candidate winning 50% or more of the vote would automatically be elected. If no candidate wins 50% of the vote, the least popular candidate would be eliminated and their second preferences redistributed. If necessary, other candidates would be eliminated until one candidate reached 50% of the vote.

4. The remaining 15-20% of MPs would be top-up MPs chosen on a city-wide or county basis depending on the overall vote of the party in the area as a whole and the number of seats a party had already won. The election of top-up MPs would ensure that parties were not under-represented to the extent that they are in the current plurality system.

Adapted from the *Guardian*, 30 October 1998.

The mechanism for electing top-up MPs

Under the Jenkins system, top-up MPs would be elected correctively - that is, on the basis of the second vote and taking into account the number of constituency seats gained by each party in each respective area. The mechanism would be as follows:

- the number of second votes cast for each party would be counted and divided by the number of constituency MPs plus one gained by each party in the area
- the party with the highest number of second votes after this calculation would be allocated a top-up MP
- any additional top-up members for an area would be allocated using the same method, but adjusting the calculation to take into account the fact that a party had already gained a top-up MP.

By-elections

In the event of a by-election being required for a top-up MP, the Jenkins Commission recommended that the vacancy be filled by the candidate next on the list of the party holding the seat.

Reaction to the Jenkins Report

The Liberal Democrats are fervent supporters of proportional representation on both pragmatic grounds (the party would gain considerably more seats under a proportional system) and on ideological grounds. On the whole, the Liberal Democrats were positive about the Jenkins Report because it went some way to meeting their concerns that there should be a higher degree of proportionality in the voting system. Similarly, those whose main concern was that the link between an MP and a constituency should be maintained were relieved that this link would remain if the Jenkins recommendations were implemented.

The Prime Minister, Tony Blair, 'warmly welcomed' the report and urged the Cabinet to help him manage the debate it was bound to bring (*Guardian*, 31 October 1998). At the time the report was published, it was common knowledge that the Cabinet was divided on the issue of electoral reform - as was the Labour Party in general. It appeared that the government's strategy was to allow a period of discussion and, through this process, to educate the electorate about the proposed changes. As noted above, the Labour Party made a pledge to hold a referendum on electoral reform.

Opposition to reform

Critics of the recommendations of the Jenkins Commission argued that the system was too complicated to operate and that it would produce two classes of MP - one superior to the other. William Hague, the Leader of the Conservative Party, said that the Conservatives would fight 'every inch of the way' to resist electoral reform for elections to the Commons. He argued that a proportional system would undermine the fundamental principle of democratic accountability and asserted that:

> 'PR is a system of unfair votes. It takes political power away from the electorate and gives it to smaller political parties.' (*Guardian*, 25 February 1998)

Some commentators have argued that one of the Jenkins Commission's underlying objectives was to find a way of marginalising the Conservatives permanently (Dunleavy & Weir 1997). This suggests that the Conservatives had pragmatic as well as ideological grounds for opposing the recommendations of the Jenkins Commission.

Main points - Sections 4.2-4.3

- Supporters of the plurality system currently used to elect MPs and councillors use the following arguments in its support: (1) it produces strong, single-party governments; (2) it ensures that there are strong links between an MP and the local community; (3) the system is easy to understand; (4) by producing an outright winner, it provides the government with a mandate; and (5) the system works.

- Opponents of the plurality system currently used to elect MPs and councillors use the following arguments against it: (1) many votes are wasted; (2) the winner is almost always the choice of a minority; (3) there are regional imbalances; (4) constituencies become over-important; (5) it ensures that Parliament is not representative of society as a whole; (6) there is a danger that a single party will become entrenched in power; (7) single-party governments are no more accountable than coalition governments; and (8) other systems are not necessarily more difficult to use.

- After a year in power, the Labour government had made five firm announcements concerning new electoral arrangements: (1) a Closed List system for European elections; (2) a version of the Additional Member system for the new Scottish and Welsh assemblies; (3) STV for the new Northern Ireland Assembly; (4) a version of the Additional Member system for the London Assembly; and (5) the Supplementary Vote system for the election of Mayor of London.

Activity 7.8 *Electoral reform*

Item A *The 1997 general election (1)*

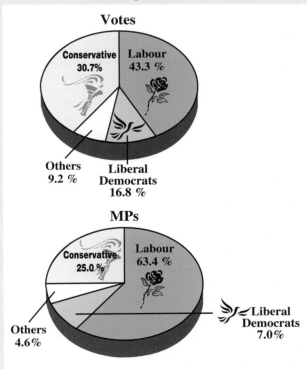

These pie charts show the percentages of votes and the percentage of seats won by parties in the 1997 general election.

Figures from Curtice 1997.

Item B *The 1997 general election (2)*

First, only one MP is elected in each constituency, so all the voters who did not vote for that candidate are not represented. Their votes do not help elect anybody and so are wasted. The voters could have stayed at home and the result would have not been altered. In the 1997 general election in Conwy, for example, the Labour MP, Betty Williams, was elected on only 35% of the vote, leaving all the people who voted Liberal Democrat, Conservative, Plaid Cymru and for the other parties unrepresented. In 1997, in Great Britain, 14.7 million voters cast ineffective votes - that is 47% of those who voted. A high proportion are the same people every time - for example, Conservative voters in County Durham or Labour voters in Sussex. Second, voters are represented unequally. In 1997, the average number of votes per MP elected was 32,318 for Labour, but 113,987 for the Liberal Democrats. If a party's support is concentrated, that gives it an advantage. In 1997, for example, Conservative support was spread thinly over most of Scotland - Conservatives won 18% of the votes in Scotland but no seats. The Liberal Democrats, on the other hand, won a smaller percentage of the Scottish vote (13%), but ten seats because they had strong support in a few constituencies and minimal support in others. Third, in 1997, Labour won 43.3% of the total vote, but 63.4% of the seats in Parliament. Although 11 out of 20 British electors voted against the government, it has complete power.

Adapted from a leaflet produced by the Electoral Reform Society in 1997.

Item C *The 1997 general election (3)*

	EXISTING PLURALITY SYSTEM	PURE PROPORTIONALITY (LIST)	ALTERNATIVE VOTE	SINGLE TRANSFERABLE VOTE	ADDITIONAL MEMBER SYSTEM	SUPPLEMENTARY VOTE
Conservative	165	202	110	114	203	110
Labour	418	285	436	342	303	436
Liberal Democrats	46	110	84	131	115	84
SNP/Plaid Cymru	10	46	10	24	20	10
Others	20*	18	19	18	18	19
RESULTS	LABOUR MAJORITY 178	LABOUR 89 SEATS SHORT	LABOUR MAJORITY 213	LABOUR MAJORITY 25	LABOUR 27 SEATS SHORT	LABOUR MAJORITY 213

* This figure includes the Speaker (a Labour MP before being elected Speaker). In the 1997 general election, she was elected unopposed by Conservative and Liberal Democrat candidates and does not count when calculating Labour's overall majority.

This study was based on a survey of 8,000 electors interviewed by the polling organisation ICM immediately after the general election in May 1997. Each respondent was asked not only how they voted in the general election but also to fill in mock ballot papers for the different voting systems. The votes were then analysed by an academic team (the so-called 'Democratic Audit'). The impact was estimated region by region for the potential make-up of the House of Commons under each of the different systems.

Adapted from Democratic Audit 1997.

Item D *The case against PR*

It is frequently assumed that, if proportional representation (PR) is achieved, this will solve most other political problems. Indeed, the usual argument in favour of a House of Commons elected according to PR principles is that the composition of the country's main legislative chamber should reflect the composition of views within the electorate, as expressed in party choice. What that case almost always fails to appreciate, however, is that proportional representation within the House will not necessarily be reflected in proportional bargaining power there. A party may get 10% of the votes cast and so be allocated 10% of the seats in the House, but does it get 10% of the political power ('power' being defined here as the ability to influence a government's legislative programme)? PR does not produce proportional power. For example, in assemblies where permanent coalitions are required, parties often bargain over the formation of a government after the election. In that bargaining process, some parties are more powerful than others because they are pivotal in more potential coalitions. Further, the distribution of bargaining power depends not just on each party's allocation of seats but also on the number of other parties and the distribution of seats among them. A small change, even in a three-party or a four-party assembly, can produce a major shift in bargaining power. A few by-election results, for example, could lead to some parties becoming much less powerful, while others find that their power increases (perhaps even without their own number of seats changing).

Adapted from Johnston 1995.

Questions

1. a) Using Items A-D, give the arguments for and against reform of the voting system used in elections to the House of Commons.
   b) Why do you think the Leader of the Conservative Party is opposed to proposals to use PR in elections to the Commons?

2. a) Write an analysis of the evidence which appears in Items A-C.
   b) Which electoral system in Item C would have produced the fairest result? Explain your answer.

3. a) Judging from Item D, what problems might PR cause if it was used for elections to the Commons?
   b) What other arguments against PR could the author of Item D have used?

4. Do you think a referendum should be held on the subject of electoral reform in Britain? Give reasons for your answer.

References

Austin (1997) Austin, T. (ed.), *The Times Guide to the House of Commons*, Times Books, 1997.

Batchelor (1992) Batchelor, A., 'Referendums and initiatives', *Politics Review*, Vol.1.3, February 1992.

Batchelor (1994) Batchelor, A., 'Lessons from the Maastricht debates: the referendum we never had', *Talking Politics*, Vol. 6.3, Summer 1994.

Beetham (1993) Beetham, D., *Auditing Democracy in Britain*, The Charter 88 Trust, 1993.

Butler & Kavanagh (1997) Butler, D. & Kavanagh, D., *The British General Election of 1997*, Macmillan, 1997.

Catt & Shaw (1990) Catt, H. & Shaw, A., 'The intelligent person's guide to electoral reform', *New Statesman and Society/Common Voice*, April 1990.

Cole (1997) Cole, M., 'Politics and youth', *Politics Review*, Vol 6.3, January 1997.

Coote & Campbell (1982) Coote, A. & Campbell, B., *Sweet Freedom: The Struggle for Women's Liberation*, Blackwell, 1982.

Cowley & Dowding (1994) Cowley, P. & Dowding, K., 'Electoral systems and parliamentary representation', *Politics Review*, Vol.4.1, September 1994.

Craig (1989) Craig, F.W.S., *British Electoral Facts 1832–1987*, Gower Publishing Company, 1989.

Curtice (1997) Curtice, J., 'Anatomy of a non-landslide', *Politics Review*, Vol. 7.1, September 1997.

Curtice & Steed (1997) Curtice, J. & Steed, M., 'The Results Analysed' in *Butler & Kavanagh (1997)*, Appendix 2.

Deacon & Lynch (1996) Deacon, R. & Lynch, P., 'New Labour and devolution for Scotland and Wales', *Politics Review*, Vol. 6.2, November 1996.

Dearlove & Saunders (1984) Dearlove, J. & Saunders, P., *Introduction to British Politics*, Polity Press, 1984.

Democratic Audit (1997) Democratic Audit, *Making Votes Count*, Scarman Trust, 1997.

Denver (1997) Denver, D., 'The General Election in Scotland', *Politics Review*, Vol.7.2, November 1997.

Denver (1997) Denver, D., 'The 1997 general election results: lessons for teachers', *Talking Politics*, Vol. 10.3, Autumn 1997.

Dobson (1998) Dobson, A., 'The 1997 general election: explaining a landslide' in *Lancaster (1998)*.

DoE (1998) Department of the Environment, *Modernising Local Government: Local Democracy and Community Leadership*, Consultation Paper, 1998 (www.local.doe.gov.uk/sponsor/democrac.htm)

Dunleavy et al. (1997) Dunleavy, P., Gamble, A., Holliday, I. & Peele, G., *Developments in British Politics 5*, Macmillan, 1997.

Dunleavy & Weir (1997) Dunleavy, P. & Weir, S., 'The true aim of electoral reform', *New Statesman*, 5 December 1997.

Evans (1997) Evans, M., 'Political participation' in *Dunleavy et al. (1997)*.

Fisher (1997) Fisher, J., 'Third and minor party breakthrough' in *Geddes & Tonge (1997)*.

Foulkes (1992) Foulkes, G., 'Face to face', *Politics Review*, Vol.1.4, April 1992.

Geddes & Tonge (1997) Geddes, A. & Tonge, T. (eds), *Labour's Landslide*, Manchester University Press, 1997.

ERS (1997) Electoral Reform Society, *What is STV?*, leaflet produced in 1997.

Hailsham (1978) Hailsham, Lord, *The Dilemma of Democracy*, Collins, 1978.

Hancock (1996) Hancock, J., 'Democracy', *Politics Review*, Vol 5.4, September 1996.

Held (1987) Held, D., *Models of Democracy*, Polity Press, 1987.

Heywood (1991) Heywood, A., 'Liberal democracy', *Talking Politics*, Vol.3.2, Winter 1990-91.

HMSO (1991) HMSO, 'Parliamentary Elections' in the *Aspects of Britain* series, HMSO, 1991.

Johnston (1995) Johnston, R., 'Proportional representation and proportional power', *Politics Review*, April 1995.

Kavanagh (1995) Kavanagh, D., *Election Campaigning. The New Marketing of Politics*, Blackwell, 1995.

King (1998) King, A. (ed.), *New Labour Triumphs: Britain at the Polls*, Chatham House, 1998.

Labour (1993) Plant, R., *Report of the Working Party on Electoral Systems*, 1993, Labour Party, 1993.

Labour (1997) *New Labour – Because Britain Deserves Better*, Labour Party manifesto, Labour Party, 1997.

Lancaster (1995) Lancaster, S. (ed.), *Developments in Politics*, Vol.6, Causeway Press, 1995.

Lancaster (1998) Lancaster, S. (ed.), *Developments in Politics*, Vol. 9, Causeway Press, 1998.

Lynch (1998) Lynch, P., 'Devolution and a new British political system', *Talking Politics*, Vol.10.2, Winter 1997-8.

Norris (1997) Norris, P., 'Political Communications' in *Dunleavy et al. (1997)*.

Norris (1998) Norris, P., 'The battle for the campaign agenda' in *King (1998)*.

Norton (1991) Norton, P., 'Parliamentary democracy', *Modern History Review*, Vol.2.3, 1991.

Paine (1791) Paine, T., *The Rights of Man*, Everyman's Library, Dent Dutton, 1979.

Parry & Moyser (1993) Parry, G. & Moyser, G., 'Political participation in Britain', *Politics Review*, Vol.3.2, November 1993.

Parry et al. (1991) Parry, G., Moyser, G. & Day, N., *Political Participation in Britain*, Cambridge University Press, 1991

Plant (1992) Plant R., 'Electoral reform and electoral systems' in *Wale (1992)*.

Robins (1998) Robins, L., *Politics Pal 1997*, Hyperion Press, 1998.

Robertson (1986) Robertson, D., *The Penguin Dictionary of Politics*, Penguin, 1986.

Rooker (1992) Rooker, J., 'Face to face', *Politics Review*, Vol.1.4, April 1992.

Scammell (1995) Scammell, M., *Designer Politics. How Elections are Won*, Macmillan, 1995.

Taylor (1965) Taylor, A.J.P., *English History 1914–45*, Penguin, 1965.

Temple (1995) Temple, M.,'Electoral reform: the consequences of change' in *Lancaster (1995)*.

Urwin (1987) Urwin, D., 'Electing representatives: proportional systems', *Social Studies Review*, Vol.2.5, May 1987.

Wale (1992) Wale, W. (ed.), *Developments in Politics*, Vol.3, Causeway Press, 1992.

Watts (1994) Watts, D., *Electoral Reform: Achieving A Sense Of Proportion*, PAVIC Publications Sheffield Hallam University, 1994.

Watts (1997) Watts, D., 'The growing attractions of direct democracy', *Talking Politics*, Vol.10.1, Autumn 1997.

Weir (1994) Weir, S., 'Crisis of confidence' in *Bite the Ballot*, a supplement in *New Statesman and Society*, 29 April 1994.

Williams (1981) Williams, R., *Parliamentary Democracy*, Spokesman Press, 1981.

Wilkinson & Mulgan (1995) Wilkinson, H. & Mulgan, G., *Freedom's Children*, Demos, 1995.

8 Political parties

Introduction

Which political party do you belong to? The chances are that the answer to this question is, 'none'. Party membership (of all three main parties) over the last 30 years has been in decline. But, that does not mean that political parties are any less important than they were 30 years ago. The British political system has developed in such a way that political parties are at its heart.

A political party is a group of like-minded people who agree to abide by a set of rules and set out to win political power in order to achieve their common goals. Normally, this means that the party puts up candidates for election. But, some parties choose to attempt to win power in other ways. That political parties aim to win power and to govern (rather than just to influence the government) is important. It is one of the factors which distinguishes them from pressure groups. Another factor is that, unlike most pressure groups which concentrate on a single issue, political parties formulate and try to implement a broad range of policies.

Most people, no matter how little interest they have in politics, could name the current leaders of the main parties because they see them regularly on the television, hear them on the radio and read about them in the newspapers. Fewer people could identify the main policies of these parties. Fewer still would feel able to discuss the parties' history, ideology or internal structure. This chapter looks at the evolution of the British party system since the 19th century and examines the history and internal structure of the three main political parties. It also examines the role of minor parties and considers whether Britain has a two-party system.

Chapter summary

Part 1 looks at the early history of British political parties and their role and functions within the British political system. It asks why political parties are necessary.

Part 2 focuses on the Labour Party. The history and organisation of the party are examined. Sections then discuss the selection of the Leader and the Leader's role.

Part 3 focuses on the Conservative Party. It follows the same pattern as Part 2.

Part 4 focuses on the Liberal Democrats and follows the same pattern as Parts 2 and 3.

Part 5 provides a survey of the minor parties.

Part 6 considers the arguments for and against the view that Britain has a two-party system.

Part 1 The development of political parties in Britain

Key issues

1. Why did political parties first develop?
2. What are the functions of political parties?
3. How are political parties financed?

1.1 Why did political parties first develop?

Historical background

Before the 19th century, political parties did exist but they were very different from modern political parties. The first political parties - the Whigs and the Tories - existed only within Parliament. These parties were rather loose groups of MPs who were drawn together by family ties or who shared similar views. It was not until the mid-19th century that mass political parties with organisations and members outside Parliament began to develop.

The key to the growth of mass political parties was the extension of the franchise (see Chapter 7, Section 1.4). Before there was a mass electorate, participation in politics was confined to a small and wealthy élite. As a result, political parties were unnecessary outside Parliament. There were so few voters that candidates could canvass their vote individually - they did not need a party machine behind them.

Impact of the Great Reform Act

The Great Reform Act of 1832 was the catalyst for change. Although the electorate remained tiny after

1832, one of the requirements of the Act was that voters must be registered. The political parties quickly realised that it was essential to get their supporters registered. To ensure that the registration process was carried out efficiently, the parties saw the need for some central control over the activities of groups of local supporters. The Tories, therefore, established the Carlton Club as their headquarters in 1832 and the Whigs established the Reform Club as their headquarters in 1836. Once this central organisation had been established, political parties began to take on new roles. The Great Reform Act, therefore, led the parties to establish the links between politicians and voters via a central organisation which are typical of the modern party.

The impact of further electoral reform

Further electoral reform between 1867 and 1918 led to a truly mass electorate and to the establishment of more rigorously democratic electoral procedures. For a party to win the support of a mass electorate, it is necessary for the party to have a reasonably clear set of policies and ideas which can be presented to the electorate. It is also necessary for a party which hopes to govern the country to have representatives and supporters in every constituency. So, the growth of the mass electorate led directly to the growth of the mass party. To survive, parties had to adapt to the new conditions. Not only did they have to ensure that party supporters actually went to the polls and voted on election day, they had to ensure that the government (when they formed it) was able to remain in office and implement its programme. This required discipline and tight organisation both in Parliament and in the constituencies.

By the early 20th century the fundamental features of modern political parties were in place. By then, the two main parties - the Liberal Party (which evolved from the Whigs) and the Conservative Party (which evolved from the Tories) - fulfilled the same key functions which are exhibited by political parties today.

1.2 The functions of political parties

Classifying the functions of parties

As Ball (1987) and Garner & Kelly (1998) point out, political parties exist because they perform functions which are essential for the working of the political system. It is possible to classify these functions in a number of ways, but the key functions of political parties in Britain can be described under the following headings.

1. The governing function

The British government is formed by the political party with an overall majority in the House of Commons or (more rarely) by the largest single party or (very rarely) by a coalition of parties. The Prime Minister is the Leader of the governing party and the Cabinet is drawn from its senior members (or, in a

coalition government, from the senior members of the governing parties). In this sense, therefore, political parties are central to the process of government.

2. The electoral function

The electoral process is dependent upon political parties. Parties choose candidates at local and national elections. They provide funds and facilities for election campaigns. They devise policies which the electorate is asked to support. They provide a label with which voters can identify. They provide a means of accountability since the electorate is able to hold them responsible for policy successes or failures.

3. The representative function

Political parties enable the views of people to be heard and they ensure that matters of public concern reach the political agenda. Some parties allow the views of key sectional interests to be represented. For example, the Labour Party has traditionally represented the views of trade unions and members of the working class. In addition, parties attempt to represent interests which go beyond these sectional concerns. For example, the Conservative Party in the 1980s tried to win the support of working-class voters by promoting the sale of council houses.

4. The policy function

In performing their representative function, political parties are led to formulate policies which relate to the sectional and more broadly based interests which they support. By formulating policies, they ensure that the electorate has a choice between different approaches at election time. This brings clarity to the political process. Parties are supposed to implement these policies if they form the government and they are held responsible by the electorate at the next election for their successes or failures.

5. The recruitment and participation function

Political parties play a key role in encouraging people to become political activists. Most political activists are members of political parties. Once people have joined a political party, the party provides a continuing means of political participation.

6. The communicative and ideological function

Political parties provide their leaders with the means to communicate with their members and vice versa. Parties are also essential in allowing the debate to take place between competing principles. For example, the early 1980s were dominated by the debate between the ruling Conservatives, whose main economic goal was low inflation, and the opposition parties, whose main concern was the high level of unemployment that this entailed.

Common criticisms of parties

Political parties are often criticised for a number of reasons. First, parties are accused of imposing a uniformity of views upon their members. Since party members are encouraged to 'toe the party line', important debate can be stifled. Second, it is argued that the existence of parties perpetuates social divisions. Since the essence of the party system is that the different parties compete against each other, it is necessary for them to emphasise their differences and, sometimes, to maintain them artificially. And third, it is claimed that parties prevent new ideas from emerging. Since the British political system is dominated by the three main parties, it is very hard for new ideas to break through into the mainstream.

Main points - Sections 1.1-1.2

- Before the 19th century, political parties did exist but they were very different from modern political parties. The key to the growth of mass political parties was the extension of the franchise.
- The Great Reform Act of 1832 was the catalyst for change. But, it was the development of a mass electorate between 1867 and 1918 that brought the need for mass parties.
- The functions of political parties can be divided as follows: (1) the governing function; (2) the electoral function; (3) the representative function; (4) the policy function; (5) the recruitment and participation function; and (6) the communicative and ideological function.
- Political parties are often criticised because: (1) they impose a uniformity of views; (2) they perpetuate social divisions; and (3) they prevent new ideas from emerging.

Activity 8.1 *Political parties in the late 1990s*

Item A *The role of political parties (1)*

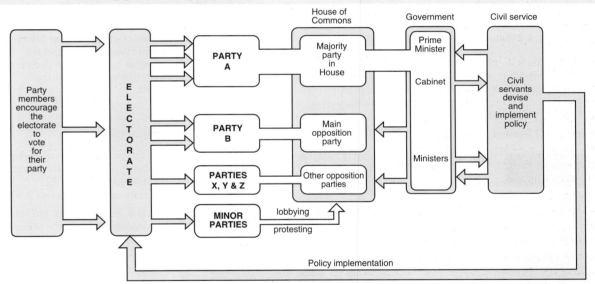

This diagram shows the role of political parties in the British political system.

Item B *New parties for a new age*

Ben Lucas, a former aide to the Home Secretary, Jack Straw, argues that the Labour Party should be like a voluntary organisation. People should pay what they want to pay to join, he argues, and the party should be more genuinely open. Between 1994 and 1997, the Labour Party increased the number of individual members by 40%. Despite this revival, however, the era of the mass party as the main vehicle for organising politics really is drawing to a close. On the one hand, a modern-day, professional, media-driven party needs to maintain discipline, unity, a coherent voice and a populist platform. On the other hand, a vibrant local political culture requires flexibility and autonomy (freedom from central control), or at least serious decentralisation. The conflict between these two needs is producing great strain. While it is impossible to see what, other than political parties, might take on the business of running democratic national government in the next century, it is becoming clear that other forms of political participation (formal and informal, structured and disorganised, funded and DIY, respectable and barely legal) are the best hope for regenerating the civic spirit upon which democracy will be sustained.

Adapted from the *New Statesman*, 25 July 1997.

Item C   *The decline in party membership*

According to Michael Pinto-Duschinsky, the main casualty of the 1997 general election campaign was the system of party politics and campaigning. Even the slight increase in Labour's individual membership, he argues, could not disguise the continuing, sharp decline in political participation in the country as a whole. The 1997 general election was the first in which the Labour Party's individual membership (406,000) exceeded that of the Conservatives. In 1979, by way of contrast, Conservative membership was five times that of Labour. In 1997, the Liberal Democrats had around 100,000 members. So, together, the three main parties had less than a million members in 1997 - two for every 100 electors - the lowest since the war. Moreover, Pinto-Duschinsky points out, the Labour Party and Liberal Democrats have introduced national computerised systems of recruitment which ensure that, in effect, an increasing number of members have little contact with their local party. This helps to explain the increasingly centralised structure of the Labour Party. The main change in terms of party funding has not been the amount of money raised but its sources. Money from rich individuals has become ever more important. Unlike in the past, these donors are not driven solely by a desire for titles. They also wish to use contributions to affect party policies - for example, Rowntree's donations were part of its campaign for constitutional reform and the animal lobby's donations to Labour were made in the hope of a government stance against hunting. The decline in party membership and activity bodes ill for politics. It will be difficult to rid politics of disillusion and of the perception of sleaze unless the decline of local party organisation and activity is checked.

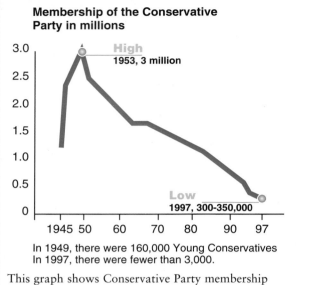

Membership of the Conservative Party in millions

High 1953, 3 million

Low 1997, 300-350,000

1945 50   60   70   80   90   97

In 1949, there were 160,000 Young Conservatives
In 1997, there were fewer than 3,000.

This graph shows Conservative Party membership during the period 1945-97.

Adapted from the *Times*, 23 April 1997.

Item D   *The role of political parties (2)*

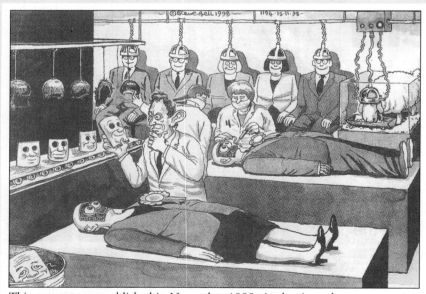

This cartoon was published in November 1998. At the time, there was a great deal of public criticism of the Labour leadership's attempts to maintain control of the party from the centre.

Questions

1. 'Political parties are at the heart of the British political system.' Explain this statement using Items A-D.

2. Use Item A to explain how parties 'provide the means for peaceful resolutions of political tensions'.

3. a) 'The role of political parties has changed'. Explain this statement using Items B-D.
   b) How might political parties deal with some of the difficulties faced in recent years?

4. What does Item D tell us about the role of political parties? How valid is the point being made?

1.3 The financing of political parties

Background

The question of how political parties are funded has become a matter of public concern since the Cash for Questions scandal in 1994 (see Chapter 14, Section 2.5) and the Formula One scandal in 1997 (shortly after Formula One motor racing was exempted from a ban on tobacco advertising in 1997, it was revealed that Formula One boss Bernie

Ecclestone had donated £1 million to the Labour Party).

The problem of how British political parties should be funded arose because political parties themselves developed in a haphazard fashion. As the franchise was broadened and parliamentary groupings found it necessary to develop into mass parties, a corresponding need to finance these parties developed. To pay for their staff and campaigns, parties turned to two principal sources. The first source was a subscription paid by all individual members. The second source was donations from wealthy individuals or institutions. In the case of the Conservative Party, donations came from landowners, businesspeople and corporations anxious for a Conservative government which would protect and further their interests. In the case of the Labour Party, donations came principally from affiliated trade unions who hoped that a Labour government would further their interests. The system of party funding which emerged was unregulated by law, inefficient in that it did not provide adequate funding for the minor parties and, potentially, subject to abuse.

The debate over state funding
Lemieux (1995) suggests that the questions relating to the funding of political parties can be summarised under two headings: the ethical issues and the political issues. The ethical issues relate in particular to the large donations made by wealthy individuals and institutions. There is a serious concern about the extent to which donations are used to buy honours or influence government policies. In the case of the donation made by Bernie Ecclestone, for example, it was alleged that his gift to the Labour Party was an important factor in deciding to exempt Formula One from the ban on tobacco advertising. There is also concern about the spiralling cost of election campaigns. The more money that is spent on campaigns, the more that needs to be raised. Some people argue that it is unethical for parties to 'buy' their way into power.

Arguments for and against of state funding
Supporters of the state funding of political parties argue that it would:
- provide a solution to the ethical concerns outlined above
- provide more equal funding for the main parties
- ensure the smaller parties receive some financial support.

Opponents of the state funding of political parties argue that it would be difficult to decide how much parties should receive and which parties should receive funding (should taxpayers' money go to the fascist British National Party, for example?). In addition, opponents argue that party activity and funding should be a voluntary activity in which individuals participate by choice.

Reports and recommendations
Consideration of the arguments outlined above led the 1975 Houghton Report and the 1981 Hansard Commission to recommend some state funding of political parties. A subsequent Home Affairs Select Committee report in 1993-94, however, concluded that the existing system was broadly satisfactory. As more was revealed by the media about large donations to the Conservative Party by wealthy individuals of questionable reputation, however, pressure grew on John Major's government to investigate the matter of party funding fully and thoroughly. The result was the Neill Report of 1998.

The Neill Report
The Neill Report emerged from the Cash for Questions scandal of 1994. Following the exposure of this scandal, John Major established a Committee on Standards in Public Life. He refused, however, to include party funding within the committee's remit. The 1997 Labour manifesto promised that the committee's remit would be extended to include party funding and, on gaining office, Labour fulfilled this promise. Since the committee's chair was Lord Neill, the resulting report was known as the Neill Report. This was published in October 1998.

The report treads a path between full state funding of political parties and a voluntary system. It recommended that a large number of regulations should be put in place, but did allow voluntary activity to continue so long as it did not break these regulations. The main recommendations of the report are outlined in Box 8.1.

Box 8.1 The Neill Report recommendations
1. Foreign donations should be banned.
2. Blind trusts should be abolished.
3. All national donations of £5,000 or more and local donations of £1,000 or more should be made public.
4. Anonymous donations of £50 or more should be banned.
5. There should be a £20 million cap on party campaign budgets at general elections.
6. There should be tax relief for parties on donations up to £500.
7. There should be the tripling of state funding to help opposition parties in Parliament and a new £2 million fund for policy research.
8. Shareholders should approve company donations and sponsorship.
9. There should be new rules for referendums including equal state funding for Yes and No campaigns.

The government's response
The government's response was to welcome the report and to promise legislation within the lifetime of the current Parliament. Ceilings on the amount allowed to be spent on the forthcoming elections to the Scottish Parliament (£1.5 million) and Welsh Assembly (£600,000) were set in place in 1998.

Adapted from the *Guardian* and *Times*, 14 October 1998.

Main points - Section 1.3

- There has been particular public concern over the funding of political parties since the Cash for Questions scandal.
- Supporters of the state funding of political parties argue that it would: (1) provide a solution to ethical concerns; (2) provide more equal funding for the main parties; and (3) ensure the smaller parties receive some financial support.
- Opponents of state funding argue that it would be

difficult to decide how much parties should receive and which parties should receive funding. Opponents also argue that party activity and funding should be a voluntary activity.
- The Neill Report recommended that a large number of regulations should be put in place, but did allow voluntary activity to continue so long as it did not break these regulations.

Activity 8.2 Party funding

Item A *Election spending in 1997*

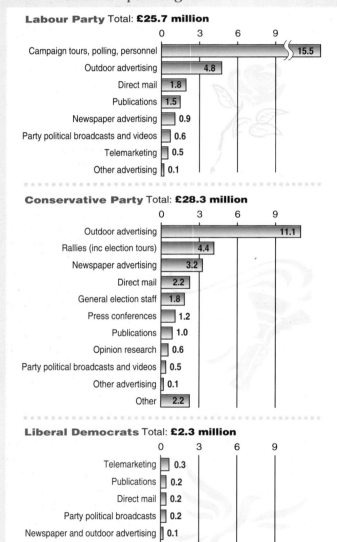

Labour Party Total: **£25.7 million**

Campaign tours, polling, personnel	15.5
Outdoor advertising	4.8
Direct mail	1.8
Publications	1.5
Newspaper advertising	0.9
Party political broadcasts and videos	0.6
Telemarketing	0.5
Other advertising	0.1

Conservative Party Total: **£28.3 million**

Outdoor advertising	11.1
Rallies (inc election tours)	4.4
Newspaper advertising	3.2
Direct mail	2.2
General election staff	1.8
Press conferences	1.2
Publications	1.0
Opinion research	0.6
Party political broadcasts and videos	0.5
Other advertising	0.1
Other	2.2

Liberal Democrats Total: **£2.3 million**

Telemarketing	0.3
Publications	0.2
Direct mail	0.2
Party political broadcasts	0.2
Newspaper and outdoor advertising	0.1
Other	1.3

Adapted from the *Guardian*, 14 October 1998.

Item B *Party funding*

Money talks. The noise of cash can be heard everywhere - except in politics. In their world, so politicians claim, money miraculously loses its voice. Margaret Thatcher and John Major denied (despite so much evidence to the contrary) that large donations to the Conservative Party could secure a knighthood or a peerage or a more serious favour. Tony Blair was horrified that anyone should connect the £1 million the Labour Party received from Bernie Ecclestone with the government's U-turn on banning the tobacco sponsorship of motor racing. It is certainly true and mildly encouraging that money does not always buy political love. Mohamed al Fayed invested thousands in the Conservative Party, yet he is still waiting for his British passport. James Goldsmith is supposed to have spent £20 million on the Referendum Party at the last election and yet it didn't buy him a single seat in Parliament. The trade unions are the lousiest investors in political influence. They have donated over £100 million to the Labour Party since 1979. For 18 years, they received no return on their money. Now that, finally, a Labour government has been elected, it does no more for the unions than it would have done anyway, and probably less. The fact that the Labour Party has received money from the unions increases Blair's fears of being seen to be influenced by them. This makes the unions model donors. They are British (unlike the foreign tycoons, jailbirds, tax dodgers and other fraudsters who financed the Conservatives in the late 1980s and early 1990s). Everyone knows where union money comes from and what they hope to gain from it. And, their cash has brought them nothing in terms of special access and privileged treatment. In a perfect world, every political donor would gain as little as the unions. It is because the world is not perfect that the Neill Inquiry is necessary.

Adapted from the *Observer*, 19 April 1998.

Item C *The Neill Report (1)*

The Neill Report amounts to a dose of sharp detergent, scrubbing away at a stain in our public life. Neill's demand for full disclosure of donations above £5,000 will draw back the veil on our political process in an instant. Suddenly, we will know before the government decides to exempt Formula One from the ban on tobacco sponsorship that Bernie Ecclestone had given £1 million to the Labour Party. We could then draw our own conclusions. And, perhaps, the government might even act differently as a result. Transparency could change everything. Once full lists matching donors to their gifts are printed in the papers, the trade in cash-for-politics will lose much of its sting. If voters know Candidate X is receiving money from Cigarette Brand Y, they will soon realise why Candidate X has started campaigning for free nicotine starter-kits for toddlers. The spending cap of £20 million is a great help too. Labour always feared being outgunned by the fund-raising powers of the Tories. The result was an 'arms race' for cash between them. The pressure to raise ever bigger amounts of cash should now ease. There are some misgivings. Some people wanted Neill to wipe out the entire problem by banning all donations and replacing them with state funding. Others fear that the Neill rules will just be too easy to break. Donors might divide their gifts up into small chunks of £4,999 and parties might be able to wriggle around the spending cap by encouraging donors to spend the money for them in a 'personal' capacity.

Adapted from the *Guardian*, 14 October 1998.

Item D *The Neill Report (2)*

This cartoon was published on 14 October 1998, the day after the Neill Report was published.

Questions

1. Using Items A-C, explain why there was a need to change the rules on the funding of political parties.
2. Judging from Items C and D, would you agree that the Neill Report adequately addressed the problem of party funding? Give reasons for your answer.
3. Give arguments for and against the view that the private funding of parties should be replaced by state funding.

Part 2 The Labour Party

Key issues

1. How did the modern Labour Party evolve?
2. What is the structure and organisation of the Labour Party?
3. How powerful is the Leader of the Labour Party?

2.1 The roots of the Labour Party

19th century origins

Electoral reform in the 19th century gave more and more working-class men the vote (see Chapter 7, Section 1.4). At first, this made little difference to the party system. The Conservative and Liberal parties both claimed that they could represent the new voters. It was not until the beginning of the 20th century that a new political party was set up specifically to represent the interests of the newly enfranchised working class in Parliament. This party - the Labour Party - owed its existence to the support of the trade union movement. Links between the Labour Party and the trade unions have remained ever since.

Socialist groups in the 19th century

Although socialist groups existed in the 19th century, they had little electoral success (see Chapter 2, Section 4.2 for an explanation of the term 'socialism'). Not only did they face competition from the established parties, they faced a number of other difficulties. First, even by the end of the 19th century less than 70% of adult men and no women had the vote. Most working-class people were, therefore, still disenfranchised in 1900. Second, the traditional way of protesting against the system was to use extra-parliamentary techniques such as demonstrations and marches. There seemed no place for working-class people within the parliamentary system and socialists felt more comfortable campaigning outside the system. Third, working-class people did not have the resources to become MPs. In 1900, MPs were unpaid and so candidates needed another source of income if they were to be able to carry out their duties as an MP. And fourth, opponents of socialism were very successful in promoting the idea that socialism would lead to bloody revolution and should, therefore, be opposed.

Trade unions in the 19th century

Although socialist groups did not gain much success by 1900, the same is not true of the trade union movement. In 1850, the trade union movement was of little consequence. But, by 1900, several million workers had joined unions, the TUC (Trades Union

Congress - the national body for all trade unions) had been established, unions had won some legal rights and a number of union leaders had become MPs. The first union leaders to be elected as MPs were elected in 1874. Alexander Macdonald and Thomas Burt were miners sponsored by their union and recruited to stand for their local Liberal Party (a few local Liberal parties decided to put up working-class candidates after the extension of the franchise in 1867 because they realised that working-class people would make up the majority of voters in their constituency). By 1884, there were nine 'Lib-Lab' MPs, as these working-class Liberals became known. The Liberal Prime Minister, Gladstone, promoted one of these Lib-Lab MPs, Henry Broadhurst, to the Cabinet in 1886. Gladstone was convinced that Lib-Lab MPs should be concerned with trade union matters alone. They should not put forward the working-class view on other issues.

Keir Hardie and the ILP
At the TUC conference held in 1887, Broadhurst came under attack from Keir Hardie. Hardie argued that working-class people should not join a political party which supported the employers against the workers. He urged workers to set up their own independent political party. Although Hardie failed to convince delegates at the conference in 1887, he continued to argue his case and brought up the question at every TUC conference in the 1890s. In 1892, Keir Hardie was invited to stand as an independent candidate in West Ham and he won the election. Hardie shocked his fellow MPs by refusing to conform to their dress code. Whilst the other MPs wore top hats and morning dress, Hardie wore a deerstalker and a checked suit. This symbolised the difference in class and ideology between Hardie and the other MPs.

In Parliament, Hardie attacked the Liberal and Conservative parties for their lack of concern for working-class people. Outside Parliament, he helped to set up the Independent Labour Party (ILP). At a conference in Bradford in January 1893, a group of socialists agreed to stand as ILP candidates in the forthcoming election. In the 1895 election, 28 ILP candidates stood but all, including Hardie, were defeated. Despite this setback, support for a working-class party which would work within the existing political system began to grow. In 1898, the ILP won a majority on West Ham's borough council.

The Labour Representation Committee (LRC)
At the TUC conference in 1899, the Amalgamated Society of Railway Servants (ASRS) put forward a proposal that a conference be organised between the ILP, the Fabians (see Chapter 10, Section 1.6), the SDF (a Marxist group) and the unions. The aim of the conference was to devise ways of securing the return of a group of working (ie 'labour') MPs in the next Parliament. The ASRS could not persuade the railway

companies to recognise it as an official union and it blamed this on the number of MPs who had shares in the railways. As a result, it saw the advantage of having a distinct group of working-class MPs in Parliament. The ASRS managed to persuade a majority of delegates at the TUC conference to support its proposal.

The birth of the Labour Party
The conference was held in London in February 1900 and it was attended by seven unions (representing a membership of 353,070), a member of the ILP, a member of the Fabian Society and a member of the SDF. None of the major unions attended. At the conference, the Labour Representation Committee (LRC) was set up. The purpose of the LRC, on a motion proposed by Keir Hardie, was to create a distinct Labour group in Parliament which would be subject to its own whips. The LRC was, therefore, to be a new political party. Six months after the LRC was set up, a general election was called. The LRC managed to put up 15 candidates. Two - Keir Hardie and Richard Bell (Secretary of the ASRS) - were elected. Although this was a modest start, it had immense consequences. Six years later, the LRC was renamed the Labour Party. The first person to act as Secretary to the LRC was Ramsay Macdonald. In 1924, he became the first Labour Prime Minister.

The Taff Vale case
In August 1900, workers on the Taff Vale railway in South Wales went on strike. The railway company sued the union, claiming damage for loss of profits. In July 1901, the House of Lords ruled in favour of the company and the union was forced to pay £23,000 in damages. This meant that any union could now be sued if it organised a strike - a disaster for unions since they would no longer be able to use their main weapon. All unions, therefore, realised that their funds would be in danger unless a new law was passed to protect them. But, the Conservative government refused to intervene and unions could not be sure what priority would be given to this issue by the Liberals. As a result, the idea of an independent party representing working-class interests began to gain wider support from the unions. By 1904, the number of union members affiliated to the LRC had more than doubled to 956,025 and the unions had agreed to charge a levy of one penny on every member to raise the funds necessary to pay Labour MPs' salaries. So, the Taff Vale case not only provided the LRC with a clear issue to campaign on (the right to strike), it also brought an increased membership and greater funds.

The Lib-Lab pact, 1903
In 1903, Ramsay Macdonald, Secretary of the LRC, made a secret pact with the Liberal Chief Whip, Herbert Gladstone. The deal was as follows. After the

forthcoming general election, LRC MPs would support the Liberals in Parliament if the Liberals agreed not to put up candidates in a number of constituencies during the election itself.

When the 1906 general election was called, no Liberal candidates were put up in 30 constituencies. This allowed LRC candidates in these constituencies to have a clear run against the Conservatives. Of the 50 LRC candidates who stood in the 1906 general election, 29 were successful. Most of these owed their success to the secret Lib-Lab pact.

Winning 29 seats was a major achievement. The LRC MPs elected Keir Hardie as their Leader and decided to take a new name - the Labour Party. The gains made in 1906 provided the platform for the new Labour Party to develop into a major party.

The Labour Party 1906-24
Between 1906 and 1916, Labour did not appear to be a great threat to the Liberal Party. The Liberals won a large overall majority in the election of 1906, so the new Labour MPs could make little impact. Between 1906 and 1916, the Labour Party failed to win any new seats. The number of Labour MPs rose to 40 in 1910 because the Miners' Federation joined the Labour Party and its Lib-Lab MPs were instructed to take the Labour whip. It was not until the Liberal Party split in 1916 that Labour's fortunes began to improve. Between 1916 and 1924, four factors combined to change Labour from a small, opposition party into a major party of government. First, the Liberal split in 1916 and its continuation after the war undoubtedly boosted Labour's support. Second, Labour MPs served in Lloyd George's wartime coalition government, providing Labour members with experience of government and bolstering the party's credibility. Third, the Representation of the People's Act of 1918 enfranchised a huge number of people. Many of the newly enfranchised came from the working classes. And fourth, in 1918, the Labour Party adopted a new constitution and its structure and organisation were shaken up. This provided it with a political platform and the organisation necessary for it to become a mass party.

The Labour Party in power
It is a measure of the Labour Party's initial success that in 1924, just 21 years after its first two MPs were elected, the Labour Party was able to form a government, albeit a minority government which relied on Liberal support to survive. The first Labour government lasted just ten months and is, perhaps, most notable for the way in which Labour ministers tried desperately to convince the public that, whatever their opponents might claim, the Labour Party was a party of moderation and respectability. Since the government relied on Liberal support, there was no chance of implementing a socialist programme even if ministers had wanted to do so.

The same points can be made about the second Labour government of 1929-31. This was also a minority government and it contained many of the same faces - for example, Ramsay Macdonald was Prime Minister and Philip Snowden Chancellor in both administrations. But, the second government ended with the Labour Party in disarray. In August 1931, Ramsay Macdonald, convinced that there was a major economic crisis, dissolved the Labour government and agreed to form a 'national' government (a coalition government containing members of all three main parties). Macdonald failed to consult with his colleagues before agreeing to this course of action and it is unlikely he would have gained their agreement if he had done so. The result was a split in the party. Macdonald and seven other MPs joined the National Government whilst the Labour Party went into opposition (in the subsequent election the number of Labour MPs was reduced from 287 to 52). Macdonald and his colleagues were expelled from the party.

The Labour Party since 1931
The Labour Party remained in opposition until it won its first overall majority in 1945. This was the first time that a Labour government had been able to set its own agenda. Despite the economic difficulties facing Britain after the war, the Labour government under Attlee embarked on an ambitious programme of nationalisation and set in place the main elements of the welfare state (see Chapter 3, Section 1.1).

In the 34 years between 1945 and 1979, the Labour Party held power for 17 years - the same number of years as the Conservatives. Between 1979 and 1997, however, the party remained in opposition. Despite doubts (especially in the late 1980s) that Labour could ever win an overall majority again, the party proved doubters wrong by winning its largest ever overall majority in 1997.

2.2 Reform in the Labour Party 1979-97

The need for reform
Since 1979, there has been extensive reform of the structure and organisation of the Labour Party. In part, this is a reflection of the party's failure to win a general election between 1979 and 1997. In part, it is a reflection of an ideological struggle between different factions within the party. Since 1979, there have been three distinct phases.

Phase 1. The Bennite challenge 1979-83
Following Labour's 1979 general election defeat, a group of Labour Party activists led by Tony Benn attempted to change the balance of power within the party. According to Kelly, these reformers argued that:

'By ignoring the wishes of Labour's activists, its parliamentary leaders had lost touch with the wishes of its natural working-class electorate, which paved the way for Mrs Thatcher's victory in 1979. Benn thus contested that organisational reform had become necessary, not just to satisfy abstract theories of party democracy, but to ensure that future Labour governments would not "betray" the socialist ideas developed in opposition.' (Kelly 1994, p.40)

According to Kelly, therefore, the internal party reforms supported by Tony Benn and his colleagues after 1979 were designed not just to ensure that the Labour Party became electable once again, they were also designed to ensure that a distinct ideological standpoint was reflected in the way in which the party worked.

Rule changes, 1980

The pressure for reform exerted by Benn and his supporters produced two main changes. First, as a result of a rule change made at the 1980 party conference, it became mandatory (compulsory) for Labour MPs to be reselected by their constituency Labour parties (CLPs) before each general election (see Chapter 11, Section 2.1). And second, the right to elect Labour's Leader and Deputy Leader was no longer the responsibility of the Parliamentary Labour Party (PLP) alone. From 1981, the Leader and Deputy Leader were to be elected by an electoral college (an electoral college is a mathematical device for measuring votes). This electoral college was made up of the PLP (which had 30% of the vote), CLPs (which had 30% of the vote) and trade unions (which had 40% of the vote). For the first time, it became possible to challenge the Leader and Deputy Leader whether they were in government or in opposition. Prior to this, it had not been possible to challenge the Leader and Deputy Leader whilst they were in government.

The aim of these reforms was to give greater power to Labour activists in the CLPs who (it was assumed) were more radical than the party's leadership and, therefore, more likely to support socialist measures. There is little doubt that these reforms encouraged the damaging split which resulted in the departure of 30 Labour MPs to the SDP (see Section 4.1 below). The culmination of this phase was the adoption of a radical manifesto for the 1983 general election.

Phase 2. Modernisation, 1983-94

Labour's poor showing in the 1983 general election resulted in a backlash against the ideas and strategy of Benn and his colleagues. After 1983, the party leadership began to reassert its authority and it introduced organisational reforms which both broadened and centralised the decision-making process within the party.

The leadership reasserts its authority

One way in which the Labour Party leadership tried to reassert its authority was by purging the party of members of the Militant Tendency in the mid-1980s.

The Militant Tendency was a Trotskyist group whose members joined the Labour Party in the hope of moving Labour policies to the left. Neil Kinnock's public battle against the Militant Tendency suggested that the party was changing direction and moving away from the hard left.

OMOV

Whilst Tony Benn and his colleagues aimed to extend the power of CLPs because that was where party activists were to be found, after 1983 the Labour leadership aimed to extend power beyond the CLPs to ordinary members. The introduction of 'one member, one vote' (OMOV) became an important part of the party's modernisation programme. OMOV extended democracy within the party by encouraging the participation not just of activists but of every ordinary member.

The Labour Party and the unions

The debate over OMOV also, most importantly, raised the question of the Labour Party's relationship with the trade unions. Traditionally, the Labour Party had been very close to the unions. The unions provided the party with most of its funds and most of its members and, in return, the unions had been given an important part in decision making within the party. During the 1980s and early 1990s, however, many union leaders joined the Labour leadership's demand for greater democratisation of the party. Since the introduction of OMOV for leadership elections and the selection of parliamentary candidates in 1993, the power of the unions within the Labour Party has declined. Significantly, due to the adoption of new fund-raising techniques, by 1997 only 46% of Labour's income came from union sources, a 20% fall from 1987.

Phase 3. Blair and New Labour since 1994

The third phase of reform began in 1994 with Tony Blair's election as Labour Leader. Blair and his colleagues began to argue that the modernisation process had not gone far enough for the party to win over enough voters to gain a majority in the forthcoming general election. In particular, he aimed to win over those people living in 'Middle England' (people in social group 'C1' - those with junior managerial or administrative posts - who mainly live in the Midlands and South East England). As a result, Blair and his colleagues set about distancing the current Labour Party (New Labour) from the Labour Party of the past (Old Labour). It was at the first annual party conference after his election as Leader that Blair first used the term 'New Labour' and it was at this conference that he first suggested that a key symbol of the past - Clause IV of the party constitution - should be abandoned (see also Chapter 2, Section 4.4). After a substantial consultation process with Labour members, a new Clause IV was unveiled by the NEC in April 1995. A special conference was held on 29 April at which 90% of constituency members and 55% of affiliated trade unions approved the change. The symbolic change brought about by abandoning the old Clause IV was then followed by changes in the structure of the party (see Section 2.3 below) and by a repositioning of the party (see Chapter 3, Section 4.1).

2.3 The structure and organisation of the Labour Party

Labour Party branches
Ordinary members of the Labour Party belong to a local branch (there is a national membership list, so members join via party headquarters and are then assigned to a particular local branch depending on their address). Members are invited to attend branch meetings and can stand for election to the branch's executive committee at the branch's annual general meeting. Individual branches are responsible for looking after their own members and finance and branches choose candidates for local elections. Branch rules are laid down in the Labour Party constitution (Labour 1999).

The Constituency Labour Party (CLP)
Each branch is able to elect a number of delegates to the local CLP's general committee (GC) and to the CLP's executive committee (EC). The number of delegates is determined by the number of paid-up members in the branch. In addition, a number of delegates are appointed to the CLP's GC by trade unions which are affiliated to the Labour Party. Ordinary branch members and union members can attend meetings of the CLP's GC, but only delegates are allowed to vote. Delegates to the CLP can stand for election to the CLP's general management committee. Rules governing the CLP are laid down in the Labour Party constitution (Labour 1999).

Until 1987, one of the key functions of the CLP was to select parliamentary candidates. But, since 1993, every ordinary member has been able to vote in the selection process (see Chapter 11, Section 2.1). Local and national election campaigns are organised at constituency level. Delegates are elected by the CLP to attend regional and annual conferences.

The National Executive Committee (NEC)
According to Clause VIII of the Labour Party constitution:

> 'There shall be a National Executive Committee of the Labour Party (the NEC) which shall, subject to the control and directions of party conference, be the administrative authority of the party.' (Labour 1999, p.8)

In 1998-99, the NEC contained 32 members. The rules stipulate that there will be 33 members once the Labour Party Black Socialist Society fulfils certain criteria - see Box 8.2.

Box 8.2 Members of the NEC

- 24 members elected by party conference
- the Leader and Deputy Leader of the party
- the Leader of the European Parliamentary Labour Party
- the Party Treasurer
- three frontbench MPs
- one youth member elected at the national Young Labour Conference
- one member elected by the Labour Party Black Socialist Society at its conference (this member to be elected once the society has 2,500 members and at least one-third of eligible trade unions have affiliated).

Adapted from Labour 1999.

Duties and powers of the NEC
The duties and powers of the NEC are laid down in the constitution and are extensive. Its general responsibility is to ensure that the party machinery runs smoothly at all levels (at constituency, district, county and regional level) and to oversee the work of the party between conferences. In practice, this involves five principle areas of activity. First, it has a policy-making role. It participates in the consideration of reports produced by the policy commissions of the National Policy Forum and in their publication prior to submission to conference. Second, the NEC is the guardian of the constitution and is responsible for ensuring that its rules and procedures are obeyed. Third, the NEC has power to discipline members if rules are breached and can expel members, subject to conference. Fourth, the NEC is responsible for party finances and running the party headquarters. Fifth, the NEC plays an important part in the selection of parliamentary candidates, especially at by-elections (see Chapter 11, Section 2.1).

Labour Party headquarters
Until 1997, the Labour Party's national office was in Walworth Road, London. Since 1997, the national party bureaucracy has been based in Millbank Tower in London. The head of the national party bureaucracy is the party's General Secretary, who is elected by the annual party conference on the recommendation of the NEC. There is no time limit on the General Secretary's tenure of office.

Greater professionalism
Following the disappointing general election result in 1983, Neil Kinnock and his NEC allies brought changes to the organisation of the party's national bureaucracy at Walworth Road. A new General Secretary, Larry Whitty, was appointed and a new post, Director of Communications, set up. By gaining the assistance of pollsters, marketing specialists and media experts, the General Secretary and Director of Communications were able (with the support of Neil

Kinnock) to rejuvenate Labour's national bureaucracy and give the party a new image. Most commentators agreed that Labour's election campaigns in 1987 and 1992 were highly slick and professional, though some party members were critical of what they described as 'designer socialism'.

Larry Whitty's successor as General Secretary, Tom Sawyer, accelerated the process of change. Offices were first rented at Millbank Tower in 1995 to house the party's communication and polling operation. By the time of the 1997 general election, this operation had grown into a complex and effective machine. Following the 1997 general election victory, the rest of the party's national bureaucracy moved over to Millbank Tower.

The annual party conference

Labour's annual party conference has a number of functions. First, formally speaking, the conference is an important decision-making body. Clause VI of the Labour Party constitution describes the power of the party conference as follows:

> 'The work of the party shall be under the direction and control of the annual party conference which shall itself be subject to the constitution and standing orders of the party. Party conference shall meet regularly once every year and also at such other times as it may be convened by the NEC.' (Labour 1999, p.7)

In real terms, however, the power of the conference has declined (see below). Second, the conference provides the opportunity for ordinary members to air their views in public. And third, the conference provides a platform for leading members of the party. Cabinet (or shadow Cabinet) ministers use the conference to make set-piece speeches designed to appeal both to party members and the wider public (since they are televised). The reception of these speeches can make (or, occasionally break) the public standing of a minister.

The voting system

Before 1993, voting was dominated by trade unions which had one conference vote for every registered affiliated member of the Labour Party (an affiliated member is a union member who pays the political levy as part of their union subscription). Each union cast all its votes in a single block (hence the phrase 'block vote'). How the union cast this vote was normally determined by the union's leaders. So, provided that Labour leaders had the support of union leaders, they were able to secure a conference majority without difficulty. In fact, they could quite easily ignore the concerns of constituency delegates at the conference since their votes were relatively so few. In 1993, however, an electoral college was introduced. This divided conference into a union section with 70% of the vote and a constituency

section with 30% of the vote. Moreover, for every 30,000 new individual members, the constituency section would gain an extra 1% of the vote (whilst the union section would lose 1%). In 1995, the proportion of votes in the union section was reduced to 50%, significantly reducing union influence over the party.

The National Policy Forum

The National Policy Forum was set up in 1990 to streamline the party's policy-making process and to produce a rolling programme of policy making. The Forum appoints various policy commissions. Each commission deals with a specific policy area, producing reports for the NEC and, ultimately, conference to approve. Each commission has around 20 members and is headed by a frontbench MP.

Policy making

Labour's annual party conference has the power to make policy. This power is laid out in Clause V of the constitution:

> 'The party conference shall decide from time to time what specific proposals of legislative, financial or administrative reform shall be included in the party programme. This shall be based on the rolling programme presented to conference by the National Policy Forum as approved by conference. No proposal shall be included in the party programme unless it has been adopted by conference by a majority of not less than two-thirds of the votes recorded on a card vote.' (Labour 1999, p.7)

Although conference has the formal power to decide policy, this power has been somewhat diluted since the setting up of the National Policy Forum and the introduction of revised procedures in 1997 (Kelly 1998, p.5). In the past, affiliated organisations were able to submit policy resolutions to conference, sometimes resulting in votes that went against the wishes of the leadership. In 1992, for example, conference supported unilateral nuclear disarmament against the wishes of the leadership. The rule changes agreed in 1997, however, mean that affiliated organisations cannot submit policy resolutions on a subject to annual conference before a commission has reported on that subject. In addition, the role of conference is limited to either approving or rejecting the recommendations of each commission. Kelly argues that these rule changes were:

> 'A clear sign that [conference] was being changed from a serious deliberative assembly into a celebration of new policies initiated by the Leader and his closest advisers.' (Kelly 1998, p.5)

It should be noted that the rule changes were opposed by 102 CLPs at the 1997 annual conference. But, despite this, they were eventually endorsed.

- It was not until 1900 that a new political party was set up to represent the interests of the newly enfranchised working class in Parliament. This party - the Labour Party - owed its existence to the support of the trade union movement. Links between the Labour Party and the trade unions have remained ever since.
- It is a measure of the Labour Party's initial success that in 1924, just 21 years after its first two MPs were elected, the Labour Party was able to form a government. It won its first overall majority in 1945 and its largest overall majority in 1997.
- Between 1979 and 1997, reform of the structure and organisation of the Labour Party went through three main phases: (1) the Bennite challenge 1979-83; (2) modernisation 1984-94; and (3) changes under Blair since 1994.
- The NEC is the administrative authority of the Labour Party. Its duties and powers are extensive. Its general responsibility is to ensure that the party machinery runs smoothly at all levels and to oversee the work of the party between conferences.
- The role of annual conference has changed. Although, formally, it is the party's decision-making body, in practice it has lost the power to initiate policy.

Activity 8.3 *The Labour Party*

Item A *Labour's electoral record*

(i) Labour Prime Ministers and general election victories since 1900

1920

J. Ramsay MacDonald
PM 1924, 1929-31

Minority government
1923

Minority government
1929

1940

Clement Attlee
PM 1945-51

1945
(Labour majority of 146)

1950
(Labour majority of 5)

1960

Harold Wilson
PM 1964-70, 1974-76

1964
(Labour majority of 4)

1966
(Labour majority of 96)

Feb 1974
Minority government

Oct 1974
(Labour majority of 3)

1970

James Callaghan
PM 1976 -79

1990

Tony Blair
PM 1997-

May 1997
(Labour majority of 178)

2000

Key

General election after which the Labour Party was invited to form the government

(ii) The development of the Labour Party

Date	MPs elected	Total votes polled
1900	2	63,304
1906	29	323,195
1910 (Jan)	40	505,657
1910 (Dec)	42	371,772
1918	57	2,244,945
1922	142	4,241,383
1923	191	4,438,508
1924	151	5,489,077
1929	288	8,389,512
1931	46	6,362,561
1935	154	8,325,491
1945	393	11,995,152
1950	315	13,266,592
1951	295	13,948,605
1955	277	12,404,970
1959	258	12,215,538
1964	317	12,205,606
1966	364	13,064,951
1970	288	12,179,341
1974 (Feb)	301	11,639,243
1974 (Oct)	319	11,457,079
1979	269	11,532,148
1983	209	8,457,124
1987	229	10,029,270
1992	271	11,559,735
1997	418	13,516,632

Adapted from Pelling 1991 and Curtice 1997.

Item B   *The structure and organisation of the Labour Party*

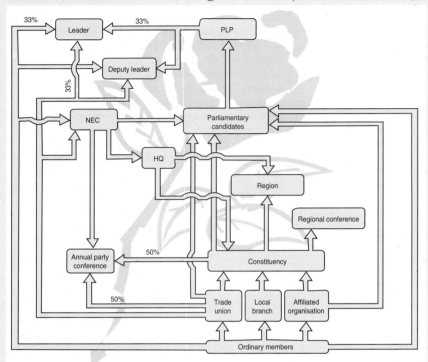

Item C   *Labour and the unions*

At the heart of New Labour has been an appeal to the middle classes. This brought into question Labour's historic links with the trade unions. Unlike previous Labour Leaders, Tony Blair had a weak emotional attachment to union-party links. As a result, there has been an attempt to weaken those links and even some talk of breaking them altogether. At the 1995 conference, the leadership engineered a 20% reduction in the union share of votes. At the same time, there was a campaign to encourage donations from wealthy individuals. By 1997, only 46% of Labour's income came from the unions. By the end of 1997, there was talk from some union leaders about voluntarily giving up their right to vote. This suggestion drew little complaint from the Labour leadership. But, the leadership should be cautious. Apart from giving the party insider advice from the workplace, the unions have always donated to Labour when others were reluctant to do so. Labour must hope that wealthy backers do not become fair weather friends. Also, Blair, like his predecessors, has had to rely on the union block vote during tricky debates at conference. Had it not been for their support in 1996, for example, he could have faced embarrassment over both child benefit and minimum wage policy. Parties made up of individual members only are far harder for Leaders to control.

Adapted from Kelly 1998.

Questions

1. 'The natural party of government'. Is this a fair description of the Labour Party? Use Item A in your answer.

2. a) What do Items B-D tell us about the structure and organisation of the Labour Party?
   b) How has the structure and organisation changed since 1980?

3. Using Items B and D, explain how policy is made in the Labour Party.

4. Give arguments for and against the view that Labour should cut its ties with the unions. Use Item C in your answer.

Item D   *Policy making in the Labour Party*

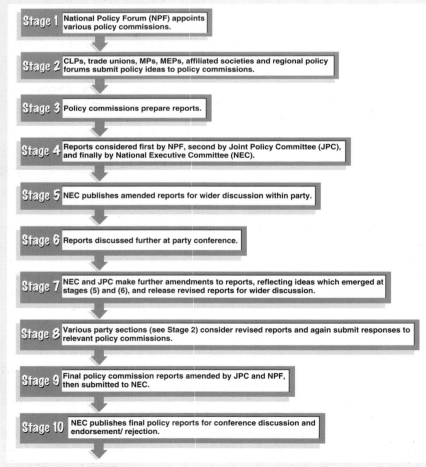

Stage 1 National Policy Forum (NPF) appoints various policy commissions.

Stage 2 CLPs, trade unions, MPs, MEPs, affiliated societies and regional policy forums submit policy ideas to policy commissions.

Stage 3 Policy commissions prepare reports.

Stage 4 Reports considered first by NPF, second by Joint Policy Committee (JPC), and finally by National Executive Committee (NEC).

Stage 5 NEC publishes amended reports for wider discussion within party.

Stage 6 Reports discussed further at party conference.

Stage 7 NEC and JPC make further amendments to reports, reflecting ideas which emerged at stages (5) and (6), and release revised reports for wider discussion.

Stage 8 Various party sections (see Stage 2) consider revised reports and again submit responses to relevant policy commissions.

Stage 9 Final policy commission reports amended by JPC and NPF, then submitted to NEC.

Stage 10 NEC publishes final policy reports for conference discussion and endorsement/ rejection.

Adapted from Kelly 1998.

2.4 The selection and role of the Labour Leader

The Leader and the Parliamentary Labour Party (PLP)

Until 1922, the Labour Party's main spokesperson was known as 'Chairman of the Party'. It was only after 1922 that the term 'Leader of the Labour Party' came into common usage.

All MPs who take the Labour whip belong to the Parliamentary Labour Party (PLP). Until 1980, the PLP alone chose the Leader in a series of ballots. The last Labour Leader to be elected in this way was Michael Foot in 1980. He defeated Denis Healey in the second ballot.

The PLP is still responsible for choosing the composition of the shadow Cabinet when the party is in opposition. Each MP has 18 votes and, since 1989, must cast at least three votes for women candidates. Those elected form a pool from which the Party Leader, Deputy Leader, Chief Whip and Chair of the Party select the shadow Cabinet. Since 1980, the Labour Leader has been obliged, following a general election victory, to form the first Cabinet from those who had served in the existing shadow Cabinet. But, the Leader is unrestricted in any future reshuffles.

Selecting the Leader and Deputy Leader

Nomination

Candidates for the posts of Leader and Deputy Leader of the Labour Party must be MPs. Between 1981 and 1988, candidates had to secure the support of 5% of the PLP before they could be nominated. Following Tony Benn's abortive challenge to Neil Kinnock in 1988, however, the rules were changed.

Since 1989, candidates have had to secure the support of 12.5% of the PLP if there is a vacancy or 20% of the PLP if there is no vacancy to the positions whilst Labour is in opposition. If Labour is in government then, whether there is a vacancy or not, challengers have to secure the support of 20% of the PLP and they also have to gain the backing of two-thirds of those who can vote at annual conference. Before 1981, challenges to the leadership whilst the Labour Party was in government were not allowed.

Electoral college

Since 1981, the Labour Leader and Deputy Leader have been chosen by an electoral college. Between 1981 and 1993, this electoral college was split as follows: the trade unions had 40% of the vote; the CLPs had 30% of the vote; and the PLP (including MEPs) had 30% of the vote. Since 1993, this electoral college has been divided equally between trade unions, CLPs and the PLP (including MEPs). Also since 1993, one member, one vote (OMOV) has been introduced. So, every paid-up member of the Labour Party is able to vote in the constituency section and every trade union member who pays the political levy and whose trade union is affiliated to the Labour Party is able to vote in the trade union section (the block vote, therefore, no longer has a place in the selection of Labour leaders).

Electoral procedure

To win, a candidate for the leadership or deputy leadership has to gain more than 50% of the vote. If no candidate wins more than 50% of the vote outright, the candidate with the least number of votes is excluded and their second preference votes redistributed (the alternative vote system - see Chapter 7, Section 4.1).

Under the rules laid down in the constitution, the election for Leader and Deputy Leader should take place at the time of the annual party conference unless for some reason the Leader or Deputy Leader becomes 'unavailable' (ie becomes ill, resigns or dies). If that happens, then the NEC can arrange for a ballot before the next annual conference is held. This happened when John Smith died in May 1994. The results of the leadership election were announced in July 1994, more than two months before the annual party conference was held.

Role of the Labour Leader

The role of the Labour Leader is not easy to determine. In theory, the Leader is subordinate to the annual party conference and to the NEC. In practice, however, this is not the case. First, the Leader is the party's main spokesperson and the public nature of the position confers them with considerable influence. Second, although, in theory, the wishes of the Leader are subordinate to the wishes of the annual party conference, in practice, on most occasions Leaders are able to manufacture the decisions they want at conference. The rule changes of 1997 (see above Section 2.3) strengthened the position of the Leader and made it easier to manufacture decisions at conference. Third, it has been regular practice for Labour Leaders to ignore or to manipulate the NEC. And fourth, although conference policy is meant to be included in the party election manifesto, Leaders are usually able (if they so desire) to dilute or to alter it in such a way that its original intentions are lost.

So, the Leader has the potential to exercise a great deal of power. Determined Leaders with clear intentions are able to wield as much power as their Conservative counterparts and can do so with a greater degree of security (between 1961 and 1994 the only time that a sitting Leader was challenged was in 1988). Tony Blair is a good example of a determined Leader. The changes he made to party organisation and policy during the period 1994-97 (see Sections 2.2 -2.3 above and Chapter 3, Section 4.1) suggest just how powerful the Party Leader can be.

2.5 The location of power in the Labour Party

McKenzie's thesis, 1955

In his classic analysis of the organisation of the Labour Party, McKenzie (1955) argued that real power in the Labour Party rested with the Labour leadership. There was, he argued, a fundamental gap between the party's constitutional theory, which suggested that real power lay with extra-parliamentary bodies such as the annual conference, and party political practice which resulted in the party leadership taking all the key decisions. McKenzie suggested that this was a consequence of the fact that the party leadership always has to perform the role of government or government-in-waiting. The government is accountable to Parliament, not to bodies outside Parliament. Equally, the government is expected to represent the wishes of the people as a whole and not just the wishes of a narrow section. In other words, members of the government have a wider responsibility than to the annual party conference and, to demonstrate that they are capable of government (ie to win general elections), the Labour leadership has to be prepared to ignore or act against the wishes of the majority of ordinary party members.

The location of power 1955-94

The fact that Labour Leaders continued to ignore or to act against the wishes of the majority of ordinary members in the years after McKenzie wrote his book in 1955 suggests that power remained with the Labour leadership. Indeed, there is good evidence that the moves towards centralisation undertaken by Neil Kinnock after 1983 strengthened the power of the leadership. Nevertheless, the power of the Leader was by no means absolute. It was restricted in two ways. First, starting in the late 1980s, there were attempts to democratise the party (see Section 2.2 above). And second, leaders were genuinely restricted by the annual party conference. Neil Kinnock could not have abandoned the policy of unilateralism without the support of conference, for example. It may be true that Labour Leaders usually won in the end, but they were always aware that failure to carry the majority of conference with them would lead to a public fight and unsightly shows of disunity.

The location of power under Tony Blair

The relationship between Leader and the wider party was given a further twist after Blair became Leader. By 1998, a debate was taking place about whether Blair's reforms had strengthened or weakened democracy in the party. Blair and his supporters argued that the new policy-making process (see Section 2.3 above) provided a more focused and, therefore, effective role for members, allowing them to influence policy during the consultation process and at party conference. Moreover, the decision to hold internal referendums on the revision of Clause IV and on the acceptance of the key principles on which Labour was to fight the 1997 general election can be interpreted as the leadership giving a greater say to ordinary individual members. Opponents place an altogether different interpretation on events. They claim that the changes to policy making place greater power in the hands of the Leader and the NEC. It is the Leader and NEC, they claim, who shape the policy that is debated at conference. In addition, they say, the two internal party referendums were presented as 'back me or sack me' issues and gave no real choice to ordinary members.

> ### Main points - Sections 2.4-2.5
>
> - Until 1980, the PLP alone chose the Leader in a series of ballots. Since 1981, the Labour Leader and Deputy Leader have been chosen by an electoral college. Between 1981 and 1993, trade unions had 40% of the vote; the CLPs 30% of the vote; and the PLP 30% of the vote. Since 1993, each of the three sections has one-third of the vote.
> - Candidates for the posts of Leader and Deputy Leader of the Labour Party must be MPs and must have the support of 12.5% or 20% of the PLP, depending on circumstances.
> - In theory, the Leader is subordinate to the annual party conference and to the NEC. In practice, however, this is not the case.
> - Traditionally, real power in the Labour Party rested with the leadership. There is a debate about whether Tony Blair's reforms have handed some power back to ordinary members.

Activity 8.4 *Power and the Labour leadership*

Item A *Labour leadership and deputy leadership contests 1976-94*

(i) Leadership election, 1976

Candidate	Ballot 1	Ballot 2	Result
Callaghan	84	141	176
Foot	90	133	137
Healey	30	38	
Jenkins	56		
Benn	37		
Crosland	17		
100% votes cast by PLP			

(ii) Leadership election, 1983

Candidate	PLP	Constituency	Trade unions	Total
Kinnock	14.8	27.5	29.0	71.3
Hattersley	7.8	0.6	10.9	19.3
Heffer	4.3	2.0	0.1	6.3
Shore	3.1	0.0	0.1	3.1

PLP section = 30%; constituency section = 30%; trade union section = 40%

(iii) Leadership election, 1994

Leader	MPs/MEPs	Ordinary members	Trade unions	Total
Blair	60.5	58.2	52.3	57.0
Prescott	19.6	24.4	28.4	24.1
Beckett	19.9	17.4	19.3	18.9

Deputy leader	MPs/MEPs	Ordinary members	Trade unions	Total
Prescott	53.7	59.4	56.6	56.5
Beckett	46.3	40.6	43.4	43.5

MPs' & MEPs' section = 33.3 %; ordinary members' section = 33.3%; trade union section = 33.3%

Item B *Power in the Labour Party*

It is difficult to manage any political party, but no political party is more difficult to manage than the Labour Party. For all its recent problems, the ideology and structure of the Conservative Party is still suited to control by a strong (or at least successful) Leader. As a result, Tories find it fairly easy to differentiate between who does the managing and who (or what) is managed. For Labour, both as a whole and even within its component parts, this is not the case. Labour is a fairly egalitarian organisation - a party which, while it may seek leadership, also distrusts it. It is a party for whose members the very idea of management smacks of top-down control and adds up to not simply a lack of consultation, but a denial of fundamental rights. The Labour Party is a federal institution. Power is located in a number of sites which can all lay claim to more or less legitimate authority. While the annual conference is theoretically supreme, for example, it is obvious that it can be and has been influenced (if not controlled) by the parliamentary leadership, the affiliated trade unions and the combination of both which (together with others) goes to make up the NEC. Outside the conference period, the NEC supposedly has control. But, while the NEC may lay claim to being the last court of appeal when it comes, for instance, to disciplinary matters, custom and practice grant the PLP considerable independence. The PLP is a 'sovereign body' - a status which also affects the extent to which it can be bound by conference decisions on matters of policy. The distribution of power within these federated sub-sections is just as complicated and unstable as that which exists between them.

Adapted from Brivati & Bale 1998.

Item C *Party discipline*

PRESS OFFICE? DO I LIKE RED OR WHITE WINE?

Labour is preparing to crack the disciplinary whip over potential rebels on the party's new-look NEC by issuing a new code of conduct designed to stifle policy clashes in the media. The party's new General Secretary, Margaret McDonagh, is seeking to bind NEC members to new rules which would require them to contact the party's press office before discussing NEC business with the media. This is bound to be seen as a warning to the four new left-wing constituency members on the NEC. Tony Blair is already embroiled in fresh allegations that staff at Downing Street and party's headquarters at Millbank are displaying 'control freak' instincts over the selection of candidates for the elections in Wales, Scotland and London. Blair will not have known about McDonagh's text. In return for abiding by the code of conduct, Labour's famously disciplined press office will respond to NEC members' requests for advice within 30 minutes, offering it 'freely and without prejudice'. This will almost certainly mean that a Blairite view will prevail on the NEC.

Adapted from the *Guardian*, 13 November 1998.

Item D   *The Leader*

After four years riding above his party, Tony Blair chose his fifth annual party conference speech to enlist his party in his enterprise. His speech at the 1998 conference was the first in which he sounded as though he really belonged to the organisation he is supposed to be leading. Another way of saying that is that he at last finds the party ready to have conferred upon it the task for which he has made it worthy. He retains his grandeur and is far and away the dominant figure. Cabinet colleagues gazed at him throughout as if with stars in their eyes. They were transfixed. But, this was his first serious attempt to convert his project into a collectivist effort. You are all responsible, he told the party. This is our shared work. Go out and deliver the message. And the party, which is now in soul as well as body his party, applauded itself to the rafters. It feels almost hideously good about itself, having completed its refit into a machine for governing. Any dissenters who have reached the rostrum have been silently hounded into being defensive. Even union barons, for the most part, came only whispering to the mike. Much of what was said here revealed a belief in a Blairite future. This view did not have to be engineered - which possibly makes it more alarming.

Adapted from the *Guardian*, 30 September 1998.

Questions

1. Using Item A, explain how the Labour Leader and Deputy Leader were selected after 1981 and how the system had changed by 1994.

2. a) Judging from Items B-D, where does power lie in the Labour Party?
   b) Using Items B-D, give arguments for and against the view that Tony Blair's reforms have ensured that the Labour Leader has complete control over the party.

3. What role is played by the Labour Leader? Use Item D in your answer.

Part 3 The Conservative Party

Key issues

1. How did the modern Conservative Party evolve?
2. What is the structure and organisation of the Conservative Party?
3. How powerful is the Leader of the Conservative Party?

3.1 The roots of the modern Conservative Party

Historical background

If a political party is judged by its ability to win elections and form governments then the Conservative Party has been by far the most successful party in Britain throughout the 20th century.

The roots of this success were laid in the 19th century. Although there is no firm date to mark the transition from Tory Party to Conservative Party, most commentators date this transition to 1834, the year in which Robert Peel became Leader (see, for example, Garner & Kelly 1998).

At the general election of 1832, the first to be held after the Great Reform Act was passed, the Tories won just 175 seats out of 658. Before 1832, the Tories had been able to appeal to the interests of the landed gentry and win sufficient seats to form a government. But, the 1832 Act enfranchised those who had become wealthy through business rather than inheritance and their interests were very different from those of the landed gentry. The 1832 Act provoked a crisis in the Tory party. This crisis was only overcome when Peel became Leader.

Robert Peel's leadership

Robert Peel's great achievement was to develop a political party which could represent the interests of all people of wealth whether that wealth was derived from property, land, industry or the professions. He managed to create this new voting alliance by advancing a new political creed - conservatism. Peel argued that social, economic and political change should not automatically be opposed. It should be welcomed, but only if it occurred slowly and if it built upon established institutions rather than sweeping them away. By encouraging change, Peel appealed to entrepreneurs and those who had become wealthy through the changes brought by the Industrial Revolution. By emphasising respect for established institutions such as the monarchy and the Church, Peel appealed to the ancient traditions of the landed aristocracy.

The crisis over the Corn Laws

In the short term, Peel was successful. The Conservatives won the general election of 1841. In the longer term, however, this new voting alliance was uneasy. In 1846, the party split over the Corn Laws or, more accurately, it split between those who supported free trade and those who supported protectionism (see Chapter 15, Section 1.2 for an explanation of these terms). The Corn Laws placed duty on imported grain. They were, therefore, protective tariffs which kept the price of grain artificially high. Whilst the landed gentry benefited from these laws (since their wealth came from agriculture) those whose wealth came from manufacturing argued for their abolition. Manufacturers argued that the Corn Laws kept the price of food artificially high. High food prices led to demands for high wages. If the Corn Laws were abolished, they argued, the price of food would come down and wages could then be reduced to enable profits to grow. Peel pushed through legislation for the abolition of the Corn Laws and in so doing divided his party. Although it was a Conservative government which abolished the Corn Laws, many Conservatives who supported free trade left to join the Whigs whilst the Conservative Party returned to its pre-Peelite position as the party of the landed gentry.

One nation conservatism
Conservative fortunes were revived by the practical and ideological contribution of Benjamin Disraeli (Conservative Prime Minister in 1868 and between 1874 and 1880). Not only was Disraeli responsible for organisational changes (Conservative Central Office was set up in 1870, for example), it was Disraeli who created 'one nation' conservatism.

Like Peel, Disraeli's aim was to broaden the electoral appeal of the Conservative Party. But, Disraeli did not restrict this appeal just to the wealthy. He aimed to unite the interests of both the wealthy and the underprivileged. Despite class differences, Disraeli maintained, the interests uniting the British people were of far greater significance than those dividing them. True, he argued, rich and poor sections in society did exist. But, the rich, because they held a privileged position in society, had a duty to look after the welfare of their inferiors. The Conservative Party, he claimed, was, therefore, the party of the whole nation - both rich and poor. It stood for the interests of the wealthy and at the same time favoured measures to support the poor.

One nation conservatism since 1865
Disraeli's ideological strategy was a great success. Between 1830 and 1865, the Conservatives had an effective parliamentary majority for only five years. But, from 1865 to 1900, the Conservatives had overall majorities for 17 years. It should be noted, however, that Conservative fortunes were aided during this latter period by a split in the Liberal Party in 1886 over home rule for Ireland (the formation of the Liberal Party is usually dated to 1859 when Whigs, Peelites and Radicals - MPs who supported reform, especially religious reform - joined together to set up a new party - see section 4.1 below). This split in the Liberal Party brought back to the Conservative Party some of those with manufacturing backgrounds who had left in 1846. By 1900, therefore, the Conservatives had been able to forge an alliance of forces which included landed and industrial wealth and whose aim was to preserve the power of property whilst maintaining social stability through paternalistic measures intended to ease the suffering of the poor.

The one nation strand of conservatism remained a key aspect of Conservative Party ideology and practice in the 20th century. It underpinned, for example, the long period of rule under Harold Macmillan whose governments demonstrated an ability to come to terms with the post-war welfare state and Keynesian economics (see Chapter 3, Section 1.1).

'Liberal' conservatism
Like most political parties the Conservative Party is a broad alliance. Not all Conservatives are one nation conservatives. Indeed, during the 1990s, the one nation conservatives were in the minority. Since the election of Margaret Thatcher as Conservative Party Leader in 1975, the Conservative Party has been dominated by those who subscribe to a different tradition - 'liberal' conservatism.

Liberal conservatism also has its origins in the 19th century and it is mainly derived from those Conservatives whose basis of wealth was manufacturing and finance rather than land. Such people had always championed the individual as well as the nation and they believed in free enterprise, individual initiative and in limited government intervention in the running of the economy. Whilst some of these liberal Conservatives came from the Liberal Party when it split over home rule for Ireland in 1886, many more came from the Liberal Party when it fell into deep decline after the First World War. The emphasis placed on individual initiative and free-market economics by liberal conservatives has informed debate within the Conservative Party throughout the 20th century. But, whereas the one nation conservatives held sway for 30 years after the Second World War, since 1975 the pendulum has swung towards the New Right, many of whose ideas draw on the liberal tradition.

Factions and tendencies within the Conservative Party
Today, few people would argue that the Conservative Party does not have an ideology. Yet that used to be the prevailing view. Stephen Ingle argues that the Thatcher governments changed this:

'Thatcherism could be said to have brought ideology into Conservative Party politics and in doing so destroyed the basis of unity, trust and loyalty which had been the party's most reliable weapon. Thus, one of the party's abiding myths, that it was not an ideological party, [has] been destroyed.' (Ingle 1993, p.3)

Within the Conservative Party, there are a number of groups or 'factions' (a faction is an organised group within a party which focuses on a particular ideological approach or particular policy). An examination of these factions suggests that the myth that the Conservative Party was not an ideological party is just that. Many of the factions existed before Margaret Thatcher became Leader. Their different aims reflect the different ideological approaches within the Conservative Party (see Box 8.3 for examples).

In addition to the formal groups mentioned above, there are informal groupings of Conservative MPs, also known as 'tendencies'. For example, in the 1980s, Conservatives were divided broadly into

Box 8.3 Examples of factions within the Conservative Party

Name of group	Date set up	Aims/ideology
Bow Group	1951	Broadly supports liberal conservative policies.
Monday Club	1961	Set up to protect right-wing principles and to oppose one nation conservatism.
Tory Reform Group	1975	Supports one nation conservatism.
No Turning Back Group	1983	Set up to protect and extend Thatcherite policies.
Bruges Group	1988	Set up after Thatcher's anti-European 'Bruges Speech' to oppose moves towards greater European integration.

'wets' (opponents of Thatcherism) and 'dries' (Thatcherites). In the 1990s, the key division was between Europhiles and Eurosceptics. Indeed, the split between Europhiles and Eurosceptics became so pronounced in the period 1992-97 that the party's reputation for unity suffered badly. Following the Conservative defeat at the general election of 1997, the division in the party between Europhiles and Eurosceptics remained central.

3.2 The structure and organisation of the Conservative Party

The structure of the party before 1998

Until the 1997 general election, surprisingly little was known about the internal workings of the Conservative Party. This was due, in part, to the fact that the Conservative Party had no official constitution:

'The arcane nature of Tory organisation owes much to the lack of any grand constitution outlining the powers and functions of its various organs. Indeed, a legal inquiry in 1982, involving Conservative Central Office and the Inland Revenue found that "the Conservative Party" did not even exist as "a compact, legally recognised organisation". It concluded that the party consisted instead of "three separate components" operating mainly on the basis of convention.' (Kelly 1994, p.52)

The three components referred to by Kelly were: the volunteers in the constituency associations (who were represented in the National Union of Conservative Associations); the party professionals at the regional headquarters and at Central Office; and, the parliamentary party (MPs and MEPs).

One reason why the Conservative Party did not exist as a 'compact, legally recognised organisation' was that, historically, the party had only existed in Parliament as a parliamentary group. The extension of the franchise in the 19th century produced the pressure to build up popular support. But, the real power in the party remained with the parliamentary leadership. To a large extent, this remained true until 1998. Writing in 1993, for example, Ingle claimed that:

'Properly speaking the Conservative Party is that body of MPs and peers who take the Conservative whips and the function of the constituency associations and regional and national structures is to support and sustain that body.' (Ingle 1993, p.3)

William Hague's reforms 1997-98

Following his election as Leader in June 1997 (a month after the Conservatives won their lowest number of MPs since 1906), William Hague argued that nothing short of a 'cultural revolution' was necessary in the Conservative Party. To achieve this, he made it clear that he intended to change the structure of the party. In autumn 1997, a green paper entitled *Blueprint for Change* was published. Following consultation, the proposals in this paper were amended and a fresh set of proposals published in February 1998 under the title *The Fresh Future*. The proposals in this paper were put to a ballot of party members and the results announced at a Special Reform Conference held on 28 March 1998. Of those who voted in the ballot, 96% supported the proposals (though only 33% of the membership voted in the ballot).

As a result of this ballot, the Conservative Party now has a written constitution, a national membership scheme and, for the first time, the party's three separate components have been united within a single party structure. Whilst constituency associations (see below) remain the key organisation at local level, the party structure has four new elements. These are outlined in Box 8.4 below.

Constituency associations

Like all political parties, the Conservative Party relies on volunteers to work on its behalf locally. These volunteers join their local constituency association, the key organisation at local level. Constituency associations are run by an executive committee which is elected at the annual general meeting (AGM). They are divided into branches which are based on local council polling districts and exist to fight local elections. The executive committee of the constituency association is made up of representatives from the

Box 8.4 Conservative Party structure

1. The Board
The Board has supreme responsibility for all aspects of party management outside Westminster. It is made up of 14 members from all three components of the party - five appointed by the Leader; five from the National Convention (see below); one member from Wales; one from Scotland; one from the Association of Conservative Councillors; and, one from the backbench 1992 Committee. It normally meets once a month and is chaired by the Party Chairman. It is responsible for organising the annual party conference and has taken over the functions which used to be performed by the National Union. It is also responsible for running Conservative Central Office.

2. The National Convention
The National Convention is made up of national, regional and area officials, officers from constituency associations and members of affiliated organisations. It is supported by a network of 11 Regional Councils and 42 Area Councils. Its function is to channel to the Leader grass-root views and to advise the Board on extra-parliamentary organisation. It meets twice a year.

3. The National Convention executive
The executive is made up of the six senior officers of the National Convention, five of whom are the Convention's representatives on the Board. It has day-to-day responsibility for voluntary activity and is accountable to the Board.

4. The Policy Forum
The aim of the Policy Forum is to allow ordinary members to play a part in devising policy by making proposals to conference. The Forum is made up of regional policy congresses which coopt experts and parliamentary spokespeople. It is chaired by the minister responsible for policy development. Like the National Convention, the Forum has advisory powers.

branches. Constituency association meetings are attended by ordinary members rather than delegates.

The functions of constituency associations
Constituency associations have three main functions. First, they provide the local organisation necessary to fight elections. Second, they play an important part in the selection of candidates for local and national elections (see Chapter 11, Section 2.1 for a description of the selection process). And third, they provide a place for like-minded people to meet and socialise. Studies have shown that the majority of members of the Conservative Party do not attend party meetings or participate in party activities. They join so that they can use the party's social facilities (Whiteley et al. 1994).

Kelly points out that, in recent years, constituency associations have declined and this was a major factor in William Hague's desire for reform:

> 'By 1997, many constituency Tory parties ("associations") were clearly dilapidated. Membership had shrunk from almost 3 million in 1952 to less than 400,000 with the vast majority of members inactive and elderly.

Owing to the related fall-off in association revenue, the number of full-time constituency agents had shrunk to less than 200 and, during the 1997 campaign, there were sundry reports of "moribund" [nearly dead] associations in key marginals.' (Kelly 1998a, p.29)

The introduction of OMOV
After being elected Leader, William Hague announced that he intended to ensure that ordinary members played a more active role in decision making. Between June 1997 and October 1998, he balloted ordinary members on three occasions (see Box 8.5) and promised to ballot them on the next Conservative manifesto. This was unprecedented. Ordinary members of the Conservative Party had never been asked for their views before.

Box 8.5 Conservative ballots 1997-98

1. Autumn 1997 - Leadership ballot
In September 1997, Conservatives were asked whether they endorsed William Hague as Leader and the reforms he was proposing. A majority (81% of votes cast) voted in favour of Hague and his reforms. The turnout was 44%.

2. March 1998 - *The Fresh Future*
In March 1998, Conservatives were asked whether they supported the proposals for reform of the party outlined in the document *The Fresh Future*. A large majority (96% of votes cast) voted in favour of adopting the proposed reforms. The turnout was 33%.

3. Autumn 1998 - Policy on Europe
In autumn 1998, Conservatives were asked whether they supported William Hague's policy on the single European currency (namely, that the party should oppose Britain's entry into a single currency during the current and next Parliament). A majority (84% of votes cast) backed the policy. The turnout was 60%.

Changes in constituency association powers since 1998
Until 1998, constituency associations were completely autonomous (free to act as they liked). This meant, for example, that John Major was unable to prevent Tatton Constituency Association from selecting, and refusing to deselect, the disgraced ex-minister Neil Hamilton as their candidate for the 1997 general election. The leadership simply had no power over constituency association candidate selection.

According to Richard Kelly (1998a), William Hague's reforms have curtailed this freedom in three ways. First, a new Ethics and Integrity Committee (overseen by the new Board) has been set up with the power to suspend or expel unsuitable members. This gives the national party some control over candidate selection (it could have forced Neil Hamilton's constituency association to deselect him in the run-up to the 1997 general election, for example, if it had been in operation then). Second, the new Board has the power to set efficiency criteria for each individual association. If an association does not meet these criteria, the Board can order it to be reorganised and force its officers to be replaced. And third, whereas associations had complete control over their local finances before 1998, they now have to submit annual accounts to Central Office. In addition, the introduction of a national membership scheme means that some membership funds automatically go to Central Office (whereas, before, all membership funds were collected and retained locally).

Since March 1998, Conservative constituency associations have had (in theory at least) a new policy-making role via the new Policy Forum. The power of the Policy Forum, however, is only advisory. In other words, the leadership can ignore its views if it so chooses.

The annual party conference

The annual party conference has no formal powers to make party policy. Decisions made at conference are advisory only. The party leadership may choose to ignore them. It is, therefore, no surprise that the traditional view of the annual party conference is that it has little political importance. Rather, it is usually seen as a rally of the party faithful where dedicated party members meet together, reinforce each others' views and enjoy an exciting social occasion. In support of this view, it should be noted that, until 1965, the Party Leader only attended the conference on the final afternoon. Although party leaders have always attended since then (which may suggest that the conference has grown in importance), they are automatically given a standing ovation regardless of their popularity or the content of their speech. This suggests that the purpose of the conference is to rubber stamp the decisions made by the party leadership.

Political significance of conferences

Annual party conferences may be carefully stage managed public relations exercises, but that does not necessarily mean that they do not have any political importance. It has long been known, for example, that a poor speech from a frontbencher can dash their hopes of promotion or even (in the case of Reginald Maudling in 1965) their hopes of party leadership. Besides, the polite surface often conceals underlying currents. Journalists often make a great deal of the length of time that standing ovations last and they attempt to 'decode' the 'mood' of the conference. A cool response to a senior figure's speech, for example, might be a sign of widespread grass-roots discontent.

Despite the fact that the annual party conference does not have a formal role in policy making, senior Conservatives often use it as a forum either to 'test the water' before devising concrete proposals or actually to announce new policies. That senior party figures use the conference for this purpose suggests that they

consider conference to be an important body.

Regional and sectional conferences

In addition, it has been suggested that, in fact, the regional and sectional conferences have a bigger influence over policy development than is generally realised. Richard Kelly (1989) has argued that much of the ground work for the annual party conference is done at these regional and sectional conferences. He notes that debates at these conferences are much more critical and frank than those at the annual party conference, and they are encouraged to be so by senior Conservatives. Kelly suggests that:

'[The annual party conference] is, in a sense, the climax of an oblique "conference system" where ministers earn their ovations only by showing some accommodation of the advice rendered by Tory activists at previous conferences held that year.' (Kelly 1992, p.27)

Conservative Central Office

The Conservative Party employs a full-time bureaucracy which has its headquarters in Smith Square, London. Conservative Central Office was set up in 1870 by Disraeli as his private office. The Party Chairman (the Conservatives refuse to use the gender-neutral term 'chair') and other party officials are appointed by the Party Leader and are answerable to the Party Leader alone. The Party Chairman is in charge of Central Office.

Structure and organisation of Central Office

In the late 1990s, the number of staff employed by Central Office declined, though it does vary according to circumstances (more staff are employed at the time of a general election, for example). In January 1994, around 250 staff were employed by Central Office whilst, in January 1999, the figure was around 100. The structure and organisation of Central Office was altered after the general election defeat of 1997. For example, the press office and research office were combined and stationed in a single, open-plan room to encourage staff to work together. According to the press office, the day-to-day set up in 1998 was that which, previously, had only been used during election campaigns, the implication being that it was necessary to run the party as if it was constantly on a campaign.

In 1998, also, regional offices which had been set up in 1993 were closed down. Instead, the UK was divided into 26 areas, each headed by an Area Campaign Director. The job of the Area Campaign Director is to liaise between the 12 or so constituency associations in their local area and Central Office.

The role of Central Office

Central Office is responsible for the party's finances and for membership policy (since 1998, it has been responsible for maintaining the national membership list). It also has a coordinating role at election time. It is responsible for national campaigning, liaising with the media and for ensuring satisfactory resources are available in the constituencies.

Central Office provides an important bridge between ordinary party members and the parliamentary party. It provides constituency associations with information and advice and trains the professional agents employed by constituencies. Whilst candidates for election are selected locally, this takes place under the supervision of Central Office. As noted above, since 1998 Central Office has had some genuine control over candidate selection (control which was lacking before).

The Party Chairman

The Conservative Party Chairman, Deputy Chairman and Vice Chairmen are appointed by the Party Leader. The Party Chairman has a dual role - to run Central Office and to publicise policies which concern the structure and organisation of the party. The Party Chairman is also responsible for running the party's national election campaigns.

Although the Party Chairman performs both a managerial and a political role, appointments to this post are decidedly political. Senior party figures, normally ex-Cabinet ministers are appointed. Michael White suggests that a pattern has emerged in the appointments made since 1979:

> 'Recent tradition tends to appoint a caretaker manager for the first half of Parliament (to

sack surplus staff and pay off the debts) and a star to help win next time.' (*Guardian*, 21 June 1994)

Main points - Sections 3.1-3.2

- If a political party is judged by its ability to win elections and form governments then the Conservative Party has been by far the most successful party in Britain throughout the 20th century.
- Within the Conservative Party, there are a number of factions and tendencies. The split between Europhiles and Eurosceptics became so pronounced in the period 1992-97 that the party's reputation for unity suffered badly.
- Before the 1997 general election, the Conservative Party had no written constitution and was not even a legally recognised body.
- Since 1997, there have been significant reforms. The party now has a written constitution and the various components have been joined together to make a single party. The extra-parliamentary party is run by the Board and the voice of ordinary members is heard via the National Policy Forum.
- The National Policy Forum and party conference have advisory powers only. The Leader can ignore their views.

Activity 8.5 *The Conservative Party*

Item A *Conservative Prime Ministers and general election victories since 1900*

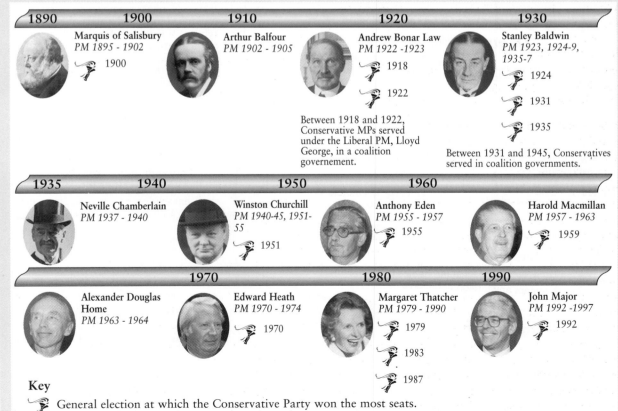

Key

General election at which the Conservative Party won the most seats.

Item B   *The structure and organisation of the Conservative Party*

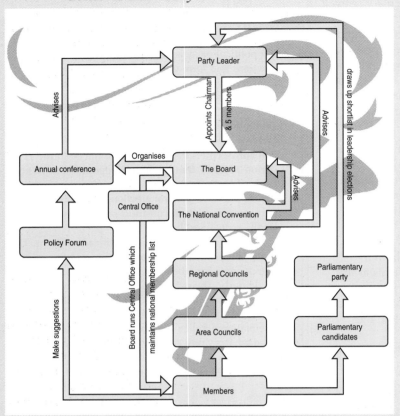

Item D   *William Hague's Six Principles*

Hague's six principles

1. UNITY: The separation of the parliamentary, voluntary and professional sides of the party no longer serves us well. There must be a single party, with one governing Board and a single constitution.

2. DECENTRALISATION: We will rebuild the party from the grassroots. Constituency associations must be the crucial building block.

3. DEMOCRACY: Our reforms will be built on the principle of giving more power to members. All members will have a say in policy making and every member will have a vote in the election of the Party Leader.

4. INVOLVEMENT: The key to mass membership and involvement is national membership. National membership will enable direct communication between Leader and members.

5. INTEGRITY: Our current disciplinary methods are outdated. New powers are needed to deal with individuals who bring the party's good name into disrepute.

6. OPENNESS: We will publish the names of all major donors and will refuse to accept any foreign donations.

The reforms to the Conservative Party proposed by William Hague in 1998 in *The Fresh Future* were based on the six principles outlined above.

Adapted from Kelly 1998.

Item C   *The Fresh Future*

The Fresh Future echoes much of what happened in the Labour Party after 1983. Both Kinnock and Blair preached the OMOV gospel while effectively strengthening central authority and Hague seems to have been impressed by New Labour's achievement. Yet, the reorganisation of the Labour Party had a clear ideological purpose - namely, to sideline socialism while furthering the 'modernising' of policy. Likewise, *The Fresh Future* has wider policy implications. Hague is expected to face a string of bitter disputes with fellow Tory MPs over Europe (at least a fifth of Conservative MPs elected in 1997 have pro-European tendencies which do not square with Hague's own ideas). If Hague can cite support from the party outside Westminster, he stands a better chance of pushing through his policies (he has already used this tactic when he organised a ballot on his European policy, announcing the result at the start of the 1998 party conference). Beyond Europe, Hague hopes to fight New Labour with New Conservatism. The details are still vague, but this involves a new Conservative brand of laissez faire morality which is seen by some as the natural partner to laissez faire economics. Among elderly Tories there is natural hostility to 'libertarian' ideas (in 1998, Hague defended 'alternative lifestyles' and 'cultural pluralism', for example). Among younger Tories, there is more enthusiasm. If these younger members could be multiplied (one of the aims of Hague's reforms was to increase the membership of the party, especially the young membership) and if their voice was amplified, this could give Hague crucial support in his battle for the party's soul.

Adapted from Kelly 1999.

Questions

1. 'The natural party of government'. Judging from Item A, is this a fair description of the Conservative Party? Give reasons for your answer.

2. What evidence is there in Items B-D that William Hague borrowed ideas from New Labour?

3. a) What do Items B-D tell us about the structure and organisation of the Conservative Party?
   b) Why do you think William Hague changed the structure of the party?

4. a) Judging from Items B and D, how has the structure and organisation of the Conservative Party changed since the party's election defeat in 1997?
   b) Where does power lie in the Conservative Party?

3.3 The role of the Conservative Leader

The power of the Party Leader

Until the resignation of Margaret Thatcher in November 1990, there was a general consensus amongst political scientists that Conservative Leaders enjoyed almost unrestrained power so long as they were able to bring electoral success (see, for example, McKenzie 1955 and Garner & Kelly 1998).

The powers of the Conservative Leader are indeed considerable. First, in theory at least, the Leader alone is responsible for choosing the Cabinet or shadow Cabinet. Second, unlike the Labour Leader, the Conservative Leader does not have to work with an elected Deputy Leader (Conservative Leaders are free to choose or not choose a Deputy Leader). Third, the Conservative Leader has sole responsibility for the formulation of the party's election manifestos (though William Hague promised in 1998 to submit a draft of the manifesto for the forthcoming general election to a ballot of all members). And fourth, the Conservative Leader chooses the Party Chairman. These powers allow Conservative Leaders to introduce the policies and style of their own choosing. With the adoption of a written constitution in 1998, the Leader's formal role was described in writing for the first time. The wording showed that the Leader was to have a great deal of freedom of movement:

> 'The Leader shall determine the political direction of the party having regard to the views of party members and the Conservative Policy Forum.' (Conservative 1998, p.6)

Why is the Conservative Leader so powerful?

There are two main reasons why the Conservative Leader has such a powerful position in the party. First, belief in hierarchy and leadership is embodied in Conservative ideology. As Ian Aitken put it, it is a 'top-down' rather than a 'bottom-up' party (*Guardian*, 14 January 1998). And second, the British electorate tends to favour parties which are united behind a strong Leader. Since electoral success is judged to be of primary importance to the Conservative Party, that helps to explain why the party encourages strong leadership.

Some commentators have argued that William Hague's reforms in 1997-98 strengthened the power of the Leader (see Activity 8.6 below).

Restrictions on the Leader's power

Before the reforms of 1997-98, it was standard to argue that, in practice, the Conservative Leader's power was restricted by the need to consider the views of two groups - senior colleagues and backbenchers (backbenchers all belong to and are represented by the 1922 committee). It was essential for the Leader to retain the support of the vast majority in these two groups, so the argument went, because it was these two groups alone which could decide to ditch the Leader and choose a new one. Since 1998, however, the position has changed. Although it is still important for the Leader to retain the support of senior colleagues and backbenchers, it is not so essential because the Leader can appeal directly to ordinary members. So, if the Leader wants to adopt a policy which is unpopular with some senior colleagues, but popular with activists at the local level, the Leader can call a ballot of the membership and then (assuming the result is decisive) argue that a mandate has been won for the policy. This is exactly what happened in autumn 1998 when William Hague organised a ballot on his policy towards the single European currency.

3.4 The selection of the Party Leader

'Emergence'

Until 1965, the Conservative Leader was chosen by what has been called 'emergence'. New Party Leaders were not selected by any formal system. Rather the new Leader would 'emerge' from meetings held between senior party members, influential backbenchers and others considered to be of importance within the Conservative Party. It is, perhaps, no surprise to learn that those senior Conservatives involved in the choice of Leader were known as the 'magic circle'.

After the resignation of Harold Macmillan in 1963 this system proved itself inadequate. There was no clear successor to Macmillan and the 'magic circle' chose Lord Home as Leader. Many Conservatives considered Home to be an inappropriate choice. This view seemed to be confirmed when Home lost the 1964 general election. Before Home resigned, however, he set up an inquiry to establish a new way of choosing the Conservative Leader.

New system, 1965

The result of the inquiry was that a new system for electing the Conservative Leader was set up. From 1965, a candidate for the post of Leader needed a nominator and a seconder. There would then be a maximum of three ballots in which Conservative MPs would be allowed to vote. In the first ballot, a successful candidate needed to gain more than 50% of votes cast and to have 15% more votes than any other candidate. Later, this was changed. A successful candidate needed more than 50% of the votes of those entitled to vote and 15% more votes than any other candidate. If the first ballot was inconclusive, a second would be held. In the second ballot, a successful candidate simply needed to win more than 50% of the votes cast. If that did not produce a winner, a third round would be held. In this ballot, the three most popular candidates (according to the results of the second round) would contest the post. The winner was the candidate who had the majority using an alternative vote system. Candidates could withdraw from the contest at any stage.

Contests under this system

The first contest to be held under this system took place in 1965. It was won by Edward Heath. Heath failed to gain the required majority in the first round but he led his opponents by such a margin that they all withdrew. Subsequent contests took place in 1975, 1989 and 1990. In 1975, Margaret Thatcher won on the second ballot. In 1989, Margaret Thatcher won on the first ballot. Then, in 1990, despite having a majority, Margaret Thatcher withdrew after the first ballot because she had failed to win an outright victory (and a number of Cabinet colleagues made it clear that she had lost their support). Her withdrawal was followed by the victory of John Major.

New rules, 1991

Following the leadership contest of 1990, changes were made to the leadership election system. From 1991, the contest had to take place within 14 days of a new Commons session or within three months of a new Parliament. Also, any challenger had to have the backing of 10% of Conservative MPs. These new arrangements were made in response to the 'frivolous' challenge of Anthony Meyer in 1989. Meyer took advantage of a rule change in 1974 which stipulated that there should be a leadership election every year whether or not the Conservatives were in power (Margaret Thatcher was elected unopposed every year between 1975 and 1989). Although Meyer had no hope of winning himself, he hoped that other more serious challengers would come forward. His actions, therefore, put the Leader under pressure. The leadership elections of 1995 (when John Major resigned voluntarily and then won a convincing majority in the first ballot) and 1997 (when John Major resigned following the general election defeat - the first time in the 20th century that a Conservative Leader resigned immediately after a general election defeat) were held under the new rules.

William Hague's reforms

The 1997 Conservative leadership contest was particularly controversial for two reasons. First, the 1997 general election had resulted in just 165 Conservatives being elected as MPs. Under the existing rules, that meant that the new Leader would be chosen by an electorate of just 164. Many within the party (and outside) argued that this was undemocratic and that ordinary party members

should have a say. And second, when opinion polls were conducted in constituency associations, it became clear that a large majority of ordinary members favoured Kenneth Clarke and yet it was William Hague who won the contest. As a result, critics questioned the legitimacy of Hague's position as Leader.

To gain legitimacy, to prevent similar criticisms being made in the future and to improve the Conservative Party's electoral prospects, William Hague announced that he intended to introduce reforms and held a special ballot of ordinary members asking them to endorse his position as Leader and to approve the principles behind the intended reforms (outlined in Section 3.2 above). The support gained in the referendum was sufficient to provide Hague with some legitimacy and paved the way to changes in the way in which the Party Leader was to be elected.

The rules introduced in 1998

The key change introduced in 1998 was the rule allowing ordinary Conservative Party members to have the final say in who should become Party Leader. In a leadership contest where only two candidates stood, there would simply be a ballot of all party members. In a leadership contest where more than two candidates stood, there would be a primary ballot (or series of ballots) of Conservative MPs to whittle down the number standing to just two candidates. Then, there would be a ballot of all party members to choose between the two remaining candidates.

Main points - Sections 3.3-3.4

- The 1998 Conservative constitution states that the role of the Leader is to 'determine the political direction of the party having regard to the views of party members and the Conservative Policy Forum'.
- Although commentators argued before Thatcher's removal that the power of Conservative Leaders was almost unrestrained, in fact it has always been restricted by the need to retain the support of senior colleagues and backbenchers.
- Since the reforms of 1997-98, the Leader has also been obliged to take into account the views of ordinary members. Some commentators argue that these reforms increased the Leader's power.
- Before 1965, Conservative Leaders 'emerged'. Between 1965 and 1998, Leaders were chosen by a ballot (or series of ballots) of MPs. The rule change in 1998 meant that, for the first time, ordinary members would have the final say on who should become Leader.

Activity 8.6 *The Conservative Leader*

Item A *Elections to the post of Conservative Leader, 1990 and 1997*

(i) Leadership election, 1990

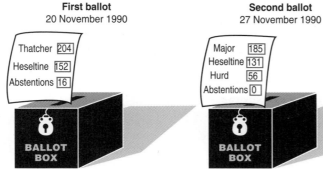

First ballot
20 November 1990

Thatcher 204
Heseltine 152
Abstentions 16

BALLOT BOX

Thatcher withdrew as she had not won an outright victory.

Second ballot
27 November 1990

Major 185
Heseltine 131
Hurd 56
Abstentions 0

BALLOT BOX

Heseltine and Hurd withdrew even though Major had not won an outright victory.

(ii) Leadership election, 1997

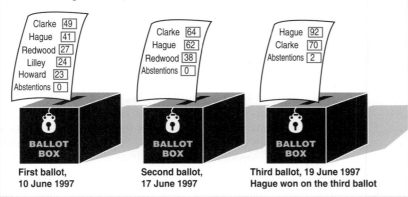

Clarke 49
Hague 41
Redwood 27
Lilley 24
Howard 23
Abstentions 0

BALLOT BOX

**First ballot,
10 June 1997**

Clarke 64
Hague 62
Redwood 38
Abstentions 0

BALLOT BOX

**Second ballot,
17 June 1997**

Hague 92
Clarke 70
Abstentions 2

BALLOT BOX

**Third ballot, 19 June 1997
Hague won on the third ballot**

Item C *New rules, 1998*

Challenging Conservative Leaders: revised rules (1998)

1. A vote of no-confidence must be proposed by no fewer than 15% of Conservative MPs.
2. If Conservative MPs vote on a no-confidence motion and it is defeated, no further no-confidence motions are allowed for another 12 months.
3. If Conservative MPs vote on a no-confidence motion and it is carried, the Leader must resign and take no part in the subsequent contest. A formal leadership contest then begins and nominations are invited by officers of the 1922 Committee.
4. Candidates require the backing of two other (named) MPs.
5. *Either* (a) If there are only two other candidates, a one member, one vote contest is immediately organised, involving all those who have been members of the Conservative Party for six months prior to the vote of no-confidence.
Or (b) If there are more than two candidates, Conservative MPs vote in first-past-the-post 'primary' elections until only two candidates remain (the bottom placed candidate being eliminated after each ballot). A one member, one vote ballot then takes place.

This diagram shows the rules for electing Conservative Leaders introduced in 1998.

Item B *The impact of Hague's reforms (1)*

Things have become so dire for the Conservatives that they have finally had to embrace democracy. Historically, they never cared much for it. Edward Burke, for example, shuddered at the thought of giving the vote to the 'swinish multitude'. The Conservatives reluctantly came to terms with universal suffrage, but expressed their real feelings about democracy by excluding it from their own arrangements. The MPs-only system of selecting a chief was discredited by the 1997 contest. Hague was not the first choice of the public (that was Clarke). He was not the first choice of Tory activists (also Clarke). He was not even his own first choice as Leader (initially he agreed to support Michael Howard, but changed his mind). Just 41 MPs voted for Hague in the first ballot (only a quarter of the parliamentary party). It is much to Hague's credit that he realised the process which produced him should never be repeated. Conservative MPs will retain the power to dispose of a failed Leader. That is important to them. Whilst Labour MPs fear their activists will be rebellious, Tory MPs are worried that their activists are too loyal. Had it been up to the activists, Heath would have remained Leader in 1975 after losing three out of four general elections. Similarly, activists would not have deposed Thatcher in 1990. So, there will still be a mechanism to throw out the Leader. MPs still have the power of assassination. What they will lose is the power of appointment. This reform will make the Tory system arguably more democratic (and certainly more straightforward) than Labour's electoral college. By the time Hague completes his reforms, he wants to be able to argue that his party is more democratic, more egalitarian and more open to debate than Blair's. It is hard to know who would be more staggered by this - Edward Burke or the average member of the Labour Party.

Adapted from the *Observer*, 11 January 1998.

Item D *The impact of Hague's reforms (2)*

A closer inspection showed that Hague's 'cultural revolution' only went so far. The Policy Forum and the National Convention were only to have the sort of advisory powers traditionally given to the Conservative annual party conference which itself gained no extra teeth. In short, the leadership was still free to ignore the wishes of extra-parliamentary Tories. In fact, there were reasons to suspect that Hague's democratisation could weaken activists while strengthening the leadership. OMOV leadership elections, for example, will allow Tory Leaders to claim a mandate from the whole party, something not available to Hague's predecessors. The new rules also make it harder for the Leader to be dethroned. Ballots of MPs take only a few weeks, inviting the prospect of a swift downfall. But, challenges involving constituency members take much longer and pose more danger to the party's public image (Labour's leadership contest of 1994 took over two months whereas the Conservative contest in 1997 took only two weeks). This, in turn, makes a challenge to the Leader much less likely - the prospect of a drawn-out and costly challenge will discourage a vote of no confidence, making stalking horse challenges of the sort launched by Anthony Meyer against Margaret Thatcher in 1989 less likely to surface. It is worth noting that, since Labour scrapped its MPs-only system in 1981, its Leader has only once been challenged - a challenge which left a strong sense of 'never again' within the Labour Party. By contrast, between 1989 and 1995, Tory Leaders were challenged three times. It is not so surprising, therefore, that Kinnock and Blair have been the boldest Labour Leaders this century having gained the extra legitimacy and security from ballots of the whole party.

Adapted from Kelly 1998a and 1999.

Questions

1. a) Using Item A, explain what procedure was used to choose a Leader in 1990 and 1997.
   b) How did the rules differ in the two contests?

2. Judging from Items A-C, what is new about the rules for choosing a Conservative Leader introduced in 1998 and what has remained the same?

3. 'William Hague has considerably strengthened his position since he became Leader in 1997'. Explain this statement using Items B-D.

4. 'All style, no substance'. Is that an accurate description of William Hague's reforms? Explain your answer.

Part 4 The Liberal Democrats

Key issues

1. How did the Liberal Democrats evolve?
2. What is the structure and organisation of the Liberal Democrats?
3. How powerful is the Leader of the Liberal Democrats?

4.1 Origins and history of the Liberal Democrats

Origins

The Liberal Democrats came into being in March 1988 when the Liberal Party formally merged with the Social Democratic Party (SDP) to form a new party. At first, this new party was known as the Social and Liberal Democrats (SLD) but, after a ballot of the members in October 1989, Liberal Democrats was adopted as the common name of the party. Although the party is, therefore, the youngest of the three main parties, its roots reach back way beyond 1988. Whilst the SDP was formed after a split in the Labour Party in 1981, the foundation of the Liberal Party is generally dated to June 1859.

The rise of the Liberal Party

Like the Conservative Party, the Liberal Party emerged from an existing parliamentary group - the Whigs. Whigs supported free trade, religious tolerance and the power of Parliament over that of the Monarch. At first, the Liberal Party was a loose coalition of Whigs, Peelites (Conservatives who had broken from their

party in 1846 because they supported free trade) and Radicals (MPs who supported reform, especially religious reform). Support for free trade and individual freedom were the main areas of agreement. But, under the leadership of Gladstone (Prime Minister 1868-74, 1880-85 and 1892-94), the Liberal Party developed into a modern political party with a mass membership and nationwide extra-parliamentary organisation.

Between 1860 and 1914, the Liberal Party was the main alternative to the Conservative Party. The two parties alternated in power and dominated Parliament. But, in the early 20th century, the Liberal Party went into rapid decline. Although the Liberals won an overall majority in the general election of 1906 and remained the party with the largest number of seats after the general election of 1910, within 20 years the party was only able to win a handful of seats and it had been replaced as the main party of opposition by the Labour Party.

The decline of the Liberal Party

Historians do not agree about when the decline of the Liberal Party started nor why it happened. But, most would agree that the following factors made an impact. First, the Liberal Party suffered from internal divisions before and during the First World War and this affected its credibility. In 1916, for example, David Lloyd George replaced Herbert Asquith as Prime Minister and in doing so split the party. In the 1918 election, Lloyd George Liberals remained in coalition with the Conservatives and they fought seats against Asquith Liberals. Second, the extension of the franchise following the Representation of the People Act of 1918 trebled the number of voters (from c.7 to c.21 million). It soon became clear that the majority of these new voters were not prepared to vote Liberal. Third, the First World War brought changed social and economic circumstances. Fourth, in the early years of the 20th century the Labour Party was becoming established and, although it had not made a significant breakthrough before 1914, the foundations for electoral success had been laid. It is significant that the Labour Party was set up specifically to provide a voice for the working class. Although the Liberal government of 1906-11 had introduced reforms which were designed to ease the suffering of the disadvantaged, the Liberal Party could not claim to represent the working class in the way that the new Labour Party could. And finally, Liberal support was evenly spread rather than concentrated in dense pockets. As a result, the 'first-past-the-post' system (see Chapter 7, Section 3.1) ensured that the Liberals gained far fewer seats than the number of votes for them would suggest they should receive.

The Liberal Party, 1920s-1980s
The general election of 1923 was the last time when the number of Liberal MPs reached three figures. In 1935, the number of Liberal MPs fell to a low of 21. Between 1935 and 1988 (when the Liberal Party was formally disbanded), it never managed to win more than 23 seats in a general election. These figures show that the decline of the Liberal Party was not just sudden and deep, it was also long lasting. By the time the Second World War broke out, the idea that the Liberal Party was a minor party was well established.

Although the Liberal Party was never able to return the significant number of MPs that it returned up until the early 1920s, the party always managed to retain a toehold in Parliament and it always managed to win votes in the millions. From the 1950s, there were signs periodically that a significant revival in the fortunes of the party was about to happen. But, despite winning 19% of the vote in February 1974, 25% of the vote in 1983 and 22.5% of the vote in 1987, the party was unable to shake the hold that the two other major parties had on the electoral system.

The SDP
In November 1979, shortly after Margaret Thatcher's election victory, Roy Jenkins (a former Labour Home Secretary and Chancellor) delivered the annual Dimbleby lecture. In his speech, he lamented the drift of Conservatives to the right and Labour to the left and called for a realignment of British politics to enable the majority of moderate voters to be represented. Jenkins allowed his Labour Party membership to lapse.

It was the organisational changes won by Tony Benn and his colleagues at the special Labour conference in 1981 (see above, Section 2.2), however, which were the catalyst for the formation of the Social Democratic

Party (SDP). Shortly after the conference, three senior Labour MPs, Bill Rogers, David Owen and Shirley Williams, together with Roy Jenkins, issued the 'Limehouse Declaration'. This was a statement which attacked the Labour Party for heading towards extremism and set up a Council for Social Democracy. Rogers, Owen, Williams and Jenkins (who became known as the 'gang of four') set up the SDP in March 1981 and the following autumn formed a formal alliance with the Liberal Party.

Initially, the prospects for the Alliance seemed excellent. By the end of 1981, the SDP was able to claim 27 former Labour MPs and one former Conservative. It received a great deal of money and many offers of support. Opinion polls suggested that the Alliance would win a majority of votes. The findings of these polls seemed to be confirmed when the Alliance won three by-election victories. But, this early enthusiasm was not translated into general election success. In the 1983 general election, although the Alliance came close to pushing Labour into third place in terms of votes cast, it won only 23 seats. Of these 23 seats, 17 were won by Liberals and six by members of the SDP. The general election of 1987 was even more of a disappointment. The number of seats and the percentage of the vote won by the Alliance dropped.

From Alliance to merger
After the 1987 general election, David Steel, the Liberal Leader, called for a complete merger of the two parties. He argued that voters had been confused about the exact nature of the Alliance. The fact that there were two Leaders (David Steel and David Owen) particularly caused problems in the 1987 election campaign. The debate over merger was fierce with both parties divided on the issue. But, after balloting the membership, a merger was agreed.

Within the SDP, however, the Leader, David Owen, and a group of supporters refused to accept this majority decision and they set up a rival party which retained the name SDP. Owen and two other MPs fought on until 1990 when successive electoral defeats demonstrated clearly that the party had little support. Similarly, disenchanted Liberals continued to struggle on under the banner of the Liberal Party.

Record since merger
Since merger, the Liberal Democrats have regularly scored 20% of the vote in local elections and higher in council by-elections. They have also won some spectacular by-election victories. Until the 1997 general election, however, they failed to win more than 25 seats. In 1992, they won 17.8% of the vote in the UK as a whole (18.3% in Great Britain) and 20 seats. In the 1994 Euro-elections, they won 16% of the vote and two seats.

The 1997 general election
The general election of 1997 was an important breakthrough for the Liberal Democrats. Despite

securing a slightly lower percentage of the popular vote than they had won in 1992 (17.2% in Great Britain, 16.8% in the UK as a whole), they won more than double the number of seats - 46 seats. This impressive rise in the number of seats was achieved largely because of the growth of tactical voting by voters anxious to remove the Conservatives and prepared to vote for either of the two main opposition parties. These voters made an assessment as to whether it was the Labour or the Liberal Democrat candidate in their constituency who was most likely to defeat the Conservative candidate and voted accordingly. In the south of England, this tactical approach was particularly beneficial for the Liberal Democrats.

Following the election, there was a second important breakthrough. The new Labour government made it clear that it was prepared to cooperate with the Liberal Democrats in those areas where the two parties broadly agreed on policy. This led to the setting up of a Cabinet committee on which senior Liberal Democrats were invited to sit together with senior ministers (see Chapter 12, Section 2.4). In addition, Roy Jenkins was chosen to head the commission set up to examine the case for electoral reform for elections to the Commons (see Chapter 7, Section 4.3).

4.2 The structure and organisation of the Liberal Democrats

A federal structure
When the members of the Liberal Party and the SDP agreed to merge in 1988, one of the key issues that had to be resolved was the structure and organisation of the new party. The result was a compromise between the centralised structure of the SDP and the federal structure of the Liberal Party. This structure is laid down in a written constitution.

A federal party is a party in which the central decision-making body of the party (the federal party) is not all-powerful. Power is devolved to area and local parties. The area and local parties remain independent with regard to local and internal affairs. Any matter of national concern is dealt with by the federal party. The federal principle survived the merger of the two parties and, as a result, considerable autonomy is granted to area and local party organisations.

In Wales and Scotland, the party has three tiers. In England, there are four. Nationally, there is the federal party. This is responsible for the preparation of policy for Britain as a whole. It also has overall responsibility for parliamentary elections and national fund raising. All other matters are delegated to the three 'state' parties - one each for England, Scotland and Wales. Scotland and Wales are then subdivided into constituency parties (known officially as 'local' parties) whilst England is subdivided into 12 regional parties and then into local parties.

The state parties
The state parties are responsible for the operation of local parties, selection procedures for parliamentary candidates, the arrangements for collecting and renewing party membership and local policy matters. In England, each regional party appoints representatives to the English Council, the state party's governing body. For its own convenience, the English state party has delegated policy-making powers to the federal party. In Scotland and Wales, members of the local parties elect representatives to the Scottish Conference and the Welsh Council, their governing bodies. The Scottish and Welsh state parties have policy-making powers.

Membership
Every member who joins the Liberal Democrats automatically becomes a member of the federal party, the relevant state party and the relevant local party. Their membership fees are divided between these three levels in the way determined by the federal conference and the relevant state conference.

Party headquarters
The Liberal Democrats' federal party headquarters is based in Cowley Street in London. In 1999, 40 full-time staff were employed there (up from 24 in 1994). The main tasks carried out by this staff are the organisation of campaigns and elections, the management of the national membership list and national finances and the organisation of federal conferences. Because of the party's federal structure, party headquarters is not the focal point of the party in the way in which the party headquarters of the Labour and Conservative parties are the focal points.

Each state party has its own headquarters and employs its own administrative staff. If ordinary members have a query, they would approach their regional party headquarters (in England) and their state party headquarters (in Scotland and Wales) in the first instance.

Advantages and disadvantages of the federal system
The Liberal Democrats' federal structure means that considerable autonomy is given to the party in the English regions, Scotland and Wales. This reflects the Liberal Democrat emphasis on community politics. The party argues that flexibility is needed to respond to the needs of a particular locality and this is best achieved by giving the local party power to respond to local needs as it sees fit.

But, giving such autonomy to local parties can also create difficulties. This can be demonstrated by reference to the actions of the Liberal Democrats in Tower Hamlets, East London. Tower Hamlets hit the headlines in 1993 when a British National Party candidate was elected to the local council. This shocked the major parties and highlighted the racial tension that existed in the area. Following this election, an internal Liberal Democrat inquiry revealed that the local party had issued an election leaflet in 1991 which encouraged racism. The inquiry's report suggested that the local Liberal Democrats had deliberately contributed to the growth of racist sentiments during the time when they had been the largest party on the local council. In addition to criticising the behaviour of local activists, the report blamed the federal nature of the party. Lack of central control, the report suggested, had resulted in inadequate supervision and discipline in the local party.

The federal conference

Twice a year (in March and September) representatives from every local party are elected on a system of one member, one vote to attend the federal conference (local parties with less than 30 members have to combine with neighbouring parties to obtain representation). The federal conference is the final decision-making body of the party. Like the annual Labour Party conference, the Liberal Democrat federal conference is sovereign.

The federal conference is responsible for making policy decisions at the federal level. In other words, it takes policy decisions which affect the country as a whole. For example, the federal conference would take decisions about foreign policy or about transport in Britain as a whole. It would not take decisions about transport in Scotland. That and other Scottish issues would be decided at the conferences organised by the Scottish Conference. But, since the English state party has delegated policy-making powers to the federal party, the federal conference does make policy decisions which only affect England. The federal conference is also responsible for electing members to the three federal committees (the executive, policy and conference committees).

The three federal committees

Each of the three federal committees contains, in addition to representatives elected by the federal conference, members of the parliamentary party, councillors and representatives from the Scottish and Welsh state parties. At least a third of each committee must be women and at least a third must be men.

1. The federal executive

The federal executive is chaired by the President of the party. The President is elected for a two-year term by all members of the party on a one member, one vote basis. The executive committee has 14 elected members. In addition, the Party Leader, President, three Vice Presidents, two other MPs, one peer, two councillors and one representative from each state party have the right to vote (Liberal Democrat Press Office, January 1999). The executive committee is responsible for overseeing and implementing the decisions made by the federal party. It has the right to initiate a ballot of all

members on any issue it considers important.

2. The policy committee

The policy committee contains 29 members: the Party Leader, four MPs, one peer, the President, three councillors, two representatives from the Welsh and two from the Scottish state parties and 15 people elected by federal conference (Liberal Democrat Press Office, January 1999). This committee is responsible for drawing up and developing policy proposals. Most of the policy proposals debated at conference are put forward by the policy committee.

3. The conference committee

The conference committee is responsible for organising the two annual conferences and for drawing up the agenda for the conferences. This committee contains 21 voting members: 12 people elected by the federal conference, two members elected by the federal executive, two elected by the federal policy committee; a representative from each state party, the party's Chief Whip and the Party President (Liberal Democrat Press Office, January 1999).

Policy making

It is the federal principle which determines Liberal Democrat policy making. Policy decisions which affect a particular locality are made locally whilst those affecting the country as a whole are made by the federal institutions.

In a federal United Kingdom, there would probably be a federal Parliament, a Scottish Parliament, a Welsh Parliament and regional Parliaments in England. Whilst the federal Parliament would make decisions about matters which affected the country as a whole, each of these state and regional Parliaments would be responsible for making decisions about local issues. The Liberal Democrat policy-making system reflects this division of responsibility.

The supreme policy-making body is the federal conference. If conference accepts the motions proposed by the federal policy committee, local, regional and state parties, then they become party policy. But, policy proposals concerning, for example, Scottish affairs would not be put forward to the federal conference. They would be proposed and debated at a conference organised by the Scottish state party and, if the proposals were passed, they would become party policy in Scotland.

Power of the party leadership

Although the federal conference is supposedly the sovereign body and it must give its formal approval to policy, the party leadership retains a great deal of control over the formulation of policy. Most major policy proposals are initiated by the federal policy committee which is dominated by the party leadership. This committee sets up working groups to study subjects in depth and, after consultation, submits these papers to federal conference for approval. Conference can amend these papers. But, if that happens, the policy committee must review them once more before they return to conference. Although representatives at conference are able to propose motions on policy issues for debate, the policy committee has the power to insist that a final decision is postponed. Also, the policy committee, together with the parliamentary party, is responsible for drawing up the party's election manifestos. So, again, the system ensures that the party leadership retains control of the policy-making process. In addition, the federal conference committee determines which motions are debated at conference. As with the policy committee, composition of this committee is such that the party leadership is able to keep a firm grip on its decisions.

Selecting the Liberal Democrat Leader

The Liberal Party was the first of the major parties in Britain to involve its ordinary members in the choice of the Leader. A system of weighted votes was first adopted in 1976. This early attempt to involve the broad range of party members was a response to the increasing emphasis that the Liberal Party placed on grassroots involvement at the local level. In 1981, the weighted votes system was replaced by a full one member, one vote (OMOV) system.

Unlike the Liberal Party, the SDP had a leadership selection system which placed much more power in the hands of the Leader and the parliamentary party. Although the Leader was elected by the whole membership, a challenge could be mounted only if the Leader was not also Prime Minister and if more than half the parliamentary party passed a motion calling for a contest within one month of a new parliamentary session.

The system adopted by the Liberal Democrats

The system adopted by the Liberal Democrats stipulates that a contest, using the Single Transferable Vote system (see Chapter 7, Section 4.1), must take place two years after every general election. A leadership election can also be called either when the current Leader resigns or is incapacitated or when a majority of MPs or 75 local parties demand it. Every paid-up member is entitled to vote in the election on a one member, one vote basis. Candidates for the leadership must be MPs, they must be proposed and seconded by other MPs and they must be nominated by no less than 200 members in at least 20 different local parties.

Main points - Part 4

- **The Liberal Democrats came into being in March 1988 when the Liberal Party formally merged with the SDP. The roots of the party, however, reach back way beyond 1988 - to the foundation of the Liberal Party in 1859.**
- **Since merger, the Liberal Democrats have regularly scored 20% of the vote in local elections and have also won several by-elections. Until 1997, the number of MPs remained under 25.**
- **Despite securing a slightly lower percentage of the popular vote than in 1992, the Liberal Democrats won 46 seats in 1997 - mainly because of a growth in tactical voting. Since the election, senior Liberal Democrats have worked closely with ministers.**
- **The federal structure of the Liberal Democrats is laid down in a written constitution. A federal party is a party in which the central decision-making body of the party is not all-powerful. Power is devolved to area and local parties.**

Activity 8.7 *The Liberal Democrats*

Item A *Liberal Prime Ministers and election victories 1900-45*

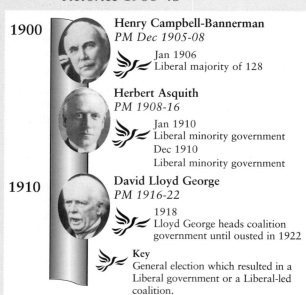

1900

Henry Campbell-Bannerman
PM Dec 1905-08

Jan 1906
Liberal majority of 128

Herbert Asquith
PM 1908-16

Jan 1910
Liberal minority government
Dec 1910
Liberal minority government

1910

David Lloyd George
PM 1916-22

1918
Lloyd George heads coalition government until ousted in 1922

Key
General election which resulted in a Liberal government or a Liberal-led coalition.

Item B *General election results 1945-97*

Election	No of candidates	MPs elected	Total votes	% of UK total
1945	306	12	2,252,430	9.0
1950	475	9	2,621,487	9.1
1951	109	6	730,546	2.6
1955	110	6	722,402	2.7
1959	216	6	1,640,760	5.9
1964	365	9	3,099,283	11.2
1966	311	12	2,327,457	8.6
1970	332	6	2,117,035	7.5
1974 (Feb)	517	14	6,059,519	19.3
1974 (Oct)	619	13	5,346,704	18.3
1979	577	11	4,313,804	13.8
1983	633	23	7,780,949	25.4
1987	633	22	7,341,633	22.5
1992	632	20	5,998,446	17.8
1997	639	46	5,242,894	16.8

Adapted from Craig 1989, the *Guardian* 11 April 1992 and Dobson 1998.

Item C *The structure and organisation of the Liberal Democrats*

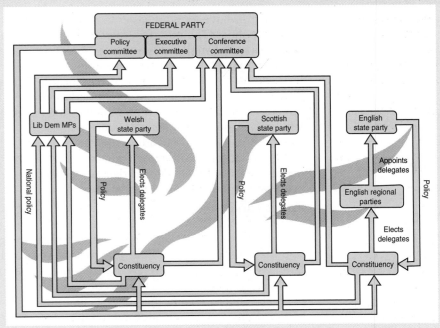

Item D *Liberal Democrat aims*

We Liberal Democrats are in politics not just to manage things better, but to make things happen and to build a prosperous, fair and open society. We believe in the market economy as the best way to deliver prosperity, but we recognise that market mechanisms on their own are not enough. We believe in a society in which every citizen shares rights and responsibilities. But, we recognise that a strong country is built from the bottom, not the top, that conformity quickly becomes the enemy of diversity and that the imposition of social blueprints leads to authoritarian, centralised government. Liberal Democrats believe that power and opportunity, like wealth, should be widely spread. Above all, Liberal Democracy is about liberty. That does not just mean freedom from oppressive government. It means providing all citizens with the opportunity to build worthwhile lives for themselves and their families and helping them to recognise their responsibilities to the wider community. Liberal Democrats believe that the role of democratic government is designed to protect and strengthen liberty and to redress the balance of power between the powerful and the weak.

Adapted from Lib Dem 1997.

Item E *Paddy Ashdown resigns*

Paddy Ashdown last night stunned Liberal Democrats when he announced that he will resign as Party Leader after the crucial local and Euro-elections in spring 1999. He resigns just as he gets closer to the reins of power than any predecessor since Lloyd George. As senior Liberal Democrat MPs warned potential successors not to start campaigning for the vacancy before the elections, Paddy Ashdown moved to quash conspiracy theories about his departure after 11 years of struggle to push third party politics towards real influence. Ashdown said that he had always wanted to go at a time when people would ask why he was going rather than why he wasn't going. He told his fellow MPs that it was a joint decision with his wife for family reasons and he insisted that the decision had been made before the 1997 general election. But, speculation immediately surfaced that Ashdown was giving up because the Blair-Ashdown 'project' for eventual Lib-Lab coalition is under terminal strain. There were also suggestions that Ashdown had failed to win his cherished referendum on proportional representation for Westminster elections. Ashdown was hoping this would be held before the next election. Liberal Democrat insiders, however, said that Ashdown's aim was to quit while the party was doing well and give his successor time to settle in.

Adapted from the *Guardian*, 21 January 1999.

Questions

1. a) What do Items A and B tell us about the changing status of the Liberal Party/Liberal Democrats in the 20th century?
   b) Would you describe the Liberal Democrats as a major or a minor party? Explain your answer.

2. Look at Item C.
   a) Where is power located within the Liberal Democrat party organisation?
   b) How does the organisation of the Liberal Democrats differ from that of (i) the Labour Party and (ii) the Conservative Party?

3. To what extent are the aims outlined in Item D reflected in the structure and organisation of the Liberal Democrats? Explain how they are connected.

4. Look at Item E.
   a) Describe how the Liberal Democrats' leadership selection process works.
   b) How do the powers of the Liberal Democrat Leader differ from the powers of the Conservative and Labour Leaders?

Part 5 The minor parties

Key issues

1. What is the significance of the minor parties?
2. What are the aims of the minor parties?
3. How much success have they had?
4. What are the main characteristics of the minor parties?

5.1 The significance of the minor parties

Why are minor parties important?

Throughout the 20th century, new parties have been set up in the hope that they would attract sufficient support to break the mould of British politics. But, with the exception of the Labour Party which was itself a minor party in the early years of the 20th century, no party has managed to achieve nationwide success. Since 1918, British politics has been dominated by the three main parties and there is little sign that this will change, certainly whilst the current electoral system survives.

But, although the three main parties dominate the political arena, that does not mean that the minor parties do not have any significance. In Wales and Scotland, for example, the nationalist parties are an important force and they regularly win seats in Parliament. Despite the small number of MPs from these parties, they can still play a crucial role in certain circumstances. Between 1993 and 1997, for example, the Major government's overall majority was eroded through deaths, by-election losses and suspensions. As a result, the government had to rely on the support of the ten Ulster Unionist MPs. This made it difficult for the government to find a peace settlement in Northern Ireland acceptable to the republicans. Similarly, in the 1974 general election, Labour won an overall majority of three whilst 11 Scottish National Party (SNP) MPs and 3 Plaid Cymru (Welsh nationalist) MPs were elected. Once the Labour government's overall majority of three disappeared as a result of by-election losses, it was forced to do a deal with the nationalist parties. In return for their support in Parliament, the government promised to hold referendums on devolution in Scotland and Wales (see Chapter 7, Section 3.7). This shows that, even within the existing electoral system, it is possible for minor parties to exert influence and to play an important political role. Besides, the setting up of the Scottish Parliament, Welsh Assembly and Northern Ireland Assembly has provided minor parties with new opportunities.

Minor parties and local politics

Whilst parliamentary success is unusual for the minor parties, they have found it easier to make an impact in local politics. The number of Green councillors has grown since the mid-1980s and even the Monster Raving Loony Party has won seats on local councils. It should be noted that success even at local level has been far harder to achieve for minor parties whose politics is located on the extreme right or the extreme left than it has been for the nationalist parties or Greens. The nationalists and Greens are generally perceived as being within the mainstream whilst the parties on the extreme left and right are generally perceived as being a threat to the system.

Parties outside the mainstream

On the few occasions when groups on the extreme right or left have achieved electoral success (winning a substantial percentage of the vote may be regarded as an electoral success, even if the candidate is not elected), this has been greeted by considerable popular concern. Again, this suggests that minor parties do have a significance even if they are unable to win seats in elections. Their role is, perhaps, as barometers of public opinion. When people are generally content with the existing party system the minor parties do badly, whilst a significant vote for a minor party can suggest that people are discontented with the existing party system. The ebb and flow of support for minor parties provides a judgement on the party system and provides a legitimate avenue for the expression of views beyond the mainstream.

5.2 Key minor parties

The Scottish National Party (SNP)

The SNP was founded in 1934 when two small nationalist parties merged. Its aim is an independent Scotland. At present, there are two distinct viewpoints within the SNP. Whilst the right wing (which has generally maintained control of the party) stresses traditional values and nostalgic nationalism, the left wing has pressed the case for a socialist Scotland as an independent country within the EU (the party's official policy at the time of the 1997 general election). Following the 1997 general election, the party temporarily suspended its demand for an independent Scotland and supported the Yes-Yes campaign (which aimed for a Scottish Parliament with tax-varying powers) in the referendum which was held in September 1997. It did this on the grounds that a devolved Parliament would be the first step on the road to independence (see Chapter 4, Sections 3.2 and 3.3 for further information on devolution).

The SNP's electoral record

The SNP won its first seat in Parliament in a by-election in Motherwell in April 1945 but lost the seat in the following general election. It was not until a by-election held in 1967 that the SNP won another seat. But, again, it lost the seat in the next general election in 1970. The 1970 general election was, however, the first general election in which the SNP managed to win a seat. This was a turning point in the party's fortunes. It has won seats in every general election since then.

The SNP's best general result came in October 1974 when it won 30.4% of the vote in Scotland and 11 seats. Although it was unable to sustain this level of support (especially in the years following the referendum in 1979), the SNP has established itself as the third party in Scotland. Voters who are disaffected with the main parties tend to register their protest with the SNP. The SNP, therefore, plays a role similar to that played by the Liberal Democrats in England. This was graphically illustrated in the by-election in the constituency of Monklands East which was held on 30 June 1994 following the death of Labour's Leader, John Smith. Whilst Labour won a majority of 15,712 in the 1992 general election, this majority was cut to just 1,640 in the by-election. The SNP vote went up from 6,554 to 15,320, a gain of 27%. This is just the sort of by-election result achieved by the Liberal Democrats in England.

In the 1997 general election, the SNP vote grew by 0.6% compared to 1992 and the party won six seats (compared to three in 1992). Once the Scottish people had voted Yes-Yes in the referendum held in September 1997, Alex Salmond, Leader of the SNP, announced that, if the SNP won an overall majority in the new Parliament, this would be interpreted as a mandate to press ahead with the necessary steps that would lead to independence.

Plaid Cymru

Plaid Cymru was founded in 1925. Its aim is an independent Wales. Following the 1997 general election, Plaid Cymru supported the Yes campaign in the referendum held on whether to set up a devolved Welsh Assembly. Like the SNP, it saw a devolved assembly as the first step towards independence. But, Plaid Cymru has always laid more stress on cultural and linguistic identity than the SNP (partly because there are many more Welsh speakers than Gaelic speakers). Plaid Cymru aims for a completely bilingual Wales and it works hard at increasing the use of Welsh in schools, broadcasting and in public administration. The problem that Plaid Cymru faces with insisting on bilingualism is that it does tend to alienate people living in Wales who do not speak Welsh. Most party members are Welsh speaking and most of the party's support comes from areas where Welsh is the first language. Between 1992 and 1997, Plaid Cymru had close links with the Green Party. In 1992, Cynog Dafis was elected as an MP on a joint Plaid Cymru/Green ticket and the Green Party agreed not to put up candidates against Plaid Cymru candidates. During the period 1992-97, however, the

Green Party split over this policy and, in 1997, some Green candidates did stand against Plaid Cymru candidates. Despite this, Plaid Cymru puts the environment high up on its political agenda.

Plaid Cymru's electoral record

Plaid Cymru won its first seat in a by-election in 1966. It lost this seat in the subsequent general election. Its best performance in terms of size of vote then came in the 1970 general election when it won 11.5% of the vote in Wales (175,016 votes). But, it did not win any seats in that election. Like the SNP, Plaid Cymru did well in October 1974. It won 10.8% of the vote and three seats. But, the disappointing referendum result in 1979 led to a decline in votes which continued until the 1992 general election when its share of the vote rose from 7.3% in 1987 to 11.1% and the number of seats captured rose from two to four. In 1997, Plaid Cymru was the second party in terms of seats captured (it retained its four seats). Its share of the vote rose by 1% compared to that in 1992.

The Green Party

The Green Party emerged from the protest movements of the 1960s and the growing environmental concerns of the 1970s and 1980s. The party's origins can be traced back to 1973 when an environmental pressure group was formed, named 'People'. As this group began to explore the connections between environmental concerns and began to formulate policies to deal with them, it transformed itself into the Ecology Party. It changed its name to the Green Party in 1985. The Green Party is committed to the broad aims of other European Green parties, namely the decentralisation of political power and the placing of environmental issues at the top of the political agenda.

Although the Greens have not enjoyed any electoral success in parliamentary elections, they have enjoyed some success in local elections. In 1998, the Green Party had 27 councillors in councils above the parish level and over 90 parish councillors (or their equivalent in Scotland and Wales). This was the party's highest number of councillors ever (Green Party Information Office, January 1999). The party's greatest electoral success, however, came in 1989 when it won 15% of the vote in the European election. Although it did not win any seats, Greens polled more of the vote nationally than the Liberal Democrats. Since 1989, support for the Greens in national elections has dropped rapidly, not least because of the internal divisions which have dogged the party.

Fascist groups

Fascist politics emerged in Britain, as in most other West European countries, in the years between the two world wars. After sitting as a Conservative MP between 1918 and 1922 and as a Labour MP between 1926 and 1931, Oswald Mosley opted out of mainstream politics and set up the British Union of

Fascists (BUF) in 1932. At its peak in 1934, the BUF had around 35,000 members. It contested elections, but never won a seat. Like other Fascist groups, the BUF was racist, militaristic and violently nationalistic. Modern Fascist groups trace their ancestry back to Mosely's group through a complex web of splits and schisms.

The National Front

Perhaps the most influential post-war Fascist group was the National Front (NF), founded in 1967. In the mid-1970s, the NF had a membership of around 20,000. Although the NF contested elections, it also maintained links with neo-Nazi paramilitary groups both at home and abroad. The NF never won a seat. But, it did poll well in some constituencies. In the London boroughs of Hackney, Newham and Tower Hamlets, for example, it gained 10% of the vote in 1977. Its support dwindled in the late 1970s and had fallen to around 6,000 by 1980. It has been argued that support for the NF fell because Margaret Thatcher's government promoted policies which attracted the support of many who had shown an interest in the far right (Ball 1987).

In the 1980s, the NF split and from this split the British National Party (BNP) emerged. The BNP hit the headlines in September 1993 when a BNP candidate won a local seat in a ward by-election in Tower Hamlets, East London. Although this seat was subsequently won back by Labour in the local elections of May 1994, the support given to the BNP in this part of London was a source of great concern to many people.

Marxist groups

Like the Fascist groups, Marxist groups have, on the whole, been marginal in British politics, though there have been periods when their influence has appeared to be growing. In the 1945 general election, for example, the Communist Party of Great Britain (CPGB), founded in 1920, won two seats and polled over 100,000 votes. But, since 1950, no Communist MP has been elected and, in 1964, the CPGB won just 0.8% of the vote in the constituencies it contested. Although the CPGB remained an important lobbying group (especially within the trade union movement), it split in the 1980s between those who followed the line laid down by the communist government in the USSR and the 'Eurocommunists' (who aimed to promote a new, independent and progressive form of Marxism). Following the collapse of communism in Eastern Europe the CPGB collapsed and dispersed.

The Trotskyist left

In the 1980s, the Trotskyist left received more publicity than the CPGB. Perhaps, the best known Trotskyist group is Militant Tendency. The activities of Militant Tendency were the subject of considerable media interest in the mid-1980s because it was revealed that members of Militant had joined the Labour Party in the hope of influencing Labour Party policy. This led Neil Kinnock to conduct a purge of Militant members from the Labour Party with the result that there was a wave of expulsions, including several MPs.

Other Trotskyist groups include the Socialist Workers Party (SWP) which was prominent in the anti-Nazi League of the 1970s (set up to combat the NF). The SWP rejects the parliamentary system, though it does sometimes put up candidates for election. Members of the SWP are expert at ensuring that their flags and posters are prominent at any demonstration or protest organised for a left-wing cause.

Other minor parties

The above survey of minor parties is by no means exhaustive. It does not include, for example, the Monster Raving Loony Party (MRLP) or the Natural Law Party, both of which put up candidates around the country in national and local elections. Those standing for the MRLP are literally joke candidates. Like those who stand for the Natural Law Party, they use elections to promote their ideas rather than to mount a serious challenge to the main parties. The Natural Law Party is a semi-religious party which supports a variety of transcendental policies to right the wrongs of the world.

According to Butler and Kavanagh (1997), a record number of political parties put up candidates in the 1997 general election. Two minor parties gained significant media coverage because of their Eurosceptical stance (shared by many national newspapers). These were the UK Independence Party and the Referendum Party.

The UK Independence Party

The UK Independence Party (UKIP) was set up in 1993. Its main aim is to campaign for the withdrawal of the UK from the EU, though it has formulated a complete political programme. It put up 24 candidates in the 1994 Euro-election, winning an average of 3.3% of the vote. Candidates from the party stood in all by-elections held between 1994 and 1997. None won more than 2.9% of the vote. Although, in 1996, the party's Leader, Alan Sked, tried to make an electoral pact with the Referendum Party, this did not materialise and Referendum Party candidates stood against UKIP candidates in 165 constituencies. In the 1997 general election, the party put up a total of 194 candidates and won an average of 1.2% of the vote. The party lacked the funds and high media profile of the Referendum Party and was outperformed by it. In August 1997, Alan Sked resigned as Leader, shortly after the party had polled just 39 votes in the Uxbridge by-election.

The Referendum Party

The Referendum Party was set up by multi-millionaire James Goldsmith in November 1995. Goldsmith said that he was prepared to spend up to £20 million backing it. The party's aim was to put up candidates in every constituency except those where the sitting MP had stated in public that they supported holding a referendum on Britain's future in the EU. The party also promised to disband once such a referendum had been held. A great deal of money was spent on advertisements (£7.2 million, compared to £13.2 million spent by the Conservatives and £7.4 million spent by Labour - Butler & Kavanagh 1997, p.242) and the party gained a number of high-profile supporters. For example, former Conservative MP, George Gardiner (who had been deselected for attacking John Major's policy towards the EU) joined the party. By the time of the 1997 general election, the Referendum Party claimed to have 230,000 supporters. The party had a headquarters in London and ten regional offices. It put up 547 candidates in the 1997 general election - the first time a fourth party had fought that many seats. Before the election, there was speculation that the Referendum Party would make serious inroads into the Conservative vote, but this did not happen:

> 'The Referendum Party had only a limited effect on the Conservatives' fortunes. Where a Referendum Party candidate stood and secured an average vote of around 3%, approximately two-thirds of that vote appears to have come from the Conservatives. However, where the Referendum Party vote was above average, the Liberal Democrats appear to have been the main losers...the net effect of the Referendum Party's and UK Independence Party's intervention is probably to cost the Conservatives only three seats.' (Butler & Kavanagh 1997, p.251)

It should be noted, however, that, according to Curtice and Steed (1997), the Referendum Party's average of 3.1% of the vote in the constituencies where it stood was the strongest performance ever by a British minor party (other than the nationalist parties or parties in Northern Ireland).

The Referendum Movement

Following the 1997 general election, the decision was made that the Referendum Party would no longer fight elections. Instead, it would act as a cross-party pressure group under a new name - the Referendum Movement. In July 1997, James Goldsmith died of cancer and former Conservative Party Treasurer, Lord MacAlpine, became Leader of the movement. In December 1997, the campaign for a referendum was relaunched by Goldsmith's widow, Annabel. The following September, the Eurosceptic multi-millionaire, Paul Sykes, joined forces with the Referendum Movement and pledged to spend up to £20 million campaigning against a single European currency.

Political parties in Northern Ireland

Between 1972 when direct rule from Britain was imposed on Northern Ireland and 1992, none of the three main political parties fielded any candidates in Northern Ireland. In the general elections of 1992 and 1997, however, the Conservative Party did put up candidates in Northern Ireland (though none was elected). Since 1972, therefore, the people of Northern Ireland have elected MPs from what, in terms of the UK as a whole, are minor parties. The results of the 1997 general election are shown in Box 8.6.

Box 8.6 The 1997 general election in Northern Ireland

Party	Seats	% vote	Seats in 1992
Ulster Unionist Party	10	32.7	9
SDLP[1]	3	24.1	4
Sinn Fein	2	16.1	0
DUP[2]	2	13.6	3
UKUP[3]	1	1.6	0

1. SDLP stands for the Social Democratic and Labour Party.
2. DUP stands for the Democratic Unionist Party.
3. UKUP stands for United Kingdom Unionist Party.
In addition, the Progressive Unionist Party (PUP), the Alliance Party, the Workers Party and the Women's Coalition put up candidates, but none was elected.

Unlike in the rest of the UK, most of the political parties in Northern Ireland are clearly divided between those supported by the Protestant community and those supported by Catholics.

The Unionists

The two main Protestant parties in Northern Ireland are the Ulster Unionist Party (UUP) and the Democratic Unionist Party (DUP). Traditionally, both opposed power-sharing with the Catholic community, though the UUP signed up to the Good Friday Agreement (see Chapter 4, Section 3.4). The UUP was the party which governed Northern Ireland from the time when it was set up as a province in 1922 until direct rule was imposed in 1972. Before 1972, the UUP was closely associated with the Conservative Party. But, it broke with them over direct rule. Despite this, UUP MPs tend to vote with the Conservatives on most issues in Parliament. The same is true of the Democratic Unionist Party (DUP). The DUP is an offshoot of the UUP, founded in 1971 by Ian Paisley. The DUP takes a more extreme position than the UUP on Northern Irish affairs. It refuses any concessions to the Catholic population of Northern Ireland and refused to sign up to the Good Friday Agreement.

The UUP and DUP played an important part in keeping John Major's government in power in the period 1992-97. By voting with the government, the UUP and DUP (with 12 MPs in all) ensured that the government maintained a majority. Since the Major government relied on Unionist votes, it found it difficult to make progress towards a peace settlement after the IRA's first ceasefire was announced in 1994.

Nationalist and republican parties

The main nationalist party in Northern Ireland is the Social Democratic and Labour Party (SDLP), founded in 1970. Although the SDLP was not set up to represent just Catholics, the vast majority of its support comes from the Catholic community. The SDLP was one of the main architects of the Good Friday Agreement. In the 1980s, the SDLP's grip on the Catholic vote was challenged by Sinn Fein, the republican party whose military wing is the IRA. Before the early 1980s, Sinn Fein boycotted elections, but the popular support for the hunger strikers encouraged the party to put up candidates for election. In the 1983 general election, Gerry Adams won Belfast West for Sinn Fein and he held the seat until 1992. In 1997, Adams was re-elected, together with Martin McGuinness, Sinn Fein's Chief Negotiator. Following the election, Adams and McGuinness were refused access to Parliament because they refused to take the Oath of Loyalty (see Activity 14.2, Item B). Like the SDLP, Sinn Fein signed up to the Good Friday Agreement.

The Alliance Party

Whilst almost all political parties in Northern Ireland appeal to either Protestants or Catholics, the Alliance Party, founded in 1970, is an exception. This party manages to gain around 10% of the vote (it won 8% of the vote in 1997) mainly from middle-class people in both communities. The party supports the Good Friday Agreement.

Main points - Part 5

- Throughout the 20th century, new parties have been set up in the hope that they would attract sufficient support to break the mould of British politics. But, apart from the Labour Party, no party has managed to achieve nationwide success.
- Minor parties do have some significance - especially if the government only has a small overall majority in Parliament (as between 1992 and 1997).
- The nationalist parties - the SNP and Plaid Cymru - both made gains in 1997. The SNP vote grew by 0.6% compared to 1992 and the party won six seats (compared to three in 1992). Plaid Cymru was the second party in Wales in terms of seats captured (it retained its four seats). Its share of the vote rose by 1% compared to that in 1992.
- Other minor parties failed to make an impact in the 1997 general election (except in Northern Ireland where five parties won seats).

Activity 8.8 *Minor parties*

Item A *General election result 1997 - the minor parties*

Party	Total votes	Candidates	MPs	Party	Total votes	Candidates	MPs
SNP	630,263	72	6	Socialist Labour Party	52,110	64	0
Plaid Cymru	152,307	40	4	British National Party	35,833	57	0
Independent candidate*	29,354	1	1	Liberal Party	44,989	54	0
Referendum Party	811,827	547	0	Pro-life Alliance	18,545	53	0
UK Independence Party	106,028	194	0	Scottish Socialist Alliance	9,740	16	0
Natural Law Party	28,073	178	0	Others	136,804	309	0
Green Party	63,452	94	0				

* Martin Bell stood as an independent candidate in Tatton, the seat where the disgraced former minister, Neil Hamilton, was standing. The Labour Party and Liberal Democrats did not put up candidates in the hope that Bell would win. Bell did win even though this was the Conservatives' fifth safest seat.

Adapted from Curtice 1997.

Item B *The SNP and Plaid Cymru in general elections 1945-97*

(i) The SNP's electoral record

Election	Candidates	MPs	Total votes	% *
1945	8	0	30,595	1.2
1950	3	0	9,708	0.4
1951	2	0	7,299	0.3
1955	2	0	12,112	0.5
1959	5	0	21,738	0.8
1964	15	0	64,044	2.4
1966	23	0	128,474	5.0
1970	65	1	306,802	11.4
1974 (Feb)	70	7	633,180	21.9
1974 (Oct)	71	11	839,617	30.4
1979	71	2	504,259	17.3
1983	72	2	331,975	11.8
1987	71	3	416,473	14.0
1992	72	3	629,564	21.5
1997	72	6	630,263	22.1

* This column shows the number of votes won by the SNP as a percentage of the total votes cast in Scotland.

(ii) Plaid Cymru's electoral record

Election	Candidates	MPs	Total votes	%*
1945	7	0	16,017	1.2
1950	7	0	17,580	1.2
1951	4	0	10,920	0.7
1955	11	0	45,119	3.1
1959	20	0	77,571	5.2
1964	23	0	69,507	4.8
1966	20	0	61,071	4.3
1970	36	0	175,016	11.5
1974 (Feb)	36	2	171,374	10.7
1974 (Oct)	36	3	166,321	10.8
1979	36	2	132,544	8.1
1983	38	2	125,309	7.8
1987	38	3	123,599	7.3
1992	38	4	156,796	8.9
1997	40	4	152,307	9.9

* This column shows the number of votes won by Plaid Cymru as a percentage of the total votes cast in Wales.

Item C *The minor parties*

According to the journalist Matthew Parris, the general election in 1997 produced a bumper harvest of joke candidates, crazy candidates and serious fringe candidates. In 1997, 3,717 people risked their £500 deposit, an average of five per constituency and 769 more than in 1992. All of the fringe candidates lost their deposits. Most expected to do so. The result, however, was that voters had a choice of such causes as the Independently Beautiful Party, the Happiness Stan's Freedom to Party Party and the Black Haired Medium Build Caucasian Male Party. In the 1994 Euro-election, Richard Huggett won some 10,000 votes standing as a 'Literal Democrat' candidate. In 1997, he chose to stand as Liberal Democrat - Top Choice candidate in Winchester and gained 640 votes. The genuine Liberal Democrats won the seat by just two votes. Not every fringe candidate represented a flight of fancy, of eccentricity, of deception or of idealism on the candidate's part. It is worth remembering that for ten counter-signatories and a deposit of £500 (lost unless the votes gained exceed 5% of the total cast), a candidate gains access to a freepost facility for contacting every voter and a good deal of free publicity in the local media. This might explain the birth and post-election disbandment of the Mongolian Barbecue Great Place to Party Party. In addition, the election results do not necessarily tell us about the seriousness of the party concerned. The Socialist Labour Party (Arthur Scargill's challenge to New Labour) scored pitifully. Scargill himself gained just 1,951 votes. Similarly, there was serious intent behind Dickon Tolson's candidature. His party name was 'None of the Above' and his name came last on the ballot paper. Tolson's election address read: 'Being frustrated and concerned at the apathy and lack of moral cohesion which makes up the current political climate, I have decided to put my life savings into standing for election.' Tolson won 368 votes.

Adapted from Parris 1997.

Item D *The Green Party*

With proportional representation (PR) on the horizon, the media will soon have to take the Green Party seriously. The Greens have got what it takes to become a 5-10% national party under PR - activists, organisation (eg a nationwide membership register, an elected executive, delegate conferences and elaborate policy-making procedures), attractive branding and a big idea able to generate mass passion. But, it is early days. Barely 200 Greens (out of a membership of c.4,000) turned up to the spring 1998 conference in Scarborough. They don't practice the art of spin doctoring yet (a spokesman's comment on the party's education policy was: 'Yeah, I know it's weak and a bit of a mess'). Their manifesto includes commitments to the abolition of angling, zoos, public examinations and NATO, a reduction in the top driving speed to 55 mph, the phasing out of urban parking, higher taxes for the better-off and a strategy of non-violent social defence to tackle Saddam Hussein. This does not matter yet. In the next few years, the Greens want a foot in the electoral door opened by PR and, in the process, they aim to exploit the growing hostility to Blairism among parts of the Labour left and Liberal Democrats. If they achieve these goals, bigger prizes may follow. The first test will be the Euro-elections of 1999. Even under PR, the Greens will need at least 8% of the vote in a region to win seats. In 1994, the best Green result was 6.5%. So, with a fair wind, they could pick up a seat or two. Any MEPs elected will be seasoned campaigners - like the top candidate in the Green list for the South East, Mike Woodin, an Oxford University Psychology lecturer who is one of five Green councillors in Oxford and the party's newly elected Leader. In the wake of their surprise 1989 Euro-election triumph, membership shot up from 4,000 to 18,000. They could easily repeat the trick if the party gains momentum.

Adapted from the *Observer*, 22 February 1998.

Item E *The Referendum Party*

According to his widow, the challenge James Goldsmith set himself was to break the mould of British politics. The Referendum Party aimed to cross all parties which explains its campaign theme - 'It doesn't matter which of the traditional parties you vote for because Westminster has already surrendered its powers to Brussels'. Goldsmith's great achievement, she claims, was to force a huge debate. As a result of his intervention in British politics, the main parties were pushed into a commitment to a referendum on the single currency - a commitment which protected Britain, stopping it from joining the single currency in the first wave. Shortly before his death, Goldsmith said that he wanted the Referendum Party to become a movement, a genuine people's campaign open to the supporters of all political parties or none, to the young and the old. As a movement (and not a party), Annabel Goldsmith argues, the Referendum Movement does not threaten or challenge traditional party allegiances. On the contrary, supporters are urged to stay and fight within their parties. With no elections and, therefore, no divided loyalties, the Referendum Movement will be able to concentrate its energies on winning the single currency referendum. It will then be able to fight for a full referendum on Britain's relationship with Europe.

The poster (right) was published by the Referendum Party during the 1997 general election campaign. It shows Tony Blair and John Major on the lap of the German Chancellor, Helmut Kohl. The Conservatives had produced a poster showing just Tony Blair on Kohl's knee.

The Iron Men of Europe..?

"UNDER MY LEADERSHIP I WILL NEVER ALLOW THIS COUNTRY TO BE ISOLATED OR LEFT BEHIND IN EUROPE."

"IN ABOUT THE NEXT TWO YEARS, WE WILL MAKE THE PROCESS OF EUROPEAN INTEGRATION IRREVERSIBLE."

"THE FUTURE FOR THE UK LIES WITHIN THE EUROPEAN UNION AND NOT BEYOND IT."

Men of unshakeable and deep rooted convictions? As the British people wake up, we witness an almost comical U-turn from our politicians.

What's more, don't be fooled by their promises of a 'referendum.' It's a phoney. It deals only with the side issue of a single currency - not whether Britain should remain a free nation or become a province of Europe.

The people of Britain must have a full referendum on Europe that is legally binding on a future government. Vote Referendum Party.

REFERENDUM PARTY
Stop the betrayal - Let the people decide

Adapted from the *Times*, 14 December 1997.

Questions

1. 'Disappointing'. To what extent is that a reasonable description of the impact made by the minor parties in the 1997 general election? Use Items A-E in your answer.
2. a) 'The minor parties face problems which the major parties do not have to face.' Explain this statement using Items B-E.
   b) Why do you think people vote for the minor parties?
3. a) Judging from Items C-E what role is played by minor parties?
   b) Would you agree that the growth of minor parties is healthy for democracy? Explain your answer.
4. 'The Liberal Democrats should be added to the list of minor parties.' Give arguments for and against this view.

Part 6 The party system

Key issues

1. How are party systems classified?
2. What are the advantages and disadvantages of the two-party system?
3. Does Britain have a two-party system?
4. Has the party system in Britain changed since 1945?

6.1 The nature of party systems

Classifying party systems

Most political scientists (see, for example, Simpson 1998) would accept that party systems can be divided into four categories: the single-party system; the dominant-party system; the two-party system; and, the multi-party system.

1. The single-party system

In a single-party system only one party puts up candidates for election. Other parties are banned. The single-party system is usually, therefore, undemocratic and authoritarian. Nazi Germany and the Soviet Union under Communism are two examples of the single-party system.

2. The dominant-party system

The dominant-party system is a system where many parties may exist and fight elections, but only one party tends to win power - either on its own or as the dominant member of a coalition. Political scientists have often cited Japan as the classic example of the dominant party system. Japan's Liberal Democratic Party (LDP) remained in government from its foundation in 1955 until August 1993.

3. The two-party system

In a two-party system, two parties compete for power on an equal or near equal basis. Other parties may stand against the two dominant parties, but in a two-party system these other parties win few seats and exercise little power. It has often been argued that Britain has a two-party system. But, some political scientists deny that this is the case.

4. The multi-party system

A multi-party system is one in which more than two parties compete on an equal or near equal basis. In such a system, power may alternate between the various parties or it may be shared in coalitions. Political scientists often used to cite Italy as the classic example of the multi-party system because proportional representation in Italy continually produced multi-party coalition governments. In April 1993, however, a large majority of Italians voted to change their electoral system to a plurality ('first-past-the-post') system.

6.2 Britain as a two-party system

McKenzie's thesis

The idea that Britain has a two-party system was given great currency by Robert McKenzie's 1955 study of British political parties (McKenzie 1955). In this study, McKenzie spent 595 out of the 597 pages discussing the Conservative and Labour parties. By dismissing the Liberal Party and the minor parties in two pages, McKenzie suggested that they were all but irrelevant to the British party system. Since 1955, political scientists have periodically returned to McKenzie's ideas and tested them in light of what happened later (see, for example, Garner & Kelly 1998).

In the two-party system described by McKenzie and his followers, the two main parties compete in elections for an absolute majority of seats. Whilst one party forms the government, the role of the other is to form an opposition which exposes government policy to scrutiny and develops its own policies. The opposition party works on the assumption that it will take over the reins of government at the next election and, more often than not, that is what happens.

The two-party system and democracy

According to this model, the two-party system is integral to the success of Britain as a democracy. It is the two-party system which ensures that the democratic process works smoothly. It does this in three ways. First, by choosing one party to govern and then another, the electorate exercises choice - a vital element of democracy. Second, since the vast majority of the electorate votes for the two main parties and it is in the interest of neither of the main parties to upset a system which favours them, the system ensures that legitimacy is maintained and political conflict is kept within limits (see Chapter

18, Section 1.1 for a definition of legitimacy). And third, the need to win an overall majority ensures that both parties shape their policies to appeal to the needs of the majority.

Another way of looking at this is to consider what would happen if the system broke down. Suppose that a single party found itself being elected time after time. Then, the ruling party would have few checks on its power since a government with an overall majority can ensure that legislation is passed even if the opposition parties are strongly opposed to it. The party in opposition would have no opportunity to put its programme into operation or to change the direction in which the government was going. In short, there would be a good case for arguing that the country's democratic process was in danger of decay.

Advantages of the two-party system

A number of other advantages of a two-party system have been isolated (see, for example, Simpson 1998, p.77). First, the two-party system presents voters with a clear choice between two rivals. Two different programmes are presented during the election campaign and it is up to the voters to choose between them. Second, the two-party system produces stable and strong government. Since the party in government normally has an overall majority in Parliament, it is able to implement the pledges made during the election campaign and the electorate can check the actions of the government against its election pledges. This may not be possible in a system which allows a coalition government to be formed after an election. Third, the seating arrangements in the House of Commons and the debates for and against a motion encourage a two-party system. British politics has an adversarial nature (the opposition is expected to criticise and make arguments against the government and vice versa). This is facilitated by the two-party system. Fourth, if the government fails or loses its way, there is always a ready-made government waiting in the wings. And fifth, supporters of the two-party system argue that the system has been proven to work and, therefore, it should not be changed.

Disadvantages of the two-party system

Critics of the two-party system have argued that it suffers from a number of disadvantages (see, for example, Ball 1987). First, critics question whether adversarial politics are constructive and desirable. In a two-party system, it is the job of the opposition party to criticise the government on all counts. But, this results in an unnecessary and harmful exaggeration of the differences between the two parties. The opposition opposes virtually all government policies, regardless of their merits. That makes it difficult for the public to judge whether policies are being opposed because they are genuinely harmful or simply because that is what politicians do. In addition, the adversarial nature of politics leads to a tendency for extremists to gain control of the two main parties. The system encourages polarisation rather than consensus. Second, the two main parties are not really representative of the majority of the electorate (most governments this century have won less than 50% of the votes) and, therefore, the party in power does not really have a mandate to govern. Third, a two-party system is wasteful because it produces huge swings in government policy. Since the two parties alternate in power and since they are diametrically opposed on many issues, there is a tendency for a new government to repeal many of the decisions made by the previous government. And fourth, the two-party system undermines the importance of the House of Commons. The government can rely on its overall majority to pass legislation, regardless of criticisms made by the opposition. Debates in the Commons rarely change anything.

Does Britain have a two-party system?
Having surveyed the historical development of British political parties between 1689 and 1989, Stephen Ingle concludes:

'Our historical survey indicates that the British political system has been dominated on and off, over the past 300 years, by two parties, but it also shows the nature of this domination and of the parties themselves to have been subject to constant and considerable change. The pattern of party politics, moreover, has changed just as dramatically, with long spells of dominance by one party and with parties constantly breaking up and regrouping.' (Ingle 1992, p.3)

This passage shows how important perspective is in considering whether or not Britain has a two-party system. If someone is living through a period in which two parties have been alternating in power for the previous 30 years, then it appears that Britain has a two-party system. On the other hand, if someone is living through a long period of government by a single party, it appears that a dominant-party system has replaced the old two-party system. Similarly, if someone chooses to examine the party system in Britain between 1945 and 1979, that will probably lead them to different conclusions from someone who looks at trends over the last 150 years.

Is a two-party system the norm?
At the time when McKenzie was writing (1955), it did indeed seem that a two-party system had established itself after the Second World War. Labour governed from 1945 to 1951 and then the Conservatives took over. And, for a while after 1955, it seemed that McKenzie's analysis was faultless. Between 1945 and 1979 - a period of 34 years - both Labour and the Conservatives held power for exactly the same number of years.

But, even this period of seeming two-party rule is open to reinterpretation. Between 1951 and 1964, Labour lost three general elections in a row. For those who, by 1964, had lived through 13 years of Conservative rule, it probably did not seem much like a two-party system. And, if a wider perspective is taken, the idea that the two-party system is the norm loses some of its credence. According to Heywood (who was writing before Labour's general election victory in 1997):

'Taking a longer perspective, it could be argued that Britain has had a dominant-party system through much of the 20th century and certainly since the old Liberal-Conservative two-party system collapsed after the First World War. The Conservatives have been in government, either alone or as the dominant member of a coalition, for 51 of the last 70 years. Two-party politics undoubtedly took place during this period but was largely confined to the 1964-79 period when Labour won four out of five general elections. The important point is that Labour has only twice, in 1945 and 1966, recorded decisive election victories and at no time has the party managed to serve two consecutive full terms in office.' (Heywood 1993, pp.86-87).

If this is the case, then the four Conservative election victories between 1979 and 1992 merely confirmed a trend (that the Conservative Party is the single dominant party) rather than indicating a turning point (from two-party to dominant-party system).

Is Britain becoming a multi-party system?
A further point needs to be examined - namely that Britain is or is becoming a multi-party system. Since the early 1970s, the Liberals (now the Liberal Democrats) have won a considerable number of votes, if only a small number of seats. Between 1945 and 1974, the combined share of the vote for the two main parties never fell below 80%. But, between 1970 and 1997, the two main parties' share of the vote declined markedly. In 1983, the Alliance won 25.4% of the vote, the biggest proportion of the vote won by a third party since 1923 (when the Liberals won 29.7% of the vote). Although the SDP failed to 'break the mould' of British politics by forming a government, the Liberal Democrats have become an important force in British politics and, in 1997, picked up the largest number of seats won by a third party since 1929. So, how do they fit in the British party system?

One way of answering this question is to consider how representative the British party system is (or is not). It is significant to note that only in the elections of 1931 and 1935 have the parties which took over the reins of government scored more than 50% of the vote. And, in both 1931 and 1935, a National Government (a coalition government formed in response to a national emergency) was elected rather than a single party. If Britain had a different electoral system which allowed the size of a party's vote to be reflected in the number of seats it won, then the Liberal Democrats would almost certainly have become partners in a governing coalition following the 1992 general election (the Conservatives won 41.8% of the UK vote, Labour won 34.4% and the Liberal Democrats won 17.8%) . Considerations such as these led Dearlove & Saunders to suggest:

'Britain can be characterised as a two-party system (in the Commons); as a multi-party system (in the country); and as a dominant-party system (in the corridors of power) because the electoral system and multi-party politics have together enabled the Conservatives to monopolise the control of the state for more than a decade in a way that has mocked the close competition in the country at large.' (Dearlove & Saunders 1991, p.55)

The impact of the 1997 general election result

The 1997 general election returned power to the Labour Party for the first time in 18 years. The fact that Labour won a substantial overall majority undermined the arguments of those who had maintained that Britain had been transformed into a dominant-party system. The Labour victory suggested that the two-party model may be appropriate after all.

The future shape of the party system in Britain will be determined by two key developments. First, since the election of a Labour government in 1997, electoral reform has risen up the political agenda. The adoption of proportional systems for elections to the new regional assemblies may produce enthusiasm for change. If the electoral system was changed, this would almost certainly change the party system. And second, the way in which the major parties respond to long-term social and economic changes will affect their electoral prospects.

Main points - Part 6

- Most political scientists accept that party systems can be divided into four categories: (1) the single-party system; (2) the dominant-party system; (3) the two-party system; and (4) the multi-party system.
- In a two-party system, two main parties are likely to win a majority of seats. Whilst one party forms the government, the other scrutinises and criticises government policy and develops its own policies, working on the assumption that it will take over the reins of government at the next election.
- There is a debate about whether Britain has a two-party system. Supporters argue that power has been shared by the Conservatives and Labour since 1945. Some opponents argue that the Conservative Party has been the dominant party throughout the 20th century. Others argue that a multi-party system has developed since 1970.
- Before 1997, many commentators argued that a dominant-party system was developing (because the Conservatives won four general elections in a row). The Labour victory in 1997 suggests that the two-party model may be appropriate after all.

Activity 8.9 *The party system*

Item A *General election results 1945-97*

General Election	Lab	Con	Lib/Lib Dem	Prime Minister
1945	393	210	12	C. Attlee (Lab)
1950	315	298	9	C. Attlee (Lab)
1951	295	321	6	W. Churchill (Con)
1955	277	345	6	A. Eden (Con) 1
1959	258	365	6	H. Macmillan (Con)
1964	317	304	9	H. Wilson (Lab)
1966	364	253	12	H. Wilson (Lab)
1970	288	330	6	E. Heath (Con)
1974 (Feb)	301	297	14	H. Wilson (Lab)
1974 (Oct)	319	277	13	H. Wilson (Lab) 2
1979	269	339	11	M. Thatcher (Con)
1983	209	397	23	M. Thatcher (Con)
1987	229	376	22	M. Thatcher (Con) 3
1992	271	336	20	J. Major (Con)
1997	418	165	46	T. Blair (Lab)

1. Eden resigned Jan. 1957 and replaced by Macmillan
2. Wilson resigned Mar. 1976 and replaced by Callaghan
3. Thatcher resigned Nov. 1990 and replaced by Major

Adapted from Craig 1989, the *Guardian*, 11 April 1992 and Butler & Kavanagh 1997.

Item B *The main parties, 1832-1997*

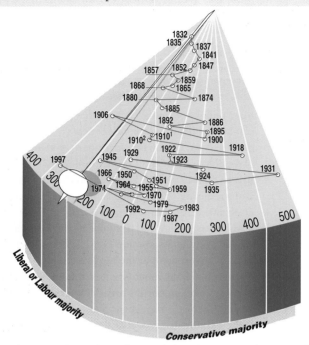

This diagram shows how the pendulum has swung between the Conservative Party and the main parties opposed to it in general elections held between 1832 and 1997. The position of the pendulum has been calculated by subtracting the number of seats won by the Liberal Party/Liberal Democrats and the Labour Party from the number won by the Conservatives. In 1918, 1931 and 1935, the figure for the Conservatives include those allies who joined the coalition government, but the figure does not include those Conservatives who remained outside the coalition.

Adapted from Craig 1989 and Simpson 1998.

Item C *The 1997 general election (1)*

Those who remained by their television sets or radios throughout the night of 1-2 May 1997, watching and listening to the results of the general election, were largely agreed about the significance of the result as they emerged, bleary eyed, into the morning. As well as the ritual complaints about tiredness and the severity of their hangovers, these people could be heard uttering words and expressions such as 'amazing', 'incredible', 'remarkable', 'once in a lifetime' and 'record breaking'. For once, the immediate, simple reactions were correct, the 1997 general election yielded results which were all these things and more. It resulted in the Conservatives' worst defeat since 1832. It unseated a record number of Cabinet ministers from their parliamentary seats. The election produced the largest swing from one party to another in history and gave Labour its largest overall majority in the 97 years of its existence. The Liberal Democrats achieved their highest number of seats ever and an independent candidate unseated a Conservative in one of the safest Tory seats in the country (Tatton). The most unlikely places saw Conservative defeats and Labour victories - even Hove on the south east coast of England saw the Conservative lose his seat. Last, but most certainly not least, the Tories lost all their remaining seats in Wales and Scotland, transforming them into a wholly English party.

Adapted from Dobson 1998.

Item D *The 1997 general election (2)*

The 1997 election marked a reversal of the long-term trend towards the geographical polarisation between a Conservative south and a Labour north. Thanks to results in 1992 and 1997, Labour now has a more even geographical spread of seats whilst the Conservative Party is more than ever a party of English shires and suburbs. Liberal Democrat support was evenly spread across the country and the party finished third in vote share in every region (except the South West where it was second and Scotland where it was fourth). The extent and direction of turnover of seats was comparable to 1945 - which also saw the defeat of a long-established party of government. But, unlike in 1945, which was a surprise even to Clement Attlee, a victory for Labour had long been predicted. The result was all the more striking considering the many analyses in the aftermath of the 1992 election which argued that the dominant-party system had arrived and that Labour faced too high a mountain to climb within the lifetime of one Parliament (Anthony King, for example, claimed that Britain no longer had two major parties. Rather, it had one major party, the Conservatives, one minor party, Labour, and one peripheral party, the Liberal Democrats). Not that the two-party system can be said to have recovered in 1997. Labour and the Conservatives shared 75% of the vote (2% less than in 1992). Between 1970 and 1992, the decline in total vote share was the consequence of Labour's decline. In 1997, however, it was due to a sharp fall in support for the Conservatives. The total of 75 third-party MPs was the highest since 1923.

Adapted from Butler & Kavanagh 1997.

Item E *The two-party system*

Questions

1. a) Using Items A-E, give arguments for and against the view that Britain has a two-party system.
   b) Why is it important to know whether Britain has a two-party system or some other system?
2. What conclusions can be drawn about the British party system using Items A and B?
3. How does the 1997 general election result affect our understanding of the British party system? Use Items C and D in your answer.
4. How accurate is the point being made in Item E?

References

Austin (1997) Austin, T., (ed.) *The Times Guide to the House of Commons May 1997*, Times Books, 1997.

Ball (1987) Ball, A., *British Political Parties*, Macmillan, 1987.

Brivati & Bale (1998) Brivati, B. & Bale T. (eds), *New Labour in Power*, Routledge, 1998.

Butler & Kavanagh (1997) Butler, D. & Kavanagh, D., *The British General Election of 1997*, Macmillan, 1997.

Conservative (1998) *Constitution of the Conservative Party*, Conservative Central Office, February 1998.

Craig (1989) Craig, F.W.S., *British Electoral Facts 1832-1987*, Gower Publishing Company, 1989.

Curtice (1997) Curtice, J., 'Anatomy of a non-landslide', *Politics Review*, Vol. 7.1, September 1997.

Curtice & Steed (1997) Curtice, J. & Steed, M., 'The results analysed', appendix in *Butler & Kavanagh (1997)*.

Dearlove & Saunders (1991) Dearlove, J. & Saunders, P., *Introduction to British Politics*, Polity Press, 1991.

Dobson (1998) Dobson, A., 'The 1997 general election - explaining a landslide' in *Lancaster (1998)*.

Garner & Kelly (1998) Garner, R. & Kelly, R., *British Political Parties Today*, Manchester University Press, 1998.

Heywood (1993) Heywood, A., 'The dominant-party system', *Talking Politics*, Vol.5.2, Winter 1993.

Ingle (1992) Ingle, S., 'The Glorious Revolution and the party system', *Politics Review*, Vol.1.3, February 1992.

Ingle (1993) Ingle, S., 'Political parties in the nineties', *Talking Politics*, Vol.6.1, Autumn 1993.

Kelly (1989) Kelly, R., *Conservative Party Conferences*, Manchester University Press, 1989.

Kelly (1992) Kelly, R., 'Power in the Conservative Party', *Politics Review*, Vol.1.4, April 1992.

Kelly (1994) Kelly, R., 'British political parties: organisation, leadership and democracy' in *Wale (1994)*.

Kelly (1998) Kelly, R., 'Power in the Labour Party: the Blair effect', *Politics Review*, Vol.8.2, November 1998.

Kelly (1998a) Kelly, R., 'Democratising the Tory Party: the Hague agenda', *Talking Politics*, Vol.11.1, Autumn 1998.

Kelly (1999) Kelly, R., 'Power in the Conservative Party: the Hague effect', *Politics Review*, Vol.8.3, February 1999.

Labour (1997) *New Labour - Because Britain Deserves Better*, Labour Party manifesto, Labour Party, 1997.

Labour (1999) *Labour Party Rule Book 1999*, Labour Party, 1999.

Lancaster (1998) Lancaster, S. (ed.), Developments in Politics, Vol.9, Causeway Press, 1998.

Lemieux (1995) Lemieux, S., 'The future funding of political parties', *Talking Politics*, Vol.7.3, Spring 1995.

Lib Dem (1997) *Make the Difference*, the Liberal Democrat manifesto, Liberal Democrats, 1997.

McKenzie (1955) McKenzie, R.T., *British Political Parties*, Heinemann, 1955.

Parris (1997) Parris, M., 'Beyond the fringe' in *Austin (1997)*.

Pelling (1991) Pelling, H., *A Short History of the Labour Party*, Macmillan, 1991.

Simpson (1998) Simpson, D., *UK Government and Politics in Context*, Hodder & Stoughton, 1998.

Wale (1994) Wale, W. (ed.), *Developments in Politics*, Vol.5, Causeway Press, 1994.

Whiteley et al. (1994) Whiteley, P., Seyd, P. & Richardson, J., *True Blues: the Politics of Conservative Party Membership*, Oxford University Press, 1994.

9 Voting behaviour

Introduction

On the face of it, any attempt to explain voting behaviour is an impossible task. The system for electing politicians in Britain involves a secret ballot. Voting is a very individual act which takes place in the privacy of the voting booth. Voters have free choice. There is no legal obligation to vote and no compulsion to vote for one candidate rather than another.

Although voting is an individual act, it does not take place in isolation. Voters are constrained and influenced by a whole host of factors. Some of the constraints are obvious. If the voter's name is omitted from the electoral register, for example, then that voter is unable to cast a vote. Similarly, illness may prevent a visit to the polls or a voter's favoured party may not put up a candidate in that constituency. Other limitations and influences on voters may be more complex, but they are equally potent. The role of the television and the press, the economic performance of the government, the policies and promises of the parties competing for power, the social origins and circumstances of the voter, the voter's family and friends - all these factors and more may help to define the context in which the voter carries out the seemingly solitary act of voting.

It is the task of political scientists to discover patterns and trends in political behaviour. As a result, various theories or models have been devised to make sense of voting behaviour. This chapter looks at a number of these models. Each model offers a different explanation of voting behaviour. But, although each model examines voting behaviour from a different perspective, not all the models are necessarily competing with each other.

Chapter summary

Part 1 looks at the social structures model of voting behaviour. To what extent is voting determined by occupational class and other social factors?

Part 2 examines the party identification model of voting behaviour. How important is party loyalty in explaining voting behaviour?

Part 3 focuses on the rational choice model of voting behaviour. Do people make rational decisions rather than emotional decisions when they vote? If so, what determines which candidate or party they choose?

Part 4 investigates the dominant ideology model of

voting behaviour. How do powerful groups attempt to set the political agenda via the media? What impact do messages in the media have on voting behaviour? What is the role and importance of opinion polls?

Part 5 analyses the voting context model. How do perceptions about the purpose of an election and the particular context in which voting takes place affect voting behaviour?

Part 6 uses a general model of voting to suggest ways in which the various models outlined earlier in the chapter are connected.

Part 1 The social structures model

Key issues

1. What connection is there between voting behaviour and social groups?
2. To what extent is class a factor in voting behaviour?
3. Do studies of voting behaviour reveal variations according to region, age, sex, ethnicity and religion?

1.1 Class and voting

Voting and class interests

One explanation for voting behaviour is that most people vote according to their objective class interests. Traditionally, class is seen in occupational terms. Those in manual jobs - the working class - are expected to vote for the Labour Party whilst those in non-manual jobs - the middle and upper classes - are expected to vote for the Conservatives.

Although the figures depend on the criteria used for measurement, between 1945 and 1970, a majority of people belonged to the working class. So, if people always voted according to their occupational class position, the Labour Party would have won every general election during this period. As this did not happen, either a considerable proportion of the working class did not bother to vote or there was some degree of cross-class voting with more manual workers not voting Labour than non-manual workers not voting Conservative - or both. In fact, survey results show that, at some general elections since 1945, a third or even more of the working-class vote has gone to the Conservatives.

Embourgeoisement

In the decades following the Second World War, various explanations were offered for working-class Conservative voting. One argument concerned people's perceptions of their own status or class position in society. If they viewed themselves as middle class rather than working class, they were more likely to vote Conservative. This argument is associated with the theory of embourgeoisement - the idea that, because of rising pay levels and living standards, the attitudes and behaviour of better-off manual workers become more like those of the middle class (including a willingness to vote Conservative).

A study in the 1960s (Goldthorpe et al. 1969), however, found no systematic evidence to support this theory. Instead, the authors found a more significant correlation: non-Labour support of manual workers was higher amongst those who had friends or family connections with non-manual ('white collar') employees. Consistent with this finding is the argument that manual workers living outside the more traditional, single-industry, working-class communities are more exposed to what Frank Parkin described as the 'dominant value system' and, therefore, less likely to vote Labour (Parkin 1972).

The string of Conservative general election victories between 1979 and 1992 led to the revival of the theory of embourgeoisement as an explanation of the decline in the working-class Labour vote. But, the theory has few supporters since it fails to account for the fall in middle-class Conservative support that also occurred during this period.

Deferential and secular Conservatives

In another study of cross-class voting, McKenzie and Silver distinguished between 'deferential' and 'secular' working-class Conservative voters. The former defer to the traditional authority represented by Conservative leaders who are seen as Britain's 'natural rulers'. The latter vote Conservative not because they are enthusiastic supporters of Conservative values, but because they believe they will be better-off, particularly financially, with a Conservative government. They are secular

Conservatives because they are not true believers in Conservative ideology (McKenzie & Silver 1968).

1.2 Class dealignment

What is the evidence for class dealignment?

Despite a significant degree of working-class Conservative voting, the voting patterns between 1945 and the 1970s seemed to indicate quite strong class alignment. In the 1945-70 period, nearly two-thirds of all voters voted for their 'natural' class party. In other words, most manual voters did vote Labour and most non-manual voters voted Conservative. But, since the mid-1970s, a number of political scientists have claimed that a process of class dealignment has been taking place. They argue that the link between occupational class and party preference at election times has diminished. This argument was first fully developed in 1977 (Crewe et al. 1977). Further studies concluded that the process of class dealignment continued in later elections (for example, Benyon & Denver 1990). It should be noted, however, that although these commentators argue that the link between class and party preference has diminished, they still consider class to be important. As Ivor Crewe put it:

> 'In the 1945-70 period, nearly two-thirds of all voters voted for their class party. From February 1974, the link slowly and fitfully weakened and, since 1983, the proportion has been under half (44-47%) with a majority voting for either the "class enemy" or for the non-class centre or nationalist parties. This trend should not be exaggerated, however: class remains the single most important social factor underlying the vote.' (Crewe 1993a, pp.99-100).

The Heath thesis

In 1985, the theory of class dealignment came under attack. The sociologist Anthony Heath and his colleagues published an article which claimed that there was no evidence that there had been a fall in working-class loyalty to the Labour Party or that the proportion of members of the working class voting Labour had fallen. Rather, the overall decline in the Labour vote reflected a reduction of the size of the working class as a whole. Class alignment was still important but the balance of the classes had changed. The long-term pattern in class voting was one of 'trendless fluctuation' rather than inevitable decline (Heath et al. 1985). This thesis was further explored in 1991 (Heath et al. 1991).

At the heart of the debate between those who support and those who oppose the theory of class dealignment is the definition of the term 'class'. Whereas conventional accounts used a simple manual/non-manual definition, Heath and his colleagues split the electorate into five categories:

> '[These different groups were] distinguished according to their degree of economic security, their authority in the workplace, their prospects of economic advancement and their sources as well as their level of income.' (Heath et al. 1991, p.66).

Other writers, however, do not accept the measures of class alignment used by Heath and his colleagues (see, for example, Denver 1993). Although most would go along with the proposition that the working class as a whole has been shrinking, they argue that Labour's declining share of the vote in the period 1979-92 was more marked than it otherwise would have been because of the process of class dealignment.

Class and the 1997 general election

In the 1992 general election, the Labour Party won 34% of the vote. In 1997, it won 43%. One explanation for this increase could be that class dealignment had gone into reverse, with members of the working class returning in large numbers to Labour. John Curtice, however, rejects this interpretation because survey data indicates that increases in Labour's support were fairly evenly spread across the different classes:

> 'The rise in Labour's support compared with 1992 was more or less the same in each social grade. The differences between the social grades were largely the same in 1997 as in 1992. Rather than being accompanied by the emergence of some long-lost relationship between class and vote, Labour's 1997 victory appears to have done little to disturb the relationship between class and vote.' (Curtice 1997, p.4)

In broad terms, this was also the conclusion reached by Pippa Norris:

> 'New Labour has triumphed by maintaining its traditional base and yet simultaneously widening its appeal to Middle England...[The] explanation lies in the changing pattern of party competition, notably New Labour's shift towards the ideological middle ground with a classless appeal.' (Norris 1997, pp.15-16)

Explanations of class dealignment

A number of explanations, often interconnected, have been suggested for the process of class dealignment.

1. Party dealignment

Some explanations of class dealignment are associated with the related phenomenon of party dealignment (a decline in party identification) and require consideration of, for example, the role of education, media coverage, ideological changes and dissatisfaction with party performance. These issues are examined in Part 2 of this chapter.

2. Changes in the occupational structure

Since the 1960s, there have been important changes in the structure and pattern of employment in Britain. A process of 'de-industrialisation' - a decline in the traditional manufacturing industries - has taken place (see Chapter 5, Section 3.1 and Chapter 15, Section 2.2). De-industrialisation has gathered pace since 1979 and it is, perhaps, no surprise that it has affected the way in which people vote.

In the traditional manufacturing industries, the workforce exhibited a strong, collective trade union identity. Historically, these unions had close links with the Labour Party and the vast majority of workers voted Labour. But, since the 1960s, several million of these workers have either lost their jobs or found work in new hi-tech or service industries. Hi-tech and service industries are not organised in the same way that traditional industries were organised. For example, the role of trade unions (if trade unions are tolerated) is often reduced. As a result, the old ties between workers and the Labour Party have been broken (the number of trade union members, for example, fell from 13.3 million - 53% of the workforce - in 1979 to 7.2 million - 28% of the workforce - in 1996). This has led to class dealignment.

Class dealignment, however, has not only affected the Labour vote. There has also been some falling away of middle-class support for the Conservatives. In part, this also can be partly explained by changes in the occupational structure. Many workers gain promotion to non-manual jobs and, therefore, move from the working class to the middle class. These 'new recruits' to the middle class, it has been shown (see, for example, Benyon & Denver 1990), often retain their allegiance to the Labour Party. The fall in middle-class support for the Conservatives in 1997, however, may well owe more to changes within the Labour Party, which made a concerted effort to capture the Middle England vote in 1997, than to changes in the occupational structure.

3. Production and consumption cleavages

Dunleavy & Husbands (1985) argue that the significance of the old manual/non-manual class divisions is being replaced by new sectoral cleavages based on public-private splits. They distinguish between:

- production sector cleavages
- consumption sector cleavages.

'Production sector cleavages' refer to the real or assumed conflicts of interest between employees in the public sector and those in the private sector. It is argued that these cleavages have resulted in the development of new political alignments, largely irrespective of whether employees are in manual or non-manual occupations.

'Consumption sector cleavages' refer to changes in the ways in which certain services are purchased and provided. Two important examples are housing and transport. Together, these constitute a significant proportion of most people's disposable incomes. It is argued that the policies of Conservative governments between 1979 and 1997 led to the growth of privately owned (as opposed to publicly rented) housing and a greater emphasis on personal rather than public transport. This created new alignments relating party choice to patterns of consumption. These new alignments cut across manual/non-manual class alignments.

It should be noted that this model is based on the traditional assumption that the Labour Party is the champion of the public sector whilst the Conservative Party is the champion of the private sector. Since Tony Blair became Leader of the Labour Party in 1994, however, priorities have changed and it has become clear that one of the goals of the Labour Party is to distance itself from its old image. This was reflected in Labour's manifesto for the 1997 general election:

> 'New Labour will be wise spenders, not big spenders. We will work in partnership with the private sector to achieve our goals. We will ask about public spending the first question that a manager in any company would ask - can existing resources be used more effectively to meet our priorities?' (Labour 1997, p.12)

4. The 'traditional' and 'new' working classes

There are some similarities between the ideas of Dunleavy & Husbands and those of Ivor Crewe. Following the major defeat of Labour at the 1983 general election, Crewe focused on what he saw as divisions within the working class (*Guardian*, 13 June 1983). Elaborating on a survey which found that only 38% of manual workers voted Labour, he claimed that the party could only rely on the shrinking traditional working class and it was losing the support of the 'new' working class. Those who belonged to the traditional working class were predominantly people who lived in Scotland and the North of England and those in other areas who lived in council houses or worked in the public sector. Those who belonged to the new working class were manual workers employed by private firms who lived mainly in the South and owned their own homes.

Following the 1987 general election, Crewe pursued his theory of a divided working class and he brought union membership into the equation (Crewe 1987). But, although the Conservatives still won the 1992 general election, the overall swing to Labour from 1987 seemed to have reversed any polarisation between the new and the traditional working classes. Crewe admitted that the gap between the two groups was 'much narrower' than previously (Crewe 1992). He attributed this change to the differential effects of the recession in the early 1990s (by the 1992 general election, the hi-tech and service industries in the South of England had been hit by recession harder than the public sector and the North).

The 1997 election and a divided working class

The result of the 1997 general election has cast doubt on Crewe's theory about a divided working class. Dorey, for example, using the Registrar General's classification (see Chapter 5, Section 2.1) points out that:

> 'Although the Labour Party increased its support amongst all socio-economic groups in May 1997, it was amongst the C1s and DEs [unskilled and semi-skilled working class] that this increase was most pronounced...Labour also won back swathes of support from the C2s, the skilled working class who had deserted the party in droves in 1979 and throughout the 1980s...In May 1997, the Labour Party was supported by almost 60% of the working class.' (Dorey 1998, pp.95-6, slightly adapted)

Not only did more working-class voters support Labour in the 1997 general election, Labour's support in the South-East of England, East Anglia and the East Midlands grew substantially. This is significant because it is in these areas that much of the new, hi-tech, non-unionised industries are based.

<table>
<tr><td colspan="2" align="center">**Main points - Sections 1.1-1.2**</td></tr>
<tr><td>

• **One explanation for voting behaviour is that most people vote according to their objective class interests. Class remains the single most important social factor in determining voting behaviour.**

• **In the 1945-70 period, nearly two-thirds of all voters voted for their 'natural' class party. Since then, there has been a debate about whether class dealignment has taken place.**

</td><td>

• **Heath argued that Labour's vote shrank between 1979-92 because the working class was shrinking. Others argue that Labour's vote fell further than can be explained by a shrinking working class.**

• **Class dealignment has been explained by reference to: (1) party dealignment; (2) changes in occupational structure; and (3) changes in production and consumption patterns.**

</td></tr>
</table>

Activity 9.1 Social class and voting behaviour

Item A   *Occupational class and party choice, 1964-97*

(i)

	1964 N/M	1964 M	1966 N/M	1966 M	1970 N/M	1970 M	1974 (Feb) N/M	1974 (Feb) M	1974 (Oct) N/M	1974 (Oct) M
Con	62	28	60	25	64	33	53	24	51	24
Lib Dem	16	8	14	6	11	9	25	19	24	20
Lab	22	64	26	69	25	58	22	57	25	57

	1979 N/M	1979 M	1983 N/M	1983 M	1987 N/M	1987 M	1992 N/M	1992 M	1997 N/M	1997 M
Con	55	36	51	35	49	37	49	35	39	25
Lib Dem	19	17	31	28	31	23	25	20	21	15
Lab	26	46	18	37	20	40	26	45	40	60

N/M = non-manual   M = manual All figures in percentages

The table above shows the percentage of manual and non-manual workers who voted for the three main parties between 1964 and 1997.

(ii)

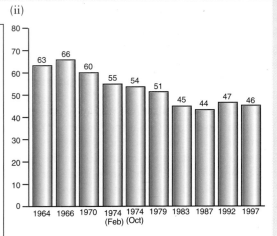

The chart above shows the percentage of voters who voted for their 'natural' party according to class.

Adapted from Benyon & Denver 1990, Crewe 1993b and Kellner 1997.

Item B   *Class voting in 1992 and 1997*

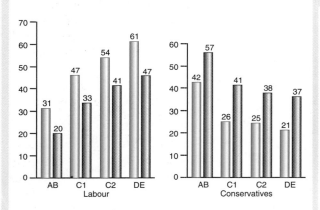

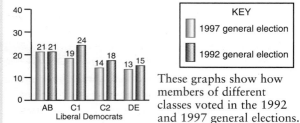

KEY
☐ 1997 general election
▨ 1992 general election

These graphs show how members of different classes voted in the 1992 and 1997 general elections.

The figures show the percentage of each class which voted for a party.

Adapted from Curtice 1997.

Item C   *Production and consumption sector cleavages*

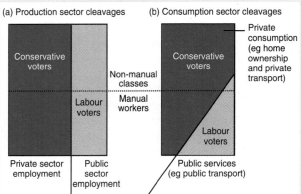

The diagrams above show how sectoral cleavages translate into support for the Labour and Conservative parties. Since the Labour Party has traditionally been associated with the public sector, their support is indicated to the right of the dividing line. Support for the Conservatives is indicated on the left of the dividing line. In employment terms, about 30% of the total working population is employed in the public sector. In consumption terms, however, most non-manual people are involved in private, individualised consumption (for example, home ownership and private transport). Dunleavy and Husbands argue that, during the post-war period, Labour lost support amongst a large group of private-sector manual workers and gained support only amongst a much smaller public sector non-manual group.

Adapted from Dunleavy & Husbands 1985.

Item D   *The problem faced by political scientists*

Questions

1. What evidence is there to suggest that 'class remains the single most important social factor underlying the vote'? Use Items A and B in your answer.

2. a) Judging from Items A and B, what is the evidence to support the view that class dealignment has taken place?

   b) Does the information on the 1997 general election cast any doubts about the theory of class dealignment?

3. a) What does Item C add to our understanding of voting behaviour?

   b) The model described in Item C was devised in 1985. How valid is it today?

4. Judging from Item D, what is the problem faced by political scientists who attempt to explain voting behaviour by reference to class?

1.3   Other social factors

Regional differences

During the 1980s, political commentators increasingly used the term 'North-South divide' to describe the geographical polarisation of support for the Labour and Conservative parties. In general terms, support for the Conservatives appeared to be declining in the North of England, Scotland and Wales whilst support for Labour declined in the South of England.

Although regional differences existed before the 1980s, two new developments have been discovered. First, whereas before 1970 the changes in party support from one election to another tended to be similar across most regions of Britain, since 1970 this has changed. Swings vary from region to region. Second, a further spatial divide has been revealed. Since 1959, electoral support for the Conservatives in general elections has shown a relative decline in urban areas whilst the vote for Labour has declined in rural areas (although, in 1997, Labour did well in rural areas).

Explanations of regional differences

1. Class differences

Although most political scientists agree that there has been a degree of class dealignment (see above Section 1.2), they still accept that the relationship between occupational class and party support is important. Likewise, some relationship between class and region is to be expected. For example, the South of England contains a higher proportion of middle-class home owners than the North. This could partly account for the Conservative predominance in the South and Labour predominance in the North during the period 1979-92 . It should be noted, however, that geographical differences in voting behaviour still show up when the class variable is held constant.

2. Cultural differences

Research carried out by Miller (1984, 1990) on constituency voting trends showed that, between 1960 and 1990, class polarisation between constituencies increased as class polarisation between individuals declined. In other words, there was an increasingly powerful 'locality effect'. People tended to adopt the dominant political norms of their locality. So, people living in predominantly middle-class areas were more likely to vote Conservative whatever their own class might be whilst people living in working-class areas were more likely to vote Labour. Put another way, local culture has an important influence on voting behaviour because:

> 'If almost everyone whom a voter meets at work, in shops, in pubs and clubs, at church or on the housing estate appears to support the same party, then there is strong pressure on the individual to support that party too.' (Denver 1993, p.66).

This cultural dimension is emphasised by Johnston & Pattie (1992) who argue that geographical variations in voting behaviour suggest that there is a growing local and regional consciousness in Britain. They argue that geographical variations in voting behaviour contradict the idea that there is a uniform British political culture - even though the parties themselves increasingly rely on the national mass media to project their images.

3. Economic circumstances

Since the 1970s, it has been possible to demonstrate a relationship between the economic fortunes of the regions and variations in party support - particularly in terms of a broad North-South divide.

Johnston & Pattie (1992) have emphasised the connection between regional voting patterns and regional economic factors. They argue that, during the 1980s, those areas of Britain that experienced economic decline saw the Conservative vote fall whilst those faring better showed a drop in the Labour vote. Furthermore, this pattern seemed to have been produced not just by people who personally were affected by the relative economic fortunes. It seems that the influence of regional economic prosperity or decline was more general than this. These findings again suggest the cultural significance of the social and economic context in which people live.

4. Support for third parties

Geographical variations in electoral support for the Labour and Conservative parties may be intensified where third parties do well. The rise of support for the Scottish National Party (SNP) and Plaid Cymru in the 1970s and the large numbers of votes cast for the Liberal/SDP Alliance in the 1980s account, in part, for the regional variations in support for Labour and the Conservatives. If Labour is weak in the South overall, for example, it is likely to do even worse in southern constituencies where the third party vote is substantial. Similarly, greater support for a third party in Scotland is more likely to be at the expense of the Conservatives than Labour. Tactical voting (see Section 5.3 below) intensifies this phenomenon.

Age

Survey data from general elections usually shows a tendency for younger people to vote Labour and older people to vote Conservative. In the October 1974 election, for example, 42% of new voters voted Labour compared to 24% who voted Conservative. Although, in 1983 and 1987, the Conservatives obtained clear majorities from the youngest voters, by 1997 the traditional pattern seemed to have reasserted itself with Labour once again winning a majority of first-time votes.

Studies have shown that swings within the 18-22 age group can be quite marked and, therefore, no party can afford to take its support for granted. Anthony Heath and his colleagues have remarked:

'The young elector tends to be rather less interested in politics, somewhat less likely to turn out and vote, less committed to any political party and somewhat more volatile.' (Heath et al. 1991, p.212)

Gender

Writing in 1967 one political scientist stated:

'There is overwhelming evidence that women are more conservatively inclined than men.' (Pulzer 1967, p.107).

Pulzer argued that, between 1945 and 1966, whilst men had given the Labour Party a victory at every general election, women had done so only twice. Similarly, in the four general elections held between 1979 and 1992, more women voted for the Conservatives than for the other parties. In 1997, however, gender differences in party choice had all but disappeared. Three factors may account for the apparent disappearance of gender differences in voting behaviour in 1997.

1. Labour's election tactics

The Labour Party made a concerted effort to win over women voters. For example, although the party was forced to drop its policy of imposing all-women shortlists, the controversy surrounding the policy gave the impression that the party was making an effort to increase women's representation in Parliament. Similarly, the emphasis on improving childcare and on education and health during the election campaign was designed to appeal to women.

2. A changing workforce

The changing nature of the workforce and women's position in it may have made an impact. It was only in the mid-1990s that the number of women in paid employment reached a similar level to that of men. This may be important for two reasons. First, there is an argument that people are more readily exposed to pro-Labour ideas and influences at work because of the collective experience of the workplace and participation in the trade union movement (though it should be noted that women tend to be employed in part-time non-unionised jobs - jobs which do not necessarily expose them to pro-Labour ideas). And second, because more women are working, family and household roles are changing. Fewer women consider it to be their role to stay at home. As a result, there is an argument that traditional values relating to the family and domestic life (which used to be emphasised in Conservative election campaigns) now have less impact.

3. Gender and age

A third theory concerning gender differences in voting behaviour emphasises the importance of age. Since women's life expectancy is higher than men's, there are always more older women than older men in the population - and older people are more likely to vote Conservative than younger people. Although the gender gap in voting behaviour amongst older women has been demonstrated in previous elections (see Lovenduski 1997, p.207), the poll evidence for the 1997 general election is somewhat contradictory. One post-election survey showed that, compared to 1992, there was an 11% increase in votes for Labour amongst the over-65s in 1997 (see Item A in Activity

9.2 below). By way of contrast, however, the NOP/BBC exit poll showed a 2% decrease among this age group (Butler & Kavanagh 1997, p.246).

Religion

Historically, there have been close links between religion and politics in Britain. In the 19th century, for example, the Church of England was described as, 'the Tory Party at prayer' and was closely identified with the political establishment. Non-conformist sects such as the Methodists and Baptists, on the other hand, were associated with support for the Liberal Party. But, although politico-religious links are still important determinants of party choice in some parts of Western Europe (including Northern Ireland), it is generally agreed that their significance in most parts of Britain has disappeared. Denver (1994) points out that religious affiliation is now rarely examined in major works on voting behaviour.

An exception to this is the work of Anthony Heath and his colleagues (Heath et al. 1991 and Heath 1992). They claim that the assumption made in the 1960s that the connection between voting preference and religious affiliation would continue to weaken may not have turned out to be totally correct. Although Heath and his colleagues find evidence of a general decline in religion, their comparison of voting patterns in 1964 and 1987 indicates that the connection between Church of England attendance and Conservative voting still persists - at least amongst the middle class - as does the connection between non-conformist sect attendance and Liberal voting. Heath and his colleagues acknowledge, however, that the reasons for any connections between religious groups and party choice might not be due to religion itself. For example, the high Labour vote among British Catholics, many of whom are of Irish descent, might be related historically to the policies of the main parties on the 'Irish question'. Similarly, the voting preferences of Sikhs and Muslims in Britain may have more to do with ethnicity than with religion.

Ethnicity

The more recent analyses of the relationship between voting behaviour and ethnicity have focused on the voting patterns of different black and Asian groups (see Chapter 5, Section 2.3 for an examination of the term 'ethnicity'). Although studies show that the majority of black and Asian people vote Labour, different levels of party support have been noted between black and Asian voters as well as differences within each of these groups. For example, in 1997, there was a difference of 16% in Asian (70%) and black (86%) support for the Labour Party (Saggar 1998, p.27). In an earlier study, Fitzgerald (1988), using data from the 1987 general election, noted markedly higher levels of support for the Conservative Party among East African Asians than

among those from the Indian sub-continent. It should be noted that such variations may have a differential effect if turnout levels also vary. Layton-Henry (1990) reports a lower turnout at elections of African-Caribbeans compared to Asians. He attributes this not to political apathy, but to a greater degree of alienation from British politics.

Three main factors have been suggested to explain why the Labour Party attracts the votes of immigrants and their descendants.

1. Class

The most common reason given by black and Asian respondents to survey questions about why they vote for the Labour Party is that Labour is for the working class (see, for example, Saggar 1993). Further analysis of the evidence, however, led Heath and his colleagues (1991) away from a simple class explanation. By itself, it would not explain, for example, why the black and Asian working-class Labour vote is much higher than the working-class Labour vote in general. Fitzgerald (1988) also doubts the validity of a simple class explanation. She claims there is no clear evidence that black and Asian people especially perceive themselves to be working class. Also, she points to the variety of socio-economic positions occupied by black and Asian people. A major survey in the 1980s showed that 22% of East African Asian men, 20% of Hindus, 11% of Muslims and 4% of Sikhs were employed in professional or managerial jobs. The comparable figure for whites was 19%.

2. Race

Although, in 1997, it pursued a 'very low key campaign towards ethnic minorities' (Saggar 1997, p.192), the Labour Party is usually seen as more liberal than the Conservatives on issues related to race and immigration. According to Denver (1994), this is one reason for the high black and Asian Labour vote. But, the majority of evidence suggests that black and Asian voters are not predominantly concerned with 'race' issues. Most surveys reveal a high similarity between black and Asian groups and whites. Differences among black voters are likely to be as significant as differences between black and Asian groups and whites.

3. Political geography

Although black and Asian voters make up c.5% of the electorate, residential concentration of some black and Asian communities means that, in some constituencies, the black and Asian vote is large enough to make a significant impact. The concentration of black and Asian voters in constituencies which have become Labour strongholds has been historically significant in forging the close two-way relationship between black and Asian communities and Labour (a link which has not developed with other political parties). Fitzgerald (1988) points out that, from the early days of post-war black and Asian immigration, black and Asian people have relied on their local Labour MPs for political support. At the same time, the most obvious and accessible route for black and Asian people who wish to play a role in public life has been through the Labour Party. Electoral geography has, therefore, functioned to strengthen the links between black and Asian people and the Labour Party.

Main points - Section 1.3

- Class is just one of a number of social factors which influence voting behaviour. Regional differences, age, gender, religion and ethnicity must also be taken into account.
- Explanations of regional differences in voting behaviour focus on class differences, cultural variations, economic circumstances, and levels of third party support.
- Survey data from general elections shows a tendency for younger people to vote Labour and older people to vote Conservative.

- In most elections, a majority of women vote Conservative and a majority of men vote Labour. In 1997, gender differences in voting disappeared - due to Labour's strategy, a changing workforce and fewer than usual old people voting Conservative.
- There is a debate about whether religious affiliation affects voting behaviour. There is some evidence that it does have some impact.
- The Labour Party wins a vast majority of black and Asian votes. This is due to class, race and electoral geography.

Activity 9.2 *Social factors and voting behaviour*

Item A   *Voting and age in 1992 and 1997*

	Con	Lab	Lib Dem
FIRST TIME VOTERS			
1992	38	35	22
1997	22	56	13
PEOPLE AGED 25-34			
1992	37	41	18
1997	25	50	17
PEOPLE AGED 35-44			
1992	38	38	21
1997	26	53	12
PEOPLE AGED 45-64			
1992	44	35	19
1997	29	44	18
PEOPLE AGED 65+			
1992	49	33	14
1997	36	44	12

This chart shows how different age groups voted in 1992 and 1997.

Adapted from Curtice 1997.

Item B   *Gender and party choice 1964-97*

Year			Con	Lab	Lib Dem
1964	Men		40	48	11
	Women		46	42	12
1966	Men		38	53	8
	Women		45	46	9
1970	Men		44	49	8
	Women		51	41	8
1974 (Feb)	Men		40	41	19
	Women		40	38	22
1974 (Oct)	Men		34	46	19
	Women		40	39	21
1979	Men		47	39	13
	Women		46	39	14
1983	Men		46	30	24
	Women		43	28	28
1987	Men		44	33	22
	Women		44	31	25
1992	Men		41	40	19
	Women		45	36	19
1997	Men		31	44	17
	Women		32	44	17

This table shows voting according to gender 1964-97. All figures are percentages.

Adapted from Denver & Hands 1990, Crewe 1992 and Butler & Kavanagh 1997.

Item C   *Voting and ethnicity 1974-97*

	1974 (Oct) %	1979 %	1983 %	1987 %	1992 %	1997 %
Labour	81	86	83	72	81	78
Conservative	9	8	7	18	10	17

This table shows the percentage of black and Asian voters who voted for the two main parties between 1974 and 1997. The figures are percentages.

	Asian	Black
Conservative	25	8
Labour	70	86
Lib Dem	4	4
Other	1	1
Undecided/refused/not voting	22	21

This table shows the voting intentions of black and Asian voters in 1996-97. The figures are percentages.

Adapted from Saggar 1997.

Item D   *Regional voting in 1997*

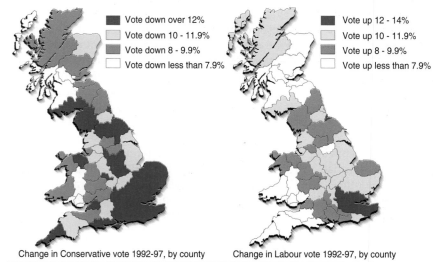

Vote down over 12%
Vote down 10 - 11.9%
Vote down 8 - 9.9%
Vote down less than 7.9%

Vote up 12 - 14%
Vote up 10 - 11.9%
Vote up 8 - 9.9%
Vote up less than 7.9%

Change in Conservative vote 1992-97, by county   Change in Labour vote 1992-97, by county

The North-South divide closed slightly in 1997 because Conservative support fell most sharply in areas where the party had been remarkably strong in the 1980s - London (-14%), the South East (-13.1%), East Anglia (-12.3%) and the East Midlands (-11.7%). In contrast and despite their loss of seats, the Conservatives experienced the smallest swings against them in Scotland and Wales. They were wiped out in these areas because they were already so vulnerable that even a modest swing against them (7.5%) was enough to ensure they did not win any seats there. The election result means that the Conservatives have become the party of southern England - almost three-quarters of their MPs come from there.

The North-South divide

	Con	Lab
1974 (Feb)	8.5	9.3
1974 (Oct)	11.9	8.4
1979	11.7	15.1
1983	14.0	13.5
1987	17.3	17.9
1992	15.8	15.8
1997	13.6	13.6

Note: The Conservative index measures the proportion of Conservative votes from the South minus Conservative support in the North. The Labour index follows the same pattern with North minus South. The South equals London, the South East, South West, East Anglia and Midlands. The North equals the remainder of Britain.

Adapted from Norris 1997.

Questions

1. You have been asked to explain why people voted as they did in the 1997 general election. Write an account using the social structures model of voting behaviour.

2. a) What conclusions can you draw from Items A-C about the importance of age, gender and ethnicity in determining voting behaviour?
   b) How did the 1997 general election affect recent trends?

3. a) Judging from Item D, what is the evidence of a North-South divide in voting behaviour?
   b) Why you think the North-South divide came about?
   c) How did the 1997 general election affect the pattern?

Part 2 The party identification model

Key issues

1. Why do people identify themselves as supporters of a political party?
2. Why has a process of party dealignment taken place?
3. Has party dealignment resulted in greater electoral volatility?

2.1 Principal elements of the model

What is the party identification model?

'Party identification' (or partisanship) refers to the attachment, over a period of time, to a particular political party. According to Miller (1990), the basic claims of this model are that:

- many voters identify themselves as supporters of a political party
- party identification is relatively stable and enduring
- party identification influences voters' attitudes towards issues, personalities and government performance
- party identification directly affects voters' voting behaviour.

The party identification model is derived from studies in the USA in the 1950s. By 'party identification', political scientists mean psychological attachment to a party rather than a rational choice based on an instrumental assessment of the party's aims, promises or practices. Party identification, therefore, has much to do with a party's public image and it should be seen as one of the long-term influences on voting behaviour. Although the assumption is that most people who identify with a party (partisans) would normally vote for the party with which they identify, the model does not claim that this is always the case. For example, some people vote tactically.

Political socialisation

Work on the party identification model in Britain in the 1960s emphasised the effects of 'political socialisation' - the process by which people acquire their political attitudes, values and ways of behaving. Most theories of political socialisation assume that the majority of people retain the party preferences and voting habits formed when they first become politically aware. The influences of childhood and early adulthood are, therefore, considered important. Family (especially parents), friends and work colleagues and the social class to which they belong are regarded as the main agencies of political socialisation. Today, political socialisation has become less central to most explanations of voting behaviour.

Recent research

Over recent years, research has focused on three areas of party identification:

- its extent
- its direction
- its intensity.

'Extent' (or incidence) refers to the proportion of the electorate that self-consciously identifies with a particular political party. Do more or less people identify with a party than did so 30 years ago? 'Direction' refers to the choice of party. How many voters are attached to the Conservative Party, for example, and has the percentage changed over time? 'Intensity' refers to the strength of an individual's support for a party. Why do some people feel strongly attached to a party whilst others do not?

If the extent and intensity of party identification are high then political scientists refer to high degrees of party alignment. If the extent and/or the intensity of party identification are low or falling then a process of party dealignment is said to be taking place.

Variations in the extent and intensity of party identification may determine the degree of electoral stability and volatility. High levels of strong party identification are likely to mean that few people switch their vote from one election to another - with the result that there is a period of electoral stability. Weak or low levels of party identification, on the other hand, are likely to mean that voters are less predictable in their party choices and so voting behaviour is more volatile. Short-term factors (such as current issues, the personalities of Party Leaders and the role of the media) tend to have a greater influence on electoral outcomes when this is the case since party loyalty has less of a role to play.

2.2 Party dealignment

What is party dealignment?

Whilst there has been a debate about the extent or even existence of class dealignment (see above, Section 1.2), there is general agreement that party (or partisan) dealignment (a drop in the number of voters identifying strongly with the main parties) has been taking place since the early 1970s.

Before 1970, the post-war period had been characterised electorally by extensive and intensive party identification with the Conservative and Labour parties. In the 1950s and 1960s, although there had been changes in government, electoral outcome varied little. Party (and class) alignment supported a stable two-party system. This electoral stability then started to give way to a greater volatility. The two-party system came under attack from other parties. The Liberal Party began to attract votes in greater numbers. The SNP and Plaid Cymru also gained support.

But, to what extent have Labour and the Conservatives lost support? Have they suffered equally? These questions can be answered in two ways - by examining the changes in the parties' share of the actual vote at election times and by analysing survey data related to party identification.

Share of the vote

Between 1950 and 1983, there was a marked decline in the share of the actual vote won by Labour and the Conservatives combined. This trend showed signs of reversal in 1987 and 1992, but dipped once more in 1997 (see Box 9.1).

Box 9.1 Votes for the two main parties

The combined share of the vote for the Conservative and Labour parties 1945-97.

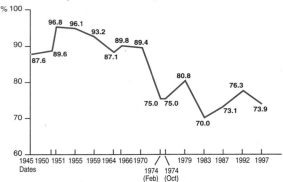

The fall in the combined Conservative-Labour share of the vote can be explained by the growth in fortunes of other parties, especially the Liberals. It is significant, for example, that the Liberals fielded just 109 candidates in 1951, but 523 in 1979. Moran (1989) argues that the willingness of third parties to field more candidates is itself a reflection of the decline in support for the two major parties. Until 1997, Labour suffered more than the Conservatives from the drop in voting support at general elections.

Party identification

Voting for a party is not the same as identifying with it. It is, therefore, necessary to add other information about party support to knowledge of the actual share of the vote. Crewe (1993b), for example, provided evidence that the percentage of Conservative identifiers held up better than Labour's in the early 1990s. If, among the identifiers, however, intensity of identification is measured, then, according to Denver (1994), both major parties have suffered from party dealignment since the 1960s. In 1964, 48% of Conservative and 51% of Labour voters identified 'very strongly' with their party. By 1992, the corresponding figures were 21% for Conservative voters and 24% for Labour voters.

Denver also found that between 1964 and 1992 the number of Liberal voters who identified 'very strongly' with their party fell from 32% to 8%. This suggested that partisan dealignment was not confined to the two major parties. It also suggested that the electoral fortunes of the Liberal Democrats could be expected to fluctuate more than the other main parties since it had fewer identifiers. One explanation for this was that the Liberal Democrats gain the votes of disaffected voters from the Conservative and Labour parties. The Liberal Democrats' record at by-elections would seem to confirm this. Their gains at by-elections are frequently wiped out in general elections.

The extent of party dealignment

Writing after the 1987 general election Crewe conceded that declining party identification should not be over-emphasised:

> 'Long-term allegiance to the Conservative and Labour parties remains the dominant fact about the British electorate, the psychological anchor of a stable, slow-moving party system.' (Crewe 1988, p.3).

Indeed, a survey carried out after the 1992 general election (Sanders 1993) revealed a noticeable increase in the respondents identifying 'very' or 'fairly' strongly with political parties. Nevertheless, the drastic reduction in voting support for the Conservatives at the 1997 general election means that any such increase in party identification is not reflected in the overall picture of combined Labour-Conservative support indicated in Box 9.1 above.

The causes of party dealignment

Political scientists have suggested a number of factors which may have contributed to party dealignment. Taken individually, however, it is unlikely that any single factor could provide a definitive and undisputed case. The reason for this is that correlative evidence (evidence which shows a connection between two variables) does not prove the existence of a causal relationship.

1. Class dealignment (see above, Section 1.2)

Most commentators recognise a connection between party dealignment and class dealignment. Crewe and his colleagues (1977), for example, suggested that a decline in the links between class and party may have helped to weaken party identification. They claimed that:

> 'Partisan decline reflected a continuing erosion of the class-party tie.' (Crewe et al. 1977, p.183)

This theory could help to explain why Labour won such a big victory in 1997. The party put a great deal of effort into attracting the support of people outside its 'natural' class (the working class). By appealing to Middle England, the Labour Party may have made it easier for voters who did not belong to the working class to vote for it.

2. The generation effect

The electorate does change from one general election to the next. New (usually young) voters enter the register for the first time whilst others (generally older) die in between elections.

The idea that a generational effect explains party dealignment has been dismissed by some political analysts, however. Evidence analysed by Crewe and his colleagues (1977) and later by Clarke & Stewart (1984), for example, indicated that a decrease in party identification was not confined to young voters, but spanned the whole range of age groups in the electorate.

3. Education

There is an argument that partisan dealignment has followed a period during which the electorate became better educated. According to this view, a better-educated electorate is better able to make rational political decisions. Voters are, therefore, less reliant on an unthinking psychological attachment to a particular party.

4. Television

As well as more formal education, some commentators suspect that party dealignment is linked to the growing and changing television coverage of political events. It was not until the 1960s that the majority of households in Britain had a television set. Since then, coverage has changed. Interviews are much less deferential today than they were in the early 1960s, for example. It has been suggested that developments in television broadcasting and a better-educated electorate have heightened political awareness and led to the questioning of traditional party loyalties. The 'political balance' of programmes and the treatment of politics as a series of events rather than a struggle between ideologies may encourage the belief that partisan positions are unreasonable. Satirical programmes, like *Spitting Image* and *Have I Got News for You*, may have contributed to, as well as merely reflected, a greater cynicism about politics. They may, therefore, have helped to reduce party loyalty.

5. Ideological disjuncture

Party loyalty is likely to be adversely affected if the attitudes, beliefs or wishes of a party's supporters become out of step with some of the basic principles or policies of the party. There is some evidence that such an ideological disjuncture affected the Labour Party in the 1960s and 1970s - over the issues of public ownership, trade union power and welfare expenditure. More recently, Conservative Party support has suffered from ideological and policy splits - especially over Europe.

6. Performance of the parties

It is sometimes argued that voters have become increasingly dissatisfied with the performance of their preferred party, particularly when that party has formed the government. Denver (1990, 1994) argues that this has been the case since the mid-1960s. High levels of satisfaction with party performance tend to go together with high levels of party identification. A decreasing faith in parties and politicians, on the other hand, is likely to accompany falling levels of partisan loyalty. What is debatable is whether growing dissatisfaction in the performance of parties is a cause or an effect of party dealignment.

Party dealignment and electoral volatility

A common argument is that party dealignment produces greater volatility in voting behaviour. This argument, however, is not accepted by all political scientists. Some argue that, although party dealignment has taken place, volatility has increased very little (see, for example, Heath et al. 1991). The different conclusions reflect, to some extent, the different ways in which electoral volatility is measured.

Measurements are able to distinguish between 'overall' and 'net' volatility. 'Net volatility' refers to changes in the parties' share of the vote from one election to another. 'Overall volatility' refers to the total amount of vote-switching which takes place in a single election campaign. It is possible to have high overall volatility and low net volatility if, for instance, votes which have switched from Labour to Conservative are matched in number by votes which have switched from Conservative to Labour. The changes cancel themselves out in terms of their net effect.

Denver (1992) drew attention to the example of the Conservative share of the vote from 1979 to 1992. The relatively small decline in the Conservative vote from 43.9% in 1979 to 41.9% in 1992 appeared to indicate stability rather than volatility. But, these figures showed only the net effect of switches in the vote between parties. According to Denver, the figures concealed a degree of overall volatility which indicated that the Conservatives as well as Labour had suffered from party dealignment. In support of this theory, Chris Game has showed that as many as 11 million voters changed their minds in both the 1992 and the 1997 general elections (Game 1995 and 1998).

Volatility and party dealignment

As well as differing interpretations about the extent of electoral volatility, there is also disagreement about the nature of its connection with party dealignment. Since party identification is a psychological attachment to a political party, those who support the idea of a causal link between party dealignment and electoral volatility explain any upsurge in electoral volatility by reference to changes in the social psychology of voters. But, Heath and his colleagues (1991) doubt the necessity to do this. They argue that changing political circumstances (for example, an increased tendency for a party to change its policies) might themselves be sufficient to lead to greater volatility. In other words, they see no reason why increased volatility and party dealignment should be linked. In fact, Heath and his colleagues doubted in 1988 that party identification had become significantly less influential in determining voter choice (Heath et al. 1988). Miller (1990) also conceded that a decline in intensity of party identification may have accompanied electoral volatility and not necessarily caused it.

Main points - Part 2

- **'Party identification' refers to the psychological attachment to a political party. This influences attitudes and directly affects voting behaviour.**
- **Party dealignment (a drop in the number of voters identifying strongly with the main parties) has been taking place since the early 1970s.**
- **Evidence for party dealignment is a drop in the share of the votes won by the two main parties and opinion polls showing that a declining number of voters identify strongly with a party.**
- **Causes of party dealignment include - class dealignment, the generation effect, education, changing television presentation, ideological disjuncture and the performance of the parties.**
- **There is a debate about whether party dealignment has caused greater electoral volatility.**

Activity 9.3 The party identification model

Item A *Party identification*

(i) Party identification 1964-87

	1964	1966	1970	1974 Feb	1974 Oct	1979	1983	1987
% With identification	92	90	89	98	88	85	86	86
% With Con or Lab identification	81	80	81	75	74	74	67	67
% 'Very strong' identifiers	43	43	41	29	26	21	20	19
% 'Fairly strong' Con or Lab	40	39	40	27	23	19	18	16

This table shows the results of surveys held between 1964 and 1987. People were asked whether they identified with one of the two main parties and, if so, how strongly.

Adapted from Benyon & Denver 1990.

(ii) Party identification 1979-92

	1979	1983	1987	1992	Change 1979-92
Con	37	40	38	39	+2
Lab	38	34	33	35	-3
Lib Dem	13	15	16	12	-1
Other	3	2	2	2	-1
None	10	9	12	12	+2

This table shows the percentage of people who identified with a particular party. The figures have been rounded, so they do not always add up to 100%.

Adapted from Crewe 1993b.

Item B *Party identification*

At election time there is an interplay between a voter's long-term party identification and short-term influences such as current political issues and campaign events. Out of this interplay comes a voting decision. A person's party identification will determine how issues and events are interpreted and evaluated. In other words, identification can serve as a filter through which political messages pass to the individual voter and it can provide a framework within which political events are understood and

evaluated. But, identifying with a party is not the same as voting for it. Voting is a behavioural act whereas party identification is psychological - it exists only in the head. Voting is also time specific (taking place only when there is an election) whilst identification can be ongoing and continuous. Unlike voting, party identification varies in intensity.

Adapted from Denver 1990.

Item C *Intra-election volatility, May 1997*

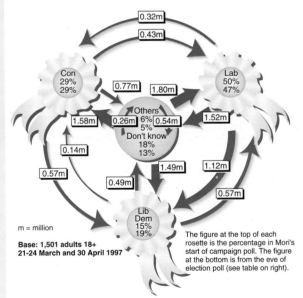

m = million

**Base: 1,501 adults 18+
21-24 March and 30 April 1997**

The figure at the top of each rosette is the percentage in Mori's start of campaign poll. The figure at the bottom is from the eve of election poll (see table on right).

Changes in voting intention during the campaign (million votes)

	Con (29%)	Lab. (47%)	LD** (19%)	Others (5%)	DK* (13%)	Start of campaign totals	Total switchers
Con (29%)	8.57 / 81%	0.43	0.57	0.14	0.63	10.34	1.77
Lab (50%)	0.32	14.73 / 84%	1.12	0.49	1.03	17.69	2.96
LD (15%)**	0.14	0.57	3.98 / 56%	0.09	0.40	5.18	1.20
Others (6%)	0.29	0.34	0.17	0.81 / 45%	0.54	2.15	1.34
DK* (18%)	1.29	1.46	1.32	0.26	3.41 / 57%	7.74	4.33 / 11.6
End of campaign totals	10.61	17.53	7.16	1.79	6.01		
less start of campaign totals	10.34	17.69	5.18	2.15	7.74		
Net campaign movement	+0.27	-0.16	+1.98	-0.36	-1.73		

Header note: Eve of election poll, 30 April; Start of campaign poll 21-24 March

* DK = Don't Know
** LD = Liberal Democrats

Intra-election mobility is a measure of electoral volatility within a single election. The diagram above shows the results of a MORI panel survey conducted during the 1997 general election campaign. It shows that over 11 million voters changed their minds during the 1997 election campaign. All figures, except where otherwise indicated, are millions of voters as projected from the percentage change figures from the panel survey. The figures in the boxes on the right show the number and percentage of non-switchers.

Adapted from Game 1998.

Item D   *Inter-election volatility*

(i)

Row	1959-64	66-70	70-74 Feb	74-79 Oct	79-83	83-87	87-92
1.	18	16	24	22	23	19	22
2.	35	34	42	37	40	37	37

Inter-election volatility is a measure of electoral volatility between successive elections. Row 1 in this table shows the percentage of voters who switched parties in successive elections. Row 2 includes those who did not vote in one election but did so in the next or vice versa. The figures are percentages.

(ii)

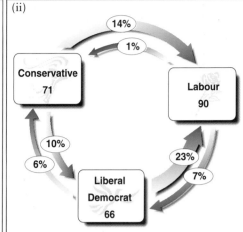

The diagram (left) shows the percentage of voters who switched votes between 1992 and 1997. The figure inside each party's box shows the percentage of votes retained in 1997. The other figures show the percentage moving between the other two main parties.

(iii)

The argument that the British electorate has become dealigned (in both class and party terms) has provoked a good deal of controversy recently. Those who support the dealignment theory argue that one of its consequences is that the electorate has become more volatile - more willing to switch parties. The figures for 1997 show conclusively that the electorate displayed a high level of volatility. By any standards, the changes in vote share were dramatic. The swing from Conservative to Labour was almost double the previous post-war record (5.3% in 1979) and the vote share for 'other' candidates was close to twice that in 1992. The Pederson index is the standard measure of net volatility in elections. It is calculated by adding the changes in the vote share of all parties and dividing by two. In 1997, it produced a score of 12.5, the second highest score (after February 1974) since 1945.

Adapted from Heath et al. 1994 and Denver 1997.

Questions

1. Using the party identification model write a short passage describing the major trends in voting behaviour between 1960 and 1997.

2. a) Using Item A, what are the trends in (i) the direction (ii) the extent and (iii) the intensity of party identification?
   b) How would you expect the pattern of party dealignment to change following the 1997 general election? Explain your answer.

3. Judging from Item B, how does the party identification model differ from the social structures model?

4. a) Judging from Items C and D, what evidence is there of increasing volatility of the electorate?
   b) Why do you think that switching between the Conservatives and Labour is the least common form of electoral volatility?
   c) Is electoral volatility a consequence of party dealignment?

Part 3 The rational choice model

Key issues

1. Is there evidence to suggest that people vote according to rational criteria rather than according to class or party loyalty?
2. How important are issues and values in determining how people vote?
3. To what extent do perceptions of the competence of parties determine whether voters will vote for them?
4. How important is the personality of Party Leaders?

3.1 Principal elements of the model

What is the rational choice model?

The rational choice model suggests that political parties cannot rely simply on the loyalty of their supporters or on particular social classes to win elections. They have to compete for votes on the basis of their policies, their past records and the credibility of their leaders.

The rational choice model focuses on the connection between the attitudes of voters and their decision to vote for a particular party. It does not concern itself with the origins or sources of these attitudes but adopts a supermarket or consumer choice view of voting behaviour. Commenting on the 1997 general election, for example, David Sanders states:

> 'Voters have become much more consumer-like in their voting decisions. They compare the policy and leadership packages that are on offer from the various parties and cast their votes according to which appears (realistically)

to promise the best deal.' (Sanders 1997, p.73) In other words, voters are seen as shopping around for the best deal and then voting accordingly. This model, therefore, emphasises the significance of **instrumental voting** (making rational decisions) rather than the **expressive voting** (making emotional decisions) portrayed in the social structures and party identification models discussed in Parts 1 and 2 above.

Since the rational choice model can encompass a number of variations according to the type of attitudes that are thought to lead to voting choice, various labels are used to indicate the possible connections. These include:

- the issue voting (or policy preference) model
- the value (or ideological voting) model
- the prospective (or investment) model
- the retrospective model
- the Leader personality model.

Each of these models is examined below.

3.2 The issue voting model

What is the issue voting model?

Supporters of the issue voting (or policy preference) model argue that class and party dealignment have been accompanied by a greater willingness on the part of the electorate to be more rational and less emotional in their voting choices. A study by Franklin (1985) attempted to measure this change statistically by analysing a collection of influences upon party preferences. The study concluded that there had been an increase in the contribution which issue options make in determining party preference - from 25% in the 1964 election to about 40% in the elections of 1979 and 1983. Referring to the 1979 election, Ivor Crewe remarked:

'It was issues that won the election for the Conservatives...The Conservatives' success came from saying the right things about the right issues.' (quoted in Benyon & Denver 1990, p.93)

Supporters of the issue voting model agree with this analysis and argue that the Conservatives won and Labour lost the general elections in 1983, 1987 and 1992 because voters supported Conservative policies which promoted individualism and self interest (such as extending share ownership, reducing income tax rates and the sale of council houses) whilst they were scared by Labour's 'left-wing' programme (such as its support for the trade unions, nationalisation and unilateral nuclear disarmament). By 1992, Labour had discarded or radically altered many of its left-wing policies. Nevertheless, so the argument goes, the memory of them lingered in the minds of the electorate and it was not until 1997 that a sufficient number of voters were once again able to find Labour policies sufficiently acceptable to vote for them.

A flawed model?

The main problem with the issue voting model is that, whilst most people would agree that issues do have some effect on voting behaviour, it is difficult to find an exact link. According to Crewe (1992), the significance of an issue in contributing to electoral swing depends upon three factors. First, how important the issue is to the voters. Second, which party is preferred and by how much. And third, how these factors have changed since the last election. This, however, assumes that voters are able to match specific policies with particular parties - an assumption which has been questioned (for example by Conley 1990). Also, for a particular issue to be influential in affecting the outcome of an election, one party must have substantially greater support on that issue than the other parties and that issue must be considered of great importance.

Even then, studies have shown, support for a party's stance on an issue or a range of issues does not necessarily result in a vote for that party. This was the case in the 1983, 1987 and 1992 general elections.

Issues and elections 1983-92

In a study of the 1983 general election, Heath and his colleagues (1985) found that, if people had voted on the issues alone, Labour and the Conservatives would have received roughly equal numbers of votes. In fact, the Conservatives won the election by a very large margin.

In a survey of the 1987 election, Ivor Crewe concluded:

'Had electors voted solely on the main issues, Labour would have won. It was considered the more capable party on three of the four leading issues - jobs, health and education - among those for whom the issue was important.' (*Guardian*, 16 June 1987)

In fact, again, the Conservatives won an overall majority.

This cartoon was produced shortly after the 1987 election. As in 1983, Labour had appeared to be ahead in terms of issues, but the Conservatives won the election.

In a study of the 1992 general election, Crewe (1992) concluded that, if electors had voted on the issues alone, the Conservatives would still have won, but their lead over Labour would have been 5% rather than 8%. Using data from the same post-election Gallup survey used by Crewe in 1992, however, Sanders (1993) concluded that, if voters had voted on the issues alone, Labour would have won the election with 44% of the vote compared to 33% for the Conservatives. The discrepancy between Crewe's account and that of Sanders indicates how difficult it is to measure the effect that support for particular issues has on a person's vote. The fact that both accounts conclude that Labour's support would have increased if issue voting had taken place, however, suggests that it was not issues which led voters to vote Conservative. It must have been other factors.

Issues and the election of 1997

The issues which Labour chose to concentrate on in the run-up to the 1997 election were those which most concerned the voters (health, education, law and order, unemployment and pensions). The Conservatives in 1997, by way of contrast, were out of touch with the voters:

> 'In the 1997 general election, it was the Conservative Party which was suffering "ideological disjuncture", wedded as it was to policies and an ideological perspective which were at odds with the views and values...of the majority of the electorate. Only a minority of the electorate in 1997 wanted more privatisation [or] were opposed outright to Britain's possible membership of a single European currency...Two of the issues which the Conservatives attempted to highlight, trade unions and devolution, were considered by voters to be the two least salient [important] issues.' (Dorey 1998, pp.112-3)

Even though Labour was ahead on issues, however, that alone did not guarantee victory - as the lessons of 1983-92 show. Rather, it would be more accurate to argue that Labour's superiority on issues helped to provide the environment in which people felt comfortable voting for the party.

Other problems with the issue voting model

There are two further problems with the issue voting model. First, it ignores the way in which the choices confronting voters are limited or manipulated by the media. Media effects may help to produce contradictory opinions on related issues within the same voter. If this occurs, then the vote itself may not be the outcome of careful, rationally thought out decision making. Second, as with other explanations of voting behaviour, there is the danger of confusing a correlation with a cause. As Rose & McAllister (1986) point out, the attempt to explain a connection between issues and voting choice through post-election (after the event) analyses is unsatisfactory since only a correlation can be shown. This problem is summed up by Benyon & Denver as follows:

> 'Does the voter pick the party because of its policies or choose the policy positions because they are favoured by the party he or she supports?' (Benyon & Denver 1990, p.93)

3.3 Ideological voting

What is the ideological voting model?

Problems with the issue voting model have led to the development of a variant - the ideological voting model. Heath and his colleagues (1985), for example, are not convinced that issue voting has increased, particularly if the model implies that voters make their choice after weighing up the parties' detailed policy proposals. They do, however, argue that there is a connection (a fit) between voters' general values or ideologies and their overall perception of what parties stand for. The closer the fit, they argue, the stronger the attachment to the party concerned and, therefore, the greater the likelihood that the voter will vote for that party.

According to Rose & McAllister (1986 and 1990) durable political values outweigh issues by more than ten to one in their importance in explaining voting behaviour. Issues on their own, they argue, are not that significant because voters' evaluation of the parties are made within the context of 'a lifetime of political learning' (Rose & McAllister 1990 p.141). At election times, a number of different influences are operating simultaneously. Family loyalties, socio-economic interests, the social and political context, and the current and recent performance of political parties and leaders all play a part in determining a person's voting behaviour. But, the most important part is played by the person's political values.

A flawed model?

One problem with the ideological voting model is that, between 1979 and 1997, opinion polls consistently indicated that a majority of people were prepared to pay higher taxes to maintain or improve standards of public service, but this support was not translated into votes for Labour. This suggests that there is a gap between people's values and their actions. Ivor Crewe (*Guardian*, 15 & 16 June 1987), however, explains away this gap by arguing that responses to opinion polls are constructed in terms of 'public problems' whilst, at the time of voting, 'family concerns' are uppermost in voters' minds. During the run-up to the 1997 general election, the Labour Party ruled out any rises in income tax rates to fund increases in public spending - despite evidence from opinion polls continuing to show that a majority would support such a move. This cautious approach suggests that the party leadership was not convinced that the poll results accurately reflected people's real desires.

3.4 Perceptions of competence

The prospective model

To what extent do perceptions of the competence of parties determine whether voters will vote for them? The answer to this question depends on how voters evaluate two factors:

- the past performance of the parties (the retrospective model)
- parties' likely future performance (the prospective model).

According to the prospective model, people vote for the party which they judge most likely to raise (or at least to protect) their standard of living. For some voters, this judgement depends not just on considerations of their personal economic wellbeing. It also depends on a wider perception of the competence of a party to manage the economy in general.

The sociology of aspirations

The prospective model fits with what political commentator Stuart Hall describes as 'the sociology of aspirations' (Hall 1992). According to this theory, the electorate thinks in terms of images rather than policies (see Box 9.2).

Box 9.2 The sociology of aspirations

When voters were asked in the 1987 election campaign which policies they supported, most preferred Labour on unemployment, health, housing and education - the welfare issues. During the campaign, these remained the most important issues for most voters. Yet, if voters were asked about image - questions like: 'Who is doing a good job?' or 'Who is making it feel good to be British again?' - the majority consistently said, 'Maggie'. Given that the Conservatives won the election, it seems that increasingly the electorate is thinking in terms of images rather than policies. This does not mean that policies do not matter. It means that policies do not capture people's imaginations unless they are constructed into an image with which people can identify. Some people argue that this trivialises politics. But, images are not trivial things. It is through images that political questions are being posed and argued through. Political imagery is not a matter of presentation but of ideology - which is a different and altogether more serious matter.

Adapted from Hall 1987.

If a party manages to project the image of economic competence, this theory suggests, then it will attract voters regardless of their existing economic circumstances.

The 1992 general election

There is, however, also a reverse side to the prospective model. Not only do voters choose parties because they believe they will be competent in the future, they also reject parties because they believe they will be incompetent in the future. This, it seems, is what happened to Labour in 1992. At the time of the 1992 general election, the economy was in recession. To deflect criticisms of its economic record, therefore, the Conservative government mounted a relentless attack on Labour's taxation plans, making it difficult for Labour to shake off its image as the party of high taxation. This strategy was adopted on the grounds that people tend to calculate their tax liabilities not so much on their current earnings, but on the income they aspire to in the near future. The strategy worked. Although the 'feel-good' score (a measure of how voters assess their current economic circumstances) was -3 in the run-up to the 1992 election (compared with +12 before the 1987 general election), the Conservatives still won an overall majority. Significantly, polls showed that, during the campaign, voters judged the Conservatives more competent (or, at least, less incompetent) to manage the economy than Labour (Crewe 1992).

The 1997 general election

By the time of the 1997 general election, perceptions of competence had changed considerably and significantly. The Conservatives were no longer perceived by many voters to be competent and Labour had managed to banish the 'fear factor' which the Conservatives had exploited so skilfully in 1992. The key to this turnaround was the withdrawal from the EU's exchange rate mechanism in September 1992 (see Box 9.3).

Box 9.3 Black Wednesday

Any adequate explanation of the 1997 general election needs to examine how the symbolic images that voters held of the parties changed during the period 1992 and 1997. One event did more than any other to change those images - 'Black Wednesday' in September 1992 when the pound was forced out of the exchange rate mechanism. Almost overnight the Conservatives' reputation as a strong, competent government that knew how to run the economy and defend Britain's interests abroad was destroyed. Until then, sterling crises and devaluations had been the prerogative of Labour governments, most recently in 1967 and 1976; from 1992 onwards, they were a Conservative problem too. As a result, the Conservatives' opinion poll ratings slumped by more than 10 points within a matter of weeks (as indeed did Labour's in 1967 and 1976) and they never recovered. The impressions of incompetence and division caused by Black Wednesday were simply reinforced by subsequent tax rises, sleaze and squabbling over Europe.

Adapted from Curtice 1997.

The retrospective model

Whereas the prospective model examines ways in which forecasts of party performance affect voting behaviour, the retrospective model focuses on voters' perceptions of the parties' past records and especially on the past record of the incumbent government. As such, the retrospective model fits more closely into a purely rational choice model since voters can base their decisions on concrete evidence.

As with the prospective model, the retrospective model suggests that voting behaviour is primarily determined by economic factors. What counts is the voters' perception of the past economic record of the government and the policies supported by the opposition parties. Although, on occasion, non-economic factors can influence voting behaviour (for example, the Falklands War was a significant factor in the Conservative election victory of 1983), this model suggests that management of the economy and economic issues determine the outcomes of most elections.

The 1992 general election

Like the prospective model, the retrospective model can be used to explain the result of the 1992 general election. The parties entered the 1992 election campaign with the economy in recession. Businesses were going bankrupt, workers were losing their jobs and many house buyers were unable to keep up with their mortgage repayments. More voters claimed that their standard of living had fallen over the previous year than those who believed it had risen (Crewe 1992). On the basis of recent past performance, therefore, it might be expected that the government would lose the election. But, it did not. Somehow, it managed to deflect the blame for the poor economic circumstances which prevailed at the time. The 1992 Harris exit poll indicated that voters (including some Labour and Liberal Democrat supporters) were much more likely to blame 'world economic conditions' or even 'Mrs Thatcher's government' than they were to blame John Major's government. Only 5% of Conservative voters and 7% of other voters gave 'John Major's government' as the reason for the poor state of the economy - despite the fact that most of John Major's Cabinet ministers had served in the Thatcher government, including Major himself as Chancellor. These figures suggest that the past record of the government was important. But, people separated the past performance of the Thatcher government from the performance of the Major government. In addition and as noted above, there is evidence that voters were afraid of Labour's economic policies, especially their policies on taxation. In other words, enough voters to ensure a Conservative victory were prepared to look kindly on the past performance of the Major government but looked unkindly on the past performance of the Labour Party.

The 1997 general election

By the time of the 1997 general election, there had been a significant turnaround. Not only had Labour made a great deal of effort to discard its reputation as the party of high taxation, the Conservatives had lost their reputation for competence (see Box 9.2 above), even though the economy was, objectively, in much better shape than it had been in 1992. Despite an economy which was booming as a whole, the 1997 BBC/NOP exit poll showed that three-quarters of voters believed that their standard of living was either worse or about the same as it had been in 1992. On the other hand, 35% believed that the economy as a whole had become stronger than it was in 1992, compared with 31% who thought it had become weaker. The political commentator Peter Kellner suggests that these figures can be explained by two factors. First, some people may have felt that they had been left behind by the economic recovery - their standard of living did not reflect national economic improvements. And second, the term 'standard of living' may have been taken not to refer just to money, but to include:

> 'A wider sense of the quality of life, including the quality of the health and education services, public transport and so on... Surveys have shown that large majorities of people feel that public services have deteriorated since 1992.' (Kellner 1997, p.112)

By the time of the 1997 general election, therefore, the record of the Conservative government counted against it whilst Labour's new image mitigated doubts about the record of past Labour governments.

3.5 Leadership and personality

Leadership and voter perceptions

Between 1945 and 1998, the Labour and Conservative parties both elected eight Leaders, an average of a new Leader about every seven years. Although some Party Leaders retained their position for considerably longer than the average (for example, Margaret Thatcher was Conservative Party Leader for 15 years and Harold Wilson was Labour Leader for 13 years), these Leaders were not typical. On the whole, Party Leaders change fairly frequently. As a result, voter perceptions of the personality or competence of a Party Leader can be classed as a short-term factor in accounting for voting behaviour. If it is correct to assume that, as a result of class and party dealignment, long-term factors have decreased in significance, then perceptions of leadership may be one of the factors which has come to play a greater role in party choice at election times.

The growing importance of Leaders' reputations

In their observations of pre-1974 elections, Butler & Stokes (1971) recognised that leadership could be an issue in voting behaviour. But, it was only one of a number of influences and, usually, only became a factor if one Party Leader stood out as being particularly more popular than another. Since 1974, the extent and style of media coverage of election campaigns has changed. Media attention on personalities, rather than on policies, is nothing new. In more recent general elections, however, the media has focused attention on the Party Leaders much more than used to be the case. By 1983, studies suggest, leadership had become crucial. Miller (1984), for example, argued that Labour lost the 1983 election not primarily because of unpopular policies, but because its divided leadership failed to give the impression that Labour was competent to rule. When asked which Leader would make the best Prime Minister, respondents to opinion polls in 1983 gave Labour's Leader, Michael Foot, very low ratings. Similarly, in 1992, Neil Kinnock's perceived lack of leadership qualities has been cited as an important reason for Labour's defeat (see Dobson 1998, p.4, for example).

Leadership and the 1997 general election
In 1997, the overall public opinion poll ratings for the three main Party Leaders closely reflected the division of the vote between the parties at the election itself (Kellner 1997, p.117). Tony Blair's rating, however, was considerably higher than Kinnock's in 1992 and may have been a significant boost to the Labour Party's performance:

> 'There is no doubt that his relative youth, dynamism, manner and televisual qualities enabled Blair to transform the negative image held of the Labour leadership when Kinnock was in command into something more popular. This, together with Major's difficulties during his premiership and consequent image as a weak leader, meant that the deficit experienced by Kinnock in relation to Major in 1992 was transformed into a significant credit for Blair by 1997...The importance of this turnaround should not be underestimated.' (Dobson 1998, p.9)

Personality and leadership qualities
These findings and observations raise a number of questions. First, if the personalities of the Party Leaders do have some effect on party choice, is the impact positive or negative - do voters tend to vote for parties whose Leaders they like most or dislike least? Second, can voters' attitudes towards Party Leaders be separated successfully from their views of the parties in general. And third, do voters tend to draw a distinction between the personality of a Leader and the Leader's leadership qualities? What is it about the Leader (if anything) which determines voting behaviour?

It is difficult to answer these questions. It may, for example, simply not be possible to disentangle voters' perceptions about personality from those concerning leadership qualities. As Benyon & Denver (1990) have noted, it may be that voters are more likely to operate in terms of generalised images which involve a combination of views on and perceptions of personalities, policies, competence and ideology. But, given that most people obtain the bulk of their information about policies and politicians from television and newspapers, media coverage is likely to feature significantly in the formation of such images.

Main points - Part 3

- The rational choice model suggests that parties cannot rely simply on loyalty or social factors to win elections. It emphasises the significance of instrumental voting (making rational decisions) rather than expressive voting (making emotional decisions).
- The issue voting model suggests that voters' analysis of issues affects their voting behaviour. The main problem with the model is that, whilst most people would agree that issues do affect voting behaviour, it is difficult to find an exact link.
- The ideological voting model suggests there is a connection between voters' durable political values and their voting behaviour. The problem is that what people say are their values does not necessarily translate into votes.
- The prospective model suggests that people vote for the party which they judge most likely to raise (or at least to protect) their standard of living. The retrospective model focuses on voters' perceptions of the parties' past records.
- The personalities of Party Leaders do have some effect on party choice, but it is difficult to find out the extent to which they influence voting behaviour. It may be that voters operate in terms of generalised images.

Activity 9.4 *The rational choice model*

Item A *Perceptions of competence (1)*

Throughout the 1980s, it had been the Labour Party which suffered from voters' perceptions that the party was deeply divided over ideology and policies. This perception reinforced the electorate's reluctance to support Labour at general elections, underpinning the widespread assumption that the party was 'unfit to govern'. In 1997, however, it was the Conservatives who suffered from voters' perceptions that the party was divided and no longer 'fit to govern'. The most obvious source of division was the EU. Whilst the Conservative Party as a whole had adopted an increasingly Eurosceptic stance, it remained the case that a number of senior and prominent Conservatives were Europhiles, wanting Britain to be at the 'heart of Europe'. As a result, the Conservatives entered the 1997 election campaign unable to conceal the deep divisions over Europe. In the BBC/NOP exit poll, 84% of respondents said that they thought that the Conservative Party was divided whilst only 34% of respondents thought that the Labour Party was divided.

Adapted from Dorey 1998.

Item B   *Perceptions of competence (2)*

How did the Conservatives manage to win the 1992 general election in the middle of the longest economic recession since the 1930s and lose the 1997 general election when inflation, unemployment and interest rates were low? One answer would be to deny that the state of the economy is a major determinant of voting behaviour. But, this would ignore the importance of people's perceptions of the economy (as opposed to official economic statistics). At the time of the 1992 general election, most voters did not blame John Major's government for the poor state of the economy. Many believed that their future personal economic circumstances would be better under the Conservatives. All this changed after the ERM crisis in September 1992. Many people no longer felt that the Conservatives were competent managers of the economy. The Conservatives never recovered from this and were unable to benefit from the upturn in economic optimism of 1996-7. Conservative difficulties were made worse by the rival attraction of the revised policies of Tony Blair's New Labour. The Conservative Party certainly benefited from moods of economic optimism at the elections of 1983, 1987 and 1992, but this had been based on public perceptions of its superior competence in managing the economy. At the 1997 election, these perceptions had disappeared. The links between economic perceptions, the 'feel-good' factor and the Conservatives - present at the previous three general elections - had been broken.

Adapted from Sanders 1998.

Item C   *Issues and the 1997 general election*

(i) Which issues were important?

```
% 80
    70 ┤ 70
       │ ▓
    60 ┤ ▓   62
       │ ▓   ▓
    50 ┤ ▓   ▓   50
       │ ▓   ▓   ▓   45  42
    40 ┤ ▓   ▓   ▓   ▓   ▓
       │ ▓   ▓   ▓   ▓   ▓   35
    30 ┤ ▓   ▓   ▓   ▓   ▓   ▓   32
       │ ▓   ▓   ▓   ▓   ▓   ▓   ▓   28
    20 ┤ ▓   ▓   ▓   ▓   ▓   ▓   ▓   ▓   24  24
       │ ▓   ▓   ▓   ▓   ▓   ▓   ▓   ▓   ▓   ▓   21
    10 ┤ ▓   ▓   ▓   ▓   ▓   ▓   ▓   ▓   ▓   ▓   ▓   12  11
       │ ▓   ▓   ▓   ▓   ▓   ▓   ▓   ▓   ▓   ▓   ▓   ▓   ▓   10  10
     0 ┴───────────────────────────────────────────────────────
```

Health care 70, Education 62, Law and order 50, Unemployment 45, Pensions 42, Taxation 35, Economy 32, Housing 28, Europe 24, Environment 24, Transport 21, Animal welfare 12, Northern Ireland 11, Trade unions 10, Devolution 10

This chart shows the percentage of people who regarded a particular issue as important in helping them to decide who to vote for. The results of the survey were first published on 6 April 1997.

(ii) Issues and image

In recent general elections, particularly 1992, the popularity of Labour's stance on a range of policy issues had been outweighed by its perceived lack of competence in economic affairs. In 1997, however, Labour was able to appeal to the electorate on economic as well as social policies, to the extent that, on a whole range of issues, the party appeared much more in tune with public opinion and values than the Conservatives. Indeed, between 1992 and 1997, voters' perceptions of Labour across the entire range of key issues had been comprehensively transformed. The Conservatives still enjoyed small leads on inflation and defence. But, in every other issue area, Labour was clearly ahead. This suggested a fundamental shift in Labour's overall image as a potential party of government.

Adapted from Sanders 1997 and Dorey 1998.

Item D   *Taxation 1992 and 1997*

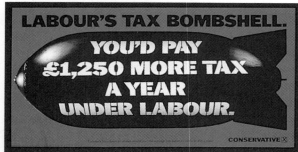

The poster on the left was produced by the Conservative Party in 1992. The poster on the right was produced by the Labour Party in 1997.

Item E *Party leadership*

(i) This chart shows the result of exit polls held in 1992 and 1997 in which people were asked who they thought would make the best Prime Minister.

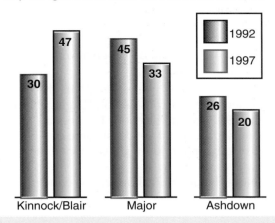

(ii) In the 1992 and 1997 exit polls, people were asked whether John Major and Neil Kinnock or Tony Blair were strong or weak leaders. This chart shows the percentage who thought each Party Leader was strong.

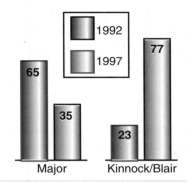

Questions

1. a) How does the rational choice model differ from the social structures and party identification models?
   b) Give arguments for and against the view that voting is a rational act.
2. a) Judging from Items A and B, how did perceptions of the competence of the main parties affect the way in which voters voted in 1992 and 1997?
   b) Explain the information in Items A and B in terms of (i) the prospective model and (ii) the retrospective model.

3. a) Using Items C and D, explain the results of the 1997 general election in terms of issue voting.
   b) What does Item D tell us about the issue of taxation in the 1992 and 1997 elections?
   c) How important are issues in explaining voting behaviour? Explain your answer.
4. Look at Item E. What impact do you think voter perceptions of Party Leaders had on the outcome of the 1992 and 1997 general elections? Explain how you reached your answer.

Part 4 The dominant ideology model

Key issues

1. What role does the mass media play in determining voting behaviour?
2. Does the media affect voting behaviour in the short term or long term?
3. How useful are opinion polls in forecasting voting behaviour?
4. Do opinion polls determine voting behaviour?

4.1 Principal elements of the model

What is the 'dominant ideology'?

The central claim of the dominant ideology model is that powerful groups in society (collectively, the 'Establishment') influence the attitudes and behaviour (including the voting behaviour) of the public. This influence is exerted by the control that these groups exercise over public institutions and through the mass media.

Dunleavy & Husbands (1985) suggest that an analysis of voting behaviour cannot be reduced to

the level of the individual voter. Instead, analysis should focus on shifts of party support in the electorate as a whole. The way in which society is organised - the social structure - and people's locations within that structure may well be significant influences on voting behaviour (see Part 1 above). The effects of such structural factors, however, are mediated in many complex ways by:

> 'A set of dominant ideological messages formulated by institutions of central social significance.' (Dunleavy & Husbands 1985, p.19)

According to Dunleavy & Husbands these 'institutions of central social significance' include:

- the mass media
- the government
- business interests
- political leaders
- the political parties.

Together, these institutions are structured in such a way that they provide an advantage to mainstream (Establishment) political parties. Traditionally, the major advantages were seen to be gained by the Conservative Party, but the model can apply to any of the main parties which are seen to serve or support the interests of the dominant groups in society.

The dominant ideology model in practice

Although the political commentator Ivor Crewe has voiced doubts about the dominant ideology model, he has also recognised the existence of institutional inequalities in some areas. For example, he examined the phenomenon of under-registration in the early 1990s (Crewe 1992). By the time of the 1992 general election, around 1 million adults were not registered to vote. This was a large increase compared with previous elections - an increase mainly due to concerns about the poll tax. Since under-registration is more common amongst groups more likely to vote Labour (such as the unemployed, the geographically mobile young and those living in inner cities), the Labour Party was disproportionately affected. It was estimated that differential under-registration was worth about eight seats to the Conservatives at the 1992 general election (Crewe 1993a). Since the poll tax was devised by those in power in the late 1980s (a product of the dominant ideology at the time), it could be argued that, in this instance, the dominant ideology had a direct impact on voting behaviour.

4.2 The mass media

The party bias of the press

Central to the dominant ideology model is the role of the mass media. It is through the mass media that groups attempt to set the political agenda and influence public opinion (see also, Chapter 19).

Most adults in Britain read a national daily and a Sunday newspaper. Until recently, the vast majority of these newspapers actively supported the Conservative Party and urged their readers, on election days, to vote Conservative. The tabloid newspapers, in particular, tend to be highly partisan with news, opinion and party propaganda mixed together.

The press and the 1992 general election

In 1992, most of the tabloid newspapers openly campaigned for the Conservatives and the *Sun* even claimed that it was single-handedly responsible for the Conservatives' victory. Whilst that boast was generally regarded as an over-simplification, the contribution played by the press in the Conservative victory was acknowledged by senior Conservatives. One, Lord McAlpine (a former party Treasurer), stated publicly that:

> 'The heroes of this campaign were Sir David English [*Daily Express* editor] and Kelvin McKenzie [*Sun* editor] and the other editors of the grander Tory press. Never in the past nine elections have they come out so strongly in favour of the Conservatives. Never has the

attack on Labour been so comprehensive...This is how the election was won.' (quoted in the *Sunday Telegraph*, 12 April 1992)

According to one study (Linton 1996), at the time of the 1992 general election, 70% of the press favoured the Conservatives, compared to only 27% favouring Labour. Linton pointed out that the Labour Party had never won an election when its press share was more than 18% behind the Conservatives.

The 1997 general election

By the time of the 1997 general election, the position had changed considerably. During the run-up to the 1997 general election, 11 national newspapers (dailies and Sundays) came out in support of Labour and just eight supported the Conservatives:

> 'Never before has Labour enjoyed the majority support of the national daily press in a general election...In the political history of the press, this was an historic moment every bit as significant as the size of Labour's majority.' (Seymour-Ure 1997, p.78)

The most notable shift in party allegiance came from the *Sun*. During the election campaign, Tony Blair was regularly given space in the *Sun* 'for his unedited views' and later thanked it for 'its magnificent support' which 'really did make the difference' (Scammell & Harrop 1997, pp.160, 183). Earlier speculation - that Blair and Murdoch (owner of the *Sun*) had arranged some sort of deal on cross-media ownership policy - received little in the way of renewed comment. In May 1997, in terms of readership of the national dailies, 21.6 million people were reading pro-Labour newspapers compared to 10.6 million reading Conservative newspapers (Scammell & Harrop 1997, p.156).

Broadcasting

Unlike the press, news and current affairs broadcasts on the television and radio operate under legal obligations to be neutral on party political matters. Broadcasters go to great lengths at election times to attempt an almost arithmetic balance in their coverage of the three main parties. Since most voters gain most of their political information from television rather than from newspapers, it could be argued that such a balance is a political necessity because:

> 'Television (in contrast to the press) is commonly found to be the most important and trusted source of political information for the public.' (Gavin & Sanders 1997, p.128)

Can balance really be achieved?

Whether a genuine balance is actually achieved, however, is open to debate. One argument is that the attempt to be balanced restricts the extent and nature of election coverage. Another is that newspapers play a significant role in setting the agenda for television news coverage. The argument goes as follows. If most of the newspapers concentrate on issues which are more favourable to one party rather than another and ignore those less favourable to that party, then television might well reflect this in its coverage of the issues. A study of the 1987 general election campaign shows how this benefited the Conservative Party (Miller et al. 1990). Television coverage in the 1987 general election campaign focused on defence and law and order (issues more favourable to the Conservatives) rather than on those issues which favoured Labour - such as unemployment, education and health. Conversely, in 1997, it was Labour that appeared to benefit (see Norris 1997).

Government advantage?
The apparent neutrality of radio and television broadcasting might also conceal another factor contributing to what Miller and his colleagues have described as 'a massive bias towards the government' (Miller et al. 1990, p.57). Although the parties might well receive equal campaign coverage, the party in power gets a good deal of additional attention through the reporting of the activities and pronouncements of the government of the day. As Crewe (1993a) has pointed out, however, this additional coverage could be a two-edged sword since news reports discuss government failures and problems as well as successes. So, for example, although the Conservatives benefited from this extra exposure in 1992, it suffered from it in 1997:

> 'The seismic rumblings of the Conservative Party's deep divisions on the European single currency, and the acrimonious squabbles between the competing factions that often came in their wake, were regularly and prominently portrayed on television, especially in the last few weeks of the campaign when Europe became the most important issue in coverage.' (Gavin & Sanders 1997, p.131)

Does bias matter?
It is one thing to show that the mass media is biased, but quite another to show that this bias does, in fact, influence voters. The traditional view is that, whilst newspapers are probably responsible for few conversions from one party to another, they do have a reinforcing effect on voting behaviour. At most, they play a role in persuading the previously uncommitted to vote for a particular party. Nevertheless, in an era of party dealignment and increasing electoral volatility (see above Section 2.2), this role may be a growing one. Since dealignment means that there are fewer committed voters, more voters should be open to persuasion and there should, therefore, be more scope for media influence. It has even been suggested that one possible cause of the decline in party identification is the balanced, non-partisan and non-ideological style of television coverage (Denver 1994).

The problem facing all social scientists in trying to assess the degree of media influence on any aspect of behaviour, however, is how to isolate the effects of all the other possible variables such as family, class, age and a whole range of other factors. Attempts to do this, though (for example, Miller 1991 and Newton 1992), have suggested that newspapers do exert some influence on electoral outcomes.

Short-term and long-term effects of bias
When Neil Kinnock resigned as Labour Leader following the 1992 general election, he blamed the election result on the anti-Labour attacks during the campaign made by the Conservative tabloid newspapers. Evidence of a noticeable swing to the Conservatives among *Sun* readers during the later stages of the campaign lends some support to Kinnock's claim. But, the late swing was not just confined to *Sun* readers (Crewe 1993a).

Although short-term effects of media bias cannot be ruled out, the traditional view that the media has limited influence is challenged more strongly by approaches and studies that take a longer-term view. The traditional claim was that people's choice of newspaper depends on their political preference rather than vice versa and so newspapers reinforce rather than convert. But, continual reinforcement over a long period may well be significant. The long-term drip by drip effect of the media may be more important than any short-term campaign or story run by a newspaper. Miller attempted to look beyond the short-term effects of newspaper coverage during elections by interviewing the same panel of respondents on a number of occasions over a 12 month period preceding the 1987 general election (Miller 1991). The results of this survey indicate that newspapers do influence their readers over the long term.

The importance of what is omitted
Even more influential in helping to produce or confirm a 'world view' among voters could be those things which the media chooses to omit. In their urge to convey news, the mass media is more likely to focus on short-term, trivial issues and events than on longer-term, larger and more underlying questions. The range of issues, beliefs and arguments projected by the media forms the context in which voters make their choices. This context also affects the behaviour of the parties. After the 1992 general election, for example, it was suggested that a Conservative-dominated press forced Labour to be extra cautious to avoid accusations of 'loony leftism' (Newton 1992). It could be argued that the subsequent emergence of New Labour was a reaction to the fact that the boundaries of what was politically acceptable and unacceptable had been drawn up by a media which was dominated by right-wingers. This would explain the changes in the organisation, image and policies of the Labour Party and, above all, its 'abandonment of socialism' (Dorey 1998).

The manipulation of news

The relationship between the media and the political parties is not a one-way affair. All political parties attempt to manipulate the ways in which political affairs are reported and presented in the media. When most of the press supported the Conservative Party, that party found the process of manipulation easier to manage (at least as far as newspapers were concerned). There is evidence, for example, of particularly close collaboration at election times between leading Conservatives and the editors of major right-wing newspapers (see, for example Benyon & Denver 1990). During the 1997 general election campaign, however, a combination of sophisticated organisation, skilful 'spin doctoring' and a much more sympathetic press gave a clear advantage to Labour:

> 'In 1997 compared to 1992, the newspapers did not set an agenda which served systematically to undermine Labour - quite the reverse. Further, the Conservative-supporting press was often lukewarm in its endorsement of the party and the support for the Conservatives in the election campaign frequently followed many months of severe criticism of the Major government. Labour also used television very effectively. The party managed to minimise bad publicity for Labour and maximise it for the Conservatives.' (Dobson 1998, p.13)

If a party favoured by most of the press is also the party in government, the advantage is heightened. Miller (1990), for example, drew attention to the way in which Conservative governments in the 1980s altered the way in which unemployment figures were calculated. These altered figures (which showed a reduction in the number of people out of work) were then reported uncritically by sympathetic elements in the media. In addition, during the 1980s, Conservative governments ran advertising campaigns to publicise certain policies even before Parliament had granted legal approval for their implementation.

Political advertising

It is at election time that party advertising is most common. All the major parties spend a great deal of effort and money on their pre-election advertising campaigns. There are legal ceilings on the amount that can be spent by parliamentary candidates at constituency level. The fact that there were no legal restrictions on what parties could spend nationally came under increasing criticism in the late 1990s. In October 1998, the Neill Report on party funds was published. This recommended a limit on the maximum amount that political parties could spend nationally. As soon as the report was published, the government agreed to implement its proposals.

During the 1997 general election campaign, the amount of paid party advertising in the press actually fell quite considerably compared to 1992. This reflected a switch to poster site advertising. Nevertheless, advertising still remained a prominent feature for the following reasons:

> 'Press and poster advertisements were often reported in the news columns and party election broadcasts were always reviewed and sometimes previewed in the papers. The Conservative advertisement portraying Blair as Kohl's dummy and Labour's "Fitz the bulldog" election broadcast became news stories with a life of their own.' (Scammell & Harrop 1997, p.183)

Scammell and Harrop go on to add that the 1997 campaign confirms the theory that the main purpose of political advertising is not to influence voters directly, but to help set the news agenda.

Negative campaigning

Not infrequently, party election broadcasts and adverts are exercises in negative propaganda which criticise the policies or leadership of opposing parties. Negative campaigning often leads to charges of media manipulation. After the 1992 general election campaign, for example, complaints were made that elements of Conservative Party advertising so distorted Labour's taxation policies that it amounted to a major misrepresentation and to an unfair electoral advantage. But, negative campaigning is not always effective and can be counter-productive. It was found, for example, that Conservative attempts to discredit Labour through political advertising in the months leading up to the 1997 general election largely failed:

> 'A dispute has broken out in the Conservative Party over two broadcasts in which a lone woman and a lion end up weeping at the prospect of a Labour government. A study suggests that Tory waverers have been put off by the negative tone...The research suggests that the 'New Labour, New Danger' campaign is failing. A monthly poll of 1,000 previously Tory voters showed that 60% said that it had made no difference. A balance of 8% said that the campaign had reduced their support for the Conservatives.' (*Times*, 21 February 1997 - slightly adapted)

Media manipulation and the dominant ideology model

Supporters of the dominant ideology model see some of the activities described above not so much as isolated attempts to secure support for or against particular policies, but as part of a wider network of control through which powerful groups, with the aid of the mass media, are able to influence the attitudes and behaviour of the public. The attempts may not always be successful, and the claims of those who detect bias in the media may sometimes seem exaggerated. Nevertheless, there may be some substance to these claims. For example, rising economic optimism was thought to have been a significant factor in maintaining the Conservative Party in power throughout the 1980s. From one perspective, this can be explained using the rational choice model - economic optimism increased and those who were optimistic voted Conservative. But why, asked Miller, did voters become optimistic? If it was because Conservative governments successfully managed to manipulate the media and the economy, then, he argues, this is evidence which supports the dominant ideology model (Miller 1990, p.60). Miller produces evidence that can be interpreted in this way. For example, before the 1987 general election, the government adjusted calculations of economic statistics, paid for political advertising out of public funds, pressurised the BBC in an attempt to manage the news and manipulated the 'real economy' to stimulate a consumer boom in time for the election.

The 1997 election and the dominant ideology model
Throughout the period 1979-97, there were political commentators who argued that the Labour Party was unlikely ever again to secure a general election victory. For these commentators, the dominant ideology model helped to explain the apparent invincibility of the Conservatives. Following the 1997 general election, these commentators had to reappraise their position. Some argued that there had been a major and significant shift in voting behaviour. Others, however, rejected this view and argued that the fact that New Labour had replaced the Conservatives in government did not fundamentally affect the validity of the dominant ideology model. To these commentators, the change in government was due more to shifts within the main parties than to shifts of belief or behaviour amongst the electorate. In other words, these commentators would argue that it was the Labour Party, not the *Sun*, which had changed its politics.

Main points - Sections 4.1 - 4.2

- The central claim of the dominant ideology model is that powerful groups in society influence voting behaviour. Central is the role of the mass media. It is through the mass media that groups attempt to set the political agenda and influence public opinion.
- In 1992, the majority of papers supported the Conservatives. In 1997, a majority supported Labour.
- Unlike the press, news and current affairs broadcasts on the television and radio operate under legal obligations to be neutral on party

political matters. Whether broadcasts are neutral is questionable, however.
- It is difficult to know the extent to which the media influences behaviour, but it seems to have a greater impact in the long term than the short term.
- The relationship between the media and the political parties is not all one-way. Parties attempt to manipulate the media and the media supports parties which uphold the media's values.
- The lesson of 1997 was that either voting behaviour changed drastically or it was the parties which had changed, not the voters.

Activity 9.5 *The dominant ideology model*

Item A *Headlines from the 1997 general election campaign*

Sun — 18 March
The Sun backs Blair

Guardian — 12 April
'CASH FOR QUOTE' ROW HITS MAJOR

Financial Times — 16 April
Tory crisis over EU rebels

Mirror — 18 April
Read this and weep- NHS destroyed

Guardian — 17 April
Major at war with his party

Financial Times — 21 April
Tory divisions on EU widen

Sun — 28 April
BLAIR KICKS OUT LEFTIES

Independent — 29 April
TORIES GIVING UP

Sun — 30 April
WHO BLAIRS WINS

Item B   *The press and the 1997 general election (1)*

(i) Analysis of the major issues covered by television and the press during the 1997 campaign shows that the conduct and progress of the election occupied a third of the coverage and the discussion of individual policy issues focused on (in descending order) Europe, sleaze, education, taxation, constitutional reform, privatisation, health, social security and Northern Ireland. During the first two weeks, sleaze stories predominated. After that, Europe rose to the top of the agenda. Both issues meant negative coverage for the government and prevented it from pushing its own message about the health of the economy.

Adapted from Norris 1997.

(ii) Referring back to its 1992 post-election headline, the *Sun* stated (on page 2, this time) - 'It's the *Sun* wot swung it'. For the second election in a row, the paper argued, the victorious Party Leader had good reason to thank the *Sun*. But, given the size of Labour's victory, the influence of the press during the campaign cannot have been that significant. The press undoubtedly helped to set the agenda and it may well, as always, have shifted some votes. But, the press was not responsible for Labour's landslide. Indeed, the shift of newspapers to Labour was as much a reflection of Labour's growing popularity as a cause of it. In the longer term, the press may have helped to shift opinion - the hostility towards the Conservatives from previously friendly papers began in 1992 after the ERM crisis.

Adapted from Seymour-Ure 1997.

(iii) British television coverage of the 1997 election campaign was extensive and detailed. Yet, it has been criticised for overkill, saturation, negativity and for being boring - with the result that many voters switched off or over or did not bother to vote. This is not entirely the fault of television journalists. Under Section 93 of the Representation of the People's Act, they are prevented from broadcasting about constituency affairs unless all candidates for the seat agree or take part in the broadcast. This restricts coverage of interesting local stories and encourages further coverage of Party Leaders. Despite its good intentions, the requirement to ensure 'balance' tends to lead to regimented soundbites and negative conflict. The restrictions on broadcasting need reforming to allow more room for creative talent and to produce more thoughtful and newsworthy reporting.

Adapted from Semetko et al. 1997.

(iv) In 1997 many voters were prepared to vote in defiance of the recommendation of their paper. For the first time ever, a majority of *Daily Express* and *Mail* readers did not vote Conservative. Many readers of pro-Conservative newspapers voted Labour because their experience of the Conservative government did not fit with what Conservative politicians and newspapers were saying. In addition, they were no longer worried about the threat of a Labour government. Many were so disillusioned with the Conservatives that they were willing to give Labour a chance, believing it was 'time for a change'.

Adapted from Dorey 1998.

Item C   *The press and the 1997 general election (2)*

	Circulation (000)		Party support	
	1992	**1997**	**1992**	**1997**
Dailies				
Mail	1,675	2.151	Con	Con
Mirror/Record	2,903	3,084	Lab	Lab
Star	806	648	Con	Lab
Telegraph	1,038	1,134	Con	Con
Express	1,525	1,220	Con	Con
Financial Times	290	307	'Not a Con majority'	Lab
Guardian	429	401	Lab	Lab
Independent	390	251	Uncommitted	Lab
Sun	3,571	3,842	Con	Lab
Times	386	719	Con	'Eurosceptic'
Total circulation pro-Conservative		4,504 (33%)		
Total circulation pro-Labour		8,533 (62%)		
Total circulation		13,757		
Sundays				
Express on Sunday	1,666	1,159	Con	Con
Independent on Sunday	402	276	'Not a Con majority'	Lab
Mail on Sunday	1,941	2,112	Con	Con
News of the World	4,768	4,365	Con	Lab
Observer	541	454	Lab	Lab
People	2,165	1,978	Lab	Lab
Sunday Mirror	2,774	2,238	Lab	Lab
Sunday Telegraph	558	909	Con	Con
Sunday Times	1,167	1,310	Con	Con
Total circulation pro-Conservative		5,490 (37%)		
Total circulation pro-Labour		9,311 (63%)		
Total circulation		14,801		

Adapted from Seymour-Ure 1997.

Questions

1. a) How does the dominant ideology model differ from the other models described in this chapter?
   b) Explain why the media is an important component in the dominant ideology model.

2. a) Using Items A-C, explain the role played in the 1997 general election campaign by the media.
   b) How did the approach of the media differ from that in 1992?
   c) How much influence do you think the press had in determining the outcome of the 1997 general election (a) in the short term and (b) in the long term? Explain your answer

3. Item B (iii) suggests that restrictions on television coverage of elections should be relaxed. What might be the positive and negative effects of doing this?

4.3 Opinion polls

The growth of polling

Opinion polls on political matters are not only carried out at election times nor are their questions confined to voting intentions. It is during election campaigns, however, that polls attract the greatest attention and scrutiny. The first British general election campaign in which opinion polls were conducted was the general election of 1945. At that time, only one polling organisation existed. Since the 1970s, the number of polls published in the media has increased sharply. Indeed, most polls are commissioned by the media. During the 45-day election campaign in 1997, 44 sets of national poll results were published in the national press (Butler & Kavanagh 1997, p.123 and Crewe 1997). This was a smaller number than the number published during the much shorter general election campaign of 1992. Opinion polls at election times typically use samples of around 1,000 adults from a range of different constituencies. Almost all polls are carried out by just five agencies - ICM, Gallup, NOP, Harris and MORI.

What are opinion polls?

Strictly speaking, questions designed to discover how people will vote are not polls of opinion but surveys of intended behaviour. Nor are poll results predictions of election results. What they provide is a snapshot of voting intentions on a certain day (or over a period if the poll is conducted over a number of days). But, the media often does present poll data as forecasts (as do the polling organisations when they present their final pre-election polls). As a result, comparisons are made with the actual election results to assess the polls' accuracy. As Conley (1993) points out, because those who study voting trends - psephologists - rely heavily on data from opinion polls, the validity of psephology depends to a large extent on the accuracy of the poll data.

Accuracy 1970-92

According to Kavanagh (1992) the polls had a reasonably good record of accuracy at general elections up to 1970, but, after 1970, polls were inaccurate in five of the following seven elections. Even so, Eatwell (1993) has calculated that the average error of the final polls between 1945 and 1987 was only 1.3%. This is an impressive record, especially given that the polling organisations themselves stress that in general elections with a sample of around 1,000 respondents there is a margin of error of plus or minus 3%. It should be noted that polls conducted during by-elections are usually less accurate because there is often a greater degree of volatility in voting behaviour compared to that in a general election.

The 1992 general election

Despite this record of accuracy the reputation of the polling organisations suffered a great deal after the 1992 general election. Throughout the election campaign, the polls suggested a narrow Labour lead. Even most of those polls conducted during the final two days of the campaign either gave Labour a marginal lead or had Labour and the Conservatives even. A hung Parliament was regarded as the most likely electoral outcome. Overall, the five major polling organisations on average gave Labour a 1.3% lead over the Conservatives. But, the actual result was a 7.6% win for the Conservatives. The verdict afterwards was that this was the pollsters' worst ever election performance and there was the suspicion that polls had been over-estimating Labour support for a long time. Complaints about the inaccuracy of the polls intensified because the polls themselves had been a major item of news throughout the campaign - perhaps because they suggested such a close-run contest between the two main parties.

Reasons for polling errors in 1992

The Market Research Society set up its own investigation into the inaccuracy of the polls in 1992. It concluded that there had been four main reasons for the errors:

- faulty sample design involving an unrepresentative selection of respondents
- a late swing to the Conservatives - too late for the polls to identify
- a 'spiral of silence' - the refusal of some voters (disproportionately Conservative) to admit to their voting preference
- non-registration - a small number of (mainly Labour) respondents had not registered to vote and, therefore, when election day came were unable to vote. (Game 1998, pp.143-4)

Did the polls misrepresent public opinion?

According to Sanders (1993), the question of the accuracy of the polls boiled down to one or both of the following - either the polls were correct at the time they were conducted (and late switching took place) or the polls unconsciously misrepresented 'true' public opinion. It is the latter idea which presented pollsters with a major problem. Much of the work of psephology involves the construction of ideas and theories about what people think and what they do. But, opinion polls only measure what people say. They cannot be expected, therefore, to take account of discrepancies that might arise between these different aspects of human behaviour. That people might say one thing yet think or do another is a possibility at any election. The 1992 election campaign was marked by the high moral tone taken by the opposition parties and by an appeal to self-interest by the Conservatives. If, as some studies suggest (for example, Kavanagh 1992), people tend to give what they feel are 'politically correct' answers to opinion poll questions whilst voting according to what they perceive to be their economic self-interest, this might account for the discrepancy between the polls and the actual election result.

Exit polls in 1992

The idea that some respondents did not tell the truth was discounted as 'unimportant' by the Market Research Society's report. Nevertheless, it could explain why the exit polls (the polls taken as people come out of the polling station) underestimated the Conservative vote in 1992. Exit polls do not ask people how they intend to vote but how they have just voted. The samples of voters questioned in exit polls are considerably larger than pre-election polls. Since samples are larger and polling takes place just after voters have voted, exit polls should be more accurate than pre-election polls. Even so, after the 1992 general election, their use as an accurate forecast of the election result began to be challenged.

The media and polls after 1992

The poor performance of polls generally in 1992 resulted in changes in the way in which the media reported poll findings. The BBC issued guidelines on the reporting of poll findings and its *Newsnight* programme announced a ban on exit polls until improved methods of polling were introduced. The media in general then gave much less prominence to the polls during the 1997 election campaign. Fewer were commissioned and those which were commissioned received less coverage (Crewe 1997).

The polling organisations after 1992

After 1992, the polling organisations themselves introduced changes and promised to make greater use of panel surveys. Panel surveys involve repeated interviews with the same sample of respondents at different stages during (and sometimes after) an election campaign. An advantage of panel surveys is that:

> 'By interviewing the same people each time, panel polls are largely immune from sampling fluctuations. Any changes in party support derive from panel members changing their minds.' (*Observer*, 27 April 1997)

In addition, polling organisations started to adjust their figures to take into account factors which had previously been ignored. The problem here was that all the polling organisations introduced their own changes in different ways and to different degrees (Crewe 1997). For example, some polls now take account of former Conservatives who are, at present, 'don't knows' or 'won't says', but might revert to the Conservatives at the next general election. Others are adjusted to ensure that the sample includes the right proportion of Conservative, Labour and Liberal Democrat voters according to the number of votes each party received in the previous general election. Some polling organisations switched from quota interviewing (where respondents are interviewed face

to face) to the greater anonymity of telephone interviewing. Others used both polling methods.

How accurate were the polls in 1997?

There is some debate about how far the polling organisations improved their performance in 1997. Given the extent of Labour's victory, it is perhaps not surprising that all the polls predicted a Labour win. Polls are not just used to forecast the winning party, however. They are also used to forecast:

- the percentage of votes won by individual parties
- the percentage lead of one party over another
- the projection of parliamentary seats.

Comparing the forecast of the polls with the actual results using these three categories, it becomes clear that the accuracy of the polls was mixed:

> 'In the 1997 general election, there was a span of 7% in the final polls' recorded support for Labour (43% to 50%), a span of 5% in the case of both the Conservatives and Liberal Democrats and one of 12% in the Labour lead. It was "the widest range of forecasts in the history of polling" (Crewe 1997, p.580). This is not, perhaps, surprising bearing in mind the pollsters' now differing methods. In turn, the projected Labour majorities ranged from 81 to 221 - a difference of 140 seats, or well over one-fifth of the whole House of Commons - which, in a much more evenly balanced contest, would not have been terribly helpful to the readers of the pollsters' respective newspapers.' (Game 1998, p.152)

Chris Game concludes that, although all the polling organisations were accurate about something, all were also inaccurate about something else:

> 'Almost every poll got at least something nearly dead right - their individual party figures (ICM), Labour's percentage lead (Gallup), or their parliamentary projections (Harris, MORI). But, equally, they all got something quite badly wrong. Next time, and certainly in a more evenly balanced election, they are unlikely to find it as easy to headline the former and hide the latter.' (Game 1998, p.153)

Do polls influence voting behaviour?

In addition to the question of polling accuracy, there is a long-running debate about whether or not the publication of opinion poll results influences voting behaviour. One view is that polls have a 'bandwagon' effect and encourage some voters to vote for the party which appears to be the most popular. An opposite view is the idea of a 'boomerang' effect - a party trailing in the polls picks up sympathy votes as the 'underdog' or supporters of the leading party become complacent and fail to turn out to vote. According to Denver (1994), however, research has found little evidence to support either view.

The 1992 general election

Although it is difficult to find evidence to support the bandwagon or boomerang effects, Ivor Crewe suggests that the publication of the polls did have a marked effect on voting behaviour in the 1992 general election. He suggests that, because the opinion polls put Labour ahead, people became afraid of a Labour government and ended up voting Conservative. He adds:

> 'There is an irony here. Had the campaign polls consistently shown the Conservatives to be ahead, as they probably were, the government might not have mobilised the anti-Labour vote so effectively and hence might not have survived in office.' (Crewe 1992, p.11)

Other ways polls influence voting behaviour

There are two other ways in which opinion polls may influence voting behaviour. First, it is possible that opinion poll results are used by some people who vote tactically (see Section 5.3 below). Since, however, effective tactical voting at a general election needs to be based on information about relative party support at constituency level, the publication of national opinion poll results is not much of a guide (though this is not to say that polls are not used by tactical voters). Tactical voting played a considerable part in the 1997 general election and so the potential influence of opinion polls was, perhaps, greater than before. Certainly, in by-elections it is easier for people to vote tactically since opinion polls are conducted locally.

Second, whatever they may say in public, opinion polls are taken seriously by politicians. Not only do parties commission private polls, to some extent they base their campaigns on information gained from polls. During the 1997 election campaign, however, although the parties continued to make use of private polling, they relied 'more heavily than before on the semi-structured discussions of small focus groups' (Crewe 1997). The results of polls, though, can have a marked effect on the morale of politicians and party workers during an election campaign.

Should opinion polls be restricted?

Because of the possible influence of opinion polls, there are those who would like to see restrictions placed on the publication of opinion poll results. The publication of poll results is banned in France and Germany during the final week of an election campaign. In 1967, the Speaker's Conference on Electoral Reform advocated a similar ban in the UK over the final three days of an election campaign. Although Parliament rejected this recommendation, the question is still raised from time to time in Parliament.

Main points - Section 4.3

- Strictly speaking, opinion poll results are not predictions of election results. They provide a snapshot of voting intentions on a certain day. But, the media often presents poll data as forecasts.
- The verdict after the 1992 general election was that this was the pollsters' worst ever election performance. The polls over-estimated support for Labour and indicated the result would be closer than it was.
- The Market Research Society concluded that inaccuracy in 1992 was due to: faulty sample design, a late swing, a 'spiral of silence' and non-registration. After 1992, the polling organisations introduced changes.
- In 1997, it became clear that the changes made by the polling organisations had not solved the problem. If the result had been closer, the polls would have produced as distorted a view as in 1992.
- There is a long running debate about whether or not the publication of opinion poll results influences voting behaviour. One view is that polls have a bandwagon effect. An opposite view is the idea of a 'boomerang' effect.

Activity 9.6 Opinion polls

Item A *Performance of the final polls in 1997*

	Conservative		Labour		Lib Dem		Others		Average error per party by poll	Labour lead		Labour majority (seats)	
	%	error	%	error	%	error	%	error	%	%	error	No.	error
Actual Result (Great Britain)	31.5		44.4		17.2		6.9			12.9		178	
Harris	31	-0.5	48	+3.6	15	-2.2	6	-0.9	1.8	17	+4.1	173	-5
NOP	28	-3.5	50	+5.6	14	-3.2	8	+1.1	3.4	22	+9.1	221	+43
MORI *(Times)*	28	-3.5	48	+3.6	16	-1.2	8	+1.1	2.35	20	+7.1	195	+17
ICM	33	+1.5	43	-1.4	18	+0.8	6	-0.9	1.15	10	-2.9	81	-97
Gallup	33	+1.5	47	+2.6	14	-3.2	6	-1.9	2.05	14	+1.1	137	-41
MORI *(Standard)*	29	-2.5	47	+2.6	19	+1.8	5	-1.9	2.2	18	+5.1	183	+5
Average	30.3	-1.2	47.2	+2.8	16.0	-1.2	6.5	-0.4	2.2	16.8	+3.9	165	-13

This table compares the findings of the final opinion polls (carried out by polling organisations between 27 and 30 April 1997) to the actual result.

Adapted from Game 1998.

Item B   *The polls in 1997*

In 1997, the polls did get it right in two senses. First, they all picked Labour as the runaway winner (and consistently anticipated that result throughout the campaign). And second, they benefited, by chance, from the exceptionally non-uniform distribution of the 10.5% national swing from Conservative to Labour. With a completely uniform swing of that size, Labour's 13% lead might have been expected to produce a parliamentary majority of nearer 130 than 180. The actual majority, however, was inflated partly by successful targeting of winnable seats and partly by the fact that Labour won a disproportionate number of the country's smaller and lower-voting constituencies. As a result, those polls that produced seriously exaggerated Labour leads made parliamentary projections which proved closer to the actual result than those whose individual figures were more accurate.
Adapted from Game 1998.

Asked how well the polls had done in 1997, Robert Worcester, chair of the polling organisation MORI, said 'Just fine, thank you for asking. British voters did not lie in 1992 or now...The British public is vindicated along with the pollsters by the accuracy of the polls in the 1997 general election.'
Adapted from the New Statesman Special Edition, May 1997.

The credibility of the polls has been restored. The 1997 election result was broadly in line with opinion poll predictions. This is an important warning to any future government that might be tempted to disregard such evidence. For all their real and imagined failings, opinion polls remain the least unsatisfactory way of gauging the state of public opinion on both specific policy issues and the parties' overall images.
Adapted from Sanders 1998.

The pollsters were lucky. In a landslide result, they are bound to pick the winner. If the actual result had been a gap between the two main parties of 6% or less, the 12% spread in forecasts in the final polls would have meant that at least one and probably more would have forecasted a win for the wrong party. Again, the Labour share of the vote was overestimated.
Adapted from Crewe 1997.

Item C   *Polls and voting behaviour in 1997*

The failure of the polls in 1992 affected political strategy over the following five years. Since the polls had under-estimated support for the Conservatives, Conservative strategists refused to believe that Labour really had the support indicated in the polls. They thought the polls merely indicated the 'political correctness' of those approached by pollsters and assumed things would turn out differently on election day. As a result, Conservatives did not seriously consider altering their policies or taking action to revive the damaged reputation of the leadership.
Adapted from Sanders 1998.

In 1992 and, to a lesser extent, in the two general elections prior to 1992, the impact of the opinion polls on the election was an important question. In 1997, the polls had little effect on the timing, course or result of the election.
Adapted from Crewe 1997.

The failure of the polls in 1992 meant that news editors were far less willing to make them the lead in news stories in 1997. The fact that the polls did not form such an important part of the media agenda in 1997 helped Labour because it minimised the risk of a late swing to the Conservatives (in 1992, voters who realised the risk of a Labour victory returned to the Conservatives at the last minute). It also reduced the risk of Labour supporters becoming complacent. *Adapted from Dobson 1998.*

Item D *Injecting 'realism' into the polls*

From May 1994, the *Guardian*'s ICM poll included adjustments to give a more realistic picture of voting intentions. Table A, the raw poll results, shows Labour with a lead of 18%. But, Table B is adjusted to take account of the many former Conservatives who were, at the time, 'don't knows' or 'won't says' but might revert at a general election. This gave Labour a more modest lead of 16%. Table C shows a different adjustment. The figures in Table C were adjusted so that they contained the right

Table A	Raw poll results				
	May	Apr	Mar	Feb	1992*
Con	26	26	24	26	42
Lab	44	48	49	51	36
LibDem	26	22	22	20	18
Others	5	4	5	4	4
Lab lead	+18	+22	+25	+25	−8

* Actual result in the 1992 general election

Table B	Adjustment (1)			
	May	Loc*	Apr	Mar
Con	27	27	29	28
Lab	43	42	46	47
LibDem	25	27	22	21
Others	4	4	4	4
Lab lead	+16	+15	+17	+19

* Local election result in May 1994

Table C	Adjustment (2)		
	May	Loc*	Apr
Con	28	27	28
Lab	41	42	43
LibDem	26	27	23
Others	5	4	5
Lab lead	+13	+15	+15

* Local election result in May 1994

Table D	Both adjustments		
	May	Loc*	Apr
Con	30	27	32
Lab	40	42	41
LibDem	26	27	23
Others	4	4	4
Lab lead	+10	+15	+9

* Local election result in May 1994

proportion of people who voted Labour or Conservative in the previous (1992) general election. This is an adjustment made in France and Germany as a matter of course. This gave Labour a 13% lead and brought the level of party support to within just 1% of the actual election result at the local elections (the ICM poll was conducted on the two days following the local elections). The problem with making this adjustment in the past was that many people forgot that they voted Liberal and polls, therefore, underestimated Liberal support. In 1994, it was argued, people were less likely to forget they voted Liberal because Liberals had a great deal of television coverage. Table D shows what happens if both adjustments are applied together. Labour's lead falls to 10%. ICM's director argued that the double adjustment was necessary to predict how people would vote in a general election.

Adapted from the *Guardian*, 11 May 1994.

Questions

1. Using Items A and B, assess the accuracy of the opinion polls in the 1997 general election.
2. Judging from Item C, what influence did the opinion polls have on the outcome of the 1997 general election?
   b) How did this differ from the 1992 general election?
   c) Give arguments for and against the view that

opinion polls affect voting behaviour.

3. a) Using Item D, explain why ICM decided to adjust its polls.
   b) Judging from Item A what were the benefits and drawbacks of making these adjustments?

4. Give arguments for and against the view that the publication of opinion poll results should be banned in the week before a general election.

Part 5 The voting context model

Key issues

1. How do the perceptions that voters have about an election and the range of options available to them affect their voting behaviour?
2. Why do some people choose not to vote?
3. Why do some people vote tactically?
4. How important is the election campaign in determining how people vote?

5.1 Principal elements of the model

What is meant by 'voting context'?

Miller (1990) claims that, unlike journalists, political scientists have paid little attention to voters' assessments of the context in which they vote. By 'voting context' Miller has in mind the perceptions

that voters have about the purpose of the election and the range of options available to them. These options include not voting (abstention), using the vote as a protest (which is more common in by-elections) or voting tactically. The range of options may be influenced by what the voter perceives to be the purpose of the election. This, in turn, may be related to the type of election. Voting behaviour varies according to whether it is a local, general, European or by-election. By emphasising the context, Miller suggests that voting is not always limited to a straightforward expression of personal preference. Voters, in considering these options, are also weighing up the likely consequences of their vote.

5.2 Turnout and abstention

Turnout

Turnout is an important factor in explaining voting

behaviour since it is, in a sense, a measure of abstention. The number of people turning out to vote at an election is expressed as a percentage of those whose names appear on the electoral register. This register is compiled by local authorities every October, comes into operation from the following February and remains in force for one year. It can, therefore, never be completely accurate. Apart from bureaucratic errors, some households do not complete the registration forms. According to Platt & Smyth (1994) the numbers not registered are increasing and include 20% of young people, 24% of black people and 15% of Asians. In addition some people die or move house in the period between registering and election day. A study by the *Guardian* suggested that as a many as 6 million people were not registered to vote at the time of the 1997 general election - 2 million failed to ensure their names were on the register and 4 million had moved house without making arrangements for a postal vote (*Guardian*, 24 June 1998).

Turnout trends

Turnout trends have been fairly consistent since 1966. Platt & Smyth (1994) compare the 73-75% turnout at general elections in the 1980s unfavourably with the 84% recorded in 1950. But, over a longer timespan, the 1950 turnout (together with 82.5% in 1951) appears as a high point. The average turnout between 1922 and 1945 was 74%. Turnout at the 1992 general election was 77.7%. This was 2.4% up on the 1987 general election and was also the highest since 1974. Butler & Kavanagh (1992) suggest that this was because the 1992 general election was the first election since 1974 whose outcome, according to the opinion polls, was in doubt. Turnout in 1997, however, dropped to 71.4%, the lowest since 1935.

Why did turnout fall in 1997?

There are five possible reasons why turnout was so low in 1997. First, the result was never in doubt. Labour was well ahead at the beginning of the campaign and remained so throughout it. Many voters may have come to the conclusion, therefore, that there was no need to vote. Second, the election campaign was very long and there is an argument that voters became bored and, by 1 May, could not be bothered to vote. Third, there is some evidence of growing disillusion with politics. This may have contributed to the low turnout, especially as there appeared to be little to choose between the parties in terms of policies. Fourth, there is the argument that many former Conservative voters had become disillusioned with the government, but did not want to vote for the other parties and so they stayed at home (on 5 May 1997, the *Guardian* alleged that 2 million non-voters fitted this category). Although this might seem to be a reasonable explanation for the low turnout, detailed studies of the election results soon dismissed it:

'One obvious possible explanation [for the low turnout] is that this was caused by disillusioned Tory voters staying at home. If this were so we would expect to find that the Conservative vote fell most where turnout fell most, but there is no such relationship in the results...If Tory voters had been staying at home, then we would have also expected to find that turnout fell most in seats where the Conservatives were previously strongest, but in fact the opposite was true.' (Butler & Kavanagh 1997, p.299)

The fifth and final reason for the low turnout is related to the first. Turnout was lowest in Labour's heartlands because some former Labour voters were disillusioned with the Labour Party and others assumed that Labour would win in their constituency and, therefore, did not bother to vote.

Differential turnout

Overall rates of turnout mask quite marked variations among different sections of the electorate. Considerable differences are found when turnout is compared constituency by constituency. For example, Denver (1994) reports that constituencies with a higher level of owner occupiers tend to show higher turnouts. Inner city areas, on the other hand, tend to have more transient populations and have a lower turnout rate. At the 1992 general election, turnout rose in most safe Conservative seats, but rose hardly at all in constituencies which Labour was defending. The same was true in the 1997 general election (Curtice & Steed 1997, p.299). Indeed, by 1997, Curtice & Steed were able to talk about a North-South divide in turnout:

'Despite the rapid growth of Labour Party membership over the last three years, the party still appears to have a significant problem in mobilising some of its traditional support into the polling station. Nowhere is this more true than in the north of England (where turnout had already risen by less than in the south of England and the Midlands in 1992); it now fell again by more than in the south of England. Quite why the new North-South gap in turnout has appeared is one of the intriguing unanswered questions of recent British electoral behaviour.' (Curtice & Steed 1997, p.300)

Investigations into districts within constituencies can also show important variations. For example, Platt & Smyth (1994) noted that there was a turnout of 20% in the West End of Newcastle Upon Tyne in the 1992 election, but a turnout of 71.3% in the constituency as a whole.

Factors relating to low turnout

Although there appears to be little in the way of variation according to gender, class, income level or education, Denver (1994) points to four factors associated with low turnout. People who are young, single, live in privately rented accommodation or are residentially mobile are less likely to vote. These four factors are frequently inter-related. Denver argues that the lower the degree of social involvement in a stable community, the less inclined people are to vote.

As might be expected, the stronger people's party identification, the more likely they are to vote. This connection is most clearly seen in local elections where overall turnout is usually substantially lower than at a general election. Denver (1994) argues that party dealignment is an important factor in the declining turnout in local elections since the 1950s.

Abstention

As with many other aspects of voting behaviour, explanations of non-voting may focus on individual motivation or on social groups. For example, at the level of the individual, a distinction can be made between passive and active abstainers (passive abstainers are also sometimes described as 'accidental', 'negative' or 'apathetic' non-voters). Whilst passive abstainers have no or very little interest in politics, active abstainers are those who refuse to vote on principle or as a protest - they may disagree with the electoral system (or indeed with the entire political system) or they may simply not be attracted to any of the parties or candidates standing in their constituency. Platt & Smyth (1994) have noted an 'increasing cynicism about politics as a whole' among sections of the electorate (for example, young people and African-Caribbean men). This was confirmed by the British Cohort Survey, a survey carried out in March 1997 of 9,000 people born in the same week in 1970:

> 'Asked whether they were interested in politics, nearly 60% of men and nearly 75% of women said they had "no interest" or were "not very interested" in politics. In a similar survey six years ago, the same question was put to 12,000 people born in 1958. Researchers found lower apathy ratings then of 45% among men and 66% among women...A significant proportion of 27 year olds who took part in the latest survey will stay away from the polling booths.' (*Guardian*, 23 March 1997)

5.3 Tactical and protest voting

What is tactical voting?

Tactical voters can be defined as those voters who, rather than voting for their preferred party, choose to vote for another party in the hope that this will help to prevent their least favoured party from winning the seat.

Miller (1990) used data from by-elections to show that the electorate can be divided into four groups. The largest group is that of core voters. Core voters already know at the start of the campaign how they will vote and they would not change their minds even if their preferred candidates had no chance of winning. This group makes up 39% of the electorate at by-elections. The second largest group is that of tactical voters. They make up 37% of the electorate at by-elections. The third largest group is that of the abstainers - people with no intention of voting. They make up about 15% of the electorate at by-elections. And, the smallest group is that of the floating voters - voters who are unsure about who they will vote for until the last minute. They make up 9% of the electorate at by-elections.

When does tactical voting take place?

Tactical voting has been particularly significant at by-elections for many years. In recent years, evidence has come to light that tactical voting has influenced the outcome of other elections too. In the 1994 local elections, for example, the Labour Party attracted by far the largest share of the votes. The Conservatives, however, were beaten, just, into third place behind the Liberal Democrats. Although the total number of votes cast for the Liberal Democrats was only marginally higher than their share in the 1992 local elections, on this occasion, their proportion of the vote delivered a large increase in the number of seats. According to Ivor Crewe (*Observer*, 8 May 1994), this was the result of tactical voting.

Similarly, there is evidence of tactical voting in recent general elections. Butler & Kavanagh (1992), for example, claim that tactical voting in 1992 reduced the Conservative majority by half. Certainly, the swing to Labour in Conservative-Labour marginals was higher than elsewhere (3.5% compared with 2% overall). This suggests tactical voting by Liberal Democrat supporters.

Tactical voting seems to have a played a particularly important role in the outcome of the 1997 general election. Indeed, it helps to explain why the Labour Party and Liberal Democrats won more seats than the percentage of the vote they won nationally would suggest they should have won:

> 'There appears to have been more anti-Conservative tactical voting than ever before. Labour's vote rose by more than the national average in those seats where it started off second to the Conservatives, while the Liberal Democrats' support fell by above the average. In contrast, the Liberal Democrat vote usually rose against the national trend in those seats where they were best placed, while Labour's rose considerably less than the average.' (Butler & Kavanagh 1997, pp.251-2)

What makes tactical voting effective?

To be effective, tactical voting needs to be based on good information about likely voting support for the different parties in that constituency. This is not always available and decisions about whether or not to vote tactically may in some cases be made on the basis of the standing of the parties nationally - a poor guide to the standing of the parties locally. Alternatively, voter perceptions about party support in their own constituency may be based on the results of recent local elections - which also may be misleading.

Protest voting

A protest vote is a negative vote. It is a vote against a policy or against the current direction of the government, rather than a vote for one of the opposition parties. Tactical voting can be seen as a form of protest voting in the sense that it is based on voters' dislikes rather than on what they like.

Protest voting is more common in by-elections and in local or Euro-elections than in general elections. Since 1979, especially, protest voting has produced some spectacular results. No matter how large the government majority at the previous general election, this majority can be eroded at a by-election. For example, in June 1994 a Conservative majority of 17,702 was overthrown in the Eastleigh by-election - a clear sign that the voters of Eastleigh wanted to protest about the government's recent behaviour. Similarly, one reason why the Conservatives did badly in local elections during the period 1979-97 was that people who voted Conservative in general elections were prepared to register a protest vote against the government in local elections.

How important is protest voting?

Governments can afford not to be too worried by protest voting. It is often short-lived and many voters revert to their usual preferences at the next general election. In 1987, for example, a general election was held only five weeks after local elections, yet only 71% of those who voted in both elections chose the same party both times. Similarly, in the 1992 election the Liberal Democrats did not retain any of the seats which they had won in by-elections during the course of the previous Parliament.

5.4 Electoral campaigns and events

The importance of election campaigns

It is difficult to measure exactly how much of an impact the election campaign makes on voting behaviour. What is clear, however, is that politicians and party workers from all parties behave as if election results are solely determined by the success or failure of the campaign.

One argument is that, if class and party dealignment has taken place, then fewer voters should have made firm voting choices before the election date is announced. So, more voters should be open to persuasion and, therefore, influenced by the election campaign. An examination of late deciders (voters who made up their minds during the

election campaign) and waverers (voters who seriously considered voting for a party other than the one they finally chose) in general elections between 1964 and 1992 shows that around a quarter of voters make up their minds during the election campaign (see Box 9.4).

Box 9.4 Late deciders and waverers 1964-92

	1964	1966	1970	Feb. 1974	Oct. 1974	1979	1983	1987	1992
Late deciders	12	11	12	23	22	28	22	21	24
Waverers	24	22	21	25	21	31	25	27	26

Adapted from Heath et al.1988 and Heath et al.1994.

The figures in Box 9.4 suggest, first, that election campaigns are an important determining factor for a significant number of voters and, second, that the proportion of hesitant voters has varied only slightly since the 1960s. It should be noted, however, that the accuracy of the above figures has been questioned. Denver (1994), for example, records the results of a panel study of voters during the 1987 general election. This found that just 13% of panelists voted for a party other than the one chosen at the start of the campaign (compared with 27% in the table above).

Even if the lower figure is correct, it still translates into a significant number of voters. This helps to explain why the main parties are prepared to spend so much money and effort ensuring that their campaigns are run professionally.

The general election campaigns of 1992 and 1997

The 1992 general election campaign came under great scrutiny because opinion polls showed Labour and the Conservatives to be neck and neck and yet the Conservatives ended up with a 7.6% lead. The immediate reaction of some commentators was to suggest that the campaign was decisive (Butler & Kavanagh 1992, p.247). Whilst Heath and his colleagues, however, agreed that the election campaign may have been decisive in ensuring that the Conservatives won an overall majority, they point out that no matter how good an election campaign Labour had fought, it would not have been enough to win Labour an overall majority:

'Butler and Kavanagh were almost certainly right in suggesting that the campaign was decisive. An error-free Labour campaign might have pushed their share of the vote up from 35% to 36% - nowhere near enough to have made them the largest party but probably enough to deprive the Conservatives of their overall majority...It is very unlikely, however, that Labour could have done anything in the campaign to have generated enough votes for an overall majority or even to have made it the largest party in a hung Parliament.' (Heath et al. 1994, p.20)

Similarly, in 1997, there was probably nothing that the Conservative Party could have done in its campaign to give it any chance of victory. As it was, Butler and Kavanagh argue that all three main parties could claim to have won the campaign:

> 'On selected criteria, each of the three parties could claim to have won the campaign...

Liberal Democrat support rose from 12% at the start to 17% on polling day, and the Conservatives cut the Labour lead from 25% to 13%. However, when voters were asked who had fought the most effective campaign, three times as many mentioned Labour as the other parties. Labour outscored the Conservatives on most campaign activities.' (Butler & Kavanagh 1997, p.238)

Main points - Part 5

- 'Voting context' refers to perceptions that voters have about the purpose of an election and the options available to them. The model suggests voting is not always about personal preference. Voters also weigh up the likely consequences of their vote.
- Turnout is a measure of abstention. In recent general elections there has been a tendency for former Labour voters in the north of England and young people to abstain.
- Rather than voting for their preferred party, tactical voters choose to vote for another party in the hope that this will help to prevent their least

favoured party from winning. Tactical voting made an impact in the general election of 1992 and a big impact in 1997.
- A protest vote is a negative vote against a policy or against the government, rather than a positive vote for a party. Governments tend to ignore protest votes as voters often go back to their former party at the next general election.
- It is difficult to measure exactly how much of an impact election campaigns make on voting behaviour, but they make more of an impact in a close-run election like that in 1992 than in a one-horse election like that in 1997.

Activity 9.7 *The voting context*

Item A *Turnout*

(i) Turnout in the 1997 general election

As in previous elections, turnout in 1997 varied markedly across constituencies. The lowest turnout was in Labour-held Liverpool Riverside (51.9%) and the highest in marginal Brecon and Radnor (82.2%) which was taken from the Conservatives by the Liberal Democrats. Only nine constituencies had a turnout of over 80%, while in 33 it was below 60%. Almost all of these 33 were inner city constituencies - including ten in inner London, four in Glasgow and four in Greater Manchester. As in previous elections, poorer urban, working-class seats with larger than average numbers of ethnic minority and young voters had much lower turnouts than wealthier suburban, small town and rural seats. In addition, the marginality of seats was important.

Adapted from Denver & Hands 1997.

(ii) Turnout at different types of election 1992-8

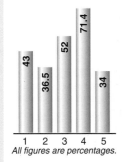

KEY
1 = Local elections, May 1994
2 = European election, June 1994
3 = By-elections*, 1992-97
4 = General election, May 1997
5 = London borough elections, May 1998
* This figure gives the average turnout from the 18 by-elections held during the 1992-97 Parliament.

1 2 3 4 5
All figures are percentages.

Item B *Tactical voting*

(i) Under Britain's 'first-past-the-post' system constituency boundaries are crucial since they define the local level of support for each party. A voter may live in an extremely safe Labour local government ward which is situated within a marginal Labour/Conservative parliamentary constituency which is part of a marginal Conservative/Liberal Democrat Euro-constituency. Clearly, the tactical voting pressures on voters depend upon what sort of election is being held. The tactical voter who wants to prevent the Conservatives winning seats will vote Labour at local and general or by-elections and Liberal Democrat at Euro-elections.

Adapted from Miller 1990.

(ii) On 27 April 1997, the *Observer* reported the findings of individual polls in 16 seats being defended by the Tories. In Enfield, the ICM poll put the Tories just 4% ahead of Labour, showing Michael Portillo could be unseated if Liberal Democrat voters switched tactically to Labour. On 2 May, Portillo admitted the poll had helped to sink him. Enfield's new Labour MP, Stephen Twigg, agreed saying: 'I started my acceptance speech by thanking the *Observer* and ICM. It showed us what could be done. As soon as your poll came out last Sunday, we put out a leaflet targeting one ward that the Liberal Democrats were campaigning very hard for.' Altogether, the Tories lost 12 of the 16 seats polled by ICM. Labour gained nine, the Liberal Democrats two and the SNP one. They included all seven seats where Cabinet ministers were defeated. Four would probably have lost anyway. The other three may well have hung on.

Adapted from the *Observer*, 4 May 1997.

Item C   *Two marginal constituencies in 1997*

HEXHAM					Con hold		
Electorate % Turnout		58,914	77.5%	**1997**	57,812	82.4%	**1992**
Atkinson, P.	Con	17,701	38.8%	-13.7%	24,967	52.4%	Con
McMinn, I	Lab	17,479	38.3%	+14.1%	11,529	24.2%	Lab
Carr, Dr P	Lib Dem	7,959	17.4%	-4.2%	10,344	21.7%	Lib Dem
Waddell, R	Ref	1,362	3.0%		781	1.6%	Green
Lott, D	UK Ind	1,170	2.6%				
Con to Lab swing 13.9%		Con majority 222			Con majority 13,438		

TEIGNBRIDGE					Con hold		
Electorate % Turnout		81,667	77.1%	**1997**	76,740	82.3%	**1992**
Nicholls, P.	Con	24,679	39.2%	-11.0%	31,740	50.3%	Con
Younger-Ross, R	Lib Dem	24,398	38.8%	+3.6%	22,192	35.1%	Lib Dem
Dann, S	Lab	11,311	18.0%	+5.0%	8,181	13.0%	Lab
Stokes, S A	UK Ind	1,601	2.5%		682	1.1%	Loony
Banwell, N	Green	817	1.3%		365	0.6%	NLP
Golding, L	Dream	139	0.2%				
Con to Lib Dem swing 7.3%		Con majority 281			Con majority 9,548		

Adapted from Austin 1997.

Item E   *The election campaigns of 1987-97*

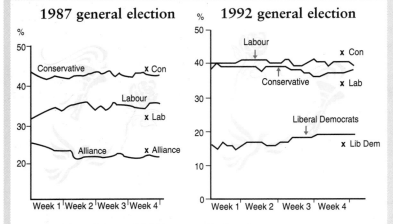

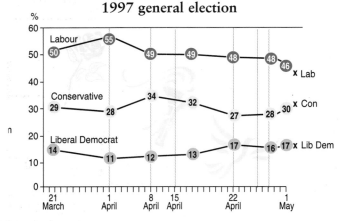

These graphs show the average daily support for each party during the 1987, 1992 and 1997 general elections (the data comes from the opinion polls held during the campaign). The X shows the actual share of votes.

Item D   *The 1997 general election campaign*

(i) The importance of Labour's campaign should not be overlooked. The campaign organisation, the main themes and the key policy decisions had all been planned months in advance of the formal campaign. In fact, the 1997 election marks a major breakthrough in modern campaigning, demonstrating the importance of technology (for rapid rebuttal and voter-targeting), of the use of focus groups (to help shape the style and language of Party Leaders) and of remaining focused on a simple message.

Adapted from Kavanagh 1997.

(ii) The campaign provided only limited support for claims that intensive local campaigning can win votes. Both Labour and the Liberal Democrats concentrated resources over a long period in a number of target seats. Liberal Democrats did perform noticeably better in their target seats, but Labour did not do any better in its target seats than in other seats where it started off second to the Conservatives.

Adapted from Butler & Kavanagh 1997.

(iii) The decline in turnout in 1997 suggests that voters were bored by the campaign. It was long, it lacked excitement and policy differences between parties were perceived to be minimal. The paradox, however, is that turnout dropped more in Labour-held seats than in Conservative areas. Those who voted Conservative in 1992 switched to another party in 1997, whereas past and potential Labour supporters showed a greater tendency to abstain. This may have been due to complacency or to Labour's ditching of traditional policies and ideology.

Adapted from Denver 1997 and Denver & Hands 1997.

Questions

1. To what extent can the voting context model be used to explain the outcome of the 1997 general election?

2. What does Item A tell us about voting behaviour in elections held between 1992 and 1998?

3. a) What are the advantages and disadvantages of voting tactically? Use Items B and C in your answer.
   b) Why do you think neither of the two main political parties publicly support tactical voting?

4. Suppose you are a Liberal Democrat supporter who wanted to prevent the Conservatives winning by voting tactically. How would you cast your vote in each of the two marginal seats in Item C if you were living there when the next general election was called? Explain your choices.

5. Judging from Items D and E would you say that the main parties are justified in spending large amounts of money and effort on their election campaigns? Give reasons for your answer.

Part 6 A general model of voting

Key issues

1. What does a general model of voting behaviour look like?
2. What are the links between the models of voting behaviour which were described earlier?

6.1 A general model of voting

Links between the models

Each of the five models of voting behaviour discussed in this chapter provides a self-contained explanation of why people vote as they do. Political scientists disagree about which are the most useful or appropriate. However, not all the models necessarily compete with each other, nor do the different models necessarily claim to provide a full or exhaustive explanation of why people vote as they do. On the contrary, it is possible to find links between the different models and elements within them which complement each other.

Short-term and long-term factors

Some political scientists make a distinction between short-term and long-term influences on how people vote. Long-term influences include factors such as class, age, gender, occupation and region. Short-term factors may be those which determine the result of a single election - specific events, issues or policies, the style of Party Leaders or the attitude of the media during the campaign, for example. It has been suggested that if long-term factors predominate, then changes in voting patterns from one election to another are likely to be slight. If short-term factors predominate, electoral outcomes are likely to be less predictable and more volatile. Such a distinction, however, should not be exaggerated. Policies and issues do not occur in a political vacuum. They may well be related to longer-term party strategy or ideology. Similarly, changes in the class or age structure of the population may occur over time and result in significant alterations in the distribution of votes to the main parties. Also, the voting system is bound to affect voting behaviour. Elections to the Scottish Parliament and Northern Ireland and Welsh assemblies, for example, have a proportional element not found in the 'first-past-the-post' system used for Westminster and local elections.

A general model of voting

William Miller (1990) has constructed a general model of voting which summarises and synthesises the models of voting behaviour discussed earlier in this chapter. His model suggests some of the possible links between the different models. It also

suggests a way in which political scientists might attempt a full explanation of why people vote as they do. This model is shown in Box 9.5. Miller explains how the various elements in the diagram in Box 9.5 are connected:

'Arrow A says that voters' social and family backgrounds influence their sense of party identification. For example, working-class children with working-class, Labour-voting parents who grow up in a working-class neighbourhood are more likely to identify themselves with the Labour Party than those who come from a different background. Links B and C suggest that voters' attitudes are influenced by their background and by this pre-existing sense of party identification. Link D suggests that the content and style of the mass media is influenced by the actions of government and the parties...The actions of government and parties influence voters' attitudes directly through personal experience (eg of inflation or unemployment) shown by link E; and indirectly through mass media reports (eg about defence policy) represented by link F. Similarly voters' perceptions of party credibility are influenced by direct experience (eg the availability of candidates,

Box 9.5 A general model

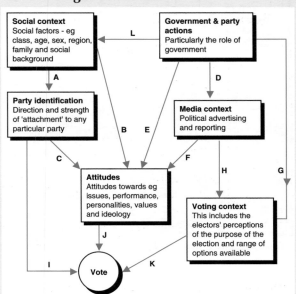

The arrows in the above diagram show how different elements link together. An arrow implies that one element influences another, but it does not imply that one element determines another.

Adapted from Miller 1990.

whether they have been leafleted or canvassed) shown by link G; and by media reports (eg opinion poll projections of the parties' chances) represented by link H. The voter's ultimate decision about which way to vote is based upon a mix of influences from party loyalty (link I), political attitudes (link J) and the voting context (link K)...Governments can also influence social background (link L). Obviously, nothing can be done to change voters' family backgrounds but it is quite easy to change their...social circumstances by selling them council houses, privatising their employers and encouraging them to rely on private healthcare organisations instead of the NHS.' (Miller 1990, pp.43-5)

Main points - Part 6

- Not all the models oulined in this chapter compete with each other, nor do they necessarily claim to provide a full explanation of why people vote as they do.
- Some political scientists make a distinction between short-term factors (those which may determine the result of a single election) and long-term influences (such as class, age, gender, occupation and region). There is greater volatility if short-term factors predominate.
- The voting system itself affects voting behaviour.
- Miller (1990) constructed a general model of voting which summarises and synthesises the models of voting behaviour outlined in this chapter. His model suggests some of the possible links between the different models.

Activity 9.8 A general model of voting

Item A   *Daily Mail cartoon, April 1989*

'Your husband's had an injection to cure his allergy and a tiny frontal lobotomy to cure his nasty voting habits'

Item B *Why I can't vote Liberal Democrat*

On reaching Cambridge University aged 19 I joined both the Liberal Party and a group called Pressure for Economic and Social Toryism (PEST). This would allow me to hear the best speakers from both sides. After a few meetings, I still saw much to recommend them both. Then came the local elections. I read the manifestos. The Liberals seemed fresh and well meaning. The Tories seemed like placemen. I entered the polling station to vote for the first time. Uncertain of the procedure, I found my way to the ballot paper and voting booth. Pencil poised above the ballot paper, I prepared to select and mark the Liberal candidates. Then something extraordinary happened. I saw a name which was attached to the words - the Conservative Party candidate. I never knew how it happened or why. The only thing I knew was that I placed a faltering cross in the box next to that name. Thus began a lifetime of voting Conservative. Ever since then I've supposed there was a suppressed idealist within and that he was a Liberal. So, it was with a clear conscience that I decided to vote Liberal in the local elections last Thursday. The Lib Dems narrowly controlled the council, Labour were challengers and the Tories had no chance. To keep Labour out you had to vote Lib Dem. Besides, the Liberals had canvassed and sent an election address. The Tories had not bothered. I approached the polling station clutching a little leaflet with the Lib Dem names on it. I held my pencil above the ballot paper. And, again, it happened. I saw the words - the Conservative Party candidate and, as if gripped by some higher force, wrote a cross in the box next to that name. It was a wasted vote. The Lib Dems lost and Labour won. I was a fool, I know. But, there's no saving me.

Adapted from the *Times*, 9 May 1994.

Item C *View from the Tory heartlands*

David Leach, 23, a computer programmer from Norwich was a first time voter in 1992 and voted Conservative. But, events over the last two years have left him disillusioned. He said that the biggest blow to him was news of the imposition of VAT on fuel. The new taxes, he argued, had been introduced through the back door. He would not have minded paying an extra penny or two on income tax. Mr Leach also criticised the government for moving Department of Health workers to Leeds. He argued that the government had got its priorities wrong because it spent so much on this when the money was needed for hospital beds. Mr Leach is a supporter of the Prime Minister, John Major, however. 'Personally', he said, 'I think he's a decent man with a good style.' Mr Leach comes from a family which has traditionally voted Labour. He and his mother, who recently set up her own business some years ago, both voted Conservative in 1992. Neither of them are as committed to voting Conservative as they were before.

Adapted from the *Daily Telegraph*, 21 March 1994.

Item D *Voting behaviour in Christchurch 1992-97*

(i) General election 1992		(ii) By-election 1993		(iii) General election 1997	
Con	63.5	Con	31.4	Con	46.4
Lab	12.1	Lab	2.7	Lab	6.9
Lib Dem	23.6	Lib Dem	62.2	Lib Dem	42.6
Other	0.7	Other	3.7	Other	4.1
Turnout	80.7	Turnout	74.2	Turnout	78.6

This table gives the results of three elections in one constituency. All figures are percentages.

Adapted from Butler & Kavanagh 1997.

Questions

1. You have been asked to explain why the 1997 general election resulted in a convincing victory for the Labour Party. Go back through the chapter and collect information relevant to each element in the general model. Use this information as the basis of a newspaper article entitled: How did Labour win in 1997?

2. How would you explain the voting behaviour of the author of Item B? Is there any evidence in this passage which could be used to link the voting behaviour of the author with any of the models which make up the general model of voting?

3. How useful are interviews like that in Item C for political scientists trying to explain voting behaviour?

4. Using your knowledge of voting behaviour, how would you explain the election results in Item D?

References

Austin (1997) Austin, T. (ed.), *The Times Guide to the House of Commons May 1997*, Times Books, 1997.

Benyon & Denver (1990) Benyon, J. & Denver, D., 'Mrs Thatcher's Electoral Success', *Social Studies Review*, Vol.5.3, January 1990.

Butler & Kavanagh (1992) Butler, D. & Kavanagh, D., *The British General Election of 1992*, Macmillan, 1992.

Butler & Kavanagh (1997) Butler, D. & Kavanagh, D., *The British General Election of 1997*, Macmillan, 1997.

Butler & Stokes (1971) Butler, D. & Stokes, D., *Political Change in Britain*, Penguin, 1971.

Clarke & Stewart (1984) Clarke, H.D. & Stewart, M.C., 'Partisan change in Britain, 1974–83' in *Denver & Hands (1992)*.

Conley (1990) Conley, F., *General Elections Today*, Manchester University Press, 1990.

Conley (1993) Conley, F., 'The 1992 general election: the end of psephology?', *Talking Politics*, Vol.5.3, Summer 1993.

Crewe (1987) Crewe, I., 'The 1987 general election' in *Denver & Hands (1992)*.

Crewe (1988) Crewe, I., 'Voting patterns since 1959', *Contemporary Record*, Vol.4.2, Winter 1988.

Crewe (1992) Crewe, I., 'Why did Labour lose (yet again)?', *Politics Review*, Vol.2.1, September 1992.

Crewe (1993a) Crewe, I., 'Voting and the Electorate' in *Dunleavy et al. (1993)*.

Crewe (1993b) Crewe, I., 'The changing basis of party choice, 1979-1992', *Politics Review*, Vol.2.3, February 1993.

Crewe (1997) Crewe, I., 'The opinion polls: confidence restored?' *Parliamentary Affairs*, Vol.50.4, 1997.

Crewe et al. (1977) Crewe, I., Sarlik, B. & Alt, J. 'Partisan dealignment in Britain 1964-1974', *British Journal of Political Science*, Vol.7.2, 1977.

Curtice (1997) Curtice, J., 'Anatomy of a non-landslide', *Politics Review*, Vol.7.1, September 1997.

Curtice & Steed (1997) Curtice, J. & Steed, M., 'Appendix 2: the results analysed' in *Butler & Kavanagh (1997)*.

Denver (1990) Denver, D., 'Elections and voting behaviour' in *Wale (1990)*.

Denver (1992) Denver, D., 'The 1992 general election: in defence of psephology' in *Talking Politics*, Vol.5.1, Autumn 1992.

Denver (1993) Denver, D., 'Elections and voting behaviour' in *Wale (1993)*.

Denver (1994) Denver, D., *Elections and Voting in Britain* (2nd edn), Harvester Wheatsheaf, 1994.

Denver (1997) Denver, D., 'The 1997 general election results: lessons for teachers', *Talking Politics*, Vol.10.1, Autumn 1997.

Denver & Hands (1990) Denver, D. & Hands, G., 'A new gender gap...', *Talking Politics*, Vol.2.3, 1990.

Denver & Hands (1992) Denver, D. & Hands, G. (eds), *Issues and Controversies in British Electoral Behaviour*, Harvester Wheatsheaf, 1992.

Denver & Hands (1997) Denver, D. & Hands, G., 'Turnout' in *Norris & Gavin (1997)*.

Dobson (1998) Dobson, A., 'The 1997 general election: explaining a landslide' in *Lancaster (1998)*.

Dorey (1998) Dorey, P., *Voting Behaviour in Britain: a More Volatile Electorate*, Sheffield Hallam University Press, 1998.

Dunleavy & Husbands (1985) Dunleavy, P. & Husbands, C.T., *British Democracy at the Crossroads*, Allen & Unwin, 1985.

Dunleavy et al. (1990) Dunleavy, P., Gamble, A., & Peele, G. (eds), *Developments in British Politics 3*, Macmillan, 1990.

Dunleavy et al. (1993) Dunleavy, P., Gamble, A., Holliday, I. & Peele, G. (eds), *Developments in British Politics 4*, Macmillan, 1993.

Dunleavy et al. (1997) Dunleavy, P., Gamble, A., Holliday, I. & Peele, G., *Developments in British Politics 5*, Macmillan, 1997.

Eatwell (1993) Eatwell, R., 'Opinion poll accuracy: the case of the 1992 general election', *Talking Politics*, Vol.5.2, Winter 1993.

Fitzgerald (1988) Fitzgerald, M., 'There is no alternative...black people and the Labour Party', *Social Studies Review*, Vol.4.1, September 1988.

Franklin (1985) Franklin, M., *The Decline of Class Voting in Britain*, Oxford University Press, 1988.

Game (1995) Game, C., 'Opinion polls: the lessons of 1992' in *Lancaster (1995)*.

Game (1998) Game, C., 'Opinion polls and the 1997 general election' in *Lancaster (1998)*.

Gavin & Sanders (1997) Gavin, N.T. & Sanders, D., 'The economy and voting' in *Norris & Gavin (1997)*.

Goldthorpe et al. (1969) Goldthorpe, J.H., Lockwood, D., Bechoffer, F. & Platt, J., *The Affluent Worker in the Class Structure*, Cambridge University Press, 1969.

Hall (1987) Hall, S., 'Blue election, election blues', *Marxism Today*, July 1987.

Hall (1992) Hall, S., 'No new vision, no new votes', *New Statesman & Society*, 17 April 1992.

Heath (1992) Heath, A., 'Social class and voting in Britain', *Sociology Review*, Vol.1.4, April 1992.

Heath et al. (1985) Heath, A., Jowell, R. & Curtice, J., *How Britain Votes*, Pergamon, 1985.

Heath et al. (1988) Heath, A., Jowell, R. & Curtice, J., 'Partisan dealignment revisited' in *Denver & Hands (1992)*.

Heath et al. (1991) Heath, A., Jowell, R. & Curtice, J., Evans, G., Field, J. & Witherspoon, S., *Understanding Political Change: the British Voter 1964–1987*, Pergamon, 1991.

Heath et al. (1994) Heath, A., Jowell, R. & Curtice, J., *Labour's Last Chance*, Dartmouth, 1994.

Johnston & Pattie (1992) Johnston, R.J. & Pattie, C.J., 'The changing electoral geography of Great Britain' in *Denver & Hands (1992)*.

Kavanagh (1992) Kavanagh, D., Polls, predictions and politics', *Politics Review*, Vol.2.2, November 1992.

Kavanagh (1997) Kavanagh, D., 'The Labour campaign' in *Norris & Gavin (1997)*.

Kellner (1997) Kellner, P., 'Why the Tories were trounced' in *Norris & Gavin (1997)*.

King et al. (1993) King, A., Crewe, I., Denver D., Newton, K., Norton P., Sanders, D. & Seyd, P., *Britain at the Polls 1992*, Chatham, 1993.

King et al. (1998) King, A., Denver, D., McLean, I, Norris, P., Sanders, D. & Seyd, P., *New Labour Triumphs: Britain at the Polls*, Chatham House, 1998.

Labour (1997) *New Labour - Because Britain Deserves Better*, Labour Party, 1997.

Lancaster (1995) Lancaster, S. (ed.), *Developments in Politics*, Vol.6, Causeway Press, 1995.

Lancaster (1998) Lancaster, S. (ed.), *Developments in Politics*, Vol.9, Causeway Press, 1998.

Layton–Henry (1990) Layton–Henry, Z., 'The black electorate', *Contemporary Record*, Vol.3.3, February 1990.

Linton (1996) Linton, M., *Was it the Sun Wot Won It?*, Nuffield College, Oxford, 1996.

Lovenduski (1997) Lovenduski, J., 'Gender politics: a breakthrough for women? in *Norris & Gavin (1997)*.

McKenzie & Silver (1968) McKenzie, R. & Silver, A., *Angels in Marble*, Heinemann, 1968.

Miller (1984) Miller, W.L., 'There was no alternative...' in *Denver & Hands (1992)*.

Miller (1990) Miller, W.L., 'Voting and the electorate' in *Dunleavy et al. (1990)*.

Miller (1991) Miller, W.L., *Media and Voters: the Audience, Content and Influence of Press and Television at the 1987 General Election*, Clarendon Press, 1991.

Miller et al. (1990) Miller, W.L., Clarke, H.D., Harrop, M., Leduc, L. & Whiteley, P.F., *How Voters Change: the 1987 British Election Campaign in Perspective*, Clarendon Press, 1990.

Moran (1989) Moran, M., *Politics and Society in Britain* (2nd edn), Macmillan, 1989.

Newton (1992) Newton, K., 'Caring and competence: the long, long campaign' in *King et al. (1993)*.

Norris (1997) Norris, P., 'Anatomy of a Labour landslide' in *Norris & Gavin (1997)*.

Norris & Gavin (1997) Norris, P. & Gavin, N.T., *Britain Votes 1997*, Oxford University Press, 1997.

Parkin (1972) Parkin, F., *Class, Inequality and Political Order*, Paladin, 1972.

Platt & Smyth (1994) Platt, S. & Smyth, G. 'Bite the Ballot', *New Statesman & Society*, 29 April 1994

Pulzer (1967) Pulzer, P.G.J., *Political Representation and Elections in Britain*, Allen & Unwin, 1967.

Rose & McAllister (1986) Rose, R. & McAllister, I., *Voters Begin to Choose*, Sage, 1986.

Rose & McAllister (1990) Rose, R. & McAllister, I., *The Loyalties of Voters*, Sage, 1990.

Saggar (1993) Saggar, S., 'Competing for the black vote', *Politics Review*, Vol.2.4, April 1993.

Saggar (1997) Saggar, S., 'Racial Politics' in *Norris & Gavin (1997)*.

Saggar (1998) Saggar, S., 'Party strategy and ethnic politics in the 1997 general election campaign', *Politics Review*, Vol.7.4, April 1998.

Sanders (1993) Sanders, D., 'Why the Conservative Party won - again' in *King et al. (1993)*.

Sanders (1997) Sanders, D., 'Voting and the electorate' in *Dunleavy et al. (1997)*.

Sanders (1998) Sanders, D., 'The new electoral battleground' in *King et al. (1998)*.

Scammell & Harrop (1997) Scammell, M. & Harrop M., 'The press' in *Butler & Kavanagh (1997)*.

Semetko et al. (1997) Semetko, H.A., Scammell, M. & Goddard, P., 'Television' in *Norris & Gavin (1997)*.

Seymour-Ure (1997) Symour-Ure, C., 'Editorial opinion in the national press' in *Norris & Gavin (1997)*.

Wale (1990) Wale, W. (ed), *Developments in Politics*, Vol.1, Causeway Press, 1990.

Wale (1993) Wale, W. (ed), *Developments in Politics*, Vol.4, Causeway Press, 1993.

10 Pressure groups

Introduction

Farmers facing riot police on the streets of Brussels; mass lobbies of Parliament; letter writing campaigns; publicity stunts; meetings between ministers and members of the Fabian Society - these are all examples of pressure group activity, a form of political action that has been growing in importance in Britain.

As the membership of political parties has fallen, that of pressure groups has increased. This may indicate a fundamental shift in the British political system. Like political parties, pressure groups want to affect the outcome of the political decision-making process. Unlike political parties, however, they do not contest elections.

As membership of pressure groups has grown, so has their professionalism. It is not uncommon today for people concerned about an issue to employ paid, professional lobbyists to promote their cause. Not that all pressure groups act or would want to act in this way. The problem with the term 'pressure groups' is that it encompasses a huge variety of organisations - from ad hoc local protest movements based in a single village to huge, international organisations. These groups promote their interests in a variety of ways with a varying degree of success. How they do this and how it is possible to distinguish between them are the two main subjects of this chapter.

Chapter summary

Part 1 asks the question, what is a pressure group? It examines the different ways in which this question has been answered.

Part 2 considers the ways in which pressure groups achieve their aims. How can we measure their success?

Part 3 examines the way in which the role of pressure groups has changed since the early 1970s.

Part 4 considers the European dimension. How has membership of the EU affected pressure groups in Britain?

Part 1 What is a pressure group?

Key issues

1. What exactly is a pressure group?
2. What are the differences between different groups? What problems are encountered in categorising them?
3. How do the aims and functions of pressure groups differ?

1.1 A definition

What is a pressure group?

Amnesty International, the Confederation of British Industry (CBI), the Worldwide Fund for Nature (WWF), Demos, the Campaign for Nuclear Disarmament (CND), the National Union of Students (NUS), Charter 88 - these are all examples of pressure groups. Whereas the number of political parties in Britain is very small (fewer than double figures if minor parties like 'Lord' Sutch's Official Monster Raving Loony party are excluded), the number of pressure groups runs into the thousands - tens of thousands if local groups are counted. In fact, any organised group that does not put up candidates for election but seeks to influence government policy can be described as a pressure group.

Pressure groups are also sometimes described as 'interest groups', 'lobby groups' or 'protest groups'. Some writers avoid the term 'pressure' groups because it implies that such groups use coercion to achieve their ends. This does not necessarily happen.

Limitations of the definition

Clearly, the definition above is far too loose to be of use for most writers. It does not distinguish between a huge organisation like the CBI (which represents 150,000 businesses) and a single issue locally based organisation like the Save Audley Campaign (Audley is a small village in Staffordshire. The Save Audley Campaign was set up in the 1970s to fight planning proposals to build factories on local farm land. The group had around 50 members and disbanded as soon as the plans were dropped). Nor does such a definition distinguish between groups on the fringes of society such as the Animal Liberation Front (whose campaigns include illegal activities such as planting bombs) and those who have the ear of decision makers such as the Institute for Public Policy Research (IPPR) which has links with the Labour government (some of the IPPR's proposals have formed the basis of government legislation and some members of the IPPR have regular contact with Cabinet ministers).

Despite this, such a definition does indicate how pressure groups differ from established political parties and how they differ from groups which make no attempt to influence government policy. It is, therefore, an adequate starting point.

1.2 Sectional groups and cause groups

Classifying groups (1)

One of the earliest attempts to classify pressure groups produced the division between 'sectional' groups and 'cause' groups (Stewart 1958). Later writers have sometimes used the same criteria but different terms - sectional groups are called 'interest' groups (which is confusing because other writers use interest groups to mean all pressure groups) and cause groups are called 'promotional' groups.

Sectional groups

Sectional groups seek to represent the common interests of a particular section of society. As a result, members of sectional groups are directly and personally concerned with the outcome of the campaigns fought by the group because (usually) they stand to gain professionally and/or economically. Trade unions, employers' associations and professional bodies are all sectional groups. The National Union of Teachers (NUT), the Society of Motor Manufacturers and Traders and the British Medical Association (BMA) are three examples of sectional groups.

Because sectional groups are solely concerned with a particular section of society, membership is usually restricted. Since the aim is to look after the interests of all people in that section of society, sectional groups tend to aim to get as many eligible members as possible to join the group.

Cause groups

Cause groups pursue a particular set of objectives (a cause), the achievement of which is not necessarily of direct professional or economic benefit to the members of the group. Shelter (whose cause is homelessness), CND (whose cause is nuclear disarmament) and the Society for the Protection of the Unborn Child (whose cause is the prevention of abortions) are three of the myriad of cause groups.

Because cause groups aim to promote a cause (which might potentially be supported by everybody, regardless of their profession or economic position),

membership is not usually restricted. However, that does not mean that cause groups have or want to have a large membership.

Some cause groups have few members but a great deal of influence. For example, Liberty (a group with around 5,000 members in 1998) put pressure on the Labour Party, in opposition and in government, to make the incorporation of the European Convention on Human Rights into UK law a priority. Then, when the 1998 Human Rights Act (which incorporated the convention) was passed, the group worked with the government to provide training for lawyers on human rights issues. Conversely, some cause groups have many members but little influence. For example, in the early 1980s over 250,000 supporters of CND marched in London on several occasions but, despite this show of popular support, CND failed to influence the government's defence policy.

Cause groups can be subdivided according to the aims they pursue (see Box 10.1).

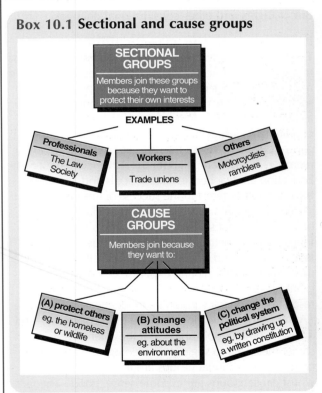

Box 10.1 Sectional and cause groups

SECTIONAL GROUPS
Members join these groups because they want to protect their own interests

EXAMPLES

Professionals — The Law Society

Workers — Trade unions

Others — Motorcyclists ramblers

CAUSE GROUPS
Members join because they want to:

(A) protect others — eg. the homeless or wildlife

(B) change attitudes — eg. about the environment

(C) change the political system — eg. by drawing up a written constitution

1. Sectional cause groups

Sectional cause groups aim to protect the interests of a section of society. For example members of Shelter work on behalf of the homeless. The Child Poverty Action Group works on behalf of children who live in poverty. The group MIND works to protect and fight for the rights of those suffering from mental illness.

2. Attitude cause groups

Attitude cause groups aim to change people's attitudes about a particular issue or policy. For example, Greenpeace, Friends of the Earth (FoE) and WWF aim to change people's attitudes towards the environment.

Box 10.2 **Insider and outsider groups**

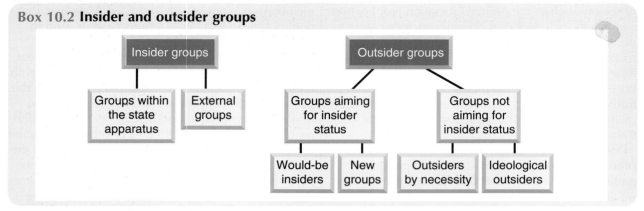

3. Political cause groups

Political cause groups aim to change the political system or political process in some way. For example, Charter 88 argues that, because our political system does not have a written constitution, strong governments can pass laws which erode civil liberties. As a result, Charter 88 campaigns for an entrenched Bill of Rights and other constitutional changes.

Problems with this classification

The first problem with this method of classification is that many groups cut across the two categories. For example, many trade unions campaign for equal opportunities in society as a whole or for a cleaner environment as well as pursuing sectional interests such as better pay and conditions in a specific industry. Equally, some cause groups pursue sectional interests. For example, many members in the Campaign for the Advancement of State Education are teachers in state schools and, therefore, have a vested interest in the success of this organisation.

Second, people using this method of classification often assume that sectional groups are generally more influential and better resourced than cause groups. In fact, a major trend since 1970 has been the growth in membership, income and expertise of many cause groups. Besides, some sectional groups are poorly resourced and lack substantial influence.

A third problem is the use of the terms 'sectional' and 'cause'. Some people argue that these terms are sometimes used to suggest an ideological preference, namely that sectional groups are in some sense 'bad' whilst cause groups are in some sense 'good'. The fact that some writers do use the terms in this way suggests that the distinction between the two types of groups is rather vague and it might be better to search for a different method of classification.

1.3 Insider groups and outsider groups

Classifying groups (2)

Rather than classifying pressure groups in terms of what motivates their members, some authors classify them in terms of their status and the strategies they adopt. The distinction here is between 'insider' and

'outsider' groups.

Insider groups

Insider groups are the groups which the government (local or national) considers to be legitimate and are, therefore, given access to decision makers. For example, insider groups might be involved in regular meetings with ministers or civil servants and they might be included on lists for circulation of new government proposals.

Insider groups are similar in one respect. Generally, they abide by the 'rules of the game'. For example, they tend to respect confidences and not to make public attacks on ministers. Insider groups can be further divided into two categories (see Box 10.2 above).

1. Institutions within the state apparatus

This category includes organisations such as the Church of England and the police force. They can be described as insider groups because they are included in the consultation process as a matter of course when government proposals relevant to their activities are discussed. For example, representatives of the police force are consulted when matters of law and order are under discussion and teachers' representatives are consulted when changes to the National Curriculum are proposed.

2. External groups

Groups in this category are in a different position from institutions within the state apparatus. Whilst institutions within the state apparatus are consulted as a matter of course when government proposals relevant to their activities are discussed, the same is not true of external groups with insider status. External groups with insider status are the independent organisations such as trade unions, charities or pressure groups which are called upon by the government to provide expertise when it is needed. The type of group selected varies according to the government's ideological orientation and other factors such as public opinion. So, the type of external groups given insider status varies from government to government. For example, Labour governments in the 1970s often included trade union representatives in the consultative process whereas trade unions certainly did not have insider status during the 1980s when Margaret Thatcher was Prime Minister. Although the Blair government was prepared, in its first 18 months, to listen to trade union views, unions did not have the close contact enjoyed in the 1970s.

Outsider groups

Outsider groups have none of the advantages of insider groups. They cannot expect to be consulted during the policy-making process, nor can they expect to gain access to ministers and civil servants. Rather, they have to work outside the governmental decision-making process and, therefore, have fewer opportunities to determine the direction of policy.

Outsider groups adopt different strategies and can be further subdivided accordingly.

1. Outsider groups aiming for insider status

Those outsider groups which do aim for insider status may be waiting for a different political climate, such as a change in government. If such a climate materialises, they might immediately gain insider status. This happened to the IPPR. Until the election of a Labour government in 1997, the IPPR was an outsider group. Once Labour was elected, however, it immediately gained insider status. Outsider groups hoping for a change in political climate often work closely with the opposition in Parliament and, generally (like existing insider groups), their strategy is to abide by 'the rules of the game'.

Alternatively, groups seeking insider status may be new groups with little experience, resources and expertise. Decision makers might support their aims but do not consult them because they are thought to have little to offer.

2. Groups not aiming for insider status

Those outsider groups which do not aim for insider status may do so out of necessity. For example, the residents of Old Milverton, a village in Warwickshire, set up a pressure group in October 1997 to prevent the siting of a telecommunications tower. The group was set up on a temporary basis to fight a particular local planning proposal. It never aimed for or was likely to gain insider status. There are many small single-issue pressure groups like this. Equally, there are larger outsider groups which do not aim for insider status out of necessity. CND is a good example. Since 1987, none of the major political parties has supported CND's aims. Out of necessity, therefore, CND has not been able to aim for insider status.

In addition there is a category of outsider groups which do not aim for insider status because they are ideologically opposed to the political system. By definition, such groups have no interest in gaining access to governmental decision makers. An example is the radical environmental group Earth First!

Problems with this model

According to Grant (1999), five separate criticisms have been made of the insider/outsider model. These can be summarised as follows.

1. Achieving insider status is not difficult

Maloney and colleagues (1994) argue that the original insider/outsider model overestimated the difficulty of achieving insider status because it did not distinguish between a group's strategy and its status. They (and others) point out that large numbers of groups are placed on government department consultation lists and asked to respond to policy proposals as a matter of course. For example, 200 different groups are consulted as a matter of course on matters concerning motorbikes. What counts, they argue, is not the strategy adopted by these groups, but their status. They divide insider groups into three according to status:

- **Core insiders** have a close relationship with decision makers over a broad range of issues (eg the National Farmers' Union, the NFU)
- **Specialist insiders** are seen as reliable and knowledgeable, but in narrower policy areas (eg British Poultry Federation)
- **Peripheral insiders** are consulted but carry little influence (eg Greenpeace).

The distinction between these categories, Maloney and colleagues claim, is more important than the general distinction between insiders and outsiders.

2. Most pressure groups have no choice of strategy

The original insider/outsider model suggested that groups have a choice about which strategy to adopt. In other words, it suggested that some groups decide to aim to be insiders whilst others decide to adopt outsider strategies. Maloney and colleagues (1994), however, argue that most pressure groups do not have a real choice between insider and outsider strategies. The strategy a group adopts is determined by the resources at its disposal, its public image and reputation, and its history. Since groups do not have a real choice, they suggest, the model is flawed.

3. Modifying the model undermines it

Some critics have argued that the two criticisms outlined above destroy the validity of the insider/outsider model since they show that the model is flawed.

4. Some groups pursue both insider and outsider strategies

Some critics have noted that some groups simultaneously pursue both insider and outsider strategies. May and Nugent (1982), for example, identify 'thresholder' groups - groups that fall between the insider and outsider labels because they might, for example, organise demonstrations and letter-writing campaigns (outsider tactics) whilst, at the same time, negotiating with government officials (an insider tactic). May and Nugent suggest that trade unions fall into this category.

5. A new political era has undermined the model

Some critics have argued that the insider/outsider model is no longer relevant because a new political era has developed. Dudley and Richardson (1998), for example, argue that politics is becoming a 'multi-level, multi-arena game' in which the use of outsider strategies by insider groups is becoming both common and acceptable. As a result, the distinction between insider and outsider groups is no longer so clear-cut.

A response to the criticisms

Grant (1999) accepts the validity of the first two criticisms, but argues that, just because the original model needs to be altered, that does not mean that it has been fatally undermined. He also accepts that some groups simultaneously use both insider and outsider tactics, but argues that simultaneously pursuing an insider and outsider strategy is a transitional phase. Eventually, a group has to opt for one strategy or the other. Finally, whilst accepting that the political landscape is changing, Grant argues that there is still much which looks like 'business as usual'. There are still insiders and outsiders and many groups which have always been powerful (such as

groups representing business interests and farmers) continue to exert great pressure on decision makers.

Main points - Sections 1.1-1.3

- Broadly, any organised group that does not put up candidates for election but seeks to influence government policy can be described as a pressure group.
- One of the earliest attempts to classify pressure groups produced the division between 'sectional' groups (groups which aim to represent the interests of a particular section of society) and 'cause' groups (groups which pursue a particular set of objectives).
- Problems with this method of classification are: (1) many groups cut across the two categories; (2) it is often assumed sectional groups are better resourced and more influential; and (3) the terms may indicate an ideological preference.
- Another method of classification divides groups in terms of their status and the strategies they adopt - insiders have access to decision makers and outsiders do not.
- Five criticisms have been made of the insider/outsider model, but Grant (1999) argues it is still useful.

Activity 10.1 *Classifying pressure groups*

Item A   *Two pressure groups*

FRIENDS *of the*
earth
for the planet for people

With the support of people like you, and backed by careful research, Friends of the Earth has:

- persuaded Parliament to pass three major environmental Acts that we first drafted
- pressured the government to speed the removal of pesticides and nitrates from water using the European and High Courts
- pioneered practical renewable energy and waste-recycling schemes
- stopped the hunting of otters in Britain
- convinced the government to cancel 32 new nuclear power stations
- saved wildlife reserves from development
- exposed health-threatening traffic pollution levels

The diagram above was devised from a leaflet produced by Friends of the Earth in 1997.

The advert above was published in March 1998 in the week before MPs voted on a Private Members' Bill to ban hunting with dogs. The Bill was withdrawn in July 1998 after failing to gain the backing of the government.

Item B *The aims, income and resources of selected pressure groups*

Group	Aims	Supporters (members and/or donors)	Income	Staff*	Government contacts?**	Uses direct action?***
Charter 88	Campaigns for a written constitution and an entrenched Bill of Rights.	79,064 supporters	£750,000	14 ft 10 vols	✓	✗
British Union for the Abolition of Vivisection	Campaigns to halt the breeding and use of animals in experiments.	5,000 members 38,000 supporters	£1,210,682	18	✗	✓
Confederation of British Industry (CBI)	Promotes the interests of business and employers.	250,000 businesses	£4,329,000	200	✓	✗
Central Area Leamington Residents Association (CLARA)	Campaigns to preserve and improve the town of Leamington Spa and the surrounding area.	280 households	£840	vols	✓	✗
British Roads Federation	Aims to focus attention for a higher standard of service from the UK road network.	15 trade associations (representing 50,000 companies) and 80 individual business members	£500,000	9 ft	✓	✗
Earth First!	Campaigns against the destruction of the environment.	63 autonornous groups	not known	vols	✗	✓
Liberty	Campaigns to defend and extend human rights and civil liberties.	c.5,000 supporters	£500,000	10 ft 3 pt	✓	✗
Unison	Trade union for public sector workers.	1.3 million members and donors	£100 million	998	✗	✗
Friends of the Earth (FoE)	Campaigns to protect and conserve the environment	200,000 members	£3,509,000	110	✓	✓

* ft = full time   pt = part time   vols = vounteers
** This column indicates whether a group has regular contacts with members of government (local or national) or with government officials (local or national)
*** This column indicates if a group uses direct action regularly

Information gathered in November 1998.

Questions

1. a) How would you classify the two pressure groups mentioned in Items A? Give reasons for your answers.
   b) Which is the better method of classification - sectional/cause or insider/outsider? Explain your answer.
2. Which of the groups in Items A and B would fit under the following headings: sectional cause group, attitude cause group, political cause group?
3. a) Which of the groups in Items A and B are insider groups and which are outsider groups? Explain how you know.
   b) Give arguments for and against using the insider/outsider model.

1.4 The role played by pressure groups

The aims of pressure groups

The aim of all pressure groups is to influence those who have the power to make decisions. Pressure groups do not seek the power of political office for themselves, but they do aim to affect the decisions made by those who have this power. If necessary, pressure groups will compete against rival groups and aim to gain an advantage over them.

How pressure groups work

Permanent and temporary groups

Some pressure groups have become permanent institutions whilst other groups cease to exist once they have achieved their aim. An example of the latter was the Snowdrop Campaign (a group which aimed at the banning of all handguns). This was launched shortly after the Dunblane massacre of March 1996 in which 16 children and their teacher were shot dead. In February 1997, Parliament agreed to a ban on all handguns over .22 calibre. In May 1997, the decision was taken to wind up the Snowdrop Campaign after the Labour government announced that it would introduce a Bill banning all handguns. This Bill was passed in the Commons in June 1997.

Coalitions

The aims of one pressure group may coincide with

another and, sometimes, this can result in two or more groups working together. For example, Friends of the Earth (FoE) and WWF have a similar aim - the protection of the environment. Often they work together using their different methods to complement each other's campaigns. One of WWF's conservation officers said:

> 'My concern is with sustainable forestry. WWF, like FoE, aims to stop the destruction of the world's forests by promoting sustainable forest management. When I am negotiating with logging companies, I often exploit the different reputations of the two groups. I will, for example, drop hints to the effect that if the loggers do not accept the moderate demands proposed by WWF, then it is likely that they will be targeted for direct action by FoE. The fact that both organisations use different methods in pursuing the same aims makes it more likely that we will achieve our goals.'
> (interview with Francis Sullivan of WWF, February 1994)

Similarly a large pressure group with a wide agenda may join forces with a small group that has a specific aim. For example, in February 1998, FoE joined forces with a local group to prevent the building of a 1,350 space park and ride site in Falconwood Field, a wild meadow situated next to an ancient woodland in South London. The campaign was successful. The local council refused planning permission for the park and ride site.

Conflict

On other occasions, two pressure groups may find themselves in direct conflict with each other. For example, when the Wild Mammals (Hunting with Dogs) Bill was introduced by Labour MP Michael Foster in November 1997, The International Fund for Animal Welfare (IFAW), the League Against Cruel Sports and the Royal Society for the Prevention of Cruelty to Animals (RSPCA) campaigned in favour of the Bill whilst the British Field Sports Society campaigned against it.

Functions of pressure groups

Although it is difficult to generalise because of the diversity of pressure groups, it is possible to identify three separate functions.

1. Enabling political participation in national politics

Pressure groups provide a means of popular participation in national politics between elections. It is true that a government with an absolute majority can be sure of passing legislation regardless of popular opinion, but pressure groups are sometimes able to mobilise sufficient support to force government to amend or even to scrap legislation. For example, when, in March 1998, around 300,000 people went to London to protest about the Labour

government's rural policies (the so-called 'Countryside March'), the government reacted by announcing that it was considering plans for a Ministry of Rural Affairs and that it would be publishing a white paper looking at all aspects of rural life. It is also generally agreed that this march helped the government to decide not to give government time to Michael Foster's anti-hunting Bill (effectively ending its chances of success).

2. Enabling political participation in local politics

Pressure groups provide a means of popular participation in local politics between elections. Just as national campaigns can affect the decisions made by Parliament, local campaigns can affect decisions that affect a locality - whether these decisions are made by local or by central government. For example, in 1994, the A452 Coordination Group (made up of nine smaller local pressure groups) set out to block plans by Warwickshire County Council to turn the A452 (which joined the towns of Kenilworth and Leamington) into a dual carriageway. Intense lobbying by the group eventually led to the council dropping the plan.

3. A source of specialist knowledge

It is a function of pressure groups to act as a source of specialist knowledge. Since most pressure groups are concerned with a single issue or a narrow policy area, they often develop expert knowledge of that issue or area. Many groups attract and bring together specialists. Some of the better-resourced groups are able to employ a team of specialists. As a result, pressure groups often have access to information which is highly valued by decision makers. Sometimes this specialist knowledge provides groups with direct access to the decision-making process. For example, specialists who work for MENCAP and MIND (groups which campaign on behalf of people with mental disabilities) are often invited to give briefings to government departments. In return, not only do these groups have an important input into the making of decisions, they also receive financial contributions. About one-fifth of MIND's total funds comes direct from the government.

1.5 Pressure groups and pluralism

Overcoming the democratic deficit

In a representative democracy, representatives are chosen infrequently and they are voted in by a majority. In theory, that means that the extent of most people's political participation is to cast a vote every few years. It also means that people have little or no influence over decision makers between elections and that the views of minorities may not be represented or supported by the elected decision makers. It means, in short, that there is a democratic deficit.

According to the pluralist view of politics, the

operation of pressure groups remedies these shortcomings. The pluralist view has four main strands.

1. Pressure groups and political participation

Pressure groups are an important means of political participation. Casting a vote does not express the strength of feelings that people may have about a specific issue. By joining a pressure group, people can express their strength of feeling and they can take active steps to influence decisions relating to the matter about which they feel so strongly. Also, joining a pressure group is a way for ordinary individuals to take part in political activity between elections.

2. Pressure groups and political parties

The work of pressure groups complements that of political parties. Individuals with strong views on a particular issue may support a political party in general terms but be unhappy about a policy on a particular issue or the lack of priority given to it. By joining a pressure group, such individuals can put pressure on decision makers in political parties. Also, pressure groups often raise questions that are not addressed in party manifestos and they ensure that issues which are of importance to people who do not belong to political parties appear on the political agenda.

3. Pressure groups and minority views

Members of pressure groups ensure that a group's views (especially a minority group's views) are heard by decision makers. This is particularly important in a democracy since the majority view tends to prevail. Without pressure groups it would be very difficult for the rights of minorities to be protected.

4. Pressure groups and decentralisation

Pressure groups help to disperse power away from central institutions. Decision makers are continually confronted by groups competing for their attention and, for every policy, there are groups for and groups against a particular point of view. Since this is the case, decisions are reached as a result of bargaining and compromise. It is the role of decision makers to arbitrate between the views presented to them.

Criticisms of the pluralist view

Pluralism is a political model, a theory. But, how well does this model translate into practice? Although few people would deny that pressure groups play an important role in British politics, critics have argued that this role may not be the one suggested by the pluralist model.

1. Decision makers have their own agenda

The idea that it is the role of decision makers to arbitrate between different interest groups is unrealistic. Decision makers have their own agenda.

Although the views of pressure groups may sometimes be considered, they are likely to be ignored if they do not conform with the ideology or agenda of the decision makers.

2. Groups are unelected and unrepresentative

Pressure groups themselves may not be representative of their members. Their officers are not usually elected. Few groups have procedures for consulting their members. As a result, the views expressed by group officials may not be those shared by the group's members.

3. Pressure groups disguise the true nature of power

Marxists argue that the pluralist view is a convenient justification used by the ruling class to disguise the true nature of its power. By claiming that decision makers merely arbitrate between the views presented by competing groups, supporters of pluralism give the impression that decision makers are somehow neutral when, actually, their primary concern is maintenance of the capitalist system. In practice, Marxists argue, there are élite pressure groups whose function is to maintain the status quo and it is these groups which gain access to decision makers. Pressure group activity gives people hope that they can make a difference. This hope is a distraction. The ruling class would rather that people put their energies into pressure group activities which do not question the fundamentals of the system than into political activity which seriously challenged the right of the élite to govern.

Main points - Sections 1.4-1.5

- The aim of all pressure groups is to influence those who have the power to make decisions.
- Pressure groups can be temporary or permanent organisations. Sometimes, they work together. Sometimes, they are directly opposed.
- The functions of pressure groups are: (1) to allow participation in national politics between elections; (2) to allow participation in local politics between elections; and (3) to provide decision makers with specialist knowledge.
- Pressure groups are important to the pluralist model because they: (1) allow political participation between elections; (2) complement the work of political parties; (3) ensure minority views are voiced; and (4) allow decision makers to arbitrate between different views.
- Critics of the pluralist model argue that: (1) decision makers are not neutral - they have their own agenda; (2) pressure groups are unelected and unrepresentative; and (3) pressure groups disguise the true nature of power.

Activity 10.2 Pressure group aims and functions

Item A *The battle over fox hunting*

The Countryside Alliance emerged in early 1997 when three groups amalgamated - the British Field Sports Society (BFSS); the Countryside Business Group (set up in 1995 to bring together people with a personal and business interest in rural sports); and, the Countryside Movement (also set up in 1995 to increase public understanding of rural issues). In July 1997, the Alliance jolted the government when 120,000 people gathered in Hyde Park. Using the BFSS's network of 320 affiliated hunts across the country and a network of some 50 other organisations, including the Country Landowners' Association, the Campaign for Shooting, the Jockey Club and the British Horseracing Board, the organisers had access to a huge base of supporters. The diversity led to some bickering about the purpose of the Countryside March which was organised in 1998. For example, the Sportsmen's Association (set up after Dunblane to reduce the impact of the anti-gun laws) complained that it was placed under strong pressure by the Alliance not to hold rallies of its own. The anti-hunting lobby has also had problems. Three powerful animal rights groups have combined against fox-hunting under the umbrella of the Campaign for the Protection of the Hunted Animal. The RSPCA has been accused of breaching its charitable status by engaging in political lobbying and has been threatened with mass infiltration by the BFSS. The American-based and hugely rich International Fund for Animal Welfare (IFAW) hit controversy when its £1 million donation to Labour was revealed before the general election. The League Against Cruel Sports (with 30,000 members) has been divided over what to do if hunting is banned. It split before, in 1995, when senior members concluded that banning fox-hunting would actually increase the suffering of foxes as farmers resorted to poison, snares and guns to get rid of them.

Adapted from the *Times*, 1 March 1998.

Item B *The Countryside Alliance*

Countryside Alliance

MANIFESTO

"To champion the countryside, country sports and the rural way of life."

✓ Preserve the freedoms of country people and their way of life

✓ Lead campaigns for country sports, their related trades and activities, and the countryside

✓ Co-operate closely with other organisations to promote and protect the rural way of life

✓ Promote conservation and the viability of the countryside as part of the national heritage

✓ Increase awareness and develop understanding of rural issues across the political spectrum

✓ Undertake research and provide authoritative information to politicians, the media and the public

✓ Develop education programmes for all ages, to promote a better understanding in town and country of the countryside and rural issues

✓ Advance animal welfare and expose the dangers of the 'animal rights' agenda

The above manifesto was produced after the Countryside March in March 1998.

Item C *The League Against Cruel Sports (1)*

Established in 1924, the League Against Cruel Sports maintains a unique approach to the protection of wildlife combining both campaigning and conservation. In Parliament, the League has cross-party support for its campaign to abolish hunting with dogs and live hare-coursing. In 1996, the League helped steer the Wild Mammals (Protection) Act through Parliament. League investigators (often undercover) regularly expose the reality of what goes on behind the respectable facade of hunting. It also looks out for tell-tale signs of (and wherever possible brings

to justice) those involved in illegal bloodsports such a badger-baiting, dog-fighting and cock-fighting. The League provides practical help to wildlife through its network of Wildlife Sanctuaries. Since 1959, it has purchased land of special benefit to wildlife and currently owns 37 sanctuaries covering an area of 2,000 acres. These are managed from the League's West Country Operations HQ. Sound conservation practices are employed to provide a safe haven for wild animals. The League believes it is vital to promote respect for wildlife and habitat conservation especially amongst young people. To this end, school talks and educational visits to the Wildlife Sanctuaries are regularly organised.

Adapted from a leaflet produced by the League Against Cruel Sports in 1998.

Item D *The Countryside March*

The affluent rural lobby re-emerged as a major force in British politics yesterday after about 250,000 people joined the march in protest against government policies on the countryside. In the largest demonstration since the CND rallies of the early 1980s, marchers descended on the capital to protest about ministerial handling of rural issues including fox hunting, farming and the right to roam. It now seems unlikely that Tony Blair will attempt to tackle the pro-hunting lobby head-on during this Parliament. Organisers claimed the demonstration had woken politicians to the strength of feeling over countryside issues. The small number of anti-hunt protesters who picketed the march claimed that most people (including a majority in the countryside) still favoured a ban on fox hunting. The government seemed deeply divided with Michael Meacher, Environment Minister, taking part on behalf of the government whilst Jack Cunningham, Minister of Agriculture, stayed away. A Countryside Alliance spokesman, Paul Latham, said: 'It shows the rural lobby is alive and a force in politics. In the build-up to the march, there have been a number of decisions taken that the countryside would welcome.' Journalist Matthew Engel overheard a debate between a marcher and picket. 'This is meant to be a democracy. But you can't do anything these days', said the marcher. 'This is a democratic country and most people don't want fox hunting', said the picket.'So what is democracy?', asked Engel, 'At what point does a majority's power end and a minority's rights begin?'

Adapted from the *Guardian*, 2 March 1998.

Questions

1. a) Using Items A-C, describe the aims of the Countryside Alliance and the League Against Cruel Sports.
   b) How do they differ?
   c) What does this tell us about the role of pressure groups?
2. Judging from Items A-D, what functions are performed by pressure groups?
3. a) What evidence is there in Items A-D to support the pluralist view that pressure groups ensure that a democracy functions smoothly?
   b) How might critics of the pluralist view interpret the evidence in Items A-D?

1.6 Think tanks

What are think tanks?

Think tanks are organisations set up to undertake research and to formulate policy ideas which (they hope) will be adopted by those who have the power to make decisions:

> '[Think tanks] are an organisational expression of the blending of ideas, politics and policy outside formal political arenas...[They] occupy an ambiguous position between the market and the state.' (Stone 1996, p.2)

'Think tank' is an American term that was first used in Britain in 1970 when Edward Heath's Conservative government set up the Central Policy Review Staff (CPRS). The CPRS was a small unit in the Cabinet Office (the civil service department in charge of administrative and secretarial work within the Cabinet system). Its aim was to serve the Cabinet as a whole by providing strategic advice on policy and by promoting interdepartmental cooperation. To achieve this aim, it undertook research and presented papers which were free from a departmental perspective. Although the CPRS survived the downfall of Edward Heath, it fell out of favour with Margaret Thatcher and was disbanded in 1983. Although the term 'think tank' has only been used since 1970, think tanks first came into existence long before this. The Fabian Society, for example, was set up in 1884.

Think tanks and pressure groups

Think tanks are different from other pressure groups in three respects. First, most think tanks aim to influence the policy decisions made by a particular political party (most other pressure groups are careful not to be too closely tied to a particular political party). Second, think tanks are interested in a whole political programme not just a single issue or narrow policy area. Third, think tanks are overtly ideological. Their ideas come from a carefully considered ideological standpoint and there is, usually, little concern with 'balance'. Think tanks often compete with each other to win over the ideological soul of a political party. Sometimes that means that they get involved in public debates about internal party matters.

These differences have led some critics to question whether think tanks are in fact pressure groups at all. But, if the definition of a pressure groups is an institution whose aim is to influence political decisions without putting up candidates for election, then think tanks qualify as pressure groups. They do not put up candidates at elections. They certainly try to influence political decisions. And, like all pressure groups, they can only exert an influence if they are in line with decision makers' current thinking.

The range of think tanks
Think tanks have grown in number since 1970. They now range right across the political spectrum. During the 1980s, it was the New Right's think tanks which gained access to government. For example, the Adam Smith Institute championed the policy of privatisation. Think tanks continue to make an impact on the political agenda. Since May 1997, the election of a Labour government has ensured that new think tanks have come into favour with ministers:

> 'Centre-left think tanks are now saying that there is no going back on privatisation while the "non-party" free-market groups traditionally seen as being on the centre-right will be hoping to influence the Labour government's policies. Those with strong Conservative links, on the other hand, will be left to reinvent the Conservative Party and its policies.' (*Labour Research*, November 1997)

The role of think tanks
As their name suggests, the role of think tanks is to employ people to do the thinking which many of the people actively involved in decision making simply do not have the time to do. It is usual, therefore, for think tanks to hold seminars, to publish research and discussion documents and to draw up policy recommendations. Political parties rely on think tanks to come up with fresh and original ideas. They also expect them to produce the relevant data and support material which will enable them to package these policy ideas in an appealing manner. Denham and Garnett argue that think tanks have two main objectives:

> 'There do appear to be two main objectives that all think tanks seek, albeit with varying degrees of emphasis. The first is to influence the "climate of opinion" within which, it is

assumed, political actors are bound to operate...The second objective is to inform public policy decisions more directly, through contact with MPs, government ministers or officials. The difference between this goal and the first one might seem rather slight, since in both cases the intention is to shape legislation. However an important difference remains; while on the first model a policy is implemented in response to public demands, the second can be seen as something of a short-cut in which an elected government, convinced by think tank arguments can, in theory at least, introduce legislation even if the general public dislikes the idea, then wait to see how voters respond to the policy in practice.' (Denham & Garnett 1998, pp.16-17 - slightly adapted)

The Fabian Society
The Fabian Society was founded in 1884 by Sidney Webb, Beatrice Webb and George Bernard Shaw. It is upon the Fabian Society that other think tanks have been modelled (in terms of organisation if not in terms of ideology). The Fabian Society was set up to promote the gradual path to socialism. It was named after the Roman general Fabius Cunctator who defeated Hannibal by delaying and avoiding a direct confrontation. The early Fabians tried to win a wide audience for their ideas by organising debates and seminars and by publishing pamphlets. Perhaps the Fabians' period of greatest influence was during the years 1900-14 when they helped to shape the new Labour Party and provided ideas which were incorporated into the Liberal government's social reforms. The Fabian Society remains an important source of ideas in the Labour Party today.

The Institute of Economic Affairs (IEA)
The IEA was founded in 1955. Its aim was to do for free-market economics what the Fabians did for socialism. Keith Joseph, Geoffrey Howe and Margaret Thatcher all learned their economic theory through the IEA. According to Wyn Grant, the IEA has had:

> 'A significant influence on the way in which the intellectual climate has changed from favouring the interventionist, neo-Keynesian ideal to support for more market orientated approaches.' (Grant 1989, p.50)

In the 1990s, its key areas of concern were the European Union and constitutional reform.

The Centre for Policy Studies (CPS)
The CPS has been described as 'the engine room of Thatcherism'. It was founded by Margaret Thatcher and Keith Joseph shortly after the Conservatives' defeat in February 1974 and quickly became one of the main vehicles for policies favoured by the New Right (see Chapter 3, Section 2.1). The CPS recruited

non-political specialists such as the economist Alan Walters. Margaret Thatcher was more inclined to take notice of Alan Walter's opinions on the economy than those of her Chancellor Nigel Lawson. This was a major factor in Lawson's decision to resign in 1989. Hugo Young says that, when Margaret Thatcher became Leader of the Conservative Party, the CPS:

> 'Effectively eclipsed the official Conservative Research Department as the source of approved intellectual activity.' (Young 1989, p.113)

The CPS is, therefore, an excellent example of just how much influence a think tank can have.

The Adam Smith Institute

The Adam Smith Institute was founded in the USA in 1978 and set up in Britain in 1981. Like the CPS, the Adam Smith Institute's ideology is that favoured by the New Right. Also like the CPS, the Adam Smith Institute made an important contribution to the policies adopted by the Thatcher governments, especially privatisation. For example, Norman Fowler's proposals for privatising the NHS ancillary services came direct from the Adam Smith Institute (*Labour Research*, February 1984).

The Institute for Public Policy Research (IPPR)

The IPPR was founded in 1988 by academics, business people, trade unionists and Labour Party supporters who were close to the former Labour Leader, Neil Kinnock. Its aim was to provide an alternative to free-market thinking and to make the idea of collectivism respectable again. Between 1992 and 1994, it organised the independent Commission on Social Justice. The recommendations made in the Commission's 1994 report made an impact on policies pursued by the Blair government:

> 'On employment, it called for help for lone parents to find childcare facilities, while on education it called for literacy and numeracy targets for seven-year-olds. A policy already taken up by Labour is the release to local authorities of receipts from council house sales.' (*Labour Research*, November 1997)

Despite this, contacts between the IPPR and the Labour government have fallen short of IPPR hopes. Denham and Garnett argue:

> 'Other bodies, notably the revived Fabian Society and Demos, enjoy more favoured status with the new regime...Despite its current problems, the IPPR might have a

healthy future as an independent think tank.' (Denham & Garnett 1998, p.184)

The Social Market Foundation (SMF)

The SMF was set up in 1989 by supporters of David Owen after the SDP was disbanded. Its primary aim was to perpetuate David Owen's ideological vision of the 'social market'. It believes in 'the vitality of the market' and 'the need for social consent'.

The European Policy Forum (EPF)

In 1992, the CPS and Adam Smith Institute were joined by a third New Right think tank - the European Policy Forum (EPF). The EPF was set up by Graham Mather and Frank Vibert, the former director and deputy director of the IEA. They left the IEA after a bitter dispute over policy and aims. The EPF's aim is to promote a free-market and anti-federalist Europe. Whilst in office, Douglas Hurd and John Major both supported the aims of the EPF and spoke at EPF meetings.

Demos

Demos (ancient Greek for 'the people') was launched in March 1993. Unlike the other think tanks mentioned above, Demos claims to be an independent, non-partisan organisation. It has three main aims:

> 'To enrich the culture of political debate that has become narrow and self referential; to develop strategic approaches to the fundamental problems faced by both the UK and other advanced societies; and to encourage radical thinking that helps to harness the inventiveness and motivation of citizens alienated from the existing political mainstream.' (Demos briefing, spring 1994)

The work of Demos is overseen by an advisory council of 23 people drawn from business, academia, the media and the public and voluntary sectors. None of the 23 members of this council is a professional politician and their political affiliation is diverse. For example, the council was originally chaired by Martin Jacques, an ex-Communist. But, John Ashworth, director of the London School of Economics, was also a member. Ashworth was once described as Margaret Thatcher's favourite academic. Demos, therefore, has close ties with no one political party and aims to appeal not just to government and opposition parties but to:

> 'Change makers in the public, private and voluntary sectors, at whatever level.' (Demos 1993, p.7)

Main points - Section 1.6

- Think tanks are organisations set up to undertake research and to formulate policy ideas which (they hope) will be adopted by those who have the power to make decisions.
- Think tanks differ from other pressure groups in that they are: (1) often partisan; (2) interested in the whole political programme, not just a single

issue; and (3) overtly ideological.
- The role of think tanks is to: (1) do the thinking politicians have no time to do; (2) come up with new and fresh ideas; and (3) produce the relevant data and support material which will enable politicians to package policy ideas.

Activity 10.3 *Think tanks under Labour*

Item A   *The growth of think tanks*

Following the 1997 general election, a large number of pro-Labour think tanks were set up. It is in these think tanks that the battle lines of future policy debates are already being formed. In the autumn of 1997, for example, the Smith Institute was set up in memory of former Labour Leader John Smith. Its aim is to prove the unremarkable proposition that 'social justice and economic progress can go hand in hand'. Also in 1997, the Foreign Policy Centre was set up to widen the input of ideas into foreign policy making. In 1996, the Centre of European Reform was set up by, amongst others, David Miliband who was appointed to the Downing Street Policy Unit in May 1997. Its goal is to add a pro-European voice to political debate. Whilst all those mentioned above are very New Labour, Old Labour also set up a think tank - Catalyst. Catalyst supports unfashionable aims like 'policies of redistribution of wealth, power and opportunity'. It has published pamphlets which accuse the government of pluralism and 'government by élite'. Think tanks played an important role in providing the intellectual ammunition for Thatcherism. But, the Conservative think tanks of the 1970s were working in opposition, aiming to equip the party with a brand new philosophy and programme, ready for 1979. The Labour Party is reversing the process. Labour gained office by shedding ideological baggage and the party is now casting around for coherent policies to sustain itself in government. That is where the new think tanks find their role.

Adapted from the *Economist*, 18 July 1998.

Item B   *Brick's view of think tanks*

Item C   *Demos (1)*

Serious new ideas need the contribution of doers as well as thinkers. We will draw on people from across the political spectrum in the belief that the best ideas have no preordained political home. The traditional think tank is organised as a pyramid with a group of the 'great and good' or an intellectual guru at the top. Demos will organise itself as a network of partners working both full and part time to encourage flexibility and openness. These partners will in turn form the hubs of much larger networks of thinkers and doers. The traditional think tanks target government and Parliament. They have no contact with people who make things and provide services. Demos will seek a close relationship with doers. Demos will not be confined to the narrow world of politicians and civil servants. Of course, we will seek to influence both government and opposition parties. But, public policy can no longer be made in charmed circles. Our primary audience will be change makers in the public, private and voluntary sectors, at whatever level. Demos will address unexpected subjects. Research will be carried out on issues that cut across professional divides and on broader issues that are ignored by the over-specialisation of policy analysis. Our work will range from the future of Parliaments to parks, from the role of religion to fiscal regimes.

Adapted from Demos 1993.

Item D *Demos (2)*

The think tank world has changed radically and Demos was one of the things that changed it. Before, there was a clear dividing line between left and right. But, following his election as Party Leader, Tony Blair made an appeal for new thinking. Demos was in the right place at the right time because it saw its role as ditching the old ideologies and producing fresh ideas. This fitted in with what was happening politically in the Labour Party. Influence is hard to quantify, but a pattern can be found. Demos' ideas on rebranding Britain, for example, at first caused uproar. Many dismissed it as ludicrous, but, in a matter of months, it was government policy. Most of Demos' work is behind the scenes. It does very detailed management consultancy work with councils, schools and businesses. Two of its researchers were on secondment to government contact departments in 1998, whilst two former members (Geoff Mulgan, one of the founders, and Mark Leonard, the researcher who wrote the pamphlet on rebranding Britain) have been appointed to work for the government full time. Demos has been accused of lacking philosophical coherence. But, one Demos writer, Charles Leadbetter, argues that everything revolves around two main themes - the nature of politics and government, and the nature of modern society. Another writer says that Demos' long-term aim is to show that the economic approach of both left and right is deeply impoverished. One of Demos' most original contributions is the idea that public policy should be shaped in conjunction with the people affected by it. So, they consult young people on youth, teachers on education and doctors on medicine.

Adapted from the *Guardian*, 30 June 1998.

Questions

1. a) How would you classify think tanks using the criteria laid out in sections 1.1-1.3 above?
   b) What are the aims and functions of think tanks? Use Items A-D in your answer.

2. a) Judging from Items A and D, how did the election of a Labour government in May 1997 affect think tanks?
   b) Why do you think the Blair government took notice of some of the ideas which emerged from Demos?

3. What does Item B tell us about the role of think tanks?

4. Look at Items C and D.
   a) What are the aims of Demos?
   b) How does Demos differ from other think tanks?
   c) How would you expect Demos to measure its effectiveness as a think tank?

Part 2 How do pressure groups achieve their aims?

Key issues

1. What tactics are used by pressure groups which campaign within the governmental system?
2. What tactics are used by pressure groups which campaign outside the governmental system?
3. What are the most effective ways for pressure groups to achieve their aims?

2.1 Campaigning within the governmental system

How do pressure groups make contact with decision makers?

In an ideal world, members of a pressure group would approach decision makers and ask them directly to incorporate their demands. In reality, of course, this rarely happens. It is often difficult to pinpoint who exactly makes a decision - most decisions are the outcome of a process rather than the work of an individual - and, therefore, it is difficult to know who to approach. Besides, decision makers do not have the time (and sometimes the inclination) to meet all the interested parties before making their decisions. As a result, pressure groups have to adopt other tactics to make sure that their voice is heard. What tactics they adopt is determined, to some extent, by the status of the pressure group.

Influencing ministers and civil servants

Ministers and civil servants are involved at all stages in the formation of government policy and the making of legislation. Many pressure groups, therefore, aim to gain access to ministers and civil servants at the earliest possible stage in the decision-making process.

Ministers and civil servants invite interested parties for consultation as a matter of course. Insider groups have a close and secretive relationship with the government. Consultation is, therefore, frequent and private. Outsider groups may also be invited for consultation. But, their effectiveness is determined by the point at which they enter the decision-making process. There are three main stages at which consultation occurs. The earlier a group is included, the greater its chance of success.

Box 10.3   How pressure groups influence the political agenda

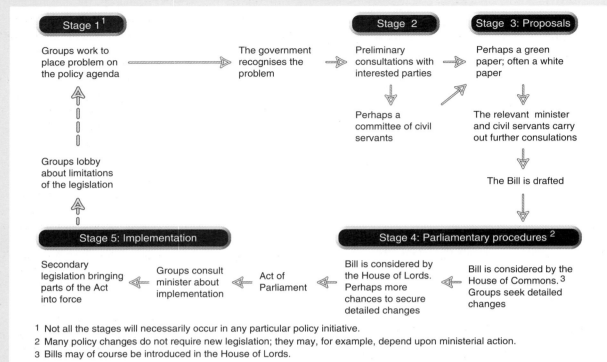

1 Not all the stages will necessarily occur in any particular policy initiative.
2 Many policy changes do not require new legislation; they may, for example, depend upon ministerial action.
3 Bills may of course be introduced in the House of Lords.

Adapted from Grant 1995.

Stage one

The earliest stage is the point at which government is working out new policy, but has not made any public statement about it. Since the government will not lose face by retreating from a publicly announced position, this is the stage at which pressure groups can exert most influence. At this point, thinking is more fluid and decision makers are open to advice.

Stage two

The second stage is the period after governmental intentions reach the public domain, but before a proposal becomes law. This stage might begin with the publication of a green paper (a consultative document setting out policy options for discussion). Once the green paper has been circulated, civil servants invite interested groups to give their views on the matters raised in it. Large numbers of groups can become involved in the consultation process. Some are taken more seriously than others.

The chances of success recede as this stage progresses. Once a white paper (a document outlining proposals for legislation) has been published, it is much more difficult to secure fundamental changes since the white paper contains firm proposals backed by the government. Nevertheless, change is possible and it is worthwhile for groups to continue to lobby MPs or civil servants right up to the point at which a proposal becomes law.

Stage three

The third stage concerns the implementation of the policy. Parliament has only a limited time in which to consider new legislation. Many Acts of Parliament are brought into force and the details of policy filled in later through secondary legislation. This means that the implementation of policy is delegated to a minister who sets out the powers, rights and duties. The timing and the detail of this secondary legislation can be very important to pressure groups.

Box 10.3 above shows the various points at which pressure groups may try to influence the political agenda.

Why do civil servants listen to pressure groups?

There are three main reasons why civil servants take the policy proposals made by pressure groups seriously.

First, consultation is regarded as an accepted and important part of the democratic process. Therefore, civil servants are obliged to consult.

Second, Britain has a generalist civil service. Although the civil service does employ all kinds of specialists, pressure groups often know more about a subject than the civil servants and can help them to make informed decisions. This trend towards a specialist dialogue has been seen as part of a professionalisation of policy making in which civil servants see themselves as talking to fellow professionals who staff pressure groups (Richardson 1990).

And third, pressure groups can help put policies into practice. For example, they might ask their members to follow a voluntary code of practice or ask them to cooperate with a new government policy on training.

Influencing Parliament

Baggott (1995) provides evidence that Parliament is an important focal point for pressure groups. In a survey carried out in 1992, for example, he found that a third of groups were in contact with MPs at least once a week, while over 60% had contact at least once a month. Miller, however, gives MPs as a group an influence score of four out of ten, rising to six if there is a small majority or an obvious public issue. Individual MPs get a score of one. This compares to eight for civil servants and seven for ministers (Miller 1990, pp.53-6).

There are three areas in which parliamentary influence on the decision-making process can be seen at work.

First, MPs who win a high place in the ballot for Private Members' Bills are likely to be approached by pressure groups. Some pressure groups have achieved their objectives through such Bills. For example the Abortion Reform Bill brought forward by David Steel was legalised by a 1967 Act.

Second, backbench committees can exert some influence over decisions - Miller gives them a six on his influence grid (Miller 1990, p.40). As a result, pressure groups may approach these committees in the hope that their demands will be adopted by the committee and presented to government.

And third, pressure groups are sometimes invited to appear before select committees (see Chapter 14, Section 2.3). The reports from these committees are often seriously considered by government. If pressure groups appear before these committees their views may find their way into the committee's report and, by appearing there, influence government policy.

Influencing political parties

Perhaps the most obvious link between pressure groups and political parties is the link between trade unions and the Labour Party. Despite the decision at the 1993 Labour Party conference to introduce OMOV (one member, one vote), trade unions still retain financial and organisational ties with the Labour Party. Labour MPs sponsored by a union are expected to support the interests of that union in Parliament and union delegates still have a voice in the formulation of Labour policy at every level. Relatively speaking, however, the unions have much less influence over Labour policy than used to be the case.

Other pressure groups have links with political parties, but on a more casual basis. Although most pressure groups are careful to maintain a non-partisan approach, some can only realistically expect to exert influence if a particular party is in power. For example, it is only since Labour came to power in 1997 that the Electoral Reform Society had any realistic chance of achieving its goals because the

Conservatives were strongly opposed to electoral reform whilst in government.

It is not always pressure groups which approach political parties. Parties sometimes approach pressure groups in the hope that they will support a policy or a campaign. Many pressure groups are widely respected and so their endorsement of a policy or a campaign can bring it great credibility. In cases like this, however, pressure groups have to consider carefully whether they are prepared to risk the charge of abandoning their political neutrality.

Using the courts

One way in which pressure groups can challenge and sometimes overturn a government decision is to take action in the courts. Legal actions are expensive and lengthy, but they are increasingly being used by pressure groups, not least because British membership of the European Union has widened the scope of legal action through use of the European Court of Justice:

'Although the primacy of European law has given pressure groups added incentive to support test cases that could lead to changes in the law, the growing use of legal processes to fight government policy decisions is in fact part of a broader trend. In recent decades, there has been a growth of judicial activism at the domestic level too.' (Baggott 1995, p.217)

Most of the larger pressure groups now have a legal representative or department. For some groups, this is a necessity. For example, environmental policies are increasingly being set by international treaties and so it is necessary for environmental groups (such as WWF) to go to court to seek better enforcement of these treaties (WWF 1991).

Sometimes winning a case is not important. The publicity surrounding a case can be sufficient for the decision makers to back down. On other occasions, however, a public outcry can be ignored by decision makers. The cost of taking legal action means that, in general, the courts are only used as a last resort when all other methods have been unsuccessful.

Using professional lobbyists

Over recent years, there has been a rapid expansion of paid political consultants who offer to act as intermediaries between pressure groups and Parliament. Although lobbyists are used mainly by sectional groups and commercial clients, some cause groups do make use of them.

Lobbyists have three main functions:
- to provide groups with political information
- to bring groups into contact with MPs or officials, or to bring MPs or officials into contact with groups
- to persuade MPs or officials to back a particular issue or cause.

As the 'Cash for Secrets' scandal of July 1998 revealed (see Chapter 11, Section 3.3), some lobbyists have access to the heart of government. Others cultivate ties with backbenchers and officials in departments:

> 'I may not have as wide contacts as any group of consultants whose whole life is to build up contacts. Nevertheless, I reckon that I know well about 120 MPs and on good friend terms. I know as acquaintances at least another 150; so I am up to a very large number of MPs. I know dozens of civil servants in all the departments that matter to us, at both senior and drafting level.' (the lobbyist Anthony Weale quoted in Maloney 1996)

It should be noted that, for every lobbying success, there is a similar story of failure, not least because consultants are frequently hired on both sides of a dispute.

2.2 Campaigning outside the governmental system

The need to attract public support

All pressure groups need to attract public support. They do this by using the media, by appealing to members of the public directly, by organising demonstrations or by other forms of direct action. There are two types of campaign:

- long-term educational and propaganda campaigns designed to produce significant shifts in public opinion
- short-term campaigns aimed at warning the public about a specific problem and trying to solve it.

Attracting public support is particularly important for outsider groups because outsider groups cannot expect to have direct contact with decision makers. Insider groups are generally reluctant to become involved in campaigns that involve direct action.

Using the media

The media plays a central role in modern politics and is used by all pressure groups. Television and newspapers are particularly important in determining which issues appear on the political agenda both nationally and locally. They can also help to create a climate of public opinion which puts pressure on decision makers. It is for these reasons that pressure groups issue press releases and cultivate contacts with the media.

The relationship between pressure groups and the media, however, does not flow one way. People working in the news media are always looking for story ideas just as pressure groups are looking for media exposure. In fact, pressure groups often do journalists' ground work for them. Suppose, for example, that an editor received a press release from a pressure group. This might be passed onto a journalist. The journalist's first action would then be to contact the pressure group. In this way, pressure groups can set the agenda. If the story is run, it is more likely that the pressure group's aims will become of concern to decision makers.

Six ways of using the media

Wyn Grant suggests that there are six ways in which pressure groups can make use of the media (Grant 1995). First, the media can provide visibility. References to a new group establish a presence in the audience's mind, making it easier to recruit new members. Constant exposure reassures a group's supporters that the group is active and helps the retention and recruitment of members. Second, the media acts as a source of information for pressure groups. Pressure groups often scrutinise the media for relevant information and are able to build campaigns around issues that are in the news or which have a local relevance. Third, the media plays a part in changing the political climate and this can have a direct effect on pressure group popularity. For example, the Abortion Reform Association was set up in 1936 but its views were ignored until a new liberal outlook emerged in the 1960s. Fourth, pressure groups may need to react to a news item. For example, when in December 1988, Edwina Currie announced that most of Britain's egg production was contaminated with salmonella, the National Farmer's Union had to react quickly to defend its members. Fifth, media coverage can demonstrate that a matter is of public concern. This is especially useful when pressure groups are presenting their case to decision makers since the decision makers are more likely to take notice of issues of public concern. And sixth, information provided by pressure groups may directly influence the content of articles or programmes.

What determines effectiveness?

Sometimes, it is advantageous for pressure groups to try and reach the largest possible audience. On other occasions, it is better to target certain strands of the media. No matter how large or small, pressure groups have to make tactical decisions about how best to achieve the publicity they desire.

The main problem with basing a campaign around media attention is that it is difficult to sustain. It may be difficult to keep a story in the news for the length of time that it takes to bring about effective change.

Resources also determine effectiveness. The Women's Environmental Network (WEN), for example, could only afford to employ one full-time and nine part-time members of staff in 1998 to cover all aspects of WEN's work whilst WWF employed three senior press and campaign officers and one assistant press and campaigns officer, one office manager and an administrative assistant in the press office alone. Some groups have even started to charge journalists for talking to campaign staff or for the use of their libraries. This may be counterproductive, however, since it might cut off the publicity upon which the groups depend not just to influence decision makers but also to gain new members and donations.

Finally, problems can arise if the media takes a negative attitude towards a group. This makes it more difficult for the group to communicate its message and the group may lose members or find it more difficult to recruit them in the future.

The timing of publicity campaigns

Publicity campaigns may be organised for the following reasons.

First, publicity campaigns are often launched to take advantage of the fact that a particular issue is in the news. For example, Greenpeace launched a campaign against genetically modified food in November 1998 to coincide with the publication of a survey showing that the number of people who believed that genetically modified food was unacceptable had risen from 35% in 1997 to 51% in 1998.

Second, publicity campaigns are designed to coincide with pre-planned summits or conferences relevant to the interests of the group. For example Friends of the Earth (FoE) ran an extensive advertising campaign to coincide with the Earth Summit in New York in June 1997 and the Climate Change Summit in Kyoto, Japan in December 1997.

And third, publicity campaigns are designed to draw attention to new pieces of legislation. When, in 1998, Deputy Prime Minister John Prescott announced that he would draw up legislation designed to ensure that Britain had sufficient housing to meet people's needs, FoE began a campaign against building on green belt land whilst Shelter (a group which aims to combat homelessness) campaigned for the building of new houses.

Campaigning techniques

1. Paying for adverts in newspapers

Paying for adverts in newspapers can attract support for the cause and bring in donations and new members. But, advertising is expensive and so only groups with large funds can afford to use this technique. Some economically powerful pressure groups pay for the services of professional advertising agencies. For example, the RSPCA uses professional lobbyists and a PR consultancy to run its campaigns. Methods of presentation vary. Some groups use shock tactics to gain support. Others focus on a success which shows that the group is able to achieve its aims.

2. Direct mail

Some groups produce mailshots which are posted direct to members of the public. This is a way of reaching a large number of people relatively cheaply. Some mailshots are designed to recruit new members. Others are designed to inform people about important developments or to ask them to take action. Greenpeace, for example, has managed to persuade nearly half a million people to write letters protesting about whaling.

3. Publicity stunts

Some groups are not viewed in a sympathetic light by the media and, therefore, cannot expect to receive good publicity as a matter of course. Other groups may find that their press releases are ignored because different issues are given a higher priority. As a result, groups often organise events that are designed to gain publicity. These events might be marches or demonstrations or they might be other forms of direct action. Some groups even use violence as a means of publicising their cause.

Direct action

Direct action has been defined as:

> 'A form of political action which operates outside the formal political process. It is (in many ways) extra-parliamentary rather than parliamentary activity. It can be characterised as a range of activities which have a number of essential qualities. They are demonstrative, obstructive, publicity seeking, increasingly illegal and sometimes violent.' (Hoad 1998, p.208)

Campaigns of direct action are often highly organised. FoE claims that successful campaigns of direct action involve local groups working with help from a central headquarters:

> 'No other environmental campaigning group has our reach at local level - there are FoE groups in 250 towns and local areas. From South Yorkshire where FoE led residents in forcing English Nature to drop plans to de-notify Sites of Special Scientific Interest on Thorne and Hatfield moors to allow expanded peat extraction, to Heathrow where FoE continues to lead the fight against Terminal Five our work in the community continues.' (FoE Annual Review 1997)

Although local campaigns of direct action might not be successful, they can still influence government policy. For example, local campaigns of direct action to prevent roads being built through Twyford Down or around Newbury were unsuccessful in that the roads were eventually built. Nevertheless, the publicity generated by the local campaigns helps to explain why, in 1997, the government scrapped and deferred a number of proposals to build new roads.

Main points - Sections 2.1-2.2

- Pressure groups have to adopt tactics to make sure that their voice is heard. What tactics they adopt is determined, to some extent, by the status of the pressure group.
- Many pressure groups aim to gain access to ministers and civil servants at the earliest possible stage in the decision-making process. The earlier their input, the more chance of making an impact on legislation.
- Pressure groups also target Parliament and political parties. Sometimes, they take action through the courts. Some groups employ lobbyists to act on their behalf.

- All pressure groups use the media. The media: (1) provides visibility; (2) provides information; (3) helps to change the political climate; (4) raises issues that require a response; (5) reveals public concerns; and (6) uses information provided by groups.
- Campaigning techniques include: (1) paying for adverts in the press; (2) paying for PR; (3) producing mailshots; and (4) organising publicity stunts.
- Direct action is a form of political action which operates outside the formal political process. It can be highly organised and effective. It may be illegal and/or violent.

Activity 10.4 *Pressure group tactics*

Item A   *Influencing the government*

(i)

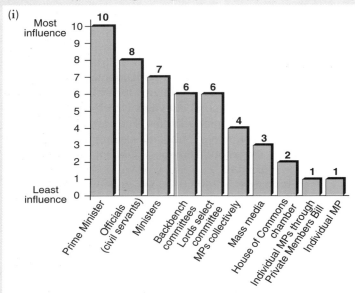

This chart shows how much influence each person or group has in the decision-making process.

(ii)

Contacts between pressure groups and decision-makers

Institution/office	% of groups in contact at least		
	once a week	once a month	once a year
Prime Minister/PM Office	1	11	53
Cabinet ministers	8	37	81
Junior ministers	11	49	86
Senior higher civil servants*	19	50	82
Junior higher civil servants**	34	67	85
MPs	31	61	89
Peers	18	50	84
Media	81	94	98

* Grades 1-4

** Grades 5-7   **For an explanation of the grades, see Chapter 13, Section 2.3**

This table shows the results of a survey carried out in 1992.

Adapted from Miller 1990 and Baggott 1995.

Item B   *Lobbying Parliament and the government*

(i) The League Against Cruel Sports is organising a mass lobby of Parliament, to be held on 11 November 1998. Members are to assemble in the early afternoon. Briefing notes will be distributed before those taking part meet their MPs. A mass lobby, the League claims, is an invaluable campaign tool. Most MPs support the abolition of hunting and they will welcome the opportunity to speak with their constituents. Those MPs who support hunting or who will not vote against it need to be reminded that they are acting against the wishes of the electors. The League's Chair, John Cooper, said: 'If every MP is lobbied it will carry a clear message to the government that the campaign for the abolition of hunting is as alive as ever.'

(ii) Elliot Morely, the Minister for Rural Affairs, has once again confirmed his support for the abolition of hunting with dogs. Members and an official of the League Against Cruel Sports accompanied Mr Morely on a visit to a planned nature reserve in West London. The Minister discussed plans for the proposed reserve with Jean Smith, a local councillor and member of the League. Ms Smith had earlier persuaded party members to incorporate an animal welfare charter into their manifesto for elections to the local council.

Adapted from *Wildlife Guardian*, issue 40, summer/autumn 1998.

Item C *A newspaper advert*

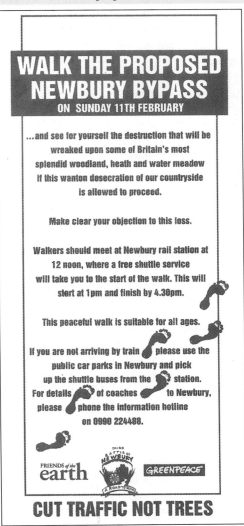

This advert appeared in the *Independent* on 3 February 1996 and in other national newspapers. The march aimed to keep up pressure on the government to abandon the proposed Newbury bypass and to show support for the protesters living in tree houses along the route. These protesters were due to be evicted in February 1996. Around 5,000 people attended the march, a record for a protest against a road.

Item D *Protesting against genetically modified food*

Nothing had been left to chance. The attack had been planned weeks before. Reconnaissance missions had taken place to check security. Studies into how long they would need and what equipment they should take with them had been carried out. Then, before deciding a time and a date, they talked between themselves. Were they ready to be arrested, charged, fined and possibly jailed for their actions? They were. Nobody spoke during the ten minute drive and, as they approached the target field, they steeled themselves. With torches and moonlight they marched into the half acre field and began 'decontamination'. 'We were absolutely methodical', said one of the group. 'We pulled up all the sugar beet plants and bagged them up. I was nervous, but I needn't have been. We got clean away.' Four days later, 30 other activists completed the second part of the operation, storming the field at dawn and setting up a camp which remained unchallenged for a fortnight. It was a significant victory - the first occupation of a 'contaminated site' and a template for the type of guerrilla activity which will distinguish this latest environmental movement. The campaign is focused on genetically modified food (it was genetically modified sugar beet that was being grown in this instance). Much has been learned from past campaigns - from the anti-road campaigns to opposition to a second runway at Manchester Airport. The new movement is supported by veteran eco-warriors - people who have dug tunnels, camped out in trees, chained themselves to fences and seen the inside of more courts than most magistrates. Last weekend, Luke Anderson, an environmentalist from Devon organised a demonstration at a local supermarket which stocked genetically modified foods. One hundred people turned up, some dressed as vegetables crossed with chickens, others in grim reaper suits. They handed out leaflets to customers saying 'Thank you for taking part in our experiment'.

Adapted from the *Guardian*, 13 June 1998.

Questions

1. What does Item A tell us about (a) the tactics which pressure groups should use and (b) the tactics they actually use?

2. How would you explain the different sort of tactics used by the pressure groups mentioned in Items B-D?

3. Why do you think that FoE and Greenpeace chose to buy the advert in the *Independent* (Item C)? Would you say it was money well spent? Explain your answer.

4. Think of an issue which you feel strongly about. Suppose you were a member of a pressure group which campaigned on this issue. What tactics would you use? Explain why you could not or would not use certain tactics.

2.3 Factors affecting pressure group success

Difficulties with measuring success

It is not easy to measure the success of a pressure group. Although there are some cause groups which have a single objective, most pressure groups have multiple objectives and it is difficult to know which has priority. Objectives may vary over time according to what is on the political agenda or there may be different factions within a group which have to be considered. Besides, even in the case of groups with a single objective it is difficult to be sure to what extent the achievement of the objective was due to the work of the pressure group. Take, for example, the Snowdrop Campaign. This group had the single objective of banning all handguns. But, how far was the banning of handguns due to the group? It could be argued that the attitude of the media or the result of the 1997 general election was more important. Similarly, the announcement, in November 1998, of a ban on the testing of cosmetic ingredients on animals in the UK might appear to be a triumph for the National Anti-Vivisection Society and the British Union for the Abolition of Vivisection, two groups which have campaigned on this issue for many years. Yet, both groups claimed that the real power for change had come from consumers who have chosen to look for products not tested on animals.

Factors other than the achievement of an objective

The following factors may affect whether or not a group is judged to be successful.

First, it is important to consider whether decision makers are responsive to a pressure group's message. If a pressure group's message fits with the decision makers' ideology, it is much more likely to be accepted and the group is, therefore, much more likely to be effective.

Second, the fact that much of the discussion about a decision often takes place in private is also important since, later, it may not be clear from the records whether a pressure group's actions have been influential.

Third, the fact that, sometimes, several pressure groups campaign for the same outcome means that it can be unclear which particular group, if any, influenced the decision makers.

Fourth, even if decision makers do not appear to be receptive, this does not mean that they have taken no notice of a pressure group's campaign. Pressure group demands may be taken on board quietly to avoid a loss of face.

Fifth, it may not always be obvious what the decision makers' policy really is. They may take a tough line in the beginning for tactical reasons so that they can give ground and appear more generous later, for example.

And sixth, although a pressure group may occasionally achieve exactly what it wanted, it should be emphasised that, generally, a degree of compromise is involved. In fact, policy often emerges as a series of compromises and it is difficult to unravel who or what exactly was responsible at each stage of the process.

Grant's classification of pressure group effectiveness

Grant (1995) argues that there are three main categories which affect pressure group effectiveness.

1. Domain organisation

Membership

The characteristics of the membership of a pressure group to some extent determine the effectiveness of the pressure group. A group whose membership is drawn from a disadvantaged section of the population is less likely to be effective than a group whose membership comes from the middle classes. This is because middle-class members tend to be educated and articulate, have organisational ability, and know how the political system works. By

definition, these qualities tend to be lacking in the disadvantaged sections of the population. So, WWF with its mass membership and middle-class activists is more likely to be effective than the Claimants Union, the bulk of whose membership is unemployed.

Electoral influence

The attractiveness of a group in terms of its electoral influence may also play a part in determining effectiveness. It is easier to arouse public concern and, therefore, the support of decision makers for the elderly than for, say, offenders or the low paid.

Competition for members

Competition for members can lead to groups becoming less effective. Rather than presenting a united front, groups representing the same interests may be fragmented by their differing ideologies and strategies. If this is the case, then decision makers are likely to adopt a 'divide and rule' policy which reduces the chance of any of the pressure groups fulfilling their objectives. This is a tactic often used by the government when dealing with unions. For example, the teaching profession is represented by six different unions and it is highly unusual for all six to take the same line on government policy. This makes it easier for the government to ignore views it does not support.

2. Resources

The finance, number of staff and the organisational structure of a pressure group has a bearing on its effectiveness.

Financial resources

Financial resources not only affect what campaigning techniques a group can use, they also determine how many members of staff a group can employ. A group which is able to employ 100 people full time is almost certainly going to be more effective than a group with the same objectives which can only afford to employ one person full time. Employees have the time and expertise to ensure that campaigns are organised in a professional, effective manner. Size in itself, however, is not a guarantee of success. During the 1980s and early 1990s, many trade unions had large financial reserves and employed many full-time officials. But, the anti-union attitude adopted by the Conservative government meant that they had little chance of achieving their objectives.

Financial uncertainty

Financial uncertainty can also affect a group's effectiveness. Most groups rely on membership subscriptions and donations. But, these sources of funds can easily dry up. Between 1989 and 1992, for example, WWF's income fell by more than £3 million because it lost a tenth of its supporters. This drop in the number of supporters was due both to the depth of the economic recession and the fact that the environment had slipped down the political agenda (Carter 1995). Between 1995 and 1997, however, the number of supporters (full members plus donors) rose by nearly 100,000 (WWF Annual Report 1996-97).

Organisational structure

A group's organisational structure also has a bearing on its effectiveness. Sectional groups tend to have a centralised structure consisting of a council which is the ultimate policy-making body and smaller specialised groups which look after individual areas or campaigns. Cause groups, on the other hand, tend to have a more decentralised structure. The advantage of a decentralised structure is that local groups and members feel that they are intimately involved in the group's decision-making process. Also, information can easily be fed back from the grassroots to the centre. The disadvantage is that local groups may decide to take action without fully consulting the rest of the organisation. Such action could embarrass the group or run contrary to group policy, possibly leading to relations with decision makers being soured.

Tactics

Every group has finite resources, but the way in which a group chooses to use these resources will help to determine that group's effectiveness. A bad choice of tactics can mean a long-term setback. Overuse of the strike tactic in the 1970s, for example, led to the anti-union legislation of the 1980s.

3. The external environment

Public opinion

Public opinion can be an important factor in determining a pressure group's effectiveness. Attitudes tend to change slowly, but a series of events or a crisis may lead to the expression of new views. Often these new views are first expressed in the media. Decision makers tend to be concerned with what the media sees as important and to give priority to these issues. That is one reason why pressure groups cultivate contacts with the media.

The environmental movement

The importance of public opinion can be seen in the way in which the environmental movement grew in the 1980s. Much media coverage was given to environmental problems such as the depletion of the ozone layer, global warming and acid rain. Public concern about environmental issues led not only to an increase in support for environmental groups (for example, the number of supporters of Friends of the Earth rose from 74,360 in 1988 to 231,211 in 1991) it also led to greater emphasis being placed on the environment by decision makers. As Friends of the Earth pointed out, politicians rarely act until public pressure forces them to do so (FoE 1992).

But, public opinion can change and it did so during the recession of the early 1990s. By June 1993, the public was tired of the gloomy messages put over by environmental groups and had begun to suffer from 'doom fatigue'. This forced environmental groups to respond to the public mood. They changed tactics and began to emphasise the solutions being delivered rather than the problems that they faced (*Observer*, 27 June 1993).

Rose's classification of pressure group values

According to Richard Rose there are six types of relationship between pressure groups and public attitudes (Rose 1974). The more acceptable that a pressure group's values are to the general public, the more chance a group has of achieving its objectives.

1. Values are generally accepted

The ideal relationship is one in which the values of a pressure group are in harmony with general cultural norms. For example, the vast majority of people agree with the RSPCA that people should not be cruel to animals. As a result, the RSPCA has a good chance of achieving its objectives.

2. Attitudes change over time

A group may support values which become increasingly acceptable over time. Fifty years ago, for example, homosexuality was illegal. In the 1960s, homosexuality became lawful over the age of 21. In 1994, the age of consent for homosexuals was lowered to the age of 18. In 1998, the House of Commons voted by a big majority in favour of a clause in the Crime and Disorder Bill reducing the age of consent for homosexuals to the age of 16 (the same as the age of consent for heterosexuals). This shows that attitudes towards homosexuality have changed considerably. Even though the House of Lords rejected the clause in the Crime and Disorder Bill, the government announced in the second Queen's Speech that it would introduce a separate Bill lowering the age of consent for homosexuals on the grounds that the Commons vote had shown that public attitudes had changed. This represented a victory for those pressure groups which had been campaigning for an equal age of consent between homosexuals and heterosexuals. Their campaign was successful because public opinion moved into line behind it.

3. Opinions are divided

On some issues, opinion is divided. Whereas most people, at all times, think it is wrong to be cruel to animals, for example, people are divided about the extent to which trade unions should be involved in governmental decision making. Some people support greater involvement. Others do not. Attitudes can fluctuate over time. For example, there was greater support for trade union involvement in governmental decision making in the 1970s than there was in the period 1979-97. Since unions were unpopular in the period 1979-97, they were less effective.

4. Cultural indifference

Some pressure groups meet with cultural indifference. The Pedestrian Association is an example. In 1998, it only had 1,000 members nationally and attracted little attention from a car-loving public.

5. Attitudes shift away from some groups

Some pressure groups have goals which aim to halt or reverse long-term cultural trends. Since the tide is moving against them, these groups have difficulty in achieving their aims. An example of this is the Lord's Day Observance Society which opposes work on Sunday. The growth of Sunday trading and the legislation on this issue mean that this group has little chance of achieving its aim.

6. Conflict between public opinion and tactics

There is sometimes conflict between public opinion and the tactics adopted by pressure groups. Some groups are not prepared to compromise in any way and they use tactics which alienate potential supporters. For example, even if they share the objectives of Earth First! or the Animal Liberation Front, most people do not agree with their use of violence. Lack of public support hinders the effectiveness of such groups.

Main points - Section 2.3

- It is not easy to measure the success of a pressure group. Even if a group's objective is achieved, that might not be due to the work of the group.
- Evaluation of effectiveness depends on: (1) the responsiveness of decision makers; (2) what happens in private; (3) how many groups are involved; (4) whether decision makers are worried about losing face; (5) what tactics decision makers use; and (6) how much compromise is involved.
- Grant (1995) argues that there are three main factors which affect pressure group effectiveness: (1) domain organisation; (2) resources and (3) the external environment.
- Rose argues that there are six types of relationship between groups and public attitudes: (1) a group's values fit with public attitudes; (2) public opinion moves towards a group's values; (3) public opinion fluctuates; (4) people are indifferent; (5) attitudes shift away from a group; and (6) people disapprove of the tactics adopted by a group.

Activity 10.5 *Evaluating pressure group success*

Item A *The anti-poll tax campaign*

The anti-poll tax movement was at its most enthusiastic in spring 1990 when it sprung into action lobbying MPs, collecting petitions and so on. All sorts of stunts were tried. In Nottingham, for example, protesters dressed like Robin Hood tried to invade the council chamber and in Exeter councillors were pelted with Cornish pasties. But, these efforts were in vain. The legislation was in place and town hall computers were preparing millions of bills. Non-payment was a better tactic. It tapped into an old tradition of civil disobedience and it had the rare advantage of combining strong moral anger with material self-interest. Non-payment was also passive. The number of non-payers was probably ten times the number of participants in the anti-poll tax movement. This was the winning strategy. Without cooperation from the public, it became apparent that the tax would never work. By the end of 1991, £1 billion (nearly 10% of poll tax revenue) remained uncollected. This compared to an average collection of 98% under the rates. The deep unpopularity of the tax led the government to announce in March 1991 that it would be abolished.

Adapted from Barr 1992.

Item B *The Howard League*

The Howard League
for Penal Reform

What is the Howard League?
The Howard League was established in 1866, named after John Howard, the first prison reformer. Its aim is to work for humane, effective and efficient reform of the penal system.

The Howard League's programme of action

- An informal settlement process should be devised to keep petty offences out of the courts.
- The prison building programme should be halted immediately, and these funds used to renovate existing establishments and to fund alternative non-custodial resources.
- Nobody should be remanded in custody unless the crime they are accused of is so serious that they are seen as a danger to the public. Bail hostels and support services for community supervision should be improved immediately.
- Tightly drawn up national minimum standards should be agreed to ensure prisoners have a decent quality of life.
- A charter of prisoners' rights should be drawn up and made enforceable.
- Prison medical facilities should be improved and specialist services provided for drug addicts and alcoholics.
- An independent tribunal should set the maximum capacity for every prison.
- People should not go to prison for failing to pay a fine.
- A review of staffing should take place to determine appropriate staffing levels and improve training.

Item C *Age Discrimination Week*

Age Discrimination Week

In January 1998, Age Concern launched a campaign in support of a Private Members' Bill aimed at outlawing age discrimination in job adverts. The campaign cost £15,000 of which 5% was allocated to research and evaluation.

PREPARATIONS

January 1998 - preparation for the campaign (behind the scenes):
(1) Age Concern's public relations team compile a report entitled *Making Age Discrimination a Thing of the Past*.
(2) Gallup is commissioned to conduct a survey on attitudes towards ageism.
(3) Age Concern joins up with an advertising agency to produce a striking image for a poster (they come up with a take-off of the Wonderbra advert, using a 56 year old model, Pearl Reed).

AGE DISCRIMINATION WEEK

2-6 February 1998 - Age Discrimination Week:
(1) Findings of Gallup survey released (70% agree there is discrimination against people over age 45).
(2) Complaints line set up for people to ring with stories of age discrimination.
(3) Poster unveiled to journalists, photographers, press and TV at Parliament.

LOBBYING PARLIAMENT

3-5 February 1998 - lobbying Parliament:
(1) Age Concern and Linda Perham MP (who introduced the Private Members' Bill) meet all-party group on ageing to discuss Bill.
(2) Early day motion in the Commons gains the signatures of nearly 150 MPs.
(3) Second reading of Bill takes place on 5 February.

RESULT

Although the Bill was talked out, the campaign raised the profile of the issue and, in August 1998, the government introduced a voluntary Code of Practice on Discrimination at Work. On 17 December 1998, the *Independent* described the campaign as 'one of the most cost effective ever run. The charity put Pearl's poster on one mobile billboard and relied on the press to do the rest. It worked splendidly. There were 2,000 responses from the public, ten solid hours of broadcasting time, hundreds of column inches and interest from as far away as Argentina, Italy and Norway.'

Item D *The Saffron Boot House Action Group*

The Saffron Lane council estate in Leicester was built in the 1920s by the Henry Boot Construction Company. Due to a shortage of bricks, houses were built using reinforced concrete columns. In the 1970s, 1,000 houses developed structural problems. The houses would have to be demolished and the residents rehoused. By 1989, 500 houses had been rebuilt, but the ten-year rebuilding plan collapsed because central government finance was withdrawn. Angry, the remaining tenants formed the Saffron Boot House Action Group (SBHAG) to campaign for the continuation of the rebuilding programme. In 1993, a compromise was reached. The houses would be replaced by a development consisting of one-third housing association homes and two-thirds council houses. Given central government's hostility to council house building, this was a significant victory for the tenants. Factors producing this success include the following. First, the group was well-organised and enjoyed the support of the local community. It met regularly and kept tenants fully informed. Second, the group worked closely with elected representatives, notably the local councillors who were active in their support. Third, the local media gave the issue a great deal of publicity, generating wider public support. Fourth, the city council and its officers were supportive and the housing department made representations to the Department of the Environment. Fifth, the group was able to put across its views to key decision makers at the Department of the Environment on a number of occasions. On one occasion, members of the group 'ambushed' the Housing Minister at a conference and put their case directly.

Adapted from Baggott 1995.

Questions

1. Using Items A-D, describe the range of tactics used by pressure groups to win the support of the public.
2. a) Why were the campaigns described in Items A and D successful?
   b) To what extent did the success of each campaign depend upon the factors referred to in Grant's classification of pressure group effectiveness and Rose's classification of pressure group values?
3. Suppose you had been asked to decide whether the work of the Howard League had been effective (Item B). What criteria would you use?
4. Would you describe the campaign described in Item C as a success? Explain your answer.

Part 3 How the role of pressure groups has changed

Key issues

1. What is corporatism and why did it fail?
2. How did the role of pressure groups change in the 1980s?
3. What are the current trends?

3.1 Corporatism

What is corporatism?

When the major pressure groups in a society work closely with the government in the hope of achieving mutually beneficial goals, this is known as 'corporatism'. In a corporatist system:

'The emphasis is on mutual cooperation; groups bargain and negotiate with government agencies while broadly agreeing on policy objectives...In return for access to key decision makers, groups cooperate with government. They may provide information and advice, help formulate policy or assist with the implementation and monitoring of policies.' (Baggott 1995, pp.41-42)

Corporatism was a feature of British politics in the 1960s and 1970s. During this period, the Trade Union Congress (TUC) and the Confederation of British Industry (CBI) formed close ties with government. They were consulted before industrial or economic policies were decided and then shared responsibility for trying to make sure that the policies were implemented. Since corporatism in Britain involved three parties (the TUC, the CBI and the government), it is also known as 'tripartism'.

The NEDC

Corporatism in Britain is usually dated from 1961 when the National Economic Development Council (NEDC) was set up. The NEDC was a forum where civil servants, members of the government, employers and trade unions could meet regularly to consider ways of promoting economic growth. This was the first time that the government had invited both employers and trade unionists into the heart of the decision-making process. It set the pattern for the next 15 years.

Corporatism and economic growth

Throughout the 1960s and 1970s Britain managed only slow economic growth compared to its competitors. It was to counter this that governments sought a corporatist solution. The assumption which was shared by Labour and Conservative governments alike was that if both employers' representatives and trade unionists agreed to cooperate with the government over prices and wages, then the economy as a whole would grow more quickly. Clearly, then, corporatism was very much a product of the post-war consensus. It was also closely associated with the incomes policies which were the centrepiece of government economic policies in the 1960s and 1970s.

The failure of corporatism

The drift towards corporatism stopped when the Conservatives under Margaret Thatcher were elected in 1979. By then, a number of criticisms had been levelled at this method of governing.

1. Parliament was being bypassed

Critics complained because tripartite decision making bypassed Parliament. Important decisions were made in private by ministers with the help of pressure group officials. This, it was argued, was detrimental to parliamentary democracy.

2. Corporatism did not work

Critics argued that corporatism simply did not work. Neither the CBI nor the TUC had sufficient control over their members to ensure that any decision they made with the government would be implemented. It seemed that government was continually making concessions in return for assurances of backing on prices and incomes policies which then turned out to have no lasting value. Employers became less enthusiastic about such policies when profits were eroded by the rules to which they had agreed. Government concessions to the unions were not sufficient to prevent strikes.

3. The system was élitist

Some critics argued that the system was bound not to work because it was élitist. Only some groups were invited to participate in the decision-making process. Many were excluded. Those which were included did not necessarily represent the true interests of their members.

4. Corporatism stifles the market

The New Right argued that corporatism was damaging because it stifled the free market and granted far too much power to trade unions. The New Right's antipathy towards corporatism was closely tied to its determination to break with the post-war consensus.

5. Corporatism weakened the unions

Critics on the left argued that, far from enhancing the power of the unions, corporatism weakened them. By including the TUC in tripartite negotiations, the government and CBI were able to extract greater concessions than they would otherwise have achieved.

3.2 Changes in the 1980s

The Thatcher government and pressure groups

The antagonism of Margaret Thatcher towards large organised interest groups ensured that close contact with both the CBI and the TUC ceased after 1979. By 1988, Lord Young, Trade and Industry Minister, could claim:

'We have rejected the TUC. We have rejected the CBI. We do not see them coming back again. We gave up the corporate state.' (*Financial Times*, 9 November 1988)

The rhetoric of the Conservatives in the 1980s, however, did not always live up to the reality. Reviewing the experience of pressure groups under Prime Minister Thatcher, Richardson (1990) claimed that, although the Thatcher governments excluded some groups from major policy decisions, they then brought them in to discussions on implementation. Also, although some groups lost out (especially local authorities and trade unions), others did not.

Richardson notes that the Thatcher governments' confrontational style was often not well thought through. Radical changes to existing policy were often proposed but not implemented swiftly enough. By the time the government got round to implementation, pressure groups had managed to organise themselves. The result was a traditional round of bargaining and consultation.

Baggot (1992), in a statistical survey of pressure group activity during the 1980s, confirms that there was a reduction of contact between labour groups and the government. But, there was also a growth in parliamentary lobbying, especially amongst labour groups.

Think tanks and cause groups

Two other phenomena must be taken into account when assessing the role of pressure groups in the 1980s. First, the growing importance of think tanks (see Section 1.6 above). And second, the huge growth in numbers and significance of cause groups. Membership increases were huge in the 1980s. For example, the RSPB grew from 98,000 members in 1971 to 561,000 in 1987 and 880,000 in 1992. Although some groups with large memberships were clearly unsuccessful in the 1980s (CND is an obvious example), others made a substantial impact (environmental groups, for example). As the unexpected success of the 'Live Aid' concert in 1985 indicates, it seems that people began to look for new ways in which to participate in politics during the 1980s.

3.3 Changes in the 1990s

John Major's government and pressure groups

As in many other areas, the Major government's attitude towards pressure groups did not differ markedly from that of its predecessor. The hostility of the Major government towards corporatism was indicated by the abolition of the NEDC shortly after the 1992 general election. There is no evidence that either the CBI or trade unions were consulted on government policy in the period 1990-97 any more than they had been under Thatcher. Nevertheless, the Major government did make a couple of gestures towards a more inclusive approach. First, in 1991, the Secretary of State for Health, William Waldegrave, offered to discuss proposed changes to GPs' contracts with the British Medical Association (BMA). The BMA had been ignored prior to this. And second, in March 1994, Stephen Dorrell (Treasury Financial Secretary) became the first Conservative minister for more than 20 years to address the TUC. These gestures, however, hardly added up to a fundamentally new approach.

The growth of direct action

Whilst there was little change at government level under John Major, there was significant change outside government. In particular, the period 1990-97 was characterised by the rapid growth of (often small and locally-based) single-issue groups which used direct action in new ways to promote their cause. Some commentators have argued that this was a reflection of growing mistrust with mainstream politics and politicians (fuelled by sleaze in Westminster and frustration with public spending cuts). It has also been suggested that new people were becoming involved in protests during the 1990s:

> 'Mass protest isn't new, but it is a bit different today in terms of the kind of people getting involved. It's quite clear that some of these people have never been involved in this sort of thing before. This could be something to do with greater participation in public life by women and the media revolution in television and electronic news gathering.' (Wyn Grant quoted in the *Coventry Evening Telegraph*, 16 February 1995)

Perhaps the best example of this phenomenon was the development of the anti-roads lobby. Most commentators agree that the Major government's decision to cut its road-building programme in 1994 was influenced by the public support attracted by anti-roads protesters. It was in the early 1990s that these protesters began to make their mark:

> 'The environment lobby failed in the 1980s when the roads lobby exploited its insider status to regain its hegemony [its position of power]. The 1990s, however, look rather different for a number of reasons, not least of which is the continuing ability of anti-roads groups to exploit the multi-arena politics of the period.' (Dudley & Richardson 1998, p.746)

The Blair government and pressure groups

The election of a Labour government in May 1997 raised the possibility of a new era of tripartism. The Labour Party still retained close links with the unions (albeit links which were weakened after Tony Blair was elected Leader) and, in opposition, New Labour had made a concerted effort to woo business. The new government quickly made it clear, however, that there would be no return to the corporatism of the 1970s. Grant (1998) points out that it was four months after the election before union leaders were invited to Downing Street. Similarly, whilst close contacts between business and government were encouraged, the CBI was not invited to advise the government as a matter of course. The government's arm's length approach was illustrated when the Union of Democratic Mineworkers called on the government to intervene after the coal mining company RJB announced that it was to close down Ashfordby colliery:

> 'The Downing Street response made it clear

that there were no IOUs to the unions and it was not the job of the government to intervene. The comment, "it is entirely a matter for the commercial company involved", could have been made by the Conservatives. Subsequently, RJB claimed that ten of its 17 deep mines were under threat of closure. Once again, they received short shrift from government - it told them to negotiate contracts to sell their coal at a more realistic price.' (Grant 1998, p.113)

Signs of tripartism
Although the government made it clear that there was to be no return to the corporatism of the 1970s, some new tripartite arrangements have emerged. For example, the government set up a Low Pay Commission to advise on the level of a minimum wage. This included representatives from both employers' associations and trade unions. It is significant, however, that when bodies with a tripartite structure have been set up, government has been sensitive to the charge that corporatism is re-emerging:

'When Trade and Industry Secretary Margaret Beckett announced plans to create industry bodies to advise on ways to improve the performance of British companies, officials were anxious to play down any comparisons with the NEDC. Although the new bodies will have a tripartite constitution, the emphasis was on their "light and flexible" character which presumably means some kind of post-modernist corporatism.' (Grant 1998, p.113)

Other developments under Labour
The change of government did mean a change in status for some groups. Groups like Charter 88 and Liberty which had called for constitutional change had been able to make little impact on policy whilst the Conservatives were in power. They had worked closely with Labour in opposition, however, and, when Labour was elected, they gained insider status. Conversely, a number of groups (right-wing think tanks, for example) which had been influential whilst the Conservatives were in power found themselves on the outside.

Whilst the status of some groups changed, there was little sign in Labour's first 18 months in power that the role played by pressure groups changed in any significant way. Grant (1999) argued that conventional interest group activity flourished during the first 18 months of Labour government and that, for all the talk of a 'new' Britain and a 'new' politics, there was much that seemed 'business as usual'. He did point out, however, that devolution would open up a new arena for pressure group activity and he suggested that the introduction of proportional representation might shift the focus of pressure group activity.

It should also be noted that the change of government in 1997 did not check the growth of direct action which had been accelerating whilst the Major government was in power. For many protesters, the election of a new government was greeted with indifference as they focused on their local campaigns. As under John Major, many of these campaigns focused on environmental issues.

Main points - Part 3

- Corporatism was a feature of British politics in the 1960s and 1970s. The TUC and CBI were consulted by government before economic policies were decided and then shared responsibility for making sure that the policies were implemented.
- Critics of corporatism argued that: (1) Parliament was being bypassed; (2) corporatism did not work; (3) the system was élitist; (4) corporatism stifled the market; and (5) corporatism weakened the unions.
- Government contact with the CBI and TUC ceased after 1979. Although some groups (notably the unions) lost out in the 1980s, others did not. The 1980s were also notable for the rising influence of think tanks and the growth of cause groups.
- As in many other areas, the Major government's attitude towards pressure groups did not differ markedly from that of its predecessor. There was one significant development in the early 1990s - a new wave of protest and new forms of direct action.
- The Labour government quickly made it clear that there would be no return to the corporatism of the 1970s, although some tripartite bodies were set up. The change of government meant a change in status for some groups, but there was little sign of the role of pressure groups changing. The growth of direct action continued.

Activity 10.6   *Pressure groups under Labour*

Item A   *The dual state model*

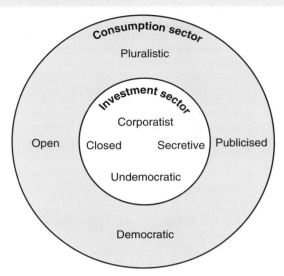

According to the dual state model, issues affecting production (in the investment sector) tend to be settled in a corporatist style (by a small number of large, organised interest groups in secret), whilst those concerning the consumption sector (welfare and moral issues) are settled by a pluralistic process (by a large number of groups of varying sizes openly competing for government attention).

Item B   *The CBI and the Labour government*

The CBI will not be resisting the government's industrial relations agenda in an aggressive way over the next 12 months. Instead, it will concentrate on helping companies raise their productivity by promoting best practice and improving employee skills in partnership with government. The Director General of the CBI, Adair Turner, said that the organisation's role would not be to block and minimise changes carried out by the Labour government. Rather, it would develop a new positive agenda which would, in the long term, prove to be more important than one which simply minimised barriers and dangers. The CBI did not welcome the Labour government's proposed new law on trade union recognition, but, Adair Turner claimed, the proposals were much better than they would have been without the CBI's intensive lobbying.

Adapted from the *Financial Times*, 31 August 1998.

Item C   *Tree battle unites middle classes and eco-warriors*

Volvo drivers and eco-warriors formed an unusual alliance on 24 March 1998 as the commuter belt came out in force to defend environmentalists camped in their trees. Bailiffs were sent to Kingston upon Thames to evict about 60 protesters clinging to trees that are to be felled. But, as the protesters were being evicted, residents gathered to express their thanks to the campaigners. 'The tree protesters are doing what we would like to be doing and that is why we support them so much' said one resident. The 48 trees planted in 1948 to shield a power station are to be cut down to free the view to the Thames for luxury flats being built there. The protesters first built tree houses in November 1997 after planning permission for the felling was confirmed by the council. One of

Eco-warriors in the trees due to be felled in Kingston upon Thames. The protestors were evicted shortly after this picture was taken.

the protesters said: 'I'm doing it because the trees belong to the people of Kingston. The only people who will benefit are the developers and that is out of order.' A petition against the felling was signed by 20,000 park users whose anger is directed against the council for failing to listen to residents' views. A council spokesperson said that the felling is part of a legal agreement granted when planning permission was approved. The eviction is thought to be costing the council £500,000.

Adapted from the *Daily Telegraph*, 25 March 1998.

Item D *The unions and the Labour government*

Having been excluded from the corridors of power during the 1980s and much of the 1990s, some trade unions hoped that the election of a Labour government might result in moves towards a 'social partnership' in which the TUC, CBI and ministers would meet on a regular basis to discuss economic policies and progress. The General Secretary of the TUC, John Monks, is a keen supporter of this, believing it would help to tackle problems such as low pay, increasing inequality of incomes, lack of investment and job insecurity. Monks admits that a return to the corporatism of the 1970s would be unwelcome, but argues that a new social partnership is necessary to combat the problems of an unregulated free market. Some trade union leaders are suspicious that social partnership would end up (like in the 1970s) as little more than a vehicle for incomes policies intended to secure wage restraints. If so, the unions would gain little. At present, however, social partnership appears highly unlikely - mainly because neither the Blair government nor the employers seem remotely interested in any institutional arrangements which might be seen as being corporatist. Blair himself has often given the impression that he finds the unions tiresome and that he feels more empathy with employers. Certainly, some union leaders have complained that, on the few occasions Blair has met them, his disdain bordered on contempt. The Blair government has also rejected an incomes policy as a means of curbing inflation or unemployment - so it does not need to gain agreement from the unions and employers. Besides, it is difficult to imagine what the unions could offer ministers.

Adapted from Dorey 1999.

Questions

1. What evidence is there in Items B-D to support the dual state model illustrated in Item A?

2. Judging from Items B-D, did the election of a Labour government in 1997 mean a significant change in relations between government and pressure groups? Explain your answer.

3. What do Items B and D tell us about the chances of a revival in corporatism?

4. What key characteristics of pressure group activity in the 1990s are illustrated by Item C?

Part 4 The European dimension

Key issues

1. Why has the European Union become an important focus for British pressure groups?
2. How can pressure groups influence policy making in the EU?

4.1 Impact of the Single European Act

The 1986 Single European Act (SEA)

Like most aspects of British politics, the role of pressure groups has changed since Britain joined the EU. Pressure groups go where the power goes. As more and more power has shifted towards Brussels, pressure groups have begun to place increasing emphasis on lobbying EU decision makers.

This has particularly been the case since the Single European Act (SEA) was passed in 1986. The SEA resulted in two major changes, both of which have encouraged greater pressure group activity in Brussels (these changes were then extended by the Maastricht Treaty and Amsterdam Treaty - see Chapter 6, Sections 1.2 and 1.3).

1. The change in voting procedures

The SEA changed the voting procedure in the Council of Ministers. Whereas a single member state had previously had the power to veto a proposal, the SEA allowed for the introduction of qualified majority voting on some matters. Since some measures can

now be passed by the Council of Ministers with just 62 of the 87 votes, pressure groups can no longer rely on the veto of a single member to stop any legislation they do not like (the maximum number of votes cast by a single member is 10 - see Activity 6.3, Items B and C).

2. Extension of the range of policies

The range of policies covered by the EU has also been extended. Policies which had previously been decided by national governments are now decided by the EU. As a result, pressure groups have been forced to lobby the EU to have any hope of influencing decisions.

Impact of the changes

The net result of these changes is that any pressure group which continues to rely exclusively on lobbying Whitehall and Westminster is adopting a high risk strategy. The trend is to put pressure on EU decision makers. A survey conducted in 1992 found that c.10,000 people were involved in lobbying the EU. By 1998, the number had increased to c.13,000. The vast majority of these people were on the staff of single firms, industry groups and non-governmental organisations (*Economist*, 15 August 1998).

4.2 Pressure groups and the EU

Lobbying the EU

It is more difficult for groups to influence EU decisions than it is to influence decisions made in Britain because the decision-making process within the EU is more complicated and more unpredictable. According to Grant (1990) and Baggot (1995) there are four main channels through which pressure groups can work.

1. Working through the national government

Many pressure groups work through contacts with the British government with the aim of persuading the government to adopt their favoured position in discussions at European level. This tactic is particularly favoured by insider groups since they can make use of previously established contacts with the government. Outsider groups supporting issues which can be presented as being in the national interest might also be able to persuade the government to adopt their point of view. The advantage with this method is that a group's position may be presented direct to the ultimate EU decision-making body, the Council of Ministers. The disadvantage is that the group relinquishes control. The group's proposals may be altered, watered down or even abandoned during the bargaining process.

A further reason for adopting this method is that even though the EU passes the legislation, it is up to the member states to implement it. By working with the national government, groups may gain the opportunity to influence the way in which EU legislation is implemented.

2. Working through Eurogroups

Many pressure groups choose to work through a federation made up of representative groups from each of the 15 members - the so-called 'Eurogroups'. Although they are more common among sectional groups, some cause groups are also organised into federations. For example, the Motorcycle Action Group is the UK representative of the Federation of European Motorcyclists. According to a survey conducted in 1992, around three-quarters of British pressure groups are in some way connected to Eurogroups (Baggott 1992). Laura Cram found evidence of a rapid growth in the number of Eurogroups in the 1990s:

> 'There has been a rapid increase in the number of Eurogroups operating at EU level, many seeking to gain information about or to influence the European political process.' (Cram 1998, p.72)

Eurogroups are recognised by the European Commission as being representative of European-wide interests. As a result, their officials are able to cultivate close ties with EU bureaucrats. Around 15,000 civil servants work for the European Commission. These civil servants rely upon outside groups to supply expertise. Pressure groups are, therefore, positively welcomed into the decision-making process.

Eurogroups often lack sufficient resources. This makes it difficult for them to respond quickly to changing events. They also suffer from the problem of gaining agreement between organisations from 15 different member states. It has been argued that their impact on EU policy is minimal because, by trying to reconcile national differences, they tend to end up with the lowest common denominator.

3. Joining direct membership associations

Some pressure groups choose to join a direct membership association. That is, rather than joining a national organisation affiliated to a federation, members join a Brussels-based organisation. For example, 40 of the largest firms in Western Europe have formed the European Round Table of Industrialists. The advantage of this is that members have direct contact with the organisation rather than going through an intermediate level or national body. Not only can a direct membership association respond quickly to changing events, it also has the authority to develop effective policies. For example the European Round Table of Industrialists was instrumental in persuading the EU to introduce a single market policy. It has access to heads of national governments and to commissioners. Although few such organisations exist, the number is likely to grow as the EU develops.

4. Setting up an office in Brussels

Some pressure groups choose to set up office in Brussels and lobby directly. This option is only open to large, well-established groups such as the CBI as it is very expensive. It has the advantage of providing direct access to decision makers.

A mixed approach

It should be noted that many groups do not rely on a single method to achieve their aims. Cram (1998) provides evidence that many groups use two or more of the strategies outlined above at the same time.

The three laws of Euro-lobbying

Mazey and Richardson (1993) identified three laws of lobbying. It is by observing these laws that pressure groups have the best chance of influencing decisions made by the EU.

1. Discover where the power lies

The first law of Euro-lobbying is to discover exactly where the power lies. Although the Council of Ministers is the ultimate EU decision-making body, much of the power actually lies with the Commission. It is the Commission which draws up policy proposals for the Council of Ministers and it is the Commission which is responsible for policy implementation. As a result, it is the Commission which is targeted by most pressure groups based in Brussels.

2. Be willing to compromise

The second law of Euro-lobbying is to be willing to compromise. Since so many different interests are at stake, it is rare for any single party to achieve its goals completely. Pressure groups need to be willing to make deals. They often have to make a concession over one clause in the hope that the favour will be returned later. Mazey and Richardson say that EU policies are:

> 'As much peace treaties between competing interests and nations as they are rational decisions.' (Mazey & Richardson 1993, p.21)

3. Intervene as early as possible

The third law of Euro-lobbying is that the most effective time to influence a decision is at the earliest possible stage. Ideally, a pressure group should be there at the start. The further along the road a policy has travelled, the less chance groups have to change it. One EU official told Mazey and Richardson that, in general, probably 80% of the initial proposal remains in a directive's final draft. That indicates just how important it is to be involved in drawing up the initial proposal. It also indicates how important advance information can be. It may be expensive to maintain an office in Brussels, but groups which do so are likely to have earlier access to the decision-making process than other groups.

Main points - Part 4

- The SEA brought a new voting procedure and extended the range of policies covered by the EU. This encouraged more pressure group activity at the European level.
- There are four main channels through which pressure groups can work at the European level: (1) through the national government; (2) through Eurogroups; (3) through direct membership associations; and (4) through an office in Brussels. Many groups do not rely on a single method to achieve their aims.
- The three laws of Euro-lobbying are: (1) discover where the power lies and target it; (2) be willing to compromise; and (3) intervene as early as possible.

Activity 10.7 Pressure groups and the EU

Item A Decision making in the EU (1)

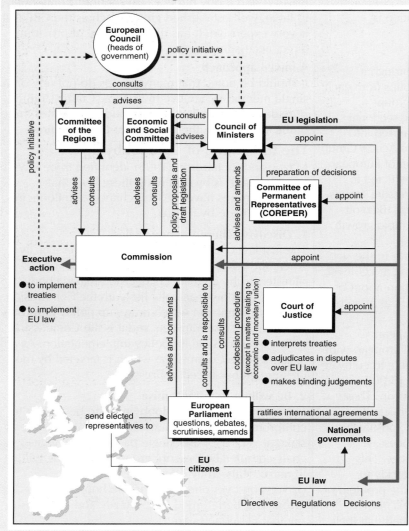

Adapted from Mazey & Richardson 1993.

Item B The Lappel Bank case

On 2 April 1979, the EU Council of Ministers approved the Birds Directive which required individual member states to designate Special Protection Areas (SPAs) to conserve wild birds whose habitat was under threat. On 21 May 1992, the Habitats Directive gave the same protection to wild flora and fauna. In December 1993, the Secretary of State for the Environment designated the Medway Estuary and Marshes as a SPA, but did not include an area known as Lappel Bank. Four years earlier, planning had been granted to expand the port of Sheerness and Lappel Bank had been earmarked to become an enormous car and cargo park. The minister's reason for excluding Lappel Bank from the SPA was that economic interests outweighed conservation interests. This was challenged by the Royal Society for the Protection of Birds (RSPB) through the courts. In 1994, the challenge was rejected by the High Court and Appeal Court, and in February 1995, it was rejected by the House of Lords, though the Lords agreed that the case could go to the European Court of Justice. Throughout this process, the courts refused to grant an injunction halting construction work. In July 1996, the European Court of Justice ruled that a member state was not permitted to take account of economic considerations when designating SPAs. But, by that time, Lappel Bank was a car park.

Adapted from Day 1998.

Item C *Trade unions lobbying in the EU*

Since 1988, Britain's trade unions have displayed an increasingly pro-European stance and strategy, although this conversion has been by no means universal (the NUM, for example, remains suspicious of the EU, regarding it as a 'capitalist club'). The 1990s have seen a number of British trade unions opening their own offices in Brussels, with full-time professional staff, the aim being to gain closer and more regular contact with the European Commission (which is widely regarded as being more open and accessible than Whitehall). Indeed, the TUC itself opened its own office in Brussels in December 1993. Other institutional forums through which unions have increasingly sought to exert influence include the European Trade Union Confederation, the Economic and Social Committee and through the many industry committees operating in various sectors (such as construction, engineering, telecommunications and transport) under the guidance of the Commission. The unions might well view the EU as a means of trying to prevent the Blair government from going back on its commitments to improve employees' rights and providing at least some social and employment protection.

Adapted from Dorey 1999.

Item D *Decision making in the EU (2)*

In Amsterdam in June 1997, the EU's 15 heads of government agreed a protocol legally binding on all member states which recognises that animals are 'sentient beings' (ie they have feelings) and this must be taken into account when formulating and implementing policies on agriculture, transport, research and the internal market. In all these areas, member states will now have to pay full regard to the welfare rights of animals. Nearly 200 British members of Compassion in World Farming (CIWF) made it to the demonstration in Amsterdam to push the case for this protocol (pictured right). At the demonstration, it was good to hear from groups from all over the EU who had come to support it and who were often fighting a tough and lonely battle for animals in their own country. Our thanks go to the junior Agriculture Minister Elliot Morley who was instrumental in winning the new status for animals. We congratulate the UK government which led the way in Amsterdam to securing this great success. Best of all, after ten years we were successful!

Adapted from *Agscene*, autumn 1997.

Questions

1. Suppose you had been asked to organise a Euro-lobby on an issue which you feel strongly about. Using Item A:
   a) describe the tactics you would use.
   b) explain which points in the EU decision-making process you would target.
   c) what factors do you think would determine the success or failure of your campaign?

2. a) What do Items B-D tell us about the different methods pressure groups use to influence decisions made by the EU?
   b) Evaluate the effectiveness of each method.

3. What does Item B tell us about the difficulties faced by groups lobbying at the EU level?

4. What lobbying techniques would you expect CIWF to have used (Item D) during its ten year campaign?

References

Baggott (1992) Baggott, R., 'The measurement of change in pressure group politics', *Talking Politics*, Vol.5.1, 1992.

Baggott (1995) Baggott, R., *Pressure Groups Today*, Manchester University Press, 1995.

Barr (1992) Barr, G., 'The anti–poll tax movement', *Talking Politics*, Vol.4.3, Summer 1992.

Carter (1995) Carter, N., 'The environment' in *Lancaster (1995)*.

Cram (1998) Cram, L., *Collective Action in the EU*, Routledge, 1998.

Day (1998) Day, M., *Environmental Action: a Citizen's Guide*, Pluto Press, 1998.

Demos (1993) *Demos Mission Statement*, Demos, 1993.

Denham & Garnett (1998) Denham, A. & Garnett, M., *British Think Tanks and the Climate of Opinion*, UCL Press, 1998.

Dorey (1999) Dorey, P., 'Trade unions and industrial relations' in *Lancaster (1999)*.

Dudley & Richardson (1998) Dudley, G. & Richardson, J., 'Arenas without rules and the policy change process: outsider groups and British roads policy', *Political Studies*, Vol.46, pp.727-47.

FoE (1992) *Earth Matters*, Friends of the Earth, November 1992.

Grant (1989) Grant, W., *Pressure Groups, Politics and Democracy in Britain*, Philip Allan, 1989.

Grant (1990) Grant, W., 'Pressure groups' in *Wale (1990)*.

Grant (1995) Grant, W., *Pressure Groups, Politics and Democracy in Great Britain* (2nd edn), Philip Allan, 1995.

Grant (1998) Grant, W., 'The economic policies of the Blair government' in *Lancaster (1998)*.

Grant (1999) Grant, W., 'Pressure groups' in *Lancaster (1999)*.

Hoad (1998) Hoad, D., 'Direct action and the environmental movement', *Talking Politics*, Vol.10.3, spring 1998.

Lancaster (1995) Lancaster, S. (ed.), *Developments in Politics*, Vol.6, Causeway Press, 1995.

Lancaster (1998) Lancaster, S. (ed.), *Developments in Politics*, Vol.9, Causeway Press, 1998.

Lancaster (1999) Lancaster, S. (ed.), *Developments in Politics*, Vol.10, Causeway Press, 1999.

Maloney (1996) Maloney, K., *Lobbyists for Hire*, Dartmouth Publishing Company, 1996.

Maloney et al. (1994) Maloney, W., Jordan, G. & McLaughlin, A., 'Interest groups and public policy: the insider/outsider model revisited', *Journal of Public Policy*, Vol.14, pp.17-38.

May & Nugent (1982) May, T. & Nugent, N., *Insiders, Outsiders and Thresholders*, Paper to the 1982 conference of the Political Studies Association at the University of Kent.

Mazey & Richardson (1993) Mazey, S. & Richardson, J., 'Pressure groups and the EU', *Politics Review*, Vol.3.1, September 1993.

Miller (1990) Miller, C., *Lobbying* (2nd edn), Basil Blackwell, 1990.

Richardson (1990) Richardson, J.J., 'Government and groups in Britain: changing styles', *Strathclyde Papers on Government and Politics*, No.69, 1990.

Rose (1974) Rose, R., *Politics in England Today*, Faber and Faber, 1974.

Stewart (1958) Stewart, J.D., *British Pressure Groups*, Oxford University Press, 1958.

Stone (1996) Stone, D., *Capturing the Political Imagination: Think Tanks and the Political Process*, Frank Cass, 1996.

Wale (1990) Wale, W. (ed), *Developments in Politics*, Vol.1, Causeway Press, 1990.

WWF (1991) *WWF Review 1991*, Worldwide Fund for Nature, 1991.

Young (1989) Young, H., *One of Us*, Macmillan, 1989.

11 Political recruitment

Introduction

It is difficult to establish accurate figures for the number of people who are politically active. Although the Conservative Party does not collect figures nationally, membership was thought to be under 400,000 in 1998. The Labour Party claimed to have a membership of 406,000 in early 1998 but this had fallen to 385,000 by June (*Guardian*, 23 June 1998). The Liberal Democrats claimed a membership of around 100,000 for 1998, the Scottish National Party 30,000, Plaid Cymru 8,000 and the Greens 4,000. However, many of these members simply pay their subscriptions and never attend meetings or other events organised by their party. For example, only 177,391 Conservative Party members (45% of the total estimated membership) voted in the referendum on the reform of the Conservative Party in 1997. Similarly, research into the behaviour of Labour Party members suggests that giving money has become the most important form of activism (Whiteley & Seyd 1998).

If the number of political activists is small, then the number of activists who seek to become candidates for local, national and European elections is even smaller. This chapter examines the type of people who stand as candidates and the procedures that are used to select them. It also considers whether councillors, MPs and MEPs are representative of the population as a whole and how the pressures on them affect the extent to which they can claim to be accountable to their constituents.

In addition to the recruitment of elected representatives, this chapter examines the recruitment of people whose work is political but who are not elected - people who are appointed to serve on quangos. What sort of people are appointed to do these jobs and why? To whom are they accountable? What does their appointment tell us about the British political system?

Chapter summary

Part 1 examines the selection and role of local councillors. Who stands for office? How representative are they? What rewards do they get from office?

Part 2 looks at the selection of parliamentary candidates. How do selection procedures differ in the main parties? What qualities are sought?

Part 3 considers whether or not MPs are representative of their constituents. What background do they have? How accountable are they? What pressures are put upon them? What

rewards do they get from office?

Part 4 looks at who stands for the European and Scottish Parliaments and the Welsh and Northern Ireland Assemblies and how they are selected. It also considers MEPs' pay and conditions and their accountability.

Part 5 focuses on the criteria used for the appointment of people to quangos. What sort of people are appointed to these posts? To whom are they accountable?

Part 1 The selection and role of local councillors

Key issues

1. Who stands for office and why?
2. How are candidates for election selected?
3. What are councillors' hours and rewards?
4. What role do councillors play?
5. How representative are councillors?

1.1 Who stands for office?

Why do people stand?
Each year thousands of individuals make the decision to stand as candidates in local elections. Their reasons for standing may vary, but it is possible to group them under the following headings: ideology; power; personal satisfaction; specific

policy interest; and ambition (Kingdom 1991).

The level and type of commitment required from candidates depends on whether they are standing at parish, district or county level, or for unitary authorities. At parish level, seats are usually contested by individuals who avoid a party political label. As parish councils have little power and are responsible for only small amounts of money, often little interest is shown in the elections. As a result, it may be difficult to persuade people to stand for office. At district, county and unitary authority level, most elections are party political contests, but independents do stand, especially in rural areas. For some who join a political party, becoming a candidate for a local council election is a product of years of political activity in their local branch. For others, it is a first step on a planned political career. All those who stand have a wish to represent their fellow citizens in some way.

The selection and election of candidates

Independent candidates make their own choice to stand and then have to find friends and supporters to help them if they decide to run an election campaign. The number of independent candidates standing in district and county council elections has fallen over the last 30 years. Before the 1974 local government reorganisation, only 46% of councils were classed as 'party authorities' (where the three main parties make up more than 50% of council membership). Immediately after the 1974 local government reorganisation, this rose to 64%. By 1997, the number of independent councillors in Britain had fallen to 2,153 compared to 20,149 councillors representing the different political parties (Rallings & Thrasher 1997).

Selection

Candidates who stand on behalf of political parties are selected at a special selection meeting. Even when there is a shortage of candidates or the seat is impossible to win and only one person agrees to stand, a selection meeting is generally held. Candidates are selected by the local branch of the party, though the party tier at district level often has an input into the process, perhaps by having an approved list of candidates. A recent development is the involvement of the major parties at national level - to weed out dissidents and those candidates with a potentially embarrassing past. The Labour Party has introduced Project 99. This requires all candidates to fill in a questionnaire and complete a written test. The questionnaire asks candidates detailed questions about their past and also, indirectly, about their political beliefs. The written test asks candidates to answer a mock constituency query. Candidates are also expected to sign a declaration of willingness to abide by the party's code of conduct. In addition:

> 'Among other hurdles the potential candidate must cross is an undertaking to meet the

standards laid down by the Nolan Committee relating to financial probity. Any rent or council tax arrears would automatically lead to deselection or disqualification from the list.' (*Guardian*, 5 May 1998)

The Conservatives have taken similar measures. New party rules demand that:

> 'In order to ensure that constituency associations have a wide choice of candidates, the Board will ensure the maintenance of a sufficiently large list of Approved Candidates... In future, all candidates on the Approved List will be required to abide by the rulings of the Ethics and Integrity Committee.' (Conservative 1998, p.10)

At the selection meeting, party members listen to potential candidates and ask them questions. Voting then takes place and a single candidate is selected for each ward.

Selection of mayoral candidates

Traditionally, the position of mayor was largely ceremonial and senior (ie long-serving) councillors took it in turns to hold the post on a fixed-term basis. Following Labour's election in 1997, however, proposals to create a new, directly elected, post of Mayor of London were approved in a referendum (in May 1998). As a result, the major parties were forced to devise a selection procedure for choosing the candidate they wished to back in the forthcoming election. In February 1998, William Hague announced that the Conservatives would throw open the selection of the Conservative mayoral candidate to a primary election of all party members in London. For the Labour Party, however, the matter caused controversy because Ken Livingstone (Leader of the GLC when it was abolished in 1986) made it clear that he wanted to stand, whilst senior Labour figures were determined to prevent him from standing because of his outspoken criticism of Blair's government. Resolution of the controversy hinged on whether or not Labour's National Executive Committee had the power to prevent candidates' names appearing on the shortlist which would be circulated to all party members in London in a ballot.

The selection procedure for choosing mayoral candidates in London assumed greater significance after the Labour government published a white paper on local government in July 1998. This laid out the requirement that councils streamline their decision-making processes by introducing a directly elected mayor or Cabinets of senior councillors. The selection procedure used in London provides a framework for other mayoral contests.

The election campaign

Having selected a candidate, the local party supports them in the election campaign. Election campaigns vary from an active campaign in which votes are canvassed on the doorstep to a 'paper' campaign where the candidate does no canvassing.

Candidates supported by political parties have the advantage of access to money (for leaflets and so on) and personnel. But, even though the major political parties try to fight every seat, some council seats are still uncontested (the number in this category is falling).

Hours

Being a councillor is a time-consuming business. A study carried out by the Joseph Rowntree Foundation showed that, in 1993, councillors spent, on average, 74 hours per month on council business (though this figure conceals considerable variation between the more and the less active councillors). Council leaders and chairs of committees are likely to spend much longer on council business than ordinary councillors. The time spent shows a small decrease compared with a study in 1976 but is considerably more than the Maud study in 1965 (52 hours per month). The Widdicombe Report (Widdicombe 1986) also revealed an average of 74 hours per month.

There is some evidence that time and commitment given to council work varies according to political party. Wood and Crawley show that Labour and Liberal councillors on average spend more time on council work than others. Conservative councillors often define their role in more limited terms than others. They tend to see council work as one of a number of leisure interests and certainly no more than a voluntary activity requiring only limited commitment (Wood & Crawley 1987).

Councillors in the key positions on district and county councils have the task of spending millions of pounds and are responsible for the delivery of efficient services to their community. As a result, meetings often have to be held during the day. This is a problem for many councillors who find it difficult to combine a full-time job with their council work. If they work in the private sector, they are dependent on the generosity of their employer to release them from work. The 1986 Widdicombe Report recommended that public sector employees be allowed up to 26 days a year leave to undertake council work. It is, therefore, not too surprising that the majority of councillors are either self-employed, working in the public sector, retired or not in full time work.

Rewards

Traditionally, councillors have undertaken their council work on a voluntary basis, not for financial reward. According to the Audit Commission's 1990 study, for example, the average amount claimed by councillors was just £2,000. Recent developments, however, suggest that this may be changing. Since 1991, all councillors have been able to claim a basic allowance. Since 1995, the upper limit on this allowance has been scrapped. The scrapping of this upper limit and the Labour government's local government reforms (the introduction of elected mayors and Cabinets of senior councillors) have provided the opportunity for some

councils to pay councillors much more than used to be the case. Research by Kirsty Milne revealed, for example, that, in 1998, the council in Fulham decided that ordinary councillors would be able to claim £7,500 per year (up from £2,000 in 1997) whilst the Council Leader would receive £22,500 (up from £8,000) and the six Executive Deputies would receive £17,500 (up from £5,000). Milne admitted that this was an extreme example, but argued that it was not an isolated one:

> 'The Labour-controlled London boroughs of Camden and Haringey recently voted to pay councillors £5,000 a year. In Conservative Kent, the county council has quadrupled members' allowances to £4,000 a year. Because these huge hikes are happening piecemeal they have attracted little attention. But, they amount to a stealthy revolution in how, and how much, councillors are paid.' (Milne 1998, p.13)

Arguments for and against full-time councillors

The main arguments in favour of these moves towards the creation of full-time, salaried councillors are as follows:

- payment will encourage higher quality candidates to stand
- payment will lead to greater professionalism and better local government
- payment will allow people to stand who, at present, cannot afford to stand
- councillors deserve to be paid the same as people appointed to quangos (members of health authorities are paid £5,000 a year and chairs earn between £15,000 and £19,000).

The main arguments against these moves towards the creation of full-time, salaried councillors are as follows:

- payment will encourage careerists (who tend to be white, male and middle class) to the exclusion of others
- payment will ensure that people stand for election for money not because they care about their local community
- the money would be better spent on local services
- payment would cause problems for councillors on benefits - perhaps even making them worse off
- payment could bring real panic at election time since councillors would be terrified of losing their income.

There is also concern because payments vary widely. Some people support the idea of national rates with councillors being paid the same throughout the country.

How representative are councillors?

It is clear from the Local Government Management Board's census of councillors in England and Wales that councillors tend not to mirror the electorate they represent socially:

> '[The typical councillor] is a white man, just short of his 56th birthday, who is also a school governor or on the board of another public body. He has a degree or a professional qualification and has sat on the council for nine years, serving on six committees and sub-committees.' (*Guardian* 20 March 1998)

Despite this, councillors often claim to represent the view of their constituents politically. The degree to which councillors can be said to represent their constituents is, to some extent, determined by the way in which they themselves perceive their role since that will determine the extent to which they consult with and take on board the views of constituents.

Kingdom's four categories

John Kingdom has suggested that the ways in which councillors perceive their role can be divided into four categories (Kingdom, 1991). First, councillors may act as delegates, directly reporting the views of their constituents to the council. Because of the small size of local government electoral units it is possible for councillors to work in this way. Second, councillors may claim a mandate if they have presented a manifesto to the electorate and won the election. Third, councillors may see themselves as leaders who should exercise personal judgement.

Fourth, councillors may be self-seeking and have minimal interest in the local community.

Low turnout

One difficulty that all councillors face in claiming to represent the community politically is the low proportion of the electorate which turns out to vote in local elections. Given that few councillors in contested seats are likely to receive much more than 20% of the total electorate's vote, they cannot easily be confident that they have the support of the public for any policy initiatives.

Main points - Part 1

- **The main reasons why people stand in local elections are ideology, power, personal satisfaction, specific policy interest, and ambition.**
- **Most candidates are party candidates and they have to undergo a selection procedure before being able to stand. Recently, national party HQs have become involved in selection.**
- **Councillors spend, on average, 74 hours per month on council business.**
- **Recently, there have been moves towards the creation of full-time, salaried councillors.**
- **Councillors tend not to mirror the electorate they represent socially.**

Activity 11.1 Councillors

Item A *The amount of time spent on council duties, 1964-93*

Average number of hours in a typical month	1964	1976	1985	1993
Attending council meetings (including committee meetings)	11	23	21	22
Preparation for meetings and travelling	18	26	25	24
Attending party meetings related to council activities	-	5	5	5
Dealing with electors' problems, surgeries, pressure groups	8	13	13	13
Meeting external organisations	5	8	8	7
Public consultation meetings	-	-	2	3
Other	10	4	-	-
Total average	**52**	**79**	**74**	**74**

This table shows how much time councillors spent on the same duties between 1964 and 1993.

Adapted from Williams 1995.

Item B *Councillor profile (1)*

(i)

Employment

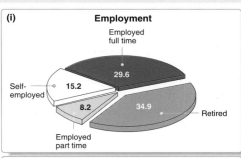

Employed full time 29.6

Self-employed 15.2

Employed part time 8.2

Retired 34.9

(ii)

Gender

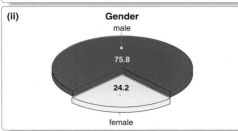

male 75.8

female 24.2

(iii)

Ethnicity

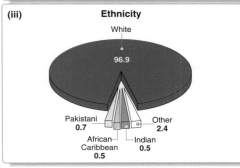

White 96.9

Pakistani 0.7

African Caribbean 0.5

Indian 0.5

Other 2.4

Compared to Britain's population as a whole, councillors tend to be:

- older - they are more likely to be retired (34.9%) than under 45 (18%).
- male - female councillors are outnumbered by three to one.
- better educated - 53% have a professional qualification.
- white - only 3% of councillors are from the ethnic minorities.
- less likely to be in full-time work as an employee - 15.2% are self employed.
- able-bodied - 10.8% are disabled.

Adapted from LGC 1998.

Item C *Councillor profile (2)*

Name	Richard Tarver
Age	45
Job	British Telecom Clerical Officer, on long-term full-time secondment as an elected official of the Communication Workers' Union, representing workers, mostly in BT.
Salary	£16500
Hours	Variable (flexitime) averaged to 37 per week
Home owner?	No
Party affiliation	Labour Party member for 16 years
Positions in local government	District Councillor in Oxford for eight years - since 1990. Re-elected 3 times. Member of Economic Development Committee, and Housing Committee. Chair of the Economic Development Committee.
Why did you become a councillor?	To try and do some useful and important things for the community of Oxford. To use my socialist principles to participate in the drawing up and implementing of policies to allow improvement in the lives of people in this community.
Hours spent on council duties	Varies from two to ten hours per week.
Rewards	Winning cases on behalf of individuals in my ward (councillors' constituency) who ask me for help, for example with their housing or planning problems. Taking decisions which benefit the community - and seeing the fruits of those decisions in improvements to the quality of life of both individuals and the general community.
Allowances	£22 for attending each official meeting. These include Council Committees, and management Committees of organisations I am elected to serve on as a councillor. There are travel allowances: a petrol allowance and a cycle allowance.
How do you see your role?	To act as a responsible community leader, collecting and representing the views and needs of both the local ward that I elected to serve, and the wider city that I represent as Chair of the Economic Development Committee and as a member of the Labour group which has political control of the City.

Adapted from an interview conducted in July 1998.

Questions

1. Look at Item A.
   a) What does this table tell us about the work done by councillors?
   b) How far do the figures support the argument that party politics takes up too much of a councillor's time?

2. Judging from Items B and C:
   a) why do you think people want to be councillors?
   b) what sort of people are likely to be elected as councillors?
   c) what are the main factors that might deter people from standing as candidates in local elections?
   d) would you agree that, on the whole, the British people are well represented at local level?

3. a) List the characteristics of the councillor in Item C which are (i) typical and (ii) not typical.
   b) Which of Kingdom's four categories best describes the councillor in Item C?

Part 2 The selection of parliamentary candidates

Key issues

1. How are parliamentary candidates selected by the major political parties?
2. To what extent should selection remain at local rather than at national level?
3. What qualities should a parliamentary candidate have?
4. Why are so few parliamentary candidates women or from the ethnic minorities?

2.1 Selecting candidates

Who are the candidates?

In the general election of 1997, there were 3,724 candidates fighting for the 659 parliamentary seats - an average of 5.6 per constituency.

In parliamentary elections, a minority of candidates are either individuals who want publicity for a particular cause or are from fringe political parties. Most are members of the three main parties. The three main parties expect to fight every seat in mainland Britain with the exception of the Speaker's seat. In the 1997 general election, Labour and the Liberal Democrats also decided not to fight the seat of Neil Hamilton (the disgraced former Conservative minister implicated in the 'Cash for Questions' row) in Tatton. This allowed Martin Bell, an independent candidate, to fight (and win) the seat. Of the three main parties, only the Conservatives put up candidates in Northern Ireland in 1997. Since the 1960s, the Scottish and Welsh Nationalists, the Green Party and other fringe parties have gradually increased the number of seats which they contest. In 1997, the Referendum Party put up 547 candidates, the UK Independence Party put up 194 candidates and the Green Party put up 95 candidates.

The selection process

Becoming a candidate for any of the parties fighting the election seriously is a competitive process. Even in a seat where a party has little chance of winning, several potential candidates invariably put themselves forward. For some political activists, fighting the election campaign as the party's official candidate is the peak of their political career. For others, an election campaign in an unwinnable seat is seen as a first step towards fighting a winnable seat later. In most parliamentary seats, there is already an incumbent MP who was elected in the previous general election and who is standing in the same seat for the same party in the subsequent general election. Generally, incumbent MPs can expect to be selected as their party's candidate for subsequent general elections and, usually, a high proportion can expect to be re-elected. In 1997, however, boundary changes meant that some sitting MPs were not selected as candidates for the newly created seats and also an exceptionally large number of MPs (117) decided to retire. Candidates who inherit a 'safe' seat, where the party's sitting MP has retired, usually have a good chance of being elected. But, challengers who are fighting a seat held by another party usually have a low rate of success. An exception to this was the 1997 general election when a high swing to Labour and tactical voting ensured that large numbers of Labour and Liberal Democrat candidates were elected in what had been thought to be safe Conservative seats.

Common features of selection

The process of selecting candidates varies from party to party. There are, however, certain common features. The process combines local political choice with an element of central control. Potential candidates must present themselves to the relevant local party organisations and attempt to win support for their candidature. Endorsement by the party headquarters is also necessary. Since, in safe seats, the choice of candidate by party members (the 'selectorate') is tantamount to choosing an MP, how the process works is of considerable importance.

Selection procedure in the Labour Party before 1993

The selection of parliamentary candidates in the Labour Party has been a controversial procedure. It has undergone a number of changes since 1980.

In 1980, a rule change passed at the annual party conference meant that a system of mandatory (compulsory) reselection should occur for all sitting Labour MPs between general elections. Before that, sitting Labour MPs could not be challenged.

In 1987, a second change was made to procedure. Before 1987, the parliamentary candidate was selected by the constituency general committee (GC). Ordinary party members had no direct vote in the proceedings (though they did vote for the delegates to the GC). After the 1987 general election, an electoral college was introduced. This consisted of 60% votes for individual party members and 40% for affiliated organisations. Members were able to cast their votes at ballots held in the branch or by postal vote.

Selection procedure in the Labour Party since 1993

The annual party conference in 1993 brought further changes to the selection procedure. Most noticeably, the franchise was extended further so that the principle of one member, one vote (OMOV) was secured.

Further changes were introduced in 1998 following a consultation exercise carried out by the NEC and a subsequent vote at the 1998 Labour Party conference. As a result, parliamentary candidates are chosen by all Labour Party members in a constituency after the GC has drawn up a shortlist from nominated candidates.

Drawing up the shortlist

The names on the shortlist can come from a number of sources. First, there is a national panel, drawn up and held by the NEC. Names on this panel are either individual party members who have applied and fulfilled selection criteria or party members nominated by nationally affiliated organisations (such as trade unions). Second, individual party members who are not on the national panel can seek nomination from branches and affiliated organisations (each branch and affiliated organisation is allowed to nominate one candidate). And third:

> 'In any constituency where one or more black or Asian members of the national panel express an interest in selection, the constituency executive shall meet to make a nomination from amongst those interested members to ensure that at least one black or Asian candidate is available for shortlisting.' (Labour 1998, p.9)

All those nominated are considered for the shortlist. If a sitting MP is nominated by a majority of all the organisations from which nominations are received, that MP is selected without a ballot. Otherwise, the GC decides how many candidates should be shortlisted (if more than four are nominated then at least four must be shortlisted) and then holds a ballot to decide which candidates should be included on the shortlist. The shortlist must meet the criteria laid out in Box 11.1.

Box 11.1 Deciding who should be shortlisted

1. Any sitting Labour MP representing a constituency that is wholly or substantially contained within the area of the CLP (the work of the Boundary Commission - see Chapter 7, Section 3.1 - means that borders of constituencies change) will be automatically included on the shortlist if they choose to contest the seat and are nominated.
2. Where no sitting MP is contesting a seat, there should be an equal number of men and women on the shortlist. If four or more are nominated, there must be a minimum of four on the shortlist and at least two men and at least two women on it.
3. There must be separate ballots between the men and women who are nominated to decide which candidates are to be included on the shortlist.
4. The ballot to decide who should go on the shortlist is to be conducted using the STV voting system.

Procedure after the shortlist has been agreed

Once the shortlist has been agreed, each candidate

on it is permitted to circulate a canvassing leaflet which must conform to certain conditions laid down by the NEC. The candidates are invited to speak at hustings meetings of party members with each candidate addressing the members in turn and then answering questions. At the end of each husting meeting there is a vote. Members who cannot attend their local selection meeting can apply for a postal ballot. The ballot is conducted by a version of the alternative vote system (see Chapter 7, Section 4.1). The ballot boxes are opened and the votes counted at a special meeting of the GC.

A change for the better?

The Labour leadership has claimed that these changes have broadened party democracy at local level. Individual party members now decide who should be the candidate rather than delegates elected to the constituency GC and local trade union branches. Critics from the left, however, have argued that democracy has been reduced because the new rules encourage 'armchair' involvement, prevent the participation of the unions and reduce the power of reselection. One unintended byproduct of the new procedure may have been to encourage the choice of local candidates:

> 'A very liberal interpretation of the right to vote postally encouraged this tendency, with members voting from home without hearing or seeing the candidates at the selection meeting, and, accordingly, voting for known local figures rather than unknown outsiders.' (Butler & Kavanagh 1997, p.189)

The NEC

Throughout this period of change at local level, the NEC has retained power at national level. Endorsement by the NEC is required once the vote has been taken at local level. This power, which includes ultimately the power to impose a candidate on a local constituency, ensures that party headquarters can keep control of events and weed out what the party leadership regards as unsuitable candidates. The NEC has used this power. For example, in 1995 the NEC decided to bar Liz Davies from standing as the candidate for Leeds North East despite her democratic selection by the local party. Labour's general secretary, Tom Sawyer, claimed that Ms Davies did not believe fully in the notion of collective responsibility. He said:

> 'It is about her perpetual opposition to the mainstream of the party and its policies over a long period of time.' (quoted in the *Guardian*, 26 September 1995)

Further evidence of NEC control came in October 1998 with the publication of an NEC procedural document which was approved by conference. This document made it clear that the national panel of parliamentary candidates would consist of only those who had met 'clear minimum standards' and who had taken part in training and assessment weekends organised by the NEC. Candidates not on the national panel would have to go through an endorsement interview. Also, tighter controls were introduced for sitting MPs. The party's Chief Whip was instructed to present a report to the NEC which listed unauthorised absences, abstentions and votes against the party whip. If necessary, MPs with exceptionally poor disciplinary records could then be interviewed by the NEC and asked to explain their behaviour. In extreme cases, they might then be refused endorsement as candidates at the following election. The information would also be made available to the MP's constituency party. The *Guardian* commented on these proposals before they were passed by conference and suggested they amounted to:

> 'Control-freakishness that borders on the obsessive.' (*Guardian*, 28 May 1998)

By-elections

In the event of a by-election, the control exercised by the NEC over candidate selection is even greater. It is the NEC that draws up the shortlist - the assumption being that it is the NEC, rather than the local party, which is in a better position to judge whether the candidates are likely to be able to stand up to the greater media scrutiny inherent in by-elections. Once the shortlist has been approved by the local party, members in the constituency then choose their candidate using the OMOV system. The final approval still rests with the NEC.

Selection procedure in the Conservative Party

Drawing up the national list

Like the Labour NEC, Conservative Party headquarters (Central Office) also draws up a list of approved candidates. Following the general election defeat of 1997, it was decided that this list should be drawn up from scratch. It is not easy to get onto this list. Procedure is as follows. First, a potential candidate must make a written application to Central Office, enclosing references from influential party figures (such as sitting MPs or the chair of a constituency association). Second, if the application is accepted, the potential candidate is interviewed by the regional agent. Third, if successful in this interview, the potential candidate is interviewed by a special adviser from Central Office. Fourth, if the special adviser is satisfied, the potential candidate is invited to attend a residential weekend where all-round abilities are assessed. Successful candidates are then placed on the approved candidates list and can apply to be candidates when vacant seats arise.

Procedure when a vacancy arises

If a vacancy arises, a constituency association informs Central Office which, in turn, informs those whose names appear on the national list. If they are interested in standing, they inform Central Office which then passes their details to the constituency association concerned. The constituency selection committee then carries out a paper sift and draws up a shortlist of (usually) about 20 potential candidates. Of these 20 potential candidates, normally between 10 and 12 are invited to be interviewed and a shortlist of at least three names is then submitted to the constituency executive council. The constituency executive council then draws up a shortlist of not less than two potential candidates and asks those on the list to attend a general meeting of the constituency association. At this meeting, the potential candidates speak and answer questions and then the ordinary members take a vote. If more than two potential candidates have been invited to the general meeting a number of ballots might be taken to ensure that the winning candidate has more than 50% of the vote. The winning candidate is then adopted as the parliamentary candidate for the constituency in the forthcoming general election.

Procedure for by-elections

Procedure for by-elections is the same as for general elections, though a special list of candidates who are thought to be particularly suitable for by-elections was introduced in the *Fresh Future* reforms (William Hague's new blueprint for party organisation introduced in March 1998 - see below).

Deselection

Unlike in the Labour Party, there is no system of mandatory reselection of MPs. But, on occasions, local MPs do lose the confidence of their local party members. In that case, a ballot of all local party members is held. For example, before the 1997 general election, Sir Nicholas Scott was deselected from his seat in Kensington and Chelsea after a number of embarrassing incidents.

The *Fresh Future*

William Hague's *Fresh Future* strengthened party headquarters' control over the whole parliamentary candidate selection procedure at national level. As a result, there is a much greater emphasis on the importance of the approved list and all candidates have to agree to abide by the rulings of the new Ethics and Integrity Committee. The permanent sub-committee responsible for candidate selection is much more proactive in creating the approved list. Its job is to ensure 'a thorough examination of potential candidates...the development of standardised curriculum vitae [and] training for all approved members of the candidates' list' (Conservative 1998, p.19).

The Liberal Democrats' selection procedure

At the regional level

Like the Labour and Conservative parties, the Liberal Democrats keep a national list of approved candidates. All candidates must be on the current national list and they are not eligible for selection until they are. The Liberal Democrats are organised on a federal basis and so it is the regional parties which organise 'assessment days' to decide whether potential candidates are eligible for the national list. At these events, there are four potential candidates, four assessors, one facilitator who chairs the meeting, and one policy assessor, normally an MP or former MP (Turner 1996, p.33).

At the constituency level

At the constituency level, selection procedure is as follows. When a vacancy arises, the local constituency party invites applications. Usually an advert is placed in *Liberal Democratic News*. A shortlist is then made of potential candidates (any members who want to be placed on the shortlist must ensure that their names appear on the national list). The shortlist for each vacant seat must contain at least one man and one woman. All constituency members are invited to a selection meeting. After each candidate has spoken and answered any questions, a ballot is held. Absent members can only have a postal vote if they make a special application (to encourage as many members as possible to be present at the meeting). Voting is by the Single Transferable Vote system (see Chapter 7, Section 4.1). The procedure is the same for by-elections as it is for general elections.

Conclusions

There are four general criteria which can be applied to the selection procedure in any party. The procedure should be:

> 'Explicit - so that applicants know the rules; fair - so that the participants feel that there has been no undue influence; thorough - so that the qualifications, experience and abilities of candidates are closely scrutinised; and open - to attract a good range of candidates.' (Geddes et al. 1991, p.19)

If there are agreed procedures which meet these four criteria then it is more likely that there will be an internal consensus within the party. The existence of an internal consensus encourages party members to work collectively for victory at the polls.

In all three main parties there has been a move towards greater centralisation and greater national control over the process of choosing candidates. At the same time, there have been moves to involve more party members in making the choice at local level.

There is an argument that the base for choosing candidates should be widened still further so that it is not only party members who are involved but also people who vote for the party. This could be achieved by introducing a system of primary elections similar to the system in the USA. People who regularly vote for a party could register as a party supporter and then be invited to vote in a primary election to choose the candidate.

Main points - Section 2.1

- **Most candidates are members of the three main parties, though the number of candidates from the smaller parties has been rising since the 1960s.**
- **Candidates must present themselves to the relevant local party organisations and attempt to win support for their candidature. Endorsement by the party headquarters is also necessary.**
- **The Labour Party's selection process has undergone a number of changes since 1980. Ordinary members now have a greater say and the NEC has greater control over the names appearing on the shortlist.**
- **Potential Conservative candidates must undergo a stringent series of tests before being placed on the national list. Once on the list, they can apply when vacancies arise. The constituency association then makes the final choice.**
- **Potential Liberal Democrat candidates must also pass a series of tests before their names are added to the national list. Members of the constituency party then make the final choice.**

Activity 11.2 Choosing parliamentary candidates

Item A   *The Uxbridge by-election of July 1997*

In the face of criticism from local party activists following Labour's defeat in the Uxbridge by-election, senior figures insisted the system of selecting by-election candidates had worked well for the past ten years and there was no reason to change it now. There was, they insisted, no intention to alter the system of using a special panel rather than the constituency party to choose by-election candidates. By-election candidates come under intense scrutiny. Also, choosing a candidate from outside moves the focus onto national issues rather than local ones. Local activists, however, claimed the party could have won if it had stuck with the candidate who fought the general election. Peter James, Chair of the Labour group on Hillingdon Council, which included Uxbridge, said: 'Far from the Tories winning this election , I think the Labour Party did a very good job at losing it. We had a very good candidate at the general election, Councillor David Williams, who should have been standing at this election.' The Deputy Prime Minister, John Prescott, said that the Labour Party lost some terrible by-elections when constituency parties selected candidates because candidates in by-elections face special pressures.

Adapted from the *Guardian*, 2 August 1997.

Item B *The selection process in the Labour Party*

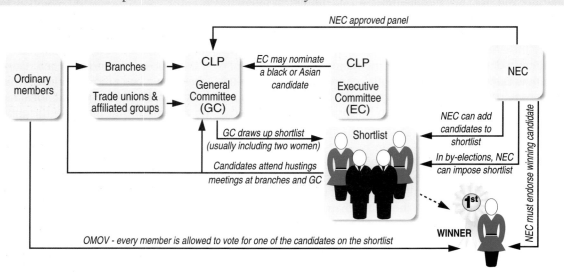

NEC approved panel

Ordinary members → Branches → CLP General Committee (GC)

Trade unions & affiliated groups →

EC may nominate a black or Asian candidate

CLP Executive Committee (EC)

NEC

GC draws up shortlist (usually including two women)

Shortlist

NEC can add candidates to shortlist

In by-elections, NEC can impose shortlist

Candidates attend hustings meetings at branches and GC

NEC must endorse winning candidate

WINNER 1st

OMOV - every member is allowed to vote for one of the candidates on the shortlist

Item C *Central Office and constituency associations*

Tatton Conservatives decide tonight whether to re-adopt Neil Hamilton. John Major claims that he has no power to intervene, arguing that, under the Conservative Party constitution, the selection of a candidate is the responsibility of the association. This argument, however, is both misleading and implausible. John Major could act if he wanted to. All Conservative candidates have to be supported by the National Union's Standing Advisory Committee. This must satisfy itself that they are loyal, financially solvent and of sound character. Otherwise, a person is not recognised as an official Conservative candidate and does not receive the Leader's message of recommendation or any Central Office facilities or speakers during the campaign. If elected, such a candidate would not be given the Tory whip and the association which defied the national party could be disaffiliated from the National Union. So, while it is true that the selection of a candidate is the responsibility of the association, it does not follow that the person selected has to be recognised as the official Conservative Party candidate. John Major could do three things to stop Hamilton fighting as an official Conservative candidate. He could ensure that Hamilton is removed from the party's Approved List of candidates. He could disaffiliate the constituency association. Or, he could announce that Hamilton will be denied the Conservative whip, if elected.

Adapted from the *Guardian*, 8 April 1997.

Item D *The selection process in the Conservative Party*

STEP 7
Members vote after hearing candidates at listings meeting. There may be several ballots to ensure winner has over 50% of the vote.

STEP 6
Constituency executive council interviews c. 10-12 candidates and draws up a shortlist of at least two candidates.

STEP 5
Constituency selection committee sifts through cvs and draws up a shortlist of c. 20 names.

STEP 4
Approved candidate list is drawn up - 700 names by Summer 1999.

STEP 3
Weekend selection board.

STEP 2
Interview with regional agent and special adviser.

STEP 1
Application form and references to Central Office.

Item E   *The deselection of George Gardiner*

At a meeting in Reigate on 30 January 1997, Sir George Gardiner (who had served as Conservative MP for 23 years) was deselected by 272 votes to 213. The fate of Sir George, a self-confessed Thatcher devotee and Eurosceptic, was sealed by what was seen by the local Conservative association as his growing, bare-faced disloyalty to Thatcher's successor John Major. Sir George was an outspoken opponent of Major's European policy and, in a newspaper article published in December 1996, described Major as a ventriloquist's dummy manipulated by his pro-European Chancellor, Kenneth Clarke. In June 1996, Sir George survived an attempt to deselect him, largely because he was backed by Central Office and because he pledged his loyalty to John Major. Significantly, Central Office withdrew its support in January 1997. Sir George was the second Conservative MP to be deselected in two months. Sir Nicholas Scott was dropped by the Kensington and Chelsea Tories after being found face down in the gutter at the 1996 party conference. In March 1997, Sir George Gardiner left the Conservative Party and joined the Referendum Party. In the 1997 general election he won 3,352 votes as the Referendum Party candidate whilst the Conservative Party candidate, Crispin Blunt, was elected with 21,123 votes.

Adapted from the *Guardian*, 15 December 1996 and 31 January 1997, the *Times*, 10 March 1997 and Austin 1997.

Questions

1. Do you think that the national party headquarters of the three major parties should have the power to veto parliamentary candidates chosen locally? Use Items A and C in your answer.

2. a) Suppose you were a Labour Party member who wanted to become a parliamentary candidate. Using Item B, explain the procedures you would follow.
   b) Explain how the selection procedure has changed since 1980. Why do you think the changes were introduced?

3. Using Items B and D compare the selection procedures used by the Labour Party and Conservative Party. What are the benefits and drawbacks of each system?

4. Look at Item E. In what circumstances do you think that it is justified for a local party to deselect a sitting MP as a parliamentary candidate?

2.2 Parliamentary candidates

The qualities sought in a parliamentary candidate

The local party members who choose the parliamentary candidate (the 'selectorate') seek to select the best candidate to win the seat for their party. Their choice is based fundamentally on two criteria - the personal qualities of the candidate and the candidate's political views.

Personal qualities

A survey carried out in 1987 (the British Candidates Survey - see Norris & Lovenduski 1989) revealed the personal qualities which the selectorate regarded as important. The findings of this survey are shown in Item A in Activity 11.3. It should be noted that, although there are some differences between the political parties, there are also a number of similarities. For example, all parties regard a candidate's speaking ability as important. In general terms, this means that more highly educated candidates are likely to be chosen since a higher education often gives people both the confidence and the ability to express their views in public.

Political views

But, it is not just personal qualities that are important during the selection process. The political views of both the candidate and the selectorate can affect the outcome. In all the major parties there is, commonly, a divide between left and right with a large centre ground which encompasses the majority. During their campaigns, candidates can be expected to temper their views to the political complexion of the particular members they are addressing. They need to exercise some care, however, to avoid the charge of political opportunism.

Data gathered for the British Candidates Survey makes it clear that social and economic policy issues dominate the questioning at interviews. Local issues and the candidates' political and personal experience generate fewer questions. Foreign policy and the candidates' family lives are usually of least concern. Particular circumstances, however, may mean exceptions to these findings. For example, the Conservative Party's 'Back to Basics' campaign brought an unusual amount of attention to MPs' family affairs during the winter of 1993-94.

Main points - Section 2.2

- The selectorate's choice of candidate is based on the personal qualities of the candidate and the candidate's political views.
- All parties regard a candidate's speaking ability as important. In general terms, this means that more highly educated candidates are likely to be chosen.
- During their campaigns, candidates can be expected to play to the audience, but they need to take care to avoid the charge of political opportunism.
- Social and economic policy issues dominate questioning. Foreign policy and the candidates' family lives are usually of least concern.

Activity 11.3 Parliamentary candidates

Item A *Qualities sought by selectors when choosing a parliamentary candidate*

Item B *The background of parliamentary candidates in 1997 (1)*

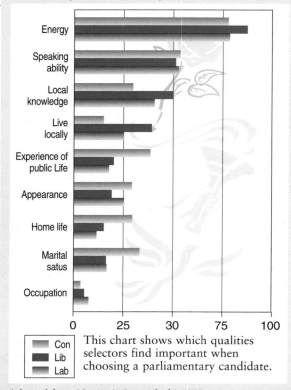

This chart shows which qualities selectors find important when choosing a parliamentary candidate.

Con
Lib
Lab

Adapted from Norris & Lovenduski 1989.

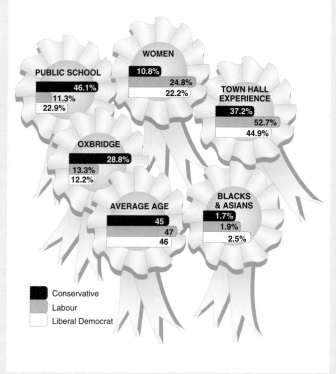

Adapted from the *Times*, 17 April 1997.

Item C *The background of parliamentary candidates in 1997 (2)*

Occupation	Labour	Conservative	Liberal Democrat
Professions	295	234	289
Business	77	276	212
Manual worker	74	10	15
Miscellaneous:			
White collar	98	18	58
Political organiser	49	35	18
Publisher/journalist	39	41	22
Others	7	26	24

This table shows what jobs candidates were doing before standing for Parliament.

The professions are well represented among all three main parties at this election. In particular, over 15% of Conservative candidates and 7% of Labour candidates have legal backgrounds. As usual, the Labour Party is well represented by teachers and lecturers. More than one in four Labour contestants hold, or have held, academic positions prior to their candidatures. Among Liberal Democrats, the figure is more than 20%. If the classroom or the lecture theatre has been home to many Labour hopefuls, business will again dominate the Conservative benches. A total of 47% of Conservative candidates have business backgrounds, compared to 16% of Labour contestants. The Conservatives have twice as many candidates in their 20s and 30s as Labour, although most of these have no real prospect of victory and are competing in the hope of securing more winnable seats next time. Local government continues to be a stepping stone to a Westminster career. This time 45% of candidates have served on local authorities. It is the area of gender, however, that reveals the most marked change in this election. In 1992, a total of 341 women candidates stood for the three main parties. This time, the overall figure is not much changed with Conservatives, Labour and Liberal Democrats fielding a total of 370 candidates. The important difference this time is that many more are in winnable seats.

Adapted from Butler & Kavanagh 1997 and the *Times*, 17 April 1997.

Questions

1. a) Using Items A-C write a profile of the ideal
      parliamentary candidate for the Labour Party.
   b) How would your profile differ for the Conservative
      Party and Liberal Democrats?
   c) Can you think of negative qualities which might
      persuade the selectorate not to choose someone?

2. Look at Items B and C.
   a) What differences are there between the parties in
      terms of (i) the educational background and (ii) the
      occupations of the candidates selected?
   b) What do the items tell us about parliamentary
      candidates in general?
   c) What is the significance of these findings?

2.3 Women parliamentary candidates

The under-representation of women

In recent years there has been a growing concern
that the number of women parliamentary candidates
is unrepresentative of the number of women in the
population as a whole and is even unrepresentative
of the number of women who are members of
political parties. There has been an improvement in
the number of women elected in recent elections.
But, the three major parties only fielded 370 women
candidates in 1997 compared to 341 in 1992.
Labour had the largest number of women candidates
with 155, followed by the Liberal Democrats with
139 and the Conservatives with 66 (Butler &
Kavanagh 1997, p.199). In the 1997 election, 120
women candidates were elected, compared to 60 in
1992 and 41 in 1987.

Between 1918 and 1997, just 2,481 women have
stood as parliamentary candidates for the three main
parties (1,918 candidates stood for the three main
parties in the 1997 general election alone). All three
main parties claim that they are taking active steps to
encourage the selection and election of more
women. The Conservatives claimed that ending the
tradition of potential parliamentary candidates being
required to bring their wives or girlfriends to
selection meetings would encourage more women to
come forward (*Observer*, 1 November 1998). The
Labour Party attempted to introduce structural
changes to increase the number of women
candidates, but were forced to back down after being
challenged in the courts (see below). It is now a
requirement to include at least some women on
shortlists. It was written into the Liberal Democrats'
constitution that at least one woman must be
included in shortlists of two to four candidates and at
least two in larger shortlists.

Time

One major factor which affects the chance of
women being selected as parliamentary candidates is
the time that a potential candidate must invest. The
British Candidates Survey carried out in 1992
discovered that:

> 'The time that candidates could devote to
> politics was the most significant factor in
> predicting which applicants would be adopted
> as candidates by both the Labour Party and

Conservatives.' (Longmate 1997, p.116).
The British Candidates Survey revealed that over
four-fifths of candidates spent more than 20 hours a
week on political activity. Some of this time was
spent on actually seeking the candidature for a
parliamentary seat (one woman candidate, Emma
Nicholson, had to travel to 42 constituencies before
she was adopted). The rest was spent on general
political activity at ward, constituency, councillor,
regional and even national level (to ensure that the
potential candidate had the right experience to have
a chance of being selected). In addition, women are
still more likely to be viewed and to view themselves
as having the primary responsibility for children and
the household. This leaves them with less time than
men to pursue a political career.

Money

A second major factor which affects the chances of
women being selected as parliamentary candidates is
money. Campaigning to be a parliamentary
candidate can be expensive. It often runs into several
thousand pounds. Potential candidates have to bear
the cost of transport, loss of earnings, childcare and
accommodation. They often have to campaign for
selection in several constituencies before they are
chosen. This adds to the cost:

> 'While the costs of seeking local selections
> more typical of the Labour Party might only be
> a few hundred pounds, candidates with more
> distant seats may spend £3,000 to £10,000,
> once adopted, on weekly travel and hotel
> expenses to nurse the constituency, with no
> guarantee of a successful or secure career at
> the end of it.' (Longmate 1997, p.118)

In addition, many potential candidates would benefit
from training (in public speaking, media management
and so on). This, too, can be costly. There is little
doubt, therefore, that some people who would make
excellent candidates (especially women who are on
low incomes or have young families) are deterred by
considerations of expense.

Other factors

Whilst having time and money is a necessary first
step for women candidates, it is not sufficient to
ensure selection. Women candidates often lack the
networks of school, employment or trade union
activity that male candidates have and this leaves
them at a disadvantage. Childcare and domestic

commitments and the tendency for politics to be seen as a masculine activity are also deterrents. In addition, women candidates have to overcome prejudice:

> 'Local activists will refuse to take the risk of nominating a woman (although there is, in fact, no evidence that women candidates now lose votes.' (Bryson 1996, p.22)

The result is that only one woman puts herself forward to be adopted as a candidate for every four men.

Women and the Labour Party

It is only in the 1990s that the Labour Party has begun to take positive action to increase the number of women MPs. To do this, efforts are being made to provide women with experience at every level of the party. At branch and constituency level, for example, it is compulsory for members to ensure that two of the four main officers on the executive (Chair, Vice Chair, Secretary and Treasurer) are women. Similarly, whenever delegates are appointed, 50% must be women. If only one delegate is appointed, then it must be a woman every other year.

These rules at branch and constituency level are designed to encourage more women to gain the experience which will help them to climb the party ladder. The more women that gain experience of the selection process, the argument goes, the more women that will eventually be selected.

All-women shortlists

At its 1989 conference, the Labour Party took the decision to implement a programme designed to ensure that half of the Parliamentary Labour Party (PLP) would be composed of women by the year 2000. In 1992, however, only 10% of candidates selected in vacant safe seats were women and, between April 1992 and October 1993, just two women were selected to fight marginal seats compared to 16 men. It was in this context that the 1993 Labour Party Conference decided that there should be all-women shortlists in 50% of vacancies in 'winnable' seats (seats which required a swing to Labour of 6% or less). As a result, between 1993 and 1996, 35 women were selected in winnable seats from all-women shortlists. During this period, however, the procedure was challenged by two male Labour Party members (on the grounds that it was illegal under the Sex Discrimination Act to prevent people applying because of their sex) and, in January 1996, an (all-male) industrial tribunal judged it to be illegal. The Labour Party immediately changed the rules, reverting to the requirement that a shortlist should simply contain one woman. However, the 35 selected candidates remained and proved to be a crucial component of the very large increase in the number of Labour women MPs in Parliament after the 1997 general election:

> 'The number of women candidates for the three main parties...was not much higher than 1992...but what was different in 1997 was the strategic placing of Labour's women candidates, only 54 of whom found themselves in unwinnable seats on the day.' (Butler & Kavanagh 1997, p.199)

Rules introduced in 1998

Following the 1998 Labour Party conference, new rules were introduced to secure more women parliamentary candidates. Where party branches nominate candidates for the shortlist, they must submit the names of at least one man and one woman. This requirement does not apply to other party units or to affiliated trade union branches, though they may submit the names of one man and one woman if they choose to do so. The selection rule should mean that women make up half of shortlists in most cases. While this falls short of some of the more radical demands for change, it is likely to increase the number of women chosen to be parliamentary candidates by the Labour Party.

EMILY's List UK

On 6 February 1993, a group of Labour women launched a campaign to raise money to support women who want to become candidates for the British or European Parliament but cannot afford to put their names forward. This campaign (EMILY's List UK) is for women who belong to the Labour Party only. The idea came from a successful campaign in the USA (EMILY's List USA) but there are no formal links between the two organisations.

EMILY is an acronym for 'Early Money Is Like Yeast' (it makes the 'dough' rise). In Britain, the name also conjures up memories of two of the best known suffragettes - Emmeline Pankhurst and Emily Wilding Davison.

The aim of EMILY's List UK is to raise £30,000 annually to sponsor women in much the same way that trade unions sponsor their candidates. Sponsored women are given grants to cover the cost of training, travel, accommodation and childcare during their campaign to gain selection. Then, once selected, EMILY-sponsored candidates can apply for funds to help cover their election expenses.

Any woman belonging to the Labour Party can apply for EMILY sponsorship. The organisation has set up a panel of 25 Labour members to interview applicants and decide which to sponsor. The only political stipulation is that applicants must support a woman's right to choose whether to have an abortion.

Other groups

While EMILY's List has been in the headlines, other organisations like the '300 Group' (named after the plan to ensure that there are at least 300 women MPs), the Fawcett Society (which campaigns for equal representation of women in Parliament), the Women's Organisation in Conservative Central Office and Labour's Women's Network also offered training and support for women seeking to become parliamentary candidates (Peake 1997).

Main points - Section 2.3

- Despite a small growth in the number of women parliamentary candidates, there has been a growing concern that the number is unrepresentative.
- A number of factors make it difficult for women to stand - factors such as time, money, lack of network, domestic and childcare responsibilities, and prejudice.
- Labour Party rules at branch and constituency level

are designed to encourage more women to gain the experience which will help them to climb the party ladder. An attempt to impose all-women shortlists failed in 1996, but new rules mean that women should make up half of most shortlists.

- EMILY's List and other organisations have been set up to encourage and help women to stand for elected posts.

Activity 11.4 *Women candidates and MPs*

Item A *Women and selection*

When assessing a woman's candidacy, the influence of the local party activists who select candidates and act as 'gatekeepers' is crucial. The lack of women MPs has been explained in terms of 'supply and demand' deficiencies in the market for parliamentary candidates. On the supply side, a shortage of sufficiently well-qualified women making applications has ensured numbers remain low. Angela Rumbold, the former Conservative Vice-Chairman in charge of candidates, argues, for example, that many professional women who would make good MPs will not give up their career for what could be a five year contract. On the demand side, the selectorate may discriminate against women, either directly or indirectly, as a result of members' own perceptions of what a candidate's background and experience should be. Jacqui Smith (Labour MP for Redditch) suggests that people have tended to select MPs who are in the image of existing MPs. Until there is a critical mass, she argues, it is difficult for the world to recognise that women can be MPs. The big change in the Labour Party has been that, whilst people used to say they would select a good woman if only they could find one, nobody would say that today since there are so many good women coming forward.

Adapted from Peake 1997.

Item B *Women candidates and MPs, 1945-97*

Year	Women candidates	Con	Lab	Women MPs Lib Dems*	Others	Total
1945	87	1	21	1	1	24
1950	126	6	14	1	-	21
1951	74	6	11	-	-	17
1955	87	9	14	-	1	24
1959	75	12	13	-	-	25
1964	89	11	17	-	-	28
1966	80	7	19	-	-	26
1970	97	15	10	-	1	26
1974 (Feb)	143	9	13	-	1	23
1974 (Oct)	150	7	18	-	2	27
1979	206	8	11	-	-	19
1983	276	13	10	-	-	23
1987	327	17	21	2	1	41
1992	568	20	37	2	1	60
1997	672	13	101	3	3**	120

* Includes all women MPs elected for Liberal and SDP parties.
**Includes the Speaker, Betty Bothroyd, who was a Labour MP before being elected Speaker.

This table shows the number of women candidates and MPs between 1945 and 1997.

Adapted from Wood & Wood 1992 and the House of Commons Information Office, July 1998.

Item C *Critical mass theory*

Feminists have used the theory of critical mass to locate the point at which the number of women in a male-dominated political organisation changes the nature of that organisation. Using the example of Scandinavian politics where women have achieved higher levels of representation than anywhere else, it has been argued that women reached a critical mass once they numbered more than 15% of the parliamentary group. This critical mass had the potential to initiate changes in the organisational structures, gender relations and political agendas. The average percentage of women in Nordic Parliaments is 36.4% with Sweden highest at 40.4%. Now that women make up 18% of MPs in Britain, it will be interesting to see whether the new critical mass will launch a programme of changes in the Commons. Three changes are needed. First, more women should be appointed as ministers and secretaries of state. Second, the attitude of male MPs has to change. Up to now, many men have not accepted that women are entitled to occupy the Commons on an equal basis with men. And third, the organisational structures and procedures of the Commons need to be reformed - to take into account that members are no longer 'gentlemen' and have very different domestic roles to fulfil outside the House.

Adapted from Puwar 1997.

Item D   *The 1997 election*

This photo was taken in May 1997. It shows the Prime Minister, Tony Blair, surrounded by some of the 101 women elected as Labour MPs in the 1997 general election. In addition, 13 Conservative MPs, three Liberal Democrat MPs, two SNP MPs and the Speaker were women.

Item E   *All-women shortlists*

In a party whose membership was two-thirds male, there were legitimate questions about the availability of enough suitable women candidates, particularly in the old industrial regions. In addition, not all Labour women were impressed with the decision that there should be all-women shortlists in 50% of vacancies in 'winnable' seats. Ann Carlton (wife of Labour MP Denzil Davies) set up the Labour Campaign For Real Equality to protest against all-women shortlists. She insisted that CLPs should be trusted, and encouraged, to pick whoever was the most able candidate and argued that the system also discriminated against the party's Asian members who were overwhelmingly male. Women members in Slough also launched a petition against 'the patronising view of women's capabilities inherent to the quota system'. One of the CLP's officers, Ann Scargu, said: 'If I want to become an MP or a councillor, I'm prepared to take on any man and beat him on merit - why make women helpless?' Slough was one of several CLPs which, by the end of 1995, had all-women shortlists imposed on them following the breakdown of their regional consensus meetings where, it was hoped, the CLP would volunteer for 'closed-list' status.

Adapted from Kelly 1996.

Questions

1. a) Using Items A-E, give the arguments for and against the view that there are likely to be substantially more women MPs by the year 2002.
   b) Suppose you were a woman who wanted to be selected as a parliamentary candidate in a safe Labour seat. What problems do you think you would face?
2. Look at Items A and B.
   a) Make a list of the conclusions that you can draw from examining Item A.
   b) How does Item B help you to explain the conclusions you have drawn from Item A?
3. a) 'It is crucial that more women parliamentary candidates are selected'. Give arguments for and against this view. Use Items C and D in your answer.
   b) Assess the validity of critical mass theory.
4. Make a list of the arguments for and against positive discrimination in candidate shortlists. Use Item E in your answer.

2.4 Black and Asian parliamentary candidates

Number of candidates

Although all the major parties claim that the ethnicity of a potential candidate has no bearing on the outcome of the selection process, the small number of black and Asian candidates selected suggests that this is not the case (see Chapter 5, Section 2.3 for an examination of the term 'ethnicity'). In 1997, just 42 black and Asian candidates were selected to fight seats for the major parties out of a total number of 1,918. Of these 42 candidates, 13 stood for Labour, ten for the Conservatives and 19 for the Liberal Democrats (Butler & Kavanagh 1997). This figure is higher than that in the 1992 election when 23 black and Asian candidates stood. Although all the main parties claimed that they wanted more black and Asian candidates, few of those selected stood for safe or winnable seats. In 1987, four black and Asian MPs were elected - the first to be elected since 1929. In 1992, all four retained their seats and the total number of black and Asian MPs rose to six. In 1997, nine black and Asian MPs were returned. All nine were Labour Party candidates. This raises two questions:

1. Why are so few black and Asian candidates selected?
2. Are there grounds to expect that more black and Asian candidates will be selected in the future?

Why are so few black and Asian candidates selected?

There are several reasons why so few black and Asian candidates are selected.

1. Discrimination

First, according to Terri Sewell:

'The most pernicious factor working against the selection of black candidates remains the popular perception that black candidates lose votes.' (Sewell 1993, p.136).

In other words, discrimination is a factor. It was observed in Chapter 5 (Item C in Activity 5.4) that 65% of people in Britain admit to being at least a little racist in their attitudes. Even if those involved in the selection process do not have racist attitudes themselves, they may decide against selecting a black or Asian candidate on the grounds that the majority of voters do have racist attitudes and might, therefore, refuse to vote for a black or Asian candidate.

2. Complacency

Second, traditionally, the Labour Party has attracted more support from black and Asian people than any other party (see Box 11.2). This means that it is easy for members of the Labour Party to justify the selection of white candidates on the grounds that black and Asian people have voted for white candidates in the past and there is, therefore, no need to make special provisions to increase the number of black and Asian candidates in the future.

Box 11.2 Black and Asian voting 1974-97

	1974 % (Oct)	1979 %	1983 %	1987 %	1992 %	1997 %
Labour	81	86	83	72	81	78
Conservative	9	8	7	18	10	17

This table shows the percentage of blacks and Asians who voted for the two main parties between 1974 and 1997.

Adapted from Saggar 1997.

3. Time and cost

Third, making a serious attempt to win a parliamentary candidature is both time consuming and costly (especially if a potential candidate is aiming to be selected in a constituency some distance from their home). Like many women (see Section 2.3 above), many potential black and Asian candidates may be deterred by the time and cost involved, especially given the low rate of success.

4. Educational and job experience

Fourth, in addition to time and cost, black and Asian people are, on average, less likely to be graduates than whites and they are under-represented in the 'brokerage' professions which are easily combined with a political career and from which many constituency parties like to select their candidates - barristers, university lecturers, trade union officials, journalists and political researchers. Media coverage may also have a deterrent effect since the images projected tend to reinforce the view that white politicians are the norm.

5. Lack of quotas

And fifth, none of the three main parties supports quotas or programmes of positive discrimination to ensure that more black and Asian people are selected. The nearest to creating any kind of structure was the Black Sections movement in the Labour Party which began in the 1980s. The aim was to create a group within the Labour Party which would enjoy the same status as the existing Women's and Youth Sections. Demands for Black Sections to have the right to nominate and select their own candidates, however, resulted in a battle within the party. This ended in compromise in 1990. Although there was no Black Section, the party set up:

'A single affiliated organisation for members of African, Caribbean and Asian descent with local and regional groups and direct representation on the National Executive Committee.' (Composite 8, Labour Party Conference 1990)

The result was the Labour Party Black Socialist Society which was allowed to elect one member of the NEC once individual membership reached 2,500 and a third of eligible trade unions affiliated to it (Labour Party Rules 1998, p.8).

Are more black and Asian candidates likely?

One way for parties to tempt black and Asian supporters away from the Labour Party might be to ensure that they select more black and Asian candidates, especially in seats where a significant proportion of the electorate is black. At the same time, if it is to retain the black vote, the Labour Party might take steps to ensure that the ethnic minorities are better represented. There is, however, little sign of this happening. Indeed, one report in 1998 suggested that black and Asian Labour councillors were being pushed out by white Blairites:

'The Labour Party is facing a high profile court case following the deselection of ethnic minority councillors in Birmingham...The Commission for Racial Equality has confirmed that it has received complaints from all over Britain as black councillors complain that they are losing out to "Blair's babes".' (*Observer*, 15 March 1998)

This report is significant because many people who are selected as parliamentary candidates have experience in local government. If the number of black and Asian councillors drops, this is likely to have a knock-on effect, perhaps even reducing the number of black and Asian parliamentary candidates in the long term.

Labour Party rule change, 1998

At national level, the Labour Party claims that it wishes to support more black and Asian candidates. Procedural changes were agreed at the 1998 conference requiring that one black or Asian candidate must be nominated by the constituency executive committee if one or more black or Asian members of the national panel expresses an interest in standing in that particular constituency. This requirement is unlikely to make a significant difference to the number of black and Asian candidates, however, since it does not guarantee a place on the shortlist, let alone selection as a parliamentary candidate.

Main points - Section 2.4

- In 1997, just 42 black and Asian candidates were selected to fight seats for the major parties out of a total number of 1,918.
- The main reason for the small number is the popular perception that black and Asian candidates lose votes. In addition, black and Asian people are deterred from standing because of time and cost or because they do not have the right experience or skills.
- None of the main parties supports quotas or programmes of positive discrimination to ensure that more black and Asian people are selected.
- There is little sign that constructive efforts are being made to increase numbers.

Activity 11.5 The selection of black and Asian candidates

Item A   *Black tribunes*

The riots of the 1980s served as a catalyst to black political participation in Britain. However unwelcome, they did raise the awareness of the nation to the needs and demands of black people. Diane Abbott specifically attributed her election to this effect. Similarly, the campaign for Black Sections in the Labour Party has also been cited by many black candidates as a factor in their selection. The best known example was the selection of Russell Profitt in Lewisham East. Profitt claimed: 'Black Sections provided a well organised group of people involved at grassroots level. Lewisham East was the first place where this tactic was successfully used to bring about the selection of someone who was black. I saw my selection as very much part of this campaign.' While it is difficult to know the extent to which black under-representation was considered by selectors in some constituencies which chose black candidates in 1987, the impact was clearly evident. This appears to have been a major consideration in the selection of Paul Boateng in Brent South, for example. 'It was very natural to choose a black candidate' confirmed one member of Brent South Labour Party: 'There was a general acceptance that Brent South should be represented by someone who truly reflected the multiracial nature of the community.'

Adapted from Sewell 1993.

Item B   *Black and Asian MPs, 1997*

Name	Party	Change in party's vote 1992 & 1997	Location of constituency	Re-elected, defeated or newly elected in 1997	Labour majority in 1992 (%)	Labour majority in 1997 (%)
D. Abbot	Labour	+6.4	London	re-elected	30.9	47.6
P. Boateng	Labour	+15.4	London	re-elected	26.5	57.1
B. Grant	Labour	+13.2	London	re-elected	26.7	53.6
P. Khabra	Labour	+14.7	London	re-elected	9.0	39.2
O. King	Labour	-7.2	London	newly elected	27.7	25.3
A. Kumar	Labour	+11.4	Middlesborough	newly elected	-2.4	19.8
M. Sarwar	Labour	+1.1	Glasgow	newly elected	15.4	9.0
M. Singh	Labour	-11.7	Bradford	newly elected	19.4	8.5
K. Vaz	Labour	+9.0	Leicester	re-elected	22.8	41.5
N. Deva	Conservative	-13.7	London	defeated	-2.8	25.7

This table shows a list of the black and Asian MPs elected in 1992 and those newly elected in 1997. One Asian MP, Nirj Deva, was defeated in 1997. All figures are percentages. The figures in the columns on the far right show the percentage lead that the candidate had over the candidate who came next.

Adapted from Saggar 1997.

Item C *The 1997 general election*

The total of 42 major party candidates from black and Asian backgrounds compares to 23 in 1992, with the Liberal Democrats accounting for most of the difference. Given that Labour was the only party with support in strength in black and Asian communities, it was clearly that party's responsibility to increase the number of non-white MPs. There were three main reasons why the gains made (from five to nine non-white Labour MPs) were proportionately large but, in real terms, slight. First, the Labour Party had a far stronger commitment to feminisation (to increasing the number of women candidates and MPs). Second, there were divisions between the various black and Asian groups. This made a

significant impact in two seats - Bethnal Green & Bow (where Conservative support rose by nearly 5%) and in Bradford West (where it fell by less than 1%). Both seats contain a significant Muslim minority and, in both seats, the Conservatives selected a Muslim whilst the Labour Party selected a black or Asian candidate who was not a Muslim. Although Labour won both seats, the swing showed that the black and Asian population had been split. And third, a large number of sitting white MPs were unwilling to give up their seats to local non-white challengers in heavily black or Asian constituencies.

Adapted from Butler & Kavanagh 1997.

Item D *Bethnal Green and Bow*

The 1997 general election presented an opportunity for the under-representation of black and Asian groups to be tackled. However, the issues associated with black and Asian representation are far from straightforward, as the case of Oona King, in Bethnal Green and Bow demonstrated. When the former Labour Cabinet minister Peter Shore announced his decision to retire, a controversial selection contest to seek his replacement followed. Eventually, Oona King was chosen. King's father is African-American and her mother a British Jew. However, although King's selection would potentially double the number of women from black and Asian groups (albeit from one to two), her selection provoked bitter resentment within the Bengali Muslim population on the grounds that a member of that community should have been selected for the seat. In the Bethnal Green and Bow

Bethnal Green and Bow		
Candidate	**Party**	**Votes**
Oona King	Lab	20,697
Kabir Choudhury	Con	9,412
Syed Nurai Islam	Lib Dem	5,361
David King	BNP	3,350
	Others	5,862
Total Vote		44,862
Lab majority		11,285
Swing Lab to Con		5.9%
Turnout		61.2%

constituency, 29.1% of the population is of Bengali origin. Both the Conservatives and Liberal Democrats chose Bengalis to contest the seat. The most significant aspect of the Bethnal Green result was the swing to the Conservative candidate, Kabir Choudhury, of 5.9%. This reveals the divisions within the local Bengali community.

Adapted from Geddes & Tonge 1997.

Questions

1. 'A significant breakthrough has been made by black and Asian candidates since the 1987 general election.' Using Items A and B, give arguments for and against this view.
2. What steps might be taken to increase the number of black and Asian candidates? Use Items A, C and D in

your answer.
3. Judging from Items C and D, and your own knowledge, what problems do black and Asian candidates have to overcome before they are selected?
4. What does Item D tell us about the difficulties black and Asian candidates might face once selected?

Part 3 How representative are MPs?

Key issues

1. What is the socio-economic background of MPs?
2. How do MPs' working conditions affect their ability to do their job effectively?
3. What pressures are there on MPs?
4. What rewards can MPs expect?

3.1 The socio-economic background of MPs.

Who becomes an MP?

The verdict of the voters translates a minority of parliamentary candidates into MPs. After each

general election, a significant number of new faces appear in the House of Commons. But, these new faces tend to look very much like those which they have replaced. If the criticism of parliamentary candidates is that they are predominantly white, male and middle-class, this criticism is even more apt for MPs.

The fact that most MPs come from a relatively narrow stratum in society is a cause of concern for those who argue that the House of Commons should be a microcosm of the nation. It patently is not. MPs are, on the whole, older and more highly educated than the general population. If the House of Commons was truly representative, 29 black MPs would have been elected in 1997 (rather than 9) and

332 women would have been elected (rather than 120).

The class background of MPs

In class terms (as judged by occupation), MPs are generally drawn from a narrow segment of society, regardless of the party in power. This is illustrated by Item A in Activity 11.6 below. Of the 629 MPs from the three main parties, only 56 have a manual working background (54 of these are Labour MPs), That makes just 8.9% of the total in a Parliament dominated by the party originally set up to provide representation for members of the working class. Indeed, in the 19th century one of the major criticisms of Parliament was that the House of Commons was made up entirely of people from the middle and upper classes. In the early part of the 20th century, this began to change as the franchise was extended and the Labour Party grew in popularity. Before the Second World War, a high proportion of Labour MPs had working-class backgrounds. The vast majority of MPs belonging to the three main parties in 1997 (546 MPs or 87%), however, have a background in social classes 1 and 2 (using the Registrar General's definition of class - see Chapter 5, Section 2.1) whilst just 9% have a background in social classes 3-5. In rough terms (classifications differ making comparisons difficult), this compares to 34% of the general population with an occupation in social classes 1 and 2 and 42% with a manual occupation (figures from Social Trends 1998, p.34).

The educational background of MPs

MPs' educational experiences are also not typical of the electorate as a whole (see Item B in Activity 11.6). For example, 440 MPs from the three main parties went to university (70%) compared to 14% of the population as a whole (figures from Social Trends 1998). Similarly, 28% of MPs from the three main parties went to public school compared to 7% of the general population (figures from ISIS 1998).

Recent figures show that the educational background of MPs is changing in the following ways:

- more and more MPs attend university
- the percentage of Labour MPs who attended university has never been higher - 66% of those elected in 1997 compared to 57% when Labour won the 1974 general election
- the percentage of Conservative MPs who attended university has never been higher (81%)
- the lowest ever number of Old Etonians was elected (15 Conservative MPs, two Labour MPs and one Liberal Democrat)
- just 9% of Conservative MPs were Old Etonians compared to 15% in 1979, 20% in 1959 and 29% in 1945.

(Adapted from Butler & Kavanagh 1997, p.204)

The age of MPs

Generally, MPs are middle-aged. The proportion of MPs aged over 60 has fallen as the work of MPs has increased. Although the voting age was reduced from 21 to 18 in 1969, the minimum age at which a person can stand as an MP remains 21.

In 1997, ten MPs under the age of 30 were elected, all of them Labour MPs (the youngest being Christopher Leslie who was 24 at the time of the election). This compares to just one MP under the age of 30 being elected in 1992. The larger number of very young candidates is a reflection of the size of Labour's win. In some cases, selectorates chose young candidates not because they expected they would win, but because they thought that fighting the seat would provide useful experience in the long term. Even so, it is clear from the small overall number of young candidates elected that selectorates are generally reluctant to select young people. As a result, many young people feel very remote from the typical MP who is a white man in his late 40s.

Why are many MPs middle-aged, white, middle-class men?

The selection process is likely to lead to the selection of candidates who are replicas of the selectorate. If most people involved in the selection process are middle-aged, white, middle-class men, then it is likely that they will choose people like themselves. Besides, the selectorate is often reluctant to choose candidates who do not conform to the stereotype supposedly popular with the voters. There are fears, often not openly expressed, that such candidates will be electoral liabilities. As noted above (Sections 2.3 and 2.4), this is particularly the case with women and black and Asian candidates. It is no surprise, therefore, that potential candidates who are untypical in some way often do not feel that it is worth pursuing their candidature.

The need for experience and skills

In safe and marginal seats, competition is usually intense and the selectorate looks for a candidate of exceptional ability. In such circumstances, previous political experience (service as a local councillor or previous nominations as a parliamentary candidate) is often a prerequisite. Such experience is almost inevitably linked to age. Young candidates have little chance of competing against more experienced colleagues.

Similarly, a university education is often regarded as a sign of a trained mind and is, therefore, taken as an indication that a person would be capable of handling the complexities of the work of an MP. Since much of that work requires communication skills, it is, perhaps, little surprise that occupations such as barrister, solicitor, teacher and lecturer are often seen as suitable training.

Political complexion and class background

The political complexion and class background of

the parties at local and national level inevitably affects the make-up of the House of Commons. Given the make-up of all the parties, it is perhaps no surprise, therefore, that most MPs are middle-aged, white, middle-class men.

Main points - Section 3.1

- 87% of MPs belonging to the three main parties in 1997 have a background in social classes 1 and 2, compared to 34% of the general population. Just 9% of MPs have a background in social classes 3-5, compared to 42% of the general population.
- 28% of MPs from the three main parties went to public school compared to 7% of the general population.
- Only ten MPs elected in 1997 were under 30.
- The selection process is likely to lead to the selection of candidates who are replicas of the selectorate. If most people involved in the selection process are middle-aged, white, middle-class men, then it is likely that they will choose people like themselves.

Activity 11.6 MPs elected in 1997

Item A   Occupations of MPs elected in 1992 and 1997

Occupation	Labour 1992	Labour 1997	Conservative 1992	Conservative 1997	Liberal Democrat 1992	Liberal Democrat 1997
Professions:	**115**	**188**	**131**	**61**	**12**	**23**
Lawyer	17	29	60	29	6	6
Civil servant/local government	16	30	10	5	0	2
Teaching (all levels)	76	111	22	8	4	7
Other professions	6	18	39	19	2	8
Business	**22**	**37**	**128**	**65**	**2**	**11**
Manual worker	**59**	**54**	**4**	**1**	**0**	**1**
Miscellaneous:	**75**	**139**	**73**	**38**	**6**	**11**
White collar	36	69	9	2	1	1
Politics*	24	40	20	15	2	5
Publisher/journalist	13	29	28	14	3	4
Other	2	1	16	7	0	1

For example, lobbyists, political agents or members of think tanks.

Adapted from Butler & Kavanagh 1992 and 1997.

Item B   Educational background of MPs, 1992 and 1997

	Labour 1992	Labour 1997	Conservative 1992	Conservative 1997	Lib Dem 1992	Lib Dem 1997
State school	43	50	19	5	2	5
State school & degree	188	301	109	51	8	22
Public school	0	2	28	9	0	1
Public school & degree	40	65	180	100	10	18
Total	**271**	**418**	**336**	**165**	**20**	**46**
Oxford or Cambridge	44	61	151	84	6	15
Other universities	122	214	94	49	9	17
All universities	**166**	**275**	**245**	**133**	**15**	**32**
%	61	66	73	81	75	70
Eton	2	2	34	15	0	1
Other public schools	38	65	174	94	10	18
All public schools	**40**	**67**	**208**	**109**	**10**	**19**
%	14	16	62	66	50	41

Adapted from Butler & Kavanagh 1992 and 1997.

Item C *MPs, members and voters, 1987*

	Conservative Party			Labour Party		
	MPs	Members	Voters	MPs	Members	Voters
	%	%	%	%	%	%
Classes 1 & 2	90	46	31	66	56	14
Class 3	9	41	39	15	18	23
Classes 4 & 5	1	12	31	19	26	63
Public schools	68	-	9	14	-	3
Further Education	82	14	13	79	32	10
University	70	-	11	56	-	6
Oxbridge	44	-	-	15	-	-
Women	5	58	52	9	41	52
Ethnic minorities	0	-	2	2	-	9

This table uses the Registrar General's definition of class (see Chapter 5, Section 2.1).

Adapted from Crewe 1993.

Questions

1. 'It is misleading to list MPs' characteristics as if they are a single species because Labour and Conservative members differ significantly along most dimensions.' Judging from Items A-D would you agree with this statement?

2. 'In social, if not political, terms Conservative and Labour MPs have more in common with each other than with the party members who selected them or the voters who elected them.' Is there evidence in Items A and B to support this view?

3. Give arguments for and against the view that the type of people becoming (i) Labour MPs and (ii) Conservative MPs has changed over the last 20 years. Use Items A-C in your answer.

4. a) Would you describe Colin Pickthall (Item D) as a typical Labour MP? Explain why.
   b) How would you expect his profile to differ if he was (i) a Liberal Democrat MP or (ii) a Conservative MP?

Item D *Profile of a Labour MP*

Name:	Colin Pickthall
Date of birth:	13 September 1944
Party:	Labour
First elected:	April 1992
Constituency:	Lancashire West
Schools:	Broughton Road County Primary 1952-56 (State School) Ulverston Grammar 1956-63 (State School)
University:	University of Wales 1963-66 (BA-English & History) University of Lancaster 1966-67 (MA-Socialism and English poetry in the 1930s &1950s)
Former employment:	Labourer in Shipyards Teacher at Ruffwood Comprehensive School, Kirkby 1967-70 Lecturer Edge Hill College 1970-92
Previous political experience:	County Councillor 1989-93 Chair of Governers, Skelmersdale College of Further Education
Parents:	Father worked in shipyards in Barrow-in-Furness Mother was a housewife

Adapted from interviews held in November 1994 and July 1998.

3.2 How accountable are MPs?

Theories of representation

Section 3.1 above established that most MPs are not representative of their constituents in terms of their class, gender, ethnicity and age. But, this does not mean that MPs cannot represent their constituents in some other way. There are three main theories of representation.

1. Trustee model

The trustee model was first articulated by Edmund Burke (who lived between 1729 and 1797). In a speech to his constituents in Bristol in 1774, Burke argued that, if they elected him as their MP, they should expect not a slavish concern to please them but the exercise of his own judgement and conscience. According to this theory of representation, although MPs have a duty to consult and to take into account the opinions of their constituents, their primary duty is to act according to their own consciences. In other words, voters hand responsibility for decision making to trustees (ie representatives). The prevalence of this view amongst British MPs explains why, for example, the House of Commons has consistently voted against the reintroduction of the death penalty even though surveys have shown that a majority of voters supports it.

2. Delegate model

The second theory is that MPs are the voters' delegates and it is their job to act as a mouthpiece through which the voters' concerns are voiced. The MPs' personal views on a matter are not relevant and should be suppressed. If MPs subscribe to this theory, therefore, they will vote according to the dictates of their constituents rather than according to the dictates of conscience. In practice, it is difficult for MPs to adhere strictly to this theory because issues arise where constituents are split and it is unclear what the majority view is. Besides, many MPs believe that it is their job to give a lead - something which a delegate cannot do.

3. Mandate model

A third theory is that MPs are not elected on their own individual merits but because they are members of a particular political party. Once elected, MPs have a popular mandate to ensure that the policies outlined in the party's manifesto are put into effect. It is, therefore, their job to support their party at all times (unless the party is failing to deliver its manifesto promises). Since loyalty to party comes first, at times it will be necessary to suppress personal views or to ignore the views of constituents.

Accountability

Accountability means explaining to interested parties why a particular course of action has been taken and being open to criticism about that course of action from those interested parties. The three contradictory views of the role of a representative described above ensure that there are different views about the parties to whom an MP is or should be accountable.

MPs who support the Burkean view of representation do not have to account for their actions, other than to explain that they voted according to their conscience. Of course, if they choose to ignore the views of their constituents completely, there is the chance that they will not be elected next time. Also, there is usually great pressure from the party whips to conform with the party line. But, if MPs are allowed a free vote, there is, in theory, no reason for those who follow the Burkean line to worry about accountability.

MPs who see themselves as delegates are much more directly accountable. It is their duty to carry out the wishes of their constituents and they must, therefore, be able to convince their constituents that they have exercised their powers and discharged their duties properly. As a result, delegate MPs tend to have a high profile in their constituency.

MPs who subscribe to the mandate model place party above constituent or conscience. They fulfil their duty by voting for their party and pressing the party leadership to fulfil its manifesto commitments. Mandate MPs are unlikely to rebel or vote against their party even if, privately, they do not agree with the decisions made. After the 1997 general election, there was some criticism that Labour backbenches were too loyal to the leadership. Many commentators argued, for example, that more MPs should have voted according to their conscience over the cutting of benefit for single mothers rather than voting according to the wishes of the party leadership.

Accountability in practice

In practice, politicians veer between the three models, depending on what seems expedient at the time. Understandably, therefore, it is difficult to determine a hard and fast rule about just how accountable MPs are or to whom they are accountable. It could be argued, however, that they are accountable to their constituents, to their party and to their conscience all at the same time and it is by the way in which they resolve any conflicts which arise from this that they are judged.

Accountability and backbench MPs

The work of backbench MPs has a direct bearing on their accountability. During the course of their work, MPs meet groups from their constituency, have meetings with party officials at both local and national level and pursue their own particular causes and interests. MPs also have access to the media and employ a secretarial staff. As a result, during the course of their work, they are able to explain to interested parties why a particular course of action has been taken and they provide opportunities for criticism about that course of action from those interested parties. All MPs hold constituency surgeries, for example, where constituents have the opportunity of airing grievances or questioning an MP's behaviour.

A growing workload

To be accountable, MPs have to be seen to be active in their constituency (to maintain the support of party members and their constituents). On average, constituencies cover 150 square miles and their boundaries are set so that there are c.65,000 constituents. It is, therefore, simply not practical for MPs to meet all or even most constituents. In addition, most constituencies are a long way away from Westminster and so MPs have to spend a great deal of time travelling to and from Parliament. This means the time spent meeting constituents is limited.

In Parliament, the volume of MPs' work has grown as the activities of government have grown. Parliamentary sessions last longer and more legislation is passed than was the case at the beginning of the century. In 1900, the average length of a public Act was 200 pages. By the 1970s, it was 2,000 pages. Similarly, the average length of a parliamentary session has risen from 129 days before 1914 to 163 days since 1945. In addition, the development of select committees (see Chapter 14, Section 2.3) has resulted in more work for the 25% of MPs who sit on them. Some MPs spend 20 hours per week preparing for and attending these committees.

MPs' hours and working conditions

In 1998, the allowances provided for office costs were £47,568 a year (Public Information Office, July 1998). As a result, most MPs can afford to pay for two or more members of staff to act as researchers and secretaries.

A survey published in 1994 of the 1992 intake of new MPs suggested that many MPs work for more than 70 hours per week when the House is sitting

(Watts 1994). It has been a longstanding criticism of the House of Commons that most MPs do not have adequate facilities to do this work efficiently. Inadequate facilities make it difficult for people to perform their duties efficiently. So, if MPs do not appear to be accountable to their constituents, inadequate facilities may be a contributory factor. This is set to change, however. In 1998, building work began on a new block of offices for MPs. Situated next to Parliament and connected to the Commons by an underground tunnel, this new block will accommodate 200 MPs and their assistants, providing 400 offices as well as rooms for conferences and select committee meetings and a 200-seat restaurant. The new offices are being built in lavish style with bronze and brass fittings. The total cost of the building has been estimated at £240 million - which works out at £10,000 per square metre (*Observer*, 13 September 1998).

The growth of 'professional' MPs

In 1981, Anthony King wrote an article identifying a new breed of 'professional' or 'career' politicians. These were MPs who had entered Parliament at a relatively young age and whose aim was to retain their seats for the whole of their working lives. These MPs, he argued, looked upon their work as a career with the same promotional prospects and the same insecurity that could be found in any profession (King 1981). After the 1997 general election, there was a total of 60 MPs who described their occupational backgrounds as 'politician or political organiser'. In addition, 37 MPs had experience of the civil service or local government (see above, Item A in Activity 11.6). Student activism was also a route for some Labour MPs. Five of Labour's new MPs had been past presidents of the National Union of Students (NUS) and others had been full-time NUS officers (*Labour Research*, June 1997). All these MPs were 'professional' politicians in the sense that it was through paid political work that they were noticed and selected as candidates. Like those MPs identified by King, these MPs hoped for continuous re-election and promotion to ministerial post and the Cabinet.

Greater professionalism is also suggested by longer-term trends. In 1945, the average length of service as an MP was just over five years. In 1974, it was ten years (Vallence 1988). Box 11.3 shows the parliamentary experience of MPs elected in 1997.

Professional politicians and accountability

The growth of professional politicians has a bearing on the question of the accountability of MPs in the sense that, if the main concern of MPs is remaining in office and gaining promotion, this will necessarily affect the way in which they perform the job. It might mean, for example, that, in the hope of being promoted, they always support the advice of party whips and never vote according to conscience or take note of the wishes of constituents. On the other hand,

Box 11.3 Parliamentary experience in 1997

First entered parliament	Labour	Conservative	Lib Dem
1950-59	2	5	-
1960-69	10	2	1
1970-74	27	23	2
1975-79	20	17	-
1980-83	29	32	6
1984-87	62	25	6
1988-92	78	28	3
1993-97	190	33	28
Total	**418**	**165**	**46**

Adapted from Butler & Kavanagh 1997.

it might mean that they are prepared to work harder for constituents in the hope of being re-elected.

Accountability and ministers?

A large minority of MPs who belong to the governing party achieve ministerial office. Government ministers are obliged to take individual ministerial responsibility for the work undertaken in their departments (see Chapter 13, Section 1.3) and collective responsibility for the work of government (see Chapter 12, Section 2.3). As a result, ministers are bound by collective decision making. This automatically reduces their leeway as representatives.

In all matters concerning their ministerial work, ministers are (in theory at least) accountable to Parliament. They must, therefore, answer questions on their brief in the House and they must reply to written questions from MPs.

Ministers work long hours and have heavy workloads. As well as their ministerial duties, they also have the normal parliamentary and constituency duties to perform. The sheer volume of work makes it difficult for a minister to be an efficient representative.

Main points - Section 3.2

- There are three main theories of representation - the trustee model; (2) the delegate model; and (3) the mandate model.
- Accountability means explaining to interested parties why a particular course of action has been taken and being open to criticism about that course of action.
- There are different views as to whom an MP is or should be accountable. In practice, politicians veer between the trustee model, delegate model and mandate model.
- The type of work done by backbench MPs and their workload has a direct bearing on their accountability.
- There is a debate about whether the growth of professional MPs has made MPs more or less accountable.
- In all matters concerning their ministerial work, ministers are accountable to Parliament.

Activity 11.7 Accountability and MPs

Item A *Professional politicians*

Critics take the view that it is unhealthy for the House to have MPs whose background is limited to politics. An experience in other spheres ensures a House that is better informed and able to appreciate concerns and problems. A second problem is that the ambition to achieve promotion might ensure slavish obedience to the whips in the House. A third is that constituents might come to see the House as an essentially closed institution, full of career politicians driven by ambition for office rather than by a desire to serve their constituents. This could undermine trust in Parliament. On the other hand, knowledge of the political world ensures that some new members already know how to use parliamentary procedures. Given the demands now made of members by constituents and pressure groups, the capacity to hit the ground running is a valuable one. Also, the rise of the career politician over the past 20 years has coincided with a rise in greater backbench dissension. Most important, however is the fact that, for the career politician, it is essential to be re-elected. Volatility in voting intentions (more pronounced since the mid-1960s) ensures that members are aware of their electoral vulnerability. To try to bolster support, tremendous effort is put into constituency activity and casework.

Adapted from Norton 1994.

Item B *Difficulties faced by MPs*

Labour's election landslide has produced some unexpected problems. First, it is difficult to manage the Parliamentary Labour Party (PLP). Many Labour MPs are becoming frustrated because there is little chance of promotion. Already, it is rumoured that ambitious Labour MPs do not get along with each other because of the highly competitive climate that exists within the PLP. Many have been told to look after the needs of their constituents and to become super-MPs, but they complain that this will merely result in them becoming super-councillors. And second, research shows that the new intake of Labour MPs are suffering from the stress of the job - the hot-house pressures, the long working hours and the travelling. Those with pre-school children or adolescent children are under particular stress, as are those whose constituencies are far away. The Labour landslide was responsible for some of the problems. Some MPs did not expect to win and arrived in the House of Commons unprepared for a massive change of lifestyle. Because so many were newcomers, they were thrown in at the deep end, with hardly enough desks and not enough people to show them around. Over 50% of new MPs complained that they had little or no training. Some didn't even know their way around the House. As many as 40% complained of lack of resources. They were told: 'Here's a desk, here's a phone, off you go.'

Adapted from Robins 1998 and the *Guardian* 28 March 1998.

Item C *A minister's workload in 1977*

Name: Tony Benn
Status: Labour MP for Bristol SE & Secretary of State for Energy

TOTAL WORKLOAD IN 1977

1. **MP for Bristol SE**
   50 public engagements; 12 speeches in the city; 16 surgeries; 5,000 letters to be dealt with.
2. **Member of Bristol SE CLP**
   4 general meetings; 20 branch meetings; a membership drive; 5 Labour Group meetings.
3. **MP in House of Commons**
   129 votes registered; The House sat for 149 days.
4. **Member of PLP**
   12 PLP Meetings; 14 Speeches to Sub-committees.
5. **Secretary of State for Energy**
   3 energy Bills; 8 Speeches to House; 5 parliamentary Statements; 154 meetings with non-government organisations; 8 meetings of energy sub-committees; 1-3 hours per night work on government papers.
6. **Member of the Cabinet**
   42 Cabinet meetings; 106 Cabinet committee meetings; 4 Cabinet papers submitted; 45 Cabinet sub-committee papers submitted; 1,750 Cabinet papers received.
7. **Member of Labour party NEC**
   15 NEC meetings; 62 NEC committee meetings.
8. **International Work**
   19 visits abroad; 32 meetings with foreign ministers; 6 EC Council meetings.
9. **General political works**
   80 speeches; 83 radio interviews; 57 television interviews; 34 press conferences; 16 articles; 30 interviews with individual journalists; 1,000 letters received or answered which did not involve constituency work.

Adapted from the *Guardian*, 11 February 1978.

Item D *An MP's workload in 1997*

Monday	
9 am	Office
10 am	Surgery in constituency
1 pm	Meeting with district councillors in Coleford.
3 pm	Meeting with Health Authority in Gloucester.
3.30 pm	Drive to London.
5.30 pm	Discussion meeting with the Road Hauliers Association.
7 pm	Vote - 3-line whip.
7.30 pm	Dinner with South West Tourist Board.
10 pm	Vote - 3-line whip.

Tuesday	
10 pm	Meeting of the Agriculture Select Committee Food Safety Investigation.
1 pm	Meeting with the UK Women of Europe.
1.30 pm	Meeting with Sky Television.
2 pm	Meeting with Talk Radio.
2.30 pm	House of Commons - Agriculture Questions followed by a debate in the chamber.
4.15 pm	Meeting of the Statutory Investments Select Committee.
6 pm	All-party group on Heritage.
7 pm	Vote - 3-line whip.
7.30 pm	Television interview on Severn Bridge Tolls.
10 pm	Vote - 3-line whip.

The information above was supplied by Diana Organ (Labour MP for Forest of Dean) in July 1998. The two days outlined are typical of her working week. She said that gaps between appointments were spent doing casework or attending sessions in the Commons. She also worked on Saturday between 11 am and 3.30 pm.

Questions

1. To whom are MPs accountable and to whom should they be accountable? Use Items A-D in your answer.

2. a) Using Item A, give the arguments for and against the view that the growth of career politicians is a cause for concern.
   b) Would you say that the growth of career politicians is likely to result in MPs becoming more or less accountable to: (i) their constituents (ii) their local party and (iii) their parliamentary colleagues? Give reasons for your answer.

3. a) Judging from Items B and D, why do you think MPs suffer from stress?
   b) How do MPs' hours and working conditions affect their accountability?

4. a) 'A minister and a backbench MP are accountable to different groups of people.' Explain this statement using Items C and D.
   b) How would you attempt to hold your own MP accountable?

3.3 Pressures on MPs - who pulls the strings?

Factors exerting pressure

MPs are not just elected to represent parliamentary constituencies. They also represent their political party. In addition, they may have trade union or business connections. They may be members of pressure groups. They are usually members of their parliamentary party (not always - Martin Bell was elected as an independent MP in 1997) and they all have their own personal and financial interests.

All these factors exert pressures on MPs, but they do not necessarily pull in the same direction. In fact, an MP can often face pressure to act in one way from one side and in the opposite way from another side. On every occasion when a decision is made, an MP has to make a choice between competing views.

Links with the community

Most MPs claim, when they have been elected, that they intend to represent all their constituents even though it was probably a minority who voted for them. In practice, however, MPs cannot possibly know the views of all their constituents. In any case, their constituents' views are likely to be divided.

Individuals do lobby their MPs by writing letters and attending constituency surgeries. Occasionally, they will go to Westminster to lobby their MP in person at the House of Commons.

MPs usually try to meet local organisations and local pressure groups to show that they are concerned about the views they hold. It is easier for them to promise to represent these views either when they are in line with broad party policy or where the issues are not party political. On occasion, very strong local feelings can present a dilemma for the

MP if those feelings do not accord with party policy.

Parliamentary pressures

At Westminster, nearly all MPs are subject to a party whip. The whips are key figures in the political parties. Not only do they work to maintain party discipline and loyalty amongst MPs, they also serve as a communication line along which views can be carried between backbenchers and the party leadership. The government's Chief Whip has been described as:

> 'A personnel manager whose job it is to keep the legislative production line running to prevent strikes at minimum expense.'
> (*Guardian*, 19 October 1992)

This is achieved through an elaborate network of information, including information on MPs' strengths and weaknesses and even some details about their private lives.

Control in the Labour Party

In the build-up to the 1997 general election, the Labour leadership tightened its grip on Labour MPs. New rules were introduced to the standing orders of the Parliamentary Labour Party which stipulated that Labour MPs should do nothing 'which brings the party into disrepute' (*Guardian*, 3 December 1996). After the election, control was further tightened with the NEC authorising the whips to send reports on sitting MPs to their constituency parties (CLPs), detailing 'their voting record and parliamentary conduct' (*Guardian*, 28 May 1998). This measure was seen as an invitation to CLPs to deselect dissident MPs.

Parliamentary arithmetic

The 1997 election resulted in a large overall majority for Labour (178 seats), making it unlikely that the government would be defeated in the Commons. A small overall parliamentary majority, however, can lead to government defeats if backbenchers rebel. But, MPs are well aware of the costs of such rebellions - defeat for the government could lead to a vote of no confidence. This, in turn, could lead to a general election in which they might lose their seats.

As well as the formal pressures from the whips there are informal pressures from colleagues and the knowledge that disloyalty could end the chance of promotion.

Sponsorship

The Labour Party operates a system of 'constituency plan agreements' between unions and selected CLPs. Money from the affiliated trade union is given to the local CLP to help finance a forthcoming general election campaign. There were approximately 100 such agreements in operation for the 1997 general election, concentrated in the marginal seats. These constituency plan agreements were introduced after the Nolan Report was published in 1995. They replaced the sponsorship of individual Labour MPs by trade unions because that system had led to accusations that sponsored MPs were in the pocket of the unions.

Nevertheless, virtually all of the 418 Labour MPs elected in 1997 were union members. Unions hope that MPs who are union members will promote the interests of unions in a general sense as well as taking up particular causes in which a union has an interest.

Members' interests

In 1965, James Callaghan commented:

> 'When I look at some members discussing the Finance Bill I do not think of them as the hon. member for X, Y or Z. I look at them and say "investment trusts", "capital speculators" or "that fellow who is the stock exchange man who makes a profit on gilt edged".'

The concern that MPs' extra-parliamentary activities influence their behaviour in Parliament has grown in recent years. Many MPs continue to have business interests which they maintain whilst serving as MPs.

Because of the fear of corruption and the possibility that MPs might be concealing vested interests when they took part in parliamentary activities, Parliament established a Register of Members' Interests in 1975. But, although MPs had to declare an interest when speaking in debates in the House, they did not have to do so when asking parliamentary questions, signing early day motions or voting - so long as they had declared their interests in the Register.

The Commons Standards and Privileges Committee

A series of scandals involving MPs' earnings, including the Cash for Questions scandal in 1994 (see Chapter 14, Section 2.5), led to the creation of a new Commons Standards and Privileges Committee with a permanent Commissioner (initially, Sir Gordon Downey). The Commissioner's job is to report on MPs' interests and conduct, and to oversee the compilation, maintenance and accessibility of the Register of Members' Interests.

Since November 1995 (when MPs voted to accept the recommendations of the Nolan Report), MPs have been required to make available for public inspection any contracts relating to the provision of services in their capacity as MPs and to declare in the Register of Members' Interests what they were paid for such services. Precise details of payment are not required, though MPs do have to declare what they were paid in bands of £5,000 (*Labour Research*, July 1996). In addition, the Parliamentary Order Paper shows if an MP has a relevant interest when signing early day motions or tabling written questions or amendments (*Guardian*, 7 November 1995).

Inadequate register?

Despite these reforms, there is growing evidence that the Register is still inadequate, does not provide enough information and leaves questions unanswered. The first Register to be published using the new guidelines came out in April 1996. This showed that:

> 'Some 80 Conservative MPs, including 25 former ministers and one Prime Minister, have

failed to declare their earnings from some or all of their extra-parliamentary activities. In addition, five Labour MPs and two Liberal Democrats did not provide earnings details from directorships...Many are doing this on the basis that they judge their work to be unrelated to their "capacity as an MP".' (*Labour Research*, July 1996)

In April 1996, the Register suggested that MPs earned up to £2.76 million from their extra-parliamentary activities. But, a year later, *Labour Research* claimed that:

> 'The big money earned by some MPs does not have to be declared in the Register... Investigations have revealed that the undeclared earnings of just three Conservative MPs amounted to more than the £2.76 million declared in the Register.' (*Labour Research*, April 1997)

Ministers' interests

On joining the government, ministers are expected to resign from any directorships that they might hold and to make sure that any investments are placed into the hands of independent advisers through 'blind trusts' so that the minister has no involvement in or knowledge of any financial transactions. If the investments are likely to impinge directly on their work, they are encouraged to dispose of them. This procedure is designed to protect ministers from conflicts of interest and possible corruption.

In the Register of Members' Interests examined by *Labour Research* in 1993, only 43 out of the 83 ministers declared that they had nil interest (*Labour Research*, March 1993). The Labour government elected in 1997 had fewer ministers with a background in business, but two ministers who did have business interests soon found themselves under attack from the opposition and the media. The Paymaster General, Geoffrey Robinson, was criticised for holding offshore trusts and for failing to make a full declaration in the Register of Members' Interests. And, Lord Simon (a former chairman of BP appointed as Minister in the Department of Trade and Industry) was criticised for holding £2.4 million worth of shares in BP at the time of his appointment.

Lobby Firms

Parliamentary consultants or 'lobbyists' who claim to have inside knowledge of the ways in which ministers, civil servants and Parliament work, sell their services to whoever can afford to pay them. They represent the views of their clients to those making political and administrative decisions and seek to influence the outcome.

During the period 1992-97, there was growing concern about the development of lobby firms, especially those which were run by MPs or employed MPs to do work for them. By 1995, there were more than 60 of these specialised companies with a turnover of over £10 million a year. In addition, major public relations companies were engaged in lobbying. The inside knowledge that these companies claimed was based partly on the fact that many of them employed or were run by MPs (in 1995, there were 167 MPs with more than 350 consultancies between them - *Observer*, 21 May 1995)

Although it was not illegal for an MP to be a paid consultant for a company, the proliferation of consultancies during the 1990s, and the links between MPs and lobby firms, became a cause for concern because any individual could set up a lobby company and begin business and there was no external or internal regulation of their activities. In 1994, Vandermark commented:

> 'Some MPs allege that a number of their colleagues' financial links with these firms, in the form of an executive directorship or monthly sponsorship payment , is tantamount to being "bought". Political commentators have shared their anxiety, believing that the many lobbyists who claim to be able to "sell influence" are achieving this by effectively paying MPs to take account of their concerns first.' (Vandermark 1994, p.34)

Growing opposition

Media exposure of the work of these lobby companies ensured that public perception of the work done by MPs suffered. In a survey conducted by Gallup in 1995, for example, two-thirds of respondents agreed that 'most MPs make a lot of money by using public office improperly'. This view was enhanced by the sleaze allegations against a number of Conservative MPs and Ministers - especially those against Tim Smith and Neil Hamilton, two junior Ministers who had taken cash and gifts from the owner of Harrods, Mohamed Al Fayed and the lobbyist Ian Greer. It was to counter this public cynicism that the Nolan Report recommended that MPs should be banned from working for lobbying firms that had more than one client and that MPs should disclose their employment contract and earnings from outside interests.

Despite opposition from some (mainly Conservative) MPs, the recommendations of the Nolan Report were accepted by the Commons and, after the 1997 general election, the number of consultancies declared on the Register of Members' Interests dropped significantly.

The 'Cash for Secrets' scandal

New concerns about the activities of lobby companies arose in 1998. In the build-up to the 1997 general election, Labour frontbenchers and top party officials had employed a large number of advisers. Some of these moved into official advisory posts when the new Labour government was formed. Some were recruited by lobby companies because they were believed to have inside knowledge about the new government's thinking and important contacts. Others formed their own lobby companies. The influence of these lobbyists was exposed by the *Observer* in July 1998. Using reporters who posed as company representatives seeking insider knowledge and introductions to key Labour ministers, the newspaper discovered lobby companies offering (for a fee):

- meetings with government ministers and special advisors
- access to advance copies of select committee reports
- help with securing a place on government task forces (whose job is to formulate policy)
- advance knowledge of the Chancellor's Mansion House speech
- lunch at 10 Downing Street
- help with winning approval for take-over bids.

Most worrying of all was the influence that the lobbyists had with key figures in the new Labour administration. Derek Draper (a lobbyist who worked for the company GPC), for example, arranged a meeting between Roger Liddle, a member of Tony Blair's Policy Unit, and an *Observer* reporter who was posing as a someone representing big United States energy concerns. The *Observer* claimed that Roger Liddle said:

'Just tell me what you want and who you want to meet and Derek [Draper] and I will make the call for you.' (*Observer*, 5 July 1998)

Draper himself boasted:

'There are 17 people who count. To say that I am intimate with every one of them is the understatement of the century.' (*Observer*, 5 July 1998)

While there were no allegations of wrongdoing by Labour ministers, the 'Cash for Secrets' scandal, as it became known, raised serious questions about the activities of lobby companies and the links between lobbyists and key Labour advisers.

Main points - Section 3.3

- **MPs come under pressure from their constituents when they meet them or receive letters from them.**
- **At Westminster, MPs come under pressure from their party whips.**
- **Financial pressures include sponsorship from trade unions and paid extra-parliamentary work.**
- **Following a number of scandals, MPs have to disclose more information in the Register of Members' Interests.**
- **Lobbyists also try to put pressure on MPs and ministers. MPs are now banned from joining lobbying companies, but there is evidence that lobbyists still have influence.**

Activity 11.8 Pressures on MPs

Item A *Members' interests*

CAMPBELL, Anne (Labour, Cambridge)

1. **Remunerated directorships**
   The Welding Institute (TWI). (£5,001-£10,000).

2. **Remunerated employment, office, profession etc.**
   Occasional fees from broadcasting and journalism. £500 fee from Barclays New Features to judge the '97 Schools' competition.

4. **Sponsorship or financial or material support**
   The assistance of Ms Lesley Bulman to work as a research assistant beginning on 21 August 1995 to 31 May 1997. Her services were donated by Consultants, Recruitment and Training (CRT) Ltd. (£20,001 - £25,000).
   Loan of a TV set and set-top box under the Cambridge Interactive Trial scheme being run by Online Media and Cambridge Cable.

5. **Gifts, benefits and hospitality (UK)**
   Gift of modem, software and subscription to Internet connection from UKnet Pipex, Cambridge.
   One year's subscription to *Research Fortnight* journal in return for writing one article for them. (Registered 13 May 1998).

6. **Overseas visits**
   23-27 June 1997, to San Francisco, to speak at GIGA conference. 'Business online 97', at the request of Andersen Consulting and paid for by the conference organisers. (Registered 6 July 1997).

8. **Land and property**
   Freehold of holiday cottage in Brittany, France. (No net income from letting this property).

10. **Miscellaneous and unremunerated interests**.
    Chair of Opportunity Links - an information service enabling welfare-to-work for parents (unremunerated).

NB There were no entries under numbers 3,7 and 9.

Adapted from the Register for Members' Interests, June 1998.

Item B *Lobbyists (1)*

A troubling parallel for the Labour government is with the sleaze which poisoned the Major administration in its final years. Then, as now, lobbyists were revealed to be swaggering around London bragging of their ability to open the doors of power to those willing to pay. For a government elected on a wave of disgust at Tory sleaze, the parallel is uncomfortable - especially Derek Draper's, 'I just want to stuff my bank account at £250 an hour' comment. The idea that profiteering followed an election victory fuelled by public hunger for clean politics is hard to stomach. But, there are two important distinctions to be made. First, the worst element in Tory sleaze was not that the lobbyist Ian Greer traded his contacts with ministers and MPs but that the politicians themselves were on the take. There is no suggestion of that here. A second distinction centres on lobbying itself. One of the companies named by the *Observer*, LLM, insists it offers only advice and analysis, not access. It guides clients through the political maze the way lawyers guide clients through the law. But one LLM executive boasted about his ability to contact Gordon Brown. This suggests LLM was crossing the line it had drawn. Many would doubtless wish lobbyists did not exist and big businesses wrote to their MPs like the rest of us. That is unrealistic, but there needs to be hard thinking on how the industry might be supervised.

Adapted from the *Guardian*, 7 July 1998.

Item C   *Lobbyists (2)*

This cartoon was published on 12 July 1998, at the time when the Cash for Secrets scandal was dominating the news.

Item D   *Pressure from the party*

Before the 1997 general election, Labour Party headquarters issued a contract (described as a 'toolbox of good practice' by officials) to all Labour candidates. In return for extra funding and support from party headquarters, candidates were issued with targets for meeting voters, organising discussions and recruiting members. That explains why Shona McIssac, a newly elected Labour MP could be found at the fish market in Grimsby at 6.45 am on 16 June 1998. Her seat had been one of 90 target seats in 1997. Not only did she receive extra funding from party headquarters, hundreds of party workers were bussed in from safer seats nearby. She won the seat with a majority of 10,000. In return, the party wants its payback. It is her job to work hard for the party - and that means making sure she has a high profile in her constituency. At party headquarters, officials point out that money is scarce. The contracts were issued to candidates, they explain, to ensure that seats with new Labour MPs are in the strongest possible position by the time of the Euro-elections in June 1999.

Adapted from the *Guardian*, 17 June 1998.

Item E   *Influencing Parliamentary decisions*

1.	Contacting members of the House of Lords	77.3
2.	Circulating documents to all or many MPs	65.4
3.	Circulating documents to Standing Committee	58.3
4.	Asking MPs to propose an amendment	53.6
5.	Asking MPs to ask parliamentary questions	53.6
6.	Asking MPs to speak in second reading debate	52.6
7.	Arranging to meet MPs or hold seminar for them	49.3
8.	Asking MP to arrange meeting with minister	31.3
9.	Direct contact with ministers or civil servants	17.5
10.	Organising lobby or letter writing campaign	7.6
11.	Using the media	1.9
12.	Cooperating with other pressure groups	1.4
13.	Not specified	0.5

This table shows the result of a 1989 survey. Lobbyists were asked which techniques they used to influence the outcome of parliamentary decisions (the figures show the percentage of those questioned who used the technique).

Adapted from Berry 1993.

Questions

1. a) Using the information in this section and Items A-E, describe the different pressures that are exerted on an MP.
   b) How do these pressures affect an MP's accountability?
2. 'The Register of Members' Interests seeks to balance the public interest against the privacy of individual MPs and their families.' Judging from Item A does it succeed? Give arguments for and against.
3. 'Lobbyists should be banned'. Using Items B and C, give arguments for and against this view.
4. a) What do Items D and E tell us about the pressures exerted on MPs and ministers?
   b) To which individuals or groups should (i) an MP and (ii) a minister pay most attention to?

3.4 The rewards of office

Backbench MPs' pay

If there is a trend towards professional politicians (see Section 3.2 above), there is still a large number of MPs who do not expect Parliament to be their sole provider. Until 1911, MPs were not paid. When pay was introduced, it was meant to be a minimum payment. David Lloyd George (the Chancellor of the Exchequer) made this quite clear:

'When we offer £400 a year as payment to Members of Parliament it is not a recognition of the magnitude of the service, it is not a remuneration, it is not a recompense, it is not even a salary. It is just an allowance, and I think a minimum allowance, to enable men to come here, men who would render incalculable loss to the state not to have here, but who cannot be here because their means do not allow it.' (Hansard 1911)

Today, many MPs still see their pay as no more than an allowance. Some claim that they need to have other sources of income in order to maintain an adequate standard of living and they combine other jobs with their parliamentary duties. This has led to the charge from the Labour MP Dennis Skinner (amongst others) that those who do this are merely part-time MPs. In mitigation, some MPs argue that poor facilities and poor pay make it impossible to represent their constituents adequately.

Pay and allowances

Backbench MPs were paid a basic salary of £45,066 in 1998-99. In addition, they were able to claim a number of allowances:

- up to £47,568 to pay for secretarial and support services
- up to £12,717 to pay for accommodation in London if their constituencies were outside Inner London (and up to £1,406 if their constituencies were inside Inner London)
- 50.1p per mile for the first 20,000 miles and 22.3p per mile thereafter to cover the cost of car travel on parliamentary business (including travel between the MP's constituency and Westminster).

In addition, MPs receive travel warrants if they need to travel on parliamentary business by air, sea or rail and they receive free stationery and phone calls for all parliamentary business conducted from the Palace of Westminster. For MPs who are defeated in an election or retire, there is a winding up allowance of £15,856 for office expenses and a resettlement grant to assist with the costs of adjusting to 'non-parliamentary life'. The amount is based on age and length of service and varies between 50% and 100% of the annual salary. All claims have to be submitted for approval to the Fees Office in the House of Commons.

Pay awards

Because MPs' pay is always a contentious issue and because MPs had always decided their own pay increase (based on recommendations of the Top Salaries Review Body), a decision was made by the House that, from April 1997, the annual updating of MPs' salaries would automatically be increased by the average percentage by which the mid-points of the Senior Civil Service pay band had increased. This, it was hoped, would defuse the row over the 26% increase that MPs awarded themselves in 1996 and prevent future rows.

Compared to legislators in other countries, British MPs are not well paid and they lack adequate support. A survey which compared the UK with the

Box 11.4 Ministerial salaries, 1998-99

Post	Amount (If in Commons)	Amount (if in Lords)
Lord Chancellor	–	£148,850
Prime Minister	£147,816	–
Cabinet Minister	£106,716	£80,107
Minister of State	£77,047	£53,264
Under Secretaries	£69,339	£44,832

Information from the House of Commons Information Office, July 1998.

USA, Belgium, Denmark, France, Germany, Italy, Portugal and Sweden concluded that:

> 'By comparison with other legislatures, our MPs are relatively deprived.' (Watts 1994, p.156)

Ministers' pay

Ministers are paid more than MPs (see Box 11.4).

When Tony Blair became Prime Minister he decided not to take the full amount of his salary, claiming £102,417. His Cabinet ministers followed suit, claiming £87,851 each. Ministers have the luxury of chauffeur-driven cars and special residences come with some ministerial posts. Otherwise, ministers are eligible for the same allowances as MPs and no more. The Leader of the opposition and the opposition Chief Whip, Deputy Chief Whip and Assistant Whip also receive higher salaries. William Hague earned £101,579 in 1998-99 (*Labour Research*, August 1998).

Some ministers argue that the pay they receive is poor recompense for the degree of responsibility they have and that it compares very badly with pay in the private sector. One minister, Lord Gowrie, resigned in 1985 because, he claimed, he could not live on his salary. He promptly found work which gave him a much higher financial reward.

Ex-ministers

Since 1979, there has been a growing trend for ex-ministers to join companies as directors. For example, Douglas Hurd, Foreign Secretary under John Major, was recruited by the Nat West Bank, three months after leaving government. Martin West, Nat West's Chief Executive, claimed that the recruitment of Mr Hurd would fill a 'skills gap'. Hurd commented:

> 'This will in many ways be a continuation of the work I have done in government in promoting British interests abroad.' (*Guardian*, 13 September 1995)

Hurd resigned as an MP in 1997 and was elevated to the Lords. Other former ministers remain MPs and still find time for other jobs. In total, 18 of the 45 Conservative ministers who retained their seats in the 1997 general election (including five from the last Conservative Cabinet) found lucrative outside interests (*Labour Research*, January 1998). Former Chancellor, Ken Clarke, for example, earned

£120,000 in 1997-98 as part-time chair of Unichem (for one and half to two days work a week). He was also employed as a part-time director of Foreign and Colonial Investment Trust where he earned about £20,000 a year. In addition, he was appointed as deputy chair of the tobacco multinational BAT Industries.

Ex-Prime Ministers
Former Prime Ministers can earn a great deal of money very quickly. By the beginning of 1998, for example, John Major had sold the rights to his autobiography for £600,000 and (like Margaret Thatcher) had begun making a series of lucrative lectures around the world. According to the *Guardian* (5 February 1998), Major earned up to £36,000 per lecture for lectures delivered in the USA (four times), Sweden and Oman. The same report noted that Major has made it a policy to speak for free at universities and public meetings and that he turned down the offer of 15 company directorships.

The Nolan Report and ex-ministers
Following the Nolan Report, rules for ministers leaving the government have been introduced. There is now a three month waiting period before ex-ministers can take up appointments. An Advisory Committee on Business Appointments can impose conditions relating to employment and can recommend that an ex-minister waits for up to two years after leaving office before taking up any appointments. In July 1998, the *Guardian* reported that more than 50 former ministers and senior civil servants had been forced to accept delays and restrictions imposed by the committee before taking up jobs (*Guardian*, 29 July 1998).

Ex-MPs
Ex-MPs can also find that their parliamentary experience has proved useful. Two days after losing his seat in the general election of 1992, for example, Roger King (ex-MP for Birmingham Northfield) found a job as the public affairs director for the Society of Motor Manufacturers. Whilst an MP, King had spoken extensively on the car industry (*Guardian*, 9 April 1993).

Patronage (see also Chapter 12, Section 1.2)
The exercise of patronage is an important part of the Prime Minister's job. On appointment to the office of Prime Minister, the incumbent has the constitutional right to choose the Cabinet and to make all other ministerial appointments. In addition, further appointments during the lifetime of Parliament are anticipated by backbenchers and their behaviour is shaped accordingly. It is the job of the party whips to identify potential talent and to make recommendations to the Prime Minister. Julian Critchley, a longstanding Conservative backbench MP has commented on this process:

'What is it the whips are looking for? It will certainly be loyalty, the cement that keeps a broad church together. It could be ability, although intelligence is not enough on its own. It might even be expertise. But, what are civil servants for? What I think they are looking for above everything else is predictability.' (Critchley 1989, p.60)

Predictability is found in loyal votes and speeches and hard, unstinting work on committees. But, even that may not be enough. At any one time, only around 100 MPs can be chosen for ministerial office. When a government has a large overall majority (like the Labour government elected in 1997), this can be a problem since many backbenchers are never invited to join the government and some who are passed over become embittered.

The Prime Minister also has the power to create peers, to appoint staff at Downing Street and to appoint people to the following posts:
- top civil servants at the permanent secretary level
- chairs of nationalised industries
- heads of the security services
- chairs of Royal Commissions.

In addition, the Prime Minister has the ultimate responsibility for recommendations of baronetcies, knighthoods, MBEs and so on in the various honours lists.

Other ministers also have powers of patronage. They appoint political advisers, members of task forces and members of quangos (see Part 5 below).

Honours
In March 1993, the Prime Minister, John Major, announced a reform of the honours system as part of his drive towards a 'classless' society. Since then, members of the public have been able to nominate candidates for minor awards, like the MBE, simply by filling in a form and sending it to the Honours Secretariat at 10 Downing Street. Nominations for the more important honours are still made by the Leaders of the three main parties. In addition, it was announced that the award of honours to senior civil servants and high ranking military officers solely on the grounds of seniority or status would be stopped after the Queen's birthday honours list in 1993. The differentiation of military medals according to the rank of the recipient was also abolished after that date. Honours now have to be approved by the Political Honours Scrutiny Committee which consists of three Privy Councillors representing the main three political parties. This committee, however, can only make recommendations and the Prime Minister is free to ignore them when making recommendations to the Queen (it is the monarch who formally grants the honour). John Major's reform did not, however, address the most controversial aspect of the honours system - the practice of giving honours as rewards for party or political services.

During the 1980s there was growing concern about the use of the honours system to reward those who had provided political support to the Conservative Party (or even, more personally, to the Prime Minister). John Major continued this tradition. By April 1993, he had awarded 17 knighthoods to private sector industrialists. Of these, 13 were connected to companies which had donated, together, £3 million to the Conservative Party since 1979 (*Labour Research*, April 1993). The concern about honours for donations to political parties was confirmed when Lord Pym, the chairman of the Political Honours Scrutiny Committee stated that party donations were a 'positive point' in the award of honours. He told the Neill Committee on investigating standards in public life that donations showed that people 'put their money where their mouth is' (*Guardian*, 14 May 1998).

New Labour and honours

In June 1997, it was announced that Tony Blair would end the convention of granting knighthoods and other honours to MPs purely for long political service. It was also announced that Blair planned a fundamental shake-up of the honours system in his first term to give it more independence from the office of Prime Minister.

Despite these announcements, however, when Blair announced the creation of 31 Labour life peers in August 1997, four of the new peers were major donors to the Labour Party and a fifth was the coordinator of a blind trust of donations that funded Tony Blair in opposition (*Guardian*, 26 January 1998). Another donor to the Labour Party, Paul Hamlyn, who gave £500,000 to Labour's general election fund, received a peerage for services to education and publishing in the honours list announced in December 1997 (*Guardian*, 31 December 1997). As a result of these appointments, the suspicion remained in some quarters that the honours system is still being used for party political ends.

Main points - Section 3.4

- Despite a basic salary of £45,066 in 1998-99 plus allowances, a large number of MPs do not expect Parliament to be their sole provider. Pay increases are now tied to civil service rates.
- Ministers earn more than backbenchers, but they cannot take up paid extra-parliamentary positions.
- Many ex-ministers win lucrative contracts three months after they leave government. Delays and restrictions may be imposed if there is a potential conflict of interest.
- The exercise of patronage is an important part of the Prime Minister's job.
- In March 1993, John Major announced reforms to the honours' system. Tony Blair has promised further reforms.

Activity 11.9 The rewards of office

Item A *Ex-ministers*

A comprehensive *Labour Research* survey of the ministers who have resigned over sleaze, been sacked or stood down from their jobs during the Major/Thatcher years reveals that three-quarters of them have lucrative directorships or consultancies. The survey was carried out in April 1997. Its main findings are that:

- 122 former ministers hold a total of over 420 directorships and consultancies
- 56 ministers (46%) hold positions at companies with which they would have had contact while they were ministers
- 17 ex-ministers have been appointed to quangos
- 16 ex-ministers have paid contacts with companies which were privatised by the Conservatives after 1979.

These findings are based on the 197 ministers who have served in government between 1979 and 1997. Out of that number, 12 remained in office in April 1997, one had defected to Labour (Alan Howarth) and 18 had died. Of the 166 remaining ex-ministers, 122 (74%) had paid directorships, consultancies or quango posts.

Adapted from *Labour Research*, May 1997.

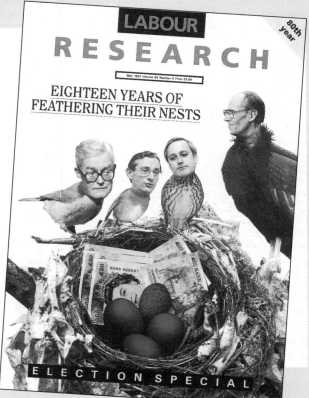

Item B   *Patronage*

It used to be rather easier. Kings and governments were expected to reward their supporters. In 1603, King James knighted 46 supporters on one morning. Between 1979 and 1992, industrialists were ten times more likely to be awarded peerages or knighthoods if they had donated to the Conservative Party. Under James, a baronetcy cost £1,000 (about £500,000 in today's money). Under Thatcher, knighthoods cost £10,000 and peerages £50,000. But, then it changed. A new morality arrived - courtesy of Conservative arrogance and sleaze, and Labour's opposition. Expectations have changed. But, what about the new Labour government? It is true that some appointments to important positions involve high-profile supporters of New Labour - for example, Gerry Robinson's appointment as chair of the Arts Council. But, many do not. For example, Peter Davis, head of Prudential Insurance, publicly supported the Conservatives before the election, but now heads the New Deal task force. Similarly, former Conservative minister, David Mellor, heads the Football task force. There are several theories. The first is that the Prime Minister believes in inclusive politics and is not driven by ideology. The second is that the new government simply cannot find enough New Labour candidates to fill the posts. And the third is that Blair is dazzled by big business and, therefore, inclined to appoint from that sector. It should be noted that, in the post-Nolan world, many more posts are being advertised. Even the most notable patronage appointment so far - that of Robinson to the Arts Council - involved advertising, headhunting, the search for a suitable woman, and Sir Len Peach (Commissioner for Public Appointments whose job it is to ensure appointments are non-partisan) sitting in on one of the shortlist interviews.

This cartoon was published in January 1998. It shows Health Secretary, Frank Dobson, Prime Minister, Tony Blair, and Minister without Portfolio, Peter Mandelson, making appointments.

Adapted from the *Guardian*, 26 January 1998.

Item C   *Honours*

In December 1997, Jonathan Freedland argued for a change to the honours system. His concern was not just about whether honours were given in return for political favours. Rather, he had a more fundamental concern. The problem with the system as it stands, he argued, was the titles because they build into society the rawest form of inequality. It is, Freedland claimed, only in societies with the most rigid hierarchy that some people have a different form of address to others, solely to indicate their superior status. By depriving a knight of his last name and a Lord of his first name, this sends the clear message that some people live on a higher plane than others. But, argued Freedland, like the notion of a hereditary head of state selected by birth not merit, this has no place in a modern society. As a progressive alternative, Freedland suggests a new set of honours - perhaps one for valour and another for public service - which are handed out by an authority other than the Prime Minister. An independent authority would ensure that the suspicion of political pay-off which sours the current system is removed. Freedland also suggests that the awards should be separated from the recipient's title. The honoured man or woman would remain Mr or Ms. The model for this is the current Companion of Honour award. In December 1997, this award was accepted by the Marxist historian Eric Hobsbawm. He remains Eric and is still Mr Hobsbawm - which, Freedland argued, is how all honours should be.

Adapted from the *Guardian*, 31 December 1997.

Questions

1. a) What does Item A tell us about the rewards of office?
   b) What objections could there be to ex-ministers joining the boards of companies?
   c) Give arguments for and against the view that backbench MPs should be allowed to have paid outside interests.

2. a) Which of the three theories outlined in Item B best explains the exercise of patronage under Tony Blair? Give reasons for your answer.
   b) 'Public appointments should be made by an independent body rather than the Prime Minister'. Give arguments for and against this view.

3. a) Using Item C, explain why Jonathan Freedland wants the honours system to be reformed.
   b) Give arguments for and against the views expressed in Item C.

Part 4 The recruitment of other elected representatives

Key issues

1. Who stands for the European Parliament and why?
2. How are candidates for the European and new regional assemblies selected?
3. How representative are MEPs?
4. Who are the representatives in the new Scottish Parliament and assemblies in Northern Ireland and Wales?

4.1 Members of the European Parliament (MEPs)

Euro-candidates

All candidates for European elections (see also Chapter 7, Section 3.5) must be over 21 and they must not be bankrupt. People holding certain posts are not allowed to stand - namely, judges, members of the armed forces, police officers, members of national governments and members of the European Commission. Peers and religious ministers can stand, even though they are disqualified from standing for election to the House of Commons. There is no rule preventing a politician from sitting as both an MP and an MEP. Obviously, however, it would be difficult for one person to perform both roles adequately.

Candidates must complete a nomination paper with the signatures of a proposer, seconder and 28 voters from the constituency in which they want to stand. Candidates can stand in countries other than their home state (for example, the British businessman James Goldsmith stood in France in 1994). Candidates can only stand in one seat, however. A £1,000 deposit must be paid. It is returned if the candidate receives 5% or more of the votes cast.

The selection of Euro-candidates

In mainland Britain in 1997, the Labour government announced that it hoped to introduce a new voting system in time for the European elections to be held in 1999. On the assumption that this new voting system would be introduced, the political parties adopted the following selection procedures. It should be noted that, under the new (proportional) voting system, the UK was to be divided into 12 regions, each returning a number of MEPs (the number would depend on the population within the region).

The Conservative Party

In 1997, the Conservative Party announced that ordinary members would have the final say in the selection of Euro-candidates. Potential candidates, however, would first have to ensure that their names appeared on the European Approved List drawn up by each Regional Selection College (a Selection College is a committee made up of senior elected officials in the region). Selection Colleges undertook a screening and selection process which resulted in a shortlist of around 20 names for each region (sitting Conservative MEPs were automatically entitled to an interview for this shortlist). Once the shortlist had been finalised, all party members in the region were invited to attend a selection meeting whose purpose was to select the candidates for the party's list for that region and to rank them in order.

The process of selection in the Conservative Party, therefore, did give ordinary party members the final say in the choice and ranking of candidates, but only after the party hierarchy had decided on an approved shortlist.

The Labour Party

The Labour Party also involved both ordinary party members and the party leadership in the process of selecting its candidates. The process, however, was the reverse of that used by the Conservatives in that ordinary Labour Party members began (rather than ended) the selection process. The selection process had two stages. The first stage was for ordinary Labour Party members to choose candidates (one man and one woman) from within their present Euro-constituency in a secret postal ballot. Any sitting MEPs who wished to stand for reselection had to put their names forward and win this ballot. Those who did win the ballot joined the party's national pool of candidates and entered the second stage of the process. The second stage was for a joint panel of NEC members and regional representatives to weed out unsuitable candidates and to rank the candidates in order on the party's list. Only those ranked near the top of the list would be likely to be elected. In 1998, the final placing of Labour's 84 candidates caused anger on the left of the party because, it was alleged, well-known left-wingers were placed low down the regional lists. The 49 sitting Labour MEPs dominated the top ends of the regional lists and 34 of the candidates were women.

It should be noted that this selection process was designed for the 1999 European election only. After the 1999 elections, new selection procedures would be introduced.

The Liberal Democrats

Unlike the other two main parties, the national leadership of the Liberal Democrats was not involved in the selection of MEP candidates. Rather, potential candidates submitted their applications to the regional committee. The regional committee considered the applications, conducted interviews and then drew up a shortlist (around twice as many candidates as there were places on the final list). Hustings meetings were held in every county and then the final list of candidates was chosen in a postal ballot of all members using the STV system. For the 1999 Euro-elections only, the Liberal Democrats introduced a system of 'zipping' - alternative places on the list were reserved for men and women, ensuring a 50:50 split between male and female candidates.

MEPs' pay

MEPs are paid the equivalent of their national parliamentary salary. So, there are considerable discrepancies between salaries received by members from different countries. In 1998, British MEPs earned £45,066 a year. By comparison, the lowest salary was paid to the Greeks (c. £15,000 a year) and the highest salary was paid to Italians (c.£80,000 a year). The salary, however, is by no means the only money MEPs receive. Further allowances mean that MEPs can receive over £100,000 a year above their salaries (*Guardian*, 17 June 1998). These allowances include:

- a daily attendance allowance of £159 for attending official meetings
- £6,400 a month for research and secretarial assistance
- £2,100 a year to fund trips around the world to investigate relevant problems
- allowances for computer courses, language courses, free taxis, life assurance and insurance.

EP's Register of Outside Financial Interests

Concern about the reputation of MEPs has led the European Parliament to introduce a Register of Outside Financial Interests. Under the rules of procedure, MEPs should register:

> 'Any support...additional to that provided by Parliament and granted to the member in connection with his political activities by third parties.' (quoted in the *Observer*, 22 March 1998)

Yet, only 290 of the 626 MEPs returned the form detailing their financial interests for 1997. The problem is that:

> 'The authorities are hamstrung in dealing with MEPs caught cheating or failing to abide by disclosure rules because Parliament has been allowed virtually no disciplinary powers by the member states.' (*Guardian*, 31 January 1998)

Working conditions

Working conditions at Brussels and Strasbourg are far superior to those at Westminster. The new Parliament building in Brussels has been built at a cost of £750 million. Each MEP's office is equipped with a shower (at a cost of £7,000), desk (£2,000), 30 channel television, computer with internet access, and a free telephone. Another new Parliament building has been opened at Strasbourg at a cost of £350 million (*Guardian*, 13 February 1998). Also, MEPs have their own reserved seats in Parliament and there are no late-night sittings.

On the other hand, there are the strains of long absences from home and an interminable round of meetings conducted in a multiplicity of European languages. A working month usually consists of three weeks in Brussels (two weeks working on parliamentary committees and one week working for political groups) followed by mass upheaval to Strasbourg where the Parliament sits for one week. Travel between the two Parliament buildings twice a month costs £80 million a year.

How representative are MEPs?

Like MPs, MEPs are not representative of the electorate as a whole (see Item B in Activity 11.10 below). In part, this is a reflection of the electoral system. The plurality system used in elections between 1979 and 1994 meant that Labour and the Conservatives secured the vast majority of seats. In 1994, for example, they secured all but four of the 84 seats in England, Scotland and Wales (the Liberal Democrats won two seats and the SNP won two). No minor party has ever won a seat (although the Green Party won 15% of the vote in 1984, it did not win a seat).

The turnout in Euro-elections also raises questions about how representative MEPs are. In 1994, 38% of the electorate voted, compared to 36% in 1989. These figures suggest a degree of indifference among the voters and allow MEPs' legitimacy as representatives to be questioned.

The ability of MEPs to represent their constituents is further restricted by the nature of party discipline in the EP (which operates in the same way as in Westminster). It is also restricted by the large geographical and population sizes of the Euro-constituencies. Most voters do not know the name of their MEP and MEPs have direct contact with a very small proportion of their constituents.

4.2 Representatives in the new regional assemblies

MSPs and MWAs

As a result of the setting up of the Scottish Parliament and Welsh Assembly, a new breed of elected politicians has been created - Members of the Scottish Parliament (MSPs) and Members of the Welsh Assembly (MWAs). The voting systems used to elect MSPs and MWAs are described in Activity 4.5, Item A.

Two types of representative

The use of the Additional Member voting system in elections to the Scottish Parliament and Welsh Assembly will result in the creation of two different types of representative.

In Scotland, there will be a total of 129 MSPs. Of these, 73 will be elected from constituencies using the 'first-past-the-post' plurality system currently employed for Westminster MPs and 56 will be elected from party lists in the constituencies (seven from each of the eight Euro-constituencies). This is to ensure that the final number of MSPs is proportionate to the votes cast for each party. In Wales, there will be 40 directly elected members of the Assembly with 20 additional members, again chosen from a party list drawn up by the party from the five Euro-constituencies in Wales.

Candidate selection - the Labour Party
In Scotland and Wales, the candidate selection process has two stages.

Stage one
In the first stage, after completing their application forms, potential candidates are subjected to a rigorous selection test by members of the Welsh or Scottish selection panel. The selection panels were set up early in 1998 by the Welsh and Scottish executive committees and are made up of five members of each of the following four groups:

- the Welsh or Scottish executive committee
- the NEC
- members of the Labour Party in Wales or Scotland
- professional advisors (for example, trade unionists and councillors).

Members of the selection panel interview potential candidates, quizzing them in particular about their commitment to the party, and they test their communication skills. Potential candidates also have to undergo a mock press conference to find out whether they have the ability to cope under pressure. The names of those successful at this stage are placed on a list which is circulated to all CLPs.

Stage two
In the second stage, constituencies are 'paired', the idea being that a pair of CLPs will select one male and one female candidate. Each branch and affiliated organisation in a constituency is allowed to nominate a potential candidate from the list drawn up by the selection panel. Then, a meeting of the General Committee of the CLP is called and a shortlist drawn up. This shortlist can contain up to four names and must contain at least one name from each gender. Since each constituency is paired with another constituency, a combined shortlist of up to eight names results. Potential candidates on this shortlist are then invited to one or more hustings meetings in the two constituencies, followed by a ballot. All members of the CLP are eligible to vote in the ballot, but they must apply beforehand for a postal vote if they are unable to attend the meeting in person (the aim being to encourage attendance). Those who take part in the ballot have two votes - one for a male candidate and one for a female candidate. If the ballot takes place at different times in the two constituencies, ballot boxes from the first vote remain sealed until the second ballot has taken place. Votes from both constituencies are then counted together. The male and female with the highest number of votes then become the candidates for the two constituencies.

Controversies
This selection system has caused some controversy in both Scotland and in Wales. In Scotland, after the first stage was completed, it emerged that a number of well-known activists (including two Westminster MPs) failed to be selected. This led to accusations that the party leadership was deliberately manipulating the selection process to exclude left-wing candidates (*Guardian*, 30 June 1998). In Wales, it was the system of pairing that came under attack from some party members.

Candidate selection - other parties
The Conservatives select candidates using the same process that was used to select Euro-candidates in 1997-98. The Liberal Democrats select the 'first past the post' candidates using the same system as for Westminster. For the additional places, however, the regional committee draws up a shortlist of candidates and the final list is chosen in a postal ballot of all members using the STV system. In effect, as Lynch (1998) points out, this is a primary contest, similar to that used by parties in the USA. The SNP uses a system similar to the Liberal Democrats. Like the Labour Party, both the Liberal Democrats and the SNP are committed to a 50:50 split between male and female candidates.

The Northern Ireland Assembly
Elections for the 108 members of the Northern Ireland Assembly took place on 25 June 1998, using the STV system. None of the three main British parties fielded candidates. The election resulted in nine parties being represented, including two members of the Women's Coalition (see also Chapter 4, Section 3.4).

Main points - Part 4

- Conservative selection of Euro-candidates in 1997-98 - a regional selection panel draws up a shortlist and the membership then selects candidates and ranks them in order.
- Labour selection of Euro-candidates in 1997-98 - members vote for one man and one woman, the winners go into a national pool and a joint panel chooses and ranks candidates.
- MEPs' allowances and conditions are superior to those of MPs. Like MPs, MEPs are untypical of the electorate. MEPs are more remote and have less legitimacy than MPs.
- Labour selection of MSPs and MWAs has two stages: a selection panel draws up a list and then members choose candidates from the list (pairing ensures an equal number of men and women candidates).
- Conservative selection of MSPs and MWAs is the same as the selection of MEPs.

Activity 11.10 How representative are MEPs?

Item A *The selection of MEPs*

In March 1998, it was revealed that Conservative efforts to secure more women candidates for the Euro-elections had failed. Only 8% of candidates on the regional lists were women. Some senior Conservatives called for positive discrimination, but this was strongly opposed. At the end of May 1998, there was further controversy amongst Conservatives. On this occasion, Eurosceptics in the party were angry that too many Europhiles were gaining top places on the regional lists. After meetings in the South East, Yorkshire and West Midlands at which ordinary members voted for candidates and ranked them in order, it became clear that only one Eurosceptic was high enough on the list to be elected (Dan Hannan). Leading Eurosceptics were angry that high-profile supporters like the former Chancellor Norman Lamont did not survive the first stage of the selection process. They also hoped that more sitting MEPs would not be reselected. Earlier in 1998, controversy over the Labour Party's selection procedure led to the expulsion of two MEPs. They and their supporters opposed the procedure because it allowed the party leadership to have the final say. Left-wingers, they argued, would therefore be rejected. Party officials, on the other hand, argued that the reason for adopting this procedure was to ensure more women and ethnic minority candidates. 'At the moment there are no women north of the Humber, and in areas with quite a high ethnic minority concentration there are no ethnic minority candidates", said a senior Labour spokesman.

Adapted from the *Times*, 9 March, 31 May and 1 June 1998 and the *Guardian*, 28 January 1998.

Item C *The youngest MEP*

Only three months ago, Elenud Morgan was a £17,000-a-year researcher at BBC Wales, sharing with two others the terraced house she bought last year. Now she is the youngest member of the EP - having won for Labour with a majority of 30,000. So, now she is busy setting up four offices in Brussels, Strasbourg, Aberystwyth and Carmarthen. She needs to find an apartment to rent in Brussels. And she needs to hire at least three full-time staff/researchers and some secretaries. Her £35,000 salary will be supplemented by around £100,000. Not that Elenud is very impressed. She says that money has never been very important to her. She was born a vicar's daughter and brought up on a council estate in Cardiff. Both her parents were local councillors. Her enthusiasm for Europe developed after winning a scholarship to Atlantic College. She joined a Cardiff Labour supporters trip to Strasbourg and then studied for a year at the university there. She now speaks French, Spanish, German and Welsh. After reading European Studies at Hull University, she worked for five months in Brussels as a researcher on regional policy for the socialist group in the EP. It was after that that she worked for BBC Wales. In a sense, much of her life has been a preparation for being an MEP. She says that it is an opportunity to use all her skills.

Adapted from the *Times*, 22 June 1994.

Item B *How representative are MEPs?*

(i) Share of the votes at Euro-elections 1984-94

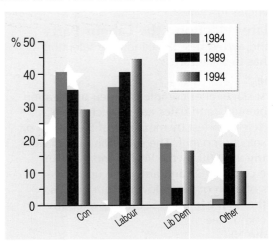

This table shows the share of the vote received by parties in Euro-elections 1984-94.

(ii) MEPs elected, June 1994

Party	Men	Women	Total	Total, 1989
Con	16	2	18	32
Lab	49	13	62	45
Lib Dem	2	0	2	0
SNP	1	1	2	1
Other	3	0	3	3
Total	**71**	**16**	**87**	**81**

This table shows the gender of the MEPs elected in June 1994.

(iii) Occupation of candidates, Euro-election 1994

Conservative		Labour	
Occupation	No.	Occupation	No.
Company director	19	Lecturer	14
Consultant	9	Teacher	13
Lawyer	9	Voluntary sector	11
Journalist	7	Council officer	7
Manager	7	Party employee	5
Party employee	6	Manual worker	5
Farmer	6	Journalist	5
Banker	4	Lawyer	2
Lecturer	4	Trade union employee	1
Other	10	Other	19
Unknown	2	Unknown	1

This table shows the occupation of candidates who stood for the Labour and Conservative parties in the European election of June 1994.

Item D   *MEPs' pay and conditions*

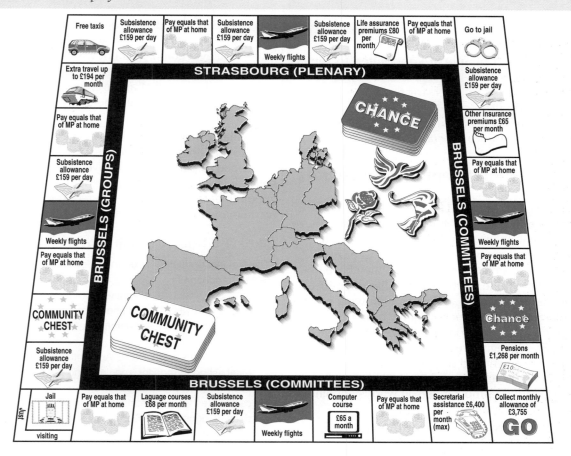

In recent years, MEPs' allowances have come under a great deal of criticism. MEPs do not have to produce any evidence of actual travel to make claims and they only have to sign in, not stay for sessions to claim the daily attendance rate of £159, for example. British MEPs can earn up to £10,000 a year just by claiming expenses on their weekly business flights to Brussels or Strasbourg because they are paid a flat-rate mileage allowance for air travel which is well in excess of the price of the most expensive ticket. In October 1997, a German documentary caught Nelio Mendonca, a Portuguese MEP, walking near his home in Brussels when he had claimed a fare home to Madeira. He said he had been taken ill at the last moment and would repay the money (the EP only has the power to request the money back). In March 1998, it was revealed that British MEPs were receiving free parking worth thousands of pounds from BAA, the owner of the UK's major airports, but only 13 of the 87 MEPs had disclosed this gift in the Register of Outside Financial Interests. At the time, BAA was lobbying MEPs to support its campaign against the planned abolition of duty-free shopping in 1999.

Adapted from the *Guardian*, 1 June 1994, 27 November 1997 and 17 June 1998 and the *Observer*, 22 March 1998.

Questions

1. 'The selection procedures used by the two main parties to choose Euro-candidates in 1997-98 were flawed'. Using Item A, give arguments for and against this view

2. a) Judging from the information in Items B, C and D, would you say that MEPs are representative of the population as a whole? Explain your answer.
   b) Are there any grounds for suggesting that they will become more representative in the future?

3. How typical a candidate would you say Elenud Morgan was (Item C)? Give reasons for your answer.

4. a) MEPs' pay and allowances must be reformed. Do you agree with this statement? Use Item D in your answer.
   b) How might an MEP justify current pay and allowances?

Part 5 Quangocrats

Key issues

1. What sort of people are appointed to serve on quangos?
2. What criteria are used for their appointment?
3. What are their pay and hours?
4. To whom are they accountable?

5.1 The appointment of quangocrats

What is a quangocrat?

It was noted in Section 3.4 above that ministers have powers of patronage. It is the job of ministers to recruit political appointees - people who have political responsibilities even though they have not been elected. In the 1990s, the number of political appointees grew rapidly, reflecting a growing number of unelected agencies such as quangos (for a full definition and description of quangos see Chapter 16, Part 5). Quangos are permanent bodies set up by central government and staffed by paid appointees rather than by elected representatives. A quangocrat, therefore, is quite simply a person who is appointed to serve on a quango.

What sort of people are appointed to serve on quangos?

Appointments under the Conservatives

According to surveys undertaken while John Major was Prime Minister, the typical quangocrat was a white, middle-aged, middle-class male who worked in business and finance and voted Conservative (see, for example, Weir & Hall 1994 and 1995). That Conservative ministers were deliberately packing quangos with Conservative supporters was revealed by Baroness Denton in June 1993. She had been responsible for 804 public appointments when she confessed that she had never knowingly appointed a Labour supporter (*Guardian*, 21 June 1993). The little information that was published on ministerial appointments between 1993 and 1997 suggested that Baroness Denton's attitude was by no means unusual. Typical was the report in April 1996 that two prominent Conservative Lords had been appointed to lucrative part-time quango posts - Lord de Ramsey was appointed as Chair of the Environment Agency, whilst Lord Bellwin was appointed as Chair of the North Hull Housing Action Trust (*Guardian*, 11 April 1996). Tony Stott, however, pointed out:

> 'Given the paucity [scarcity] of publicly available information on appointments and a lack of systematically researched evidence of party connections in appointments made to non-elected bodies, the appointments process

appears closed, secretive and unrepresentative. It is naive to think that governments of whatever colour will not want to place people sympathetic to their views and policies in organisations that are responsible for the delivery of the government's policies.' (Stott 1996, p.125)

The Nolan reforms

The Nolan Report (published in May 1995) responded to public concern over both sleaze in general and the political nature of many quango appointments in particular. The report made the recommendations outlined in Box 11.5.

Box 11.5 Nolan Committee recommendations

The Nolan Committee made the following recommendations:

- all appointments to executive non-departmental public bodies and NHS bodies should be made on the advice from a panel or committee which contains an independent element
- a Commissioner for Public Appointments should be established to monitor, regulate and approve appointments procedures
- candidates for appointment should be required to declare significant political activity (such as holding an office in a political party, public speaking on behalf of a party or standing as a candidate for election)
- quangos should adopt codes of conduct for members and staff
- the government should review the legal framework governing the propriety and accountability of quangos

Adapted from Baggott 1995.

The government accepted these recommendations in November 1995, but there was little evidence of substantial change by the time the 1997 general election took place. Stott argued:

> 'Although the government accepted the idea of a Public Appointments Commissioner and the use of more independent advice and assessments in making appointments...the Nolan Committee's approach does not address the fundamentally party political nature of some key appointments.' (Stott 1996, p.126)

Of particular concern is the limited powers of the Public Appointments Commissioner. The Commissioner can only monitor appointments and deal with complaints, not initiate investigations. Also, the Commissioner's terms of reference only cover the c.8,000 appointments made directly by ministers.

Although quangocrats now have to declare party political activity, this is restricted to activities carried out in the past five years.

Appointments under the Labour government

According to the Commons Committee on Public Administration, the typical quangocrat was still, in 1998, a 'white, middle-aged, middle-class male' (*Times*, 19 February 1998). A survey published in April 1998 revealed that just 35 out of 2,005 people appointed to quangos by the Labour government in 1997-98 were Asians. Asians make up 3.5% of the population as a whole, but made up just 1.7% of appointments (*Observer*, 5 April 1998). Figures published in June 1998 then showed that in 1,100 quangos and public bodies, there were 12,200 women and 26,000 men (*Guardian*, 30 June 1998). In this sample, therefore, 31% of quangocrats were women compared to 69% men. There are some signs of change, however. For example, in June 1998, it was announced that:

> 'The government is to search out 7,000 women to replace men to serve on 1,100 quangos and public bodies...Women are to be given parity [equality] with men in future appointments for government bodies as part of a move to make the bodies more accountable and representative of society. There is also to be a drive to increase the number of ethnic minority members serving on quangos.' (*Guardian*, 30 June 1998)

Under Labour, there have also been charges that ministers are biased towards Labour supporters:

> '[Frank Dobson, the Health Secretary] now faces Conservative charges of "packing" NHS trusts with Labour placemen by handing seats on the boards to Labour councillors and others.' (*Guardian*, 30 December 1997)

Also, since many quangocrats were appointed in the last years of the Conservative administration, there is some concern that Conservative supporters are still over-represented. The difficulties in finding out whether this remains the case were revealed in the 1997 Public Appointments Annual Report for the NHS. In this report, 75.1% of appointees failed to provide any information about their political affiliations and a further 20.8% claimed not to have undertaken any political activity in the last five years. In total, therefore, 95.9% of appointees claimed no active political affiliation. Yet, closer analysis of those who failed to provide any information on political affiliation revealed that many had held office in the Conservative Party at local or national level. Even among those who claimed no political affiliation, a significant number were partners of Conservative MPs, past Conservative MPs or even past Conservative Cabinet Ministers (Belton 1997).

What criteria are used for the appointment of quangocrats?

Whatever criteria are used for counting quangocrats (different authors have different definitions and, therefore, come up with different figures), it is clear that there are substantially more quangocrats than locally elected councillors. Before the Nolan Report, recruitment procedure was as follows. People who wanted to serve on quangos applied to central government. Those whose applications were accepted were then invited to an interview. If successful, their names were placed on a central register from which appointments could then be made. Ministers were also free to 'maintain their own lists, consult interested bodies, make personal suggestions or use head-hunters' (*Observer*, 10 July 1994).

Since the Nolan Report, selection methods have been made more open and accountable with many posts being advertised. Also, in 1995, a Commissioner for Public Appointments was appointed for the first time to scrutinise ministerial appointments to about 1,000 non-departmental bodies. The aim is to extend the 'merit' principle used in civil service appointments. In February 1998, however, the Commons Committee on Public Appointments claimed that too many individuals were still appointed because they 'play golf and know the chairman of the board' (*Guardian*, 19 February 1998). The problem is that ministers are often only responsible for appointing the chair of the quango. The chair is then responsible for appointing the other members of the board. The board then, in turn, employs other staff.

Pay and hours

Many quangos are organised so that policy decisions are made by a board of directors which meets infrequently, whilst the day-to-day work is undertaken by a full-time chief executive and staff. For example, at local level, the governors of a Further Education College might meet only every two months or so while the Chief Executive, usually the Principal, runs the college on a day-to-day basis.

In general, the payment of board members and chief executives of the larger quangos is generous. Certainly, it is more than most local councillors can expect to claim for expenses. In 1997, for example, Brandon Gough, Chair of the Higher Education Funding Council received £37,000 for two days work a week and Richard Simmons, Chair of the Countryside Commission, earned £39,000 for two days work a week (Milne 1997). The Chair of the Port of London Authority, City Banker Sir Brain Shaw, was the highest paid quangocrat in 1996 earning £150,000 for 36 days work. This amounted to £4,000 a day (*Guardian*, 11 April 1996).

Such amounts are not unusual and they are not confined to London-based appointments. Members of a district health authority/board, for example, are required to work for one day a week and receive £5,000 a year. Since membership of a quango is often not very time consuming, some individuals are able to hold multiple appointments.

To whom are quangocrats accountable?

Although quangocrats are appointed by ministers or ministerial appointees, ministers have no control over the day-to-day running of quangos. Quangocrats are not, therefore, accountable to ministers. Also, unlike elected representatives, quangocrats are not obliged to explain or justify their actions to the public. Quangos can meet behind closed doors. There are no formal mechanisms that concerned members of the public can use to take quangocrats to task if they feel that they have acted improperly. Whereas, in an elected council, there are members of opposition parties who do their best to seek out corruption and inefficiency, quangos are not challenged in this way.

Whilst critics argue that the growth of quangos means a growing 'democratic deficit', supporters of quangos argue that quangocrats are, in fact, accountable for their actions. It is just that they are accountable in a different way from elected representatives. The Conservative minister William Waldegrave, for example, argued that quangocrats are accountable to the consumers of the public services they administer in the same way that the people who manage a shop are accountable to their customers (*Observer*, 20 March 1994). Christopher Thomas, Chair of the Bristol Development Corporation, added further justifications for political appointments. He argued that it was actually an advantage that quangocrats were not elected because that ensured they acted independently of any political party. He also claimed that he was accountable to the local community because he was a local. If quangocrats made bad decisions, he argued, they would lose respect in the eyes of that local community. This, he suggested, was enough to ensure that quangocrats acted in the best interests of the community (quoted in Jones 1994).

The Labour government elected in 1997 recognised that there was a problem of accountability and announced that it would consider a number of options to increase accountability. These included:

- a greater role for select committees of the House of Commons
- the requirement that annual reports should be published
- meetings to be held in public perhaps on an annual basis
- a greater role for local authorities, the Scottish Parliament and Welsh Assembly
- publication of more information by quangos about their work
- a greater role for the Parliamentary Ombudsman.
  (Government 1997)

Main points - Part 5

- The typical quangocrat is a white, middle-aged, middle-class male. The Conservatives were accused of packing quangos with supporters, as were Labour after May 1997.
- The Nolan Committee's recommendations on quango appointments were accepted in November 1995, but they had made little impact by 1998.
- Often a minister appoints the chair of a quango and the chair then appoints members of the board. Too often, it is alleged, this means members are simply friends of the chair.
- In general, the payment of board members and chief executives of the larger quangos is generous. One quangocrat received £150,000 for 36 days work in 1996.
- Quangocrats are not accountable to an electorate (as nobody elected them), they are not obliged to respond to criticisms made by members of the public and they are only indirectly accountable to the minister who appointed them.
- Supporters argue that quangocrats are accountable in the same way that people who manage a shop are accountable to customers and that quangocrats are free of party restraints.

Activity 11.11 *The recruitment of quangocrats*

Item A *Lord Wade of Chorlton*

According to his official biography, Lord Wade of Chorlton is: 'A farmer and cheesemaster who, having developed a number of cheese companies and holding a number of directorships, became Chairman of the Cheese Export Council.' These, it appears, are perfect credentials for a role in today's NHS. Lord Wade is a non-executive director of an NHS trust hospital in Chester who receives £5,000 for his work of one day a week. The hospital says non-execs were chosen for a variety of reasons - commitment to healthcare, living locally, ability to devote time to the trust and specific expertise and experience to complement that of the five executive directors. Lord Wade is a local who lives just outside Chester. His interests include 'politics, reading, shooting, food, travel'. He was also joint Treasurer of the Conservative Party from 1982-90.

Adapted from the *Guardian*, 19 November 1993.

Item B *Sir Leonard Peach*

The first Public Appointments Commissioner is Sir Leonard Peach. It is his job to ensure that all future quango appointments are non-partisan and that a much wider number of people, including more women and members of ethnic minorities, are encouraged to apply for the top jobs. Peach himself, however, is a classic example of the quango type. Educated at a grammar school and Oxford, he was a corporate personnel manager and company director in the private sector until joining the NHS in 1985. He has served as Chief Executive, NHS Management Board (1986-89), Member of the Data Protection Tribunal (from 1985), Chairman of the Policy Studies Institute (from 1991), Chairman of the Police Complaints Authority (1992-95), Chairman of the University of Westminster (from 1993) and Commissioner for Public Appointments (from 1995). In February 1998, he was attacked by members of the Commons Committee on Public Administration after asserting that nine out of ten appointments to the 1,000 bodies he oversees were given to people with no active party political involvement. The committee urged a wider definition of 'political activity' and more stringent tests to identify it. Sir Leonard was described as 'unambitious and complacent'.

Sir Leonard Peach

Adapted from the *Times* and the *Guardian*, 19 February 1998.

Item C *Political affiliations of appointees to the NHS quangos*

Political affiliations of appointees

	INC*	None	Con	Lab	Lib Dem	Other
Executive non-departmental bodies	102	0	0	0	0	0
District health authorities	133	389	44	37	6	3
NHS trusts	2,091	309	39	7	6	2
Special health authorities	253	15	0	0	0	0
Total	2,579	713	83	44	12	5
Total as percentage	75.1	20.8	2.4	1.3	0.4	0.2

* Information not collected

This table shows the results of survey asking members of quangos to provide information on their political affiliation.

Adapted from Belton 1997.

Item E *The Committee on Women's Rights*

"The committee on women's rights will now come to order".

Item D *View of a quangocrat*

Martin Wainwright, a journalist for the *Guardian*, is also a quangocrat (Chair of a Regional Advisory Board of the Lotteries Charities Board). He says that sitting on a quango results in the sort of nagging pain associated with the princess and the pea. Something irritating niggles away at a sensitive part of your anatomy, and it doesn't take very long to realise what it is - your conscience. Certain questions keep springing to mind, such as 'Why me? Who put me there? Who elected me?'. Of course, he concludes, there is no democratically justifiable answer to these basic challenges, and no amount of Nolan rulings can put that right. Even if, as the government is likely to suggest, quangos were to meet in public, publish their minutes and operate a clear rotation of membership with limited terms of office, they would still lack the legitimacy that comes from election. One way of improving matters, Wainwright argues, would be to use a jury system so that, in a quango made up of 12-18 members at least two would be randomly selected from the public at large. This would allow the bulk of the quango to be made up of experts, but it would breathe some legitimacy into them.

Adapted from the *Guardian*, 27 October 1997.

Questions

1. a) Why do you think Lord Wade (Item A) was chosen to serve on a quango?
   b) Is it likely that somebody like him would be appointed to a quango today? Explain your answer.

2. 'Sir Leonard Peach was not the best person to appoint as Public Appointments Commissioner'. Using Item B give arguments for and against this view.

3. What does Item C show? What conclusions can be drawn from this information?

4. a) Using the information in Items A-E, write a report on the recruitment of quangocrats which answers the following questions: (i) What sort of people are appointed to serve on quangos? (ii) What criteria are used for their appointment? (iii) To whom are quangocrats accountable? (iv) What are the advantages and disadvantages of this recruitment system?
   b) How might the system be improved? Use Item D in your answer.

References

Austin (1997) Austin T. (ed.), *The Times Guide to the House of Commons*, Times Books, 1997.

Baggott (1995) Baggott, R., 'Putting the squeeze on sleaze?: the Nolan Committee and standards in public life', *Talking Politics*, Vol.8.1. Autumn 1995.

Belton (1997) Belton, T., 'Beyond quangocracy', *New Statesman*, 18 July 1997.

Berry (1993) Berry, S., 'Lobbying - a need to regulate?', *Politics Review*, Vol.2.3, February 1993.

Bryson (1996) Bryson, V., 'Women in British politics', *Politics Review*, Vol.6.2, November 1996.

Budge & McKay (1993) Budge, I. & McKay, D. (eds), *The Developing Political System: the 1990s*, Longman, 1993.

Butler & Kavanagh (1992) Butler, D. & Kavanagh, D., *The British General Election of 1992*, Macmillan, 1992.

Butler & Kavanagh (1997) Butler, D. & Kavanagh, D., *The British General Election of 1997*, Macmillan, 1997.

Conservative (1998) *The Fresh Future*, Conservative Central Office, 1998.

Crewe (1993) Crewe, I., 'Parties and electors' in Budge & McKay (1993).

Critchley (1989) Critchley, J. *Palace of Varieties*, John Murray, 1989.

Geddes et al. (1991) Geddes, A., Lovenduski, J. & Norris, P., 'Candidate selection', *Contemporary Record*, April 1991.

Geddes & Tonge (1997) Geddes, A. & Tonge, J., *Labour's Landslide*, Manchester University Press, 1997.

Government 1997 HM Government, *Opening up Quangos: a Consultation Paper*, HMSO, 1997 (Chapter 3: 'Can we make quangos better?').

ISIS (1998) Independent Schools Information Service, August 1998.

Kelly (1996) Kelly, R., ' Selecting parliamentary candidates: some recent developments', *Talking Politics*, Vol.9.2, Autumn 1996.

Jones (1994) Jones, B., 'The unknown government: government by quango', *Talking Politics*, Vol.6.2, Winter 1994.

King (1981) King, A., 'The rise of the career politician in Britain - and its consequences', *British Journal of Political Science*, Vol.11, 1981.

Kingdom (1991) Kingdom, J., *Local Government and Politics in Britain*, Philip Allan, 1991.

Labour (1998) *Labour's Future: Keeping a Strong Voice in Parliament* (NEC Parliamentary Selections Working Group Procedural Document), Labour Party, 1998.

Lancaster (1997) Lancaster, S. (ed.), *Developments in Politics*, Vol.8, Causeway Press, 1997.

LGC (1998) Local Government Management Board, 'Census of councillors in England and Wales', *Local Government Chronicle*, 20 March 1998.

Longmate (1997) Longmate, J., 'Women and representation' in *Lancaster (1997)*.

Lynch (1998) Lynch, P., 'Devolution and a new British political system', *Talking Politics*, Vol.10.2, Winter 1997-8.

Milne (1997) Milne, K., 'Opening a can of quangos', *New Statesman*, 27 March 1997.

Milne (1998) Milne, K., 'An end to democracy on the cheap', *New Statesman*, 31 July 1998.

Norris & Lovenduski (1989) Norris, P. & Lovenduski, J., 'Pathways to Parliament', *Talking Politics*, Vol.1.3, 1989.

Norton (1994) Norton, P., 'A "new breed" of MP?', *Politics Review*, Vol.3.3, February 1994.

Peake (1997) Peake, L., 'Women in the campaign and in the Commons' in *Geddes & Tonge (1997)*.

Puwar (1997) Puwar, N., 'Gender and political élites: women in the House of Commons', *Sociology Review*, Vol. 7.2, November 1997.

Rallings & Thrasher (1997) Rallings, C. & Thrasher, M., 'The 1997 local election results', *Politics Review*, Vol.7.1, September 1997.

Robins (1998) Robins, L., *Politics Pal 1998*, Hyperion Press, 1998.

Saggar (1997) Saggar, S., 'The dog that didn't bark? Immigration, race and the election' in *Geddes & Tonge (1997)*.

Saggar (1998) Saggar, S., 'Party strategy and ethnic politics in the 1997 general election campaign', *Politics Review*, Vol.7.4, April 1998.

Sewell (1993) Sewell, T., *Black Tribunes: Black Political Participation in Britain*, Lawrence & Wishart, 1993.

Social Trends (1998) Office for National Statistics, *Social Trends*, Vol. 29, HMSO, 1998.

Stott (1996) Stott, J., 'Evaluating the quango debate', *Talking Politics*, Vol.8.2, Winter 1995-6.

Turner (1996) Turner, R., 'The politics of parliamentary candidates selection', *Politics Review*, Vol. 6.2, November 1996.

Vallence (1988) Vallence, E., 'The job of a backbencher', *Contemporary Record*, Vol. 2.3, 1988.

Vandermark (1994) Vandermark, A., 'Lobbying and registration: biting the bullet or shifting the focus?', *Talking Politics*, Vol. 7.2, Autumn 1994.

Watts (1994) Watts, D., 'The debate over members' pay and facilities', *Talking Politics*, Vol 6.3, Summer 1994.

Weir & Hall (1994) Weir, S. & Hall, W. (eds), *Ego Trip: Extra-governmental organisations in the UK and their accountability*, The Charter 88 Trust, 1994.

Weir & Hall (1995) Weir, S. & Hall, W. (eds), *Behind Closed Doors: Advisory Panels in the Corridors of Power*, Channel 4 Television, 1995.

Whiteley & Seyd (1998) Whiteley, P. & Seyd, P., *New Labour: New Grass Roots Party*, ESRC, 1998.

Widdicombe (1986) Widdicombe, D., *The Conduct of Local Authority Business*, Cmnd 9797, HMSO, 1986.

Williams (1995) Williams, J., 'Power and politics', *Sociology Review*, September 1995.

Wood & Wood (1992) Wood, A.H. & Wood, R. (eds), *The Times Guide to the House of Commons 1992*, Times Books, 1992.

Wood & Crawley (1987) Wood, T. & Crawley, G., 'Equal access to political power - a principle in danger', *Local Government Chronicle*, 21 August 1987.

Part 4
Decision making

12 Prime Minister and Cabinet

Introduction

Most people would agree that the most powerful individual in the British system of government is the Prime Minister. The exact extent of the power exercised by the Prime Minister, however, is not easy to calculate since Prime Ministers do not govern alone. Strategic policy decisions, for example, are made (or at least discussed) by the Cabinet, a group of senior ministers appointed by the Prime Minister. If most matters of substance are discussed in the Cabinet, it is possible to argue that power is exercised collectively, by the Cabinet as a whole. On the other hand, since the Prime Minister appoints (and sacks) members of the Cabinet and since many policies are initiated outside the Cabinet, it is also possible to argue that the Cabinet has little real power.

To some extent, of course, the exact relationship between the Prime Minister and the Cabinet is determined by the personalities of those involved. A Prime Minister with a forceful, authoritarian character, for example, is less likely to listen to and take note of the views of Cabinet colleagues than a Prime Minister with a passive, cooperative character. In addition, it should be noted that power is not necessarily static. The location of power in one government may be very different from its location in another government.

This chapter looks at the role played by the Prime Minister and the Cabinet and examines the relationship between them. In particular, it considers who has the central position in decision making - the Prime Minister, the Cabinet or other groups? This is an important question since its answer may reveal a great deal about the way in which British government functions.

Chapter summary

Part 1 looks at the role played by the Prime Minister. What powers does the Prime Minister have? What limits these powers? How does the leadership style of Prime Ministers vary? Is there a need for a Prime Minister's department?

Part 2 considers the role of the Cabinet. What is collective responsibility? What is the purpose of Cabinet committees? How much power does the Cabinet have? Indeed, where does power lie within the 'core executive'?

Part 1 The Prime Minister

Key issues

1. How did the post of Prime Minister develop and what is the Prime Minister's role today?
2. What are the sources and limitations of prime ministerial power?
3. How does the leadership style of different Prime Ministers vary and what impact does this make?
4. Is there a need for a Prime Minister's department?

1.1 The development of the post of Prime Minister

Historical origins

Following the 'Glorious Revolution' of 1688 (see Chapter 4, Section 1.2), Parliament passed the Bill of Rights in 1689. The Bill of Rights curbed the powers of the monarch by making it illegal to raise money through taxation or to dispense or execute laws without the consent of Parliament. The monarch still remained the head of the executive and appointed a group of ministers (the Cabinet) to govern the country. These ministers, however, had to have the support of a majority in the House of Commons or they would be unable to pass legislation or raise taxation.

It was not until the reign of George I (1714-27) that the monarch stopped attending meetings of the Cabinet. When the monarch did stop attending Cabinet meetings, they were chaired by the First Lord of the Treasury who was later to become known as the Prime Minister. 'First Lord of the Treasury' remains one of the Prime Minister's official titles.

Robert Walpole

Historians have traditionally agreed that Robert Walpole who was First Lord of the Treasury from 1721 to 1742 was Britain's first Prime Minister. But, Wilson (1977) notes that, at that time, the departments of state were still individually answerable to the monarch and, in this sense, the monarch could still be regarded as head of the executive. In addition, the term 'Prime Minister' was applied to Walpole as a term of abuse, implying that he was the monarch's favourite. It may have been true that Walpole was 'first minister' and enjoyed predominance over other heads of department, but he was not a Prime Minister in the modern sense.

19th century developments

By the beginning of the 19th century, William Pitt the Younger was arguing that there was:

'An absolute necessity...that there should be an avowed and real minister possessing the chief weight in the Council and the principal confidence of the king.' (quoted in Wilson 1976, p.17)

But, it was not until 1878 that the term 'Prime Minister' was used in an official document for the first time (by Disraeli) and it was not until 1917 that the office was recognised for the first time in statute.

Although the term 'Prime Minister' was not established until late in the 19th century, it has been argued that the first Prime Minister in the modern sense was Robert Peel, who held office from 1841 to 1846. By then, it was Parliament rather than the monarch which chose the government.

Impact of the extension of the franchise

Wilson (1976) argues that the Great Reform Act of 1832 (see Chapter 7, Section 1.4) was the turning point since the widened franchise meant that the monarch's patronage which was exercised through the First Lord of the Treasury, could no longer be decisive in buying seats. After 1832, the House of Commons could (a little) more legitimately claim to represent the voice of the people and, as a result, it was the Commons rather than the monarch which determined the composition of government and whether or not the government should stay in office. When the franchise was widened further in 1867, political parties became established on a national basis and elections came to be fought as much on the personality of the Party Leader as on the government's or the party's policies. The Leader of the party with a majority in the Commons automatically became Prime Minister with the rights of appointment previously held by the Crown.

1.2 The role and powers of the Prime Minister

Key questions

What role does the Prime Minister play in the British system of government and how has this role changed? Have recent Prime Ministers exercised more power than their predecessors? Would it be reasonable to say that the British Prime Minister had presidential powers?

Prime ministerial duties

The role played by the Prime Minister is governed far more by convention than by law or by rules and regulations. It is, for example, by convention that the Prime Minister always sits in the House of Commons. Similarly, a number of formal duties have evolved:

'The Prime Minister presides over the Cabinet, is responsible for the allocation of functions among ministers and informs the Queen at regular meetings of the general business of the government. The Prime Minister's other responsibilities include recommending a number of appointments to the Queen. These include:

- Church of England arch-bishops, bishops and other Church appointments
- senior judges, such as the Lord Chief Justice
- Privy Counsellors
- Lord Lieutenants.

They also include certain civil appointments, such as...Poet Laureate, Constable of the Tower and some university posts; and appointments to various public boards and institutions, such as the BBC.' (HMSO 1994, p.37)

The way in which particular Prime Ministers carry out the job depends to some extent on their individual leadership style and personality, but, as James (1992) points out, it is also likely to be significantly determined by the day-to-day events and problems facing the government and by the capabilities of and relationships with political colleagues.

Prime ministerial powers

According to the former Cabinet minister Tony Benn, the powers enjoyed by the British Prime Minister can be classified into ten separate categories. The first of these is the power to appoint, reshuffle or dismiss ministers. Benn argues that this is the Prime Minister's most important power:

'The authority to appoint and dismiss ministers without any constitutional requirement to get these changes approved by Parliament or the party, is the most decisive [power]. For, by the use, or threat of use, of this authority, all the other powers described below fall into the hands of the Prime Minister alone; to exercise as he or she thinks best.' (Benn 1981, p.26)

Benn's categories are outlined in Box 12.1 below.

A growth in prime ministerial power?

During the late 1980s, it became increasingly common for political commentators to argue that the Prime Minister had gained power at the expense of the Cabinet. This was not a new argument. Indeed, the classic case for this view was provided by Richard Crossman in his introduction to Bagehot's *The English Constitution*, published in the 1960s.

Box 12.1 Prime Ministers' powers

1. Power to appoint, reshuffle or dismiss ministers.
2. Power to create peers.
3. Power to give out honours.
4. Power to appoint chairs of nationalised industries.
5. Power to make other appointments (eg top civil servants, ambassadors, bishops, judges).
6. Power over ministerial conduct (rules are laid out in the *Ministerial Code* (Cabinet Office 1997) - see Section 2.3 below.
7. Powers relating to government business (eg setting the agenda for Cabinet meetings, setting up Cabinet committees and choosing whether or not to circulate minutes or papers).
8. Powers over information (eg deciding whether or not to inform Parliament about government. activities and using the lobby system to inform the media).
9. Powers in international relations.
10. Power to terminate a Parliament or government.

Adapted from Benn 1981.

Crossman's thesis

In his introduction to Bagehot's *The English Constitution*, Crossman traced the changes in the way in which the UK was governed between the time when the Second Reform Act was passed in 1867 to the end of the Second World War. There had, he argued, been a shift from Cabinet government to prime ministerial government which came about for two main reasons. First, the party system had developed in such a way that the party machinery had been centralised under the control of the Prime Minister. And second, the civil service had grown too large to be controlled by the Cabinet and, instead, had developed into a centralised bureaucracy with the Prime Minister ultimately in control. The combined effect of these changes, Crossman argued, was that the Prime Minister came to stand at the apex of the administrative and the political arms of government. As a result, the role played by Prime Ministers was complicated by the fact that they were both head of government and Leader of the dominant party in Parliament.

Recent developments

In addition, recent developments may suggest that the UK now has prime ministerial government. Prime Ministers are now closely involved in foreign and economic affairs. The electorate, through the mass media, is now more than ever encouraged to identify parties, governments and their policies with Party Leaders. The formal structure of Cabinet and its committees has been downgraded by the practice of 'pre-cooking' policy in informal meetings between the Prime Minister and a few other ministers (see Section 2.6 below). Business tends to flow through the Prime Minister's Office at least as much as through the Cabinet Secretariat.

Presidential powers?

Some commentators have argued that the British Prime Minister is becoming 'presidential'. During the 1980s, this development was associated with Margaret Thatcher's premiership. Johnson, for example, argued that:

> 'It is hardly exaggerating to describe Thatcher's premiership as not merely presidential but quasi-monarchical. This is not just a matter of verbal usage - the royal "we are a grandmother" or "I as government" (both things even monarchs would blench to say), or Thatcher's habit of making policy on the hoof, or the record reduction in the number, duration and documentation of Cabinet meetings, or even the fact that, last year, for the first time, the cost of the PM's department was higher than the Queen's household. It is all these things and more: the huge devotional pictures of Thatcher at Tory meetings, her endless taking of the salute on military occasions, the overt tensions with the palace, the mother-of-the-nation act at national tragedies, and so on.' (Johnson 1990, p.8)

In his analysis of 'presidential' politics in Britain, Foley explains that Thatcher's perceived domination of government revived interest in the traditional debate between prime ministerial and Cabinet power:

> 'In order to maximise the point of executive centralism, references were often made to the comparability of the British Prime Minister with the American Presidency. The association of the personal authority of the Prime Minister as the "focal point of the modern Cabinet" and the evident individual stature of an American President proved too close and too appealing a linkage to ignore.' (Foley 1994, p.137)

Arguments against

Some writers, however, are sceptical about such a comparison. Burch (1990), for example, notes that there are practical restrictions on the Prime Minister's formal power to hire and fire ministers, there are limits on the involvement of a Prime Minister in the initiation of policy and there are constraints on the capacity of the Prime Minister to control government business. Jones (1985 & 1990) concedes that Prime Ministers can be in a powerful position, but only so long as they can carry their colleagues with them - they are only as strong as their colleagues allow them to be. The significance of this statement was underlined by the downfall of Margaret Thatcher in November 1990 (see Chapter 3, Section 3.1), especially as she was regarded as the most powerful post-war Prime Minister. It was also underlined by the position of her successor, John Major - who suffered from a small parliamentary majority, a divided party and a press which branded him as weak and dithering. Unsurprisingly, talk of a presidential Prime Minister subsided until Tony Blair became Prime Minister with a huge majority in Parliament and an energetic leadership style.

Limits of the debate

The conventional debate about the move towards

prime ministerial government or towards a presidential premiership has been based on the assumption that the power of the Prime Minister has increased whilst that of the Cabinet has declined. But, this may ignore other, perhaps wider, analytical frameworks through which the location of power might be explored (see Section 2.7 below). Furthermore, the presidential analogy glosses over the very different constitutional position of an American President compared to a British Prime Minister. The American President, for example, has a much weaker hold on the legislature.

Foley's thesis

Foley (1994) argues that some features of the American presidency can be employed to analyse some of the changes in the role of the Prime Minister which have taken place since the late 1970s. He isolates four features of the American presidency which, he claims, have been adopted by British Prime Ministers.

1. Spatial leadership

The term 'spatial leadership' refers to the attempts made by American Presidents to distance themselves politically from the presidency when it is expedient to do so. John Major's Citizen's Charter initiative is a good example of the way in which this idea has been adopted in the UK. By publicly criticising bureaucratic elements of government, Major gave the impression that he was on the side of the ordinary citizen, battling against oppressive bureaucracy. Similarly, in his first year of office, Tony Blair shook off reports of political corruption involving Labour MPs and Labour councils 'by disowning both MPs and councils before anything is proven against them' (Lloyd 1997).

2. The cult of the outsider

Just as Presidents Nixon, Carter, Reagan and Clinton all claimed to be outsiders (both politically and socially) and, therefore, not to have the vested interests of government insiders, this has also been the stance of Prime Ministers from Callaghan onwards. Thatcher, in particular, maintained close ties with the party rank and file and engaged in populist politics which circumvented the Whitehall machine. Even before he became Prime Minister, Tony Blair used a similar strategy when reforming the Labour Party. The success of those reforms has ensured that the same approach has continued in government.

3. Public leadership

American Presidents have increasingly appealed for support directly to the public over the heads of Congress:

> 'Presidents exploit the individuality of office to project themselves as the focal embodiments of popular concern and the public interest.' (Foley 1994, p.139)

Foley argues that British political leadership has developed in a similar way:

> 'With the emergence of a much less hierarchical social order and with the establishment of television as the primary medium of news information and political exchange, a Leader's relationship with the public is now central and decisive.' (Foley 1994, p.139)

4. The personal factor

As in the USA, an integrated image of a party and its programme is being routed through its Leader. In this way, differences between parties tend to become personalised. It is assumed that the personal qualities of the Prime Minister and other party leaders are central to public evaluations of political leadership and performance.

Conclusion

Together, Foley argues, these developments have resulted in a new kind of British premiership. He concludes that:

> 'Given the scale, depth and implications of these largely unacknowledged changes, it is no exaggeration to declare that British premiership has to all intents and purposes turned not into a British version of the American presidency, but into an authentically British presidency.' (Foley 1994, p.141)

The Cabinet Secretary, Sir Richard Wilson, would disagree with this conclusion, however. Whilst appearing before the Commons Public Administration Committee in June 1998, he pointed out that executive powers were legally vested in individual departments, with the Prime Minister's only executive power being in relation to the civil service. This, Wilson argued, meant that the Prime Minister had to work through colleagues, preventing the development of a presidential Prime Minister (*Times*, 17 June 1998).

Main points - Sections 1.1-1.2

- Robert Walpole is usually said to have been Britain's first Prime Minister (1721-42), but historians argue that the first Prime Minister in the modern sense was Robert Peel (1841-46).
- It was only after the franchise was extended that the Commons gained the power to choose the composition of the government and to decide whether the government should stay in office.
- Prime ministerial duties include presiding over the Cabinet, allocating jobs to ministers, informing the monarch of government business and recommending appointments.
- According to Tony Benn, Prime Ministers have ten separate powers. There is a debate about whether Prime Ministers' powers have increased at the expense of the Cabinet.
- Some commentators have argued that British Prime Ministers are becoming increasingly 'presidential'. There are some signs that Tony Blair has a presidential style.

Activity 12.1 *The Prime Minister's powers*

Item A *A Prime Minister's diary*

1975

Audiences of the queen	8
Cabinet meetings	11
Cabinet committees	24
Other ministerial meetings	43
State visits	1
Other head of government visits	5
Other foreign VIP visits	8
Visits abroad	2

Visits to Northern Ireland	1
Meetings with industry, prominent industrialists, etc	28
Official meetings	27
Ministerial speeches	17
Political speeches	9
Visits within Britain	13
Official lunches and dinners	20
Political meetings - no speech	11
TV or radio broadcasts	8

This diagram shows an analysis of Harold Wilson's diary for the last three months of 1975. Wilson noted: 'Christmas apart, I was not able to record a single private or social engagement.'

Adapted from Wilson 1976.

Item B *Constraints on the Prime Minister*

There are a number of constraints on the Prime Minister. First, ministerial appointments require some recognition of the need for political balance and administrative competence. Also, there is pressure (from colleagues or the media) to appoint certain people - all Prime Ministers at least listen to advice from senior colleagues before making appointments. Second, the Prime Minister's ability to control the flow of business is restricted. It would simply be impractical for a Prime Minister to intervene constantly in the drawing up of agendas or the composition of Cabinet minutes. Third, apart from drawing up the party manifesto, most Prime Ministers do not initiate policy - they have a small staff and most expertise and detailed information is located in individual departments. So, it is difficult for Prime Ministers to interfere constantly in the work of a department. Anyway, it is simply beyond the ability of a single person to be everywhere and to know everything. Different Prime Ministers have different opportunities. John Major, for example, made much less use of his powers of direction and management than Margaret Thatcher did. Also, Major was much more reluctant to hire and fire ministers than Thatcher. Those Major did sack were often dismissed with reluctance and in response to outside pressure. Major, however, was constrained by political factors (ideological splits in his party making it hard to manage, especially as it had a small majority) and economic factors (in the early 1990s Britain suffered a bad economic recession - recessions lead to falling popularity which, in turn, creates stronger political constraints).

Adapted from Burch 1990 and 1994.

Item C *A presidential Prime Minister?*

One of the clearest impressions from this year's party conference is that New Labour is the tale of one man. All the conference oxygen is sucked up by the Leader. 'It's all about him, he's the only one who can excite them', said one delegate. Tony Blair does little to discourage this sentiment. Yesterday, he gently belittled the Cabinet with a joke at their expense - to show that his underlings did not mean much to him. Then, in his speech, he used the first person far more than he referred to the party ('The people entrusted me with the task of leading their country...That is the Britain I offer you' and so on). He uses presidential imagery as well as language, including the now familiar trumpeted entrance and post-speech pose for the cameras with the First Lady. All heads of government hope to escape party and acquire power that transcends politics.

Mitterand did it successfully in France in 1988 and Clinton did it in the USA in 1996. But, unlike Mitterand and Clinton, Blair is not a President. He is not directly elected, but owes his job to his party's majority in Parliament. With that one restraint, however, he is seeking to be his own man. And, so far it is working.

Adapted from the *Guardian*, 1 October 1997.

Questions

1. 'The office of Prime Minister has long been overrated.' In what ways and to what extent are the powers of the Prime Minister limited? Use Items A-C in your answer.

2. Using Items B and C explain why there is much more to the role played by Prime Ministers than the performance of their formal duties.

3. Does the British Prime Minister have presidential powers? Use Item C in your answer.

1.3 Prime ministerial styles

Studying leadership styles

As Norton (1987) has noted, the formal powers of a Prime Minister are a necessary but not a sufficient condition for the effective application of prime ministerial power. Other variables come into play - such as the political circumstances of the time and relationships with Cabinet colleagues. How these variables are handled depends to some extent upon the political skills and personality of the Prime Minister. It depends, in other words, on the style of leadership which the Prime Minister chooses to adopt.

Most commentators (but not all) would agree that leadership style is important. To what extent, however, does it account for the variations in the role which Prime Ministers play in the policy-making process? Although there have been studies of the style adopted by individual Prime Ministers (for example, King (1985a) examines the style of Margaret Thatcher), the subject has rarely been examined systematically. Burch (1994) suggests that attempts to analyse prime ministerial power and style purely in terms of the personality types of those who hold the office are severely limited. There is no single generally accepted method of classifying personalities and few political analysts, commentators or psychologists are sufficiently close to a Prime Minister to be able to build up an accurate personality profile. This limitation is all the stronger since, during the time Prime Ministers are in office, personal aspects and characteristics are filtered through, and probably distorted by, the party image makers and organs of the mass media.

Norton's fourfold typology of prime ministerial style

Despite the drawbacks mentioned above, Norton (1987) argues that it is possible to classify Prime Ministers according to a fourfold typology. He argues that different Prime Ministers seek or end up in office for different reasons and these different reasons then have a bearing on how they behave in office. The four categories he suggests are: innovators, reformers, egoists and balancers.

1. Innovators

Innovators seek power in order to achieve some future goal (they are, in other words, ideologically motivated). They are prepared to risk unpopularity in order to achieve that goal. The goal is not necessarily formulated and agreed by their party. It bears the personal imprint of the innovator.

2. Reformers

Reformers also seek power in order to achieve some future goal (they are also ideologically motivated). But, this goal has been previously formulated and agreed by their party. The goal does not necessarily bear their personal imprint.

3. Egoists

Egoists seek power simply in order to exercise and retain power. They are, in other words, motivated by self-regard, not by ideology. Since their main aim is to retain power for themselves, they are principally concerned with the present and not with some future goal.

4. Balancers

Balancers seek power to ensure that peace and stability are maintained - both within their party and within society as a whole. Balancers fall into two sub-categories - those who actively seek office and those who do not. Those who do not actively seek office tend to be compromise candidates in leadership elections. Norton describes them as 'conscripts'.

5. Applying the models

Whilst these categories are not mutually exclusive, Norton argues that their value is that all Prime Ministers exhibit a preponderance of characteristics of a particular type. For example, he describes Margaret Thatcher as an innovator, citing her address to the 1979 Conservative conference when she said:

> 'We have to move this country in a new direction - to change the way we look at things, to create a wholly new attitude of mind.'

Thatcher had a radical vision and she was prepared to lead from the front, hoping that her party would follow. In this, she was very different from other radical Prime Ministers. Norton contrasts Thatcher's style with that of the post-war Labour Prime Minister Clement Attlee. Like Thatcher, Attlee had a radical vision, but he was careful to ensure that he had the backing of the party before agreeing on a course of action.

Norton is careful to point out that this typology must be used carefully. He emphasises in particular two qualifications. First, Prime Ministers cannot be rigorously 'boxed' - an individual may straddle two or more types. And second, even though most individuals do fall preponderantly within a type, there is no rule that they must remain there. Norton describes Churchill, for example, as an innovator in wartime and a balancer in peacetime.

Despite these qualifications, Norton claims that his typology provides a focus for inquiry. By looking at 'purpose' (the reason why Prime Ministers seek power), it is possible to go beyond a study of prime ministerial powers themselves and towards an examination of the 'why of prime ministerial power' (Norton 1987, p.345).

Political skills

Most analyses of prime ministerial styles, however, have focused on the political skills required by Prime Ministers and the effectiveness with which different

Prime Ministers have selected and applied such skills. In the article mentioned above, for example, Norton (1987) identifies a number of skills which a Prime Minister may need, depending on political circumstances. First, at a general level, Prime Ministers need to develop the skill of 'impression management'. They need to give the appearance that they are suited to the role of Prime Minister. Second, they should have and sustain a 'feel for the office' - an intuitive grasp of when to deploy and when not to deploy the specific skills that they need in order to achieve their purpose in office. And third, they need to know when to lead and when to react. To do this, a successful Prime Minister knows when to command, when to persuade, when to manipulate and when to 'hide' (to keep a distance from a crisis).

Margaret Thatcher's style of leadership

The idea that Britain had prime ministerial government gained support in the 1980s because of Margaret Thatcher's style of leadership. In particular, Thatcher gained the reputation of being a Prime Minister with a dominant personality (see Chapter 3, Section 2.2). She described herself as follows:

> 'I'm not a consensus politician or a pragmatic politician: I'm a conviction politician. And I believe in the politics of persuasion: it's my job to put forward what I believe and try to get people to agree with me'. (Interview in the *Observer*, 25 February 1979)

As such, she appeared to meet with some success in pushing through innovative policies in the face of some opposition from members of her government and party.

In terms of political skills, Thatcher seems to have deployed a number of those identified by Norton above. Certainly she knew how to 'hide'. King (1985a), for example, notes that she sometimes distanced herself from her own government by referring to it as 'they' rather than the more usual 'we'. In addition, she was generally effective in getting her own way when the government appeared to be enjoying popular support, though the reverse applied when popular support ebbed, as it did on a number of occasions between general elections. This suggests that Burch was right to state that:

> 'While Prime Ministers may increasingly be given more of the credit for the success of a government, they must also take more of its blame for its failure'. (Burch 1985, p.356)

John Major's style of leadership

Every Prime Minister brings their own style to the job or develops it during the course of their premiership. Since this is the case, there is no reason to assume that any radical alterations in the way in which one Prime Minister carries out the role will have an impact beyond the term in which that individual holds office. Thatcher's style was very different from

that of her immediate predecessors, but did the job of Prime Minister change as a result of that? Did any of the innovations made by Thatcher become institutionalised or, at least, did her successor John Major attempt to emulate elements of her style or to incorporate her skills into his way of working?

The circumstances of Thatcher's downfall (see Chapter 3, Section 3.1) dictated that Major needed to adopt a different style. It is no surprise, therefore, that Major's first months as Prime Minister were characterised by a consensus-seeking, less strident, less decisive and more pragmatic approach than that exhibited by his predecessor. At the time of the 1992 general election, Major was described in the newspapers as 'honest John' whose government had shown the 'caring face of capitalism'. The contrast with the style of Thatcher was quite deliberate.

Innovations under John Major

Yet, on an organisational level, Major did formalise some of the practices introduced or developed by his predecessor. For example, according to Burch (1994), Major introduced a 'political' session after most Cabinet meetings (a meeting of Cabinet ministers and other senior party members without the presence of civil servants). Meetings like this had been held occasionally under Thatcher, but under Major they became a regular event. In addition, when Major became Prime Minister, the Chief Whip, Leaders of both Houses and the Party Chairman met the Prime Minister at the beginning of each week to review the political and parliamentary developments expected in the week ahead. This way of bringing party management more closely into the formal structure of the Cabinet system had been practised by Thatcher, but in a less formal way.

In terms of policy direction and executive action also, there is evidence that Major's premiership continued and accelerated the radical reforms which were a feature of Thatcher's third term:

> 'It was not until [Thatcher's] third term that policy changes began to exhibit major signs of radicalism. Most importantly, this radicalism has rolled over into the Major period, with the result that Major has presided over many of the structural changes often associated with Thatcher. Thus, it would be wrong to see policy in the Major period as a pale reflection of the reforms introduced by Thatcher.' (Kerr et al. 1997, p.14)

Tony Blair's style of leadership

In terms of Tony Blair's prime ministerial style, the consensus that had emerged by the end of his first 18 months in office was that there were notable differences between Blair and Major, but some striking similarities between Blair and Thatcher. In part, this reflected Blair's strong parliamentary position. For much of his premiership, John Major had a wafer thin majority, allowing small groups of MPs to exert pressure on him. By contrast, Blair (like Thatcher) won a comfortable majority, allowing him greater freedom of manoeuvre.

Parallels between Thatcher and Blair

The parallels between Blair and Thatcher are as follows. First, although, according to McCrum (*Observer*, 28 September 1997), Blair carries 'no ideological baggage whatsoever', he has nonetheless been described as a 'conviction politician'. Second, the two Prime Ministers share a common approach. Blair's premiership has been described, for example, as being characterised by 'strong leadership' and 'charismatic control' (Draper 1997, p.42), characteristics shared by Thatcher. Third, like Thatcher, Blair has been described as 'the most commanding of premiers' who drives the system from the centre (Hennessy 1998). And fourth, like Thatcher, Blair has shown the ability to shake off crises. In the first 18 months, for example, the government faced a number of crises. Yet, judging from opinion poll findings, these crises made absolutely no impact on Tony Blair's personal popularity ratings.

Blair - a distinctive leader?

Although there is, therefore, good reason to point to parallels between the leadership styles of Blair and Thatcher, it should also be recognised that Blair's style is distinctive. For example, Blair publicly apologised when it was revealed that the government had exempted Formula One racing from a ban on tobacco sponsorship following a million pound donation to Labour Party funds. It was not Thatcher's style to apologise. Also, Blair has shown a willingness to experiment with a wide range of methods and approaches to policy making and advice, especially those involving the numerous task forces which draw heavily on people from outside the government machine (see Section 1.4 below). Thatcher did not experiment in this way. As Jonathan Freedland pointed out, although Thatcher is the obvious parallel to Blair, there is cause to argue that Blair's leadership is more complete:

'Blair's charisma, together with an uncanny ability to divine and personify the public mood, has given him a mastery rare in British politics. Margaret Thatcher is the obvious parallel. She, too, towered above her colleagues and enjoyed a charisma that cast all others in her shadow. Yet, Blair has a much tighter grip than Thatcher had at the same

stage. She had to deal with a group of wets (see Chapter 3, Section 2.3) in her Cabinet and a majority of Heathites [supporters of the former Prime Minister Edward Heath] in her parliamentary party. Today's Prime Minister has only a couple of wobblers in his Cabinet and a healthy Blairite majority among Labour MPs. He is fully in charge.' (*Guardian*, 1 October 1997- slightly adapted)

The impact of prime ministerial style

Any examination of variation in styles should not be taken in isolation from the political structures and the political context within which Prime Ministers operate. Margaret Thatcher's downfall (which has been described as 'the most shocking political event of modern times' - see Watkins 1998, p.211) demonstrates the need for Prime Ministers to maintain the support of their Cabinet colleagues. It is partly this requirement which allows King (1985b) to argue that, although British Prime Ministers are often described as political 'leaders', most in fact rarely lead. It is, in other words, not often that Prime Ministers make decisions entirely on their own and it is not often that they are able to steer Cabinet colleagues in directions that they do not want to take. This observation suggests that the power of Prime Ministers to make a major and systematic impact on decision making is limited. Nevertheless:

'[Although] there are limitations to ways in which individual [leaders] can behave...there is still some scope for personality differences to impact on the decision-making process.' (Elgie 1997, p.230)

Main points - Section 1.3

- The way in which Prime Ministers deal with the political circumstances of the time and relationships with Cabinet colleagues is determined by their leadership style.
- Norton argues there are four main styles - innovators, reformers, egoists and balancers.
- The skills Prime Ministers need include impression management, feel for the office, and knowing when to lead and when to react.
- Margaret Thatcher gained the reputation for being a Prime Minister with a charismatic and dominating style, whereas John Major was criticised for being weak and dithering.
- Like Thatcher, Tony Blair's style is charismatic and dominating.

Activity 12.2 Leadership styles compared

Item A *Margaret Thatcher's style (1)*

In 1985, Anthony King argued that Margaret Thatcher's prime ministerial style was very different from that of her predecessors. She was very much an activist who was in politics not 'to be' but 'to do'. Since she was elected Conservative Leader not because of her economic views but despite them, she had to lead from the front if she was to achieve her goals. In part, this was a matter of personality. But, it was also a reflection of the political situation in which she found herself. She was forced to act as an outsider because she was an outsider. The style she adopted can be seen most clearly in her dealings with the Cabinet. According to King, most Prime Ministers play a waiting game, only intervening in a discussion at a fairly late stage. Their aim in acting this way is to see whether a consensus emerges. If it does, then that usually settles the matter. If there is no consensus, then the Prime Minister's intervention may sway feelings one way or another. Thatcher's style, however, was very different. She stated her views at the outset, often thought aloud and interrupted ministers with whom she disagreed. In other words, she did not simply chair Cabinet meetings, she actively participated in them and often dominated them. The result was twofold. On the one hand, she got her own way more often than is normally the case with Prime Ministers. On the other hand, she was sometimes defeated in the Cabinet and was seen to be defeated.

Adapted from King 1985a.

Item B *Margaret Thatcher's style (2)*

Changing the orchestra won't affect the tune - they're only there for appearances.

This cartoon appeared in the *Guardian* on 26 July 1989.

Item C *John Major's style (1)*

In an article written in April 1994, Hugo Young argued that whilst John Major's prime ministerial style was a source of strength when he was first elected, by 1994 it had become a source of weakness. Major's rise to power, Young claimed, was due to his ability to soothe very many and enrage very few members of his party. He did this by being neither opinionated nor autocratic. He gave the impression that he was prepared to listen and to proceed by consensus. Whilst this was just the contrast that was needed in 1990, by 1994 it had come to be seen as weak leadership personified. This reputation for weakness persisted until the 1997 general election. Writing after the election, Richard Brooks reported that Major's colleagues thought he was a poor general with no real desire for office, who dithered and was uncertain of his own views. David Mellor (former Heritage Secretary) said he was 'fed up with the quality of generalship', whilst Tristan Garel-Jones (former Foreign Office Minister) argued that, thanks to Major's indecision, the government 'bled to death' over Europe. Douglas Hurd (former Foreign Secretary) claimed that Major 'had no lust for office' whilst Malcolm Rifkind (Hurd's successor) recalled Major 'sometimes not expressing any view at all until he has allowed all of his colleagues to express them'.

Adapted from the *Guardian*, 29 April 1994 and the *Observer*, 21 September 1997.

Item D *John Major's style (2)*

By 1997, John Major had gained the reputation for dithering, as this cartoon illustrates.

Item E *Tony Blair's style (1)*

Writing in June 1998, Andrew Rawnsley argued that, when Tony Blair announced in May 1997 that he had 'campaigned as New Labour and will govern as New Labour', he meant that he would continue to hand down decisions from a tight group at the centre and everyone else was meant to march in step. According to Rawnsley, Blair believes the job of Labour backbenchers is to support the government - it is not their role to hold ministers to account but to spread the New Labour message in their constituencies. The Chief Whip, Rawnsley claims, is to report on the behaviour of Labour MPs and interview those with a poor record - the aim being to purge MPs for thought crimes against Blairism. Peter Hennessy also sees evidence of centralisation. He notes that paragraph 88 of the *Ministerial Code* (issued in July 1997) instructs ministers to submit speeches, documents and requests to do interviews to Downing Street for clearance. Whilst some people criticise Tony Blair's 'control freak' style, Hennessy argues that such an absolutist approach is unrealistic in the long term. The trouble with solo decision making is that the buck stops with the decision maker. The blame cannot be shared unless the responsibility is genuinely collective. John Lloyd, on the other hand, admires Blair's 'charismatic modesty, impatient niceness and tousled efficiency'. The difference between Blair and Major, he argues, is one of certainty. Blair and his allies are convinced they are in control of history.

Adapted from the *Observer*, 7 June 1998, Hennessy 1998 and the *New Statesman*, 26 September 1997.

Item F *Tony Blair's style (2)*

This cartoon was drawn to mark the Blair government's first anniversary in power. The men carrying the throne are spin doctors.

Questions

1. a) Judging from Items A-F, how do the prime ministerial styles of Margaret Thatcher, John Major and Tony Blair differ?
   b) To what extent would you say that a difference in style means a difference in substance? Give reasons for your answer.

2. a) Using Norton's typology of prime ministerial styles, how would you describe (i) Margaret Thatcher (ii) John Major and (iii) Tony Blair? Give reasons for your answer.
   b) What are the benefits and drawbacks of Norton's typology?

3. Compared to other factors affecting the exercise of power, how much importance would you place on the question of prime ministerial style?

1.4 Prime Minister's staff

The Prime Minister's Office

There is no Prime Minister's department. Unlike most ministers in the Cabinet, Prime Ministers do not have their own ministry to run. There is, however, a Prime Minister's Office. This Office includes political appointees and advisers (some of whom are employed as 'temporary civil servants') as well as permanent civil servants. All are there primarily to serve the Prime Minister. According to the *Guardian* (30 June 1998), a total of 152 staff was employed in the Prime Minister's Office in 1998. By contrast, in 1998, the Department for Education and Employment employed 4,600 civil servants in its headquarters and regional government offices and even a small government department like the Department for Culture, Media and Sport employed 372 civil servants.

Since 1974, there have been at least four identifiable functional groups within the Prime Minister's Office. Although in practice the dividing lines between their respective functions are not always clear-cut, these groups are: the Prime Minister's Private Office, the Political Unit, the Press Office and the Policy Unit. In addition, the Labour government created a new group in November 1997 - the Strategic Communications Unit. Prime Ministers also sometimes make use of external advisers and task forces.

1. The Private Office

The Prime Minister's Private Office is mainly staffed by permanent civil servants 'on loan' from other government departments. These officials deal with the Prime Minister's official engagements and with the Prime Minister's relations with Parliament and the government departments. Conventionally, the head of the Private Office is a civil servant - the

Prime Minister's Principal Private Secretary - who remains in almost constant contact with the Prime Minister. During the first 18 months of Blair's premiership, however, many of the more important functions of a Principal Private Secretary (such as 'gatekeeping' - deciding who should have access to the Prime Minister) were performed by Jonathan Powell, the Chief of Staff. Powell ran Blair's office in opposition and Blair wanted him to have the post of Principal Private Secretary, but Sir Robin Butler, the then Head of the Civil Service, vetoed this move. Instead, John Holmes was appointed Principal Private Secretary and Powell given the post of Chief of Staff.

A central function of the Private Office is control of the flow of information. The Private Office acts as a filter for the mass of information which converges on the Prime Minister's Office from all branches of the Cabinet system, including all the government departments. If its job is done properly, the Prime Minister should have sight of all important policy initiatives at an early stage in their development. Such knowledge should, therefore, aid the potentially powerful position of the Prime Minister at the centre of the government apparatus.

2. The Political Unit

The Prime Minister's Political Unit often contains young people who later progress to senior political positions. For example, Nigel Lawson (who later became Chancellor of the Exchequer) worked in the Political Office (as the Unit was then called) when Alec Douglas Home was Prime Minister (1963-64) and Douglas Hurd (who later became Foreign Secretary) worked in the Political Office when Edward Heath was Prime Minister (1970-74). Following the Labour election victory in May 1997, Sally Morgan (previously Head of Campaigns at Labour Party headquarters) was appointed as Tony Blair's Political Secretary.

The main function of the Unit is party liaison. It deals with the Prime Minister's party and constituency affairs and is, therefore, in close contact with the headquarters of the party in power as well as with the party's supporters and MPs. The Unit may also assist with the Prime Minister's speeches and offer general advice of a political nature. According to James (1992), however, such advice is frequently ignored and the Political Unit has little influence on policy.

3. The Press Office

The Prime Minister's Press Office looks after the Prime Minister's relations with the media. During Margaret Thatcher's premiership, Bernard Ingham, the Press Secretary, gave the Press Office a formidable 'up-front' role - particularly in his handling of lobby correspondents (see Chapter 19, Section 2.2). Traditionally, with the occasional

exception (such as Harold Wilson's Press Secretary Joe Haines who is said to have exercised considerable influence over incomes policy in the mid-1970s), the staff of the Press Office have been more likely to affect the presentation than the content of policy. Under Blair, however, the presentation of policy has assumed great importance and the Chief Press Secretary, Alastair Campbell, has been described as:

> 'A key figure in an increasingly politicised post. He [sees] Blair several times a day, controls access to him and travels with him. All requests for ministerial interviews have to be cleared through him.' (*New Statesman* Wallchart, 6 June 1997)

4. The Policy Unit

A recent addition to the Prime Minister's Office is the Policy Unit. Created by Harold Wilson in 1974, it has been used by Prime Ministers ever since. The function of the Policy Unit is to advise the Prime Minister on particular aspects of government policy - mainly providing policy advice for the medium and long term, but also providing more immediate policy advice if required. The Policy Unit is usually made up of outside specialists taken on as temporary civil servants, though Thatcher brought in officials from government departments. A complete change of staff occurs with each new Prime Minister. On becoming Prime Minister in May 1997, Tony Blair appointed David Miliband as Director of Policy and Derek Scott as Financial Adviser and (by July 1998) ten others - the so-called 'Downing Street Dozen' - 11 political advisers and one civil servant (*New Statesman*, 24 July 1998). Previously, Miliband had worked as a researcher for a think tank (the IPPR) and as Secretary of the Social Justice Commission. Scott had been Blair's economic adviser in opposition.

The role of the Policy Unit

The Policy Unit can strengthen Prime Ministers in their dealings with other ministers because it is somewhat distanced from the civil service machine (which operates on a departmental basis, providing advice to individual government ministers). As a result, it can provide Prime Ministers with an alternative source of policy advice. In July 1998, Kirsty Milne assessed the role of the Policy Unit as follows:

> 'The Policy Unit gets the blame for all sorts of evils, from the watering down of this week's transport white paper to the absence of a policy on mental health...[The staff] have far more face-to-face contact with Blair than the average minister. They see Cabinet papers, they attend Cabinet committees. "If the Prime Minister wants something to happen, you are his foot soldier around Whitehall" explains the Tory MP, Damien

Green, who was a member of John Major's Policy Unit. "That's a powerful position"...But most of No 10's time is taken up with day-to-day surveillance duties: ploughing through a departmental document here, querying a controversial policy there. One Tory Minister used to call Damien Green "the spy in the cab".' (*New Statesman*, 24 July 1998)

Policy initiatives

The Policy Unit puts forward its own policy initiatives, sometimes promoting ideas from outside specialist advisers, from think tanks and from other countries. James (1992) reveals, for example, that the notion of an 'internal market' for the NHS was apparently suggested to Prime Minister Thatcher by her Head of the Policy Unit, John Redwood. His suggestion was, in turn, based on an idea proposed by an American academic.

Overseeing ministers

Kirsty Milne notes that, under Tony Blair, members of the Policy Unit are given particular areas of policy to oversee. For example, in 1998 it was the job of Liz Lloyd (the only woman member of the Policy Unit in 1998) to oversee agriculture, environment and home affairs and the job of Geoffrey Norris to oversee trade and industry, transport and regional policy. One of the reasons for overseeing these areas is to ensure that ministers follow the line set by the Prime Minister:

> 'Often the degree of interference is inversely proportional to the "reliability" of the minister concerned. With Jack Straw so instinctively "on-message", there is no need for Lloyd to reach for the tiller. But, Norris intervenes routinely at the Department for Trade and Industry where Margaret Beckett is hard-put to match Blair's desire to please the business community.' (*New Statesman*, 24 July 1997)

5. The Strategic Communications Unit

The Strategic Communications Unit was set up in November 1997 with a staff of six - a mix of civil servants and special advisers (who are political appointees). The aim of the new unit is to pull together the government's media work:

> 'The unit is intended to spot pitfalls... coordinating ministerial announcements and thinking well ahead, keeping the big picture in mind.' (*Guardian*, 28 November 1997)

Critics complained that the creation of this unit was a sign of further centralisation and the politicisation of civil servants. There were also complaints when it was revealed that, partly as a result of creating this new unit, in 1997-98 Labour had spent £1.5 million more on staff at Downing Street than the Conservatives did in 1996-97. It should be noted,

however, that the amount spent (c.£5 million) was far less than that spent by the President in the USA or France.

Political advisers and task forces

In addition to those advisers placed in the five groups described above, Prime Ministers also sometimes appoint special advisers on specific policy areas. Although she did not initiate this practice, Margaret Thatcher made considerable use of special advisers. Most famously, she appointed Professor Alan Walters as her economic adviser (policy differences between Walters and Nigel Lawson, the Chancellor, were a major factor in Lawson's decision to resign in 1989). During the first 18 months of his premiership, Tony Blair drafted in outside advisers and made use of seminars in which academics and members of think tanks were invited to present their views. Extensive use was also made of 'task forces'. These task forces contained outsiders (often from the business world) who were assigned to advisory and review groups, each concentrating on a specific area or aspect of policy. Within three months of the Blair government taking office, more than 50 of these task forces had been set up. A year later, there were 75 (*Observer*, 28 June 1998).

A Prime Minister's department

Over the years, the number of staff employed in the Prime Minister's Office has increased. There is an argument that, taken together, the Prime Minister's Office and the Cabinet Office now constitute a formidable alternative power base to that of the Cabinet. Bearing in mind that the Prime Minister and the Cabinet Secretary have a close working relationship (see below, Section 2.5), this implies that in effect, if not in name, a Prime Minister's department has emerged. This argument was considerably strengthened by the development of a closer relationship between the Prime Minister's Office and the Cabinet Office following the election of Tony Blair's government. The central role in forging this link was played by Peter Mandelson, the Minister without Portfolio based in the Cabinet Office. Mandelson's remit was:

> 'To assist in the strategic implementation of government policies and their effective presentation to the public.' (Draper 1997, p.19)

Peter Hennessy (1998) claims that all Prime Ministers have toyed with the idea of setting up a Prime Minister's department. Under Blair, he argues, this is already happening. He cites a former top civil servant Peter Kemp who asserted that 'all the things I've called for are coming true - a Prime Minister's department in all but name.'

Against this, however, is the view that most Cabinet ministers have the administrative support of vast government departments and receive advice from their senior permanent officials. Some leading Cabinet ministers also appoint their own special advisers. Cabinet committees, especially those not chaired by the Prime Minister, can be seen as alternative centres of power to the Prime Minister's Office. The sources of advice and support to a Prime Minister, on the other hand, are more transitory and more difficult to control. For these and other reasons (see Item A in Activity 12.3 below), it is still sometimes suggested that Prime Ministers need their own department of state.

Main points - Section 1.4

- There is no Prime Minister's department. There is, however, a Prime Minister's Office.
- The job of the Private Office is to control the flow of information to the Prime Minister. The Political Office deals with party liaison. The Press Office looks after the media. The Policy Unit develops policy and scrutinises the work of departments. The Strategic Communications Unit pulls together Downing Street's media work.
- Prime Ministers also employ special advisers. Tony Blair has set up a number of task forces to deal with particular issues.
- Some people argue that, in reality, a Prime Minister's department already exists. Others argue that Prime Ministers would have greater control over government if a formal department was set up.

Activity 12.3 *Downing Street and reform*

Item A   *The case for and against a Prime Minister's department*

Arguments in favour of a Prime Minister's Department	Arguments against a Prime Minister's Department
<ul><li>The powers and duties of the Prime Minister have grown and will continue to do so. As a result, it is necessary for the Prime Minister to have an adequate support system.</li><li>Prime Ministers have to be able to strike a balance between departmental and wider strategic objectives. They have to be able to provide Parliament and the media with a ready answer to almost any aspect of government action. The globalisation of political affairs means that they need to be well briefed on issues in their international context.</li><li>Prime ministers need an advice system of their own and one which has the time and the personnel to provide advice based on knowledge and study at a reasonable depth across the range of government activities. This could only be provided by a department set up to serve the Prime Minister.</li></ul>	<ul><li>A Prime Minister's department would be a revolution in the constitution, a move from a ministerial and Cabinet system to prime ministerial government.</li><li>The existence of such a department might actually weaken the powers of the Prime Minister because what Prime Ministers need are flexible arrangements rather than a rigid bureaucratic structure. The current system is responsive to the political control and direction taken by the Prime Minister. If it became a bureaucratic structure, it would develop a momentum of its own, have a view of its own and put to the Prime Minister a certain line.</li><li>The current system prevents the emergence of one person who has the Prime Minister's ear. Rather, several people are in constant daily touch with the Prime Minister.</li><li>A department would generate a large amount of paperwork. The Prime Minister would find it difficult to keep on top of this paperwork.</li></ul>

Adapted from Berrill 1985 and Jones 1985.

Item B   *Special advisers under Blair*

One of the biggest transfers of political staff into Whitehall was confirmed in June 1997 when the Cabinet Office published a list of special advisers employed since the general election. In addition to special advisers working with civil servants in each department, Labour moved almost its entire core election campaign team into government. Key decisions on presentation of policy were taken by an inner team - Peter Mandelson (Minister without Portfolio), Jonathan Powell (Prime Minister's Chief of Staff) and Alastair Campbell (Chief Press Officer) - which met early in the morning. Other frequent attenders were Mr Campbell's deputy and Tim Allan (a special adviser attached to Downing Street). The Chancellor, Gordon Brown, sent his special adviser and press officer, Charlie Whelan. The Foreign Secretary, Robin Cook, was represented by his special adviser, David Clark. Deputy Prime Minister John Prescott sent his special adviser Joe Irvin. A civil servant from the office of the Cabinet Secretary was also present. The plan, drawn up before the election, was for a stronger No 10 in which an enhanced Policy Unit would work closely with a more proactive Cabinet Office to drive the machine as a whole. Peter Mandelson was a key figure. He was located in the Cabinet Office and had a seat on nearly all the Cabinet groups that counted. No 10 was represented in all the serious policy reviews. A member of the Policy Unit sat on all the comprehensive expenditure review teams. Blair used his Policy Unit briefs and his lawyer's questioning skills to great advantage in his discussions with individual departmental ministers.

Adapted from the *Guardian*, 3 June 1997 and Hennessy 1998.

Item C Setting up the Prime Minister's Office

In his account of Tony Blair's first 100 days in power, Derek Draper pointed out that being physically close to the person in charge ensures power and patronage. He then described the setting up of the Prime Minister's Office. Jonathan Powell was located in the Principal Private Secretary's Office, next to the Cabinet room. Alastair Campbell moved into the Press Secretary's office, to the right of the front door. Tim Allan (Campbell's deputy) and Hilary Coffman (a special adviser) were given desks in the press room next to Campbell's office, working alongside civil service press officers. Kate Garvey, keeper of Blair's diary, shown to a desk at the back of the outer Private Office, was no longer within shouting distance of her boss. David Miliband opted for a bare room across the corridor from the Private Office. Sally Morgan and her team in the Political Unit had an artificially partitioned room along the corridor that leads to the Cabinet Office. After running Blair's office for 11 years, Anji Hunter was thwarted by officials who knew they must take over most, if not all, of her functions. But, after a weekend of manoeuvring, she was back - as Special Assistant to the Prime Minister, with responsibility for planning external events. In truth, she continued to act as the gateway for many Labour figures and for Blair's friends and contacts. A word in her ear beats any Whitehall formality.

Adapted from Draper 1997.

Item D The Policy Unit

This cartoon was first published in the *New Statesman* on 24 July 1998.

Questions

1. a) 'The establishment of a Prime Minister's department is unnecessary.' Using Item A, give arguments for and against this view.
   b) How would the establishment of a Prime Minister's department affect the way in which Prime Ministers do their job?
2. a) Using Items B-D, explain how the changes made after May 1997 might be used to strengthen Tony Blair in his dealings with other ministers.
   b) 'The greater use of special advisers is a cause for concern'. Give arguments for and against this view.
3. a) What role is played by the Policy Unit under Blair? Use Items B and D in your answer.
   b) How accurate is the view of the Policy Unit portrayed in Item D?

Part 2 The Cabinet

Key issues

1. What role is played by the Cabinet?
2. What is 'collective responsibility' and how does it work?
3. What role is played by Cabinet committees?

2.1 The Cabinet

Origins of the Cabinet

The element of the executive now known as the Cabinet first emerged at the end of the 17th century, following the curbing of the powers of the monarch after the 'Glorious Revolution'. When the Bill of Rights was passed in 1689, the monarch at first remained at the centre of the executive:

'To enable the Sovereign [monarch] and Parliament to work together to carry on the government of the country, a group of ministers, or Cabinet, became the link between the executive and the legislature. Although the ministers were appointed by the Sovereign, they had to have sufficient support in the House of Commons to enable them to persuade Parliament to pass legislation and vote for taxation.' (HMSO 1994, p.3)

From the reign of George I (1714-27), the monarch ceased to attend meetings of the Cabinet. Instead, the Cabinet was chaired by the First Lord of the Treasury, later known as the Prime Minister. The Cabinet developed into its modern form during the 19th century when the extension of the franchise and the evolution of the party system resulted in governments (and, therefore, the Cabinet) relying on the support of the House of Commons. From this requirement grew the convention of collective responsibility (see below, Section 2.3).

The role played by the Cabinet

A changing role

Although the Cabinet may have developed into its modern form in the 19th century, the role played by the Cabinet then was very different from that which it plays today. James notes that:

'Many studies explore the Cabinet's genesis and evolution in past centuries: this can be unhelpful and even misleading. The post-1945 Cabinet is very different from its ancestors...[After the Second World War] the character of Cabinet government changed markedly. The volume of work grew enormously, this work became complex and detailed, and departments' problems became more closely interrelated, particularly in the economic and social fields. Ministerial life became frantic and high-pressured...A huge network of Cabinet committees developed to cope with the load. It became less easy for the Cabinet to exercise full control over the government's main policies. Inevitably, the Cabinet's role was eroded.' (James 1992, p.2)

Despite this, the Cabinet is still typically seen as one of the central institutions of the British political system. Although its methods of operating have changed over time, the Cabinet is normally portrayed as occupying the apex of the executive arm of government.

The Cabinet's functions today

The Cabinet's functions have been described as follows:

'The functions of the Cabinet are policy making, the supreme control of government and the coordination of government departments.' (HMSO 1994, p.39)

The Cabinet, therefore, has a dual role:

- to propose legislation
- to supervise administration.

Constraints on the Cabinet

Full meetings of the Cabinet take place only once or twice a week and most have finished within a couple of hours. It is simply not feasible for the full Cabinet, therefore, to carry out detailed policy making over all areas covered by government policy.

In any case, the Cabinet's dual role rests upon the party system. Elections are party contests. The outcome of elections determines the party balance in the House of Commons and, therefore, which party (or parties, if there is a coalition) forms the government. In so far as the government then has a mandate to implement party policy as presented in its election manifesto, the Cabinet's policy-making

role clearly has a party political dimension. The Cabinet also depends on party support in the House of Commons for its continued existence.

The size and structure of the Cabinet

In the period since 1945, Cabinets have generally consisted of around 20 ministers, chaired by the Prime Minister. Most Cabinet ministers are responsible for particular government departments. Since they are expected to explain and defend their policies in Parliament, most Cabinet ministers are MPs, though a few sit in the House of Lords. Outsiders may be appointed to the Cabinet, but they would normally be made a peer or would be expected to fight and to win a by-election - the businessman David Young was made a life peer when he was appointed as Employment Secretary under Margaret Thatcher whilst the trade unionist Frank Cousins fought and won a by-election in 1964 after being appointed Minister for Technology.

The structure and size of the Cabinet, therefore, are prime ministerial decisions. But, the fact that the number of Cabinet ministers at any one time has varied so little since 1945 suggests that there are practical limitations to prime ministerial discretion.

Cabinet hierarchy

Certain departments, because of their centrality to key areas of government policy are now always represented - the Treasury, Home Office and Foreign Office, for example. The fact that the ministers representing these three departments are usually placed at the top of the list published when a new Cabinet is formed suggests that there is a hierarchy within the Cabinet. But, the order of ministers in the hierarchy is not fixed. The exact positioning in the list is likely to reflect the relative political status of the holder of the post as well as the post itself. Ministers new to the Cabinet are normally first appointed to junior positions within the hierarchy.

Personnel

The Prime Minister's choice of Cabinet ministers may be influenced by the expectations of the parliamentary party, though this constraint is often exaggerated. There are numerous examples of senior party figures who have been left out of Cabinets. The former Prime Minister, Edward Heath, for example, never served in a Cabinet under Margaret Thatcher or John Major.

Is the Cabinet too big?

It has been suggested that a Cabinet of 20 or more members is too large for a decision-making body to operate effectively. Also, it has been argued that, if most of the Cabinet's members have departmental responsibilities, there is a danger that departmental concerns, rather than overall matters of policy planning, tend to dominate proceedings. As a result, it is sometimes argued that a much smaller Cabinet, composed of perhaps six to eight ministers who have no departmental responsibilities, would be more effective. Members of such a Cabinet would be free from the administrative workload current heads of departments have to undertake and would, therefore, be able to give their full-time attention to overall matters of policy planning and its coordination.

Experiments with smaller Cabinets

Experiments this century with much smaller cabinets have largely been confined to the emergency conditions of wartime. During the second half of the First World War, for example, Lloyd George headed a Cabinet that varied in size from five to nine members. Similarly, in 1940, Churchill's War Cabinet initially only contained five members, though it was soon expanded to eight. Churchill's experiment with 'overlords' (coordinating ministers) in 1951 reduced the size of the Cabinet to 16, but within two years it had grown to 19 and the experiment was abandoned.

Arguments against small Cabinets

Those who argue against the idea of small Cabinets say that it is based on the false assumption that policy and administration can be separated. They claim that the two are closely enmeshed, with the details of policy merging with matters of administration so that it is not practical to exclude heads of major government departments from the Cabinet. Attempts to separate policy making from administration could also interfere with the principle of ministerial responsibility (see Chapter 13, Section 1.3). In other words, which minister would be answerable to Parliament for which matter might become less clear.

Other means of improving efficiency

Whatever the validity of the arguments for and against smaller or larger Cabinets, the fact remains that for most of the 20th century Prime Ministers have looked to other ways to facilitate coordination or otherwise improve the efficiency of the decision-making process. Rather than focusing on Cabinet size, they have, for example, sought to expand the Cabinet Secretariat (see below, Section 2.5), amalgamated government departments (or, on occasions, split them) and made greater use of Cabinet committees (see below, Section 2.4).

Reshuffles

From time to time, Prime Ministers reshuffle their Cabinets. This might be necessitated by a death, illness or resignation from government. In such cases, the changes could be slight, involving only one or two alterations to the team. Alternatively, the Prime Minister might wish to weed out incompetent or unpopular ministers, alter the balance of views in the Cabinet, or to discourage the formation of alternative power bases. In such cases, new members may be appointed with some Cabinet ministers being promoted, moved sideways or

dropped. In the biggest reshuffle of recent times, Harold Macmillan sacked a third of his Cabinet in a single reshuffle in 1962. This reshuffle became known as the 'night of the long knives' after Hitler's purge of the SA (the military wing of the Nazi Party) in 1934.

2.2 The shadow Cabinet

Definition and role

Although it is not part of the structure of government, a shadow Cabinet operates in the British political system. In a predominantly two-party system, the shadow Cabinet is composed of frontbench politicians from the official opposition party (the leading opposition party in Parliament). Though not necessarily identical, the posts of the shadow Cabinet normally mirror quite closely those in the Cabinet itself. So, for example, there is a shadow Chancellor, a shadow Home Secretary and so on.

Not only does the existence of a shadow Cabinet ensure that an opposition spokesperson is available to put the opposition's side in any political debate, it also means that a team of opposition politicians gains some expertise across the range of policy areas. Since the shadow Cabinet is the centre of a government in waiting, the performance of its members can be closely scrutinised by political commentators and the media in general. When the government has a large majority, however, the significance of the shadow Cabinet as an alternative government is much diminished - particularly in the early stages following a general election.

The key difference between the Cabinet and shadow Cabinet is that, although the shadow Cabinet formulates policies, it is unable to implement them. The shadow Cabinet, therefore, has no executive support in the form of a shadow civil service.

Main points - Sections 2.1-2.2

- The Cabinet first emerged at the end of the 17th century. Today, it has a dual role - to propose legislation and to supervise administration.
- Full meetings of the Cabinet take place only once or twice a week and most are over within a couple of hours. The size of the Cabinet (over 20 ministers) makes discussion difficult. Some people argue for a smaller Cabinet.
- From time to time, the Prime Minister reshuffles the Cabinet to weed out incompetents, alter the balance of views or to discourage the formation of alternative power bases.
- The shadow Cabinet is composed of frontbench politicians from the official opposition party. Its members put the opposition's side in any political debate and gain expertise.

Activity 12.4 *The Cabinet*

Item A *The Cabinet room (1)*

This photograph shows the Cabinet room which is located at 10 Downing Street.

Item C *In favour of a smaller Cabinet*

Reshaping the Cabinet would not just be smart politics, it would bring government closer to the lives of real people. A Cabinet of 22 ministers is simply too large and unwieldy. When was the last time you had a meaningful conversation with 22 people around the table? Whereas Major aimed at collegiate government, Blair prefers the Thatcher method - consulting a few colleagues and then delivering a fait accompli to the full Cabinet. There is little discussion under Blair. The whole business takes just half an hour. Anyway, the Cabinet has lost relevance. Individual posts are positively redundant. The following posts could be dropped:

- the Department of Social Security could become part of the Treasury - experts have long agreed that tax and benefits should be integrated and the Treasury already supervises the Inland Revenue
- the Ministry of Defence should be absorbed into the Foreign Office along with the Department of International Development (which used to be there anyway) - military spending should be driven less by institutional self-preservation and more by foreign policy
- if devolution works, there is no need for separate Scottish and Welsh Offices - a settlement in Northern Ireland makes the Northern Ireland Office redundant
- for a government of life-long learning, Culture and Education should no longer occupy separate addresses
- in a global economy, trade might sit better in the Foreign Office, watching out for Britain's relations with the world
- a wide-ranging Rural Affairs Ministry could deal with problems currently dealt with by Agriculture, Transport and Education.

The result would be a handful of mega-ministries, each charged with seeing society as an interconnected whole. Two more changes would be required to make this work. First, a beefed-up Prime Minister's department to ensure the work of the ministries is coherent. And second, a proper system of parliamentary scrutiny to ensure the ministries behave.

Adapted from the *Guardian*, 4 March 1998.

Item B *The Cabinet room (2)*

Writing in 1992, Simon James argued that the physical layout of a meeting room often affects the quality of discussion and the layout of the Cabinet room is particularly unhelpful. Ministers sit around a long table with the Prime Minister at the centre of one of the long sides. The Cabinet Secretary sits to the right of the Prime Minister and the most senior colleagues sit to the left and opposite. Other ministers are allocated seats by the Cabinet Office in such a way that the more senior a minister, the closer that minister's seat is to the centre. Junior ministers, therefore, sit at the far extremities of the table. The acoustics of the Cabinet room are bad. There is a constant rustling of papers and murmuring between ministers. When ministers speak, they naturally turn their heads to face the Prime Minister. The result is that those at the end of the table can hear little. Cabinet meetings under John Major were conducted in a formal style. Remarks were addressed to the Prime Minister and ministers referred to each other by their formal titles. Shortly after the 1997 general election, however, it was revealed that Tony Blair was breaking with the formality of his immediate predecessors. As under Harold Wilson in 1974, Cabinet colleagues were to address each other by their first names, rather than by their formal titles. Blair also refused to stick to a formal agenda.

Adapted from James 1992, the *Times*, 9 May 1997 and the *Guardian*, 10 May 1997.

Questions

1. Judging from Items A-C, why might Cabinet ministers find it difficult to perform their role satisfactorily?

2. Using Items B and C, describe how the Cabinet works under Tony Blair.

3. 'The ideal Cabinet would consist of five or six ministers who do not have departmental responsibility.' Using Item C, give arguments for and against this statement.

2.3 Cabinet collective responsibility

The *Ministerial Code*

One of the first documents given to new ministers on their appointment is the *Ministerial Code* (until 1997, called *Questions of Procedure for Ministers* - QPM). QPM was first made public in May 1992. Over the years, the document has been changed and added to, but there is always a section on collective responsibility. The July 1997 edition of the *Ministerial Code* states:

> 'Decisions reached by the Cabinet or ministerial committees are binding on all members of the government...Collective responsibility requires that ministers should be able to express their views frankly in the expectation that they can argue freely in private while maintaining a united front when decisions have been reached... Ministers cannot speak on public affairs for themselves alone. In all cases...they speak as ministers; and the principle of collective responsibility applies. They should ensure that their statements are consistent with collective government policy and should not anticipate decisions not yet made public. Ministers should exercise special care in referring to subjects which are the responsibility of other ministers.' (Cabinet Office 1997, paragraphs 16, 17 and 93)

Within Cabinet and its committees, therefore, ministers can express their own views and disagree with each other. The doctrine of collective responsibility, however, requires that, once a decision has been reached, all ministers must accept it and must not publicly disagree with it.

Collective responsibility and resignations

According to the traditional interpretation of the doctrine of collective responsibility, any minister either unable or unwilling to support a Cabinet decision publicly must resign from government. This has important implications. Some commentators, for example, argue that, since ministers only resign as a last resort, the doctrine of collective responsibility strengthens the hand of Prime Ministers. Prime Ministers can push a line knowing, first, that dissenting ministers are unlikely to resign when it is accepted and, second, that, once it has been agreed, no minister will be able to criticise it in public. Other commentators, however, argue that the doctrine encourages constructive collective decision making. Under the doctrine, views expressed within Cabinet and its committees are completely confidential. That means that, even if ministers vehemently oppose measures in Cabinet meetings, their opposition remains unknown to everyone except those present at the meeting (who are themselves obliged to keep silent). As a result, when dissenting ministers are later asked to defend the measures they have criticised, they can do so without losing face. Also, since confidentiality is ensured, ministers are more likely to be critical and this, in theory at least, should have the effect of improving the quality of the decisions made.

Recent trends

According to Dorey (1995), the application of the doctrine of collective responsibility has been subject to two trends in recent years - it has been applied more widely and it has been applied less stringently. The result is that the traditional interpretation needs to be updated.

1. Wider application of the doctrine

Dorey notes that, when the Prime Minister Lord Salisbury described the doctrine of collective responsibility in 1878, he was referring only to collective responsibility within the Cabinet. Other ministers were exempt. During the 20th century, however, the doctrine has come to be more widely applicable. Today, the rules make it quite clear that the doctrine applies not just to Cabinet ministers, but also to all junior ministers and even to parliamentary private secretaries (those just below ministerial level - see Chapter 13, Section 1.1).

Implications

The result of this development is that junior ministers are asked to support, without question, decisions which are made without consulting them. From the executive's point of view, this is clearly desirable since it means that the government can present a united face in public and dissent can be minimised. From the point of view of the individuals concerned, however, it may mean that they feel obliged to go along with decisions about which, in private, they have grave reservations. This, it seems, is what happened, for example, with the poll tax. Privately, ministers had grave reservations, but publicly they presented a united front.

Further evidence of wider application of the doctrine of collective responsibility is the fact that the doctrine is now adopted by the shadow Cabinet. Just as the government wants to present a united front, so too does the government in waiting. It is, therefore, no surprise that public dissent is prohibited on the opposition frontbench.

2. Less stringent application of the doctrine

Whilst ministers do still, on occasion, resign because they feel unable to toe the government line, there is some evidence that the traditional assumption that a dissenting minister must resign (or be sacked) is weakening. Indeed, Dorey argues that, on a number of occasions, ministers who have resigned on the grounds that they could no longer maintain collective responsibility have used this as a pretext to cover ulterior motives.

The Westland Affair

Dorey cites Michael Heseltine's resignation over the Westland Affair in 1986 as a prime example of this tendency. In January 1986, Heseltine, the Defence

Secretary, stormed out of a meeting of the Cabinet claiming that he was unable to support the government's policy over Westland helicopters. Heseltine wanted the company (which was in financial trouble) to be taken over by a European consortium whilst the official Cabinet line was one of neutrality between the European consortium and an American bid (it was well known that the Prime Minister and Secretary of State for Trade and Industry favoured the American bid). Dorey argues that, although Heseltine claimed he was forced to resign because he was unable to support government policy, this was really a pretext. Heseltine aimed to make a bid for the leadership of the Conservative party and realised he would be unable to do so while he remained as part of the government team.

Geoffrey Howe and Europe

Similarly, Dorey argues, Geoffrey Howe said that he was resigning from the Cabinet in November 1990 because he could no longer support the government's policy on Europe. The timing of his resignation, however, suggests that his real pretext was to ensure that a serious leadership contest took place that year (he resigned in time for a leadership challenge to be mounted at the beginning of the parliamentary session, the only time it could be done under Conservative Party rules). Dorey concludes that:

> 'Some of the recent resignations by ministers ostensibly in accordance with the doctrine, have raised doubts about whether such resignations were primarily concerned with policy disagreements or whether they were really manifestations of personality and power struggles within the government, with collective responsibility being invoked in order to legitimise and give credence to the actions of resigning ministers.' (Dorey 1995, p.105)

Further evidence of weakening

Dorey goes on to provide three further indications of the weakening of the doctrine of collective responsibility. First, he claims that the publication of a growing number of ministerial diaries and memoirs suggests that confidentiality is no longer as secure as was once the case. Second, he notes that, on three occasions this century, Prime Ministers have suspended the doctrine of collective responsibility, allowing members of the Cabinet to talk against and vote against government policy - in 1932, 1975 and 1977. In 1975, the Prime Minister allowed members of the Cabinet to support both sides in the referendum over membership of the EC. In 1977, the Prime Minister allowed a free vote over the type of electoral system to be used in European elections. The third indication of the weakening of the doctrine of collective responsibility was the growing tolerance of public dissent from Cabinet members which was permitted by John Major after the 1992 general election. In 1994, for example, Michael Portillo made a number of speeches which appeared to criticise the official government line. Although Major appealed to his ministers to avoid the public airing of differences over policy, no member of the Cabinet resigned or was dismissed.

Main points - Section 2.3

- **The doctrine of collective responsibility requires that, once a decision has been reached, all ministers must accept it and must not publicly disagree with it.**
- **Some people argue that, since ministers must resign if they are unable or unwilling to accept a Cabinet decision, this strengthens the power of the Prime Minister. Others argue that it ensures constructive decision making.**
- **In recent years, the doctrine of collective responsibility has been applied more widely. It now applies to all ministers and PPSs.**
- **There is some evidence that the traditional assumption that a dissenting minister must resign (or be sacked) is weakening.**

Activity 12.5 *The Westland Affair*

Item A *A civil servant's view*

Margaret Thatcher is very clear about her views, very much a leader. Because of that she doesn't need or want to resolve things by collective discussion. She knows what she wants to do about almost everything. But, it is a collective machine because they must all sink or swim with her. She uses the Cabinet as a sort of sounding board. It restrains her when restraint is necessary. She has her own instinct when she cannot carry her colleagues with her. She lets them know what she thinks. Then, they try to adapt and mould it. She has very acute antennae. She's very quick to take the signals if she can't carry it.

Senior civil servant quoted anonymously in Hennessy 1986.

Item B *Thatcher's view*

There was a period when the Cabinet did not seem and, in fact, was not acting with collective responsibility because one person [Michael Heseltine] was not playing as a member of the team. The press was very critical of me in many ways before that. Some said that I should have asked Mr Heseltine to go earlier.

Margaret Thatcher quoted in Hennessy 1986.

Item C   *The Westland Affair*

This cartoon shows Michael Heseltine storming out of the Cabinet room after failing to convince the Prime Minister and the rest of the Cabinet to follow his line. It was first published in the *Guardian* on 10 January 1986.

Item D   *A political commentator's views*

Ministers who feel unable to overcome personal doubts about the nature of government policy, as agreed in full Cabinet or in one of its committees, should under normal circumstances resign if they wish to criticise such policy. Concerning the Westland affair, Thatcher's argument was that she had stretched the doctrine of collective responsibility to its absolute limit in an attempt to accommodate Heseltine. She claimed that the government policy of neutrality was the result of collective discussion between ministers on nine occasions whilst Heseltine was in the Cabinet. Heseltine's view was completely different. He believed that the majority of his colleagues might well have supported the bid by the European consortium if he had been given a chance to explain it properly. Neutrality, he claimed, was a sham used by the Prime Minister and her allies to give the impression that Cabinet was united behind a collective policy.

Adapted from Pyper 1987.

Questions

1. 'Collective responsibility is absolutely essential for good government.' Do you agree with this statement? Explain your answer.
2. Judging from Items A-D, why was the Westland Affair an important milestone in the history of collective responsibility?
3. Is the doctrine of collective responsibility a way of checking personal ambition or a means of furthering it? Use Items A-D in your answer.

2.4 Cabinet committees

Evolution of the Cabinet committee system

Although Cabinet committees were in use in the 19th century, primarily on an ad hoc basis, their existence on something like their present scale only dates back to the 1940s. During the Second World War, Cabinet committees took on much of the work usually done by the Cabinet, allowing the small wartime Cabinet to concentrate on matters concerning the war effort. After the war, the system of Cabinet committees was developed further in response to the expansion of government activity arising out of the setting up of the welfare state and the interventionist economic and social policies pursued by the Labour government (see Chapter 3, Section 1.1).

The current system

According to the Cabinet Office, Cabinet committees play the following role:

> 'Cabinet committees provide a framework for collective consideration of and decisions on major policy issues and issues of significant public interest. The committees meet to resolve disputes and make difficult decisions. Non-contentious issues can generally be agreed in correspondence. Cabinet committees relieve the pressure on Cabinet itself by settling business in a smaller forum or at a lower level, when possible, or at least by clarifying issues and defining points of disagreement. Committees enable decisions to be fully considered by those ministers most closely concerned, in a way that ensures that government as a whole can be expected to accept responsibility for them. They act by implied devolution of authority from the Cabinet and their decisions, therefore, have the same formal status as decisions by the full Cabinet.' (Cabinet Office 1998)

All Cabinet committees are composed of ministers. Some are made up just of ministers of Cabinet rank. Some include junior ministers. Some include senior civil servants and some do not. A Cabinet committee set up after the 1997 general election includes senior Liberal Democrats as well as Labour ministers (see below). Ministerial committees are usually mirrored by so-called 'official' committees composed entirely of civil servants. Official committees are significant because they often meet in advance to prepare the ground for ministerial meetings.

There are two main types of Cabinet committee - standing and ad hoc. **Standing committees** are referred to by code names or letters. They deal with a specific policy area and are relatively permanent. **Ad hoc committees** are set up to deal with specific short-term problems and issues or are committees which meet irregularly. For example, Dorey (1991) notes that while Margaret Thatcher was Prime Minister, ad hoc committees were set up to prepare for the 1984 miners' strike, to prepare for the abolition of the Greater London Council and to investigate the replacement of Polaris nuclear submarines by Trident. By their nature, ad hoc committees are not formal structures and it is, perhaps, no surprise that the Cabinet Office refuses to reveal details about the number of ad hoc committees in existence under Tony Blair.

The extent to which Cabinet committees are used

The composition and even the existence of Cabinet committees were supposed to be secret until 1992 when, for the first time, a list of all Cabinet standing committees (together with their membership and terms of reference) was made public. Before 1992, editions of *Questions of Procedure for Ministers* argued that such secrecy was a necessary part of collective responsibility. Despite the secrecy, however, the evidence suggests a great deal of variation under different Prime Ministers.

Thatcher and Major compared

From the information available, it seems that Margaret Thatcher made less use of the formal Cabinet committee system than did her predecessors. For example, Burch (1994) notes that 941 meetings of Cabinet committees were recorded in 1978, compared to 340 in 1989. Similarly, he notes that, although Thatcher was Prime Minister for much longer than Attlee, she set up less than half the number of ad hoc Cabinet committees and only one sixth of the standing committees he set up in the immediate post-war era. According to Burch & Holliday (1996, p.45), Thatcher cut Cabinet committee meetings by a third between 1979 and 1990. Instead, she organised informal meetings with ministers.

There seems to be a consensus that, although the number of Cabinet committees declined from 26 to 19 in the period 1992-96, John Major made more use of the Cabinet committee system than Thatcher (see, for example, Burch & Holliday 1996, p.280 and Hood & James 1997, p.181). Burch (1994) claims that Major streamlined the system and gave committees a more strategic, wide-ranging remit. For example, whereas Thatcher had chaired four substantive domestic committees, Major chaired just one - a new overarching committee which covered the whole range of domestic policy (known as 'EDP').

Cabinet committees under Blair

Tony Blair's first list of Cabinet committees was published in June 1997. The list revealed that there were 20 committees and a change in emphasis:

'The list of Cabinet committees signals a number of changes of emphasis within government, with the scrapping of four committees from John Major's premiership. Committees on nuclear defence policy, on competitiveness and on the coordination and presentation of government policies have been disbanded, together with the ministerial sub-committee on terrorism.' (*Times*, 10 June 1997)

Blair set up new committees on devolution, constitutional reform, the incorporation of the European Convention on Human Rights and food safety. Blair himself chaired four committees - constitutional reform, Northern Ireland, defence and overseas policy, and intelligence (Thatcher and Major also chaired the latter two).

By July 1998, the number of Cabinet committees had grown to 26 (committees were set up to deal with matters such as reform of the House of Lords, Freedom of Information and the 'millennium bug' - the problems that might occur if computers are unable to deal with the change of date on 1 January 2000). Despite this growth in number, however, there were signs that less use was being made of the Cabinet committee system:

'Cabinet committees rarely meet - except when they absolutely have to. One Cabinet minister believes "the only Cabinet committee to work in a traditional way is that for devolution. This is chaired by Derry Irvine [the Lord Chancellor] and is necessary because of the interdepartmental and legislative complexities of constitutional change"...The rest hardly meet.' (Draper 1997, pp.35-6)

The role of the Prime Minister

The shape - and even the use - of the Cabinet committee system, therefore, appears to depend on the particular style of the Prime Minister. It is the Prime Minister who decides which committees should be set up, what their terms of reference should be, who should chair them and who should sit on them. There may be practical and political restrictions on the Prime Minister's choice - the nature of an issue may require the inclusion of ministers from certain departments, for example. But, there is still considerable room for manoeuvre.

The Lab-Lib Cabinet committee

Two months after the 1997 general election, Tony Blair announced the setting up of a Cabinet consultative committee which would take the unusual step of including leading members of another party. In addition to Blair (who would chair the meetings), the committee was to be composed of five other Labour ministers and five leading Liberal Democrats. The Cabinet Secretary would also attend. The Liberal Democrats on the committee are not bound by collective responsibility, though they do have to sign the Official Secrets Act (and are, therefore, unable to disclose any information they obtain as members of the committee). It was agreed that the committee would meet at least once every two months. The first meeting was held on 17 September 1997. There are only two precedents for this type of committee - a ministerial group on disarmament in 1931 and one on defence research in 1935-37. In November 1998, it was announced that the brief of the joint Lab-Lib Cabinet committee would be widened. Initially, the committee only considered constitutional reform. From November 1998, it considered other areas of mutual concern such as health and education policy.

Cabinet committees and policy making

Despite the variations in the way in which different Prime Ministers use the system, there appears to be considerable scope for the exercise of power by the ministers chairing the committees and by any minister who is a member of several different committees. But, although decisions may be reached in Cabinet committees and they may, therefore, represent what Burch (1990) describes as 'the points at which major policies are determined and decided', these committees are less likely to initiate policy.

Main points - Section 2.4

- Since the 1940s, considerable use has been made of Cabinet committees. It is in these committees that some key decisions are made.
- There are two main types of Cabinet committee - standing and ad hoc. It is only since 1992 that a list of standing committees has been published.
- It seems that John Major made more use of Cabinet committees than Margaret Thatcher. Under Blair,

there has been a change of emphasis. This suggests the shape and role of the committee system depend on the style of the Prime Minister.

- In July 1997, Tony Blair invited senior Liberal Democrats to join a consultative Cabinet committee. Initially, it only considered constitutional reform, but, in November 1998, its brief was widened.

Activity 12.6 *Cabinet committees*

Item A   *Cabinet committees*

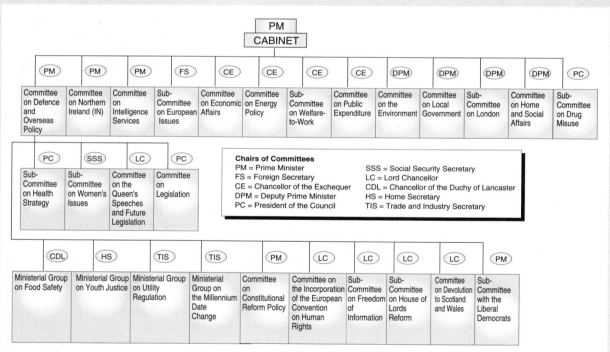

Some Cabinet Committees have sub-committees. They do not normally take final decisions on policy, but they enable the collective discussion of issues ranging across several departments' responsibilities - such as women's issues, drugs, London and EU business. Ministerial Groups are also set up. Their role is to carry out a particular task - for example, the task of the Ministerial Group on the Millennium Date Change is 'to drive action across the public and private sectors to ensure that the national infrastructure is not damaged by the failure of electronic systems related to the year 2000 date change'.

Adapted from information from the Cabinet Office, July 1998.

Item B *Cabinet committees - for and against*

(i) Cabinet committees are the most private and well protected parts of our democracy. Power ought to reside where the public can see it in Parliament, but in fact it hides in these committees. The Prime Minister appoints their members and is, therefore, able to pack them to achieve a desired result. Cabinet committees often present the full Cabinet with a fait accompli.

Adapted from Cockerell et al. 1984.

(ii) Some critics have argued that Cabinet committees enhance the power of the Prime Minister, but, to Harold Wilson, this was a facile view - Cabinet committees make government more effective and prevent the Cabinet being bogged down in detail. Wilson claimed that the role of the Prime Minister is to ensure that the Cabinet committee system works smoothly by delegating authority to the committees and by being sufficiently sensitive to know when to respond to an appeal by a dissatisfied minority or to spot a case which should go straight to Cabinet. He said that it did not increase prime ministerial power since it would be difficult even for a megalomaniac Prime Minister to ignore a decision made by a committee of Cabinet colleagues.

Adapted from Wilson 1976.

(iii) The new regime has been impatient with the traditional structure of Cabinet committees which Peter Mandelson (Minister without Portfolio, based in the Cabinet Office) has said, had 'sometimes been allowed to become excessively slow moving and bureaucratic, and a recipe for delays and non-decision as they failed sufficiently to confront powerful departmental vested interests'. One result has been an increased use in task forces involving a mixture of civil servants and outsiders on issues crossing departments such as welfare-to-work, standards in schools, youth justice and, now, skill shortages'.

Adapted from the *Times*, 10 November 1997.

Questions

1. a) 'The Lord Chancellor is in a very powerful position in the Cabinet'. Explain this statement using Item A.
   b) What does Item A tell us about the Blair government's priorities?
2. a) Judging from Item B, what are the benefits and drawbacks of the use of a system of Cabinet committees?
   b) Do you think the Blair government should ensure that Cabinet committees meet more regularly? Explain your answer.

2.5 The Cabinet Secretariat

What is the Cabinet Secretariat?

The administrative and secretarial work connected with the flow of policy business within the Cabinet system is carried out by the Cabinet Secretariat. The Secretariat forms a major part of the Cabinet Office which is headed by the Cabinet Secretary. In June 1998, the Cabinet Office had a total staff of 1,875 (*Guardian*, 30 June 1998). According to the Cabinet Office:

> 'The Cabinet Secretariat is non-departmental in function and purpose. It services the Cabinet itself together with its Cabinet committees and sub-committees. The Secretariat aims to ensure that the business of government is conducted in a timely and efficient way and that proper consideration takes place when it is needed before policy decisions are taken.' (Cabinet Office 1998)

The job of the Secretariat is to arrange the times of meetings and, in conjunction with the chairs of Cabinet committees, to prepare agendas. The Secretariat also briefs committee chairs and records and circulates the minutes of the meetings of the Cabinet and its committees.

The four Secretariats

Following the election of a Labour government in 1997, the Cabinet Office was divided into four smaller Secretariats - Economic and Domestic affairs, Defence and Overseas, European (EU), and Constitution:

> 'The four Secretariats...are accountable to the Prime Minister through the Cabinet Secretary and to ministers who chair committees. The Economic and Domestic Secretariat also deals with legislative and parliamentary matters. The Constitution Secretariat coordinates work on constitutional reform including devolution to Scotland, Wales and the English regions and the incorporation into UK law of the European Convention on Human Rights.' (Cabinet Office 1998)

Blair's reforms of July 1998

When Sir Richard Wilson was appointed as Cabinet Secretary in January 1998, Tony Blair asked him to draw up plans to strengthen the Cabinet Office. His report was completed by Easter 1998 and then delayed to coincide with Tony Blair's first reshuffle. When this reshuffle took place, in July 1998, Tony Blair simultaneously announced a shake-up of the Cabinet Office. The measures are outlined in Box 12.2 below.

The Cabinet 'enforcer'

When Jack Cunningham was placed in charge of the Cabinet Office, he was described in the media as the 'Cabinet enforcer'. Interviewed by the *Times* on the day after his appointment, however, he was at pains to make it clear that he would work with Sir Richard Wilson as 'joint partners'. His view of his role was as follows:

> 'The Cabinet Office is not just the powerful engine of government; in future, it is going to be involved in key policy initiatives. If I see problems looming, it is my responsibility to

make the Prime Minister aware of them. Everyone is asking me what levers of power I have to deal with difficulties. Well I say there are two. One is that I can say "Tony says so" and the second is "I have taken advice from the Cabinet Secretary and this is what he says...".' (*Times*, 29 July 1998)

The Performance and Innovation Unit

The Performance and Innovation Unit is staffed by civil servants and experts recruited for short stints to review specific policies (its first task was to look at policies for older people, for cities and for the regions). According to the *Independent*:

'Mr Blair said the new unit would have the right to range across Whitehall departmental boundaries, to propose new policies, and to improve the delivery of existing objectives. It will also seek to secure increased coordination and improved practical delivery of policy and services which involve more than one government organisation.' (*Independent*, 29 July 1998)

The creation of the unit was widely interpreted as a challenge to the Treasury since the Treasury already monitored departmental programmes and took an overview of policy.

The power of the Cabinet Secretariat

The traditional view of the power of the Cabinet Secretariat is that it does have considerable potential influence simply because it is the job of the Cabinet Secretary and other senior officials in the Secretariat to attend meetings of the Cabinet and its committees and to spend a great deal of time with the Prime Minister and senior ministers. That does not mean that the Secretariat has a political agenda. Rather:

'[The Secretariat] is mainly concerned with the smooth running of business and, if it has any influence, it is exercised through shaping and handling rather than the content of policy and through briefing committee chairmen and the Prime Minister.' (Burch 1990, p.106)

Developments since the election of the Blair government, especially the reforms of July 1998, suggest that the power of the Cabinet Secretariat is growing.

2.6 Informal groups

What are informal groups?

Whilst the Cabinet, its committees and the Cabinet Secretariat constitute the Cabinet system in formal terms, the system also involves many meetings and contacts of a less formal nature. Informal groups are not necessarily subject to the same procedures of official agenda setting and minute taking as formal groups, though some informal meetings are more organised than others. Informal meetings range from the casual chat in the corridor to the regular gathering of an inner circle of senior colleagues. Such inner circles are by no means uncommon. Prime Ministers use them:

- to discuss the main issues of the day
- to sound out colleagues
- to make deals
- to initiate or shape policy
- to consider strategy.

Informal groups are by no means confined to ministers. They may include advisers or civil servants. They may be bilateral - an informal discussion between the Prime Minister and one other minister, official or adviser, for example.

Informal groups under Thatcher

The use of groups outside the formal structure is not a particularly recent development. There is, however, little doubt that informal meetings of groups of ministers outside the formal Cabinet committee system increased substantially during Margaret Thatcher's premiership. Burch (1990a), for example, notes that this way of conducting business was actively encouraged, with many matters being decided interdepartmentally outside the formal Cabinet structures, often by ministerial correspondence. In addition, Thatcher herself made extensive use of such informal networks. Seldon, for example, explains that:

'When there was a particularly sensitive issue, or one which gave rise to a good deal of controversy, Margaret Thatcher liked to have a multilateral (non-Cabinet committee) meeting with small groups of ministers...to allow her to clarify her mind. It also allowed her to prepare a caucus ahead of full Cabinet or Cabinet committees...A multi- or bilateral meeting with the PM would usually have an official from the Cabinet Office in attendance.' (Seldon 1990, p.115)

Informal groups under Major

When John Major became Prime Minister there was some movement back towards the greater use of formal structures, but Burch argues that this did not result in a restoration of fully collective government:

'Under Major, the informal structure is still used extensively, though its complexion is quite different from that which operated under his predecessor. Its most noticeable feature is that it is less singular, less focused solely on the Prime Minister. Major has a tendency to rely on an informal inner group of senior ministers and confidants whom he may call upon for advice and to clear particular decisions. This varies according to the task and issue at hand...Moreover, Cabinet and key committee meetings are often still a bit of a fix, with tricky issues being dealt with on a one-to-one basis beforehand.' (Burch 1994, p.30)

Informal groups under Blair

The tendency to use informal groups to initiate policy, to decide its content and to present it to the public was a feature of the Blair government in its first 18 months. Derek Draper (a lobbyist who had close ties with Downing Street in the first few months after the 1997 general election) asserted that, although Tony Blair considered setting up a formal Inner Cabinet, he quickly rejected the idea because a formal structure might entrench the power of its members. Instead, he relied on two informal groups. The first was ministerial in composition and involved the Prime Minister, Deputy Prime Minister, Chancellor and Foreign Secretary. This group met each Thursday before the full Cabinet met. Anderson and Mann refer to this group as the 'Big Four' and claim that the meetings were the continuation of a practice which began when Labour was in opposition. These meetings, they argue, had great significance:

'These meetings became the place where key decisions were made, and remain a key feature of the Labour government.' (Anderson & Mann 1997, p.53)

Draper agreed that this group was significant. He argued that:

'The chances of a lone Secretary of State outside this group taking it on and winning are clearly slim.' (Draper 1997, p.35)

The second key group (see Item B in Activity 12.3) met daily. Until the reshuffle in July 1998, it was chaired by Peter Mandelson, the Minister without Portfolio. Afterwards, it was chaired by the Minister for the Cabinet Office. The group was connected to the Strategy Group which met weekly and performed a similar function to a committee chaired by Michael Heseltine in the previous government which dealt with the presentation of policy (Hood & James 1997, p.181).

Implications

The trend towards dealing with business in smaller, less formal groups at the centre of government cannot be explained simply by reference to the style of an individual Prime Minister. The trend may be the result of greater concern about secrecy. It may be because the formal structure of the Cabinet system has proved to be too unwieldy to handle many of the sensitive or urgent issues facing modern governments. Or, it may be a reflection of, as well as a contribution to, the centralisation of power around the office of the Prime Minister.

Whatever the reasons for the increased use of informal groups, one conclusion is clear. The formal structure of the Cabinet system now plays less of a policy-formulating and policy-coordinating role than used to be the case. The formal structure may still be used to ratify or confirm decisions, but policies are determined elsewhere.

2.7 The place of the Cabinet within the government structure

Where does power lie?

Cabinet government can operate in a number of ways, depending on:

1. The approach of the particular Prime Minister.
2. The complexion of government.
3. The nature of the policy issues under consideration.
4. The prevailing political circumstances.

These and other factors need to be taken into account when dealing with the question of where power lies within the Cabinet system.

The traditional view

The traditional view is that the Cabinet is the seat of power in terms of policy initiation and decision making. It is not just that Cabinet decides all important issues, it also coordinates and controls government policy as a whole. In this way, it plans overall strategy. Rush notes that the 19th century political commentator Walter Bagehot regarded the Cabinet as the crucial institution of government, describing it as the 'efficient secret':

'What he meant by this was that government was still carried on in the name of the monarch - a role to which he assigned the term "dignified" - but that in reality it was the Cabinet that made political decisions. He described its role as "secret" because of the monarchical facade by which it operated, and "efficient" because having the support of a majority in the House of Commons, it could provide firm and effective government and yet remain sensitive to criticism through its constitutional responsibility to Parliament. Bagehot was writing just as the modern party system was beginning to emerge, however, and he did not fully anticipate the strong, disciplined parties that would come to dominate the political system.' (Rush 1984, pp.15-16)

The assumption behind the traditional view (which also underlies the principle of collective responsibility, see above, Section 2.3) is that Cabinet ministers meet together to thrash out all major issues of policy before coming to a collective decision which then binds all members of government. Burch summarises this view as follows:

'Cabinet does not make all the decisions, but it does make all the major ones and it sets the broad framework within which more detailed policies are initiated and developed.' (Burch 1990, p.103)

The core executive

In recent years, some commentators have argued that the old debate over Cabinet government versus prime ministerial government is too simplistic. It is not sufficient merely to examine the relationship between the Prime Minister and the Cabinet and to decide which of the two has most power. Such an approach, it is claimed, is subject to a number of limitations.

Limitations on the traditional debate

First, compared to the amount written about the other institutions of government (such as Parliament), it is only recently that:

'The Cabinet system...has begun to be subjected to the degree of analysis that its importance in the British system warrants.' (Burch & Holliday 1996, p.2)

Writing in 1985, King notes that academic literature on the Prime Minister and Cabinet simply did not exist:

'Biographies and memoirs abound, but works by academic political scientists are few and far between. All of the books on the prime ministership can easily be held in one hand; the books on the prime ministership and Cabinet together can easily be held in two hands' (King 1985, p.1)

This is due in part, King argues, to research difficulties as few academics have access to the Prime Minister or Cabinet ministers and, therefore, few studies are based on primary source material.

Second, despite some small moves towards openness, the operations of the Prime Minister and the Cabinet remain surrounded by secrecy. It is difficult to provide up-to-date information about the inner workings of government when, for example, all Cabinet records are subject to the 30 year rule. The traditional reluctance of senior civil servants to discuss their work also helps to preserve a remoteness and inaccessibility.

Third, the wrong questions have been asked. The traditional debate between Cabinet government versus prime ministerial government tended to ignore the wider economic and political context - which to some extent determines the freedom within which a Prime Minister or Cabinet can act. It also oversimplified the distribution of power and the nature of decision making within the British government.

What is the core executive?

Dunleavy & Rhodes, in an influential article published in 1990, suggested that the focus should be broadened to include the whole of the **core executive** which they define as:

'A complex web of institutions, networks and practices surrounding the Prime Minister, Cabinet, Cabinet committees and their official counterparts, less formalised ministerial "clubs" or meetings, bilateral negotiations and interdepartmental committees. It also includes some major coordinating departments - chiefly the Cabinet Office, the Treasury, the Foreign Office, the law officers and the security and intelligence services...All those organisations and structures which primarily serve to pull together and integrate central government policies or act as final arbiters within the executive of conflicts between different elements of the government machine.' (Dunleavy & Rhodes 1990, pp.3-4)

The aim of Dunleavy and Rhodes was to shift the ground not only on what is studied, but also on how it is studied. They wanted to see, for example, more case studies of top level decision making. They also suggested that greater attention be paid to influences such as the variations of leadership styles and personalities. The key question was (and is):

'Who is coordinating whom to do what?' (Rhodes 1997, p.14)

Where does power lie in the core executive?

An examination of the core executive as a whole reveals that:

- power is not located in any single place. It can be found throughout the core executive, though it is not found in equal measure at its various locations
- the nature of this power varies
- where power does exist, it varies over time and according to the particular environment which exists at a particular time.

By focusing on the core executive as a whole rather than on the Cabinet or on the Prime Minister (or the relationship between the two), it is possible to construct new models to explain how the complex machinery of the executive works.

Main points - Sections 2.5-2.7

- The Cabinet Secretariat aims to ensure that the business of government is conducted in an efficient way and that proper consideration takes place before policy decisions are taken.
- The shake-up of the Cabinet Office announced in July 1998 strengthened it, giving it a strategic role.
- Since 1979, increasing use has been made of informal groups. The Blair government uses such groups to initiate policy, to decide its content and to present it to the public.
- The traditional view is that the Cabinet is the seat of power in terms of policy initiation and decision making. Critics argue that power may be located elsewhere.

Activity 12.7 *The core executive*

Item A *A model of prime ministerial power*

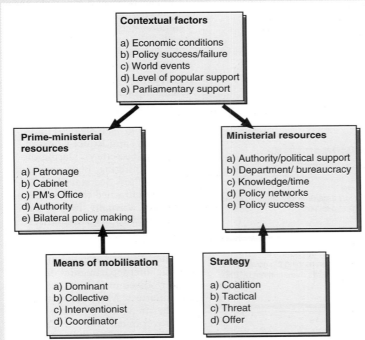

The diagram left is an attempt to draw up a model of prime ministerial power which is aware of the complexities of power and of the need to place the relations between Prime Ministers and Cabinet in context. In this model, both the Prime Minister and the Cabinet have resources. The authority of the Prime Minister derives from the Cabinet. Ministers owe their positions to the Prime Minister. The freedom to use these resources, however, depends on external circumstances and policy area. In making a decision, the Prime Minister has to exchange resources with one or more minister. Prime Ministers have a range of different strategies of exchange - they may be dominant, collective, interventionist or coordinators (or a mixture). They are constrained, however, by the resources of ministers. Ministers have specialist skills or political authority which makes it difficult for the Prime Minister to override them. Also, ministers may build coalitions or threaten to resign. By mobilising their resources like this, they can defeat the Prime Minister.

Adapted from Smith 1994.

Item B *The Cabinet Office shake-up*

The aim of the changes announced on 28 July 1998 is to turn a weak Cabinet Office into an organisation with the clout to monitor, advise and force the delivery of public services across government. Although nobody would admit it publicly, the new-look department under Jack Cunningham (the so-called 'Cabinet enforcer') effectively becomes the Prime Minister's private office, an alternative power base to the Treasury. The Performance and Innovation Unit is, in effect, a crisis command centre (it will examine interdepartmental topics, monitor departmental progress and conduct the 'forward thinking' at which ministers are no longer considered competent) whilst the Centre for Management Policy Studies is a think tank (the centre will circulate guidance to central and local government and groom the high flyers with top business management courses). Jack Cunningham, the minister who is to oversee the changes, will attend Tony Blair's weekly planning meeting at No 10 with Jonathan Powell, his Chief of Staff, David Miliband, the Head of the Policy Unit, Sir Richard Wilson, the Cabinet Secretary, and the heads of the various Cabinet Secretariat divisions. Cunningham will also chair the daily strategy meeting to discuss the government's presentation of policy. This is a serious undermining of Cabinet government. Mr Blair is bureaucratising Cabinet government at the top.

Adapted from the *Guardian*, 29 July 1998 and the *Times*, 29 July 1998.

Item C   *The Cabinet system*

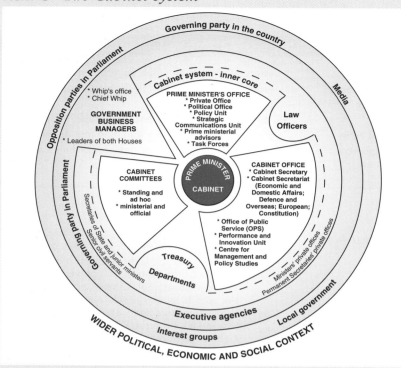

Adapted from Pyper & Robins 1995.

Item E   *Models of core executive decision making*

Type	Characteristics/issues
1. PM government	- PM has virtual monopoly of power - PM able to decide on policy in any area or in key strategic areas, or by determining the ideological direction - most associated with Thatcher - limited value as a model.
2. PM clique	- PM's power derived from inner group of advisers - fits with reality of difficulty of one person running big government - recent emphasis on degree to which news management by PM's Press Office is key to power of clique.
3. Cabinet government	- traditional notion of how UK system works - in reality Cabinet can't take all decisions - even under Thatcher, Cabinet was a court of appeal, means of holding PM in check constitutionally and a final authoritative forum for the resolution of policy.
4. Ministerial government	- political and administrative departmentalism, a federation of more or less equal agencies which marks out UK government - PM and Cabinet government limited by this constraint - ministers have their own power resources and are deemed to be responsible for activities in their domain.
5. Segmented decisions	- PM and Cabinet operate in different policy areas - PM control strong on defence, foreign and important economic issues - Cabinet and ministers dominate in all other areas of domestic policy - implies that the core executive has limited control over government.
6. Bureaucratic coordination	- core executive has very limited control - PM, Cabinet and ministers have a minimal role - emphasis here on civil servants as a power élite (left-wing view) or as monopoly suppliers of information and maximisers of budgets (New Right view).

Adapted from Thain 1993.

Item D   *The Cabinet under Tony Blair*

The Cabinet is no longer a central organ of government. Cabinet ministers still matter as heads of departments, but Cabinet meetings no longer really count. The system is no longer collective. It is a centralised system directed by 10 Downing Street. John Major held lengthy discussions on awkward topics like Europe so that all had their say and were committed to the policy. But, Blair prefers an informal approach without a set agenda. The court of appeal is now the sofa of his small office rather than the Cabinet table. There is even little left of the Cabinet's role as a reporting and reviewing body. The Cabinet minutes may give an impression of order. For example, they say that the Cabinet decided on 17 July 1997 to use a system of proportional representation at the next European elections. In reality, however, Blair had already made the decision on the basis of a paper from Jack Straw (Home Secretary) and Robin Cook (Foreign Secretary). During the Cabinet meeting, Blair announced that his Press Secretary had already informed the press of this decision. Virtually none of the government's major initiatives have been discussed by the full Cabinet. Issues are discussed bilaterally with affected ministers while interdepartmental disputes are resolved in Cabinet committees. Most important of all is the strengthening of the centre of government with the Cabinet Office and No 10 Policy Unit working more closely. The aim is for 'proactive initiatives' (Peter Mandelson's phrase) to come from the centre. Some of these changes are desirable to give direction to government, but they also have their risks. The government's self-inflicted problems over the single currency and Formula One, for example, might have been avoided if the issues had been properly discussed with the ministers concerned. The decline in the Cabinet's function puts a strain on the cement which binds the government together.

Adapted from the *Times*, 10 November 1997.

Questions

1. a) What advantages does the model in Item A have over more traditional approaches to the study of decision making?
   b) Apply the model to what you know about the functioning of the government under Tony Blair.

2. a) What are the advantages and disadvantages of policy formulation by informal groups? Use Items B and D in your answer.
   b) 'Cabinet government is dead'. Is that a realistic assessment of the position of the Cabinet under Tony Blair? Use Item D in your answer.

3. Why do you think Tony Blair decided to appoint a 'Cabinet enforcer' and to strengthen the Cabinet Office? Use Item B in your answer.

4. Using Item C, explain where power lies in the Cabinet system.

5. Which of the models outlined in Item E best explains the way in which Tony Blair's government worked after the 1997 general election? Give reasons for your answer.

References

Anderson & Mann (1997) Anderson, P. & Mann, N., *Safety First: the Making of New Labour*, Granta Books, 1997.

Benn (1981) Benn, T., *Arguments for Democracy*, Penguin, 1981.

Berrill (1985) Berrill, K., 'Strength at the centre - the case for a Prime Minister's department' in *King (1985)*.

Burch (1985) Burch, M., 'The demise of Cabinet government?', *Teaching Politics*, Vol.14.3, September 1985.

Burch (1990) Burch, M., 'Power in the Cabinet system', *Talking Politics*, Vol.2.3, Spring 1990.

Burch (1990a) Burch, M., 'Cabinet government', *Contemporary Record*, Vol.4.1, September 1990.

Burch (1994) Burch, M., 'The Prime Minister and Cabinet from Thatcher to Major', *Talking Politics*, Vol.7.1, Autumn 1994.

Burch & Holliday (1996) Burch, M. & Holliday, I., *The British Cabinet System*, Harvester Wheatsheaf, 1996.

Cabinet Office (1997) Cabinet Office, *Ministerial Code: a Code of Conduct and Guidance on Procedures for Ministers*, July 1997.

Cabinet Office (1998) Cabinet Office website, www.open.gov.uk/co/review.htm, 29 July 1998.

Cockerell et al. (1984) Cockerell, M., Hennessy, P. & Walker, D., *Sources Close to the Prime Minister*, Macmillan, 1984.

Dorey (1991) Dorey, P., 'The Cabinet committee system in British government', *Talking Politics*, Vol.4.1, Autumn 1991.

Dorey (1995) Dorey, P., 'Widened, yet weakened: the changing character of collective responsibility', *Talking Politics*, Vol.7.2, Winter 1994/95.

Draper (1997) Draper, D., *Blair's 100 Days*, Faber and Faber, 1997.

Dunleavy et al. (1997) Dunleavy, P., Gamble, A., Holliday, I. & Peele, G., *Developments in British Politics 5*, Macmillan, 1997.

Dunleavy & Rhodes (1990) Dunleavy, P. & Rhodes, R.A.W., 'Core executive studies in Britain', *Public Administration*, Vol.68.1, Spring 1990.

Elgie (1997) Elgie, R., 'Models of executive politics: a framework for the study of executive power relations in parliamentary and semi-presidential regimes', *Political Studies*, Vol.XLV, pp.217-31, 1997.

Foley (1994) Foley, M., 'Presidential politics in Britain', *Talking Politics*, Vol.6.3, Summer 1994.

Hennessy (1986) Hennessy, P., *Cabinet*, Blackwell, 1986.

Hennessy (1998) Hennessy, P., 'The Blair style of government: an historical perspective and an internal audit', *Government and Opposition*, Vol.33.1, Winter 1997-8.

HMSO (1994) Central Office of Information, *The British System of Government*, HMSO, 1994.

Hood & James (1997) Hood, C. & James, O., 'The central executive' in *Dunleavy et al. (1997)*.

James (1992) James, S., *British Cabinet Government*, Routledge, 1992.

Johnson (1990) Johnson, R.W., 'The president has landed', *New Statesman and Society*, 30 November 1990.

Jones (1985) Jones, G., 'The Prime Minister's aides' in *King (1985)*.

Jones (1990) Jones, G., 'Mrs Thatcher and the power of the PM', *Contemporary Record*, Vol.3.4, April 1990.

Kerr et al. (1997) Kerr, P., McAnulla, S. & Marsh, D., 'Charting late-Thatcherism: British politics under John Major' in *Lancaster (1997)*.

King (1985) King, A. (ed.), *The British Prime Minister*, Macmillan, 1985.

King (1985a) King, A., 'Margaret Thatcher: the style of a Prime Minister' in *King (1985)*.

King (1985b) King, A., 'Introduction: the textbook prime ministership' in *King (1985)*.

Lancaster (1997) Lancaster, S. (ed.), *Developments in Politics*, Vol.8, Causeway Press, 1997.

Lloyd (1997) Lloyd, J., 'Schmaltz and the right stuff', *New Statesman*, 26 September 1997.

Norton (1987) Norton, P., 'Prime ministerial power: a framework for analysis', *Teaching Politics*, Vol.16.3, September 1987.

Pyper (1987) Pyper, R., 'The Westland affair', *Teaching Politics*, Vol.16.3, September 1987.

Pyper & Robins (1995) Pyper R., & Robins, L. (eds), *Governing the UK in the 1990s*, Macmillan, 1995.

Rhodes (1997) Rhodes, R.A.W., *Understanding Governance*, Open University Press, 1997.

Rush (1984) Rush, M., *The Cabinet and Policy Formation*, Longman, 1984.

Seldon (1990) Seldon, A., 'The Cabinet Office and coordination', *Public Administration*, Vol.68.1, Spring 1990.

Smith (1994) Smith, M.J., 'Reassessing Mrs Thatcher's resignation', *Politics Review*, Vol.3.4, April 1994.

Thain (1993) Thain, C., 'The core executive' in *Wale (1993)*.

Wale (1993) Wale, W. (ed.), *Developments in Politics*, Vol.4, Causeway Press, 1993.

Watkins (1998) Watkins, A., *The Road to Number 10: from Bonar Law to Tony Blair*, Duckworth, 1998.

Wilson (1976) Wilson, H., *The Governance of Britain*, Michael Joseph and Weidenfeld & Nicholson, 1976.

Wilson (1977) Wilson, H., *A Prime Minister on Prime Ministers*, Michael Joseph and Weidenfeld & Nicholson, 1977.

13 Ministers and civil servants

Introduction

Although all members of the Cabinet are ministers, not all ministers are members of the Cabinet. There is a ministerial hierarchy with the Cabinet at its apex. By convention, ministers are drawn from Parliament, with the vast majority of ministers being drawn from the Commons. Each minister is appointed by the Prime Minister and may be replaced at any time. Ministerial appointments, therefore, lack security.

Ministers play both a political and an administrative role. Politically, all ministers are members of the government team and each is responsible for an area of government policy both in Parliament and in public. Administratively, ministers are responsible for overseeing the implementation of government policy. The administration of government takes place through government departments. Ministers instruct their departmental officials (civil servants) who then deal with the day-to-day running of each department. Ministers are also responsible for building links between their own department or, when necessary, defending their departments against attacks from outside. This chapter examines the career structure and role of ministers.

The civil service also consists of a hierarchy. But, unlike ministers who rely on the good will of the Prime Minister to retain their position, civil servants are permanent officials. The range of jobs performed by civil servants is immense. Whilst a small number of high ranking civil servants work closely with ministers, many thousands of civil servants are employed to process claims and deal with administrative matters which arise from government decisions. Since 1979, the structure of the civil service and the scope of its activities have changed fundamentally.

The group of civil servants which is of most interest to political scientists is that at the very top of the hierarchy. This is because it is this small group (sometimes referred to as the 'mandarins') which is closely involved with ministers on policy issues. This chapter examines the characteristics of mandarins and the role they perform.

Chapter summary

Part 1 examines the qualities that a person needs to be chosen for ministerial office and the duties performed by ministers. It considers the reasons why ministers resign and examines the convention of ministerial responsibility.

Part 2 focuses on the structure of the civil service and the impact of recent reforms. To what extent are civil servants involved in policy making? Can they be described as 'neutral'? How is policy implemented?

Part 3 analyses the relationship between ministers and high-ranking civil servants.

Part 1 Ministerial careers

Key issues

1. What special qualities are required to become a minister and what makes a successful minister?
2. Who is held responsible if a mistake is made in a government department and who has to take the blame? For what reasons does a minister have to resign?
3. What duties do ministers perform? How does a minister's personality affect the way in which a department is run?

1.1 The ministerial hierarchy

Departments

The administration of government takes place through departments. Each department is responsible for a particular area of government policy and is headed by a Secretary of State who is a Cabinet minister. Ministers are responsible for the work of their departments. The role of the department is to prepare legislation and, when passed, to put that legislation into effect.

Departments vary in size. The most important

department is the Treasury. Madgwick (1991) describes the Treasury as the 'super department' and the Chancellor as the 'super minister'. This is because the Treasury manages the economy and controls public expenditure. All other departments depend on the Treasury for approval of their spending plans.

Changing the organisation of departments

From time to time, changes are made in the organisation of departments. For example, John Major created a new National Heritage Department in 1992 (its name was changed to the Department of Culture, Media and Sport after the 1997 general election). Similarly, Tony Blair combined the Department of the Environment and the Regions with the Department of Transport to form the Department of Environment, Transport and the Regions, even though the two departments were situated in different buildings. If government departments are amalgamated, this might reduce the number of ministers in Cabinet.

The route to the top

There is a hierarchy of ministers ranging from the Prime Minister at the top down to (unpaid) private parliamentary secretaries (PPSs) at the bottom. Senior ministers are those who have a place in Cabinet. All other ministers below that level hold junior posts.

Most departments are headed by a Cabinet minister (it is up to the Prime Minister to decide which departments are represented in Cabinet). The Treasury (since it is regarded as the most important department) has two ministers in Cabinet - the Chancellor of the Exchequer who is head of the department and the Chief Secretary to the Treasury who is responsible for the control of public expenditure (see Chapter 15, Section 4.1).

The private parliamentary secretary (PPS)

Strictly speaking, PPSs are not ministers:

> 'PPSs are backbench MPs from the government party who are chosen by individual Cabinet ministers or ministers of state to assist them in their parliamentary duties. They act as a channel of information between backbenchers and ministers, for example. They are not paid a salary and are not ministers of the Crown. However, they are not expected to vote against government policy, serve on select committees or take part in debates on their minister's subjects of responsibility.' (Silk & Walters 1998, p.42)

To be chosen as a PPS is often the first step on a ministerial career. The appointment provides an MP with useful experience of ministerial work and ensures that the MP has frequent contact with ministers and senior civil servants.

At one time, only Cabinet ministers were entitled to have a PPS, but now any minister can, except for the lowest rung of the ministerial ladder (the

parliamentary under secretary of state). The whips like to have large numbers of PPSs because they need to be aware of the opinions and feelings of MPs over an issue before an important vote takes place. Also, a large number of PPSs guarantees a large number of government votes - PPSs are obliged always to vote with the government. They must resign rather than abstaining or voting against the government.

Pairing

One of the functions of the PPS is to find a 'pair' for the minister. If a member of the government is unable to attend Parliament for an important vote, then a backbencher from the opposition must be found who will also be absent. They then form a 'pair' cancelling out each other's vote. One former member of Margaret Thatcher's government remembers his role and responsibilities as a PPS as rather a miserable one:

> 'The task [of the PPS] is to act as the private bagman of his minister, [by] listening to his critics among the troops at Westminster and finding him a pair from the opposition parties...In return, he is allowed to sit in on meetings at his boss's department (as long as nothing significant or confidential is under discussion). He is unpaid and mostly unconsulted.' (Bruce-Gardyne 1986, p.14)

Junior ministers

Parliamentary under secretaries of state

The post of parliamentary under secretary of state (or 'pussy' as it sometimes called) is usually an 'up or out' post. That is, successful parliamentary under secretaries of state are likely to be promoted within a few years whilst those not regarded as a success return to the backbenches with the hope of a knighthood. About half of those who serve as parliamentary under secretaries of state go no further. The number of parliamentary under secretaries of state in each department varies. For example, after the reshuffle in July 1998, the Home Office and the Department for Education and Employment had three each whilst the Department of International Development had one.

Ministers of state

The next rung up is the post of minister of state. The post dates back to the 1830s, but has only existed in its modern form since 1955. It was first confined to those departments where senior ministers were likely to be away from London for some time due to wider geographical commitments and, therefore, needed someone to stand in for them. Today, most departments have ministers of state because of the increasing workload and wider range of responsibilities of many departments. For example the Department of Trade and Industry has four ministers of state, each being responsible for a particular area (energy, industry, trade, and consumer affairs and small firms).

A quarter of ministers of state go no further. Sideways movements are more common at this level but the 'up or out' principle usually prevails eventually. Around 20% of all junior ministers eventually become Cabinet ministers (see Chapter 12 for further information on Cabinet ministers).

The appointment of ministers

Prime Ministers are solely responsible for appointing and dismissing ministers. Normally, the vast majority of ministers are chosen from the Commons and a minority from the Lords. Occasionally, however, outsiders are appointed. If outsiders are appointed, it is usual for them to be given a life peerage or to seek election as quickly as possible. In August 1998, the appointment of Gus Macdonald as Scottish Industry Minister was controversial because he was not an MP or a Lord at the time (he was promised a life peerage, but this could not be confirmed until after the end of the summer recess - three months after his

appointment). Critics argued that, because he was not an MP or a Lord, Macdonald would not be accountable to Parliament. Some also complained because Macdonald's appointment suggested that none of Labour's Scottish MPs had been considered to be suitable for the job.

Main points - Section 1.1

- **Ministers are responsible for the work of their departments - namely, preparing legislation and, when passed, putting that legislation into effect.**
- **There is a hierarchy of ministers ranging from the Prime Minister at the top down to (unpaid) private parliamentary secretaries (PPSs) at the bottom.**
- **Junior ministers are ministers not in the Cabinet.**
- **Most ministers are MPs. Some may be Lords. Outsiders are sometimes appointed. Usually, they are given a peerage to ensure they are accountable to Parliament.**

Activity 13.1 *The post-war consensus*

Item A *The ministerial hierarchy*

This cartoon shows the number of each type of minister (after the July 1998 reshuffle). The figures come from the House of Commons Information Office, 2 November 1998.

Item B *A need for fewer ministers?*

In Attlee's 1945 government, there were 33 junior ministers. When Labour came to power in May 1997, Tony Blair appointed 59 junior ministers. Attlee's government was responsible for setting up the health service, for running the Empire and for running much of industry. Between 1979 and 1997, however, the Conservatives sold off many nationalised industries and transferred many of the operational tasks of central government from departments to semi-independent agencies (responsible for the day-to-day running of services). The Labour government has continued the trend. Gordon Brown transferred control over interest rates from the Treasury to the Bank of England and legislation was passed in 1997 devolving power from Westminster to the Scottish Parliament and Welsh Assembly. In such a world, ministers (especially junior ministers) increasingly appear to be little more than public relations agents for a service someone else is providing. So, why has the number of junior ministers not declined? The answer has to do with party management. Unless one third of the parliamentary party is in government and another third has expectations, the condition of the final third (mainly sour and disillusioned) might infect the party as a whole. The government is bloated because patronage is the only way to keep it afloat.

Adapted from the *Guardian*, 11 January and 13 January 1994, and 8 May 1997 and Loughlin & Scott 1997.

Item C   *Ministers on the way up*

Whenever there is speculation about Tony Blair's first reshuffle, the two junior ministers most often tipped for promotion to the Cabinet are Alan Milburn (age 40) and Stephen Byers (age 45). Both are ministers of state - Milburn at Health and Byers at Education. Both came to the Commons in 1992. Both share a left-wing background. Both have been marked out - Byers is attached to the Social Exclusion Unit which Blair chairs and Milburn was one of the few junior ministers to travel with Blair to Washington in February. Of the two, Milburn is the more instantly impressive because of his obvious energy and easy, intimate charm. Byers is sharp and refreshingly direct. Both have been given hefty responsibilities by their bosses in the Cabinet. The pair have travelled a long way politically. Byers' roots are in local government, Milburn's in the trade unions. Today, however, both are loyal Blairites. They first gained notice at Westminster by ferreting out information through parliamentary questions and government leaks. At this stage, there is little to choose between them. Milburn is better in the chamber, but Byers is a good committee man. The question people are asking is whether loyal Blairites like these two are capable of independent thought. The Prime Minister is keen for junior ministers to write articles pushing out the boundaries. It is difficult to imagine Milburn or Byers risking more than a glorified departmental press release.
Note: in the July 1998 reshuffle, Stephen Byers was promoted to the Cabinet as Chief Secretary to the Treasury whilst Alan Milburn remained Minister of State for Health.

Adapted from the *New Statesman*, 8 May

This cartoon shows Stephen Byers (left) and Alan Milburn as ministers and as young left-wingers.

Item D   *Appointing outsiders*

It is surprising that a government that has done much to extend democracy (Scottish Parliament, Welsh Assembly, Mayor of London) has a blind spot when it comes to the allocation of key jobs. With the appointment of Gus Macdonald, the Prime Minister granted executive power to a man who has never faced the voters. The government can argue that he has great talent and is ideally qualified, but, if that's the standard, we might as well abolish elections altogether and let a recruitment agency choose the government from talented businesspeople. Gus Macdonald is not a one-off. New Labour is making a habit of appointing ministers from unelected business. David Sainsbury and David Simon are both now ministers at the Department of Trade and Industry Neither has ever stood for election. A key player in government is Charles Falconer, a lawyer friend of Blair's who was rapidly enrobed last year and promoted in last week's reshuffle. As deputy 'Cabinet enforcer', he will order around Cabinet ministers who, unlike him, have won a mandate from the people. Scottish MPs have been slighted by Macdonald's appointment, but the real snub is to those who voted for them. By looking outside Parliament for ministers, Labour is telling the nation that Parliament no longer matters.

Adapted from the *Guardian*, 5 August 1998.

Questions

1. a) Using Items A and B, explain why the number of junior ministers has grown since 1945.
   b) Give arguments for and against the appointment of fewer ministers
2. What does Item C tell us about the qualities necessary to rise up the ministerial hierarchy?
3. a) What does Item D tell us about the appointment of ministers under Tony Blair?
   b) How might a Prime Minister justify the appointment of outsiders?

1.2 Ministerial turnover

Why do ministers move on?

Ministers may move or be moved for a number of reasons. They may lose their seat at a general election (as happened with seven Cabinet ministers in 1997, for example). They may choose to resign for personal reasons or out of principle. They may resign in connection with individual or collective responsibility. As Pyper (1993) found in a study of ministerial moves since 1964, however, by far the most common reason for moving is a reshuffle by the Prime Minister. In reshuffles, ministers may find that they have been moved to another post or that they have been dropped altogether. It should be noted that reshuffles are a relatively recent phenomenon. Until 1945, they were rare - ministers tended to serve as long as their health permitted, they agreed with government policy or remained in power (*Guardian*, 23 July 1996).

Ministerial reshuffles

A great deal of secrecy surrounds a ministerial reshuffle. Although ministers are aware that a reshuffle is in the offing, most are not informed of the actual date. The Prime Minister usually seeks opinions over particular appointments. The Chief Whip is normally consulted, as is the Leader of the House and the Chancellor (if the appointments affect economic departments). But, it is the personality of the Prime Minister which determines procedure. Both Richard Crossman and Barbara Castle (former Labour ministers) record in their diaries, for example, that Harold Wilson sounded out opinions before finalising changes whereas James Callaghan tended to keep his plans to himself. Margaret Thatcher refers to conversations she had with William Whitelaw and

John Wakeham before her 1985 reshuffle (Thatcher 1993, p.418). Before making his first reshuffle in July 1998, Tony Blair sounded out the opinions of senior civil servants, asking them to appraise ministers' competence and efficiency. This was the first time civil servants had been asked for their opinion by a Prime Minister (*Guardian*, 14 July 1998).

Who is affected?
A minor reshuffle may only involve a small number of ministers. A large reshuffle, however, can radically alter the complexion of the government. In 1962, Harold Macmillan removed a third of his Cabinet colleagues in what came to be called 'the night of the long knives'. This was the biggest change of the Cabinet in modern times. The reshuffle in July 1998 affected 52 ministers. Three were promoted to the Cabinet, two promoted and three moved sideways within the Cabinet, and four sacked from the Cabinet (the Cabinet was reduced in size by one). One junior minister resigned and nine were sacked. Ten new junior ministers were appointed from the backbenches, 16 junior ministers were promoted and four moved sideways (*Times*, 29 July 1998).

Other consequences of reshuffles
Reshuffles may also result in structural reorganisation. For example, in July 1995, the Department of Employment was split between the Department of Education (to link training with employment), the Department of Trade and Industry (whose role was to look after industrial relations and pay) and the Department of the Environment (whose role was to deal with health and safety issues). Similarly, the reshuffle in July 1998 resulted in a reduction in the size of the Cabinet from 23 members to 22 (the Transport Minister was no longer a member of the Cabinet) and the reorganisation of the Cabinet Office - with the creation of the new post of 'Cabinet enforcer'.

A further reason for reshuffling is to change the political balance of the Cabinet and to avoid rival power bases being built. A number of political commentators argued that Tony Blair's first reshuffle in July 1998 was designed to strengthen his own position at the expense of Gordon Brown. Supporters of Gordon Brown, it was argued, were sacked or moved sideways whilst those loyal to Blair were promoted (*Guardian*, 28 July 1998).

Are British ministers reshuffled too much?
Compared to other ministers in Europe, British ministers have relatively short periods in a particular job. Rose (1991) found that, between 1964 and 1990, the average length of tenure of office was two years, regardless of which party was in government. Junior ministers are more likely to be reshuffled than senior ministers. Turnover also differs between departments. Chancellors last longest (on average $4^1/_2$ years) whilst, between 1983 and 1993, there

were seven Environment Secretaries, on average a new one every 19 months. This led David McKie to comment:

> 'It's a huge and complex department, and if sometimes they don't seem to be on top of every aspect of it, no wonder.' (*Guardian*, 25 July 1994)

The seventh of these Environment Secretaries, John Gummer, broke the trend, however. He remained in post between May 1993 and May 1997.

The implications of rapid turnover
Rose (1991) argues that this rapid turnover has important implications for two main reasons.

First, rapid ministerial turnover is an important factor when considering the balance of power between ministers and civil servants. Permanent secretaries (the chief civil servants in government departments) have longer terms of office than the ministers they serve. A top civil servant may spend 20 to 30 years before reaching an important post, in some cases spending all that time in a single department. This means that civil servants often have a greater knowledge of the working of the Whitehall machinery than their political masters.

And second, Britain reshuffles its Cabinet ministers more often than other European governments. As the EU makes more of an impact on British policy, British ministers are expected to work more and more closely with their European counterparts. This task will not be made any easier if the personnel is continually changing. Also, in comparison with British ministers, other European ministers are far more likely to have greater specialist knowledge of the department in which they work. In France, the Netherlands and Norway ministers must resign their seats when they take office as ministers. Many have come to the post with experience in administration gained at local or regional level. On the other hand, it should be noted that British ministers tend to have more parliamentary experience than their European counterparts.

1.3 Resignation issues

Why do ministers resign?
According to Woodhouse:

> 'Ministerial resignations are an important element of accountability... justified in a system in which routine accountability is weak.' (Woodhouse 1993, p.278)

Resignations reassure the public that, beneath the adversarial party politics and the dramatic performances which take place in Parliament, moral values and a sense of responsibility are upheld by those in power.

Factors leading to resignation
It should be noted, however, that ministers do not

automatically resign when a mistake has been made. Resignation depends on a variety of factors. First, it depends on the issue responsible for the pressure to resign. Some issues are certainly resigning matters whilst others are not so clear-cut. Second, it depends on the Prime Minister's attitude. If the minister concerned is close to the Prime Minister, there may be a timely reshuffle to avoid resignation. New ministers cannot then be blamed for the mistakes of their predecessors. Third, it depends on the position of the minister in the party. If backbenchers are supportive of a minister's stance, the minister is less likely to resign. Fourth, ministers who are popular in the country or who have powerful friends are less likely to resign. And fifth, it depends on the minister's personality. Some are more reluctant to resign than others.

Five paths leading to resignation

Pyper (1993) suggests that five different paths can lead to resignation:

1. Changes in government structure and personnel (ie reshuffles).
2. Electoral defeat of a minister.
3. Miscellaneous personal reasons (including age, health, family factors, career development outside government).
4. Factors concerned with the convention of collective responsibility.
5. Factors concerned with the doctrine of individual ministerial responsibility. (Pyper 1993, p.66)

Collective responsibility is discussed in Chapter 12 (Section 2.3). It should be noted that, when ministers resign because they disagree with government policy, they resign as a result of the doctrine of collective ministerial responsibility, not individual ministerial responsibility. So, it is collective ministerial responsibility (not individual ministerial responsibility) which explains why, for example, the Social Security Minister, Frank Field resigned in July 1998 (he disagreed with government policy on welfare reform).

Individual ministerial responsibility

The official definition of individual ministerial responsibility is as follows:

> 'The individual responsibility of ministers for the work of their departments means that they are answerable to Parliament for all their department's activities. They bear the consequences of any failure in administration, any injustice to an individual or any aspect of a policy which may be criticised in Parliament, whether personally responsible or not. Since most ministers are members of the House of Commons, they must answer questions and defend themselves against criticism in person. Departmental ministers in the House of Lords are represented in the Commons by someone

qualified to speak on their behalf, usually a junior minister.' (HMSO 1994, p.42)

Pyper (1993 and 1994) argues that the doctrine of individual ministerial responsibility has two strands which he describes as 'role responsibility' and 'personal responsibility'.

1. Role responsibility

By 'role responsibility' Pyper means that ministers are responsible for four areas which he describes as:

> 'Policy leadership in their departments; managing departments; piloting legislation through its various parliamentary stages; [and] representing departmental interests in Cabinet, with pressure groups and with departmental clients.' (Pyper 1994, p.12)

These are, in other words, areas of responsibility connected with the role played by ministers. On occasion, ministers are forced to resign due to failings in the performance of their role as head of a government department or part of a government department.

Ministers are expected to be aware of and to be prepared for any eventualities that may arise in the area of government covered by their department (or their part of a department if they are junior ministers). They are responsible not only for the decisions they take, but also for those which they should have taken. An error of judgement can lead to resignation (though, in practice, it rarely does). This is as true with senior ministers as it is with junior ministers.

In theory also, since they are political heads of department, ministers are held responsible for the actions of all subordinates as well as for their own acts:

> 'Viewed simplistically - as it often is - the doctrine of individual ministerial responsibility tells us that it is ministers, not civil servants, who are accountable to Parliament for the work of government departments and, correspondingly, it is ministers who take the blame when things go wrong. It is, however, not difficult to show the superficiality of such assumptions.' (Pyper 1994, p.13)

2. Personal responsibility

By 'personal responsibility' Pyper means that ministers are responsible for their own personal conduct:

> 'Naturally, like all other citizens they are expected to obey the law. Like all other MPs, they are expected to obey the rules and conventions of Parliament, such as those relating to possible conflicts of interest between private and parliamentary activities. As ministers, they are subject to a further set of rules of conduct...These establish guidelines on issues such as the holding of company shares and directorships. Less tangibly,

ministers are also expected to act in accordance with an unwritten moral code.' (Pyper 1994, p.12)

All MPs are under public scrutiny, but this becomes even greater once they become ministers. An irregularity in an MP's private life might bar that MP from being considered for ministerial office in the first place. The media is only too eager to pick up on any event which might suggest that the MP has been dishonest or hypocritical. In recent years, media campaigns and exposés have led to a relatively large number of resignations. The ministers are forced to resign because of some personal failing which is not necessarily related to their performance as head of a government department or part of a government department. Personal responsibility explains the resignation of the Welsh Secretary, Ron Davies, in October 1998 and the majority of resignations during John Major's premiership.

It should be noted, however, that publicity surrounding a minister's personal life does not necessarily lead to resignation. For example, when, in 1997, newspapers revealed that the Foreign Secretary, Robin Cook, had been having an extra-marital affair with his research assistant, Cook divorced his wife and married his research assistant. He did not resign.

Does individual ministerial responsibility really exist?

In practice, the convention of individual ministerial responsibility does not work predictably. Individual ministers may be shielded against the consequences of serious errors by their departments or by collective ministerial responsibility. Whether or not a particular minister is required to resign over a particular issue becomes a political rather than a constitutional question.

If the Prime Minister wishes or party solidarity applies, the issue may be made into a test of confidence in the government as a whole. Norman Lamont came under severe criticism after 'Black Wednesday' when Britain withdrew from the ERM in September 1992, for example, but he did not resign because he was shielded by the Prime Minister.

Gray (1989) draws attention to the fact that the doctrine of ministerial responsibility has grown out of Britain's uncodified constitution. This makes it difficult to define exactly what the responsibilities of ministers are:

'Ambiguities which arise may allow an individual minister to escape censure because principles may be unclear.' (Gray 1989, p.42)

Passing the buck

Woodhouse pointed out in the *Economist* (1 October 1994) that, in the 19th century, ministers could be expected to know everything that went on in their departments. Today, however, no minister can expect

to know about even a small proportion of the work that is done. This situation has been further complicated by the delegation of government tasks to quasi-autonomous agencies. As Pyper points out:

'There were fears from the outset that, if policies were formulated in the parent department but implemented by the agencies, this was a recipe for the type of buck passing which had stalled many attempts to enforce accountability in the old nationalised industries, where ministers would decline to take responsibility on the grounds that: "This is a matter of day-to-day management", while members of the board would claim in turn that: "It is really a matter of strategic policy - ask the minister".' (Pyper 1994, p.14)

This happened in 1995 when the Home Secretary, Michael Howard, dismissed Derek Lewis, Head of the Prison Service Agency, on the grounds that he was responsible for prison security and, therefore, for a recent spate of escapes. It later emerged that:

'[Howard] failed to provide Parliament with information which, if known at the time, might have resulted in his being forced to resign.' (Simpson 1998, p.70)

The Scott Report and evasion of responsibility

In 1992, an inquiry was set up under the judge Richard Scott to find out whether government ministers had deliberately not informed, or set out to mislead, Parliament (see also Activity 17.4). The Scott Report was published in February 1996 and concluded that ministers were guilty of concealing the truth and that they had been aided in this by senior civil servants. Two ministers who remained in office were singled out for particular criticism - William Waldegrave, a Foreign Office minister at the time and Nicholas Lyell, the Attorney General. In the days after the report was published:

'[These ministers] were portrayed by the government as victims of a smear campaign who had been "cleared" by the report...With the full support of their ministerial colleagues and all but a few maverick backbenchers, [they] took refuge in the fact that Scott had not found them guilty of malicious intent.' (Adams & Pyper 1997, p.172)

After a debate in Parliament two weeks after the report was published, the majority of MPs sided with the government. As a result:

'A majority of MPs voted, in effect, to be repeatedly misled by ministers and civil servants...Ministers conceded only that there had been some cock-ups and that the fault for those lay with officials.' (Norton-Taylor et al. 1996, p.197)

No ministers resigned in response to the Scott Report.

Main points - Sections 1.2-1.3

- **Reshuffles may: (1) change the political complexion of the government; (2) result in structural reorganisation of government; and (3) prevent rival power bases being built.**
- **Rapid turnover of ministers affects the balance of power between ministers and civil servants and makes it difficult for ministers to work with their European counterparts.**

- **There are five main reasons for ministerial resignations: (1) reshuffles; (2) electoral defeat of a minister; (3) personal reasons; (4) collective responsibility; and (5) individual ministerial responsibility.**
- **Ministers are supposed to resign if their department makes a mistake (role responsibility) or if they make a mistake (personal responsibility). Often, however, they try to evade responsibility.**

Activity 13.2 Turnover of ministers

Item A *Shuffling the pack*

The highly charged drama of reshuffles makes them seem more important than they usually are. In his final years, John Major conducted several. None helped the government recover in the polls or perform more competently. In his first reshuffle, Blair should focus on reforming the structure of government. Rightly, he has been worried about the number of ministers with 'departmentalitis' (viewing policy and strategy from the perspective of their department rather than thinking in terms of the government as a whole). This is not the fault of individual ministers, but an inevitable consequence of a system which encourages departmental rivalries. However many reshuffles take place, the Foreign Office will continue to view the Department for International Development with resentment and the Department of International Development, in turn, will continue to feel threatened by the Department of Trade and Industry (DTI) whilst the DTI

will continue to be wary of the Department of Transport, Environment and the Regions. Some of these tensions are unavoidable and perfectly healthy. But, not all of them. The government has already set up a number of bodies, for example the Social Exclusion Unit, to encourage a more holistic approach to government. The creation of further 'super-ministries' which recognise that several smaller departments have common interests is under consideration - as is reform of the Cabinet Office. Institutional reform is more difficult than moving ministers (although less personally painful - most Prime Ministers dread the prospect of sacking colleagues). But, structural changes are more of priority than a big reshuffle. That can wait until next year. At least.

Adapted from the *New Statesman*, 17 April 1998 and *Guardian*, 16 July 1998.

Item B *Resignations 1945-98*

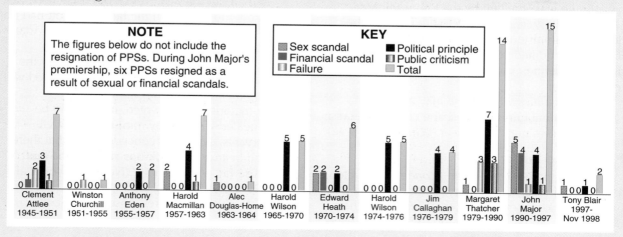

NOTE
The figures below do not include the resignation of PPSs. During John Major's premiership, six PPSs resigned as a result of sexual or financial scandals.

KEY
- Sex scandal
- Financial scandal
- Failure
- Political principle
- Public criticism
- Total

Item C *Resignations*

In October 1998, the Secretary of State for Wales, Ron Davies, resigned after being robbed at knifepoint following a late-night walk on Clapham Common. He said that 'a moment of madness' had resulted in 'a serious lapse of judgement'.

In 1954, the Minister of Agriculture, Thomas Dugdale, resigned after the Crichel Down Affair. A public inquiry revealed that officials in his department had used underhand tactics in order to prevent landowners regaining possession of land which had been compulsorily purchased during the Second World War. Dugdale was not himself involved in the case, but resigned after pressure built up in the media.

In October 1994, the Under Secretary of State for Northern Ireland, Tim Smith, and the Under Secretary for Corporate Affairs, Neil Hamilton were forced to resign following allegations that they had taken bribes.

In December 1988, the Parliamentary Under Secretary of State for Health, Edwina Currie, was forced to resign two weeks after making a statement on television claiming that most of Britain's egg production was affected by salmonella. This resulted in a slump in egg sales and an outcry from egg producers. The government was forced to pay compensation of several million pounds.

RESIGNATION

In June 1993, the Minister of State for Northern Ireland, Michael Mates was forced to resign after newspapers revealed that he had given a watch to Asil Nadir, a Cypriot businessman who jumped bail and returned to Northern Cyprus to avoid answering charges of fraud.

On 11 December 1996, David Willets resigned as Paymaster General after it was revealed that he had lied to the parliamentary inquiry into the Cash for Questions Affair.

In 1947, the Chancellor of the Exchequer, Hugh Dalton, resigned after breaking parliamentary etiquette by revealing details of his Budget to a lobby journalist just before delivering it to the Commons.

On 23 July 1996, the Treasury Minister David Heathcoat-Amory, resigned over the government's policy towards a European single currency.

When Argentina attacked the Falkland Islands in 1982, the Foreign Secretary, Lord Carrington, the Lord Privy Seal, Humphrey Atkins, and the Minister of State in the Foreign Office, Richard Luce, resigned. They accepted that they had failed to anticipate the Argentinian invasion and failed to assess Argentinian intentions correctly.

On 3 June 1996, the Parliamentary Under Secretary for Wales, Rod Richards, resigned after a newspaper revealed that he had been having an affair. Rod Richards was leading a campaign in his constituency for a return to traditional family values.

Item D *The non-resignation of Waldegrave and Lyell*

The Scott Report provides an example of accountability avoidance. Scott concluded that the government statements made in 1989 and 1990 about arms exports to Iraq failed to fulfil the obligations imposed by the constitutional principle of ministerial accountability. Yet, no minister resigned after publication of the report. The two ministers who might have been expected to resign were William Waldegrave and Nicholas Lyell. Waldegrave, Scott concluded, misled Parliament about government policy on numerous occasions, although he did not deliberately set out to deceive MPs. Lyell, Scott found, was personally at fault over the preparation of Public Interest Immunity (PII) certificates for the Matrix Churchill trial and was to blame for failing to inform the prosecution that one minister, Michael Heseltine, was reluctant to sign a PII certificate. They both fulfilled the constitutional requirement for resignation because there was a departmental fault in which the minister was involved or of which he knew or should have known. There may also have been an element of personal fault (since the ministers made misjudgements). From another point of view, however, the ministers' conduct could be defended - Scott did not argue that Lyell was responsible for a cover-up or that Waldegrave misled Parliament intentionally. Ultimately, however, their survival was due to the political circumstances at the time. In particular, they retained the solid support of the Prime Minister, Cabinet and most Conservative backbenchers.

Adapted from Simpson 1998 and Gray 1997.

Questions

1. a) Judging from Items A-C, why do ministers lose their jobs so frequently?
   b) Give arguments for and against the view that there should be a rapid turnover of ministers.

2. a) Describe the trends shown in Item B.
   b) Why do you think the number of resignations has grown since 1979?

3. a) Did each of the ministers mentioned in Item C resign because of role responsibility, personal responsibility or neither?
   b) Describe the factors that might lead a minister to resign.

4. What does Item D tell us about individual ministerial responsibility?

1.4 What makes a successful minister?

Qualifications and qualities

In theory, the qualifications for becoming a minister are minimal. Any MP or peer who is prepared to support the government can be appointed. In practice, however, there are a number of qualifications and qualities which help a person to succeed as a minister.

Long working hours

Probably the most important qualification for all ministers at any level is a considerable capacity for hard work. Theakston (1987) notes that for a junior minister:

> 'A 12 to 15 hour working day is common. Often starting in the office or leaving on a visit before nine o'clock in the morning and not finishing until well after ten o'clock at night if there is a vote in the House of Commons.' (Theakston 1987, p.77)

Nor can ministers who are MPs relax at the weekend since, like all MPs, they have to look after their constituency affairs. Joel Barnett, Chief Secretary to the Treasury in the 1970s, recalled:

> 'I soon found that good health and an ability to manage on little sleep - I am fortunate in only needing five or six hours - were invaluable assets in my new job. Having always been accustomed to working seven days a week, I was not troubled by the actual volume of work, although it was soon clear that not only would I be working seven days but also much of the evenings and nights too.' (Barnett 1982, p.16)

Although long hours are the norm for ministers, there is some scope for flexibility:

> 'One Downing Street insider reports that the Prime Minister [Tony Blair] likes to keep a light schedule - a nine to five day broken by lunch with friends or family and an early knock-off for quality time with the kids. [Chancellor] Brown, meantime, had new locks fitted at the Treasury so he could start work at 6 am and stay there past midnight.' (*Guardian*, 26 November 1997)

As this passage indicates, the nature of the post and the personality of ministers determine how hard they work.

Public speaking

Second, a talent for good organisation and the ability to put over a good argument in public are advantageous. A good performance in the Commons is important, particularly in the early stages of a minister's career. An impressive speech can help make a junior minister's reputation and a poor performance can help to break it. The chances of success are improved if junior ministers keep in touch with specialist backbench committees since junior ministers are more likely to gain support if they are putting over what backbenchers want to hear. Also, at a more senior level, the reception given to a speech at the party conference can do much to boost or undermine a minister's reputation.

Handling legislation

Third, ministers' reputations are judged on how well they handle pieces of legislation (this is particularly so at Cabinet level) and how well they defend their interests in inter-departmental battles. If legislation passes through Parliament smoothly and seems to be working well, a minister's reputation tends to be enhanced. Similarly, ministers with a reputation for being tough fighters for their departments tend to be promoted. Conversely, ministers whose proposed legislation does not pass through Parliament smoothly have less chance of promotion.

Loyalty

Fourth, ministers need to show loyalty if they are to advance their career. Ministers are often appointed as a reward for their loyalty to the Party Leader. For example, Norman Lamont was appointed as Chancellor in 1990 after playing a prominent role in John Major's leadership campaign. Similarly, Gordon Brown was rewarded with the job of shadow Chancellor and then Chancellor after he agreed not to fight against Tony Blair in the Labour Party leadership contest of 1994. Tony Blair's other leadership rivals John Prescott and Margaret Beckett were also appointed to senior positions in the Cabinet in May 1997, having proved their loyalty to Blair between the leadership election and the 1997 general election.

Alliances

Fifth, it can be advantageous for junior ministers to gain the backing of formal and informal groups of backbenchers, especially if these groups do not represent mainstream opinion. For example, it has been argued that Clare Short's appointment to a Cabinet post in May 1997 was made in response to pressure from backbenchers.

Teamwork

And finally, ministers at any level need to build a good working relationship with other members of their department. Since ministers tend to be in post for a relatively short time they cannot possibly know all the answers. As a result, they need to be able to listen to their civil servants and yet to be decisive when they have heard what options are available. They need to be able to draw a fine balance between what their government wants, what their department wants and what other interests want.

1.5 Ministerial roles

The role of junior ministers

Before 1830, departments were small and all

ministers below Cabinet rank were undifferentiated:

> 'They were all alike in their legal, administrative and political subordination to their ministerial chiefs.' (Theakston 1987, p.1)

By 1830, government business had increased in volume and this led to a gradual change in the structure of departments. From 1914 onwards, departmental work not only increased but became more complex. This led to duties being broken down into particular areas of responsibility.

The trend of appointing a number of junior ministers with specific responsibilities began in 1964 when Alec Douglas Home was Prime Minister and has continued ever since. During the 1970s:

> '[It gradually] became the practice to assign to named ministers specific areas of departmental work to oversee rather than delegating to them miscellaneous duties on an ad hoc basis.' (Theakston 1987, p.87)

The job

Today, some junior ministers are appointed to a specific job by the Prime Minister. Alternatively, the allocation of a junior minister's duties is left to the minister who heads the department. The job allocated to a junior minister depends on that minister's experience, abilities and the particular circumstances at the time. Areas of responsibility are not fixed and:

> 'There may be frequent adjustments as ministers enter, leave or change their posts and as changing circumstances push issues up or down the political agenda.' (Theakston 1987, p.87)

In general terms, however, because junior ministers tend to have greater responsibility today than used to be the case, they have moved more into the political limelight. They now defend their particular area of work at Question Time and in the media. On occasion, this greater exposure can lead to greater criticism. For example, in November 1997, the Public Health Minister, Tessa Jowell, came under attack after announcing that the government had decided to exempt Formula One motor racing from a ban on cigarette advertising.

Ministerial decision making

Ministers are responsible for the policy initiated in their departments. They must study the different options presented to them by their civil servants and then use their political judgement to decide what policies or options should be decided upon or rejected. Decisions are made on ideological grounds or financial grounds (or both). Ministers also liaise with Parliament, the public and outside bodies on behalf of their department.

According to Madgwick, much of the work in a department is routine. He compares the role of Cabinet ministers with those of managing directors. Cabinet ministers oversee the work of their departments and are:

> 'Semi-detached, at the top but not in touch, on a cloud rather than a mountain.' (Madgwick 1991, p.22)

They rely on their officials to keep them up-to-date with what is happening.

The way in which junior ministers handle their role largely depends on their previous experience and personality. For example, a junior minister with business experience is likely to be used to dealing with administrative pressures, whilst a minister with journalistic experience is likely to be familiar with the communication requirements of the job. Sideways movement from one ministerial post to another helps ministers gain a wide range of experience and tests their abilities.

Constraints on ministers

Norton (1998) points out that constitutional, legal and organisational constraints tie ministers' hands. The 'constitutional' constraints he identifies are as follows:

- the doctrine of collective responsibility
- the knowledge that the Prime Minister can promote or sack ministers
- the necessity of answering questions and defending actions in the Commons.

The 'legal' constraints he identifies are:

- the necessity of acting within the limits of the powers provided by Parliament (in other words, ministers need to be sure that actions are not ultra vires)
- membership of the EU (since this limits the scope of actions which can be taken unilaterally by ministers).

The 'organisational' constraints boil down to a single factor - lack of time. In addition to their ministerial duties, ministers remain MPs with parliamentary and constituency responsibilities. They also remain party members who must attend Parliament and local party meetings. The sheer volume of work and the need to juggle different roles mean that ministers have to prioritise and leave some matters undone.

Relationships between ministers

Generally, Cabinet ministers have little say as to who their junior ministers should be. They may inherit an existing team when they move to a department or the Prime Minister may decide to shuffle junior ministers to spread their experience.

Relationships between ministers vary according to the role adopted by the Cabinet minister. Some Cabinet ministers have regular team meetings. Others do not. In the Treasury, for example, although each minister has a separate area of responsibility, the whole team is brought together for the annual Budget. The extracts in Box 13.1 below illustrate the importance of cultivating good relations between ministers working in the same department.

Seven ministerial categories

Philip Norton (1998) argues that the role played by ministers is determined to some extent by the personality and goals of the minister. What a minister

Box 13.1 Ministerial teamwork

(i) In July 1962, William Whitelaw was appointed as a junior minister in the Department of Labour. His experience there provided him with the model he used when later appointed to the Cabinet:

'I found a fascinating ministry under John Hare whom I came to admire as a most skilful and sensitive minister. He was an ideal minister to serve under as he brought his junior minister in on all discussions and once he had delegated work he left you to get on with it without interference. Subsequently, as a minister myself, I have tried to follow that example and it must be the right way to run a government department. It is, alas, more difficult today since government departments are much larger and there are so many more ministers involved with whom to keep in touch.'

Adapted fromWhitelaw 1990

(ii) In 1970, Peter Walker was asked by the Prime Minister, Edward Heath, to set up the new Department of the Environment. Every morning, he briefed the whole ministerial team:

'These daily meetings did mean that all ministers knew what was happening throughout the whole department. Civil servants could never go to a junior minister and get him to agree to something that the Secretary of State would turn down. It led to more cohesion and enthusiasm. There was another important advantage. PPSs could attend, so I had, in fact, 15 ministers and PPSs going around the Commons explaining why we had adopted this or that policy. In this way you were able to make a big impact on the parliamentary party where so much strength ultimately lay.'

Adapted from Walker 1991

wants out of the job, he argues, determines how that minister does the job. A minister whose main goal is promotion to higher office, for example, is likely to do the job rather differently from a minister whose main aim is to achieve particular policy outcomes. After interviewing a number of ministers who served in government during the period 1979-97, Norton identified seven main types of minister:

1. Team players - those who believe in collective decision making and want the government to work as a team.

2. Commanders (self-driven) - those who have very clear ideas about what they hope to achieve and whose ideas come from their own personal preferences and goals.

3. Commanders (ideologues) - those who have very clear ideas about what they hope to achieve and whose ideas are based on a particular ideology.

4. Managers - ministers whose decisions are pragmatic rather than being driven by a particular ideology.

5. Agents (prime ministerial) - ministers whose aim is to ensure the Prime Minister's wishes are carried out.

6. Agents (civil service) - ministers who

do what the civil servants in the department advise.

7. Agents (European Union) - ministers who do what they can to fulfil Britain's EU treaty obligations.

Norton found that most ministers were either self-driven commanders or managers. Few ministers fitted into the other categories.

Pressures on ministers

Pressures on time

There are immense pressures on the time of ministers, especially Cabinet ministers. They are expected to run their departments and to perform their constituency duties as MPs. They are also expected to speak in public for both government and party.

Departmental work has increased considerably in recent years and ministers cannot possibly watch over all the day-to-day work carried out by a department. It should be noted, however, that the vast majority of work done by a department is routine and uncontroversial. Ministers need to learn the art of delegation, as former Conservative minister Norman Fowler explained:

'I regularly started work at 5.30 am when I had just taken over the DHSS [Department of Health and Social Security] and every issue - big, small and minute - appeared to run through my office...Whitehall would feed you red boxes as long as you wanted to eat. If you were not careful, you simply ended up with the interdepartmental prize for letter signing and a reputation for seeing every piece of paper in circulation at the time. I found it better to devolve.' (Fowler 1991, pp.318-19)

Lack of specialist knowledge

It is not just the amount of work that brings pressure to bear on ministers, it is also the nature of the work. On his first day as Under Secretary of State in the Department of the Environment, Alan Clark complained that:

'The subject matter is turgid: a mass of "schemes" whose purpose, plainly, is not so much to bring relief to those out of work as to devise excuses for removing them from the Register...The Enterprise Allowance Scheme, the Job Release Scheme, the Community Scheme. Convoluted and obscure even at their inception, they have since been so picked over and "modified" by civil servants as to be incomprehensible. I ought to welcome these devices, and must try to master their intricacies. But, my head is bursting.' (Clark 1993, p.10)

So, as well as lack of time, ministers are constrained by a lack of specialist knowledge. The constant reshuffling of ministers prevents many of them from acquiring any detailed knowledge and understanding of the work of their department. The result, according to Madgwick, is that:

'Some ministers stay for two years or more in one office, learn fast and master enough of their subject to be reasonably effective. Others can be no more than visiting amateurs, reading a brief on the way to a meeting, hoping not to be found in error in public.' (Madgwick 1991, p.42)

Access to information

A further problem is access to information. Theakston (1987) suggests that less than 1% of a department's work is seen by a minister and that information is rationed on a 'need to know' basis. In some cases junior ministers do not even know what is going on in their own department outside their own area of work.

Pressures from interested parties

There is also constant pressure on ministers from their own party, from the opposition parties, from pressure groups, from other lobbyists, from the media and from members of the public. This pressure can become particularly intense if there is disagreement within the government ranks. The split between the pro-Europeans and Eurosceptics in John Major's Cabinet after 1994, for example, added to the pressure on the government at all levels.

Main points - Sections 1.4-1.5

- In theory, the qualifications for becoming a minister are minimal. In practice, however, a successful minister needs to be: (1) hardworking; (2) a good public speaker; (3) able to handle legislation; (4) loyal; (5) popular on the backbenches; and (6) a team worker.
- Ministers are responsible for the policy initiated in their departments. They also liaise with Parliament, the public and outside bodies on behalf of their department.
- Constitutional, legal and organisational constraints tie ministers' hands
- Norton (1998) argues that the role played by senior ministers is determined to some extent by the personality of the minister. He found that most ministers were either self-driven commanders or managers.
- The main pressures on ministers are: (1) lack of time; (2) lack of specialist knowledge; (3) gaining access to information; and (4) the need to satisfy interested parties.

Activity 13.3 *What makes a successful minister?*

Item A *Advice to ministers*

How to be a good minister

1. Beware of 'departmentalitis' - ministers are split up and isolated.
2. Don't become big-headed (tempting though that might be after 18 years in opposition).
3. Remember you are still an MP - treat backbenchers courteously and pay attention to what they say.
4. Remember you are a Labour Party member - talk to and listen to other party members (sometimes they have ideas worth taking up).
5. Remember your constituents - do not take them for granted or you'll be out at the next election.
6. Stand up for yourself - always listen to advice, but do not always follow it.
7. Never take no for an answer - the official machinery is capable of stitching ministers up.
8. Control your diary - time is of the essence in ministerial work.
9. Don't sign documents unless they are exactly as you want them.
10. Do your boxes and know your stuff.
11. Remember you are politically mortal - the day will inevitably come when you are no longer a minister.

Adapted from Kaufman 1996 and 1997.

Item B *Mo Mowlam*

Mo Mowlam was first elected to Parliament in 1987. In 1988, she was given a junior job on the team shadowing Northern Ireland. A year later she moved to Trade and Industry. She then achieved a rare double by being elected to both the shadow Cabinet and the NEC, a demonstration of her popularity in the party. She used a good memory to political effect. One Labour activist commented: 'Whenever I meet Mo she knows who I am, what I do and when we first met. There are other members of the Cabinet to whom I have to introduce myself each time we meet.' The most common criticism of Mowlam is that she tends to be all things to all people. She does not surround herself with cronies from any particular group and she is difficult to place within the party. One party worker described her as a 'moderniser' and another as 'an ally of the left'. In fact, she encourages such uncertainty, admitting: 'People say that I stuck close to Kinnock, then Smith, then Blair and that I can switch my personality to suit whatever audience I'm with. There's an element of truth in that.' Through hard work and shrewd positioning, Mowlam assembled a strong hand in difficult circumstances. She wooed the unionists without alienating the republicans and maintained good relations with Dublin and the USA. Throughout the negotiations on Northern Ireland in the spring of 1998, she managed to keep the parties talking. The result was the Good Friday Agreement. Just how much party members appreciate her was demonstrated at the 1998 party conference. At the mention of her name in Tony Blair's keynote speech, she was given a standing ovation - the first time that a Leader's speech had ever been interrupted by a standing ovation for a colleague.

Adapted from the *Independent on Sunday*, 6 July 1997 and the *Guardian*, 30 September 1998.

Item C   Alan Clark, Minister for Trade

In his diaries, Alan Clark (who was Minister for Trade between 1986 and 1989) complained about the time ministers waste meeting delegations because there are so few occasions when a minister's mind is altered during a discussion. Despite this complaint, however, he reveals that a delegation from the charity Lynx convinced him to draft legislation which would force fur traders to label garments made of the skins of animals that had been caught in leg-hold traps. Clark felt so strongly about this measure that he spent enormous time and energy on it. He even admitted that: 'Sometimes I think that all I want is to stay in office here long enough to get my fur legislation on to the statute book.' To prepare the path for the legislation, Clark met, threatened and cajoled all sorts of people - such as lawyers, ambassadors, senior civil servants from several departments, eskimos, furriers and small shopkeepers. By June 1988, it seemed that the legislation would be adopted. On 14 June, however, Clark was summoned to see Prime Minister Thatcher. She wanted Clark to drop the scheme. After four and a half minutes, Clark realised he had lost. The meeting was scheduled for 15 minutes, but lasted 55. About three quarters of the way through the meeting Clark said: 'Well, if that's what you want, I will obey you.'

Adapted from Clark 1993.

Item D   Pressures on ministers

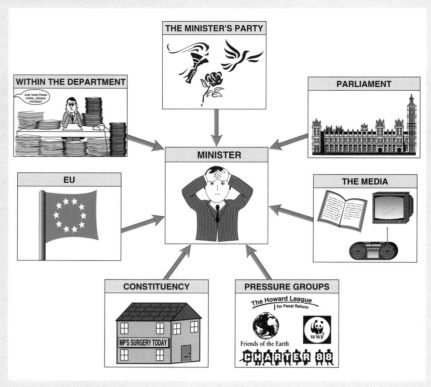

Questions

1. Judging from the criteria in Item A, would you say that Mo Mowlam (Item B) and Alan Clark (Item C) have the sort of qualities necessary to make a successful minister? Explain your answer.

2. Suppose you had been asked to give advice to a minister who complained that there were too many pressures pulling in different directions. What advice would you give? Use Items A, C and D in your answer.

3. Which of Philip Norton's seven ministerial categories (see Section 1.5 above) best describes (a) Mo Mowlam (Item B) and (b) Alan Clark (Item C)? Explain how you reached this conclusion.

Part 2 The civil service

Key issues

1. What is the civil service?
2. What sort of people become civil servants?
3. What role does the civil service play in theory and in practice?
4. How have recent reforms affected the civil service?

2.1 What is the civil service?

A definition

The civil service is an administrative system which consists of a body of government officials who are employed in civil (non-military) occupations. According to a government publication:

'Civil servants are servants of the Crown. For all practical purposes the Crown in this context means, and is represented by, the government of the day...The civil service as such has no constitutional responsibility separate from the government of the day which it serves as a whole, that is to say Her Majesty's ministers collectively. The duty of an individual civil servant is first and foremost to the minister of the Crown who is in charge of the department concerned. A change of minister for whatever reason does not involve a change of staff.' (HMSO 1994, pp.47-48)

This may be the official view, but, in practice, the role and responsibilities of civil servants are more complex than this suggests (see Sections 2.5-2.6 below for a discussion of the role of civil servants).

Historical background

The earliest recorded civil service existed in China 2,000 years ago under the Ch'in dynasty (221-206 BC). It consisted of a centralised bureaucracy of talented people whose role was to serve the state. Entry into the civil service was by examination. Officials were called 'mandarins', a term still used to describe the small élite at the top of the British civil service today.

According to Hennessy (1989) the term 'civil service' was coined by the East India Company which ran India on behalf of the British government from 1599 to the mid-19th century. The term was introduced to distinguish civilian employees from those serving with the military.

Before the 19th century, a civil service in the modern sense did not exist. The state's administrative system was not regarded as a single service and the number of full-time staff was small (in the 1820s, for example, the total number of civil servants employed by the Home Office was just 17). What appointments there were, were made by nepotism or patronage rather than on merit. Ministers tended to look after their own departmental affairs whilst officials performed tasks which today would be considered political. It was not until the mid-19th century that an attempt was made to establish an efficient and organised civil service.

The Northcote-Trevelyan Report (1854)

The impetus for civil service reform came from the Treasury. The Chancellor, Gladstone, set up an inquiry in April 1853 under Northcote and Trevelyan. Trevelyan had served in the Indian civil service (set up by the East India Company) and he aimed to bring the British civil service up to the high standard of administration for which the Indian civil service was known. The Northcote-Trevelyan Report was published in 1854. Its five main recommendations are outlined in Box 13.2.

Box 13.2 Main recommendations of the Northcote-Trevelyan Report

1. Civil service posts should be divided between superior and inferior categories, creating a distinction between intellectual and mechanical tasks.
2. Entrants into the service should, in general, be young men who would receive on-the-job training for their duties (it rejected recruiting mature men who had acquired experience elsewhere).
3. Recruitment should be through open competitive examination - one for graduates to higher posts, one for junior posts.
4. The examination should in all cases be in liberal arts rather than professional or technical subjects.
5. Promotion should be on the basis of merit, not favouritism.

Adapted from Drewry & Butcher 1991.

The report was welcomed by Gladstone but was opposed by his colleagues and by top civil servants who saw it as a threat to the system of patronage. Although entrance examinations were conducted by the Civil Service Commission set up in May 1855, open competition was not fully established until the Playfair Report was published in 1875.

The Fulton Report (1968)

Although there were a few small inquiries and adjustments to the civil service after 1875, its structure remained virtually unchanged until 1968 when the Fulton Report, commissioned by Prime Minister Harold Wilson was published. This report was commissioned in response to growing concern over the continuing tradition of employing recruits with a generalist rather than a specialist background.

The Fulton Report found that civil servants still came from a narrow background and had little real experience of the outside world. It also found that they were poorly trained, lacked expertise and had few managerial skills. The report made recommendations designed to professionalise the service by making civil servants more accountable. Greenaway notes that Fulton was:

> 'Concerned with three areas of the civil service - its structure and grading, recruitment procedures and in-service training...One of the key recommendations [was the introduction of a] single, unified grading structure...linked to a desire to abolish the dividing lines between the generalist administration and specialist classes.' (Greenaway 1992, pp.176-7)

Changes following the Fulton Report

The report made a number of recommendations, but only a few were implemented (partly because civil servants themselves had to implement the reforms and they only implemented those acceptable to them). The main changes were as follows:

- a civil service college was set up (but most training was still done in departments)
- a civil service department was set up (but it was abolished in 1981)
- civil service jobs were slightly restructured and a new Administrative Trainee grade was set up
- civil service pension rules were modified
- some departmental functions were hived off
- some planning units were set up (but not on the Fulton model).

2.2 Reforms since 1979

Next Steps

By the time that the first Thatcher government was elected in 1979 it was clear that the Fulton reforms had largely failed. Soon after her election, Margaret Thatcher began to argue that the civil service was too large, wasteful of resources and did not provide value for money. The result was a new attempt to reform the service.

Certainly the civil service had grown. In 1961, it employed 640,000 people, but, by 1979, this had grown to 732,000. On taking up office, Thatcher froze civil service recruitment (compulsory redundancies were avoided by not replacing those who retired). She notes that this policy was not readily accepted by civil servants themselves:

> 'Departments came up with a range of ingenious reasons why this principle should not apply to them. But, one by one they were overruled.' (Thatcher 1993, p.94)

The work of the Efficiency Unit

The drive for reform was managed from Downing Street. Sir Derek Rayner (a leading businessman brought in from the private sector) was given a small unit within the Cabinet Office (the Efficiency Unit) whose job was to scrutinise the civil service from within. As a result of this initiative, the Management Information System for Ministers (MINIS) was introduced into the Department of the Environment in 1980 and this led to the introduction of the Financial Management Initiative (FMI) in 1982. The FMI covered all departments and was the first real attempt at streamlining the civil service. Its aim was to improve efficiency by initiating a change of attitude and introducing new management practices. Civil servants were to become the equivalent of line managers in business by being held directly responsible for particular policies in their departments. They were to be given a clear view of their objectives and encouraged to use their initiative to make the best use of resources available to them.

Tackling the culture of bureaucracy

Margaret Thatcher also argued that a great deal of potential talent in the civil service was being wasted because of the culture of bureaucracy which was fostered by Whitehall. She argued for performance related pay to improve efficiency. But, introduction of performance related pay did not prove easy:

> 'The difficulties of introducing pay rates related to merit proved immense...It took several years and a great deal of pushing and shoving.' (Thatcher 1993, p.46)

The Ibbs Report

The Rayner reforms were intended to produce long-term changes, but, by 1987, many of the supporters of the new managerialism remained disappointed. Three main criticisms were made. First, experimentation with budgeting and performance related pay had not gone far enough. Second, devolution of responsibility had not been achieved in practice. And third, promotion to the top continued to be from too narrow a base.

These concerns led to the setting up of a new

efficiency scrutiny into management practice right across government. This was carried out by Sir Robert Ibbs. Ibbs began work under Margaret Thatcher and continued when Major became Prime Minister. The Ibbs Report *Improving Management in Government: the Next Steps* was first presented to Margaret Thatcher before the 1987 general election. The document's contents were so sensitive, however, that it was kept secret until after that election. It was finally published in February 1988.

The Ibbs Report made three main points. First, it argued that the civil service was too vast both in scale and in size to carry out its role in an efficient manner:

> 'A single organisation of this size which attempts to provide a detailed structure within which to carry out functions as diverse as driver licensing, fisheries protection, the catching of drug smugglers and the processing of parliamentary questions is bound to develop in a way which fits no single operation effectively.' (HMSO 1988, para.10)

Second, it criticised civil servants for playing safe rather than taking an enterprising outlook. Third, it complained that the civil service was still spending too much and not providing value for money.

Next Steps agencies

The Ibbs Report recommended a programme which would lead to substantial changes in the structure of the civil service. Its most important recommendation was that semi-autonomous agencies should be set up:

> 'As far as is practicable, the executive functions of government, that is service delivery undertaken by departments (as distinct from policy), should be carried out by executive units clearly designated within departments, referred to as "agencies", with responsibility for day-to-day operations delegated to a chief executive responsible for management within policy objectives and to a resources framework set by the responsible minister.' (quoted in Simpson 1998, p.64)

The main recommendations made by the Ibbs Report were accepted in February 1988 and, since then, steps have been taken to implement them. At first, progress was slow. By April 1990, just 12 agencies had been set up. Since then, however, the number of agencies has grown rapidly. By 1 April 1998, 124 agencies, employing 77% of all permanent civil servants had been set up. The long-term plan is that 95% of civil servants should be employed by agencies, leaving the other 5% employed by ministries at the central level.

The agencies retain links with their government department, but have a degree of autonomy:

> 'Next Steps agencies are located within government departments and staffed by civil servants. They operate under framework agreements which delegate authority and

responsibilities to the chief executive who is then accountable to the minister.' (Simpson 1998, p.64)

From Citizen's Charter to Service First

In response to concerns over the provision of public services, John Major launched the Citizen's Charter in 1991 (see also Chapter 17, Section 1.3). The idea was that, because many civil servants are in contact with the general public (for example, issuing passports, dealing with benefit claims or collecting income tax), charters could be drawn up which describe the sort of service which the public is entitled to. By setting targets, the government would make civil servants more accountable to members of the public and improve standards of service provision. Although the Citizen's Charter was criticised at the time of its launch, by the time that Labour came to power in 1997 elements of the scheme had proved popular. In particular, the awarding of Charter Marks for the provision of high quality public services gained public support (nominations from the public rose from 4,000 in 1995, the year the scheme was launched, to 25,000 in 1997).

In June 1998, the government announced that the Citizen's Charter programme would be replaced by the Service First programme. The new scheme would differ from the old in that:

> 'The success of each organisation will be judged on the views of those who use it rather than on how fast it can answer the telephone or reply to letters.' (*Times*, 30 June 1998)

As a result of this new initiative, public bodies were told to canvass opinion about the quality of the service they provide by using local focus groups, sending out questionnaires or holding public meetings - the idea being that feedback from this consultation would result in action to improve the service.

Like the Citizen's Charter, the Service First programme is run by a team in the Cabinet Office. The job of this team is also to monitor the quality of public services and to offer advice on how standards could be improved.

Contracting-out and privatisation

In the same way that many of the services in local government were contracted-out to private contractors in the late 1980s and early 1990s (see Chapter 16, Section 2.6), steps were taken under the Conservatives to introduce market forces into the civil service. This took two main forms - contracting-out services to the private sector and selling them off (privatising them). Whilst the selling off of services proved relatively straightforward (for example, to cut running costs in departments, the Major government

sold off departments' information technology (IT) services to private companies), contracting-out was less so. An initiative in 1991, for example, aimed to introduce 'market testing' by opening up civil service work to outside contractors. Although the Major government required government departments to identify 30% of their work for market testing, there was little take-up by departments and the scheme was dropped in 1994 (Hood & James 1997). Similarly, the 1992 Private Finance Initiative (designed to enable private companies to carry out public sector work by putting in place a flow of payments) did not achieve its targets (*Times*, 10 March 1998).

During its first 18 months in power, the Labour government made no attempt to reverse Conservative initiatives. Indeed, some proposals made by the Major government were implemented after Labour came to power. For example, the Department of Social Security's property estate (including 700 local benefit offices), 740 computer systems and the Benefits Agency Medical Services were sold off to the private sector in August 1997 (*Guardian*, 1 August 1997). Nevertheless, there was a clear change in priorities under Labour. Whereas John Major's government had focused on farming out the day-to-day work of departments to agencies, the Blair government concentrated on changing the government machinery at the centre. Changes in the structure of the Cabinet Office were particularly significant (see Chapter 12, Section 2.5).

Main points - Sections 2.1-2.2

- The civil service is an administrative body with no constitutional responsibility separate from that of the government. It is the duty of civil servants to serve the minister in charge of their department. A change of minister does not involve a change of staff.
- Attempts to reform the civil service took place in 1854 (the Northcote-Trevelyan Report) and 1968 (the Fulton Report). It is only since 1979, however, that substantial changes have taken place.
- The drive for greater efficiency in 1979-97 led to the creation of semi-autonomous Next Steps agencies, the Citizen's Charter initiative and to parts of the civil service being contracted-out or privatised.
- During its first 18 months in power, the Labour government did not attempt to reverse these changes, though it did make it clear that it had different priorities from the previous government.

Activity 13.4 A new type of civil service

Item A   Next Steps

The Next Steps initiative is the most far-reaching reform of the civil service in the 20th century. The term 'Next Steps' is used because it is the successor to a whole range of other changes in the management and financial control of government departments that have taken place since 1979. The creation of agencies which are responsible to ministers for the execution of policy will transform public administration and public policy in the UK. The first agency was the Vehicle Inspectorate launched in August 1988. The largest agency is the Social Security Benefits Agency which employs 63,000 staff and the smallest is Wilton Park, employing 30 staff. The aim of the Next Steps initiative is to improve the efficiency and quality of service delivered by public agencies. Agencies do not decide what these services should be. The Vehicle Inspectorate, for example, performs tests, but only has an advisory role in deciding what the structure and parameters of the tests should be. Transport policy, road safety and the links between vehicle testing, driver licensing, vehicle registration and motorway design all remain the responsibility of the Department of Transport. Similarly, although the Benefits Agency costs £2 billion to run and distributes over £50 billion in benefits, the structure and levels of benefits and the agency's objectives are set by the Department of Social Security - the agency is one adviser amongst many.

Adapted from Thain 1993.

Item C Performance related government

Tough new standards are to be imposed on Britain's public services in what the government is describing as 'performance related government'. In December 1998, the Treasury will announce more than 100 separate annual targets for individual Whitehall ministries, agencies and cross-departmental initiatives. Ministers believe that an electorate opposed to higher taxes can be persuaded to support funds for public services such as health and education if there is this new form of public accountability. Departments will be expected to meet their targets by April 2002, the end of the three year period for which Treasury funding is guaranteed. Meanwhile, they will be expected to measure annual progress towards targets and publish a report setting out the relevant statistics. Ministers believe that this process will raise standards across the public sector. Whilst extra cash will be given to departments which perform well, the Treasury will provide managerial advice on improving performance to those which fail. The Chief Secretary to the Treasury, Stephen Byers, will require independent government agencies (eg Inland Revenue and the Forestry Commission) to publish their own targets. Expected targets include a Foreign Office requirement to secure 250,000 extra jobs through inward investment, a Home Office goal of cutting car crime by a third in three years, and a Health Department objective of reducing cancer. Controversially, the Department of Social Security may be required to cut relative poverty.

Adapted from the Observer, 8 November 1998.

Item B   Setting up a Next Steps agency

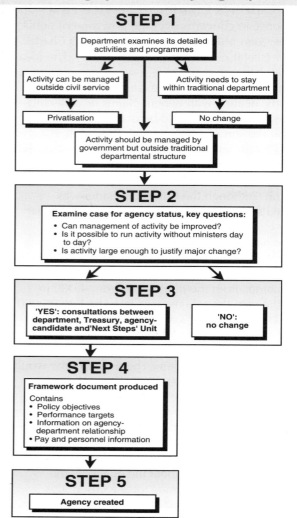

Adapted from Pyper 1992.

Item D   Brick's view

Questions

1. a) Judging from Items A and B: (i) what is the Next Steps initiative; (ii) how does it work; and (iii) what are its benefits and drawbacks?
   b) Explain why the Next Steps initiative has been described as 'the most far-reaching reform of the civil service in the 20th century'.
2. Does Item C provide evidence of continuity with or change from the previous government? Explain your answer.
3. What does Item D tell us about the way in which the civil service has changed since 1979?

2.3 The structure of the civil service

Classes, grades and groups

Following the Northcote-Trevelyan reforms in 1854, the civil service was based on three 'classes' - the **administrative class** (which advised ministers on policy), the **executive class** (which was concerned with the implementation of policy) and the **clerical class** (which carried out detailed routine tasks). By the 1960s, however, these three broad classes had been subdivided into 47 different general classes and 1,400 departmental classes (Greenwood 1989).

The 1968 Fulton Report suggested that classes should be renamed 'grades' since the word 'class' suggests inferior and superior groups. This, it was argued, could inhibit mobility and restrict opportunities for people to advance within the structure. The idea was that there would be a single unified grading system - around 20 grades which covered all jobs from top to bottom. This, it was hoped, would simplify the structure of the service. But, by 1977, there were still 38 general classes and 500 departmental classes.

Today, the non-industrial civil service can still be divided roughly into three groups:

1. Service-wide groups
Service-wide groups are made up of generalist administrators who operate in various or all departments. The main service-wide group is the Administration Group (see below).

2. Service-wide specialist groups
Service-wide specialist groups are made up of specialists who operate in various or all departments. These groups have their own grading and qualification systems. Examples are the Economist, Information Officer, Librarian and Statistician Groups.

3. Departmental groups and agencies
Departmental groups are made up of civil servants peculiar to a single department. Different departments have different pay and qualification structures. Many civil servants (77% in 1998) who used to work for departmental groups now work for executive agencies - for example, prison officers are now employed by the Prison Service Agency. They used to be employed by the Home Office.

The structure

The structure of the civil service can, therefore, be broken down as follows:

'About half of all civil servants are engaged in the provision of public services. These include paying sickness benefits and pensions, collecting taxes and contributions, running employment services, staffing prisons and providing services to industry and agriculture. Around a quarter are employed in the Ministry of Defence. The rest are divided between: central administrative and policy duties [the Administration Group]; support services; and largely financially self-supporting services, for instance, those provided by the department for National Savings and the Royal Mint...Four-fifths of civil servants work outside London.' (HMSO 1994, p.48)

The Administration Group

By far the biggest service-wide group is the Administration Group. At the top of the Administration Group is the 'Open Structure'. Below it are the lower administrative levels.

The Open Structure

The top seven grades in the civil service make up the Open Structure (see Box 13.3). Until 1996, Grades 1-3 made up the Senior Open Structure. In April 1996, however, a new structure - the Senior Civil Service - was set up. This incorporated Grades 1-5, though the new structure moved away from describing senior civil servants by their grade (instead, there are wide, overlapping pay bands). Whereas there were c.600 people in the Senior Open Structure, there were c.4,000 in the Senior

Box 13.3 The seven grades in the Open Structure

Grade 1	First Permanent Secretary	Senior Civil Service (SCS) since 1996
Grade 1A	Second Permanent Secretary	
Grade 2	Deputy Secretary	
Grade 3	Under Secretary	
Grade 4	Executive Directing Bands	
Grade 5	Assistant Secretary	
Grade 6	Senior Principal	
Grade 7	Principal	

Civil Service in 1998.

The Open Structure, therefore, includes those civil servants at the very top of the hierarchy. These civil servants are involved in the policy-making process and make up just 5% of the non-industrial civil service as a whole.

As far as the policy-making process is concerned, the key advisers to ministers are drawn from Grades 1-4. Grade 5 civil servants are responsible for a section of a department's work and may make a significant input into policy making (though their views are normally filtered through more senior officials). Grades 6 and 7 are more concerned with the finer details of potential legislation. For example, they are the civil servants who deal with pressure groups. There are roughly 1,000 civil servants in Grades 1-4.

The administrative levels

Those civil servants who work for the Administration Group but are not on Grades 1-7 belong to the administrative levels. The range of tasks varies from middle management to routine clerical jobs.

Industrial civil servants

The number of industrial civil servants is small. They make up around 6% of the overall total. Industrial civil servants work in government-controlled industrial concerns, such as the navy shipyards in Scotland.

2.4 Recruitment

Career pathways

At its peak in 1976, the civil service employed a total of 746,000 people. By 1979, this number had fallen to 732,000. Since 1979, efforts to slim down the service have resulted in a substantial decrease. By April 1998, the total number of civil servants had fallen to 463,300 - a fall of 38% since 1979.

Civil servants are recruited to different levels according to their academic qualifications. Those whose only qualifications are GCSE passes can apply to be Administrative Assistants. Those with A levels but no degree can apply to be Administrative Officers. For graduates, there are two types of entry. Either they can apply to join the Executive grade (middle management with the prospect of gaining promotion up the hierarchy) or they can apply to join the 'fast stream'. If their application is successful, they enter the Administration Group as an Administrative Trainee at the Higher Executive Officer grade.

The Oughton Report

In 1993, the Cabinet Office Efficiency Unit produced a report under the leadership of Sir John Oughton. The Oughton Report made recommendations in three areas:

- internal training and development
- selection and appointment
- terms of employment.

Since 1993, there have been some changes in all

three areas. The most significant changes are:

- the extension of open competition for posts
- the introduction of greater flexibility in pay
- the introduction of greater flexibility in the grading of senior posts
- changes to contractual arrangements
- the introduction of performance related pay.

The main aims were to introduce new, more efficient management techniques and to broaden the base from which senior civil servants are recruited.

The fast stream

As the term implies, the 'fast stream' is the route to the top of the civil service hierarchy. Candidates are appointed only if they succeed in passing the rigorous tests and interviews set by the Civil Service Selection Board (whose methods are based on techniques pioneered by the War Office in the Second World War). As well as tests and interviews, candidates take part in a series of exercises designed to test their ability to handle work they might encounter on a day-to-day basis in a government department - exercises such as sifting through a bundle of documents within a set time and deciding which are most urgent and what action to take, simulating the briefing of a minister or producing a policy recommendation in a limited period of time.

The theory is that any civil servant with potential can rise up the hierarchy. Employees entering with A levels, for example, are encouraged to take part-time degrees to improve their prospects. In reality, however, those recruited in the fast stream have a distinct advantage. Once recruited, fast stream appointees are moved from department to department to broaden their experience and to gain an overview of how the Whitehall machinery works. Training is given on the job. After about 18 months as a HEO(D) - Higher Executive Officer (Development) - a fast stream recruit can expect to be promoted to the post of principal, the bottom rung of the Open Structure. Although anyone within the civil service can apply for promotion into the Open Structure, in practice, those who enter via the fast stream monopolise appointments.

The fast stream and senior appointments

Traditionally, a position in the civil service meant a job for life (barring accidents or gross misconduct):

> 'Traditionally, civil servants have enjoyed security of tenure. Once appointed they cannot easily be removed. This provides continuity and the characteristic of permanence - in contrast to ministers who spend much less time in the department before they are moved on.' (Bayliss & Dargie 1998, p.84)

Under the traditional system, promotions at the higher levels were centralised and advancement depended on the opinions of colleagues, ministers and, in some cases, the Prime Minister. Promotion was, in other words, an internal matter. Senior posts were not advertised.

Since 1993, efforts have been made to change this. Three main techniques have been used.

1. Open competition

First, there has been pressure for jobs to be subject to 'open competition'. Jobs subject to open competition are advertised and people from outside the civil service are able to apply for them. Most senior posts for executive (Next Steps) agencies are filled using open competition and the idea was that this practice would be extended to departmental senior civil servants. By 1998, more senior jobs were subject to open competition, but the number of outsiders actually being appointed was declining (Bayliss & Dargie 1998).

2. Opening up the SASC

Second, in 1995, the Senior Appointments Selection Committee (SASC) was opened up. Since then, the First Civil Service Commissioner has sat on the committee. The First Civil Service Commissioner is responsible for:

- advising on whether posts should be subject to open competition or to internal appointment
- approving all appointments made to senior civil service posts from outside the civil service.

Also, the committee is required to include both a woman and an outsider.

3. Changing the terms of employment

And third, there have been attempts to change the terms of employment. Most senior staff in executive agencies are on fixed-term contracts and performance related pay. Although the Major government rejected fixed-term contracts for departmental senior civil servants (on the grounds that they are demotivating and inhibit career development), it did propose that they should have to sign written employment contracts. It also introduced individually determined pay (greater flexibility) and an element of performance related pay in an attempt to bring civil service practice into line with the private sector:

'Senior civil servants are now appraised on their managerial skills and part of their pay is performance based. However, the government, in rejecting fixed-term contracts, has maintained the distinction between departmental senior civil servants and the heads of executive agencies.' (Bayliss & Dargie 1998, p.84)

Appointments at the top of the hierarchy

It still remains the case that, formally, the Prime Minister must approve all appointments at permanent and deputy secretary level (Grades 1 and 2) on the recommendation of the Head of the Home Civil Service, with departmental ministers being consulted before such recommendations are made. How much influence ministers have over such appointments is debatable. Whilst the former Conservative minister Patrick Jenkin claimed in 1986 that he won his preferred choice on all three occasions a permanent secretary was appointed to his department, the Head of the Civil Service at the time, Robert Armstrong, argued that there was normally a balance between the wishes of the minister, Prime Minister and the Head of the Home Civil Service. Certainly, the personality and attitude of the Prime Minister is an important variable. Proactive Prime Ministers (like Margaret Thatcher) are more likely to veto names put forward by the Head of the Home Civil Service whilst reactive Prime Ministers are more likely to rubber stamp the decisions made for them.

The fast stream - education and class

Recruitment to the fast stream has been criticised on the grounds that it favours candidates whose background is middle-class, public school and Oxbridge - as was demonstrated in a 1986 BBC documentary which followed two candidates through the selection process and showed that:

'[The] charming and beautiful ex-public schoolgirl [was] admitted to the Foreign Office despite demonstrating appalling ignorance of foreign affairs and the spiky ex-comprehensive schoolboy brimming with passionate views [was] turned down for the home civil service.' (Hennessy 1989, p.513)

Recruitment figures indicate that this trend remains. Information from the Cabinet Office published in 1996, for example, shows that 42% of those on Grades 1-3 had been to public school and 49% had a degree from Oxford or Cambridge. Bayliss and Dargie note that this gives the impression that members of the senior civil service are:

'Removed from the needs and concerns of the general public - as top public servants, they are not representative of the population they serve.' (Bayliss & Dargie 1998, p.88)

It should be noted, however, that a number of defences can be offered for this apparent bias. First, it could be argued that the most able students go to Oxbridge anyway and, therefore, if the civil service is to recruit the most able civil servants, it is bound to find most of its recruits there. Second, it is the case that Oxford and Cambridge colleges have a long tradition of encouraging their students to apply for civil service positions. Certainly, the number of applications from Oxbridge is proportionately higher than elsewhere. And third, although Oxbridge provides proportionately more candidates than other universities, the success rate of other universities is statistically higher.

The fast stream - gender, disability and ethnicity

Criticisms of fast stream recruitment have also been made because very few women and even fewer disabled people or people from black and Asian groups are selected. Women tend to be over-represented at the bottom of the civil service hierarchy and under-represented at the top. Disabled people and black and Asian people rarely reach the highest grades.

Theakston & Fry (1989) found that out of 304 permanent secretaries appointed between 1900 and 1979 only two had been women (they both held office between 1955 and 1963). Between 1992 (the year in which the government announced an initiative to increase the number of women in senior civil service posts) and 1996, the number of women in Grades 1-3 increased by 4%. In 1996, there were three women on Grade 1 (9%), eight women on Grade 2 (7%) and 55 on Grade 3 (12%). In all, women made up 11% of the total posts for Grades 1-3 (Bayliss & Dargie 1998).

Figures for disabled people and black and Asian people show that they, too, are under-represented in the Senior Civil Service. For example, only 1% of civil servants in Grades 1-5 are Asians and 0.34% are African-Caribbean (*Observer*, 12 October 1997). The Cabinet Office records that the proportion of black and Asian staff in the civil service as a whole has increased from 4.2% in 1989 to 5.7% in 1997 (1989 was the first year in which ethnic origin data was collected). In April 1997, disabled people made up 3.8% of all civil service staff (Cabinet Office 1998).

The fast stream - generalists not specialists
Those in the top civil service grades tend to have a generalist rather than a specialist background. For example, civil servants working in the Treasury would not be expected to have an expertise in accounting or economics. The idea is that high fliers have such good brains that they are able to pick up the relevant strands of an argument, whatever the subject area, without needing specialist knowledge themselves. If specific information is required, then it is obtained by consulting with an expert in the field. Indeed, the very fact that most top civil servants are generalists ensures that the views of a range of interest groups and individuals with specific areas of expertise are listened to during the decision-making process.

There has been debate about whether so many generalists should be at the top of the civil service since the publication of the Fulton Report in 1968 (the report argued that generalists were amateurs at worst and all-rounders at best and proposed that more specialists be appointed to the top of the civil service). Clearly, this debate is important in relation to recruitment. As a former civil servant, Clive Ponting, put it, the civil service selection process reflects:

> 'Qualities prized by the civil service - a touch of greyness, ability to turn out work for any purpose, no strong beliefs and an ability to fit in amongst other "good chaps" in the service.' (Ponting 1986, p.73)

There is no evidence that the domination of generalists in the senior civil service has changed since 1993.

Impact of changes since 1993
Selection procedures and senior appointments are important because the system used makes an impact both on the character of the civil service and on relationships between civil servants and politicians. Although there have certainly been changes since 1993, there is little evidence of significant structural change. In practice, open competition has led to the appointment of few outsiders. Although there is greater awareness of the need to appoint more women, disabled people and people from ethnic minority groups, relatively few (as yet) have worked their way to the top of the hierarchy. Most senior civil servants remain generalists not specialists. As is often the case with the civil service, the pace of change is slow:

> 'Despite significant shifts in policy focus and the implementation of significant government reports on recruitment and selection, there has been little change to the fast stream process which sustains the senior civil service. Open competition shows a declining influence... Most senior civil servants do well in performance schemes and civil servants remain on indefinite, rather than fixed-term, contracts.' (Bayliss & Dargie 1998, p.85)

Main points - Sections 2.3-2.4

- In terms of policy making, the relevant part of the civil service is the Administration Group. At the top is the 'Open Structure' (the top seven grades in the civil service). Below are the lower administrative levels.

- The key advisers to ministers are drawn from Grades 1-4. Those on Grade 5 are responsible for part of a department's work and may make an input into policy making.

- Although, in theory, any civil servant can rise up the hierarchy, those recruited to the fast stream have a distinct advantage.

- The Oughton Report (1993) recommended changes in internal training and development, selection and appointment, and terms of employment. The aims were to increase efficiency and to broaden the recruitment base for senior civil servants.

- Traditionally, senior civil servants had a job for life. Promotion was an internal matter. Senior posts were not advertised. Since 1993, open competition has been introduced, the SASC has changed and employment contracts and performance related pay have been introduced.

- Despite these changes, most senior civil servants remain white, middle-class males and most are generalists not specialists.

Activity 13.5 Recruitment to the civil service

Item A *The non-industrial civil service in 1990 and 1996*

The Open Structure

Grade	No. 1990	No. 1996	Men 1996	Women 1996	% Women 1990	% Women 1996
1-4	1,026 }	*3,930	3,440	490	5 }	*12.5
5	2,800 }				11 }	
6	5,200	5,170	4,370	800	10	15
7	16,200	17,630	14,060	3,570	12	20

Administrative levels

Grade	No. 1990	No. 1996	Men 1996	Women 1996	% Women 1990	% Women 1996
SEO	23,900	23,490	19,590	3,900	10	17
HEO	73,100	73,050	56,180	16,870	18	23
EO	121,000	111,990	60,550	51,440	40	46
AO	154,400	154,950	51,920	103,030	66	66
AA	91,600	68,170	23,040	45,130	73	66

KEY
SEO Senior Executive Officer   AO Administrative Officer
HEO Higher Executive Officer   AA Administrative Assistant
EO   Executive Officer
* In 1996, Grades 1-5 became the Senior Civil Service (SCS)

Figures supplied by the Cabinet Office.

Item C *Sarah Tiffin*

At school, Sarah Tiffin said that she wanted to work for the Foreign Office (FO) (she had a friend whose father was a diplomat in Bonn). After school, she studied modern languages at Pembroke College, Cambridge. She was then accepted into the fast stream at the FO. It was not a problem that she was no foreign affairs expert because the FO taught her what she needed to know. What the FO wants, she says, is people who are prepared to argue British policy and not waver. After two week's training, Sarah became Desk Officer for Thailand and Laos and Assistant on Vietnam and Cambodia. Her job was to keep ministers briefed on those countries and to answer any questions MPs received from their constituents. As she spoke French, she was then asked to go to France's top civil service college. From there, she was posted to the British embassy in Paris where she was Private Secretary to the ambassador for two and half years. The following year she returned to London to head a section in the FO's Human Rights Policy Department, with particular responsibility for keeping ministers informed of UN resolutions. She then became part of a team advising on all UK foreign policy issues, specialising in Asia. Her next post was as First Secretary (Political) in India. Her aim is to spend three years in India, to return as Deputy Head of a department and then to go overseas as Head of a section in one of the bigger embassies. Her ambition is to be an ambassador by her mid-50s.

Adapted from the *Guardian*, 18 January 1997.

Item B *The glass ceiling*

(i) In February 1996, Dame Pauline Neville-Jones, the highest ranking woman in the Foreign Office (FO), resigned after being passed over for the post of ambassador in Paris. Against convention, she was offered Bonn (where she had previously been deputy), a much less prestigious post. If Dame Pauline cannot make it over the final FO hurdle, what hope is there for other women? Her departure was accompanied by a whispering campaign which suggested she was 'difficult' and 'not quite top-drawer academic' - the classic male attack on a confident woman. In this looking-glass world, those qualities which are admired in men at the top (drive, aggression, ambition) are seen as negative in women. Ironically for Dame Pauline, the FO in its lower levels is proud of its equal opportunities record. More than 50% of fast stream entrants were women in 1996, for example. Right at the top, however, there is a block. Charlotte Eagar calls it 'Hansard's Law' - the clubbier the culture, the less likely women are to make the top.

Adapted from the *Observer*, 11 February 1996.

(ii) A survey published in October 1997 suggested that it would be 20 years before an Asian would reach Grades 1-2 in the civil service. One Asian civil servant on Grade 7 said: 'If my branch is anything to go by, things are pretty dire. There certainly is a glass ceiling. Asians are put under more pressure by their managers than their white counterparts and their careers are not as developed as much. You're not seen as good, no matter how hard you work and an old boy network definitely still operates.' Asians make up 3.3% of the population as a whole and are the largest non-white ethnic group, but provide only 2% of the civil service. They are trapped in secretarial and lower grades, with only a few involved in policy making. The Cabinet Office said it was setting up an advisory panel on equal opportunities at senior levels and organising an action programme. A statement said: 'We are concerned that ethnic minorities tend to be concentrated in the lower grades. We accept time alone will not deal with this.'

Adapted from the *Observer*, 12 October 1997.

Item D *The civil service and equal opportunities*

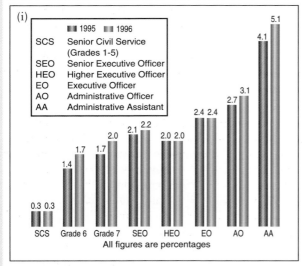

This graph shows the percentage of disabled people working in each grade in the civil service in 1995 and 1996.

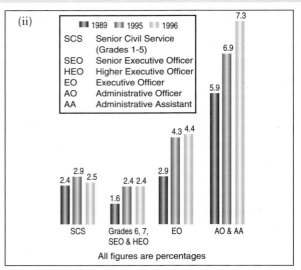

This graph shows the percentage of black and Asian people working in each grade in the civil service in 1989, 1995 and 1996.

Questions

1. Look at Items A and D.
   a) Describe the main features of the structure of the civil service.
   b) How has the structure changed since 1979?
   c) How did staffing change between 1990 and 1996?

2. 'Since the early 1980s, a great deal of progress has been made by women and minority groups in the civil service.' Using Items B-D, give arguments for and against this statement.

3. a) What does Item C tell us about recruitment and career development in the civil service?
   b) 'A typical product of the civil service system'. Is that a fair description of Sarah Tiffin? Explain your answer.

4. What conclusions can be drawn from the graphs in Item D?

2.5 The formal role of civil servants

The job done by senior civil servants

Most of the work done in a government department is never seen by the minister in charge. It is carried out by the department's civil servants. In theory at least, the British civil service is apolitical (not political). Appointments are supposedly not made on political grounds, for example, and promotional prospects are not supposed to be affected by a change in government. As Ridley (1986) notes, this is in contrast to some other European countries where key officials are appointed because they are sympathetic to their government's policies.

The traditional role of civil servants

The traditional role of senior civil servants is to provide advice to ministers, regardless of which party is in power:

> 'All civil servants are bound by the civil service pay and conditions service code which demands that they deliver duties of confidentiality and loyal service "for all practical purposes" to the minister of the day. An individual's duty to the courts, Parliament

and the public is subsumed in [secondary to] their primary duty to their minister.' (Elizabeth Symons, Leader of the top civil servants' union writing in the *Guardian*, 2 April 1993)

The terms of the civil service pay and conditions service code were clarified by a memorandum written by the Head of the Home Civil Service, Sir Robert Armstrong, in 1986. This memorandum was published in the 1986 Treasury and Civil Service Select Committee Report. It outlines the role that civil servants should play:

> 'The determination of policy is the responsibility of the minister...In the determination of policy the civil servant has no constitutional responsibility or role distinct from that of the minister. It is the duty of the civil servant...to give the minister honest and impartial advice, without fear or favour, and whether the advice accords with the minister's view or not. Civil servants are in breach of their duty and damage their integrity as servants of the Crown...if they seek to obstruct or delay a decision simply because they do not agree with it. When, having been given all the relevant information and advice, the minister has taken a decision, it is the duty of civil

servants loyally to carry out the decision with precisely the same energy and goodwill, whether they agree with it or not.' (HMSO 1986, pp.7-8)

There are, then, three main elements in the traditional role played by civil servants.

1. Impartiality

Civil servants are expected to be impartial - that is, they must not be seen to be politically active in any way. It is the role of the government to take decisions and the role of civil servants to implement policy loyally regardless which party is in power.

2. Neutrality

Civil servants must remain neutral - even if they personally disagree with a particular government policy. Senior civil servants who wish to participate in national politics or stand for a party must resign. Civil servants must not express their own opinions in the media or before parliamentary committees.

3. Anonymity

Civil servants should remain anonymous. They work behind the scenes and must not discuss what takes place in their department with outside agencies or with the media. In addition, they must not reveal written information. If something is in an official file, it is an official secret (all civil servants working in government departments sign the Official Secrets Act).

Maintaining confidentiality

It can be argued that the preservation of the confidentiality of discussions and documents is a crucial part of the preservation of a neutral civil service. In theory at least, it is for ministers to decide what the public should or should not know and civil servants to remain silent and neutral, even if they do not agree. The reasoning behind this view is that ministers are held responsible for any errors of judgement that take place in their departments and it is they who take the blame, not the civil servants.

Has the traditional role changed since 1979?

In their review of recent reforms affecting the senior civil service, Bayliss and Dargie argue that the role of senior civil servants has begun to change. In 1979, they argue, senior civil servants were 'traditional public administrators' fulfilling (in theory at least) the traditional role described above. By 1998, however, there was a trend towards a new role - that of the 'new public manager':

'The development of the new public manager is part of a worldwide change in the organisation and management of public services. The new public manager adopts generic management skills that can be used to manage any organisation or service, rather than particular public service skills. This new type of civil servant asks what is to be done, why, and how much it costs...The new public

manager also requires training in specific management skills, mobility in careers with flexible labour markets, and competition for recruitment, promotion and retention.' (Bayliss & Dargie 1998, p.76)

In other words, new public managers run public services in much the same way that managers in the private sector run businesses.

What impact have recent changes made?

Evidence in support of the growth of new public management techniques can be found in the recent changes in recruitment and pay structures, and in the setting up of executive agencies to deliver public services. These reforms have clearly made an impact on the role played by senior civil servants. Nevertheless, it would be wrong to conclude that the role has changed fundamentally:

'There has been extensive change to the recruitment, retention, promotion and pay structures of senior civil servants that are evidence of managerialism. However, the senior civil service remains a careerist, centrally recruited and internally sustained system. Open competition and increased external mobility are threats to the cohesion and common culture of the civil service, but, so far, they have achieved only a marginal impact. The senior civil service has preserved more of its traditional characteristics than it has adopted new ones.' (Bayliss & Dargie 1998, p.96)

2.6 Are civil servants really neutral?

Public interest and neutrality

Civil servants are servants of the Crown. They should, therefore, act in the interests of the state. But what if they believe that a government policy is not in the interests of the state? Should they loyally implement such policies without question? And, in particular, what should they do if they believe that a minister is deliberately misleading the public?

Clive Ponting

An example of the sort of dilemma faced by civil servants was revealed in 1984-85 during the trial of Clive Ponting, a civil servant who worked for the Ministry of Defence during the Falklands War. After the Falklands War there were allegations that the *General Belgrano* (an Argentinian ship sunk by the British navy during the war) had been sunk for unnecessary political reasons, not on military grounds. The government denied these allegations, but Ponting had information which contradicted the public line taken by the government. He chose to leak this information to a Labour MP on the grounds that the public ought to know what had actually happened. When it was revealed that Ponting had leaked the document, he was prosecuted for breaking the Official Secrets Act. In his trial, Ponting argued that it was his duty to inform an MP about a major constitutional impropriety. In other words, he placed his duty to the state (the public interest) above his duty to his minister. The judge instructed the jury to find Ponting guilty since it was up to ministers to define what was in the public interest. But, the jury acquitted him. After the trial Ponting wrote:

'A number of questions remained unsolved. Why did Parliament not have the right to know this information? Why had the old Official Secrets Act been wheeled out yet again when national security was not involved and the only matter at risk was the political reputation of certain government ministers?...Before the trial there had been much debate about the role and duties of civil servants. Were they just blind servants of ministers, doing only what they were told, or could there be circumstances when they might have a higher loyalty either to Parliament or possibly the public interest?' (Ponting 1985, pp.3-4)

Steps taken after the Ponting trial
In 1989, the Thatcher government passed the new Official Secrets Act (see Chapter 19, Section 5.2). This was designed to prevent any disclosures about security or intelligence matters by making such disclosures a criminal offence. It also prevented defendants using a public interest defence. One of the aims was to prevent leaks like that made by Ponting. Leaks have continued to be made, however. During the period October 1994 and December 1996, for example, there were 64 leaks from Whitehall or government sources. The Conservative MEP, Graham Mather claimed:

'Leaks by civil servants to opposition politicians, trade unions and direct to newspapers are running at epidemic proportions. The leakers are often sophisticated in their choice of material and timing. Motives range from internal hostility to a government policy, to fear of public spending cuts; or sometimes simply a desire to embarrass.' (*Independent*, 22 October 1995)

Self-interest and neutrality
As a result of the Scott Inquiry, it became clear that the neutrality and impartiality of civil servants is sometimes compromised not because civil servants act against the wishes of ministers but because they collude with them. The inquiry revealed that, not only did civil servants advise ministers on ways to get round government guidelines forbidding the sale of arms and military equipment to Iraq in the late 1980s, they also helped ministers to misinform Parliament and the public. That there were occasions on which it was necessary for civil servants to lie or tell half truths was actually admitted during the

course of the inquiry when Sir Robin Butler, the Head of the Home Civil Service, said:

'Only in the most exceptional of cases should one mislead...but there is a wider category of cases where it is necessary to give an incomplete answer.' (quoted in Adams & Pyper 1995, p.93)

This admission casts doubt on the traditional view that civil servants are impartial and neutral officials. As Sue Cameron pointed out:

'The real issue Scott raises is not who knew what and when. It is whether civil servants have an allegiance to the public interest beyond their duty to ministers. The inquiry has found disturbing indications that the proper relationship between civil servants and ministers has become blurred. There is uncertainty about when officials can and should say no to ministers...Now the risk is that civil servants will be regarded less as people of goodwill serving the public interest from above the political fray and more as mercenaries who can be put into the front line of the political battle.' (*Times*, 14 February 1996)

The Arms-to-Sierra Leone Affair
Whilst the Scott Inquiry revealed that civil servants and ministers had colluded in the hope of keeping information from Parliament, the Arms-to-Sierra Leone Affair which broke in May 1998 suggested that, on occasions, civil servants keep information from ministers and follow their own agenda. After it had been revealed that Britain had broken an arms embargo by sending arms to Sierra Leone, one former senior diplomat stated:

'Given the main elements of policy laid out at the top, the condemnation by Britain at the UN of the military coup, the welcome given by Tony Blair to the exiled President at the Commonwealth summit, and the fact that ministers are often difficult to get hold of, officials may have just got on with helping President Tejan Kabbah back to power. Not bothering ministers with all the details would have been understandable behaviour by the Africa department.' (*Financial Times*, 13 June 1998)

Political pressure and neutrality
Between 1992 and 1997, a number of civil servants made public their disquiet at the increasing political pressure which they felt they were under. This pressure, they argued, made it harder for them to be impartial. It had two main sources.

1. Conservative monopoly of power
First, the pressure resulted from the Conservatives' monopoly of power between 1979 and 1997. Over time, government matters and party matters became

blurred and there was an increasing tendency for ministers to use civil servants for what previously had been considered as party political matters.

2. Civil service reforms

Second, the pressure resulted from the changes in the structure and organisation of the civil service. On the one hand, some civil servants felt obliged to do what ministers demanded because they were worried that they might lose their job or their prospects for promotion. On the other hand, the setting up of executive agencies changed the relationship between ministers and officials:

> 'Ministers argue that they cannot be responsible for all the decisions taken in their department. However, there are fears that, as ministers distance themselves from agencies, the link between responsibility and accountability becomes weaker - the so-called "accountability gap". In the case of the Child Support Agency and the Prison Service, it was the senior civil servant who was forced to take responsibility for agency failures.' (Bayliss & Dargie 1998, p.93)

If senior civil servants rather than ministers have to take responsibility for matters, then their role as impartial and neutral advisors may be compromised. Also, agency chiefs are not anonymous - they have a high public profile.

Political pressure under Labour

During the Blair government's first 18 months in power, there were further charges of creeping politicisation of the civil service. These charges were based on two related pieces of evidence. First, the Labour government appointed the largest ever number of political advisers (69 had been appointed by the end of 1997, compared to 36 appointed by the previous administration and just five under Margaret Thatcher) as well as setting up numerous task forces and policy reviews (more than 500 people were appointed to task forces and policy reviews in 1997). This brought the accusation that the government was intending to bypass the civil service, using party supporters and others not bound by the civil service code of practice rather than neutral officials. And second, a relatively large number of senior civil servants resigned in the months after Labour's general election victory - leading to the charge that only civil servants sympathetic to Labour's policies were acceptable to the new government. The government denied these charges, arguing that its aim was greater professionalism not greater politicisation (*Times*, 17 June 1998).

The civil service code

In response to the criticisms that the civil service's reputation for impartiality was suffering, the all-party Treasury and Civil Service Select Committee recommended in its 1994 report that a statutory code of ethics should be agreed. This code set out civil servants' duties and ministers' responsibilities. It was launched in October 1995 and came into operation in 1996.

The code gives civil servants the right of appeal to a Civil Service Commissioner if they believe that they are being asked to act in illegal, improper or unethical ways. It also makes it clear that:

- the leaking of information is a disciplinary matter that could result in dismissal
- civil servants must not abuse their position of confidence
- civil servants must not frustrate the policies or actions of government.

General Election Guidance

In March 1997, at the start of the general election campaign, the Cabinet Office published *General Election Guidance*, a code of conduct for ministers and senior civil servants during the campaign. This was the first time such guidance had been published:

> 'An indication that Sir Robin Butler, the Cabinet Secretary and Head of the Civil Service, is acutely aware of the potential for controversy and allegations of political abuse of Whitehall officials after so many years of one-party rule'. (*Guardian*, 18 March 1997)

The document included the following guidelines:

- during the campaign, the government should only clear up business already underway
- the role of civil servants was to be limited to providing 'factual business'
- senior civil servants were debarred from national political activities
- ministers were not to use official cars or government buildings for election-eering purposes.

Main points - Section 2.5-2.6

- There are some signs that the traditional role of senior civil servants may be changing as new public management techniques are adopted.
- By leaking information, civil servants break confidentiality. After Clive Ponting successfully argued it was in the public interest to leak documents, the 1989 Official Secrets Act was passed. Leaks have continued since then, however.
- The Scott Inquiry showed that the neutrality and impartiality of civil servants can be compromised if civil servants collude with ministers. The Arms-to-Sierra Leone affair shows that civil servants sometimes keep information from ministers.
- There is a debate about whether the civil service is becoming politicised. Critics argue that Labour's use of political advisers, task forces and policy reviews has led to greater politicisation.

Activity 13.6 An impartial and neutral civil service?

Item A   The blurring of party and government matters (1)

Papers leaked in November 1996 showed that Michael Heseltine wanted civil servants to collect lists of non-political people who could be recruited as cheerleaders for government policies the country did not value enough. When he was told by the Head of the Civil Service that it was unacceptable for neutral civil servants to do this, Heseltine gave in, saying that that proved how well the system worked. This was not the view of political commentator, Hugo Young. He argued that what the episode proved was how much the system had changed since 1979. It was by no means the first time Heseltine had used civil servants for political ends - in 1983, for example, he tried to get an MI5 agent, Cathy Massiter, to collect evidence linking the Labour Party to CND. By the time Heseltine returned from political exile in 1990, Young says, Whitehall had endured a culture shift and the blurring of private and public was well advanced. As Deputy Prime Minister in 1996, Heseltine appeared before the Commons Public Service Committee. On being asked about the distinction between party and government matters he admitted there were few rules. It was all a blur - 'I just have to have a feel based upon some experience of our profession, as to what I can ask civil servants to do and what I cannot ask them to do', he said. He just knew when 'things were moving into a party-political dimension' and had to be halted.

Adapted from the *Guardian*, 14 November 1996.

Item B   Civil servants and the 1997 general election

Whitehall's mandarins would never admit it in public, but they seek and expect a Labour victory in May 1997. Party neutrality, integral to the training and culture of the senior civil service, is the root cause of this enthusiasm for Labour. 'We are politically impartial, you understand, so it would be nice to work for more than one party per generation', says one top official. The political commentator Peter Hennessy suggests that the mood in Whitehall is similar to that in 1964. 'Most of Whitehall's top brass want a change - not because they are a bunch of lefties, but for the health of the system and boredom avoidance', he says. Claims that the senior civil service has been 'Toryfied' are unfounded. In the 1980s, it is true, some officials were crusaders for bitterly partisan policies from privatisation and the poll tax to the assault on the unions and the miners. But, such issues are now either ancient history or (in the case of privatisation) conventional wisdom. Today, the mentality of many mandarins is 'in many respects pretty New Labour and planets away from Portillo and Howard', as one top official put it. The Foreign Office, in particular is desperate for a 'Euro-confident' government. British diplomats in Brussels have virtually abandoned their trade so distrusted are the Conservative government's motives.

Adapted from the *Observer*, 16 March 1997.

Item C   The blurring of party and government matters (2)

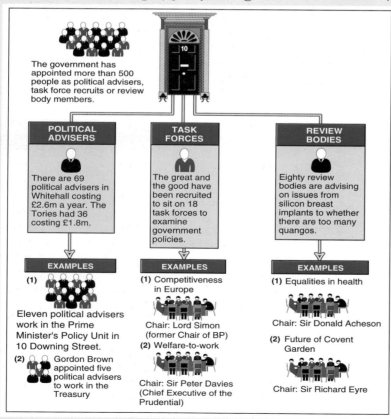

The government has appointed more than 500 people as political advisers, task force recruits or review body members.

POLITICAL ADVISERS

There are 69 political advisers in Whitehall costing £2.6m a year. The Tories had 36 costing £1.8m.

EXAMPLES

(1) Eleven political advisers work in the Prime Minister's Policy Unit in 10 Downing Street.

(2) Gordon Brown appointed five political advisers to work in the Treasury

TASK FORCES

The great and the good have been recruited to sit on 18 task forces to examine government policies.

EXAMPLES

(1) Competitiveness in Europe

Chair: Lord Simon (former Chair of BP)

(2) Welfare-to-work

Chair: Sir Peter Davies (Chief Executive of the Prudential)

REVIEW BODIES

Eighty review bodies are advising on issues from silicon breast implants to whether there are too many quangos.

EXAMPLES

(1) Equalities in health

Chair: Sir Donald Acheson

(2) Future of Covent Garden

Chair: Sir Richard Eyre

Labour more than any government this century wants its party machine to operate in tandem with the Whitehall one. The aim is to create something similar to the American model where a whole tier of government is removed with each incoming administration and replaced with political sympathisers determined to get policies implemented. A Labour source ridiculed the traditional idea of a dividing line between politicians and a neutral civil service, saying: 'Whitehall has to wake up to the real world. Everything is politics. The idea that you can cut off politics from the officials does not work. Let's stop pretending'. By December 1997, nine government information officers (career civil servants) had been removed and their jobs taken over by special advisers, attached to ministers. Some supporters of the traditional system resented this, arguing that government information officers provided objective information. Opponents of the traditional system, on the other hand, argued that, if Labour wanted a second term, it could not afford to mess around.

Adapted from the *Guardian*, 29 October 1997 and the *Sunday Times*, 30 November 1997.

Item D *The blurring of party and government matters (3)*

A bitter row over the political role of Alastair Campbell, Tony Blair's Chief Press Secretary, broke out in August 1998 when it was learned that a draft report on the government's press service had been 'shredded' by Labour MPs. The key issue which divided the Commons Public Administration Committee was a refusal by Labour MPs to call for tighter controls over Mr Campbell's overtly partisan role at the heart of government and over his authority to manage civil servants. In one of the few areas of agreement, however, the committee did express fears that Tony Blair's new public relations command centre in Downing Street could work to the Labour Party's advantage. The new Strategy and Communications Unit is made up of a seven-person team, a mix of civil servants and political advisers, and there was concern that this could blur lines between civil servants and political aides. The committee called on the government to explain 'how it distinguishes between legitimate activity on behalf of government and activities which could unduly advantage the party of government'.

Adapted from the *Times*, 7 August 1998.

Item E *No, minister*

Questions

1. 'In the last few years, the civil service has become over-politicised.' Is there any evidence in Items A-D to support this statement?

2. What do Items A, C and D tell us about the difficulties civil servants face when trying to maintain impartiality and neutrality.

3. 'Labour's victory in May 1997 means that the politicisation of the civil service is no longer a problem'. Give arguments for and against this view using Items B-D.

4. Look at Item E.
   a) When should civil servants say 'No, minister'?
   b) What might prevent a civil servant from saying 'No, minister'?

Part 3 Ministers and civil servants

Key issues

1. What is the ideal relationship between ministers and civil servants?
2. What sort of relationships exist in practice?
3. Have relationships between ministers and civil servants changed?

3.1 Ministers and civil servants - ideally and actually

What is the ideal relationship?

According to Norton (1989) the civil service is a:
> 'Well-oiled machine, manned by public servants of integrity and serving loyally successive governments of whatever political persuasion.' (Norton 1989, p.82)

The role of the minister is to determine the policies of the government. The role of civil servants is to advise ministers on how best to implement those policies which they wish to introduce.

In the ideal world, therefore, both ministers and civil servants are motivated by a sense of public duty and a genuine desire to act in the public interest. Both ministers and civil servants know their place and the role they should play. Civil servants brief ministers impartially and objectively. Ministers listen carefully to what their civil servants have to say and make decisions after weighing up this advice. Civil servants expect the minister in charge of their department to fight courageously for funds during the annual spending round and to defend the actions of the department in public. Ministers expect to be kept informed of what is happening in the department and they expect civil servants to implement, with a good grace, decisions with which they disagree. Although ministers are members of a political party, they would never dream of asking their civil servants to undertake party political matters. Similarly, whatever their personal views, civil servants would never act in a partisan manner.

The relationship in reality
In reality, a number of factors affect the relationship between ministers and their civil servants.

1. Ministers have limited information
Ministers may have little knowledge of the area covered by their departments. On taking up their new post they do not see the papers of their predecessors, but are supplied with a briefing document by their officials. From the outset, therefore, there is the chance for civil servants to shape the way in which ministers view their job.

2. Ministers have other commitments
Ministers have other commitments - in Parliament and in their constituencies, for example. They, therefore, have less time to devote to decision making than their full-time officials. For this reason, they rely on the experience and administrative expertise of their civil servants. Often, this advice is shaped by the internal culture of the department. Senior civil servants will often have been steeped in this internal culture for many years. Headey quotes one permanent secretary who said:

> 'In effect, it was just a question of getting my ministers to take on board policies that we had in hand anyway. Of the six ministers I worked with closely, it would be hard to say that any of them made even a minor contribution to policy.' (Headey 1974, p.109)

It should be noted, however, that this quote comes from the 1970s, before the civil service reforms instigated by Margaret Thatcher had been enacted. The May 1998 Arms-to-Sierra Leone Affair, however, suggests that civil servants are still sometimes willing to take the initiative and may even keep ministers in the dark.

3. Civil servants outnumber ministers
Civil servants outnumber ministers. There are about ten civil servants for every one minister in the top policy-making grades and 40 civil servants to every one minister if all civil servants who make an input into policy making are included. If all these officials take a similar line, this adds weight to the line taken.

4. Top civil servants meet by themselves
Although civil servants outnumber ministers, there is still a sufficiently small number of permanent secretaries at the top of the hierarchy (about 40 in all) for them to meet together often both formally and socially. A permanent secretary having 'problems' with a minister might, therefore, be able to persuade a colleague in another government department to persuade a more compliant minister to put pressure on the minister causing the 'problems'. In this way, top civil servants might be able to agree upon and engineer certain policies.

5. Time spent with civil servants
Ministers spend more time with civil servants than they do with other politicians:

> 'In an average week, a Cabinet minister is likely to see at least two civil servants - his permanent secretary and his private secretary - far more frequently than he sees the Prime Minister or any of his or her party colleagues. The significance of this simple fact should not be underestimated as a source of pressure on ministers to conform to civil service expectations.' (Headey 1974, p.153)

6. Avoidance tactics
Civil servants often outlast ministers and can use various tactics to avoid having to implement a policy they do not like. According to Norton (1989), there are three ways in which civil servants can reverse a minister's decision. First, they can wait for a change of ministers - new ministers may be open to the advice they are offering. Second, they can brief officials in other departments to ensure that their ministers are primed to oppose the minister's decision (as suggested above). Or third, they can leak a document to the media in the hope that this will undermine the minister's credibility.

Theakston's models
Theakston (1992) argues that four separate models are used by political scientists to describe the relationship between ministers and civil servants.

1. The formal-constitutional model
This model defines the civil service as a non-political neutral bureaucracy whose sole aim is to serve loyally the interests of the government of the day. Civil servants make sure that ministers are fully aware of all the constraints and options open to them before making decisions. Once decisions have been taken, civil servants loyally work to implement the policy which has been laid down.

2. The adversarial model
This model sees the relationship between ministers and civil servants as a constant struggle for power. Both Richard Crossman and Tony Benn (Labour ministers) claimed that their civil servants were only concerned with preserving the status quo and were less than helpful when it came to implementing the Labour government's policies. Similar criticisms have been expressed by ministers on the New Right.

3. The village life in the Whitehall community model
This model sees a cosy relationship in which both sides work together in harmony. The civil servants provide the expertise acquired through long experience in the department, whilst the minister provides the ideological energy.

4. The bureaucratic expansionism model
This model claims that bureaucrats are self-centred

and only interested in expanding their own areas of power - an attitude which leads to waste and inefficiency. Top civil servants are, in other words, more interested in empire building than in what is best for the country. It is up to ministers to find ways of improving efficiency (in the period 1979 to 1997, for example, by introducing competition and market testing). This theory originated in the USA, but was adopted by the New Right.

Conclusion
In essence, therefore, there are two contrasting views of the relationship between ministers and civil servants. One view is that civil servants are neutral advisers. The other view is that it is civil servants who make the policy, expecting ministers to go along with what the department already has in hand.

3.2 Ministers and civil servants since 1979

The impact of reforms 1979-90
The civil service reforms enacted during the period 1979-90 took their toll on the relationship between ministers and civil servants. Willman noted:

'The arrival of Mr Major in Downing Street in late 1990 was greeted with relief by many civil servants. They hoped it would bring to an end 11 years of permanent revolution in Whitehall, with privatisations, staff cuts, pay restraint, efficiency drives and institutional reform. They could hardly have been more mistaken. Majorism has intensified the pace of change in the civil service.' (Willman 1994, p.64)

Ministers and civil servants 1990-97
Before 1979, many commentators complained that the civil service had its own policy goals and was able to manipulate ministers into taking a certain direction. By 1997, however, the relationship between ministers and civil servants had changed. There were a number of reasons for this.

1. Conservative monopoly of power
A single party remained in power for 18 years. By 1994, Plowden could note:

'The promotion of every single occupant of a Grade 1 or Grade 2 has been approved by Mrs Thatcher or Mr Major. In that sense, they could be said to owe their positions to the Conservatives. Probably every occupant of a Grade 3 has reached that position during the Conservative years. No administrator aged 35 or less will have worked for ministers of another party.' (Plowden 1994, pp.101-2)

This, in itself, is not enough to change the relationship between ministers and civil servants, but, combined with other factors, that has been the net result.

2. Ministers and appointments
Although, according to Plowden (1994), ministers have rarely taken action to secure the appointment of a particular individual in a top position, they manipulate the promotion process and use their influence to prevent the promotion of individuals:

'Some individuals, for ill-defined reasons, fail to make progress. Speaking of a senior official whose promotion to permanent secretary was widely felt to have been unduly delayed, a former minister commented, almost in passing, "Yes, his card was marked for some reason, wasn't it?"' (Plowden 1994, p.101)

The net result was that, during the period 1979-90, senior positions were filled with civil servants who were compliant and unlikely to disapprove of ministers' ideological goals.

3. Ministers' attitudes towards civil servants
Third, and perhaps most important, ministers' attitudes towards officials changed during the 18 years of Conservative rule. In any relationship, mutual respect is important. But, many ministers lost their respect for their officials:

'The root of today's problem lies in the Thatcherite attitude towards civil servants. Too many ministers feel that if civil servants were any good, they would not be in Whitehall. Their advice is vitiated [corrupted] by their professional weaknesses. Unadventurous by nature and unenterprising by habit, they exaggerate the difficulties and risks of ministers' proposals rather than concentrating on putting them into practice. A good minister will not be deflected by their ingenious objections. Indeed - this line of thinking continues - a determined minister will not use them as advisers on policy but, as they should be used, as instruments for implementing his/her own original intentions.' (Plowden 1994, p.103)

Conclusion
The relationship between ministers and civil servants in the period 1990-97 was, in other words, by no means a relationship between equals - ministers appeared to be very much in charge. As a result, during this period, civil servants were accused of weakness and of lacking impartiality. Yet, ministers were not necessarily all-powerful. They simply did not have the time or specialist knowledge to determine every last detail. They set the parameters, but it was the civil servants who did the spade work. By doing this, civil servants were able to exercise some control over the policy-making process.

Labour ministers and civil servants
Meetings between top officials and Labour shadow ministers began several months in advance of the 1997 general election campaign (as they had done

before the 1992 general election - see Pyper 1995, p.85). As a result, most commentators agree, the change from Labour to Conservative ministers in May 1997 was regarded as a smooth operation.

After the election, the Labour government inherited a civil service which was very different to that which had operated when Labour was last in power. Labour's 1997 general election manifesto contained no proposals to reverse the structural changes which had taken place in the previous 18 years. Some commentators suggested that this was just as well:

> 'There is no prospect of the Blair government being able to reverse most of the changes, even if it wanted to. But that still leaves Labour ministers with plenty of scope for selective unpicking and re-engineering of the machinery of government to achieve different emphases.' (Hood & James 1997, p.184)

In its first 18 months, a number of developments in the relationship between ministers and civil servants came to light.

1. David Clark's statement, June 1997

On 17 June 1997, the Chancellor of the Duchy of Lancaster, David Clark, made a keynote speech in which he emphasised that senior civil servants had 'an essential leadership role' in their departments, but made no reference to their policy role. This led Bayliss and Dargie to conclude:

> 'The new government seems to be consolidating and extending many of the reforms of the previous administrations...There is a commitment to more managerialism without confirmation of the senior civil servant's policy role.' (Bayliss & Dargie 1998, p.95)

This suggests that the new government saw senior civil servants more as administrators (people who implement the policies of ministers) rather than as policy advisers.

2. The appointment of political advisers

As noted above (Section 2.6), the appointment of a large number of political advisers led to concerns that senior civil servants would be bypassed or the relationship between senior civil servants and ministers would be politicised.

3. Discontent with the quality of advice

By September 1997, some ministers had begun to criticise the quality of advice being provided by senior civil servants:

> 'After an initial honeymoon with the civil service, Labour ministers have begun questioning the quality of the briefings they are being given by officials. Some have criticised

"Tory holdovers" and have complained that officials have not adjusted to Labour ways of thinking.' (*Independent on Sunday*, 14 September 1997)

This criticism was voiced again by Nigel Griffiths after he was sacked in the July 1998 reshuffle (*Guardian*, 29 July 1998 - see Activity 13.7, Item C).

4. Ministers who bully

In March 1998 and then, again, in June, officials complained to newspapers about the way in which they were being treated by some ministers (see Activity 13.7, Item B). Harriet Harman and Robin Cook were singled out in particular. Harman was then sacked in the July 1998 reshuffle.

5. Concerns about constitutional reform

Before the 1997 general election, concerns about Labour's proposed constitutional reforms were raised both by (Labour) shadow ministers and by senior civil servants. Shadow ministers were worried that senior officials would block the reforms or try to water them down. Senior civil servants, on the other hand, were worried that a Freedom of Information Act might affect their traditional anonymity (if the public gained access to ministerial papers, for example). By the autumn of 1998, the fears on both sides had been addressed. In Labour's first year in power, a number of constitutional reforms were implemented speedily (for example, devolved assemblies and an elected mayor in London), whilst other reforms reached an advanced stage of planning. At the same time, measures were taken to appease senior officials' fears about a Freedom of Information Bill. The minister responsible for the Bill, David Clark, was sacked in the reshuffle of July 1998 and responsibility for a Freedom of Information Bill was handed over to the Home Office. Then, on 30 September 1998, it was announced that freedom of information legislation would not be included in the next Queen's Speech because David Clark's draft Bill needed more work on it. This was widely interpreted as a victory for senior officials reluctant to open up the machinery of state to public scrutiny (see also Chapter 19, Section 5.4).

Conclusions

Although the day-to-day work of ministers and civil servants, and their relationship, is rarely reported, the above examples show that the transition from a Conservative to a Labour government was not as smooth as first suggested. To some extent, this was a matter of clashes of personality. More important, perhaps, there are some signs that the structural upheaval which took place under the Conservatives did not come to an end in May 1997.

Main points - Part 3

- In the ideal world, ministers and civil servants are motivated by a sense of public duty. Civil servants brief ministers impartially. Ministers listen carefully to their civil servants and make decisions after weighing up this advice.
- In reality, their relationship is affected by - (1) ministers' access to information; (2) ministers' other commitments; (3) the number of civil servants; (4) meetings between top civil servants; (5) the time ministers spend with civil servants; and (6) civil servants' avoidance tactics.
- Theakston (1992) argues that four models describe this relationship: (1) the formal-constitutional model; (2) the adversarial model; (3) the village life
- in the Whitehall community model; and (4) the bureaucratic expansionism model.
- Before 1979, it was argued that the civil service had its own policy goals and was able to manipulate ministers. By 1997, however, the relationship between ministers and civil servants had changed because of: (1) the Conservative monopoly of power; (2) appointments to the senior civil service; and (3) changing attitudes of ministers.
- Although the day-to-day work of ministers and civil servants, and their relationship, is rarely reported, the transition from a Conservative to a Labour government was not as smooth as first suggested.

Activity 13.7 Ministers and civil servants

Item A Alan Clark

It was 8.56 am on Monday 20 June 1983. The phone rung and Alan Clark (Under Secretary of State at the Department of Employment) overheard Jenny Easterbrook, his private secretary, telling someone that, yes, he had arrived. She then came into Clark's office. 'Have you read the brief on the revised conditions for the Job Splitting Scheme?', she said. 'Yes', replied Clark (he was lying). 'Good', she said (meaning good that she had caught him out), 'because Donald Derx would like to come round to discuss it with you.' When Clark asked when Derx, Deputy Secretary at the Department of Employment would come, he was told that he was due in five minutes (enough time for Clark to skim-read the brief). But, Derx arrived in just 80 seconds and proceeded to raise a number of points about the brief. Clark just managed to keep the discussion going by glancing surreptitiously at the brief. In Clark's opinion, the meeting was an ambush. Derx wanted to know at what time Clark arrived in his office and he wanted to find out the extent to which Clark was reading the contents of his ministerial red boxes. The brief under discussion had been hidden a quarter of the way down the box. But, Clark was wise to this trick - he didn't take the papers out in the order in which they were arranged. He had learned that the little photocopied documents marked 'PUSS to see', with Jenny's initials, were the difficult items.

Adapted from Clark 1993.

Item B Ministers who are bullies

According to senior civil servants there has been a spate of bullying by Labour ministers which amounts to some of the worst treatment they have ever experienced. 'The pressure is coming from ministers; people are snapping under the stress', said Jonathan Baume, Leader of the First Division Association (the top civil servants' union), 'They are being shouted at, singled out and picked on. The bullies isolate people and have, on occasion, reduced officials to tears'. Officials admit that the problem has spread to all levels of Whitehall and their own members are guilty of bullying more junior staff. But, they believe that some ministers are fostering a climate of blame and intimidation by expecting instant results and demanding unrealistic deadlines. Those identified as bullies are Harriet Harman, Robin Cook and Gordon Brown. Harman had a showdown and then sacked a senior official after a mix-up about whether or not she was taking a pay rise led to negative stories in the tabloids. Cook has a reputation for arrogance and upset officials by demanding absolute discretion over his private life whilst failing to defend officials against accusations on Sierra Leone. Gordon Brown is described as 'very brusque'. On one occasion, people sitting at desks around one official were phoned by Brown one by one and called into a meeting. Soon only this official was left - even his deputy had been called in. He has not been consulted since. A loyal adviser defended Brown, saying that most officials enjoyed dealing with somebody who likes to get things done. 'Under Ken Clarke, there were too many long lunches. Now they have more of a challenge'.

Adapted from the Times, 31 May 1998.

Item C A disgruntled ex-minister

The day after being sacked as Minister for Consumer Affairs at the DTI, Nigel Griffiths wrote an article in the Guardian in which he discussed his relationship with civil servants. He argued that, when Labour was elected in 1997, it had a packed programme and a strong vision. As a result, it was bound to clash with a demoralised and under-staffed civil service. The long years of Conservative rule meant that many old methods and systems had become entrenched. Some Whitehall press offices, he said, were 'fossilised' with draft press notices omitting key facts and ministers having to vet news releases to ensure that important details were included. For Griffiths, the clash came early - when he was told to give a 'somewhat dry and lifeless response' to an important press enquiry. From his first day, he was told by civil servants not to deal with problems affecting other departments, but there was no way of ensuring other departments returned journalists' calls. A network of Labour ministers developed, but this was a poor substitute for efficient government press offices. Griffiths also noted that barriers were put in the way of ministers consulting colleagues on policy issues. When he tried to consult an MP with expertise in firework safety, he was told that ministers could under no circumstances show a colleague a DTI briefing paper. So, he asked for a legal opinion - which supported his approach. On another occasion, a lawyer told Griffiths there was no legal barrier to him endorsing a price-cutting campaign. The lawyer then circulated a memo saying he completely disagreed with Griffiths' (political) decision.

Adapted from the Guardian, 29 July 1998.

Item D *The minister's workload*

1 What do Items A-C tell us about the relationship between ministers and civil servants?

2. Using Theakston's models describe the relationship between ministers and civil servants found in Items A-C.

3. a) 'Civil servants have too much power'. Using Items A-D, give arguments for and against this view.

   b) How have relations between ministers and civil servants changed since 1979?

4. Judging from Items A, C and D, how can civil servants manipulate the decisions made by ministers?

References

Adams & Pyper (1995) Adams, J. & Pyper, R., 'A guide to the Scott Inquiry', *Talking Politics*, Vol.7.2, Winter 1994-5.

Adams & Pyper (1997) Adams, J. & Pyper, R., 'Whatever happened to the Scott Report?', *Talking Politics*, Vol.9.3, Spring 1997.

Barnett (1982) Barnett, J., *Inside the Treasury*, Andre Deutsch, 1982.

Bayliss & Dargie (1998) Bayliss, R. & Dargie, C., 'The senior civil service in the 1990s' in *Lancaster (1998)*.

Bruce-Gardyne (1986) Bruce-Gardyne, J., *Ministers and Mandarins*, Sidgwick and Jackson, 1986.

Cabinet Office (1998) Cabinet Office, *Equal Opportunities in the Civil service: a Progress Report 1995-7*, Cabinet Office Home Page, November 1998.

Clark (1993) Clark, A., *Diaries*, Weidenfeld & Nicolson, 1993.

Drewry & Butcher (1991) Drewry, G. & Butcher, T., *The Civil Service Today*, Blackwell, 1991.

Dunleavy et al. (1997) Dunleavy, P., Gamble, A., Holliday, I. & Peele, G., *Developments in British Politics 5*, Macmillan, 1997.

Fowler (1991) Fowler, N., *Ministers Decide*, Chapman, 1991.

Gray (1989) Gray, A.G., 'The individual accountability of ministers' in *Jones (1989)*.

Gray (1997) Gray, P., 'When ministers won't resign', *Talking Politics*, Vol.9.2, Winter 1996-7.

Greenaway (1992) Greenaway, J., 'The civil service - 20 years of reform' in *Jones & Robins (1992)*.

Greenwood (1989) Greenwood, J., 'Managing the civil service - from Fulton to Ibbs', *Talking Politics*, Vol.1.2, Winter 1988-89.

Headey (1974) Headey, B., *British Cabinet Ministers*, Allen & Unwin, 1974.

Hennessy (1989) Hennessy, P., *Whitehall*, Secker & Warburg, 1989.

HMSO (1986) Seventh Report of the Treasury and Civil Service Committee 1985–86, *Civil Servants and Ministers: Duties and Responsibilities*, HMSO, 1986.

HMSO (1988) Efficiency Unit, *Improving Management in Government: the Next Steps*, report to the Prime Minister, HMSO, 1988.

HMSO (1994) Central Office of Information, *The British System of Government*, HMSO, 1994.

Hood & James (1997) Hood, C. & James, O., 'The central executive' in *Dunleavy et al. (1997)*.

Jones (1989) Jones, W.D.A. (ed.), *Political Issues in Britain Today* (3rd edn), Manchester University Press, 1989.

Jones & Robins (1992) Jones, B. & Robins, L. (eds), *Two Decades of British Politics*, Manchester University Press, 1992.

Kavanagh & Seldon (1994) Kavanagh, D. & Seldon, A. (eds), *The Major Effect*, Macmillan, 1994.

Kaufman (1996) Kaufman, G., 'Master of arts', *Talking Politics*, Vol.8.3, Spring 1996.

Kaufman (1997) Kaufman, G., 'How to be a minister', *Politics Review*, Vol.7.1, 1997.

Lancaster (1998) Lancaster, S. (ed.), *Developments in Politics*, Vol.9, Causeway Press, 1998.

Loughlin & Scott (1997) Loughlin, M. & Scott, C., 'The regulatory state' in *Dunleavy et al. (1997)*.

Madgwick (1991) Madgwick, P., *British Government: the Central Executive Territory*, Philip Allan, 1991.

Norton (1989) Norton, P., *The Constitution in Flux*, Blackwell, 1989.

Norton (1998) Norton, P., 'Leaders or led? Senior ministers in British government', *Talking Politics*, Vol.10.2, Winter 1997-8.

Norton-Taylor et al. (1996) Norton-Taylor, R., Lloyd, M. & Cook, S., *Knee Deep in Dishonour. The Scott Report and its Aftermath*, Victor Gollancz, 1996.

Plowden (1994) Plowden, W., *Ministers and Mandarins*, Institute for Public Policy Research, 1994.

Ponting (1985) Ponting, C., *The Right To Know*, Sphere, 1985.

Ponting (1986) Ponting, C., *Whitehall: Tragedy and Farce*, Sphere, 1986.

Pyper (1992) Pyper, R., 'A new model civil service?', *Politics Review*, Vol. 2.2, November 1992.

Pyper (1993) Pyper, R., 'When they have to go...why ministers resign', *Talking Politics*, Vol.5.2, Winter 1992-3.

Pyper (1994) Pyper, R., 'Individual ministerial responsibility', *Politics Review*, Vol.4.1, September 1994.

Pyper (1995) Pyper, R., *The British Civil Service*, Prentice Hall/Harvester Wheatsheaf 1995.

Ridley (1986) Ridley, F., 'Political neutrality in the civil service', *Social Studies Review*, Vol.1.4, March 1986.

Rose (1991) Rose, R., 'Too much reshuffling of the Cabinet pack?', *Institute of Economic Affairs Inquiry*, No.27, 1991.

Silk & Walters (1998) Silk, P. & Walters, R., *How Parliament Works* (4th edn), Longman, 1998.

Simpson (1998) Simpson, D., *UK Government and Politics in Context*, Hodder & Stoughton, 1998.

Thain (1993) Thain, C., 'The core executive and central government under John Major' in *Wale (1993)*.

Thatcher (1993) Thatcher, M., *The Downing Street Years*, HarperCollins, 1993.

Theakston (1987) Theakston, K., *Junior Ministers in British Government*, Basil Blackwell, 1987.

Theakston (1992) Theakston, K., 'Ministers and mandarins', *Talking Politics*, Vol.4.2, Winter 1991-2.

Theakston & Fry (1989) Theakston K. & Fry, G.K., 'Britain's administrative élite: permanent secretaries 1900–86', *Public Administration*, Vol.67.2, Summer 1989.

Wale (1993) Wale, W., (ed.), *Developments in Politics*, Vol. 4, Causeway Press, 1993.

Walker (1991) Walker, P., *Staying Power*, Bloomsbury, 1991.

Whitelaw (1990) Whitelaw, W., *The Whitelaw Memoirs*, Headline, 1990.

Willman (1994) Willman, J., 'The civil service' in *Kavanagh & Seldon (1994)*.

Woodhouse (1993) Woodhouse, D., 'When do ministers resign?', *Parliamentary Affairs*, Vol.46.3, 1993.

14 Parliament

Introduction

Parliament is the UK's legislative authority. Strictly speaking, it has three elements - the monarch, the House of Lords and the House of Commons - and all three elements must be in agreement before a proposal can become law. The legislative role of the monarch, however, has largely been taken over by government ministers (see Chapter 4). Usually, therefore, when people talk about 'Parliament', they are referring to the Palace of Westminster where the House of Commons and the House of Lords are located. Parliament, in this sense, is perhaps the most visible of Britain's political institutions. Its proceedings are reported in the press and broadcast on radio and television. Whether or not Parliament is the focal point of political power in the UK, however, is debatable. Although some commentators argue that the work done by the House of Commons and the House of Lords makes an important contribution to the shaping of legislation, others argue that, in reality, Parliament is little more than a talking shop where ambitious politicians polish their egos and their public speaking skills.

This chapter looks at the role played by the House of Commons and the House of Lords in the decision-making process. It traces the development of the two chambers and examines the work they do and the procedures they follow. It also considers arguments for and against reform. By concentrating on these areas, it should be possible to form a judgement about exactly how powerful and how effective Parliament is and how (if at all) its power and effectiveness have changed in recent years.

Chapter summary

Part 1 examines the evolution, composition and functions of Parliament.

Part 2 looks at the composition and work of the House of Commons. It also discusses the legislative process, the work of committees and procedures for debates and questions in the House. A section on the Cash for Questions scandal and its consequences is included.

Part 3 discusses the composition of and work performed by the House of Lords. It also considers the arguments for and against abolishing or reforming the House of Lords.

Part 4 considers the debate about the effectiveness of Parliament. What criteria are used to judge Parliament's effectiveness and are these criteria fulfilled?

Part 1 Parliament

Key issues

1. What were the key events in the development of Parliament?
2. What are the functions of Parliament?
3. What role does Parliament play?

1.1 The evolution of Parliament

Early history

The origins of Parliament can be traced right back to the 11th century when Saxon monarchs established the principle that advice should be sought from the 'Witangemot' (the assembly of the wise). The Witangemot was made up of powerful landowners and church leaders. It was the forerunner of Parliament in the sense that proposed laws and new taxes were discussed by its members.

After the Norman invasion of 1066, monarchs took advice from the Great Council of barons. This Council:

'Met three or four times a year at the summons of the king to help him decide policies of state, to review the work of the administration, to sit as a high court of justice and to take part in making and amending laws...Medieval kings were expected to meet all royal expenses, private and public, out of their own revenue. If extra resources were needed for an emergency, such as war, the Sovereign would seek to persuade his barons, in the Great Council, to grant an aid.' (HMSO 1994, pp.10 & 12)

In 1254, Henry III's brother (acting regent whilst the king was abroad) was unable to raise sufficient funds from the barons and, therefore, summoned two knights from each English shire to the Great Council in the hope that they would be able to raise funds for the king. Ten years later, not only knights but also two leading citizens from each city and borough were summoned. The Great Council, therefore, came to contain two groups - those summoned by name (the barons and clergy - Lords) and those who were representatives of local communities (the knights and leading citizens - Commoners). These two groups formed the basis for what were to become the House of Lords and the House of Commons.

The term 'Parliament'

The term 'Parliament', from the French 'parlement' meaning 'speaking', was first used in Britain in 1236 and applied, in general terms, to meetings called for the purpose of discussion. It was only later in the 13th century that the term began to refer to meetings of the Great Council. Later, in the 13th century, monarchs began to call Parliaments regularly. Edward I, for example, held his first general Parliament in 1275 and held 30 Parliaments during his 25 year reign. Commoners, however, were not always summoned to these Parliaments (Edward I summoned them just four times). It was only after 1325 that commoners were summoned regularly.

Developments in the 15th century

Two important developments regarding the Commons took place in the 15th century. First:

'In 1407, Henry IV pledged that, henceforth, all money grants should be approved by the House of Commons before being considered by the House of Lords.' (HMSO 1994, p.14)

And second, the Commons began to play an important role in law making:

'During the 15th century, [the Commons] gained the right to participate in giving their requests - or Bills - the form of law. The costs of government and war forced the king   to turn with increasing frequency to Parliament for supplies. Before supplies were granted, he was often called upon, through petitions, to redress stipulated grievances. Since this usually resulted in some kind of legislation, the law-making power, as well as the power to raise taxes passed into parliamentary hands.' (HMSO 1994, pp.14- 15)

The impact of the English civil war

Conflict between the monarchy and the Commons resulted in civil war in the mid-17th century. Defeat of the royalist forces led to the execution of Charles I (in 1649) and the abolition of the monarchy and the House of Lords (though this was short-lived). British government was dominated by the Lord Protector, Oliver Cromwell. In 1660, two years after Oliver Cromwell died, Charles II returned from exile and was restored to the throne, having given the guarantees the Commons demanded. But, although the monarchy was restored (as was the House of Lords), the relationship between the monarch and the Commons had changed for good.

The Glorious Revolution

When James II (who succeeded Charles II in 1685) tried to reassert the dominance of the monarchy, he was deposed and replaced by William of Orange (the so-called 'Glorious Revolution' of 1688). William was granted the throne on condition that he agreed to the introduction of a Bill of Rights which limited the royal prerogative. By accepting this Bill of Rights, William effectively ended the monarch's claim to absolute power and accepted the notion of parliamentary government. From this point onwards, the monarch ruled through Parliament. In practice, this meant that the monarch increasingly delegated the task of government to ministers. It is in the 18th century, for example, that the post of Prime Minister and the Cabinet emerged for the first time (although not in the same forms as today - see Chapter 12, Section 1.1).

The impact of industrialisation

Parliamentary politics in the 18th century was dominated by a political élite. This élite was made up of the aristocracy and large landowners. It did not include those whose wealth was created through industry. One result of the growth of industry in the late 18th century was the development of a commercial middle class. Members of this middle class had economic power, but lacked political representation. By the beginning of the 19th century, members of this middle class had begun to demand the vote and, after a long political struggle, the Great Reform Act of 1832 was passed (see Chapter 7, Section 1.4). Not only did this Act extend the vote to a number of middle-class men, it also established the principle that those who contributed to the development of society deserved the right to have a say in the make-up of the government. Later in the 19th century, the vote was extended in further Electoral Reform Acts (in 1867 and 1884). By 1900, about 70% of men (but no women) could vote.

Impact of a mass electorate

The development of a mass electorate had a profound effect on Parliament. First, it necessitated the development of the party system. The party apparatus came to dominate parliamentary activity. And second, there was a growing divide between the House of Commons with its members elected by the mass of the people and the House of Lords which remained unelected. In the early 20th century, this divide led to a struggle between the two Houses from which the Commons emerged victorious. Not only has the convention developed that the Prime

Minister should be chosen from the Commons rather than the Lords, the legislative and financial powers of the House of Lords were restricted by the Parliament Act of 1911 and its ability to delay the passage of legislation was curtailed further in 1949.

1.2 The role of Parliament

Changing functions

Philip Norton notes that:

> 'The functions ascribed to Parliaments...are not static. The form of Parliaments may remain, but what is expected of them will change as political conditions change.' (Norton 1985, pp.1-2)

It is clear from Section 1.1 above that political conditions have certainly changed during Parliament's long history. Relations between Parliament and the monarchy and indeed the House of Commons and the House of Lords today are very different from those which existed in the 19th century or earlier. Perhaps the most important development in the last hundred years is the growth of the power of the executive (the government). Today, it is the government which sets the legislative agenda and, since it is formed from the majority party (or parties) in the Commons, it is usually able to gather a majority in favour of its proposed laws, regardless of the strength of feeling of opposition MPs. But, even if the executive has the upper hand, the House of Commons still performs a number of functions.

1. Legitimation

The House of Commons is the elected part of Parliament. As such, it can be said to confer legitimacy on the exercise of political power by governments and on public policy in general. Following a general election, the majority party in the House (or coalition of parties, if there is a hung Parliament) forms the government. By supporting the government (primarily by giving their assent to government proposals to change the law), MPs of the governing party (or parties) provide the government with legitimacy. That is why the government is thrown into crisis if it loses a vote in the Commons - the loss of the vote is a loss of legitimacy which can only be restored if a subsequent vote of confidence in the government is passed.

In addition, since assent to legislative proposals is based on majority voting, a further dimension to the process of legitimation comes from Parliament as a whole. This is the (at least tacit) agreement from all sides in Parliament that once parliamentary approval has been given to a change in the law, that new law should be obeyed unless and until Parliament assents to the law being changed again.

2. Scrutiny and influence

The policy proposals, executive actions and expenditure of governments are all legitimate subjects for examination and criticism by Parliament. They are of particular concern to the opposition parties, but a government's own supporters (whose loyalty is needed by the government) are also involved in the process of scrutiny.

3. Representation

The representative part of Parliament is the House of Commons. Each MP represents a particular geographical area in the UK. Although MPs are elected on a party platform, after the election they are expected to represent the interests of all their constituents, regardless of party affiliation. One of the functions of MPs, therefore, is to look after the interests of their constituents in Parliament and to take up their grievances (see Chapter 17, Section 3.2). In this sense, Parliament is often seen (realistically or not) as an institution able to give expression to public opinion or sentiment.

4. The recruitment of government ministers

Parliament is the recruiting ground for the vast majority of government ministers. Some members of government are still chosen from the House of Lords, but most ministers are selected from among MPs of the governing party in the House of Commons. Many MPs ('career politicians') have ambitions to become government ministers and see their backbench parliamentary role as a preparation for future promotion to office.

The Prime Minister can bring into government individuals from outside Parliament, but they would normally be expected to win a seat in the Commons at a subsequent by-election or to be given a seat in the House of Lords (see Chapter 13, Section 1.1).

5. Law making

Much of the work done by Parliament involves the scrutiny of legislative proposals put forward by the government. As far as the government is concerned, it is Parliament's job to give assent to the government's legislative programme. The process of scrutiny prior to assent, however, can provide MPs in the Commons and members of the House of Lords with the possibility of influencing the content of legislation.

6. Deliberation

Both Houses of Parliament are debating chambers and debates are held on, for example, topical issues or on specific matters of policy.

Main points - Part 1

- The origins of Parliament lie in the 11th century, but it is only in the 13th century that the term 'Parliament' began to be used.
- The House of Commons and House of Lords emerged out of the monarch's Great Council. In the 15th century, the Commons began to play a role in law making. The Glorious Revolution of 1688 ended the monarch's claim to absolute power and parliamentary government was established.
- Industrialisation led to the growth of a middle class which demanded political representation. During the 19th century, the electorate grew,

leading to mass parties and conflict between the Commons and the Lords.
- The functions of Parliament are not fixed. They change over time.
- Today, Parliament has six main functions: (1) to provide the government and political process with legitimacy; (2) to oversee and criticise executive actions and policies; (3) to represent the interests of constituents; (4) to serve as a recruiting ground for ministers; (5) to scrutinise and amend legislative proposals; and (6) to debate key issues and policies.

Activity 14.1 The role of Parliament

Item A   The MP, the House and the constituency

Item B   Lord Irvine and Lord Richard

Lord Irvine   Lord Richard

Lord Irvine (the Lord Chancellor) and Lord Richard (Leader of the House of Lords) were the only two members of Tony Blair's first Cabinet who were also members of the House of Lords. Taking the government as a whole, there were 88 ministers in Tony Blair's first government (including 23 Cabinet ministers). Of the 65 non-Cabinet ministers, ten were members of the House of Lords (see table below).

Item C   Newspaper headline, March 1979

LABOUR GOVERNMENT LOSES NO-CONFIDENCE VOTE IN THE COMMONS - GENERAL ELECTION TO BE CALLED

Name	Position
Baroness Hayman	Minister for Roads
Baroness Symons of Vernham Dean	Foreign Office Minister
Lord Williams of Mostyn	Minister for Constitutional Issues
Baroness Blackstone	Minister of State for Further and Higher Education
Lord Clinton Davies	Minister of State in the Board of Trade/DTI
Lord Donoughue	Minister for Farming and the Food Industry
Lord Sewell	Minister for Agriculture, Environment and Fisheries
Baroness Jay of Paddington	Minister of State for Health
Baroness Hollis of Heigham	Minister for Social Security
Lord Dubs	Minister in the Lords for Environment, Agriculture

Questions

1. a) To which function of Parliament does Item A refer?
   b) What point is the cartoon making about this function?

2. Using Items A-C, explain in what ways and why the House of Commons and the House of Lords have different functions and play different roles.

3. Item B shows that most ministers in Tony Blair's first government were selected from the House of Commons
   a) Why do you think this is the usual practice?
   b) Give arguments for and against recruiting ministers from the Lords.

4. a) To which function of Parliament does Item C refer?
   b) What does Item C tell us about the role of Parliament?

Part 2 The House of Commons

Key issues

1. What is the composition of the House of Commons?
2. How does the House of Commons work?
3. What part does the Commons play in the legislative process?
4. What is the composition and role of committees in the Commons?
5. What is the function of debates and Question Time in the Commons? What procedure is followed?
6. Why was the Cash for Questions scandal significant?

2.1 The House of Commons today

Composition

The House of Commons is an assembly elected by universal adult suffrage. It is composed of Members of Parliament (MPs), each of whom represents a geographical area (a constituency) in the UK. At the time of the 1997 general election, there were 659 seats in the House of Commons (the number varies as constituency boundaries are altered - see Chapter 7, Section 3.1). This total of 659 seats was divided as follows:

- 529 seats for England
- 40 seats for Wales
- 72 seats for Scotland
- 18 seats for Northern Ireland.

  Since 1945, the vast majority of MPs have stood for and won an election under a party label.

Seating arrangements

The importance of parties, including the division into governing and opposition parties, is emphasised in the seating arrangements of the House of Commons chamber. Government ministers occupy the front benches on one side of the House. They face the frontbench team of the opposition party (or parties) on the other side. The seating arrangements, therefore, serve to favour a two-party system and a confrontational (or 'adversarial') style of party debate. The seating in other Parliaments is organised differently. The European Parliament, for example, is arranged almost in a circle. This makes a symbolic as well as a practical difference to the way in which the proceedings in the European Parliament work.

Business

After each general election, a new Parliament begins. This new Parliament has a life of up to five years - the Parliament Act of 1911 stipulates that five years should be the maximum time between general elections. Each Parliament is divided into sessions with each parliamentary session normally lasting about a year (from November to November). At the start of each session, the Queen's Speech is delivered. This speech is written by the Prime Minister and outlines the legislative proposals which the government intends to put before Parliament during the year ahead. There are annual breaks, when the House is in recess - at Christmas, Easter, Spring Bank and during the summer.

Daily business

Until 1995, the daily business in the House of Commons began at 2.30 pm on Mondays to Thursdays and at 9.30 am on Fridays (it began earlier on Fridays to enable MPs to travel back to their constituencies for the weekend). The amount of business to be covered, however, meant that the House frequently sat past its official closing time of 10.30 pm. There were complaints of unsociable working hours (all-night sittings were not uncommon) and members whose constituencies were distant from London had little time to spend in their constituencies. Growing demands from some MPs for reforms in working practices eventually led to the introduction of some changes which were designed to reduce the number of late-night sittings and, generally, to rationalise the hours of business. The changes, agreed in November 1995, included the following:

- sessions from 2.30 pm to 10.30 pm on Mondays to Thursdays (with the

possibility of late-night sittings) and a session from 9.30 am to 3 pm on Fridays
- a session from 9.30 am to 2 pm on Wednesdays (for Private Members' debates) followed by business as usual from 2.30 pm
- Prime Minister's Questions to be moved from Tuesday and Thursday (at 3.15 to 3.30pm) to a single session on Wednesday (at 3.30 to 4 pm)
- ten Friday sitting days to be dropped from each session
- MPs not required to attend after 7.30pm on Thursdays.
  (Information from the House of Commons Information Office, 20 May 1998)

The usual channels

The weekly business of the House is arranged by the government and opposition Chief Whips. The Speaker is informed about which leading speakers from each party would like to address the House during debates. This is termed 'arranging business through the usual channels'. Other matters may be agreed 'through the usual channels'. The business for the two weeks ahead is announced each Thursday by the Leader of the House. The Leader of the House also arranges the Commons' programme for the entire parliamentary session.

The Speaker

The proceedings in the chamber of the House of Commons are chaired by the Speaker or one of the Deputy Speakers. Speakers are chosen by their fellow MPs at the start of each new Parliament or when the previous Speaker retires or dies. Although Speakers are elected MPs, they are not permitted to speak on behalf of their constituents in the Commons and they do not take part in debates since they are supposed to be impartial. The Speaker only votes in the House in the event of a tie and, even then, is guided by precedent - by the decisions of Speakers in similar previous cases.

As well as representing the House of Commons on ceremonial and formal occasions, it is the Speaker's job to see that the procedural rules of the House (contained in the Standing Orders) are followed and to decide which MPs are called upon to speak. In attempting to preserve order, there are a number of sanctions at the Speaker's disposal. First, MPs can be directed to withdraw remarks made in 'unparliamentary language'. Second, if these instructions are ignored, MPs can be suspended from the House. Third, in the event of a serious general disorder in the chamber, the Speaker can suspend the entire proceedings. This happened in 1985, for example, when the then Speaker, Bernard Weatherill, suspended proceedings for 20 minutes following continued protests from a group of opposition Labour MPs against the government's refusal to agree to a debate on the dispute in the coal industry.

Main points - Section 2.1

- **The House of Commons is an assembly elected by universal adult suffrage.**
- **The layout of the Commons favours a two-party system and an adversarial style of debate.**
- **A Queen's Speech is delivered at the start of each parliamentary session. Written by the Prime Minister, it outlines the government's programme.**
- **Complaints about the Commons' working hours led to changes being agreed in 1995.**
- **The weekly business of the House is arranged 'through the usual channels'.**
- **Proceedings in the Commons are chaired by the Speaker or Deputy Speakers. It is their job to ensure that the procedural rules of the House are followed and order is maintained.**

Activity 14.2 Business in the House of Commons

Item A *The Speaker (1)*

Yesterday, the Labour MP for West Bromwich West, Betty Boothroyd, ended more than 700 years of male tradition by being elected Parliament's first woman Speaker by an overwhelming majority of MPs. More than 70 Conservative MPs were among the 372 votes in her favour. She obtained 134 more than her nearest rival the former Conservative Cabinet minister, Peter Brooke. This was only the sixth time that an open election for a new Speaker had been held. It is the third election this century and the first since 1951. The usual pattern has been to arrange matters behind the scenes. The Prime Minister, John Major, said: 'The holder of the office of Speaker must know when to turn a blind eye and when not. She needs a quick mind and a ready wit. She must be unfailing in her impartiality. She will sometimes need the wisdom of Solomon and, if I am strictly honest, she will sometimes need the patience of Job'.

Adapted from the *Guardian*, 28 April 1992.

Item B   *The Speaker (2)*

The Sinn Fein MPs Gerry Adams and Martin McGuinness are to contest in the European Courts the refusal yesterday of the Speaker, Betty Boothroyd, to grant them the same facilities as other MPs. The two MPs are being denied the use of Commons facilities because they refuse to swear the oath of allegiance to the Queen. Explaining her decision, the Speaker said: 'You are in effect asking for associate membership of this House. Such a thing does not exist. There can be no halfway house.' In the Commons, Tony Benn, a former Cabinet minister, took the rare step of challenging her decision, protesting that the oath could be changed just as it had been changed in the past (it was last changed in 1888 so agnostics and atheists did not have to swear allegiance to God). The Speaker, however, argued that primary legislation would be needed to change the Parliamentary Oaths Act or the form of the oath and it was the refusal to swear or affirm that prevented the two MPs taking their seats - not any action by her. Tony Benn replied that the Speaker's statement was of such major constitutional importance that the House should have the chance to reach a decision 'rather than rely solely on a statement from the chair'.

Adapted from the *Guardian*, 5 December 1997.

Item D   *The layout of the House of Commons*

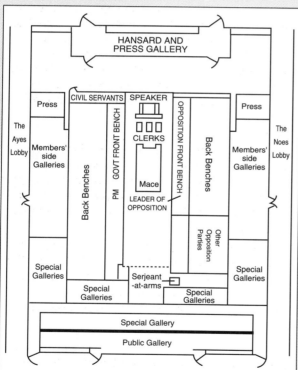

Facilities at Westminster include: a gym; a hair salon; a rifle range; two souvenir shops and a kiosk; a police cell; 14 bars; cafes and restaurants; and, the Members' Smoking Room. In February 1998, 178 MPs signed a motion urging the government to set up a creche for MPs and staff working at Westminster. A proposal in 1994 to turn the rifle range under the Lords into a creche was defeated.

Adapted from the *Guardian*, 20 February 1998.

Item C   *House of Commons daily timetable, Monday to Thursdays*

9.30-2.00pm (Wednesdays only)	**Private members' debates**
2.30pm	Prayers
	Preliminary business -such as motions or new writs for by-elections, or unopposed private bills
2.35-3.30pm	**Question Time** - questions to ministers from MPs
3.30-4.00pm (Wednesdays only)	**Prime Minister's Questions**
3.30pm (other days)	**Public business** - the main debates of the day, including those concerning proposed new laws
10.00pm	Public business ends*
	Adjournment debate - on a topic raised by backbench MPs
10.30pm	House adjourns

(* If the House fails to complete its business by 10 pm it may continue to sit. All-night sittings are not uncommon.)

The House of Commons timetable for Mondays to Thursdays, based on information from the House of Commons Information Office, 20 May 1998.

Item E   *Modernising parliamentary procedure*

A report from the cross-party Modernisation Committee (set up after the 1997 general election) yesterday made a number of recommendations. Perhaps the most important was to allow some government Bills to go through Parliament more slowly - taking two parliamentary sessions rather than one. In addition, it was recommended that the following practices should be ended:

- wearing an opera hat when making a point of order during a vote (until now, the rule was that an MP must be 'seated and covered' to make a point of order and opera hats are kept at strategic points around the chamber)
- shouting 'I spy strangers' to force a vote and disrupt business (a practice which was important in previous centuries when anyone who was not an MP was excluded during debates for fear that they might carry tales to the monarch)
- continuing to be paid when suspended for bad behaviour
- allowing Privy Councillors to have precedence in debates
- tolerating the shouting of 'reading' in an attempt to put off MPs who consult their notes.

Rituals which are to continue, however, include the following:

- addressing the Speaker not each other
- calling MPs not by their names but their title ('the honourable member for...' etc)
- voting in person, not electronically.

Adapted from the *Guardian*, 10 March 1998.

Questions

1. a) Judging from Item A, what are the qualities required by the Speaker? Which qualities are most important?
   b) What does Item B tell us about the difficulties the Speaker is likely to face? Can you think of other difficulties the Speaker might face?

2. Look at Items C-E.
   a) What changes have recently been made to the way in which business is conducted in the Commons?

   b) Why do you think these changes were made?
   c) Can you think of any reasons why MPs might still not be happy with the way in which business is conducted in the Commons?

3. What are the arguments for and against moving the House of Commons to a new, purpose-built, semi-circular chamber outside London? Use Item D in your answer.

2.2   The legislative process

Private Bills

Private Bills play only a minor role in legislation today. They are intended to apply only to a particular area, a specific organisation or a certain section of the population. They are sometimes promoted for large capital projects on behalf of private companies or by public bodies (such as local authorities) as a means of avoiding long and costly public inquiries. Private Bills were popular in the 19th century when local authorities sought means to improve their facilities. Large-scale projects, such as the Manchester Ship Canal and the Birmingham Municipal Bank, were set into motion by private Bills. The Transport and Works Act of 1992 has restricted the scope of private Bills by changing the basis on which statutory authority for major infrastructure developments is granted:

> 'Projects such as railways, tramways, ports, harbours and barrages will in most cases no longer come before Parliament for approval by way of a private Bill, but by ministerial orders following, in most cases, public local enquiries conducted by professional departmental inspectors.' (HMSO 1994, p.75)

Public Bills

The vast majority of Bills passing through Parliament are public Bills (they are aimed at the public as a whole). Most public Bills are sponsored by the government and therefore referred to as 'government Bills'. But around 10% of Commons' time is spent on a second type of public Bill - the Private Members' Bill. Private Members' Bills are introduced and promoted by backbench MPs.

Private Members' Bills

Since Private Members' Bills encounter special difficulties in their passage through Parliament, the vast majority fail and do not become law. Out of 741 Private Members' Bills introduced between November 1990 and May 1997, for example, only 173 were successful in the sense that they received royal assent (House of Commons Information Office, 20 May 1998). Many of those which were successful were either politically uncontentious or received government support.

There are three ways of introducing a Private Members' Bill into Parliament - the ballot; the 'Ten Minute Rule' procedure; and Standing Order 58.

1. Ballot Bills

At the start of each parliamentary session, MPs can enter their names in a ballot from which 20 names are drawn. Only 12 Fridays in each parliamentary session are normally set aside for discussion of 'Ballot Bills', however, and half of these tend to be taken up with the later stages of Bills already in the pipeline. Attendance at the House on Fridays is usually low (many MPs return to their constituencies for the weekend on Thursday evening) and the MP promoting a Ballot Bill might well see it delayed or pushed off the Commons timetable because an insufficient number of MPs are present in the chamber for a division (vote) to take place. Even so, the chances of success for a Ballot Bill are much higher than Private Members' Bills introduced in other ways.

2. The Ten Minute Rule

Under the Ten Minute Rule an MP is allowed ten minutes to outline the case for a new piece of legislation. MPs frequently use this procedure to gain publicity for ideas they wish to express rather than in hope of getting new legislation on the statute book.

3. Standing Order 58

MPs have a slightly higher chance of success with the procedure laid down in Standing Order 58. This allows a Bill to be introduced without debate if a day's notice is given to the Speaker. The vast majority of Bills introduced in this way, however, fail.

Why Private Members' Bills fail or succeed

Overall the majority of Private Members' Bills fail because the government does not provide the support necessary for their successful passage through the House. The main requirement is that of time. Without the provision of extra time by the government, a Bill has little chance of success. Controversial Private Members' Bills (such as the anti-hunting Bill proposed by Michael Foster in 1997) are especially vulnerable to hostile tactics. For example, filibustering is a common tactic - an opponent of a Bill carries on speaking (often about unrelated matters) simply to use up time and to prevent a vote being taken. Similarly, the tabling of new clauses and amendments can keep a debate going until time runs out (as happened with Michael Foster's Bill).

Some Private Members' Bills, however, do receive government (and even bi-party) support. These Bills are sometimes used as a means of introducing social reforms with which the government does not wish to be directly identified. In the 1960s, for example, reforms to the law on abortion and homosexuality were achieved through Private Members' Bills. Similarly, in 1994 the age of consent for homosexuals was lowered to 18 after the government supported a Private Members' Bill.

Michael Foster's Ballot Bill

Pressure groups often target MPs who have been successful in the ballot in the hope that they will introduce a Bill in support of their cause or interest. For example, as soon as it became known that Labour MP Michael Foster had come top of the ballot in May 1997, he was approached by a number of anti-hunting pressure groups in the hope that he would introduce an anti-hunting Bill. When Foster announced on BBC Radio 4 that he would introduce a Bill which was 'in the best interests of the city of Worcester [his constituency] and the people of this country', one of these pressure groups - the International Fund for Animal Welfare - paid for a MORI poll in Worcester which showed that 70% of his constituents supported a ban on hunting (*Guardian* 8 June 1997). This poll undoubtedly helped to persuade the MP to choose to introduce an anti-hunting Bill. Having agreed to introduce an anti-hunting Bill, Foster then consulted closely with a number of pressure groups in drawing up the Bill:

> 'The Bill has been drawn up by animal welfare groups, including the Royal Society for the Prevention of Cruelty to Animals, the International Fund for Animal Welfare and the League Against Cruel Sports.' (*Times*, 17 June 1997)

Although the Bill was not successful, it passed its second reading in the Commons with a majority of 260 (411 in favour and 151 against) and the Prime Minister, Tony Blair, hinted that the government might take action to ban hunting before the next general election (*Times*, 29 November 1997).

Government Bills

Some types of government Bill are introduced in every parliamentary session - for example the Finance Bill containing the provisions of the Budget. Some are brought in to deal with emergencies (wars or civil strife, for example) or in response to pressure. Others are planned as part of the general process of implementing government policy. Often, such Bills relate to manifesto promises.

Consultation

Consultation takes place between the sponsoring government department and other departments (especially the Treasury). There may also be consultation with outside organisations. Sometimes the consultation process involves the publication of a **green paper** in which the government outlines its ideas, presents policy options and invites comments. The 1993 Ripon Commission report, however, noted that green papers were becoming rare. The trend was to produce less formal 'consultation papers'. In addition to, and sometimes instead of, an initial consultation stage, the government publishes a **white paper** which states its policy on a particular topic or view. In effect, a white paper is a statement of intended legislation and may be the subject of parliamentary debate. Once the Cabinet decides to go ahead with the proposals, a date is fixed for their introduction into Parliament and a draft Bill is drawn up.

Passage of a Bill

A government Bill is usually given its first reading in the House of Commons, though it can begin in the Lords. It then goes through further stages - second reading, committee stage, report stage, third reading. It then passes to the other House where it goes through a similar series of stages. Once the Bill has received royal assent, it becomes law in the form of an Act of Parliament.

Legislative function of the Commons

The function of the Commons with regard to law making, therefore, is:

- to debate the proposed legislation
- to scrutinise it at the committee stage
- to suggest amendments
- to agree on its final shape.

It should be emphasised, however, that it is the government (on the whole) which decides what matters require legislation and the government is normally able to command a majority in any vote taken in the House. The scope for opposition MPs (and indeed for government backbenchers) to make an impact on legislation which comes before the House is, therefore, limited.

The role of the whips

Each of the main parties in the Commons appoints a Chief Whip and assistant whips. The role of government whips in the legislative process is to ensure that the government maintains its majority in votes taken in the House. The opposition whips organise their supporters to mount an effective challenge to the government.

MPs receive weekly printed instructions from their party whips indicating when they should attend the House to vote. These instructions are also referred to as 'whips'. A **three-line whip** means attendance is essential. A **two-line whip** means that MPs must attend unless arrangements have been made under the 'pairing' system (government and opposition whips can agree for an MP on each side to 'pair' up and be absent at the same time - see Chapter 13, Section 1.1). A **one-line whip** merely requests the attendance of MPs.

When the governing party in the Commons has a large majority, there are insufficient partners in the main opposition party for the pairing system to work properly. When this happened after the 1997 general election, an alternative system was introduced. Labour backbenchers were organised into groups of around 50 and, taking it in turns, these groups were allowed a 'constituency week' in which they were not obliged to attend the House for one-line or two- line whips.

Applying pressure

Whips can apply pressure to rebellious MPs in a number of ways. Normally a stiff talking to is enough to secure the MP's loyalty. But, if an MP votes against the government in a motion with a three-line whip, the whip may be withdrawn from the MP - the equivalent of being expelled from the party. This is what happened to eight Conservative MPs in November 1994 when they voted against the government Bill increasing Britain's contributions to the EU (this was the first time this century that such a large number of Conservative MPs had been disciplined in this way at one time). Withdrawal of the whip, in practice, is often only a temporary punishment for disloyalty, but permanent expulsion is a possibility. In 1997, the Conservative Party withdrew its whip from one of its MPs - Peter Temple-Morris - after he had opposed his party's line on the single European currency. Temple-Morris' response was to resign from the party but to continue to take his seat in the Commons as an 'independent Conservative'.

Other functions

Maintaining party support and party discipline form only part of the managerial role of the party whips

(see Alderman 1995). The government's Chief Whip attends Cabinet meetings and has the status of a senior minister. The Chief Whips arrange the weekly business of the House. Whips arrange 'pairs' and allocate offices in Westminster. Also, whips provide an important means of communication between the party leadership and backbenchers.

Main points - Section 2.2

- Proposed legislation come in the form of private Bills and public Bills. Private Bills play only a minor role today.
- Bills introduced by backbench MPs are called 'Private Members' Bills'. These can be introduced using the ballot, the Ten Minute Rule or Standing Order 58. Few Private Members' Bills succeed, often because they run out of time.
- Most public Bills are sponsored by the government. Government Bills may follow the publication of a green paper and/or a white paper. They pass through three readings, a committee stage and a report stage in each House before receiving royal assent and becoming law.
- The role of government whips is to ensure that the government maintains its majority in votes taken in the House. The role of opposition whips is to mount an effective challenge to the government.
- The term 'whips' also refers to instructions issued to MPs. A three-line whip means attendance at the House is essential. A two- line whip means MPs must attend unless paired or on a constituency week. A one-line whip means attendance is only requested.

Activity 14.3 *Legislative machinery*

Item A *A whip*

PRIVATE & CONFIDENTIAL   **PARLIAMENTARY LABOUR PARTY**

MONDAY, 7th JULY 1997 - The House will meet at 2.30pm

1. Home Office Questions
   Tabling for National Heritage and Lord Chancellor's Department.
2. Ten Minute Rule Bill: Hair Dressers Registration (Amendment) - Austin Mitchell.
3. Conclusion of the Budget Debate (Rt. Hon. Frank Dobson and Rt. Hon. Alistair Darling).

YOUR ATTENDANCE BY 9.00PM AND UNTIL ALL THE BUDGET RESOLUTIONS HAVE BEEN OBTAINED IS ESSENTIAL.

PRIVATE & CONFIDENTIAL   **PARLIAMENTARY LABOUR PARTY**

TUESDAY, 8th JULY 1997 - The House will meet at 2.30pm

1. Foreign and Commonwealth Questions Tabling for Health.
2. Ten Minute Rule Bill: Film Classification Accountability and Openness - Julian Brasier
3. Local Government Finance (Supplementary Credit Approvals) Bill: Remaining Stages (Hilary Armstrong and Nick Raynsford). Local Government Contracts Bill: Remaining Stages (Hilary Armstrong and Nick Raynsford).

YOUR ATTENDANCE FROM 3.30PM IS ESSENTIAL.

PROVISION WILL BE MADE FOR THE 10.00 PM RULE TO BE SUSPENDED.

Information provided by the House of Commons Information Office.

Item B   *League for the Introduction of Canine Control (LICC)*

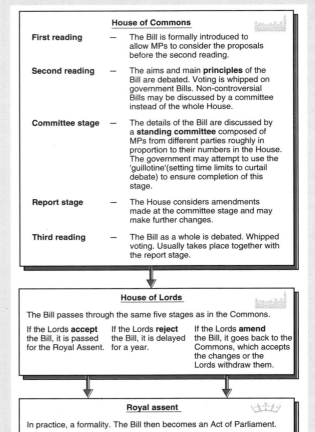

Did you know...

● *That dogs' excrement can be loaded with diseases that can maim or even kill human beings.*

● *That surveys show 6% of apparently healthy people HAVE ALREADY BEEN INFECTED.*

● *There is evidence on record to show that human illnesses and deaths earlier attributed to other causes actually stemmed from virulent diseases passed on by dogs.*

● *There is good reason to believe that 12% of this country's 6.5 MILLION dogs are already disease carriers.*

● *That ¾ MILLION infected "samples" are deposited by dogs every day in the United Kingdom.*

● *That some diseases live in soil for so long that 1500 MILLION infected samples are thought to be present in the soil of Britain at any one time.*

● *That treatment can arrest these diseases in humans.*

League for the introduction of
CANINE CONTROL

P.O. Box 326
London NW5 3LE

Campaign copyright
reserved by
Crawley Borough Council

Item C   *The passage of a Bill through Parliament*

House of Commons

First reading	— The Bill is formally introduced to allow MPs to consider the proposals before the second reading.
Second reading	— The aims and main **principles** of the Bill are debated. Voting is whipped on government Bills. Non-controversial Bills may be discussed by a committee instead of the whole House.
Committee stage	— The details of the Bill are discussed by a **standing committee** composed of MPs from different parties roughly in proportion to their numbers in the House. The government may attempt to use the 'guillotine'(setting time limits to curtail debate) to ensure completion of this stage.
Report stage	— The House considers amendments made at the committee stage and may make further changes.
Third reading	— The Bill as a whole is debated. Whipped voting. Usually takes place together with the report stage.

House of Lords

The Bill passes through the same five stages as in the Commons.

If the Lords **accept** the Bill, it is passed for the Royal Assent.	If the Lords **reject** the Bill, it is delayed for a year.	If the Lords **amend** the Bill, it goes back to the Commons, which accepts the changes or the Lords withdraw them.

Royal assent

In practice, a formality. The Bill then becomes an Act of Parliament.

Questions

1.   How does the role of the whips affect the way in which the Commons performs its functions? Use Item A in your answer.

2. a)   Suppose a minister agreed to meet LICC (Item B) and to sponsor a Bill imposing heavy fines on dog owners whose pets fouled the pavement. Using Item C, describe the process to be undertaken before the Bill became law.

b)   How much influence would backbench and opposition MPs have on the final form of the Bill?

c)   Suppose ministers refused to sponsor such a Bill. Advise LICC on the best way to proceed to achieve legislation.

3.   'The House of Commons' most important function is to participate in the law-making process.' Give arguments for and against this view.

2.3   Commons Committees

Official and unofficial Committees

Philip Norton explains that:

> 'Within the House of Commons there are basically two types of committee: official and unofficial. Each can be further subdivided. The two principal types of official committees are the standing and select committees, though the House also makes use of a form of hybrid, known as special standing committees. Unofficial committees comprise essentially party committees and all-party groups. The official committees are established by the House under its Standing Orders. They are subordinate bodies: the House retains the final say on all matters. Unofficial committees are, as the name indicates, not bodies established formally by the House: they are created within the parliamentary parties or by groups of Members.' (Norton 1991, p.5)

Norton points out that, although the use of committees can be traced back to the 14th century, the current, extensive use of committees in the House of Commons is a recent development. Since 1907, the sending of Bills to standing committees has been normal practice. It is only since 1979, however, that select committees have been appointed to investigate the activities of government departments.

Standing committees

When a Bill has received its second reading, it

reaches its committee stage. The Bill is then usually sent to a standing committee for consideration - unless the House decides otherwise (the committee stage of uncontentious Bills or Bills of constitutional importance, such as the Maastricht Bill, are taken on the floor of the House). Standing committees examine the details of a Bill within the confines of the Bill's general principles which were approved at the second reading. The job of standing committees is to debate and consider amendments to the Bill.

Despite their name, standing committees are ad hoc committees. They are set up specifically to examine a particular Bill and are then disbanded. No collective identity (which might lead to a stronger, more investigative, role) is, therefore, likely to develop.

Standing committees' origins lie in the 19th century. Two standing committees, each of 60-80 MPs, were established in 1883. The present structure, however, dates from 1907. Since then, the number of committees has increased and the numbers serving on each committee has decreased.

Membership

Standing committees do not have distinctive names, but are referred to as Standing Committee A, B, C and so on. Members come from different parties in rough proportion to the party political make-up of the House as a whole. A government with a secure majority can, therefore, normally expect to secure acceptance of its proposals, although during the detailed consideration of a Bill it may wish to make minor amendments.

The Committee of Selection, composed of senior MPs, decides which MPs should sit on each standing committee (after consulting with party whips). The relevant minister and opposition spokesperson is included as a matter of course and members with a special interest or expertise in the subject of the Bill are normally considered. Most standing committees have between 18 and 25 members, but it is up to the Committee of Selection to decide exactly how many should serve on the committee. The committee's work is presided over by a senior backbencher appointed by the Speaker from the 'Chairman's panel' (they are supposed to be impartial). It should be noted that:

> 'The committee meets in a similar adversarial format to the House itself, the government supporters sitting on one side of the committee room and the opposition parties on the other side.' (Norton 1995, p.23)

Procedure

Standing committees examine Bills by considering each clause in turn. Amendments can be put forward by any member of the committee, but, unless they are moved by the minister, they usually fail (clauses of government Bills which are voted on tend to be

whipped). In order to reduce the time a committee spends on a Bill, the government may seek to apply the guillotine. This involves setting a time limit for debate on each clause. Its use is not restricted to the committee stage and it is used particularly for those occasions when it has not been possible to reach agreement with the opposition 'through the usual channels' (see above, Section 2.1).

The general pattern in standing committees is for opposition members to begin by tabling numerous amendments. These are usually rejected. Since little progress has been made, the government then calls for a guillotine to be imposed. This restricts the opportunity for significant changes to be made.

Standing committees have been criticised for taking excessive time to carry out their work and because they operate on adversarial party lines. As a result, the outcome of their deliberations is, generally, predictable. In addition, it is argued that these committees have inadequate information at their disposal since they are not permitted to take evidence from outside bodies or individuals.

Possible reforms

In response to these criticisms, Norton (1995) has identified four possible reforms.

1. Fixed timetable

First, the House of Commons Procedure Committee suggested that Bills should be given a fixed timetable. This would prevent the imposition of the guillotine and allow more balance since each part of the Bill would be given a certain amount of time for scrutiny.

2. Permanent committees

Second, the Hansard Society Commission recommended that standing committees should be set up on a permanent basis. A core of permanent members would be supplemented by the cooption of extra members for each Bill. This would allow a body of knowledge to develop and help to reduce the partisan nature of committees.

3. Earlier stage

Third, Norton (1992) has suggested that the committee stage should precede the Bill's second reading. This would allow the committee to consider wider issues since the principles upon which the Bill is based would not have been established.

4. Additional powers

And fourth, the report of the Ripon Commission in 1993 recommended that, where appropriate, standing committees should be able to take on the powers of 'special standing committees' which can spend up to three public sessions questioning witnesses and considering particular aspects of a Bill before carrying out the clause-by-clause examination. The advantage of this would be that committees could obtain adequate information to scrutinise the Bill properly. Also, outside groups would be able to make representations in an open environment, rather than relying on the secret or private contacts that are normally made with government departments during the legislative process.

Merge standing and select committees?

One further suggestion (see Downs 1985) is to amalgamate the work of standing committees with that of select committees. Select committees are responsible for scrutinising and reviewing the work of government departments (see below). An amalgamation would result in the committee reviewing the work of a particular department, including the legislation produced by that department.

Select committees

According to a government pamphlet:

> 'Select committees are generally set up to help Parliament with the control of the executive by examining aspects of public policy and administration. They may also undertake more specific responsibilities related to the internal procedures of Parliament. They examine subjects by taking written and oral evidence and, after private deliberation, present a report to the House.' (HMSO 1994, p.80)

Drewry (1989) explains that select committees were used a great deal before the mid-19th century, but the development of a disciplined party system in Parliament and greater control by the executive led to their decline. A number of non-departmental select committees have a long history, but it is only since 1979 that departmental select committees have been in operation.

Non-departmental select committees

Perhaps the most important non-departmental select committee is the Public Accounts Committee, first set up in 1861. This committee has a large staff of auditors working under the Comptroller and Auditor General. It checks the government accounts, attempts to ensure that money has been spent in properly authorised ways, and also assesses whether value for money is achieved. Other non-departmental select committees include the Committee on the Parliamentary Commissioner for Administration (which supervises the work of the Ombudsman - see Chapter 17, Section 3.2) and the Select Committee on European Legislation (which scrutinises legislation proposed by the European Union). There are also non-departmental select committees which deal with the House's internal affairs (such as the Select Committee on Standards and Privileges, and ad hoc committees set up to investigate particular issues - such as the Select Committee on Standards in Public Life which was set up in 1995 to consider the recommendations of the Nolan Committee (see Section 2.5 below).

Departmental select committees

In 1979, despite ministerial reluctance, MPs voted to set up a number of departmental select committees whose task would be to examine the expenditure, administration and policy of individual government departments and to report back to the House. Initially, 14 departmental select committees were set up. Two more were set up in 1992 and one for Northern Ireland was set up in 1994.

Departmental select committees each have 11 members (except for the Committee on Northern Ireland Affairs which has 13). Members are chosen by the Committee of Selection. Apart from the Committee on Northern Ireland Affairs (which includes five MPs from Northern Irish parties), membership of select committees (as with standing committees) roughly reflects the relative party sizes in the Commons as a whole. Unlike standing committees, however, no government ministers or frontbench opposition members are included and no whips attend. Select committees do not tend to operate on the adversarial party lines of standing committees. Party-based differences may still occur, but select committees, generally, aim to produce unanimous reports at the end of their investigations.

Powers

Most departmental select committees meet once a week. In theory, they can investigate any issue within the scope of the work of the relevant department, but time places severe limits on what a small group of backbench MPs (who have the support only of a small administrative staff) can achieve. The committees do have, however, the power to send for 'persons, papers and records'. Witnesses can be interviewed (in public unless confidential or security matters are discussed), evidence taken and specialist advisers appointed.

Limitations

Despite such powers, however, the committees may not obtain the information they require. The tradition of government secrecy makes it difficult to obtain information from ministers and civil servants. Without the express permission of the House as a whole, committees cannot compel ministers or other MPs to attend, although they generally do. More important is the difficulty some committees have in persuading ministers and other witnesses to give straight answers to direct questions. Committees do not have automatic recourse to departmental papers and records (though concern is normally expressed in the House and increasingly by the media if evidence is refused on unreasonable grounds). Norton (1995a) also notes the pressures of time on individual members. Although each committee typically meets once a week for up to two hours, preparation time can add an estimated eight hours per week to a committee member's already busy schedule.

It should be noted that the government is not

obliged to act upon the recommendations of select committees and there is no guarantee that their reports will even be debated in the House. The government usually responds to reports with a detailed memorandum.

Reasons for popularity

Membership of select committees is more popular than membership of standing committees. In part, this is because MPs believe that the work done by such committees is important (if nothing else, ministers and civil servants are aware that a select committee can investigate any aspect of a department's work and so the committee acts as a deterrent against arbitrary government). In part, it also reflects the media attention which is sometimes given to the work of committees (for example, the 1991-92 Trade and Industry Committee's inquiry into the sale of arms to Iraq). Select committees allow backbenchers to engage in investigative work and, in some cases, this is a substitute for ministerial office.

Select committees and the executive

When departmental select committees were set up in 1979, some people hoped that this would alter the balance between Parliament and the executive. But, given the strength of the party system, the idea that the Commons could in some way control the government is unrealistic. Rather, the effectiveness of select committees should be judged by the extent to which they influence the executive. Norton argues that:

'The impact of committees on government policy has been modest. Some policies have been affected by committee reports; many have not. The Prime Minister in 1986 identified 150 recommendations from select committees that the government had accepted in the period from March 1985 to March 1986. However, many of the recommendations were essentially minor and constituted a minority of the recommendations emanating from the committees. Nonetheless, those accepted were proposals that otherwise would probably never have seen the light of day.' (Norton 1991, p.9)

Concern was also expressed that the setting up of select committees would reduce interest in and attendance at meetings of the full House. These concerns, however, appear to have been largely unfounded. Adonis argues that, if anything, the committees have:

'Enhanced the profile and reputation of the House of Commons among policy formers and the media.' (Adonis 1993, p.170)

Norton agrees that there have been advantages, but points out that the system also has limitations:

'The committees have proved of value to the House and to MPs individually. They have acted as a means of specialisation, as deterrents, as agents of open government, as safety valves and as policy influencers. The combination is an impressive one...Against the advantages one has to put the limitations. The committees stand accused of having inadequate resources, an amateurish approach, limited powers, little linkage with the floor of the House, limited influence and of wilting under the pressure of political interference and of other demands on MPs' time.' (Norton 1994, pp.29 & 31)

Main points - Section 2.3

- Standing committees are ad hoc committees which examine a Bill clause-by-clause within the confines of the Bill's general principles (as approved at the second reading).
- Members of standing committees are taken from parties in rough proportion to the size of each party in the House as a whole, so the government has an in-built majority. Proceedings are adversarial and often whipped. No outside information is available.

- Select committees are set up to help Parliament with the control of the executive by examining aspects of public policy and administration.
- Non-departmental select committees include the Public Accounts Committee which checks that the government has spent money in properly authorised ways.
- Proceedings in departmental select committees are not adversarial and the committees can call for 'persons, papers and records'.

Activity 14.4 Committees in the House of Commons

Item A　Select committees

Might the rise of select committees be a check against Tony Blair's massive majority? Certainly a mutinous spirit stalks the Commons committee corridor. Both the Health Committee and Committee on European Legislation have attacked the government's handling of the Formula One tobacco sponsorship affair. The Treasury Committee set up American-style 'confirmatory hearings' for members of the Bank of England Monetary Policy Committee and the Education Committee is to do the same with appointments to the Office for Standards in Education. All these committees have Labour chairs. But, there's the rub. The governing party has to empower party backbenchers to give ministers a hard time. Committee powers only mean anything if other MPs back them up and that depends on the whips - who have a wonderful armoury of patronage, bribery and threats. Using these means under John Major, they neutralised a select committee investigating the Supergun Affair (the same inquiry revealed another weakness - Alan Clark, a key actor, simply refused to answer questions). Similarly, when, under Major, the Health Committee chaired by Tory Nicholas Winterton criticised the internal market within the NHS, the whips invented the 'Winterton rule' preventing a committee chair serving more than two terms. To subvert 'independent' committees, the Tories showed, you turn committee chairs into ministers or even whips. Anyway, select committees are wildly varied in the quality of their members and output. The Public Accounts Committee, for example, is a model of effectiveness. Through it, MPs are able to conduct regular, professional and thoroughgoing investigations on the public's behalf. But, too many select committee inquiries verge on the farcical. Questions are asked which are merely statements of prejudice. MPs don't follow up questions. Civil servants and ministers spend hours preparing. MPs, however, often don't bother to prepare at all. Complaisant members are easy meat for whips and, above all, whips control committee membership, seeking to ensure that there is never a majority of difficult MPs. Hard and fast evidence of committee influence on government policy is hard to find.

Adapted from the *Guardian*, 7 July 1998.

Item B　Record of select committees 1986-96

1986 - The Defence Select Committee
This committee investigated the 'Westland Affair' - see Chapter 12, Section 2.3.
- Thatcher refused to allow the committee to interview key civil servants.
- The committee failed to discover if Thatcher was responsible for the improper leaking of a letter from the Attorney General.

1990 - The Agriculture Select Committee
This committee investigated the outbreak of BSE.
- The committee failed to uncover the dangers of weak controls on contaminated offal.
- The committee did not monitor the possibility of mad cow disease spreading to humans.

1992 - The Trade & Industry Select Committee
This committee investigated the 'supergun' arms sales to Iraq.
- Key civil servants were refused permission to testify.
- The addresses of retired civil servants were not disclosed to the committee
- The Conservative MP at the centre of the affair, Hal Miller, refused to testify.
- The committee failed to uncover MI6 errors and secret government support for Iraq.

1996 - The Trade & Industry Select Committee
This committee investigated naval gun sales to Iran.
- The committee was denied access to intelligence documents and Ministry of Defence information about Iranian weapons.
- The chief executive of BMARC, the company involved, did not testify.
- The committee failed to allocate responsibility for the scandal, claiming insufficient powers and time.

1996 - Home Affairs Select Committee
This committee investigated the need for a ban on handguns (even though Lord Cullen's inquiry was underway at the same time).
- The committee did not hear evidence from victims of the Dunblane shootings.
- The committee concluded that no ban was necessary.
- The report issued by the committee was rejected by the Labour minority on the committee and by police, doctors, parents and even the government.

Adapted from the *Observer*, 14 August 1996.

Item C　The standing committee on the Social Security Bill in the 1997- 98 parliamentary session

	Number
Sittings of committee	14
Amendments made to Bill	131
Ministerial amendments carried	131
Amendments moved by government backbenchers	0
Amendments moved by opposition MPs	173
Opposition amendments carried	0
Votes on opposition amendments	10
Hours of deliberation in committee	28 hrs 27 mins

Information from the House of Commons Information Office, 5 November 1998.

Item D *The record of standing committees*

The most shocking thing about the Commons is the way in which laws are made. If you want to see what it is like, sit on a standing committee. A Bill is produced and that Bill has to be defended. At the same time, it has to go through the committee stage. The government has a majority on that committee and it selects the members of the committee. It doesn't pick people who are going to be difficult - it picks a tame majority which can be relied on to defend the measure and uncritically see it through the process. And then, ministers will say, 'Parliament has decided'. I'm not easily shocked, but I was in respect of what became the 1993 Education Act. Members of the government party on that Bill spent their committee time writing their Christmas cards. This is the reality of how legislation is scrutinised in standing committee. People stay out of the room, except for crucial votes. Government MPs are told to say nothing so that a Bill can go through as quickly as possible. The opposition simply engages in a tactic called 'delay' - talking about anything remotely connected to the Bill in the vain hope of extracting some political benefit. David Butler has described the committee stage as a 'futile marathon'. He cites a standing committee which met for two months in 35 separate sessions for a total of 120 hours. Yet, no fewer than 35 hours were spent on the first two clauses and, when only 17 of the 129 clauses had been examined, a guillotine was applied, depriving most of the details of the Bill from any scrutiny at all. There were 173 votes on the committee stage and, surprise surprise, the government won them all. You could replay the same story for any major piece of legislation. This is why we have such bad legislation. It is a shocking state of affairs.

Adapted from Wright 1997 (at the time of writing, Tony Wright was Labour MP for Cannock and Burntwood).

Questions

1. To what extent and in what ways is the select committee system able to act as a check on the executive? Use Items A and B in your answer.
2. Do you agree with the following statements? Use Items A and B in your answer.
   (i) Select committees are to be welcomed because of their emphasis on consensus rather than party division.
   (ii) By questioning ministers and civil servants, select committees make the executive more accountable to Parliament.

   (iii) Select committees give backbenchers more power.
   (iv) Select committees lead to more open government.
3. a) Judging from Items C and D, why do you think standing committee work is unpopular with (i) opposition MPs and (ii) government backbenchers?
   b) What are the drawbacks with the existing standing committee system? What improvements would you recommend? Use Items C and D in your answer.

2.4 Debates and questions

Debates

Rules for the conduct of debates

The House of Commons is a debating chamber and an elaborate set of rules for the conduct of debates has developed over time. Some of the rules are laid down in Standing Orders (the regulations governing the House of Commons' procedures). Others operate by convention:

'The subject for debate starts off as a proposal or "motion" made by a member. When a motion has been moved, the Speaker proposes the question (in the same terms as the motion) as the subject for debate...In both Houses, members speak from wherever they have been sitting and not from a rostrum (although frontbench members usually stand at one of the dispatch boxes on the Table of the House). They may not read their speeches (although they may refresh their memories by referring to notes...). Generally, no member may speak twice to the same motion, except to clarify some part of a speech that has been misunderstood, or by leave of the House.' (HMSO 1994, pp.60-61)

Procedure

Major debates are normally opened and closed either by government ministers or members of the opposition front bench and frontbenchers are generally given more time than backbenchers to make their speeches. MPs wishing to make contributions to a debate must first 'catch the Speaker's eye', although this is usually done by notifying the Speaker before the beginning of the debate. Until 1998, Privy Councillors were given priority in debates (Privy Councillors are mainly existing and former Cabinet ministers or leading members of the opposition parties). Unlike ordinary MPs who are referred to as 'honourable' members, Privy Councillors are referred to as 'right honourable' members.

Although the purpose of debates is, in theory, to decide upon government policy and administration, a government can usually rely on its majority in the House to gain approval for its actions (see Box 14.1 for the range of debates). The division (vote) at the end of a debate is, therefore, generally a foregone conclusion (it is called a 'division' because MPs divide up into those going into the 'ayes' lobby and those going into the 'noes' lobby). Commons debates are perhaps more accurately seen as a device for expressing government, opposition and dissenting views.

Box 14.1 Debates in the Commons

1. **Debates on white papers**
2. **Debates on Bills**
3. **Debates on ministerial statements**
4. **Debates on reports of parliamentary committees**
5. **Debates on the Queen's Speech**
   The Queen's Speech is the annual address to Parliament, written by the Prime Minister, outlining the government's legislative programme for the forthcoming session. The subsequent debate takes place over a number of days and is one of the few occasions during the year when a major Commons speech is delivered by the Prime Minister.
6. **Daily adjournment debates**
   These take place during the final half hour of each day's sitting when an MP can raise almost any subject. These debates are often used to air constituents' grievances or draw attention to matters in which individual backbenchers are personally interested.
7. **Government motions**
   About 20 days per session are devoted to debates on government motions.
8. **Opposition days**
   There are 20 days per session for debates on subjects chosen by the opposition.
9. **Motions of no-confidence (in the government)**
   No-confidence debates are more likely to be called for by the opposition when the government's majority is small. If defeated, the government must resign or call a general election, but this has occurred only once this century - James Callaghan's Labour government was defeated on a no-confidence vote in March 1979.
10. **Private Members' motions**
    About 10 days per session are reserved for debates on these motions, together with the final day before each recess (holiday). These debates are usually poorly attended.
11. **Emergency debates**
    Requests for emergency debates are rarely granted by the Speaker, but opposition requests for them can secure media attention.

Modernising procedure

After the 1997 general election, the Labour government set up a cross-party Modernisation Committee. It was set up:

> 'To consider a range of ideas for making the Commons more user friendly.' (*Guardian*, 10 March 1998)

In June 1997, this committee recommended that a third desk be placed in the division lobbies to speed up divisions (which were taking up to 10 minutes longer than before the election because of the large number of Labour MPs going through the same lobby). This recommendation was accepted and implemented by the Speaker (*Times*, 27 June 1997). It was also the Modernisation Committee which recommended the changes to procedure noted in Activity 14.2, Item E above.

Quality of debates

Debates vary in quality, but are frequently little more than a series of speeches which make party political points to a sparsely attended chamber. Unless the government has a small majority, most debates make little impact on government policy. Even if the government only has a small majority, it is not often the quality of the points made in a debate which result in government action. For example, in the first few months after the 1992 general election, the government made policy concessions over its plans to close coal mines and over its intended timetable for ratification of the Maastricht Treaty. Both of these concessions were made, however, in response to backbenchers' threats not to vote with the government rather than because of the content or quality of the debates themselves (see Adonis 1993, p.144).

Occasionally, a debate on a matter of crucial national or international significance can prove to be an exception. In September 1990, for example, Parliament was summoned to meet before the end of the recess so that a debate could be held on the crisis in the Gulf following Iraq's occupation of Kuwait. Immediately after the debate, a Labour frontbencher claimed that this was one of those rare occasions when a parliamentary debate may have influenced the government (in this case, by showing the strength of feeling in the House about the need to maintain international consensus on any future action in the crisis).

Coverage of debates

Lengthy sessions of the September 1990 debate referred to above were covered live on radio and television, bringing the views expressed to a much wider audience. Yet, the broadcasting of the proceedings of the House is of fairly recent origin. Regular radio coverage began in 1978 and television cameras were first allowed into the Commons in 1989 (see Chapter 19, Section 3.3).

Importance of debates

The performance in debates can help to determine the direction of an MP's career. A reputation as a poor performer in the Commons does not help an MP to gain promotion to the front bench, nor does it make it easy for an MP to retain such a position.

In general, as a means of scrutinising the executive or of influencing policy, debates have their limitations. But, they may have some effect in forcing the government to explain its policies and to justify its actions. They also bring conflicting political views to the attention of the electorate.

Question Time

Procedure

Question Time is held in the Commons each weekday (except Fridays) from 2.35 pm to 3.30 pm. The Prime Minister now answers questions in a single session lasting for half an hour - from 3.30 to 4 pm every Wednesday when Parliament is in session (between 1961 and May 1997, the Prime Minister answered questions from 3.15 to 3.30 pm on Tuesdays and Thursdays each week). Other government ministers take turns to answer questions (a rota system is used to determine which minister answers at which time):

> 'Questions are usually handed in at the Table Office in writing, but may be sent by post. Usually at least two days' notice must be given to allow time for an answer to be prepared. If an oral answer is required, the question must be marked with an asterisk; questions without asterisks are answered in writing. An MP may ask up to two oral questions and any number of written questions a day. No more than eight questions requiring oral answers may be tabled by any MP during a period of ten sitting days. An MP may ask only one oral question of any one minister on any day.' (HMSO 1994, p.88)

The Table Office

The Table Office (which consists of four clerks under the control of a principal clerk) scrutinises proposed questions to ensure that they conform to the parliamentary rules. They may edit the questions. The admissibility of questions is determined by whether they conform to principles established by the rulings made by successive Speakers. They must conform to five broad criteria:

> 'A question must be framed as a genuine question and not as a statement or a speech in the interrogative; it must not seek the interpretation of a statute or legal opinion; it must not ask for information already published or for the confirmation of a rumour or press report; it must not be "tendentious, controversial, ironic, vague, frivolous or repetitive"; and, it must be concerned with a matter for which a minister is officially responsible.' (HMSO 1994, p.89)

Supplementaries

Before each Question Time, ministers work with their civil servants to prepare their responses. In particular, they try to anticipate the **supplementary** questions which follow each initial answer. Each questioner is permitted to ask one supplementary question and the Speaker may then allow further supplementaries from other MPs. Supplementaries from opposition MPs are often, therefore, designed to test the ability and efficiency of the minister. The purposes behind questions are summarised in Box 14.2.

Prime Minister's Questions

Supplementary questions must be confined to matters for which the answering minister has responsibility. Since the Prime Minister is in charge of no department in particular, during the 1980s and and 1990s the

---

> ### Box 14.2 Why are questions asked at Question Time?
>
> 1. To gain information (but more effective ways, such as writing to the appropriate government department, are usually available).
> 2. To press for action on an issue.
> 3. To raise a grievance on behalf of a constituent or group.
> 4. To give publicity to the aims or interests of a pressure group.
> 5. To impress constituents, constituency party or party managers.
> 6. To embarrass the government (particularly the Leader of the Opposition's questions to the Prime Minister).
> 7. To attempt to show government policy or actions in a favourable light (including the 'planted' question, about which the opposition complains from time to time).

convention developed of tabling 'open' questions at Prime Minister's Questions (PMQs). Usually, these took the form of asking the Prime Minister what their engagements were for the day. On 20 March 1997, for example, nine of the ten questions on the order paper were identical, each asking what the Prime Minister's engagements were for the day (*Guardian*, 10 May 1997). Having asked the open question, questioners could then ask what they really wanted to ask in the form of a supplementary question. One of the problems with this was that the whole process became rather ritualistic and time consuming. Each questioner would ask the same question and, after actually listing the day's engagements to the first questioner, the Prime Minister would then respond to each further questioner with the formula: 'I refer the honourable member to the reply I gave some moments ago.'

By the time of the 1997 general election, there was a consensus amongst the leadership of the three main parties that the quality of PMQs should be improved (*Times*, 10 May 1997). Sessions had become set pieces in which the Leaders of the main parties attempted to score points against each other - with the result that sessions often deteriorated into rowdy slanging matches. The fact that clips from these confrontations were often shown on prime time television news caused concern that the reputation of Parliament might suffer. As a result, one of the new Labour government's first actions was to introduce changes. Not only were the two 15 minute slots on Tuesday and Thursday combined to make a single session on Wednesday, changes were also made to procedure. To save time, for example, once the Prime Minister had listed the day's engagements in response to the first questioner, later questioners were allowed to ask their supplementary question immediately without having to go through the ritual of asking the open question. In addition, questioners who placed substantive questions in advance were then allowed to ask a follow-up question (*Times*, 22 May 1997). According to a Downing Street official:

'[The aim of the reforms was] to replace entertainment politics with good politics.' (*Guardian*, 10 May 1997)

The importance of Question Time

For opposition members, Question Time is an opportunity for political point scoring whilst government ministers and their civil servants tend to regard it as an exercise in damage limitation and reveal as little as possible. Ministers are not obliged to answer questions. If they refuse to answer a question, they do not even have to supply a reason, although they usually do. Referring to the carefully prepared responses of ministers which are provided by civil servants, one backbench MP declared:

> 'Most of the words they say haven't even passed through their own brains.' (quoted in Jordan & Richardson 1987, p.72)

Question Time and accountability

MPs on both sides agree that, regardless of the limitations, Question Time is an important means of scrutinising the work of ministers:

> 'In an average length session between 1945 and 1985, the number [of oral questions] tabled would not exceed 15,000 and sometimes would be closer to half that figure. Since then the number tabled in an average session has exceeded 20,000 and is usually closer to 25,000...In some recent sessions the number [of written questions] tabled has exceeded 45,000...One recent survey of some MPs on both sides of the House found that there was general agreement that questions were important for holding ministers to account...Oral questions were seen as marginally more important than written questions in this context. Written questions were deemed more important than oral questions for obtaining information that would otherwise be difficult to acquire.' (Norton 1993, p.96-97)

Question Time may not be a mechanism for obtaining detailed, informative and open answers to searching political questions, but it can help to publicise party political positions and conflicts and, as with debates, it has a part to play in securing a degree of ministerial accountability to Parliament.

Written questions

In addition to oral questions, MPs can also put questions to ministers for written answer. Indeed, any question written by an MP and directed to a minister must be answered (so long as it meets the criteria laid down by the Table Office). These written questions and answers are published in Hansard and there are around 50,000 written questions per year (House of Commons Information Office, November 1998).

Main points - Section 2.4

- **An elaborate set of rules for the conduct of debates in the House of Commons has developed over time. Some of the rules are laid down in Standing Orders. Others operate by convention.**
- **Although the purpose of debates is, in theory, to decide upon government policy and administration, a government can usually rely on its majority in the House to gain approval for its actions.**
- **It is only on rare occasions that debates make an impact on government policy. They do sometimes force the government to explain and justify its actions and bring issues to the public's attention.**
- **Government ministers take it in turns to answer questions in the Commons at Question Time each weekday (except Friday). PMQs now take place on Wednesday (3.30-4 pm).**
- **MPs on both sides agree that Question Time is an important means of scrutinising the work of ministers and in securing a degree of ministerial accountability to Parliament.**

Activity 14.5   *Questions and debates*

Item A   *PMQs (1)*

It used to be claimed that Prime Minister's Questions (PMQs) were one of the glories of Parliament. No longer. In March 1967, Harold Wilson was called to answer specific questions. What was his view on textile imports? Had he plans to meet the Polish Foreign Minister? Seven narrowly targeted questions to which answers had been prepared. Ten years later, Jim Callaghan faced only three. In each case, there were several supplementaries, but all were closely tailored to the question on the order paper. Many MPs thought the system let Leaders have it too easy. As questions were tabled in advance, they were rarely topical, and questions aimed at the Prime Minister were often transferred to other departments. So, a practice grew up of asking more general questions which opened the way to a supplementary about a hot local issue. The turning point came in Thatcher's premiership. By allowing the so-called 'open' question and encouraging supporters to plant questions, PMQs became a propaganda platform. The televising of proceedings resulted in the trivialisation and barbarisation of PMQs. John Major attempted a more relaxed style, but was anxious to introduce a successful soundbite for the evening news. By May 1997, both Major and Blair backed changes because PMQs had become so stage-managed and rowdy that it was bringing the House into disrepute.

Adapted from the *Guardian*, 10 and 21 May 1997 and the *Times*, 10 May 1997.

Item B *PMQs (2)*

Yes, it was dull, but it was meant to be. The new, responsible, non-confrontational PMQs reminded me of one of those political interviews from the 1950s which usually went like this: 'Prime Minister, thank you for coming to the studio. I believe you have a Bill connected with unemployment.' 'Yes I do.' 'Could you describe it?' ' Certainly, it is our intention to abolish unemployment, insofar as that proves practicable.' 'I am sure the country will be delighted to hear that, Prime Minister. Thank you for coming here tonight.' Tony Blair was slightly more forthcoming. When the Tory, Ian Taylor, thanked him sarcastically for sparing time to attend the House, he replied that he had had a busy day because, unlike the last government 'we are actually governing'. But, that was about as confrontational as it got. Stuart Bell, a Labour MP, told us how excited the whole country was by the 26 Bills in the Queen's Speech. 'What will you do for an encore?' An awful truth dawned: there are going to be as many Labour greasers as there were Tories. It's just that their style will be different, consisting of theatrical, luvvie-style flattery.

Adapted from the *Guardian*, 22 May 1997.

Item C *PMQs (3)*

BLAIRCOCK'S HALF HOUR

This cartoon was published the day after Tony Blair had taken part in the first reformed session of PMQs. Blair is portrayed as the comedian Tony Hancock who starred in a radio show called 'Hancock's Half Hour' in the 1950s.

Item E *Debates (2)*

As a new backbench MP, you will probably only have three and possibly four chances to speak in a debate each year - and then, not in the great debates. The Speaker usually ensures that yesterday's statesmen (former Cabinet ministers and time-servers) are called in the great debates. Despite the abundance of lackwits in Parliament, you should always prepare your speech on the assumption that there will be at least one person present who, unlike yourself, is a real expert on the discussion. You must also get used to speaking in an empty chamber - as a newcomer you will probably be called to speak between 7 and 9pm when most MPs are having dinner or attending meetings that mean far more to them than what you have to say. Finally, you should remember that your purpose in speaking is not to convince anyone to act other than they would have done anyway. Still less can you hope to change people's minds. Your purpose is to let those who count know you exist. Once the debate is over, you will be in the corridors conspiring to move upwards. The corridors are far more important these days than the chamber itself. Private words in ears, accompanied by promises and threats, are far more effective than grand public gestures in helping you climb the greasy pole.

Adapted from Sedgemore 1995.

Item D *Debates (1)*

The Commons debates endlessly into the night. After all, politicians' only qualification is being able to talk. The Commons is supposed to be the great meeting place of the nation where ideas and issues are thrashed out and, in some sense, that is what happens. But, debates in the Commons do not necessarily reveal what the public needs to hear. It is fair to say that an exchange on *Newsnight* is far more revealing and important than an exchange in the House. The House is an echo chamber. It used to be the other way round - the media used to reflect issues raised in the Commons. I remember when those of us who were elected in 1992 had a celebration after the first year. John Smith (Leader of the Labour Party until his death in 1994) came to cut the cake and made a speech in which he said: 'I know some of you think this place is not very effective, but what you must remember is that this place is an intimate theatre.' I like that phrase. It is about play-acting.

Adapted from Wright 1997.

Questions

1. Judging from Items A-C:
   (a) how has PMQs changed since the 1960s?
   (b) why was PMQs in need of reform by May 1997?
   (c) have the changes to PMQs introduced in May 1997 increased or decreased ministerial accountability to Parliament?

2. What point do you think the cartoonist is making in Item C?

3. What are the main purposes of debates in the Commons? Use Items D and E in your answer.

2.5 The Cash for Questions Affair and its consequences

Background

In July 1994, the *Sunday Times* revealed that two Conservative MPs, David Tredinnick and Graham Riddick, had each accepted £1,000 in return for tabling a written question to a minister (see Section 2.4 above for information on written questions). The *Sunday Times* had set up an undercover operation in which a journalist posed as a businessman and approached 20 MPs - ten Labour and ten Conservative. Of these 20 MPs, four Conservatives agreed to ask questions. One asked for the money to be sent to charity, a second agreed to ask a question for nothing, whilst Tredinnick and Riddick asked for the money to be sent to their home addresses.

Technically, Tredinnick and Riddick would have done nothing wrong so long as they declared the payment in the Register of Members' Interests (see Chapter 11, Section 3.3) within a month. But, the news that the two MPs had accepted cash for questions caused great public outrage because of the moral issues it raised. In this case, the MPs were not offering their expertise (for which they might legitimately have charged a fee), but had taken advantage of their privileged position as MPs.

Further allegations

This outrage was then fuelled by reports in the *Guardian* in October 1994 that junior ministers Neil Hamilton and Tim Smith had also received money in return for tabling parliamentary questions between 1987 and 1989 (when they were both backbenchers). Smith resigned from the government immediately. Hamilton resigned soon afterwards, but denied receiving cash for tabling questions. He was also accused of accepting other benefits not declared in the Register of Interests.

Further allegations of misconduct were then levelled at other, more senior, ministers, including Jonathan Aitken. Together with a growing unease about decline in standards in public life generally, these developments were considered by many commentators to have had an adverse effect on the reputation of Parliament and the government. They added to a general atmosphere of 'sleaze' which the newspapers, in particular, were happy to comment on repeatedly.

The Nolan Committee

In response to these allegations, an investigation was launched by the Commons Select Committee on Privileges and the government set up a Committee on Standards in Public Life under Lord Justice Nolan. The Nolan Committee was given the following brief:

> 'To examine current concerns about the standards of conduct of all holders of public office, including arrangements relating to financial and commercial activities, and to make recommendations as to any changes in present arrangements which might be required to ensure the highest standards of propriety in public life.' (quoted in the *New Statesman and Society*, 4 November 1994)

The Nolan Committee, then, was not confined to examining concerns about MPs, but had a remit which also included the conduct of: ministers, civil servants, UK MEPs, quango officials, local councillors and officials.

The Nolan Report

The Nolan Committee submitted its first report in May 1995. This report recommended that:

- MPs should be barred from working for lobby companies
- MPs' earnings should be fully disclosed
- an independent Parliamentary Commissioner for Standards should be appointed
- a code of conduct for MPs should be introduced.
  (Borthwick 1997)

Many MPs (mostly Conservatives) were very unhappy about these recommendations (Baggott 1995). The government's response was to set up a Select Committee on Standards in Public Life to examine those recommendations of the Nolan Report which affected Parliament. Following this, the House introduced, in November 1995, some changes to its rules:

- the introduction of an 'advocacy ban' by which MPs are not now permitted to initiate debates, introduce Bills or ask parliamentary questions about matters which concern their own commercial interests
- the appointment of a Select Committee on Standards and Privileges to replace the former Privileges Committee and the Committee on Members' Interests
- the appointment of a Parliamentary Commissioner for Standards - Sir Gordon Downey.

The Downey Report

Downey investigated the Cash for Questions allegations and, in July 1997, reported that he found 'compelling' evidence that Neil Hamilton had taken cash from Mohamed Al Fayed, the owner of Harrods. Four months later, a majority of the members of the Standards and Privileges Committee endorsed the Downey Report. The committee also argued, however, that the relationship between the roles of the Commissioner and the committee, in terms of the House's self-regulation procedures, needed reviewing. The crucial question was whether the committee should function as a judicial tribunal (a court able to issue punishments directly) or whether it should be there to oversee the work of the Commissioner and to issue any punishments to MPs who were found, by the Commissioner, to have behaved incorrectly.

The full House subsequently backed the committee's report and Ann Taylor, Leader of the House, announced that a new parliamentary committee on privilege with members from both Houses would consider new legislation concerning bribery and corruption relating to MPs.

Main points - Section 2.5

- In July 1994, the *Sunday Times* revealed that two Conservative MPs had accepted £1,000 in return for tabling a written question to a minister.
- This caused public outrage on the grounds that the MPs had not offered their expertise (for which they might legitimately have charged a fee), but had taken advantage of their privileged position as MPs.
- After further allegations of misconduct had been made, the Nolan Committee was set up to examine the conduct of people holding public office. The

Nolan Report recommended that: (1) MPs should be banned for working for lobbying companies; (2) MP's earnings should be disclosed; (3) an independent Parliamentary Commissioner should be appointed; and (4) a code of conduct for MPs should be introduced.

- Although some changes were made before 1997, it was only after the Downey Report was published in July 1997 that legislation was promised to combat bribery and corruption in Parliament.

Activity 14.6 Cash for Questions

Item A *Cash for Questions (1)*

Reporter: Hello David. Thanks so much. I got your message on the answerphone when I got back. You tabled questions this evening, did you?

Tredinnick :Yes.

Reporter: Fine, brilliant.

Tredinnick: So you will get an answer on Tuesday.

Reporter: Right. OK.

Tredinnick: That's unless they can't get the information in time. It went down as it was written, without change.

Reporter: I will send you the £1,000 in the post now then.

Tredinnick: That's very kind of you.

Reporter: You checked that this is all above board and everything, didn't you?

Tredinnick: Oh yes, that's fine.

Reporter: There's no problem about that?

Tredinnick: I probably will declare an interest, but I don't have to be specific on that and it's confidential between the two of us.

Reporter: Right. OK, fine. The address I have is the correct address to which to send the cheque?

Tredinnick: Yes, it's my home address.

Adapted from the *Times*, 12 July 1994.

Item B *Cash for Questions (2)*

This cartoon was inspired by the first reports of the Cash for Questions allegations. It appeared in the *Guardian* on 12 July 1994.

Item C *What's new?*

Allegations of corruption and misconduct in British public life are older than Parliament itself. Attempts to control and set standards of conduct also have a long history. In 1410, Parliament introduced legislation to prohibit the King's officers from receiving gifts for carrying out their duties. During the 20th century, various inquiries have been set up in the wake of public scandals, some of which resulted in changes to the rules governing the behaviour of politicians and officials. A series of scandals in the first two decades of the 20th century, for example, led to the Prevention of Corruption Acts of 1906 and 1916, and, in the 1920s, a Political Honours Scrutiny Committee was set up following a scandal over the sale of honours. Parliament was forced to strengthen its system of self-regulation in the 1970s following the Poulson Affair which revealed a network of corruption involving civil servants, MPs, councillors and local government officials. This episode resulted in new rules about MP's declaration of financial interests and the introduction of a Register of Members' Interests.

Adapted from Baggott 1995.

Item D *MPs and self regulation*

In December 1997, following the resolution of the Hamilton Affair, Dale Campbell-Savours, a Labour MP and member of the Standards and Privileges Committee wrote an article in the *Guardian*, arguing that he no longer believed that it was the job of MPs to try other MPs. 'I am neither judge, juror nor lawyer', he wrote, 'and I do not believe that a committee of Parliament stuffed with MPs is capable of conducting the investigative and cross-questioning aspects of an inquiry into members' conduct'. He pointed out that in the Hamilton case, there were over 14,000 documents to consider as well as a large number of oral accounts. MPs on the committee, he argued, simply did not have the resources to conduct an investigation on this scale. In addition, he alleged, a great deal of political interference took place during the course of the investigation. The 'inescapable truth', he concludes, is that politicians 'go native. Political pressures are too great'. Campbell-Savours called for the role of the Committee on Standards and Privileges to be limited to ensuring that:

- investigations made by the commissioner are properly conducted
- a periodic review of the parliamentary code of conduct is undertaken
- appropriate reports are published.

Adapted from the *Guardian*, 16 December 1997.

Questions

1. 'A storm in a tea cup'. Is this a fair reflection of the Cash for Questions scandal that broke out in 1994? Use Items A-D in your answer.

2. What is the point being made in Item B?

3. a) Using Items A-D, examine the claim that the House of Commons is not fit to regulate the activities of its own members.
   b) What are the alternatives to self-regulation?

Part 3 The House of Lords

Key issues

1. How does the House of Lords work?
2. What does the House of Lords do?
3. What are the arguments for and against the abolition of the House of Lords?

3.1 The composition and organisation of the Lords

Composition of the Lords

In the Queen's Speech of November 1998, the Labour government promised to introduce a Bill ending the right of hereditary peers to sit and vote in the Lords. If this Bill comes into effect, it will affect the composition, organisation and role of the Lords. The following section describes the composition, organisation and role of the Lords in operation at the beginning of 1999.

At the beginning of 1999, nobody was elected to the House of Lords (which is also known as the 'upper House'). The House of Lords was composed of the **Lords Temporal** and the **Lords Spiritual** (Lords are also known as 'peers'). The Lords Spiritual were the 26 bishops of the Church of England (including the two archbishops). The vast majority of Lords were the Lords Temporal:

'Temporal peerages (both hereditary and life) are created by the Sovereign [monarch] on the advice of the Prime Minister. They are usually granted either in recognition of distinguished service in politics or in other walks of life, or because one of the political parties wishes to have the recipient in the upper House. The House of Lords also provides a place in Parliament for people who offer useful advice but who do not wish to be involved in party politics. Unlike the House of Commons, there is no fixed number of members in the House of Lords. Relatively few are full-time politicians.' (HMSO 1994, pp.28-29)

Hereditary and life peers

At the beginning of 1999, therefore, Lords Temporal fell into two categories - hereditary peers and life peers.

By far the largest category was that of hereditary peers (those who inherited a title and automatically became members of the House of Lords once they reached the age of 21). In May 1998, there were 759 hereditary peers. In addition, there were the life peers (those who were appointed to be members of the House of Lords for life but whose heirs would not succeed to a peerage). In May 1998, there were 487 life peers. This figure does not include the 26 bishops, but it does include the 12 Law Lords - 'Lords Appeal in Ordinary'- whose major role was to listen to cases when the House of Lords sat in its capacity as the highest court of appeal. In such cases, only the Law Lords take part.

Including bishops, the total number of peers in May 1998 was, therefore, 1,272. Of these, just 96 were women. It should be noted, however, that 68 Lords were not entitled to seats in the House of Lords because they had not been issued with a Writ of Summons (it was the job of the Lord Chancellor to issue hereditary peers with a Writ of Summons when they had proved that they were the legitimate heir to the title. Legitimate heirs under the age of 21 and those who could not prove they were legitimate heirs were not granted a Writ of Summons). Also, a further 65 peers were on leave of absence and, therefore, unable to take part in proceedings during the lifetime of the Parliament. So, a total of 1,139 peers was eligible to attend the proceedings of the House in 1998. Yet, a large number of these peers rarely or never attended the Lords. Average daily attendance, which increased after 1957, when peers were first able to claim an attendance allowance, was 378 in the 1993-94 parliamentary session, 372 in the 1995-96 parliamentary session and 412 in the 1997-98 parliamentary session (all the above figures come from the House of Lords Information Office).

Organisation and procedure

At the beginning of 1999, there were a number of similarities with the Commons in the way in which the House of Lords was organised. In the chamber, peers supporting the government sat on benches opposite those who supported the opposition parties. There was also the distinction between the front and back benches which is found in the Commons. Between May 1997 and July 1998, 12 peers were members of the government. It was their job to explain and defend government policy in the Lords. They were shadowed by opposition peers who sat on the opposition front bench.

Business in the Lords

At the beginning of 1999, the business of the House was arranged by the party leaders and party whips through the usual channels (see Section 2.1 above). Proceedings, however, were presided over by the Lord Chancellor who acted as a Speaker (the Lord Chancellor was appointed by the Prime Minister and sat in Cabinet). The Lord Chancellor had a less active role than the Speaker in the Commons. Peers were expected to regulate their own proceedings. They decided themselves who was to speak and when, for example. The Lord Chancellor merely 'put the question' to the House when a decision was required:

> 'In the House of Lords, the Speaker...has no authority to check or curtail debate. Members of the House of Lords do not address themselves to the Speaker during debates, but to all their fellow members in the House. If two peers rise to speak at the same time during a debate, the House itself, not the Speaker, determines who shall speak.' (HMSO 1994, p.61)

Guidance on procedural matters came from the Leader of the House of Lords, a government minister of Cabinet rank.

The activity of the House grew considerably in the second half of the 20th century. The total number of hours in which the House sat increased from 294 in 1950 to 1,072 in 1990 (Rush 1994). In the 1995-96 parliamentary session, it had dropped to 935 hours (House of Lords Information Office, May 1998). In 1950, the average daily sitting was just under three hours. In 1990, it was just over seven hours. And, in 1995-96 it was just under seven hours (Rush 1994 and House of Lords Information Office, May 1998). Peers

have never received a salary for their parliamentary work, but, since 1957, they have been able to claim expenses.

Party composition

Although, at the beginning of 1999, there was a party system in the Lords, including party whips, a major difference between the two Houses of Parliament was the significant number of **crossbenchers** in the Lords. They did not take the whip of the main political parties and, in this sense, were independent. In practice, however, about two-thirds of crossbenchers always voted with the Conservatives (though crossbenchers did not attend the Lords as regularly as party peers). Party allegiance for any peer, however, was ultimately a voluntary affair. They were not elected and, therefore, did not represent constituents. As a result, the ultimate sanction of withdrawal of the whip for disloyalty lacked the severity it has in the Commons.

At the beginning of 1999, therefore, even if, on paper, there was not a Conservative overall majority, in practice Conservative supporters dominated the House. So, Conservative governments could expect their legislative programme to have a smoother passage through the Lords than governments formed by other parties. This was one reason for the Labour government's determination to end the right of hereditary peers to sit and vote in the Lords.

Powers of the House of Lords

The extension of the franchise through the Reform Acts passed in the 19th century (see Chapter 7, Section 1.4) increased the authority of the Commons. The Parliament Act of 1911 removed the Lords' veto over public legislation, replacing it with the weaker power of delaying the passage of a Bill for two years. The 1911 Act also effectively removed the Lords' power over money Bills (which give approval for raising taxes, for example). The Parliament Act of 1949 reduced the Lords' power of legislative delay to one parliamentary session. At the beginning of 1999, the House of Lords still had an absolute veto over any proposal to extend the life of a Parliament beyond five years. This gave the Lords some significance as a 'residual guardian of the constitution' (Richards 1988, p.173).

3.2 Functions of the House of Lords

The Lords and the Commons

At the beginning of 1999, some of the functions of the House of Lords appeared similar to those performed by the Commons, but there were differences both in the range of activities and how they were carried out. Rush (1997) argued that:

> 'The classic statement of the functions of a second chamber is found in the Bryce Report of 1918 which suggested four functions which have continued to be widely accepted. The subsequent development of the House of Lords,

however, especially after the introduction of life peers in 1958, suggests that a further four can usefully be added.' (Rush 1997, p.25)

These eight functions are outlined in Box 14.3.

> **Box 14.3 Functions of the House of Lords in 1998**
>
> In 1998, it was the function of the House of Lords to:
> - cause sufficient delay to enable the government or the public, or both, to reconsider legislation passed by the House of Commons
> - examine and revise Bills passed by the House of Commons
> - initate non-controversial legislation
> - hold debates on major issues and policies in a less partisan atmosphere than in the House of Commons
> - consolidate existing legislation
> - deal with private legislation
> - deal with delegated legislation, including European legislation
> - scrutinise policy and administration.

At the beginning of 1999, therefore, the role of the unreformed House of Lords, could be divided into five separate areas.

1. Legislative role

Although some non-controversial Bills were introduced into the Lords first, conventionally the role of the upper House was to amend and revise Bills sent from the Commons. The more leisurely pace and less partisan nature of the Lords' proceedings allowed more time to be spent on a detailed examination of a Bill than in the Commons. As a result, peers could point out problems which may not have been foreseen by the government and they could pass amendments to clauses in Bills before returning them to the Commons for reconsideration. When this happened, however, the government often relied on its overall majority in the Commons to overturn the amendment.

The Salisbury doctrine

Since it was unelected, the House of Lords rarely rejected a Bill in its entirety. Also, it usually accepted the principle that it should not defeat a government Bill at second reading if the proposed legislation was meeting a manifesto commitment of the governing party. This was known as the 'Salisbury doctrine' after the Conservative Leader of the Lords, Lord Salisbury, who, in 1945, suggested such a response to the legislative proposals of the newly elected Labour government. Lord Salisbury argued that, since the new Labour government had a clear mandate to introduce its nationalisation and welfare state measures, the Lords should not oppose them at second reading.

2. Scrutinising role

In 1998, the House of Lords examined the work of government through questions and select committees.

Although the Lords had no structure of departmental select committees on the Commons model, it could and did set up committees to investigate particular policy areas or subjects.

The Select Committee on European Communities

Particularly significant was the Select Committee on the European Communities. Through its six sub-committees, it investigated and reported on those European proposals which appeared to raise important questions of policy or principle, or other matters to which the committee felt the House should be alerted. These terms of reference were wider than those for its counterpart in the Commons since the Lords' committee could consider the merits of the proposals before it. The committee and its sub-committees had an administrative and secretarial support staff and could employ specialist advisers to assist in their investigations. The work done by the committee was widely admired by European decision makers and was often cited as a model that other EU members should follow (see Norton 1995).

Joint committee for scrutinising delegated legislation

In addition, there was a joint committee consisting of members of both Houses which played a scrutiny role over the form of delegated legislation known as 'statutory instruments':

> 'In order to reduce unnecessary pressure on parliamentary time, primary legislation often gives ministers or other authorities the power to regulate administrative details by means of secondary or 'delegated' legislation, most of which takes the form of Orders in Council, regulations and rules known as statutory instruments. These instruments are as much the law of the land as the Act of Parliament from which they are derived...There are about 2,000 statutory instruments each year.' (HMSO 1994, pp.77-78)

The limited powers of this joint committee, however, led to the criticism that Parliament's scrutiny over the growing volume and scope of delegated legislation was too weak. Following a proposal in 1992, the upper House set up a Delegated Powers Scrutiny Committee to consider the proposed powers to be delegated to ministers under new Bills. According to Rush, this was:

> 'An important development, extending significantly Parliament's scrutiny of secondary legislation.' (Rush 1994, p.33)

Question Time in the Lords

The House of Lords did have a daily Question Time in 1998, but the procedure was different from that in the Commons. For example, it was briefer (30 minutes maximum) and up to four starred questions were answered per day (but no more than one question tabled by a particular Lord):

> 'Starred questions are so-called because they appear on the order paper with an asterisk against them. They are asked in order to obtain

specific information, and not with a view to making a speech or raising a debate, although supplementaries may be asked. In addition "unstarred" (debatable) questions may be asked at the end of business on any day, when speeches may be made.' (HMSO 1994, pp.91-92)

3. Deliberative role

In 1998, debates were held on specific matters of policy or on topical issues, but, although there were whips, party lines were not so rigidly adhered to as in the Commons. By 1998, the House of Lords had a reputation for holding high level debates - though some commentators were sceptical about this and claimed that such a view was held most strongly by the peers themselves who had a vested interest in maintaining their privileged position. Politically, it was not the quality of the debate that was significant but the extent to which a debate had an effect or influence. Adonis suggested:

'Lords debates may not entirely be without influence, but they rarely make an impact which is more than minor and indirect.' (Adonis 1993, p.216)

4. Legitimating role

As an elected body, it was the House of Commons which had the chief legitimating role in Parliament. But, according to Rush (1994), the House of Lords also contributed to legitimacy in the sense that it also gave formal approval to Bills which passed through it.

5. Judicial role

Unlike the Commons, in 1998 the House of Lords had a judicial function. It should be noted, however, that this was a specialised role, divorced from the main proceedings and functions of the House. It was also a role in which the vast majority of peers could take no part. When the House sat as the highest court of appeal, only the Law Lords, including the Lord Chancellor, could take part.

Main points - Sections 3.1-3.2

- At the beginning of 1999, the House of Lords was an unelected body composed of Lords Temporal (hereditary and life peers) and Lords Spiritual (bishops).
- The layout of the Lords was similar to that of the Commons and business in the Lords was carried out 'through the usual channels'. The Lord Chancellor chaired sessions in the Lords, but peers regulated their own proceedings.
- Although there was a party system in the Lords, there were many crossbenchers. In practice, about two-thirds of crossbenchers voted with the Conservatives.
- The role of the House of Lords could be divided into five: (1) legislative role - delaying, revising and initiating Bills; (2) scrutinising role - checking government policies and administration; (3) deliberative role - holding debates on major issues and policies; (4) legitimising role; and (5) judicial role - acting as the highest court of appeal in the UK.

Activity 14.7 The functions of the Lords in the 1990s

Item A The House of Lords in session

This photograph shows the House of Lords during a debate held in 1994.

Item B The functions of Parliament in 1994

Function	Performed by	
	House of Commons	House of Lords
Legitimising	X[a]	x
Representative	X	x
Financial	X	x
Redressing of grievances	X	x
Legislative	X	x
Recruitment of ministers	X	x
Scrutinising and informing	X	x
Judicial		X[b]

a X indicates the more important of the two Houses in performing a particular function, x the less important.
b performed exclusively by Law Lords.

This table shows the functions performed by Parliament as a whole and the relative importance of each House.

Adapted from Rush 1994.

Item C   *The Lords in the 1990s*

(i) Educational and social background of peers in 1997

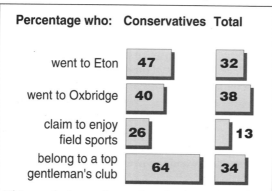

This graph shows the results of a survey into the educational and social background of peers conducted in 1997.

(ii) Labour peers by age, 1995

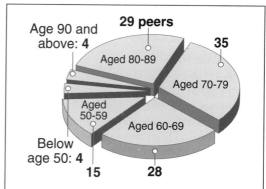

This graph shows the results of a survey into the age of Labour peers conducted in 1995.

According to House of Lords statistics, attendance by hereditary peers in 1996-97 was very patchy with nearly one-third (198) failing to attend on even one day during the 1996-97 session. A *Labour Research* analysis of peers' educational background shows that nine out of ten hereditary peers attended public school. There were 290 Old Etonians among the 561 hereditary peers whose educational origins could be identified. Over half (283 out of 591) of hereditary peers were educated at Oxford or Cambridge universities with the Royal Military Academy, Sandhurst, proving a popular alternative. A *Labour Research* analysis of the 2,000 or so Stock Exchange companies shows that a Lord on the board is very desirable, with overall 119 Lords holding 201 directorships in such companies. Although backbench peers are not paid for being members of the House of Lords, they can claim expenses for each day's attendance. These include a maximum of £78 overnight subsistence, £34.50 daily subsistence, £33.50 secretarial assistance and, depending on where they live, certain travel expenses.

Adapted from *Labour Research*, December 1997.

Item D   *Activity in the House of Lords 1950-96*

Activity	1950	1959-60	1989-90	1995-96	Percentage increase 1950-60	Percentage increase 1959-90	Percentage increase 1990-96
Average daily attendance	86	136	318	372	58	134	17
Sitting days	100	113	147	136	13	30	-7.5
Sitting hours	294	450	1,072	935	53	138	-13
Length of sitting (hrs.mins)	2.57	4.00	7.21	6.53	36	84	-9
Sittings after 10pm	1	1	74	60	0	7,300	-19

This table shows how active peers were in the period 1950-96.

Adapted from Rush 1994 and the House of Lords Information Office, May 1998.

Item E   *Party affiliation in the House of Lords*

Party	Life peers	Hereditary peers of first creation	Hereditary peers by succession	Lords Spiritual	Total
Con	168	4	302		**474**
Lab	139	1	16		**156**
Lib Dem	43	0	24		**67**
Crossbench	118	4	201		**323**
Other	11	0	82	26	**119**
Total	**479**	**9**	**625**	**26**	**1,139**

This table shows the party strengths in the Lords in May 1998.

Information from the House of Lords Information Office, May 1998.

Questions

1. How did the powers and procedures of the House of Lords differ from those of the Commons in the 1990s? Use Items A, B and D in your answer.

2. Using Items A-C, give arguments for and against the view that the House of Lords played an important role in the British political system in the 1990s.

3. a) What does Item C tell us about the nature of the House of Lords in the 1990s?
   b) How might the composition of the Lords have affected the way in which it functioned?

4. a) What does Item E tell us about the balance of power within the House of Lords in 1998?
   b) What are the political implications of this?

3.3 The Lords and reform

Criticisms of the Lords

Dissatisfaction with the composition, and even the existence, of the unreformed House of Lords is not new. The main criticism has been that, as an unelected body which is not accountable to the electorate, it is an undemocratic institution.

Two further criticisms have been made of the unreformed House of Lords. First, some people object to the fact that life peers are appointed on the recommendation of the Prime Minister (since this gives the Prime Minister the power of patronage). And second, some people argue that the hereditary principle is outdated and not appropriate in the modern world. Not only is the hereditary principle outdated, they argue, it also helps to restrict the social composition of the House (peers tend to be wealthy, white, privately-educated males with a narrow range of interests, as Item C in Activity 14.7 shows). Heredity and patronage, critics argue, can no longer be justified as the basis for choosing part of the legislature. In other words, it is a matter of political principle that those chosen to make political decisions should be chosen by the electorate in an election since elections ensure that representatives are, in some sense, accountable for their actions. Unelected decision makers are accountable to nobody but themselves.

Reform of the Lords - the alternatives

Those who agree that the House of Lords needs to be reformed fall into two categories:

- those who support the idea of outright abolition (in which the second chamber is dismantled and not replaced)
- those who support reform of the House of Lords (but the retention of a second chamber).

1. Outright abolition

Those who argue that the House of Lords should simply be abolished (and not replaced) emphasise that Britain would not be alone if it only had a single legislative chamber. A number of other countries, such as Denmark, Israel, New Zealand and Sweden operate in this way. After all, the only formal legislative power exercised by the current House of Lords is the power to delay the passage of a Bill. If the House of Commons is determined that a piece of legislation should reach the statute book, there is nothing that the Lords can do about it in the long term. Given that the House of Lords' main function is to provide a checking mechanism, there is no reason why a similar checking mechanism could not be built into a single chamber system.

An alternative argument used by abolitionists is as follows. The Lords' power of delay, coupled with what, in effect, is an in-built Conservative majority in the Lords, could prevent a government from completing its legislative programme in the year before a general election. The way to prevent this happening is to abolish the second chamber.

A third argument relates to the fact that Britain is a unitary state and not a federal state (see Chapter 4, Section 3.1):

> 'One of the commonest rationales for having a second chamber is in federal systems, in which the lower house is popularly elected in proportion to the distribution of the population and the upper house represents, usually though not always on an equal status, the states or constituent parts of the federation. The most well known case is the United States' Senate which consists of 100 members, two from each state, regardless of population or geographical size.' (Rush 1994, p.35)

Since Britain does not have a federal system, there is, therefore, no need for a second chamber.

2. Retention but reform

Those who argue that the House of Lords should be reformed but retained fall into two main groups:

(i) All members should be elected

One group argues that a second chamber should be retained and should perform pretty much the same functions that are performed by the unreformed House, but its members should be elected (perhaps by a system of proportional election). Since the members of this new, elected second chamber would not be Lords, most supporters of this type of reform support the idea that this new chamber should be given a new name (such as 'Senate'). Those in favour of this type of reform argue that it is the only way to ensure that the second chamber is democratically accountable.

(ii) At least some members should be appointed

The second group argues that what is needed is reform but not abolition. One view is that hereditary peers should be banned from voting, leaving the legislative function of the Lords in the hands of life peers (the majority of whom would be distinguished former MPs with a wealth of experience). A second view is that the House should be made up of a mixture of elected and unelected peers. Such a solution was favoured by a committee of Conservative peers, chaired by Lord Home, in 1978. This committee recommended that two-thirds of members should be elected on a regional basis and the remaining third should be appointed on the advice of the Prime Minister. Supporters of this line argue that this is a pragmatic stance (it has a better chance of being brought into practice than outright abolition or replacing the Lords with a completely elected second chamber). They also argue that it solves the main problem with the Lords (namely, the hereditary element). Finally, they argue that retention of life peers is beneficial since these peers provide a wealth of experience which would be lacking if all members were elected to the second chamber.

Arguments against a unicameral Parliament

Those who agree that it is necessary to have a second chamber argue that a second chamber performs a number of important functions which would either not be performed or would be performed inadequately if there was no second chamber:

> 'It is not difficult to demonstrate that the House of Lords performs a number of useful functions. None could be described as vital to the body politic, but, equally, it is not difficult to demonstrate that its health would suffer were these performed less adequately or not at all. Were the House of Lords abolished and Westminster became a unicameral Parliament - Labour's policy in its 1983 election manifesto - then the burden of work carried by the upper House would fall on the House of Commons or not be done at all...As it is, the Commons meets as frequently or more frequently than any other legislative chamber in the world.' (Rush 1997, p.26)

Labour's intended reforms

The Labour government elected in 1997 made a manifesto commitment to reform the House of Lords:

> 'The House of Lords must be reformed. As an initial, self-contained reform, not dependent on further reform in the future, the right of hereditary peers to sit and vote in the House of Lords will be ended by statute. This will be the first stage in a process of reform to make the House of Lords more democratic and representative. The legislative powers of the House of Lords will remain unaltered...A committee of both Houses of Parliament will be appointed to undertake a wide-ranging review of possible further change and then to bring forward proposals for reform.' (Labour 1997, pp.32-3)

In January 1998, the new Cabinet committee set up to discuss reform of the Lords met for the first time. In November 1998, it was announced in Labour's second Queen's Speech that a Bill would be put forward to abolish the right of hereditary peers to sit and vote in the House of Lords.

Attempts to reform the Lords in the past have met with concerted opposition. In 1969, for example, Harold Wilson's government sponsored a Bill which proposed the phasing out of hereditary membership of the Lords and its eventual replacement with an entirely nominated membership. This Bill failed because an unusual alliance of Labour backbenchers on the left (who argued that the Bill did not go far enough) and Conservative backbenchers on the right (who argued that the Bill went too far) was able to

squash the Bill as it went through its committee stage.

Some of those who favour abolition of the House of Lords are fearful of the Labour government's decision to attempt reform in stages. Roy Hattersley, himself appointed as a life peer in 1997, for example, supports a 'big bang' approach:

> 'The appointment of life peers is almost as bad as hereditary peers since they rely on the patronage of party leaders. I have always been a unicameralist. The House of Lords should be abolished or totally replaced. There are better things for the House of Commons to do than fight the Lords.' (*Guardian*, 30 September 1997)

Arguments against reform

Arguments against reform of the Lords can be divided into two main categories:

- negative arguments - arguments which focus on the problems that might arise from an elected second chamber
- positive arguments - arguments based on the idea that the current system works well and any other system might not work as well.

1. Negative arguments

The Commons would lose legitimacy

First, it is argued that the House of Commons derives its seniority and legitimacy, in part, from being the only elected chamber. If both chambers were elected, then this would detract from the legitimacy of the Commons:

> 'The House of Commons is acknowledged as the superior of the two Houses of Parliament precisely because it is the elected chamber; an elected second chamber would secure a significant degree of democratic legitimacy which the House of Lords, at present, inevitably lacks. Second, if elections for the second chamber were held at a different time, possibly on a staggered basis with a proportion of the membership retiring at regular intervals (as with the US Senate), then the more recently elected chamber might claim or be seen to have greater legitimacy because it reflected a more recent expression of public opinion.' (Rush 1994, pp.36-7)

Parties would dominate

A second argument is that, if the second chamber were elected, it would almost certainly become dominated by the political parties. This would change the nature of the second chamber. At present, it is argued, partisanship in the Lords is limited and, as a result, mature and rational examination of government proposals and policy is possible. If party politics became more intense, there would be less room for the development of consensus and constructive criticism.

Constituents would apply pressure

And third, it is argued that, if the second chamber were elected, then its members would have constituents. These constituents would put pressure on the members and these pressures might conflict with the pressures put on MPs by their constituents. This could lead to conflict between the two chambers.

2. Positive arguments

An unreformed House of Lords is supported by some because they believe it works well and there is a danger that any alternative system would not work as well. This argument is put forward in a variety of ways.

A revival since 1958

First, supporters of an unreformed House of Lords claim that there has been a revival of the Lords since the introduction of life peers in 1958. Norton notes that:

> 'In the 1940s, the House [of Lords] had a membership of over 800, but of those "only about 100 attend regularly and of these about 60 of them take an active part in its business" (Gordon 1948, p.139). The House rarely met for more than three days a week and on those days would often sit for no more than three hours. Votes were rare and when they were taken peers voted on party lines...Limited powers and limited activity led to little interest in the House.' (Norton 1993, p.26)

Norton goes on to argue that, since the early 1970s, there has been a major revival in the activities performed by the House:

> 'Over the past 20 years the daily attendance has increased...The House now sits on more days and, for longer hours, than it did in previous decades. Votes have also become more frequent, as have government defeats... From 1979 to 1990, the Thatcher government suffered just over 150 defeats at the hands of their Lordships.' (Norton 1993, p.27)

This revival in the activities performed by the Lords, it is argued, proves that the House of Lords can perform an important role.

Advantages over the Commons

Second, it has been argued that an unreformed House of Lords has a number of advantages over the Commons:

- the House of Lords is able to deal with the details of legislation more thoroughly than the Commons and has the opportunity to scrutinise delegated legislation
- the House of Lords examines proposed European legislation more closely than the Commons
- the quality of debates and select committee work in the Lords is high
- the Lords perform a crucial role as a check on the executive.

The 'real opposition'

And third, during the 1980s and early 1990s supporters of an unreformed House of Lords argued that, while the Conservatives remained in power between 1979 and 1997, the Lords became the 'real opposition' to government. Since Margaret Thatcher and then John Major were able to rely on overall majorities in the Commons, opposition in the Commons often appeared to be impotent. There was, after all, nothing the Labour Party could do to prevent the passage of legislation so long as the Conservative government managed to retain the support of all its MPs. Whilst the opposition in the Commons was unable to inflict parliamentary defeats on the government, the Lords did occasionally vote against the government (not that this made much difference in the long term since the government could rely on its Commons majority to overturn Lords' amendments). Ironically, therefore, supporters of an unreformed (undemocratic) House of Lords used the argument that it was the House of Lords which had protected and strengthened democracy during a long period of one-party rule.

Main points - Section 3.3

- **The main criticism of the unreformed House of Lords is that, as an unelected body which is not accountable to the electorate, it is an undemocratic institution.**
- **Some people argue that the House of Lords should simply be abolished and Britain should be governed by a single chamber.**
- **Those who argue that the House of Lords should be reformed but retained fall into two main groups: those who believe all members of the second chamber should be elected and those who believe**

- some or all members should be nominated.
- **The Labour government elected in 1997 made a manifesto pledge to reform the House of Lords. A Bill abolishing the right of hereditary peers to vote in the Lords was included in the Queen's speech in November 1998.**
- **The arguments against reform of the Lords can be negative (anything that replaces the current system would be worse) or positive (the Lords is doing a good job).**

Activity 14.8   Reforming the Lords

Item A   *In support of reform by stages*

Only one thing might yet come to the rescue of the hereditaries. It is what has saved them from every other attempt at reform - lack of agreement about what to put in their place. Labour's present plan is to put nothing in their place. Not immediately, anyway. A Cabinet committee chaired by the Lord Chancellor is currently considering what powers a reformed upper House is to enjoy. This raises the age-old problem. If a second chamber agrees with the first, it is useless. If it disagrees, it is dangerous. The more democratic Labour makes the upper House, the more likely it will be to challenge the supremacy of the Commons and the more legitimacy and authority it will claim. This has prevented reform in the past. The lesson of the 1960s is that it is best to proceed in stages. That leaves Labour open to the charge of creating a mega-quango of prime ministerial stooges. This charge can be answered by taking the power of appointment away from the Prime Minister and giving it to a robustly independent body. The half-reformed Lords will be a quango. But, better a quango of the living than a quango of the dead. Stripping out the hereditaries is an imperfect staging post to full reform. There's a risk that the government will find seductive reasons to stop there. But, we should not permit the perfect to become the enemy of the good. I can think of few more appropriate ways of celebrating the new millennium than removing from Parliament people whose seats depend on their birth certificates.

Adapted from the *Observer*, 8 February 1998.

Item B   *Against reform by stages*

If the power of hereditary peers is illegitimate because it has never been subject to democratic consent, then the same formula surely applies to the power of appointed peers. The trouble is that, once hereditary peers have been stripped of some of their powers, the wider reform of the House of Lords looks likely to be quietly dumped. A second chamber controlled by appointees is simply too convenient to discard. Yet, with a few striking exceptions, appointments to the House of Lords amount to a monumental role of dishonour. Life peerages are handed to people who have performed 'political services' (stuffing their party's pockets), 'services to wealth creation' (stuffing their own pockets), or 'public services' (stuffing the rest of us). When hereditary peers have been stripped of their voting rights, the gigantic, politically-appointed quango which remains is likely to regard its power over the life of the nation as doubly legitimate. So how should we replace it? Should we encourage the government to establish an elected second house as soon as possible? This carries the danger of constructing a rival decision-making body, rather than an effective revising chamber. If a second chamber is to perform as a corrective to the excesses of power, might it not be appropriate to fill it with the utterly powerless, those who would never be chosen by a party machine or for a grace and favour appointment? Ordinary citizens could, like members of a jury, be selected at random. We might even discover a socially useful role for the Lottery - a booby prize of a year's attendance in the upper House which would be recognised not as a privilege but as a terrible duty.

Adapted from the *Guardian*, 29 July 1997.

Item C   *Brick's view of the House of Lords*

Item D *Does Britain need a second chamber?*

Does Britain need a second chamber?

NO

**(a) How could the Commons cope with the extra work currently done by the Lords?
(b) Who would act as a check on the Commons? For example, what if the government wanted to prolong its own life indefinitely?**

YES

Should it be elected?

NO

How would you defend the undemocratic nature of an unelected second chamber?

YES

**(a) Who would choose the candidates?
(b) An elected second chamber could claim equivalent legitimacy and authority to the Commons. What problems would this produce?**

Questions

1. a) Using Items A and B, give arguments for and against reform of the Lords by stages.
   b) Draw up a paper outlining the issues that the Cabinet committee considering Lords reform should discuss.
   c) What would be the merits and drawbacks of implementing the jury system of appointment suggested in Item B?

2. Describe the three types of second chamber illustrated in Item C. Which does the cartoonist favour? Explain how you know.

3. Follow your preferred pathway through Item D answering the questions you encounter. Explain why you did not choose one of the other pathways.

Part 4 How effective is Parliament?

Key issues

1. What criteria are used to judge Parliament's effectiveness?
2. Using these criteria, how effective is Parliament?

4.1 Limits on the power of Parliament

Expectations and effectiveness

Whether or not Parliament is judged to be effective depends on what expectations are held about Parliament's role in British politics today. It is not unusual now for Parliament to appear to be bypassed and, therefore, to have less of an essential function than in earlier periods. The growth, specialisation and professionalisation of the civil service, the increased influence of pressure groups on ministers and departments and the impact of the mass media have all contributed to this apparent decline. Given the party system in Parliament, it is certainly unrealistic for Parliament to govern the country or to control the government. But this is nothing new. It is doubtful if Parliament has ever really been in such a position to govern the country or control the government. Even in the 'golden age' of Parliament in the early 19th century (before the extension of the franchise led to the development of the party system), Parliament's power was limited. Yet, given these limits on the powers of Parliament, it is still pertinent to consider how effective Parliament is in carrying out its functions - especially its legislative and scrutiny functions:

Changing the law

All proposals to change the law have to be passed by Parliament. Yet, in the main, what this means is that Parliament gives its approval to measures that have been drawn up elsewhere - either by the British government or by the European Union. As far as domestic legislation is concerned, Parliament is, at most, a reviser of Bills that are prepared in Whitehall and given priority by the government.

Maintaining the government's majority

The operation of the party system means that Parliament functions to maintain the government's majority. Parliament does have the power to throw a government out, but it rarely uses this power. In fact, it can be argued, sustaining a government has become the prime task of Parliament and it is true to say that most members of Parliament (especially in the Commons) act as party politicians most of the time. In other words, most MPs (and peers) who support the government are likely to regard their primary role as supporting the government.

Scrutinising the executive

It is also the job of Parliament to scrutinise the executive, and this gives rise to something of a paradox. How can Parliament scrutinise the executive effectively when most of its members see their primary role as maintaining a majority for their government? One way round this problem is for Parliament to gain a degree of independence from government and, in recent years, there have been signs that this is happening. For example, the work done by select committees (see Section 2.3 above) and the readiness of the House of Lords to amend government Bills (in the initial stages of a Bill's passage through Parliament at least) are both signs that Parliament is willing to investigate and object to the work of government. The upper House has also set up mechanisms to scrutinise European legislation and the work of the EU bureaucracy - though few people would pretend that parliamentary scrutiny in this increasingly important area is anywhere near satisfactory. Indeed, greater European integration in the future (whether economic or political) is likely to decrease the influence and relevance of Parliament (see, for example, Norton 1995).

Parliament and finances

Perhaps the limits to parliamentary effectiveness are best illustrated by Parliament's lack of any real say in financial matters. The House of Lords' influence over financial matters has long since disappeared, but does the House of Commons fare any better? There are, of course, the formal processes in the Commons where MPs give approval to the Budget proposals (in the form of the annual Finance Bill) and to the government's 'estimates' (which set out the amounts required for each government department for the following year). On occasion, these formal processes can yield change - for example, the debate over the Budget in 1994 resulted in a government climbdown over an increase in VAT for fuel after Conservative backbenchers voted against the measure. But, such rebellions are unusual and they can only bring a government defeat if the

government commands a small overall majority (or is extremely incompetent). For the most part, the government's financial proposals are rubber stamped by Parliament. In addition, it is true that it is the role of the Public Accounts Committee to find out whether public money has been spent wisely and to investigate cases of overspending. Nevertheless, it is the government (not Parliament) which has, in the words of Harold Wilson, 'complete control' over expenditure. Ordinary MPs, for example, cannot formally propose an increase in taxation.

Main points - Part 4

- In practice, it is unrealistic to expect Parliament to govern the country or to control the government. Rather, its effectiveness should be judged by considering how well it performs its legislative and scrutinising functions.
- In recent years, there is some evidence of Parliament gaining a degree of independence from government.
- Nevertheless, on the whole, Parliament is restrained by the government's ability to command a majority (in all but exceptional circumstances). This is particularly true when it comes to financial matters.
- Commentators are divided about how effective Parliament is today, though few would argue for its abolition.

Activity 14.9 How effective is Parliament?

Item A Peter Riddell's view

According to those who argue that Parliament is ineffective, the House of Commons is a rubber stamp - a loud, self-indulgent sideshow whose actors are kept in line by the party whips. Peter Riddell, however, argues that the idea that Parliament is ineffective is false. On the contrary, he claims, Parliament remains as central as it ever has been. This conclusion is reached by considering Parliament's role. According to Riddell, Parliament's central role is to set up a government which meets the wishes of the voters (as expressed at general elections) and to put that government's programme into practice. In addition, Parliament has other functions - to provide an outlet for public opinion, to teach and inform society and to legislate, for example. These functions are still performed by Parliament. Even a government with a clear overall majority has to listen to its supporters (and critics), make concessions and respond to demands. Similarly, the government cannot avoid dealing with issues that are raised in Parliament (albeit mainly in the Commons) - the Commons provides an arena in which the issues of concern to the nation are voiced. But, most crucially, political careers are built up and broken down in Parliament. Parliament provides the pool from which members of the government are chosen. It also ensures that the executive is accountable in the sense that ministers are answerable to Parliament for their actions.

Adapted from Riddell 1989.

Item B Andrew Adonis' view

Andrew Adonis argues that Parliament performs an important scrutiny role which has been strengthened in recent years by the development of the committee system (in both the Commons and the Lords) and by the rise of a new generation of full-time and more independent-minded MPs. He claims that what makes Parliament effective is that, although it does not govern itself, government takes place through Parliament. As a result, parliamentary committees are able to scrutinise the work of government, whilst the televising of Parliament means that ordinary voters can themselves scrutinise the behaviour of government and parliamentary activity. Adonis notes that, despite popular cynicism about politicians, social attitude surveys show a significant increase in people's readiness to attempt to influence decisions and in the perception of their ability to do so. This activity is focused on Parliament and, therefore, suggests that Parliament has an important role to play. Adonis does concede, however, that there is widespread public discontent with the quality of parliamentary representation and government, and that less and less government is taking place through Parliament because of the growing influence of European institutions.

Adapted from Adonis 1993.

Item C *Brick's view of the effectiveness of Parliament*

Item D *Philip Norton's view*

Philip Norton evaluates the effectiveness of Parliament by asking a number of questions. What would the British political system be like if Parliament did not exist? How would the government be chosen? Who or what would represent citizens and confer legitimacy on the actions of government? Who would champion the views of ordinary citizens? What forum would allow for the expression of conflicting views? Norton acknowledges that, in answering most of the above questions, it is possible to come up with an alternative to Parliament. The press, for example, champions the views of ordinary citizens. The National Audit Office and the media scrutinise the action of government. Ministerial actions can be challenged in court. Conflicting views can be expressed through opinion polls, television debates and referendums. Despite this, Norton argues, what makes Parliament distinctive and indispensable is the fact that it enjoys the popular as well as the formal legitimacy to undertake all these tasks. This legitimacy, he claims, has been enhanced by the greater degree of scrutiny undertaken by Parliament over recent years and the greater willingness of MPs to take on greater amounts of constituency casework and a more active role as interrogators of government.

Adapted from Norton 1985 and 1993.

Item E *Tony Wright's view*

Tony Wright asserts that, after four years in the House of Commons, he believes that Parliament doesn't really exist at all. He notes that a Labour MP recently remarked that it wasn't the job of the opposition to scrutinise and improve government legislation. Neither is it the business of government backbenchers - otherwise the whips would soon be all over them. So, he asks, whose job is it? His stark answer is that it is nobody's job. Parliament does not exist collectively at all. What exists is government and opposition - engaged in a never-ending election campaign on the floor and in the committee rooms of the House of Commons. The only rules of the game are those agreed by the players themselves and lubricated by the 'usual channels' of the party managers. There is nobody to speak for the public interest or to suggest that people are not well served by this cosy self-regulation. Government and opposition conspire to prevent reform to the system, Wright concludes, as they both benefit from it. The only losers are the public.

Adapted from Wright 1997.

Item F *Hugo Young's view*

Who governs Britain - Parliament or people? This is the question which Hugo Young posed in October 1997. According to Young, New Labour's incessant references to 'the people' are a dangerous ploy. The idea of a 'People's Britain' runs against the grain of British life and the British constitution. 'The people' is an entity which sits easily with direct democracy but is out of place in a parliamentary system where the popular will works through the filter of representative democracy. Parliament, not 'the people', is sovereign - an arrangement which constrains the power of demagogues (politicians who do what is popular not what is in the public interest) and protects minorities. Young concedes that greater consideration of the popular will can be beneficial and he applauds the Blair government's record use of referendums. But, he warns, the desire to bypass Parliament has a dangerous side. The Commons, he points out, is an elected body whilst the new focus group set up to keep ministers in touch with what the people are really thinking is not (this focus group is made up of 5,000 nominees and paid for by government funds). The people, Young concludes, are being told what is good for them and then being praised as the authors of policies they've had none but the vaguest role in putting together. The problem is that all critics, including those in Parliament, are in danger of being swept aside by a version of democratic bullying.

Adapted from the *Guardian*, 2 October 1997.

Questions

1. 'Parliament is no longer central to British politics'. Do you agree? Use Items A-F in your answer.
2. Identify points of agreement and disagreement amongst Items A-F.
3. Which of Items A and B. D, E and F support the view expressed in Item B? Explain how you reached your answer.
4. In what ways could Parliament be reformed to ensure that it performed its functions more effectively?

References

Adonis (1993) Adonis, A., *Parliament Today*, Manchester University Press, 1993.

Alderman (1995) Alderman, K., 'The government whips', *Politics Review*, Vol.4.4, April 1995.

Baggott (1995) Baggott, R., 'Putting the squeeze on sleaze? The Nolan Committee and standards in public life', *Talking Politics*, Vol.8.1, Autumn 1995.

Borthwick (1997) Borthwick, R.L., 'Changes in the House of Commons', *Politics Review*, Vol.6.3, February 1997.

Downs (1985) Downs, S.J., 'Select committees: experiment and establishment' in *Norton (1985)*.

Drewry (1989) Drewry, G., 'The new select committees - nine years on', *Social Studies Review*, Vol.4.4, 1989.

Gordon (1948) Gordon, S., *Our Parliament* (3rd edn), Hansard Society, 1948.

HMSO (1994) Central Office of Information, *Parliament*, HMSO, 1994.

Jordon & Richardson (1987) Jordon A.G. & Richardson, J.J., *British Politics and the Policy Process*, Allen & Unwin, 1987.

Labour (1997) *New Labour - Because Britain Deserves Better*, Labour Party manifesto, Labour Party, 1997.

Lancaster (1997) Lancaster, S. (ed.), *Developments in Politics*, Vol.8, Causeway Press, 1997.

Norton (1985) Norton, P. (ed.), *Parliament in the 1980s*, Blackwell, 1985.

Norton (1991) Norton, P., 'Committees in the House of Commons', *Politics Review*, Vol.1.1. September 1991.

Norton (1992) Norton, P., 'A reform Parliament?', *The House Magazine*, 22 June 1992.

Norton (1993) Norton, P., *Does Parliament Matter?*, Harvester Wheatsheaf, 1993.

Norton (1994) Norton, P., 'Select committees in the House of Commons: watchdogs or poodles?', *Politics Review*, Vol.4.2, November 1994.

Norton (1995) Norton, P., 'Standing committees in the House of Commons', *Politics Review*, Vol.4.4, April 1995.

Norton (1995a) Norton, P., 'Resourcing select committees', *Talking Politics*, Vol.8.1, Autumn 1995.

Richards (1988) Richards, P.G., *Mackintosh's The Government and Politics of Britain* (7th edn), Hutchinson, 1988.

Riddell (1989) Riddell, P., 'In defence of Parliament', *Contemporary Record*, Vol.3.1, Autumn 1989.

Rush (1994) Rush, M., 'The House of Lords, end it or mend it?', in *Wale (1994)*.

Rush (1997) Rush, M., 'Thinking about the Constitution', in *Lancaster (1997)*.

Sedgemore (1995) Sedgemore, B., *An Insider's Guide to Parliament*, Icon, 1995.

Wale (1994) Wale, W. (ed), *Developments in Politics*, Vol.5, Causeway Press, 1994.

Wright (1997) Wright, T., 'Does Parliament work?', *Talking Politics*, Vol.9.3, Spring 1997.

15 Management of the economy

Introduction

The management of the economy is a central task of modern government. Indeed, it is often the yardstick by which a government is judged. The ability to manage the economy in a way which is perceived as being successful is one of the keys to re-election. Governments, therefore, give a very high priority to the development of economic policies.

Since 1945, public (government) spending has risen dramatically because central government has become responsible for the financing of the welfare state. The National Health Service and Social Security, for example, both require the expenditure of huge sums of public money. Exactly how much money should be raised to be spent on these and on other areas of the economy is a key problem that must be faced by every government. The decisions that are taken affect every person in the country - whether they are taxpayers faced with a larger or smaller tax burden or people who rely on state benefits.

This chapter looks at the economic theories which have dominated post-war economic policy and at the ways in which these economic theories have been translated into practice. It examines the ways in which economic decisions are made and the pressures that are exerted on decision makers both from within the governmental system and from outside.

Chapter summary

Part 1 looks at different economic theories and how British governments have attempted to translate the theory into practice.

Part 2 examines Britain's economic decline. When did it start, what caused it and what consequences has it had?

Part 3 analyses the development of economic policy since 1985. What were the main features of economic mangement under John Major and during the Labour government's first 18 months in power? How have moves towards a single

European currency affected Britain?

Part 4 focuses on the way in which economic decisions are made. What is the role of the Treasury and the Chancellor? Why is the Budget so important? What are the external influences on economic decision making?

Part 5 discusses the raising of taxes. What is the difference between direct and indirect taxation? How is the money raised from taxation used? Should income tax be higher or lower?

Part 1 Economic theories and their translation into practice

Key issues

1. What is laissez faire economics?
2. How does Keynesian economics differ from laissez faire economics?
3. What is Monetarism?

1.1 Industrialisation

The first industrial nation

Britain was the first country to become industrialised. In the short term, this gave Britain an economic advantage. In the longer term, it proved to be a burden.

It is impossible to date the beginning of the Industrial Revolution precisely. There is no single event that can be said to have sparked it off. Rather, it was a process that gathered momentum as it became established. By 1750, this process was underway. By 1900, Britain was an industrial nation.

The Industrial Revolution brought immense change to Britain. Perhaps the key development was the growth of mass production which was made possible by the increasing use of mechanisation. The invention of new machines and new methods of powering them encouraged the growth of industry, new modes of transport and new ways of working. A rapid growth of population, linked to changes in agriculture and the growth of industry, resulted in the expansion of towns and cities. This brought a new way of life and new problems.

Industrialisation did not just have an impact domestically. Mass production produced a surplus which could be sold abroad. Britain's trade with other countries grew rapidly. Also, the need to secure new markets overseas (as well other factors such as a mission to 'civilise' newly discovered areas) led to the growth of a huge overseas Empire.

Since Britain was the first country to become industrialised, its manufacturing output in the late 18th and early 19th centuries far exceeded that of other countries. But, as other countries developed industries of their own, their output grew and they were able to compete with and sometimes overtake Britain (see Box 15.1). This experience - of leading the field and then being caught up and overtaken by competitors - had an important effect on economic thinking in Britain in the 20th century.

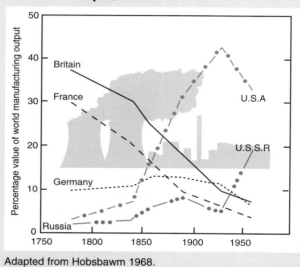

Box 15.1 Share of world manufacturing output, 1750-1960

Adapted from Hobsbawm 1968.

A capitalist economy

Industrialisation in Britain was piecemeal. It relied upon individual initiative. New industrial enterprises were set up and owned by private individuals. On the whole, central government did not encourage or attempt to organise economic development. It certainly did not attempt to gain ownership of the new industrial enterprises.

An industrial country whose wealth (ie land, raw materials and businesses) is owned mainly by individuals rather than by the state is a capitalist country. In simple terms, those who own and control the wealth are capitalists whilst the people they employ are workers. Although the capitalists are fewer in number than the workers, they tend to acquire political as well as economic power. As a result, the economic beliefs of capitalists usually determine the economic policies adopted by governments.

Capitalists have a particular interest in how much the government intervenes in the management of the economy because government regulations often add to the costs of running businesses. The government's

decision to impose a minimum wage, for example, means that employers paying very low wages are forced to pay out more money in wages. Those capitalists who want minimal government intervention can be said to support 'laissez faire' economics.

1.2 Laissez faire economics

What are laissez faire economics?

Laissez faire is French for 'leave alone'. Supporters of laissez faire economics oppose government intervention. They want a free market in which the government leaves them alone. The case for a laissez faire approach to economics was first expressed in the 18th century by Adam Smith in his *An Enquiry into the Nature and Causes of the Wealth of Nations* (Smith 1776). He argued that producers should not be subject to any restrictions. They should be free to supply products at the price consumers are willing to pay. Provided that competition was fair, he argued, the 'invisible hand' of the market would allocate resources to everyone's advantage.

Supporters of laissez faire or 'free-market' economics accept that producers are primarily motivated by the desire to make profits. But, they argue, producers employ people, create wealth and distribute it. By employing people, they provide them with a means to live. By creating and distributing wealth they ensure that society as a whole becomes richer.

Laissez faire economics can be applied on a larger scale, too. The question of whether or not the British government should support a policy of free trade with its overseas trading partners has often been the cause of fierce debate.

Free trade versus protectionism

A country practising free trade refuses to protect its economy by imposing quotas limiting the number of goods which can be imported or by charging a tariff (a tax or duty) on goods which are imported into the country. So, suppose that Britain and France were practising free trade. If Britain imported cheese from France, no limit would be imposed on the amount of cheese that France could send over for sale, nor would a tariff be charged when that cheese arrived in Britain. Similarly, British firms producing beer would be able to export as much beer to France as they liked and they would not have to pay a tariff when it arrived in France.

The problem with free trade between countries is that it can affect domestic markets. Suppose, for example, that British people stopped buying British cheese because they preferred imported French cheese. Should the British government then intervene and protect the jobs of British cheese manufacturers? Supporters of free trade would argue against intervention. They would argue that the market should determine whether or not the British cheese manufacturers should survive. Besides, they argue, if the British government chose to protect British cheese manufacturers by imposing a quota or a tariff, then it is likely that the French would respond by imposing their own quotas and tariffs - on British beer, say. British beer exported to France would then rise in cost (because only a certain amount could be sold in France and because of the duty paid on it). This would adversely affect the British beer industry. In other words, by intervening the government would artificially protect an uncompetitive industry (the cheese manufacturers) whilst jeopardising the future of a competitive one (the beer industry). Free trade, on the other hand, would ensure that only those companies which are truly efficient and competitive survive.

Arguments in favour of protectionism
Supporters of protectionism use the following arguments to justify the imposition of tariffs and quotas. First, tariffs are a good way of raising revenue for the government without burdening voters with greater taxation. Second, the imposition of quotas or tariffs tends to raise the final price of a product (unless the foreign producer absorbs the extra cost). If the final price is higher, then it is easier for domestically produced products to compete. Quotas and tariffs, therefore, help domestic producers to remain viable. Third, a truly free market is a utopian idea. Since the economies of countries are so interlinked, every country in the world would have to agree not to impose any trading restrictions before a truly free market could be achieved. In reality, all countries choose to adopt protectionist policies to some extent. Rather than aiming for something that is simply unattainable, it is better to be realistic and to plan accordingly.

The choice
The debate between free trade and protectionism presents a choice between two ways of managing the economy. On the one hand, those who support free trade argue for a laissez faire approach. On the other hand, those who support protectionism believe that government has a positive role to play in the management of the economy.

1.3 Keynesianism

What is Keynesianism?
For much of the post-war period, British economic policy was based on the theories put forward by the economist J.M. Keynes (1883-1946). During the Great Depression of the 1930s, capitalist economies all over the world had slumped and millions of workers had lost their jobs. In 1936, Keynes published his *General Theory of Employment, Interest and Money* which put forward a theoretical framework to explain why the recessions which periodically hit capitalist economies happened and how they could be overcome.

Keynes rejected laissez faire policies which left the market to regulate wages and prices. He argued that, if it was left to itself, the market would stabilise at a point below its full capacity (ie in recession). Since companies tended to lay people off and to reduce wages during a recession, unemployment was then bound to rise and people were bound to have less money to spend. As a result, there would be an inevitable fall in demand for new goods. This fall in demand would intensify the recession. Even more people would be laid off and demand would fall still further. In other words, a vicious circle would take hold of the economy.

Keynes also rejected the socialist view that the economy could be stimulated by simple redistribution of wealth to the poor. He argued that redistribution of wealth would destroy any incentive to achieve.

Demand management
Keynes' solution was to argue that recessions could be overcome by government intervention. The government, he argued, should direct investment into new economic activity. Extra government spending and/or lower taxes would stimulate the economy. Instead of saving during a recession, governments should take the lead and borrow money to invest in new projects. These new projects would provide jobs and create wealth. The people who did these new jobs would have money to spend and, by spending this money, they would stimulate the economy. As a result of this stimulation, demand would increase and the economy would come out of recession.

So, what Keynes proposed was a 'demand management' in a mixed economy. He proposed a capitalist economy in which the government was prepared to intervene to achieve full employment and planned economic growth. In this mixed economy, if there was a rise in unemployment, the government would, if necessary, increase the Budget deficit by investing in new projects and lowering taxes. But equally, when there was full employment and demand was threatening to rise too much (ie the economy was beginning to overheat), the government would reduce the Budget deficit, for example by raising taxes. This would dampen down demand.

Butskellism
The term 'Butskellism' comes from the amalgamation of the names of two Chancellors of the Exchequer in the 1950s - R.A. Butler, Conservative Chancellor from 1951 to 1955, and H. Gaitskell, Labour Chancellor from 1950 to 1951. Although from different parties, both Chancellors pursued the same broad 'Keynesian' economic policies. Having established a consensus in the early 1950s, governments continued to work within it until the late 1970s. 'Butskellism', therefore,

is a term used to describe the management of the economy during the period of the post-war consensus (see also Chapter 3, Part 1).

The fundamental aim of governments during the period 1945-79 was to keep unemployment to a minimum and to maintain and improve the welfare state through increases in public expenditure. Keynesianism, therefore, became the economic orthodoxy. But, as Grant points out, the application of Keynes' theory was not undiluted:

> 'When discussing Keynesianism in Britain it is important to remember that what is being referred to is not the undiluted application of Keynes' ideas as set out in his *General Theory*, but rather a particular interpretation of Keynesian ideas by the Treasury. What the Treasury particularly liked about Keynesianism is that it offered the possibility of managing the economy without getting one's hands dirty. By manipulating the level of aggregate demand in the economy by increasing or decreasing taxes, it was seen as possible to influence key economic indicators, notably the trade-off between inflation and unemployment.' (Grant 1992, p.99)

Keynesian economics in the 1950s and 1960s

During the 1950s and 1960s, unemployment tended to fluctuate between 1% and 2% of the working population. There were never more than 1 million people unemployed at any one time during this period. And, whilst the unemployment figure remained low, other economic indicators remained favourable. Between 1950 and 1970, the rate of inflation averaged at 4.5% and, until 1969, stayed in single figures (inflation is a general sustained rise in the price level). During the same period, wages grew in real terms by 20% and, although Britain's rate of economic growth was lower than that of many of its rivals in Western Europe, it still remained at 2% a year on average. In June 1957, the Prime Minister Harold Macmillan felt able to boast:

> 'Let's be frank about it. Most of our people have never had it so good. Go around the country, go to the industrial towns, go to the farms and you will see a state of prosperity such as we have never had in my lifetime - nor indeed ever in the history of the country.' (Extract from a speech made in Bedford, 20 July 1957)

The successes Macmillan referred to were achieved by the application of the Keynesian mechanism of demand management.

The Stop-Go cycle

The problem with the system of demand management was that it was impossible to maintain a stable level of low unemployment over the long term. The economy still tended to move from mild boom to mild recession. When unemployment was low, growth was high. But, this brought higher inflation and a growing balance of payments deficit. By reducing demand, the balance of payments deficit was reduced and inflation curbed, but the economy then moved into mild recession and unemployment grew. A recession encouraged the government to intervene to increase the level of demand. As a result, the whole cycle began again. This process is known as the 'Stop-Go cycle'.

The breakdown of Keynesianism

The Stop-Go cycle was made worse in Britain by the existence of a fixed exchange rate in the 1950s and 1960s (an exchange rate is the price at which one currency is convertible into another). A strong pound made imports relatively cheap. As a result, when the economy moved into boom, consumers spent surplus income on imports. This produced an alarming balance of payments deficit which forced the government to intervene and slow down the economy. The problem was eased in 1967 when the pound was devalued (with the result that exports became cheaper and imports dearer). It remained, however, until a floating exchange rate was introduced in the 1970s.

Full employment and inflation

It could be argued that the Stop-Go cycle was an inevitable product of the application of Keynesian economics. The goal of Keynesian economics is full employment. When there is full employment, labour is, by definition, in short supply. This pushes up its price. If the price of labour increases then so does the price of goods. Suppose, for example, an employer grants a 10% wage rise, then, assuming that all other factors remain constant and assuming that wages make up 50% of the company's costs, the company's costs rise by 5%. These higher costs are then usually passed on to the customer in the form of higher prices. Higher prices lead to demands for higher wages. Higher prices and higher wages on a large scale produce inflation. So, Keynesian policies with their goal of full employment inevitably produce an inflationary spiral.

The economy 1960-79

During the period 1960-79, the link between wage levels and inflation led to increasingly close links between government, management and unions. This was the era of corporatism and tripartite agreements (see Chapter 10, Section 3.1). Although both Labour and Conservative governments attempted to negotiate incomes policies in the hope that wage restraint would keep inflation down, this proved particularly difficult. Agreements were broken by management and unions alike. Industrial action was a frequent occurrence. The failure to produce a workable incomes policy meant that the inflationary spiral described above could not be broken.

When oil prices quadrupled in 1973-74, a world recession began and the economic growth that had continued since 1945 came to an end. Britain's trade deficit soared to £5,351 million in 1974. The following year inflation reached nearly 25% whilst unemployment grew to almost 1 million. Over the next five years, unemployment continued to grow whilst inflation remained high (so-called 'stagflation'). Under Keynesian theory, inflation and wage demands should have come down as unemployment went up. That, however, simply did not happen. By the end of the decade, opponents of Keynesianism were able to argue that the theory had failed and it was time to try something new.

Main points - Sections 1.1-1.3

- Britain was the first industrial nation. By 1900, however, Britain was no longer the biggest industrial producer in the world.
- Supporters of laissez faire economics oppose government intervention. They want a free market in which the government leaves them alone.
- Supporters of protectionism argue that tariffs help raise government revenue and make it easier for locally made products to compete.
- Keynes argued that recessions could be overcome by government intervention. He supported a capitalist economy in which the government intervened to achieve full employment and planned economic growth.
- From 1950 to 1976, governments pursued broadly Keynesian policies. By the mid-1970s, however, Keynesian policies seemed unable to prevent stagflation (the coincidence of rising unemployment and rising inflation).

Activity 15.1 Keynesianism

Item A *Affluent Britain*

In the second half of the 1950s, Britain seemed to be changing fundamentally and for the better. This was due to unprecedented prosperity and full employment. Unemployment had disappeared in the war and remained minimal throughout the 1950s. Better still was the fact that earnings rose faster than prices. There had also been a reduction in the working week. The new affluence was measured in consumer durables. By 1965, 88% of households in Britain had TVs, 39% had fridges and 56% had washing machines. The number of TV licences grew from half a million in 1950 to over 12 million in 1964. In 1951, there were 2.25 million cars on the road. In 1964, this figure had risen to over 8 million. Growth in ownership was made easier by hire purchase and the lowering of purchase tax as well as higher earnings. Home ownership also grew between 1955 and 1964. By 1964, over 40% of the population owned their own homes. In addition, the Conservatives cut income tax five times between 1955 and 1964.

Adapted from Childs 1992.

Item B *The Stop-Go cycle*

This cartoon shows how the Stop-Go cycle works.

Item C *Inflation and unemployment 1970-79*

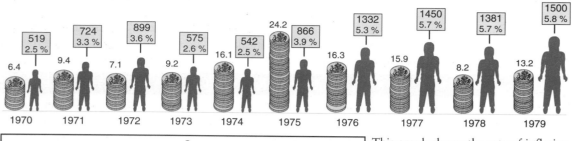

519 2.5%	724 3.3%	899 3.6%	575 2.6%	542 2.5%	24.2 866 3.9%		1332 5.3%	1450 5.7%	1381 5.7%	1500 5.8%

6.4 · 9.4 · 7.1 · 9.2 · 16.1 · 16.3 · 15.9 · 8.2 · 13.2

1970 1971 1972 1973 1974 1975 1976 1977 1978 1979

Price Inflation (annual rate of increase) in percentages

Unemployment (thousands) and the percentage of the labour force unemployed

This graph shows the rate of inflation and level of unemployment between 1970 and 1979.

Item D *The limitations of demand management policies*

Assume that the government announces a £500 million increase in civil servant salaries and a £500 million increase in road building. The increase in civil servant salaries will work through the economy relatively quickly. Civil servants will increase their spending within months of receiving their pay increase. The road building programme, however, may take years even to start. So, a government needs to be careful to take account of lags in spending when using active fiscal policy (manipulating government expenditure) to fill or remove deflationary or inflationary gaps. In the past, governments were accused of destabilising the economy by using active fiscal policy. In 1972, for example, the Chancellor reflated the economy at a time when (arguably) the economy was moving into a boom of its own accord. The combination of extra private and public spending then created an inflationary gap. An active fiscal policy assumes that the Chancellor knows the current state of the economy. But, statistics are notoriously unreliable and have become more so over time. If the balance of payments is in deficit the Chancellor will not know how much is due to genuine deficit and how much is due to inaccurate recording of statistics. Further, some economists argue that it is impossible to predict changes in variables to the last few per cent. Yet, many of the variables governments wish to control are small numbers. For instance, the government may wish to reduce economic growth by half. To do so, it might have to cut the growth in national income from 3% to 1.5%. Active fiscal policy, however, is unlikely to be sensitive enough to achieve exactly that 1.5% fall.

Adapted from Anderton 1995.

Item E *Why Keynesianism failed*

By the mid-1980s, Keynesianism was everywhere in retreat and the free-market right triumphant. So, what went wrong? The problem is easy to identify - the arrival of 'stagflation' (the coincidence of rising unemployment and rising inflation) in the late-1960s. The causes of stagflation, however, were (and are) hotly contested. The free-market right argued that the Keynesian relationship between unemployment and inflation ceased to work as soon as people started taking inflation for granted. Constant boosting of demand simply fuelled inflation without having any effect on unemployment. Keynesians blamed factors outside governments' control - the oil price shock of 1973-74, the explosion of industrial strife after 1968 and the collapse of the system of managed exchange rates. At first, most governments tried to maintain demand while dampening inflation with incomes policies. When that did not work, they allowed unemployment to rise to counter inflation. When, in turn, that became painful, they allowed inflation to rise to counter unemployment. By the mid-1970s, it had all spun out of control. Faced with rampant inflation, rising unemployment and a currency crisis, the Labour government asked the IMF for a loan. The IMF insisted on severe spending cuts. This unlocked the door back to the forgotten world of laissez faire economics.

Adapted from Anderson & Davey 1996.

Questions

1. Judging from Item A, why do you think there was little criticism of the Keynesian model before the late 1970s?

2. a) Using Item B, describe how Keynes' economic theory was put into practice.
   b) How did the Keynesian system differ from the laissez faire approach adopted by earlier governments?

3. a) Using Items C-E, describe the limitations of the Keynesian economic model.
   b) Why do you think criticism of Keynesianism grew during the 1970s?

1.4 Monetarism

What is monetarism?

Monetarism is an economic theory which completely rejects the aims and techniques of economic management proposed by Keynes. Whilst the primary goal of Keynesianism is to maintain full employment, the primary goal of monetarism is to keep inflation under control - even if that means maintaining a high level of unemployment. Whereas Keynesian economists argue that the government should play an active role by managing demand, monetarists argue that the government's only role should be to control the money supply (the money supply is the total amount of money circulating in the economy).

Monetarism is based on the quantity theory of money, one of the oldest economic theories. It dates back at least 500 years. The quantity theory of money states that increases in prices are caused solely by increases in the money supply and the speed of its circulation (the frequency with which money changes hands). In other words, there is a causal link between the money supply and inflation.

Today, monetarism is most often associated with the economist Milton Friedman. He argued that the economy is not really affected by the level of public expenditure or the level of taxation. Rather, what matters is the money supply. As he put it in 1968, 'inflation is always and everywhere a monetary phenomenon.' Friedman argued that the money supply can be measured and controlled and that it was the government's job to measure and control it. It was his theory that, if the government restricted the money supply, inflation would fall.

1.5 Applying monetarism in Britain

New economic thinking

By the mid-1970s, stagflation was a major problem in Britain and Keynesianism had come under attack. After approaching the IMF for a loan, the Labour government of 1974-79 was forced to move away from Keynesianism. The Prime Minister, James Callaghan, signalled this change in a speech made at the Labour Party conference in 1976 when he said:

> 'We used to think that you could spend your way out of recession by cutting taxes and boosting government spending. I tell you in all candour that this option no longer exists and insofar as it ever did exist, it injected a higher dose of inflation and a higher level of unemployment. Unemployment is caused by pricing ourselves out of jobs.' (quoted in Anderson & Davey 1996, p.30)

Whilst the turning point came in 1976, it was not until a Conservative government was elected in 1979 that the Keynesian goal of full employment was openly abandoned. From 1979, the reduction of inflation, not the reduction of unemployment, was the Conservative government's main goal. To achieve this goal, the government relied on monetarism.

Monetarism and laissez faire economics

In practice, the British experiment with monetarism in the early 1980s was far more than an attempt to control the money supply. The Thatcher governments favoured a laissez faire economic approach and their support for monetarism was used to justify this. The aim was to reduce government spending and borrowing and to provide the conditions in which the market could regulate itself. Clearly, this went against Keynesian thinking, but it fitted well with monetarism. Monetarists argued that the government's only role was to control the money supply. Otherwise, the government should play a minimal role in economic management. In other words, monetarism provided an ideological framework within which the government could dismantle the structures set up during the period of Keynesianism and replace them with its own free-market solutions.

There were three main strands to British monetarism in the early 1980s:

- each year the government attempted to control the supply of money in the economy
- each year the government attempted to reduce the level of government spending
- the government actively set out to take away government controls and to create a free-market economy.

1. Attempting to control the money supply

There is no single method of calculating money supply. In Britain during the early 1980s, two main measures were used by the government to calculate money supply:

- **M0** is a narrow definition of money supply (it is equal to the notes and coins in circulation together with the balances held by banks with the Bank of England)
- **M3** is a broad measure of money supply (it is equal to all the notes and coins in circulation plus money in current accounts in banks plus monies in deposit accounts in banks plus private sector holdings of certificates of deposit).

The Medium Term Financial Strategy

Despite Milton Friedman's confidence that the money supply could be measured and controlled, experience in Britain in the early 1980s shows that this is more difficult in practice than in theory. By means of its Medium Term Financial Strategy, the government set annual targets for the rate of monetary growth over four year periods (using M3 as the measure of money supply). These targets were first published with the 1980 Budget.

A reduction in money supply was to be achieved by three means. First, the government should set interest rates high enough to lower the demand for money. Second, the government should finance the Public Sector Borrowing Requirement (PSBR) - the Budget deficit - without printing money. And third, the government should allow the exchange rate to float - to prevent the buying and selling of foreign currencies from affecting the money supply.

Failure to control the money supply

Unfortunately for the government, these policy instruments were unsuccessful. In the early 1980s, the money supply grew at around twice the rate set by the government. Despite the government's attempts to control it, M3 sterling remained at a higher level between 1979 and 1985 than it had been at any time during the period of the previous Labour government. It is ironic to note that inflation did fall during this period, but it fell while money supply was increasing. Therefore, the monetarists' claim that inflation would only fall if the money supply was restricted was proved false.

In November 1985, the government abandoned M3 sterling as a measure of money supply and replaced it with M0, the narrower measure. Most economists dismissed M0 as an entirely unrealistic measure of true money supply because today's society is relatively cashless (the M0 measurement does not
· take that into account). The experiment with orthodox monetarism, therefore, was over by 1986. From 1986, control of the money supply was no longer a main priority of the government.

2. Reducing the level of government spending   ·

The second main strand in the Thatcher governments' monetarist policy was the reduction of government spending. The argument was that if public spending exceeded public income, the result would be an increase in the money supply. Unlike Keynesians, therefore, monetarists were not prepared to stimulate the economy by investing government money if that investment resulted in a deficit. Indeed, Margaret Thatcher argued that the nation's economy should be run like a household economy.

Until 1979, governments rarely balanced their Budgets. Most years they ran Budget deficits by spending more than they received. As a result, governments borrowed money.

Geoffrey Howe's Budgets

In his first Budget, just three weeks after the general election in 1979, Geoffrey Howe, the Chancellor:

- placed cash limits on the public sector
- raised the minimum lending rate to 14%
- sold some public assets to help finance the PSBR
- switched the emphasis from direct taxation to indirect taxation (direct taxes are taxes raised directly from an individual or an organisation. Indirect taxes are taxes on goods or services. Income tax is an example of direct tax. VAT is an example of an indirect tax). Income tax was lowered to 30% whilst VAT was raised.

This Budget signalled a move away from Keynesian demand management. Whereas Keynesians would have attempted to keep unemployment down by allowing a deficit, the 1979 Budget was designed to reduce the Budget deficit even if that meant higher unemployment and a recession in the short term. This policy was tightened in 1981. The 1981 Budget imposed huge increases in indirect tax (for example a 20p per gallon increase on petrol) and a total of £3,500 million was taken out of the PSBR.

Public spending

By the mid-1980s, the government had managed to achieve a Budget surplus. Despite this, however, public spending rose every year from 1979. One reason for this was the huge growth in unemployment. A growth in unemployment means that the Social Security bill increases (since state benefits have to be paid to those out of work). It also means that the government receives less in both direct and indirect taxes. When unemployment grows less income tax is collected since people out of work do not pay it and less indirect tax is collected since unemployed people cannot afford to buy as many goods and services which contain indirect taxes.

3. Creating a free-market economy

The third main strand in the Thatcher governments' monetarist policy was the attempt to create a free-market economy. This is closely linked to the policy of reducing government spending. By definition, a free-market economy is an economy in which government intervention is minimal.

The election of the Thatcher government in 1979 meant an end to income policies. Wage settlements were to be made by employers and their workers. The market would decide the level of settlements, not the government. The refusal to consider income policies marks a break with the Keynesian past. In addition, the programme of privatisation which gained momentum after 1983 marks an important break with the past. Privatisation is attractive to monetarists for two reasons. First, it allows the government to raise money without having to borrow it. Money raised by privatisation does not affect the money supply and, therefore, is not inflationary. Money raised from privatisation was an important contribution to the Budget surpluses of the mid-1980s. Second, privatisation reduces the state's direct involvement in the economy. By selling state-owned assets to the private sector, the government reduces the size of the public sector and, therefore, allows market forces to exert more influence over the economy.

Main points - Sections 1.4-1.5

- The main goal of monetarism is to keep inflation under control (even if that means maintaining a high level of unemployment).
- Monetarists argue that the government's only role should be to control the money supply.
- There were three main strands to British monetarism in the early 1980s: (1) controlling the supply of money in the economy; (2) reducing the level of government spending; and (3) creating a free-market economy.
- The Thatcher governments failed to control the money supply and to reduce public spending. Steps were taken, however, to create a free-market economy (ending incomes policies and implementing a programme of privatisation).

Activity 15.2 Monetarism

Item A   Conservative economic strategy in the early 1980s

The Medium Term Financial Strategy published with the 1980 Budget laid down monetary supply targets. These were to be achieved by:
- setting interest rates high enough to lower the demand for money
- financing the PSBR without printing money
- allowing the exchange rate to float.

Interest rates, the PSBR and the exchange rate, therefore, became the government's monetary instruments. In the early 1980s, however, the money supply grew at around twice the rate set by the government. In part, this was due to the government's deregulation of financial markets. When exchange controls were abolished in June 1980, there was a sudden jump in the money supply as hidden money returned to the official banking system. This led to an increase in bank borrowing which, again, increased the money supply. The economy was already moving into recession when the Conservatives took office. Their strategy pushed the economy into deflation. Between 1979 and 1986, unemployment rose from 1.3 million to 3.4 million. Each addition to the unemployment register added several thousand pounds to the PSBR as a result of extra benefit rates and lost tax revenue. The recession, therefore, raised the PSBR just as the government was trying to reduce it. The only way the government could reduce the PSBR was to bring forward in each Budget a new package of expenditure cuts and/or tax increases. These measures, however, inevitably made the recession worse. By the mid-1980s, most people agreed that there was no simple connection between the rate of interest, increases in money supply (however measured) and the rate of inflation.

Adapted from Hall & Jacques 1983 and Anderton 1995.

Item B   Monetary targets 1980-85

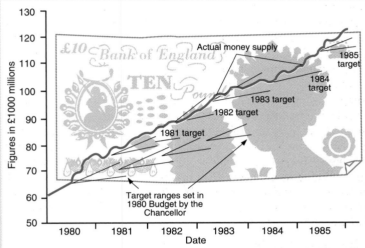

This graph shows the monetary targets set in 1980 and the actual money supply.

Adapted from the *Guardian*, 24 October 1985.

Item C   Inflation rate 1978-92

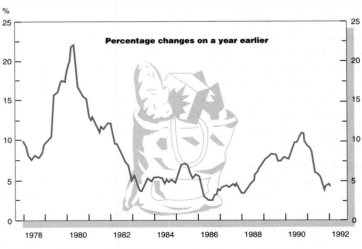

This graph shows the inflation rate in the period 1978-92.

Adapted from Anderton 1992.

Item D *Unemployment 1970-90*

Date	Unemployed (1,000s)	Date	Unemployed (1,000s)
1970	628	1980	2,244
1971	868	1981	2,772
1972	929	1982	3,097
1973	785	1983	3,225
1974	628	1984	3,284
1975	1,152	1985	3,346
1976	1,440	1986	3,408
1977	1,567	1987	3,297
1978	1,608	1988	2,722
1979	1,464	1989	2,074
		1990	1,850

Unemployment figures fluctuate from month to month. The figures in the table above show the highest monthly total each year.

Adapted from Butler & Butler 1994.

Item E *Government expenditure as a proportion of GDP, 1963-91*

Date	% GDP	Date	% GDP
1963-64	36	1983-84	46.5
1968-69	41.5	1984-85	47
1973-74	43.5	1985-86	45
1978-79	44	1986-87	44
1979-80	44	1987-88	41.75
1980-81	46.5	1988-89	39.25
1981-82	47.25	1989-90	39.75
1982-83	47.5	1990-91	40.25

This table shows government expenditure as a proportion of GDP. GDP or gross domestic product is a measure of the amount of income generated as a result of a country's economic activity, excluding net property income from abroad.

Adapted from McKie 1993 and Anderton 1994.

Questions

1. Using Items A-E, explain how economic management in the early 1980s differed from economic management in the previous 30 years.
2. Judging from Items B-E, what were the consequences of the pursuit of a monetarist economic policy in the early 1980s?
3. From the point of view of a monetarist, how successful would you say that the economic management of the economy in the early 1980s was?

Part 2 Britain's economic decline

Key issues

1. When did Britain's economic decline begin?
2. How has Britain's economy changed since the 19th century?
3. What are the indications of decline?

2.1 When did the economic decline begin?

Two perspectives

In 1860, Britain was known as the 'workshop of the world'. It was in Britain that new and exciting ways of work had developed. Britain had a large share of world trade and each year increased its industrial output. Other countries regarded Britain as advanced and modern. Indeed, Britain set the standards by which other countries measured their own development. Britain was truly a major world player.

In the 1990s, Britain was no longer top of the economic league. Although the British economy generally continued to grow in absolute terms, the growth was smaller than that achieved by many of Britain's competitors. Although Britain remained the world leader in some fields (for example, pharmaceuticals), often British industrialists looked abroad for inspiration - to the USA, to Germany or to Japan.

Today, few people would deny that Britain has suffered an economic decline. It is, however, difficult to pinpoint exactly when this decline began and what was responsible for it. It is possible to isolate two perspectives.

1. Decline since 1900

First, there is the long-term view. This suggests that because Britain was the first industrial nation, it was inevitable that other countries would catch up and overtake it in terms of output and trade. By the end of the 19th century, Britain's machinery was old and its ways of work outdated. Other countries had the advantage that their industrial revolutions began later and they could, therefore, select what was best and most up-to-date. This gave them an advantage over Britain. By the turn of the century, Britain had lost the initiative. The First World War disrupted Britain's trading patterns. And, the Second World War was an enormous financial burden from which Britain was unable to recover.

2. Decline since 1945

Second, there is the short-term view. This suggests that Britain has been badly managed since the Second World War. According to this view, Britain had an excellent chance to regain its status as a major world player in 1945, but it failed to take its chance. The setting up of the welfare state and the adoption of Keynesian economic policies led to low growth, inefficiency and poor industrial relations.

Ideology and the two perspectives

Explanations of Britain's decline depend in part on ideological preference. It is no surprise to learn, for example, that supporters of laissez faire economics are particularly critical of Britain's economic performance between 1945 and 1979 whilst opponents of laissez faire economics tend to argue that Britain's decline had begun long before 1945 (before 1945, British governments took a laissez faire approach to economic management).

From industrialisation to de-industrialisation

Economists divide the British economy into three sectors:

1. In the primary sector, raw materials are extracted and food is grown. This sector, therefore, includes farming and coal mining.
2. In the secondary sector, raw materials are made into goods. This sector, therefore, includes all manufacturing and construction industries.
3. In the tertiary sector, services are provided. Transport, banking, education and the health service all fall into this sector.

Britain's wealth in the 19th century was mainly derived from the development of manufacturing industries such as textiles, iron and steel and shipbuilding. These industries required the development of new transport systems (canals and then railways) and the exploitation of natural resources (such as coal). The majority of the working population was employed in manufacturing rather than service industries.

The inter-war years

The productivity of those industries upon which British wealth had been based (cotton, iron, shipbuilding and coal) declined during the inter-war period (see Box 15.2). There were two main reasons for this. First, by 1918, British production methods had become relatively old fashioned and uncompetitive. And second, established trading patterns were disrupted by the First World War. Japan, for example, managed to increase its trade with the USA by 700% during the war. Much of this trade was taken from Britain.

Box 15.2 Cotton and coal production

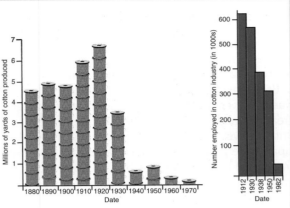

The graphs above show the amount of cotton produced (1880-1970) and the number of people employed in the cotton industry (1912-82).

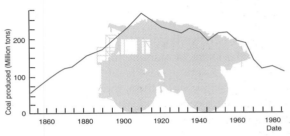

The graph above shows the amount of coal produced in Britain between 1850 and 1985.

Adapted from Cook & Stevenson 1988.

Despite this, the British economy as a whole continued to grow at an average rate of 2% per year during the inter-war period. This was due in part to the growth of new industries. The production of cars, electrical goods, plastics and chemicals, for example, all increased during the inter-war period. It should be noted, however, that these new industries, unlike the older industries, tended to be located in the Midlands and the South of England rather than the North of England, Wales and Scotland. This regional diversity led to talk in the 1930s of a North-South divide.

When the world depression hit Britain in the 1930s, the North of England, Wales and Scotland suffered higher unemployment rates than the Midlands and the South of England.

The Second World War

In the late 1930s, preparations for war stimulated manufacturing industries such as steel and aircraft production. Then, the outbreak of war led to full employment and emergency economic measures. During the war, the government intervened in the economy much more than had been the case in peacetime. Government intervention and the feeling of solidarity which came from fighting a common enemy brought a new political climate at the end of the Second World War. It was this new political climate which provided the basis of the post-war consensus.

The post-war consensus

Central to the post-war consensus was the setting up of the welfare state and the nationalisation of key industries such as coal, steel and electricity. At first, it seemed that there would be a revival in the fortunes of British manufacturing industries. Full employment was achieved and post-war reconstruction brought a great demand for goods. By the 1960s, however, Britain's Western European competitors, the USA and Japan were growing at a much faster rate than Britain. Traditional British industries had become uncompetitive and new technologies were being developed elsewhere. The loss of an Empire had economic as well as political consequences. Increasingly, Britain seemed to be falling behind.

2.2 De-industrialisation

What is de-industrialisation?

By 1950, the share of manufacturing output in Britain's total output was 34% whilst the share of services was 49%. Since then, the share of manufacturing has declined whilst the share of services has increased. In addition, manufacturing has not just declined in relative terms, it has declined in absolute terms. Between 1973 and 1976 manufacturing fell by 6% and between 1979 and 1981 it fell by 14%. By 1989, manufacturing output was only 20% higher than in 1969 whilst during the same period there had been a 70% increase in the output of services.

This process of both relative and absolute decline in manufacturing has been termed 'de-industrialisation' (see also Chapter 5, Section 3.1). Although there was a trend towards de-industrialisation before 1980, it is only since then that the process has become marked. Its most obvious manifestation is the change in the structure and pattern of employment. As a result of the economic policies pursued in the early 1980s, thousands of businesses were forced to slim down or close down. This resulted in a huge rise in unemployment. Manufacturing industries which faced harsh competition from abroad were especially badly hit. Consequently, the traditional manufacturing regions of Britain (Northern England, Scotland and Wales) have suffered higher rates of unemployment than Southern England which has a greater number of service industries.

The causes of de-industrialisation

De-industrialisation has not only occurred in Britain. Britain remains one of the G7 countries (the G7 are the seven largest industrial economies in the world). Other G7 countries show signs of de-industrialisation (for example, falling employment in the 1980s), though at a slower rate than in Britain. Britain, however, experienced the largest fall in manufacturing amongst the seven countries between 1960 and 1988. Also, Britain was the only country to show a consistent fall in employment over that period.

One cause of this fast rate of de-industrialisation is the failure of British manufacturing industry to satisfy domestic demand for manufactured goods. In the 1980s, consumer spending rose by 30% whilst manufacturing rose by only 7.8%. During this same period, imports grew to satisfy this demand whilst exports fell. This suggests that British manufacturing industries failed to compete on the world market.

A second reason for the fast rate of de-industrialisation is the British government's low rate of investment. Since 1960, Britain's level of investment (measured as a percentage of GDP) has been the lowest of all G7 countries. Japan's level of investment has been the highest and its growth has also been the highest.

A third reason for Britain's fast rate of de-industrialisation is the nature and organisation of its workforce. Not only is there a long history of poor industrial relations, the British government has failed to train and educate its workers to the level of other G7 countries. In 1988, for example, Germany was spending $3,500 per trainee, Canada was spending $2,300 and France and Japan were spending $1,000 whilst Britain was spending just $400.

Does de-industrialisation matter?

There are three main reasons why de-industrialisation matters. First, the fast rate of de-industrialisation has resulted in high unemployment. The growth in service industries has failed to provide sufficient job opportunities for all those who have lost their jobs in manufacturing industries. As a result, there is a large body of long-term unemployed people, especially in areas where manufacturing industries were traditionally based. This trend has been made worse by the introduction of labour-saving devices (increased computerisation and so on) within those manufacturing businesses which have survived.

Second, the fast rate of de-industrialisation has increased Britain's balance of payments difficulties. Countries with a strong manufacturing base are able to achieve a balance of payments surplus. In Britain, however, imports have regularly exceeded exports and this produces a deficit. Government action to reduce such a deficit (raising taxes or interest rates) dampens demand and encourages a further fall in manufacturing output. The fast rate of de-industrialisation, in other words, produces a downwards spiral.

Third, a growth in manufacturing translates into a growth in living standards. By contrast, low manufacturing output means low growth and a poorer standard of living. Britain's fast rate of de-industrialisation means that, relatively speaking, British people are becoming poorer than people living in countries with successful manufacturing industries and high growth rates.

Main points - Part 2

- In 1860, Britain was known as the 'workshop of the world'. In the 1990s, however, Britain was no longer top of the economic league.
- Some people argue that Britain's economic decline had begun by 1900. Others argue that it was the result of bad economic management since 1945.
- There is evidence that Britain's manufacturing base declined in the inter-war years, though the economy continued to grow. There were hopes of a

- manufacturing revival after 1945, but, from the 1960s, Britain grew more slowly than its competitors.
- The process of both relative and absolute decline in manufacturing has been termed 'de-industrialisation'. This process began before 1980, but has only become marked since then.
- De-industrialisation has brought high unemployment, balance of payments difficulties and low growth.

Activity 15.3 *Britain's economic decline*

Item A *UK exports and imports 1955 and 1997*

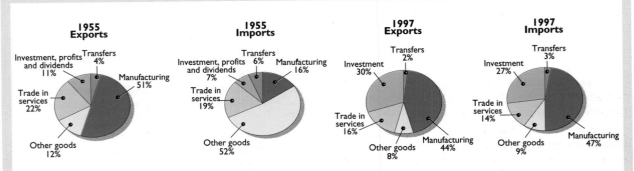

These charts show that, between 1955 and 1997, the contribution to exports made by manufacturing fell from 51% to 44%, whilst the contribution to imports rose from 16% to 47%. This is important because there is little that the government can do to influence the rest of the current account. Interest, profits and dividends are fixed. Other goods are mainly food and raw materials. Trade in services could fill the gap, but the value of trade in services is only about a third of that of manufacturing.

Adapted from Anderton 1997.

Item B *Employment in manufacturing and services*

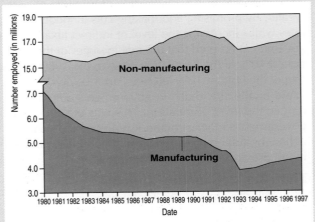

This graph shows the number of people employed in manufacturing and service industries in Britain between 1980 and 1997.

Adapted from Chambers 1993 and ONS 1998.

Item C *Manufacturing and service output 1950-93*

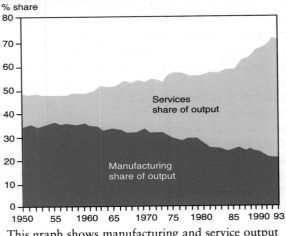

This graph shows manufacturing and service output as a share of GDP.

Adapted from Anderton 1995.

Item D *The G7 countries, 1960-88*

(i)	Manufacturing output as % of GDP			Annual % growth in employment				(ii)	Economic growth				
	1960	1979	1988	1960-67	1968-73	1974-79	1980-88		1960-67	1968-73	1974-79	1980-88	1960-88
United States	28	23	19	1.9	1.0	1.5	0.0	United States	4.5	3.2	2.4	2.8	3.3
Japan	35	29	29	4.0	2.5	-0.4	0.8	Japan	10.2	8.7	3.6	4.1	6.5
Germany	40	34	31	-0.2	0.9	-1.8	-1.0	Germany	4.1	4.9	2.3	1.7	3.1
France	29	26	21	1.1	1.6	-1.1	-2.0	France	5.4	5.5	2.8	1.9	3.7
United Kingdom	**32**	**25**	**21**	**-0.3**	**-1.1**	**-1.2**	**-2.7**	**United Kingdom**	**3.0**	**3.4**	**1.5**	**2.2**	**2.5**
Italy	29	28	23	0.8	0.4	0.3	-1.2	Italy	5.7	4.5	3.7	2.4	4.0
Canada	n.a.	19	17	2.5	2.2	1.9	0.5	Canada	5.5	5.4	2.7	2.8	4.4
								Average G7	**5.0**	**4.4**	**2.7**	**2.8**	**3.7**

Table (i) compares the annual growth in manufacturing and employment in the G7 countries between 1960 and 1980. Table (ii) compares the annual rate of economic growth. The G7 are the seven largest economies in the world. All figures are percentages. n.a. stands for 'not available'.

Adapted from OECD, Historical Statistics.

Questions

1. a) Judging from Items A-D what is the evidence that a process of de-industrialisation has been taking place in Britain since the 1960s?
   b) Can you think of any reasons why this process speeded up in the 1980s?
   c) What have been the consequences of this process?
2. 'De-industrialisation is proceeding at a faster pace in Britain than in other developed economies.'
   a) Explain this statement using Item D.
   b) Explain how this is likely to affect Britain in the long term.
3. Suppose you were invited to advise the government on what to do about the process of de-industrialisation. What advice would you give?

Part 3 Management of the economy since 1985

Key issues

1. What have been the main developments in economic policy since 1985?
2. Did the resignation of Margaret Thatcher lead to a fundamental change in economic policy?
3. What direction has been taken by the Labour government elected in 1997?
4. How have moves towards a single European currency affected Britain?

3.1 Economic policy 1985-90

Thatcher's economic aims

Management of the economy under Margaret Thatcher had four main aims. First, the Thatcher governments aimed to change the structure of ownership by transferring the ownership of industries and services from the state to private individuals. Privatisation, it was argued, would increase efficiency. Privatisation also had two other advantages from the government's point of view. It generated a great deal of money for the Treasury (which helped to finance tax cuts). And, the sale of shares to the public encouraged large numbers of ordinary people to become shareholders for the first time. By increasing the number of people with a vested interest in the capitalist system, the government hoped to increase the number of Conservative voters. The same idea lay behind the selling off of council houses to tenants at reduced rates.

The second aim was to cut public expenditure. At the heart of the Thatcher view of the economy was the idea that the nation's economy should be managed in the same way that a good housekeeper would manage a household budget. In other words, the Budget should be balanced and the nation should not live on credit.

The third aim was to change the distribution of wealth. By promising and making cuts in income tax rates whilst increasing the level of indirect taxation, the government ensured that the real incomes of the richest 10% of the population grew in the 1980s whilst that of the bottom 10% fell (see Part 5 below).

And finally, the Thatcher governments aimed to reduce the level of inflation. This was the government's main aim and it replaced the goal of achieving full employment which had been pursued by all previous post-war governments.

Thatcher's economic policies

Although the aims of the Thatcher governments remained constant, the policies employed to achieve the aims changed. As noted above (Section 1.4), there was a concerted effort in the early 1980s to translate monetarist theory into practice in the hope that this would bring down inflation. By October 1985, however, this experiment had failed. The suspension of the M3 measure of money supply signalled a change in direction.

Rather than using measures of money supply to control inflation, the Chancellor, Nigel Lawson, argued that British monetary policy was constrained by the exchange rate of the pound. Between 1985 and 1989, the main levers with which Lawson attempted to manipulate the economy were the exchange rate and the level of interest rates.

It was concern about the exchange rate which led to Lawson's public argument with Margaret Thatcher. Earlier in the 1980s, Thatcher had favoured a form of alignment with the dollar. Lawson, however, saw greater benefit in a closer relationship with Europe because Europe was much more important for trade than the USA. This led to a public debate about whether or not Britain should join the European Community's ERM - Exchange Rate Mechanism (see Section 3.4 below). Lawson favoured participation whilst Thatcher, egged on by her adviser Alan Walters, did not. The resignation of Lawson in 1989 and the ensuing debate over Britain's role in Europe were important ingredients in the chain of events which led to the resignation of Margaret Thatcher in November 1990.

3.2 Management of the economy under John Major

Major as Chancellor
John Major replaced Nigel Lawson as Chancellor in 1989 and, in late 1990, he replaced Margaret Thatcher as Prime Minister. As Chancellor, Major distanced himself from orthodox monetarism, saying:

'That used to be the theory...the government may have followed some time ago. It certainly has not been the theory that the government have followed during any period I have been at the Treasury.' (quoted in Johnson 1991)

Major also distanced himself from his predecessor, arguing that Lawson should not have allowed demand to rise as sharply as it did in 1987 and 1988. Major became Chancellor at the tail-end of the boom engineered by Lawson. He was, therefore, keen not to be blamed for the decline in economic fortunes which followed Lawson's so-called 'economic miracle'. He was, perhaps, fortunate that he only presented a single Budget (in 1990). By then, the economy was moving into recession. If the leadership crisis had come later, he might not have been so popular. It is ironic, given that Major was determined to distance himself from Nigel Lawson, that it was while he was Chancellor that Britain joined the ERM.

Main goals under Major
Once Major became Prime Minister, he immediately promised to continue to pursue policies which followed the general direction taken by Margaret Thatcher. Under Major the main goals of economic policy remained:

- encouraging the development of a free-market economy
- lower direct taxation and public spending
- the maintenance of low inflation.

The main instrument for constraining inflation was to remain membership of the Exchange Rate Mechanism (the ERM - see Section 3.4).

That Major's government should have the same broad economic goals as the Thatcher governments is not perhaps surprising. Major was regarded as a loyal Thatcherite who had been groomed by Thatcher as her successor. Also, most of the members of Major's Cabinet had served in Thatcher's Cabinet.

Policy adjustments 1990-92
The initial problem faced by the new Prime Minister was to show that he was 'his own man'. This was achieved partly by projecting a 'caring' image and partly by making policy adjustments before the 1992 general election. Of these policy adjustments, perhaps the two most important were the abandonment of the poll tax and the willingness to increase public expenditure even though that meant running up a large Budget deficit. Since the economy remained in recession right up to the 1992 general election and beyond, the scope for government action was limited. Even so, public spending was increased and tax cuts - the traditional Thatcherite pre-election 'sweeteners' - were made in the 1992 Budget.

Economic policy 1992-97
Inflation and the ERM
The measures described above were sufficient to secure a Conservative victory in 1992. Before the end of that year, however, the Major government had suffered an economic blow from which it never really recovered. As noted above, the government's priority was to maintain a low level of inflation. A run on the pound in September 1992, however, forced Britain to withdraw from the ERM. This severely damaged the government's reputation for economic competence and reduced its economic strategy to tatters:

'The ERM debacle was a unique moment of political and economic crisis, the first time since 1945 that a Conservative government was forced to devalue.' (Kelly 1997, p.281)

During the 1992 general election campaign, the government had argued that membership of the ERM was central to its strategy of maintaining a low level of inflation. Membership of the ERM meant maintaining a high value of the pound. This, it was argued, would produce a downwards pressure on prices and ensure that wage rises remained in line with other European countries. Following withdrawal from the ERM, however, the government was forced to think again. Between 1993 and 1997, the main weapon used to control inflation was manipulation of interest rates.

Taxation and public spending
In 1993, the government announced plans to increase taxes in the period 1994-96 in order to stem the high level of government borrowing. Borrowing

in the period 1990-92 had resulted in a huge Budget deficit of £28 billion in 1992-93 and £50 billion in 1993-94. The problem for the government was that the Conservatives' main message in the 1992 general election campaign had been that the Conservatives would protect tax cuts whilst Labour would increase taxes. By raising taxes, the government appeared hypocritical. In addition, the second phase of imposing VAT on fuel had to be abandoned after a backbench revolt in 1994. So, although the Budget deficit was reduced in the years 1994-97, it was only at a substantial political cost.

The development of a free-market economy

The Major government used two main strategies to encourage the development of a free-market economy. First, the government continued with the programme of privatisation begun in the 1980s. Notably, the railways were privatised in 1993. And second, the government pushed ahead with a programme of deregulation. Michael Heseltine's promise in 1992 that there would be a 'bonfire of red tape' was followed by the 1994 Deregulation and Contracting Out Act. This Act gave ministers important powers:

> '[The Act] empowered ministers to amend primary legislation through statutory instruments whenever such modification reduced unnecessary regulatory burdens.' (Loughlin & Scott 1997, p.211)

Between 1994 and 1997, ministers used these new powers to review and modify many pieces of legislation. In 1996, the Organisation for Economic Cooperation and Development (OECD), a group set up to promote economic growth and to aid developing countries, reported that:

> 'The UK market is now one of the least regulated among OECD countries, as regards restrictions on terms and conditions of employment, working times and hiring and firing rules.' (OECD 1996, p.89)

The state of the economy 1992-97

In 1992, the economy was in recession. Between 1990 and 1993, GDP fell in absolute terms. Unemployment grew from 1.8 million in 1990 to just over 3 million in 1993. The PSBR grew from -1% of GDP in 1990 to 7% of GDP in 1993. During this recession, inflation fell from just over 10% in 1990 to 1.2% in June 1993 (all figures from Anderton 1996).

Between 1993 and 1997, however, the economy recovered. Although growth rates fell back in 1995, GDP grew in absolute terms between 1993 and 1997. Unemployment also fell - from just over 3 million in 1993 to 1.6 million in May 1997. The PSBR fell from 7% of GDP in 1993 to 1% of GDP in 1997. Inflation remained within the government's target range of 1-4% between 1993 and 1997 (all figures from Anderton 1997).

3.3 Management of the economy under Tony Blair

The inheritance

Labour inherited an economy from the Conservatives which was booming:

> 'The level of unemployment as measured by the numbers claiming benefit was down to 1.6 million and falling - not far from its lowest point at the end of the 1980s boom. Consumer spending was on the increase, house prices were rising and inflation appeared to be edging up. The pound, meanwhile, was soaring in value against other European currencies, leading to worries among manufacturers that they would soon be priced out of many of their most important export markets.' (Anderson & Mann 1997, p.60)

Although the economy was booming, in addition to the potential problems outlined above, a number of long-term problems lurked behind the surface. First, there was a growing number of long-term unemployed people, mainly male. Second, there had been an explosion of part-time work (work mainly taken up by women), but many part-time workers lacked the security and rights of full-time workers. And third, Britain was lagging further and further behind its rivals in terms of education and training. In Maths, for example, British 13 year olds ranked 25th out of 26 countries (*Observer*, 20 April 1997).

Once elected, the Labour government made it clear that its priorities would be as follows:

- maintaining low inflation
- improving education and training
- creating jobs and improving working conditions
- improving public services.

New Labour and Old Labour

The economic approach of the Labour government elected in 1997 was very different from that adopted by previous Labour governments (see, for example, Brivati & Bale 1998). Before 1997, the Conservative Party had successfully been able to depict Labour as a 'tax and spend' party responsible for the bad old days of high inflation, boom and bust, and industrial strife. By 1997, however, internal Labour Party reforms, a new-look leadership and new economic policies had combined to dispel this reputation. Indeed, during the 1997 election campaign, the tables had turned to such an extent that the Labour leadership was able to make convincing attacks on the Conservatives for excessive tax rises and economic incompetence.

One reason for this change was the Labour leadership's determination to break with its old ideological commitments. Abolishing the old Clause IV meant abandoning an ideological commitment to public ownership. In its stead, the Labour leadership adopted a pragmatic approach:

> 'They have shifted the role for the active state from Keynesian demand management to supply-side interventions. The supply side here means not economic or industrial planning, but the provision of education and training. Because of globalisation, as Labour perceives it, national governments can no longer manage demand. Instead, they must intervene on the supply side. Capital is mobile and cannot be controlled. But, governments can enhance labour.' (Driver & Martell 1998, pp.32-3)

Perhaps the most telling sign of a break with Old Labour was the decision, announced in June 1998, to sell off government shares in air traffic control, the Tote, the Royal Mint and the Commonwealth Development Corporation. Although the government denied that this amounted to a programme of privatisation (since the government retained 49% of shares plus a golden share), such a policy would have been unthinkable under Old Labour (owing to its ideological commitment to public ownership).

New Labour and the Conservatives

Before the 1997 general election, some critics (especially on the left) argued that the Labour leadership's abandonment of old ideological commitments and its acceptance of market economics meant there was no real difference between the economic policies of the two main parties. To some extent, this point of view was justified. In the 1997 election campaign, for example, the Labour leadership - like the Conservatives - emphasised that:

> 'Inflation should be kept low...The disruptive state of industrial relations needed tackling and Tory trade union legislation was mostly desirable. And Conservative Chancellor Lawson was right to focus on the medium rather than the short term in economic decision making.' (Driver & Martell 1998, p.62)

Despite these points of agreement between the two main parties, however, a number of measures suggest that the Labour government's economic approach differed from that adopted by previous Conservative administrations in significant ways.

1. The welfare-to-work programme

A manifesto pledge made it clear that a Labour government would stick with Conservative spending commitments for two years:

> 'For the next two years, Labour will work within the departmental ceilings for spending already announced.' (Labour 1997, p.13)

In order to finance the government's 'welfare-to-work' programme, the Chancellor, Gordon Brown, imposed a one-off 'windfall tax' on what were seen as the excess profits of the privatised utilities. This tactic allowed the government to maintain its commitment to strict public spending limits whilst, at the same time, providing

funds for programmes designed to help young people and the long-term unemployed back to work. The welfare-to-work programme was evidence of a greater commitment to tackling long-term unemployment than was found in the previous administration. Certainly, it reflected a long-standing belief that more needed to be done. As Tony Blair put it in 1995:

> 'The Tories' indifference to the climb in long-term unemployment in the 1980s and 1990s is indefensible.' (quoted in Grant 1998, p.15)

2. The minimum wage

Previous Conservative governments consistently rejected the introduction of a minimum wage on the grounds that it would increase both unemployment and unnecessary red tape. The Labour government's adoption of a minimum wage suggested a break with previous Conservative administrations in two respects. First, it showed that the government was prepared to intervene to reduce the widening of wage inequality. The previous government argued that the market should decide wage levels. And second, it was evidence of the government's belief that, in a global economy, it might not be possible to control capital, but it is possible to 'enhance labour'.

3. Interest rates and the Bank of England

The Labour government's decision to hand control over the level of interest rates to the Bank of England (see Section 4.2 below) was designed to ensure that decisions about interest rate levels would be made on economic rather than political grounds. This can be interpreted as a guarded criticism of previous administrations which had changed interest rate levels for political reasons (lowering levels before a general election, for example). Certainly, it marked a change in approach.

4. Education and training

Unlike previous administrations, the Labour government did not start from the premise that competitiveness in a global economy would be secured by deregulation and low labour costs. Rather, the government aimed to play a role in building a skills base by engineering public-private partnerships and improving education and training programmes. Government initiatives in these areas, it was argued, would allow the unemployed to return to the workforce and would build the skills base for economic success.

5. Single European currency

Like the Conservatives, the Labour Party made a pledge to hold a referendum before joining the single European currency. Also like the Conservatives, the Labour government ruled out joining the single currency before the end of their first term. Announcing this decision in October 1997, however, Gordon Brown also made it clear that the government was strongly in favour of joining the single currency at some point. This was a sign that the Labour government was much less sceptical about the single currency than previous Conservative administrations.

Main points - Sections 3.1-3.3

- Thatcher had four main economic aims: (1) to change the structure of ownership by privatising publicly owned companies; (2) to cut public expenditure; (3) to change the distribution of wealth; and (4) to reduce the rate of inflation.
- Major had the same broad economic goals as Thatcher. Before 1992, however, the poll tax was abolished and public expenditure raised.
- In September 1992 Britain was forced to withdraw from the ERM. Then, in 1993, the government was forced to announce tax rises. By 1997, the economy had come out of recession and was booming.
- In 1997, the Labour government's priorities were: (1) maintaining low inflation; (2) improving education and training; (3) creating jobs and improving working conditions; and (4) improving public services.
- The Labour government has broken with Old Labour's commitment to public ownership and planning. Its economic policies are also different from those pursued by the previous administration.

Activity 15.4 *The Labour government and the economy*

Item A *Labour's new economics (1)*

Gone are Keynesian demand management, nationalisation, planning, tax-and-spend policies and interventionist industrial policy. Few would have predicted in the 1970s, or even 1980s, a Labour Party quite so committed to prudent economics, low inflation and stability. Few would also have predicted a party which attacked the Tories for inflationary policies and tax rises and celebrated cutting business taxes, mobilising the enthusiasm of the private sector and keeping the unions at arms length. Such beliefs are far distant from what Labour stood for pre-Blair. Gone as well is the belief in redistribution and in greater equality of outcomes secured through changes to progressive income tax or through public ownership. Those who see New Labour as aping the Tories have a little more to back up their arguments. On the fundamentals, New Labour has moved on to Tory economic ground. It is on details - the competence and unity of government and the freshness and imagination of ministers to carry out what they promise - that Labour is confident that it is different. Labour's stress on community, inclusion and the interests of the many and not just the few sets a different tone. This is reflected in new policies on welfare-to-work, the minimum wage (and the EU Social Chapter) and education and training which both mark a break with the Conservative years and demonstrate serious thinking on long-term unemployment and welfare reform.

Adapted from Driver & Martell 1998.

Item B *Labour's new economics (2)*

On the day after Gordon Brown announced the results of the Comprehensive Spending Review (which set public spending for three years beginning in 1999), the leading article in the *Guardian* argued that the Chancellor appeared to have pulled off the impossible - by promising sharply increased spending on education and health, but only within a tight fiscal framework. The article noted that education spending would rise by 5.1% a year (compared to an average of 1.4% between 1979 and 1997) and health spending would rise by 4.7% a year (compared to an average of 2.5% between 1992 and 1997). Yet, it pointed out, this extra spending would be tied to performance so it did not leak out into what are regarded as less desirable objectives - such as inflationary pay settlements. Also, the increase would take place against predictions of a steadily growing Budget surplus of £30 billion over three years. As for potential problems, the *Guardian* noted that there would be cutbacks in other departments (notably defence, agriculture and trade and industry), but these would be unlikely to make an impact. Only if the economy fell into recession would the Chancellor's plans come unstuck.

Adapted from the *Guardian*, 15 July 1998.

Item C *Labour's new economics (3)*

The critical challenge is to connect our goals to a world that has undergone a revolution of change. Technology, trade and travel are transforming our lives. Our young people will work in different industries, often those of communications and design rather than old mass production. Many will work in or own small businesses. Jobs for life are gone. Nine to five working is no longer universal. Women work, which brings new opportunities but new strains on family life. Money is traded across international boundaries in vast amounts 24 hours a day. New, new, new, everything is new. There is an urgent task to renew the social democratic model to meet this change. Labour's old values remain the same (community, inclusion, fairness, social justice), but the world has changed so much that the old policy instruments of the left (Keynesianism, public ownership, planning) are no longer relevant.

Adapted from a speech made by Tony Blair on 6 June 1997.

Item D *Labour's new economics (4)*

This cartoon appeared in the *Guardian* on 15 July 1998, the day after the Chancellor, Gordon Brown, announced the results of the Comprehensive Spending Review.

Questions

1. a) Judging from Items A-C, what were the economic goals of the Labour government in 1997-98?
   b) How did the Blair government's economic approach differ from (i) previous Labour governments and (ii) the Major government?

2. What point is being made by the cartoon in Item D? How accurate is it?

3. 'A Third Way'. Is that an accurate description of the way in which the Labour government has managed the economy since May 1997? Use Items A-D in your answer.

3.4 Britain and the single European currency

EMU

The long-term aim of the European Union is to achieve economic and monetary union (EMU). This will have occurred when a single European currency has been adopted by all the member countries. Since 1990, the question of whether Britain should adopt a single European currency has been at the top of the political agenda. It was this issue which divided the Conservative Party under John Major:

> 'The government's belated entry into and ignominious forced departure from the Exchange Rate Mechanism in 1992 increased antagonism to the whole European project and turned the prospect of a single European currency into the issue on which the right was determined to make a stand...For many Conservatives, a single European currency undermines their core beliefs in national independence and sovereignty.' (Leach 1998, p.32)

Whether or not the UK should join the group of countries going ahead with a single European currency in the first wave (beginning in January 1999) was a decision that had to be made shortly after Labour won power in 1997. As Philip Stephens noted:

> 'This was the most momentous decision facing Tony Blair's government. Economic and monetary union is the point where economics, politics and Europe collide with maximum potential for disaster.' (*Financial Times*, 28 October 1997)

The ERM

The first stage in the process towards EMU was for member countries to agree to peg their exchange rates within a band of a weighted average of European currencies. This was done by means of the Exchange Rate Mechanism (ERM). The ERM was neither a fixed nor a floating exchange rate system, it combined elements of both. On the one hand, currencies in the ERM were fixed in value against each other. On the other hand, currencies could move up and down within a narrow band against each other and the whole currency bloc could fluctuate freely against other world currencies such as the dollar or the yen. The ERM was created in 1979 by six member countries. Britain joined in October 1990 and withdrew in September 1992.

The British government and the ERM, 1979-92

Nigel Lawson was a supporter of Britain's entry into the ERM from the outset. In 1979, he wrote an article in *Financial Weekly* supporting Britain's ERM membership. His advice was rejected partly on the grounds that inflation was too high to join. Two years later, when inflation had fallen, he wrote to the Chancellor, Geoffrey Howe, suggesting that the right time to join had arrived. Again, his advice was rejected in the Cabinet by those who argued that stability against the dollar was more important than stability against European currencies.

When Lawson became Chancellor he was able to convince Margaret Thatcher that, in principle, Britain should join the ERM. He used two arguments to persuade her. First, he argued that because Britain was a member of the European Community, it was important for the Prime Minister to be seen to show some commitment to it. Second, he argued that greater economic stability would result from having a single European currency. Although agreeing in principle, however, Thatcher continued to use delaying tactics.

From the end of 1987, Chancellor Lawson and the Treasury let the pound shadow the Deutschmark in preparation for joining the ERM. They sold sterling whenever the pound threatened to go over the three Deutschmark level. In March 1988, however, strong upward pressure on the pound led to this policy being abandoned.

Lawson's resignation in October 1989 was closely linked to the delay in entry into the ERM. Margaret Thatcher's economic adviser, Alan Walters, strongly opposed entry into the ERM and she accepted his, rather than her Chancellor's, advice on this matter. As a result, Lawson had little choice but to resign. Ironically, a year later, John Major, Lawson's successor, finally persuaded the government to join the ERM.

The wrong time and the wrong rate?

At the time when Britain joined the ERM, it was experiencing high inflation (7% above that in Germany), it had a high balance of payments of deficit and was steadily moving into recession. It was, in short, a less than ideal moment to join the ERM. At the time, many commentators argued that Britain had joined the ERM at too high an exchange rate. They suggested that, since the exchange rate was too high and Britain was moving into recession, it would be difficult for Britain to grow out of recession without having a balance of payments problem (since, once Britain was within the ERM, its exchange rate would be fixed within a band). The government, however, decided that a high exchange rate would help in the fight against inflation since British exporters and British firms competing against imports would have to cut costs and lower prices if they wanted to survive. When John Major became Prime Minister, he made it clear that membership of the ERM was the key to his economic strategy. This commitment was explicitly stated during the run up to the general election in April 1992:

> 'Membership of the ERM is now central to our counter-inflation discipline.' (Conservative 1992, p.6)

'Black Wednesday'

Despite the reservations of some economists, the pound traded comfortably within its broad bands until July 1992. From July 1992, however, the pound (together with the French franc and Italian lira) came under intense selling pressure. The foreign exchange markets decided that Germany was overcoming the problems produced by reunification and the Deutschmark was not sufficiently strong. As a result, they wanted either the Deutschmark to be revalued or the pound, franc and lira to be devalued. Pressure on the pound, franc and lira grew so strong that by 13 September the Italian government had decided to

devalue the lira by 7%. The revalued lira remained within the ERM. Attention then turned to the pound. There was such strong selling pressure on the pound that, despite spending up to £10 billion of government reserves in an effort to avert the crisis (the actual figures have not been revealed), the government was forced to devalue on 16 September ('Black Wednesday'). On the same day, the government decided to leave the ERM. Britain's withdrawal from the ERM was a major blow to European monetary union. In the past, member countries stayed within the ERM even when forced to realign their currencies. Britain was the first member to withdraw from the system.

Why did Britain leave the ERM?

One reason why the British government decided to leave the ERM was that it was felt that being tied to the ERM had prolonged the recession. Whilst it remained in the ERM, the government was unable to make large interest rate cuts because they would result in the pound falling out of its band. After it left the ERM, the government was able to cut interest rates without worrying if the level of the pound fell. As a result, the government was able to encourage growth and ease the economy out of recession. A second reason for leaving the ERM was a coolness towards European integration and a desire to appease the Eurosceptics.

Although the British government was able to ease Britain out of recession, withdrawal from the ERM was a severe blow to its credibility. It was, after all, just five months before withdrawal that the government had been elected on a platform which stressed that membership of the ERM was central to its economic strategy.

The timetable for monetary union

The timetable for monetary union was first laid out in the Delors plan of 1989 and then incorporated into the Maastricht Treaty. The Maastricht Treaty also laid out the convergence criteria (debt levels, inflation rates and interest rates) which members had to meet if they were to qualify to join the single currency. When the heads of government of EU members met in Brussels on 1 May 1998 to decide who would join the single currency, 14 out of the 15 members met the convergence criteria (only Greece did not). Britain, Denmark and Sweden, however, all decided not to join the single currency in the first wave. That meant that, initially, 11 states would participate in the single currency. On 1 January 1999, the euro became a currency in its own right and conversion rates were locked. National banknotes and coins remain legal tender until the end of 2002, but they must be withdrawn from circulation by January 2003:

> 'As part of the switch-over to the euro, the exchange rates of national currencies will be irrevocably fixed against each other at the start of 1999. But euro notes and coins will not

replace them in people's wallets and purses until 2002. This is just as well. There are some 13 billion notes and 76 billion coins in circulation in Europe that will need replacing in three years. The cost will be enormous, and mostly met by the banks. Germany's Deutsche Bank calculates that it will take 2,000 "cashier months" to exchange its private customer's holdings. The risk of things going badly awry will be huge.' (*Economist*, 2 January 1998)

Britain and EMU since 1993

John Major's tiny overall majority ensured that Eurosceptic backbenchers were able to exert a great deal of pressure on the government between 1993 and 1997. By the time of the 1997 general election, John Major had pledged to hold a referendum before joining a single currency (a pledge which Labour also made) and he had adopted a cautious 'wait and see' approach.

In the run-up to the 1997 general election, the Labour leadership was cautious:

> 'There are formidable obstacles in the way of Britain being in the first wave of membership, if EMU takes place on 1 January 1999. What is essential for the success of EMU is genuine convergence among the economies that take part, without any fudging of the rules. However, to exclude British membership of EMU forever would be to destroy any influence we have over a process which will affect us whether we are in or out. We must, therefore, play a full part in the debate to influence it in Britain's interests.' (Labour 1997, pp.37-8)

Labour's dilemma

The dilemma faced by the Labour leadership was that it genuinely wanted to play a leading role in Europe after the election, but it was aware that the public was sceptical about EMU and the press was, on the whole, hostile to it. The only way a British government could play a leading role was to join the single currency in the first wave. This, however, would mean risking hostility from the public and the press.

Gordon Brown's statement, October 1997

Following press speculation that the government was thinking about joining the single currency in the first wave, the Chancellor, Gordon Brown, made a statement to Parliament on 27 October 1997:

> 'The spin described this as the most pro-European statement by a Chancellor in a generation and certainly the unequivocal support he offered for the principle of entry is an important milestone in the history of British economic policy. However, it was also stated that entry in the current Parliament was "not realistic", meaning that membership was probably not feasible before 2005.' (Grant 1998, p.110)

In his speech, Chancellor Brown set out five economic tests that would have to be satisfied before Britain would join a single European currency. There would have to be:

- sustainable convergence between Britain and the other economies
- sufficient flexibility for Britain to be able to withstand economic shocks
- evidence that joining would create better conditions for investment
- evidence that the impact on the financial services industry would be favourable
- evidence that joining would be good for prosperity and jobs.

William Hague and EMU

Shortly after the 1997 Conservative Party conference, the new Leader, William Hague, ruled out joining the single currency in both the current Parliament and the next. In effect, therefore, he ruled out joining the single currency for at least 10 years.

Arguments for a single European currency

According to Grant (1996), the main arguments in favour of joining the single European currency are as follows. First, joining would mean an end to the costs which both companies and individuals have to pay (for converting currency) as they move goods or themselves from one country to another. Second, the risk of currency fluctuations is removed. This encourages investment. Third, without EMU, competitive devaluations might undermine the single market. Fourth, the City of London would be likely to lose business if Britain remained outside the single currency. Fifth, EMU would help to keep interest rates and inflation rates low. Sixth, whilst it remains outside the single currency, Britain will become less attractive to foreign investors. And seventh, without EMU, the momentum for European integration would be lost and tensions within Europe might rise.

Arguments against a single European currency

The main argument against joining the single European currency is that joining will lead to a loss of political and economic sovereignty. There would be a loss of political sovereignty because some power over economic decisions would be transferred from British to European decision-making bodies. The Bank of England, for example, would lose power to a new European Central Bank. There would be a loss of economic sovereignty because Britain would lose some control over interest rates, exchange rates and its Budget. Sterling would disappear, interest rates would be set by the new European Central Bank and the British government would have limited powers to alter taxes or run up Budget deficits. It should be noted, however, that, even without joining the single currency, Britain has limited control over policy because foreign trade is so important to its economy. Successive post-war governments have found that they cannot run large-scale Budget deficits. As a result, their hands have been tied. It could be argued, therefore, that joining a single currency would merely formalise an existing arrangement.

Other arguments against joining the single European currency are as follows. First, there is not enough real economic convergence between member states to allow monetary union to work effectively. Second, there would be a loss of flexibility. Britain would not be able to devalue in a crisis. Third, there would be greater restraints on public expenditure which would damage welfare programmes. Fourth, more aid would have to be given to poorer regions. This would result in tax rises in Britain. And fifth, European integration is not necessarily desirable.

Main points - Section 3.4

- The EU's long-term aim of economic and monetary union (EMU) will have been achieved when a single European currency has been adopted by all member countries.
- The first step towards EMU was setting up the ERM. This was neither a fixed nor a floating exchange rate system - it combined elements of both.
- Britain did not join the ERM until 1990. It was forced to withdraw in September 1992.
- By May 1998, 14 member states met the convergence criteria necessary to join a single currency and 11 states agreed to join (Britain chose not to join). The single currency came into existence on 1 January 1999.
- In October 1997, the Labour government ruled out joining the single currency within the current Parliament, but it supported joining in principle.

Activity 15.5 Britain and EMU

Item A *Britain's economy compared*

According to Wyn Grant, there was, in 1997, too much divergence between British and continental economies for Britain to contemplate joining the single currency. By 1997, Britain was in its sixth year of recovery while the rest of Europe, affected by German reunification, was still in the early stages of recovery. This difference was reflected in British interest rates of 7.2% in October 1997 compared to just over 3% in France and Germany. Britain, Grant argues, is more prone to boom and bust cycles than its European neighbours and its economy could still be out of sync in 2002 or 2003. In terms of patterns of trade, oil and company finance, the British economy has a different structure. Its labour market is more flexible than those in France or Germany. Housing finance depends much more on variable rate mortgages (and levels of home ownership are higher anyway). As a result, the UK could not join EMU when EU interest rates were higher than domestic ones because that would push up UK rates, hurting home owners who are an important sector of the electorate. Conversely, if UK rates were significantly higher, lowering them would be inflationary. There are also political problems. Public opinion remains opposed - for example, 61% opposed EMU in the 1997 British Social Attitudes Survey. If a referendum was called, a cross-party campaign in favour, backed by the CBI and TUC, could make an impact. But, an important counter-factor would be the hostility of the tabloid press.

Adapted from Grant 1998.

Item B *Meeting the convergence criteria*

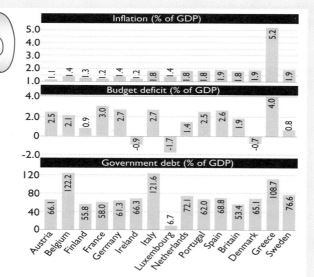

Convergence criteria

1. The inflation rate must be within 1.5 % of the average rate in the three lowest inflation countries in the EU.

2. Long-term interest rates must be no more than 2% above the average rate in the three lowest interest countries in the EU.

3. A member state's currency must have been in the narrow band of the ERM for at least two years with no realignments for 'severe tensions'.

4. A member state's fiscal Budget deficit must be no more than 3% of GDP and the national debt must be less than 60% of GDP.

The graphs above show that not all 11 states which agreed to join the single currency in May 1998 satisfied the convergence criteria perfectly. Italy and Belgium, for example, had national debts greater than 60%. Italy had also not been in the narrow band of the ERM for two years previously. Nevertheless, it was accepted that these countries were making good progress towards meeting the convergence criteria.

Adapted from Anderton 1998.

Item C *Eurocreep*

As the deadline approaches, it is increasingly clear that, although Britain will stay out of the single currency, the single currency won't stay out of Britain. Mortgage lenders, shops, businesses and even pay packets could be converted to the euro. People will be able to live and work in Britain without ever coming across a pound coin. They will earn in euros, spend in euros and even pay their taxes in euros. Just as the dollar has become a parallel currency in South America, so the euro could become a parallel currency in Britain - by a process termed 'Eurocreep'. Already shops are converting - for example, Marks and Spencer will accept euro notes and coins when they come into circulation. People returning from holiday will want to spend left-over euros. Northern Ireland will be flooded with euros from the Republic. Sainsbury's in Northern Ireland will definitely accept euros. The main force for change will be foreign tourists. Harrods and Selfridges will accept euros, as will shops in all airports. British shoppers will have to get used to dual pricing quoting both euros and pounds. And it won't just affect shops. Large numbers of businesses intend to convert to reduce their exchange rate risk. Multinationals which do a great deal of trade with the continent will do their internal accounting in euros. Every week, industries are announcing they want suppliers to bill them in euros. Some companies have even considered paying their staff in euros. For companies with branches across Europe this would make the transfer of staff a great deal easier.

Adapted from the *Observer*, 26 April 1998.

Item D *The consequences of EMU*

(i)

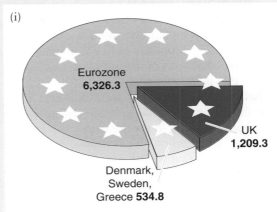

(ii)

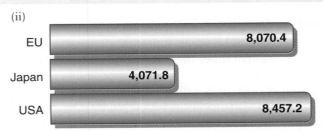

The pie chart (i) shows the relative size of 1998 GDP of those states in and out of the single currency (based on ERM central rates in $billion). The bar chart (ii) shows how the EU's economy would compare with the USA and Japan if the four states currently outside the single currency were to join. The figures are 1998 GDP based on ERM central rates in $billion.

Adapted from the *Guardian*, 30 April 1998.

Item E *Selling the idea*

In January 1998, the *New Statesman* asked an advertising company to come up with some ideas for a campaign to persuade British people to vote for a single European currency in a referendum. The three members of the shadow Cabinet in the poster - Michael Howard, William Hague and John Redwood - are known to be opposed to joining the single currency at least before 2008.

Questions

1. Should Britain join the single European currency and, if so, when? Use Items A-E in your answer.

2. 'The convergence criteria were fudged so that EMU would go ahead as planned.' To what extent does the evidence in Item B support this statement?

3. Was Britain right not to join the single currency in the first wave? Using Items A-D, give arguments for and against.

4. What point is being made in Item E? What other arguments might have been used in support of a single currency?

Part 4 Economic decision making

Key issues

1. Who makes the key economic decisions?
2. What role do these people play in the decision-making process?
3. What factors restrict the scope of the decision makers?
4. How are economic decisions made?

4.1 The key economic decision makers

The hierarchy

One of the most important functions of government is to raise money from the public and to decide how this money should be spent. Although all members of the government make decisions which involve the spending of public money, overall responsibility for economic strategy rests with the Chancellor of the Exchequer. The Chancellor is supported by a team of junior ministers and civil servants in the Treasury and by a fellow Cabinet member, the Chief Secretary to the Treasury. In addition, the Chancellor works closely with the Prime Minister. This section looks at the role of the Chancellor and other economic decision makers within the governmental system.

The role of the Chancellor

It is the Chancellor's job to determine how much public money should be raised and how it should be spent. Although the Chancellor does not make such decisions alone, it is upon the Chancellor that final responsibility for these decisions rests. Since economic success, or the perception of it, tends to be translated into electoral success, the Chancellor is, therefore, often regarded as the architect of the government's success or failure.

The Budget Statement

The Chancellor's most prominent role is the presentation of the annual Budget Statement. In the Budget speech, the Chancellor explains how the government intends to raise the money it needs to run public services during the following year. Until 1993, the Budget was announced in early spring (usually March) whilst public expenditure plans were announced separately in the Autumn Statement. Between 1993 and 1997, this changed. The two statements were joined together and a unified Budget Statement was made in November. This system changed again after Labour was elected to government in 1997. In June 1997, it was announced that a Comprehensive Spending Review (CSR) would be undertaken, examining public spending in all government departments. Then, in June 1998, a month before the results of the CSR were revealed, the Chancellor announced that all public expenditure (except that for the Department of Social Security) had been set for the forthcoming three years (1999 to 2002). As a result, there was no need for the equivalent of the old Autumn Statements (since public expenditure was fixed). Gordon Brown made an ad hoc Budget Statement in July 1997, but since then the main Budget statement has reverted to early spring. Each Budget is preceded by a pre-Budget Report in the previous November.

Other duties

Before May 1997, it was the responsibility of the Chancellor to set interest rates. In May 1997, however, Gordon Brown transferred that responsibility to the Bank of England's Monetary Policy Committee. Since May 1997, it has been the Chancellor's job to set an inflation target. The Monetary Policy Committee then has to decide what level of interest rates is necessary to achieve that inflation target.

The Chancellor's other duties are as follows:

- the Chancellor has overall charge of policy making in the Treasury
- the Chancellor is responsible for exchange rate policy
- the Chancellor is responsible for liaising with finance ministers from other countries.

According to the former Chancellor Nigel Lawson British Chancellors have a broader role to play than their counterparts from overseas:

> 'In other countries [the different] jobs are normally divided up. In the United States, for example, the Treasury Secretary is responsible for tax; the director of the Office of Management and the Budget (OMB) for public expenditure; and the Chairman of the Federal Reserve for the monetary side.' (Lawson 1992, p.272)

Nigel Lawson argues that the broader role played by the British Chancellor is healthy since it allows a coherence of policy. It can, however, put the Chancellor under great strain. Denis Healey, Labour Chancellor from 1974 to 1979, recalled that:

> 'It was exceptionally hard and frustrating work. The Chancellor of the Exchequer's is a lonely job, particularly in a period like mine when he was obliged to disappoint the hopes of his party and the aspirations of his colleagues - not to speak of his own.' (Healey 1989, p.388)

The Chancellor's influence

Since the Chancellor is responsible for the government's overall economic strategy, there is a great deal of scope for influencing policies which are not the direct responsibility of the Treasury. Nigel Lawson admitted that:

'If somebody had managed to penetrate security and called on me at a random hour of the working day, he would probably have found me, not considering interest rates or exchange rates or government borrowing - the issues so beloved of financial commentators - but playing a substantial role on a Cabinet Committee on a vast range of subjects...The Chancellor, if he proceeds with care and caution, can affect the content and not merely the cost of other Ministers' policies and, in a limited number of carefully selected areas, generate the ideas which decisively influence the direction of government policy...This is exemplified by the long-standing rule that any minister who has a proposal to put before Cabinet must first submit it to the Treasury.' (Lawson 1992, p.273)

The Chancellor and the Prime Minister

According to Wyn Grant:

'The relationship between the Prime Minister and the Chancellor is the most crucial one in British economic policy making.' (Grant 1998, p.114)

Indeed, the close relationship between Chancellor and Prime Minister is symbolised by the unlocked connecting door between 10 and 11 Downing Street. It is now well established that, regardless of the personalities involved, prime ministerial involvement in economic decision making is now part of established procedure. And, it should not be forgotten that it is the Prime Minister who appoints the Chancellor.

Grant argues that there are four basic types of relationship (see Box 15.3) and that the relationship between Gordon Brown and Tony Blair fits the top left hand corner (Number 1).

Grant's argument is based on the following assessment of Brown's qualities and the relationship between Brown and Blair:

- Brown has clear ideas about what needs to be done
- Brown is an effective parliamentary performer
- Brown and Blair trust one another
- Brown and Blair meet frequently.

Some commentators, however, have argued that there are significant tensions between Brown and Blair. These, they argue, surfaced after the publication of a biography of Brown in January 1998 (it was alleged that Brown was still bitter that Blair and not he had become Leader of the Labour Party in 1994) and at the time of Blair's first reshuffle in July 1998 (it was alleged that Blair moved firm allies into key strategic posts to offset the influence of Brown).

The Treasury

The importance of the Treasury is indicated by the fact that it is the only government department to be represented in the Cabinet by two members (the Chancellor of the Exchequer and the Chief Secretary to the Treasury). Although the Treasury stands at the centre of the economic decision-making process it is a small, intimate department with around 350 officials at the rank of principal and above and around 1,000 employees in total. Like other government departments, the Treasury is hierarchical and is staffed jointly by ministers and civil servants. It is headed by the permanent secretary, one of the most high ranking posts in the civil service.

The role of the Treasury

The Treasury has three main functions. First, it provides senior ministers (notably the Prime Minister and Chancellor) with policy advice concerning the general management of the economy. Second, the Treasury is the key institution in which decisions about the raising and spending of public money are made. Third, together with the Bank of England, the Treasury is responsible for designing policies relating to financial markets and international economic institutions (such as the International Monetary Fund and the European Union).

In practice, this means that the central tasks of the Treasury are:

- the preparation of the annual Budget (which determines how much public money will be raised)
- the allocation of public expenditure to government departments (with the exception of the Department of Social Security, now decided on a three year cycle).

Box 15.3 The relationship between the Prime Minister and the Chancellor

	Chancellor is a political figure in own right	Chancellor lacks an independent base
Harmonious relationship	1. Chancellor enjoys autonomy but also support from Prime Minister	2. Chancellor faithfully executes Prime Minister's policies
Difficult relationship	3. Clashes over policy and ultimate breakdown in relationship	4. Prime Minister lacks confidence in Chancellor and dismissal likely

Adapted from Grant 1998.

In addition, the Treasury provides information and advice to ministers on matters such as the control of the money supply, the level of exchange rates and the management of the government's debt.

The 'Treasury view'

Although Treasury officials, like any other civil servants, are supposed to be politically neutral, critics have argued that there is a distinct 'Treasury view' of the British economy and Chancellors are put under pressure to conform to this view. For example, Denis Healey has accused the Treasury of:

> 'Misleading the government, the country and the world for so many years about the true state of public spending in Britain. Indeed I suspect that Treasury officials were content to overstate public spending in order to put pressure on governments who were reluctant to cut it.' (Healey 1989, p.402)

In an attempt to change the culture of the Treasury, Gordon Brown arranged a meeting with all Treasury staff in October 1997 in which he outlined a new role for the Treasury:

> 'Officials will be told that Mr Brown's plans will give them far more clout in Whitehall and their role will no longer be confined to paring public spending. While still committed to rooting out inefficiency and waste, the Chancellor wants his department to help other departments to find ways of releasing resources for Labour's priorities. Creating high and stable levels of growth has been made the centre of the Treasury's rewritten mission statement, and Mr Brown will say that he wants officials to explore ways of creating more jobs, increasing educational opportunities and removing barriers to expansion.' (*Guardian*, 14 October 1997)

The role of the Chief Secretary to the Treasury

Until 1998, the main job of the Chief Secretary to the Treasury was to take charge of the annual spending round. It was the Chief Secretary who conducted the 'bilaterals' - separate meetings with each minister in charge of a government department. It was at these bilaterals that the amount of money to be allocated to a particular department was finally decided.

In June 1998, however, Gordon Brown announced that all public expenditure (with the exception of that allocated to the Department of Social Security) was to be set for the next three years. As a result, a major part of the role of the Chief Secretary has disappeared. On 18 June 1998, the *Times* suggested that, because of this, the position should lose its Cabinet status. By way of contrast, the political commentator Steve Richards argued that, despite the Comprehensive Spending Review (CSR), the government's work on public spending was nowhere complete (especially regarding welfare reform):

> 'If it were, there would be little point in having a Chief Secretary to the Treasury...The CSR was not quite as comprehensive as its billing suggests.' (*New Statesman*, 17 July 1998)

When Tony Blair announced his first reshuffle on 27 July 1998, the post of Chief Secretary to the Treasury retained its Cabinet status.

Main points - Section 4.1

- Overall responsibility for economic strategy rests with the Chancellor of the Exchequer. It is the Chancellor's job to determine how much public money should be raised and how it should be spent.
- In the Budget Statement, the Chancellor explains how the government intends to raise the money it needs to run public services during the following year. The Budget Statement is made in early spring. It is preceded by a pre-Budget Statement in November.
- Under Labour, public expenditure has been earmarked three years in advance (except for the Department of Social Security).
- The relationship between the Prime Minister and the Chancellor is the most crucial one in British economic policy making.
- The Treasury's main functions are: (1) to provide senior ministers with policy advice on the management of the economy; (2) to help make decisions about the raising and spending of public money; and (3) to design policies relating to financial markets and international economic institutions.

Activity 15.6 The role of the Chancellor

Item A *The financial year 1997-98*

1 May 1997	Labour victory at general election.
7 May	Chancellor announces Bank of England to have 'operational independence'.
11 June	Chief Secretary to the Treasury announces launch of Comprehensive Spending Review.
2 July	Gordon Brown's first Budget - windfall tax; VAT on fuel reduced to 5%.
27 October	Chancellor rules out joining single European currency during this Parliament.

25 November	Chancellor's pre-Budget statement.
17 March 1998	Gordon Brown's second Budget - overhaul of taxes and benefits to encourage work and enterprise.
11 June 1998	Chancellor announces public spending will be fixed for three years from 1999.
14 July 1998	Results of Comprehensive Spending Review announced.

Item B *Changing the rules*

In November 1997, political commentator Jonathan Freedland overheard a wedding guest using the term, 'I wanted to Gordon Brown it'. What they were referring to was Gordon Brown's refusal to wear full dinner dress when giving his Mansion House address. Brown wore a regular suit instead - and clearly made an impression. This rebel image, Freedland argues, took deeper root when the Chancellor broke with custom on Budget day by posing for photographers with a shiny red briefcase instead of the tattered old bag used by his predecessors. Then, on 25 November 1997, he broke with tradition a third time by delivering a first ever pre-Budget Report and inviting members of the public to offer their own views on tax, benefits and the way Britain pays for itself. The temptation, argues Freedland, is to see Brown as the left's conscience inside the Labour government. But, this misses the point. Brown is not an Old Labourite in Blairite drag. Rather, he and Blair are equal supporters of New Labour - with Brown offering substance and Blair providing style. It is the Chancellor who is steering through the flagship policies of the government (the welfare-to-work programme, for example, or preparations for the single currency). Blair works from nine to five (to have quality time with his children), whilst (childless) Brown works at the Treasury from 6 am to midnight. Despite their different working habits, however, the two are ideologically in sync - as much soulmates as Lawson and Thatcher in their heyday.

Adapted from the *Guardian*, 26 November 1997.

Item C *A revolutionary Chancellor?*

Gordon Brown, suggested political commentator Steve Richards in July 1998, was in a position to go on holiday until the next election. After all, public spending had been settled for the next three years. Interest rates were no longer the Chancellor's responsibility. And, income tax could not be increased because of manifesto commitments. The workaholic Chancellor, Richards argued, had no work - at least none that previous Chancellors would recognise. Whilst they had spent their summers negotiating public spending levels, worrying about interest rate levels and whether to raise or cut income tax, Brown had revolutionised the role of Chancellor. Richards had particular praise for Brown's decision to scrap the formal annual spending round. These, he said, had become a ritual in which individual ministers tried to prove their machismo by putting in excessive bids - a system which had as much to do with Whitehall infighting and political reputations as it did with the need for public services. Richards also praised the fact that the Treasury would be keeping an eye on departments to make sure that the money allocated to them in the Comprehensive Spending Review was spent properly. This, Richards said, was a novel but legitimate function for a Chancellor with a genuine interest in policy across the board. The only problem was a danger of too many meddlers. As well as Brown and Blair, there would be the 'Cabinet enforcer' and Party Chair, both of whom would inevitably take a keen interest in policy. Departmental ministers, Richards asserted, would not get a moment's rest.

Adapted from the *New Statesman*, 17 July 1998.

Questions

1. Judging from Items A-C, would you agree that Gordon Brown has 'revolutionised the role of Chancellor'? Explain your answer.

2. 'Today, power lies in Number 11, not Number 10, Downing Street'. Judging from Items B and C would you agree with this statement? Explain your answer.

3. How significant was Gordon Brown's decision to scrap the annual spending round? Use Item C in your answer.

4.2 External influences on economic decision making

Sources of pressure from outside

In addition to the pressures and advice which come from within the governmental system, economic decision makers have to take account of the views of individuals and institutions outside the governmental system. Although the weight attached to particular pieces of advice varies according to the personality and overall strategy of the decision maker, there are three main sources of pressure and advice outside the governmental system - economic advisers, the Bank of England and international institutions.

1. Economic advisers

Although the major economic decision makers (the Chancellor and the Prime Minister) receive a great deal of advice from economic advisers working within the governmental system (for example, from the hundred or so members of the Government Economic Service who are spread across the government departments), economic advisers outside the governmental system also exert pressure on economic decision making. Financial experts are employed by the mass media to comment on every move made by the Chancellor and often media campaigns are launched to try and alter the direction in which the government's economic strategy is moving. A good example of external economic advisers trying to put pressure on the government was a letter published in the *Times* shortly after Geoffrey Howe's Budget in 1981. This letter protested against the folly of government economic policy and was signed by 364 British economists.

Advisers with insider status

As with pressure groups (see Chapter 10, Section 1.3), economic advisers who manage to gain insider status have a better chance of influencing the outcome of the decision-making process than those with outsider status. It is normal for the Chancellor and the Prime Minister to listen to independent economic advisers (usually academics seconded from universities or members of think tanks) whose ideological stance is compatible with their own. On occasions, this can cause problems. When Margaret Thatcher's economic adviser, Professor Alan Walters, publicly disagreed with the view of the Chancellor Nigel Lawson in 1989, for example, this led to Lawson's resignation.

2. The Bank of England

The Bank of England is Britain's central bank. Although the Bank is a public body (it was nationalised in 1946 and is, therefore, owned by the government), it has always retained a degree of independence from government. Its Governor, for example, is nominated by the Prime Minister but is usually an independent figure. Employees of the Bank are not civil servants. They are recruited independently and paid more than civil servants. On 7 May 1997, the Chancellor, Gordon Brown, announced that the Bank was to be given 'operational independence' by law (see below).

The role of the Bank

When the Bank was nationalised, no clear guidance was given as to what its role should be. It ended up, however, performing a wider role than other central banks. Today, the Bank has a number of functions. First, it is responsible for the issue of notes and coins. Second, it manages the Exchange Equalisation Account - the account used to buy and sell foreign currency. The Bank's role is to maintain a given level of sterling in the foreign exchange markets. Third, the Bank acts as a banker to the government. It manages the National Debt and arranges government loans. Fourth, it acts as a banker to the banking system. All banks have to keep 0.5% of their liabilities with the Bank of England and, if banks are short of cash and other liquid assets, the Bank of England arranges loans for them. And fifth, since May 1997, the Bank has had 'operational independence'.

Operational independence

The key feature of operational independence is that a new Monetary Policy Committee has control over the setting of interest rates. The full extent of the new arrangements is as follows:

- the monetary policy objective of the Bank will be to deliver price stability (in terms of the government's inflation target) and it is also expected to support the government's economic policy and its growth and employment objectives
- the Bank has the responsibility for setting short-term interest rates so as to achieve the government's inflation target
- the government will continue to be responsible for exchange rate policy, another important economic lever

- the new Monetary Policy Committee will be made up of the Governor, the two Deputy Governors and six members (two of the six members are appointed by the Governor after consultation with the Chancellor and the remaining four are appointed by the Chancellor).

(Grant 1998, p.105)

Until May 1997, the Bank was responsible for regulating the banking sector. In May 1997, however, the Chancellor stripped the bank of this responsibility. A new body, the Securities and Investments Board, now regulates the banking sector.

A semi-independent Bank

The degree of independence granted to the Bank of England in May 1997 falls short of that granted to some other central banks. Indeed, the Bank has been described as 'semi-independent' by some commentators. This is because central banks elsewhere (in the USA, Italy, France and Germany, for example) have the power to set both interest rates and policy targets. The Bank of England, on the other hand, is constrained in a number of ways:

- the Bank must work within an inflation target set by the government
- the government has 'national interest power' - in extreme circumstances, the government can set interest rates for a limited period
- the majority of members of the Monetary Policy Committee are appointed by the Chancellor
- the Bank has to make reports to the Commons
- the Governor has to appear before the Treasury Select Committee four times a year
- the Monetary Policy Committee has a statutory duty to publish details of any interventions that the Bank makes in the foreign exchange market.

Arguments for an independent Bank of England

The main arguments in favour of an independent Bank are as follows. First, an independent Bank ensures that monetary policy is formulated by economic experts rather than amateur politicians with a political axe to grind. Second, the removal of political pressures enables greater cooperation between the Bank of England and other central banks. And third, de-politicising the Bank not only de-politicises interest rates, it also increases the Bank's credibility with the market and prevents governments from manipulating the economy just before a general election:

'Monetary policy needs to be insulated from political influence. The experience of the last 20 years in Britain has been that interest rates rise after the election and fall before the next one, regardless of the underlying state of the economy.' (Grant 1998, pp.106-7)

Arguments against an independent Bank of England

The main argument against an independent Bank of England is that elected representatives should have control over economic decisions rather than professional bankers. Elected representatives are accountable to the electorate whilst professional bankers are not. As Victor Keegan put it:

'Interest rate policy is at the centre of economic policy, especially in this country, where it has always been closely linked to exchange rate policy. To leave interest rate policy to unelected officials is an insult to democracy.' (*Observer*, 11 May 1997)

There are two further arguments against the Bank of England having the power to set interest rates. First, the Bank is likely to be more cautious about inflation and, therefore, more likely to raise interest rates. And second, there is the argument that there is likely to be a shift in power away from the manufacturing sector because higher interest rates strengthen the pound, making exports more difficult to sell.

The former Chancellor, Kenneth Clarke, opposed Gordon Brown's decision to hand the setting of interest rates to the Bank, saying:

'As a Chancellor, I found myself in a strong position. On the one hand, I could call on the very best advice from the Treasury and the Bank. On the other, as an active politician, I was in a position to keep my finger on the pulse of the real economy by talking to people who work in industry and business. In short, I was able to pursue the best policy for the hard-working man in the street.' (quoted in the *Financial Times*, 7 May 1997)

3. Globalisation and international constraints

As economic barriers between countries break down, individual countries have less freedom of manoeuvre. Since 1945, there has been greater economic interdependence and, as a result, economic management in Britain has increasingly been affected by external constraints.

Globalisation

One constraint is the increasing globalisation of financial markets. Modern methods of communication have linked together stock exchanges in different parts of the world and this has made an impact on the economies of individual countries. For example, if Britain is going through a difficult period economically, traders on the London exchanges will be up early to hear how sterling has been faring in Tokyo. Movements in Japan will influence the value of sterling against other currencies on the London market and this, in turn, will affect the price of shares in London. If the pound falls sharply and shares begin to tumble, the British government may have to intervene - for example by asking the Bank of England to buy sterling.

The Prime Minister, Tony Blair, is particularly aware of how globalisation has affected economic management. Indeed, it is because of accelerating globalisation that the Labour Party has moved away from the old economic policy instruments of the left (such as, Keynesianism, public ownership and planning the economy):

> 'In the global economy, it is argued, capital is mobile and demand is affected by factors beyond national boundaries. Governments cannot, therefore, control capital but can intervene to improve the capacities of labour. They have limited control over demand but can be active on the supply side, through education and training. This can provide for a skilled and flexible labour force to attract investment and ensure competitiveness. Countries like Britain and the USA cannot compete with less developed countries on low wages so they must focus on providing a more skilled workforce.' (Driver & Martell 1998, p.42)

The IMF

A second constraint is the influence of international economic organisations, notably the International Monetary Fund (IMF). The IMF was set up at the end of the Second World War. Its function is to stabilise exchange rates and to lend money to its members when they need foreign currency. Members pay a regular sum into the pool on the understanding that they can borrow from the pool when they have balance of payments problems. When the IMF makes a loan, however, it does so only if the government requesting the loan meets certain conditions. A request for assistance from the IMF by the Labour government in 1976, for example, led to significant changes in government policy (so that the IMF conditions were met). The Chancellor, Denis Healey, abandoned Keynesian demand management policies and introduced measures designed to control the money supply.

The World Trade Organisation

During the Great Depression of the 1930s, many countries devalued their currencies and set up trade barriers to save and create jobs in their domestic markets. Because many countries did this, the result was a fall in overall trade and a deeper depression. It was to prevent a repetition of the Great Depression of the 1930s that the General Agreement of Tariffs and Trade (GATT) was set up in 1947. In 1995, GATT's successor, the World Trade Organisation (WTO), took over its work (see also Chapter 6, Section 4.1).

The job of the WTO is to establish and enforce a system of rules governing international trade. One rule is that member nations are not allowed to increase the degree of protection given to their domestic producers. A second rule (the most favoured nation clause) is that a country which offers a cut in tariffs to one country has to offer it to all members. To encourage countries to reduce tariffs and quotas, the WTO organises a series of negotiations ('rounds'). At the first round of talks in Geneva in 1947, there were just 23 members. At the Uruguay round which ended in 1994, there were 125 members. Each round builds on the work of earlier talks. In the early days, the main job was cutting tariffs. More recently, rules against dumping exports (the sale of a product in an export market at a cheaper price than that charged in the domestic market) have been introduced. Since Britain is a member of the WTO, Britain's economic decision makers are obliged to conform to the rules established by the WTO.

The European Union

Similarly, British economic decision makers are constrained by membership of the European Union. The creation of a single internal market in 1992 has led to greater uniformity and standardisation. The need to conform to European standards has restricted individual member states' freedom of manoeuvre. Whilst membership of the EU brings many trading advantages, concern about the extent to which economic decision makers in member states should be able to determine their own economic future is at the heart of the sovereignty debate which has preoccupied many British politicians since the late 1980s.

Main points - Section 4.2

- The views of individuals and institutions outside the governmental system - such as economic advisers - affect economic decision making.
- The functions of the Bank of England are: (1) issuing notes and coins; (2) managing the Exchange Equalisation Account; (3) acting as a banker to the government; (4) acting as a banker to the banking system; and (5) setting interest rates.
- Some people argue that the Bank of England is 'semi-independent'.
- The main arguments in favour of an independent Bank are: (1) monetary policy is made by economic experts rather than amateur politicians; (2) greater cooperation with other central banks; (3) the Bank's credibility with the market is increased; and (4) governments cannot manipulate the economy.
- The main arguments against an independent Bank are: (1) elected representatives should have control over economic decisions; (2) caution is likely to lead to high interest rates; and (3) the manufacturing sector will lose power because a high pound makes exports more difficult to sell.
- International constraints on economic decision making include globalisation, the IMF, the WTO and the EU.

Activity 15.7 The Bank of England

Item A *Setting interest rates*

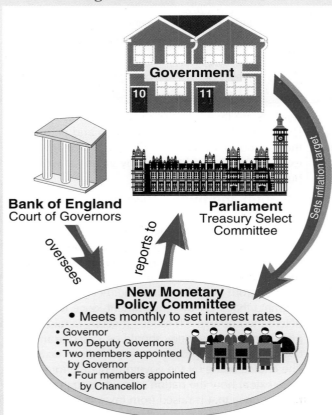

This diagram shows the economic decision-making structure for setting interest rates which came into effect in May 1997.

Adapted from the *Guardian*, 7 May 1997.

Item D *The Monetary Policy Committee*

Committee member	Dec 1997	Jan 1998	Feb	Mar	Apr	May	June	July
Sir Alan Budd	Hold	Up	Up	Up	Up	Hold	Up	Hold
Willem Buiter	Hold	Up	Up	Up	Up	Up	Up	Hold
Mervyn King	Hold	Hold	Up	Up	Up	Hold	Up	Hold
Charles Goodhart	Hold	Up	Up	Up	Hold	Hold	Up	Hold
Eddie George	Hold	Hold	Hold	Hold	Hold	Hold	Up	Hold
David Clementi	Hold	Hold	Hold	Hold	Hold	Hold	Up	Hold
Ian Plenderleith	Hold	Hold	Hold	Hold	Hold	Hold	Up	Hold
DeAnne Julius	Hold	Hold	Hold	Hold	Hold	Down	Up	Hold
John Vickers	-	-	-	-	-	-	Down	Hold

This table shows how the nine members of the Monetary Policy Committee voted on whether to lower, raise or hold interest rates between December 1997 and July 1998. All votes were for a change of $1/4$% up or down. Eddie George was Governor of the Bank of England and Mervin King Deputy Governor.

Adapted from the *Financial Times*, 11 June 1998 and 13 August 1998.

Item B *The reformed Bank of England*

On 6 May 1997, Gordon Brown announced that the Bank of England would be given operational independence by law. The Chancellor would set an inflation target (an average of 2.5%), but the Bank would manipulate interest rates to ensure that it was met. Brown said that he wanted to end the days of boom and bust economics, to provide the stability which would encourage British business to invest more and, to become more competitive, more productive and better capable of creating jobs. This, he argued, was only achievable if the markets believed that the government would no longer be open to the temptation to manufacture an unsustainable economic upturn ahead of every general election. Politicians, it was implied, could not be trusted. The result is that, today, the crucial power point in the Bank is its Monetary Policy Committee. The nine members (including four 'independent' members) have access to all the Bank's intellectual resources, but are accountable individually to Parliament. It is by the effectiveness and wisdom of the Monetary Policy Committee that Eddie George, Governor of the Bank, will be judged. He chairs the committee and, already, has been called upon to deliver a casting vote. Establishing the credibility of the new monetary arrangements will not be easy. The idea of an independent Bank sits uneasily with a sovereign Parliament and a mighty executive.

Adapted from the *New Statesman*, 10 April 1998.

Item C *A truly independent Bank*

The political commentator Simon Heffer argues that the only way to make the Bank of England truly independent is to privatise it - for six main reasons. First, the Bank's role in meeting the government's inflation target would not alter. It could not do so, because, if it did, the whole banking system and the currency itself might collapse. In other words, the continued existence of the Bank and the welfare of its shareholders would depend on it behaving responsibly. Second, privatisation would allow the Bank to expand commercially. The Bank would be more encouraged to supply commercial and investment services if it was a properly commercial business. Third, if the Bank's shares were held by the clearing banks, this would ensure that those who owned stock would also be the ones who ran the risk. Any bank bailed out by the Bank of England would be bailed out by its own money. Fourth, privatisation would, in effect, levy a windfall tax as it would mean the new shareholders paying for their share of the action. Fifth, as it would be in none of the shareholders' interests to adopt a strategy which led to financial chaos, the public would have an assurance that, even though the body which set interest rates was a private concern, its shareholders had every reason to ensure that it behaved sensibly. And sixth, it would be left to the shareholders to appoint the directors and Governor, and settle their earnings, removing another painful and delicate problem from the shoulders of the Chancellor.

Adapted from the *New Statesman*, 9 January 1998.

Questions

1. a) Judging from Items A, B and D, how did the role of the Bank of England change in May 1997?
   b) To what extent can the Bank of England be described as an 'independent central bank'?
2. a) Using Items A, B and D, describe the role of the Monetary Policy Committee.
   b) Give arguments for and against the view that interest rates should be set by the Monetary Policy Committee.
3. a) Judging from Item C, what arguments can be made in favour of privatising the Bank of England?
   b) What arguments might be used against privatisation?

Part 5 Taxation and public spending

Key issues

1. What is the difference between direct and indirect taxation?
2. Why is the level of taxation important?
3. Why has taxation been a crucial issue in recent elections?

5.1 Why is taxation important?

Direct taxation

Taxes can be raised in two ways - either directly or indirectly. Direct taxation is a tax levied directly on an individual or an organisation. Income tax is one form of direct taxation. Everyone earning more than a minimum amount pays a percentage of their earnings to central government in income tax. The rate of income tax is fixed by the Chancellor and announced in the Budget Statement each year. Income tax is the single most important source of revenue for the government. Other examples of direct tax are:

- corporation tax (a tax on company profits)
- inheritance tax (a tax on the value of assets left by an individual on their death)
- capital gains tax (a tax on real capital gains - the difference between the buying price and selling price of an asset after adjustment for inflation). Most goods and services are exempt from capital gains tax. It is paid mainly on stocks and shares.

In addition, National Insurance Contributions (NICs) are, in effect, a form of direct taxation (strictly speaking NICs are not taxes because they are a form of insurance premium, but they have come to be seen and used by government as a form of taxation). All workers have to pay NICs to qualify for state benefits. Employers also pay NICs for each worker they employ.

Indirect taxation

Indirect taxation is a tax levied on goods or services. The tax is indirect since it is only paid by those people who buy the goods or use the services which are subject to it. The main indirect tax is VAT (Value Added Tax). This is a tax on expenditure. 'Essential' goods and services such as food and children's clothes are exempt from VAT. All other goods and services are taxed. Excise duties - such as the taxes levied on alcoholic drinks, tobacco and petrol - are the second main type of indirect tax. The level of excise duty is calculated not by value (as with VAT), but by volume sold.

Taxation and public spending

Since all but 5% of government revenue is gained from taxation, the levels at which the various taxes are set is of crucial importance. Each year the government needs to raise a certain amount of revenue to finance public services and the government's programme. This money is raised from both direct and indirect taxes. The dilemma that faces the government, once it has determined how much money it needs to raise, is what proportion of this money should be raised from direct taxation and what proportion from indirect taxation. The choice made by the government determines to a large extent how the nation's wealth is shared out. The money that is raised from taxes is spent on public services. The more money that is raised, the more money there is for spending on education, the health service and so on. But, against this, the more money that is raised in taxes, the less money that people have to spend themselves. If the level of direct taxes is high, people's take-home pay is low. If the level of indirect tax is high, goods and services become expensive.

For Keynesians the level of taxation is important since it helps to determine demand. The raising or lowering of taxes slows down or boosts demand and is, therefore, a tool used to manipulate the economic cycle.

Taxation can also be used to influence consumption patterns. By placing large duties on tobacco and spirits, for example, the government discourages people from buying these products.

5.2 Taxation 1979-98

Taxation and general elections

Between 1979 and 1997, the Conservative Party attempted to promote itself as the party of low taxation and sound economic management. Low taxation (which, in practice, means low rates of direct taxation and high rates of indirect taxation) has electoral appeal, as the former Chancellor Nigel Lawson made clear in his autobiography:

'There are large numbers of people in this country who have been conditioned to believe that it sounds better to say that they would like to see more money spent on worthy public services - however doubtful they may be about whether the worthy public services will improve as a result - than that they would like to receive a tax cut. But, when it comes to casting a vote which might determine which of the two takes place, it is a different matter altogether. This was clearly demonstrated, to my complete lack of surprise, by the outcome of the 1987 general election.' (Lawson 1992, p.377)

The electoral appeal of low taxation was further illustrated in the 1992 general election when Conservative warnings that a vote for Labour would mean higher taxes helped the party to win an unexpected electoral victory.

Taxation under the Conservatives 1979-97

The Conservative government elected in 1979 attempted to shift the burden from direct to indirect taxes. In the 1979 Budget, the rate of VAT was increased from 8% to 15% and the extra revenue raised was used to finance cuts in income tax (the top rate of income tax was reduced from 83% to 60%). This set the trend. Between 1979 and 1997, the top rate of income tax fell from 83% to 40% whilst the bottom rate fell from 33% to 20%. Between 1979 and 1990, the amount of government income raised from income tax dropped from 31% to 26.6% whilst the amount of government income raised from indirect taxes (excise duties and VAT) rose from 27.9% to 30.6%. This shows that the tax burden was shifting from direct to indirect taxes. During the same period, NICs paid by employees increased as a percentage of tax revenue whilst contributions paid by employers declined. It could be argued, therefore, that part of the reduction in income tax has effectively been paid for by the overall increase in NICs.

Distribution of wealth

The result of these changes was a change in the distribution of wealth in the country. Between 1979 and 1994, the richest 10% of the population became over 60% better off whilst the poorest 10% of the population became 3% worse off (Anderton 1997). One reason for this was the shift in taxation. A rise in indirect taxes hits people on low incomes hard because the lower the income of a family, the greater the proportion of that income which is spent on goods and services which charge indirect taxes. When Norman Lamont, the Chancellor, announced in 1993 that VAT would be charged on domestic fuel, one Conservative backbench MP admitted that the consequence of this would be that:

'People on lower incomes will pay a higher proportion of income in tax than those earning more...In the case of food or domestic heating... such a tax would bear disproportionately on lower income earners.' (*Independent*, 29 November 1993).

Taxation 1993-97

Although the Conservatives pledged in their 1992 election manifesto not to raise taxes, they were forced to break this pledge in 1993. This was necessary to stem the high level of government borrowing that had developed during the recession of 1990-92 (the deficit had grown to £50 billion). In January 1994, the Labour Party was able to provide evidence that, for the first time since 1979, tax levels under a Conservative government exceeded the tax levels of the previous Labour government. Since the main thrust of the Conservatives' 1992 general election campaign had been that a vote for Labour would mean a vote for higher taxes whilst a vote for the Conservatives would not, Labour was able to charge the government with hypocrisy and to dent the Conservative Party's image as a party of low taxation.

Taxation and spending under Labour

Traditionally, the Labour Party has favoured a greater emphasis on direct rather than indirect taxation. Direct taxes, it is argued, are fairer because they are determined by the ability to pay. If VAT is added to a product, the same price is paid by a person on income support and a millionaire. It is better to raise public money from those who can afford it. Therefore, it is better to raise public money by taxing the income of the millionaire. As a result, under pre-1997 Labour governments, income tax rates were graduated to ensure that high earners paid high rates of income tax. The effect of this was to redistribute wealth from the rich to the poor - exactly what might be expected from a party whose aims included the commitment:

'To secure for the workers by hand or by brain the full fruits of their industry and the most equitable distribution thereof.' (Clause IV of the Labour Party constitution until 1995)

Taxation and spending under New Labour

By 1997, the Labour leadership had replaced the old Clause IV with a new one (see Chapter 2, Section 4.4) and it was determined to avoid the charge that Labour was a tax and spend party. As a result, it pledged to keep to spending targets set by the Conservatives during its first two years in office and it also pledged not to raise income tax rates and not to extend VAT throughout its term in office.

Despite this self-imposed straitjacket, the government managed to finance its welfare-to-work scheme by imposing a one-off 'windfall' tax on the privatised utilities. In addition, the Comprehensive Spending Review (completed in July 1998) resulted in a reallocation of public funds - with extra money being allocated in particular to health and education whilst some other departments faced cuts. By fixing public spending allocations for the years 1999 to 2002, the Chancellor, Gordon Brown, aimed to produce a period of stability in which the pressure to raise new taxes was avoided. Certainly, the spending allocations announced in July 1998 did not require extra taxes to fund them.

Main points - Part 5

- Direct taxation is a tax levied directly on an individual or an organisation.
- Indirect taxation is a tax levied on goods or services. It is indirect since it is only paid by those people who buy the goods or use the services which are subject to it.
- Since 95% of government revenue comes from taxation, the levels at which taxes are set is important. The more money that is raised, the more money there is for spending on public services, but the less money people have to spend on themselves.

- The Conservative government elected in 1979 attempted to shift the burden from direct to indirect taxes. Although the Conservatives pledged not to raise taxes in 1992, they were forced to break the pledge in 1993.
- Pre-1997 Labour governments favoured direct taxes - such as graduated income tax. In 1997, however, the Labour government pledged not to raise income tax or to extend VAT. It did, however, carry out its pledge to impose a one-off windfall tax on privatised utilities.

Activity 15.8 *Taxation under New Labour*

Item A *Indirect taxation*

In the July 1997 Budget, Gordon Brown cut VAT on domestic fuel from 8% to 5% (VAT was first imposed on fuel in 1993). He argued that the tax hit lower income households harder than higher income households because they paid more in tax as a percentage of their income. The graph (right) shows that the bottom fifth of households paid 30% of their income in indirect taxes compared to only 16% for the top fifth of households. Local taxes such as the council tax and water charges also hit the poor harder. The bottom fifth of households in 1994-95 paid £570 in taxes compared to £790 for the top fifth of households.

Adapted from Anderton 1997.

United Kingdom
Percentages

Percentage of income paid in indirect taxes

Bottom fifth	Next fifth	Middle fifth	Next fifth	Top fifth
30				
20			All households	
10				
0				

Item B *Labour's 1997 manifesto commitments*

Taxation is not neutral in the way it raises revenue. How and what governments tax send clear signals about the economic activities they believe should be encouraged or discouraged and the values they wish to entrench in society. New Labour will establish a new trust on tax with the British people. There will be no return to the punishing tax rates that existed under both Labour and Conservative governments in the 1970s. To encourage work and reward effort, we are pledged not to raise the basic or top rates of income tax throughout the next Parliament. Our long-term objective is a lower starting rate of income tax of ten pence in the pound. This will benefit the many, not the few. It is in sharp contrast to the Tory goal of abolishing capital gains and inheritance tax, at least half the benefit of which will go to the richest 5,000 families in the country. We will cut VAT on fuel to 5%, the lowest level allowed. We renew our pledge not to extend VAT to food, children's clothes, books and newspapers and public transport fares.

Adapted from Labour 1997.

Item C *Taxation 1978-79 to 2002-03*

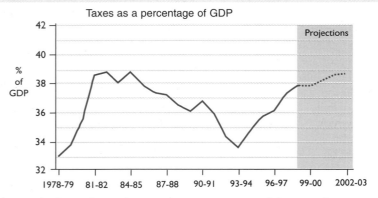

Taxes as a percentage of GDP

The graph above shows that taxes as a percentage of GDP are forecast to rise by 2002-03, according to government Budget projections in 1998. Various Budget measures, such as increases in tax on holiday insurance, cuts in tax allowances for mortgage tax relief and continued increases in taxes on petrol would lift the amount of tax raised at any given level of income. Since GDP was forecast in 1998 to grow by 2% a year for the next five years, however, the government would also gain tax revenues.

Adapted from Anderton 1998.

Item D *Poster from the 1997 general election campaign*

Questions

1. a) What is the difference between direct and indirect taxes? Use Item A in your answer.
   b) Why do you think Gordon Brown reduced the rate of VAT on fuel in July 1997?
2. Judging from Items A-D, how does the Labour government's approach to taxation differ from (a) previous Labour governments and (b) Conservative governments 1979-97?
3. Look at Item B. Why might Labour's manifesto pledges on tax be difficult to fulfil?

References

Anderson & Davey (1996) Anderson, P. & Davey, K., 'A farewell to Keynes?', *New Statesman*, 23 February 1996.

Anderson & Mann (1997) Anderson, P. & Mann, N., *Safety First: the Making of New Labour*, Granta, 1997.

Anderton (1992) Anderton, A., *The Student's Economy in Focus 1992/3*, Causeway Press, 1992.

Anderton (1994) Anderton A., *The Student's Economy in Focus 1994/5*, Causeway Press, 1994.

Anderton (1995) Anderton, A., *Economics* (2nd edn), Causeway Press, 1995.

Anderton (1995a) Anderton, A., *The Student's Economy in Focus 1994-5*, Causeway Press, 1995.

Anderton (1996) Anderton, A., *The Student's Economy in Focus 1996-7*, Causeway Press, 1996.

Anderton (1997) Anderton, A., *The Student's Economy in Focus 1997-8*, Causeway Press, 1997.

Anderton (1998) Anderton, A., *The Student's Economy in Focus 1998-9*, Causeway Press, 1998.

Brivati & Bale (1998) Brivati, B. & Bale, T. (eds), *New Labour in Power: Precedents and Prospects*, Routledge, 1998.

Butler & Butler (1994) Butler, D. & Butler, G., *British Political Facts 1900-94*, Macmillan, 1994.

Conservative (1992) *The Conservative Manifesto 1992*, Conservative Central Office, 1992.

Chambers (1993) Chambers, I. (ed.), Hall, D., Jones, R. & Raffo, C., *Business Studies*, Causeway Press, 1993.

Childs (1992) Childs, D., *Britain Since 1945*, Routledge, 1992.

Cook & Stevenson (1988) Cook, C. & Stevenson, J., *Modern British History 1714-1987*, Longman, 1988.

Driver & Martell (1998) Driver, S. & Martell, S., *New Labour: Politics after Thatcherism*, Polity Press, 1998.

Dunleavy et al. (1997) Dunleavy, P., Gamble, A., Holliday, I. & Peele, G., *Developments in British Politics 5*, Macmillan, 1997.

Grant (1992) Grant, W., 'Management of the economy' in *Wale (1992)*.

Grant (1996) Grant, W., 'Making economic policy in a global economy', *Politics Review*, Vol.6.1, September 1996.

Grant (1998) Grant, W., 'The economic policies of the Blair government' in *Lancaster (1998)*.

Hall & Jacques (1983) Hall, S. & Jacques, M. (eds), *The Politics of Thatcherism*, Lawrence & Wishart, 1983.

Healey (1989) Healey, D., *The Time of my Life*, Penguin, 1990.

Hobsbawm (1968) Hobsbawm, E., *Industry and Empire*, Pelican, 1968.

Johnson (1991) Johnson, C., *The Economy under Mrs Thatcher 1979–90*, 1991.

Kelly (1997) Kelly, G., 'Economic policy' in *Dunleavy et al. (1997)*.

Labour (1997) *New Labour - Because Britain Deserves Better*, Labour Party manifesto, Labour Party, 1997.

Lancaster (1998) Lancaster, S. (ed.), *Developments in Politics*, Vol.9, Causeway Press, 1998.

Lawson (1992) Lawson, N., *The View from No. 11*, Bantam Press, 1992.

Leach (1998) Leach, R., 'Political Ideas' in Lancaster (1998)

Loughlin & Scott (1997) Loughlin, M. & Scott, C., 'The regulatory state' in *Dunleavy et al. (1997)*.

McKie (1993) McKie, D. (ed.) *The Guardian Political Almanac 1993/4*, Fourth Estate, 1993.

OECD (1996) *OECD Economic Surveys 1996: United Kingdom*, OECD, 1996.

ONS (1998) Office for National Statistics, *Annual Abstract of Statistics*, HMSO, 1998

Smith (1776) Smith, A., *An Enquiry into the Nature and Causes of the Wealth of Nations*, Pelican, 1970.

Wale (1992) Wale, W. (ed.), *Developments In Politics*, Vol.3, Causeway Press, 1992.

16 Sub-national government

Introduction

In Britain, politics tends to be seen and understood in national political terms. The focus is on the world of Westminster and Whitehall. But, it is the various agencies of sub-national government (whether local authorities or other bodies) which most often impinge on the lives of ordinary citizens. The services provided by these agencies range from education to refuse collection and from roads to healthcare. They are, therefore, services which are of vital importance to the whole population. It is, however, not only because sub-national government is responsible for a wide range of services that it is important. There is a political principle to consider - the extent to which, in a parliamentary democracy, there is a need for a system of local democracy to counterbalance the power of a centralising state. It is the balance between the demands of centralised power and the needs of local autonomy which is at the heart of a discussion of the role and functions of sub-national government.

In recent years, major changes have taken place in sub-national government. Local government services have been privatised, for example, and local finance has been brought under strict central control. At the same time, there has been a striking growth in the number of unelected bodies (quangos), many of which are responsible for spending public money and making decisions which used to be made by local authorities. Since these changes were initiated by central government and are opposed by many who work in local government, the relationship between central and local government is fraught with a strong sense of crisis.

This chapter looks at the changes that have taken place in sub-national government over the past 25 years and considers what impact these changes have made and where sub-national government is heading.

Chapter summary

Part 1 looks at the organisation and structure of local authorities. Special attention is paid to the changes that have taken place since 1945.

Part 2 examines policy and decision making in local authorities. The range of activities and the functions local authorities perform are considered.

Local authority financing is reviewed.

Part 3 considers the changes in central-local government relations.

Part 4 charts the growing importance of quasi government with particular emphasis on the development of quangos.

Part 1 The structure of local government

Key issues

1. How did the modern system of local government develop?
2. How did the past shape the present?
3. What were the key developments between 1945 and 1990?
4. How did local government organisation change in the 1990s?

1.1 Origins

Early history
Although local government can be traced back to Saxon times, strong central control by the monarch was a feature of its early history. The three basic units of local government today date back to the 15th century:

- the parish (the area served by the local church)

- the county (or shire)
- the town (also known as the borough or burgh).

Before the 19th century, there was little uniformity and little local democracy in Britain. Roughly speaking, there was a two-tier system by 1800. At one level, counties were administered by unelected Justices of the Peace (JPs) who were agents of the monarch. JPs delegated duties to officials in the parishes. At a second level, boroughs (towns which had been granted a Royal Charter) were autonomous local units administered by unelected mayors or aldermen. Bribery and corruption were common.

The Industrial Revolution brought the momentum for change. Rapid urbanisation led to overcrowding, disease, poor housing and crime. These problems led to demands for change, especially from the growing urban middle classes.

Municipal Reform Act 1835

The first phase of reform began with the Municipal Reform Act of 1835. This established elected town councils for the first time, but only applied to 178 boroughs in England and Wales. In many towns, progressive leaders had already campaigned for special Acts of Parliament to deal with problems such as water supply or street lighting. The new elected councils took over these projects. The 1835 Act was important in the long term since it set the standard pattern of local government. It established the principle that elected members should be responsible to those who paid local taxes and it gave the council responsibility for maintaining local services.

Local Government Acts in the 1880s and 1890s

The second phase of reform came with the first Local Government Act of 1888. Elected county councils were created and towns with populations above 50,000 became 'county boroughs' independent of the county.

The second Local Government Act of 1894 set up a further tier of local government - urban and rural district councils. District councils had responsibility for health, housing and highways. The 1894 Act also set up 7,000 parish councils.

By 1900, therefore, England and Wales were divided into 82 county boroughs and 58 counties (see Box 16.1). The county boroughs provided services for larger towns, whilst county councils and district councils served other areas. This was the 'golden age' of local government. The new councils took over services which had been provided by voluntary agencies on an ad hoc basis (if they had been provided at all). They also bought out public utility companies and began to administer basic services. This system remained unchanged for over 60 years.

London

Any description of the organisation of local government in England should include the warning, 'with the exception of London'. The size and extent of the city has meant that a system appropriate for other cities is not workable in London.

The London Government Act of 1889 set up an entirely new London County Council (LCC). This was supplemented in 1899 with a second tier of 28 metropolitan boroughs and 3 county boroughs. By 1901, the LCC covered an area which contained 4.5 million people.

1.2 Changes in organisation since 1945

Pressure for change

Although the organisation of local government remained fundamentally unchanged until the 1960s, even before World War II the system had come under pressure, mainly because of population growth and demographic change. After 1945, four main criticisms were made. First, there were too many authorities and they were too small to deliver their services efficiently. Second, size varied enormously even amongst authorities of the same type. Boundaries did not reflect social and economic realities. Third, the two tiers of county and district did not allow accountable, democratic government since the division of functions between the two tiers was piecemeal and often illogical. And fourth, there was no tier to deal with the special problems of major conurbations outside London (especially, Birmingham, Liverpool and Manchester).

The London Government Act, 1963

To examine the problem of local government in London, the Herbert Commission was set up in 1957. It recommended that old boundaries be redrawn and a new two-tier system be set up consisting of the Greater London Council (GLC) and 32 new borough councils. The GLC would plan on a London-wide basis and the boroughs would provide services within their locality. These recommendations were accepted by the government and the London Government Act of 1963 came into operation in 1965. The system

Box 16.1 The system of local government at the end of the 19th century

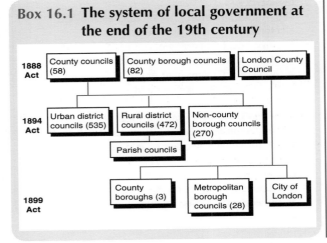

survived until the mid-1980s.

The Local Government Act, 1972

The Maud Commission was set up in 1966 to investigate local government in England and Wales. The majority report of 1967 supported a unitary solution. England (apart from Birmingham, Liverpool and Manchester) was to be divided into 58 unitary areas in which a single authority would carry out all functions. The three conurbations were to be organised in the same way as London. One member of the Commission did not agree with this and submitted a minority report arguing for two tiers (35 city regions and 135 districts).

The Labour government fell before legislation was passed on these recommendations and the new Conservative government rejected the unitary solution. As a result, the Local Government Act of 1972 provided a two-tier system. In the higher tier, the 58 counties of England and Wales became 47 shire counties and six metropolitan counties. In the lower tier, 1,249 districts were reduced to 333 rural (shire) districts and 34 metropolitan districts. Whereas metropolitan districts had responsibility for providing important services such as social services and education, in rural (shire) districts, these services were provided by the county council. This Act came into force in 1974. Critics claimed that the changes made local government more remote and less accountable.

The Scottish Local Government Act, 1973

In 1973, a separate Local Government Act was passed for Scotland. This Act also provided a two-tier system. It created nine regional councils and three island councils in the higher tier and 53 district councils in the lower tier. In addition, communities were given the option of establishing their own community councils, with minor responsibilities for matters such as traffic management. Around 1,300 were created in total.

Minor councils

Town, parish and community councils in existence before the Acts of 1963, 1972 and 1973 remained untouched and still survive. There are more than 10,000 of such bodies in operation outside London. They undertake minor functions and act as a mouthpiece for public opinion.

Abolition of the GLC and metropolitan counties

The Widdicombe Committee was set up in 1985 to examine the practices and procedures governing the conduct of local authority business in Britain with particular reference to the rights and responsibilities of elected councillors and to the relationship between councillors and officers. The subtext was that the Conservative government was worried about Labour councillors' activities and hoped that the Widdicombe

Committee would find ways of stopping them. In fact, the Widdicombe Report (which was published in 1986) failed to do this.

The government then came up with its own solutions. In 1986, it abolished the GLC and metropolitan county councils on the grounds that they were an unnecessary burden on public resources. Ministers argued that these councils performed few functions which could not be performed at district or borough level. These few functions (for example, fire, police and public transport), they argued, would be better performed by new joint boards (composed of representatives from borough and district councils).

Criticisms of the abolition

Critics accused the government of acting in a partisan manner since all these councils had a Labour majority and the GLC, in particular, had developed a high public profile and a record of support for causes which the Conservative Party found unacceptable. Critics also argued that abolition would not really remove a tier of government because many of the functions of metropolitan counties would be transferred to the new joint boards. These new boards would be more remote from the public and, therefore, less accountable. Third, critics pointed out that there was no guarantee that neighbouring districts or boroughs would cooperate (especially if they were dominated by different parties) - with the result that services might suffer. And fourth, they argued that metropolitan counties made savings through economies of scale. Abolition would neither improve efficiency nor save money.

The abolition of ILEA

The abolition of the GLC was followed by the abolition of ILEA (Inner London Education Authority). ILEA had been responsible for organising education in the inner London boroughs. Responsibility was devolved to the individual boroughs.

Main points - Sections 1.1-1.2

- Three basic units of local government (the parish, county and borough) date back to the 15th century. Before 1800, there was little uniformity or local democracy.
- The Municipal Reform Act of 1835 established elected town councils for the first time.
- The first Local Government Act of 1888 created elected county councils and county boroughs. The second Local Government Act of 1894 set up a further tier of local government - urban and rural district councils.
- After 1945, pressure grew for local government reform, resulting in Local Government Acts in 1972 which provided a two-tier system in England, Scotland and Wales.
- In 1986, the government abolished the GLC and metropolitan counties on the grounds that they were an unnecessary burden on public resources.

Activity 16.1 *Local government reform*

Item A *The (majority) Maud Commission Report*

England should be divided into 61 new local government areas. In 58 of them, a single authority should be responsible for all services. In the three very large metropolitan areas around Birmingham, Liverpool and Manchester, responsibility for services should be divided between a metropolitan authority whose key functions would be planning, transport and major development and 20 metropolitan district authorities whose key functions would be education, social services, health and housing. These 61 new local government areas should be grouped together with Greater London into eight provinces, each with its own provincial council. The key function of these councils would be to settle provincial strategy and the planning framework within which the main authorities must operate.

Adapted from Maud 1967.

Item B *Organisation of local government after 1974*

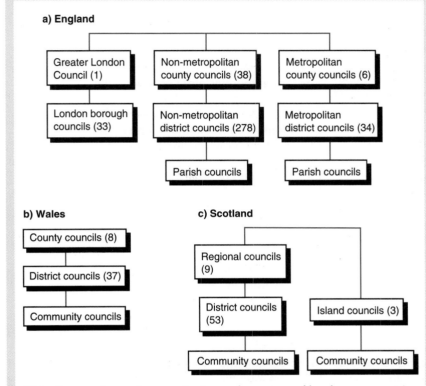

This diagram shows the organisation and structure of local government in England, Wales and Scotland after the Local Government Acts of 1972 and 1973 were passed. The numbers of each type of council are shown in brackets.

Item C *Streamlining the cities*

The basic principle of earlier reorganisation was that there was a need for a two-tier system of local government throughout the country: a lower tier providing essentially local services and an upper tier dealing with a wider area of administration. The GLC and metropolitan county councils (MCCs), however, have full responsibility for only a limited number of services. In many areas, they share powers with the borough and district councils. A strict interpretation of the role of the GLC and MCCs would leave them with too few real functions. As a result, they search for a 'strategic role' which may have little basis in real needs and which often brings them into conflict with the lower tier authorities. It may also lead them to promote policies which conflict with national policies. The abolition of the GLC and MCCs will streamline local government in the metropolitan areas. It will remove a source of conflict and tension. It will save money after some transitional costs. It will also provide a system which is simpler for the public to understand since responsibility for virtually all services will rest with a single authority.

Adapted from HMSO 1983.

Questions

1. a) Use Item A to draw a diagram showing what the organisation and structure of local government would have been if the majority Maud proposals had been adopted.
   b) What would have been the advantages and disadvantages of the system proposed by the Maud Commission?
   c) Can you think of any reasons to explain why the Maud proposals were not accepted?

2. Using Item B, explain how the organisation and structure of local government (a) differed from the system that existed before 1974 and (b) changed in the 1980s.

3. Before the proposals in Item C became law, there was consultation with interested groups. Write a consultation paper putting forward the arguments for and against abolition of the GLC and MCCs.

1.3 Change in the 1990s

The local government review, 1990-91

McNaughton argues that the abolition of the GLC and metropolitan county councils meant an end to an experiment with the idea of regional government:

'Britain's first serious flirtation with the idea of regional government had ended. Abolition was not the result of any long-term vision, however, rather it was a political expediency resulting from local-central tensions.' (McNaughton 1998, p.22)

In 1990, the Secretary of State for the Environment, Michael Heseltine, announced his intention to review three local government issues:

- local government finance
- internal management
- the structure of local government.

In a white paper published in 1991, it was argued that a unitary structure was the best system for organising local government. A unitary system would mean that all functions of local government would be delivered from a single body. In practice, this would mean the abolition of county councils and the transfer of their responsibilities to district councils. The idea of a uniform unitary structure was dropped, however, after warnings of civil war within the Conservative Party. Instead, the government decided that the pattern of local government in each county should be decided locally in England. This would be achieved by various groups making representations to a Local Government Commission. The groups making representations would include both national bodies (eg professional associations) and local bodies (eg local councils, voluntary associations and local businesses).

The Local Government Commission for England

The Local Government Commission was set up in 1992 under John Banham and was instructed to issue reports county by county. Government guidance to the Commission stressed that the following criteria should guide its work:

- efficiency
- accountability
- responsiveness
- local needs.

The Commission's first report proposed a unitary authority for the Isle of Wight. Whilst this report was uncontroversial, that was not the case with the next three reports for Humberside, Avon and Cleveland. Most district councillors were hoping that a unitary authority would mean the same district boundaries, but greater powers. The reports, however, recommended the amalgamation of several district councils into a single unitary authority (and the abolition of the county council). Overall, that would mean fewer councillors. As a result, many councillors protested about the recommendations.

In 1993, the appointment of a new Secretary of State for the Environment, John Gummer, caused further difficulties. Gummer put pressure on the Commission to recommend single-tier authorities in all but 'exceptional' cases, an approach which sparked a great deal of anger:

> 'This seemed to challenge the independence of the Commission and angered many local government politicians. Two councils - Derbyshire and Lancashire - claimed that Gummer was acting unlawfully in interfering, and instituted legal proceedings. But, even

though they won the case in the High Court in January 1994, the minister made only a cosmetic retraction and continued to press for the unitary solution.' (McNaughton 1998, p.23)

Arguments in favour of abolishing county councils
The government's arguments in favour of the abolition of county councils were as follows. First, two tiers are confusing. It would be better if services were provided from a single focal point. Second, the government hoped that many schools would opt out of local authority control. If they did so, county councils would have a reduced role. Third, the other services run by county councils could easily be transferred to district councils or be run by joint boards.

The Commission's work since 1993
Relying heavily on public opinion surveys, the Commission moved away from its earlier support for unitary authorities and began to make recommendations which either allowed the existing two-tier system to remain or proposed new 'hybrid' solutions (a combination of unitary status for one or two parts of a county and the retention of the two-tier system in the rest of the county). The response of John Gummer (who favoured unitary authorities on the grounds of efficiency and cost) was to refer three recommendations to retain two-tier systems back to the Commission. This resulted in confrontation with the Commission's chair, John Banham, and, in 1995, Banham's resignation. Banham was replaced by David Cooksey.

The position in 1998
By 1998, 46 new unitary authorities had been created in England, covering about a quarter of the non-metropolitan population. Four of the 39 counties had been abolished completely (Avon, Cleveland, Humberside and Berkshire) and the Isle of Wight had become a unitary authority. In the remaining 34 counties, the two-tier system was retained and the old county of Rutland (which had been abolished in 1974) was restored. The result of the Commission's work, therefore, was to create a mixed system of local government in England. In general, rural areas still tend to have two-tier systems whilst unitary authorities are more common in urban areas.

The work of the Commission continues:

> 'As for the Local Government Commission, it will continue in existence, to undertake what are known as periodic electoral reviews. These authority-by-authority reviews will examine the total number of councillors, the number in each electoral division or ward, the ward boundaries, their names and the timing of elections. It will also consider the idea of councils being allowed for the first time to have paid, full-time executive councillors. It will not, however, re-review the boundaries between councils or their functions.' (Wilson & Game 1998, p.62)

Scotland and Wales

In Scotland and Wales, the process of reform was swifter and did not involve a Local Government Commission. Consultation, therefore, was minimal. The Welsh Secretary, David Hunt, made a statement on 3 March 1993 announcing that 22 unitary authorities would replace the existing district and county councils in Wales. Similarly, the Scottish Secretary, Ian Lang, announced that the existing regional and district councils would be abolished and replaced by 25 unitary authorities (the three existing island councils would remain as unitary authorities). During the committee stage in Parliament, four new unitary authorities were added, making a total of 32 in Scotland as a whole. The population of these unitary authorities would vary widely. For example, the largest authority, The City of Glasgow Authority, would have a population of 600,000 whilst Orkney and Shetland Authority would have a population of 20,000. In both Wales and Scotland, there would be joint boards to cover areas such as policing, water supply and tourism. The plans came into effect on 1 April 1996.

Results of the reform

In a review of the changes in Scotland and Wales, the Joseph Rowntree Foundation pointed out that, although the government had aimed to make government more local:

- the number of local authorities had fallen
- there would be an increase in the population per authority
- the number of local councillors had been reduced.

In addition, the review suggested, the reorganisation had, in practice, replaced a two-tier system with a three-tier system. This is because, although there are unitary authorities, there are also supra-unitary joint boards (boards with members from two or more unitary authorities) responsible for the police and fire services and sub-unitary area committees (committees with members from part of the unitary authority) responsible for providing some other services (Rowntree 1995).

Local government after devolution

Devolution is bound to make an impact on local government in Wales and Scotland. In Scotland, the new Parliament will have legislative and executive control over local government as well as over many other areas which affect local government - such as health, education and the environment. The Parliament will also have tax-varying powers of 3p in the pound (Lynch 1998). In Wales, similar powers will be devolved, but the Assembly will not raise any of its own taxation nor will there be separate Welsh laws (McNaughton 1998).

Northern Ireland

Before 1972, Northern Ireland had its own devolved government, based in Stormont Castle. In 1972, however, the outbreak of violence resulted in the British government imposing direct rule. As a result, a two-tier structure of local government was set up in Northern Ireland with nine area boards delivering some services and 26 district councils delivering others. Between 1972 and 1999, district councillors were directly elected, but membership of the area boards was made up of Northern Ireland Office appointees and delegates from the district councils.

Under the peace deal agreed in Northern Ireland in 1998, a directly elected Assembly was set up with full legislative and executive authority for those matters which were the responsibility of the six departments of the Northern Ireland Office. The Assembly, therefore, is now responsible for the provision of local government.

London

Following the abolition of the GLC, there was no London-wide authority. Yet, according to the Joseph Rowntree Foundation (1997), there were four good reasons why such an authority should be set up:

- to provide a voice for London as a whole
- to introduce local democratic control to a number of public services that were being provided by government agencies, joint boards and departments
- to increase the capacity of local government in London to achieve particular policy objectives
- to override local parochial interests for the good of the capital as a whole.

In its 1997 general election manifesto, the Labour Party made the following pledge:

'London is the only Western capital without an elected city government. Following a referendum to confirm popular demand, there will be a new deal for London, with a strategic authority and a mayor, each directly elected. Both will speak up for the needs of the city and plan for its future. They will not duplicate the work of the boroughs, but take responsibility for London-wide issues.' (Labour 1997, p.34)

Following its election, the Labour government issued green and white papers on London and then, in May 1998, held a referendum in London. This supported the government's proposals, though the turnout was low (see Chapter 7, Section 3.7). The Yes vote in the referendum means that a mayor will be elected and a new Greater London Assembly will come into operation. Together, the Mayor and Assembly will make up the Greater London Authority (GLA). The GLA will have a budget of £3.3 billion, most of which will come from central government (the remainder will come from a redistribution of business and council tax rates). The GLA will not, however, have tax-raising powers.

The introduction of an elected mayor for London suggests a new approach to local government. It is possible that this approach might be repeated in other large cities, if it is seen to be a success in London.

The position of the 33 London borough councils remains unaffected by the new plans.

Main points - Section 1.3

- In 1992, a Local Government Commission was set up to review the structure of local government in England. Although the government hoped that it would recommend unitary authorities, in some counties it favoured the status quo or a hybrid system.
- By 1998, 46 new unitary authorities had been created. Four of the 39 counties had been abolished completely and the Isle of Wight had become a unitary authority. In the remaining 34 counties, the two-tier system was retained. Rutland was restored.

- In Scotland and Wales, unitary authorities were imposed by central government. They came into operation on 1 April 1996.
- Local government in Northern Ireland has a two-tier structure. Under the 1998 peace deal, an elected Assembly has been set up with responsibility for local government.
- The Labour government's proposals to set up a Greater London Authority were approved in a referendum held in May 1998.

Activity 16.2 *Local government in the 1990s*

Item A   *In support of unitary authorities*

In 1991, the Conservative government published a document outlining its reasons for reviewing local government organisation. This document admitted that changing the structure of local government would not solve all the problems. Nevertheless, it suggested, unitary authorities would bring improvements. First, the document argued, it was important that people should be able to identify a single authority responsible for providing services for their area. Second, a single tier would reduce bureaucracy and improve the coordination of services, increasing quality and reducing costs - even if the county council and district councils in a county were efficient already. Third, a single tier would bring proper financial accountability. People must know who is responsible for setting a budget and achieving value for money in services in their area. Fourth, introducing unitary authorities would also offer the opportunity of relating the structure of local government more closely to communities with which people identify. This should increase interest in local affairs and make for more responsive and representative local government. The document made it clear that the government did not intend that county or district councils be abolished wholesale. In some places, it suggested, it might be best for existing authorities to be merged. In others, the best approach might be to create or recreate quite different authorities. In some areas, there could be a case for two tiers.

Adapted from HMSO 1991.

Item B   *Elected mayors*

In December 1997, the political commentator Andrew Adonis predicted that, within ten years, most of Britain's major cities would have elected mayors and that the post of mayor would be more sought after than membership of the House of Commons. He based this theory on two main pieces of evidence. First, the Local Government (Experimental Arrangements) Bill had begun its passage through Parliament. Among its provisions, this Bill allows councils to modify existing committee systems and to transfer executive power to a directly elected mayor. All the council has to do is to vote to do this by a majority. And second, the first Mayor of London is to be elected in 1999. Boasting the votes of a million or more Londoners, the victor will be among the four or five most prominent politicians in Britain. With profile and popularity, Adonis argues, go influence. The fact that the Mayor's powers are to be tightly restricted will not prevent the holder of the office from being outspoken on issues outside their direct responsibility. This will encourage other councils to opt for a high-profile figurehead. It will not be long, Adonis predicts, before Birmingham, Manchester, Liverpool, Newcastle and dozens of smaller cities want their mayor too. And, if councillors are unwilling to give them one because they oppose what they see as presidential leadership at their expense, local media and public pressure will do the job.

Adapted from the *Observer*, 14 December 1997.

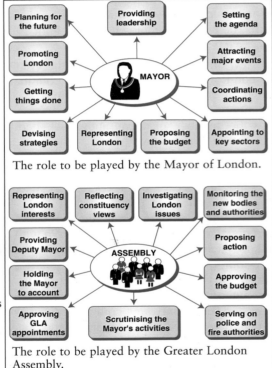

The role to be played by the Mayor of London.

The role to be played by the Greater London Assembly.

Item C *Against unitary authorities*

For once, it is not financial cutbacks which are responsible for the threat to Somerset's nine mobile and 35 static libraries, though they have certainly made their mark. This time it is the restructuring of local government which may undo much of the hard work put into the county's bookshelves. Under the government's plans for unitary authorities, Somerset is to be divided into three. Accordingly, the management of the county's library service will follow suit. But, if the county's libraries are split into three separate bodies, the book stock available to local people will be immediately diluted by two thirds. It will be too costly, impracticable and bureaucratic to rotate books from one end of the county to another. The money spent on administration will increase threefold. Nor is this impending disaster restricted to the south west. Librarians throughout the country know that small units will never be able to afford the more expensive and specialist material good libraries need. Few units will have the infrastructure for static branches, let alone mobiles.

Adapted from the *Guardian*, 8 April 1994.

Item D *Local government at the end of the 20th century*

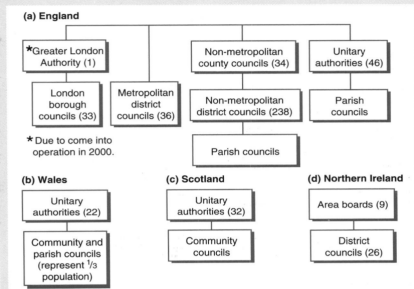

Questions

1. 'Unitary authorities will result in better local government.' Using Items A, C and D, give arguments for and against this view.

2. a) Judging from Item B, why are directly elected mayors likely to become more common?
   b) What are the advantages and disadvantages of moving to a system of directly elected mayors?

3. a) Using Item D, explain how the organisation of local government has changed in the 1990s.
   b) Would you say that the organisation of local government has been improved? Explain your answer.

Adapted from Wilson & Game 1998.

Part 2 Decision making in local authorities

Key issues

1. How is policy formulated and how are decisions made in local authorities?
2. What role is played by councillors and council officers?
3. Why have party politics become important in local government?
4. How is local government finance organised?
5. What changes have resulted from privatisation?

2.1 The range of local authority activities

A wide range of functions

Local government in 1997-98 cost £46.4 billion. This amounted to about a quarter of all public expenditure and a tenth of the UK's gross domestic product. Local government is a major employer. It employs about one in ten of the working population.

Councils provide a wide range of services. For example, Manchester City Council's *A-Z Guide* contains information about its services under more than 700 headings. This huge range of activities is a product of the two main functions of local authorities: their political or representative function and their administrative or executive function.

Political function of local authorities

Local authorities are democratically elected bodies. They provide an opportunity for people to stand for political office as councillors (see Chapter 11, Part 1). One of the functions of local authorities, therefore, is to provide a forum in which elected representatives can determine how local affairs should be run. Equally, because the local authority is a democratically elected body, it is (in theory at least) directly accountable to local people.

Administrative function of local authorities

The range of activities carried out by local authorities is determined by law and, therefore, ultimately by Parliament. A number of Acts of Parliament, some of which are specific to local government and some of which are more general, lay down the parameters within which local government can operate. It is the function of local authorities to implement and to administer the decisions made by central government.

For example, metropolitan districts, unitary authorities and county councils are obliged by law to provide, without charge, adequate primary and secondary education for all children between the ages of five and 16. Central government determines overall education policy and circulates detailed regulations on educational matters. Local authorities are obliged to comply with these regulations. This is not just the case with education. Most of the activities performed by local authorities are mandatory (compulsory).

Local authorities do have some room for manoeuvre, however. The Local Government Act of 1972 states that councils may do anything which is:

'Calculated to facilitate or is conducive or incidental to the discharge of their mandatory activities.'

To use the example of education again, it is not mandatory for local authorities to provide nurseries for children under the age of five. But, under the terms of the 1972 Local Government Act, they may choose to do so.

Although local authorities can choose to carry out additional functions, they may not take action which is not sanctioned by law or which exceeds their lawful authority. If they do, they are deemed to have acted 'ultra vires' (beyond their legitimate powers). When a court finds that a local authority has acted ultra vires, it declares its actions illegal and may punish its councillors or officers.

The full council and committees

The full council is the supreme decision-making body in a local authority. Elected representatives - councillors - make decisions in the full council. Their decisions are implemented by officers who are full-time council employees. Since it would be impossible to deal with all council business at full council, detailed work is delegated to committees.

Before the Bains Report of 1972 committees liaised between the full council and the relevant local authority departments (departments are teams of officers whose job is to implement policy). So, for example, a county council would delegate matters concerning education to its Education Committee. The Education Committee would then be responsible for the county's overall education policy (within the parameters set by central government) and the allocation of resources. Decisions made by the Education Committee would be implemented by the council's Education Department.

The Bains Report 1972

In 1971, the Bains Committee was set up to consider how the new system of local government (which was to be introduced by the 1972 Act) should be managed. The Bains Report of 1972 recommended a new system of 'corporate management'. The aim was to encourage councillors and officers to focus on the corporate good rather than on their own specific area of interest. To achieve this, the two main innovations were:

- the creation of a Principal Chief Officers' Management Team under the control of a Chief Executive
- the setting up of a Policy and Resources Committee.

It was the job of both of these new structures to take an overview of council policy.

The result of these innovations was a change in the way that the committee system worked. Instead of reporting direct to full council, committees now reported to the Policy and Resources Committee which, in turn, reported to full council. Also, instead of liaising directly with local authority departments, committees now relayed their decisions to the Principal Chief Officers' Management Team which then passed them on to individual departments.

Case study - Oxford City Council

Oxford is divided into 17 wards (geographical areas). Each ward elects three councillors who sit for four years. Oxford City Council, therefore, has 51 councillors (for the number of councillors from each political party on the council see Section 2.3 below).

The council's work is shared among committees which meet either every month or every two months. There are seven main committees (including the Policy and Resources Committee) and, generally, 12 councillors sit on a committee. The Leisure Services Committee, for example, is responsible for:

- providing sports and leisure facilities
- managing the Ice Rink
- looking after parks and countryside facilities
- organising leisure events.

In 1997-98, it was responsible for the net expenditure of £8.06 million.

Most of the business of committees is held in public. The main decisions and recommendations of the committees are submitted to the meetings of the full city council, after consideration by the Policy and Resources Committee. There are ten meetings of the full city council each year. To support the committees there is a series of sub-committees, working groups and advisory groups, many of which coopt their members from the community. Most sub-committees are advisory, although a small number have statutory powers. All committees and sub-committees are advised by council officers. The number of councillors from a political party on each committee must, by law, reflect the number of councillors of that party elected to the council as a whole.

Oxford City Council employs about 1,000 people to carry out the day-to-day work of the council. Laws govern the council's responsibilities in areas such as litter collection, traffic management, road maintenance, planning and building control, housing, the environment, and leisure and recreation. The level of services and the allocation of resources, however, are the responsibility of the elected councillors.

Case study - Oxfordshire County Council

A total of 70 councillors (or 'members') sit on Oxfordshire County Council, each member representing a different part of the county. Elections for all seats on the council are held every four years. After the 1997 county council elections Oxfordshire County Council was 'hung'. No political party had overall control. The Conservatives were the largest party with 27 seats. Labour had 22 seats. The Liberal Democrats had 19 seats. There were two Green Party councillors.

Meetings of the full county council take place five times each year. These meetings determine the overall policy and direction to be taken by the county. In particular, the full council agrees the annual budget and takes responsibility for seeking new or amended legislation.

Committees and sub-committees are responsible for specific areas of the council's work. The size of each committee varies, but its composition reflects the relative numbers of councillors belonging to each of the political parties on the council as a whole. Some committees also include people coopted because of their particular knowledge or experience. Coopted committee members have speaking and voting rights even though they are not councillors. The Education Committee, for example, includes people representing the teaching profession and the churches.

Committees and their sub-committees consider detailed policy issues. They also review existing policies, examine efficiency and recommend budgets for services. A statement of the business dealt with by each committee is considered at meetings of the full county council.

Meetings of the full council, its committees and sub-committees are normally open to the public. A limited number of subjects, however, are dealt with in private. For example, cases involving named individuals are usually discussed in private.

Main points - Section 2.1

- **About a quarter of all public expenditure is spent by local authorities. They provide a wide range of services.**
- **One of the functions of local authorities is to provide a forum in which elected representatives can determine how local affairs should be run.**
- **It is also the function of local authorities to implement and to administer the decisions made by central government.**
- **Although most of the activities performed by local authorities are mandatory (compulsory), they do have some room for manoeuvre.**
- **Councillors' decisions are implemented by officers (full-time council employees). Detailed work is delegated to committees.**
- **Since 1972, councils have been controlled by a Principal Chief Officers' Management Team under the control of a Chief Executive and a Policy and Resources Committee (which receives reports from committees and itself reports to full council).**

Activity 16.3 *Areas of responsibility and decision making*

Item A *Local authorities' areas of responsibility (1)*

The man (left) lives in a council house (behind him). He wants his two children to attend the local primary school, but it is full. He relies on public transport, but finds it difficult to walk to the bus stop following an injury at work.

Item B *Local authorities' areas of responsibility (2)*

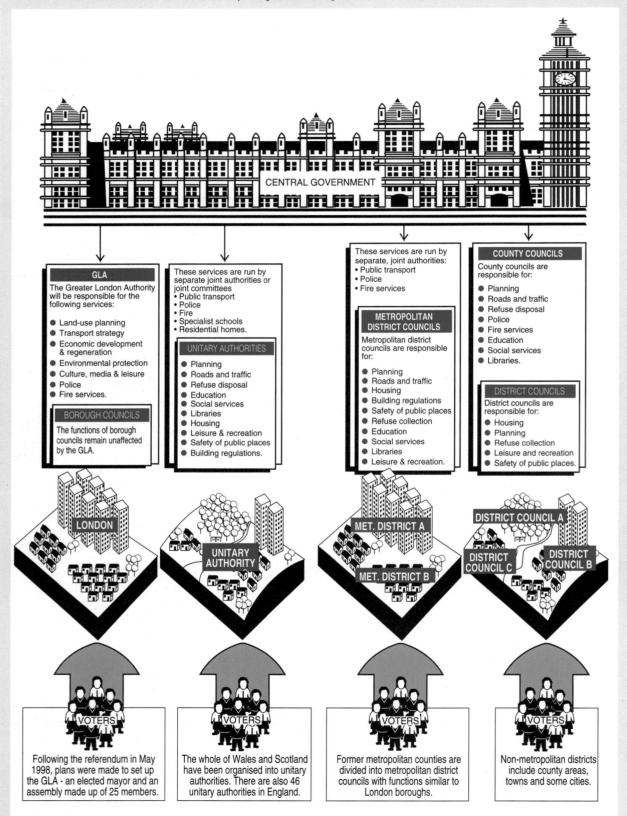

CENTRAL GOVERNMENT

GLA

The Greater London Authority will be responsible for the following services:

● Land-use planning
● Transport strategy
● Economic development & regeneration
● Environmental protection
● Culture, media & leisure
● Police
● Fire services.

BOROUGH COUNCILS

The functions of borough councils remain unaffected by the GLA.

These services are run by separate joint authorities or joint committees
• Public transport
• Police
• Fire
• Specialist schools
• Residential homes.

UNITARY AUTHORITIES

● Planning
● Roads and traffic
● Refuse disposal
● Education
● Social services
● Libraries
● Housing
● Leisure & recreation
● Safety of public places
● Building regulations.

These services are run by separate, joint authorities:
• Public transport
• Police
• Fire services

METROPOLITAN DISTRICT COUNCILS

Metropolitan district councils are responsible for:

● Planning
● Roads and traffic
● Housing
● Building regulations
● Safety of public places
● Refuse collection
● Education
● Social services
● Libraries
● Leisure & recreation.

COUNTY COUNCILS

County councils are responsible for:

● Planning
● Roads and traffic
● Refuse disposal
● Police
● Fire services
● Education
● Social services
● Libraries.

DISTRICT COUNCILS

District councils are responsible for:

● Housing
● Planning
● Refuse collection
● Leisure and recreation
● Safety of public places.

LONDON

UNITARY AUTHORITY

MET. DISTRICT A

MET. DISTRICT B

DISTRICT COUNCIL A

DISTRICT COUNCIL C

DISTRICT COUNCIL B

VOTERS

VOTERS

VOTERS

VOTERS

Following the referendum in May 1998, plans were made to set up the GLA - an elected mayor and an assembly made up of 25 members.

The whole of Wales and Scotland have been organised into unitary authorities. There are also 46 unitary authorities in England.

Former metropolitan counties are divided into metropolitan district councils with functions similar to London boroughs.

Non-metropolitan districts include county areas, towns and some cities.

Adapted from the *Guardian*, 5 March 1991, Wilson & Game 1998 and McNaughton 1998.

Item C *Management structure before and after the Bains Report*

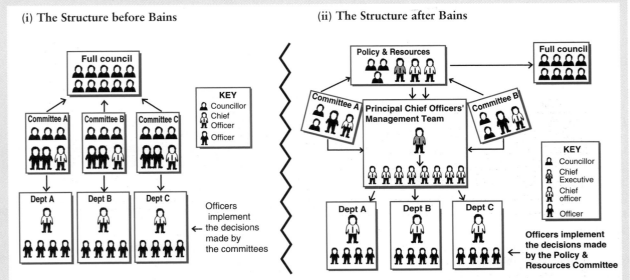

(i) The Structure before Bains

This diagram shows the management structure which existed in local authorities before 1972.

(ii) The Structure after Bains

This diagram shows the management structure which existed in local authorities after 1972.

Item D *Decision making by committee*

- Meetings are often overwhelmed with detail. They should instead focus on deciding major or controversial issues.
- Insufficient attention is paid to following up previous decisions and monitoring performance.
- Committees take up the bulk of members' time. Many councillors, however, believe they should perform a wider representative role.
- The value of time spent in formal committee is undermined, in many cases, because the ruling group agrees its line in advance.
- Committees can consume a great deal of management time. They can slow down decisions and duplicate each other's work.
- In one council, a decision to change the structure of administrative staff was put to the Neighbourhood Services Committee, cross-referenced by the Personnel Committee and then had to be ratified by the Policy and Resources Committee. This process took four months with 30 councillors considering the decision (some councillors considered it more than once because they sat on more than one of the committees concerned).

Adapted from Audit Commission 1997 and Wilson 1997.

Questions

1. Suppose the man in Item A lived where you live. Which departments in which type of council would be responsible for solving the problems he faced?

2. Judging from Item B, what are the main differences between the four types of local authority?

3. a) What does Item C tell us about the way in which decision making in local authorities changed after 1972?
   b) Where was power located before 1972? Where is it located now? Give reasons for your answer.

4. What are the benefits and drawbacks of making decisions by committee? Use Item D in your answer.

2.2 Councillors and officers

Personnel

In the UK as a whole, there are over 23,000 elected councillors and more than 2 million local authority employees. Of these 2 million employees, only 500,000 can be described as local government 'officers' (professional, technical and clerical staff). This section examines the relationship between councillors and officers.

The traditional view and its variants

The traditional or formal view of the relationship between councillors and officers is that councillors make policy and officers implement it. So, power rests with the elected councillors.

An alternative view is that administration actually involves policy making. Since officers have technical and professional expertise which councillors lack, they help to set the agenda and give advice. Since they do this, they play an important role in determining policy outcomes and exercise power.

As the traditional view is contradicted by its alternative, it is perhaps no surprise to find that a third view has developed. According to this view, developing and administering policy is a joint activity of both officers and councillors. This view was supported by the Bains Committee (see above,

Section 2.1). The Bains Report stated that:

> 'If local government is to have any chance of achieving a corporate approach to its affairs, members (elected councillors) and officers must both recognise that neither can regard any area of the authority's work and administration as exclusively theirs.' (Bains 1972)

Élite theory

During the late 1970s, some political commentators argued that local government had fallen into the hands of an élite made up of senior officers and senior councillors (Cockburn 1977 and Saunders 1979). This élite, it was claimed, was a direct result of the Local Government Acts of 1972 and 1973. Reorganisation of local government meant the adoption of new management structures. These new structures had produced an élite.

According to this theory, before the Acts of 1972 and 1973, a loose assembly of council committees had determined policy which was then administered by a large number of small departments. Reorganisation after the Bains Report of 1972 brought streamlining and a hierarchical structure. The Principal Chief Officers Management Team became, in effect, a board of directors under a single head (the Chief Executive). Only senior councillors sat on the new Policy and Resources Committee. The net result was that power became concentrated in the hands of a small group - the Chief Executive, the senior officers and the senior councillors.

The pluralist model

Élite theory has been criticised on the grounds that it is too simplistic (Wilson 1997). Supporters of the pluralist model argue that the relationship between officers and councillors is such that the balance of power is varied and changes according to the issues, the personalities, the strength of the political parties and the particular local authority.

Councillors, it is argued, are rarely united in their objectives. Alliances, therefore, develop between certain councillors and officers who then compete against other councillors and officers over particular policies. This is especially likely to happen when members of one committee have to compete with another committee for funds.

Second, attention must be paid to the ruling party group as a whole rather than just the senior councillors. Junior or 'backbench' councillors can exert influence through the party caucus meetings where policy priorities are discussed. If the party caucus meetings decide on a particular policy, senior as well as junior councillors must pursue this policy. On occasions, therefore, senior councillors may be overruled. Two recent examples illustrate this:

> 'Two majority group Leaders - Stewart Foster in Leicester and Valerie Wise in Preston - were overthrown following votes of no-confidence by their respective Labour groups.' (Wilson 1997, p.27)

Third, policy disagreement and rivalry can exist both between departments and even within departments of the council. So, it is misleading to suggest that the officers are a united group with a uniform view. For example, the interests of officers working in the Treasury Department are unlikely to be the same as those working in a spending department like Housing.

Fourth, the fact that individual councillors represent a particular geographical area should not be ignored. Although the constraint of party discipline makes it difficult for councillors to take an independent line, there are occasions when ward interests predominate and party discipline is broken or modified.

A symbiotic relationship?

So, in theory, the relationship between officers and councillors is symbiotic. The councillors need the officers to develop and implement policy, whilst the officers need the councillors to provide their actions with political legitimacy. Neither could survive without the other. In practice, a number of factors combine to determine which of the two has the upper hand.

Officers' technical knowledge

First, the technical knowledge of local government officers undoubtedly affects their relationship with councillors. There is a danger of the full-time professionals (the officers) dominating the part-time amateurs (the councillors) who are often elected with low turnouts and who rely on electoral fortune to retain their position. The professionals, after all, know what can and cannot be achieved and that knowledge could easily be translated into power. Nevertheless, officers do not always have their own way. For example, if one party has a majority on the council, then it is likely that there is a clear policy manifesto and a mandate from the electorate. Councillors from the majority party can expect officers to implement their programme (so long as none of their commitments are ultra vires) whether the officers approve of the policies or not.

Political climate

Second, the political climate can be an important factor. For example, in the 1980s, the New Urban Left (Labour-controlled local councils with radical political ideas) set out to challenge the government by developing a new approach to local politics. Councillors began to use the corporate structures set up after the Bains Report to advance their political causes. Officers were required to provide support for these policies. By the mid-1980s, according to the Widdicombe Report (which, amongst other things, was instructed to examine the relationship between councillors and officers), councillors became more dominant in local government than they had been before because they became clearer about their political objectives (Widdicombe 1986).

Central government intervention
A third factor is the intervention of central government. Between 1987 and 1997, for example, the Conservative government set out to change the role of local authorities. Councils should no longer provide services directly, it was argued. Rather, they should be 'enabling authorities', bodies which regulate the services provided by outside organisations. Legislation passed between the mid-1980s and 1997 ensured that more and more services provided by councils were contracted-out. This undoubtedly affected the relationship between officers and councillors, though it was not clear exactly how it changed it. One theory was that the changes provided an opportunity for councillors to reassert their authority because officers were no longer responsible for delivering services. As a result, councillors were not so reliant on officers' technical expertise. A second theory suggested that the power of officers was enhanced because the awarding of contracts was increasingly seen as a technical matter and, therefore, not the job of councillors.

Hung councils
Finally, attention should be paid to 'hung' councils where no party has overall control. The number of these councils has grown since the mid-1980s, creating a new balance of power. Since many of these newly hung councils had been used to a long period of majority party control, the new arrangements upset the long-established officer-councillor relationships. Since no single party has control in a hung council, inter-party deals have to be struck. Officers find that they are responsible in a very real way to all political parties and not just to a ruling group. As a result, officers need to cultivate the vote of all councillors. They can no longer rely upon a ruling group to rubber stamp decisions already agreed in private. Also, although the creation of some hung councils has resulted in more open and democratic decision making, in others confusion has allowed officers to gain greater control over the decision-making process.

Alternative models of management
Beginning with the publication of a consultation paper *The Internal Management of Local Authorities* in 1991, central government began to suggest alternative models of management. *The Internal Management of Local Authorities* suggested that the existing committee structure was time-consuming and cumbersome and that, whilst it was not necessary to create a uniform system throughout the country, local experimentation with alternatives would be desirable. Six options were suggested:
1. Retention of the existing system.
2. Adaptation of the current system by allowing councils to delegate decision making to the chairs of committees.
3. A Cabinet system in which an executive of elected members would be chosen from the council as a whole.
4. A council manager who would be appointed to take over day-to-day responsibility for running the council.
5. An executive which would be elected in separate elections.
6. A directly elected mayor to take over the council's executive responsibilities.

Local authorities were generally hostile to change - and especially opposed the sixth option because they saw it as a threat to the representative nature of local government (Wilson 1995).

Proposals for change under Labour
During the Blair government's first 18 months in power, there was continuing pressure for change. In March 1998, Tony Blair called for:
- more directly elected mayors
- the abolition of many committees
- strengthening the role of backbench councillors.
(*Guardian*, 4 March 1998)

Then, in July 1998, a white paper was published under the title *Modern Local Government, in Touch with the People*. The white paper (which outlined a ten year programme of change) criticised the committee system on the grounds that, too often, it was not clear who, exactly, was responsible for making decisions. Since this was the case, it was difficult to hold particular individuals to account. To address this problem, the white paper proposed that councils should adopt new approaches to decision making - approaches which would provide for a separation of powers between an executive and an assembly. The white paper suggested three models:
- a directly elected mayor with a Cabinet made up of councillors
- a Cabinet with a Leader elected by fellow councillors - the Cabinet would be made up of councillors either appointed by the Leader or elected by councillors
- a directly elected mayor with a full-time council manager appointed by councillors.

A Local Government Bill was included in the Queen's Speech of November 1998, but the Bill did not include the provisions laid out in the white paper of July 1998. The *Guardian* reported that:
'Plans for a radical shake-up of local councils, including the creation of elected mayors in provincial cities, have been put on hold by ministers.' (*Guardian*, 25 November 1998)

Decentralisation
Concern about the dominance of élite groups (whether officers or councillors or both) has led

some Labour-controlled and Liberal Democrat-controlled councils to introduce a more decentralised system of decision making. The aim was that, by decentralising service provision to area or community offices, accessibility to the services and the responsiveness of council staff would be improved. Managerial decentralisation, it was hoped, would allow local people to have access to 'one-stop shops' where all services provided by the council could be accessed. In addition, there would be an opportunity for members of the local population, as consumers of local government services, to make their voice heard about the quality of the services provided. To achieve this:

> '[Some local authorities] went a stage further and established neighbourhood fora or committees in an attempt to secure increased participation by local citizens in the government of their communities. Such political decentralisation was an attempt to develop local citizenship as opposed to consumerism.' (Elcock 1997, p.40)

Parallels between chief officers and senior civil servants?

At first sight, it might seem that the relationship between local government chief officers and councillors is similar to that between senior civil servants and Cabinet ministers (see Chapter 13, Part 3). After all, the role of senior local authority officers, like that of senior civil servants, is to provide policy advice and to implement the decisions made by elected representatives. Also, like civil servants, officers are supposed to be politically neutral. On closer inspection, however, two important differences appear.

First, unlike the generalist civil servants at Whitehall local government officers are specialists. Their technical knowledge is extensive, usually much greater than that of councillors. On the other hand, councillors, unlike Cabinet ministers, are part-time, amateur politicians.

Second, unlike senior civil servants, chief officers are often publicly identified with particular policies and projects and they are sometimes prepared to make public statements in support of such policies and projects. For example, many Chief Education Officers in the 1970s supported the adoption of a comprehensive system of education and they publicly encouraged local councils to convert their schools to that system. Most senior civil servants would avoid such publicity.

Decision making

At full council meetings, the main business is to finalise the council's policy on all matters which have been through committees. Councillors have their last chance to make changes after examining reports from the main committees. The full council has four choices when it has examined the committee minutes. First, it may receive a committee minute. This means it approves the action taken. Second, it may accept a recommendation as it is. Third, it may change a minute in some way before accepting it. And fourth, where a minute records a decision taken by the committee on behalf of the full council, the council can rule that it is not happy with the decision and send the matter back to the committee for further consideration.

At committee or sub-committee meetings, the main business is to consider reports from the officers. Normally, these contain recommendations for action. After considering the officers' reports, committees or sub-committees have three choices. First, they can accept the officers' recommendations or advice as they are. Second, they can change them in some way. And third, they can decide to do something different.

At both full council meetings and at committee meetings, decisions are reached by members suggesting a course of action. For example, a member might propose that an officer's recommendation is accepted by the whole meeting. Other members might then propose amendments. When all the amendments have been dealt with, the proposal as it then stands is voted on.

Main points - Section 2.2

- The traditional view is that councillors make policy and officers implement it. A second view is that officers' expertise ensures they often make policy. A third view is that developing and administering policy is a joint activity of both officers and councillors.
- During the late 1970s, some people argued that local government had fallen into the hands of an élite made up of senior officers and senior councillors. The pluralist model suggests that the balance of power between officers and councillors is varied.
- Officers' specialist knowledge, the political climate, action by central government and the council's political make-up affect the relationship between officers and councillors.
- Since 1991, central government has pushed alternative models of management. The Labour government wants to separate the executive role of councillors from the representational role.
- Officers differ from senior civil servants in two important ways - they are specialists and they often publicly support particular policies.

Activity 16.4 Decision making and power

Item A *Councillors, officers and the public*

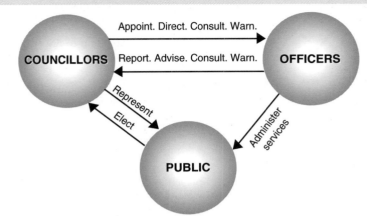

Appoint. Direct. Consult. Warn.

Report. Advise. Consult. Warn.

COUNCILLORS

OFFICERS

Represent

Elect

Administer services

PUBLIC

This diagram shows the relationship between councillors, officers and the public.

Adapted from Roberts 1986.

Item C *Decision making*

As with most organisations, the way in which local authorities actually make decisions is as much dictated by discussions behind the scenes as it is by the formal process of a committee's deliberations. Each council has its own way of working and, within each council, the different departments may have quite individual styles in the way that they handle business. In some cases, a committee may discuss an item without there being a preconceived view on it. On other occasions, the decision will have been made long before the matter was placed on the committee agenda. Sometimes, the views of the officers are all-important, whereas, at other times, individual councillors dominate decision making. When a single party is in control, it will usually hold all the important positions - such as chair of all the committees. Under the Local Government Housing Act of 1989, councillors from all political parties represented on the council must be appointed to committees in the same proportion to the number of seats they won in the election. By controlling the chairs of committees and by virtue of their strength in numbers on the committees, the party in control can exercise considerable power.

Adapted from Hutt 1990.

Item D *The role of senior local government officers (2)*

The various roles of senior officers can be categorised under three headings. First, they are the professional managers of local authority service departments. As such, they have day-to-day responsibility for major budgets and a large staff. Second, they are advisers responsible for ensuring that the council and its committees are informed of the facts, the law and all other relevant considerations before they make decisions. They are also responsible for proposing and advising on policy options. Third, they are arbitrators who stand outside the political conflicts between councillors and ensure that council business is conducted fairly. Skilled officers are able to carry out all three roles. But, some officers are only able to concentrate on one or two of their roles. For example, officers who place very strong stress on their professional judgement and on their legal duty to serve the council might fail to satisfy the need to advise the majority party leadership. This might result in pressure for the appointment of officers sympathetic to the majority party's political views. On the other hand, officers who spend too much time with the majority party leadership might neglect their duties as professional managers and fail to retain the confidence of the minority parties.

Adapted from Widdicombe 1986.

Item B *The role of senior local government officers (1)*

Chief officers have overall responsibility for implementing council policies relating to their departments. Though highly trained, professionally qualified and well paid, they are as much employees of the council as any manual worker. Unlike councillors (who are often far less well educated and usually less well paid), they have not been elected. Their role is to ensure that the policy laid down by the councillors is implemented and that all their reasonable and lawful instructions are carried out. Most local authorities have a Chief Executive who is the chief officer in charge of the council and its departments - the 'head of the paid service'. Often, the Chief Executive acts as the council's 'monitoring officer' whose job is to check the council operates within the law (a compulsory appointment since 1989). The Chief Executive is a kind of officers' team leader and will generally chair (weekly or fortnightly) a Principal Chief Officers' Management Team which ensures effective liaison and policy co-ordination across departments. The internal organisation of departments is characterised by two main elements - professionalism and hierarchy. Senior positions are held by the dominant profession in that department. In parallel, there is a strong commitment to formal accountability and hierarchical control. A typical service department will have a hierarchy of accountability running from field worker to chief officer. So, the span of control of any one officer is limited. In some authorities, over a dozen tiers could separate chief officer from the staff providing the service.

Adapted from Wilson & Game 1998.

Item E *The location of power inside local authorities*

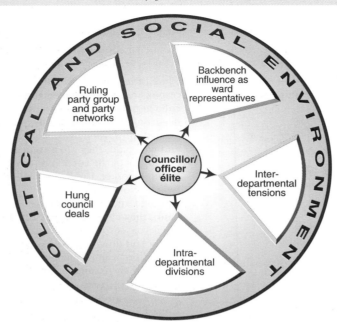

This diagram shows the various factors which determine where power is located within local authorities.

Adapted from Wilson & Game 1998.

Questions

1. a) Does the diagram in Item A illustrate the traditional view of the relationship between officers and councillors or one of its variants? Explain how you know.
   b) Redraw the diagram to illustrate one of the other models mentioned in this section.

2. a) Using Items B-D, explain what factors determine how decisions are made and implemented by local authorities.
   b) What factors constrain the powers of (i) officers and (ii) councillors?

3. Using Items B and D, describe the role played by (i) senior officers and (ii) the Chief Executive.

4. Using Item E, explain where power is located in local authorities.

5. Look in your local newspaper for a piece of news which mentions a decision made by a local council. Find out as much as you can about this decision and write a piece explaining the various steps taken before this piece of news was released.

2.3 Party politics and local government

A new development?

Local government is now dominated by party politics. Some commentators have argued that this is a new development (for example, Barber 1978). Others claim that it is a return to the political climate in which local government operated before the Second World War (for example, Alexander 1985 and Stoker 1988). Those who subscribe to the latter theory claim that, during the period 1945 to 1970, local authority officers managed to depoliticise local government.

The growth of party politics

There is good evidence to suggest that party politics has grown in importance since 1970. The Maud Report of 1967 found that 50% of local authorities were under independent control whereas the Widdicombe Report of 1986 found that just 16% of local councils (mainly in rural areas) were dominated by independent councillors.

As the number of independent councillors has declined, so the number of councillors standing on a party ticket has increased. According to the Widdicombe Report, 83% of councillors in 1985 stood on a party ticket. The result of this is an inevitable growth in party discipline, party caucuses and party voting both at full council meetings and on committees.

This trend has continued since the Widdicombe Report. Local government is increasingly conducted on party lines with the majority party (or sometimes a coalition) forming a government and the minority parties forming an opposition. The allocation of committee chairs and the make-up of committees are determined by the overall strength of a party in the council as a whole. Issues are increasingly defined in party political terms.

Whilst this pattern has been quite common in the cities for a number of years, it is a recent phenomenon in the shire counties. In particular, the growth of the Liberal (now Liberal Democrat) vote since the early 1980s means that all three main parties now have a real opportunity of exercising power.

Hung councils

After the 1997 county council elections, 15 out of 34 county councils were left with no overall control. Of the remainder, Labour controlled nine county councils, the Liberal Democrats controlled two and the Conservatives controlled eight. Amongst the unitary authorities, there were eight councils with no overall control. In a council where no overall control exists, effective party discipline is essential if alliances are to be forged between parties which seek to share power.

State of the parties

Following the local elections in 1998, Labour had 10,417 councillors, the Conservatives 4,770, the

Liberal Democrats 4,632 and the Nationalists 304. In addition, there were 2,160 independent councillors or councillors from minor parties (Rallings & Thrasher 1998).

One of the most remarkable developments in recent years has been the collapse of the Conservative Party in local government. In 1979, there were 12,100 Conservative councillors. By 1987, the number had dropped to 9,100 and, in 1992, it was down to 8,300. In 1996, the Conservatives were overtaken by the Liberal Democrats as the second biggest party in local government (they remained in third place until 1998 when they overtook the Liberal Democrats again). In 1997 and 1998, the Conservatives controlled no councils in Scotland and Wales. There was a small sign of a Conservative revival in the 1998 local elections, but it was not a significant revival:

> 'The pattern of transfer of seats between parties confirms the absence of any clear national swing in 1998. While the Conservatives emerged with net gains, both Labour and the Liberal Democrats enjoyed some success in different parts of the country. The Conservatives' gain of 343 seats, in almost equal proportion from Labour and the Liberal Democrats represents only a modest recovery and much more will need to be done before the party can mount a serious challenge.' (Rallings & Thrasher 1998, p.40)

Case Study - party politics in Oxford City Council

After the 1998 local government election, Oxford City Council had a Labour majority. There were 33 Labour councillors, no Conservative councillors, 14 Liberal Democrat councillors and four Green Party councillors.

Since it had a majority in 1998, the Labour group could be sure of winning all the votes taken at full council meetings and at committees. A Labour councillor held the position of Leader of the Council in 1998. Also Labour councillors were chairs and vice chairs of all the council committees.

A large number of Labour councillors would have to defy the party whip and vote with the opposition to defeat the ruling group on any issue. But, Labour councillors were unlikely to do this since they would risk being expelled from the Labour group in the council and even from the Labour Party.

In 1998, the Labour group met regularly to determine what view the group should take on particular issues. There were often heated discussions at these meetings with different points of views being advanced. Once a majority position was established, however, all Labour councillors were expected to follow the agreed line. This agreed line was also expected to be in accord with national

Labour Party thinking. The Labour Party organises national conferences which are attended by local councillors.

In 1998, there was a close link between the Labour group and the DLP (District Labour Party). Observers from the DLP (which represents all Labour Party members living in the area of the City Council) attended the Labour group meetings. Their role was to inform Labour councillors of views expressed by members of the DLP and to report back to the DLP the decisions made by the Labour councillors. The relationship between the two bodies was similar to the relationship between the Labour Party at national level with the PLP (Parliamentary Labour Party). The Labour Party's election manifesto for the Oxford City Council elections in 1998 was debated by the DLP and had to be approved by that body. Although the choice of candidate to fight council seats was made by the local party branch, it had to be endorsed by the DLP.

The benefits of party involvement

Greater party involvement in local government is supported on the following grounds. First, it helps to define the issues placed before the electorate. Parties stand on a manifesto which clearly distinguishes their different policies. Second, policies tend to be based on principles rather than personalities. This leads to greater consistency. Third, there is greater coherence because of party discipline. Fourth, more seats are contested and there is a slightly higher turnout at elections. Fifth, there is greater accountability because the electorate is able to comment on a party's performance by re-electing it or voting it out of office. Sixth, there is better coordination between local and national politics. Seventh, the democratic structure of parties allows party members to participate in decision making. So, as a result, political participation increases.

The drawbacks of party involvement

Greater party involvement in local government has been criticised for the following reasons. First, party involvement is not desirable because most local issues are not party political. Local issues are neglected because party concerns predominate. Second, real decisions are no longer taken in council chambers but in party meetings. Decisions are made by party activists behind the scenes rather than by democratically elected councillors. Third, the electorate votes on party lines rather than on the quality of candidates. Fourth, council decisions are made in an adversarial climate (two hostile groups debate angrily). This is neither the most effective nor the most efficient way to make decisions. Fifth, wholesale reversal of policies takes place when party control changes hands. Sixth, independent councillors find it much harder to be elected because they do not have a party machine behind them.

The 'nationalisation' of local politics

In addition to the growth of party politics, some

commentators claim that there has been a growing 'nationalisation' of local politics (see, for example, Schofield 1977). By this, they mean that local government is perceived less in local terms and more in terms of national government and national political issues. In other words, local elections are seen as judgements on the performance of parties nationally rather than as a test of local opinion or as a judgement on the performance of local politicians.

Some doubts, however, have been expressed about the extent of the 'nationalisation' of local politics. The Widdicombe Report of 1986, for example, claimed that local matters can still determine local election results, especially at ward level. Research for the report indicated that 56% of those interviewed claimed to be influenced more by local issues than by national issues in local elections. Also, 39% of those interviewed claimed that the quality of the individual was more important than the party in local elections and 20% voted for different parties in local elections and national elections.

The findings of the Widdicombe Report were confirmed by Rallings and Thrasher in 1997. They claimed that:

'It seems clear that many more electors cast votes for different parties at the 1997 general and local elections than had done so at the comparable contests in 1979. We have long suspected, using evidence from the annual local elections, that for many voters making a choice of party at local level is something to be done independently of, and even in contradiction to, their national party preference. We now know this to be true.' (Rallings & Thrasher 1997, p.182)

Main points - Section 2.3

- **Party politics has grown in importance since 1970.**
- **The growth of the Liberal Democrat vote since the early 1980s means that all three main parties now have a real opportunity of exercising power, though Labour has by far the most seats.**
- **One of the most remarkable recent developments has been the collapse of the Conservative Party - from 12,100 seats in 1979 to 4,770 in 1998.**
- **The benefits of party involvement are: (1) policies are clearly outlined; (2) policies are based on principle not personality; (3) greater coherence; (4) more seats contested; (5) greater accountability; (6) better local/national coordination; and (7) greater participation.**
- **The drawbacks of party involvement are: (1) local issues neglected; (2) decisions made by activists not elected councillors; (3) voting for party not candidate; (4) adversarial climate; (5) can be major policy reversals; and (6) difficult for independents to be elected.**
- **Some commentators claim there has been a growing 'nationalisation' of local politics. Others have found evidence that people vote differently in local and national elections.**

Activity 16.5 *Party control of local authorities*

Item A *Party control of local authorities, 1979-98*

Party	1979	1989	1994	1998
Con	262	169	80	25
Lab	79	163	156	204
Lib Dem	1	12	44	42
Other	39	12	6	4
Independent	57	32	19	23
No overall control	77	127	144	142

Adapted from Chandler 1991, the *Guardian*, 6 May 1994 and Rallings & Thrasher 1998.

Item B *The impact of party politics*

In the metropolitan areas, in most of the counties and unitaries and in the larger shire districts, there are now fully developed party systems. Some 80% of all councils fall into this category and, because this figure includes nearly all county and unitary councils, party systems affect nearly all voters. Whether people like it or not, party politics at local level is not only here to stay, but has received a boost with the spread of large unitary authorities. The significance of party politics might not feature on formal policy-making charts inside local authorities, but its centrality is real enough. Party group discipline and loyalty affects the way in which councillors conduct local representation. Most councillors place loyalty to the group above loyalty to those they represent. But, the loyalty demanded by the group and the willingness of councillors across the political spectrum to give that loyalty sets the stage for an increasing alienation of the community from its own representatives. This process will continue unless party groups locally and political parties nationally recognise the legitimate claims for responsive representation made by local communities. Whilst the party group system restricts councillors' willingness and ability to act on community demands, democratic renewal would allow greater participation in the representative process.

Adapted from Wilson 1997 and Copus 1998.

Item C *Hung councils*

In 1979, one in seven councils was hung. In 1997-98, the figure was nearly one in three. On twice as many councils, therefore, party groups now have to take account of each other's policies and actions. Otherwise, any proposal they put forward might be defeated. First, though, they need to decide how council business is going to be conducted. There are three main approaches:

1. Minority administration
One party (usually the largest) is allowed by the others to take all committee chairs and vice chairs and to govern as if it had an overall majority. Clearly, the ruling party is expected to listen carefully to the other parties.

2. Power sharing
Two or more parties agree to share committee chairs, but do not have any more far-reaching agreement on a shared policy programme. In other words, a deal is made rather than a formal coalition.

3. Rotating chairs
No party permanently chairs a committee. Rather, the chairs are rotated for procedural purposes among two or more parties. The rotation has no policy significance.

All three forms of administration involve extensive contact and negotiation between the parties, of a sort rarely seen in majority-controlled councils. Officers, too, have to assume different roles as they have to work with and brief members of several parties rather than just one. Sometimes, they play a brokerage role - bringing parties together to negotiate a policy or procedural agreement. Backbench councillors' positions may also be enhanced as every vote is precious. Bargaining is the order of the day.

Adapted from Wilson & Game 1998.

Item D *Rotten boroughs*

(i) Local government is in a bad state. Council meetings are often a farce, with decisions already taken in closed party meetings. Local newspapers are gradually dropping coverage of councils (except scandals), adding to the sense of disconnection between councillors and their communities. Too many cases of corruption occur, many involving Labour one-party states. Latest estimates suggest that a single party has 80% of seats in 20% of local authorities. Turnout for local elections is well below 40% - the worst in Europe. In Salford, only one in five members of the public voted in May 1997.

(ii) Labour faces serious allegations against councillors or local authority officials in at least eight areas. Yet, with 10,000 Labour councillors dominating 470 local authorities, the party can argue that corruption is

1 Glasgow
Nine senior councilllors, including Labour leader and Lord Provost, suspended in trips-for-votes affair.

2 Paisley
Local party suspended after allegations of illegal gains, linked to drugs.

3 South Tyneside
Labour's NEC conduct an inquiry into membership irregularities and intimidation.

4 Hull
NEC investigates city council's Labour group. Former chaiman of local party suspended.

5 Doncaster
Five councillors suspended. Police probing expense claims and links with developers.

6 Birmingham
Three constituency parties suspended. Allegations of queue jumping for housing grants.

7 Coventry
Labour council launches inquiry into claims of irregularities in contracts.

8 Hackney
Power struggle in left results in Labour losing control. Government sends in team to improve borough's schools.

rare. Significantly, the Local Government Association Chair, Jeremy Beecham (Labour's leading town hall voice), has suggested voting reform to give the opposition a chance to make a comeback. He says that the disappearance of Conservatives from most city councils is unhealthy for democracy.

Adapted from the *Observer* 21 June 1998 and *Guardian*, 27 October 1997.

Questions

1. a) Judging from Items A and B, what evidence is there of greater party political control of local government since 1970?
   b) Why do you think this has happened?
2. Using Items B and C, explain how the political complexion of councils affects the way in which decisions are made.
3. Judging from Items B and D, should the electorate be concerned about the growing involvement of party politics in local government?
4. 'The Labour Party's dominance of local government is unhealthy.' Give arguments for and against this view. Use Item D in your answer.

2.4 Local finance

Background information

Local government costs a great deal of money. This money comes from a number of sources. First, fees and charges are made for some local authority services. Car parking charges, swimming pool entrance fees and council house rents are all examples. Second, councils also raise money to pay for local services through local taxation. Since 1993, this local taxation has been the council tax - a tax based on property. Third, councils receive money from business rates paid by the owners of offices, shops and factories in the area. Fourth, councils receive central government grants which are earmarked for specific services. And fifth, councils can acquire money by borrowing for capital expenditure (for example, for building schools or houses). Loans are raised from banks, from finance houses and from central government's Public Works Loan Board.

The money raised by local authorities is used to provide a range of services (see above, Section 2.1). This money is spent both on running services (current expenditure) and on buildings, roads and equipment (capital expenditure). A significant part of current expenditure is the salaries of council employees. Teachers, social workers and trading standards officers are all examples of people employed by a local authority. The actual cost of running the council (the cost of meetings, members' allowances and so on) is a very small proportion of the total.

Raising finance 1945-76

Between 1945 and 1976, the main political parties agreed that local authority spending was an important and worthwhile expense. There was all-party support for the welfare reforms introduced after the Second World War. These reforms gave local authorities an expanded role which was financed by larger central government grants. In addition, local authorities raised money locally through the rates - a local property tax.

During this period, each local authority was free to decide upon the quantity and quality of the local services it provided. According to one commentator the main restraint on spending was:

> 'The extent to which local electors would vote for councillors who increased rate demands.' (Chandler 1991, p.60)

Tighter restraint after 1976

The oil crisis of the mid-1970s led to a balance of payments problem. The Labour government elected in 1976 was forced to approach the International Monetary Fund (IMF) for a loan. One of the stipulations made by the IMF when providing this loan was that public expenditure should be cut. The result was that central government had to reduce the amount of money granted to local government. As the minister responsible for local government, Anthony Crosland, put it in 1975:

> 'We have come to terms with the harsh reality of the situation which we inherited. The party's over.' (Crosland 1983, p.295)

The Thatcher governments which followed in the 1980s had no interest in lifting the financial restraints imposed by the Labour government. They saw local government as an unnecessary evil. According to John Kingdom, the New Right thought that local expenditure:

> 'Created a dependency culture, a post-war funk in which wasteful councils elected by non-ratepaying voters, served by empire-building bureaucrats dispensed lavish patronage to working-class scroungers.' (Kingdom 1991, p.174)

Government grants

Between 1979 and 1990, central government grants as a proportion of local authority expenditure fell from 58% to 42% with a corresponding increase in the burden on local taxpayers. Also, within budgets, the overall proportions spent on the different services changed. Less money was spent on education, for example, and more on law and order.

To ensure that local authorities reduced public spending, the first Thatcher government passed the Local Government Planning and Land Act of 1980. This fundamentally changed the system by which grants were allocated to local authorities. From 1980, grants were allocated on the basis of an assessment prepared by the Department of the Environment. At first this was known as the Grant Related Expenditure Assessment (GREA). It is now called the Standard Spending Assessment (SSA). This assessment determines how much money a council needs to provide its services at the existing level. A grant is then paid up to that amount. The introduction of this system gave central government a great deal of control over local finances.

The Audit Commission

Tighter financial control was also achieved through the activities of the Audit Commission. An audit is an investigation of financial accounts to check whether money has been spent legally, efficiently and in line with stated policies. Local authorities had always been subject to an annual external audit by impartial district auditors. But, after 1984, the Local Government Finance Act set up the Audit Commission to take over this work. The Audit Commission has a chief officer appointed by central government. Its brief is not only to ensure that councils spend money legally, but also to ensure that they achieve value for money in commercial terms. Many local authorities have seen the Audit Commission as a device to ensure more control from the centre.

2.5 Local taxation since 1945

The rates

Until the late 1980s, local authorities raised revenue by means of a property tax - the rates. The rates were an ancient form of taxation, first introduced in 1601 to raise money for the new poor law. The advantage of the rating system was that it was easy to administer and difficult to avoid. Money was raised by charging an annual rate for each piece of property in the locality. The size of the fee was determined by the size and standard of the property. Businesses paid a special business rate on their property.

The rates had a number of disadvantages. First, the rates hit poorest people hardest. The poor paid a larger proportion of their income in rates than the wealthy. Second, the rates were not related to ability to pay but on the size and standard of the property. Third, the tax took no account of how much use was made of the services provided by the local authority. A single property of low rateable value might house five people who made use of local services a great deal whereas a property of high rateable value might house a single person who made very little use of local services. Fourth, there was no incentive to improve properties because improvements led to higher rates being charged. And, finally, only about half the electorate paid rates. The other half received rebates.

Opposition to the rates

From the time when Margaret Thatcher was shadow Environment Minister in the mid-1970s, she supported the abolition of the rates. It was not until the mid-1980s, however, that this became a serious proposition. By then, Conservative think tanks were arguing that many of those who voted in local elections did so without having to consider the rates burden since they did not have to pay it themselves. This, they argued, was particularly hard on businesses. Businesses paid over 50% of rates but were given no right of representation.

The reduction of central government finance after 1976 forced many local authorities to put up the rates so that services could be maintained. When the Thatcher government introduced the Grant Related Expenditure Assessment in 1980 (see above), councils began to use 'creative accountancy' to avoid the impact of central government's squeeze on their resources.

Rate capping

In response to this, further Acts of Parliament were passed in the 1980s. These Acts increased central government's control over local government finance and plugged the loopholes which councils had exploited. Especially contentious was the introduction of 'rate capping' in 1984. Rate capping permitted central government to control the expenditure of overspending councils by setting upper limits on the amount they could spend and limiting the amount they could raise in rates. This led to 18 councils being rate capped in 1985-86 and another 12 in 1986-87. Despite the protests against ratecapping, all except Liverpool and Lambeth councils eventually complied with the law. Liverpool budgeted to overspend and refused to reduce services. As a result, 49 councillors were surcharged and disqualified from office for five years.

The poll tax or Community Charge

The Conservatives were anxious to produce an alternative to the rates and, in 1985-86, decided to opt for the 'Community Charge'. This tax was to be based on residence. Almost all adult residents, some 35 million people, would have to pay this tax - about double the number who had paid the rates. The government claimed that this was the best alternative to the rates because it meant that all adult consumers of local authority services would pay something towards them and this would increase local accountability. Although the tax was not based on the electoral register, it rapidly became known as the 'poll tax'.

As well as reforming the domestic rates the government also changed the rating system for businesses (the non-domestic rates). Local businesses would no longer pay rates set by councils. They would pay a uniform business rate set by central government. The money collected from non-domestic rates would then be distributed by central government in grants to local authorities.

Opposition to the poll tax

The poll tax plans met with significant opposition. Before the new tax had been introduced, critics raised the following objections. First, the tax was regressive (individuals in an area would pay the same amount regardless of income). Second, many people, and especially those families with adult families living at home, would find that their poll tax bills were much bigger than the rates. Third, it would be expensive and complicated to collect the tax because it would involve tracing people rather than property.

The poll tax was initially introduced in Scotland in April 1989, and in England and Wales a year later. It soon became the focus of a huge protest movement. A mass campaign of non-payment was launched. This was based on two principles - that people could not afford to pay and that some should not have to pay. By the end of the 1990-91 financial year, £1 billion - nearly 10% of poll tax revenue remained uncollected in England and Wales (*Guardian*, 7 March 1991). This compared to an average collection of 98% under the rates.

Poll tax capping of 21 Labour-controlled authorities in 1990 and a further 17 in 1991 added to the criticism of the tax. The capping negated the argument that the poll tax would bring greater local accountability.

The deep unpopularity of the tax led the government to announce in March 1991 that the tax would be abolished.

The council tax

Announcing the abolition of the poll tax in March 1991, Michael Heseltine, Secretary of State for the Environment, said that he would introduce:

> 'A new local tax under which there will be a single bill for each household comprising two essential elements, the number of adults living there and the value of the property.' (*Guardian*, 22 March 1991)

He insisted that the new local tax would be fair and

linked to the ability to pay, but it would include the poll tax principle that most people would make some contribution for the use of services.

The change was seen as a major climbdown by the government and a reversal of Thatcherite policies. The council tax came into operation in April 1993. The title of the tax was carefully chosen so that those facing new bills would be conscious that they were paying for local authority services. The tax itself, however, only accounts for about 15% of local government expenditure.

It should be noted that the business rates (the national non-domestic rates) are still set and distributed by central government. All the money raised from businesses is collected into a national pool. Central government decides how much each district and county council or unitary authority should receive from that pool.

Developments since May 1997

Like its predecessor, the new Labour government was wary of giving local authorities greater financial freedom. In its first 18 months in power, the Labour government introduced only minor modifications to controls over the use of receipts to fund capital spending. In addition, the capping system remained in place:

> '[The government] has set the financial arrangements for the financial year 1998-99 with all the bells and whistles of control still in place. It would have required no new legislation to get rid of capping. But, what Prescott [Secretary of State in charge of local government] has regularly called "crude and universal" capping remains, though with the promise that a less crude version will be introduced in the next year or two.' (*Guardian*, 29 April 1998)

In the Queen's Speech of November 1998, it was announced that measures would be taken to end the 'crude and universal' capping of council finances. These measures would be included in the forthcoming Local Government Bill.

In June 1998, as part of the Comprehensive Spending Review (see Chapter 15, Section 4.1), the Chancellor, Gordon Brown, announced an increase in council grants up to the year 2002. He warned, however, that the Treasury would be prepared to cut council grants if local council tax rises were 'excessive'. The Local Government Association Chair, Jeremy Beecham, argued that this meant that services provided by councils would remain under financial pressure:

> 'Despite the extra money for headline services, there is a danger that other important services, especially those provided by district councils, will still be under extreme pressure.' (*Local Government Chronicle*, 17 July 1998)

Main points - Sections 2.4-2.5

- **The money spent by local authorities comes from fees and charges, local taxation, business rates, central government grants, and loans.**
- **From 1976, central government grants to local authorities fell in real terms and tighter financial controls were imposed (including 'capping').**
- **Until the late 1980s, local authorities raised revenue by means of a property tax - the rates.**
- **In 1989-90, a tax based on residence - the poll tax - was introduced. This tax met with significant opposition, including a non-payment campaign. Its abolition was announced in 1991.**
- **A new tax - the council tax - came into operation in 1993. This tax takes into account the value of the property and the number of adults living in it.**
- **The Labour government elected in 1997 has not loosened the financial restraints imposed on local authorities by the Conservatives. Government grants, however, have been set to increase between 1999 and 2002.**

Activity 16.6 *Local government finance*

Item A *Income for 1998-99 - Oxford City Council*

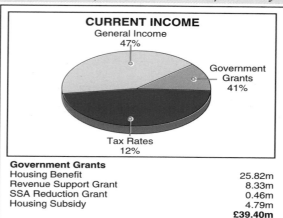

CURRENT INCOME

- General Income 47%
- Government Grants 41%
- Tax Rates 12%

Government Grants

Housing Benefit	25.82m
Revenue Support Grant	8.33m
SSA Reduction Grant	0.46m
Housing Subsidy	4.79m
	£39.40m

Tax and Rates

Council Tax	6.88m
Business Rates	4.41m
	£11.29m

General Income

Council Housing - rents	22.78m
Council Housing - other income	1.78m
Leisure	1.22m
Estates	9.13m
Housing Benefit Administration	0.37m
Homelessness	0.41m
Other Housing	0.04m
Highways	4.77m
Financial Services	0.56m
Planning, Economic Development & Environmental	1.38m
Other services	1.91m
	£44.35m

TOTAL £95.04m

Item B *Changes in council spending 1980-95*

(i) Sources of expenditure 1989-90

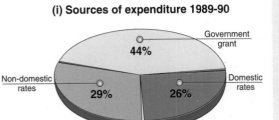

Locally-determined expenditure = 55%
(Domestic and non-domestic rates)

(ii) Sources of expenditure 1991-92

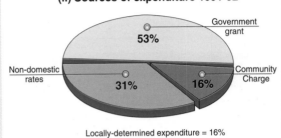

Locally-determined expenditure = 16%
(Community Charge)

(iii) Sources of expenditure 1994-95

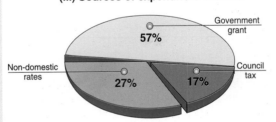

Locally-determined expenditure = 17%
(Council tax)

These charts show how the source of English local authorities' expenditure has changed over time. Before the poll tax (Community Charge) was introduced, local authorities collected and spent both domestic and non-domestic rates. Since 1990, non-domestic rates have been paid into a central pool and then redistributed by central government.

Adapted from HMSO 1996.

Item C *The provision of selected services by councils 1981-98*

Service	1981-82	1991-92	1997-98
Education	45.5	42.74	39.03
Housing	6.26	3.40	– *
Transport	9.89	7.11	4.36
Law & Order	12.49	13.51	16.40
Social Services	2.20	10.21	19.68

* Figure so low that it did not merit a separate category in CIPFA's figures.

This table shows the percentage of total income spent on selected services by councils between 1981 and 1998.

Adapted from information supplied by CIPFA (Chartered Institute of Public Finance and Accountancy).

Item D *The council tax*

The council tax is a local tax set by local councils to pay for local services. There will be one bill per dwelling whether it is a house, bungalow, flat, maisonette, mobile home or houseboat and whether it is owned or rented. The bill will be based on the relative value of your property compared to others in your local area. There will be discounts, including where only one adult lives in the dwelling. Bills will also be reduced for properties with people on low incomes, some people with disabilities and some other special cases. The value of your home has been assessed by the Valuation Office Agency (part of the Inland Revenue), not by your council. Your home will be placed in one of the eight council tax valuation bands. Your home's value is based on its estimated sale price on 1 April 1991, taking account of any significant change to the property between then and 1 April 1993 (such as an extension). Your home was valued in order to establish its relative value compared with other homes. The fact that homes may be worth more or less today does not itself mean that they have been put in the wrong band.

Adapted from a leaflet produced by the Department of the Environment, September 1992.

Item E *The poll tax*

Every voter now faced with paying their share of council expenditure will have a powerful incentive to consider the possible costs of their candidate's policies before they cast their vote. Officials will have to take account of the effect of their recommendations on the public they deal with. Councillors will have to consider the impact of their decision on their voters. Accountability and responsibility will reappear in many communities where, in recent years, both have been lacking. This will create substantial pressure on authorities to reduce their expenditure.

Adapted from ASI 1989.

Item F   *How the council tax is used*

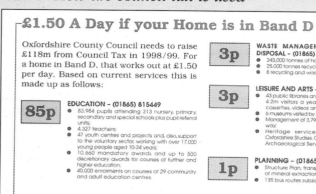

£1.50 A Day if your Home is in Band D

Oxfordshire County Council needs to raise £118m from Council Tax in 1998/99. For a home in Band D, that works out at £1.50 per day. Based on current services this is made up as follows:

85p

EDUCATION – (01865) 815449
- 83,984 pupils attending 313 nursery, primary, secondary and special schools plus pupil referral units;
- 4,327 teachers;
- 47 youth centres and projects and, also, support to the voluntary sector, working with over 17,000 young people aged 10-24 years;
- 10,660 mandatory awards and up to 500 discretionary awards for courses of further and higher education;
- 40,000 enrolments on courses at 29 community and adult education centres.

34p

SOCIAL SERVICES – (01865) 375515
- works with 23,000 people each day;
- receives 65 new referrals each day;
- purchases 24,834 hours of home care per week, helping 3,535 households;
- supports 759 residential places for elderly people in 20 County homes and a further 656 in nursing and independent homes;
- undertook 1,042 child protection investigations each year by which 406 children were registered in 1997;
- looks after 400 children each day in foster placements and in children's homes.

7p

HIGHWAYS – (01865) 815700
- 3,951 kilometres of roads, 861 road bridges, 50,764 street lights maintained.

5p

FIRE SERVICE – (01865) 842999
- 51 vehicles from 24 fire stations attended 10,600 incidents in 1997;
- 229 Full-time, 278 Part-time firefighters;
- 34 fire prevention officers dealt with over 12,000 fire safety responsibilities in 1997.

3p

WASTE MANAGEMENT, RECYCLING & DISPOSAL – (01865) 815796
- 243,000 tonnes of household waste disposed of;
- 25,000 tonnes recycled at County Sites;
- 8 recycling and waste centres provided.

3p

LEISURE AND ARTS – (01865) 815520
- 43 public libraries and 8 mobile libraries with over 4.2m visitors a year and issues of 5m books, cassettes, videos and disks;
- 6 museums visited by 312,000 people in a year;
- Management of 3,790 kilometres of public rights of way;
- Heritage services including Centre for Oxfordshire Studies, County Archives and County Archaeological Services.

1p

PLANNING – (01865) 815700
- Structure Plan, transportation planning, control of mineral extraction;
- 135 bus routes subsidised.

7p

CAPITAL FINANCING & INTEREST
- The costs of servicing the Council's debt, after deducting interest earned on surplus balances.

5p

MISCELLANEOUS SERVICES – (01865) 815352
- A wide range including probation, courts, emergency planning, flood defence, registrars and Trading Standards.

TRADING STANDARDS – (01865) 815000
- 'Our business is fair trading' - ask for our 'Service Standards' leaflet;
- Working for 608,000 residents; Working with 20,000 businesses;
- Quality assured (ISO 9002), Charter Mark winner and 'Investor in people'.

What do Houses in other Bands pay?

The most that your household will be asked to pay per day for County Services is:

Band A	£1.00	Band E	£1.83
Band B	£1.17	Band F	£2.17
Band C	£1.33	Band G	£2.50
Band D	£1.50	Band H	£3.00

Working for Oxfordshire

In December 1997 15,672 people were working for Oxfordshire County Council. 6,615 were full-time and 9,057 part-time. This was the equivalent of 10,900 full-time employees, which is how the figures below are shown.

December 1996		December 1997
6,236	Education - schools	6,295
346	Education - other	323
2,520	Social Services	2,396
283	Environmental Services	270
304	Leisure and Arts	292
298	Fire Service	290
244	Miscellaneous Services	231
10,231	SUB-TOTAL	10,097
880	Commercial Services	803
11,111	TOTAL	10,900

Staffing levels for many services have been reduced because of budget cuts. Education staffing levels have increased because of the growing number of school children. But the growth in teacher numbers has not kept pace with the growth in pupil numbers so class sizes have been rising. Some staff reductions have resulted from reorganisation, and other steps to improve efficiency.

Like to Know More?

The County Council constantly reviews the performance of its service and publishes a range of service standards and performance indicators. As well as the telephone numbers for services listed opposite, more information is available:

- **At your Local Library**
  Check the OXCIS free information point. Ask for our publications for reference.
- **By telephone or letter**
  County Treasurer's Office (01865) 815622. For general information or a list of councillors telephone (01865) 815266.
- **By attending Council Meetings at County Hall**
  You are welcome to attend and in some cases make your points to the meeting.
- **On the Internet**
  Visit our web sites (www.oxfordshire.gov.uk and www.oxon-tss.org.uk for Trading Standards);

Published by: Oxfordshire County Council County Hall, Oxford OX1 1ND – Tel: (01865) 792422
Typeset & printed by: Commercial Services Print Unit – Tel: (01865) 815672   RECYCLED PAPER

A leaflet produced by Oxfordshire County Council in 1998.

Questions

1. Look at Items A-C.
   a) Explain how the system of local government finance works.
   b) How has local government expenditure changed since 1981?
   c) Do you think that councillors should be responsible for spending such large amounts of money? Give arguments for and against.

2. Look at Items D-F.
   a) Why do you think the poll tax was introduced?
   b) How does the council tax differ from the poll tax?
   c) Why do you think there was a mass campaign against the poll tax but not against the council tax?

3. Judging from Items D and F, what are the advantages and disadvantages of the council tax?

2.6 The privatisation of local government

Pressure since 1979

Until the 1980s, it was taken for granted that local authorities were themselves responsible for providing services. Between 1979 and 1997, however, there was increasing pressure on local authorities to introduce market mechanisms - to 'privatise' their services. The long-term aim was nothing short of a fundamental change in the role played by local authorities. The idea was that local authorities would no longer be responsible themselves for providing and managing services. Instead, they would be 'enabling authorities', bodies which regulated the services provided by outside organisations.

Enabling authorities

The 'enabling authority' was a concept developed after the Conservatives' third successive electoral victory in 1987. Nicholas Ridley, the minister who first promoted the idea, suggested in 1988 that the role played by councils should change. No longer should councils have a monopoly on service provision. Their spending should be limited to the provision of essential services contracted-out to private firms. Councils should give up ownership of leisure centres, recreation grounds, retail centres, factory units, workshop and land. Instead of actually providing services, it should be the role of councils to identify markets, to devise strategies to meet consumer demands and to monitor services once they had been contracted-out.

So, no longer would a local authority run its own

refuse collection service. Instead, the council's job would be to find out what refuse services were required by local citizens and then to contract a private refuse collection company to undertake the work. The company contracted would be the company that could do the work at the lowest possible cost whilst maintaining the standards required by the council. Having contracted-out the work, it would then be the job of the council to monitor the delivery of the service. If standards were not maintained, then the council would be able to refuse to renew the contract or to impose penalties.

This change in the role of local authorities from 'provider' to 'purchaser' has been described by the Joseph Rowntree Foundation as a 'fundamental change' in the way in which local authorities work (Rowntree 1992).

Privatisation

The creation of enabling authorities depended upon the widespread privatisation of local government services. Privatisation was supported for two main reasons.

First, it was argued that privatisation increases efficiency. A common criticism of local government, especially in the late 1970s, was that it was over-bureaucratic, inflexible and inefficient. By allowing private firms to bid for public service contracts, it was argued, local people would get better value for money.

And second, it was argued that privatisation increases direct accountability to the consumers of services. According to this view, local government public service provision operates not in the interest of those who receive the service, but in the interest of those who administer it. Private sector provision, on the other hand, is more genuinely controlled by the public. Private companies have to satisfy public taste or they will not survive. Privatisation, therefore, increases accountability because, although not everyone participates in local elections, everyone is a consumer. Consumer pressure determines whether a company succeeds or fails.

During the 1980s and early 1990s, the privatisation of local authority services took a number of different forms.

1. The sale of assets

One of the consequences of the setting up of the welfare state after 1945 was a change in local government responsibilities. Before 1945, local authorities had been responsible for the provision of public utilities such as water, gas and electricity. After 1945, these public utilities were nationalised and transferred from local authority control into the hands of public corporations.

Having lost control in some areas, local authorities gained responsibility for a new range of social and welfare services - such as education and housing. In the 20 years after 1945, education and housing

expenditure dominated local government budgets. Whereas education and housing amounted to 35% of local authority expenditure in the 1940s, it had increased to 60% in the 1950s. By 1961, there were 4.2 million council houses and flats, 27% of all households.

Although the sale of council houses had been permitted since before the Second World War, most council tenants could not afford to buy their houses. The Housing Act of 1980, however, offered tenants a major discount if they agreed to buy their council house within a certain period (long-term tenants could receive a discount of as much as 60% of the market price of the house). The result was the sale of over a million council houses by 1987.

The Conservative Party had promised council tenants the 'right to buy' in their 1979 election manifesto. This was not just a ploy to win the votes of council tenants. The policy reflected the Conservatives' belief in owner occupation and their concern about public spending. By selling council houses, they argued, public expenditure would be reduced since the new owners would be responsible for their upkeep.

Some of the revenue received from the sale of council houses was used to finance new house building. But, councils were only allowed to reinvest a proportion of it in new buildings. At first, this proportion was 50%. Later, it was reduced to 20%. As a result, much of the money raised from council house sales remained locked up by central government controls on capital spending.

Council houses are not the only local government assets to be sold off since 1979. Local authority land has also been sold off. Perhaps the most notorious example of this was Westminster Council's decision in 1987 to sell three cemeteries for 15 pence. After the ombudsman declared that 'maladministration causing injustice' had taken place, the council bought back the cemeteries in 1992 for £5 million.

2. Deregulation

Whilst some local authority assets were sold off, others were 'deregulated'. An example of this is the provision of bus services. Until 1980, strict licensing of bus transport meant that, in practice, private operators found it hard to compete with bus companies run by local authorities. Changes in legislation in 1980 made it easier for private companies to obtain licences. This broke the public monopoly. Then, the Transport Act of 1985 forced public sector operators to form private companies and to operate in line with market criteria. The National Bus Company was broken up and privatised. Routes were deregulated so that a single route might have buses from several companies running on it. On such a route, different companies could charge different fares for the same distance. The market would determine how many buses would run how often and which companies would survive to operate them.

3. Compulsory competitive tendering (CCT)

Compulsory competitive tendering (CCT) was also introduced. Rather than simply employing their own staff to provide services, councils were forced to allow private companies to bid for contracts. To facilitate this, council employees were detached from the local authority's main management structure and set up as free-standing companies (direct service organisations). If a private company made a bid which was lower or, in some way, better than that made by the council's direct service organisation, then the council was expected to award the contract to that private company. The 1980 Local Government and Land Act required CCT in the areas of highways and building construction and maintenance. The Local Government Act of 1988 extended this requirement to refuse collection, street cleaning, catering, cleaning buildings and vehicle maintenance. The Local Government Act of 1992 extended this requirement still further to professional, financial and technical services.

CCT has been criticised because, when local authority workers have won contracts, they have often found that their pay and working conditions have suffered. Also, the quality of work provided by private companies is not always of a sufficiently high standard. It was on these grounds that the introduction of CCT was fiercely opposed by the Labour Party.

4. Greater provision of services outside local authority control

In a number of areas, the Conservative government encouraged the transfer of services from local authority control to the private sector. First, in education, City Technology Colleges and Grant Maintained schools were encouraged to opt out of the local authority system and, instead, to be controlled and financed directly by central government. Second, central government encouraged private housing corporations at the expense of local authority council housing. And third, under the terms of the Community Care Act which came into operation in April 1993, local authorities were expected to dispose of most of their own residential homes, day care centres and other facilities to the private and voluntary sectors. It would then be the job of the local authority to award contracts to the private and voluntary providers of the services.

Privatisation under the Conservatives

The changes brought about by privatisation under the Conservatives varied widely. Some 'flagship' Conservative-controlled councils such as Wandsworth and Westminster embarked enthusiastically on privatisation drives. In an interview in 1987, for example, Wandsworth Council

Leader, Paul Beresford, described his strategy as:

'The efficient management of services; to cut waste; to ensure high quality; to test all council services, where possible, against the private sector; to contract-out where appropriate; and to promote a vigorous sales policy involving (a) the sale of land and buildings where such action proves economically efficient and (b) the sale of houses to families on low incomes, thus breaking up enormous housing estates and providing a stimulus to the maintenance of such housing.'

When the Conservatives briefly took over control of Bradford in the late 1980s, they introduced competitive tendering across a wide range of council services, they ended council provision of a number of services and they increased council house rents.

In local authorities controlled by Labour or the Liberal Democrats, however, considerable efforts were made to minimise the impact of privatisation. Even in some Conservative-controlled councils, the changes were minimal.

The battle over CCT

The imposition of CCT was particularly controversial and, at first, there is evidence that many councils (especially Labour-controlled councils) tried to avoid it. In 1992, between 75% and 80% of contracts were awarded to councils' direct service organisations (Wilson 1993). Four years later, there were over 120 local authorities in which the councils' direct service organisations had won 100% of contracts whilst there were 26 authorities (mainly non-metropolitan districts) where the direct service organisations had not won any contracts. By the 1997 general election, the impact of CCT was described as follows:

'The private sector has not rushed into this "new" market and totally transformed service provision overnight as some hoped and others feared. In many cases still, there are no private sector bids and in-house direct service organisations win by default. The overall picture is...extremely varied from one council to another, depending upon their size, type and, perhaps above all in this instance, their political inclinations.' (Wilson & Game 1998, p.345)

New Labour and privatisation

Despite the Conservative government's determination to privatise locally-run services, popular satisfaction with council-run services remained high. For example, 61% of those surveyed by MORI in an opinion poll for the National Consumer Council in 1995 expressed satisfaction with the quality of council-run services. Also, people were more satisfied with their local council than with any other major institution in Britain. In 1998, another MORI poll showed a high level of support for local government and local decision making (LGA 1998).

Since Labour's election in May 1997, the future of privatisation has looked less certain. Labour's election manifesto stated:

> 'Councils should not be forced to put their services out to tender, but will be required to obtain best value. We reject the dogmatic view that services must be privatised to be of high quality, but equally, we see no reason why a service should be delivered directly if more efficient means are available.' (Labour 1997, p.34)

The Best Value initiative

From the beginning, the Labour Party was suspicious of CCT, believing that it forced workers to accept very low wages so that their employers would secure the contract. Following the 1997 general election, the Labour government set up a pilot scheme designed to replace CCT with 'Best Value'. Councils taking part in the Best Value pilot scheme escaped CCT by setting steadily rising performance targets and then achieving them. These councils had to use open competition for service delivery unless they could show, to the satisfaction of the district auditor, that competition was inappropriate (*Local Government Chronicle*, 25 July 1997). This suggested that Labour no longer had a fixed ideological commitment to local government provision of services. Rather, its approach can be described as 'pragmatic'. Services might be delivered by either local authorities or private contractors, depending on local circumstances. A major criticism of CCT was that issues of quality were always secondary to issues of cost. In the 'twelve principles of Best Value' set out by the Local Government Minister in June 1997, the Labour government made it clear that:

> 'Best Value is about effectiveness and quality, not just economy and efficiency.' (*Local Government Chronicle*, 6 June 1997)

In the Queen's Speech of November 1998, it was announced that the Local Government Bill would replace compulsory CCT with a Best Value regime.

A different type of enabling authority

The original concept of the enabling authority was developed by the New Right. According to that model, local authorities would play only a minor role in providing services. The main role of local authorities would be to decide which contractor should be awarded a contract and then to monitor and regulate the work performed by contractors. The New Right model is not the only model of the enabling authority, however. Another view of the enabling authority is that:

> 'The role of an enabling council is to use all the means at its disposal to meet the needs of those who live within the area.' (Clarke & Stewart 1988, p.1)

This definition allows a much broader interpretation of the role of local authorities:

> 'The starting point here is the identification of community needs. The enabling authority in this sense uses a wide range of powers and resources, including the powers of civic leadership, influence and campaigning, to meet those needs. Pro-active negotiation with the private sector to stimulate economic activity, empowerment of local communities, imaginative use of regulatory powers, and the positive use of links with other public sector organisations are all means to this end.' (Wilson & Game 1998, p.354)

Wilson & Game point out that this broader interpretation is the one preferred by many local authorities, and it is close to the 1997 Labour Party manifesto's emphasis on 'partnership working'. What this means in practice is that, although local authorities have lost their traditional function of providing services, they have developed a new role, namely that of coordinating the work of other agencies. So, whereas, for example, local authorities no longer control further education colleges (they are now controlled by a quango - the Further Education Funding Council), they can (and do) play the lead role in bringing together agencies to bid for European money (John 1997).

Main points - Section 2.6

- Until 1979, it was taken for granted that local authorities should provide services. Between 1979 and 1997, however, the Conservatives aimed to create 'enabling authorities' - councils which contracted-out services and monitored them.
- Creating enabling authorities depended upon the privatisation of local government services. This, it was argued, would improve efficiency and accountability.
- Privatisation took four different forms: (1) selling assets; (2) deregulation; (3) CCT; and (4) transferring services to the private sector.
- The changes brought about by privatisation under the Conservatives varied widely. The imposition of CCT was particularly controversial - the use of outside contractors varied widely, depending on the size, type and political inclinations of the council.
- The Labour government's approach is pragmatic, allowing either local authorities or private contractors to deliver services - whichever suits local circumstances.

Activity 16.7 Local authorities and privatisation

Item A Refuse collection

This picture shows a dustcart owned by West Lancs District Council. Since 1988, council employees have had to compete with private companies.

Item B Arguments in favour of CCT

Allowing the private sector to compete to provide local authority services can bring significant improvements in value for money either because the in-house workforce improves its efficiency (to match the competition) or because the private firm which wins the contract can beat the in-house staff on price and/or quality. Some local authorities have led the way in using the private sector to deliver services to the consumer. These authorities are free to concentrate on planning the future direction of service delivery, setting quality standards and monitoring the service to ensure that the standard required is achieved. But, a number of other authorities have persisted in retaining all work in-house. We have, therefore, had to introduce compulsory competitive tendering for a significant number of services, to ensure that local taxpayers in all areas share in the benefits which competition brings. Much remains to be done. The government is looking urgently at ways of extending competition further. We intend to ensure that private firms have a fair chance to compete for local authority work. The government already has powers to prevent the local authority's own workforce carrying out certain activities where it fails to meet its financial obligations or seeks to gain an unfair advantage over the private sector by other means. This could also be appropriate where an authority demonstrably fails to provide an acceptable level of service.

Adapted from the *Citizen's Charter* 1991.

Item C Arguments against CCT

The main arguments against the extension of compulsory competitive tendering in local government are as follows. First, the costs of setting up CCT are high both in terms of time and in terms of money. Second, recurrent costs will be increased. Inspectors will have to be recruited, extra work will be generated for lawyers and costly court cases are likely. Third, there is the likelihood that redundancies will result from CCT. Fourth, downward pressure on wages and conditions of service will occur. The experience of 1980 to 1988 shows that this is likely. Fifth, there are high risks of lower standards of service provision. Damage may be done before penalty clauses can have a real impact on a rogue contractor. Sixth, services will be run for profit not to meet social needs. Flexibility will be lost. Seventh, elected councillors will come close to losing control over key areas of local authority work. And, finally, the character of the 'competition' in CCT is inherently unfair.

Adapted from Pyper 1990.

Item D Privatised and deregulated buses

Ten years ago, bus services were run by the state. Over the last ten years, however, the state has been rolled back in a new, deregulated bus market. The reasoning behind this is familiar - private is best and competition is the best way of ensuring efficiency. Yet, the results have not been quite as predicted. Because capital and running costs of buses cannot be altered (after all, a bus is a bus with wheels and an engine, and a route is a route), the efficiency gains can only come from four sources:

- allowing the bus fleet to age
- cutting wages and wider employment costs, such as employers' pension contributions
- cutting out unprofitable routes
- putting up fares.

By 1997, Britain's buses were older and more prone to breakdown. Staffing had been lowered, wages cut and overheads reduced. Services at quieter times of the day and to outlying regions had been cut or scaled down.

Adapted from Hutton 1997.

Item E   *The public's view of local government*

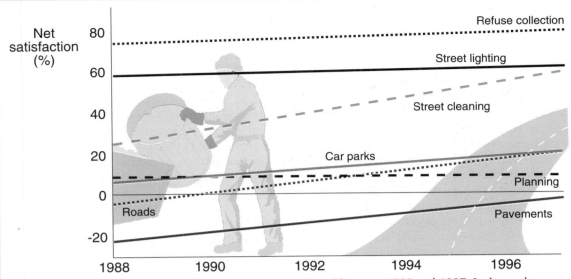

The chart above shows the results of MORI surveys conducted between 1988 and 1997. It shows the average level of satisfaction with a range of services provided by or overseen by local authorities. In a MORI survey, published in June 1997, more than twice as many people were satisfied with the way their local council was doing its job (52%) than with how Parliament was working (23%). Also, nearly two-thirds of people surveyed (61%) agreed they would like the government to allow their local council to set the council tax at the level it feels it needs to deliver good local services.

Questions

1. Look at Item A. Find out who is responsible for refuse disposal at your home. How would you judge whether this service is efficient?

2. How has privatisation changed the role played by local authorities? Use Items A-D in your answer.

3. Judging from Items A-E, would you say that CCT was a positive or a negative development? Give reasons for your answer.

4. 'CCT is very popular with the public'. Is there any evidence in Item E to support this view? Give reasons for your answer.

Part 3 Relations between central and local government

Key issues

1. Is there a need for a system of local government?
2. What changes have taken place in local-central relations?
3. What are the likely future directions?

3.1 Is there a need for local government?

Origins of the debate

Between the mid-19th century and the 1980s, few people seriously challenged the need for local government. As in many other areas, however, the breakdown of the post-war consensus stimulated a new debate about existing local government arrangements. Opponents of local government argued that local authorities were inefficient and unrepresentative whilst supporters complained that the powers of local authorities were being eroded by central government. The question of whether, and if so why, local government is necessary has increasingly been debated. The arguments on both sides can be summarised as follows.

Arguments against the need for local government

In theory, of course, there is no absolute need to have a system of local government. Services could be delivered locally, but administered and controlled by central government. This happens today with social security. Social security is delivered locally through offices located all over the country. Control, however, rests with the Department of Social Security in London. All services provided by local government could be organised in this way. Some critics of local government favour this approach. They point out that there is a great deal of variation in the standard, range and quality of services which are offered by local authorities. If all services were controlled from the centre, they argue, then provision would be uniform throughout the country.

Other reasons for doing away with local government are as follows. First, some local authorities are inefficient. The services they provide cost more than the same services provided by other local authorities. Abolition of local government would increase efficiency. Second, local government itself is a cost. Meetings of councillors and the full range of support services they require does not come cheap. Third, local government can be narrow and introspective. Local authorities are often concerned only with local issues. How these local issues fit into the national picture, or even how they relate to what is happening just over the authority's border, is simply ignored. Central government is better able to plan. Fourth, since local government has become dominated by political parties, narrow party self-interest has become the crucial determinant of policy decisions. Fifth, there is a marked lack of interest in local democracy. This is reflected in the low turnout in local elections and in the public's lack of knowledge about councils' functions. The public only cares about the efficient delivery of services, it does not care about local democratic control. Sixth, local councillors are amateur politicians who lack the detailed knowledge to run complex modern bureaucracies. Seventh, there is such wide central government control that the scope for local autonomy is so small that it is hardly worth bothering with a system of local government. And eighth, since local government reorganisation in 1974, local government has become remote to many people.

Arguments in support of the need for local government

Supporters of local government (for example, Byrne 1990) have countered these criticisms with the following arguments. First, all but the smallest democratic states have systems of local government. The tendency elsewhere is to increase not to erode the powers of local government. The setting up of a tier of local government in Spain, for example, was seen as an important step in the transition from Franco's fascism to democracy. Second, local government is an efficient method of administering certain services since local authorities are run by local people who know local needs. What works in one area may not work in a different area, so it is better to retain local control. Control exerted from the centre tends to be rigid and inflexible. Third, there is no indisputable evidence to suggest that services could be provided more cheaply without local government. Fourth, local authorities are multi-purpose bodies and can, therefore, ensure policy coordination across a range of departments. They are not necessarily narrow or introspective. Fifth, local authorities can experiment with ideas because they have a degree of independence. An individual authority can introduce a pilot scheme, which, if successful, may be adopted elsewhere. Sixth, local government encourages democracy because local

representatives run councils and local people are given the opportunity to vote in local elections. Low turnout is not a good reason for doing away with local democracy. It could be a sign that people are generally happy with the way local affairs are run. Also, local government reflects the different political balance of different parts of the country. The North of England, for example, is a Labour stronghold. During the 1980s, however, Conservative victories in general elections meant that the majority view of the North of England was not represented by central government. It was represented at local level, however. Seventh, local authorities can be seen as a barrier or defence against an all-powerful central government. Eighth, an important function of local government is to hold public servants accountable. The conduct and misconduct of teachers, police officers, social workers and so on produces complaints and grievances which need to be investigated. MPs simply would not have time to investigate all these complaints. It is better that this is left to elected local politicians. And ninth, local government is part of our heritage and culture. It ensures that the important principle of 'no taxation without representation' is maintained.

3.2 Relations between central and local government

The power of central government

Legislative power
From a constitutional point of view, local government would appear to be entirely at the mercy of central government. Parliament has the power to reform or reduce the functions performed by local government and it could even pass a law abolishing all local authorities outright. Although at one time it was assumed that any changes in the local government system would only occur with the agreement of local authorities, this idea was dismissed as long ago as 1956. In that year, a white paper issued by the government included the following sentence:

> 'The government naturally does not take the view that no changes in the structure and functions of local government should be proposed to Parliament except with the agreement of local authorities.' (Cmnd 9831 1956)

Since then, both Labour and Conservative governments have passed laws affecting the responsibilities of local authorities without the agreement of the local authorities concerned.

Central government's power is also boosted by the power of ministers to impose statutory instruments on local authorities:

> 'Acts of Parliament are often referred to as "primary legislation". Many Acts, however, delegate law-making powers to appropriate

government ministers...The Statutory Instruments Act 1946 requires that all such secondary legislation is published and laid before Parliament. But, with some 3,000 statutory instruments currently issued each year, the detailed scrutiny most of them receive is inevitably limited, and they constitute a significant means by which ministers can "flesh out" their own primary legislation and thereby strengthen, if they choose, their control over local authorities' actions and activities.' (Wilson & Game 1998, p.100)

Inspections

In addition to wielding the powers described above, some ministers are responsible for appointing chief inspectors and responding to the work of inspectorates. For example, the Education Secretary is responsible for appointing the Chief Inspector of the Office for Standards in Education (Ofsted) and may take action if an Ofsted report shows that a school is failing. Part of the job of the various inspectorates is to ensure that local authorities maintain standards in particular areas. For example, schools are regularly inspected by Ofsted and fire services are inspected annually by the Home Office Fire Service Inspectorate. Inspectors do not just perform a policing role, however. It is also their job to spread examples of good practice.

The doctrine of ultra vires

It is not only by legislation that central government can control the behaviour of local authorities. The freedom of local authorities is also restricted by the doctrine of ultra vires (see above, Section 2.1). Whereas individuals are free to do anything which is not illegal, local authorities are only allowed to do what is specifically authorised by law. Anything else may be judged to be ultra vires. Government departments circulate advice and guidance to local authorities to help them fulfil their responsibilities within the law.

Default powers

Some legislation provides ministers with 'default powers' - a minister who is dissatisfied with the performance of a local authority can, as a last resort, step in and take over the running of a service or transfer it to another body. This happened in July 1995, for example, when a government 'hit squad' (as the media termed it) was sent in to run Hackney Downs Comprehensive School, following a highly critical Ofsted report. After May 1997, it became clear that the Labour government also favoured this type of action, especially in relation to education:

> 'Nationally-prompted intervention is set to become a key policy instrument of Labour's Education Secretary, David Blunkett. The first announcement of his department's Standards and Effectiveness Unit, emphasising its zero tolerance of poor standards, was a list of 18 allegedly failing schools that could receive visitations...from what the government prefers to call "help squads".' (Wilson & Game 1998, p.103)

A complex network

Constitutionally, central government has the upper hand. But, that does not mean that central-local relations are straightforward. It is not just a question of central government issuing directives directly to local authorities. There is a complex network of relationships:

> 'The very term "central-local government relationship" can be misleading if it encourages a narrow focus on the interaction between central government departments and local authorities. In practice, a range of other organisations cuts across the relationship including local authority associations, professional organisations, party institutions, quasi-government organisations and trade unions.' (Stoker 1988, p.146)

The complex nature of the interaction between all these groups has produced a number of theoretical models which attempt to show how the system works.

1. The agency model

The agency model sees local government as the servant or agent of central government. According to this model, local government has little autonomy. Its role is to implement policies devised by central government.

2. The partnership model

The partnership model sees central government and local government as partners working towards common ends. Even though the two partners do not have equal power, local government is not entirely subordinate. Local government has some freedom to develop its own policies.

3. The power-dependence model

The power-dependence model stresses that central government and local authorities continually negotiate and bargain with each other. Both have resources which they control. Both use these resources to try and get their own way. In terms of power, local government is not as powerless as the agency model supposes nor is there as much agreement as the partnership model suggests.

The erosion of the power of local government

Central-local government relations have changed considerably since 1979:

> 'The arrival in office in May 1979 of a new, crusading New Right Conservative government led by Margaret Thatcher was to bring huge changes to local government. The Thatcher government was determined,

above all, to reduce the role of the state in British society and, as part of this crusade, it was to attack local government.' (Elcock 1996, p.47)

To support this thesis, Elcock goes on to describe a 'war on three fronts'. The opening of these three fronts, he argues, coincided roughly with each of Thatcher's terms of office and pressure on all three fronts continued when John Major came to power. These 'three fronts' are considered elsewhere in this chapter:

1. The Conservative governments' attacks on local authorities' financial autonomy (see Section 2.5 above).

2. The Conservatives' abolition of the GLC and six metropolitan county councils because they had become the focus of opposition against central government (see Section 1.2 above).

3. The devolution of services which had been provided by local authorities to outside bodies - either to private contractors (through CCT - see Section 2.6 above) or to other bodies such as joint boards or quangos (see Part 4 below).

Between 1979 and 1997, over 200 Acts of Parliament modified the powers and responsibilities of local authorities (Wilson & Game 1998). The vast majority increased the power of central government.

Why was power curbed?

There are a number of reasons why central government set out to curb the power of local authorities.

First, the growth of party political control of local government was an incentive for central government intervention. Between 1979 and 1997, the Labour Party controlled a growing number of local authorities, whilst the Conservatives retained control of central government. This led to conflict because Labour local authorities were reluctant to carry out central government policies. Central government intervened, therefore, to ensure that its major policies were implemented.

Second, the prime concern of central government between 1979 and 1997 was to control local authority expenditure. The withdrawal of central government grants, a system of targets and penalties and rate capping were all measures designed to force local authorities to conform to central government's policy of reduced public spending. Since central government held the purse strings, it had the power to impose economies on local authorities.

Third, central government had an interest in ensuring that standards of services provided by different local authorities were roughly similar. To ensure that local authorities provided a basic minimum standard, it was sometimes necessary for central government to intervene in local affairs.

And fourth, ideology played a part in central government intervention. The imposition of market mechanisms and the development of the enabling authority, for example, reflected the ideological agenda set by the New Right.

Local government and the Labour government

The election of a Labour government in 1997 was welcomed by those who favoured a revitalisation of local government, not least because, in its general election manifesto, the Labour Party promised to lean less heavily on local government:

'Local decision making should be less constrained by central government, and also more accountable to local people.' (Labour 1997, p.34)

What this might mean in practice became clearer after the publication of the white paper in July 1998 (see Section 2.2 above). In addition to proposing new models of political management, an end to 'crude and universal' capping and the replacement of compulsory CCT with a Best Value regime, this white paper included the following proposals:

- a scheme to establish beacon councils to serve as pace setters and centres of excellence
- new ways of voting - electronic voting, increased postal voting, voting on different days, and mobile polling stations
- central government to retain control of the business rates, but councils to be able to set a supplementary rate or receive rebates.

Whilst these proposals suggest that central government is prepared to restore some independence to local authorities, it will still clearly retain a tight grip on local authorities.

Moves towards regional government

Whereas Scotland, Wales and Northern Ireland have separate offices headed by a Cabinet minister, there is no equivalent structure for England. In their 1992 election manifesto, however, the Conservatives made the following pledge:

'We will strengthen the machinery for coordination in the regions. New, integrated regional offices of the appropriate Whitehall departments will be established so that businesses and local government have only one port of call.' (Conservative 1992, p.39)

This resulted in the setting up of integrated regional offices (IROs) in April 1994. Although these offices were described as 'integrated', they do not include all government departments:

'Health is not included, nor is the Department of Heritage...The IROs do not even include the Next Steps agencies of the departments they oversee - so major arms of government like the employment service and Highways Agency are left out too.' (Wilson & Game 1998, p.114) For the government departments which are incorporated into the IROs, it has been necessary for them to agree on common regional boundaries. Before 1994, different government departments split England into regions with different boundaries.

Hogwood (1995) argues that, although the IROs have brought some integration, local authorities in England still have to deal with very many different government bodies and government-funded agencies.

Labour and regional government

While in opposition, Labour developed plans for elected regional government throughout England. As the 1997 general election approached, however, these plans were modified. In 1997, the Labour Party made the following pledge in its manifesto:

'The Conservatives have created a tier of regional government in England through quangos and regional offices. Meanwhile, local authorities have come together to create a more coordinated regional voice. Labour will build on these developments through the establishment of regional chambers to coordinate transport, planning, economic development, bids for European funding and land use planning...In time we will introduce legislation to allow the people, region by region, to decide in a referendum whether they want directly elected regional government.' (Labour 1997, pp.34-5)

As the first step towards fulfilling this pledge, the Regional Development Agencies Bill was included in the Labour government's first Queen's Speech. The Bill was designed to set up regional agencies which would work with the existing IROs in promoting investment, helping small businesses and coordinating regional economic development.

Main points - Part 3

- During the 1980s, opponents of local government argued that it was inefficient and unrepresentative, whilst supporters complained that its powers were being eroded by central government.
- Constitutionally, local government is entirely at the mercy of central government - Parliament has the power to reform or reduce local government functions.
- Although central government has the upper hand, central-local relations are not straightforward. There is a complex network of relationships.
- Three models are used to explain central-local government relations - the agency model, partnership model and power-dependence model.
- Central-local government relations have changed considerably since 1979. Over 200 Acts of Parliament modified the powers and role of local authorities 1979-97.
- The Labour Party promised to lean less heavily on local government. In July 1998, it published a white paper proposing a ten year programme of change.

Activity 16.8 *Central-local government relations*

Item A *A changing role*

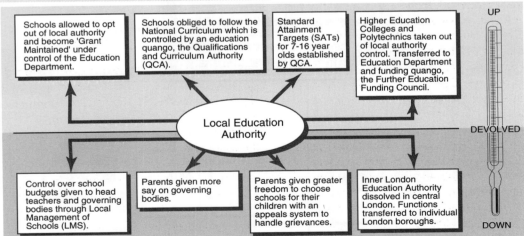

Since 1980, services which used to be provided by local authorities have been devolved either upwards to government departments, quangos or regional bodies, or down to lower tier authorities or voluntary bodies (see diagram above). Similar processes have occurred for other services such as housing, transport, the police, urban development, road maintenance and environmental services. At the same time, however, local authorities have been asked to take on some new responsibilities - for example, the Children's Act 1989 increased local authorities' responsibility for the protection of children in special need. These new responsibilities do not balance the loss of other services. Also, they are generally regarded as 'Cinderella' services - they are not glamorous and are not wanted by other bodies.

Adapted from McNaughton 1998.

Item B *Central-local government relations (1)*

Central government might try to control local government, but its influence is limited by the scale and fragmented character of local government. Working relationships are far from simple. They vary over time, from authority to authority and from one service area to another. Local authorities differ from one another, have their own political outlooks, their own policy agendas, different spending priorities and different histories and traditions. Also, despite the UK's centralist political culture, central government is by no means a single uniform entity. Different departments have different traditions, cultures and ways of working as well as different approaches to local government. Party political considerations are important, too. Between 1979 and 1990, for example, the government was not really interested in environmental health and, as a result, local authorities were allowed a great deal of discretion over this are. By 1990, however, the environment had risen up the political agenda and central government began to impose restraints. So, central-local government relations are very complex. And, it is not just a question of central government relating to local government. Account must be taken of a host of intermediate agencies (such as quangos, pressure groups and professional associations).

Adapted from Wilson & Game 1998.

Item C *Central-local government relations (2)*

For 18 years under the Conservatives, local government suffered tighter controls and ever more centralisation. The 'imperial' centre removed council powers, capped their taxing capabilities and transferred £30 billion of services to unelected quangos. In opposition, all these changes were opposed by the Labour Party - which presented itself as the defender of local democracy. But, battered and bruised local councillors remained suspicious of what would happen once office was won. They now have their answer. Yesterday, on 7 April 1998, the government published its sixth and final green paper on local government reform. The message is clear. Labour is ready to make radical reforms, but this depends on whether local councils accept change, demonstrate competence and fight corruption. The Prime Minister seems genuine in his desire to make local government more popular. Elected mayors will certainly help. The government is right to campaign for annual elections, local referendums, citizens' juries. It is also right to seek new ways of pushing up local election turnouts which, at barely 40%, are among the lowest in Europe. But, the government is still reluctant to let go of Whitehall's reins when it comes to finance. Although crude capping will end, there will still be capping controls. Also, the business rate will not go back to local councils. A local government system which is dependent for 80% of its finance from the centre is neither free nor independent. Whitehall may now use nice words ('democratic renewal'), but imperialism still reigns.

Adapted from the *Guardian*, 8 April 1998.

Item D *Central-local government relations (3)*

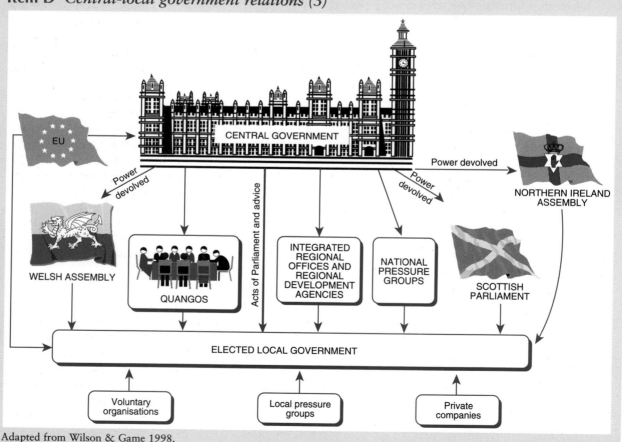

Adapted from Wilson & Game 1998.

Questions

1. What factors have affected central-local government relations in the 1990s? Use Items A-C in your answer
2. Does the agency model, partnership model or power-dependence model best fit central-local government relations today? Use Items A-D in your answer.
3. Judging from Items B and C, to what extent are changes under Labour likely to affect the independence of local government?

Part 4 Quasi government

Key issues

1. What is quasi government?
2. Why has the number of public corporations declined since 1979?
3. Why has the number of quangos grown since 1979?
4. What are the consequences of the growing number of quangos?

4.1 Quasi government

What is quasi government?

When people use the term 'public sector', they are usually referring to the areas of the economy which are financed by central government and to the agencies through which decisions made by central government are implemented. Local authorities make up one branch of the public sector. The civil service makes up another. But, local authorities and the civil service are not the only agencies to be financed by central government. Nor are they the only organisations to implement decisions taken by central government. The public sector has a third main branch. This branch can be described as 'quasi government' or 'government at arm's length'.

The main characteristic of quasi governmental organisations is that they are run by governmental appointees, not by elected representatives. They are described as 'quasi' governmental organisations because, although they are not actually branches of the government, their role is to perform a specific function or range of functions laid down by central government.

Quasi government and accountability

Since quasi governmental organisations are set up on a statutory basis and since they are run by government appointees, they retain close ties with central government. But, since ministers have no control over their day-to-day running and since those who run them are not elected, they differ from the other agencies in the public sector. The key difference is their lack of accountability. The actions performed by local authorities are the responsibility of elected representatives who are directly accountable to the electorate. Similarly, the actions performed by civil servants are the responsibility of ministers who are accountable to Parliament and ultimately to the electorate. The actions of quasi governmental organisations, however, are the responsibility of those who are appointed to run the organisation. They are accountable neither to an electorate nor to a minister. It is this lack of democratic accountability that is the root cause of criticism of quasi governmental organisations.

Two main types

Although different political commentators use different classifications, most would agree that there are two main types of quasi governmental organisation - public corporations and quangos.

4.2 Public corporations

What are public corporations?

Public corporations are organisations set up by statute (Act of Parliament) to run services or industries on behalf of the government. All public corporations have a written constitution which lays down their terms of reference. This constitution can only be modified by Act of Parliament. Each public corporation is run by a board appointed by the minister in charge of the department responsible for sponsoring the corporation. The minister has the right to approve capital investment programmes, the right to information and the power to issue directions of a 'general character' in relation to matters which affect the public interest. The day-to-day running of the corporation, however, is left to the board. Although the assets of public corporations are owned by the state, public corporations trade and are expected to derive the greater part of their revenue from customers.

The BBC

An example of a public corporation is the BBC. Initially, the BBC was a private company (the British Broadcasting Company). But, late in 1926, the company ceased to exist. It was replaced by the British Broadcasting Corporation which was granted a Royal Charter 'to provide broadcasting services as public services'. The BBC is financed largely through licence fees paid by consumers and run by a board of directors nominated by the Prime Minister. Formally, this board of directors is politically independent. But, the Prime Minister (through patronage) and other members of the government (by making public statements) may influence its policies informally.

The rise and fall of public corporations

The BBC was one of a small number of public corporations set up before the Second World War. This number grew rapidly once the Labour government elected in 1945 began its programme of nationalisation. Between 1945 and the 1980s, much of British industry was nationalised and, therefore, run by public corporations. According to a report published in 1976, nationalised industries are public corporations with four characteristics. First, there are no private shareholders. Assets are publicly owned. Second, members of the board are appointed by a secretary of state. Third, the board members are not civil servants. And fourth, these public corporations are mainly engaged in industrial or other trading activities (National Economic Development Office Report 1976).

By the late 1970s, however, Conservative Party policy had turned against public corporations. Two main criticisms were made. First, many public corporations had monopoly status which, it was argued, reduced efficiency. Second, relations between ministers and boards were unsatisfactory. Since ministers could intervene in the 'national interest', they could prevent corporations succeeding commercially. The Conservative solution in the 1980s was to privatise more than 20 public corporations, including key services such as the Central Electricity Generating Board, British Telecom, British Gas and the water authorities. Further privatisation (notably the privatisation of British Rail) has taken place in the 1990s. Once privatised, industries and services move out of the public sector and it becomes much harder for central government to regulate their activities.

The regulatory state

During the 1990s, there was a move away from direct control of industries or services and towards regulation at arm's length. This trend continued after Labour was elected in 1997. The initial aim was to create a framework of rules and regulations which ensured that privatised utilities and industries provided services in an acceptable manner. Bodies such as Ofgas (set up in 1986 to regulate the gas industry) or Ofwat (set up in 1990 to regulate the water industry) were set up to make sure that the rules laid down by government or by the relevant industry were being followed. The aim was to protect the consumer, but these regulatory bodies have been accused of lacking teeth:

> 'Regulatory bodies...have also been criticised for their ineffectual performance. Too often they have appeared unable to enforce compliance or punish other than with small fines. These regulatory bodies have also been

criticised for having "tunnel vision" when it comes to deciding what is in the public's interest. In particular, the insistence of regulators on the promotion of competition has resulted in short-term advantages for the consumers at the cost of problems in the future.' (Robins 1998, p.45)

Loughlin & Scott (1997) note, however, that the regulatory bodies themselves have countered these criticisms by claiming that they have been given insufficient powers by central government.

Regulation has spread beyond the privatised sector to the public sector. Some commentators suggest that this has occurred for ideological reasons - the aim being to 'restructure' or 'hollow out' the state by transferring activities traditionally performed by public bodies either to quangos or the private sector. Ideology, however, is only one reason for growing regulation. Loughlin & Scott (1997) note that fiscal stress and the requirements of the EU are important factors.

Regulation and the Third Way

Whilst the Conservative Party generally favours minimal regulation, the Labour government has used regulation as a means of bringing privatised enterprises back into public control. Regulation is a key component of the Third Way (see Chapter 3, Section 5.3) since the economy is run neither by the free market nor by public corporations.

4.3 Quangos

What are quangos?

According to some commentators, quango is an acronym for **qu**asi **a**utonomous **n**on **g**overnmental **o**rganisation. Others replace the non with national or argue that the term 'quango' should be replaced with QGA (quasi governmental agency). Quangos are also sometimes called 'non-departmental public bodies'.

Commentators do not just disagree about what the term 'quango' stands for. They also disagree about what it means. Some use the term loosely to mean any organisation set up and funded by central government but not run by civil servants or local authorities (under this definition, public corporations are quangos). Others are more specific. They suggest that quangos are unelected agencies that have one thing in common - they are all responsible for spending public money (this definition excludes public corporations since they are responsible for providing a service or running an industry, not for spending public money). It is in this latter sense that the term is used below.

The procedures used to recruit and appoint personnel to quangos are discussed in detail in Chapter 11, Part 5.

The Pliatzky Report, 1980

According to the 1980 Pliatzky Report on Non-

Departmental Public Bodies, there are three different types of quangos: those with an executive function; those with an advisory function; and, tribunals (Pliatzky 1980).

1. Executive quangos

Executive quangos tend to be permanent bodies with large staffs whose role is to regulate a particular area of the law, to disseminate information or to distribute funds. The Commission for Racial Equality (CRE) is one example. The function of the CRE is to monitor race relations and to work for, 'a just society which gives everyone an equal chance to learn, work and live free from discrimination and prejudice and from the fear of racial harassment.' (CRE mission statement). It has an annual budget of c.£14 million and a staff in its five regional offices and headquarters of c.200 (information from the CRE press office). A second example is the Higher Education Funding Council (HEFC). The function of the HEFC is to advise on the distribution of public funds to institutions of higher education. In 1996-97, it was responsible for distributing £3.4 billion to English universities (Milne 1997). The council consists of 14 members appointed by the Education Secretary. None is elected. Meetings of the council are closed to the public.

2. Advisory quangos

The function of advisory quangos is to examine specific problems and to make recommendations. Some are permanent bodies, others are set up on a temporary basis. The Overseas Projects Board is an example of a permanent advisory quango. This board, made up of 16 representatives of British companies and an academic, helps the government to formulate export policy and helps to coordinate joint British bids for projects in developing countries by providing 'expert advice' to the Department of Trade and Industry (*Independent on Sunday*, 20 February 1994). There are many hundreds of similar advisory quangos working on all aspects of government policy.

3. Tribunals

The function of the third category of quangos, tribunals, is to arbitrate between people who feel aggrieved and government officials. Some tribunals operate on a permanent basis - such as supplementary benefits appeal tribunals and rent tribunals. Others are set up to address a particular complaint. The work of tribunals is considered in greater detail in Chapter 17, Section 3.1.

The quango explosion

When Margaret Thatcher was elected in 1979, she made a pledge to reduce the number of quangos on the grounds that they were an unnecessary layer of bureaucracy. She said in 1980:

> 'There will always be pressure for new bodies. We shall be robust in resisting them.'

But, although the number of public corporations was decimated during the 1980s, there is evidence to suggest that, far from reducing the number of quangos, the Thatcher administration sowed the seeds for what has been described as 'the quango explosion'.

It is not easy to establish exactly how many quangos there are, not least because some exist only temporarily. According to figures from the Cabinet Office, in 1979 there were 2,167 non-departmental public bodies (the government does not officially recognise the term 'quangos'). By April 1992, this number had fallen to 1,412. This figure, however, is based on an exclusive definition of quangos which fails to take into account the huge changes in the public sector that were initiated in the late 1980s.

Changes in the late 1980s

First, changes in the organisation of the National Health Service led to the creation of quangos. The new Trust hospitals are run by quangos - boards of directors who are appointed, not elected. Also, district health authority boards no longer include local authority representatives and so have become quangos.

Second, reforms of the education system resulted in the creation of quangos. Quangos such as the Higher Education Funding Council were set up to distribute funds, for example, and the national curriculum is overseen by the Qualifications and Curriculum Authority.

Third, quangos have taken over activities which used to be run by local authorities. For example, between 1980 and 1988, ten Urban Development Corporations (UDCs) were set up with budgets ranging from £26 to £160 million. These UDCs are responsible for regenerating a targeted area by investing in the environment, housing and local business. The boards which run UDCs are not elected. They are nominated by the Secretary of State for the Environment, Transport and the Regions. Similarly, training programmes have been removed from local government control and placed into the hands of quangos - TECs (Training and Enterprise Councils) in England and Wales and LECs (Local Enterprise Councils) in Scotland.

And fourth, privatisation has led to the development of a new type of regulatory quango. As noted above, quangos such as Oftel, Ofgas and Ofwat have been set up to ensure that the privatised essential services carry out their functions and operate economically.

The real number of quangos

If these changes are taken into account, the real number of quangos in 1992 was well over 2,000. Figures from the Democratic Audit, using an inclusive definition (that quangos are executive bodies of a semi-autonomous nature which effectively act as agencies for central government and which carry out government policies), suggested that there were 5,521 quangos in 1995, compared to the government's figure of 1,227 (Wilson 1996). Another survey carried out in 1996 claimed that 5,207 quangos existed (Hall & Weir 1996).

Arguments in favour of quangos

Placing responsibility into the hands of quangos has a number of advantages for central government. First, there are political advantages for ministers. Often, it is in the interest of ministers not to be directly responsible for performing tasks. By delegating tasks to quangos, ministers can distance themselves from controversial issues and avoid awkward questions in Parliament. Also, ministers are responsible for appointing people to sit on quangos. They can, therefore, choose people who will support their political objectives and ensure, by this means, that government decisions are implemented in the way in which members of the government desire. Second, quangos may be a more efficient way of administering governmental decisions. Quangos have a free hand to fulfil their remit. They are not bound by the conventions and ways of work normally followed by civil servants. They have the time and resources to concentrate on tasks which might not gain so much attention in a government department. Third, since specialists rather than generalist civil servants can be appointed to undertake tasks, quangos can provide expert advice to ministers on technical or specialised issues. Fourth, quangos bring a large number of ordinary people into public life. Fifth, quangos can provide a quick and flexible response to matters of public concern. For example, the Nolan Committee was set up to address concerns about sleaze in public life and it was able to begin work as soon as its members were appointed. And sixth, quangos provide an alternative to elected local government. The Conservative governments of 1979-97 were hostile to elected local government and made a concerted effort to control it. By farming out responsibilities to quangos, government increased its control over local affairs from the centre, reducing the powers and responsibilities of local authorities. The creation of quangos, therefore, helped central government to achieve one of its strategic aims.

Public money administered by quangos

According to figures from the Cabinet Office, during the period 1979 to 1992, the amount of public money administered by non-departmental public bodies rose from £6,150 million to £13,750 million per year. But, following the Democratic Audit's independent survey of quangos (including those not counted in the official figures), it has been established that, actually, quangos have been responsible for spending a great deal more public money than official figures suggest. In 1996, for example, it was found that quangos were responsible for spending £60.4 billion of taxpayers' money - 35% of total public spending. These quangos were staffed by 60,000 members - outnumbering democratically elected councillors three to one (Hall & Weir 1996).

Sefras

Over the last few years a new type of quango has come into existence - the Sefra. Sefra stands for **se**lf-**f**inancing **r**egulatory **a**gency. These agencies do not just have powers of regulation over industries, they are expected to pay their own way by levying charges. According to Christopher Booker:

> 'There are hundreds of thousands of businesses in this country which can only operate by permission of a Sefra. These have the power to "authorise" anything from running a chemical plant to the discharging of water into a river, from the manufacture of a drug to running an insurance company, from storing electronic data to the right to take a fishing boat to sea. All this must be paid for by way of licences or authorisation charges, fees for inspections and the imposition of penalties for non-compliance.'
> (*Daily Telegraph*, 7 March 1994)

An example of a Sefra is the Medicines Control Agency (MCA) which controls the quality, safety and efficacy of drugs prescribed by doctors. Until 1991, this was the responsibility of civil servants working for the Department of Health. But, as a result of the Next Steps programme (see Chapter 13, Section 2.2), responsibility was transferred to the newly formed MCA. The MCA is required to finance its own activities from charges levied on the drugs producers. In the year after it came into operation, the profits raised by the MCA rose from £9 million to £18 million. This was good news for those who worked for the MCA. Their salaries rose by up to 60%. But, it was not such good news for the drugs producers who had to pay for this. Other examples of Sefras are the Driver and Vehicle Licensing Agency, the Data Protection Agency and the Child Support Agency.

The argument in favour of Sefras is that they save taxpayers' money because they are self-financing. The extra financial burden they place on the companies they regulate has two effects, however. First, some companies are forced out of business by the additional costs. And second, the extra costs are passed back to customers (who are taxpayers) indirectly as higher prices for goods or services.

Criticisms of the growth of quangos

The growing number and influence of quangos has brought two major criticisms. The first is that quangos are beyond democratic control (see Box 16.2). The second criticism is linked to the first. Between 1979 and 1997, the Conservative Party won four general elections and, therefore, had continuous control of central government. During the same period, however, the number of Conservative councillors fell dramatically and many local councils

Box 16.2 Quangos and democratic control

(i) Just over 100 years ago, the counties of England were governed by the magistrates, the Justices of the Peace who not only administered justice, but every quarter met together in quarter sessions to determine how the country should be run, how its roads should be built, how its police should be run. But, 100 years ago, we took power away from them and we gave it to elected representatives. We removed the lay élite and replaced it by councillors. Now, just 100 years on, we're doing exactly the opposite: we're taking power away from the elected representatives and giving it to a new lay élite, a group of appointed people who now run an increasing range of services. They run health, they run Training and Enterprise Councils, they increasingly run parts of education, and they are what I call the unknown government of the country, because nobody really knows how they are appointed. If you ask a member of the public who is a member of the local health authority nobody will know. You cannot hold the government to account if people do not know who is running that government.

John Stewart quoted in Jones 1994.

(ii) Speaking last year, William Waldegrave, the Minister for Open Government, declared that the transfer of services from local government yielded a democratic gain because public services became directly accountable to their 'customers'. Grant Maintained schools, for example, would increase parental choice and be responsive to consumers in the same way that the supply of cars or compact discs responds to demand. There is a fundamental flaw in this argument. Neither in Britain nor in any other democracy has a market for education, police services, inner city developments or training arisen spontaneously as it has for cars and compact discs. Any market in public services, therefore, must be an artificial one that is created and regulated by government.

Adapted from an article by Vernon Bogdanor in the *Observer*, 20 March 1994.

spokesman in Birmingham. Neither he nor his party has been in power in Birmingham since 1984, but there he is, on the funding council in control of a £2.62 billion budget - almost twice as much as the budget in Britain's second biggest city.' (*Independent on Sunday*, 3 April 1994)

New Labour and quangos

Soon after its election in May 1997, the Labour government issued a consultation paper critical of quangos. The paper argued that quangos are:

- unelected and unaccountable
- secretive (they do not always produce annual reports, their meetings are not open to the public and there is no access to the minutes of meetings)
- unresponsive and remote from the communities they serve
- unfair in terms of the way in which members are appointed.
(HMSO 1997)

In order to deal with these criticisms, the consultation paper suggested that the government take the steps outlined in Box 16.3.

Box 16.3 Opening up quangos

The Labour government's consultation paper on quangos, published in 1997, made the following recommendations:

1. Lack of accountability should be dealt with by select committees considering quangos' annual reports.
2. The publication of annual reports should become compulsory for all quangos.
3. Where practicable, quangos should hold annual open meetings.
4. Summary reports of such meetings should be issued.
5. The forthcoming Freedom of Information Act should cover all public bodies and the Parliamentary Commissioner for Administration (see Chapter 17, Section 3.2) should have a wider remit, covering quangos.
6. Details of quango appointments should be made public.
7. Ministers should attempt to reduce the numbers of quangos and all should be subject to a five year review.
8. Appointments should follow the Nolan Committee principles and the Commissioner for Public Appointments' remit should be extended

Adapted from HMSO 1997.

were controlled by other political parties. Understandably, local councils controlled by the Labour Party, say, had different priorities to councils controlled by the Conservative Party. So, although the Conservatives had power centrally, they did not have power locally in many parts of Britain. This, it is alleged, was frustrating for Conservative strategists and explains why so many of local councils' responsibilities were stripped away and handed over to quangos. Although firm evidence to support the view that quangos have been set up for party political purposes is difficult to establish, circumstantial evidence certainly exists, as the following extract shows:

'One member [of the Further Education Funding Council] is Les Lawrence, a Conservative councillor and education

As these recommendations suggest, there were no plans to abolish quangos altogether. Rather, it was argued that quangos have become a permanent part of the political landscape:

'Non-elected bodies will remain a significant feature of the governmental structure in Britain.' (Stott 1996, p.127)

The main reason for this is that, despite the criticisms that are sometimes voiced, governments find quangos to be very useful instruments. The debate has now shifted away from the existence of quangos to what is perceived as abuses of the patronage system and lack of accountability to the public.

Main points - Part 4

- Quasi governmental organisations are run by governmental appointees, not by elected representatives. They are accountable neither to an electorate nor directly to a minister. Their job is to perform functions laid down by central government.
- Public corporations are organisations set up by statute to run services or industries on behalf of the government. An example is the BBC. The programme of privatisation 1979-97, reduced the number of public corporations.
- During the 1990s, there has been a move away from direct control of industries or services and towards regulation at arm's length.
- Quango is an acronym for quasi autonomous non (or national) governmental organisation. There are different definitions, making it difficult to know how many quangos there are.
- Since the late 1980s, there has been an explosion in the number of quangos. Many activities formerly performed by local authorities are now performed by quangos. This has led to complaints about a democratic deficit and abuse of patronage.

Activity 16.9   The quango explosion

Item A *Number of quangos and public expenditure*

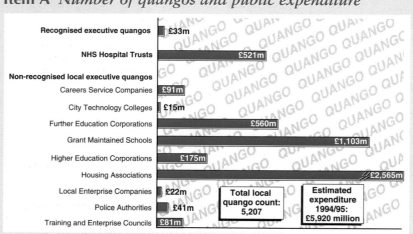

Recognised executive quangos	£33m
NHS Hospital Trusts	£521m
Non-recognised local executive quangos	
Careers Service Companies	£91m
City Technology Colleges	£15m
Further Education Corporations	£560m
Grant Maintained Schools	£1,103m
Higher Education Corporations	£175m
Housing Associations	£2,565m
Local Enterprise Companies	£22m
Police Authorities	£41m
Training and Enterprise Councils	£81m

Total local quango count: 5,207

Estimated expenditure 1994/95: £5,920 million

Adapted from Hall & Weir 1996.

Item C *Living with quangos*

Karen and Mick Etheridge live in Lewisham with their three children. When they applied to send their 10-year-old son to Kelsey Park, a Grant Maintained school, the school failed to inform them that it had been criticised two years running for failing its pupils. When Karen discovered this, she complained to the Local Government Ombudsman. He replied that he had no power to investigate grievances about schools which had opted out. Parents cannot demand improvements from the local council because councillors have no powers over opted-out schools. There is no elected official on the school's board of governors. It is answerable only to the Funding Agency for Schools. Despite public protests, a clinic near the Etheridges' home is being closed down. The area's £34.5 million budget for basic health care is controlled by the Optimum Health Trust. But, the Trust's directors cannot be voted out of office - none has been elected. They are accountable only to the Health Secretary. The Etheridges' local hospital is run by an NHS Trust which controls a £64 million budget. No members of the board are elected and the public is barred from its meetings. The Etheridges' local FE College has also been removed from local authority control. The quango which runs it is administered by businesspeople. If the Etheridges' children need vocational training, they will have to go to another quango - the South London Training and Enterprise Council. Like all TECs, it has a majority of businesspeople on the board. None is elected. The board is now self-perpetuating - it nominates a council of 100 prominent local people who then select board members.

Adapted from the *Observer*, 14 July 1998.

Item B *New Labour and quangos*

(i) According to John Osmond, director of the think tank the Institute of Welsh Affairs, the Welsh quangocracy (which runs everything from industrial development to the Welsh Language Board) has steadily undermined the democratic process. 'They were packed with Tory appointees on a scale which has not been replicated elsewhere in Britain', Osmond said. He is in no doubt that growing disenchantment with the network of 80 quangos (double the number in 1979) speeded up the government's Welsh Assembly plans.

Adapted from the *Guardian*, 17 September 1997.

(ii) By next spring, nine regional development agencies (RDAs), super quangos with a modest collective budget of under £1 billion and limited powers, should be up and running. The RDAs, covering areas with an average population of around 9 million will consist of 'very tight business-led boards' of 12 members. For the time being, councillors will be in the minority on the boards - six members from commerce, four councillors and two from voluntary agencies or the universities. Rather than simply appointing boards from the usual list of party hacks, ministers decided to advertise for membership. They received more than 2,000 applications.

Adapted from the *Guardian*, 13 May 1997.

Item D *Government by quango*

Neither the local nor the national politicians seem to be in charge as the great machinery of state progressively falls into the hands of unelected, unaccountable quangos. Nothing less than the future of our nation is at stake as a once democratic society is falling into the hands of faceless bureaucracy. It is time our politicians recognised this growing threat and clawed back power from these monsters, restoring it to elected bodies at the lowest level at which decisions can be taken.

Adapted from the *Guardian*, 19 November 1993 and the *Daily Mail*, 25 March 1994.

Questions

1. Look at the information in this section.
   a) Why do you think the number of public corporations has declined since 1979 whilst the number of quangos has grown?
   b) What are the advantages and disadvantages of government by quango? Use Items A-C in your answer.
2. Are there any signs in Item B that the Labour government has adopted a different approach towards quangos?
3. a) Use Item C to explain the term 'democratic deficit'.
   b) How might members of any of the quangos encountered by the Etheridges justify the work of their organisation?
4. What does Item D tell us about quangos? Why do you think the cartoonist chose these images?

References

Alexander (1985) Alexander, A., *Borough Government and Politics: Reading 1835–1985*, Allen & Unwin, 1985.

ASI (1989) Adam Smith Institute, *Wiser Counsels: the Reform of Local Government*, Adam Smith Institute, 1989.

Audit Commission (1997) Audit Commission, *Representing the People*, HMSO, 1997.

Bains (1972) Bains, M.A., *The New Local Authorities*, HMSO, 1972.

Barber (1978) Barber, M.P., *Local Government*, MacDonald and Evans, 1978.

Byrne (1990) Byrne, T., *Local Government in Britain*, Penguin, 1990.

Chandler (1991) Chandler, J., *Local Government Today*, Manchester University Press, 1991.

Clarke & Stewart (1988) Clarke, M. & Stewart, J., *The Enabling Council*, Luton:LGTB, 1988.

Cockburn (1977) Cockburn, C., *The Local State*, Pluto Press, 1977.

Conservative (1992) Conservative Party election manifesto, *The Best Future for Britain*, CCO, 1992.

Copus (1998) Copus, C., 'Herd instincts', *Local Government Chronicle*, 3 July 1998.

Crosland (1983) Crosland, S., *Tony Crosland*, Coronet, 1983.

Dunleavy et al. (1997) Dunleavy, P., Gamble, A., Holliday, I. & Peele, G., *Developments in British Politics 5*, Macmillan, 1997.

Elcock (1996) Elcock, H., 'Local government: managing in a time of uncertainty' in *Lancaster* (1996).

Elcock (1997) Elcock, H., 'Local government: becoming a backwater or heading for renewal?', *Talking Politics*, Vol.10.1, Autumn 1997.

Hall & Weir (1996) Hall, W. & Weir, S., 'Rise of the quangocracy', *Local Government Chronicle*, 30 August 1996.

HMSO (1983) Department of the Environment, *Streamlining the Cities*, HMSO, 1983.

HMSO (1991) Department of the Environment, *The Structure of Local Government in England*, HMSO, 1991.

HMSO (1996) Central Office of Information, *Local Government*, HMSO, 1996.

HMSO (1997) *Opening up Quangos: a Consultation Paper*, HMSO, 1997.

Hogwood (1995) Hogwood, B., 'The integrated regional offices and the single regenerational budget', *Commission for Local Democracy Research Report 13*, Municipal Journal Books, 1995.

Hutt (1990) Hutt, J., *Opening the Town Hall Door*, Bedford Square Press, 1990.

Hutton (1997) Hutton, W., *The State to Come*, Vintage, 1997.

John (1997) John, P., 'Local governance', *Developments in British Politics*, Macmillan, 1997.

Jones (1994) Jones, B., 'The unknown government: government by quango', *Talking Politics*, Vol.6.2, Winter 1994.

Kingdom (1991) Kingdom, J., *Local Government and Politics in Britain*, Philip Allan, 1991.

Labour (1997) *New Labour - Because Britain Deserves Better*, Labour Party manifesto, Labour Party, 1997.

Lancaster (1996) Lancaster, S. (ed.), Developments in Politics, Vol.7, Causeway Press, 1996.

LGA (1998) Local Government Association, *Modernising Local Government - Local Democracy and Community Leadership: a Response*, LGA, 1998.

Loughlin & Scott (1997) Loughlin, M. & Scott, C., 'The regulatory state' in *Dunleavy et al. (1997)*.

Lynch (1998) Lynch, P., 'The Scottish devolution referendum 1997: the road to a Scottish Parliament', *Politics Review*, Vol.7.4, April 1998.

Maud (1967) Maud, J., *Management of Local Government*, HMSO, 1967.

McNaughton (1998) McNaughton, N., *Local and Regional Government in Britain*, Hodder and Stoughton, 1998.

Milne (1997) Milne, K., 'Opening a can of Quangos', *New Statesman*, 27 March 1997.

Norris & Gavin (1997) Norris, P. & Gavin, N.T. (eds), *Britain Votes 1997*, Oxford University Press, 1997.

Pliatzky (1980) Pliatzky, L., *Report on Non–Departmental Public Bodies*, Cmnd 7797, HMSO, 1980.

Pyper (1990) Pyper, R., 'Compulsory Competitive Tendering', *Social Studies Review*, Vol.5.5, May 1990.

Pyper & Robins (1995) Pyper, R. and Robins, L., *Governing the UK in the 1990s*, Macmillan, 1995.

Rallings & Thrasher (1997) Rallings, C. & Thrasher, M., 'The local elections' in *Norris & Gavin (1997)*.

Rallings & Thrasher (1998) Rallings, C. & Thrasher, M., 'The 1998 local election results and democracy', *Talking Politics*, Vol.11.1, Autumn 1998.

Roberts (1986) Roberts D., *Politics a New Approach*, Causeway Press, 1986.

Robins (1998) Robins, L., *Politics Pal*, Hyperion Press, 1998.

Rowntree (1992) Joseph Rowntree Foundation, 'Changes in the role and function of local authorities', *Local and Central Government Relations Research Findings*, No.18, September 1992.

Rowntree (1995) Joseph Rowntree Foundation, 'The process of local government reform', *Local and Central Government Relations Research Findings*, No.34, April 1995.

Rowntree (1997) Joseph Rowntree Foundation, 'The new government of London', *Local and Central Government Relations Research Findings*, No.56, March 1997.

Saunders (1979) Saunders, P., *Urban Politics*, Hutchinson, 1979

Schofield (1977) Schofield, M., 'The nationalisation of local politics', *New Society*, 28 April 1977.

Stoker (1988) Stoker, G., *The Politics of Local Government*, Macmillan, 1988.

Stott (1996) Stott, T., 'Evaluating the quango debate', *Talking Politics*, Vol.8.2, Winter 1995-6.

Widdicombe (1986) Widdicombe, D., *The Conduct Of Local Authority Business*, Cmnd 9797, HMSO, 1986.

Wilson (1993) Wilson, D., 'Central–local government relationships', *Talking Politics*, Vol.5.3, Summer 1993.

Wilson (1995) Wilson, D., 'Elected local government and central-local government relations' in *Pyper & Robins (1995)*.

Wilson (1996) Wilson, D., 'Quangos in British politics', *Politics Review*, Vol.5.1, September 1996.

Wilson (1997) Wilson, D., 'Politics and policy making within local authorities', *Politics Review*, Vol.6.2, November 1997.

Wilson & Game (1998) Wilson, D. & Game, C., *Local Government in the United Kingdom*, Macmillan, 1998.

Part 5
Citizenship

17 Citizenship & redress of grievances

Introduction

Suppose you overheard the following statement: 'Britain is a free country. Everybody has rights here. That's why it is a privilege to be a British citizen'. Is it a statement you would agree with? Is it true? The statement makes reference to two terms which are at the heart of this chapter - 'citizenship' and 'rights'. Most people living in the UK are British citizens. That means that most people living in the UK have certain rights. They have the right to vote in elections if they are over the age of 18, for example, the right to free education from the ages of five to 16 and the right to say or to write whatever they like (so long as they do not break the laws of libel or slander). But, what exactly are rights? Where do they come from and what has shaped them? How do they relate to the concept of citizenship? This chapter begins by considering these questions.

In the ideal world, citizens would never have any problem exercising their rights. In the real world, however, citizens often feel that their rights have been denied or infringed. Whilst some disputes are settled amicably, many are not. When a dispute cannot be settled amicably or when citizens have grievances which they feel should be redressed, it may be necessary for an independent judgement to be made on the merits of the case of each side. This chapter also, therefore, examines the legal, non-legal and quasi-legal mechanisms which exist in the UK for the purpose of settling disputes and redressing grievances.

Chapter summary

Part 1 examines what is meant by the term 'citizenship'. What rights and liberties are enjoyed by British citizens? What has been the impact of the Citizens' Charter and the rise to power of New Labour?

Part 2 looks at the administration of justice in the UK. How does the legal system work? Who becomes a judge? How independent is the judiciary?

Part 3 focuses on the quasi-judiciary. What is it? What role is played by administrative tribunals, judicial inquiries and ombudsmen?

Part 4 considers the proposals that have been put forward for judicial reform. What are the arguments for and against a Bill of Rights? What other reforms have been suggested and why?

Part 1 Citizenship

Key issues

1. What is citizenship?
2. What rights and liberties are enjoyed by British citizens?
3. What has been the impact of the Citizens' Charter?

1.1 Citizenship

What is a citizen?

A citizen is any member of a state who is formally recognised as a citizen by that state. The concept of citizenship is, therefore, legalistic. Citizens are individuals who have some sort of legal status within a state - they have been granted certain rights by the state and are expected to perform certain duties:

'The citizen should be understood in the first instance not as a type of person...but as a position in the set of formal relationships defined by democratic sovereignty.' (Donald 1996, p.174)

The precise range and balance between the rights granted to citizens and the duties they are expected to perform varies from time to time and from state to state. In times of warfare, for example, the duties a state expects its citizens to perform may be very great and the rights and liberties enjoyed by citizens may be very few. When peace returns, however, the situation may be reversed. The precise balance between rights, liberties and duties is a matter to be resolved, either by negotiation or through conflict, by the citizens living in a particular society at a particular time.

Where exactly do political rights come from?

The question of where political rights come from has concerned political philosophers for many centuries. Whilst no single satisfactory answer has been found, the distinction is often made between natural rights and positive rights.

1. Natural rights

Political theorists who acknowledge that there are natural rights argue that certain rights are universally applicable to all societies. The origin of these rights, it is generally argued, is to be found in the essential nature of human beings or in laws given by God. The classic statement of this theory is to be found in the writing of John Locke who argued in his *Second Treatise on Government* of 1690 that, before the creation of political societies, human beings existed in a state of nature in which God-given natural laws and rights existed. These laws and rights were to be the basis of political societies when they were eventually created. Locke claimed that life, liberty and property were natural rights.

2. Positive rights

Despite the attraction of natural rights theories, a number of problems arise. It is difficult to prove that a state of nature ever existed, for example, or that rights are derived from God. It is also difficult to work out which rights are natural and which are not. As a result, some political philosophers have abandoned the idea of natural rights altogether in favour of a theory which asserts that the only rights which exist are positive rights granted by a state to its citizens. This avoids the problems associated with natural rights theories, but it raises questions about:

- why citizens should be given rights
- which rights (if any) they should be given
- how extensive these rights should be.

Also, if rights are not granted by God or nature, there is also the problem of whether they are absolute or whether they can be taken away by the state in certain circumstances (for example, in a national emergency).

1.2 Rights and liberties in the UK

The development of rights and liberties in the UK

People living in the UK are both citizens and subjects. They are citizens because they have certain defined rights and liberties, but they are also subjects of the monarch. Unlike in the USA and many other states, the rights and liberties of British citizens are not set out in a single constitutional document. Rather, they are part of the British uncodified constitution (see Chapter 4 Section 1.1). Some of these rights and liberties are the product of custom and convention. Others are contained in written documents, namely Acts of Parliament. The rights and liberties contained in these Acts are the result of struggles waged by people and their representatives against the absolute power of their rulers. The key events were as follows.

Magna Carta, 1215

In 1215, King John was forced to sign the Magna Carta. This was the first time in the UK that the power of an absolute ruler had been limited by law. The Magna Carta established that laws made by the monarch were to be within the common law (see Chapter 4, Section 1.1), the monarch could only levy certain taxes with the permission of the council and no person could be imprisoned except by a process of law involving the lawful judgement of their peers.

Habeas Corpus, 1679

In 1679, the Habeas Corpus Act was passed. This Act insisted that people should be told the reason for their arrest and should be informed of the charges against them. A person who was arrested had to be brought before a court and charged with a specific offence within three days. This Act was particularly important since it limited the arbitrary power of rulers.

Bill of Rights, 1689

In 1689, the Bill of Rights was passed. Unlike such Bills in other countries, the British Bill of Rights had no special status - it was an ordinary Act of Parliament. Nonetheless, it did increase the rights enjoyed by citizens. The Bill guaranteed the supremacy of Parliament over the monarch and prevented the monarch from imposing taxation unless this was agreed by the House of Commons. The Bill also guaranteed freedom of speech and the right of citizens to petition both the monarch and Parliament.

Further Acts

Subsequently, a number of Acts were passed extending the rights and liberties of British citizens. The right to worship freely, for example, was established by a number of Acts such as the Catholic Emancipation Act of 1829 (which also allowed Catholics to stand for Parliament for the first time). Slavery was abolished in 1833. Sex discrimination Acts were passed in 1975 and 1987. A Race Relations Act was passed in 1976. The Data Protection Act was passed in 1984.

International agreements

In addition to these pieces of domestic legislation, three international agreements have a bearing on rights in the UK. The first is the United Nations Declaration of Human Rights, agreed in 1948. The Declaration sets out a number of general rights which governments are meant to grant to their citizens and more detailed guidelines stipulating specific rights and types of treatment. The second is the European Convention on Human Rights, signed in 1950. This treaty not only set out the rights which all citizens in Europe could expect, it also established a Commission of Human Rights and a European Court of Human Rights to enforce the treaty (see Section 4.1 below). And the third is the Maastricht Treaty which had been ratified by all EU member states by the end of 1993. This gave citizenship a new dimension since workers' rights and voting rights are now guaranteed throughout the EU.

As a result of the above developments, British citizens enjoy the following basic rights and liberties:
- freedom of movement
- freedom from arbitrary arrest or unjustified police searches
- freedom of conscience in matters of religion and politics
- freedom of expression
- freedom of association, including the right to protest peacefully
- social freedoms - such as the right to marry, divorce, procure abortions or enjoy homosexual relations
- the right to vote and to stand for election
- the right to a fair trial
- the right not to be coerced or tortured by agents of the state
- the right not to be subjected to surveillance without due legal process
- the right to own property.

1.3 Citizenship in the UK in the 1990s

The growing importance of Citizenship
Since the late 1980s, a debate about what citizenship is and what it should be has risen up the political agenda. There are three main reasons for this. First, there was a campaign by the Conservative government under John Major to promote 'active citizenship'. Second, there was public concern that legislation passed in the 1980s and early 1990s resulted in the erosion of many of the rights and liberties enjoyed by British citizens. And third, the Labour government elected in 1997 promised to take the debate in a new direction:

'The millennium symbolises a new era opening up for Britain...Our aim is no less than to set British political life on a new course for the future.' (Labour 1997, p.1)

1. Active citizenship
The idea of active citizenship came out of the Conservatives' experience of government in the 1980s. According to Oliver:

'By the end of the 1980s, the Conservative government had itself become disillusioned with the potential for government to solve problems with any real or lasting success.' (Oliver 1993, p.26)

Since, Oliver argues, governmental policies had, for example, failed to solve the problem of rising crime and rising public spending levels, the government began to look for solutions to these problems which did not involve governmental intervention. One solution was to suggest that responsibility for society's problems did not lie with the government, but with the whole community. Every British citizen, in other words, had a duty to take an active part in solving society's problems:

'Active citizens, according to the Conservative view, would themselves take responsibilities for some of the things that needed doing in society, rather than expect the state to do them: charitable and voluntary work, housing associations, neighbourhood watch schemes and the like are seen as alternatives to expensive and often unsuccessful state provision.' (Oliver 1993, p.26)

Not only did this fit with the predominant ideology in the Conservative Party, it also presented the government with a means of deflecting criticism.

The Citizen's Charter
To promote the idea of active citizenship, John Major launched the Citizen's Charter initiative in the summer of 1991. This contained three central provisions. First, public services had to set themselves performance targets which were then published as individual charters and made available to the public. Second, provision was made for redress where services failed to achieve the standards laid out in a charter (an independent inspectorate was established to monitor the performance of public services against their charter standards and to make judgements in cases where citizens were seeking redress for failures). And third, a Charter Mark Scheme was set up to give recognition to those public services which performed well consistently.

The notion of active citizenship and the Citizen's Charter demonstrate the dual nature of citizenship - its concern both with the responsibilities of citizens towards each other and with what can be expected as a right from the state. McInnes notes, however, that:

'The Citizen's Charter uses the language of empowerment. However, it relies on redressing the grievances of the individual...There is little attempt to invite citizens to determine the optimum [best] level of services. It is paternalist [father-like] and reactive rather than pro-active. The citizen is consumer, not participant.' (McInnes 1996, p.25)

The Labour government's adoption and extension of the Citizen's Charter is discussed in Chapter 13, Section 2.2.

2. Liberties under attack
The second reason for the prominence of the debate over citizenship is the concern expressed by some pressure groups and opposition parties that, between

1979 and 1997, Conservative governments eroded and even destroyed basic rights which used to be enjoyed by citizens.

At heart, this concern is derived from the nature of the British constitution. Since Parliament is sovereign, Parliament can pass laws which take away (or add to) any or all of the rights enjoyed by citizens. This means that the rights and responsibilities enjoyed by British citizens are entirely dependent on the government of the day. Citizens have no right of appeal if the government chooses to take away a right or liberty which they hold dear. This, it has been argued, is especially unsatisfactory when a single party holds onto power for a prolonged period, especially given that, in all the general elections held since 1945, no single party has won 50% of the vote.

There were a number of occasions in the 1980s and early 1990s when opponents of the Conservative government were outraged by the government's erosion of civil liberties. During the miners' strike of 1984-85, for example, the police prevented miners (or those suspected of being miners) from travelling freely around the country. In 1985, the government banned employees at the Government Communications Headquarters (GCHQ) from belonging to trade unions. And, in 1990, many protesters at an anti-poll tax demonstration in London complained that they were being denied their right to protest peacefully in public. According to the pressure group Liberty (which campaigns on a wide range of civil rights issues), however, the greatest threat to civil liberty since the Second World War was the Criminal Justice Act of 1994 (see Chapter 18, Section 2.6).

3. New Labour and citizenship

It was clear from Labour's 1997 general election manifesto both that Labour had a new approach to citizenship and that citizenship was high on its agenda. In the manifesto, for example, a number of pledges were made which were clearly designed to strengthen the rights of British citizens:

- a Freedom of Information Act
- the incorporation of the European Convention on Human Rights into British law
- the promise of legal aid for those seeking to enforce their rights
- improved rights for workers through a minimum wage and signing the Social Chapter of the Maastricht Treaty
- statutory trade union recognition.

The fact that the Labour Party was committed to strengthening citizens' rights suggested that it had a different approach from the previous Conservative administration.

At the same time as promising to strengthen citizens' rights, the Labour government placed emphasis on the idea that citizens have responsibilities. For example, when the welfare-to-work legislation was proposed, ministers stressed that people had a responsibility to work since, by working, they would be able to make a valuable contribution to society as a whole. Similarly, the 1998 Crime and Disorder Act introduced community safety orders to deal with threatening neighbours and child protection orders to deal with young children neglected by their parents. These measures were designed to make it clear that neighbours and parents have responsibilities to others and that society cannot tolerate failure to carry out these responsibilities. Some commentators have argued that ideas like this are evidence that New Labour is heavily influenced by 'communitarianism' (see Chapter 2, Section 4.4).

White paper, July 1997

In July 1997, the government published a white paper which gave the commitment to 'strengthen education for citizenship'. To investigate how this was to be achieved, the Advisory Group on Citizenship and Democracy in Schools was set up. This produced interim proposals that the education of pupils in the principles and practice of citizenship and democracy should be a statutory duty for schools. By accepting these proposals in principle, the government made it clear that it recognised that the goal of active citizenship could only be achieved if people knew about, understood and were able to debate their rights and responsibilities (*Times Educational Supplement*, 27 March 1998). The government's commitment to education for citizenship indicated that citizenship was high on its agenda.

Main points - Part 1

- **Citizens are individuals who have some sort of legal status within a state - they have been granted certain rights by the state and are expected to perform certain duties.**
- **Some theorists argue that rights are natural (granted by God or nature). Others argue that the only rights which exist are positive rights granted by a state to its citizens.**
- **In Britain, some rights and liberties are the product of custom and convention and others are granted by Acts of Parliament.**
- **Since the late 1980s, a debate about citizenship has developed because: (1) Major's government promoted 'active citizenship'; (2) opponents argued that the 1979-97 Conservative governments eroded citizens' rights; and (3) citizenship is high on New Labour's agenda.**

Activity 17.1 *Citizenship in the late 1990s*

Item A *A definition*

Citizenship is a relationship between the individual and the state in which the two are bound together by rights (such as voting and the protection of the law) and duties (such as paying taxes and obeying the law). Citizens differ from subjects and aliens in that they are full members of their political community or state because they possess basic rights. Citizenship is viewed differently depending on whether it is shaped by individualism or communitarianism. Individualism emphasises individual rights. It places particular stress on what individuals are entitled to and on their freedom to act independently. Communitarianism emphasises duties. It places particular stress on the role of the state as a moral agency and the importance of community. In most countries, citizenship can be acquired by birth or by naturalisation. The UK has five different categories of citizenship with varying rights. Only full British citizenship provides a person with the right to live in the UK. British citizenship is automatically granted to anyone born in the UK to a parent who is a British citizen, or to a parent who is lawfully settled in the UK. The four other categories of citizenship are: British dependent territories citizenship, British overseas citizenship, British subject and Commonwealth citizen. The right to live in the UK differs widely for each.

Adapted from Heywood 1997.

Item B *An active citizen (1)*

Item C *An active citizen (2)*

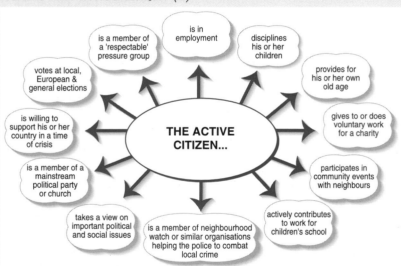

Item D *Education for citizenship*

Bernard Crick, Chair of the Advisory Group on Citizenship and Democracy in Schools, argues that most of the world has recognised that citizenship is a great educative force, and not something that can just be bolted on as an extra, since the time of Aristotle (4th century BC). The Advisory Group's terms of reference, he says, were precise - to provide advice on effective education for citizenship in schools. This should include:

- the nature and practices of participation in democracy
- the duties, responsibilities and rights of individuals as citizens
- the values to individuals and society of community activity.

As a result, Crick claimed, citizenship is by no means just political education. Education about the community and about community service is equally important. There are, in short, three strands of citizenship:

- social and moral responsibility
- community involvement
- political literacy.

Adapted from the *Times Educational Supplement*, 27 March 1998.

Questions

1. a) Using Item A, explain what it means to be a full British citizen.
   b) Explain how the definitions of citizenship favoured by the two main parties differ.
2. a) Judging from Items B and C, what is an active citizen?
   b) What are the benefits and drawbacks of active citizenship?
3. a) Give arguments for and against the view that every student should spend 5% of their time at school or college learning about citizenship. Use Item D in your answer.
   b) What should be taught in citizenship lessons? Give some concrete examples.

Part 2 The administration of justice

Key issues

1. How does the legal system work in the UK?
2. Who becomes a judge?
3. How independent is the judiciary?

2.1 The legal system in the UK

Citizens and the law
A key characteristic of citizenship is that citizens are subject to and protected by the laws of the state. When citizens are accused of breaking the law or when disputes arise between citizens which cannot be solved by mutual agreement, it may be necessary for the matter to be settled in court. In the UK, this is complicated by the fact that there are three separate legal systems in operation - one which operates in England and Wales, a second which operates in Scotland and a third which operates in Northern Ireland. To some extent, therefore, the justice that British citizens receive depends on where they live or where they commit their crime. It is, however, a characteristic common to all three legal systems that they distinguish between criminal law and civil law.

Criminal law
Criminal law is concerned with behaviour which is disapproved of by the state and has, therefore, been made illegal by statute. Since criminal offences are regarded as offences against the state, most cases in England and Wales are brought by the Crown Prosecution Service on the state's behalf. People accused of theft or murder, for example, are tried in criminal courts. Those found guilty may be punished in a variety of ways, depending on their past behaviour and the seriousness of the offence. Punishment ranges from fines and community service to long-term imprisonment.

Civil law
Civil law, on the other hand, is concerned with the relationships between individuals and groups. It deals with disputes which arise over matters such as the making of contracts or wills, accusations of libel and slander or the custody of children after divorce. Individuals (or organisations) who lose a case in a

civil court are not punished in the same way as in a criminal case. Rather, they are ordered to recompense the other party in some way - for example, by paying damages or by handing over the rights to property or the custody of children. As a consequence of their different objectives, the criminal and civil systems operate within different court structures, though these structures come together at the highest level.

2.2 The legal system in England and Wales

A hierarchical system
The legal system in England and Wales is organised hierarchically. Superior courts hear more serious cases and re-examine, on appeal, cases which were first brought to the lower courts.

The civil courts
County Courts
At the bottom of the hierarchy are the 270 County Courts. These deal with relatively minor civil actions and, therefore, deal with the majority of civil actions. County Courts are able to make judgements about disputes over contracts to the value of less than £5,000, repossessions of property by building societies, disputes between tenants and landlords, most cases involving wills and legacies and most matrimonial matters (especially divorce cases). County Courts are presided over by Circuit Judges (in August 1998, there were 560 Circuit judges in total) or by District Judges (in August 1998, there were 365 District Judges).

The High Court
The next step up the hierarchy is the High Court. Confusingly, the High Court is not one court, but three. It is made up of three divisions which have jurisdiction over separate, though occasionally overlapping, areas of law.

The largest division is the **Divisional Court of the Queen's Bench Division** (the King's Bench when the monarch is male). This division hears cases which are referred from County Courts either because the amount of money involved is too large or because the dispute involves a complex point of law. In addition, it plays the important role of judging writs of Habeas Corpus (deciding whether a person has been unlawfully detained). This court is also responsible for reviewing administrative decisions made by public bodies such as local authorities, government departments and health authorities.

The second largest division is the **Family Division**. This has responsibility for adjudicating on all matters relating to the family and the legal side of people's personal relations.

The smallest division is the **Chancery Division**. This is responsible for considering issues involving taxation and wills, issues which are often complex and involve large sums of money. Proceedings in the High Court are presided over by one or more High Court Judges (in August 1998, there were 97 High Court Judges in total). High Court Judges are officially responsible to the Crown.

The Civil Division of the Court of Appeal

Above the High Court is the Civil Division of the Court of Appeal. This court is responsible for adjudicating when the High Court gives permission for a case to go to appeal or when those in dispute successfully request such a right from the Appeal Court itself. The Master of the Rolls presides over this court. Judgements are made by the Lord Justices of Appeal (in August 1998, there were 35 Lord Justices of Appeal in total). They do not hear witnesses except in exceptional circumstances. The three judges who preside over each appeal make their decisions on the basis of documents and the arguments of barristers. Their interpretations of law set precedents which the lower courts must follow.

The House of Lords

At the apex of both the civil and the criminal legal systems is the House of Lords. Cases which reach the House of Lords are heard by the Law Lords or 'Lords of Appeal in Ordinary' as they are officially known:

> 'The Law Lords consist of...senior judges made life peers and salaried with a duty to sit on the appeals committees of the House of Lords.' (Davis 1995, p.64)

Normally, two Scottish members are included. Current and past Lord Chancellors may sit in judgement in the House of Lords. The Law Lords only accept cases referred to them by the Court of Appeal. They sit in judgement in a House of Lords committee room, without wigs or robes, and deliver their decision not as a judgement, but after a vote on whether the appeal should be accepted or dismissed. Each appeal, of which there are around 1,500 a year, is normally heard by five Law Lords (in exceptionally controversial cases - such as the second hearing on the extradition of General Pinochet - a panel of seven sits). In August 1998, there were 12 Law Lords in total.

The criminal courts

Magistrates Courts

At the bottom of the hierarchy lie the Magistrates

Courts. These courts have two roles. First, they pass judgement on the 98% of criminal cases which are not 'indictable' (not serious enough to be tried in a Crown Court). Second, they are responsible for the committal proceedings of those cases which are indictable and will go to the Crown Court if the magistrates decide that the evidence appears strong enough. There are around 700 Magistrates Courts in England and Wales. They are presided over by lay magistrates or 'JPs' (Justices of the Peace) as they are also known. JPs are members of the public who are trained, but not legally qualified. They sit in court part time. In January 1998, there were 30,361 JPs (15,713 men and 14,648 women). In areas with a heavy workload, legally qualified, full-time stipendiary magistrates provide lay magistrates with assistance. In August 1998, there were 48 metropolitan stipendiary magistrates, 40 provincial stipendiary magistrates and 114 acting stipendiary magistrates. The post of stipendiary magistrate was created in the late 18th century to give a professional gloss to the magistracy at a time when it was falling into disrepute.

The main responsibility of magistrates is to pass sentence upon minor offences. Most people brought before Magistrates Courts plead guilty. In cases where a not guilty plea is registered, three magistrates have to weigh the evidence and make a decision. Occasionally, a Magistrates Court will refer a case to the Crown Court for sentence because Crown Courts are able to impose stiffer sentences than Magistrates Courts. As well as committal, trial and sentencing, magistrates are also responsible for remanding or bailing defendants and for granting or withholding licences from pubs, betting shops and casinos.

Crown Court

All serious crimes are tried in a Crown Court. The Crown Courts were established in 1972 to replace the outdated quarter sessions and assize courts. Offences such as murder, rape, manslaughter and robbery are tried in the Crown Court. Where defendants plead not guilty, they are entitled to a jury trial. In this case, the role of the judge is confined to advising the jury on points of law and providing a summing up of the evidence presented and the legal situation relating to it. If the jury finds a defendant guilty, it is the responsibility of the judge to pass sentence.

Less serious cases are heard by a Recorder. Recorders are part-time judges drawn from the ranks of the barristers. In August 1998, there were 833 Recorders, 403 Assistant Recorders and 133 Recorders in Training. More serious offences are heard in front of a Circuit Judge and the most serious offences are heard in front of a High Court Judge. There are 94 Crown Court centres in England and Wales. The best known is the Central Criminal Court or Old Bailey in London. Like most other Crown Court centres, the Old Bailey contains several court rooms.

Appeals

Appeals against both sentences and convictions in the Magistrates Court go to the Crown Court. Appeals against Crown Court decisions go to the Criminal Division of the Court of Appeal and then, with the permission of the Appeal Court, to the House of Lords.

Behind this apparently simple procedure lies a process for criminal appeals which has been much criticised (because of the string of miscarriages of justice which have been revealed since the late 1980s).

There are three categories of appeals which are referred back to the Court of Appeal as a matter of course:

'Those where the evidence is flawed or tainted although the person may be guilty of the crime; those where the accused is innocent of the specific offence but guilty of other, similar offences; and those who are innocent of the charge for which they were found guilty.'
(*Guardian*, 19 August 1998)

Until 1997, it was the responsibility of the Home Office to decide whether cases should go back to the Court of Appeal. Since 1997, however, the Criminal Cases Review Commission (CCRC) has taken over this responsibility (see Section 3.2 below).

If an appeal is allowed, the Appeal Court can either order a retrial or acquit the accused. Acquittal does not have to come via the Court of Appeal, however. The Home Secretary can recommend to the monarch that a pardon be granted or that part or all of a sentence be removed.

2.3 The legal system in Scotland

The Scottish system

Unlike Wales, Scotland did not become part of the United Kingdom through conquest. As a result, it was able to preserve a degree of independence from the rest of the UK. One example of this independence is its legal system.

The system of criminal justice in Scotland differs in organisation and procedure from the English system.

Prosecutions in Scotland

For legal purposes, Scotland is divided into districts. All criminal investigations in a particular district are overseen by an officer called the Procurator Fiscal. The Procurator Fiscal can request the police to make further enquiries before allowing a prosecution to go ahead and has the right to interview witnesses. Procurators Fiscal make the final decision about whether a case should go to court. They perform, therefore, the same function as that performed by the Crown Prosecution Service in England and Wales. In overall charge of the Procurators Fiscal is the Crown Agent, based in Edinburgh. The Crown Agent oversees the work of Procurators Fiscal and helps them to decide whether to prosecute in difficult cases. The Crown Agent is responsible to the Lord Advocate, the senior criminal lawyer in Scotland.

Scottish courts

Minor criminal cases in Scotland are tried in District or Sheriff Courts (the name varies). More serious cases are tried at the High Court of Justiciary. There is, in other words, no intermediate level of court, equivalent to the Crown Court. In Scotland, all appeals are heard by the High Court of Justiciary in front of three judges. No further appeal to the House of Lords is permitted.

Juries in Scotland

The relationship between judge and jury in Scotland is different from that in England and Wales. In Scotland, the judge decides on questions of law, whilst the jury decides on matters of fact. Juries in Scotland contain 15 people (compared to 12 in England and Wales). At the conclusion of trials, juries in Scotland are able to give the verdict of not proven as well as that of guilty or not guilty.

The civil system in Scotland

The civil court system in Scotland also differs in organisation and procedure from the English system. Most civil litigation in Scotland is dealt with by the Sheriff Courts (the same courts which also deal with criminal litigation). With very few exceptions, there is no upper limit on the value of contracts dealt with by the Sheriff Courts. There is the right to appeal in some cases from the Sheriff to the Sheriff Principal (the head of the judiciary in each sheriffdom) and in other cases from the Sheriff to the Court of Session.

The Court of Session is the supreme civil court in Scotland. There is, however, the right of appeal from the Court of Session to the House of Lords. A leading principle of the Court of Session is that cases are first decided by judges sitting alone and are then reviewed by several judges. The total number of judges is 25, of whom 17 (the Lords Ordinary) mainly decide cases in the first instance. This branch is called the Outer House. The eight other judges are divided into two divisions of four judges each. This branch is called the Inner House. The main business of each division of the Inner House is to review the decisions of the Lords Ordinary or inferior courts which have appealed to it (SOID 1993).

The two systems compared

Despite differences in organisation and procedure, the two systems are not that far apart. Madgwick & Woodhouse (1995) noted, for example, that under John Major the Lord Chancellor was a Scottish lawyer, Lord MacKay. They also pointed out that the House of Lords is the final court of appeal for the UK as a whole, creating precedents which have a general application.

2.4 The European dimension

The two European courts

Two courts outside the UK now play an important

part in its legal system. They have entirely distinct functions, but are frequently confused.

The European Court of Justice

The European Court of Justice is the highest court of the European Union. It sits in Luxembourg (see also, Chapter 6, Section 2.1). In matters relating to EU law, the European Court of Justice is the most senior court and, in its areas of competence, its judgements override even those of the House of Lords.

The European Court of Human Rights

The European Court of Human Rights sits in Strasbourg. This court was established by the European Convention on Human Rights. Appeals can be made to this court if people believe their rights under the European Convention have been violated. Two conditions, however, are placed on such appeals. First, the appellant (the person making the appeal) must have exhausted all the procedures for justice in their own country. Second, appeals cannot be made directly. They go to court via the Commission of Human Rights. The Commission first decides whether the case is admissible and, if it is,

tries to achieve an agreed settlement before referring it to court. Of the 26 signatories to the treaty, the third highest number of cases to go to court have come from the UK - 99 between 1960 and 1998. Of these, the British government was judged to have violated the treaty on 52 occasions.

Main points - Section 2.1-2.4

- In the UK, three separate legal systems are in operation, but they all distinguish between criminal law and civil law.
- Criminal law is concerned with behaviour which has been made illegal by statute. Civil law is concerned with disputes between individuals and groups.
- The three legal systems are organised hierarchically. Superior courts hear more serious cases and re-examine on appeal cases which were first brought to the lower courts.
- Two courts outside the UK now play an important part in its legal system - the European Court of Justice and the European Court of Human Rights.

Activity 17.2 The British legal system

Item A *The legal system in England and Wales*

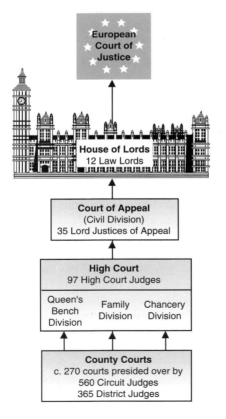

(i) The criminal courts in 1998

House of Lords
12 Law Lords

↑

Court of Appeal
(Criminal Division)
35 Lord Justices of Appeal

↑

Crown Courts
94 Crown Court centres (cases heard by High Court Judges, Circuit Judges, Recorders or Assistant Recorders)

↑

Magistrates Courts
c. 700 Magistrates Courts
(30,361 JPs and 88 stipendiary magistrates)

(i) The civil courts in 1998

European Court of Justice

↑

House of Lords
12 Law Lords

↑

Court of Appeal
(Civil Division)
35 Lord Justices of Appeal

↑

High Court
97 High Court Judges

| Queen's Bench Division | Family Division | Chancery Division |

↑

County Courts
c. 270 courts presided over by
560 Circuit Judges
365 District Judges

Item B *The jury system (1)*

In July 1998, it emerged that a new Crime Bill, due in Autumn 1998, would include a clause removing the right to a jury trial from cases affecting about 22,000 defendants a year (around 20% of cases heard in Crown Courts). Instead, these cases would be heard by a bench of magistrates. At present, the right of defendants to choose a jury trial covers a wide range of middle-ranking offences - such as theft, handling stolen goods and indecent assault. It is these offences which have been targeted for change. The main arguments in favour of this change are the savings that can be made both in terms of money and time. In 1998, the average cost of a contested jury case was £13,500 compared to £2,500 for a case tried by magistrates. Supporters of reform also claim that magistrates and judges are better

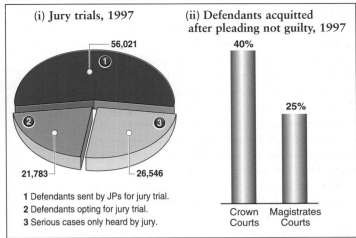

(i) Jury trials, 1997

56,021 ①
21,783 ②
26,546 ③

1 Defendants sent by JPs for jury trial.
2 Defendants opting for jury trial.
3 Serious cases only heard by jury.

(ii) Defendants acquitted after pleading not guilty, 1997

40% Crown Courts
25% Magistrates Courts

able to understand and, therefore, evaluate complex cases. Opponents, on the other hand, argue that trial by jury is more likely to be fair. Magistrates, they argue, tend to be on the side of the police. Also, trial by jury allows decisions to be made which might be wrong in law but right in common sense. Besides, the removal of juries from some offences is likely to be the first step in the complete removal of jury trials. Research evidence shows that magistrates are more likely to convict than a jury when a defendant pleads not guilty. But, Home Office research shows that over 70% of those opting for a jury trial plead guilty and judges are three times more likely to send defendants to prison, and for $2\frac{1}{2}$ times longer, than magistrates in similar cases.

Adapted from the *Guardian*, 29 July 1998.

Item C *The jury system (2)*

"*The jury will ignore that last remark…*"

Questions

1. What factors might determine whether justice is done in the legal system in England and Wales? Use Items A-C in your answer.
2. a) Using Item A write a paragraph explaining the principles which lie behind the legal system in England and Wales.
   b) Using Item A as a model, draw a diagram of the Scottish legal system.
3. Discuss the advantages and disadvantages of the jury system in the administration of justice. Use Items B and C in your answer.

2.5 How independent is the judiciary?

The role of the judiciary

The role in theory

According to the principle of the separation of powers (see Chapter 4, Section 1.1), the judicial task of law enforcement (of deciding whether laws have been broken and, if they have, of dispensing punishment) is separate from the executive and legislative tasks of devising and making laws. It is, therefore, the role of judges (known collectively as 'the judiciary') to examine cases where citizens or organisations are accused of breaking the law and to make judgements about whether or not they have done so. In theory at least, the principle of the separation of powers means that the judiciary is quite independent of the executive. Its judgements are not subject, for example, to ministerial direction or control. Equally, it is the role of the judiciary to interpret the law as it stands, not to determine what the law should be.

The role in practice

How far this theory is carried out in practice, however, depends upon a number of factors.

First, it is the job of judges to interpret general laws in specific instances:

> 'The law consists of general rules (rules which relate to all persons or to wide categories of persons). These general rules (laws) are laid down by the legislature. Laws are then given effect through policies chosen and enforced by the executive. Like the laws to which they relate, such policies apply in general, rather than specific, terms.' (Davis 1995, p.63)

By applying the general rule or policy to a particular case, judges decide on the meaning of the law in a particular instance. When an interpretation is made in a senior court, all lower courts are then bound by that interpretation in future similar cases (this is known as the 'principle of precedent'). In essence, therefore, judges in senior courts are actually making the law through their interpretations of what Parliament has laid down. Law made by judges is known as 'common law' (see Chapter 4, Section 1.1).

Second, judges play an explicitly political role in that they are asked, through the process of judicial review (see below), to consider whether local or national government has acted lawfully.

Third, senior judges play a formal role in the other two branches of government. Not only do Law Lords participate in debates and votes when the Lords sits as the legislature, but the Lord Chancellor straddles all three branches of the government as a member of the Cabinet (part of the executive), a member of the House of Lords (part of the legislature) and head of the judiciary.

Fourth:

> 'Senior judges make public speeches or publish articles which contribute to the debate on controversial government policies, particularly those which affect them directly...Similarly, it is common practice to appoint judges to lead inquiries into controversial or difficult matters and for their conclusions to be taken into account in legislation.' (Davis 1995, p.64).

And fifth, the incorporation of the European Convention on Human Rights into British law means that, for the first time in British history, judges will have the right to suggest changes to legislation if it conflicts with the aims of the convention.

How should judges interpret the law?

Given the political dimension to the making of judgements, should a judge interpret the law to ensure that the law reflects current public thinking or should the judgement go beyond current thinking in the hope of altering the consensus? This is the question that leading judicial practitioners and thinkers have asked and three schools of thought have developed from their answers.

First, according to Lord Devlin, the judiciary should be creative but not dynamic. It is, in other words, not the role of the judge to make what is effectively new law, nor should judges act as social reformers.

Second, Lord Denning has argued that it is the role of the judge to achieve justice. If this means overturning precedent or interpreting legislation very widely, that indeed is the proper role of the senior judge. Supporters of this 'dynamic' judicial role argue that, if the law is not clear, then what Parliament intended to do should be taken into account. Intention, however, is difficult to establish and this perspective gives the senior judiciary a vastly extended role in shaping laws.

And third, according to Griffith, whether or not judges choose to adopt a dynamic role is not that important:

> 'More important are their reactions to the moral, political and social issues in the cases that come before them.' (Griffith 1991, p.261)

If this is the case, then the factors which determine how senior judges apply the law depend heavily on who is appointed to be a judge and how they are appointed.

Judicial appointments

Before September 1994, all judicial appointments were made secretly by the Lord Chancellor and the Lord Chancellor's staff. Decisions were made on the basis of 'soundings' taken from other judges and senior lawyers (the Lord Chancellor's Office describes them as 'extensive consultations' rather than 'soundings'). According to a pamphlet produced by the Lord Chancellor's Department in

1986, the following selection criteria were used:

> 'The Lord Chancellor's policy is to appoint to every judicial post the candidate who appears best qualified to fill and perform its duties, regardless of party, sex, religion or ethnic origin. Professional ability, experience, standing and integrity alone are the criteria, with the requirements that the candidate must be physically capable of carrying out the duties, and not disqualified by any personal unsuitability.' (LCD 1986)

Clearly, such criteria allow for a wide range of interpretations and, by 1994 when the system was changed, it was accepted that this system was flawed for the following reasons. First, the secrecy meant that the system was open to abuse by those with personal agendas. Second, the system lacked objectivity and openness, a particular problem given that, by 1994, the Conservatives had been in power for 15 years and were under suspicion of appointing supporters to judicial posts. Third, since the system was based on soundings taken from other judges, it was no surprise that those appointed were usually people with similar backgrounds and interests to those who recommended them. In other words, the system ensured that judges were selected from only a narrow band of people. And fourth, the system did not allow those who might be interested in promotion to apply for a position. They had to hope that their ambitions would be noticed by those taking the soundings.

Changes since 1994

A new system for junior judicial appointments (those below the level of High Court Judge) was introduced in September 1994. Since then, junior judicial posts have been advertised, all those with appropriate qualifications have been encouraged to apply, and non-lawyers have taken part in the selection process (shortlisted applicants are interviewed by a panel of three comprising a Circuit Judge, a non-lawyer and a senior civil servant from the Lord Chancellor's Office). It should be noted, however, that only barristers and solicitors with 10 year's experience are eligible and they must have experience as Recorders. Since Recorders are appointed by the Lord Chancellor's Office in the first place, competition for appointment at the level of junior judge is still by no means open to all who work in the legal professions.

In February 1998, the Lord Chancellor, Derry Irvine, announced that the system used for junior judicial appointments would be broadened to include High Court Judges. Yet, whilst posts for the High Court are, therefore, advertised and shortlisted applicants are interviewed by a panel of three (a High Court Judge sits on the interview panel rather than a Circuit Judge), the Lord Chancellor does not have to select those chosen by the panel. The system of soundings remains in place and the Lord Chancellor reserves the right to appoint people even if they have not applied for the post. Furthermore, the most senior judicial posts are not advertised. Senior judges continue to be appointed using the old system.

Who are the judges?

When you picture in your mind a judge, what do you see? Do you see a young, black woman who speaks with a strong regional accent or an old, white male whose accent suggests an expensive public school and a university education at Oxford or Cambridge? If your mind conjures up the latter image, then, according to a survey published by *Labour Research* in July 1997, that image is not far from the truth. *Labour Research* examined the background of 690 senior judges (Circuit Judges and above) and found that:

- Britain's judges are still overwhelmingly an élite group in terms of educational background
- they are older on average than they were 10 years ago
- the vast majority are white males
- they are more likely to have been involved in politics than they were ten years ago.

(*Labour Research*, July 1997, p.13)

The social background of judges

Senior judges are drawn from the ranks of barristers. Traditionally, those training to become barristers have required a private income to survive the first few years of practice. Becoming a barrister is an expensive process. As a result, large sections of the population are excluded. The result is that most barristers and, therefore, most judges come from a small section of society, move in rarefied circles, and share the values of the privileged few. Whilst the 1997 *Labour Research* survey found that just 41 senior judges (6%) were female and only five (0.7%) were black, it found that 82% had attended a public school and 88% went to Oxford or Cambridge Universities. It also found that a significant minority of judges (25) were involved in party politics and 14 had stood for parliamentary election at some time in their careers. A further 12 judges were identified as freemasons whilst 61 judges said they belonged to two exclusive private clubs - the Garrick Club and the MCC. Some judges are notoriously out of touch with ordinary people. The High Court Judge, Mr Justice Harman, for example, had never heard of the footballer Paul Gascoigne, the band Oasis and the singer Bruce Springsteen (*Guardian*, 25 February 1998). It is no surprise, therefore, that according to the 1996 British Crime Survey (which interviewed 16,438 people) four out of five people believe that judges are out of touch with what ordinary people think.

The importance of social background

This combination of social characteristics, it can be argued, inevitably affects the outlook of judges and, therefore, affects the way in which they do their job. The capacity to make informed, fair judgements must be hampered when judges live at such a distance from the ordinary people they are judging. Their privileged white male characteristics are likely to make them sympathetic to some groups (the rich and well educated, for example) and not sympathetic to others (the poor and blacks and Asians, for example). Their background is also likely to make them conservative. That is not to say that many judges are active supporters of the Conservative Party. Rather, it suggests that, given the need to decide between the new and radical or the ancient, tried and tested, many judges opt for the latter. This has raised serious questions about the genuine impartiality of judges.

Judicial review

British courts are not only responsible for interpreting the precise meaning of an Act of Parliament, they are also responsible for reviewing the actions of public agents (including ministers) to find out whether their actions are 'ultra vires' (beyond their powers). The government can be brought to court on the same grounds as an ordinary person or organisation. So, when a person or organisation feels aggrieved at the actions of some ministerial, government department or local authority action, they can then apply for a judicial review. Since a judicial review requires judges to make a judgement about decisions made by politicians, the political views of the judges may have a bearing on whether the review should be granted and what verdict should be delivered:

> 'Judicial review is a direct challenge to the lawfulness of the government's action and clearly involves the courts in judgements which have political fall-out.' (Davis 1995, p.66)

Procedure

For a judicial review to take place, the aggrieved individual or organisation must apply for a judicial review at the High Court. The right to judicial review is not automatic. Only when leave to proceed has been granted, can a case be heard in front of two or three judges in the Divisional Court of the Queen's Bench Division. Leave is granted on three grounds. First, a judicial review is granted if it seems that there is sufficient evidence to suggest that a public authority may have exceeded its statutory power (ie an act performed by a public agent may have been ultra vires). Second, a judicial review is granted when there appears to have been procedural impropriety (where actions taken by a public body have contravened 'natural justice'). A public body acts according to 'natural justice' if it has acted in a way that is fair and free from bias (Griffith 1991, p.125). And third, a judicial review is allowed if it

appears that a public body has acted 'irrationally' (in a highly 'unreasonable' way). Clearly, these three grounds give judges a great deal of discretion. Different judges interpret 'fair and free from bias' and 'acting irrationally' in different ways.

Remedies

If leave to apply for judicial review is granted and the judges find against the public agent, five possible remedies are available to the court. First, the court can quash decisions made by public agents who have been acting outside their lawful jurisdiction. A planning authority, for example, which had rejected a planning application for reasons not specified in the legislation which gave it the authority to act, could be ordered to change its decision. Second, a tribunal can be prevented from considering matters outside its authority. Third, a public body can be compelled to perform a specified function by law - for example, a local authority can be compelled to provide schooling. Fourth, any public body can be ordered not to carry out or to stop carrying out an action which the court decides is unlawful. In other words, the court can issue an injunction. Injunctions played a major part in the miners' strike of 1984-85, for example - judges ruled that the strike was illegal as no ballot had been held and issued injunctions against the NUM. And fifth, the judges can choose to clarify the legal position in a particular case. This is a stronger remedy than it might appear since any public body acting against a newly clarified legal position would certainly have judgement made against them in future legal action.

Problems with judicial review

Pyper (1998) argues that citizens using judicial review to redress grievances face a number of problems:

- access to the system is limited
- only a third of actions reach a final hearing
- some judges are more likely to grant leave for cases than others (some grant leave to 80% of applicants whilst others only grant leave to 20%)
- only one in six cases results in a ruling against the public agent.

Other problems include the following. First, the growing number of cases means there is an increasing willingness on the part of the judiciary to intervene in the day-to-day business of government (Griffith 1991, p.63). Second, some critics have questioned whether unelected judges from an élite social background should be responsible for scrutinising and ruling upon the legality of the actions of elected governments and local authorities. And third, the question has been raised as to whether judges, regardless of their background, are sufficiently well trained to take legal decisions in a highly politicised environment and whether the principles valid in court are appropriate.

What cannot be doubted is that the process of judicial review necessarily involves judges in decisions of a political nature. The greater use of judicial review may be evidence that people are making greater use of the legal remedies available to them when they feel that their rights are being infringed or it may be that there has been a growth in the abuse of rights by public bodies.

Main points - Section 2.5

- In theory, the principle of the separation of powers means that the judiciary is quite independent of the executive. In practice, judges do have to make political decisions.
- There is a debate about whether judges should interpret the law dynamically or not.
- Before September 1994, all judicial appointments were made secretly by the Lord Chancellor on the basis of 'soundings' taken from other judges and senior lawyers.
- Since September 1994, junior judicial posts have been advertised, all those with appropriate qualifications have been encouraged to apply, and non-lawyers have taken part in the selection process. In 1998, this process was extended to High Court Judges.
- Most judges are old, white males with a privileged background. Some people argue that this affects the judgements they make.
- Since judicial reviews require judges to judge decisions made by politicians, the political views of the judges may have a bearing on cases.

Activity 17.3 *The independence of the judiciary*

Item A *The background of the judiciary*

(i) Judges by gender and ethnicity, 1998

Judges	Men	Women	Blacks & Asians
House of Lords	12	0	0
Court of Appeal	34	1	0
High Court	90	7	0
Circuit	512	30	5
Recorders	780	69	13
District	295	38	4
Assistant Recorders	283	61	10

(ii) Senior judges (Circuit Judges upwards) by educational background and age, 1987-97

Judges	Public School (%)			Oxbridge (%)			Age (years)	
	1987	1994	1997	1987	1994	1997	1994	1997
House of Lords	90	91	73	80	82	100	65.7	65.8
Appeal Court	83	77	78	86	87	89	63.4	62.8
High Court	62	80	84	78	80	86	58	59.9
All senior judges*	**70**	**80**	**82**	**80**	**82**	**88**	**-**	**-**

* *These figures include Circuit judges*

The table (left) shows the number of male, female and ethnic minority judges in February 1998. The table above shows the educational background and age of senior judges in the period 1987-97.

Adapted from the *Guardian*, 25 February 1998 and *Labour Research*, July 1997.

Item B *Who are the judges?*

Hello. I'm white, elderly, bigoted - and male. What are you going to do about it?

Item C *Can we trust the judges? (1)*

The Lord Chief Justice, Thomas Bingham, was appointed by John Major's Lord Chancellor, Lord Mackay. Educated at public school and fitting comfortably in the privileged world of the Bar, Bingham was 65 in 1998. According to one lawyer, Geoffrey Bindman who represents the *New Statesman* (a pro-Labour magazine), Bingham has a liberal and humanitarian outlook. The journalist Nick Cohen, however, dismisses the idea that Bingham is in any way progressive. He cites three pieces of evidence. First, during the Gulf War, Bingham allowed 90 Arabs to be imprisoned without trial on the strength of rumours from M15. He was unapologetic when the Home Office later revealed that all 90 were completely innocent. Second, he protected the security services from public scrutiny by dismissing the charges made by M15 whistleblowers that M15 agents bugged government opponents. And third, in October 1998, Bingham threw the case in favour of General Pinochet's extradition out of the Court of Appeal. Nick Cohen points out that the Law Lords are all commercial lawyers trained in dealing with wills, corporations and trusts. None has knowledge of human rights law. They are so conservative, he claims, that a desperate legal profession can only hail one senior judge as a great 'liberal'. That judge, of course, is Lord Bingham.

Adapted from the *New Statesman*, 21 November 1997 and the *Observer*, 1 November 1998.

Item D   *Can we trust the judges? (2)*

When, in July 1998, the Lord Chancellor, Derry Irvine, appointed two new Law Lords, their promotion was strongly criticised on the following grounds. First, although the new Law Lords would decide matters of life and liberty, their roots were in commercial law and they had little experience in the field of human rights. Second, the two judges who were retiring had moderate views whereas the two to be promoted were known to be right-wingers. This would tilt the court in an illiberal direction. Third, one of the new Law Lords was a senior freemason who had resisted the Home Secretary's threat to force eminent people to disclose their links with the masons. Fourth, both were middle-aged, white men. This is of particular concern at a time when the European Convention on Human Rights is due to become part of British law because judges will no longer be able to claim to be impartial technicians. They will be more like judges in the US Supreme Court, making decisions of principle. And fifth, it is an insult in a supposedly democratic country that people who will be making decisions which affect everybody have been chosen in the dark by somebody who was elected by nobody.

Adapted from the *Guardian*, 21 July 1998.

Item E   *Judicial reviews*

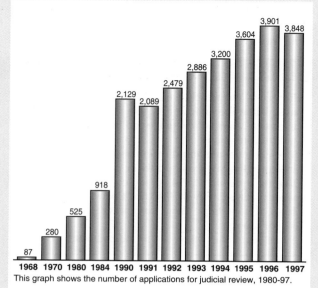

This graph shows the number of applications for judicial review, 1980-97.

Questions

1. Consider the extent to which British judges undertake a political role and assess their suitability to do so. Use Items A-E in your answer.

2. Is there any evidence in Item A to support the point made by Item B?

3. a) Using Items C and D, give arguments for and against changing the system used for selecting senior judges.
   b) Why is the selection process important?

4. 'The increasing use of judicial review means an increasingly political role for judges.' Explain this statement using Item E.

Part 3 Redress of grievances

Key issues

1. What role is played by the quasi-judicial system?
2. What are administrative tribunals and how effective are they?
3. When and why are judicial inquiries set up?
4. What role do MPs and the Ombudsman play in enabling citizens to gain redress for their grievances?

3.1 The quasi-judicial system (i)

Administrative justice

If a state is to be properly accountable to its citizens then it needs to provide a satisfactory means of investigating complaints or grievances and redressing them:

> 'In any meaningful system of accountability, there must be mechanisms designed to facilitate the redress of citizen's grievances. Democracy, accountability and redress are

inextricably linked.' (Pyper 1998, p.28)
When citizens have a complaint or grievance about an administrative action (an action taken by central government, local government or organisations funded by public money), there are three ways in which they can seek redress:

- through judicial means (the courts)
- by using the various quasi-judicial methods which are available
- through political means (for example, asking an MP to take up the case).

It is often not possible or practical to go to court. Courts refuse to hear certain cases. Besides, for most people it is usually far too expensive to take a case to court. Instead, a number of other channels have developed to enable the citizen to obtain redress from the state. Since these channels are not part of the mainstream judicial system, they can be described as 'quasi-judicial'.

In some countries, a separate system of administrative courts exists specifically to hear complaints about the actions taken by the government. In the UK, however, such cases are dealt with in one of three ways - by administrative tribunals, by the setting up of a judicial inquiry or by the involvement of the citizen's local MP (see next section).

Administrative tribunals

As the role of the state expanded after 1945 with the development of the welfare state, a system of administrative tribunals grew up:

> 'There are now about 2,000 tribunals, not all statutory and not all actually called "tribunal", concerned with the adjudication of disputes between the state and the citizen in the administration of regulatory legislation and welfare provision...Matters dealt with include disputes over tax assessments, compensation for the compulsory purchase of land, the grant of welfare benefits and pensions, appeals related to disability allowances, mental health and immigration. Tribunals are also used extensively to resolve employment and landlord/tenant disputes, which may or may not involve government agencies.' (Madgwick & Woodhouse 1995, p.291)

Composition and procedure

Each tribunal differs in its membership and procedures, but the proceedings are carried out in accordance with legal principles. In general, tribunals are less formal, less costly and less time-consuming than the courts. Tribunals are normally composed of a Chair who has legal training (usually a solicitor) and two lay members. The lay members generally have experience in the area with which the tribunal is concerned. Since tribunals are mainly set up by statute (Act of Parliament), they are the responsibility of ministers and tribunal members are often appointed by ministers. Although, therefore, those who sit on tribunals are supposedly independent, they may have a vested interest in opposing grievances. Hearings are held in public and the decisions made by the tribunal are binding. The reasoning behind a decision may be made public, but there is no obligation to make it public. As a result, the decisions made by tribunals cannot form the basis for a body of law, as happens in the courts. Appeals are only possible on points of law and some tribunals do not allow appeals in any circumstances - for example, NHS and immigration tribunals. The panel can award compensation if the grievance is judged to be justified. Alternatively, matters can be settled between the disputing parties before the hearing is held.

Effectiveness

According to Pyper, the advantages of tribunals are their 'relative simplicity, accessibility, informality and cheapness compared with courts' (Pyper 1998, p.30). Recent research, however, has led to a number of criticisms being levelled at the tribunal system. First, success in tribunals (as in the courts) often depends on the quality of advice and legal representation available to the complainant. Second, tribunal decisions show signs of inconsistency, partly because there is no formal system of precedent to govern decision making. And third, access to some types of tribunal is increasingly slow. Appeals to the Social Security Tribunal, for example, take an average of 23 weeks (Pyper 1998). It should be noted that some government departments have removed the right to take a grievance to a tribunal, relying instead on internal reviews.

Public inquiries

In general, inquiries are set up for two reasons. The first reason is to help the government make a decision about a particular issue. Legislation which provides for a new motorway to be built, for example, might make provision for a public inquiry to be held into the route which it should follow (some Acts of Parliament, especially those which deal with town and country planning, make provision for a public inquiry to be held before a final decision is made). The second reason for setting up a public inquiry is to investigate the past conduct of ministers, MPs or other public officials.

Public inquiries are set up by ministers. Normally, an inspector or a judge is appointed by the minister to conduct the inquiry. This inspector or judge then invites those with an interest to appear before the inquiry as witnesses. The report produced by the inquiry is published and reasons are given for the inquiry's recommendations. Public inquiries, however, do not make a final decision. They advise the minister. The minister is obliged to consider the advice of the inquiry, but may choose to ignore it.

There are two types of public inquiry into the conduct and behaviour of public officials - statutory inquiries and judicial inquiries.

Statutory inquiries

A Tribunal of Inquiry (also known as a 'statutory tribunal') is a body established under the 1921 Tribunals of Inquiry Act. Statutory tribunals have substantial powers - they can, for example, demand statements and evidence from witnesses. Their procedures, however, tend to be ponderous. Each party has the right to be represented by a lawyer who, in turn, has the right to cross examine every other party. This takes time and is expensive. Referring to the statutory tribunal which looked into the Crown Agents Affair (a financial scandal which affected a central government agency in the 1970s), the barrister Anthony Lester complained:

> 'The inquiry took years and years, cost the taxpayer millions of pounds and was completely obsolete by the time that the report was published.' (*Guardian*, 14 January 1994)

Judicial inquiries

Judicial inquiries do not have the power to demand statements and evidence from witnesses and, unlike statutory tribunals, they report to a specific government department. They are less formal than statutory tribunals, with witnesses speaking for themselves rather than being represented by lawyers. An example of a judicial inquiry is the Scott Inquiry into the Arms to Iraq scandal (see Activity 17.4 below and Chapter 13, Section 1.3)

How effective are inquiries?

Inquiries headed by senior judges can be an important means of investigating actions taken by government. A clear set of recommendations may pressure the government into taking action to prevent similar events happening again. If, however, the judge refuses to rock the boat, the issues and responsibilities can become clouded. As in other areas in which senior judges are involved, much depends on their individual views and competence. In general, judicial inquiries are rather a blunt instrument when it comes to securing redress because they rarely result in action being taken against individuals found to be responsible for wrongdoing.

Main points - Section 3.1

- It is often not possible or practical to go to court. Instead, a number of other 'quasi-judicial' channels have developed to enable the citizen to obtain redress from the state.
- Administrative tribunals settle disputes between the state and the citizen which arise over the administration of regulatory legislation and welfare provision.
- The advantages of tribunals are their simplicity, accessibility, informality and cheapness. But, decisions are inconsistent and procedure slow.
- Public inquiries are set up to help the government make a decision about a particular issue or to investigate the past conduct of ministers, MPs or other public officials.
- Inquiries can persuade government to take action, but, in general, they do not provide redress in the sense that those responsible for wrongdoing are rarely punished.

Activity 17.4 The Scott Inquiry

Item A Timeline and key participants

Diary of events

1980 Iran-Iraq war begins.

1984 Geoffrey Howe, Foreign Secretary, issues guidelines on exports to Iran and Iraq. Subsequently these are ignored by ministers and companies, including Matrix Churchill (MC), a machine tool manufacturer based in Coventry.

1987 The Iraqi government becomes a majority shareholder of MC.

1988 Ministers approve MC exports to Iraq. Iran-Iraq ceasefire ends war. Three ministers - Alan Clark (DTI), William Waldegrave (Foreign Office) and Lord Trefgarne (Defence) relax the Howe guidelines without informing Parliament.

1989 MC exports to Iraq continue.

1990 Iraq invades Kuwait just as export guidelines about to be relaxed. MC raided by customs officials.

1991 Three MC executives charged with exporting goods in contravention of controlling orders issued in 1987 and 1989.

1992 During the trial, the judge allows the defence to see witness statements made by ministers and civil servants. Trial collapses after Alan Clark admits ministers were aware of the intended use of MC tools.

1992 Scott Inquiry set up to investigate exports of weapon parts to Iraq (1984-90) and the attempt by ministers to conceal crucial evidence from the defence by signing Public Interest Immunity (PII) documents.

1993 Inquiry takes evidence.

1996 Scott Report published.

Item B *An assessment*

The Scott Inquiry was set up after the collapse of the Matrix Churchill trial in November 1992. During this trial, it emerged that ministers had suppressed important evidence by signing Public Interest Immunity certificates (which prevented government documents becoming available to the defence). When, a former minister, Alan Clark, admitted that the government had been aware that the machine tools exported to Iraq by Matrix Churchill would be used in weapon production, there was the suspicion that ministers had been involved in a cover-up. This led to the setting up of the inquiry under Lord Justice Scott. The scale of the inquiry can be demonstrated by the fact that the inquiry sat for over 400 hours in open session and for 50 hours in closed session. In addition, it took written evidence from 160 witnesses and scrutinised over 200,000 pages of documentation. When the Scott Report was published on 15 February 1996, it contained 1,800 pages bound in four volumes with a fifth volume of appendices. In other words, it examined the Arms to Iraq scandal in the minutest detail. The effectiveness of the inquiry, however, is questionable. On one level, it was successful. Ministers and civil servants were called to answer in public for their policies and actions, and detailed explanations of events were placed on the record. On another level, it was a failure. With the notable exception of one civil servant who resigned (and, therefore, imposed a sanction on himself), none of the official or ministerial participants in the Arms to Iraq affair were subjected to sanctions of demotion, dismissal or resignation.

Adapted from Adams & Pyper 1997.

Item C *Key findings*

The Scott Report - key findings

- Geoffrey Howe's guidelines governing exports to Iran and Iraq were changed without Parliament being informed.

- Failure to inform Parliament was a deliberate act. The government knew that any relaxation in export policy to Iraq would face fierce parliamentary opposition.

- The three Matrix Churchill executives should not have been prosecuted.

- Government action to prevent the release of documents to the trial was wrong.

- Geoffery Howe, William Waldegrave, the Attorney General, Nicholas Lyell, and a number of senior civil servants were severely criticised for their part in the affair.

Item D *A hostile verdict*

Writing in February 1996, the journalist John Pilger pointed out that British arms supplied to Iraq had been used to kill many innocent people. Yet, far from bringing those responsible to account, the Scott Report merely 'normalised the unthinkable' by clouding the issues and limiting the truth. Scott judged that Cabinet ministers acted honestly and in good faith. He said that they did mislead Parliament, but they did not mean to mislead it. By reaching these conclusions, Pilger argues, Scott let those responsible off the hook. Pilger also accuses Scott of watering down his report (ministers were given advance copies and allowed to suggest amendments). For example, in the draft report, Pilger says, Scott accused William Waldegrave of writing letters in: 'terms that were apt to mislead the readers as to the nature of the policy on export sales to Iraq...Mr Waldegrave was unquestionably in a position to know that that was so'. In the final version, it reads: 'Mr Waldegrave was in a position to know that that was so although I accept that he did not intend his letters to be misleading and did not so regard them'. Scott's job, Pilger says, was not just to listen, it was to consider all the available evidence and to draw clear conclusions for the nation. In this, he failed. A full and open inquiry might well have led to criminal prosecutions across the top level of government. Scott, in effect, contained this threat.

Adapted from Pilger 1996.

Item E *A cartoon*

I am not going outside and I may not be for some time.

This cartoon portrays Lord Justice Scott as Scott of the Antarctic. It parodies the famous last words of Captain Oates (a member of Scott's expedition) who said 'I'm just going out. I may be some time' before leaving camp to die in the hope that, by sacrificing himself, the others would reach the South Pole. Those pictured in the cartoon are (left to right) William Waldegrave, Nicholas Lyell, Lord Justice Scott, Geoffrey Howe and John Major.

Questions

1. Judging from Items A-E, would you say that judicial inquiries are an effective means of redressing grievances? Explain your answer.
2. a) Using Items A-D, explain why the Scott Inquiry was set up and what it discovered.
   b) How do judicial inquiries work?
   c) Give arguments for and against the view that a senior judge is the best person to investigate the working of a government department.
3. What point is being made by the cartoon in Item E? How valid do you think it is? Explain your answer.

3.2 The quasi-judicial system (ii)

The role of councillors and MPs

In many cases, the local councillor or constituency MP is the person to call upon if a right seems to have been infringed or a grievance requires redress. Since many complaints are concerned with the activities of local rather than central government, people often turn to their local councillor first. The next port of call might be the local MP. Whether the local MP will agree to take on a case, however, depends on a number of factors. First, the MP has to decide whether the matter is important enough to raise. Second, MPs are extremely busy and may have insufficient time to take on new cases or to pursue the cases they have taken on with sufficient vigour to ensure that a positive outcome is achieved. Third, party discipline in Parliament is strong and MPs on both sides might be discouraged from raising issues which could cause embarrassment to their party. Fourth, MPs have only limited office, research and secretarial facilities. And fifth, MPs vary enormously in terms of interests and ability.

Possible action

Once they have agreed to take on a case, MPs can take action in a number of ways in support of their constituent. First, if the problem is local, the MP can write to the person or organisation concerned and, perhaps, liaise with local councillors. Second, if the problem relates to central government, the MP can write to the minister concerned and request assistance. Third, the MP can issue a written or an oral question to a relevant government minister (the government minister is obliged to answer such questions). And fourth, the MP can request that the Parliamentary Commissioner for Administration, also known as the 'ombudsman', investigates the complaint. The term 'ombudsman' is Scandinavian, meaning 'complaints person'.

Ombudsmen

Since administrative tribunals have grown up on an ad hoc basis (see Section 3.1 above), there are areas of public administration where no tribunal exists to hear complaints. To bridge this gap and to create a mechanism for dealing with complaints of maladministration, a Parliamentary Commissioner for Administration (PCA) was first appointed in 1967. It is the job of the PCA to investigate complaints of maladministration which occur in the departments of central government. In 1987, the range of bodies included within the PCA's jurisdiction was extended to include the Equal Opportunities Commission, Sports Council, Legal Aid Board, Charity Commission, Royal Mint and Scottish Tourist Board. The PCA is supported by a staff of around 55.

Since 1967, ombudsmen have been established for Northern Ireland (1969), the health service (1973), local government (1974), Scottish local government (1975), housing association tenants (1993) and, the prison service (1994).

Some sectors of private industry have also established ombudsmen schemes, but these should not be confused with the statutory schemes.

Procedure

Members of the public cannot refer cases directly to the PCA. They must be passed on through an MP. Since 1988, however, the Local Government Ombudsman has been directly accessible to members of the public. This direct access is also available to those with complaints for the Health, Housing and Prisons Ombudsmen.

Once a complaint is received, it is acted upon only if no other form of redress exists and if the complaint satisfies the provisions of the 1967 Act, namely that a person has good reason to claim 'to have sustained injustice in consequence of maladministration' (Section 5.1 of the Act). A major problem is that 'maladministration' is not defined in the Act, though De Smith & Brazier claim that ombudsmen define maladministration as:

> 'Corruption, bias, unfair discrimination, harshness, misleading a member of the public as to his rights, failing to notify him properly of his rights or to explain the reasons for a decision, general high handedness, using powers for a wrong purpose, failing to consider relevant materials, taking irrelevant material into account, losing or failing to reply to correspondence, delaying unreasonably before making a tax refund or presenting a tax demand or dealing with an application for a grant or licence and so on.' (De Smith & Brazier 1989, p.649)

Thompson (1993) noted that only about 20% of cases referred to the PCA were investigated in the period up to 1993, though Madgwick & Woodhouse (1995) point out that over half the complaints were rejected because they did not concern administrative actions.

Powers

Once an investigation does begin, ombudsmen have wide powers. Although hearings are in private, they can compel witnesses to attend and can inspect relevant files and papers. After the investigation, a report is submitted to a House of Commons select committee. The report is also published. If maladministration has taken place, the ombudsman recommends an appropriate remedy. Although the government department found to be guilty of maladministration is not obliged to accept the ombudsman's recommendation, it is under strong pressure to do so. In most cases, an apology or financial compensation is offered. In some cases, changes to administrative procedures are implemented.

Criticisms

A number of criticisms have been made of the way in which the ombudsman system works. First, it is claimed that ombudsmen are under-used - for three reasons:

- complaints to the PCA have to be channelled through MPs
- all complaints must be placed in writing
- the system is not well publicised.

Second, the large number of rejected complaints is a cause for concern. Ombudsmen have to be satisfied that both maladministration and injustice have occurred before a complaint is considered. Some critics argue that this should be considered in the course of an investigation, not as a condition of its beginning. Third, the passive nature of the system has been criticised - ombudsmen must await complaints, they cannot make inquiries themselves. Fourth, the background of those appointed as ombudsmen is a cause of concern. Most have civil service or local government backgrounds and there is a concern that, consequently, their sympathies are with those being investigated. Fifth, there is often a long delay before a decision is reached - investigations by the PCA take, on average, over 70 weeks (Pyper 1998). And sixth, critics argue that ombudsmen ought to be given powers to enforce the recommendations made in reports. Although the recommendations are usually adopted, the gravity of the investigation is reduced because the recommendations are not enforceable. Two recent examples illustrate why this is of particular importance. In both the Barlow Clowes case of 1989 and the Channel Tunnel Rail Link case of 1995, the government publicly rejected the ombudsman's conclusion that maladministration had taken place. In the Barlow Clowes case (which involved the collapse of an investment company), the government nonetheless compensated investors. In the Channel Tunnel Rail Link case (concerning property prices along the proposed route), the government refused to pay compensation.

Advantages

Despite these criticisms, the system has its advantages. Pyper (1998) lists the following advantages:

- ombudsmen reach parts of the system other mechanisms do not reach and they cover a wide range of public bodies
- they are cheap to use
- there is no need for legal advice
- the process is not adversarial, it is conciliatory
- recommendations are almost always implemented
- the finding in one case may affect others.

Madgwick & Woodhouse point out that:

> 'The very presence of the Commissioner with his authority to conduct in-depth investigations has made departments think more carefully about their administration.' (Madgwick & Woodhouse 1995, p.289)

The Criminal Cases Review Commission (CCRC)

In October 1989, the Court of Appeal overturned the convictions of the 'Guildford Four' (three men and a woman who had been jailed in 1975 after being found guilty of bombing a pub in Guildford). These convictions were overturned on the grounds that the evidence against them had been based on police lies and false confessions. The release of the Guildford Four was of great importance. In the words of Paul Foot:

> 'The Guildford case broke the dam. Month after month, wrongful convictions were set aside: the Birmingham Six, the Broadwater Three, the Cardiff Three, the Swansea Two, the East Ham Two, Judy Ward, Stefan Kisko, the Taylor sisters, Eddie Browning. All had been convicted of murder and all were, in the proper sense, victims of miscarriages of justice - they didn't do it.' (*Guardian*, 4 July 1994)

This steady stream of miscarriages of justice in the 1990s severely shook the public's faith in the judicial system and led to demands for change. Until 1997, it was the responsibility of the Home Office to decide whether cases should go back to the Court of Appeal. Since March 1997, however, the Criminal Cases Review Commission (CCRC) has taken over this responsibility.

The CCRC is based in Birmingham with a staff of 13 commissioners, 25 case workers and a total staff of 65. In 1997-98, its budget was £4.19 million. To have a case heard by the CCRC, the appeals procedure must have been exhausted and it is necessary to present new evidence which was not available at the time of the trial or was not disclosed to the defence.

Between March 1997 and August 1998, 1,805 applicants applied to the CCRC claiming to have been wrongly sentenced. By August 1998, 20 cases had been referred back to the Court of Appeal, 61 cases had been rejected and 1,026 were awaiting review (*Guardian*, 19 August 1998).

Main points - Section 3.2

- In many cases, the local councillor or constituency MP is the person to call upon if a right seems to have been infringed or a grievance requires redress.
- MPs are busy, under pressure and lack facilities. They might, however, question a minister or complain to the Parliamentary Commissioner for Administration (PCA).
- The job of the PCA is to redress grievances in areas where no tribunals exist and to deal with complaints of maladministration. Other

- ombudsmen are responsible for specific areas of government work.
- The ombudsman system is under-used, passive and slow, with a low success rate and lacking in teeth. But, it does cover a wide range of public bodies, is cheap and conciliatory, and its recommendations are usually implemented.
- The job of the Criminal Cases Review Commission is to decide whether cases should be referred back to the Court of Appeal.

Activity 17.5 *MPs and ombudsmen*

Item A   *Complaints received and investigations completed by the PCA*

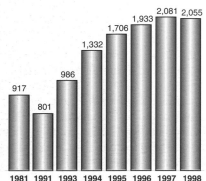

This graph shows the number of complaints received by the PCA, 1981-98.

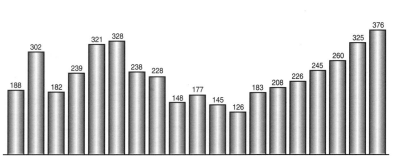

This graph shows the number of investigations completed by the PCA, 1967-98.

According to the PCA, the significant increase in cases since 1993 is largely due to two new factors - the impact of the Child Support Agency (25% of all cases in 1995) and civil service staff cuts which have resulted in a lower quality of service.

Item B   *The Barlow Clowes affair*

In 1988, around 18,000 people who had invested in the company Barlow Clowes found that their investments had failed because funds had been misappropriated by Peter Clowes. Since the company was licensed by the Department of Trade and Industry (DTI), several hundred of these investors approached the PCA (via their MPs), alleging that the DTI had been negligent in fulfilling its regulatory function. The PCA, Anthony Barrowclough, joined the claims together into one action and found that there had been 'significant maladministration' on five counts and that the DTI was liable for compensation. The Secretary of State at the DTI, Nicholas Ridley, refused to accept that there had been maladministration, saying: 'In the government's view, the department's handling of the case was within the acceptable range of standards reasonably to be expected of a regulator.' The PCA, however, was not willing to be disregarded and replied that: 'The grounds for questioning my findings have left me unconvinced.' In the end, the government paid £150 million compensation because of the 'exceptional circumstances' and in deference to the PCA. This compensation may not have been paid if pressure had not been applied by Conservative backbenchers whose constituents' were affected. It should be noted, however, that Barlow Clowes was just one of three high-profile cases to raise significant political issues since 1967. Most of the cases handled by the PCA concern accusations of relatively low-level managerial or administrative failure.

Adapted from Madgwick & Woodhouse 1995 and Pyper 1998.

Item C MPs and the redress of grievances

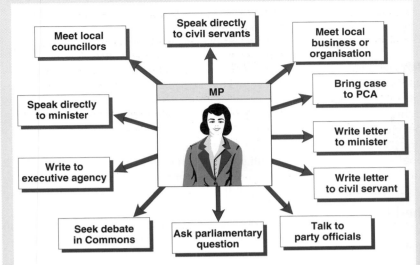

Item D The PCA

Questions

1. 'An energetic MP with a determination to fight for justice is all that a constituent with a grievance really requires.' Do you agree with this statement? Use Items A-D in your answer.
2. 'A toothless tiger'. Assess this judgement of the powers of the PCA using Items A, B and D.
3. Would you agree that the various methods for the redress of citizens' grievances in the UK are inaccessible and weak? Give reasons for your answer.

Part 4 Judicial reform

Key issues

1. What is a Bill of Rights?
2. What arguments have been used for and against the introduction of a Bill of Rights?
3. What other judicial reforms have been proposed and why?

4.1 A Bill of Rights

What is a Bill of Rights?

According to current British constitutional theory, there is no difference between constitutional laws and ordinary laws. Any law can be repealed or replaced at any time using normal parliamentary procedures. There is, in other words, an absence of any procedural protection or 'entrenchment' of constitutional legislation. In this respect, the UK differs from many other liberal democracies. In the USA and in most EU countries, for example, some basic rights are entrenched in the constitution. At present, this is not the case in the UK. British citizens have the freedom to act in any way which is not prevented by law. This is very different from having certain rights and liberties guaranteed by law.

A Bill of Rights, therefore, is usually a special law which sets out the basic rights and freedoms to be shared by every citizen. It is a special law because it is entrenched in the constitution and has a different status from other laws. It would be much more difficult for Parliament to repeal an entrenched Bill of Rights, for example, than an ordinary law. Clearly, if such a law was passed in the UK, it would have important constitutional implications.

It should be noted, however, that a Bill of Rights does not have to be an entrenched law. By passing the 1998 Human Rights Bill, Parliament in effect passed a Bill of Rights with the same status as any other law (see below).

Arguments in favour of an entrenched Bill of Rights

According to Grant (1997) there are seven main arguments in favour of an entrenched Bill of Rights:

1. The current political system ensures that, because of elective dictatorship, basic civil rights are under threat at all times. A Bill of Rights would end this threat by making it clear where rights and obligations lay.
2. A Bill of Rights would impose legal limits on a government's actions (at present they are only limited by convention).
3. The rule of law demands a clear and

enforceable statement of citizens' rights and duties. A Bill of Rights would provide this.

4. Without a Bill of Rights, it is often necessary to take cases to the European Court of Human Rights, but this is costly and slow. A Bill of Rights would provide the mechanism to gain redress if rights were violated.

5. Assuming a Bill of Rights was entrenched, it would not be easy for Parliament to pass laws contrary to it.

6. A Bill of Rights has educational value.

7. A Bill of Rights works well in other countries.

Arguments against an entrenched Bill of Rights

Philip Norton sums up the arguments against an entrenched Bill of Rights as follows:

'A judicially enforceable Bill of Rights, by which I mean a Bill of Rights enjoying some degree of entrenchment, is undesirable, unnecessary, unachievable, and - even if it were achievable - offers the unattainable.' (Norton 1993, p.149)

He argues that an entrenched Bill of Rights is undesirable for two main reasons. First, a Bill of Rights would inevitably reflect the prevailing values of the time. As a result, it would become dated. Because of its entrenchment, it would be difficult to modify the Bill without a major constitutional upheaval. And second, since judges would be called upon to decide if the Bill of Rights had been infringed in individual cases, judges would be forced to take on a much more overtly political role than is the case at present. Political decisions (he argues) should rest with Parliament not with the judiciary. Another way of putting this is to claim that an entrenched Bill of Rights is dangerous because it would undermine parliamentary sovereignty, currently the main source of the British constitution.

Other arguments against

Opponents of an entrenched Bill of Rights also use the following arguments:

- an entrenched Bill of Rights is inappropriate given the organic growth of the UK's flexible constitution
- there are problems about which rights to entrench in a Bill of Rights
- it is not clear how entrenched a Bill of Rights should be
- many existing laws would conflict with a Bill of Rights
- all governments are reluctant to put limits on their power
- left-wingers are suspicious of a Bill of Rights which might entrench right-wing principles (such as property rights) and

vice versa

- the judges might not interpret and enforce a Bill of Rights in a liberal and progressive way
- every Bill of Rights has a qualifying clause allowing for the restriction of rights and some are worthless as a result
- rights are adequately protected already.
- good methods for redress already exist. (Grant 1997, pp.100-01)

In addition, there are two further arguments. First, the adoption of an entrenched Bill of Rights might lead to endless litigation which could clog up the courts for years on end. And second, the introduction of an entrenched Bill of Rights would upset the balance of the British constitution by introducing an unfamiliar (entrenched) element. Whilst some might hope that this would lead to full-scale constitutional reform, others oppose an entrenched Bill of Rights on the grounds that it would lead to full-scale constitutional reform.

New Labour and a Bill of Rights

The Labour Party's 1997 election manifesto contained the following pledge:

'Citizens should have statutory rights to enforce their human rights in UK courts. We will by statute incorporate the European Convention on Human Rights into UK law to bring these rights home and allow our people access to them in their national courts. The incorporation of the European Convention will establish a floor, not a ceiling, for human rights. Parliament will remain free to enhance these rights, for example by a Freedom of Information Act.' (Labour 1997, p.35)

Once the Labour government began to frame legislation after winning the election, two main questions arose. The first question concerned whether the new Bill was to be entrenched. The answer that emerged was that it would not - it would have the same status as any other Act of Parliament. The second question concerned the powers the courts would have if a piece of legislation was found to contravene the convention. There were three options:

- allow the courts to strike down the offending legislation
- oblige Parliament to re-examine any legislation which the courts judged to contravene the convention
- allow the courts to issue a ruling, but do not oblige Parliament to re-examine the offending legislation.

It was the third option which was incorporated into the 1998 Human Rights Bill (the other two options were considered to be too radical and to place too much power in the hands of the judiciary).

The 1998 Human Rights Bill

The 1998 Human Rights Bill proposed the measures outlined in Box 17.1.

Box 17.1 The 1998 Human Rights Bill

The 1998 Human Rights Bill included the following provisions:

1. The European Convention on Human Rights should be incorporated into British law.
2. The higher courts should acquire the right to declare any Act of Parliament incompatible with the convention.
3. A fast track to legislation should be made available when a government department wishes to amend legislation judged to be incompatible with the convention.
4. Until legislation is amended by Parliament, it should remain in force, even if it is judged to be incompatible with the convention.
5. The courts should be able to offer 'remedy', including financial compensation, to those affected by legislation judged to be incompatible with the convention.
6. All ministers tabling Bills should declare that, to the best of their knowledge, their proposals are compatible with the convention.

The Human Rights Bill was given royal assent in November 1998. The provisions of the Act come into effect in 2000 (the delay was built in to ensure that there was sufficient time to allow magistrates and judges to undergo a training programme).

4.2 Other proposed judicial reforms

A Department of justice

At the top of the judicial system, one proposal is to replace the Lord Chancellor's Department with a Department of Justice. This has been suggested because, although Lord Chancellor is one of the most powerful positions in the British government, at present it is also one of the least accountable. The Lord Chancellor is not elected, for example, and is not accountable to any committee in the House of Commons. Labour MP Graham Allen suggests that:

> 'A Department of Justice should be considered in place of the Lord Chancellor's Department, with a Legal Affairs Select Committee through which it would be answerable to Parliament in the same way as every other government department - enabling effective democratic scrutiny of British legal policy for the very first time.' (Allen 1993, p.2)

Allen suggests that the new department be headed by a Secretary of State for Justice, appointed in the same way as any other member of the Cabinet. Allen also notes that the Secretary of State for Health does not have to be a doctor and so there is no reason why the minister responsible for the administration of the law should be a lawyer.

A Supreme Court

A second proposal is to move the court of final appeal from the House of Lords to a new Supreme Court whose members would be selected by an independent commission. There are two main arguments in favour of this. First, Law Lords are selected by the Lord Chancellor and tend to be drawn from an extremely narrow section of society. Judges chosen by an independent commission would be better able to make impartial decisions. And second, the setting up of a Supreme Court separate from the House of Lords would strengthen the separation of the powers and provide a new and potentially powerful safeguard for citizens' rights.

The election of judges

A third proposal is that judges should be elected. This, it is argued, would ensure that a range of people from wider backgrounds would be encouraged to enter the legal profession. In addition, the need to secure election would make judges more responsive to public opinion and less isolated from mainstream society. Such changes would also inject an element of public choice into a key area of the UK's constitutional arrangements. On the other hand, the introduction of elections might encourage judges to make decisions which were popular rather than just. Also, the insecurity of elected office might deter some people from seeking election. An alternative to outright election is to set up an open judicial commission which contains lay as well as professional representatives. This commission would be responsible for the appointment of judges. Judges would then retain their position unless they made gross errors of judgement.

Reducing the costs of legal action

Calls for reform not only concern the top levels of the judicial system. A major problem with the British judicial system is its cost. Solicitors are expensive to hire and, in most court cases, it is necessary to hire a barrister (who is more expensive to hire than a solicitor). The system is such that legal action is generally only a realistic option for the very rich, big organisations or those on legal aid (legal aid is granted to people who cannot afford to pay their legal fees, but it is only granted to certain people for certain cases). Between 1991 and 1997, however, the cost of legal aid grew by 115% from £682 million to £1.47 billion, despite a 9% fall in the number of people helped. Concerns about cost have led to two main proposals:

- reforming the legal aid system
- removing barristers' monopoly in court.

In October 1997, the Lord Chancellor announced that legal aid would be removed from all civil claims for damages or money and, instead, these cases would be fought on a 'no win, no fee' basis. Then, in June 1998, the Lord Chancellor announced that barristers were to lose their monopoly on representing clients in the higher courts. Instead, salaried lawyers working for law firms and for the Crown Prosecution Service would be able to represent clients in court.

Main points - Part 4

- A Bill of Rights is usually a special, entrenched law which sets out the basic rights and freedoms to be shared by every citizen.
- The main arguments in favour of a Bill of Rights are that it would define and protect citizens' rights and impose legal limits on government action.
- The main arguments against a Bill of Rights are that it is difficult to know which rights to include, that it would give judges too much power and that

adequate protection already exists.
- By incorporating the European Convention on Human Rights into UK law, the Labour government introduced a Bill of Rights, but it is not entrenched.
- Other proposed judicial reforms include a Justice Department, a Supreme Court, the election of judges, cutting legal aid and ending barristers' monopoly in the courts.

Activity 17.6 *Judicial reform*

Item A *Ten ways to reform the legal system*

1. Replace the adversarial system which encourages artificial competition between lawyers (judges act as referees) with an inquisitorial system. Judges would lead the court in a quest for truth (as in the French legal system).

10. Provide computer-based systems in libraries and advice centres for self-diagnosis of legal problems.

9. Make it easier for cases to be brought by groups of people with a common cause.

8. Create a group of para-legal advisors who would provide cheap advice, leaving court action to fully qualified lawyers.

JUDICIAL REFORM

2. End the division between solicitors and barristers.

3. Abolish wigs, gowns and the rank of Queen's Counsel.•

4. Create a specialist track for becoming a judge (a system used in Germany). Young lawyers would choose specialist training courses instead of becoming solicitors or barristers.

5. Draw up league tables assessing judges' performances. Indicators might include the speed of making judgements and skills in managing the courts.

7. Deal with more petty offences out of court - by on-the-spot fines except where people plead 'not-guilty'.

6. Take away more cases from the courts and place in arbitration.

* Those barristers whose work meets with the approval of the Lord Chancellor may be promoted to the rank of Queen's Counsel (QC). This is an honorary title, but it ensures that QCs are able to charge much higher fees than other barristers.

Item B *The 1998 Human Rights Act*

The Human Rights Act could bring about a dramatic constitutional and cultural change because, for the first time, the courts will be responsible for protecting citizens against infringements of their rights by any public authority, even the government itself. Success, however, depends to a large extent on funding. Yet, there is little prospect of adequate funding since the Bill makes no special provision for legal aid in human rights cases. Legal aid will be available for some criminal cases, but, under current rules, legal aid for civil cases will be means tested and only granted if there is a greater than 75% probability of success. As a result, it will simply not be granted in cases which seek to break new ground. Further, the change to 'no win, no fee' agreements will mean that most cases are not taken up because there will be no damages or costs to make them worthwhile. A major problem is that claims can only be made by a 'victim'. This is a narrower test than that used in judicial review proceedings where complaints can be brought by anyone with a 'sufficient interest'. That allows expert bodies to bring proceedings that raise issues of general importance even when no individual is willing to accept the strain of being the complainant (or is bought off by a settlement). One solution would be a Human Rights Commission which would bring cases affecting groups. The commission could also undertake much needed educational programmes - so far, no money has been set aside to train the public or public authorities about their new rights and responsibilities.

Adapted from the *Times*, 21 April 1998.

Item C *The European Convention on Human Rights*

The European Convention on Human Rights

Article 2   Right to life.
Article 3   Freedom from torture or inhuman or degrading treatment or punishment.
Article 4   Freedom from slavery or forced labour.
Article 5   Right to liberty and security of person.
Article 6   Right to a fair trial by an impartial tribunal.
Article 7   Freedom from retroactive criminal laws.
Article 8   Right to respect for private and family life, home and correspondence.
Article 9   Freedom of thought, conscience and religion.
Article 10   Freedom of expression.
Article 11   Freedom of peaceful assembly and association, including the right to join a trade union.
Article 12   Right to marry and found a family.
Article 13   Right to an effective remedy before a national authority.
Article 14   Freedom from discrimination.

Protocol 1
Article 1   Right to peaceful enjoyment of possessions.
Article 2   Right to education; and to education in conformity with religious and philosophical convictions.
Article 3   Right to take part in free elections by secret ballot.

Protocol 4
Article 1   Freedom from imprisonment for debt.
Article 2   Freedom of movement of persons.
Article 3   Right to enter and stay in one's country.
Article 4   Freedom from collective expulsion.

Examples of Cases brought by UK citizens and upheld by the European Court of Human Rights

- Illegal imprisonment of poll tax non-payers.
- Corporal punishment in state schools.
- Press censorship (eg in the *Sunday Times* thalidomide drug story and the '*Spycatcher*' cases).
- Phone tapping by government agencies.
- Retrospective seizure of assets of alleged criminals.
- Prisoners' conditions and treatment in Britain and torture of prisoners in Northern Ireland.
- Discrimination against homosexuals in Northern Ireland.
- Birching of criminal offenders in the Isle of Man.
- Discrimination against women, ethnic minorities and immigrants.
- The rights of workers against closed shops.
- Protection of secrecy of journalists' sources.
- The right to life, in the case of the shooting in 1988 of three unarmed IRA members by the SAS in Gibraltar.

Questions

1. a) Is there any need to reform the judicial system? Explain your answer
   b) Which (if any) of the reforms in Item A should be adopted? Give reasons for your answer.
2. Judging from Items B and C, what impact is the incorporation of the European Convention on Human Rights into UK law likely to have?
3. 'A flawed piece of legislation'. Give arguments for and against this view of the 1998 Human Rights Act. Use Items B and C in your answer.

References

Adams & Pyper (1997) Adams, J. & Pyper, R., 'Whatever happened to the Scott Inquiry?', *Talking Politics*, Vol.9.3, Spring 1997.

Allen (1993) Allen, G., 'Reform of the judiciary', *Labour and the Constitution*, Issue No.2, consultation paper produced by Graham Allen MP, March 1993.

Davis (1995) Davis, H., 'The judiciary' in *Lancaster (1995)*.

De Smith & Brazier (1989) De Smith, S. & Brazier, R., *Constitutional and Administrative Law* (6th edn), Penguin, 1989.

Donald (1996) Donald, J., 'The citizen and the man about town' in Hall & Dugay (1996).

Grant (1997) Grant, M., 'Citizenship' in *Lancaster* (1997).

Griffith (1991) Griffith, J.A.G., *The Politics of the Judiciary*, Fontana, 1991.

Hall & Dugay (1996) Hall, S. & Dugay, P. (eds), *Questions of Cultural Identity*, Sage, 1996.

Heywood (1997) Heywood, A., *Politics*, Macmillian, 1997.

Labour (1997) *New Labour - Because Britain Deserves Better*, Labour Party manifesto, Labour Party, 1997.

Lancaster (1995) Lancaster, S. (ed.), *Developments in Politics*, Vol.6, Causeway Press, 1995.

Lancaster (1997) Lancaster, S. (ed.), *Developments in Politics*, Vol.8, Causeway Press, 1997.

LCD (1986) *Judicial Appointments*, Lord Chancellor's Department, 1986.

Madgwick & Woodhouse (1995) Madgwick, P. & Woodhouse, D., *The Law and Politics of the Constitution*, Harvester Wheatsheaf, 1995.

McInnes (1996) McInnes, P., 'Citizenship', *Politics Review*, Vol. 5.3, February 1996.

Norton (1993) Norton, P., 'The case against a Bill of Rights', *Talking Politics*, Vol.5.3, Summer 1993.

Oliver (1993) Oliver, D., 'Citizenship in the 1990s', *Politics Review*, Vol.3, No.1, September 1993.

Pilger (1996) Pilger, J., 'Getting off Scott free', *New Statesman*, 23 February 1996.

Pyper (1998) Pyper, R., 'Redress of grievances', *Politics Review*, Vol.7.3, February 1998.

SOID (1993) Scottish Office Information Directorate, *Scottish Courts (factsheet 9)*, The Scottish Office, October 1993.

Thompson (1993) Thompson, K., 'The role of the ombudsmen', *Talking Politics*, Vol.1, Autumn 1993.

18 Law and order

Introduction

From *Dixon of Dock Green*, through *The Sweeny* and *Inspector Morse*, to *The Bill*, British TV audiences have shown a fascination with the work of the police force. But, this fascination is not confined to fiction. Opinion polls have shown time and again that most people put the issue of law and order high on their political agenda. A majority supports the allocation of greater resources to the police force in the hope that this will lead to the conviction of more offenders. Most people also support harsher regimes for those convicted of crime. Generally, there has been greater concern with law and order than with our rights and liberties. But, the maintenance of a free society involves the preservation of a precarious balance between the demands for individual freedom and the limits placed upon that freedom by the rule of law and the powers given to the forces responsible for enforcing that law.

This chapter examines the reasons why order - and the law to enforce it - are necessary in society. It considers the basis upon which law and order are either accepted or imposed and the major controversies which surround the role of the police and other law enforcement agencies in modern Britain. These are crucial issues since they impinge upon every aspect of our lives and upon our conception of the society in which we live.

Chapter summary

Part 1 describes the controversy surrounding the breakdown of legitimacy in Britain. It includes a section on the breakdown of order and recent developments in Northern Ireland.

Part 2 looks at the organisation of the police force. What are the recent trends in policing? To whom are the police accountable?

Part 3 investigates the role of other law enforcement agencies - the armed forces and the security services.

Part 4 discusses the policies of the main political parties on law and order.

Part 1 Law and order in Britain since 1945

Key issues

1. What is legitimacy?
2. What are the arguments for and against the view that Britain has experienced a decline in legitimacy since 1945?
3. How does the disorder in Northern Ireland relate to this debate?

1.1 Legitimacy and the law

The functions of the law

The law and the institutions which enforce it are intended to fulfil two functions. The first is to arbitrate between people who are in dispute and to enforce the outcome. An example of this was the libel action brought by the athlete Linford Christie against the journalist John McVicar in June 1998. In September 1995, McVicar had written an article in the magazine *Spiked* which suggested that Christie had taken anabolic steroids. Christie vehemently denied ever taking drugs to enhance his performance and sued McVicar and the magazine's printers and distributors for libel. The court's function was to decide which of the two sides was telling the truth. In this case, the jury found by a majority of ten to two that McVicar had libelled Christie and his allegations were untrue. The court then awarded Christie £42,000 in damages (*Guardian*, 4 July 1998).

The second function of the law is to lay down and to enforce the rules by which all members of a particular society are expected to abide. At the heart of this second function lies a paradox. So long as people accept that the law, the law makers and the law enforcers are legitimate, the need to enforce the law rarely arises. If a person considers that a law is fair (legitimate) then that person is unlikely to break the law. It is only when the legitimacy of the law and the institutions which make and enforce it come into question that people actually break the law. So, the paradox is this: only when the law fails does the need to enforce it arise.

In most circumstances, only a small proportion of the population breaks the law. As a result, the forces of law and order are able to catch and prosecute transgressors - by this means punishing actual, and deterring potential, law breakers. But, if the legitimacy of the law, the law makers and the law enforcers is called into question by a large proportion of the population, the result is an ever-increasing willingness to break the law and to tolerate those engaged in so doing.

1.2 A breakdown of legitimacy in Britain since 1945?

A decline in legitimacy?

Looking at the post-war period in Western Europe, some writers have noted trends and events which could signify a decline in the legitimacy of the regimes which govern these countries. Indeed, such has been the depth and breadth of this apparent decline that some writers have been led to discuss a 'legitimation crisis' (for example, Habermas 1973).

Habermas' view

When examining developments in modern industrial societies, Habermas uses a definition of legitimation which goes beyond the simple idea that legitimation means a willing acceptance of the authority of those who rule. This passive definition must be rejected, he argues. It should be replaced with a more active definition. Legitimacy should be seen as the means by which a justification is provided for a whole range of social actions, institutions and arrangements.

Take, for example, relations between men and women. The traditional arrangement was that men were breadwinners whilst women looked after the home. For many years, the legitimacy of this traditional relationship was provided by reference to the work of God or nature. People justified the role of women by arguing either that it was God's will that they should stay at home or that, by nature, women were weaker than men and, therefore, not suited to undertake the work done by men. It was, in other words, by exploiting people's religious sensibilities and by using a pseudo-scientific rationale that legitimacy for the traditional arrangement was secured.

These arguments, however, no longer have popular appeal. Britain is a predominantly secular society. Most women now work. Although some people still subscribe to the traditional view that a woman's place is in the home, very many do not. The traditional justification has collapsed. The idea, therefore, lacks legitimacy.

Habermas argues that when traditional justifications collapse, people turn to the government to provide solutions to the difficulties caused by the collapse. But, in general, governments have failed to provide long-term solutions. This gives the impression that

governments are ineffective or out of touch with the wishes of the people. Indeed, it seems that the political system itself is inadequate. The result is a legitimation crisis. Once governments lack legitimacy, this lack of legitimacy threatens the stability of the political system.

Arguments in support of Habermas' theory

Writers sympathetic to Habermas' thesis can point to a number of examples in the political, economic and social sphere which demonstrate the way in which Western European governments' failure to solve problems has undermined the legitimacy of the political system.

Student disturbances in 1968-9

Perhaps the most obvious example is the student disturbances of 1968-69. Especially in France, but also in Britain, students directly challenged the authority of the government and, by so doing, attempted to undermine its legitimacy. Although the students' movement failed to achieve its political goals (not least because of the use of force by the government), social change followed in its wake. The growing popularity of anti-Establishment values and the development of a youth subculture since the 1960s could be interpreted as a fundamental, if temporary, breakdown in legitimacy.

Civil disobedience since 1970

Further evidence in support of Habermas' theory might be derived from the outbreaks of civil disobedience in Britain which have happened periodically since 1970. Opposition to the government's Industrial Relations Act in 1971 and 1974, the inner city riots which took place in the early 1980s and the mass campaign against the poll tax between 1988 and 1990 all indicate a breakdown in legitimacy. It is significant that both the Industrial Relations Act and the poll tax were eventually abolished. In both cases, the government realised that their unpopularity was undermining the legitimacy of the government as a whole.

A rise in crime since 1945

In addition to the specific examples mentioned above, it could be argued that a rise in crime in Britain since 1945 suggests a more general collapse of legitimacy. In 1951, there was just one notifiable criminal offence per hundred people in England and Wales. This had risen to two by 1961, to six by 1981 and to ten by 1991 (it was just under ten in 1996). Although these figures may reflect changing police procedures or a greater willingness to report crimes, it does seem that there has also been a growing willingness to break the law. As was argued above, people only break the law when that law lacks legitimacy. A rise in crime, therefore, suggests a breakdown in legitimacy.

Arguments against a legitimation crisis

The belief that a legitimation crisis exists is based upon two fundamental claims. The first claim is that, at some point since 1945, there has been a significant collapse in people's willingness to give loyal support to the law and to those who make and enforce it. The second claim is that this represents, both in scale and severity, a new political and social development. Both these claims can be challenged.

When exactly did legitimacy break down (if at all)?

A problem with the first claim is that of identifying precisely when the crisis point occurred. Different authors suggest different times - immediately after the Second World War, in the late 1960s, in the late 1970s or in the early 1980s (Leys 1983). It is difficult to talk about a crisis when the crisis point cannot be identified with any accuracy.

Also, the very idea that a collapse in legitimacy has taken place is open to question. It has been argued, for example, that the student disturbances in 1968-69 were short-lived, lacked support from large sections of the population and, in reality, posed no genuine threat to the political system (Childs 1992). Similarly, it has been argued that, although the Industrial Relations Act and poll tax did produce a great deal of opposition, this was not a sign of a general collapse in legitimacy. Rather, these protests were examples of the successful operation of the democratic political system. Besides, it is argued, the rising crime rates do not mean there is a crisis. The rise has been gradual and the explanation for this is more complex than the legitimacy theory would allow.

Has behaviour really changed since 1945?

The trouble with the second claim is that it assumes a significant change in behaviour since 1945. But, whatever indicator is chosen, problems of at least comparable severity to those experienced in post-war Britain can be found much earlier in British history. For example, some supporters of the legitimation crisis theory argue that the inner city riots in the early 1980s are evidence of a breakdown of legitimacy. But, as John Benyon points out, the Gordon riots of 1780 and the Captain Swing outbreak of 1830-31 are two of many examples of serious law breaking and civil unrest on a scale comparable with the modern riots. Yet, these disturbances took place over 100 years ago (Benyon 1986, pp.3-4).

Conclusion

Although it is difficult to find incontrovertible evidence that a legitimation crisis has arisen since 1945, it is clear that at least some sections of society have little confidence in the law and those who enforce it. Rising crime figures and sporadic occurrences of civil unrest produce a climate in which the public and the media express concern about the balance between freedom and order in society. It is this concern which fuels much of the current debate on law and order.

Main points - Sections 1.1-1.2

- **The law and the institutions which enforce them have two functions: (1) to arbitrate between people who are in dispute and resolve their conflicts; and (2) to enforce the rules which all members of society are expected to obey.**
- **Habermas argues that rising crime, public disorder and the inability of governments to tackle major social problems are evidence of a crisis of legitimacy.**
- **Opponents of Habermas' theory argue that it is impossible to find a point at which the supposed crisis began and that, anyway, evidence of the development of a crisis is hard to find.**
- **Even if there is not a crisis of legitimacy, there is evidence that at least some sections of society have little confidence in the law and those who enforce it.**

Activity 18.1 *A breakdown in legitimacy?*

Item A *The number of offences committed per 100 people, 1951-96*

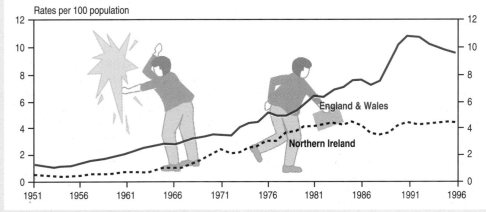

This graph shows the number of offences committed per 100 of the population between the years 1951 and 1996.

Adapted from Social Trends 1994 and 1998

Item B *The 1996 British Crime Survey*

(1) Number of recorded and unrecorded serious crimes, including burglaries with loss, vehicle thefts, wounding and robbery

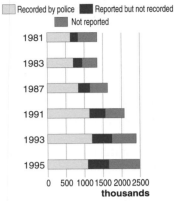

(2) Percentage of people who feel unsafe when out alone at night

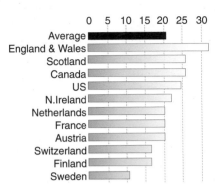

(3) Percentage of British people by gender and age feeling unsafe when out alone at night

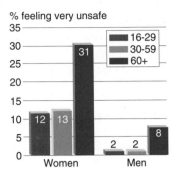

The 1996 British Crime Survey (BCS) involves interviews with nearly 16,500 adults about their experiences as victims of crimes. The BCS estimates a total of just over 19 million crimes in 1995, of which just 41% were reported to the police. Even looking at serious crime, it is clear that in 1995 less than half this crime was recorded by the police, though 67% was reported to them (see Figure 1 above). In fact, since 1981, the number of serious crimes brought to police attention has fallen, particularly in 1995. The BCS also covers the issue of fear of crime, which is almost as debilitating for some groups as crime itself. Figure 2 above shows that, in an international study, the biggest proportion of people who feel unsafe when they are out alone at night is found in England and Wales. Figure 3 confirms that older women tend to be most afraid and that younger men (who are most likely to end up in a violent or criminal incident on the street) are least likely to admit fear. The BCS also finds that fear of crime is highest in areas where the risk of victimisation is greatest. The survey found that 11% of all females said that they never went out after dark (5% of males). Of these, 31% said they always stayed in at night specifically because of fear of crime. In inner city areas, 17% of women over 60 always stayed at home because of crime fears. But, fewer women in 1996 felt insecure out on their local streets after dark than in 1982 when the first survey was conducted. Then, 21% felt 'very unsafe'. Now the figure is 18%.

Adapted from Williams 1998.

Item C *Measuring crime*

Criminal Statistics are not straightforward tabulations of the number of crimes committed in the community. They are the outcome of a series of human decisions. Between an event which might be defined as a 'crime' and a Home Office statistic which defines it as a crime, there is a complicated process of decision making. By far the majority of criminal events do not end up in the official statistics. This is because the path which leads to the official records is littered with holes through which the offence might fall. The most obvious point at which this can happen is the initial identification of the event. The crime may not be observed by anybody except the offender. Small-scale pilfering, for example, may not come to anyone's attention. There are, however, other junctures at which the offence may be lost from official records. Most criminologists agree that there is a huge 'dark figure' of crime which represents crimes committed but not officially recorded. Only a certain percentage of total crimes recorded by the police become part of the Home Office Annual Criminal Statistics. The 1992 British Crime Survey, for example, estimated that the number of crimes committed exceeded the numbers recorded by the police as follows: twice as many burglaries, three times as many thefts from vehicles, four times as many woundings, seven times as many acts of vandalism and eight times as many robberies and thefts from the person.

Adapted from Brearley 1996.

Item D *Anti-poll tax demonstration (1)*

The trouble began in Whitehall. The police didn't know what they were doing. Their horses were galloping around and the foot police looked just as likely to get trampled as we were. Then I saw what to me was a wonderful sight. Union Jacks from in front of an MOD building were pulled down and set alight. The crowd was jubilant at the sight of the Union Jack burning by Downing Street. We walked on to Trafalgar Square and joined the crowd. Some time later the police began to charge the crowd. People began to panic and this led to fights with the police. We cheered every time a blood-spattered policeman was helped to safety. Bigger, better missiles began to fly. The crowd was delirious, maniacal smiles all round. Suddenly I found a rock in my hand and hurled it at the police line. Power surged through me. I was beyond any law the police could impose. To dismiss this riot as politically inspired or as 'criminal' misses the point by a mile. While it's seen as such the police won't come to terms with the fact they're distrusted. It wasn't even about the poll tax. It was a young person's riot, a spontaneous outburst. I did what I did because I could.

Adapted from *New Statesman and Society*, 6 April 1990.

1.3 Northern Ireland

The breakdown of legitimacy

The beginning of the 'Troubles'

When legitimacy breaks down completely, very often the result is violent conflict. This is what happened in Northern Ireland in the late 1960s. The breakdown in legitimacy in Northern Ireland occurred after the growth of the Civil Rights movement in 1968. This movement aimed to win civil rights for Catholics by mass demonstration. Civil Rights marches were non-violent, but Protestants saw them as a challenge to their dominance. The result was a series of violent clashes. In July and August 1969, following the annual Orange parades, riots broke out. These riots culminated in the 'Battle of the Bogside'. When police tried to take control of the Bogside (a Catholic area in Londonderry) Catholics set up barricades and fought them off declaring the area 'Free Derry'. Since the police were unable to keep order, the British government decided to send in troops. By the end of 1969, 6,000 British troops had been sent to Northern Ireland. This figure grew to 7,500 in 1970 and 16,827 by 1972.

The decision to send in troops was an admission that legitimacy had collapsed. It indicated that normal security measures were no longer sufficient to keep the peace. This collapse in legitimacy was confirmed in 1972 when the Northern Irish government (based in Stormont castle) was suspended and direct rule from Britain began.

What a breakdown of legitimacy means

Between 1969 and July 1997 (when the IRA restored the ceasefire that had first been announced in 1994), a violent conflict was fought between loyalist paramilitary groups (whose aim was to ensure that Northern Ireland remained part of Britain and that Protestant dominance survived) and republican paramilitary groups (whose basic aim was a united Ireland). Although the majority of people in Northern Ireland did not support the means used by the paramilitary groups, the community was (and remains) divided along religious, sectarian and class lines. These divisions ensured that it was very difficult to draw up a set of constitutional arrangements which could be accepted as legitimate by all sections of the community.

An example of the sort of dilemma which faced those who tried to restore legitimacy is suggested by a survey carried out in 1978. This found that 69% of Catholics regarded their national identity as Irish whilst 67% of Protestants regarded themselves as British. The findings in this survey help to explain why it was so hard to find an acceptable political settlement. To many Catholics, British involvement in Northern Irish affairs was illegitimate. On the other hand, to many Protestants, Irish involvement in Northern Irish affairs was equally illegitimate.

Class also played a crucial role. Throughout the period 1969-97, Protestants were more than twice as likely to fall into Class 1 of the Registrar General's classification (the richest class) than Catholics. Catholics were nearly twice as likely to fall into Class 5. In 1984, Catholics were twice as likely to be unemployed than Protestants. So, economic grievances and insecurities were enmeshed with religious and national differences. This produced a climate in which the creation of a legitimate law-making authority is difficult.

The security forces in Northern Ireland

The job of the security forces in Northern Ireland, as elsewhere, is to ensure that peace is maintained, that people obey the law and that people who break the law are caught and punished. The lack of legitimacy between 1969 and 1997, however, meant that a greater degree of coercion was necessary in Northern Ireland than in a state where consent to the law is high. But, what level of coercion was acceptable? The answer to this question depended on two main factors. First, it depended on a person's outlook. As noted above, Protestants and Catholics living in Northern Ireland had, in general, very different outlooks. As a result, a Protestant would be likely to answer the question in a very different way from a Catholic. And second, the law which sanctioned the use of force by the security forces was regarded as illegitimate by many people. This meant that acceptability of the use of force was lower. As a result, if the security forces used too much coercion they ran the risk of creating further polarisation in the community.

The Royal Ulster Constabulary (RUC)

The RUC was set up in 1922 when Ireland was partitioned. In recognition of the difficulties that were likely to arise in policing the new state, the Northern Irish government encouraged both Catholics and Protestants to join the new organisation. But, because many Catholics refused to accept partition, they were unwilling to do so. The result was a police force composed overwhelmingly of Protestants. As late as 1969, the Hunt committee found that only 11% of the RUC's membership was Catholic (Farrell 1976).

The lack of Catholic recruits meant that the RUC encountered great difficulty in appearing to be an impartial force - particularly after the riots broke out in 1969. By then, the RUC was an organisation which lacked legitimacy with a significant minority of the population (the Catholics). Not only that, but the laws it tried to enforce also lacked legitimacy. For example the RUC was required to enforce regulations banning marches and demonstrations. If these took place, members of the RUC were ordered to disperse them as swiftly as possible and to detain the leaders. Often this meant the use of excessive force. The result was a vicious circle. The RUC used force to disperse peaceful demonstrators. This alienated and enraged the demonstrators who felt that they had the right to march. Because the demonstrators were alienated and angry, they became more inclined to break the law and had less respect for the RUC. So, the actions of the RUC had the opposite effect to that which was intended - they brought an escalation of violence and a speedier breakdown of order.

Internment

The security problems in Northern Ireland led, in 1971, to the introduction of internment - a system of detention without trial. Such a practice contradicts a central principle of liberal democracy, namely that no person should be imprisoned without due process of the law. It was argued, however, that this contravention of the usual conventions of British justice was acceptable as a means of restoring order because it would remove the IRA leaders from circulation.

This decision was flawed in two ways. First, internment was perceived by the Catholic population as blatant victimisation. No paramilitary loyalists were arrested and nor were any of their sympathisers. Second, it was ineffective. Most IRA leaders escaped from Northern Ireland before they could be detained.

The plan backfired. Instead of restoring order, internment served to undermine further the legitimacy of the legal system, the law makers and the law enforcers. The immediate consequence was the outbreak of riots. In the four days after internees were first detained, 22 people died in the rioting.

In the longer term, internment fuelled anger against the security forces and, therefore, hastened the collapse, rather than the restoration, of legitimacy. After the internees were released they made allegations that they had been beaten and even tortured by the security forces. These allegations led to the British government being taken to the European Court of Human Rights in Strasbourg and being found guilty of 'inhuman and degrading treatment'. The security forces had subjected some internees to an in-depth interrogation method known as 'sensory deprivation'. The aim was to cut off outside stimuli to produce a temporary episode of insanity in which the prisoner was responsive to questioning. To achieve this, prisoners were hooded, kept in isolation and put in a fixed position against a wall. Any movement resulted in a beating from the guards. Prisoners were deprived of sleep and food and subjected to loud and constant background noise. This treatment lasted for up to seven days.

Diplock Courts

If internment was one serious consequence of the absence of legitimate law-making and enforcing bodies, the loss of trial by jury in cases involving suspected terrorist violence was another.

Northern Ireland was such a sharply divided society in the early 1970s that it was extremely difficult to find impartial jurors. Also, it was very difficult to persuade witnesses to testify in open court, for fear of reprisals. As a result, Lord Diplock was asked to report on judicial arrangements in Northern Ireland and to make proposals for change, if necessary. The Diplock Commission published its report in 1972. Its key recommendations were:

- trial by jury should be suspended and cases involving terrorist violence be tried by a judge alone
- the period of time suspects could be held on remand should be extended.

Both recommendations were implemented.

Diplock Courts, however, were bitterly criticised on two grounds. First, it was argued that judges could not be impartial - their background and beliefs would preclude the suspect from having a fair trial. And second, convictions were often obtained on the basis of confessions extracted after prolonged interrogation. These confessions, it was argued, were made under duress and, therefore, should not have been admissible as evidence. Like internment, the introduction of Diplock Courts did nothing to rebuild legitimacy in Northern Ireland. Diplock Courts were abolished in 1975.

Criminalisation

The way in which trials were conducted and the methods used by the RUC in interrogation gave weight to the argument that those convicted of 'terrorist' offences were somehow different from ordinary criminals. At first, such prisoners were given

Special Category status as political prisoners. This meant they had the right to wear their own clothes, to be excused prison work, to be segregated from other prisoners, to have free association with their colleagues and to receive unlimited mail.

The granting of special status, however, drew attention to the abnormal political conditions existing in Northern Ireland. In 1975, therefore, the Labour government introduced a policy which has continued ever since - the policy of **criminalisation**. The idea behind this was to portray the violence in Northern Ireland as an extreme crime wave. Those who took part in 'terrorist' activity were, therefore, no different from any other group of organised criminals.

The institutional framework for the policy of criminalisation was set up in 1975 when internment was ended and Diplock Courts were abolished. It was then announced that, from March 1976, Special Category status was to end. Anyone convicted of a terrorist offence would be considered as a common criminal and would not be granted any special privileges. Since most prisoners who had been granted Special Category status were members of the IRA, it is no surprise that the IRA attempted to resist this measure.

The first prisoner to be denied political status was Ciaran Nugent. He refused to wear a prison uniform and was left with only his blanket to cover him. Others followed his example. Since these prisoners had been deprived of their privileges and were not allowed out of their cells with their blankets, they were, in effect, in solitary confinement. When chamber pots were upset after scuffles with prison warders, the prisoners began to smear excrement on their walls. The 'blanket' protest, therefore, turned into the 'dirty' protest. Then, in October 1980, some of the prisoners went on hunger strike. By the time the hunger strikes finished, ten prisoners had died. But, a political solution was no nearer.

The Anglo-Irish Agreement

A further attempt to produce a negotiated settlement was initiated in 1985. The Anglo-Irish Agreement aimed to stimulate peace talks, but it failed to win over the the loyalist political parties, and paramilitaries on both sides. As a result, the violence continued.

Attempting to restore legitimacy 1991-98

The Anglo-Irish Agreement was suspended in 1991 to allow further talks to take place, but, ultimately, these also broke down. In 1993, however, pressure began to build for a new attempt to reconcile the interests of the two communities. John Hume, Leader of the SDLP, and Gerry Adams, Leader of Sinn Fein, reached an agreement which (although it was not actually published) was felt to provide the basis for a possible cessation of violence by the IRA.

The Hume-Adams agreement, together with an upsurge in both loyalist and IRA violence, prompted the British and Irish governments to negotiate what became known as the Downing Street Declaration in December 1993. This declaration (see also Chapter 4, Section 3.4) was an attempt to reconcile the conflicting interests of nationalists and loyalists. It was, in other words, an attempt to find peaceful means by which legitimate authority could be established in Northern Ireland.

The Downing Street Declaration was followed in August 1994 by an IRA ceasefire which, in turn, was followed by a loyalist ceasefire. At the beginning of 1995, British troops were removed from the streets of Northern Ireland during daytime (the beginning of a return to normality), and, in March 1995, the first British troops were withdrawn. When the British and Irish governments produced the 'Framework Document' (see Box 18.1) in February 1995, however, it was rejected out of hand by unionist politicians.

Further attempts to secure a lasting agreement in 1995 and 1996 stumbled over the question of when the paramilitary groups (on both the nationalist and

Box 18.1 The Framework Document

The document published by the British and Irish governments on 23 February 1995 contained the following main proposals:

- A single chamber Assembly of about 90 members elected by proportional representation.

- A charter to protect civil, political, social and cultural rights.

- An end to the Irish constitutional claim to the territory.

- Changes to British law to recognise the right of the people to decide their future.

- A cross-border body of elected representatives made up from the new Assembly and from the Irish Parliament.

- A parliamentary forum of representatives from North and South to hold wider discussions.

- Increased cooperation between London and Dublin through a standing Intergovernmental Conference.

- An elected panel of three people to act as advisers to the Assembly.

Adapted from the *Guardian*, 24 February 1995.

unionist sides) would begin to decommission their weapons. Also, due to defections and by-election defeats, John Major's government became increasingly reliant on the vote of Unionist MPs to secure a majority in the House of Commons. In return, the government was reluctant to press Unionists into making significant concessions. As the prospects for a restoration of legitimate government became increasingly remote, the IRA finally put an end to this round of the peace process by detonating a large bomb at Canary Wharf in London on 9 February, 1996. The failure to take advantage of the ceasefire made it very clear that, once lost, legitimacy is difficult to regain.

The Good Friday Peace Agreement, 1998

The election of a new British government on 1 May 1997 gave renewed impetus to the attempt to restore legitimacy in Northern Ireland. Perhaps surprisingly after 18 years in opposition, the Prime Minister, Tony Blair, and his Northern Ireland Secretary, Mo Mowlam, decided that securing an agreement over new constitutional arrangements in Northern Ireland was to be a priority. Blair began by travelling to Belfast on 17 May to reassure unionists that no 'sell-out' to the nationalist community was being planned. On 13 June, the conditions which would have to be fulfilled if Sinn Fein was to secure entry into all-party talks were announced and, on 4 July, Blair held talks with the Irish Prime Minister, Bertie Ahern. This injection of energy into the process paid off in the summer. On 19 July 1997, the IRA announced that it was to restore its ceasefire (the British government accepted that the restoration was genuine on 29 August) and, on 10 September, it formally renounced violence.

The all-party peace talks began on 15 September and, by the end of the month, Sinn Fein and the Unionists were sitting round the same negotiating table. Two historic meetings quickly followed. On 13 October, Tony Blair met Gerry Adams in Belfast (the first time a British Prime Minister had met a republican leader since 1921) and on 11 December, Gerry Adams went with a Sinn Fein delegation to Downing Street to hold talks with Tony Blair (the first time republican leaders had gone to Downing Street since 1921). Although a series of shootings threatened to derail the peace process during the last few days of 1997 and the first few months of 1998, the government managed to maintain dialogue and it succeeded in ensuring that neither the Protestant nor the Catholic extremists in the population returned to generalised violent conflict. Both the Ulster Democratic Party and

Sinn Fein were suspended from the talks following allegations that they had been involved in violent incidents, but both were allowed back into the talks. On 26 March, the talks assumed a new urgency when US Senator George Mitchell (who chaired the talks) set a 15 day deadline and, eventually, a deal was announced on Good Friday, 10 April 1998 - the 'Good Friday Peace Agreement'. This deal was put to the Northern Irish people in a referendum on 23 May 1998 with 71% of those who voted accepting the agreement.

Criminal Justice (Terrorism and Conspiracy) Bill, 1998

Following the Omagh bombing in August 1998 (29 people died after the explosion of a bomb planted by the 'Real IRA'), the government recalled Parliament from its summer recess in order to debate and pass Criminal Justice (Terrorism and Conspiracy) Bill. This Bill was then rushed through Parliament at the beginning of September 1998. Although the Bill was passed by a large majority in Parliament, it was criticised by some groups. In particular, the clause allowing a person to be convicted on the word of a senior police officer was criticised as an important erosion of liberty:

> '[The Bill] allows the word of a senior police officer to count as evidence of a suspect's membership of a proscribed organisation. If the officer is asked to substantiate his hunch, he can refuse, claiming that to reveal intelligence matters would damage national security. He can hide behind the dreaded Public Interest Immunity certificates, a tool of the state routinely abused for political ends. A suspect has lost further rights: he cannot remain silent to avoid self-incrimination and nor can he have a solicitor by his side. These are basic human rights, removed with barely a day's reflection by our elected representatives.' (*Guardian*, 3 September 1998)

Conclusion

The problems experienced in maintaining law and order in Northern Ireland clearly demonstrate the complex relationship between coercion and consent that exists in every society. Where a high level of consent exists, relatively little coercion is required to enforce the law. Once the level of consent breaks down, however, ever greater levels of coercion are often used. When consent to the political arrangements in a society falls to a very low level or collapses entirely, coercion is often seen as the only way of maintaining a basic level of social stability.

Main points - Section 1.3

- The violent conflict which raged in Northern Ireland between 1969 and 1997 is an example of a breakdown in legitimacy.
- The origins of the conflict lie in the divided nature of Northern Irish society. These divisions led to a series of violent clashes in 1969.
- The deep-rooted nature of these divisions then made it difficult for a deal to be struck that was acceptable to both sides.
- From the late 1960s, the security forces lost legitimacy. Experiments with internment and

Diplock courts only managed to intensify the crisis. The policy of criminalisation resulted in the 'blanket' protest, 'dirty' protest and the death of ten hunger strikers.
- Political initiatives failed to make any impact until the mid-1990s. The Downing Street Declaration paved the way to a ceasefire, but the process ran out of steam. The new Labour government revitalised the process which resulted in the Good Friday Peace Agreement.

Activity 18.2 Northern Ireland and legitimacy

Item A   *Deaths in Northern Ireland 1969-98*

Date	Total deaths	Date	Total deaths	Date	Total deaths
1969	13	1979	113	1989	62
1970	25	1980	76	1990	76
1971	174	1981	101	1991	94
1972	467	1982	97	1992	85
1973	250	1983	77	1993	84
1974	216	1984	64	1994[1]	62
1975	247	1985	54	1995	9
1976	297	1986	61	1996	15
1977	112	1987	93	1997[2]	22
1978	81	1988	93	1998[3]	44

(1) The IRA ceasefire began on 1 September 1994 and lasted until February 1996. There were 58 deaths between 1 Jan and 31 Aug 1994.
(2) The IRA renewed its ceasefire in July 1997.
(3) The Omagh bomb accounted for 29 of the deaths in 1998.

This table shows the number of people killed in Northern Ireland between 1969 and 1998.

Item C   *Re-establishing legitimacy (1)*

The people of Northern Ireland voted for the Good Friday Peace Agreement yesterday with 71% in favour. The result brought jubilation to the Yes camp and paved the way for the creation of an administration based on cross-community consensus and power-sharing. This was the most momentous poll since the division of Ireland in 1921 and the first time that unionists and nationalists voted with one accord. The 71% in favour suggests that a majority of unionists had endorsed the agreement, together with almost all nationalist voters. Tony Blair welcomed the result, saying: 'The people have said: we will resolve our differences not by the gun and the bomb, but by persuasion and democracy, in a climate of tolerance, peace and respect'. The Yes campaigners believe that the historic vote will draw a line under the division, violence and sectarianism of the past and lay the basis for a more harmonious and pluralistic society. The deal is not perfect. It will not simply dissolve the ancient problems. It will face many stiff challenges. But, it has allowed the main paramilitary groups and most politicians to subscribe to an agreement which is nobody's ideal but everybody's second choice. This result doesn't mean we have seen the last dead body or heard the last bomb, but from now people are entitled to expect violence to be increasingly sporadic. It doesn't mean that the paramilitary groups will disband and hand in their weapons - paramilitarism is a symptom of distrust and that still abounds. But, it does mean that the people have made it clear they want an end to violence.

Adapted from the *Independent on Sunday*, 24 May 1998.

Item B   *The turn of the road gang*

We were the 'turn of the road' gang. There were about a dozen of us, all in our mid-teens. We were all Protestants - except for an Italian, and he didn't count. Day in, day out we'd go and stand outside the chip shop. Now and again, we'd get into a little trouble. First, it was raiding apple orchards. Everybody noticed who went in first and who hung back. Then a few people wanted to break into shops. Two of the best orchard raiders broke into a chemist's shop 'for the drugs'. They had no idea what they were looking for or what to do with it. My nights of homework paid off. I went to university in England. But I came back in the holidays. It was the mid-1970s. 'There's going to be a civil war', they told me. Everyone was asking: 'Who will save Ulster?' The answer is the same in any war. On whom does responsibility always fall? Who actually fights? The kind of lads who hang round on corners. And so it turned out. Three of the gang who became Ulster Volunteer Force (UVF) members are serving life sentences now. The pub beside the chip shop, owned by a Catholic, was burned down. The owner of the fruit shop on the other side of the chip shop was shot dead. My friend Tampy had his throat cut and two other members of the gang were assassinated. Looking back I can see that the lads from the turn of the road were always an easy target.

Adapted from the *Observer*, 11 July 1993.

Item D   *A British soldier in Northern Ireland*

My saddest moment in Northern Ireland wasn't being shot at or bombed or attacked by rioting crowds but the first time I was spat at. That was the biggest shock, just being spat on, by an extremely pretty girl. If you're shot at it's detached. They're doing it for military advantage, to create political pressure or whatever. But, if someone spits at you, it's hate, pure hate, and that's a very strong emotion to inflict on someone.

Adapted from Arthur 1987.

Item E *Re-establishing legitimacy (2)*

One of the few political parties to boycott the all-party talks and to campaign for a No vote in the referendum of May 1998 was Ian Paisley's Democratic Unionist Party. Ian Paisley, a reverend, is pictured above. When the referendum result was declared, he argued that a majority of unionists did not back the Good Friday Agreement. He reached this conclusion by claiming that 52% of voters were unionists and the No vote of 28.8% was more than half of the 52%. The cartoon appeared in the *Observer* on 12 April 1998.

Questions

1. What evidence is there in Items A, B and D to suggest that legitimacy broke down in Northern Ireland?
2. How do the attitudes in Items B and D help us to explain why legitimacy broke down?
3. a) What evidence is there in sources C and E to suggest that legitimacy has been restored in Northern Ireland.
   b) Are there good reasons to argue that legitimacy has not really been restored yet? Explain your answer.
4. What point is being made by the cartoon in Item E?

Part 2 The organisation of the police force

Key issues

1. How is the police force organised, staffed and funded?
2. What sort of people join the police force?
3. How has policing changed during recent years?

2.1 Historical context

Early history

The modern police force dates from the 1829 Metropolitan Police Act, piloted through Parliament by Sir Robert Peel. This Act set up the first professional civilian police force in London. The first police officers wore blue frock coats and top hats and were armed with wooden truncheons. They were known as 'Bobbies' or 'Peelers' after their founder.

Over the next 30 years, other large towns and cities followed the pattern established in London. But, it was not until the County and Borough Police Act was passed in 1856 that a national police force was established. This Act made all police forces subject to Home Office inspection and made grants dependent on efficiency.

The fact that the modern police force developed in a piecemeal fashion goes some way to explaining the stress which is still laid upon the decentralised, local basis of British policing.

Origins of the modern police force

Before the 1829 Metropolitan Police Act, local authorities relied upon two groups to preserve law and order. First, in the event of major civil disturbances such as riots, there was the professional army. But, the intervention of the army often had disastrous results. During the Gordon riots of 1780, for example, 700 people were killed. Second, there were the privately paid (and often corrupt) Watchmen and Constables. They were appointed by Justices of the Peace (JPs) and were responsible for combating crime and catching criminals.

A considerable controversy has raged between academics who have tried to explain why a professional police force emerged when it did (see Reiner 1992, pp.12-56). Robert Peel himself argued in the House of Commons that rising crime and civil disorder had led to the need for a new force. But, recent research indicates that there was neither a rapid rise in crime nor an increase in civil disorder in the years immediately preceding the Act. Some academics have argued that the setting up of the first police force was an inevitable consequence of urbanisation and the growth of capitalism. Others suggest that it was the product of the entrepreneurial zeal of reformers who had become dominant in central government.

The new police force

The new police force encountered considerable opposition at first. Many members of the upper and middle classes were worried that their individual freedom and their rapidly developing privileges would be undermined. Sections of the working class, on the other hand, were afraid that the new police force would be used to aid their oppression.

The extent of this opposition, however, should not be exaggerated. As early as 1838, J. Grant could write:

'The large reduction in the amount of crime committed has become sufficient to remove the feelings against the new force and to make it popular with the public.'

By the 1850s, the idea of a professional police force had gained fairly widespread acceptance. By the 1870s, the police enjoyed a high level of legitimacy.

The reason for this rapid rise to acceptability was probably not that the police were required to work in a society with widely shared values and lacking in serious divisions - Britain was rife with such divisions in the 19th century. Rather, the pressure exerted by those opposed to the creation of a professional force ensured that the police adopted an organisation and methods which made them acceptable. For example, the bureaucratic organisation of the police, their subjection to the rule of law, their use of minimal force in dealing with suspects, their politically non-partisan role, their image as a service as well as a force and, above all, their effectiveness all helped to achieve a high level of legitimacy.

By 1960, when a Royal Commission was set up to investigate the police, public and political concern had begun to develop about each of the areas mentioned above. Since then, these concerns have continued to trouble the public, politicians, academics and the police themselves.

2.2 Police organisation today

Policing in the UK

In a formal sense, policing in Britain is a function of local government. England and Wales have 43 separate police forces. Scotland has eight separate police forces. Northern Ireland has a single police force (the Royal Ulster Constabulary - RUC). With the exception of the Metropolitan Police Force of Greater London (which comes under the direct control of the Home Office), each force is answerable to a Police Authority.

The 1994 Police and Magistrates Courts Act

The 1994 Police and Magistrates Courts Act had two main objectives:

- to implement proposals to reform the organisation of the police force
- to implement proposals to reform police responsibilities and rewards.

Officially, the aim of the Act was as follows:

'The Act is designed to change the relationship between central government, Police Authorities and Chief Constables - to improve the management of the police and to reduce cumbersome central controls, devolving more power and decision making to the local level.' (HMSO 1995, p.15)

Police Authorities

A Police Authority is a committee whose job is to oversee the work of the police in a particular locality. The duties of Police Authorities were laid down in the 1964 Police Act and revised in the 1994 Police and Magistrates Courts Act. In general terms, it is the duty of Police Authorities to secure the maintenance of an adequate and sufficient police force for the locality. Specifically:

'The Police Authorities appoint the Chief Constable and Assistant Chief Constable. They also fix the maximum strength of the force, and provide buildings and equipment.' (HMSO 1995, p.14)

Until 1994, Police Authorities in England and Wales elected their own members (one-third being local magistrates and two-thirds being local councillors - councillors being given a majority on the committee because they were elected representatives and, therefore, directly accountable to the local electorate). After the 1994 Police and Magistrates Courts Act came into effect, there were changes to the composition of Police Authorities:

'The legislation [Police and Magistrates Courts Act] provides for the appointment of independent members to Police Authorities in England and Wales outside London, in addition to councillors and magistrates. The standard size of a Police Authority is set at 17 members, comprising nine councillors, three magistrates and five independent members. The Home Secretary may increase the size of an authority beyond 17 if local circumstances make it desirable...A new 12-member Metropolitan Police Committee assists the Home Secretary, who acts as Police Authority for the Metropolitan Police.' (HMSO 1995, pp.15-16)

The selection procedures for Police Authorities in England and Wales are as follows:

'Police Authorities may now elect their own chair and local selection panels are being established to select a number of non-elected members. The rationale behind this move was to recruit to the Police Authorities people with business or other administrative experience. The selection panel consists of a Home Secretary's appointee, a member selected by the Police Authority and one selected by both. The panel draws up a shortlist of candidates which is then subject to further scrutiny by the Home Secretary. From this, the magistrate and councillor members select the successful candidates.' (Brearley 1996, p.80)

Police Authorities in Scotland are composed entirely of elected local councillors. The RUC is responsible to a Police Authority appointed by the Secretary of State for Northern Ireland (HMSO 1995, p.16).

Police Authorities expect to receive an annual report from their Chief Constable. But, this can be refused if the Chief Constable decides it would be inappropriate to circulate such a document. In cases of dispute, the matter is decided by the Home Secretary. Since the 1994 Police and Magistrates Courts Act came into effect, Police Authorities have been responsible for setting local policing objectives, in consultation with their Chief Constable and the local community.

Chief Constables

The Chief Constables of the 43 forces, together with the Commissioner of the Metropolitan Police, occupy a central position in the organisation of the police force of England and Wales. These officers have complete operational control over their forces and they are responsible for allocating human and financial resources. Chief Constables are officers of the Crown. It is this which secures their independence from political control since, in theory, they are only responsible to the monarch. An attempt by the Bains Committee in 1972 to place Chief Constables in the same position as other local government chief officers was fiercely resisted with complete success. Chief Constables retained their independence. Since the 1994 Police and Magistrates Courts Act came into effect, Chief Constables have become responsible for formulating local police plans which set priorities and allocating resources. The plan must take into account the national policing objectives set by the Home Secretary.

Police personnel

The number of police officers has risen from 87,000 in 1961 to 126,798 in 1997. But, the force remains overwhelmingly male, white and working class. Between 1961 and 1997 the number of women

police officers rose from 3% to 15%. In 1987, there were just 1,105 black and Asian officers in England and Wales. By 1992, the number had risen to 1,730 and, by 1997, it had risen to 2,150. By 1987, the number of graduates had risen to 12% of the force. In 1996, more than 40% of Assistant Chief Constables and above had degrees (all figures from the Home Office, June 1998).

The Sheehy Report

The Sheehy Report, published in July 1993, proposed a new career and pay structure for the police force. It was the first inquiry into police responsibilities and rewards to be carried out since 1964. Perhaps the most important break with the past was the proposal that police recruits should no longer expect a job for life.

The report argued that the police force's management structure was 'top heavy' and should be simplified. It also proposed a new salary structure whereby officers could be rewarded financially without necessarily having to seek promotion. A Police Constable, for example, might earn £20,952 per year whilst a Sergeant (the next rank up) might earn £17,214. This would be achieved by the introduction of performance related pay.

In addition, the report argued that the starting rate for Constables should be cut and that new recruits should be appointed on fixed-term contracts (initially for ten years and then renewed for five year periods). It recommended that many existing officers face 'compulsory severance' by 1996 and new disciplinary procedures be introduced.

When the Sheehy Report was published, there was great opposition to its recommendations from within the police force - 20,000 police officers held a demonstration at Wembley Stadium, for example, and resignation threats were made by several Chief Constables. This opposition persuaded the Home Secretary, Michael Howard, to reject many of the recommendations (see Box 18.2 below).

Career structure

Every new recruit in the police force starts at the same level (Constable) with the same basic training. Normally recruits can expect promotion to the rank of Sergeant within five years. But, there are fast track courses for recruits showing exceptional potential. For example, those who pass a special 12 month course at the Police Staff College at Bramshill are promoted to the rank of Sergeant in their third year and can be promoted to the rank of Inspector two years later. All promotion is dependent on examination success.

Promotion is strictly hierarchical. Sergeants learn the basic principles of management and deployment of officers and equipment. It is their job to ensure that their officers work efficiently and as a team. The ranks above Sergeant are progressively more competitive. The Sheehy Report recommended the abolition of three senior ranks - Deputy Chief

Box 18.2 The Sheehy Report and the Major government's reaction to it

Proposals in Sheehy Report	Michael Howard's reaction to the Sheehy Report
1. **Abolition of ranks** - the ranks of Deputy Chief Constable, Chief Superintendent and Chief Inspector should be abolished with 5,000 jobs to go within three years.	1. **Abolition of ranks** - Michael Howard (Home Secretary) initially agreed to abolish the three ranks, though he wanted the job losses to be phased. Parliamentary pressure, however, forced Howard to retain the post of Chief Inspector.
2. **Fixed-term contracts** - should be introduced for all ranks, renewable every 10 years to end 'jobs for life' culture.	2. **Fixed-term contracts** - the recommendation was rejected.
3. **Local rates of pay** - should be introduced.	3. **Local rates of pay** - the recommendation was rejected.
4. **Pensions** - full pensions should only be available for those who complete 40 years service. Other changes associated with fixed-term appointments should be introduced.	4. **Pensions** - the recommendations were not implemented.
5. **Performance Related Pay** - Should be introduced with a national 'matrix' indicating how each officer should be assesed.	5. **Performance-related pay** - a pilot scheme failed and the recommendation was not implemented.
6. **Starting pay** - should be cut because it was out of line with market rates for people aged 18-22.	6. **Starting pay** - the pay of new, trained officers was cut by £5,000 in September 1995.
7. **Allowances** - a wide range of allowances, including housing allowance worth £5,000 per year, should be abolished.	7. **Allowances** - housing allowance was abolished for new officers in September 1994 and it was frozen for those who already received the allowance. The future of other allowances is a matter for the discretion of the Chief Constable.
8. **Overtime** - should be abolished for all ranks.	8. **Overtime** - abolished for inspectors and above.

Adapted from the *Guardian*, 29 October 1993.

Constable, Chief Superintendent and Chief Inspector. Members of the House of Lords objected to this idea and, to head off a parliamentary defeat, Michael Howard agreed to retain the post of Chief Inspector. The posts of Deputy Chief Constable and Chief Superintendent were duly abolished when the 1994 Police and Magistrates Courts Act came into effect.

Funding of the police force

Until 1994, funding for the police came from the local police committee (which was allocated money raised from the council tax) and from the Home Office (which used money raised from general taxation). The 1994 Police and Magistrates Courts Act, however, gave the Home Office almost complete (99%) control over funding (Section 15 of the Act allows local police forces to raise up to 1% of their budgets through sponsorship).

Expenditure on the police increased substantially after the Conservatives came to power in 1979 and continued to increase in real terms throughout the 1980s and 1990s. In 1981, £2,445 million was spent on the police force (c.4% of total government spending). By 1997, this figure was up to to £6,682 (c.6% of total government spending). This increase in expenditure was used in three main ways. First, the number of officers was increased. Second, the force was substantially re-equipped (see Section 2.4 below). Third, forces such as Special Branch which are responsible for the detection of criminally subversive activities against the state were expanded.

It should be noted, however, that more than half of expenditure is accounted for by salaries and:

> 'Increasingly, savings are made by shifting clerical duties to non-police staff who are cheaper to employ.' (*Guardian*, 24 April 1998)

Main points - Section 2.1-2.2

- The first professional civilian police force was set up in London in 1829. At first, it encountered hostility, but by the late 19th century it had gained legitimacy.
- Policing in England and Wales is a function of local government. There are 43 separate police forces in England and Wales, eight in Scotland and one in Northern Ireland.
- The Police Authority is a committee whose job is to oversee the work of police in a particular locality. The Police Authority works closely with the Chief Constable (who is in charge of all operational matters).
- The police force remains overwhelmingly male, white and working class.
- The Sheehy Report recommended a major shake-up of police organisation, but most of its recommendations were not implemented.
- The 1994 Police and Magistrates Courts Act gave the Home Office almost complete control over police funding.

Activity 18.3 Police organisation

Item A *Two Chief Constables*

Since Sir James Anderton quit as Chief Constable last summer, Greater Manchester Police has been headed ('ruled' would be too harsh a word) by an inconspicuous 48 year old Sociology and Politics graduate who believes in consensus and community policing, David Wilmot. Wilmot certainly has his work cut out. During Anderton's era, Greater Manchester sported the worst figures in almost every category of crime and policing outside London. Wilmot is keen to emphasise that, since his promotion, detection rates have improved significantly. Anderton thrived on controversy. Who could forget his rants against homosexuality, adultery, Aids sufferers, drug taking and left-wing subversion? David Wilmot prefers moderation. Anderton saw himself as part of a crusade to sweep the streets of sin and, with it, crime. Wilmot sees himself as a manager, charged with a duty to uphold the law, not make it or reinterpret it. Anderton claimed that he might have been answerable to God. Wilmot admits he is answerable to the public.

Adapted from Glinert 1992.

Item B *Councillors and police officers*

'Nothing to bother about councillor---purely an operational matter'.

Item C *Career opportunities in the police force*

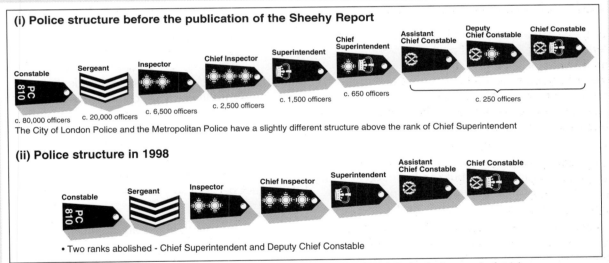

(i) Police structure before the publication of the Sheehy Report

Constable PC 810 — c. 80,000 officers
Sergeant — c. 20,000 officers
Inspector — c. 6,500 officers
Chief Inspector — c. 2,500 officers
Superintendent — c. 1,500 officers
Chief Superintendent — c. 650 officers
Assistant Chief Constable / Deputy Chief Constable / Chief Constable — c. 250 officers

The City of London Police and the Metropolitan Police have a slightly different structure above the rank of Chief Superintendent

(ii) Police structure in 1998

Constable PC 810 — Sergeant — Inspector — Chief Inspector — Superintendent — Assistant Chief Constable — Chief Constable

• Two ranks abolished - Chief Superintendent and Deputy Chief Constable

These diagrams shows the rank structure of police forces in England and Wales before and after the implementation of parts of the Sheehy Report.

Item D *Raising funds for the police*

With Merseyside's population in decline, it stands to lose up to £19 million because of a new Home Office funding formula which distributes cash according to head counts. Basic policing must be protected, leaving little spare cash for community work and crime prevention. Extra funding from outside sources would help, but Merseyside has reacted cautiously to section 15 of the 1994 Police and Magistrates Courts Act which allows forces to raise up to 1% of their budgets through sponsorship - that is £2 million pounds for Merseyside. This is an opportunity for Outreach, managed by a low-ranking officer with a commitment to community policing. In Merseyside, Outreach is managed by Constable Collette Walsh who says that it is an example of a policy which emphasises role not rank - 'I've been given a Chief Inspector's role', she says. Merseyside's police areas are free to fix up deals worth up to a total of £10,000 per year without referring back to HQ. Constable Walsh explains: 'We don't want them to go round with begging bowls. They know their patch and what their local needs are. I anticipated that they might be cynical and there were fears that they might have to patrol with company logos on their jackets. But, they have come up with a lot of ideas.' Deals include vehicle loan arrangements and a scheme to provide specialist equipment for victims of domestic violence.

Adapted from the *Guardian*, 29 November 1995.

Item E *The organisation of the police force*

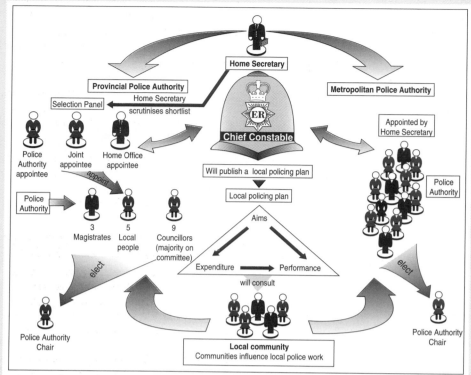

This diagram shows how the police force was organised in 1998.

Questions

1. a) What do Items A and B tell us about the role of the Chief Constable?
   b) Do you think it is right that Chief Constables have complete operational control over their local police force? Give arguments for and against.

2. a) Using Items C and E, explain how the police force is organised in England and Wales.
   b) What impact did the 1994 Police and Magistrates Courts Act make on the organisation of the police force?

3. What are the benefits and drawbacks of allowing local police forces to raise their own funds? Use Item D in your answer.

2.3 'Cop culture'

What is 'cop culture'?

Policing is a demanding and highly pressured occupation. In response to this, a dominant 'cop culture' has developed. This 'culture' is particularly marked in the lower ranks but can be found at senior levels too. According to Reiner (1992, pp 109-13), this 'culture' has seven key characteristics.

1. A mission

The first characteristic is the sense that the police force has a mission to fulfil. Policing is seen as a worthwhile occupation since it provides the means of protecting the weak in society and of gaining retribution for victims. As a result many police officers regard their work as a struggle to keep anarchy at bay. This sense of mission provides an incentive for many officers. But disappointment often leads to cynicism and pessimism. As a result, many police officers have a low opinion of human nature.

2. Suspicion

Second, police work can breed in officers an excessive level of suspicion. This may be directed against particular social groups, types of people or activities.

3. Social isolation

Third, because of irregular hours, the demands of work and the authority they are seen to wield, police officers can lead socially isolated lives. Many spend little time socialising with people outside their working environment. This, combined with the reliance on colleagues at work, tends to create a sense of solidarity between officers, particularly those working at the operational level. Conversely, the hierarchical structure of the force may ensure that junior officers lack a sense of solidarity with senior colleagues because they are seen as 'management'.

4. Conservatism

Fourth, most police officers are politically conservative in both their attitudes and their voting behaviour. In addition, many exhibit a moral conservatism in relation to such issues as homosexuality and drug taking.

5. Sexism

Fifth, within the police force there is a 'macho' atmosphere where sexism and sexual boasting are commonplace and physical strength, aggression and daring are seen as highly commendable attributes.

The evidence of sexual harassment in the workplace is well documented. There are even cases where male colleagues have been accused of raping women police officers (*Guardian*, 6 February 1993). In addition, it appears that there is discrimination in both employment and in promotion. Not only is the proportion of women employed as police officers small (15% in 1997), few women reach senior posts. The much publicised case of Alison Halford, Assistant

Chief Constable of Merseyside, highlighted the problems faced by women who aim for promotion in the police force. She alleged that she had been discriminated against when she applied for promotion. After counter accusations were made concerning her private life, she retired on the grounds of ill health at the end of August 1992. In 1995, a woman was appointed to the post of Chief Constable for the first time. In 1997, a second woman Chief Constable was appointed.

6. Racism

Sixth, there is evidence that some police officers are racists. It should be emphasised, however, that, generally, those who join the police force do not exhibit substantially more racist attitudes than those in the social classes from which they are drawn. The PSI report of 1983, for example, found that prejudice was rarely converted into discriminatory behaviour. The key point is that racism forms part of the overall power structure in British society and this is reflected in the police force.

The 1998 inquiry into the death of Stephen Lawrence, a black teenager murdered by a gang of white youths in 1993, graphically exposed this element of cop culture. Many of the police officers interrogated during the inquiry claimed not to be racists, but their language and their account of their actions suggested that this was not the case. Take for example, the comments made by Inspector Stephen Groves, the man who took charge at the scene of the murder:

'I am in a sort of quandary here: he [pointing to Edmund Lawson, counsel for the inquiry] is a white man; that [pointing to Margot Boye-Anawoma on the Lawrence's legal team] is a coloured woman. What else can I say? I have to make some description. I do not think that's being racist. He [pointing to Lawson again] is a white man; that [pointing this time to Stephen Lawrence's father] is a coloured man.' (Cathcart 1998, p.8)

7. Pragmatism

Seventh, police culture demonstrates a high level of pragmatism. The practical completion of tasks and the achievement of goals are highly valued. As a result, many police officers are distrustful of innovatory theoretical approaches.

Main points - Section 2.3

- In response to the demands and pressures on police officers, a dominant 'cop culture' has developed.
- This culture has seven key characteristics: (1) a mission; (2) suspicion; (3) social isolation; (4) conservatism; (5) sexism, (6) racism; and (7) pragmatism.
- Whilst there is considerable evidence of continuing sexism (eg research published in September 1997) and racism (eg at the 1998 Lawrence Inquiry), there are also some signs that the culture is shifting.

Activity 18.4 Cop culture

Item A Life in the police force

Personally I don't like policemen. I don't think we are very nice people. We're bound to be warped by the horrible incidents in which we are involved. We're bound to get our hands dirty. We make horrible jokes to keep the horror at bay and, yes, we are racist and probably a lot more sexist and ageist too. But, we are also what you, society at large, makes us. And, when you attack us, we take it personally. We draw in on ourselves. You force us to see ourselves as different. On holiday, I don't tell people what I do for a living. But, why should I, after 17 years, feel that defensive? All right, so some of us joined to strut about in our uniforms. But, most want to do something for the public. Society devalues the work we do.

Adapted from an interview conducted with a senior detective in *New Statesman and Society*, 2 February 1990.

Item B Racism and the police

A lot of country lads who join the Met have never seen a black face before. In the same way that the unemployed coloured youth gets fed up with being stopped all the time by horrible policemen, you've got the young policeman who's fed up with coloured lads who spit at him, verbally abuse him and, if they can, beat him up. It's Catch 22. Even experienced policemen, blokes who have got the same amount of service as me, still don't know how to deal with it properly. One person overreacts, the other overreacts and it builds up. The thing about coloureds is that they're naturally more excitable. They shout and jump about. That's the way they are.

Adapted from an interview with a Metropolitan Police Inspector in Graef 1989.

Item C Sexism and the police (1)

Male police officers do not like taking orders from women, according to research published in September 1997. Although a small number of women have reached the senior ranks, most others find it difficult to gain acceptance as detectives or as specialists. Jennifer Brown, a forensic psychologist who has made studies of women in the police service, told a conference that women police officers were less likely to be promoted and less likely to receive training than male colleagues. Her studies also found that women officers were denied access to male-dominated areas such as detective investigations and high speed driving. On the rare occasions when women were promoted to senior positions, male colleagues found it difficult to take orders from them. Some junior male officers were insolent. Some excluded the female officer from information. Others questioned an instruction in a way that they would not if the instruction had been issued by a male officer.

Adapted from the *Guardian*, 1 October 1997.

Item D *Sexism and the police (2)*

A police officer who was moved to different duties because he complained about a superior's racist and sexist behaviour won £7,500 compensation and an apology from the Metropolitan Police. The case sets a precedent for officers who complain about racism and sexism even though they are themselves male and white. In March 1996, Sergeant David Harris wrote a letter to the officer in charge of his area explaining why he was unhappy with the behaviour of his immediate superior, an Inspector. He then found himself transferred away from his team without being consulted. Mr Harris, with the backing of the Police Federation, then claimed victimisation and was due to take the case to an industrial tribunal, but an agreement was reached before evidence was taken. Mike Bayliss from the Police Federation said that the Federation would support officers who fought racism or sexism in the workplace. It was very important for officers to feel that, if they made a complaint, their career would not suffer.

Adapted from the *Guardian*, 13 October and 3 December 1997.

Item E *Cop culture?*

Questions

1. What do Items A-D tell us about 'cop culture'?
2. How good a justification of 'cop culture' is provided by Items A and B?
3. Would you expect the Met Inspector interviewed in Item B to be impartial when dealing with black and Asian people? Explain your answer.
4. 'Cop culture is beginning to change'. Give arguments for and against this statement using Item D.
5. a) What point do you think the cartoonist is making in Item E?
   b) What does this tell us about cop culture?

2.4 Recent trends in policing

The traditional image

The image of the police officer on the beat armed only with a truncheon, a whistle to call colleagues and a bicycle for rapid response never provided a complete picture of police work. Today, such an image has little grounding in reality. Over the last 30 years, the police force has employed a variety of new techniques which have transformed the nature of police work.

The impact of technology

Cars

The most widespread innovation is the growth in the use of cars both to patrol local areas and to respond speedily to actual or suspected criminal acts. Although there have been sporadic campaigns to get police officers back onto the beat (since, it was felt, valuable personal contact between the police and the public was being lost), the importance of motorised patrols has remained.

Communications

A second development is a great improvement in the methods of communication between officers on patrol and between officers and their police station. Better communication enables colleagues to be summoned more quickly to the scene and allows officers to receive intelligence and information held at the station.

Police National Computer

A third innovation is the Police National Computer (PNC). This is based in Hendon, near London. The PNC holds information supplied by and accessible to every force in the country. Subjects include missing persons, stolen vehicles and their owners, known criminals and fingerprints. The development of the PNC has enabled police forces which are located far apart to obtain and share information. Though there is nothing sinister about this in the case of, for example, a nationwide murder inquiry, its use becomes questionable when the police are engaged in overtly political activities such as policing the miners' strike in 1984-85. Those who support the cooperation made possible by the PNC maintain that it makes a major contribution to the ability of local forces to apprehend criminals. Its opponents argue that it has been instrumental in allowing the development of a national police force by the back door. They claim that this raises problems of local responsiveness and accountability.

The militarisation of the police

Although it is difficult to prove that Britain is a more violent place today than it was 30 years ago, many people believe that this is the case. In a sense, the truth of the matter is irrelevant. Because many people believe that there is a rising tide of violence, they are ready to accept measures which, they are told, will combat it. One such measure is the growth of 'militarisation' of the police. Since 1979, the police force has acquired and used a selection of hardware which is more usually associated with the military than with a civilian police force. This militarisation has affected the way in which the police fulfil two of their major roles - dealing with crime and maintaining public order.

Dealing with crime

In the fight against crime, two developments suggest greater militarisation.

First, the increasing use of firearms. It is difficult to establish an accurate appraisal of this increase because the method of counting changed in 1983. Before 1983, the number of **occasions** when firearms were issued was counted. After 1983, the number of **operations** in which firearms were issued was counted (firearms may be issued on a number of occasions during a single operation). Between 1970 and 1972, police were issued with firearms on 5,244 occasions - an average of 1,748 occasions per year. In 1991, firearms were issued for 3,783 operations. These figures suggest that there has been a substantial increase in the issuing of firearms.

The danger of greater reliance on firearms was demonstrated in 1983 when armed officers shot and seriously wounded Steven Waldorf. Waldorf was entirely innocent of any crime. He was mistaken for a wanted criminal. Since then, training in the use of firearms has changed, but the trend towards greater reliance on armed officers has continued.

A second sign of greater militarisation of the police force was the decision made in 1993 by Michael Howard, the Home Secretary, to allow the experimental introduction of two-handed batons, similar to those used by the American police. Michael Howard sanctioned this experiment on the ground that there was a rising number of violent attacks on police officers. In 1997, the Home Office gave its approval to the use of these batons, leaving it to individual police forces to decide what kind of baton they should use.

The maintenance of public order

It is in the maintenance of public order that the increased militarisation of the police has been most evident. During the 1970s and 1980s, large numbers of police officers were trained in riot tactics. The use of baton charges in the miners' strike of 1984-85 was particularly militaristic and seen by many as a turning point. Also during the 1980s, the police began to use new riot gear such as long shields and helmets and they began to arm themselves with CS gas ('tear' gas) and rubber bullets. In April 1995, the Home Secretary, Michael Howard, announced that, from 1 March 1996, a new CS gas spray would be issued to Constables. This spray is now issued routinely.

The acquisition of new hardware was seen by senior police officers as a necessity if the police were to deal with what was perceived as the growing breakdown of public order. Those concerned about civil rights, however, argued that the deployment of this type of equipment would encourage the police to initiate action rather than to react to it. Police officers would, the argument goes, be more likely to restrict the legitimate right to picket, demonstrate and march and would be more likely to use excessive force if events got out of hand.

The growing use of CS gas sprays illustrates this point. Police officers are only supposed to use the spray in self-defence and as a last resort. There is growing evidence, however, that officers are using it as an easy way out of potentially violent confrontations. Whereas, before the spray was issued, officers would have tried to negotiate a peaceful solution, it is now easy for them to spray first and ask questions later. Unease with the use of the spray came to light at a trial of a police officer in June 1998. The police officer used the spray on a 67 year old pensioner who refused to explain why he had parked on double yellow lines. Although the jury acquitted the police officer of assault, the trial judge refused to award him costs and suggested that he had over-reacted (*Times*, 3 June 1998). Some commentators have also suggested that the gas spray is issued to save money. A single police officer with a canister of CS gas spray can diffuse a potentially violent confrontation whereas an unarmed officer would have to call for back-up. Using the spray, therefore, cuts costs.

Increased police specialisation and centralisation

Since the 1970s, a number of police functions have become the preserve of specialised groups of officers. For example, all forces now have units of officers who are specialists in dealing with terrorism and public order problems.

Police Special Units (PSUs)

Specialisation may in itself result in centralisation. This can be demonstrated by reference to Police Special Units (PSUs). PSUs (created in 1974) ensure that each local police force has a number of officers specially trained in the control of strikes, crowds and demonstrations. Each unit contains 23 officers (an Inspector, two Sergeants and 20 Constables). These officers are engaged on ordinary police duties but can be mobilised speedily when required. They are also available to deal with problems arising outside their own force.

The National Reporting Centre (NRC)

When a large number of PSUs are mobilised in an emergency, they are coordinated by the National Reporting Centre (NRC) at Scotland Yard in London. The NRC is a large, adapted conference room. It is not a permanent centre. It is only activated when its controllers judge that police forces in more than one area are likely to require reinforcements to deal with major public order events. The most controversial example of such coordination was during the miners' strike of 1984-85. PSUs from all over the country were called to mining areas to maintain order. Some journalists claimed that the NRC became an operational centre during this dispute, though this was vehemently denied by the police officers in charge of the NRC. They claimed that:

> '[The NRC was] purely an efficient convenience for administering the long established mutual aid system between local forces' (Kettle 1985, p.27)

Specialist Units

There are several specialist units within the police force which are entirely centralised. For example:

- the National Criminal Intelligence Service (which is divided into several intelligence units - such as the National Drugs Intelligence Unit and the Football Intelligence Unit)
- the National Identification Bureau
- the Serious Fraud Office.

In March 1997, a National Crime Squad (NCS) was set up. It came into operation in 1998. The function of the NCS is to prevent and detect serious crime of relevance to more than one police area in England and Wales. It also has powers to support other police forces. It is supervised by the NCS Service Authority.

In recent years, national police units have increased in importance. For example, the number of officers in Special Branch grew from c.350 in the 1960s to 1,750 in 1984. There has been concern about this development, however. The main criticism is that national units are centrally controlled and, therefore, lack local accountability.

Amalgamations

There is also a tendency towards amalgamation of police forces. In 1963, there were 117 local police forces in England and Wales. In 1998, the number of police forces was 43. Clearly, the connection between a large force covering a large geographical area and the locality it serves is less pronounced. It is also less easy to make a large organisation accountable or responsive.

The implications of centralised control

The growth of centralised control has been justified on the basis of efficiency. Disorder can cross local Police Authority boundaries and it can escalate to a level beyond the capabilities of the local force. Because of this, it is argued, a mobile, specialised force is necessary. Also, in the case of serious law breaking, such as that related to drugs or fraud involving complex criminal conspiracies, skilled and specialised officers are more likely to be successful.

Critics of centralisation, however, claim that, even though this argument has some merit, local control prevents the growth of a monolithic centralised force which would be open to direct political manipulation. It preserves some degree of accountability between the local force and the community it is supposed to serve. In addition, local control creates the possibility of diversity and responsiveness to local conditions.

Main points - Section 2.4

- **Over the last 30 years, the police force has employed many new techniques which have transformed the nature of police work.**
- **Increasing use of cars, better communications and the PNC have helped to alter the way in which policing is performed.**
- **Since 1979, there has been a growing militarisation of the police force. Firearms are increasingly used, new batons have been introduced and many police officers are trained in riot tactics.**
- **There is evidence of a trend towards greater specialisation and centralisation. Critics argue that, as a result, there is less local accountability.**

Activity 18.5 *The militarisation of the police force*

Item A *Policing the miners' strike (1)*

In the first few days of the miners' strike the NRC (National Reporting Centre) sent some 8,000 men from the Police Support Units to the main target areas. Of these, 1,000 had been mobilised in the first four hours. The first aim was to seal off the Nottinghamshire coalfield. Road blocks were set up, spotter aircraft, helicopters and dog patrols were deployed. A reserve of 3,000 riot-trained police stayed in army barracks. During the following days, stories of aggressive and arbitrary police behaviour were commonplace. This initial high-profile policing did much to set the tone for the dispute. Orgreave, a coking depot in South Yorkshire, was the scene of a series of set-piece battles with the police. The police lined up in military formation - some mounted, some in full riot gear and some in normal uniforms with helmets. They were drawn from 10 counties. Reserves were kept on National Coal Board land while others were deployed against the pickets. Baton charges took place. A Barnsley miner said, 'When the lads resort to the only weapons they've got - throwing stones, Oh it's terrible. But it's OK when they're bashing you about the head with a bit of wood.' The same man explained how the police provoked pickets by holding £10 notes up to the windows of vans and coaches as they passed by.
Adapted from Fine & Millar 1985.

Item B *Policing the miners' strike (2)*

Item C *Photograph taken during the miners' strike*

This photograph shows one of the battles between the police and strikers at Orgreave in South Yorkshire in June 1984. The police are lined up in formation on the left whilst the pickets are gathered on the right.

Item D *Police and firearms*

Officers are trained never to fire unless their life or somebody else's life is in danger. That means that if some villain has a shotgun and it's pointing at the floor when we come in, we can't shoot. We've got to challenge him, tell him to drop the gun and do as he's told. There was a case when a member of the tactical firearms team was shot. It happened within months of the Waldorf shooting. This chap had a sawn off shotgun in a plastic bag. They challenged him to put the bag down but he didn't. He put his hand inside, squeezed the trigger and killed a police officer. At the time the PC didn't know there was a gun in the bag. I'm sure he was thinking: 'This is dangerous, yet I can't do anything unless I see a gun.' I sometimes think that the criticisms of the police after the Waldorf affair were perhaps made in haste. If Waldorf hadn't happened, we might have done something different and that PC would never have died.

Adapted from an interview with a Chief Inspector in Graef 1989.

Item E *The number of offences involving firearms*

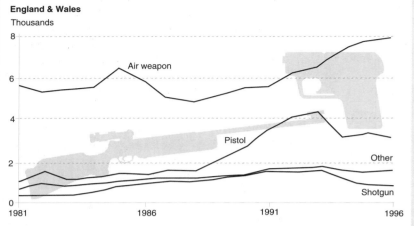

England & Wales
Thousands

This graph shows the number of offences involving firearms in England and Wales between 1981 and 1996. Between 1972 and 1996, there was more than a sixfold increase in offences involving firearms, but these offences came to just 0.3% of all recorded offences in 1996.

Adapted from Social Trends 1998.

Questions

1. Using Items A-E examine the arguments for and against the idea that greater militarisation and specialisation have fundamentally altered the role of police officers as neutral upholders of the law.

2. Why do you think the miners' strike of 1984-85 has been described as 'a turning point in the history of post-war policing'?

3. Do you think police officers should carry guns as a matter of course? Give arguments for and against. Use Items D and E in your answer.

2.5 The accountability of the police

What is accountability?

An accountable organisation is an organisation whose members are answerable to a person or a body that can exercise some form of power over them. In the case of the police force, two questions arise. First, for what actions are the police accountable and for what actions should they be accountable? Second, to whom should they be accountable?

Accountability and operational matters

Operational matters are the everyday activities of maintaining order, catching criminals and so on. Chief Constables have full responsibility for these operational matters. Individual police officers are, therefore, accountable to their Chief Constable for the execution of operational duties. But, if the wider problem of to whom or to what the police force as a whole is accountable is considered, the matter becomes more complex.

Accountability and the law

One consideration is that the police force as a whole is accountable to the law. Police officers must act within the law and, like every other citizen, officers who break the law are liable to prosecution through the proceedings of the judicial system. Officers suspected of criminal misconduct, for example, can be prosecuted. Civil actions for cases of wrongful arrest or trespass can be brought. A writ of habeas corpus can be issued to end an illegal detention. Judges can exclude evidence from court cases if they believe that it has been obtained by questionable means.

In practice, however, these legal processes of accountability frequently break down. Until recent cases which undermined the credibility of police evidence, magistrates and juries tended to believe the testimony of police officers, assuming that officers were honest and upright. It has become clear, however, that some officers are willing to perjure themselves in court to gain a conviction. At the successful appeal of the Guildford Four, for example, the Appeal Court judge, Lord Lane, maintained that new evidence showed that Surrey detectives 'must have lied' at the original trial.

In addition, it is often difficult to enforce accountability through the courts. The Crown Prosecution Service demands higher standards of evidence before prosecuting a police officer than in other cases. For example, in 1986 a group of police officers in a mobile police van stopped and assaulted a group of boys walking along the Holloway Road in London. It was several years before sufficient evidence was gathered to enable prosecutions to be made partly because of a police cover-up. Eventually, three officers were sent to prison.

A further point should be made in this context. Some judges do not regard it as a proper function of the judiciary to enforce accountability on the police force. For example, Lord Diplock said in 1979:

> 'It is not a part of a judge's function to exercise disciplinary powers over the police.'

Internal disciplinary procedures, 1964-76

The Police Act of 1964 placed a statutory obligation upon Chief Constables to investigate all complaints against police officers made by the public. Officers from other forces could be brought in if the Chief Constable so wished. If, in the opinion of the Chief Constable, an officer had committed a criminal offence, a report was to be sent to the Director of Public Prosecutions (DPP). The DPP would decide whether or not to prosecute.

This system drew a great deal of criticism because police officers were given the power to investigate complaints against fellow officers and to conduct their own disciplinary procedures.

The Police Complaints Board (PCB)

The first attempt to improve the complaints procedure was the setting up of the Police Complaints Board (PCB) in 1976. Police officers were still responsible for investigating complaints. But, at the conclusion of an internal investigation, the PCB received a copy of the report and was informed by the Deputy Chief Constable whether disciplinary charges, prosecution or both should be undertaken. The PCB then had the power to insist on charges being made if it felt that the report warranted it. In practice, members of the PCB questioned the decisions of Deputy Chief Constables only very rarely. As a result, the PCB failed to gain the trust of those who wanted independent investigations, whilst the police were angry that their professional judgement should be questioned.

Members of the PCB themselves became aware of the problems they faced in providing a credible means of ensuring police accountability. In their 1980 report, they advocated a number of changes to procedure and practice, arguing that a national team of officers should be established on secondment from their regular duties for two or three years. This team would look into serious allegations against police officers, especially those involving assault. The officers in the team would be responsible to a senior lawyer or a judge.

These recommendations were rejected by the government. Nevertheless, Lord Scarman's report into the 1980 riots and the House of Commons Home Affairs Select Committee also called for independent investigation of complaints.

The Police and Criminal Evidence Act 1984 (PACE)

The 1984 Police and Criminal Evidence Act (PACE) was partially based on the report of the Royal Commission on Criminal Procedure published in 1981. PACE has made a major impact on police procedure.

Since PACE came into operation, police officers have a statutory obligation to tape record all interviews and they must be able to produce a complete and contemporaneous account of the entire interview process. Also, since suspects have the right to have a solicitor present, police cannot, on the whole, afford to detain and interrogate anyone unless they have sufficient evidence to win a committal to a Magistrates Court. In other words, procedure is designed to prevent the police

presenting cases based on a forced confession. Confessions are only permissible as evidence if they are tape recorded and voluntarily made.

It is important to note that the recent spate of acquittals in the Court of Appeal following wrongful convictions based on forced confessions (the Birmingham Six, Guildford Four, Maguire Seven and so on) all stem from the days before PACE.

The Police Complaints Authority (PCA)

The 1984 Police and Criminal Evidence Act replaced the PCB with the Police Complaints Authority (PCA):

> 'The PCA consists of a chairman (paid £73,780 a year), deputy chairman (on £52,593) and 11 members (paid £44,957 each) whose backgrounds include, at present, the law, the armed services, community relations and local government. The authority gets just over £2 million a year; its budget has recently been squeezed.' (*Guardian*, 26 June 1998)

The investigation of complaints remains in the hands of the police (when it takes over a case, the PCA appoints a police officer to take charge of the investigation), but the PCA has the power to supervise investigations either in serious cases leading to death or injury or where it is felt that the public interest could be served by supervision. When carrying out supervision, the PCA can reject any investigating officer it feels is unfit. Also, the PCA has to certify that it is happy with an investigation once it has been completed. Legal representation is guaranteed to police officers who could lose their job or rank as a consequence of the investigation. In cases of minor complaints where both sides agree, the PCA is involved in the informal resolution of the matter.

The lack of an independent investigatory body was a matter of great regret in 1984. Many were convinced that this would prejudice the effectiveness and legitimacy of the new arrangements. Evidence of the PCA's success or failure is inconclusive, however. On the one hand, it is generally considered that procedures for resolving minor complaints have worked well. On the other hand, many commentators argue that, for serious accusations, only a fully independent system will secure public confidence in accountability and police confidence in fairness.

The work of the PCA

The work of the PCA is designed to deal with officers who fail in their professional duties, regardless of whether this failure has resulted in a criminal case. The internal disciplinary procedures which are followed have frequently been the subject of criticism not only from those outside the force (who are concerned to ensure that officers who fail in their responsibilities are disciplined), but also from senior police officers (who see current arrangements as an impediment to removing officers who are corrupt or incompetent). Criticism centres on two main areas of weakness in the system. First, the procedures are very slow. Those accused of misconduct are entitled to legal representation at hearings and there is a complex appeals procedure. Sometimes, hearings are not conducted at all if an accused officer is absent from work on health grounds. And second, the standard of proof required is the same as in criminal cases - the police officer must be found guilty 'beyond reasonable doubt'. This makes it difficult to discipline officers as there is often some doubt about their guilt. In addition, officers often escape punishment by taking early retirement on ill-health grounds (by this means avoiding disciplinary hearings and yet retaining their full police pension rights).

New measures
In March 1998, the Home Secretary, Jack Straw, announced that the following measures would come into effect in April 1999:

- the burden of proof would be lowered from 'beyond reasonable doubt' to that used in civil cases where it is sufficient to show a 'balance of probabilities' in order to gain a conviction
- a 'fast track' dismissal procedure would be introduced, enabling the worst officers to be dismissed within six weeks
- the 'double jeopardy' rule (which allowed officers acquitted at a criminal trial automatically to escape a disciplinary hearing) would be abolished
- officers claiming to be too ill to attend hearings would be dealt with in their absence
- officers' right to silence during disciplinary hearings would be ended
- the Home Secretary would automatically assess the right of an officer convicted of a criminal offence to have a full pension.

These measures were welcomed by the Association of Chief Police Officers, but the Police Federation (which represents junior officers) argued that they would damage confidence and morale.

Accountability and policy making
There are three channels through which police policy making is made accountable - the Home Secretary, the Chief Constable and the local Police Authority.

The Home Secretary
As well as being directly responsible for policing in London, the Home Secretary controls funding and, therefore, has an indirect overall control over policing policy nationally. In theory, the Home Secretary is accountable to the public through Parliament, but the power of ministers tends to

frustrate attempts by backbench MPs to question them. As a result, attempts to ensure accountability through Parliament are largely ineffective.

Chief Constables and Police Authorities
Chief Constables have complete operational control over their forces and are, therefore, responsible for local police policy. Although Chief Constables are answerable to their local Police Authority, the power of the Police Authority to examine in detail or to enforce policy changes is very limited. The key point is that, in cases of dispute between the Police Authority and the Chief Constable, the matter is referred to the Home Secretary. From the early 1980s, however, Home Secretaries have been noticeably unresponsive to the wishes of Police Authorities. Perhaps the best example of this with regard to policy was the policing of the miners' strike in 1984-85. Police Authorities dominated by Labour councillors sought to limit spending on the strike or to alter the manner of policing the strike. The Chief Constables protested to and received support from the Home Secretary. The opposition of the Police Authorities was ignored. In 1988, the powers of Police Authorities were further eroded by a Court of Appeal judgement. This gave the Home Secretary authority to override the views of Police Authorities on matters of equipment and expenditure.

The already tenuous link between local democracy and the police, through which some degree of accountability is supposed to be ensured, was further undermined by the 1994 Police and Magistrates Courts Act. Michael Howard (who steered the Bill through Parliament) aimed to alter the structure of Police Authorities by reducing the number of elected representatives and including nominees appointed directly by the Home Secretary. During the passage of the Bill, however, he was forced to make concessions. When the Act came into effect, nominees were included, but they were selected by a special panel (see Section 2.2 above). Also, the proportion of elected representatives on Police Authorities was reduced, but they still remained a majority (see Activity 18.3, Item E).

Accountability and the use of resources
Until 1994, funding for the police came from the local police committee (which was allocated money raised from the council tax) and from the Home Office (which used money raised from general taxation). The 1994 Police and Magistrates Courts Act, however, gave the Home Office almost complete (99%) control over funding (Section 15 of the Act allows local police forces to raise up to 1% of their budgets through sponsorship).

Before 1979, the assumption was that accountability would be achieved through the local Police Authority (Chief Constables would report to the Police Authority, explaining how resources had been used). Since 1979, however, controls have been placed on local government expenditure and conditions have been imposed on central government grants. The result is that financial control over the police has been centralised. There is, therefore, little local accountability.

Although extra resources for the police were made available in the 1980s, they were conditional upon the police force providing value for money. In 1983, a Home Office circular was issued making new money available only if existing resources were being used at full capacity. Tighter regulations followed in 1988 when a circular instructed Chief Constables to specify the precise objectives to be met when the establishment of new posts was requested. Similarly, when, in 1996, it was announced that a new National Crime Squad (NCS) was to be set up, one of the justifications for the new organisation was as follows:

> '[The NCS would allow] a move towards a more coordinated approach by police to buying expensive equipment including radio systems, computers and other technology. It would also work on national projects such as computer networks and systems.' (*Times*, 2 November 1996)

In terms of resources, therefore, accountability has not been a priority. If police forces are accountable to anyone, it is to central government. That means that the police force is far removed from the public which it serves.

Main points - Section 2.5

- Individual police officers are accountable to their Chief Constable for the execution of operational duties.
- Police officers must act within the law. Officers who break the law are liable to prosecution.
- If complaints are made about the police, they are investigated by the PCA.
- Investigations undertaken by the PCA are not independent (other police officers conduct the investigation). Critics argue that this prejudices the effectiveness and legitimacy of the work of the PCA.
- There are three channels through which police policy making is made accountable - the Home Secretary, the Chief Constable and the local Police Authority.
- In terms of resources, if police forces are accountable to anyone, it is to central government.

Activity 18.6 Accountability and the police

Item A *Organisation and accountability*

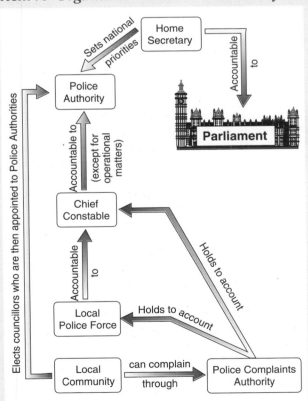

Item B *Police corruption*

In 1995, a businessman reported a theft from his home in central London. Detective Sergeant Tom Bradley was assigned to investigate. He contacted the victim and later agreed to chauffeur him and his family and to provide protection for a fee (it was later discovered that several thousand pounds was paid). Bradley and a colleague, Detective Sergeant Ian Martin, acted as bodyguards. This breach of discipline was uncovered and the two officers were suspended in November 1995. These two officers, together with a third who faced similar charges, then reported sick. In September 1996, the Chief Medical Officer for the Metropolitan Police recommended that Bradley be retired on medical grounds (other doctors confirmed he had a 'psychiatric disorder'). He was granted ill-health retirement and the Met 'reluctantly' dropped the charges. The other two officers were also granted ill-health pensions. In evidence to the Commons Home Affairs Select Committee, the Metropolitan Police said that there was real concern that individuals who were mentally strong before their suspension suffer severe psychiatric illnesses immediately afterwards and then (once they begin receiving their pension) suddenly recover and are able to work again. In November 1997, Bradley and Martin launched HomeCheck, a company which checks out neighbours and the area for prospective house buyers.

Adapted from the *Guardian*, 16 January 1998.

Item C   *Reasons why people complain against the police*

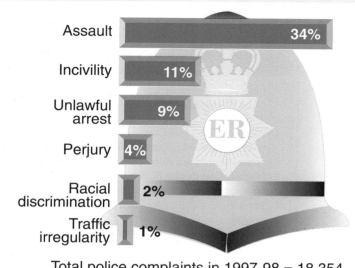

Assault	34%
Incivility	11%
Unlawful arrest	9%
Perjury	4%
Racial discrimination	2%
Traffic irregularity	1%

Total police complaints in 1997-98 = 18,354.

Adapted from the *Guardian*, 26 June 1998.

Item E   *The Lawrence Inquiry*

In August 1997, four years after the black teenager Stephen Lawrence was stabbed to death by a gang of white youths, the government finally agreed to set up an independent judicial inquiry (the previous government had refused such an inquiry despite a vigorous campaign by Stephen Lawrence's parents). The official terms of reference asked former judge Sir William Macpherson to 'inquire into matters arising from the death of Stephen Lawrence in April 1993' and to 'identify the lessons to be learned for the investigation and prosecution of racially motivated crime'. In June 1998, following several months in which the inquiry had gradually uncovered a trail of police incompetence and outright racism, the Metropolitan Police Commissioner made an unprecedented apology to the parents of Stephen Lawrence. The apology was delivered by the Assistant Commissioner, Ian Johnston. He said: 'On behalf of myself and the Commissioner, who specifically asked me to associate himself with these words, I offer my sincere and deep apologies to you...I am very very sorry and very very sad that we have let you down. Looking back now I can see we could have and should have done better. I deeply regret that we have not put his killers away.' In a statement, Neville Lawrence, Stephen's father, stated: 'The Commissioner now accepts that the first investigation was flawed and incompetent. What will happen to those officers? Will they be disciplined? Will those now retired lose their pensions?'

Adapted from the *Guardian*, 1 August 1997 and 18 June 1998.

Item D   *The PCA*

The function of the PCA is to supervise or review all complaints about the police from the public and matters of gravity referred by the police themselves, such as fatal shootings by officers. In 1997-98, there were 18,354 complaints, down from the highest ever total of 19,953 in 1996-97. In 1988, the total was 12,523. People can complain either to the police station concerned or via their MP, local councillor or lawyer or, as in 2,000 cases in 1996-97, directly to the PCA. But, does the complaints system work? Recent inquiries into corruption in the Metropolitan Police, together with a series of high-profile cases involving sexual harassment within the forces, have focused attention on how alleged malpractice gets investigated. Can complainants trust investigators who are professional colleagues of those complained against? Should the PCA employ its own investigators, be they ex-officers, customs officials or private detectives? Critics argue that the relatively small proportion of punishments handed out is an indication that officers have a good chance of escaping censure and that they will always be given the benefit of the doubt. Time and again, anxiety attaches to the fact that police officers investigate themselves. The PCA, however, defends the practice of using police officers arguing that the police are best placed to know how their colleagues might cover their tracks. Outside investigators, it says, would have even greater problems discovering the truth.

Adapted from the *Guardian*, 26 June 1998.

Questions

1. 'Accountable only to themselves at every layer of the hierarchy'. Use Item A to explain how far this is true of the police in England and Wales.

2. a) Using Items B and E, explain why it is important for police officers to be held accountable for their actions.
   b) Are the disciplinary mechanisms which currently exist sufficient to ensure that the public has confidence in the police force? Give reasons for your answer.

3. Using Items B-D, give arguments for and against the view that PCA investigations should be conducted by independent investigators.

2.6   The Criminal Justice Act 1994

Background

After their fourth election victory in a row (in 1992), Conservative ministers could no longer argue with any conviction that rising crime figures resulted from failed Labour policies. So, when, in 1993, opinion polls began to show that Labour was gaining support for its ideas on law and order, the Conservative government decided to respond.

The Conservative Party conference in 1993 pushed the issue of law and order to the top of the political agenda. In his speech to the conference, Michael Howard, the Home Secretary, announced 27 measures which he intended to put in place. The Prime Minister, John Major, also made it clear that law and order was to be a central plank in his 'Back to Basics' campaign.

The 1993 Queen's speech included the commitment by the government to introduce 17 of Michael Howard's 27 measures. Two major pieces of legislation were proposed - the Police and Magistrates Courts Bill (see Section 2.2 above) and the Criminal Justice Bill.

After a difficult passage through Parliament, during which several amendments were made (particularly in the House of Lords), the Criminal Justice Act became law in November 1994.

Provisions of the Act

Four key provisions of the Criminal Justice Act were controversial because, critics argued, they tilted the balance of the law too far in favour of the police and too far against the freedom of the individual.

The right to silence

The first of these provisions concerned the right to silence traditionally enjoyed by a person accused of a crime. This right was meant to protect an accused person from being put under pressure by the police to answer questions which might incriminate them. It was also meant to deter the police from applying undue pressure on suspects. Before the Criminal Justice Act came into effect, courts were not allowed to infer anything from a suspect's refusal to answer police questions. The new law, however, effectively abolished the right to silence by allowing judges to direct juries in criminal trials to take into account the fact that a person chose to remain silent. It should be noted that this provision was included in the new law despite the fact that a Royal Commission (which had been set up following the exposure of the miscarriage of justice which led to the release of the Birmingham Six) recommended that the right to silence be maintained.

The Criminal Justice Act also included a provision that if a defendant failed to provide the police with information which was later used by the defence, the judge could direct the jury to draw conclusions from this. As a result of this, and the effective abolition of the right to silence, the caution recited by police officers when making an arrest has been changed.

Stop and search

The second controversial provision of the Act related to police powers to stop and search people. Prior to the Act, the police could only stop and search people if they had some reasonable suspicion that a crime had been or might be committed. The 1994 Act, however, removed this restriction, making it lawful for police officers to stop and search anyone 'they think fit' (Puddephatt 1995, p.60). The aim was to enable the police to be proactive - to prevent crime before it took place. Critics argue, however, that it opened the way for police officers to abuse their powers by stopping and searching anyone who fitted their own stereotypes of a likely criminal 'type'. Given cop culture (see Section 2.3 above), there is a danger, critics argue, that the young, black and Asian people and working-class men will be subjected to undue police attention.

Protests

The third controversial provision related to the right to protest. The Conservative government had been much alarmed by the activities of hunt saboteurs and anti-road protesters and was determined to frame legislation which curbed their activities. As a result, the Criminal Justice Act created the offence of 'aggravated trespass'. This made it a criminal offence (with stiff penalties) to trespass on the property of another person with the intention of causing disruption to others. Whilst the aim was to combat the activities of those who protested in a violent and intimidatory manner, critics pointed out that this offence potentially restricted the right to protest in general (since any protest, by its very nature, causes disruption and since any gathering in a public place could be considered a trespass - on the roads of the Highway Authority, for example, or on public squares owned by local authorities).

Non-conformists

The fourth area of controversy concerned the raft of provisions intended to deal with the perceived 'problem' of raves, 'New Age' travellers and squatters. First, the Criminal Justice Act gave the police the powers to prevent raves going ahead, to seize any equipment being used and to create an 'exclusion zone' of up to five miles around the site of a rave. Second, it became illegal for travellers:

- to occupy local authority land after they had been asked to leave
- not to leave private land if damage had been done or if the travellers were travelling in a convoy of more than six vehicles and were asked to move by a senior police officer.

And third, the Act laid down that a prison term of up to six months could be imposed for squatting for more than 24 hours after an eviction order has been gained and the Act gave landlords (or their representatives) the right to force an entry into a squat to regain possession.

Two main criticisms

These measures have aroused debate because of two key characteristics: First, they place considerable discretionary powers in the hands of police officers (who may not be the best people to exercise such powers given what is known of their beliefs and prejudices). And second, many of the measures make it difficult for British people to protest or to practise an unorthodox lifestyle. For many supporters of civil liberties and cultural diversity, such developments are profoundly disturbing.

During its first 18 months in power, there was no sign that the Labour government intended to repeal the provisions in the Criminal Justice Act.

Main points - Section 2.6

- The Criminal Justice Act became law in November 1994.
- Four key provisions of the Criminal Justice Act were controversial: (1) the effective abolition of the right to silence; (2) extending police officers' right to stop and search; (3) restricting the right to protest; and

(4) restricting the rights of those who do not have a mainstream lifestyle.
- Critics argue that these measures have tilted the balance of the law too far in favour of the police and too far against the freedom of the individual.

Activity 18.7 *The Criminal Justice Act*

Item A *The Criminal Justice Act 1994*

The right of silence

At present, the prosecution may not draw conclusions from a person's choice to remain silent in police custody or as a defendant in a trial. Under the new legislation this will no longer be the case. The Government argues that hardened criminals hide behind the right to silence. Civil rights organisations say that it puts the burden on defendants to prove their innocence rather than on the prosecution to prove their guilt.

Secure Training Centres

At present, offenders who are under 14 cannot be locked away except for very serious crimes. The Government proposes setting up special centres for offenders between the ages of 12 and 14 who have three or more previous convictions.

Terrorism

The police in Britain will be given special powers to stop and search people suspected of terrorist activity in a particular area for up to 28 days. They will be able to stop and search even if there are no grounds for suspicion. It will be a criminal offence to refuse to cooperate.

Ravers

If an outdoor festival or rave has not been licensed the police can stop it. It will be a criminal offence (with a maximum sentence of three months) if a person refuses to leave the site of such an event. Police will also be able to arrest someone whom they believe is going to one within a 5-mile radius.

Hunt saboteurs/peaceful protest/road blocks

A new offence of "aggravated trespass" will be introduced. Trespassers will now be committing a criminal offence if they are intending to disrupt a legal activity. This measure has been introduced to outlaw hunt saboteurs, but might easily apply to other forms of protest such as demonstrations against road-building, trade union pickets or demonstrations outside foreign embassies. The Bill also bans assemblies which are held on land without the permission of the owner and gives the police the power to stop people they suspect of travelling to such an assembly.

Travellers

Local authorities will no longer have to provide travellers with sites. It will now be a criminal offence for them to camp after a local authority has asked them to leave. It also becomes a criminal offence not to leave land when asked to do so by a senior police officer if there has been damage to land or if there are more than 6 vehicles on the land.

Squatters

It will become a criminal offence with a sentence of up to six months to occupy a squat for more than 24 hours after a landlord has gained an eviction order. It will also be possible for landlords or their representatives to force entry into squats to gain repossession. Appeals can only be made after the eviction.

This diagram was published in the *Guardian* on 12 July 1994, before the Criminal Justice Act came into effect (it came into effect in November 1994).

Item B *Demonstrating*

In November 1997, Susan Dickens wrote to the *Independent* newspaper describing what it was like to take part in a demonstration. She had attended a demonstration the previous weekend at a farm in Oxfordshire which breeds cats for vivisection. Most of the demonstrators, she noted, were middle-aged and elderly people. On their arrival, all demonstrators were stopped and told that they would not be allowed to use a public footpath unless they had a slip of paper showing they had been searched. Luckily, she said, everybody knew that they should not give their names and addresses. The demonstrators were then photographed and videoed throughout the day. After the demonstration was over, the coach carrying the demonstrators was stopped as it tried to leave for home. Police officers boarded it and told the demonstrators that they would have to be searched. It was only after several of the demonstrators had objected to this and threatened legal action that the police officers agreed to look at the slips of paper issued previously. The video team then moved down the coach, turning people's heads and lifting their heads if they tried to avoid being filmed. That, Susan Dickens concludes, is the state of policing in Britain today.

Adapted from the *Independent*, 20 November 1997.

Item C *Aggravated trespass*

On 4 November 1994, as the Criminal Justice Act became law, a group of protesters on a crane in Manchester were arrested and charged with aggravated trespass - one of the new offences created by the Act. Section 68 of the 1994 Act provides that: 'A person commits the offence of aggravated trespass if he trespasses on land in the open air and, in relation to any lawful activity which persons are engaging in on that land, does anything which is intended by him to have the effect of disrupting that activity'. Since 1994, it has been used extensively against hunt saboteurs and against people protesting against the Newbury bypass (between January 1996 and January 1997, more than 900 people were arrested - most for obstructing the Sheriff or aggravated trespass). At first sight, the offence might not seem unreasonable. The problem is that, in reality, for much of our daily lives we are on land owned by private or public bodies - be it roads, pavements, fields, hills or town squares. Furthermore, almost any protest committed by numbers of people can be considered as having the intention of disrupting the activities of others. If a group of people stands on a pavement, walks along a road or occupies a square, there is potential disruption. Much of the peaceful protest in this country is, therefore, potentially criminalised by this Act. To ban meetings if they can be classified as 'trespassory assemblies' is a sign that our right to protest is being eroded.

Adapted from Puddephatt 1995 and the *Times* 14 August 1996 & 12 January 1997.

Questions

1. a) Judging from Items A-C, how has the Criminal Justice Act changed policing in Britain?
   b) How has the Act affected police accountability?
   c) Give arguments for and against the view that the Criminal Justice Act is a fundamental attack on civil liberties.

2. Which provisions in the Criminal Justice Act are relevant to the events described in Items B?

3. a) Why do you think criticisms have been made against the introduction of the offence of aggravated trespass? Use Item C in your answer.
   b) How might supporters of the Criminal Justice Act justify the introduction of this offence?

Part 3 Other law enforcement agencies

Key issues

1. What organisations, other than the police, play a role in enforcing the law?
2. What is the structure and function of these organisations?
3. To what extent and through what channels are these organisations accountable?
4. Does the operation of these organisations pose a threat to civil liberties?

3.1 The armed forces

The armed forces and law enforcement

The armed forces are only ordered to enforce the law as a last resort in exceptional circumstances. But, law enforcement is one of their functions. It is a function which has roused considerable political controversy.

Between January 1990 and July 1998, the strength of the armed forces was reduced from 315,000 to 220,000 (in July 1998, there were 45,500 people serving in the navy, 119,000 in the army and 56,054 in the air force). This fall of 30% was due mainly to the end of the Cold War and government drives to reduce public expenditure (*Observer*, 5 July 1998). The main function of the armed forces is to protect Britain from aggression by foreign countries and to fight for British interests abroad.

In constitutional terms, control of the armed forces is vested in the Crown. In practice, this means that government ministers exercise control using the royal prerogative. Ministers in charge of the armed forces are advised by senior civil servants and the Chiefs of Staff of the armed forces. The opinion of these senior advisers has a significant impact on decisions - especially concerning tactical matters. This means that at the heart of the decision-making process is a group of unelected and unaccountable people. While this may be entirely justifiable on the basis of efficiency, it fits poorly the requirement that in a democratic society people who make decisions should be answerable to those affected by them.

Enforcing the law

In terms of law enforcement, the armed forces' most prominent recent role has been played in Northern Ireland. Troops have shared responsibility for security since 1969 (see above Section 1.3). Between 1969 and 1994 (when the IRA first announced a ceasefire) the armed forces were considered the only force capable of ensuring even a minimal degree of adherence to the law.

But, it is not just in Northern Ireland that members of the armed forces have been given the duty of enforcing the law in the UK. In the 1960s, senior officers were apparently engaged in plots to destabilise the Labour government headed by Harold Wilson. It is even alleged that, in certain circumstances, they would have staged a coup (Wright 1987). In addition, rumours circulated during the miners' strike of 1984-85 that the army was used to bolster the number of police officers on picket duty. It is alleged that army personnel wore police uniforms without the customary identity number given to Constables.

Problems with army involvement

A number of problems arise when members of the armed forces become involved in law enforcement.

First, members of the armed forces are not subject to the same laws as police officers. Rather their activities are governed by rules of engagement which determine the levels of force they can employ in particular circumstances. Second, there exists no formal channel through which the accountability of the armed forces can be obtained. And third, members of the armed forces, owing to their training, are more likely to use greater levels of force than police officers.

Bloody Sunday

All these problems are exemplified by the events which became known as 'Bloody Sunday' in Northern Ireland. On Sunday 20 January 1972, troops from the Parachute Regiment fired at demonstrators on a civil rights march in Northern Ireland, killing 13 demonstrators. The troops opened fire because, according to their rules of engagement, they could do so if their lives were threatened. Indeed, they claimed at a subsequent inquiry that they believed that they were under threat from armed terrorists and that they fired in reply to this threat. The report of the first inquiry, chaired by a judge, broadly accepted the story given by the troops (a second inquiry was set up in 1998). The fact that two inquiries were set up to examine this incident points to the lack of accountability of the army when it is undertaking a policing role. Also, it suggests that there was concern about the army's rules of engagement in such circumstances. Moreover, the high death toll demonstrates the tendency of members of the armed forces to use fatal force more readily than police officers might in similar circumstances.

Since the first inquiry, evidence has emerged that it is unlikely that the troops responded to a genuine threat to their lives. Some of the victims were found to have been shot in the back, for example and there is no evidence that the victims were armed. This new evidence led to the setting up of the second inquiry.

3.2 The role of the security services

Spies and secrecy

The popular image of the officer in the security services comes from fiction. Whether it is the fantastic exploits of James Bond or the more mundane activities of George Smiley (the Secret Service agent created by John Le Carré), the spy is seen to occupy a shadowy world of evil villains and their righteous enemies.

Until the Security Services Act 1989, there was little public information to contradict this view. Indeed, until then, no government had even admitted that the security services existed. Since 1989, more information has gradually become available and, in one respect at least, the fictionalised accounts and official statements are in agreement. Both suggest that the security services are a necessity if law and order, democracy, freedom and the British way of life are to be preserved against the wicked activities of spies, terrorists and subversives who can be found both at home and abroad. The ordinary law-abiding citizen, it is implied, has nothing to fear from the activities of the security services.

The structure of the security services

Although the structure of the security services is a state secret, five organisations can be identified:

1. **Special Branch** which is responsible for the policing of terrorism and subversion within the UK.
2. The **Defence Intelligence Staff** which is responsible for security within the armed forces.
3. **MI5** which is charged with the task of maintaining internal security (secret investigation and monitoring of subversive and terrorist activity within the UK).
4. **MI6** which undertakes the same tasks as MI5 but in respect to activities outside the UK.
5. **GCHQ** which monitors a wide variety of communications for intelligence purposes.

With all these organisations a central political question arises. Given the secrecy of the security services, how can sufficient scrutiny and accountability be enforced to ensure that their activities are confined to enforcing the law and investigating those who pose a genuine threat to the state?

Aims of the security services

The 1989 Security Service Act defines the objective of the service as:

> 'The protection of national security [against attempts to] undermine parliamentary democracy by political, industrial or violent means'.

The key point, therefore, is the dividing line between what is defined as a 'threat' and what is considered to be legitimate activity. The difficulty is that these are vague, ill-defined ideas.

In extreme cases, no problem arises. Suppose a terrorist organisation was planning to plant bombs in the House of Commons. Most people would agree that such people should be the target of the security forces. But, problems arise in less clearly defined cases. For example, is a trade union which organises a strike against the express wishes of the government subverting national security by industrial means? What about an organisation like the Campaign for Nuclear Disarmament (CND). In the 1980s, CND campaigned to abolish British nuclear weapons, a policy opposed by the government and most members of the armed forces. Was CND detrimental to national security? CND organisers acted lawfully. But, even though the law had not been broken, did the security forces have the right to intervene on the grounds that national security was under threat? Suppose that many members of CND were also members of the Labour Party. Would that give the security services the right to investigate the Labour Party as a threat to national security?

Spycatcher

The questions raised above are not hypothetical. In *Spycatcher* (which the government attempted to ban), former MI5 officer Peter Wright claimed that plans had been laid to prevent the Labour Party winning the October 1974 general election on the grounds that a Labour victory was not considered conducive to national security. This episode reveals two key points. First, it is the security services themselves which define what is and what is not a threat to national security. And second, members of the security forces tend to have a conservative viewpoint. Any activity of the political left, constitutional or otherwise, is viewed as a potential threat.

The Security Services in the 1990s

In the 1990s (since the end of the Cold War), the role of each branch of the security services has come under scrutiny. For example, in the early 1990s there was an internal battle over which branch should take the lead in dealing with terrorism in Northern Ireland. This had been the responsibility of Special Branch, but, after some significant failures, the lead role was transferred to MI5. Throughout the 1990s, MI6 and GCHQ have been searching for a significant role. Officially, fighting international terrorism and the international drugs trade is their primary function, though it has emerged that spying on members of the EU also falls within their remit (*Guardian*, 5 May 1998).

Lack of transparency

If the deliberations of the security services were open to public scrutiny they could be debated and challenged. But, because they are secret, they are not. As a result, anything that senior security service officers regard as a threat to national security can form the basis of covert action without any check or balance being placed upon such actions. So, granted that some secret service activity is necessary in a democratic society, how is the necessary degree of secrecy to be preserved whilst the freedom to engage in legitimate political activity is maintained?

Main points - Part 3

- Although the armed forces are only ordered to enforce the law as a last resort in exceptional circumstances, law enforcement is one of their functions.
- Law enforcement by the armed forces differs from that by the police in that soldiers have different rules of engagement, there are no channels to make them answer for their actions and they are more likely to use greater levels of force than police officers.
- Until 1989, hardly any information was available on the role and organisation of the security services.
- Because of the secrecy surrounding the security services, it is difficult to scrutinise the work of these services and to hold them to account. As a result, there is a danger that they will work for their own vested interest rather than for the public interest.

Activity 18.8 The security services

Item A *MI5 comes in from the cold*

MI5 came in from the cold yesterday carrying a glossy prospectus and carefully posed photographs of its director general, Stella Rimington. The object, says Mrs Rimington in a signed introduction to the 36 page brochure, is to dispel some of the more fanciful allegations surrounding the work of the most secret of security services in the Western world. MI5, the brochure tells us, employs 2,000 people (more than at the height of the Cold War). Over half are women. Over half are under the age of 40. Only a quarter are Oxbridge educated. The brochure explains that 70% of MI5's resources are devoted to countering terrorism. Only 5% is now spent looking for political subversives. In 1992, MI5 took control of anti-IRA intelligence-gathering in mainland Britain. The brochure is the government's reply to media reports about the activities of MI5. It paints a picture of an efficient organisation under the control of the Home Secretary.

Adapted from an article in the *Guardian*, 17 July 1993.

Item B *Security services' resources*

Budgets

Annual budgets, 1998/99

GCHQ	£440m
MI6	£140m
MI5	£120m

(not including Defence Intelligence Staff with a budget of approximately £150 million and expenditure on air reconnaissance and the police Special Branch)

US Intelligence Agencies	£16.6bm
German Intelligence Agencies	£237m

Number of staff

GCHQ	4,500
MI6	2,000
MI5	1,860

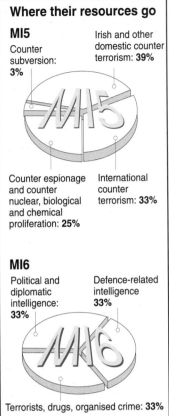

Where their resources go

MI5

Counter subversion: **3%**

Irish and other domestic counter terrorism: **39%**

Counter espionage and counter nuclear, biological and chemical proliferation: **25%**

International counter terrorism: **33%**

MI6

Political and diplomatic intelligence: **33%**

Defence-related intelligence **33%**

Terrorists, drugs, organised crime: **33%**

These figures were published by the government in 1996.

Questions

1. 'The security services play an important role in law enforcement.' Give arguments for and against this statement using Items A-C.
2. a) What do Items A-C tell us about the organisation and role of the security services?
   b) Using Items B and C, give arguments for and against the idea that the MI5, MI6 and GCHQ should be merged.
3. Why is the existence of the security services a problem in a democracy? Use Item C in your answer.

Item C *The security services in the late 1990s*

Too often secrecy has distorted the security services' view of the real world, encouraging tunnel vision and a closed political culture - they ignore what they don't want to hear. MI5 failed to predict the end of the IRA ceasefire in 1996. MI6 failed to predict the fall of the Shah of Iran, Saddam Hussein's invasion of Kuwait and, momentously, the end of the Cold War. Now, we are told, the agencies are more disciplined and, after a Whitehall initiative following the Scott Inquiry (which investigated the Arms to Iraq affair - see Chapter 13, Section 1.3 and Activity 17.4), more effective systems are in place to ensure that intelligence is passed to those who need it. Since the end of the Cold War, security service employees have been trying to find new tasks. Certainly, there have been new threats and new priorities - such as attempts by rogue nations (notably Libya, Iran and Iraq) to acquire chemical, nuclear and biological weapons, the growth of terrorist groups, drug-traffickers, money launderers and of international organised crime. But, should there continue to be three separate agencies chasing the same targets? David Bickford, former legal adviser to MI5 and MI6, thinks not and points to the 'triplication of management, bureaucracy and turf battles'. The agencies, however, argue that, although they may have similar targets, they have different functions. The dangers to democracy, however, in providing agencies with more and more technological and financial resources are obvious. Britain lags behind many countries in oversight arrangements. A parliamentary Security and Intelligence Committee meets in private and its annual reports are censored almost to the point of incomprehensibility. There is no effective scrutiny of the aggressive operations of MI6 whose agents are by law immune from prosecution if they commit acts abroad which would be illegal here.

Adapted from the *Guardian*, 5 May 1998.

Part 4 Party policy on law and order

Key issues

1. What are the main parties' policies on law and order?
2. How do these policies differ?

The Conservative Party

Traditionally, the Conservative Party has presented itself (and has been presented by the media) as a party which is 'strong' on law and order.

Conservative thinking on crime is based on two main beliefs. First, Conservatives believe that individuals must be held responsible for their own actions. Conservatives do recognise that the circumstances in which people find themselves may mitigate the wickedness of their actions. For example, a poor mother who steals food for her baby is less wicked than a poor mother who steals to support a drug habit. Nevertheless, Conservatives argue, it is wrong to break the law and people must accept the consequences if they choose to do so.

The second belief springs from the first. Conservatives believe that those who are personally responsible for crime should be punished for their actions and that their punishments should be severe and certain. They believe this, partly, because they hope that criminals and potential criminals will be deterred from committing similar crimes in the future and, partly, because they believe it is right for wrongdoers to pay for their crimes. These two beliefs have been the basis upon which the Conservatives' stance on law and order has been grounded.

Conservative policies 1992-97

As noted above (Section 2.6), the Conservative stance on law and order was particularly tough after the 1992 general election. Three Acts in particular embodied Conservative assumptions about personal responsibility and punishment - namely, the 1994 Police and Magistrate's Act, the 1994 Criminal Justice Act and the 1997 Police Act. In addition, a law was passed in 1997 introducing automatic minimum sentences for repeat violent offenders, persistent burglars and dealers in hard drugs (*Times*, 22 March 1997).

The Conservative Party's 1997 election manifesto (Conservative 1997) also reflected the two fundamental principles outlined above. Under the heading 'A safe and civil society', a complete section of the manifesto was directed to the question of law and order. The pledges made in this section of the manifesto are outlined in Box 18.3.

Box 18.3 The 1997 Conservative manifesto

In its 1997 general election manifesto, the Conservative Party made the following pledges:

- to support Chief Constables who develop local schemes to crack down on petty crime and improve public order
- to extend the use of close circuit television (CCTV) in public places
- to introduce a voluntary identity card scheme
- to enable courts to impose parental control orders on parents who refuse to keep their children under control (the order would force them to keep the children under control)
- to give courts the power to impose speedy sanctions on youngsters
- to set up a national crime squad
- to extend electronically monitored curfew orders
- to introduce new sentencing guidelines - anyone convicted of a second serious sexual or violent crime would be sentenced to life imprisonment, persistent burglars and drug dealers would receive a mandataory minimum sentence
- to modernise systems for dealing with fraud.

Adapted from Conservative 1997.

The policies of the Labour Party

Until the mid-1990s, the Labour Party did not place a great deal of emphasis on the issue of law and order. Labour's 1992 manifesto, for example, devoted only a single paragraph to the subject. But, the rise in crime in the early 1990s and a new approach by Labour's frontbench team led to a great deal more energy being devoted to this policy area during the Conservatives' fourth term in office. By the time the Labour government was elected in May 1997, the party's opinion poll approval ratings on law and order had overtaken those of the Conservatives.

Labour's traditional view

Labour's traditional policy on law and order had two main strands. The first strand was the assumption that crime is as much a result of poor social conditions as it is a result of individual wickedness or weakness. As a result, those who break the law deserve not only criticism and punishment, but also understanding and the chance to reform their ways. The second strand leads from the first. Since crime is, in large part at least, the result of poor social conditions, then resources should be used to improve these social conditions rather than simply to punish criminals (since improving social conditions will automatically reduce crime). Similarly, since criminals deserve understanding and the chance to reform themselves, resources should be used to provide the facilities for rehabilitation. Punishment has its place, but it is only part of the solution to the law and order problem.

The traditional Labour emphasis on socio-economic causes of crime can be seen in the commitments made in Labour's 1992 manifesto. In this manifesto, the Labour Party promised:

- to work in cooperation with local authorities to remove many of the causes of crime, especially crime in inner city local authority housing estates
- to provide central government assistance in modernising these estates by improving street lighting, demolishing derelict buildings and fencing in waste land
- to ban the sale of replica guns, to place more officers on the beat and to promote non-custodial sentences.

This last point highlighted a significant difference between the ideology of the Labour and Conservative parties on this matter. The Conservatives stressed the punitive aspects of punishment (for example, a prison building programme) whilst Labour stressed the element of rehabilitation and community service in punishment (for example, the emphasis on non-custodial sentences).

New Labour and law and order

Since 1993, Labour's thinking on law and order has changed fundamentally. In particular, a stress has been placed on the duties and responsibilities that individuals have as citizens. As shadow Home Secretary, Tony Blair argued that policy should not be determined by consideration of socio-economic factors alone. Individuals, he argued, have a moral duty to take responsibility for their own actions and for their community as a whole. This greater emphasis on individual responsibility meant a corresponding reduction in the role ascribed to social factors in explaining criminal behaviour. As a result, Labour policy became far more concerned with how to deter, control and punish individuals responsible for crime. As shadow Home Secretary, Blair coined the slogan 'tough on crime, tough on the causes of crime' and, once he became Labour Leader, this was the foundation upon which New Labour constructed its law and order policies.

Labour's 1997 election manifesto

The shift in emphasis was evident in the 1997 Labour Party election manifesto which included a section entitled 'Be tough on crime and the causes of crime'. Labour's approach to law and order is described as follows:

> 'We propose a new approach to law and order: tough on crime and tough on the causes of crime. We insist on individual responsibility for crime, and will attack the causes of crime by our measures to relieve social deprivation.' (Labour 1997, p.22)

The pledges made in this section of the manifesto are outlined in Box 18.4. The only reference in the manifesto to the rehabilitation of criminals was a pledge to attack the drug problem in prisons.

Labour in power

After 18 months in power, the Labour government had taken a number of steps towards fulfilling its manifesto pledges. In October 1997, for example, former Chief Constable Keith Hellawell was appointed as a 'drug czar' (coordinator of the battle against drugs). Most notable, however, was Jack Straw's Crime and Disorder Bill which was published in December 1997 (see Items B-D in Activity 18.9 below) and received royal assent on 31 July 1998.

In July 1998, Jack Straw announced that the government was prepared to accept plans drawn up by Chief Constables to allow private security guards to patrol public spaces. This was a significant departure since the use of private security guards in a role traditionally performed by the police had always been rejected in the past. Four main arguments were used to support the idea. First, it would reduce costs since private security staff are cheaper to employ than police officers. Second, it would allow the police to use their skills more efficiently since they would not have to spend so much time on the beat.

Box 18.4 The 1997 Labour manifesto

In its 1997 general election manifesto, the Labour Party made the following pledges:

- to move police officers from the office to the beat
- to introduce fast-track punishment for persistent young offenders
- to decentralise the Crown Prosecution Service to make it more effective in prosecuting criminals
- to implement an effective sentencing system to ensure greater consistency and stricter punishment for repeat offenders
- to crack down on small-scale crime and disorder
- to introduce community safety orders to deal with threatening neighbours
- to introduce child protection orders to deal with young children neglected by their parents
- to create new offences of racial harassment and racially motivated violence
- to appoint a 'drugs czar' to coordinate the battle against drugs
- to provide greater support for victims of crimes
- to allow MPs a free vote on a Bill to ban handguns.

Adapted from Labour 1997.

Third, it would increase security since there would be more people on patrol. And fourth, it would usefully employ people - helping to combat unemployment.

Policies of the Liberal Democrats

Liberal Democrat thinking on law and order reflects a philosophical commitment to the idea of community. In the Liberal Democrats' 1992 general election manifesto, they placed great emphasis on the rebuilding of communities, arguing that this was the most effective means of avoiding many crimes. The emphasis on community was also apparent in their policies on sentencing. The manifesto stressed the importance of making available to courts effective community service sentences. The idea behind this was that those who committed crimes such as burglary and theft against the community were forced to serve their sentence in the community. This, it was hoped, would rebuild a commitment to the community.

This approach was repeated in the 1997 general election manifesto (Lib Dem 1997). Alone of the major parties, the Liberal Democrats' proposals on law and order were contained in a chapter of the manifesto not solely devoted to crime and punishment, but to 'building secure communities'. As this title suggests, the Liberal Democrats believe that the best way to combat crime is to build a physical and an ideological sense of community by improving housing, fighting homelessness and developing community policing initiatives. Community-based sentences again featured in the manifesto as a means of ensuring that criminals repay their debt to the communities they have damaged.

Main points - Part 4

- **Conservative thinking on crime is based on two main beliefs - that individuals must be held responsible for their own actions and that those who are personally responsible for crime should be punished for their actions.**
- **Labour's traditional view was that crime is as much a result of poor social conditions as it is a result of individual wickedness or weakness. As a result, resources should be used to improve social conditions rather than simply to punish criminals.**

- **Since 1993, the Labour Party's position has changed. Labour now accepts individual responsibility for crime. Tackling social problems is seen as only part of the solution.**
- **Liberal Democrat thinking on law and order reflects a philosophical commitment to the idea of community. Liberal Democrats believe that the best way to combat crime is to implement policies which build a sense of community.**

Activity 18.9 *New Labour and law and order*

Item A *Tony Blair's view*

Crime is quintessentially a problem the individual cannot tackle alone. Crime demands that communities work as communities to fight it. There is a growing and open determination in the Labour Party to make crime a genuine 'people's' issue, a national campaign for better and safer communities. We are moving beyond the old debate which suggested there were only two sides - those who want to punish the criminal and those who point to poor social conditions in which crime breeds. The obvious common sense is that the choice is false and misleading. People have a right to go about their business without being attacked or abused or having their property stolen. They have a right, society has a duty, to bring those who commit crimes to justice. Equally, the purpose of any system of punishment should not just be to punish and deter but also to rehabilitate, for the good of society as well as the criminal. Above all, any sensible society will recognise that poor education and housing, inadequate or cruel family backgrounds, low employment prospects and drug abuse will affect the likelihood of young people turning to crime. We should be tough on crime and tough on the underlying causes of crime.

Adapted from Blair 1993.

Item B *The 1998 Crime and Disorder Act (1)*

The 1998 Crime & Disorder Act - main points

- Anti-social behaviour orders to tackle harassment by children over ten, nuisance neighbours and others.
- Parental orders for the parents of delinquent children.
- Sex offender orders - will ban 100,000 known sex offenders from loitering near schools and playgrounds.
- Supervision orders for sex and violent criminals lasting for up to ten years when they leave prison.
- Child safety orders which place children below the age of ten under official supervision.
- Curfew orders which ban children below the age of ten from being out alone after a specified time.
- Abolition of 'doli incapax' which assumed that a child under the age of ten could not commit a crime.
- New system of police warnings and young offender programmes to replace cautions.
- Courts to be able to remand children over age 12 directly to secure accommodation.
- Reparation orders to make young offenders apologise to or compensate their victims.
- New racially aggravated offences covering assaults, public order and harassment.
- Treatment and testing orders allowing compulsory drug testing and treatment for addicts over 16.
- Early release under curfews enforced by electronic tags for up to 6,000 prisoners a year.
- Time taken to deal with young offenders by courts to be halved.
- TV links between courts and prisons.

The Crime and Disorder Bill received royal assent on 31 July 1998.

Item C *The 1998 Crime and Disorder Act (2)*

At the launch of the Crime and Disorder Bill on 3 December 1997, the Home Secretary, Jack Straw, said that his aim was to implement a 'zero tolerance strategy'. He wanted to give power back to people in law-abiding communities and to undermine and disrupt gangs, drug dealers, criminal families and people whose sport is baiting their neighbours. He emphasised that the legislation did not mean that more offenders would be jailed - for example, the measures for dealing with young offenders should eventually prevent them from reaching adult prisons. The provisions of the Bill, he claimed, reflected the frustrations felt by the police, communities and local authorities who were unable to deal with high levels of disorder, harassment and racial attacks. The planned anti-social behaviour orders would cover anyone aged ten or over. They were aimed at offenders who harass neighbours or cause persistent trouble on council housing estates. Police and local authorities will be able to use the lower burden of proof required in civil cases to obtain restraining orders and breaches could be punished by up to five years in prison. Parents whose children are subject to an order will have to attend counselling or parenting sessions. Parents whose children regularly play truant will face parenting orders. For the first time, the proposal to introduce a period of extended supervision for violent offenders after they leave prison was spelled out. Summing up, Jack Straw said: 'It's not a magic wand. There are no magic wands about dealing with human behaviour. The more I am able to make people feel safer, the better it is.'

Adapted from the *Guardian* and the *Times*, 4 December 1997.

Item D *The 1998 Crime and Disorder Act (3)*

Laws which seek to regulate the way in which people behave tend towards extremes. On one level, the Home Secretary's Bill is a straightforward response to public concern about social disorder. But, it also greatly extends the powers of the authorities. It enables the police to arrest people for causing alarm or distress; forces councils to devise anti-disorder strategies; requires parents to ensure children attend school and are home by fixed times. All this may catch the headlines, but it is unlikely to improve behaviour. Rather, it is likely to lead to a deterioration in relations with the police. It is the police who will have to interpret, then impose the new laws. Three further criticisms can be made. First, the antisocial behaviour clause is vague and could be used against people who are simply different. Second, the detention and training order means that a child as young as 12 could be held in prison. And third, the abolition of 'doli incapax' (which presumes a child under the age of ten is incapable of committing a criminal offence) means that primary school age children will be treated the same as adults by the courts. The Bill could turn out to be one of the most sweeping attacks on civil rights this century.

Adapted from the *Times*, 4 and 16 December 1997.

Item E *Photo montage*

Questions

1. Judging from Items A-D, how does Labour's approach to law and order differ from that adopted by (a) the Conservative Party and (b) the Liberal Democrats?

2. a) Judging from Items B-D, what were the aims of the Crime and Disorder Act?
   b) Which manifesto pledges were fulfilled by the Act?
   c) What does this Act tell us about the Labour government's attitude towards law and order?

3. 'The government got it right with the Crime and Disorder Act'. Using Items C and D, give arguments for and against this view.

4. Look at Item E. How can the problems illustrated by this picture be solved? Answer this question from the perspective of (a) a Labour politician (b) a Conservative politician and (c) a Liberal Democrat politician.

References

Arthur (1987) Arthur, M., *Northern Ireland: Soldiers Talking*, Sidgwick & Jackson, 1987.

Benyon (1986) Benyon, J., 'Turmoil in the cities', *Social Studies Review*, Vol.1.3, January 1986.

Blair (1993) Blair, T., 'Why crime is a socialist issue', *New Statesman and Society*, 29 January 1993.

Brearley (1996) Brearley, N., 'Law and order in England and Wales' in *Lancaster (1996)*.

Cathcart (1998) Cathcart, B., 'Murder in the Dark', *New Statesman*, 10 April 1998.

Childs (1992) Childs, D., *Britain Since 1945*, Routledge, 1992.

Conservative (1997) *You Can Only Be Sure With The Conservatives*, Conservative Party manifesto, Conservative Party, 1997.

Farrell (1976) Farrell, J., *The Orange State*, Pluto Press, 1976.

Fine & Millar (1985) Fine, B. & Millar, R. (eds), *Policing the Miners' Strike*, Lawrence & Wisehart, 1985.

Glinert (1992) Glinert, E., 'The force of calm after the crusades', *New Statesman and Society*, 17 January 1992.

Graef (1989) Graef, R., *Talking Blues*, Fontana, 1989.

Habermas (1973) Habermas, J., *Legitimation Crises*, Heinemann, 1973.

HMSO (1995) Central Office of Information, *Criminal Justice*, Aspects of Britain series, HMSO, 1995.

Kettle (1985) Kettle, M., 'The National Reporting Centre and the 1984 miners' strike' in *Fine & Millar (1985)*.

Labour (1997) *New Labour - Because Britain Deserves Better*, Labour Party manifesto, Labour Party, 1997.

Lancaster (1996) Lancaster, S. (ed.), *Developments in Politics*, Vol.7, Causeway Press, 1996.

Leys (1983) Leys, C., *Politics in Britain*, Verso, 1983.

Lib Dem (1997) *Make the Difference*, Liberal Democrat manifesto, Liberal Democrats, 1997.

Puddephatt (1995) Puddephatt, A., 'The Criminal Justice and Public Order Act and the need for a Bill of Rights', *Talking Politics*, Vol.8.1, Autumn 1995.

Reiner (1992) Reiner, R., *The Politics of the Police*, Harvester Wheatsheaf, 1992.

Social Trends (1994) Central Statistical Office, *Social Trends Vol.24*, HMSO, 1994.

Social Trends (1998) Central Statistical Office, *Social Trends Vol.28*, HMSO, 1998.

Williams (1998) Williams, J., 'Crime trends and the fear of crime', *Sociology Review*, Vol.7.4, April 1998.

Wright (1987) Wright, P., *Spycatcher*, Viking Press, 1987.

19 Political information

Introduction

Most people gain their information about politics through the mass media - television, radio and newspapers. The media decides what is newsworthy and then explores the issues which are thrown up by the news. Furthermore, the media controls the way in which news items are presented. Reports are edited. Speeches are reduced to 'soundbites'. As a result, the media does not just keep people informed about what is happening in the world. It offers a particular interpretation of what is happening.

Because people often have no way of checking the validity of what they see, hear or read, they are, to a large extent, reliant on the mass media to shape their view of the world. If the mass media can shape people's view of the world, then it may be able to influence their political behaviour. This is one of the reasons why the way in which the media works and who controls it are issues of great importance. This chapter considers how much influence the mass media has - both upon the political behaviour of the individual citizen and upon the political culture of the UK.

A frequent criticism of the mass media is that it lacks objectivity and impartiality. Often, this criticism comes from politicians. Yet, politicians rely on the mass media to communicate their point of view. This chapter considers the pressures on the different media outlets and asks whether there is any justification for the criticism that the media is subjective and partial. It also considers the extent to which government intervenes to suppress the dissemination of political information. Can restrictions on the freedom of information ever be justified? If so, in what circumstances?

Chapter summary

Part 1 defines the term the 'mass media' and describes its historical development. It considers why the dissemination of political information is important in a democracy.

Part 2 examines the ownership and control of the press. It considers whether there is political bias in the press.

Part 3 examines the ownership and control of radio and television.

Part 4 asks how much influence the mass media has. It looks at the different ways in which this question has been answered and considers the future of the media in Britain.

Part 5 focuses on secrecy and whether or not there is a genuine move towards open government.

Part 1 The mass media

Key issues

1. What do we mean by the 'mass media'?
2. How did the mass media develop?
3. Why is political information important in a democracy?

1.1 Development of the mass media

What is the mass media?

The mass media can be defined as:

> 'The methods and organisations used by specialist social groups to convey messages to large, socially mixed and widely dispersed audiences.' (Trowler 1988, p.5)

Television, newspapers, radio, cinema, magazines and books are all part of the mass media. Usually, however, the term is used to refer to television, the radio and newspapers (the press). The growth of the mass media is a 20th century phenomenon. In 1900, books and newspapers were available, but were too expensive for most people to buy regularly. Radio and cinema had been discovered, but were not widely available. Television had not been invented.

The development of the mass media was only possible because of the development of modern technology. As Barratt puts it:

> '[Mass communication] is a product of industrial techniques such as the steam powered printing press, cinematography and

radio and television broadcasting and receiving equipment.' (Barratt 1986, p.14). The development of the mass media is, in other words, a product of the process of industrialisation that took place in Britain in the 19th century. New technology combined with new ways of work and new social conditions to provide the conditions for the growth of the mass media.

The Press

The first media outlet to develop was the newspaper industry. Modern newspapers have been published since the 18th century. The first daily newspaper, the *Courant*, began publication in 1702. The *Times* began publication in 1785. But throughout the 18th and early 19th centuries the content of newspapers was restricted by Parliament. Until 1771, newspapers were forbidden to report parliamentary proceedings and there were frequent bans on the reporting of subjects regarded as 'political'. In addition, a stamp duty was imposed on newspapers in 1725 (a tax which added to the price of each newspaper). This was designed to restrict circulation of the radical press by making their newspapers too expensive for ordinary people. The abolition of stamp duty in 1855 is regarded as a major step on the road to a free press. However, in the 19th century, low standards of living and low levels of literacy combined to ensure that it was mainly the better-off members of society who read newspapers.

The growth of a mass readership

It was not until the beginning of the 20th century that newspapers actively sought a mass readership. The turning point was the decision of Alfred Harmsworth (Lord Northcliffe) in 1896 to buy the *Daily Mail*. Newspapers in the 19th century looked dull. No pictures were included and the columns were filled with long reports of political speeches in minuscule text. The *Mail* under Harmsworth (Northcliffe) changed all this by using large headlines and pictures, by no longer including long reports of political speeches and by covering sport. These changes appealed to people. The *Mail*'s circulation grew from 200,000 in 1896 to 980,000 in 1900 to 1.48 million in 1920. As the readership grew, so did the revenue generated from printing adverts. The success of the *Mail* (especially its financial success) was noted by the other newspapers and most began to copy the new formula. The new appearance of newspapers combined with their cheap price resulted in a growing readership. By 1920, two newspapers sold over a million copies per day. By 1930, five newspapers sold over a million copies per day. And, by 1939, two newspapers sold more than 2 million copies per day.

Radio and the BBC

The period during which newspapers began to attract a mass audience was also the period in which radio became established in most homes. The 1920s have sometimes been described as the 'golden age of wireless' (radio was called 'wireless' in its early years to differentiate it from the telephone). It was in the 1920s that radio first gained a mass audience in Britain. This was facilitated by the ability of radio manufacturers to mass produce cheap radios. The number of radios in Britain rose from 35,000 in 1922 to three million in 1929 and over nine million in 1939.

The birth of the BBC

At first, private companies were allowed to apply to the post office for licences to broadcast radio programmes and to sell radios. By 1922, over 100 companies had submitted applications. The government then persuaded these companies to join together into a single organisation - the British Broadcasting Company. This operated as a private company until 1926 when a Royal Charter changed its status. From 1926, the company became a 'corporation' (see Chapter 16, Section 4.2). Its aim was no longer to make a profit but to provide a public service. To ensure that the British Broadcasting Corporation (BBC) was politically independent, a board of directors, not the government, had control over what was broadcast and the BBC was financed not by adverts but by a licence fee paid by each owner of a radio.

The first director-general of the BBC was John Reith. He had very firm ideas about the sort of values that should be promoted by the BBC. For example, Reith was a Christian and he only allowed religious and 'serious' programmes to be broadcast on Sundays. Also, he refused to allow people with regional accents to talk on the radio. Reith said in 1926:

'Our responsibility is to carry into the greatest possible number of homes everything that is best in every human department of knowledge, endeavour and achievement, and to avoid the things which are or may be hurtful. It is occasionally said that we are apparently setting out to give the public what we think they need and not what they want. But, few know what they want and very few what they need. There is often no difference.'

Radio remained the main broadcasting medium until the 1950s when television replaced it. Commercial radio was introduced for the first time in the 1970s.

Television

The first demonstration of television was organised by John Logie Baird and took place in London in January 1926. Ten years later the BBC began to broadcast television programmes. The BBC, however, did not use Baird's system. It used a system based on the cathode ray tube and developed by EMI in 1935. The first television programmes could only be seen in the London area. By 1939, just 12,000 people owned television sets. Whilst radio broadcasts were used as an important means of imparting information and maintaining morale during the Second World

War, television broadcasting shut down when war was declared and did not resume until 1945. It was only in the 1950s that television began to become a mass medium.

Television after the war

The turning point was the broadcast of the Queen's coronation in 1953. In 1950, just 10% of homes had television sets. But, neighbours crowded into homes with televisions to see the coronation and what they saw caught their imagination. By 1963, just ten years after the coronation, 90% of homes had television sets.

Since the 1950s, television technology has improved tremendously and there is a growing choice of programmes and channels. The Independent Television Authority (ITA) was set up in 1954 and commercial television (television funded by revenue from advertising) began to be broadcast in 1955. Colour televisions replaced black and white sets in the 1970s. In the early 1980s, Channel Four was set up to cater for minority interests and, in the late 1980s, cable and satellite television became available. By 1992 over 99% of households had at least one television set. Nearly 10% of homes had three or more colour television sets. By 1997, over 82% of households owned a video recorder and over 4 million homes could receive satellite television (Social Trends 1998). By 1998, the introduction of digital television (and, with it, the possibility of hundreds of channels) was imminent.

1.2 The impact of the growth of the mass media

A second-hand version of reality

The growth of the mass media has brought a new era in the conveying of political information. In effect, it has resulted in the manufacture of a second-hand version of reality. By the time a news item appears on the television or in the newspaper, what actually happened at the original event has necessarily been altered by the involvement of media professionals. No matter how long the real event, for example, the news item on television will probably be over within five minutes and it is unlikely to be allotted more than a page in a newspaper. That means that what happened has to be edited down to fit the slot. So, only part of a politician's speech is given verbatim. The remainder of the speech is summarised by the reporter. And, by summarising, the reporter is providing a particular viewpoint or interpretation.

Limited feedback

Not only does the media's intervention produce a second-hand version of an event, it also encourages apathy rather than active political participation. Whilst someone who attends a political meeting is able to respond to what is said by asking questions, applauding or heckling, the mass media's audience

has limited feedback - letter writing, phone-in programmes and, very occasionally, open access slots. And even with the limited feedback which does exist, audience responses nearly always have to pass through an editing system with the media professionals acting as 'gate-keepers'.

A major source of information

Despite these drawbacks, the various media outlets have become a major source of information in general and of political information in particular. People receive news of political events and developments much more quickly than they did 50 or 100 years ago. Political information is much more widely available than was ever the case in the past. And, people certainly take advantage of the various media outlets which are available - for example, on average in 1996, people in Britain spent around 25 hours a week watching television and 15 hours a week listening to the radio (Social Trends 1998).

Whether or not people are better informed about politics, however, is a matter of debate. The media provides entertainment, not just information, and some critics claim that the amount of serious political reporting as a proportion of total media output has diminished (see, for example, Curran & Seaton 1997).

Political ignorance and manipulation of information

Hillyard & Percy-Smith argue that:

> 'Effective political participation at all levels depends crucially on access to information. Decisions about which party to support or which policies to endorse, and judgements about the capabilities of decision makers require that people have the facts about those parties, policies and decisions. But, access to information in Britain is severely limited.' (Hillyard & Percy-Smith 1988, p.111)

Democracy requires the informed participation of the people. Yet, the sum total of many people's political participation is to cast a vote every five years. Between elections, only a minority of people take an active interest in politics (see Chapter 7, Section 2.1). It is, therefore, perhaps no surprise to find that political ignorance is widespread, particularly amongst young people. A British Youth Council survey carried out in 1998, for example, found that 60% of young people did not know that William Hague was the Leader of the Conservative Party and 76% did not know the name of their local MP (*Guardian*, 3 July 1998). If people are not well informed, they are unable to tell when information is being manipulated for certain ends.

Explanations of political ignorance

Explanations of political ignorance vary according to ideological stance. Those on the left tend to argue that people in power have a vested interest in maintaining ignorance and trivialising political matters to avoid debate. They claim that conscious efforts are made to limit information and to control what individuals can be told. Those on the right, however, tend to argue that most people have no need to develop a political understanding. Indeed, many people are not capable of so doing. The right claims that politics should be left to those who are really concerned about it.

News management
Taking a historical perspective, it is clear that those in power have sought to limit the amount of political information that is available to ordinary people. What was blatant control of political information in the 18th and 19th centuries has evolved into more varied and perhaps more subtle forms of what is now known as 'news management' or 'spin'. Sir Angus Maude, Paymaster General in Margaret Thatcher's first government, was responsible for policy on information. He argued:

> 'News management, when it means representing the facts in a way that reflects most favourably on the government, is a perfectly fair process and it is one which has been undertaken by all governments since the beginning of time.' (Cockerell et al. 1984, p.52)

Information and the 'national interest'
Information is itself rarely neutral. Whether the information is made available, the way in which it is presented, the context of the ideas, the emphasis that is given - all these factors help to dictate what sense is or is not made of political developments. Those who present political information are themselves rarely disinterested observers. In a 'free' society, it tends to be assumed that there should be a free trade in ideas. This, however, ignores the fact that some individuals, groups or institutions may be in a more powerful position than others to give their definitions of reality.

Governments, in particular, are in a powerful position to provide their version of reality and in so doing they often justify their actions by claiming to have acted 'in the national interest'. This claim is frequently made during times of conflict - such as in the middle of a major strike or during a war. During the Falklands War, for example, the government was able - through censorship and tight control over what information should be made publicly available - to present a view of events which fitted with its own political position. The government was undoubtedly supported in this by the popular press which launched a tide of jingoism (extreme patriotism). When the BBC, attempting to maintain its reputation for independence, questioned aspects of military policy, it came under attack from the government. On this occasion, the national interest became the same as the government's interest and, therefore, the same as the Conservative Party's interest. Indeed, some critics have argued that this confusion between

national and partisan interests is not confined to times of crisis. Robert Harris, for example, in a review of information policy and the media in the Falklands War, concluded:

> 'The instinctive secrecy of the military and the civil service; the prostitution of sections of the press; the lies, the misinformation, the manipulation of public opinion by the authorities; the political intimidation of broadcasters; the ready connivance of the media in their own distortion...all these occur as much in normal peacetime in Britain as in war.' (Harris 1983, p.151)

The role of the mass media
The above discussion suggests that a number of different interpretations of the role which the mass media should and does play are possible. According to Miller (1991), there are three contrasting interpretations - the media's role is:

- mobilising
- libertarian
- public service.

First, if the media plays a mobilising role, it is subordinate to the state. The government is the guardian of the national interest and the media promotes this national interest. Second, if, on the other hand, the media plays a libertarian role, it has freedom to publish and to broadcast what it likes, with only very few constraints. And third, if the media plays a public service role, it has a duty to scrutinise the government, to hold it to account for its actions and to respond to demands from the public.

Main points - Part 1

- **The growth of the mass media is a 20th century phenomenon. Usually, the term is used to refer to television, the radio and newspapers (the press).**
- **The growth of the mass media has resulted in the manufacture of a second-hand version of reality. Actual events are edited and interpreted by media professionals.**
- **Although people receive news much more quickly than they did in the past and more political information is available, the work of the media encourages apathy rather than active political participation.**
- **Democracy requires the informed participation of the people, yet there is evidence of widespread political ignorance. This allows media outlets and politicians to manipulate information.**
- **Governments restrict the flow of information by claiming that it is not 'in the national interest' to allow the public access to some information.**
- **The media can play one of three roles - a mobilising role, a libertarian role or a public service role.**

Activity 19.1 The impact of the growth of the mass media

Item A Greater access to information

Before the mass media existed, a child growing up in a slowly changing village built his or her model of reality out of images received from a tiny handful of sources - the teacher, the priest, the chief or official and above all the family. There was no television or radio in the home to give the child a chance to meet many different kinds of strangers from many different walks of life and even from different countries. Very few people ever saw a foreign city. The result was that people had only a small number of different people to imitate or model themselves on. Their choices were even more limited by the fact that the people they could model themselves on were themselves all of limited experience. The images of the world built up by the village child, therefore, were extremely narrow.

Adapted from Toffler 1980.

Item B Political ignorance

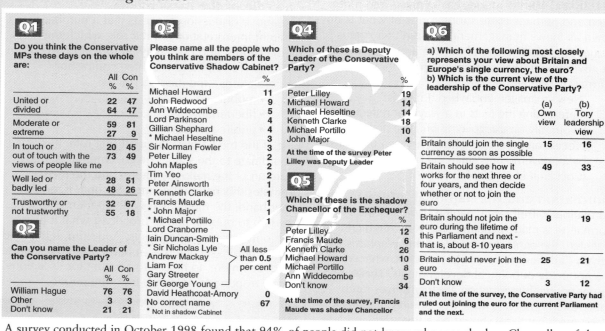

A survey conducted in October 1998 found that 94% of people did not know who was shadow Chancellor of the Exchequer (Francis Maude), 81% of people did not know who was Deputy Leader of the Conservative Party (Peter Lilley) and 24% of people did not know who was Leader of the Conservative Party. Asked to name people who were members of the shadow Cabinet, 67% of people could not think of a single correct name. Whilst just 19% of people knew what the Conservative Party's policy was on Europe, only 3% both knew what the policy was and supported it.

Adapted from the *Observer*, 4 October 1998.

Item C Depoliticisation of the news

A few years ago, a BBC focus group aimed to find out people's attitudes towards political news. Although the members of the group at first said that political news was very important, it gradually emerged that most found it boring and inaccessible. At this point, the discussion stopped and the BBC researchers went back to report their findings that the audience did not like political news - a conclusion also reached by the other main television channels. As a result, radio and television programming has gradually been depoliticised. This has serious implications for the quality of the national political debate because it has been mirrored by similar trends in the national press. News programmes on all channels have scaled down their political coverage. There are four reasons why this process has accelerated since May 1997. First, after the saturation coverage of the general election, producers (quite sensibly) welcome a reduction in political output. Second, the government's highly efficient media managers have succeeded in making politics extraordinarily dull. Third, even when there is media interest in a political story, the government spin team simply denies the media access to the important people. And fourth, the culture of depoliticisation has had an effect on the minds and actions of BBC producers and executives. Yet, the conclusions drawn from the BBC focus group were wrong. If researchers were to tease out viewers' genuine values, they would find that people recognise the importance of allowing politicians access to the airwaves to put their case. They also recognise that the public has the right to hear politicians questioned about their policies and actions in ways which don't allow them to deliver soundbites in reverential silence.

Adapted from the *New Statesman*, 31 July 1998.

Item D *Manipulating information*

(1) Should Britain stay in the EU?

58 — Stay in
42 — Leave

(2) On balance, should Britain join the European single currency?

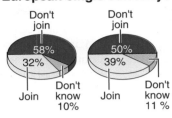

Don't join 58% / 32% Join / Don't know 10%

Don't join 50% / 39% Join / Don't know 11%

April 1996   November 1997

(3) Should Britain join a single currency:

(a) as soon as possible?
(b) after waiting to see if it works?
(c) never?

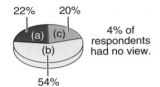

22% (a)   20% (c)
54% (b)
4% of respondents had no view.

Sun   *November 1997*

You don't want Euro bankers to run Britain

Huge snub for EMU in dramatic MORI poll

Worried voters last night gave the European single currency a massive thumbs down and warned

Tony Blair not to gamble on scrapping the pound...

Judging from the headlines and story in the *Sun* (left), it might be assumed that the poll commissioned by the newspaper had found that public scepticism towards the EU had scaled new heights and that supporters of a single currency were a tiny and shrinking minority. In fact, the poll found the opposite and a more relevant headline would have been 'Eurosceptics in retreat as voters back Chancellor Brown'. Graph (1) above shows that 58% of people wanted to remain in the EU. What the *Sun* failed to mention was that this was the highest pro-EU figure MORI had found since 1994. Graph (2) above shows that the 26% lead for the anti-euro camp in April 1996 had fallen to 11% by November 1997. In other words, it had halved in 19 months. But, the *Sun* only mentioned the figures from November 1997. Similarly, the *Sun* claimed that the figures in Graph (3) above amounted to 'a snub to pro-Europeans' and revealed 'support for William Hague's hardline rejection of EMU'. A more realistic assessment, however, is that most people (54%) share the government's pragmatic policy towards the euro - join if it works and stay out if it does not.

Adapted from the *Guardian*, 23 November 1997.

Item E *Government intervention*

A BBC television *Panorama* special was blocked by the government on 6 August 1998, hours before it planned to reveal further details of an alleged plot by MI6 officers to assassinate the Libyan Leader Colonel Gadaffi. The injunction followed the breakdown of protracted talks between the BBC's top executives and government officials. It is understood that the investigation sheds new light on the circumstances surrounding the alleged plot against Gadaffi. On 6 August, the *Guardian* published allegations made by the MI5 agent David Shaylor (currently in jail in Paris) that there was an attempt to assassinate Gadaffi in 1996. The allegations were first published in the *New York Times* on 4 August. The BBC said that it was anxious to establish that nothing it proposed to broadcast would threaten the safety of security personnel. It said it was urgently considering the next step 'in the belief that the public interest now requires full examination of the allegations made by Mr Shaylor'. The government earlier moved quickly to rubbish Mr Shaylor's allegations, though ministers were careful not to deny an unauthorised operation. Lord Williams, the Home Office minister, denied on BBC Radio 4's *Today* programme that there was an 'official plot' to kill Gadaffi.

Adapted from the *Guardian*, 7 August 1998.

Questions

1. Judging from Items A-E, what have been the benefits and drawbacks of the growth of the mass media?
2. What do Items B and C tell us about political ignorance in the late 1990s? What, if anything, should be done to counter this? Explain your answer.
3. 'The growth of the mass media has not necessarily led to greater democracy.' Explain this statement using Items B-E.
4. Using Items D and E, explain how information is manipulated.
5. Would you say that the British media plays a mobilising, libertarian or public service role? Give reasons for your answer.

Part 2 The press

Key issues

1. Who owns the press?
2. Why is ownership important and what role do owners of the press play?
3. What other factors affect newspapers' dissemination of political information?

2.1 Ownership and the press

Who owns the press?

The press in Britain is privately owned and controlled. It is free to print whatever it likes within the laws of libel and the requirements of official secrecy. This section looks at who owns newspapers and considers why ownership is concentrated into so few hands.

The quality and the tabloid press

A distinction is commonly made between the quality press (the 'broadsheets') and the tabloid press (the 'popular' press). The quality daily press is made up of the *Times*, *Daily Telegraph*, *Financial Times*, *Independent* and *Guardian*. The other dailies are all tabloids. Unlike the tabloid press, the quality press relies more heavily on advertising than sales for its commercial success.

The press barons

When newspapers first gained a mass readership in the early part of the 20th century, they were owned by wealthy individuals who are referred to collectively as 'press barons'. Three men dominated the press before the Second World War - the brothers Alfred and Harold Harmsworth (who became Lord Northcliffe and Lord Rothermere) and William Aitken (who became Lord Beaverbrook). Not only did the style of newspapers change under their ownership (see above, Section 1.1), all three imposed their own (right-wing) political viewpoints on their newspapers. For example, in the 1930s, for a short time, Rothermere decided to support the British Union of Fascists (BUF). As a result, the *Daily Mail* carried headlines such as: 'Give the Blackshirts a helping hand'. When Rothermere changed his mind about the BUF, so did the *Daily Mail*. That newspapers were being used as a vehicle to promote personal political views was freely admitted by Beaverbrook who said in 1948:

> 'I run the *Daily Express* purely for the purpose of making propaganda, and with no other motive.'

Multinationals

Today, much of the press is owned by multinational, multimedia corporations. These huge companies operate in a number of countries, tend to own a range of media outlets (for example, television stations as well as newspapers) and some have business interests which are nothing to do with the media. For example, News International which owns the *Times*, *Sunday Times*, *Sun* and *News of the World* newspapers in Britain also owns a large number of other newspapers, television stations and other operations (see Box 19.1). News International is the creation of Rupert Murdoch. Murdoch is a modern 'press baron'. But, as Box 19.1 suggests, his business interests are so wide that he has less time to become actively involved in the day-to-day running of his newspapers than was the case with press barons such as Northcliffe and Rothermere.

That does not mean that Murdoch (or the heads of the other multinationals) never intervene. When Harold Evans, editor of the *Times*, did not follow Murdoch's preferred line, he was dismissed. Evans claimed that Murdoch frequently sent him:

> 'Articles marked "worth reading" which espoused right-wing views [and he jabbed] a finger at headlines which he thought could have been more supportive of Mrs Thatcher.' (Evans 1984, p.296)

Negrine (1994) has pointed out that owners do appoint editors and chief executives. They decide budgets and staffing levels and they put their imprint on the organisations they own. As a result, editors and journalists work within already defined structures.

Exceptions to multinational control do exist. The *Guardian*, for example, is owned by a Trust which appoints the editor and guarantees editorial independence.

The concentration of ownership

Concentration of ownership of the press is nothing new. In 1908, for example, in addition to the *Daily Mail*, Northcliffe owned the *Daily Mirror*, the *Times*, the *Observer* and the *Dispatch*, as well as several periodicals and evening newspapers (Wagg 1989). Not only is concentration of ownership of the press nothing new, it has long been a cause of concern as this comment, made by a Labour MP in 1946, makes clear:

> 'For years we have watched this freedom [of the press] being whittled away. We have watched the destruction of great papers. We have watched the combines come in, buying up and killing independent journals and we have seen the honourable profession of journalism degraded by high finance and big business.' (quoted in Hansard, 29 October 1946)

Ownership of the press is narrower and more concentrated in Britain than anywhere else in the

Box 19.1 News International's holdings around the world

Television

United States
Fox Broadcasting Company
Fox Television Stations
WNYW - New York, NY
KTTV - Los Angeles, CA
WFLD - Chicago, IL
WFXT - Boston, MA
WTTG - Washington, DC
KRIV - Houston, TX
KSTU - Salt Lake City, UT
WHBQ-TV - Memphis, TN
WBRC-TV - Birmingham, AL
Acquisition pending
WHGP-TV - Greensboro, NC
Sale Pending
WATL - Atlanta, GA
Fox News
Australia
Seven Network (10)

Cable and Satellite Television

United States
IX Networks
IX
IXM: Movies from Fox
Latin America
News Corporation/Globo
Joint Venture (3)
Canal Fox
United Kingdom
British Sky Broadcasting (7)
Germany
VOX (4)
Australia
FOXTEL (3)
Asia
Star TV
ZEE TV (4)

Filmed Entertainment

United States
Fox Filmed Entertainment
Twentieth Century Fox
Fox 2000
Fox Searchlight
Fox Family Films
Fox Animation Studios
Twentieth Century
Fox Television
Twentieth Television
Australia
Fox Studios Australia

Magazines and Inserts

United States
TV Guide
The Weekly Standard
News America FSI
Canada
News Canada FSI
Coupon Clipper
Plan and Save
United Kingdom & Europe
The Times Educational
Supplement
The Times Literary
Supplement
The Times Scottish
Educational Supplement
TV Hits (UK) (5)
Hit (Germany) (5)
Inside Soap (UK) (5)
Sugar (UK) (5)
Australia & Pacific Basin
Brisbane News
Pacific Islands Monthly
Australian Post
Australian Home Beautiful (5)
Best Bets (5)
Disney Adventures (5)
Girlfriend (5)
Hit Songworks (5)
HM (5)
New idea (5)
Super Models (5)
That's Life (9)
TV Hits (5)
Your Garden (5)
TV Week (9)

Newspapers

United States
New York Post
United Kingdom
The Times
The Sunday Times
The Sun
The News of the World
Today
Australia & Pacific Basin
National
The Australian
New South Wales
The Daily Telegraph Mirror
The Sunday Telegraph
Sportsman
Cumberland Newspaper
Group (21 various titles -
Sydney suburbs and regional)
Victoria
Herald Sun
Sunday Herald Sun
The Times Weekly
The Sporting Globe
Leader Newspaper Group
(31 various titles - Melbourne
suburbs and regional)
Queensland
The Courier-Mail (6)
The Sunday Mail (6)
Gold Coast Bulletin Group (6)
Gold Coast Bulletin
Gold Coast Sun
Hinterland Sun
The Cairns Post Group (6)
The Cairns Post
Tablelands Advertiser
Pyramid News
Douglas Times

Northern Beachcomber
Travel Cairns
Rural Post
North Queensland
Newspaper Group
Townsville Bulletin (8 various
titles - regional)
Quest Community
Newspapers (17 various
titles - Brisbane suburbs
and regional)
Northern Territory
Northern Territory News
Sunday Territorian
Centralian Advocate
The Suburban
Tasmania
The Mercury
The Sunday Tasmanian
Tasmanian Country
Treasure Islander
Derwent Valley Gazette
South Australia
The Advertiser
Sunday Mail
Messenger Press Group
(11 various titles - Adelaide
suburbs)
Western Australia
Sunday Times
New Zealand
Independent Newspapers (3)
Fiji
The Fiji Times
Nai Lalakai (Fijian language)
Shanti Dut (Hindi language)
Papua new Guinea
Post Courier (2)

KEY

News Corporation holds

(1)	71%	(6)	41.7%
(2)	63%	(7)	40%
(3)	50%	(8)	26%
(4)	49.9%	(9)	22%
(5)	45%	(10)	15%

Book Publishing

**United States,
United Kingdom & Europe,
Australia & Pacific Basin**
HarperCollins Publishers

Commercial Printing

Australia & Pacific
Streetfile (5)
Progress Printers &
Distributors (5)
Keppell Printing (5)
Pac-Rim Direct (5)
Wilke Color (5)
Wilke Directories (5)
Griffin Press (5)
Griffin Paperbacks (5)
Prestige Litho (5)
Mercury Walch (5)
Argus & Australasian (5)
Westernport Printing (5)
West Web Printers (5)
Southweb (5)
Pacweb (5)
Swanweb (5)
Asher & Co. (Hong Kong) (5)
Basklands (Christchurch) (NZ) (5)
Basklands (Auckland) (NZ) (5)
Circular Distributors (NZ) (8)

Other Operations

United States
Etak
News Electronic Data
News Corporation/MCI World
Wide Joint Venture (3)
Delphi Internet Service
Kesmai Corporation
United Kingdom
Broadsystem Ltd.
Convoys Group
News DataCom Ltd.
News MultiMedia Ltd.
Sky Radio (1)
Australia & Pacific Basin
Ansett Australia (3)
Broadsystem (Aust)
Computer Power (8)
Festival Records
FS Faulkner & Sons
Lamray Industries (6)
(Sunshine Plantation)
Mushroom Records (3)
PDN Xinren Information
Technology
Super League

Adapted from the *Guardian*, 16 July 1996.

Western world. In 1998, all 20 national daily and Sunday newspapers were owned by just seven companies (Peak & Fisher 1998). News International alone accounted for 35% of all newspapers sold in Britain and the Mirror Group for 26%.

Developments in the 1980s

In the early 1980s, there was the suggestion that ownership would diversify because new printing technology was becoming available. This, however, did not happen. The start-up costs for a new newspaper are prohibitive. For example, it cost £20 million to launch the *Independent* in 1986. Most of the new newspapers launched in the late 1980s - the *Sunday Correspondent, News on Sunday* and the *Post* - were forced to close down because they were unable to generate high enough sales and sufficient advertising revenue. Others - such as *Today* - were taken over by existing owners. The man who launched *Today*, Eddie Shah, spent £22.5 million in the first 10 weeks before selling it to Rupert Murdoch's News International (Wagg 1989). Even News International, however, could not ensure *Today's* long-term survival and it closed in 1995.

Until the launch of the *Independent*, no new national quality daily had been launched for 113 years. The *Independent* itself has only survived because its owners (Newspaper Publishing plc) were given a cash injection by one of their major shareholders - Mirror Group Newspapers (*Guardian*, 31 January 1998).

Growing concentration

Anti-monopoly legislation has failed to prevent the growing concentration of ownership of the press. News International's takeover of the *Times* in 1981 and *Today* in 1987, for example, were not referred to the Monopoly and Mergers Commission by the government. Similarly, the legislation has not prevented the *Independent* and *Independent on Sunday* being part-owned by the Mirror Group. In 1900, there were 21 national dailies. In 1998, this number had shrunk to 11. And it is not just the national newspapers which are owned by the multinationals. Most regional and local newspapers, and even many of the free broadsheets, are controlled by the large corporations. In the case of the local press, some 120 newspaper companies found themselves the subject of takeovers by large press companies between 1965 and 1993. All but four takeovers took place - despite the danger of greater concentration of ownership and the requirements of the 1973 Fair Trading Act (Curran & Seaton 1997). In 1995, the Conservative government relaxed the rules on referral to the Monopolies and Mergers Commission. This allowed more takeovers to go ahead.

It should be noted, however, that the development of multinational corporations is not just a phenomenon associated with the mass media. The growth of multinationals has resulted in concentrated ownership in many business areas - motor manufacture, for example, is dominated by multinationals like Ford and Volkswagen, whilst multinationals like Matsui and Sony produce electrical goods.

2.2 The press and political information

The impact of market forces

The press does not simply represent the political views of its owners. Newspapers are owned by capitalist organisations and so the creation of profit is an important motivation. Negrine points out that:

> 'It is unlikely that such proprietorial power will be exercised without reference to commercial considerations or market considerations.' (Negrine 1994, p.64)

In other words, newspapers need to make money by selling copies to the general public. And, unless they provide what the public (or at least a sufficiently large section of the public) wants, they will not survive. This was confirmed by Lord Rothermere, owner of the *Daily Mail*, who was asked whether Paul Dacre, editor of the *Daily Mail*, could maintain the paper's Eurosceptic line. Rothermere said:

> 'It is a free country and he is entitled to have his views and to express them. But, of course, if they start to affect circulation, that would be different.' (*Times*, 24 May 1997)

Reflecting the view of the readers

There is evidence that newspapers reflect the views of their readers rather than vice versa. For example, when, in August 1994, Rupert Murdoch publicly stated that he (and, therefore, his papers) might be able to support a Labour government under Tony Blair, opinion polls showed that *Sun* readers were moving back to the Labour Party and Labour was over 30% ahead of the Conservatives. By supporting Labour in the 1997 general election, the *Sun* ensured it was on the winning side and, therefore, that it reflected the majority view that there should be a Labour government. Then, having broken with the Conservatives in 1997, the *Sun* went a step further in October 1998. On the first day of the Conservative

Party conference, it published a front page showing William Hague, Conservative Leader, as a dead parrot and including the headline: 'This party is no more...it has ceased to be...this is an ex-party'. The decision to launch this attack was made by the *Sun*'s editor, David Yelland. Commenting on this decision, Roy Greenslade wrote:

> 'Yelland's explanation for his four page assault on the party which his paper supported so fervently for 20 years from the late 1970s is deceptively simple. "It's funny but true", he says. "Britain's most popular paper cannot afford any longer to be associated with the Tory Party. What this betrays is the *Sun*'s passion for populism. It not only loves a winner: it cannot stomach the idea of being linked with failure.' (*Guardian*, 7 October 1998)

The depoliticisation of the press

Since newspapers are in competition with each other, their actions (and, to some extent, their content) are determined by the need to maintain or improve their market share. One result of this is that much of what newspapers cover has a minimal political content. This is especially the case with the tabloid press. But, even the quality press has reduced its political coverage, especially its coverage of Parliament (as noted in Item C in Activity 19.1 above).

The press and political values

Unlike radio and television which are bound by rules designed to ensure that their dissemination of political information is balanced, the press does not have to be balanced. The partisan nature of the press is most evident during general election campaigns. On the day before the election, most newspapers suggest that their readers vote for a particular party. Until 1997, a majority of national newspapers urged their readers to vote Conservative (see Box 19.2). In 1997, however, that changed. As a result, the 1997 general election has been described as:

> 'A landmark in the history of Britain's press. It was the first campaign in which Labour secured the support of most national daily newspapers.' (Scammell & Harrop 1997, p.156)

Box 19.2 Circulation and political support of newspapers

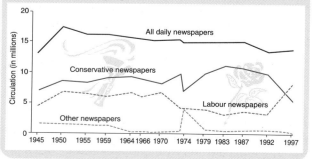

The press and the 1997 general election

Of particular importance in 1997 was the switch of the *Sun* away from its usual support for the Conservatives to Labour. The *Sun* announced its decision to back Labour the day after John Major announced the date of the general election - timing which was designed both to generate maximum publicity for the newspaper and to inflict maximum damage on the Conservative Party. In total, Labour was supported by six national daily newspapers with a combined circulation of 8.61 million (although the *Guardian*, *Independent* and *Mirror* also urged tactical anti-Conservative voting) and by five Sunday newspapers with a combined total of 9.32 million. The Conservatives, by contrast, were supported by three daily newspapers with a combined circulation of 4.5 million and four Sunday newspapers with a combined circulation of 5.49 million.

The stance of the press was in marked contrast to that in 1992. In 1992, six daily and five Sunday newspapers had backed the Conservatives, whilst just three daily and three Sunday newspapers had backed Labour.

The press and the Conservatives in 1997

In 1997, the newspapers which did continue to support the Conservatives did so with little conviction. The *Daily Telegraph* and *Daily Mail*, for example, pushed a Eurosceptic line and were critical of John Major for not moving far enough in that direction. In addition, Conservative-supporting newspapers allowed sleaze to dominate the early stages of the campaign, an issue most likely to damage the Conservatives. Golding and colleagues (1997) point out that the main focus of media coverage during the campaign was on three issues:

- the conduct of the campaign itself
- sleaze
- Europe.

None of these three issues was particularly helpful to the Conservatives.

Election coverage in 1997

Whilst Labour secured significant support from the press, the press itself provided less coverage of the election than in previous campaigns - perhaps because the campaign was so long and because the outcome never seemed in doubt. The broadsheets gave 34% of news space to the election, but the tabloids only gave it 11% of news space. In addition, the tabloids only gave 9% of leaders to the election whilst the broadsheets gave 90% (Wring 1998).

Broader Conservative values

Of course, a general election campaign is unusual because it is a time when newspapers feel able to canvass support for their chosen party openly. The rest of the time their support for their chosen party is generally more subtle. But, whether or not newspapers are wearing their party allegiance on their sleeves, they generally play a conservative role.

On the whole, the mainstream press (unsurprisingly) approves of business and the creation of wealth. It tends to condemn excessive trade union power. It generally supports the monarchy (apart from some criticism at the time of Diana's death). It is suspicious of feminists, black people, young people, the working class, radicals and protesters. And, it is often fiercely nationalistic.

Non-political articles and conservative values

Political information is not necessarily communicated in 'political' articles. Many of the attitudes described above are the premises upon which general or 'non-political' articles are based. In other words, fundamentally conservative values are dressed up as 'common sense'. For example, an article on the background and career of a rich and famous film star may, on one level, be a 'human interest' story. But, on another level, it may suggest support for the status quo and opposition to fundamental change.

Furthermore, Wagg has argued that the tabloids produce:

> 'Daily doses of undisguised racism and sexism [which make it harder for parties] committed to greater equality, particularly parties of the left, to be elected because they are felt to be peddling "weird" views on cultural matters.' (Wagg 1989, p.21)

Conservative values and the 1997 general election

Even in the 1997 general election campaign, the support which the *Sun* gave the Labour Party was tempered by coverage in the campaign which was more pro-Conservative than pro-Labour (Golding et al. 1997). In addition, it could be argued that, by the time of the 1997 general election, the Labour Party had abandoned its socialist principles and so support from the press was entirely consistent with the press' support of conservative values:

> 'The sea change in party politics, with Tony Blair's shift to the centre left, abandonment of the socialist trilogy of nationalisation, unilateralism and trade union rights, and his modernisation of the party may have convinced journalists, commentators and leader writers that New Labour did provide an attractive, energetic, fresh and newsworthy alternative to the overfamiliar and tired faces on the government front bench.' (Norris 1998, p.120)

The role of editors

It should be noted that each day most newspapers cover many of the same stories. What is different is the weight given to a particular news item and the way in which that item is used. What appears with a large headline on the front page of the *Guardian*, for example, might only feature as a small paragraph on page 7 of the *Sun* and vice versa. Similarly, an item used as an example of misgovernment in the *Times* might be used to illustrate the impotence of the opposition in the *Daily Mirror*. So, both the editorial process (the selection of items and weighting given to them) and the editorial 'line' (both the overt stance taken in editorials and the underlying values supported by the newspaper) help to determine how political information is presented.

The role of journalists

Whilst editors make strategic decisions, it is journalists who translate raw political information into the articles which the public rely on for their knowledge of the outside world. The way in which journalists perceive their role is therefore important since it is likely to determine how they present political information. Two contrasting views are suggested by Franklin:

> 'Sidney Jacobson, editor of the now defunct left-wing *Daily Herald*...argued that "relations between the government and the press are bad, getting worse and should under no circumstances be allowed to improve". [This suggests] that journalists should be independent and highly critical reporters of the political process and the behaviour of politicians...But, this view of journalists' relationship with politicians has always been contested by those who are sceptical about media independence of politicians. Marxists, for example, argue that the media is the servant rather than the master of politicians. The media does not criticise and challenge politicians but, in various ways, sustains them in power.' (Franklin 1993, p.1 - slightly adapted)

Politicians and journalists

Since politicians have a vested interest in gaining publicity for their views, much political information is brought to the press. Politicians hold press conferences and send out press releases, for example. In addition, a great deal of information is gathered simply by placing reporters in the right place - for example sending journalists to watch proceedings in the House of Commons or to wait outside Number 10, Downing Street. For further information, journalists are sent to interview people - to get their views 'on the record'. In addition to these sources of information, some journalists have access to the lobby system.

The lobby system

Traditionally, the 'lobby system' was the system which allowed selected political journalists special and privileged access to government ministers and officials on condition that they did not reveal the source of their information. Until November 1997, it was never officially admitted that the lobby actually existed, even though lobby briefings took place twice daily. The information given at these briefings was always 'unattributable' - the source of it could not be mentioned by the journalists. As a result, journalists had to use phrases like 'government sources' or 'Whitehall sources'. Any journalist who revealed the source of information given at lobby meetings was banned from attending future meetings of the lobby.

Protests against the lobby

Between 1986 and 1990, the *Independent*, *Guardian* and *Scotsman* refused to participate in the lobby system in protest at the way it was used by Margaret Thatcher and her chief press officer, Bernard Ingham. As a result, these newspapers received no information about the Prime Minister from the Press Secretary's office. Even the most routine enquiries about the Prime Minister's whereabouts were unanswered. These newspapers only returned to the lobby in 1991 when John Major's government offered a compromise allowing journalists to identify information as 'coming from Downing Street'.

Arguments for and against the lobby system

Whilst supporters claimed that the lobby was an important means of obtaining information the public otherwise would not receive, the lobby system was criticised for its secretiveness and because there was scope for manipulation and misinformation. Members of the government, for example, could use the lobby to float ideas which - if they proved unpopular - were then dropped. Since the information about such an idea was given via the lobby, the member of government responsible for floating it could not be identified. Critics also argued that the lobby system:

- resulted in lazy, uncritical journalism since journalists tended to use lobby press releases rather than their own sources of information
- allowed the Prime Minister to dictate what should be the main news items for the following week.

Changes to the lobby system

In November 1997, the Labour government not only officially admitted that the lobby system existed, it also announced changes in the way that it would work. Rather than providing 'off the record' unattributable briefings, briefings were to be 'on the record'. If information came from the Prime Minister's Chief Press Secretary, journalists were to be allowed to attribute it to the 'Prime Minister's official spokesman' (or 'spokeswoman' if a woman was appointed to the post). The same would be true of briefings given by the press officers for other Cabinet ministers. Despite this greater openness, however, the Prime Minister's official spokesman, Alastair Campbell, admitted that there would still be some occasions when briefings would have to go 'off the record':

> 'Mr Campbell admitted yesterday that in spite

of the new rules, there will still be times when some press officers, advisers and ministers - including, no doubt, himself, will still want to go off the record. In which case, they would become "a Labour source".' (*Guardian*, 28 November 1997)

Main points - Sections 2.1-2.2

- Today, much of the press is owned by multinational, multimedia corporations - such as News International whose owner, Rupert Murdoch, is a modern 'press baron'.
- Ownership of the press in Britain is narrower and more concentrated in Britain than anywhere else in the Western world. In 1998, the 20 national daily and Sunday newspapers were owned by just seven companies.
- In addition to the views of the owner and market forces, the newspaper's editorial 'line', the editorial process itself, the aims and attitudes of journalists and the lines of communication between politicians and journalists all help to determine what appears in a newspaper.
- The 1997 general election was the first when a majority of the press supported the Labour Party. Despite this, newspapers continue to promote conservative values.
- Traditionally, the 'lobby system' was the system which allowed journalists secret access to ministers and officials on condition that they did not reveal their sources. Since November 1997, most briefings have been 'on the record'.

Activity 19.2 *Political information and the press*

Item A *Political information and the Sun*

(i) Last Monday, Rupert Murdoch overrode the objections of his senior staff to order his flagship newspaper, the *Sun*, into battle on the side of New Labour with a headline which took up almost the whole of Tuesday's front page - 'The Sun backs Blair'. One insider said: 'It was a bolt from the blue for everyone, including the editor. We had planned our election coverage, then suddenly the atmosphere changed. Staff felt angry and betrayed.' As late as Monday afternoon, Stuart Higgins, the editor of the *Sun*, flatly denied that the paper was on the point of switching allegiance. But, for weeks, his proprietor had constantly intervened in how news stories were chosen or presented, demanding that the paper be more favourable to Blair.

Adapted from the *Observer*, 23 March 1997.

(ii) 18 March 1997   (iii) 24 June 1998   (iv) 6 October 1998

Item B   *The 1997 general election campaign (1)*

Newspaper	1997		1992	
Dailies				
Sun	Labour	(3.84)	Conservative	(3.57)
Mirror/Record	Labour	(3.08)	Labour	(3.66)
Daily Star	Labour	(0.73)	Conservative	(0.81)
Daily Mail	Conservative	(2.15)	Conservative	(1.68)
Express	Conservative	(1.22)	Conservative	(1.53)
Daily Telegraph	Conservative	(1.13)	Conservative	(1.04)
Guardian	Labour	(0.40)	Labour	(0.43)
The Times	Eurosceptic	(0.72)	Conservative	(0.37)
Independent	Labour	(0.25)	None	(0.39)
Financial Times	Labour	(0.31)	Labour	(0.39)
Sundays				
News of the World	Labour	(4.37)	Conservative	(4.77)
Sunday Mirror	Labour	(2.24)	Labour	(2.77)
People	Labour	(1.98)	Labour	(2.17)
Mail on Sunday	Conservative	(2.11)	Conservative	(1.94)
Express on Sunday	Conservative	(1.16)	Conservative	(1.67)
Sunday Times	Conservative	(1.31)	Conservative	(1.17)
Sunday Telegraph	Conservative	(0.91)	Conservative	(0.56)
Observer	Labour	(0.45)	Labour	(0.54)
Ind. on Sunday	Labour	(0.28)	None	(0.40)

All figures in millions

This table shows which political party (if any) each newspaper supported in the 1992 and 1997 general election campaign. The numbers in brackets are the number of newspapers sold at the time of the election. The information was supplied by the Audit Bureau of Circulation in 1997.

Item D   *The 1997 general election campaign (2)*

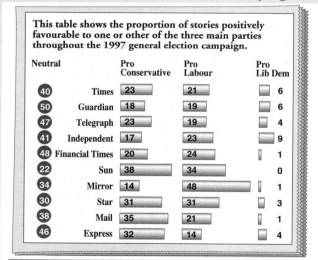

This table shows the proportion of stories positively favourable to one or other of the three main parties throughout the 1997 general election campaign.

Neutral		Pro Conservative	Pro Labour	Pro Lib Dem
40	Times	23	21	6
50	Guardian	18	19	6
47	Telegraph	23	19	4
41	Independent	17	23	9
48	Financial Times	20	24	1
22	Sun	38	34	0
34	Mirror	14	48	1
30	Star	31	31	3
38	Mail	35	21	1
46	Express	32	14	4

Percentage of stories in newspapers during the 1997 general election campaign, in which the following issues appeared:

Election conduct	32
Europe	15
Sleaze	10
Education	7
Taxation	6
Constitution	5
Privatisation	4

Information from Loughborough University's Communications Research Centre team.

Item C   *Full and truthful news*

(i) The *Daily Telegraph* has recently decided to lecture us on the purpose of serious journalism. 'Newspapers', it stated, 'especially broadsheet newspapers, must do their best to give full and truthful news'. But this mission statement rings especially hollow from the editorial columns of the *Daily Telegraph*. Let's take its coverage of Northern Ireland for instance and see how close it comes to giving 'full and truthful news'. Last week, two men were shot dead by loyalists in a pub in County Armagh. That story, a gut-wrenching human tragedy which underlines the callousness of unionist extremists who have carried out a series of random attacks on Catholics, was not thought important enough for page one on Thursday, when most other broadsheets gave it huge coverage. Yet, nine days before, when a bomb went off in nearby Portadown and nobody was hurt, the event was considered worthy of the front page. The reason for these twisted news values is clear. As a unionist paper, the *Telegraph* promotes stories of republican violence and plays down those involving unionist violence. So ingrained is this bias that it infects the reporting and sub-editing staff too.

(ii) Last week, the *Telegraph* criticised Rupert Murdoch (an Australian with an American passport) for forcing his papers to follow his anti-euro line. Yet, there is no difference between Murdoch and Conrad Black, the Canadian owner of the *Telegraph*, or between the *Times* and the *Telegraph*. Both are private companies owned by proprietors who want their papers to reflect, at least in general if not in specific terms, their political, economic and social views. They select as editors people who they know will reflect those views so well that they don't need to telephone them every day with orders. This is hardly new. The oddity is that Black's *Telegraph* should throw up its hands in alarm at Murdoch behaving to type. Rather than point-scoring over a business rival, the *Telegraph* should have highlighted what is, in fact, the important issue here - the contradiction between the free market and the freedom of speech which is exposed by private ownership of the press and publishing.

Adapted from the *Guardian*, 8 March 1998.

Questions

1. a) Judging from Items A–C, would you agree that the concentration of ownership of the press is a threat to democracy? Give reasons for your answer.
   b) Does it matter that ownership of the press in Britain is private?

2. 'Modern press barons have too much power'. Using Items A and C, give arguments for and against this statement.

3. Does the fact that newspapers openly support and campaign for political parties matter? Use Items A, B and D in your answer.

4. 'Don't believe what you read.' Would this be good advice to someone who reads a British newspaper? Give reasons for your answer.

5. Obtain three or more newspapers on the same day.
   a) Go through the newspapers and make a list of stories which appear in two or more of the newspapers.
   b) How does the treatment of each story differ in the different newspapers?
   c) What does this tell us about the way in which political information is conveyed.

2.3 Press regulation

Regulation and a free press
By definition, a 'free' press is not regulated by government or anyone else. A free press is free to print whatever it likes within the laws of libel and the requirements of official secrecy. There is no need for regulation.

The Press Council
In practice, the press in Britain is self-regulating. The Press Council - a body made up of representatives from within the newspaper industry - was set up in 1953 to protect press freedom and to promote and ensure responsible journalism by eradicating bias and inaccuracies from press coverage. In 1963, it was given the power to consider complaints about the press or conduct of persons or organisations towards the press. But, it proved incapable of controlling the excesses of the tabloid newspapers, especially with regard to the invasion of privacy, and it ceased activity in 1990. This followed the report of Sir David Calcutt and his colleagues whose inquiry into press regulation was set up by the Home Secretary.

The Press Complaints Commission
The Calcutt Report threatened a statutory regulation body if the press did not achieve effective self-regulation. As a result, the Press Council was replaced in 1991 with the Press Complaints Commission (PCC), another self-regulating body. The PCC consists of:
- an independent chair
- eight independent members with no press connections
- seven senior press editors.

The main task of the PCC is to deal with complaints made by members of the public against newspapers and, if necessary, to require newspapers to publish the findings of the PCC.

The PCC's code of conduct
The PCC drew up a code of conduct for the press. But, a review of the work of the PCC by the Calcutt Committee, published in 1993, argued that it had been a failure. Sensational coverage of the breakdown of royal marriages and the press coverage of the 1992 general election campaign had not, according to Calcutt, been responsive to voluntary self-regulation (again the issue of invasion of privacy was of greatest concern). The Calcutt Review recommended:

'The establishment of a regulatory body for the press which, among other things, would have the power to fine newspapers which broke the code of conduct and award compensation to claimants.' (quoted in Kuhn 1994, p.186)

This recommendation was rejected by Lord Wakeham, chair of the PCC. He preferred the press to take action voluntarily, though he warned the press that excesses could force the government into formal press regulation (*Guardian*, 6 April 1995). In the end, the Calcutt Committee's recommendations were not implemented and the press was given another chance to regulate its own activities.

The Di-spy case
On 7 November 1993, the *Sunday Mirror* published secretly taken photographs of Princess Diana working out in a gym. The following day, further pictures were published in the *Daily Mirror*. The publication of these photographs clearly breached Clause 4 of the PCC's voluntary code of practice which states:

'Intrusions and inquiries into an individual's private life without his or her consent including the use of long lens photography to take pictures of people on private property without their consent, are not generally acceptable and publication can only be justified in the public interest.'

The Mirror Group's action provoked a storm of protest, to which it responded by announcing that it was leaving the PCC. Since self-regulation is only credible if all newspapers agree to the rules, this provoked a crisis. Eventually a compromise was reached. Whilst the PCC withdrew its call for an advertising boycott of the Mirror Group, the Mirror Group apologised to the Princess and to the PCC, made a donation to charity, and rejoined the PCC. In an attempt to strengthen self-regulation, the PCC agreed to appoint a commissioner to deal with breaches of privacy and to write the PCC code of practice into editors' contracts.

As Bob Franklin noted in an article which examined the 'Di-spy' incident:

'The case illustrates the tension between a newspaper's need to compete for readers and advertisers, and their commitment to comply with the PCC code.' (Franklin 1996, p.43)

The incident raised serious questions about the ability of the press to regulate its own actions and it provoked calls for a privacy law.

A revised code
The issue of the invasion of privacy again reached crisis point after the death of Princess Diana in August 1997 (the car in which she was killed was being pursued by journalists). In response to criticism, the PCC announced a tougher privacy code and stronger action on harassment by journalists and on 'cheque book' journalism (*Guardian*, 25 September 1997). Newspapers remained free to use the argument that publication was in the public interest, however, and the PCC remained a voluntary, non-statutory body.

A privacy law?
Despite calls for a privacy law on a number of

occasions during its first 18 months in office, the Labour government consistently denied that it had any plans to legislate. Nevertheless, some commentators have argued that incorporation of the European Convention on Human Rights into British law will mean that a privacy law is introduced 'by the back door' since Article 8 of the convention explicitly protects the right of privacy. Other commentators, however, have pointed out that Article 10 of the convention protects freedom of

expression and argue that Article 10 is likely to prevail:

> 'The counterbalancing right to freedom of expression in Article 10...has always been more jealously guarded as the watchdog of a democratic society in Strasbourg than in Britain. In several notable cases...the Strasbourg court has found that British courts paid too little regard to free speech.' (*Guardian*, 19 December 1997)

Main points - Section 2.3

- By definition, a 'free' press is not regulated by government or anyone else. It is free to print whatever it likes within the laws of libel and the requirements of official secrecy.
- The British press is self-regulating. Between 1963 and 1990, complaints were dealt with by the Press Council. Since 1991, they have been dealt with by the PCC.
- The 'Di-spy' incident in November 1993 and the death of Diana in August 1997 provoked calls for a privacy law and an end to self-regulation.
- Incorporation of the European Convention on Human Rights might mean a privacy law is introduced 'by the back door'.

Activity 19.3 Regulation of the press

Item A   *The PCC*

(i)

The Press Complaints Commission's new code of practice

Clause 3: Privacy

i) Everyone is entitled to respect for his or her private and family life, home, health and correspondence. A publication will be expected to justify intrusions into any individual's private life without consent.

ii) The use of long lens photography to take pictures of people in private places without their consent is unacceptable.
Note: Private places are public or private property where there is a reasonable expectation of privacy.

Clause 4: Harassment

i) Journalists and photographers must neither obtain nor seek to obtain information or pictures through intimidation, harassment or persistent pursuit.

ii) They must not photograph individuals in private places without their consent; must not persist in telephoning, questioning, pursuing or photographing individuals after having been asked to disist, must not remain on their property after having been asked to leave and must not follow them.

iii) Editors must ensure that those working for them comply with these requirements and must not publish material from other sources which does not meet these requirements.

There may be exceptions to both clauses where it can be demonstrated to be in the public interest.

(ii) **(a) Number of complaints**

Number of complaints made against the PCC's privacy code provoked by various papers, January 1995-August 1997.

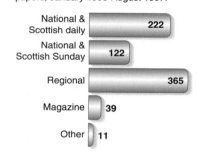

National & Scottish daily	222
National & Scottish Sunday	122
Regional	365
Magazine	39
Other	11

(b) Source of complaints

High-profile people 6.9%
Organisations 6.9%
Members of the public 86.2%

41% of privacy complaints were resolved on average within 13 weeks.

Adapted from the *Guardian*, 19 December 1997.

Item B   *Regulation under the PCC's new code*

(i)

The dilemma
A football star who is going out with a pop star is seen kissing and canoodling with another 17-year-old girl at a table outside a restaurant. Can the press use pictures?

The verdict
Yes. Although the new code extends the right of privacy to restaurants and churches, sitting at a public table on a public street does not come within the code's rules as a place where a public figure could reasonably expect privacy to be respected.

(ii)

The dilemma
A politician makes a speech arguing for a return to traditional family values. His former mistress sells her story of their affair to a Sunday tabloid. The politician and his wife simply make a one-line statement saying he regrets the affair. Up to 30 journalists are camped outside their house. How long can they stay there?

The verdict
Under the new code, the journalists would be allowed outside the house for a period unlikely to be more than a day, using the public interest defence that they were exposing a misleading statement. If the politician were to make a further statement and reiterate that he would not be adding anything else then the journalists would be expected to disperse.

Adapted from the *Guardian*, 26 September 1997.

Item C   *The European Convention on Human Rights*

The European Convention on Human Rights.

Article 8
1 Everyone has the right to respect for their private and family life, their home and their correspondence.
2 There shall be no interference by a public authority with the exercise of this right except such as is in accordance with the law and is necessary in a democratic society in the interests of national security, public safety or the economic well-being of the country, for the prevention of disorder or crime, for the protection of health or morals, or for the protection of the rights and freedoms of others.

Article 10
1 Everyone has the right to freedom of expression. This right shall include freedom to hold opinions and to receive and impart information and ideas without interference by public authority and regardless of frontiers. This Article shall not prevent states from requiring the licensing of broadcasting, television or cinema enterprises.
2 The exercise of these freedoms, since it carries with it duties and responsibilities, may be subject to such formalities, conditions, restrictions or penalties as are prescribed by law and are necessary in a democratic society, in the interest of national security, territorial integrity or public safety, for the prevention of disorder or crime, for the protection of health or morals, for the protection of the reputation or rights of others, for preventing the disclosure of information received in confidence, or for maintaining the authority and impartiality of the judiciary.

Item D   *Incorporation of the European Convention on Human Rights*

Unlike in many countries, English law has never given individuals a right to privacy. That will change when the European Convention on Human Rights is incorporated into English law (see Item C). To what extent will this impinge on the media's right to report the private foibles of politicians? And will it further hamper the task of the responsible press (which is already constrained by the Western world's most draconian libel laws) in exposing corruption and wrongdoing in public life? The way the courts enforce the new law will only become clear after it takes effect in April 1999. The Bill speaks of interference by a 'public authority'. The consensus is that this includes the PCC and the BBC. But, newspapers and commercial broadcasting companies are not included. Anyone whose rights are infringed by a public authority will be able to take court proceedings against it. But, where does the Bill leave newspapers? Individuals will not have a new right to sue papers for interfering in their private lives. Those who want to stop a newspaper publishing private information will still have to invoke existing laws (such as breach of confidence, trespass, harassment or bugging). Senior judges have been keen to develop these laws to create an enforceable right to privacy. The Lord Chief Justice, Lord Bingham, has said that judges will act if Parliament does not. The Human Rights Bill, which will require courts to take regard of the European Convention, will be a further (and powerful) spur in that direction.

Adapted from the *Guardian*, 19 December 1997.

Part 3 Radio and television

Key issues

1. Who owns and controls radio and television?
2. What is public service broadcasting?
3. Are radio and television politically neutral?
4. What impact has the televising of Parliament made?

3.1 Ownership and control of radio and television

Who controls radio and television?
Radio and television broadcasting is controlled by two bodies - the British Broadcasting Corporation (BBC) and the Independent Television Commission (ITC). The radio and television stations run by the BBC are publicly owned, whilst those provided by the ITC are owned by private individuals or companies.

The BBC
The BBC is controlled by a Board of Governors appointed by the Home Secretary. This Board of Governors appoints a Director General who has day-to-day control of the BBC. In 1998, the BBC was responsible for the running of two television stations, five national radio stations and 38 local radio stations. The BBC is mainly funded from the money paid by the public in the form of a licence fee. In 1948, 125,567 licences were sold. In 1998, over 20 million licences were sold. The BBC also raises money from its commercial enterprises (it sells programmes to other countries, for example, and raises money from the publication of books and toys).

Under the terms of the BBC's Royal Charter, first granted in 1926 (see above Section 1.1), advertising has been forbidden and the BBC has been bound to be impartial in all matters of party politics. However, since the government sets the level of the licence fee and the terms of the Royal Charter and since the Home Secretary is responsible for appointing the Board of Governors, potentially the government has a great deal of power over the way in which the BBC is organised and run.

The Independent Television Commission
Commercial broadcasting was first established in 1954 when the Independent Television Authority (ITA) was set up. Like the BBC, the ITA (which later became the Independent Broadcasting Authority - IBA) was controlled by a Board of Governors appointed by the Home Secretary. The 1990 Broadcasting Act replaced the IBA with a new body, the Independent Television Commission (ITC). Although, like the IBA, the ITC is controlled by a Board of Governors appointed by the Home Secretary, the ITC has a different role from the IBA. It lacks the IBA's detailed involvement in scheduling, but has wider powers to enforce licence conditions and ownership rules. In commercial broadcasting, therefore, it is the individual companies granted licences which are responsible for the day-to-day running of the stations. Competition for licences (also called franchises) is correspondingly fierce.

In 1998, commercial broadcasting included ITV (Channel Three), Channel Four, Channel Five, three national and 77 local commercial radio stations. In addition, 1,600 restricted services licences for temporary, low-powered radio stations were issued and 124 franchises for cable broadcasting were granted (Peak & Fisher 1998). Commercial broadcasting is funded by the revenue raised from advertising. It should be noted that companies granted licences to broadcast by the ITC operate on a commercial basis and, therefore, their aim is to make a profit for their shareholders. It should also be noted that government's control of commercial broadcasting has been reduced since the introduction of satellite television in 1989.

The concentration of ownership
A major concern about the ownership and control of broadcasting in Britain is that it is in the hands of a relatively small number of people from a narrow segment of society. This concern was voiced in a discussion paper published by the European Commission and entitled *Pluralism and Media Concentration in the Internal Market*:

> 'The media sector is characterised by a fairly high level of concentration compared with other sectors and by a complex web of shareholding and media ownership networks centred around a few national operators...The UK is alone in the EU in not having a written

constitution from which an obligation to safeguard media pluralism could be deduced.' (quoted in Peak 1994, pp.14-15)

Since the 1990 Broadcasting Act came into effect, the concentration of ownership has gathered pace as constraints on multiple ownership have been reduced. This can be illustrated by two examples.

BSkyB

The first example concerns the introduction of satellite television in Britain. When it was introduced in 1989, two companies - BSB and Sky - competed for trade. But, in early November 1990, just after the 1990 Broadcasting Act became law, Rupert Murdoch's News International (see Section 2.1 above), which owned Sky, announced that it was merging with BSB. BSkyB now, effectively, has a monopoly in the delivery of satellite television in Britain.

Channel Three licences

The second example concerns what happened after the ITC awarded Channel Three licences in 1991. These licences, awarded on the basis of competitive tender, permit companies to broadcast in the 15 regions of the ITV network. It should be noted that, under the terms of the 1990 broadcasting Act, licences must be awarded to the highest bidder amongst those passing a 'quality threshold'. Wagg explains that:

'In 1993, the Secretary of State for National Heritage, Peter Brooke, relaxed the rules governing takeovers in the British media, opening the way for major mergers among the ITV companies and for more cross ownership between media. More specifically, Brooke had ruled that any ITV companies could now hold two licences.' (Wagg 1994, p.102)

The result of this was a greater concentration of ownership:

'This resulted in three major takeovers - Carlton TV of Central; Meridian of Anglia and Granada of London Weekend Television. However, there was then a clear imbalance in the size of ITV companies - Yorkshire TV, for example, who had taken over Tyne Tees in 1992 had less than half the audience share of either Carlton or Central, who were now merged. This led, in March 1994, to the ITC submitting to the Department of National Heritage that further mergers be permitted, simply to make the smaller companies stronger. The market share of each ITV company should now be limited to 25% of the total advertising revenue and there should be less restriction on the involvement of newspapers in commercial television.' (Wagg 1994, p.102)

Cross ownership

Cross ownership of press and broadcasting had been discouraged in the 1980s, but the policy was reversed by the 1996 Broadcasting Act. This allowed newspaper groups to expand into terrestrial television. Also, the rules about cross ownership of local press and local radio were relaxed. The result was that, in February 1996, MAI (which owned the Anglia and Meridian ITV franchises) merged with United News and Media (which owned the *Daily* and *Sunday Express*, *Evening Standard*, and over 100 provincial newspapers). However, newspaper companies with over 20% of national newspaper circulation (News International and the Mirror Group) were prevented from buying into terrestrial television (Curran & Seaton 1997). This did not, however, stop Channel Five and BSkyB setting up a joint venture to broadcast teletext on Channel Five - News International's first foothold in British terrestrial television (Peak & Fisher 1997).

3.2 Broadcasting and bias

Public service broadcasting

According to the Broadcasting Research Unit (BRU 1985), public service broadcasting is broadcasting which follows a set of principles. These principles have evolved from a number of sources - broadcasting legislation, committee and commission reports and the views expressed by various Director Generals of the BBC - particularly John Reith, the first Director General. They are summarised in Box 19.3.

Box 19.3 Public service broadcasting

Public service broadcasting aims to follow seven main principles:

1. Programmes should be available to the whole population regardless of how remote or inaccessible the places in which people live.
2. Programmes should appeal to a broad range of tastes.
3. One main broadcasting organisation should be financed by a licence fee or tax paid by everyone who uses a television and/or radio.
4. Some institutional mechanism must distance broadcasters from vested interests (whether commercial or political) and must protect broadcasters from intrusion upon their activities.
5. Public service broadcasters should reflect national concerns, interests and culture. The emphasis on national concerns should not be at the expense of minority interests.
6. Broadcasting should be organised in such a way that there is competition to produce quality programming rather than competition for audiences.
7. The public guidelines for broadcasters should liberate rather than restrict programme makers.

Public service broadcasting under Labour

The BBC faces new challenges as a result of the introduction of digital broadcasting. In particular, the digital revolution will mean more channels and radio stations and, therefore, more competition for audiences. This has led top executives at the BBC to call for a significant increase in the licence fee to fund new investment (*Guardian*, 16 July 1998).

Before the 1997 general election there was some debate about whether the BBC should continue to be the main public service broadcaster. In its 1997 general election manifesto, however, the Labour Party pledged support for the BBC and its public service broadcasting role:

> 'We will ensure that the BBC continues to be a flagship for British creativity and public service broadcasting.' (Labour 1997, p.31)

Although the BBC's Royal Charter will come up for renewal in 2006, it seems likely that the BBC will continue to provide public service broadcasting :

> 'The BBC has stood, and still stands, as a witness to the fact that broadcasting can play an important public service role and thereby strengthen the civic society against the state.' (Eldridge et al. 1997, p.59)

Regulation

The 1990 Broadcasting Act gave statutory recognition to two regulatory bodies:

- the Broadcasting Complaints Commission (BCC), originally set up under the 1980 Broadcasting Act
- the Broadcasting Standards Council (BSC), originally set up in 1988.

The BCC was set up to consider and make judgements on complaints received from individuals who felt that they had been treated unfairly or that their privacy had been infringed. The BSC was responsible for drafting a code of conduct for broadcasters, offering guidance on portrayals of violence, portrayals of sex and 'matters of taste and decency generally'. In 1994, the government announced that the BCC and BSC would merge to create a new body - the Broadcasting Standards Commission. This new body came into operation in 1997.

Are radio and television politically neutral?

The terms of the BBC's Royal Charter and the Television and Broadcasting Acts place a requirement on the BBC and the ITC to maintain political impartiality. This is in contrast to the press where there is no such requirement. The 1990 Broadcasting Act strengthened this requirement by imposing a new code of impartiality.

Accusations of bias

The new code of impartiality was included in the 1990 Broadcasting Act mainly because of pressure from Conservatives who claimed that broadcasters had flouted existing rules on impartiality. In particular, the Conservatives' Media Monitoring Unit attacked the *Today* programme on Radio Four for anti-government bias. In 1995, charges of bias were again made by Conservatives, with the Chief Secretary to the Treasury, Jonathan Aitken, accusing

the BBC of 'open partisanship' (*Independent on Sunday*, 26 March 1995). Ironically, the same criticisms that had been made by Conservatives when they were in power were soon made by Labour officials after they came into power. In December 1997, for example, John Humphrys (presenter of the *Today* programme) was bitterly criticised for the way in which he handled an interview with Social Security Secretary Harriet Harman and, a few days later, Alastair Campbell, Tony Blair's Chief Press Secretary, claimed that the *World at One* news programme on Radio Four was 'consistently biased against the government' (*Guardian*, 17 December 1997).

Are broadcasters biased?

Broadcasters use two main arguments against the charge that they are biased. First, they argue that, since they are criticised by both the right and the left, that suggests that they must be successful in achieving impartiality. And second, they claim that they offer a wide variety of independent, objective sources of information which leads to an essentially balanced presentation. For example, at election times, broadcasters are scrupulous in ensuring that the different political parties are given equal amounts of air time.

Against this, however, it can be argued that broadcasters have to operate with certain basic assumptions:

> 'Broadcasters are operating within a system of parliamentary democracy and must share its assumptions. They should not be expected to give equal weight or to show impartiality which is not due to those who seek to destroy it by violent, unparliamentary or illegal means.' (Annan 1977, p.268)

Due impartiality

The notion of 'due impartiality' means that there can only be objectivity and impartiality within the boundaries of what is generally agreed and acceptable in society. So, for example, broadcasters describe members of the IRA as 'terrorists' rather than 'freedom fighters'. At the same time, however, they are expected to describe the activities of members of the IRA as accurately as possible to avoid the danger of propaganda.

The notion of 'due impartiality' also implies that the television and radio should not consistently present one viewpoint to the exclusion of others. A range of views and a variety of opinions should be given - though, over time, there should be a balance of views from those on the left and those on the right who believe in parliamentary democracy. If there is not the variety of different views, then there is the danger that the audience has no alternative sources of information on which to base its understanding.

There is tension about how this should work in

practice, especially when controversial events like industrial disputes or military conflicts involving Britain are covered. This tension is compounded by the fact that the government of the day has the power to intervene in broadcasting.

Government intervention

Since the early 1980s, a great deal of concern has been expressed at the extent of the government's intervention in broadcasting and the failure of the Boards of Governors to stand up to pressure from politicians. This concern is derived from a number of sources.

1. Appointing governors

First, the government has the power to make appointments to the Boards of Governors. When the Conservatives were in government, a number of prominent Conservative supporters were appointed to these boards. Under Margaret Thatcher, for example, one Managing Director of the BBC noted:

> 'The government has tended to put people [on the Board] who are sympathetic to its views in greater numbers than has been the practice in the past. There is a question that the PM is said to ask about every appointee to a public body: is he one of ours?' (*Guardian*, 25 August 1985)

This trend continued under John Major. In 1996, for example, Christopher Bland was appointed to be Chair of the BBC. Bland had served on the Greater London Council (GLC) as a Conservative councillor and as chair of a Conservative pressure group (*Guardian*, 10 January 1996). The Labour government has also made political appointments. For example, Lady Young was appointed as Vice Chair of the BBC's Board of Governors in 1998. At the time of her appointment, she was a working Labour peer (*Guardian*, 11 July 1998). Obviously, if a Board of Governors is packed with government supporters, it is less likely to stand up to pressure from ministers.

2. Refusing franchises

Second, some authors have suggested that the government has put pressure on the ITC, encouraging it to refuse to renew franchises because a company has been involved in making programmes perceived as having an anti-government bias. In 1988, for example, Thames Television made a programme called *Death on the Rock* which examined the shooting of three members of the IRA in Gibraltar. The IRA members were later found to be unarmed and the programme challenged the official version of the incident. According to Franklin:

> 'Politicians, like elephants it seems, have long memories. Three years later when Thames Television was refused the renewal of its franchise to broadcast, Peter Kellner described the process of allocating new television licences as, "an exercise in ideological

vengeance" used by the government, 'to punish the company that made *Death on the Rock*.' (Franklin, 1993, p.6)

3. Power of the Home Secretary

Third, the broadcasting laws allow the Home Secretary ultimate control over all broadcasting content. For example, it was the Home Secretary who in 1988 announced a ban on the broadcasting of all interviews with or speeches by representatives of eleven Northern Irish organisations, including Sinn Fein. This ban was not lifted until the IRA announced its ceasefire in August 1994.

4. State secrecy

Fourth, legislation concerned with state secrecy - such as the Official Secrets Act and the Public Records Act (see Part 5 below) can restrict broadcasting output.

5. Direct intervention

And fifth, there are ways in which the government can intervene directly. It can impose direct censorship - as, for example, happened during the Falklands War when no demoralising pictures of wounded British soldiers could be shown until after the war ended. Or, it can make objections about the broadcasting of certain programmes and put pressure on programme schedulers to block or change them. For example, in December 1997, the government threatened to suspend cooperation with the *Today* programme as a protest against the robust interviewing techniques used by John Humphrys when interviewing Harriet Harman.

Main points - Sections 3.1-3.2

- Radio and television broadcasting is controlled by the BBC and ITC. The BBC is publicly owned and mainly funded by licence fees. Radio and televisions stations controlled by the ITC are privately owned and mainly funded by advertising.

- Since the 1990 Broadcasting Act came into effect, the concentration of ownership of radio and television stations has gathered pace. The 1996 Broadcasting Act allowed cross ownership of press and broadcasting.

- Public service broadcasting means producing programmes which fulfil a number of criteria which ensure they are of interest to and beneficial to large sections of the public.

- The terms of the BBC's Royal Charter and the Television and Broadcasting Acts place a requirement on the BBC and the ITC to maintain political impartiality. The 1990 Broadcasting Act imposed a new code of impartiality.

- Broadcasters argue that broadcasting is impartial and balanced. The notion of 'due impartiality', however, influences programmes. Also, the government intervenes to block or change programmes.

Activity 19.4 Broadcasting and bias

Item A *Changes in broadcasting*

Since 1986, there have been major changes to the structure, ownership and regulation of the media. Concentration of media ownership, both within and across different media, has increased considerably. Statutory regulations and restrictions on concentration have kept only a minimal check on the creation of huge media groups. The opportunities for large companies to move across media from print to broadcasting to telecommunications have expanded. In broadcasting, the UK has witnessed the restructuring of the sector away from public service obligations and towards dependence on the market as a main force in regulating activities. Commercially-driven cable and satellite television companies are now expanding and are, through force of money, increasingly buying up the major sporting events which had previously been available to viewers for the price of a licence fee. The new media, financed through pay-per-view and subscription is growing dramatically, and new alliances between media groups will stimulate this.

Extract from the manifesto of the Campaign for Press and Broadcasting Freedom, 1996.

Item B *Television news*

(i)

	BBC1	BBC2	ITV	Channel 4	Channel 5
Accurate	56	73	51	87	64
Interesting	35	71	51	54	56
Informative	46	59	65	60	40
Balanced	31	48	49	89	41

This table shows the results of a survey (conducted at the end of the 1997 general election campaign) in which people were asked to what extent they thought various news programmes were accurate, interesting, informative and balanced. The figures are the percentage of respondents who answered 'just about always' or 'most of the time' rather than 'some of the time' or 'hardly ever'.

(ii)

Proportion of stories positively favourable to one or other of the main parties throughout the 1997 general election campaign.

	Neutral	Pro Con	Pro Lab	Pro Lib Dem
BBC1	55	14	10	9
News at Ten	59	11	12	10
Channel 4	70	12	9	5
Radio 4 *Today*	60	16	2	2

This table shows the proportion of stories on television and radio which were either neutral or positively favourable to one of the three main parties during the 1997 election campaign.

Information from Loughborough University's Communications Research Centre team.

Item C *Language and broadcasting*

(i) The language used by broadcasting institutions indicates their implicit viewpoint. For example, in news broadcasts during 1984-85, the National Union of Miners (NUM) always 'claimed' whilst the National Coal Board, police or government 'said'. 'Claiming' implies a degree of doubt whilst 'saying' implies certainty. Also, the very phrase 'miners' strike' is not neutral. It puts the blame firmly, if implicitly, on the miners' shoulders and, therefore, masks the real reasons for the dispute and the government's role in it. Consider for example the following statement on ITN *News at Ten* on 13 February 1985: 'Electricity loses £2 billion because of the miners' strike'. This implies that the miners are to blame for this loss, not the NCB which tore up the 'Plan for Coal' or the government which was determined to prevent a negotiated settlement.

Adapted from CSE 1985.

(ii) During the Falklands War, BBC broadcasters insisted that, in the interests of balance and detachment, British soldiers should be referred to as 'British' troops rather than 'our troops' or 'our boys' (phrases which were popular in the tabloid press). This brought angry complaints from Conservative backbenchers and the Prime Minister, Margaret Thatcher, said she shared, 'the deep concern...that the case for our country is not being put with sufficient vigour on certain - I do not say all - programmes.' When *Newsnight* tried to piece together what was happening in the South Atlantic using reports from the USA and Argentina, Thatcher told the Commons: 'Many people are very concerned indeed that the case for our British forces is not being put over fully and effectively. There are times when it seems that we and the Argentines are being treated almost as equals and on an almost equal basis. I can only say that, if this is so, it gives offence and causes great emotion among many people.'

Adapted from Franklin 1993.

Item D   *The government and the governors*

Questions

1. Using Items A-D, explain how radio and television coverage of political events differs from that of the press.
2. Look at Item A. Does it matter that broadcasting is increasingly subject to 'market forces'? Give reasons for your answer.
3. Using Items B-D, give the arguments for and against the view that broadcasting is politically biased.
4. During the course of a single evening listen to a news bulletin broadcast by a BBC radio station and a commercial radio station and watch the news on the BBC and on a commercial station.
   a) Make a list of stories covered by each bulletin.
   b) How did the treatment of each story differ in the different broadcasts?
   c) How did the treatment of each story differ from the way it would be treated in the press?
   d) Would you say the broadcasts met the criteria laid down for public service broadcasting? Give reasons for your answer.

3.3 Televising the House of Commons

Why were the cameras introduced?

Although radio broadcasts from the House of Commons began in 1975 and the televising of the House of Lords began in 1985, it was not until February 1988 that MPs (in a free vote) voted by a majority of 54 to allow cameras into the House of Commons as an experiment.

By 1988, there was a great deal of pressure on the Commons to introduce television coverage. By then, 58 other countries allowed cameras to televise the proceedings of their legislative bodies. The experiment in the House of Lords had been judged a success. And, recent debates in the House of Commons suggested that it was only a matter of time before a majority in favour could be mustered (in 1980 and 1983, Ten Minute Rule Bills were accepted by a majority only to fall because of lack of parliamentary time and, in November 1985, a majority of 12 voted against televising the Commons only after a number of MPs in the 'aye' lobby tried to change their vote when they realised that the Prime Minister, Margaret Thatcher, had voted 'no').

Opposition

Despite the pressure on MPs to introduce the cameras, there was still a large number of opponents. In the debate in February 1988, 231 Conservative MPs and 28 Labour MPs voted against televising the Commons. This did not just reflect the conservative nature of Conservative MPs. It also indicated a genuine fear of misrepresentation on television. It is significant that, during the 1980s, whilst Labour MPs claimed bitterly about their treatment by the tabloid newspapers, Conservatives complained equally bitterly about the bias of television (especially the BBC). Nevertheless, 116 Conservatives voted for the cameras and, combined with the support of 176 Labour MPs and 26 MPs from the Liberal Democrats and minor parties, this was sufficient to secure a majority.

Arguments against MP-TV

There were five main objections to televising the Commons. First, some MPs argued that the practical and technological difficulties of installing cameras were insurmountable. Second, others claimed that the reputation of the House would be damaged because television would misrepresent and trivialise its proceedings. This was a view favoured by the Prime Minister, Margaret Thatcher, who claimed that radio broadcasting of the Commons had damaged the reputation of the Commons. Third, some were afraid that the reputation of the House would be damaged because the public would see low attendances and boring debates. Fourth, there was concern that television might favour certain photogenic or controversial MPs, or it might favour leading politicians or even one or more parties. And fifth, it was suggested that the proceedings of the House would be distorted by television coverage.

Arguments in favour of MP-TV

Those who favoured televising the Commons argued that it would mean an extension of democracy since the communications gap between MPs and citizens would be closed. They claimed that the House would become more accountable to the public and that an educational role would be performed since members of the public would be alerted to the key issues of the day. Supporters also argued that broadcasting would allow many more people to participate in the political process:

> 'During an experiment in televising the proceedings of the Lords in 1985, ITN compared television to an electronic extension of the public gallery. ITN calculated that if the gallery seated 65 people for the 140 days of the parliamentary session, the *News at Ten* on 3 April 1985 with 12,136,000 viewers watching the debate on unemployment was equivalent to filling the public gallery for 1,333 years. Such figures represent an unrealistic extrapolation, of course, but they indicate the possibilities for television to enhance accountability and participation.' (Franklin 1993, p.12)

Control of Commons broadcasting

The broadcasting of the Commons is under the control of the Television Select Committee. It was this select committee which finally reported in May 1989. Its report was accepted in June 1989 and broadcasting finally began when the new parliamentary session was opened on 21 November 1989. The experimental period of televising lasted from then until July 1990. On 19 July 1990, MPs voted in favour of television

broadcasting for the foreseeable future.

The television pictures of the Commons are provided by what was an independent company - Broadcast Communications. This company is now owned by the Guardian and Manchester Evening News plc (another example of the growing concentration of ownership in the media).

Rules on what can be seen

At first, the rules concerning what the camera could show were quite strict. No close ups or pictures of MPs being drunk, disorderly or asleep were permitted. At the slightest hint of disorder, all the viewers saw was the Speaker calling for order. The following extract indicates the limitations:

> 'The cameras should normally remain on the member speaking until he has finished; and during questions...the director should only show the member asking a question and the minister replying to it. At other times, cutaway shots to illustrate reaction are not normally to be allowed except to show a member who has been referred to by the member speaking. However, medium angle shots, including over the shoulder shots, are permissible where the director wishes to show both the member who has the floor and other members intervening or seeking to do so.' (HC 141, 1989, paragraph 39.iv)

After the experimental period, the rules were relaxed so that wide camera shots were permitted. This allowed for more interesting coverage. After an initial period of curiosity, the audiences for programmes showing proceedings at length have been small. When extracts are used on main news broadcasts, however, large audiences inevitably do see (albeit briefly) major events in the House.

The effect of televising the Commons

Most observers agree that the behaviour of MPs has been altered by the arrival of the cameras. Not only do MPs tend to dress more smartly and not put their feet up on the seats, they also tend to make their interventions in the House in a more media friendly way by providing soundbites rather than long, rambling speeches. There has been some training - for example Harvey Thomas, a Conservative public relations adviser, coached more than 100 Conservative MPs on how to appear concise, interesting and sincere in their contributions (Franklin 1994). There has also been the growth of practice known as 'doughnutting' - surrounding speaking MPs with a group of attentive supporters to ensure that they appear to have support for their views when they are seen on television. In addition, some MPs intervene in the House or sit next to speakers so that they are seen by their constituents. Franklin notes that during election times:

> 'Whips may try to give air time to backbenchers who have not been "overly

active" in their constituencies and need to make a parliamentary showing. Members with seats in very marginal constituencies might similarly receive a publicity fillip by being seen on television questioning the Prime Minister.' (Franklin 1993, p.19)

Who benefits?

In general, television favours the government of the day since parliamentary procedures push the government of the day to the forefront. Much parliamentary time, for example, is taken up with ministers answering questions from other MPs. This gives the impression that the ministers are highly knowledgeable and have great authority whilst the questioners are minor players. Franklin (1993) notes that there has been an increase in the length of frontbench speeches and that techniques have been developed to ensure that ministers appear in a good light at set pieces such as Prime Minister's Questions (for example, friendly questions are put by backbenchers). A further consequence of televising Parliament is that it bolsters the impression that Britain has a two-party system. The Liberal Democrats and minor parties gain much less coverage than the Conservatives and Labour, partly because of the layout of the chamber and partly because of procedure.

Other broadcasts

Apart from televising Parliament, the BBC also broadcasts a number of radio and television programmes which report and comment on events at Westminster (for example, Radio Four's *In Committee* and *Yesterday in Parliament*). In 1998, however, the BBC came under attack for 'dumbing down' its coverage. A House of Commons Select Committee chaired by the Labour MP Gerald Kaufman claimed that changes in programming would:

'Inevitably reduce the number of people who

will have access to programmes that are distinct from the opinionated and soundbite offerings we hear so often from the BBC.' (*Guardian*, 27 February 1998)

Some commentators have expressed concern that political information is becoming over-packaged:

'We are seeing a parting of the ways so that politics has to compete against other newsworthy items in order to get reported...Has the secondary interpretation of political debate become more important than the factual account?' (Negrine 1997, p.25)

Main points - Section 3.3

- It was not until February 1988 that MPs voted to allow cameras into the House of Commons. Since then, there has been little opposition to the televising of the Commons.
- Objections to televising the Commons were: (1) technical difficulties; (2) TV might misrepresent and trivialise proceedings; (3) the public might not be impressed; (4) TV might favour certain MPs or parties; and (5) proceedings would be distorted.
- Supporters argued that TV would: (1) extend democracy; (2) increase accountability; (3) educate the public; and (4) encourage political participation.
- At first, the rules on what the camera could show were quite strict. But, after the experimental period, the rules were relaxed.
- The behaviour of MPs has changed - they dress more smartly and use tactics to give a good impression on camera.
- In general, the government and two main parties gain most from TV. There have been concerns, however, that political coverage is being 'dumbed down'.

Activity 19.5 *Televising the Commons*

Item A *Televising the House*

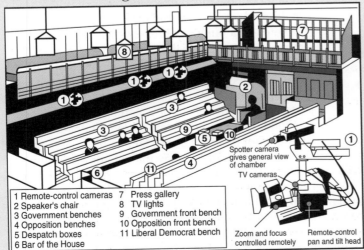

1 Remote-control cameras
2 Speaker's chair
3 Government benches
4 Opposition benches
5 Despatch boxes
6 Bar of the House
7 Press gallery
8 TV lights
9 Government front bench
10 Opposition front bench
11 Liberal Democrat bench

Spotter camera gives general view of chamber

TV cameras

Zoom and focus controlled remotely

Remote-control pan and tilt head

Item B *MP-TV*

What is remarkable about television is how little it has changed the House of Commons. All those MPs who trooped off to charm schools should be demanding their money back. Hair is a bit better combed. Dresses are slightly less dour. But, there are still plenty of MPs who do not realise that if they wear checks it will have a strobing effect on television and that constituents are not impressed to see their representative wearing his lunch down his tie. Those who have been good on MP-TV tend to be those who were already good on TV. For example, Labour's Gordon Brown was never a slouch at producing the pithy 20 second quote for the news bulletin. He can now construct a Commons speech of soundbites.

Adapted from the *Guardian*, 11 July 1990.

Item C   *Party contributions to broadcast items*

Party	Number of contribution occasions	Total number of contributions	Average no. of contributions per occasion
Conservative	1182	3873	3.27
Labour	885	2274	2.56
Liberal Democrats	230	395	1.71
SDP	18	25	1.38
Plaid Cymru	16	24	1.50
SNP	28	45	1.60
SDLP	19	32	1.68
Ulster Unionist	17	19	1.11
DUP	18	24	1.33

This table shows the results of research undertaken during the trial period of televising the Commons (November 1989 to July 1990). It shows the number of occasions on which a party was able to contribute to parliamentary programmes and the number of contributions made on each occasion.

Item D   *Broadcasting and political balance*

The party of government can expect greater television coverage because the government initiates political events. Besides, there is the argument that parties should not receive equal air time because they do not have equal numbers of seats. Rather, they should gain airtime proportionate to the size of the party in the Commons. Another way of looking at this issue is to ignore the numbers in each party and to concentrate on the issues. If this was done, what would count would not be which party a speaker came from, but what opinion was articulated. The aim would be to make sure that opinions for and against an issue were covered evenly. There are also regional considerations to be considered. During 1989-90, for example, all 58 MPs in the TVS region were Conservatives whilst Scotland and the North of England had large Labour majorities. Should regional programmes reflect the local or national political balance or a mixture of both?

Adapted from Franklin 1993.

Questions

1. Watch a TV news bulletin in which footage from the Commons is shown and then, the next day, read a newspaper account of the proceedings. What similarities and differences are there?

2. a) Judging from Items A and B, how far do you think the cameras affect the behaviour of MPs?
   b) Suppose you were a backbench MP. What would you do to ensure that you appeared on television coverage of the Commons?

3. a) Why is it difficult to achieve political balance when broadcasting from the Commons?
   b) Would you say that balance had been achieved? Use Items C and D and information from the news bulletin you watched in your answer.

Part 4 The influence of the media

Key issues

1. Why is it difficult to measure the media's influence?
2. How can the media's influence be interpreted?
3. What is the media's role in setting the political agenda?

4.1 The media and political understanding

Why is it difficult to measure the media's influence?

There is much debate about exactly how much effect the media has on people's political views. Simply demonstrating that the media has a right-wing or a left-wing bias, for example, does not in itself prove that the media determines how people perceive political events. Although much research has been undertaken to find out how much effect the media has, the results of this research are contradictory and inconclusive.

There are a number of reasons why it is difficult to measure the effect of the media on the individual. First, most people have access to more than one media outlet and so it is difficult to isolate, for example, the effect of reading a particular newspaper compared to the effect of watching the television. Second, there is a range of other influences on people (for example social factors like class, age and education) and these may mitigate or distort the effects of the media. Third, there may be a difference between the short-term effects and the long-term effects of exposure to the media. And fourth, most people's opinions are shaped to some extent by friends and relatives. These 'significant others' may affect the way in which an individual interprets what the media has to say.

Further examination of the influence of the media is undertaken in Chapter 9, Part 4. There, the impact of the media on voting behaviour is considered.

4.2 Theoretical Models

Viewing the media in different ways
In order to study the way in which the media works in society, a number of different theories have been developed. These theories can be grouped into five models. Each of the five models views the media in a fundamentally different way.

1. The Marxist model
According to Karl Marx and Friedrich Engels:
> 'The class which has the means of material production at its disposal has control, at the same time, over the means of mental production, so that thereby, generally speaking, the ideas of those who lack the means of mental production are subject to it...Insofar, therefore, as [members of the ruling class] rule as a class and determine the extent and compass of an epoch, it is self evident that they, among other things, regulate the production and distribution of the ideas of their age: thus their ideas are the ruling ideas of the epoch.' (Marx & Engels 1976, p.64)

This passage suggests that, ultimately, the power, control and direction of ideas lie with those who own and control the means of production. In a capitalist society, this means the capitalist class and, more specifically, the owners and controllers of the mass media. The owners and controllers of the mass media use the media to project the views of the ruling class and these views come to dominate the thinking of the mass of the population. In other words, the owners and controllers of the mass media exercise ideological domination. Ideological domination is crucial to the survival of capitalism since means of physical coercion are limited.

False consciousness
The Marxist model emphasises the way in which a narrow range of conservative values dominates the messages given out by the media. The media works against change and, therefore, against the interest of the mass of the population. It promotes a false consciousness which prevents people seeing the harsh reality of their place in society.

Miliband argues that it is not just the owners and controllers who are responsible for ideological domination:
> '[Owners and controllers] may confidently rely on editors, journalists, producers and others who work for them to remain well within a well understood ideological spectrum of thought which stretches from mild social

democracy at one end to far right conservatism at the other.' (Miliband 1989, p.145)

Equally, it is not only 'political' reporting which projects the ideology of the ruling class. Programmes that are supposedly designed just to entertain have a role to play. They suggest that all is well with the status quo. By doing this, they contribute to the promotion of false consciousness.

2. The pluralist model
The pluralist model claims that, contrary to what the Marxists suggest, a large range of ideas is expressed in the media and, because of this variety and diversity, no single view can predominate. Consumers, after all, are free to choose what they watch, listen to or read. Alternative views are always available if people are prepared to buy them. The mass media simply responds to the demands of the market.

According to the pluralist view, the media does have an influence and it is biased. But, it exerts its influence by reflecting and reinforcing views that are already held. So, Conservative supporters will find much to agree with if they read the *Daily Telegraph* whilst they may well be outraged by the views expressed in the *Guardian*. Conservative supporters will, therefore, either not read the *Guardian*, or they will read it only to find out what 'the other side' is thinking.

Shared power, diversity and choice
The pluralist model assumes that no one group dominates society. Power is shared by a range of groups. The mass media reflects this diversity and presents the audience with a wide ranging choice. Most people who work in the media tend to subscribe to the pluralist model. For example, Max Aitkin, a former Chair of Beaverbrook newspapers, claimed:
> 'Newspapers of today offer the public a complete range of opinion and expression.' (quoted in Trowler 1988, p.39)

The theory is that the media provides what the public wants (not that the public gets what the media gives it). Those who own and control the market are, therefore, serving the market not dictating to it. For example, Alistair Hetherington, former controller of BBC Scotland, argued:
> 'The BBC and ITV enjoy a near monopoly, but they too must try to gauge the interests of their audiences if viewing figures are to be maintained.' (quoted in Trowler 1988, p.40)

In the late 1990s, the BBC and ITV enjoyed less of a monopoly because of the growth of cable and satellite television. The introduction of digital television is likely to increase competition still further. As a results, pluralists will be able to draw on new evidence to support their case.

3. The mass manipulation model
The mass manipulation model suggests that the media plays an all-powerful role because the public is incapable of resisting the messages presented by the

media. The media itself is seen as monolithic (a single block rather than a diverse group). This model came into existence in the 1930s when, in both Germany and the Soviet Union, it was believed that the media played a key role in indoctrinating the people.

Within this model there are two alternatives. The left-wing version argues that the media is run in the interests of the ruling class. It is used to corrupt the working class (by encouraging people to worship materialist things, for example) and it helps to make sure that members of the working class do not rebel. The right-wing version sees the media as a damaging influence in society. It lowers cultural standards, produces a dull uniformity by pandering to the lowest common denominator, and encourages permissiveness. Both versions agree that the media has a great deal of influence and that people can be manipulated and controlled by the media.

4. The consensus model

The consensus model claims that what is produced by the media is produced within the framework of a consensus invented by the media. The media defines and structures reality for consumption by the general public. It plays an important role, therefore, in setting the political agenda. But, the media does this within the parameters of a selective framework which defines what should be included and excluded. Within the consensus, there is a hierarchy with some groups being better placed to meet the expectations raised by the consensus than others. Those groups outside the consensus are portrayed as being marginal or extreme. Critiques from outside the consensus may appear in the media, but they appear spasmodically and are the exception.

According to this model, the media is controlled by powerful groups in society, but direct manipulation by these groups is rare. Much more important are the routine practices of the media professionals and the technical constraints of media production.

5. The post-modern model

The most recent theory that has been developed to explain the role of the media is the post-modern model. The post-modern view can be defined as:

'An approach...which stresses the uncertain nature of societies, in which all certainties have been challenged and undermined, so that the conditions of lived existence occur in a global and fractured society in which there are no absolute rules or explanations.' (Lawson & Garrod 1996, p.205)

The current period of post-modernity is seen in contrast to a period of modernity which lasted from the so-called period of 'enlightenment' in the 18th century to the middle of the 20th century. The characteristics of the period of modernity are contrasted with those of the period of post-modernity in Box 19.4 below.

Post-modernism and the media

In the specific context of the media, post-modernists emphasise not only the huge growth in the importance of the media, but also its great diversity. For example, they note that, during the 1950s, the British population had access to only one television channel, whilst today it has access to a whole range of terrestrial channels as well as teletext and satellite and cable television. Similarly, they point to the growth in new technology and in consumerism which has allowed many people to buy personal computers and to gain access to the internet, further widening their choice of information. Instead of broadcasting to the population as a whole, stations 'narrowcast' to self-selecting audiences and this leads to:

'A greater fragmentation of media outlets, messages and audiences.' (Norris 1998, p.87)

In addition, technological developments have allowed time and space to be compressed. In an instant, people have access to events all over the world, 24 hours a day. In this 'pick and mix' society:

'[Individuals can be seen] making choices rather than being pushed about by forces outside their control.' (Best 1997, p.17)

According to the post-modern model, therefore, the influence of the mass media is limited for the following reasons. First, there is such great diversity and variety that there is a multiplicity of views. Second, individuals are able to pick and choose the information they receive. And third, individuals are even able to create their own version of reality by,

---

Box 19.4 Modernity and post-modernity

Modernity

During the period of modernity, there was an emphasis on:

- progress
- rational science
- hierarchical bureaucratic organisation
- industrial manufacturing
- the nation state
- class divisions
- politics linked to economic group interests.

Post-modernity

The period of post-modernity has the following features:

- no vision of a better future
- a variety of explanations of the world
- a diversity of social institutions operating in a variety of ways
- a post-industrial economy based on information technology
- globalisation in which marketing, advertising and consumerism play a central part
- a range of different identities based on gender, etnicity, age and sexual orientation as well as class
- a political process which has been transformed into non-institutional forms through the growth of new social movements (roads protestors, for example).

for example, making their own video or setting up their own website.

Criticisms of the post-modern model

Some critics claim that the post-modern model has failed as a theory. For example, Goldman argues:

'As post-modernism makes its way into mass culture, it becomes little more than a fetishised fascination with the image, the edit, the jump cut.' (quoted in Eldridge 1997, p.107)

In other words, the criticism is that the post-modern model is more concerned with the way in which messages are put across than with the impact that is made by the messages. So, just because there is a great variety of views available, that does not mean that people are better informed. Nor does it necessarily mean that the ruling class has lost its control over the flow of information.

4.3 The media and the political agenda

Who sets the political agenda?

It should be clear from the above discussion that the different theoretical models have different ideas about how powerful the media is and, therefore, how much effect it has on what people think and how they behave. In answer to the question - is it the media or the politicians who set the political agenda? - three contradictory answers have been given.

1. The media sets the agenda

Those who claim that the media sets the political agenda point to examples where concerted media campaigns lead to political action. For example, during the period April 1992 to May 1997, 12 government ministers were forced to resign following newspaper allegations either about corruption or their personal lives. In some cases, these media campaigns were protracted (as in the case of David Mellor who resigned from the Cabinet in September 1992). In other cases, a single exposé was enough to force resignation (as in the case of Welsh Minister Rod Richards who resigned in June 1996, the day after the *News of the World* printed a story alleging that he had been having an extra-marital affair). In all 12 cases, however, it was clear that ministerial resignations would not have taken place if the press had not exposed the allegations against the ministers in the first place. There are other ways in which the media appears to set the political agenda, too. In October 1997, for example, Gordon Brown made a speech in the Commons effectively ruling out membership of the European single currency until after the next general election. This followed several weeks of speculation in the press about Labour's plans regarding the single currency. Although government officials attempted to manage the news,

on this occasion they failed, forcing Brown to clarify his position:

'On 18 October, the *Times* published an interview with the Chancellor. On the face of it, this seemed to say nothing more than that the government would not repeat the Conservative mistake of allowing speculation about EMU [economic and monetary union] to dominate its whole term of office. However, newspaper headlines interpreted the interview as ruling out membership for the whole of Labour's first term. It transpired that this resulted from a "steer" provided by Gordon Brown's press secretary...Facing criticism of government by spin doctor, Gordon Brown made a comprehensive policy statement to Parliament about EMU on 27 October 1997.' (Grant 1998, p.110)

Given their anti-EMU stance, most newspapers had a vested interest in EMU being ruled out until after the next general election. Without pressure from the press, it is unlikely that Gordon Brown would have clarified the government's position on EMU as early as October 1997.

Lack of media coverage

Evidence that the media sets the political agenda also comes from examining events of importance which are not reported by the media. The fact that they are not reported implies that it is the media which is deciding what is important. In other words, it is setting the agenda. An example of this is the lack of media coverage of the Deregulation Bill which became law in 1994. Although this law gave the government sweeping new powers to alter existing regulations, it was hardly mentioned by the media. One BBC producer (who wished to remain anonymous) admitted that the reason why the BBC did not provide more coverage of the passage of this Bill was:

'Because the programmers did not think that deregulation was a "sexy" enough issue to interest viewers and listeners. I brought forward proposals for a programme on this subject, but the idea was rejected.' (interview with the author, May 1994)

News values

Those who support the view that the media sets the political agenda argue that the media operates with a set of news values which informs its judgement as to which stories to cover. So, for example, if a police officer is wounded or killed, that will generate many more column inches than if a former prisoner is wounded or killed. It should be noted that even though the television and radio are less partisan than the press:

'It has long been argued that newspapers are significant in establishing the national news agenda which is adopted by broadcasters...

Both in setting the agenda and establishing the main issues, and also in creating the images of the parties and leading personalities, newspapers play a key role.' (Benyon & Denver 1990, p.95)

2. The politicians set the agenda

Those who claim that the politicians set the agenda argue that the media is merely the servant of politicians. Franklin points out that politicians:

'Control the funding of public sector television, they make appointments to regulatory bodies, they can intervene directly when programming affects national security, they can censor programmes and ultimately it is politicians who drive the legislative process which enables them to restructure the wider environment in which broadcasters and journalists operate.' (Franklin 1994, p.14)

According to this view, therefore, politicians use the media to their own advantage to promote themselves and their policies and to pass their message on to the general public.

Spin doctors

Politicians do not rely entirely on their own devices to promote their message. They employ press officers or 'spin doctors' (so-called because they doctor information so that it has a sympathetic angle or 'spin'). In a bid to promote the message favoured by the politicians they serve, these spin doctors liaise with journalists and, in return, gain exposure in the media (Wring 1998). Whilst the term 'spin doctor' gained great currency in the run-up to the 1997 general election and after it, there has been a long history of the main political parties using press officers and political marketing techniques to ensure that their messages are presented in the best possible light. What is, perhaps, new is the scale of spin doctors' activity and the public attention focused on key individuals like Alastair Campbell (Tony Blair's Chief Press Officer) and Peter Mandelson (who worked as the Labour Party's Campaigns and Communications Director before serving as a minister).

The main techniques used by spin doctors are summarised in Box 19.5 below.

Spin doctors at work

In 1995, Alastair Campbell sent a fax to the BBC demanding that Tony Blair's keynote conference speech and not the verdict of the OJ Simpson trial should be the lead item in news bulletins (*Guardian*, 23 September 1996). Similarly, in December 1997, following the notorious interview between John Humphrys and Harriet Harman, David Hill (the Labour Party's Communications Chief), wrote to Jon Barton, editor of the Radio 4 *Today* programme, threatening to suspend cooperation with the programme. The tone of coverage in the media that the spin doctors try to set was described in the *Guardian* as:

'Centralised, picture-driven and presentational rather than concerned to dot the "i"s of policy detail. Its instincts are tabloid in tone. Thus, when Tony Blair wants to convey a peace message to Northern Ireland and the world, he gets photographed with 12 year old Margaret Gibney from Belfast whose letter so moved him.' (*Guardian*, 7 July 1997)

Why have spin doctors gained in importance?

The attempt to manage the news has become more professional and more important as news coverage has grown and become more immediate. Mistakes by politicians - a slip of the tongue, for example - can be seen round the world within hours. It is hardly surprising, therefore, that politicians should use spin doctors in an attempt to manage the news. As Peter Mandelson explained:

'It depends what you mean by news management...If you are accusing me of getting the truth across about what the government has decided to do, that I'm putting the very best face or gloss on government policies, that I'm trying to avoid gaffes or setbacks and that I'm trying to create the truth

---

Box 19.5 What spin doctors do

According to Jones (1996), spin doctors use the following techniques:

- they give advice on the content of speeches and the likely implications of votes and decisions
- they make themselves available to journalists after major political developments - so that there is an authoritative voice giving an instant interpretation of what has happened and background guidance on the likely political consequences
- they engage in private conversations with journalists, in an attempt to persuade them of a particular line (especially if the journalist has a line which is damaging)
- if a tricky political development is about to occur,

they guide and distort the focus of news coverage by slipping out some well-placed leaks
- they predict how journalists might react in any given set of circumstances so that, if necessary, a more favourable interpretation can be pushed on a story
- they pay special attention to particular journalists and give then inside information in the hope of gaining their favour
- they provide soundbites for journalists to use so that the message can easily be understood
- they complain to news organisations if they feel there has been unfair treatment - in the hope of undoing some of the damage and intimidating journalists.

Adapted from Jones 1996.

- if that's news management, I plead guilty.'
(*Guardian*, 9 August 1997)

Of course, journalists understand what spin doctors are trying to do and they are not necessarily taken in by the spin doctor's art.

3. Neither the media nor the politicians set the agenda

The third view is that neither the media nor the politicians are the servants or the masters. Instead, there is a symbiotic relationship between them. Each relies on the other and each makes an effort to accommodate the needs of the other. So, politicians hold press conferences or give interviews so that their views will be communicated to the general public. What happens at the press conference or interview then provides information which journalists can use in their reports. Without press conferences and interviews, it would be more difficult for politicians to get across their views. Equally, it would be more difficult for journalists to gather news.

Those who subscribe to this view emphasise that neither the media nor politicians are a homogenous group. There is a great deal of difference between what is reported in the *Independent* and what is reported in the *Sun*, for example. Similarly, the Leader of the Conservative Party has a very different agenda from the Leader of the Labour Party. As a result there is no single political agenda, but a number of agendas which surface at different places at different times.

Main points - Part 4

- **It is difficult to measure the effect of the media because: (1) people have access to several media outlets; (2) people are not just influenced by the media; (3) it is difficult to separate the short-term and long-term effects of exposure to the media; and (4) opinions are also shaped by 'significant others'.**
- **Five main models have been developed to explain the way in which the media works in society - (1) the Marxist model; (2) the pluralist model; (3) the mass manipulation model; (4) the consensus model; and (5) the post-modern model.**
- **The different models have different ideas about how powerful the media is and, therefore, how much effect it has on people. Who sets the political agenda - the media, the politicians (and their spin doctors) or neither?**

Activity 19.6 Who sets the political agenda?

Item A *Newspaper headlines on 3 November 1998*

The Daily Telegraph   3 November 1998
Britain now a step closer to the euro

The Guardian   3 November 1998
DAVIES: bitter and defiant

The Sun   3 November 1998
Outed: at last Brown and Mandelson admit they really do back the euro

The Star   3 November 1998
Carey Spice

The Mirror   3 November 1998
Ron was whipped by evil father

The Independent   3 November 1998
Britain edges closer to euro as calls grow for early referendum

The Mail   3 November 1998
Tax relief for share buyers

The Express   3 November 1998
DAVIES: we are what we are

Item B   *Media influence*

(i) Newspapers reinforce rather than create opinion - particularly as most people rely on television for most of their news. Indeed, the legal and other obligations on broadcasters to offer balanced coverage in large part offset the biases and partisan views of some newspapers. Newspapers cannot argue against the instincts and direct experiences of their readers. It would, for example, have been impossible for even the most pro-Tory newspaper to argue during the 1997 general election campaign that Tony Blair was an extremist. If a newspaper had done this, it would simply not have been believed. So, in many ways, the media follows as much as it leads.

Adapted from Riddell 1998.

(ii) The political commentator Martin Harrop is unhappy with the conclusion of many studies which suggest media influence tends to reinforce rather than change voters' political attitudes. The media and voters, he argues, are highly varied categories. The media includes cinema, radio, television and newspapers. The press, in turn, may be classified into local and national, or tabloid and broadsheet. Similarly, voters can be distinguished according to variables such as the strength of their political commitments, the extent of their political knowledge and the intensity of their interest in political affairs. Each of these factors might prove significant in enhancing or limiting media effects. As a result, it is necessary to undertake a number of distinctive inquiries before it is possible to unravel relations between the media and voters. According to Harrop, media influence depends on the nature of the voter, the society, the message and the type of effect being considered.

Adapted from Franklin 1994.

Item C   *Cartoons and theoretical models*

YOU SCRATCH MY BACK AND I'LL SCRATCH YOURS EH, RUPERT?

These cartoons illustrate two of the models described in Section 4.2 above. The top cartoon (published in the *Guardian* on 26 March 1998) shows the Prime Minister, Tony Blair, and the owner of News International, Rupert Murdoch. The bottom cartoon shows the cartoonist Brick's view of the media at the end of the 20th century.

Item D   *Spin doctors*

(i) Peter Mandelson's lasting value to the Labour leadership has been his understanding of the factors which motivate political journalists. He seemed to have a sixth sense. On seeing a group of journalists gathering in the members' lobby or chatting away in the press gallery, for example, he would guess quite accurately what they were up to and which of the day's stories they were likely to be discussing. His knowledge of the inner workings of television (he was a former London Weekend Television producer) and radio news rooms and the background information he acquired about the likes and dislikes of individual lobby correspondents was of enormous benefit as he helped the Labour Party to develop well-rehearsed routines for publicising policy initiatives. As the years went by, he was to become increasingly proficient at what, for a spin doctor, amounted to sheer artistry - the ability to determine which journalists were likely to be of use to him and could, therefore, achieve the greatest impact in return for the information he had to offer.

Adapted from Jones 1996.

(ii) In the world of political communications, there are straightforward press officers whose job used to be simply to give out information. Next, there are the public relations people who put a bit of a gloss on a subject, but most people know what the gloss is. And then, there is the modern breed of spin doctors. Their job seems to be to distort - to give a serious political issue a populist appeal and slant in a way which is often simplistic or even offensive to those who have spent their political lives trying to get difficult points across. The spin doctor is trying to convert everything into 25-second soundbites fit for televisual consumption.

The view of Brian Sedgemore, a Labour MP, quoted in the *Guardian*, 19 August 1996.

Questions

1. a) Judging from Items A-D, who sets the political agenda?
   b) What does your answer tell us about the influence of the media?
2. Explain how the information in Items A and C could be used as evidence in support of the five models outlined in Section 4.2 above.

3. 'It is difficult to measure the exact extent of media influence'. Explain this statement using Item B.
4. a) What part do spin doctors play in setting the political agenda? Use Item D in your answer.
   b) Give arguments for and against the view that the growing influence of spin doctors is unhealthy.

Part 5 Official information

Key issues

1. What are the justifications for secrecy in a democracy?
2. What are the mechanisms by which secrecy is maintained?
3. What steps have been taken to make information more freely available?

5.1 Secrecy and the state

Arguments for and against secrecy

According to Hennessy:

> 'Secrecy is the bonding material which holds the rambling structure of central government together. Secrecy is built into the calcium of a British policy maker's bones...It is the very essence of the Establishment view of good government, of private government carried on beyond the reach of the faction of political party, the tunnel vision of pressure group and the impertinent curiosity of the journalist.' (Hennessy 1989, p.346)

There is, in other words, a strong tradition of secrecy in Britain and this tradition is supported and strengthened by the actions of governments and civil servants.

Arguments in favour of secrecy

Those in power and supporters of the status quo advance the following arguments to justify this secrecy. First, they emphasise the need to maintain security. It is claimed that the government needs wide powers to prevent enemies within the UK and abroad from discovering secrets important to the nation's security. Second, it is argued that policy issues are generally too complex for the general public to understand and secrecy is needed to prevent them from being misunderstood. Third, it is argued that the wider spreading of information would be costly and difficult to administer. If there was access to information at every point in the decision-making process, then government would become inefficient. And fourth, it is argued that the doctrine of ministerial responsibility (see Chapter 13, Section 1.3) relies upon secrecy. If there was less secrecy, unelected and, therefore, unrepresentative groups might gain power at the expense of elected representatives.

Arguments against secrecy

Most critics accept that a certain amount of secrecy is essential if security (both internal and external) is to be maintained. But, they argue, the British government is much too secretive - for three main reasons:

- Whitehall conservatism
- the vested interests of the state security apparatus
- the fact that members of the government and civil servants are hostile to change for fear of jeopardising their own position.

Greater openness, they argue, would lead to greater accountability and greater efficiency.

5.2 Official secrets

What are official secrets?

Governments have a number of official tools which they can use to prevent information reaching the public. These include the Official Secrets Act, the Public Records Act and the Privy Counsellor's oath.

The 1911 Official Secrets Act

The first Official Secrets Act was passed in 1911 after a debate which lasted less than an hour. At the time there was a great deal of public anxiety about spying. The main provisions are outlined in Box 19.6.

Box 19.6 The 1911 Official Secrets Act

Section One
Section One of the Act made it an offence, punishable by up to 14 years imprisonment, to disclose information which might be of use to an enemy or to engage in conduct which was 'prejudicial to the safety or the interests of the state'.

Section Two
Section Two of the Act made it an offence, punishable by up to two years imprisonment, for a person employed by the state to pass on any official information to anyone not authorised to receive it. The 'catch all' nature of this section of the Act meant that, theoretically at least, the release of information such as the number of cups of tea drunk in a government department could be an offence.

Key steps towards reform

The Aitken case, 1970

Jonathan Aitken was a journalist who was prosecuted for handling a confidential report which seemed to show that statements by government ministers were inaccurate. The outcry against his prosecution led to the setting up of the Franks Committee on Official Secrecy. The report published by this committee in 1972 condemned the breadth and uncertainty of the 1911 Act and recommended its repeal (Franks 1972). Although the Labour government which came to power in 1974 promised to reform the Official Secrets Act, nothing was done. The Aitken case is widely regarded as the first sign that reform of the 1911 Act was inevitable.

The ABC trial

A second important trial was the 'ABC trial' of 1977 (so-called after the initials of the three defendants Aubrey, Berry and Campbell). Aubrey and Campbell were journalists arrested whilst interviewing Berry, a former Corporal in Signals Intelligence, about his work. The trial descended into farce when it became clear that information described as 'secret' by the prosecution was available from public sources. Although the defendants were convicted, their light sentences were taken as a further sign that reform was necessary.

Tisdall, Ponting and Spycatcher

In the 1980s, three further cases added pressure for reform. First, in 1984, Sarah Tisdall, a clerk at the Foreign Office, was prosecuted under the Official Secrets Act for leaking documents to the *Guardian* which showed that Cruise Missiles had arrived at Greenham Common. Tisdall pleaded guilty and was sentenced to six months in prison. Then, in 1985, Clive Ponting was prosecuted under the Official Secrets Act for passing information to a Labour MP about the sinking of the Argentine ship, the *General Belgrano*, during the Falklands War (see also Chapter 13, Section 2.6). Ponting believed that the government refused to release this information because it was seeking to save itself from political embarrassment. Unlike Tisdall, Ponting fought his case and he was acquitted by a jury who agreed with his defence that his actions were in the public interest. And third, there was the *Spycatcher* trial in 1987-88. *Spycatcher* was a book written by a former MI5 agent, Peter Wright. The government tried to ban the book's publication in Britain, even though it was available abroad, on the grounds that it breached the oath of confidentiality taken by MI5 employees. Copies of the book, however, were brought in from abroad because the government had failed to place an import restriction on the book and public readings were held. As a result, the book became the focus for the struggle to gain greater freedom of information. When the House of Lords, sitting as the final court of appeal rejected the government's case, the government moved quickly to introduce new legislation.

The 1989 Official Secrets Act

The new Official Secrets Act, passed in 1989, was designed to prevent any disclosures about security or intelligence matters by making such disclosures a criminal offence for current and past members of the security services, crown servants or government contractors. Anybody found guilty of disclosing 'damaging' information could face up to two years in prison. Disclosure is defined as 'damaging' if it prejudices the capability of the armed forces to carry out their tasks or leads to loss of life, injury, damage of equipment or installation. In addition, disclosure of information about foreign policy, police operations and relations with other countries or international organisations is an offence and civil servants may only disclose information when it is in accordance with their duty (they must not keep documents and must take steps to prevent unauthorised disclosures).

There are two other important elements in the Act. First, it is no longer a defence to argue that information is disclosed in the public interest or that it is available abroad. And second, the Act also covers the disclosure of information by journalists. Editors who encourage journalists to publish information they have reason to believe has been divulged without lawful authority are in breach of the law.

The 1994 Intelligence Services Act

The 1994 Intelligence Services Act set up the Intelligence and Security Committee, a committee of MPs and peers whose job is to monitor the work of the security services. Critics, however, argue that it is, in effect, a toothless watchdog since it is an advisory body (it advises the Prime Minister on security matters) which does not even have the power to question the heads of the security services. In October 1998, Yvette Cooper MP, a member of the committee, complained that the security services could not properly be held to account because it was they who decided how much information to provide to the committee. She argued that the committee should have access to all the security service's staff and documents (*Guardian*, 22 October 1998).

Criticisms of the 1989 Act

Critics of the new Act have argued that it has been designed to close the loopholes in the 1911 Act and, therefore, ensures there is greater secrecy rather than greater freedom of information. Also, the new Act makes conviction more likely since defendants cannot claim that it was in the public interest to reveal information.

A further criticism of the Act is that it has failed to prevent the leaking of secret information by civil servants. That governments do hide behind official secrecy was admitted by Robin Butler (Cabinet Secretary until January 1998). At the Scott Inquiry he agreed that the more secretive the decision-making process, the greater the likelihood of leaks.

The 1958 Public Records Act

Under the British Public Records Act of 1958, government papers are not available to historians, journalists and members of the public until 30 years have elapsed 'or such other period as the Lord Chancellor may provide'. There are 40 categories of government paper that are automatically kept away from public view for longer than 30 years. These 40 categories make up c.5% of all government papers. They include papers containing distressing or embarrassing personal details about living persons; papers containing information received by the government in confidence; state papers on Ireland; and papers which affect the security of the state.

The leading barrister and campaigner for greater freedom of information, Geoffrey Robertson, noted that:

'The government refused to incorporate into its 1989 reforms of the Official Secrets Act a legal right of access to information collected or generated by civil servants - at a time when such access (through Freedom of Information Acts) has become almost a defining characteristic of democratic government elsewhere in the world... [There is] an urgent need to reform the Public Records Act and to provide a legal right to appeal against over-secretive bureaucratic decisions to close files to public inspection for immeasurable times.' (Robertson 1993, p.2)

The Privy Councillor's oath

One of the earliest recorded mechanisms for ensuring secrecy is the Privy Councillor's oath. This dates from 1250 and is still used today. The oath is shown in Box 19.7.

Box 19.7 The Privy Councillor's oath

You will in all things to be moved, treated and debated in Council faithfully and truly declare your mind and opinion according to your heart and conscience; and will keep secret all matters committed and revealed unto you, or that shall be treated of secretly in Council. And if any of the said treaties or counsels shall touch any of the councillors, you will not reveal it unto him but will keep the same until such time as, by the consent of Her (His) Majesty, or the Council, publication shall be made thereof.'

Quoted in Hunt 1992.

Originally, the Privy Council was a group of advisers to the monarch. It was from the Privy Council that Charles II chose the first Cabinet and the modern Cabinet remains, formally, a committee of the Privy Council. Only senior members of government and leading opposition figures are made members of the Privy Council. Membership is for life. All new members of the Privy Council are required to swear the oath quoted in Box 19.7 in the presence of the monarch.

Ministers who are Privy Councillors are more likely to receive papers classified as 'top secret'. Occasionally, members of the opposition who are Privy Councillors are given secret material on the basis of the Privy Councillor's oath (on the understanding that they will not divulge the contents). This binds leading opposition figures to secrecy and, therefore, stifles democratic debate.

5.3 Unofficial secrets

Introduction

As well as the formal, legal mechanisms for ensuring secrecy and maintaining closed government, there are also a number of informal mechanisms which work to the same end.

1. D Notices

Much secrecy and mystery surrounds the operation of D Notices (Defence Notices). D Notices are issued to prevent the publication of articles or the broadcast of programmes harmful to national defence or security. They are issued by the D Notice Committee.

The D Notice Committee was established in 1912, a year after the Official Secrets Act was passed. The committee is composed of four senior civil servants and 11 press and broadcasting representatives. Whilst the full committee usually meets annually, the day-to-day work is carried out by the Secretary (who is usually a Ministry of Defence employee).

Matters covered by D Notices

D Notices have no legal force whatever and merely serve as guidance for the media. According to Robertson (1989), there are eight D Notices in operation, covering areas such as defence plans and equipment, nuclear weaponry, codes and communication interception, the security services, civil defence and the photography of defence installations. For example, D Notice number one on defence plans and equipment covers:

'Information relating to...defence policy or plans...actual service manpower strengths or specialities, categories or trades...future movements or intended destinations of HM ships...current or projected tactics or trials. In case of doubt, you are requested to seek advice through the appropriate government department.' (*New Statesman*, 4 April 1980)

Admiral Higgens, the Secretary to the D Notice Committee in 1992, described the system as:

'A voluntary advisory service and like pregnancy testing, its consultations are confidential.' (quoted in the *Guardian*, 21 February 1992)

Extent and effectiveness

According to a further report in the *Guardian*, Admiral Higgens gave positive advice to editors, urging them not to publish about a dozen times a year. He received about 100 inquiries a year from editors and publishers (*Guardian*, 24 September 1992). Compliance with the Secretary's advice, however, does not guarantee immunity from prosecution under the 1989 Official Secrets Act.

In practice, the media does explore areas covered by D Notices. There is evidence, however, that some areas are not explored because of fear of D Notice intervention. The fact that the system is informal has probably been responsible for the lack of outcry or reaction from the media. The D Notice system encourages the media to accept that there are sensitive areas which should not be probed.

2. The lobby system

Secrecy and control of information is enhanced by the lobby system. Although the Labour government elected in 1997 introduced changes to the system to make it less secretive (see above Section 2.2), some briefings are still non-attributable. For example, when the Social Security minister Frank Field resigned from the government in July 1998, he was attacked in 'background briefings from Cabinet sources' (*Guardian*, 3 August 1998).

3. Controlling government information

Public interest immunity certificates

Until 1996, ministers were able to sign public interest immunity (PII) certificates - so-called 'gagging orders' - blocking the release of documents to court on the grounds that their release was not in the public interest. This allowed them to block a large range of documents - for example, any documents relating to arms exports could be blocked. During the Scott Inquiry (see also Chapter 13, Section 1.3 and Activity 17.4), however, it was revealed that PII certificates had been wrongly issued, the implication being that ministers used them to cover up their own involvement in the export of arms to Iraq rather than to protect the public interest. In December 1996, nearly a year after the Scott Report was published, the government announced that blanket PII claims on documents irrespective of their content would, in future, no longer be issued. Rather, they would only be issued when disclosure of a particular document would cause 'real damage or harm'.

Labour spin doctors and civil servants

After Labour came to power in May 1997, concern was expressed that government information was being manipulated for party gain. This concern focused on the 60 or so special advisers who were appointed to work with ministers. Since many were working, in effect, as spin doctors, critics argued that party appointees were taking over work that had previously been done by impartial civil servants. Unlike special advisers, the 1,000 or so official press officers are civil servants and part of the Government Government Information and Communication Service. They are,

therefore, bound by civil service rules which demand that they provide objective information and that they are politically neutral. News that 25 senior official press officers had resigned or moved post in Labour's first 15 months in power fuelled these concerns (*Observer*, 2 August 1998). A number, it was alleged, had left after disputes with ministers. In some cases, they were replaced by advisers who were given civil service status (for example, Gordon Brown's adviser Charlie Whelan replaced Jill Rutter as Director of Information at the Treasury).

Putting across the government's message

In October 1997, Alastair Campbell, Tony Blair's Chief Press Secretary, wrote to all information directors stating that four key messages should be built into all areas of activity:

1. This is a modernising government.
2. The government is delivering its promises.
3. The government's policies are in the mainstream.
4. The government is providing a new direction for Britain.

To ensure that the public received these messages, the government spent £43 million in 1997 on advertising and promoting their policies and, in 1998, £11 million was spent on promoting the New Deal programme. In addition:

> 'The Government Information Service has set up a 24 hour media monitoring unit to supply duty press officers with immediate warnings of emerging stories so they can, if necessary, be rebutted. Campbell has also established a Strategic Communications Unit to send out messages of the day to all government departments.' (*Observer*, 2 August 1998)

Attacks on Alastair Campbell

In April 1998, the Conservative Party attacked Alastair Campbell for breaching civil service rules on political neutrality. It then emerged that, although Campbell had a civil service contract imposing civil service regulations, the contract exempted Campbell from being bound by 'those aspects which relate to impartiality and objectivity' (*Guardian*, 2 April 1998). Two months later, the Commons Select Committee on Public Administration accused Campbell of manipulating journalists, leaking government announcements, releasing information designed to damage certain ministers, bullying ministers and politicising the civil service. In response, Campbell said that his role was 'to put the government's agenda and prevent journalists from wresting control of it' (*Guardian*, 24 June 1998).

Control from the centre

The Labour government has made a concerted effort to control government information from the centre. This is made very clear in the *Code of Conduct and*

Guidance on Procedure for Ministers, the official guidelines laid down for ministers (see Box 19.8).

Box 19.8 *Procedure for Ministers*

In order to ensure the effective presentation of government policy, all major interviews and media appearances, both print and broadcast, should be agreed with the Number 10 Press Office before any commitments are entered into. The policy contents of all major speeches, press releases and new policy initiatives should be cleared in good time with the Number 10 Private Office. The timing and form of announcements should be cleared with the Number 10 Press Office.

Cabinet Office 1997.

The appointment in July 1998 of Jack Cunningham as 'Cabinet enforcer', was a further sign of centralisation. Whilst centralisation helps to ensure that ministers do not inadvertently contradict each other, the emphasis on positive stories, the release of selective information and the timing of the release of information to ensure that bad news is concealed by good all contribute to the maintenance of secrecy.

4. Refusal to answer questions in Parliament

Ministers can refuse to answer questions in the House of Commons or they can choose to give incomplete answers to MPs' questions. The Table Office which receives MPs' questions and decides which can be submitted, holds a list of topics which will not be accepted. This list has developed out of the rulings made by successive Speakers. In 1972, it was revealed that there were 95 taboo subjects (Hillyard & Percy-Smith, 1988). Ministers can refuse to answer any question on the grounds of national security.

5. The routine operation of government business

The principles of collective Cabinet responsibility (see Chapter 12, Section 2.3) and individual ministerial responsibility (see Chapter 13, Section 1.3) help to ensure that secrecy begins at the top. Little is left to chance. The *Code of Conduct and Guidance on Procedure for Ministers*, the official guidelines laid down for ministers (revised after Labour came to power), explains in some detail how secrecy is to be maintained and how the public is denied the right to know. The *Guardian* claimed:

> 'The emphasis on the rigid control of information is shocking and runs completely counter to the continuing protestations that Labour is genuinely interested in passing an effective Freedom of Information Act.'
> (*Guardian*, 1 August 1998)

The routine operation of government business is, in other words, structured to ensure that secrecy is the norm.

Main points - Sections 5.1-5.3

- There is a strong tradition of secrecy in Britain and this tradition is supported and strengthened by the actions of governments and civil servants.
- Governments have a number of official tools which they can use to prevent information reaching the public including the Official Secrets Act, the Public Records Act and the Privy Counsellor's oath.
- The 1989 Official Secrets Act made disclosure about security matters a criminal offence for government employees and blocked the use of public interest defence.
- Governments also have unofficial means of preserving secrecy: (1) D notices; (2) the lobby system; (3) controlling government information; (4) refusing to answer questions in Parliament; and (5) the routine operation of government business.

Activity 19.7 Closed government

Item A *The D Notice system*

According to a Commons Defence Committee report, newspapers simply do not use the D Notices. Some have not consulted them for years. One newspaper had lost its copy of them. The committee also notes that some categories of sensitive information are not covered by the system, that both foreign and fringe press are excluded and that the wording of the D Notices is so broad that it is almost meaningless. The report states that there were four main criticisms of the system. First, it was a form of censorship which could be used by the government to suppress information for political convenience. Second, the freedom of the press was compromised. Third, there was confusion between the D Notice system and the law. And fourth, the system was little used and, therefore, unnecessary. The report notes that D Notices have been little altered in nine years and in the last six months there were just 30 minor inquiries to the committee.

Adapted from the *Guardian*, 8 August 1990.

Item B *Secrecy and the security services*

(i) Those who wish to damage the state will naturally organise themselves and make plans in secret. So we will have to use secret means to investigate them. With the proper legal authority we may need to tap their telephones, open their letters or eavesdrop on their conversations to find out their intentions. We may have to observe their movements secretly or recruit members of these organisations as agents to tell us from the inside what is being planned. Then we have to analyse and assess the information and use our findings to counter the harm which is being considered.

Part of the Dimbleby lecture given by Stella Rimington, head of MI5, in 1994.

(ii) The Home Secretary, Jack Straw, revealed yesterday that MI5 holds 440,000 files on individuals it has targeted since it was set up in 1909. Details were announced as MI5 published a glossy brochure to dispel 'myths and misunderstandings' about its activities. Straw made it clear that individuals targeted by MI5 would not have access to their files. These individuals include the Home Secretary himself (who was targeted when President of the National Union of Students in 1969-71), the Trade and Industry Secretary, Peter Mandelson and the Economic Secretary to the Treasury, Patricia Hewitt. 'I have no idea what happened to my file', said Mr Straw, 'It has never caused me any worry.' Of 440,000 individual files kept by MI5, 25,000 are active. Of these, 7,000 relate to foreign nationals including spies and terrorists. Another 13,000 identify British citizens, more than half connected with terrorism. Other files contain information on organisations 'studied' by MI5. MI5 officers have access to a further 230,000 files on individuals no longer being investigated. It was also revealed that 285,000 files had been destroyed since 1909 (over 100,000 of which had been destroyed since the collapse of Communism). Straw said that decisions on which files should be destroyed in the future and which retained for eventual release at the Public Record Office was a matter for MI5, taking into account their 'operational value' and 'historical significance'.

Adapted from the *Guardian*, 30 July 1998.

(iii) Richard Tomlinson, the first MI6 agent to be prosecuted for secrets offences since the Soviet spy George Blake 36 years ago, said that he had no alternative but to plead guilty even though the information he supplied was 'trivial'. He said that he had wanted to plead not guilty, but the draconian nature of the Official Secrets Act made it impossible - there was no public interest defence. 'I would have been guilty even if I had disclosed the colour of the carpets in the office', he said. After leaving MI6 in 1995, Tomlinson notified his former employers that he wanted to commit his experiences to writing. Their response was to take out an injunction preventing material from being published. The prosecution told Bow Street Magistrates Court that Tomlinson had prepared a seven page synopsis of a proposed book. This was obtained by Special Branch officers. They then passed it on to MI6 who said it contained confidential information about training, operations, sources and methods. In reply, the defence said that the synopsis 'posed no substantial or realistic danger to national security'. Tomlinson was sentenced to 12 months in prison.

Adapted from the *Times*, 4 and 9 November and 19 December 1997.

Item C *Controlling government information*

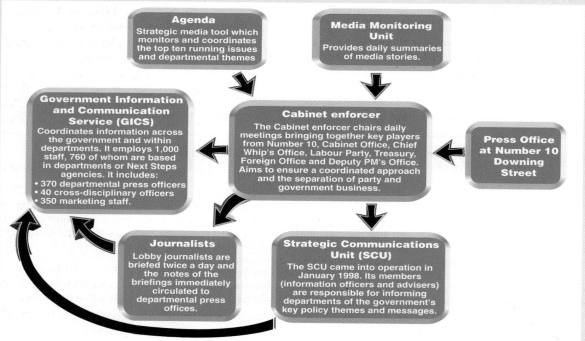

This diagram shows how the Labour government attempts to keep control over its flow of information. For further information on the 'Cabinet enforcer' see Chapter 12, Section 2.5. It should be noted that the Government Information and Communication Service is the routine external face of government departments.

Adapted from the *Guardian*, 6 August 1998.

Item D   *Parliament and secrecy*

In February 1997, a year after his Report into the Arms-to-Iraq scandal was published, Richard Scott called on MPs to step up their attack on excessive government secrecy. As a first step, he suggested, MPs should insist that the 'real harm' test (which now applies to the issuing of PII certificates) should apply to questions to ministers from MPs. Parliament, he argued, had been far too subservient. MPs should insist on their right to know - unless the information would cause grave harm to international relations or commercial interests. One way of measuring progress would be to monitor all questions which ministers have refused to answer. The Commons Public Service Committee has suggested such a move backed up by a proposal for a new senior officer of Parliament who could pass judgement when information was witheld by ministers. Ministers from both main parties, Scott claimed, have been obsessed with secrecy. There are far too many ways in which Whitehall can evade its obligations.

Adapted from the *Guardian*, 17 February 1997.

Questions

1. 'British government is too secretive'. Using Items A-D, give arguments for and against this statement.
2. a) Can you think of any reasons why people might oppose the views put forward by Stella Rimington in Item B?
   b) Is there any reason to be concerned about the files held by MI5?
   c) Give arguments for and against reforming the Official Secrets Act.
3. 'Informal mechanisms are an effective means of maintaining secrecy'. Explain this statement using Items A, C & D.

5.4 Freedom of information

Open and closed government

Governments claim that they represent the national interest. If governments do represent the national interest and they argue that secrecy is a crucial means of defending the state, then (logically speaking) secrecy must be in the interest of everybody living in that nation. This, in effect, was the argument advanced by the British government during the Cold War. Secrecy, so the argument went, was necessary to protect British citizens from the threat posed by communism, especially Soviet communism.

Whilst the above argument was used to justify 'closed' (secretive) government, some people have argued for 'open' government - government which minimises the areas of secrecy and maximises the availability of information. According to the Labour MP Tony Benn, an open government is a more participatory and a more democratic government:

> 'If we accept that the control of information about decisions and how they are arrived at is a prerogative of the government, then we are accepting that democracy cannot be mature enough to allow people to share even the thinking that precedes these decisions.' (Benn 1979, p.129)

As a result of the collapse of communism in Eastern Europe, the perceived threat to national security from abroad has been reduced. This has resulted in new interest in and new demands for open government.

The Campaign for Freedom of Information

The Campaign for Freedom of Information is a pressure group set up in 1984. Since then, this group has managed to win the support of many leading politicians and ex-civil servants. The group plays a watchdog role, checking on the proposals made by government in areas which might involve secrecy. All-party support and the backing of senior civil servants have helped to give the group legitimacy. Supporters of the Campaign

for Freedom of Information aim to give the public the right of access to official information with very few exceptions. Their case is strengthened by comparing the position in Britain with examples of freedom of information legislation in other countries - for example, the USA has had a Freedom of Information Act since 1966 and, in Sweden, it has been a legal right to inspect government documents (apart from those covered by a Secrecy Act) since 1809.

Margaret Thatcher and freedom of information

The Campaign for Freedom of Information was set up to put pressure on a government which appeared reluctant to lessen the degree of state secrecy. Indeed, the Prime Minister, Margaret Thatcher, argued against freedom of information on constitutional grounds. In a letter to the Campaign for Freedom of Information she said:

> 'Under our constitution, ministers are accountable to Parliament for the work of their departments and that includes the provision of information...A statutory right of access would remove this enormously important area of decision making from ministers and Parliament.' (quoted in Wilson 1984, pp.134-5)

John Major and freedom of information

Whilst Margaret Thatcher refused to consider more open government, her successor, John Major claimed to take a different view. His government began to promote the idea that government should be more open. This new approach was allied to the development of the Citizen's Charter (see Chapter 17, Section 1.3). The Citizen's Charter, it was claimed, would make available more information on the services provided by government. This idea was taken up in the 1992 Conservative election manifesto:

> 'Government has traditionally been far too reluctant to provide information...We will be less secretive about the workings of

government. For example, when the Committees of the Cabinet are reconstituted after the election, we will, for the first time, set out their names and membership. We will update and - for the first time - publish the guidance for ministers on procedure.' (Conservative 1992, p.16)

These manifesto promises were developed in a white paper published in 1993 and entitled *Open Government*. This white paper proposed a new Whitehall code of practice on access to official information. The government claimed that three themes would govern its approach:

- handling information in a way which promotes informed policy making and debate
- providing timely and accessible information to the citizen to explain the government's policies, actions and decisions
- restricting access to information only when there are good reasons for doing so.

This code of practice came into force in 1994.

Limitations of government policy 1990-97

Critics - for example, the Campaign for Freedom of Information - argued that the 1993 white paper and subsequent code of practice were a weak set of instruments which allowed ministers a wide measure of discretion. Many areas were exempt from disclosure and the policy-making process, internal opinion, discussion and advice all still remained secret. Crucially, the government gave people the right of access to information, not the right to see correspondence, documents or reports.

In addition, the credibility of John Major's government's support of open government was undermined by three developments. First, the Minister for Open Government, William Waldegrave, told a cross-party committee of MPs that, in exceptional circumstances, it was necessary for ministers to tell lies in the House of Commons. He also vigorously defended the use of blocking answers by ministers - the device where half truths or half answers are used in Parliament to avoid spelling out the true picture.

Second, evidence given by ministers at the Scott Inquiry (see Chapter 13, Section 1.3 and Activity 17.4) revealed just how secretive the working of government was and it became clear that much crucial information had not been revealed to the House of Commons.

And third, the response of the government to European plans for more open government suggested a continuing desire for secrecy. In January 1994, for example, a new information code drawn up by the Council of Ministers called for the widest possible access to documents. But, attempts to make use of the code were blocked (*Guardian*, 18 April 1994).

These three developments, combined with the criticisms outlined above, led critics to argue that the Major government's claims to support more open government were largely rhetorical - a change of style rather than substance.

The Labour government and freedom of information

The Labour Party's 1997 general election manifesto included the following pledge:

> 'Unnecessary secrecy in government leads to arrogance in government and defective policy decisions...We are pledged to a Freedom of Information Act, leading to more open government.' (Labour 1997, p.33)

The minister given the job of drafting a freedom of Information Bill after the election was David Clark. He was responsible for the white paper which was published in December 1997. The proposals made in this white paper are outlined in Box 19.9.

Box 19.9 The white paper on freedom of information, December 1997

- Everyone will have the legal right to see information held by national, regional and local government and some other organisations working on behalf of government - including government agencies, the NHS, quangos, privatised utilities, and private sector organisations working for government.
- Information about the security and intelligence services and the special forces, personnel files, and information vital to crime prevention will be exempt from the Act.
- Information will be witheld if documents have a bearing on: (1) national security, defence and international relations; (2) internal discussion of government policy; (3) law enforcement; (4) personal privacy; (5) commercial confidentiality; (6) the safety of individuals; and (7) the public and the environment. In addition, references, testimonials and matters given in confidence will be witheld.
- In each case, there would need to be the risk of 'substantial harm' for information not to be released.
- In the case of civil service advice to ministers, a simple test of 'harm' will be applied.
- Members of the public will be able to contact the relevant public body for information.
- A fee will be levied for the service.
- If access to information is denied, there will be the right to appeal to an Information Commissioner who will decide whether to not to grant access.

Adapted from HMSO 1997.

The Campaign for Freedom of Information's response

Maurice Frankel, Director of the Campaign for Freedom of Information, gave the proposals a cautious welcome. Describing the proposals as 'surprisingly radical', he was pleased that 'arms length' organisations (like quangos and privatised utilities) were included, but was concerned about the scope for making exemptions, potential conflict between the Official Secrets Act and Freedom of Information legislation, and the proposed fees (information from the Campaign for Freedom on Information Press Release, 11 December 1997).

Developments in 1998

Although supporters of freedom of information legislation hoped that provision for a Bill would be included in the Queen's Speech for the 1998-99 session, the government delayed its introduction. In July 1998, David Clark was sacked in Tony Blair's first Cabinet reshuffle and responsibility for the Bill handed over to the Home Secretary, Jack Straw (who, from May 1997, was a member of the Cabinet committee considering the legislation). Then, in September 1998, it was announced that Jack Straw intended to delay the implementation of legislation until 2001 and was fighting for changes in some of the provisions suggested in the white paper:

> 'He is said to be determined to maintain full exemption for the security services and police work. He is also to examine whether the present rules, which say that information must be released unless it causes "substantial harm" should be weakened to ensure that social

security staff can be protected. This is to meet Whitehall lobbying that fraud investigations could be damaged by premature disclosure under the Bill. Mr Straw claims that the Cabinet Office has failed to resolve how to match the need for disclosure of information with the need to protect the privacy of the individual. He has called a fresh team of civil servants and lawyers to re-examine the provisions under the Bill.' (*Guardian*, 30 September 1998)

Main points - Section 5.4

- Supporters of open government have called for freedom of information legislation. Whilst this was rejected by Margaret Thatcher, John Major accepted a need for open government, though little progress was made during his premiership.
- The Labour Party pledged to introduce a Freedom of Information Act if elected in 1997.
- In December 1997, a white paper was published, but, in the summer of 1998, introduction of legislation was delayed and the proposed provisions reconsidered.

Activity 19.8 Closed government

Item A *Freedom of information under Labour*

" WE PROPOSE A FREEDOM OF INFORMATION ACT..."

We can't blame the sheep-like 'bleepies' of New Labour, the electronically-tagged foot-soldiers who do whatever their pagers tell them. Nor can we condemn outright the control-freaks of the Labour high command. It's not their fault. The blame rests with parliamentary democracy itself. Westminster's rules require intense discipline. To remain in power, the government must retain its majority - and that takes iron party discipline. The leadership couldn't possibly allow backbenchers to vote according to their consciences or, perish the thought, the needs of their constituents. That would create chaos, with governments vulnerable to defeat at any moment.

Adapted from the *Times*, 9 May 1997 and the *Guardian*, 12 December 1997.

Item B   *A Freedom of Information Act (1)*

Questioned for the first time by MPs from the Public Administration Select Committee on the government's proposals for a Freedom of Information Act, David Clark, the minister responsible, conceded that officials and ministers could attempt to bypass the Act by writing comments on sticky labels which could be removed when documents were requested. Rhodri Morgan, the Labour MP who chairs the select committee, expressed concern that the Act could encourage civil servants not to commit on paper their advice to ministers. They would be likely to resort to using 'lunches at the Reform Club', he said. Clark acknowledged that exchanges might take place in corridors or over the phone, but said that the solution was to bring about a cultural change in Whitehall.

Adapted from the *Guardian*, 17 December 1997.

Item C   *A Freedom of Information Act (2)*

Freedom of information (FOI) is in trouble. The reform has been dropped from next year's legislative programme and responsibility has been transferred to the Home Secretary, Jack Straw, reportedly the leading critic of David Clark's proposals. The first signs of retreat have already been seen - the privatised utilities were going to be covered by the Act, but most of their functions will now be excluded. Ministers have also decided to introduce a new appeals tribunal, making it easier for government and business to challenge unfavourable decisions by the Freedom of Information Commissioner (this approach was rejected in the white paper). In addition, Jack Straw is on record as opposing the proposal that departments could only withold disclosure on the grounds of 'substantial harm' - a much stricter test than plain 'harm'. Removing this clause would blunt the Act's cutting edge. By backpedalling, the government will harm its public standing. Tony Blair has said FOI is a way of combating public disillusion with politics. Delay will only fuel that disillusion. Blair also said that FOI is 'not some isolated constitutional reform', but, 'a change that is absolutely fundamental to how we see politics developing in this country over the next few years.' Why then is it not at the heart of the forthcoming legislative programme?

Adapted from an article written by Maurice Frankel, Director of the Campaign for Freedom of Information, 18 August 1998.

Questions

1. 'Britain is moving towards more open government'. Using Items A-C, give arguments for and against this statement.

2. What does Item A tell us about the Labour government's attitude towards freedom of information?

3. Using Items B and C, explain why freedom of information became an important and controversial political issue in the 18 months after Labour was elected in 1997.

References

Allan et al. (1994) Allan, P., Benyon, J. & McCormick, B., *Focus on Britain 1994*, Perennial Publications, 1994.

Annan (1977) Annan Committee, *Report of the Committee on the Future of Broadcasting*, Cmnd 6753, HMSO, 1977.

Barratt (1986) Barratt, D., *Media Sociology*, Tavistock, 1986.

Benn (1979) Benn, T., *Arguments for Socialism*, Penguin, 1979.

Benyon & Denver (1990) Benyon, J. & Denver, D., 'Mrs Thatcher's electoral success', *Social Studies Review*, Vol.5.3, January 1990.

Best (1997) Best, S., 'Postmodern politics', *Social Science Teacher*, Vol.26.3, Summer 1997.

BRU (1985) Broadcasting Research Unit, *The Public Service Idea in British Broadcasting - Main Principles*, Broadcasting Research Unit, 1985.

Butler & Kavanagh (1997) Butler, D. & Kavanagh, D., *The British General Election of 1997*, Macmillan, 1997.

Cabinet Office (1997) *Ministerial Code: a Code of Conduct and Guidance on Procedures for Ministers*, Cabinet Office, July 1997.

Cockerell et al. (1984) Cockerell, M., Hennessy, P. & Walker, P., *Sources Close to the Prime Minister: Inside the Hidden World of the News Manipulators*, Macmillan, 1984.

Conservative (1992) *The Conservative Manifesto 1992*, Conservative Central Office, 1992.

CSE (1985) *Politics and Profit*, monthly newsletter of the Conference of Socialist Economists, June 1985.

Curran & Seaton (1997) Curran, J. & Seaton, J., *Power without Responsibility* (5th edn), Routledge, 1997.

Eldridge et al. (1997) Eldridge, J., Kitzinger, J. & Williams, J., *The Mass Media and Power in Modern Britain*, Oxford University Press, 1997.

Evans (1984) Evans, H., *Good Times, Bad Times*, Coronet, 1984.

Franklin (1993) Franklin, B., 'Packaging politics: politicians and the media' in *Haralambos (1993)*.

Franklin (1994) Franklin, B., *Packaging Politics*, Edward Arnold, 1994.

Franklin (1996) Franklin, B., 'Mass media' in *Haralambos (1996)*.

Franks (1972) Franks, O., *Departmental Committee on Section 2 of the Official Secrets Act 1911*, Cmnd 5104, HMSO, 1972.

Golding et al. (1997) Golding, P., Deakin, D. & Bilig, M., *1997 Election Study*, Loughborough University Communications Research Centre, 1997.

Grant (1998) Grant, W., 'Economic policies' in Lancaster (1998).

Haralambos (1993) Haralambos, M. (ed.), *Developments in Sociology*, Vol.9, Causeway Press, 1993.

Haralambos (1996) Haralambos, M. (ed.), *Developments in Sociology*, Vol.12, Causeway Press, 1996.

Harris (1983) Harris, R., *Gotcha: the Media, the Government and the Falklands Crisis*, Faber & Faber, 1983.

HC 141 (1989) *First Report from the Select Committee on Televising of Proceedings of the House*, HC 141, 1988–89, 1989.

Hennessy (1989) Hennessy, P., *Whitehall*, Fontana Press, 1989.

Hillyard & Percy-Smith (1988) Hillyard, P. & Percy-Smith, J., *The Coercive State*, Fontana, 1988.

HMSO (1997) Freedom of Information White Paper - *Your Right to Know*, HMSO, Cmnd 3818, 1997.

Hunt (1992) Hunt, S., 'State secrecy in the UK', *Politics Review*, Vol.1.4, April 1992.

Jones (1996) Jones, N., *Soundbites and Spin Doctors*, Indigo, 1996.

King (1998) King, A. (ed.), *New Labour Triumphs: Britain at the Polls*, Chatham House, 1998.

Kuhn (1994) Kuhn, R., 'The Media' in *Allan et al.* (1994).

Labour (1997) *New Labour - Because Britain Deserves Better*, Labour Party manifesto, Labour Party, 1997.

Lancaster (1998) Lancaster, S. (ed.), *Developments in Politics*, Vol.9, Causeway Press, 1998.

Lawson & Garrod (1996) Lawson, T. & Garrod, J., *A-Z Sociology Dictionary*, Hodder & Stoughton, 1996.

Marx & Engels (1976) Marx, K. & Engels, F., *Collected Works*, Laurence and Wishart, 1976.

Miliband (1989) Miliband, R., *Divided Societies*, Oxford University Press, 1989.

Miller (1991) Miller, W.L., *Media and Voters: the audience, content and influence of press and television at the 1987 general election*, Clarendon Press, 1991.

Negrine (1994) Negrine, R. *Politics and the Mass Media in Britain*, Routledge, 1994.

Negrine (1997) Negrine, R., 'Politics and the media', *Politics Review*, Vol.6.4, April 1997.

Norris (1998) Norris, P., 'The battle for the campaign agenda' in *King (1998)*.

Peak (1994) Peak, S., *The 1994 Media Guide*, Fourth Estate, 1994.

Peak & Fisher (1997) Peak, S. & Fisher, P., *The 1997 Media Guide*, Fourth Estate, 1997.

Peak & Fisher (1998) Peak, S. & Fisher, P., *The 1998 Media Guide*, Fourth Estate, 1998.

Riddell (1998) Riddell, P., 'Media and elections', *Talking Politics*, Vol.10.3, Spring 1998.

Robertson (1989) Robertson, G., *Freedom, the Individual and the Law*, Penguin, 1989.

Robertson (1993) Robertson, G., 'The cure for the British disease', *Violations of Rights in Britain No.4*, Charter 88 Enterprises, 1993.

Scammell & Harrop (1997) Scammell, M. & Harrop, M., 'The press' in *Butler & Kavanagh (1997)*.

Social Trends (1998) Central Statistical Office, *Social Trends 28*, HMSO, 1998.

Toffler (1980) Toffler, A., *The Third Wave*, Collins, 1980.

Trowler (1988) Trowler, P., *Investigating the Media*, Unwin Hyman, 1988.

Wagg (1989) Wagg, S., 'Politics and the popular press', *Social Studies Review*, Vol.5.1, September 1989.

Wagg (1994) Wagg, S., 'Politics and the media' in *Wale (1994)*.

Wale (1994) Wale, W. (ed.), *Developments in Politics*, Vol.5, Causeway Press, 1994.

Wilson (1984) Wilson, D., *The Secrets File: the Case for Freedom of Information in Britain Today*, Heinemann, 1984.

Wring (1998) Wring, D., 'Political communication', *Talking Politics*, Vol.10.3, Spring 1998.

Index